As a Scientologist I have the technology to handle life's problems and I have used this to help others in life as well.

John Travolta
Actor

Scientology is such a key part of my life today that it really constitutes an approach to living that is optimum for me as an individual, as a member of a family, as a member of the groups I belong to, and as a citizen of the world.

Terry Jastrow
Emmy Award–winning
Producer/Director
ABC Sports

Scientology makes people free, sane and able. It makes it possible to be more oneself, with the ability to create and change anything being a natural and expected phenomenon. It puts you at cause over your life.

Anne Archer
Actress

Scientology has been a tremendous asset for my brothers and me as individuals, as a family and in our highly successful firm. Being happy with oneself, one's family, one's business activities and life generally is a fantastic accomplishment and the knowledge that one can improve from there still, is incredible; yet we have found it truly achievable with Scientology.

Matt Feshbach
Feshbach Brothers
Investment Managers

Scientology changed my life because it gave me a direction that I believe in and it gave me truth.

Julia Migenes
Opera Star

Scientology answered many questions that I had been asking for a long time. As a result I have a much more stable and enjoyable personal and family life, as well as a booming career as an artist.

Jim Warren
Fine Artist and Illustrator

Scientology has enabled me to see clearly what my goals in life are. Before I became a Scientologist I was a professional race car driver but quit. Through Scientology I was able to rekindle my purpose in life and return to my profession. My capabilities increased and I became more certain. As a result I won the 24 hours of Le Mans. Without Scientology I would never have accomplished this nor found the happiness I now have in life.

Phillipe de Henning
Champion Racer & Winner
of the 1987 Le Mans

From Scientology, I've gotten a freedom to learn whatever I want to learn in life and I'm gaining new abilities all the time.

Chick Corea
Eight-time Grammy Award–
winning Jazz Musician and
Composer

For the past twenty years, Scientology has provided me and my family spiritual and intellectual growth which I thought unattainable. I played professional football for eight years in the NFL, captained my university football team and hold a master's degree.

I highly recommend the works of L. Ron Hubbard to my associates to help better their lives and improve conditions. Scientology technology works.

Bob Adams
President, Software Firm

WHAT IS SCIENTOLOGY?

WHAT IS SCIENTOLOGY?

A guidebook to the world's fastest growing religion

Bridge
PUBLICATIONS, INC.

Compiled by staff of the Church of Scientology International

Published by **Bridge Publications, Inc.** 4751 Fountain Avenue, Los Angeles, California 90029

ISBN 0-88404-850-0

Published in other countries by **NEW ERA Publications International ApS** Store Kongensgade 55, 1264 Copenhagen K, Denmark

ISBN 87-7336-945-4

Grateful acknowledgment is made to L. Ron Hubbard Library for permission to reproduce selections from the copyrighted works of L. Ron Hubbard.

Photography by Golden Era Productions except as listed (company and page number): Culver Pictures—18; ©1993 Sygma, Photographer: Bagglioni—21; The Bettman Archive—15, 21; ©1993 FPG International, Telegraph Colour Library—70.

Printed in the United States of America

That public interest in Scientology is mounting rapidly is undeniable. This volume was compiled to fill that need for information by introducing the subject to those who wish to know more about it. The full body of knowledge that comprises Scientology is contained in more than forty million spoken and written words—all by L. Ron Hubbard, the source and founder of Scientology. Contained herein, however, is a complete description of Scientology: its religious philosophy, its organization, its activities and its influence on society.

Church of Scientology International

TABLE OF CONTENTS

FOREWORD

Despite this century's torrent of technological advances, our civilization is in dire need of help. Since the advent of an atomic age which spawned the distinct possibility that all life on Earth could be extinguished at the push of a button, two generations have grown up under that specter. Partially in consequence, life in our society has taken many strange twists: Children are forcibly administered tranquilizing drugs in schools in the name of control; workers are taxed one hour's wages for every three on the job; and our youth emerge from their schools unable to read or write. Whole populations are directed what to think, what to believe or what attitudes to hold through media manipulation. Such is the world that would be encountered by a time traveler from the start of this century; and surely he would find it strange.

It is not easy to live with purpose, dignity and happiness in a world so engrossed in materialism and so utterly blind to man's spiritual needs. Half an hour's walk through any urban landscape would convince virtually anyone that life could be a happier proposition.

Which brings up this relevant question: What is Scientology?

Scientology is an applied religious philosophy.

The fastest growing religious movement on Earth, Scientology has become a firmly established and active force for positive change in the world in less than half a century.

The Scientology religious philosophy contains a precise system of axioms, laws and techniques, exhaustively researched and documented as workable; as such, it provides the individual with the ability to dramatically improve conditions, not only in his own life but in the world around him.

In a word, Scientology works.

And this is why millions of people the world over use its principles in their daily lives, why a growing number of people find such relevance in Scientology for themselves, their families, their organizations, their nations and this entire civilization.

You will learn about Scientology in this book, about its basic principles, its history, its organizations, what it is doing to improve life in a troubled world and about the remarkable man who researched and developed Scientology—American philosopher and humanitarian L. Ron Hubbard.

Fundamentally, Scientology is about the individual man or woman. Its goal is to bring an individual to a sufficient understanding of himself and his life and free him to make improvements where he finds them necessary and in the ways he sees fit.

Scientology is a workable system. Evidence of this may be seen in the lives of millions of Scientologists and the positive effects they create. People improve their lives through Scientology. As Scientologists in all walks of life will attest, they have enjoyed greater success in their relationships, family life, jobs and professions. They take an active, vital role in life and leading roles in their communities. And participation in Scientology brings to many a broader social consciousness, manifested through meaningful contribution to charitable and social reform activities. Through hundreds of separate community outreach programs, Scientologists help the needy and disadvantaged on every continent.

Scientology contains effective answers to society's most crucial problems, among them drug abuse, crime, education and decay of moral values.

All Scientologists are drug free, and spearhead effective actions in countries around the world to get others off drugs. Scientologists have helped millions of underprivileged children to dramatically improve their reading level, vocabulary and comprehension, and the record of Scientology's fight for human rights is unparalleled.

Scientology is not authoritarian. There is no enforced belief. Rather, a maxim in Scientology is that only those things which one finds true for himself are true. In Scientology you learn to think for yourself—it is a voyage of self-discovery.

In the interests of making *What Is Scientology?* useful to as many as possible, it has been organized with the assumption that the reader has little or no familiarity with the subject. Consequently, the

Scientology is about the individual man or woman. Its goal is to bring an individual to a sufficient understanding of himself and his life and free him to improve conditions in the ways that he sees fit.

book is best read in sequence, since more advanced concepts build upon information in earlier chapters. The primary purpose was to produce a book that fully answers the question "What is Scientology?" Millions of words have been written on the subject of Scientology, and in this volume we present the fundamentals. Photographs, diagrams and graphs illustrate many points of importance.

Thus, as a broad overview of Scientology, this book will be a useful reference text, both to those with specific questions about the subject and, through the selected writings of L. Ron Hubbard, to those who

CHURCH OF SCIENTOLOGY
THE L. RON HUBBARD LIFE EXHIBITION

wish to generally know more about his philosophy and principles.

The Scientology religion consists of a growing worldwide network of churches, missions and groups. And like any great movement that has advocated change for the better, it has not been a stranger to controversy, attracting media attention in many countries. *What Is Scientology?* both examines and explains this phenomenon, chronicling the history of its battles against vested interests and correcting much of the misinformation that has been manufactured in an attempt to hinder its forward progress.

Scientology is a dynamic, expanding religion. Even as this book is going to press, it is expanding into more and more countries, cities, towns and hamlets of Earth. Soon, the chapters describing Scientology's influence in society will need augmentation. But the basic ideas of Scientology, the benefits it offers, will not change and so, if this volume succeeds in answering the question posed by its title, the intention for its publication will have been well served.

A civilization without insanity, without criminals and without war, where the able can prosper and honest beings can have rights, and where man is free to rise to greater heights, are the aims of Scientology.

In less than fifty years, Scientology has become an indelible part of this civilization's fabric. It is here to stay.

How has this happened in so short a time? The answers are contained within.

The headquarters of the Church of Scientology International in Los Angeles, California

This half-million square foot facility serves tens of thousands of Scientologists living in the greater Los Angeles area.

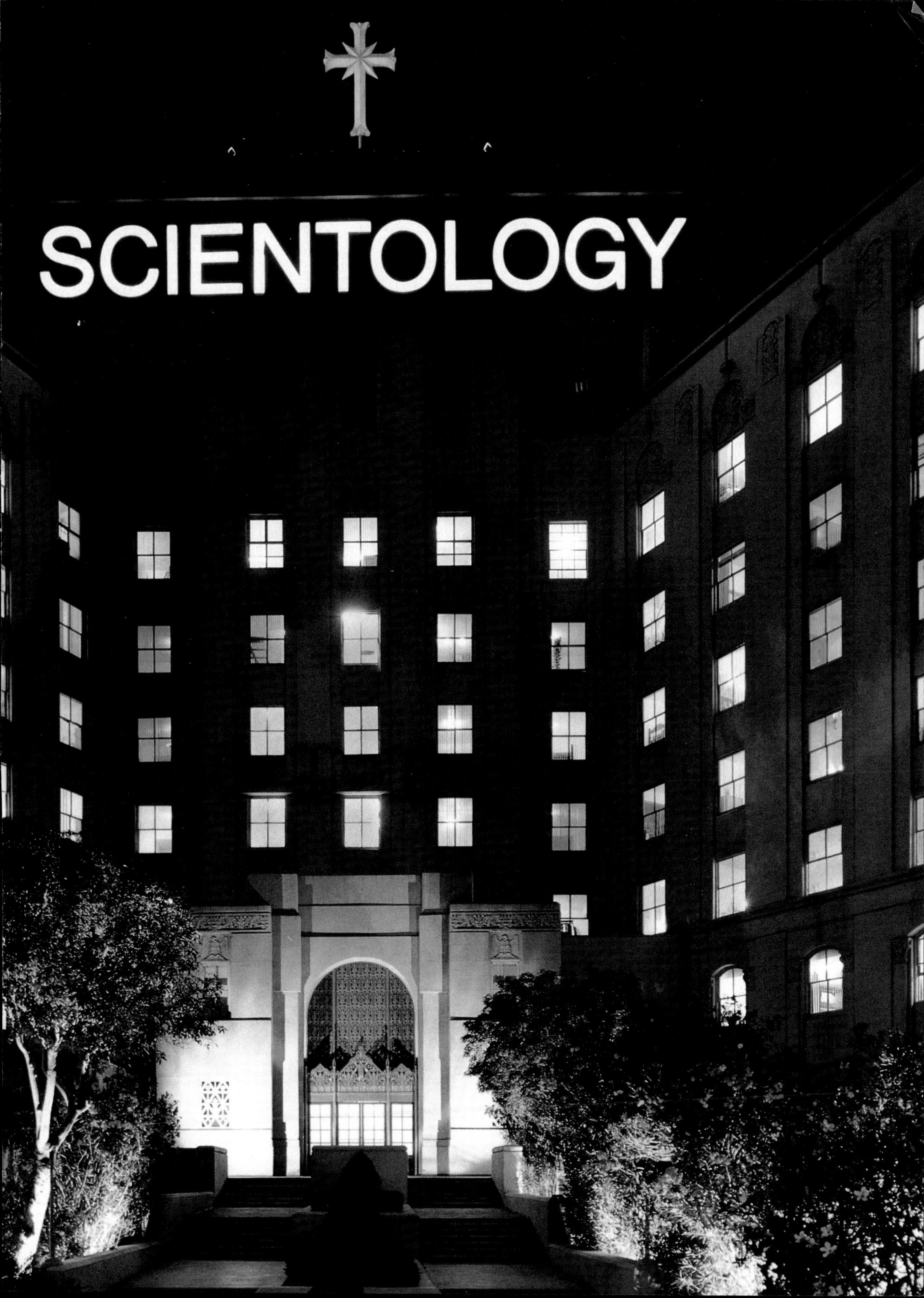
SCIENTOLOGY

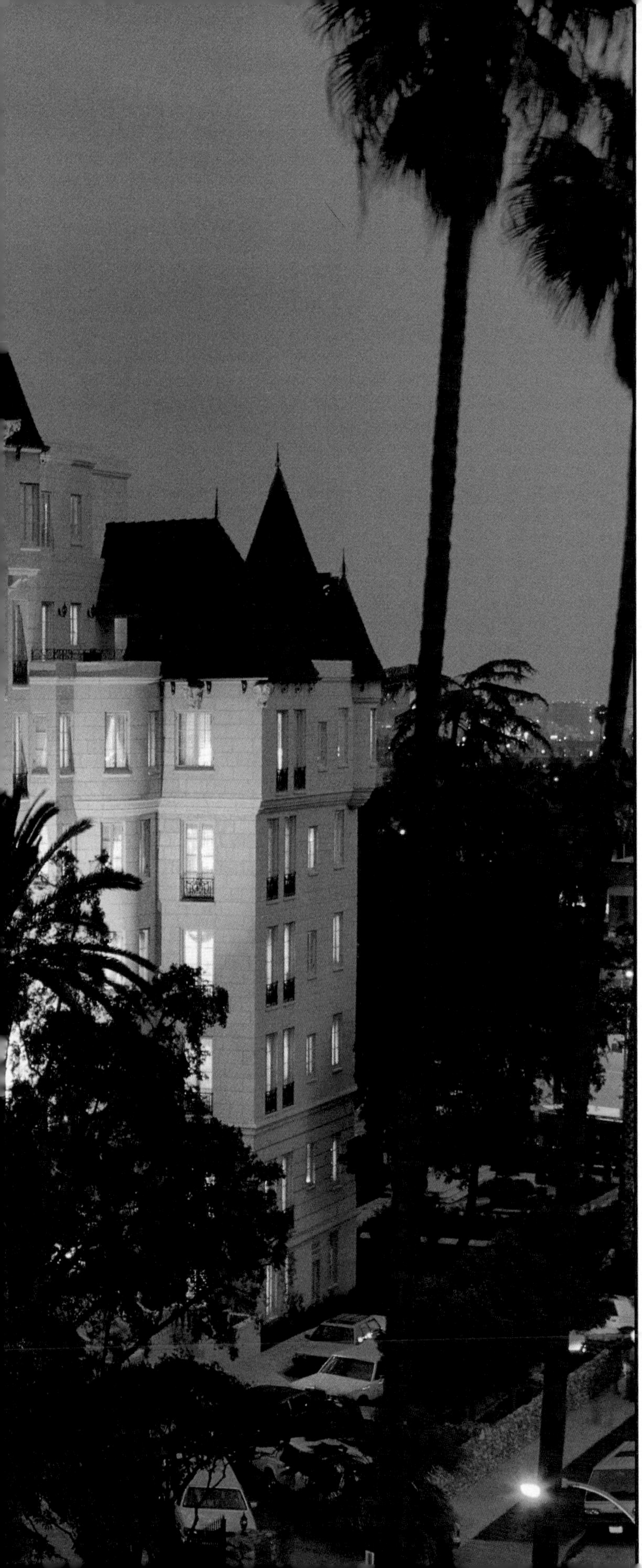

Celebrity Centre International, located in Hollywood, California, heads a worldwide network of organizations which help the many Scientology artists, athletes and business professionals. Scientology Celebrity Centres can be found in many major cities including Paris, Vienna, Hamburg, Düsseldorf, Munich, London, New York, Las Vegas, Nashville and Washington, DC.

Tokyo, Japan

Zurich, Switzerland

Toronto, Canada

Scientology churches exist in most major cities around the world. Some of them are shown here.

Hamburg, Germany

Johannesburg, South Africa

Frankfurt, Germany

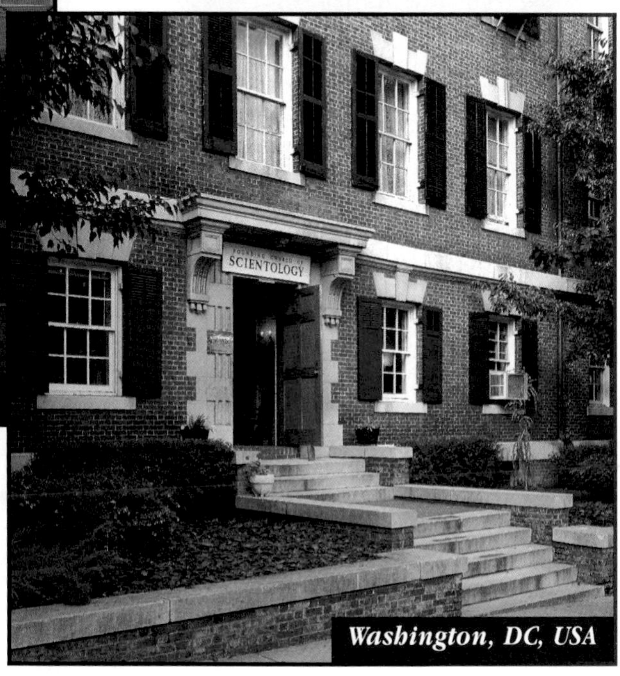

Washington, DC, USA

Los Angeles, USA

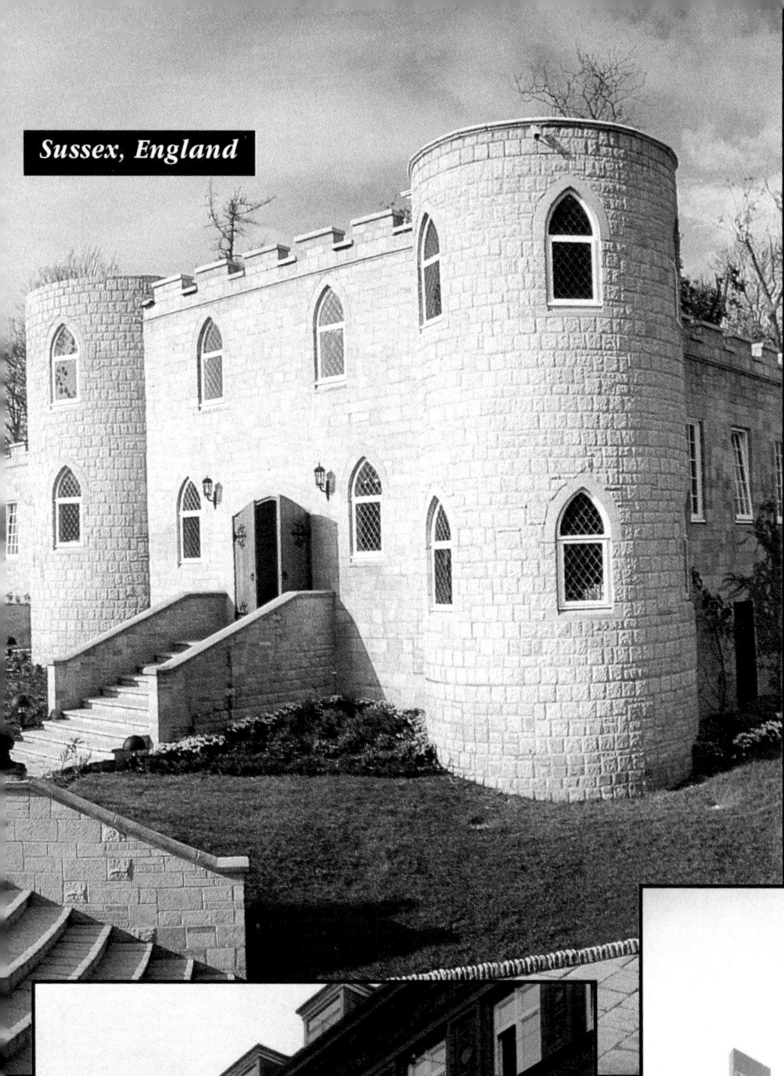

Sussex, England

The Saint Hill College for Scientologists is situated on fifty-five acres of rolling countryside in Sussex, England. Students from many countries come here to study the advanced graduate courses it offers. Church members also do these courses at similar advanced Scientology organizations in the United States, Denmark and Australia.

Sydney, Australia

Copenhagen, Denmark

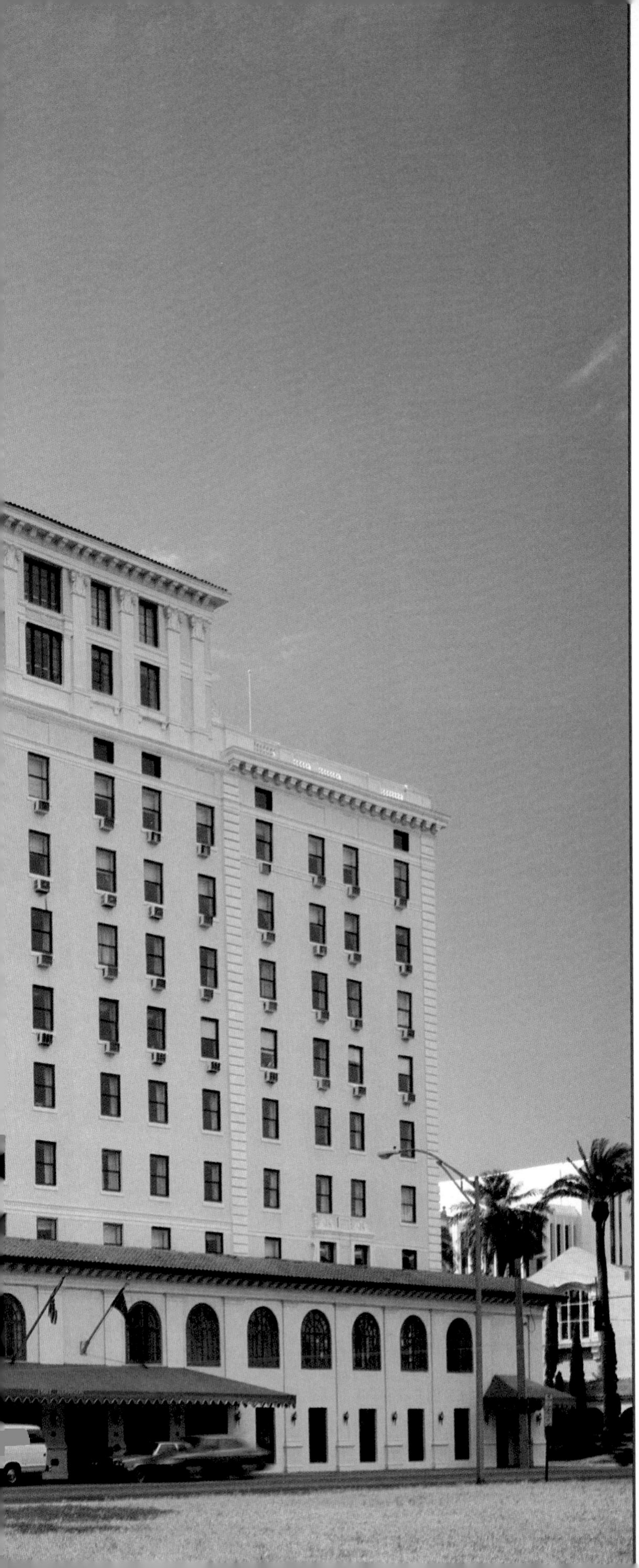

Located in Clearwater, Florida, this is one of thirteen buildings comprising the Scientology religious retreat known as the Flag Land Base.

Students from around the world study advanced Scientology courses in this building at the Flag Land Base.

Freewinds

The ***Freewinds****, operating out of her home port in the Caribbean, offers Scientologists the highest levels of spiritual advancement, off the turbulent crossroads of the world.*

Part One

Scientology: Its Background and Origins

Scientology follows a long tradition of religious philosophy and practice. Its roots lie in the deepest beliefs and aspirations of all great religions, thus encompassing a religious heritage as old and as varied as man himself.

Though drawing upon the wisdom of some 50,000 years, it is factually a new religion, one which has isolated fundamental laws of life and, for the first time, developed a workable philosophy that can be applied to help one achieve a happier and richer existence. Scientology is therefore something one *does,* not merely something one believes in—an important point which will be greatly clarified as you read on.

That Scientology's development and rapid promulgation was made possible, in part, by advances in the physical sciences through the first half of the twentieth century is significant. For Scientology constitutes man's first real application of scientific methodology to spiritual questions.

Part One of this volume provides a firm grounding on the subject of Scientology. This covers three topics, with chapters devoted to each. The first provides a brief introduction to the Scientology religion and a basic explanation of its philosophy. The second traces the history of religious thought in order to place Scientology into its proper context and clarify the path it follows. The third chapter introduces the reader to the Founder of Scientology, L. Ron Hubbard.

CHAPTER 1

INTRODUCTION TO THE SCIENTOLOGY RELIGION

Thanks to scientific and technical advances over the last hundred years, most people are today materially wealthier than their forebears. Yet, by their own accounts, the quality of their lives has not kept step. In fact, it may be argued that people were once happier and more fulfilled. For some, material affluence breeds anxiety, a gnawing fear that if someone doesn't take away their hard-earned acquisitions, the end of their days will prematurely arrive to finish the job. Others find death easier to face than a lifetime of assembly-line slavery, while most, in a less dramatic fashion, simply buckle down to lives of quiet desperation.

As the twenty-first century dawns, most have no real grasp of those factors governing their existence. And yet, simply stated, had they a greater understanding of themselves and their fellows they would be able to improve conditions and thus live happier lives. This, then, is the function of Scientology: to enable man to improve his lot through understanding.

Before Scientology, the tremendous scientific advances of this era were not matched by similar advances in the humanities. Man's knowledge of the physical universe had far outdistanced his knowledge of himself. The resulting pressures from such an imbalance account for much that has unsettled society and threatens the future. In part, therefore, what Scientology represented to many when it appeared in the early 1950s, was a restoration of the balance.

Despite its many successes, science has not provided answers to questions man has been asking himself since time immemorial: Who are we? What do we consist of? Where do we come from? Where are we going? What are we doing? Indeed, these questions have always been the province of philosophy and religion, but traditional answers seemed immensely inadequate in the face of the H-bomb. Scientology, however, drawing on the same advances in knowledge that led to nuclear physics, supplied modern answers to these questions. And it supplied *workable* methods of application which made it possible for man to reach the ancient goal he has been striving toward for thousands of years: to know himself and, in knowing himself, to know and understand other people and, ultimately, all life.

Scientology is an *applied* religious philosophy. It holds in common many of the beliefs of other religions and philosophies, and considers man to be a spiritual being, with more to him than flesh and blood. This, of course, is a very different view to that espoused by prevailing scientific thought which views man as but a material object, a complex combination of chemical compounds and stimulus-response mechanisms.

Scientology believes man to be basically good, not evil. It is his experiences that have led him to commit evil deeds, not his nature. Often, he mistakenly solves his problems by considering only his own interests, which then causes trouble for both himself and others. Scientology believes that man advances to the degree he preserves his spiritual integrity and values, and remains honest and decent. Indeed, he deteriorates to the degree he abandons these qualities.

But because man is basically good he is capable of spiritual betterment, and it is the goal of Scientology to bring him to a point where he is capable of sorting out the factors in his own life and solving his own problems. Other efforts to help man often try to solve his problems *for* him and in this respect Scientology is different. Scientology believes that an individual placed in a position where he has higher intelligence, where he can confront life better, where he can identify the factors in his life more easily, is also in a position to solve his own problems and so better his own life.

Life has tended to force the individual into certain values. The stresses of existence have tended to fixate his attention to a point where his awareness of himself and his environment has been greatly diminished. Attendant to this lowered awareness are problems, difficulties with others, illness and unhappiness. The goal of Scientology is to reverse this diminishing awareness and, in that sense, wake the individual up. As one becomes more and more alert, his intelligence rises and he is capable of greater understanding and thus better able to handle his life. Scientology, then, contains solutions to the problems of living. Its end result is increased awareness and freedom for the individual and rehabilitation of his basic decency, power and ability. It can and does accomplish these ends routinely, daily, all over the world.

The word *Scientology* is taken from the Latin *scio*, which means "knowing in the fullest sense of the word," and the Greek word *logos*, meaning "study of." Scientology means literally "knowing how to know."

The source and founder of the Scientology religion is L. Ron Hubbard, who devoted his life to finding answers to questions that have troubled mankind for millennia. Mr. Hubbard's curiosity and boundless spirit of adventure inspired his search, even as a boy. However, the first fruits of his researches did not result in Scientology, but another subject, "Dianetics." The word *Dianetics* comes from the Greek words *dia*, meaning "through" and *nous*, meaning "soul."

Dianetics constituted L. Ron Hubbard's first breakthrough, and it was these initial discoveries which led to further researches and the exact isolation of the source of life itself. Man does not *have* a spirit. He *is* a spirit. Dianetics addresses and handles the effects of the spirit on the body and thus helps provide relief from unwanted sensations and emotions, accidents, injuries and psychosomatic illnesses (ailments caused or aggravated by mental stress). Scientology, on the other hand, addresses man directly, as a spirit, with the goal of increased awareness and ability as a spiritual being and the full realization of his immortal nature.

In over half a century of investigation, Mr. Hubbard isolated many, many fundamental truths about life, leading to his development of the Scientology philosophy and the subsequent growth of the Scientology religion.

A testament to the truths contained in Scientology lies in the fact that in less than two generations, the movement now flourishes on every continent with thousands of churches, missions and groups touching millions of lives daily. Part of every facet of society, Scientologists are businessmen, housewives, students, artists, celebrities, working people, scholars, soldiers, doctors, policemen and on and on.

Ever involved in the world around them, Scientologists naturally share with others that which they have learned in Scientology. Seeing that it could have relevance in their lives too, these people also become interested in what Scientology can offer *them.* And so Scientology grows, much the same as every great religion in history has grown, from individual to individual, bringing knowledge, wisdom and hope for a better life.

With Scientology, millions know life can be a worthwhile proposition, that men can live fulfilling lives in harmony with others and that the world can be a happier place. Scientologists work to create such a world every day, constantly joined by others who share this dream. The undeniable relevance of Scientology to the lives of these millions assures its permanence in our society. And that millions upon millions more will follow in this quest to create a better world.

CHAPTER 2

THE RELIGIOUS HERITAGE OF SCIENTOLOGY

The dream of making the world a better place has long been embraced by every religious movement in history. Indeed, religion has served as the primary civilizing influence on the planet.

The knowledge that man is a spirit is as old as man himself. Only recently, with the advent of Western psychology, have notions cropped up that man is merely another animal, a stimulus-response mechanism. Such espousals stand at odds to every religious tradition, which variously speak of the "soul," the "spirit" or the "life force"—to encompass a belief held by all civilized men.

The Scientology religion follows just this tradition of man's search for his spiritual identity. In Scientology, the individual himself is considered to be the spiritual being—a thetan (pronounced "thay'-tn"). The term is taken from the Greek symbol or letter *theta* which has long served as a symbol for thought or spirit. Thus, although a new movement, Scientology is heir to the understanding of thinking men since the beginning of human history that man is a spiritual being who aspires to understand and improve life. The search was long, but it has been successful and answers now exist in Scientology for anyone who wishes to reach for them.

In Lascaux, France, 15,000 years before Christ, early man painted bulls and other images deep inside the walls of caves. His underlying belief held that such representations would bring the living animal within their grasp, and so guarantee a successful hunt.

Like this ancient man with his primitive spear, in his attempt to conquer the raging bull, human beings have been trying to understand themselves and their relationship to other living things and the physical universe for countless eons. That which has been recorded in cave paintings, on stone tablets and in ancient myths stands as a testament to this search.

For all the mystery surrounding himself, one of the first things man has innately known was that he was more than merely another beast of the forest, more than mere muscle and bone, but that he was somehow endowed with a spark of the divine, a spiritual being.

Such wisdom formed the basis of the first great civilization—the Egyptian, whose culture endured for twenty-seven centuries. As the earliest people to conquer man's deep-rooted fear of ancestral spirits, they were also among the first to propose that each man must provide for his own happy afterlife.

Despite considerable advances in the physical sciences, their gift of organization and their monumental art and architecture, the Egyptians still lacked the means to reverse the internal decay of their society. Beset with immorality and decadence, they were soon too enfeebled to resist the onslaught of Rome.

About 10,000 years ago, the early Hindu philosophers were also wrestling with life's most basic questions. Their revelations were first recorded in the Veda.

The doctrine of transmigration (the ancient concept of reincarnation)—that life is a continuous stream which flows ceaselessly, without beginning and without end—initially seemed to explain much of what plagued India. But such a belief offered little succor to the multitudes of impoverished. And so, as that misery continued to spread, concerned religious leaders began to challenge traditional doctrine.

Siddhartha Gautama, son of a wealthy Hindu rajah, declared that man is a spiritual being who can achieve an entirely new state of awareness which he termed **bodhi.** *For this reason, he is remembered today as the Buddha, revered for civilizing most of Asia. Unfortunately, however, he left no real means for others to actually attain those states of which he spoke.*

In Persia and much of the ancient world, philosophers and religious men continued their quest to divine the true nature of man, even studying the movements of the sun and stars in hopes of unlocking the mysteries of life.

In the seventh century B.C., Zoroaster, born into a priestly family, came to believe himself a prophet. Forced to flee his native land for what he taught, he found asylum with King Vishtaspa in eastern Iran. There, the Persian religion of Zoroastrianism was born around the belief that only by defining "good" and "evil" could one hope to free himself of ignorance and achieve true happiness in the afterlife.

A century later, the Chinese philosopher Lao-tse believed the world moved according to a divine pattern, one reflected in the rhythmic and orderly movements of nature. Saddened by the corruption of politicians and general social decay, he saw man ***striving*** *to be good, rather than let his inherent goodness come naturally from within. Eventually, so great was his disillusionment, he called for a return to a simpler golden age, and set out for the secluded countryside. Yet upon reaching the city's edge, Lao-tse was beseeched by the gatekeeper not to leave before recording his ideas for posterity.*

His manuscript, the ***Tao Te Ching,*** *became the basis of Taoism and held out yet another hope of higher states to which man could aspire.*

Tao *means simply "way" or "way to go." It is the way the universe moves—a universe to which man is inextricably linked. When men are most natural, they move according to the laws of interdependence and interaction of all universal laws, and so maintain a perfect harmony and balance. According to the* ***Tao,*** *it is* ***the*** *way—there is no other.*

Unfortunately, Taoism too did not provide a ***workable*** *means to reach that perfect harmony. Nor was any attempt made to provide such a means. For intrinsic in the Way, was the conviction that its basic truths were beyond words and could only be experienced. Hence the principles remained in the realm of esoteric knowledge.*

When the Delphic Oracle proclaimed the Greek philosopher, Socrates (470?–399 B.C.) to be the "wisest man in the world," Socrates countered that he was wise only in that he knew that he did not know. He believed man had a right to search for his own truth and that through increased understanding would become happier and more tolerant.

Socrates believed himself charged with a mission from God to make his fellow men aware not only of their own ignorance but also that knowledge could redeem them.

Socrates held that neither he nor anyone else had the right to force opinions on others. Rather, through systematic questioning, he sought to lead others to cast aside preconceptions and reach their own conclusions.

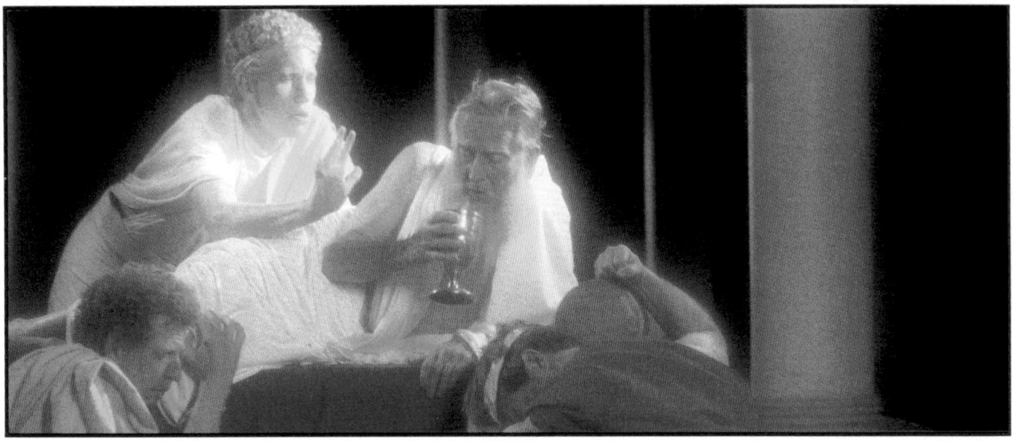

He challenged falsehoods and pomposity, but his ironic criticisms and intellectual honesty were misunderstood by the authoritarians of his time.

Like many philosophers before him, Socrates' methods challenged established beliefs. As a result, in 399 B.C. he was convicted of both "denying the gods" and corrupting youth. Sentenced to drink a cup of hemlock, a bitter poison, he chose to die rather than compromise his stand against tyranny and suppression of the truth.

Prejudice and a general deviation from the road to philosophic truth about man sent even the highly learned Greek civilization to an inevitable and untimely end. First conquered by the Roman Empire, its cities were then mercilessly sacked by barbarians.

Like the philosophers of Greece, India and China, the Hebrews, too, sought to define the meaning of life. According to Jewish tradition, it was Abraham who first gained a special understanding of what lay at the heart of the universe and from that revelation came a belief in a personal god. He further believed that beneath the seemingly endless variety of life lay a single purpose, a single reality.

Judaism is the mother religion of both Christianity and Islam—the three dominant faiths in the Western world.

Two thousand years ago, Jesus of Nazareth brought new hope to man by preaching that this life was not all men might hope for, that man was more than only flesh and would continue to live, even after death. Implicit in his message was the promise of salvation from suffering and a promise of eternal peace.

At odds with the teachings of Jesus was traditional rabbinical belief that salvation would not come until the advent of a distant Messiah. Hence, the special appeal of Christ's message that the Kingdom of God was not only at hand, but lay within all those with faith.

Long fearing popular revolt, the Romans equated Christ's words with political insurrection.

Rome had decreed that nothing should be held above imperial order and thus viewed Christ's wholly spiritual message as dangerously revolutionary, particularly his talk of the coming Kingdom.

Though crucified, the hope that Christ brought to man did not die. Instead, his death became symbolic of the triumph of the spirit over the material body and so brought a new awareness of man's true nature.

The Romans, however, continued to insist that man was just a material object. The psyche (a word meaning "spirit" or "breath of life") was thought to be given up when the man "himself," his body, had perished.

For all their military strength, the Romans never acknowledged or found ways to develop man's true potential and so, as did so many empires before them, they too perished.

About the same time Christ was teaching in the Middle East, the first Buddhist monks arrived in China. The Buddhism that first became popular in China during the Han dynasty (206 B.C.–A.D. 220) taught the indestructibility of the soul, the theory of karma and the values of charity and compassion. Buddhism spread through China, incorporating some of the practical and this-worldly philosophy of ancient China. It taught man a way to spiritual enlightenment despite resistance from the Taoists and later suppression by the state, when hundreds of monasteries were destroyed, and hundreds of thousands of monks and nuns were forced to return to lay life.

Despite such suppression, belief in the spiritual nature of man received even more impetus in the sixth century when the prophet Mohammed preached that there was only **one** *God and attempted to civilize an entire nation. He taught about the supremacy of the spiritual over the material, and beseeched man to seek his own salvation. His message was seen as a threat to the revenues of Mecca, and eventually led to his banishment.*

Within eight years, however, he returned triumphant and began his "Holy War" against infidels. He built the great Mohammedan Empire, which eventually reached from Spain to the borders of China.

The Crusades, the subsequent wars "in the name of religion" which swept Europe for hundreds of years, involved tens of thousands of people in continuous bloodshed. Nonetheless, with the Crusades came a vital cultural exchange.

Toward the end of this period, in 1215, English barons forced King John to sign the famous Magna Carta. This historic document, a formal recognition of the rights of others, was built on the belief that the basic nature of man was good, not evil, and that he was capable of determining his own destiny.

The provisions included the guaranteed freedom of the church, respect for the customs of towns, protection of the rights of subjects and communities, and what would later be interpreted as a guarantee of the right of trial by jury. These represented the triumph of law over king, and thus reason over force.

But the late fifteenth century ushered in the Inquisition, which again sought to quell man's sense of reason and his reach for spiritual enlightenment. Those subscribing to beliefs unacceptable to the Catholic church were tried and tortured until they renounced their "heretical views."

Anyone thought to have "strange" or "different" ideas could be labeled a blasphemer or even a witch, then burned at the stake if they refused to accept the established beliefs.

But man's desire to understand himself and the world around him could not be stopped and men like Leonardo da Vinci pursued their studies in the hope of finding the answers. A brilliant painter, engineer, astronomer and botanist, Leonardo helped launch the Renaissance and a new age of scientific discovery in the face of ridicule from the ignorant and bigoted. Even the most seemingly innocuous studies had to be undertaken with discretion, as the watchful eye of the Inquisition was ever present. In fact, many of his notes were written out so they could only be read in a mirror.

In the sixteenth century, Galileo dared to challenge long-held beliefs by publicly endorsing the Copernican theory that the Earth revolved around the sun and not the reverse. This was considered heresy by the still-active Inquisition.

Galileo was sentenced to an indefinite prison term by the Catholic church for his "crime." Only when he subsequently renounced Copernican theory was he allowed to return to his villa where he lived out the remainder of his life under house arrest by authority of the Inquisition, a broken man.

Fleeing suppression and intolerance in Europe, pilgrims of several faiths set sail for the New World where their aspirations of freedom were probably best summed up by Thomas Jefferson's Declaration of Independence. He wrote, ". . . that all men are created equal, that they are endowed by their Creator with certain inalienable Rights, that among these are Life, Liberty and the pursuit of Happiness." The light of spiritual freedom was once again burning bright.

There were some however, like Charles Darwin, who had a very different message: Man was but another rung on the evolutionary ladder, and could never hope to raise himself to greater levels of awareness. Darwin's man-from-mud theory, the idea that life was a chance happenstance resulting from a chain reaction in a sea of ammonia, soon took hold in the scientific community. Ironically, however, that very same theory may be traced to an ancient Egyptian myth wherein man was seen as emerging from a primordial ocean.

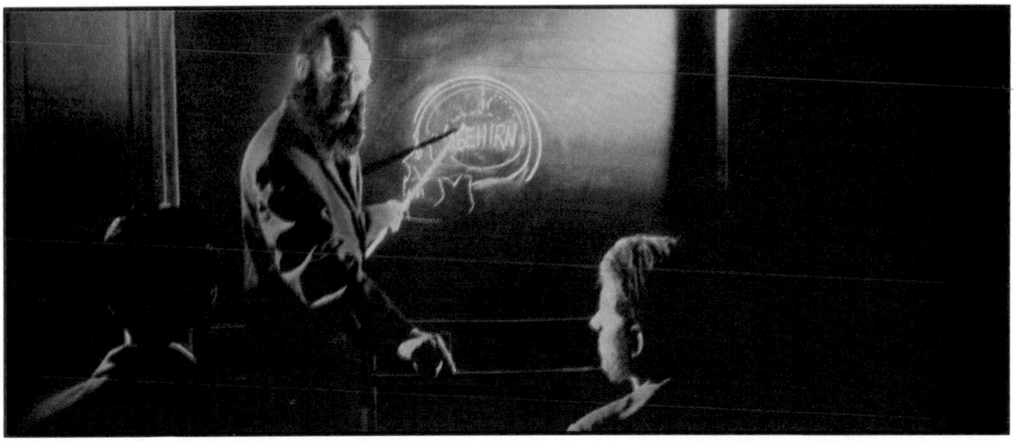

Professor Wilhelm Wundt, a German psychologist and Marxist at the University of Leipzig, proclaimed that man's soul—if indeed he had one—was irrelevant, as man could only be understood in terms of physically observable phenomena. A search for the spiritual nature of man, he reasoned, was a waste of time as there was no psyche. Thus psychology became the study of the spirit which denied the spirit. The subject of psychology thereafter became prevalent in universities.

Sigmund Freud further reinforced this "modern" concept of man, arguing that all impulses stemmed from his repressed and uncontrollable sexual desires. Such impulses were then "analyzed" as primitive and instinctive, not that different from those which drive an animal.

Although Freud himself broke new ground with his recognition that man could overcome physical ills through addressing the mind, the real value of his work was soon buried in a hodgepodge of theories from others.

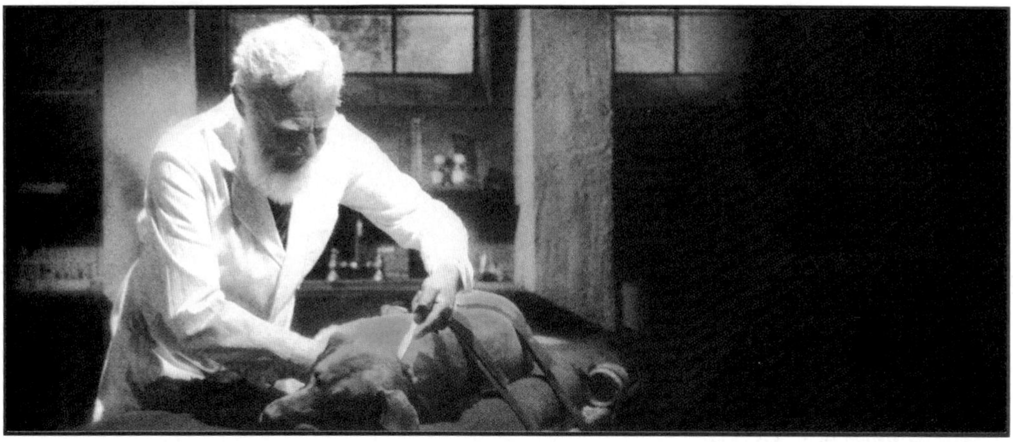

In Russia, former veterinarian Ivan Petrovich Pavlov served the dictator Stalin with experiments to discover how man could be controlled to better serve the state. He reasoned that if dogs could be made to slaver on command, so could human beings. Man had now been reduced to the level of a mindless animal—and thus psychiatry was born, as a tool for tyrannical governments.

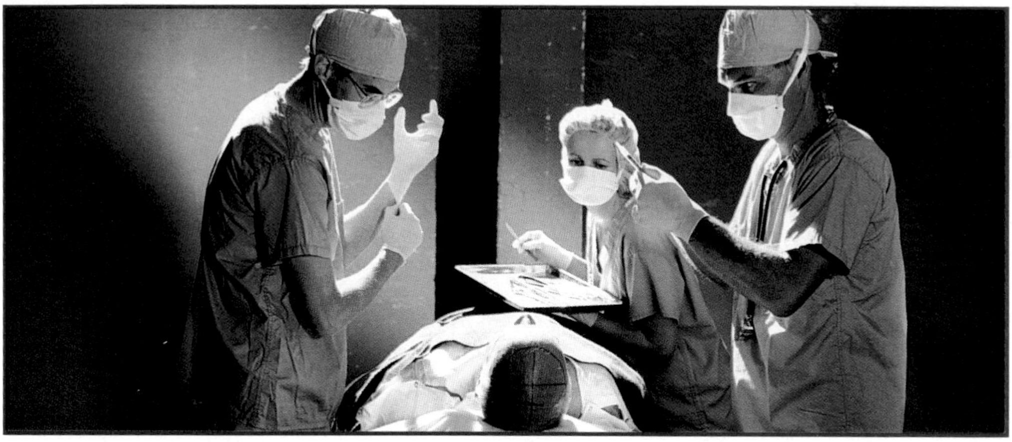

Convinced that man is only a body, psychology and psychiatry have forwarded the idea that there is no soul, merely a physical brain, an aggregation of tissue and nerve cells.

And since man no longer has a soul, he can be degraded still further through all manner of barbaric "treatments." In fact, the array of primitive methods dreamed up by "modern" psychiatrists includes hypnotic drugs, lobotomies, electric shock and bolts to the brain while a person is drugged and comatose—each of which leaves a person little more than a vegetable.

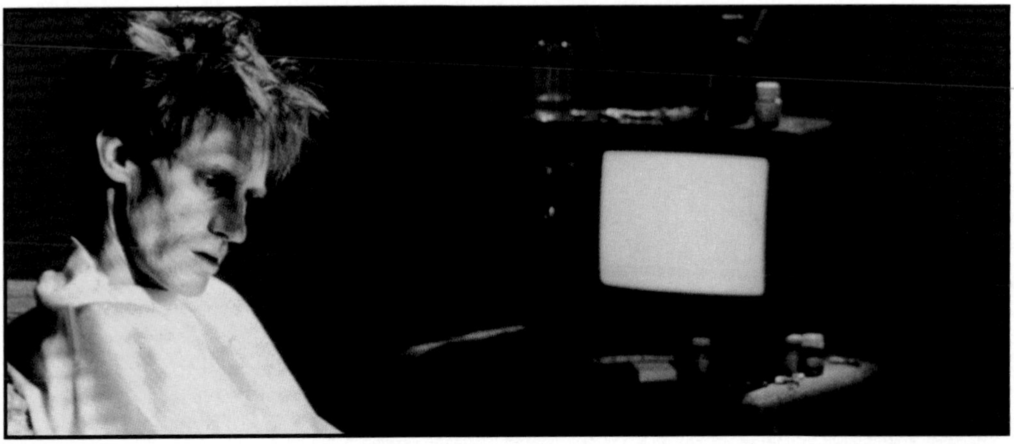

The psychologist believes in materialism. This is the principle that all is purely matter—hopes, dreams, love, inspiration—all just chemical reactions in the brain. Following from this theory, he has attempted to create a society where the body is glorified over the spirit, and where material possessions are more important than one's spiritual well-being.

In such a society, where spiritual values are no longer given credence, man soon loses touch with both his past and his future. Religion, then, becomes an "opiate," while the new high priests of psychiatry, handsomely supported by taxpayers, conduct worthless government studies that provide no solutions.

Even today, new ideas are fought by totalitarian states, and learning is restricted to the privileged few, in an attempt to keep the majority ignorant. Book burnings are another phenomenon of our own time, reminiscent of the Inquisition.

But wisdom and spiritual values cannot be suppressed. All men at all times have sought spiritual release. All individual quests and all philosophies and religions have one goal and one goal only: to discern the true essence of man and his relationship to the universe.

Unfortunately, the humanities have failed to keep pace with scientific developments. A preoccupation with all things physical has left the humanities far behind.

Science advanced to where it could send rockets into space. But, until now, the greatest challenge of all was ignored, the improvement of man himself.

At this point in the history of our civilization we have, frighteningly enough, developed the capabilities to destroy all life on the Earth.

One madman in a position of power could wreak the ultimate destruction for all living things. Lacking a real understanding of man or a workable technology to improve man, governments are unable to forge their own destinies and the potential for chaos is very real.

Perhaps it has taken the potential for ultimate destruction to bring about the ultimate in hope for mankind: a twentieth-century religion, utilizing a truly workable technology to bring man to an understanding of himself and his fellows. Both the atom bomb and this technology were born at the same time—in the crucible of the last world war. Fortunately, we can now end not only war, but crime and insanity on Earth, once and for all. We can reverse the dwindling spiral of life on this planet.

Man can find answers to his timeless questions and gain true spiritual freedom—with Scientology.

Chapter 3

L. Ron Hubbard: The Founder of Scientology

L. Ron Hubbard is the Founder of Scientology. He has described his philosophy in more than 5,000 writings, including dozens of books, and in 3,000 tape-recorded lectures. Those who regularly employ his teachings to improve themselves and help their fellows come from all walks of life, while Scientology missions and churches have been established on six continents.

The universal acclaim for the man—including thousands of awards and recognitions from individuals and groups and the unprecedented popularity of his works among people from all walks of life—is but one indicator of the effectiveness of his technologies. More importantly, there are millions of people around the world who consider they have no greater friend.

Although long celebrated as a writer, novelist and explorer, it was the 1950 publication of *Dianetics: The Modern Science of Mental Health* that initially focused world attention on L. Ron Hubbard. That book, which marked a turning point in history, provided the first workable approach to solving the problems of the mind, the first hope that something could be done about the causes of irrational behavior—war, crime and insanity. Dianetics is something that anyone can use to help improve himself and his fellows. Hence, when the book was released, Amherst College Political Science Professor, Dr. Frederick L. Schuman's declaration in the *New York Times:* "History has become a race between Dianetics and catastrophe. Dianetics will win, if enough people are challenged in time to understand it."

Although most men might have been satisfied with such an accomplishment, L. Ron Hubbard did not stop at Dianetics. Yes, he had solved the riddle of the human mind, but there still remained unsolved questions regarding the nature of the human being himself, outstanding puzzles concerning that long-sought-after "something" we call *life.* And from his methodical and wholly scientific research into this problem came the applied religious philosophy of Scientology, offering not only greater happiness and ability but also solutions to such seemingly hopeless social problems as drug abuse, the decline of moral standards and illiteracy—always providing effective and workable solutions as he found them.

The story of Dianetics and Scientology began long before the publication of Mr. Hubbard's first book on the subject. Indeed, even in his early youth he exemplified a rare sense of purpose and dedication which, combined with his adventurous spirit, made him a living legend. His life-long search for answers to the human condition was equally adventurous; for unlike other philosophers content to view events from an ivory tower, he knew that to really understand one's fellow man, one had to be part of life. One had to rub elbows with all kinds and types of people. And, one had to explore the nooks and crannies of all existence.

This chapter will cover the key incidents that shaped L. Ron Hubbard's life, and the important milestones on the road to his discoveries. By any measure, it was an immensely full and interesting life, but the true value of it lies in the legacy that he left mankind.

Son of naval commander Harry Ross Hubbard and Ledora May Hubbard, L. Ron Hubbard was born on March 13, 1911 in Tilden, Nebraska. At the age of two, he and his family took up residence on a ranch outside Kalispell, Montana, and from there moved to the state's capital, Helena.

As a young boy he learned much about survival in the rugged Far West—with what he called "its do-and-dare attitudes, its wry humor, cowboy pranks, and make-nothing of the worst and most dangerous." Not only could he ride horses at the age of three and a half, but was soon able to rope and break broncos with the best of them.

L. Ron Hubbard's mother was a rarity in her time. A thoroughly educated woman, who had attended teacher's college prior to her marriage to Ron's father, she was aptly suited to tutor her young son. Under her guidance, Ron was reading and writing at an early age, and soon satisfying his insatiable curiosity about life with the works of Shakespeare, the Greek philosophers, and other classics.

When his father's naval career necessitated that the family leave Montana for a series of cross-country journeys, Ron's mother was also on hand to help him make up what he missed in school.

It was also through these early years that Ron first encountered another culture, that of the Blackfoot Indians, then still living in isolated settlements on the outskirts of Helena. His particular friend was an elderly medicine man, commonly known as "Old Tom."

Establishing a unique friendship with the normally taciturn Indian, Ron was soon initiated into the various secrets of the tribe, their legends, customs and methods of survival in a harsh environment. At the age of six, he became a blood brother of the Blackfeet, an honor bestowed on few white men.

In early 1923, when Ron was twelve, he and his family moved to Seattle, Washington, where his father was stationed at the local naval base. He joined the Boy Scouts and that year proudly achieved the rank of Boy Scout First Class. The next year he became the youngest Eagle Scout ever, an early indication that he did not plan to live an ordinary life.

At the end of that year, young Ron traveled to the nation's capital via the Panama Canal, meeting Commander Joseph C. Thompson of the US Navy Medical Corps. Commander Thompson was the first officer sent by the US Navy to study under Sigmund Freud, and took it upon himself to pass on the essentials of Freudian theory to his young friend. Although keenly interested in the Commander's lessons, Ron was also left with many unanswered questions.

In 1927, at the age of sixteen, Ron took the first of his several voyages across the Pacific to Asia. There, both on his own and in the company of an officer attached to the British legation, he took advantage of this unique opportunity to study Far Eastern culture. Among others he befriended and learned from was a thoroughly insightful Beijing magician who represented the last of the line of Chinese magicians from the court of Kublai Khan.

Although primarily renowned as an entertainer, Old Mayo was also well versed in China's ancient wisdom that had been handed down from generation to generation. Ron passed many evenings in the company of such wise men, eagerly absorbing their words.

It was also through the course of these travels that Ron gained access to the much talked-about but rarely seen Buddhist lamaseries in the Western Hills of China—temples usually off-limits to both local peasants and visiting foreigners.

Among other wonders, Ron told of watching monks meditate for weeks on end, contemplating higher truths. Once again then, he spent much of his time investigating and questioning, seeking answers to the human dilemma.

Beyond the lamasery walls, he closely examined the surrounding culture. In addition to the local Tartar tribes, he spent time with nomadic bandits originally from Mongolia. He further traveled up and down the Chinese coast exploring villages and cities, delving into the fabric of the nation. And everywhere he went, one question was uppermost in his mind: "Why?" Why so much human suffering and misery? Why was man, with all his ancient wisdom and knowledge accumulated in learned texts and temples, unable to solve such basic problems as war, insanity and unhappiness?

By the age of nineteen, long before the advent of commercial airplane or jet transportation, he had traveled more than a quarter of a million miles, including voyages not only to China but also Japan, Guam, the Philippines and other points in the Orient. In a very real sense, the world itself was his classroom, and he studied in it voraciously, recording what he saw and learned in his ever-present diaries, which he carefully preserved for future reference.

Everywhere he went, he also took the time to help and teach others. On a remote Pacific island, for example, he proved to the terrified natives that the groans of a ghost in a supposedly haunted cave were nothing more than the rushing of underground water.

In the South Pacific islands, Ron continued his search by venturing deep into the jungles of Guam where he located an ancient Polynesian burial ground, a place steeped in the tradition of heroic warriors and kings. Though his native friends were fearful for him, he explored the sacred area—his initiative drawn from the ever-present desire to know more.

These sojourns in Asia and the Pacific islands had a profound effect, giving Ron a subjective understanding of an Eastern philosophy that had predated even the Greeks.

Yet for all the wonders of these lands and all his respect for those whom he encountered, he still saw much that concerned him: Chinese beggars willing themselves to die above open graves in Beijing, children who were less than rags, widespread ignorance and despair. And in the end, he came to the inescapable conclusion that despite the wisdom of its ancient texts, the East did not have the answers to the miseries of the human condition. It remained evident in the degradation and sorrow of its people.

Returning to the United States in 1929, Ron resumed his formal education. After attending Swavely Prep School in Manassas, Virginia, he was graduated from the Woodward School for Boys in Washington, DC.

He enrolled at George Washington University. His university subject should probably have been ethnology, since he was already an expert in many different cultures—from the Philippine pygmies to the Kayan shamans of Borneo to the Chamorros of Guam. But fate and his father placed him, fortunately, in mathematics and engineering instead. With his knowledge of many cultures and his growing awareness of the human condition, his background in engineering and mathematics would serve him well in undertaking a scientific approach to solving the riddles of existence and man's spiritual potential.

Theorizing that the world of subatomic particles might possibly provide a clue to the human thought process, he enrolled in one of the first nuclear physics courses taught in the United States. Moreover, he was concerned for the safety of the world, recognizing that if man were to handle the atom sanely for the greatest benefit, he would first have to learn to handle himself.

His aim, then, was to synthesize and test all knowledge for what was observable, workable and could truly help solve man's problems. And to that end, he set out to determine precisely how the mind functioned.

In one of his first pioneering experiments on the subject, he employed a sound wave measuring device called a Koenig photometer. Two students read poetry from extremely different languages—Japanese and English—into the device. He found that the device identified the speech as poetry regardless of language. When haiku was read in the original Japanese, the wavelengths produced by the Koenig photometer were the same as those produced when English verse was read.

Here, then, he concluded, was scientific evidence that people were not so different as he had been led to believe, that there was indeed a meeting ground, and all minds did in fact respond identically to the same stimuli.

Reasoning that questions arising from his experiments would best be answered by those who were paid to know about the mind, Ron took these discoveries to the psychology department. Rather than answers, however, he found that the George Washington University psychologists had no comprehension or understanding of the results—but more importantly—they weren't even interested in such things.

Stunned, he soon came to the realization that no one knew how the mind worked. And furthermore, no one in the fields of psychology or psychiatry was about to find out.

Not only were there no answers in the East, there were none to be found in any Western center of culture.

"To be very blunt," he put it, "it was very obvious that I was dealing with and living in a culture which knew less about the mind than the lowest primitive tribe I had ever come in contact with. Knowing also that people in the East were not able to reach as deeply and predictably into the riddles of the mind as I had been led to expect, I knew I would have to do a lot of research."

Deciding that formal study had nothing more to offer, L. Ron Hubbard left college in the depths of the Depression, again taking his quest to learn about life out into the world. He said of this period, "... my writing financed research and this included expeditions which were conducted in order to investigate primitive peoples to see if I could find a common denominator of existence which would be workable."

He directed two expeditions, the Caribbean Motion Picture Expedition, a two-and-a-half month, 5,000-mile voyage aboard the four-masted schooner, **Doris Hamlin,** *and the West Indies Mineralogical Expedition, which completed the first mineralogical survey of the island of Puerto Rico under US rule. Upon his return to the United States, and with scientific grants few and far between, he began to write his way to fame and fortune, supporting his research by becoming one of the most popular writers of the 1930s.*

As the editor of ***Thrilling Adventures*** *magazine, one of the more than 30 magazines he headlined, wrote in October 1934, "L. Ron Hubbard needs no introduction. From the letters you send in, his yarns are among the most popular we have published. Several of you have wondered, too, how he gets the splendid color which always characterizes his stories of the faraway places. The answer is: He's been there, brothers. He's been and seen and done. And plenty of all three."*

While continuing to write for his New York editors as well as screenplays for Hollywood such as ***Secret of Treasure Island,*** *he never stopped his vital researches into man.*

L. Ron Hubbard was searching for a principle which would lead to the unification of knowledge and explain the meaning of existence—something other philosophers had set out to find in the past with varying degrees of success. In fact, many Western philosophers had given up on the idea that different peoples held anything in common and were no longer even asking questions about the life force or the essence of life. Man had become just another animal, mere flesh and bones.

Yet Mr. Hubbard saw man in a very different light. Although he had no name for it yet, he felt certain that life was more than a random series of chemical reactions, and that some sort of intelligent urge underlay our actions. Organizing the tremendous body of data he had acquired—from his travels, research and experiments—he embarked upon a new experimental path, this time to determine how cells functioned. And following an elaborate series of experiments in early 1938, he made a breakthrough of magnitude: he isolated the common denominator of existence: SURVIVE.

That man was surviving was not a new idea. That this was the single basic common denominator of existence was.

The predominant theory of the time held that life was simply a chance chain reaction in a sea of ammonia. Disproving this materialistic belief and forming the basis for all his later work, his findings were compiled into a philosophic manuscript, "Excalibur," written during the first weeks of 1938.

He wrote: "I suddenly realized that survival was the pin on which you could hang the rest of this with adequate and ample proof. It's a very simple problem. Idiotically simple! That's why it never got solved. Nobody has ever looked at anything being that simple to do that much. So what do we find as the simplicities of solution? The simplicities of solution lie in this: that life, all life, is trying to survive. And life is composed of two things: the material universe and an X-factor. And this X-factor is something that can evidently organize, and mobilize the material universe."

Recalling the writing of "Excalibur," the first of his many manuscripts on the subject of life, he noted, "I began to hammer out that secret and when I had written ten thousand words, then I knew even more clearly. I destroyed the ten thousand and began to write again."

The response of those who read this manuscript was dramatic, and more than a few publishers eagerly sought to publish it. He declined. "'Excalibur' did not contain a therapy of any kind but was simply a discussion of the composition of life. I decided to go further," he added.

Ron continued to fund his research by his ever more popular fiction writing. His stories and novels spanned every genre from adventure and travel to mystery, western, romance, science fiction and fantasy. Writing not of machines and robots but of real men and real adventures, he pioneered a whole new era of science fiction writing, as one of the creators of what came to be known as the "Golden Age of Science Fiction."

His expeditions continued as well. Elected a member of the prestigious Explorers Club in New York City, he was bestowed custody of their flag, a high honor in the field of exploration, for the Alaskan Radio Experimental Expedition in May, 1940. This expedition greatly assisted in the codification of the coastal charts of British Columbia and Alaska, while augmenting his knowledge of more cultures—the Tlingit, the Haida and the Aleut Indians of Alaska.

In December 1940, L. Ron Hubbard earned his "License to Master of Steam and Motor Vessels" from the US Department of Commerce. Three months later, he obtained a second certificate attesting to his marine skill: "License to Master of Sail Vessels, Any Ocean."

Throughout all of this, however, Ron was continuing in his quest to answer the riddles of man. His writings and explorations had the purpose of financing his researches and expanding his knowledge of the world and life.

Then came the war.

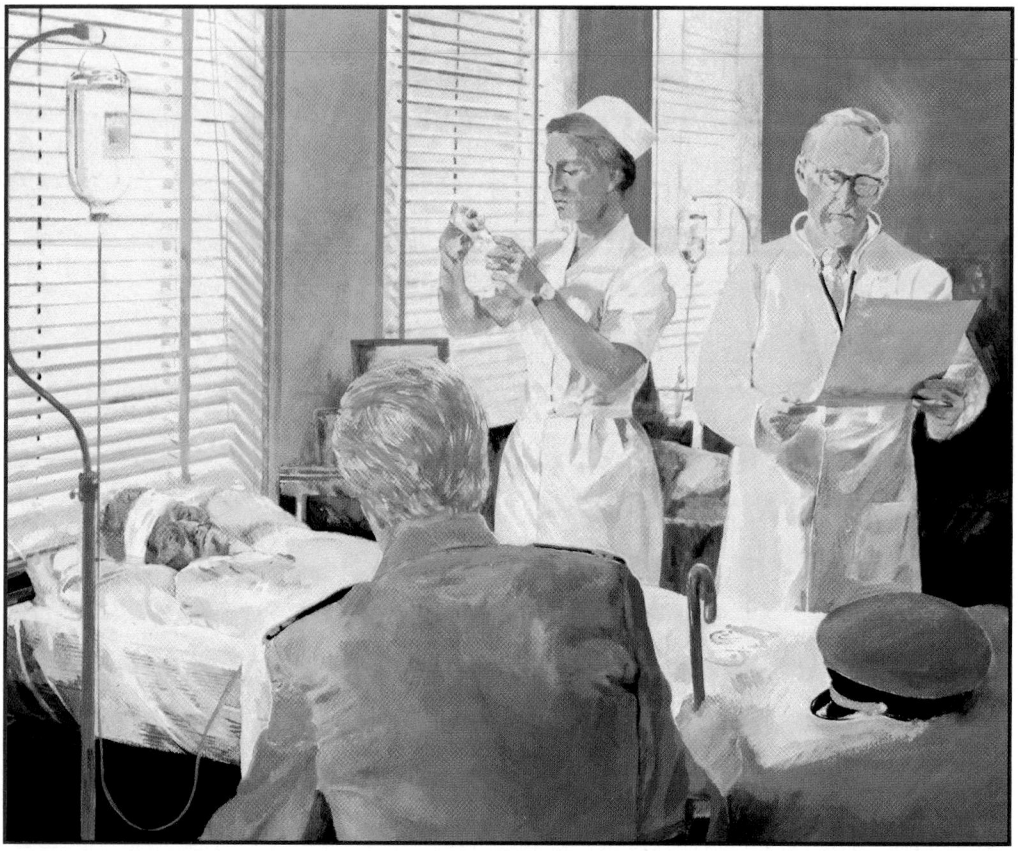

At the outbreak of World War II, Mr. Hubbard was commissioned as a lieutenant (junior grade) in the US Navy and served as a commander of corvettes. He saw action in both the Atlantic and Pacific, and thoroughly distinguished himself in the eyes of those who served beneath him. Yet he was not a man who enjoyed war, and having seen enough killing to last him a lifetime—and the effects of that bloodshed on men's sanity—he vowed to redouble his efforts to create a saner world. With this same sense of compassion, he also did all he could to safeguard his crews, prompting one of his men to write:

"I feel I owe you a tremendous debt of gratitude. First for your acquaintance. Secondly because you have portrayed to me all the attributes of a 'story book' naval officer. I can see for myself that you were an officer and a gentleman long before Congress decided so."

In 1945, left partially blind with injured optic nerves and lame from hip and back injuries, Mr. Hubbard was hospitalized at Oak Knoll Naval Hospital in Oakland, California. Among the 5,000 naval and Marine Corps patients at Oak Knoll were hundreds of former American prisoners liberated from Japanese camps on South Pacific islands. Many were in terrible condition from starvation and other causes, unable to assimilate protein.

In an attempt to resolve this problem, Navy physicians were administering testosterone, a male hormone. This medical treatment, however, was not getting effective results on all patients, and Mr. Hubbard utilized the opportunity to not only help his fellow servicemen, but to test a theory he had developed in application.

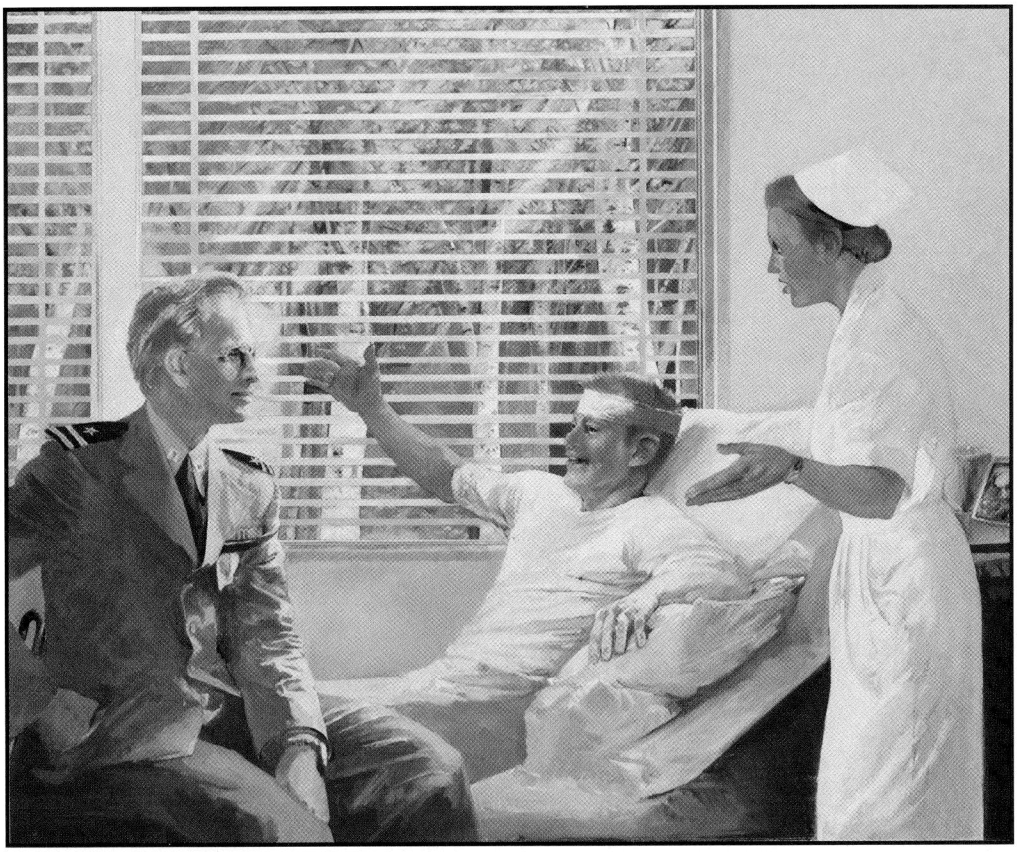

"All I was trying to establish," he wrote, "was whether or not the mind regulated the body or the body regulated the mind. Therefore, if on some of these patients hormones did not work and on some of them they did, there might be a mental reason. If those patients on whom it did not work had a severe mental block, then it was obvious that regardless of the amount of hormone or medical treatment the person received, he would not get well. If the mind were capable of putting this much restraint upon the physical body then obviously the fact that was commonly held to be true, that structure monitors function, would be false. I set out to prove this. . . . I was not interested in endocrinology but in resolving whether or not function monitored structure or structure monitored function."

In case after case, he found that by utilizing techniques he had developed, previously unresponsive patients immediately improved with medical treatment once the mental blocks were removed.

In fact, function did monitor structure. As Ron noted at the time, "Thought is boss."

This was a revolutionary concept, cutting across misconceptions which had plagued Eastern philosophy and science for centuries.

With peace restored at war's end, Mr. Hubbard immediately set out to further test the workability of his breakthroughs. This was intensive research. For subjects he selected people from all walks of life—in Hollywood, where he worked with actors and writers; in Savannah, Georgia, where he helped deeply disturbed inmates in a mental hospital; and in Washington, DC, New York City, New Jersey, Pasadena, Los Angeles and Seattle. In all, he personally helped over four hundred individuals before 1950, with spectacular results. And he used the same procedures to cure injuries and wounds he himself had received, fully recovering his health by 1949.

So complete was his recovery, that officers from the Naval Retiring Board reviewing Lt. Hubbard's case were actually upset. After all, they reasoned, how could a man physically shot to pieces at the end of the war pass his full physical examination? The only answer, they concluded, was that L. Ron Hubbard must be somebody else. And when they found that all was in order, they designated him fit for active duty.

Returning to Washington, DC, Ron compiled his sixteen years of investigation into the human condition, writing the manuscript "The Original Thesis" (today published under the title ***The Dynamics of Life****), a paper outlining the principles he was using. He did not offer it for publication. He gave a copy or two to some friends, and they promptly duplicated it and sent it to* ***their*** *friends who, in turn, made copies and sent it to others. In this way, passed hand to hand, Dianetics on its own became known the world over. Word spread that he had made a revolutionary breakthrough. L. Ron Hubbard had found the source of human aberration and had developed a technique of the mind that worked. Dianetics was born.*

The first published article on Dianetics, entitled "Terra Incognita: The Mind," appeared in the Winter/Spring 1949–1950 issue of the ***Explorers Club Journal.*** *Shortly thereafter, Ron found himself literally deluged with letters requesting more information on the application of his breakthroughs. Hoping to make his discoveries available to the broad public, and at the insistence of those working with him at the time, he offered his findings to the American Medical Association and the American Psychiatric Association. The response was most enlightening. Not only did the healthcare establishment claim no interest in his work, they declined to even examine his results.*

Thereupon a new lesson was learned.

A workable technology of the mind, that anyone could use to help himself and others, was totally at odds with the entrenched medical and psychiatric establishment. They preached that the mind was so complex it could only be understood by "experts" (themselves). They depended upon government appropriations and research grants and perceived Dianetics as a threat to these vested interests (ignoring the fact that Mr. Hubbard had always funded his own research). A technology that anyone could use posed a threat to their monopoly and their billions of dollars. They not only refused to accept Dianetics, they tried to suppress its use. If helping others was their sole purpose, certainly they would have embraced a new, completely proven technological breakthrough and assisted its release for the benefit of society. But they did not, and thus one can only conclude that their true motives were more sordid—the control of others toward their own interests, or, in one word, greed.

L. Ron Hubbard's friends and associates were aghast at the responses from the bastions of healing. On the one hand were hundreds of case histories with rave testimonials from those who had studied and used Dianetics and thousands of letters from people wanting to know more. On the other hand were the few "experts," who had resorted to 220 volts of electricity to cure problems of the mind, who had never studied the subject of Dianetics but nonetheless, didn't want it.

And so the decision was made. L. Ron Hubbard would go directly to the public with a handbook, detailing his discoveries and the techniques he had developed. Never before had there been such a text on the mind, a work expressly written for the man on the street.

The announcement was made, and all across the nation people eagerly anticipated its release.

"There is something new coming up in April called Dianetics," *wrote national columnist Walter Winchell on January 31, 1950.* ***"A new science which works with the invariability of physical science in the field of the human mind. From all indications, it will prove to be as revolutionary for humanity as the first caveman's discovery and utilization of fire."***

Winchell's prediction proved correct.

Dianetics: The Modern Science of Mental Health *was published on May 9, 1950. The response was instantaneous and overwhelming. Almost overnight the book became a nationwide bestseller, with 25,000 letters and telegrams of congratulation pouring in to the publisher. The book hit the* ***New York Times*** *bestseller list where it remained week after week, month after month, forever changing L. Ron Hubbard's life and, as we shall see, the lives of millions.*

A NEW ERA FOR MANKIND

The publication of *Dianetics* ushered in a new era of hope for mankind, and with it a new phase of L. Ron Hubbard's life. Although from this point forward, his life would prove just as adventurous as the previous 39 years, it is not the details that are most important, but the accomplishments which form the subject matter of this book.

The first indication that he was to be a public figure came immediately after the release of *Dianetics.* Although Ron had originally planned yet another expedition following the completion of *Dianetics,* so great was the popular response to his work that he had to change those plans. Thus, instead of exploring islands off Greece, he soon found himself lecturing on Dianetics to packed halls across the nation. It was also at this time that the first Hubbard Dianetics Research Foundation was formed in Elizabeth, New Jersey, and people began arriving in droves to study the new techniques and find out more about Dianetics.

By late fall of 1950, there were 750 groups across the country applying Dianetics techniques, while newspaper headlines proclaimed, "Dianetics Taking US by Storm," and "Fastest Growing Movement in America."

Ron's research continued, and in March 1951 he completed his next book, *Science of Survival.* In this 500-page work, he further explored the nature of thought and life, offering readers an understanding of, and a new means to predict human behavior. The book is oriented around a chart, the Hubbard Chart of Human Evaluation, which explains the various emotional tones of individuals, exactly delineated, and with the precise procedures to bring anyone to the highest level and thus ultimate survival.

In 1951 he wrote a total of six books, continuing to research and perfect the technologies of Dianetics with which he had resolved the problems of the human mind. But this still left many unanswered questions, questions which man had been pondering since the beginning of recorded history. "The further one investigated," he wrote, "the more one came to understand that here, in this creature *Homo sapiens,* were entirely too many unknowns."

And so, within a year and a half of the release of *Dianetics: The Modern Science of Mental Health,* L. Ron Hubbard had embarked upon another journey of discovery—entering the realm of the human spirit. This track of research, begun so many years earlier as a young man traveling the globe in search of answers to life itself, was to span the next three decades. And as breakthrough after breakthrough was codified, the philosophy of Scientology was born, giving man, for the first time, a route to higher levels of awareness, understanding and ability that anyone could travel.

Given the inherently religious nature of Mr. Hubbard's work through these years, it was only natural that those surrounding him would come to see themselves, not only as students of a new philosophy but also as students of a new religion. And so, in 1954, Scientologists in Los Angeles established the first Church of Scientology. L. Ron Hubbard founded the subject—early Scientologists began the Church.

As more and more people discovered Ron's breakthroughs, Scientology churches sprang up rapidly around the world. Meanwhile, through his writings and lectures, he continued to make his discoveries available to all those seeking answers.

In 1959, Mr. Hubbard and his family moved to England, where he purchased the Saint

Hill Manor in East Grinstead, Sussex. This was to be his home for the next seven years, and the worldwide headquarters of the Church of Scientology.

There, in addition to his constant writing and lecturing, he began intensively training Scientologists from around the world so that they, in turn, might return to their homelands and teach others. The mid-1960s saw him develop a step by step route for anyone to reach states of higher awareness. He also codified administrative principles for the operation of Scientology organizations—work which brought about the expansion of Scientology into a global network.

On September 1, 1966, with Scientology established as a worldwide religion, Mr. Hubbard resigned his position as Executive Director of the Church and stepped down from the boards of all Church corporations in order to fully devote himself to researches into the highest levels of spiritual awareness and ability. On the threshold of breakthroughs that had never before been envisaged, he returned to the sea, in part to continue his work in an undistracted environment.

On board ship for the next seven years, he again traveled extensively, while devoting his attention to ever-worsening problems facing society through the late 1960s and early 1970s. Of special note from this period is the drug rehabilitation program he developed, recognized today by government studies around the world as the most effective in existence. It was also during this period that he developed the highest levels of Scientology, refinements of application, new administrative principles, and advances in the field of logic—all of which are explained later in this book.

Returning to shore in 1975, Ron continued his travels—first from Florida to Washington, DC and Los Angeles before finally settling in the southern California desert community of La Quinta near Palm Springs, his home until 1979. There, searching for new ways to make Dianetics and Scientology more easily accessible, he wrote dozens of training films on the subjects to visually demonstrate proper application of technical principles. He directed many of these films himself.

Long concerned with accelerating social decay, Mr. Hubbard wrote a nonreligious moral code based on common sense in 1980. Published in booklet form, it is entitled *The Way to Happiness.* In explanation of this work, L. Ron Hubbard said, "Reading the papers and wandering around in the society, it was pretty obvious that honesty and truth were not being held up to the standards they once had. People and even little kids in schools have gotten the idea that high moral standards are a thing of the past. Man has in his hands today a lot of violent weapons. He doesn't have the moral standards to go with them."

Loudly applauded by community and civic groups around the world, *The Way to Happiness* spread across the planet. An entire grassroots movement formed to disseminate and use the booklet to uplift the decency and integrity of man. To date, 35 million copies have been distributed with millions more being demanded each year.

In 1980, he celebrated his 50th anniversary as a professional writer by again turning his prodigious energy to the field of fiction. He wrote *Battlefield Earth: A Saga of the Year 3,000,* an epic science fiction novel, followed by the ten-volume *Mission Earth* opus, a satirical romp through the foibles of our civilization. All eleven books went on to become *New York Times* and international bestsellers, a consecutive bestseller record unmatched by any writer in history.

Returning to his more serious work with continued research into man's spiritual potentials, Mr. Hubbard traveled extensively through California in the early 1980s. In 1983, he finally resided in the town of Creston, near San Luis Obispo. Here he completed his research and finalized the Scientology technical materials he had spent most of his life developing.

Today, those materials are recorded in the tens of millions of words on the subject of the human spirit which comprise Dianetics and Scientology philosophy. The over 25 million words of his lectures—just those that are on tape—are enough to fill over 100 volumes of text.

In fact, it may well be that L. Ron Hubbard's works include more literature, recorded research and materials than any other single subject of philosophy, the spirit or religion. All of these materials are available to anyone who desires an improvement in his life. Well over 100 million of his books are in circulation today.

Having fully completed his research and seen its broad application expand to six continents and over 60 countries around the world, improving the lives of millions of people, L. Ron Hubbard departed this life on January 24, 1986. Instead of an end, however, it marked the beginning of an unprecedented expansion of Scientology around the world, as more and more people continue to benefit from his technologies.

As just one indication of Mr. Hubbard's continued popularity, fully 38 years after its initial publication, *Dianetics: The Modern Science of Mental Health* achieved the unheard of, returning to the top of the *New York Times* bestseller list in 1988. It still rides on bestseller lists around the world to this day and has thus far sold 15 million copies.

No less dramatic was the popular acceptance of Mr. Hubbard's other discoveries. To date, for example, more than 100,000 people have been freed from drugs, utilizing his rehabilitation methods, in centers across the globe, including the world's largest drug rehabilitation and training facility in Oklahoma.

For many more throughout the world—two million in South Africa alone—the name L. Ron Hubbard means literacy and an ability to learn any subject, thanks to his developments in the field of study.

Mr. Hubbard's breakthroughs in administration have enabled thousands of professionals in industry, business and community affairs to bring sanity and stability to their workplaces and their groups.

Thousands of people each year discover Dianetics and Scientology in L. Ron Hubbard's books. They are available in over 30 languages and in bookstores around the world. Each individual book in this photograph is a separate work of Mr. Hubbard's, including 3 encyclopedic series: 18 volumes of his technical writings, 100 volumes of transcripts of his public lectures, and a 12-volume set of his administrative works.

KNOWINGNESS
L. RON HUBBARD
TECHNICAL BULLETINS
The Hope of Man
L. Ron Hubbard
THE HUBBARD LIFE ORIENTATION COURSE
The International #1 Self-Help Bestseller
DIANETICS
The Modern Science of Mental Health
L. RON HUBBARD
L. RON HUBBARD
FUNDAMENTALS OF THOUGHT
HAPPINESS
14. BE WORTHY OF TRUST
The Goal of Man
#1 Bestselling Self Help Author
L. RON HUBBARD
CLEAR BODY
CLEAR MIND

Every day, Mr. Hubbard's discoveries on the subject of ethics help bring new order into people's lives, into their families, their communities and their environment. A long-confused subject, it has been endowed with new clarity and workability.

The accolades for his work would alone fill a volume, awards recognizing his literary works, his humanitarian contributions, his discoveries including Dianetics. In 1988, *Publishers Weekly,* the prestigious journal of the book and publishing industry, bestowed on Mr. Hubbard their Century Award in recognition of *Dianetics* being on its bestseller list for over 100 weeks. No wonder *Magazine and Bookseller,* a leading publication of the US book trade wrote, "*Dianetics* by L. Ron Hubbard seems to go on and on."

But the greatest reward, particularly in Mr. Hubbard's mind, were the lives he was able to touch through Dianetics and Scientology. Today, millions of people are using his principles and are finding they work. And through this application, L. Ron Hubbard's dream, a dream that perhaps summarizes the hopes of thinking men throughout the ages—"a civilization without insanity, without criminals and without war, where the able can prosper and honest beings can have rights, and where man is free to rise to greater heights"—is not only possible but attainable.

What you are about to read in this book will provide a firm appreciation of L. Ron Hubbard's contributions to mankind, and everything contained in these pages derives from his work. Although one can enjoy the benefits of Scientology without fully knowing Mr. Hubbard, one cannot understand the man without understanding Scientology—for it is his work and his work alone.

Every few hundred or a thousand years, some genius rises and man takes a new step toward a better life, a better culture. Such a man is L. Ron Hubbard, the Founder of Scientology.

L. Ron Hubbard's many accomplishments have earned him thousands of acknowledgments and recognitions from around the world, a few of which are pictured here.

PERSONAL INTEGRITY BY L. RON HUBBARD

WHAT IS TRUE FOR YOU is what you have observed
yourself
And when you lose that you have lost
everything.

What is personal integrity?
Personal integrity is knowing what you know—
What you know is what you know—
And to have the courage to know and say what you have observed.
And that is integrity
And there is no other integrity.

Of course we can talk about honor, truth, all these things,
These esoteric terms.
But I think they'd all be covered very well
If what we really observed was what we observed,
That we took care to observe what we were observing,
That we always observed to observe.

And not necessarily maintaining a skeptical attitude,
A critical attitude, or an open mind.
But certainly maintaining sufficient personal integrity
And sufficient personal belief and confidence in self
And courage that we can observe what we observe
And say what we have observed.

Nothing in Dianetics and Scientology is true for you
Unless you have observed it
And it is true according to your observation.
That is all.

Part Two

Scientology Principles and Application

The full story of the development and codification of Scientology can be found in scores of books, more than 15,000 pages of technical writing and more than 3,000 taped lectures. All told, these works represent a lifetime of research by L. Ron Hubbard to discover a workable means to set men spiritually free—to replace ignorance with knowledge, doubts with certainty and misery with happiness.

Today, the fruits of L. Ron Hubbard's work are available to anyone who wishes to reach for them. And no matter how different Scientologists may be—whether teachers and businessmen, housewives and athletes, artists and secretaries—they hold one vital factor in common: having significantly bettered their lives, they know that Scientology works.

Nothing in Scientology, however, need be taken on faith. Its truths are self-evident, its principles are easily demonstrable and its technology can be seen at work in any church of Scientology. One need only open the door and step through.

Chapter 4

A Description of Scientology

Scientology: *Scio* (Latin), know, *logos* (Greek), the word or outward form by which the inward thought is expressed and made known. Thus, Scientology means knowing about knowing.

Scientology is a twentieth-century religion. It comprises a vast body of knowledge extending from certain fundamental truths, and prime among those truths: Man is a spiritual being endowed with abilities well beyond those which he normally envisages. He is not only able to solve his own problems, accomplish his goals and gain lasting happiness, but also to achieve new states of awareness he may never have dreamed possible.

In one form or another, all great religions have held the hope of spiritual freedom—a condition free of material limitations and misery. The question has always been, however, how does one reach such a state, particularly while still living amidst a frantic and often overwhelming society?

Although modern life seems to pose an infinitely complex array of problems, Scientology maintains that the solutions to those problems are basically simple and within every man's reach. Difficulties with communication and interpersonal relationships, nagging insecurities, self-doubt and despair—each man innately possesses the potential to be free of these and many other concerns.

Scientology offers a pathway to greater freedom. While the *hope* for such freedom is ancient, what Scientology is *doing* is new. The way it is organized is *new.* The technologies with which it can bring about a new state of being in man are likewise *new.*

Because Scientology addresses man as a spiritual being, it stands completely apart from other philosophies which see man as a product of his environment or his genes—fixed in the limitations under which he was born.

Rather, Scientology is the *study and handling of the spirit in relationship to itself, universes and other life.* Based upon the tradition of fifty thousand years of thinking men, it is built upon the fundamental truths of life. From these principles, exact methods by which one can improve conditions were derived; and unlike other efforts of improvement, which offered only rules by which men should live, Scientology offers real tools for use in everyday life. Thus, it does not depend upon a system of beliefs or faith. The emphasis is squarely on an exact *application* of its principles toward the improvement of one's life and the world in which we live.

To understand exactly how Scientology is utilized, something should be known of the track of research L. Ron Hubbard traveled and the antecedent of Scientology—Dianetics.

Dianetics: Understanding the Mind

Dianetics: *Dia* (Greek) through, *nous* (Greek) soul.

Prior to 1950, prevailing scientific thought had concluded man's mind to be his brain, i.e., a collection of cells and neurons, and nothing more. Not only was man's IQ considered to be unimprovable, but with the formation of his cerebral cortex, his personality was likewise established. These theories were, however, inaccurate and consequently science has never evolved a workable theory of the mind nor a means to resolve problems of the mind.

L. Ron Hubbard changed all that with *Dianetics: The Modern Science of Mental Health.* Its publication in 1950 marks a watershed in the history of man's quest for a true understanding of himself.

Dianetics is a methodology which can help alleviate such ailments as unwanted sensations and emotions, irrational fears and psychosomatic illnesses (illnesses caused or aggravated by mental stress). It is most accurately described as *what the soul is doing to the body through the mind.*

Like Scientology, Dianetics rests on basic principles, easily learned, clearly demonstrated as true, and every bit as valid today as when first released in 1950.

The Goal of Life

The concise statement of the goal of life itself was one of the most fundamental breakthroughs of Dianetics. This, the dynamic principle of man's existence, was discovered by L. Ron Hubbard and from this many hitherto unanswered questions were resolved.

The goal of life can be considered to be *infinite survival.* That man seeks to survive has long been known, but that it is his primary motivation is new. Man, as a life form, can be demonstrated to obey in all his actions and purposes the one command: "SURVIVE!"

This is the common denominator of all life, and from it came the critical resolution of man's ills and aberrations.

Once "Survive!" was isolated as the primary urge which explained all of a life form's activities, it was necessary to study further the action of survival. And from that research it was discovered that when one considered pain and pleasure as part of the equation, he had at hand the necessary ingredients with which to understand all of life's actions.

Survival is not only the difference between life and death. There are various levels of survival.

The better one is able to manage his life and increase his level of survival, the more he will have pleasure, abundance and satisfaction.

Pain, disappointment and failure are the result of actions which do not promote survival.

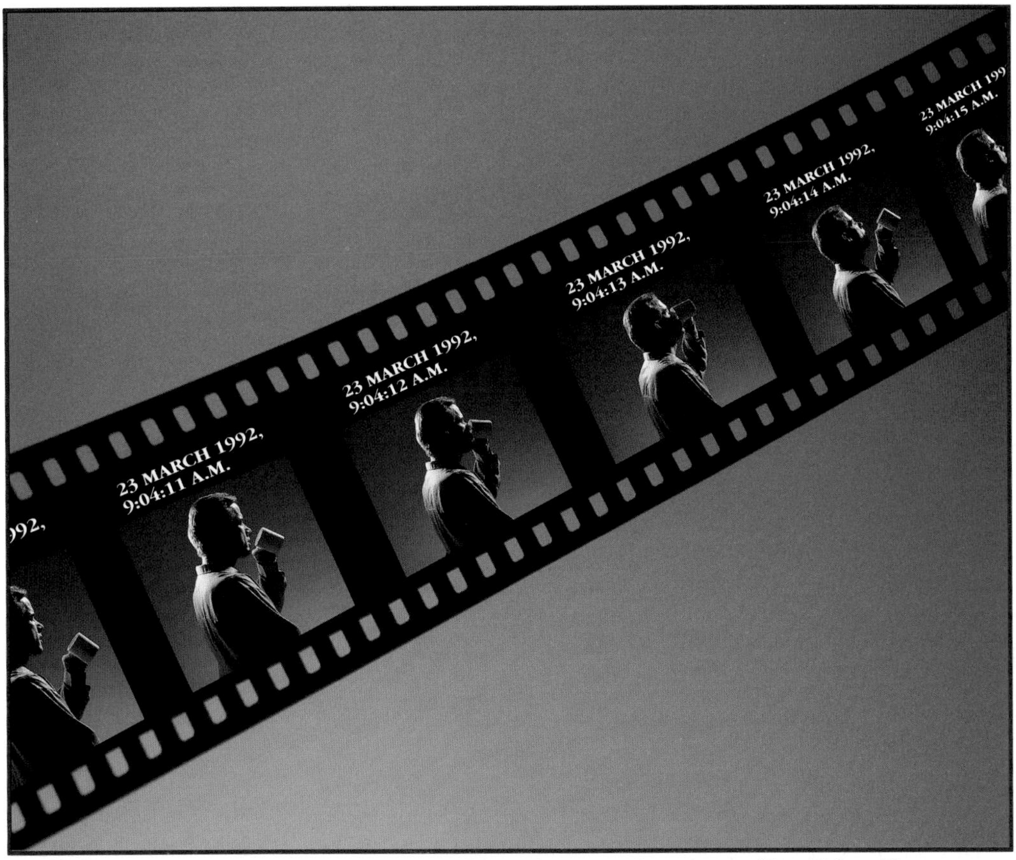

As a rough analogy, the time track could be likened to a motion-picture film, if that film were three-dimensional, had fifty-two perceptions and could fully react upon the observer.

SURVIVAL AND THE MIND

Dianetics states that the purpose of the mind is to solve problems relating to survival.

The mind directs the individual in the effort of survival and bases its operations upon the information that it receives or records. The mind records data using what are called *mental image pictures.*

Such pictures are actually three-dimensional, containing color, sound and smell, as well as other perceptions. They also include the conclusions or speculations of the individual. Mental image pictures are continuously made by the mind, moment by moment. You can, for instance, examine the picture of what you had for breakfast this morning by recalling breakfast; and similarly recover a picture of an event which occurred last week by recalling it; or even recall something which happened a much longer time ago.

Mental image pictures are actually composed of energy. They have mass, they exist in space, and they follow some very, very definite routines of behavior, the most interesting of which is the fact that they appear when somebody thinks of something. If you think of a certain dog, you get a picture of that dog.

Mental image pictures are recorded in the analytical mind.

But those mental image pictures containing physical pain and painful emotion are recorded in the reactive mind.

The consecutive record of mental image pictures which accumulates through a person's life is called the *time track.* The time track is a very accurate record of a person's past. As a rough analogy, the time track could be likened to a motion-picture film—if that film were three-dimensional, had fifty-two perceptions and could fully react upon the observer.

The mind uses these pictures to make decisions that promote survival. The mind's basic motivation, even though a person might fail in an undertaking or make a mistake, is *always* survival.

That being the case, why don't all of the actions dictated by the mind result in enhanced survival? Why do people sometimes experience irrational fears, doubt their own abilities or entertain negative emotions which seem uncalled for by circumstances?

The Parts of the Mind

L. Ron Hubbard discovered that the mind has two very distinct parts. One of these—that part which one consciously uses and is aware of—is called the *analytical mind.* This is the portion of the mind which thinks, observes data, remembers it and resolves problems. It has standard memory banks which contain mental image pictures, and uses the data in these banks to make decisions that promote survival.

However, two things appear to be—but are not—recorded in the standard banks: painful emotion and physical pain. In moments of intense pain, the action of the analytical mind is suspended and the second part of the mind, the *reactive mind,* takes over.

When a person is fully conscious, his analytical mind is fully in command. When the individual is "unconscious" in full or in part, the reactive mind cuts in, in full or in part. "Unconsciousness" could be caused by the shock of an accident, anesthetic used for an operation, the pain of an injury or the deliriums of illness.

When a person is "unconscious," the reactive mind exactly records all the perceptions of that incident, including what happens or is said around the person. It also records all pain and stores this mental image picture in its *own* banks, unavailable to the individual's conscious recall and not under his direct control. Though it may appear that a person knocked out in an accident is unconscious and unaware of happenings around him, his reactive mind is actually industriously recording everything for future use.

The reactive mind does not store memories as we know them. It stores particular types of mental image pictures called *engrams.* These engrams are a complete recording, down to the last accurate detail, of every perception present in a moment of partial or full "unconsciousness."

This is an example of an engram: A woman is knocked down by a blow to the face. She is rendered "unconscious." She is kicked in the side and told she is a faker, that she is no good, that she is always changing her mind. A chair is overturned in the process. A faucet is running in the kitchen. A car is passing in the street outside.

The engram contains a running record of all these perceptions.

The problem with the reactive mind is that it "thinks" in *identities,* one thing *identical* to another. The equation is A=A=A=A=A. A reactive mind computation about this engram would be: the pain of the kick *equals* the pain of the blow *equals* the overturning chair *equals* the passing car *equals* the faucet *equals* the fact that she is a faker *equals* the fact that she is no good *equals* the fact that she changes her mind *equals* the voice tones of the man who hit her *equals* the emotion *equals* a faker *equals* a faucet running *equals* the pain of the kick *equals* organic sensation in the area of the kick *equals* the overturning chair *equals* changing one's mind *equals* . . . But why continue? Every single perception in this engram *equals* every other perception in this engram.

In the future, when this woman's present environment contains enough similarities to the elements found in the engram, she will experience a reactivation of the engram. For example, if one evening the faucet were running and she heard the sound of a car passing outside and, at the same time her husband (the man in her engram) was scolding her about something in a similar tone of voice as used in the original engram, she could experience a pain in the side (where she was kicked earlier). And the words spoken in the engram could also become *commands* in the present: She might feel that she was no good, or get the idea that she was always changing her mind. The reactive mind is telling the woman that she is in dangerous quarters. If she stays, the pain in the areas where she was abused could become a predisposition to illness or a chronic illness in themselves. This phenomenon of "awakening" the old engram is called *restimulation.*

The reactive mind can cause unknowing and unwanted fears, emotions, pains and psychosomatic illnesses that one would be much better off without.

Dianetics can effectively "erase" the contents of the reactive mind and free a person from its adverse influence.

The reactive mind is not an aid to a person's survival for the excellent reason that though it is sturdy enough to hold up during pain and "unconsciousness," it is not very intelligent. Its attempts to "prevent a person from getting himself into danger," by enforcing its engram content, can cause unevaluated, unknowing and unwanted fears, emotions, pains and psychosomatic illnesses that one would be much better off without.

THE SOLUTION TO THE REACTIVE MIND

Having discovered the existence of the reactive mind and its engrams, L. Ron Hubbard developed very precise techniques to address it. These techniques can effectively "erase" the contents of the reactive mind and eliminate the ability of such recordings to affect the person without his conscious knowledge. Furthermore, it makes these formerly hidden memories available to the individual as memory in the analytical mind. The effectiveness of these techniques, astonishing in many cases, has been documented in a multitude of case histories over nearly a half-century of application.

THE CLEAR

The goal of Dianetics is a new state for the individual, sought throughout history but never attainable before Dianetics. This state is called "Clear." A Clear is a person who no longer has his own reactive mind and therefore suffers none of the ill effects that the reactive mind can cause.

The Clear has no engrams which, when restimulated, throw out the correctness of his computations by entering hidden and false data.

A person who no longer has his own reactive mind is called a Clear. What he is left with is all that is really him.

Becoming Clear strengthens a person's native individuality and creativity and does not in any way diminish these attributes. A Clear is free with his emotions. He can think for himself. He can experience life unencumbered by inhibitions reactively dictated by past engrams. Artistry, personal force and individual character are all residual in the basic personality of the person, not the reactive mind.

Clears are self-confident, happy and generally successful—in both careers and interpersonal relationships. It is a highly desirable state for any individual and is attainable by virtually anyone. In fact, thousands upon thousands of people have achieved the state of Clear, a living tribute to the workability of L. Ron Hubbard's discoveries and the technology he developed.

THE ATTRIBUTES OF CLEAR

Clear is a state that has never before been attainable in man's history. A Clear possesses attributes, fundamental and inherent but not always available in an uncleared state, which have not been suspected of man and are not included in past discussions of his abilities and behavior. The Clear is:

- *Freed from active or potential psychosomatic illness or aberration*
- *Self-determined*
- *Vigorous and persistent*
- *Unrepressed*
- *Able to perceive, recall, imagine, create and compute at a level high above the norm*
- *Stable mentally*
- *Free with his emotion*
- *Able to enjoy life*
- *Freer from accidents*
- *Healthier*
- *Able to reason swiftly*
- *Able to react quickly*

Happiness is important. The ability to arrange life and the environment so that living can be better enjoyed, the ability to tolerate the foibles of one's fellow humans, the ability to see the true factors in a situation and resolve problems of living with accuracy, the ability to accept and execute responsibility, these things are important. Life is not much worth living if it cannot be enjoyed. The Clear enjoys living to a very full extent. He can stand up to situations which, before he was cleared, would have reduced him to a shambles. The ability to live well and fully and enjoy that living is the gift of Clear.

Scientology: A Knowledge of Life

For all that Dianetics resolved in the field of human behavior and the mind, there still remained one outstanding question. When someone was looking at a mental image picture, *who* was looking at that picture?

The breakthrough came in the autumn of 1951, after Mr. Hubbard observed many, many people using Dianetics and found a commonality of experience and phenomena. After carefully reviewing all relevant research data, Mr. Hubbard isolated the answer: Man was neither his body nor his mind, but a spiritual being. This was the source of all that is good, decent and creative in the world: the individual being himself. With this discovery, L. Ron Hubbard founded the religion of Scientology, for he had moved firmly into the field traditionally belonging to religion—the realm of the human soul.

The term *soul,* however, had developed so many other meanings from use in other religions and practices that a new term was needed to connote precisely what had been discovered. The term Mr. Hubbard chose was *thetan,* from the Greek letter *theta,* θ, the traditional symbol for thought or life.

A thetan is the person himself, not his body or his name or the physical universe, his mind or anything else. It is that which is aware of being aware; the identity which IS the individual. One does not *have* a thetan, something one keeps somewhere apart from oneself; he *is* a thetan.

Very pertinent to Mr. Hubbard's research at this juncture was his examination into the phenomena known as exteriorization. Although various religious texts make mention of it, no one had ever considered the matter with such careful scrutiny. From this research, Mr. Hubbard concluded that the thetan is able to leave the body and exist independent of the flesh. Exteriorized, the person can see without the body's eyes, hear without the body's ears and feel without the body's hands. Man previously had very little understanding of this detachment from his mind and body. With the act of exteriorization attainable in Scientology a person gains the certainty he is himself and not his body.

The Parts of Man

From this discovery, Mr. Hubbard went on to precisely delineate the parts of man.

First there is the body itself. The body is the organized physical composition or substance of man, whether living or dead. It is not the being himself.

Next, there is the mind, which consists essentially of pictures.

Finally, and most important, there is the thetan. The thetan is not a thing. It is *the creator of things.*

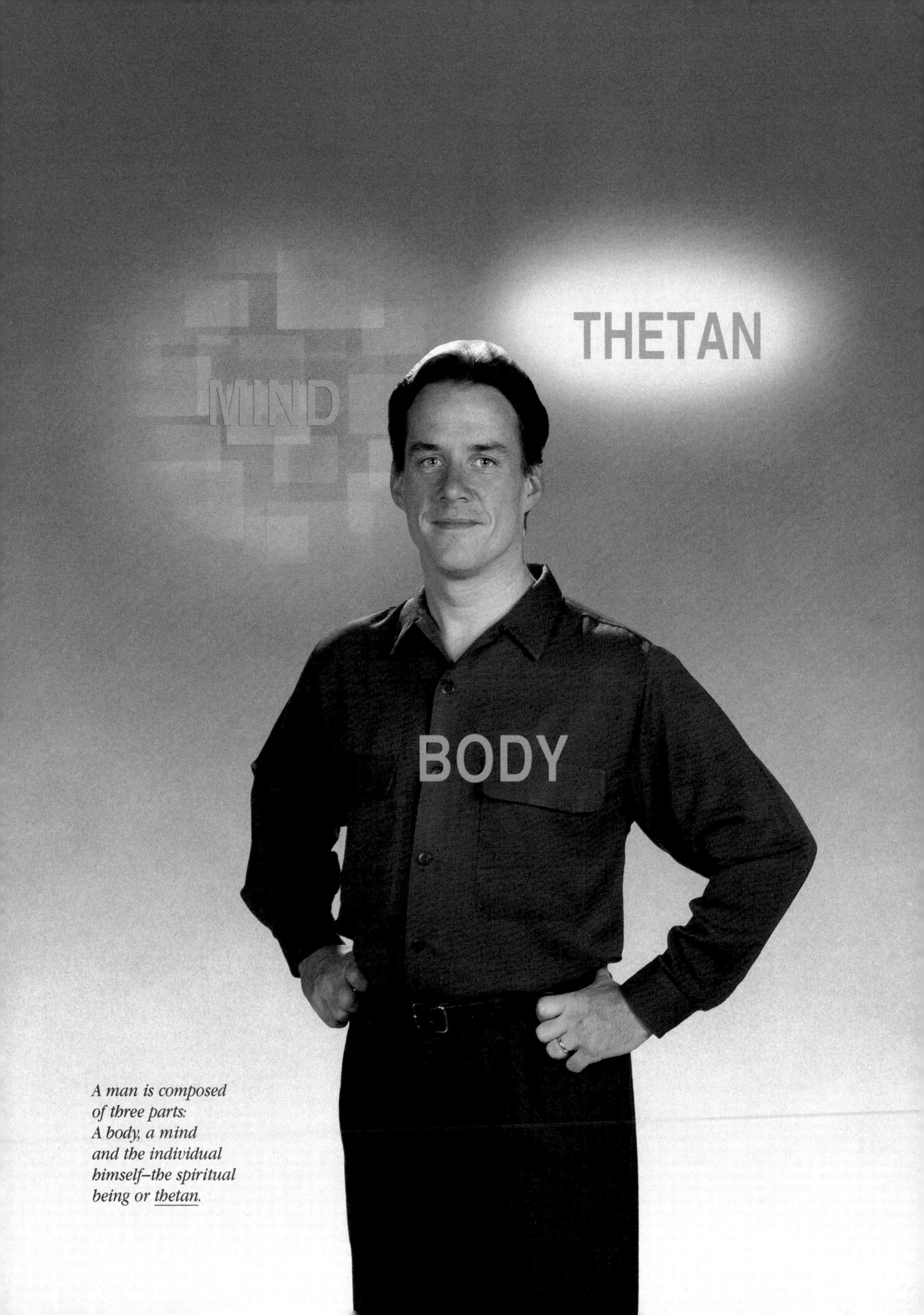

A man is composed of three parts: A body, a mind and the individual himself–the spiritual being or thetan.

The thetan is the identity which IS the individual; it is not the body. In Scientology, it has been found that a thetan can leave the body and exist independent of the flesh. This phenomenon is called exteriorization. After exteriorization, a person gains certainty he is himself and not his body.

The seniormost of the three parts of man, obviously, is the thetan, for without the thetan there would be no mind or animation of the body, while without a body or a mind there is still animation and life in the thetan.

The thetan utilizes his mind as a control system between himself and the physical universe. The mind is not the brain. The brain is part of the body and does not determine intelligence. It can be likened to a switchboard. If one said that a telephone switchboard was the intelligence of the corporation it served, this would be like saying the brain was the intelligence of the person. It is just not true. The brain is simply a conduit that, like a telephone wire, carries messages. The mind accumulates recordings of thoughts, conclusions, decisions, observations and perceptions of a thetan throughout his existence. The thetan uses his mind in the handling of life and the physical universe. The body (including the brain) is the thetan's communication center. It is a physical object, not the being himself.

The thetan is the source of all creation and *is* life itself. It becomes fully apparent for the first time in man's experience that the spirit is immortal and possessed of capabilities well in excess of those hitherto predicted. The exteriorization of the thetan from his body accomplishes the realization of goals envisioned—but questionably, if ever, obtained—in spiritualism, mysticism and such fields.

Recognition of the thetan makes possible gains in ability and awareness—improvements which are not attainable in any practice holding man to be only a body and thus entirely subject to physical universe limitations. Psychology, for instance, had worked itself into a dead end. Having no concept of the existence of an animating factor to life, it had degenerated into a practice devoted solely to the creation of an effect on living forms.

In Scientology, however, the thetan himself is directly addressed. Such an approach to improvement accomplishes increased spiritual freedom, intelligence and ability for the individual, and clarifies any part of life.

The basic command "Survive," obeyed by all life, is subdivided into eight compartments called the eight dynamics.

The Eight Dynamics

Because the fundamentals upon which Scientology rests embrace all aspects of life, certain key principles can be broadly employed to better any condition. Scientologists use these principles in their daily lives, and their use alone can often make the difference between success and failure. Moreover, the principles greatly clarify what is so often confusing and bewildering.

Suppose, for example, life could be correctly compartmentalized so that its many activities, often confused and blurred, could suddenly assume a new clarity. Suppose, for instance, that all the activities in one's varied life could not only be understood for what they really are, but harmonized with all others.

This is possible in Scientology through delineation of the eight dynamics.

The basic command "Survive!" obeyed by all of life is subdivided into eight compartments so that each aspect of life can be more easily inspected and understood. These eight compartments are called the eight *dynamics* (*dynamic* meaning urge, drive or impulse). L. Ron Hubbard had observed and delineated the first four of these dynamics in Dianetics. When his research led him into the realm of Scientology, he was able to amplify these first four and delineate the remaining four dynamics.

Through Scientology, a person realizes that his life and influence extend far beyond himself. He becomes aware also of the necessity to participate in a much broader spectrum. By understanding each of these dynamics and their relationship, one to the other, he is able to do so: and thus increase survival on all these dynamics.

*The **first dynamic** is SELF. This is the effort to survive as an individual, to be an individual. It includes one's own body and one's own mind. It is the effort to attain the highest level of survival for the longest possible time for self. This dynamic includes the individual plus his immediate possessions. It does not include other people. It is the urge to survive as one's self. Here we have individuality expressed fully.*

*The **second dynamic** is CREATIVITY. Creativity is making things for the future and the second dynamic includes any creativity. The second dynamic contains the family unit and the rearing of children as well as anything that can be categorized as a family activity. It also incidentally includes sex as a mechanism to compel future survival.*

*The **third dynamic** is GROUP SURVIVAL. This is the urge to survive through a group of individuals or as a group. It is group survival, the group tending to take on a life and existence of its own. A group can be a community, friends, a company, a social lodge, a state, a nation, a race or in short, any group. It doesn't matter what size this group is, it is seeking to survive as a group.*

*The **fourth dynamic** is SPECIES. Man's fourth dynamic is the species of mankind. This is the urge toward survival through all mankind and as all mankind. Whereas the American nationality would be considered a third dynamic for Americans, all the nationalities of the world together would be considered the fourth dynamic. All men and women because they are men and women seek to survive as men and women and for men and women.*

*The **fifth dynamic** is LIFE FORMS. This is the urge to survive as life forms and with the help of life forms such as animals, birds, insects, fish and vegetation. This includes all living things whether animal or vegetable, anything directly and intimately motivated by life. It is the effort to survive for any and every form of life. It is the interest in life as such.*

*The **sixth dynamic** is the PHYSICAL UNIVERSE. The physical universe has four components. These are matter, energy, space and time. The sixth dynamic is the urge to survive of the physical universe, by the physical universe itself and with the help of the physical universe and each one of its component parts.*

*The **seventh dynamic** is the SPIRITUAL DYNAMIC, the urge to survive as spiritual beings or the urge for life itself to survive. Anything spiritual, with or without identity, would come under the heading of the seventh dynamic. It includes one's beingness, the ability to create, the ability to cause survival or to survive, the ability to destroy or pretend to be destroyed. A subheading of this dynamic is ideas and concepts and the desire to survive through these. The seventh dynamic is life source. This is separate from the physical universe and is the source of life itself. Thus there is an effort for the survival of life source.*

*The **eighth dynamic** is the urge toward existence as INFINITY. The eighth dynamic is commonly supposed to be a Supreme Being or Creator. It is correctly defined as infinity. It actually embraces the allness of all.*

Simply delineating these dynamics clarifies and brings order into existence. One can observe these dynamics in one's own life, note which one or ones need improvement and, through Scientology, bring these factors into greater harmony.

THE TONE SCALE

Another tool drawn from the body of Scientology and commonly used in everyday life is the Tone Scale. Codified from many, many hours of exhaustive testing and observation, the Tone Scale plots emotions in an exact ascending or descending sequence. Until Mr. Hubbard's examination of this matter, emotions were something we all suffered or enjoyed, but never fully understood.

Have you ever attempted to raise the spirits of someone mourning a recent loss with a cheerful word? The response is usually a fresh outpouring of tears.

Or someone whose outlook and response to life is a chronic apathy, no matter what is happening around him? The person seems to be in good health, has a loving family and an enviable job, but nothing makes any difference. The person just isn't interested.

The Tone Scale precisely illuminates what is occurring with individuals such as these, how best to communicate with them and how to help them.

One can find himself or any individual on this Tone Scale and thus know how, using Scientology, he may best be moved up to the higher tones where increased beingness, competence, self-esteem, honesty, well-being, happiness and other desirable attributes are manifested.

These emotional levels are thoroughly detailed in Scientology, but this simplified version will serve to show different emotions and their relative positions on the scale:

40.0 Serenity of Beingness
30.0 Postulates
22.0 Games
20.0 Action
8.0 Exhilaration
6.0 Aesthetic
4.0 Enthusiasm
3.5 Cheerfulness
3.3 Strong Interest
3.0 Conservatism
2.9 Mild Interest
2.8 Contented
2.6 Disinterested
2.5 Boredom
2.4 Monotony
2.0 Antagonism
1.9 Hostility
1.8 Pain
1.5 Anger
1.4 Hate
1.3 Resentment
1.2 No Sympathy
1.15 Unexpressed Resentment
1.1 Covert Hostility
1.02 Anxiety
1.0 Fear
0.98 Despair
0.96 Terror
0.94 Numb
0.9 Sympathy
0.8 Propitiation
0.5 Grief
0.375 Making Amends
0.3 Undeserving
0.2 Self-Abasement
0.1 Victim
0.07 Hopeless
0.05 Apathy
0.03 Useless
0.01 Dying
0.0 Body Death

4.0
Enthusiasm

3.0
Conservatism

2.5
Boredom

2.0
Antagonism

1.5
Anger

1.1
Covert
Hostility

1.0
Fear

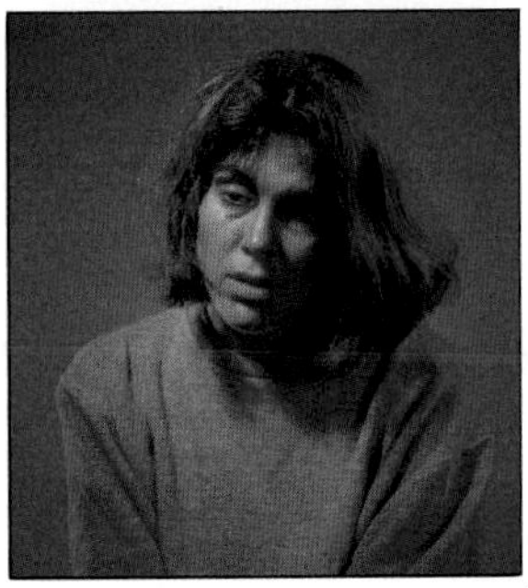

0.5
Grief

0.05
Apathy

An abbreviated version of the Tone Scale, which plots emotions in an exact sequence. Through knowledge of the scale, one can understand and predict the actions of others.

From knowledge of a man's level on the scale, much can be determined about his attitudes, behavior and survival potential.

When a man is nearly dead, he can be said to be in chronic *apathy.* And he behaves in certain specific ways. This is 0.05 on the Tone Scale chart.

When a man is chronically sad about his losses, he is in grief. And, once again, behaves in a predictable manner. This is 0.5 on the chart.

When a person is not yet so low as grief but realizes losses are impending, or is fixed chronically at this level by past losses, he is in *fear,* around 1.0 on the chart.

Just above fear, past or impending losses generate hatred in the person. However, he dare not express this as such, so the hatred comes forth covertly. This is 1.1, *covert hostility.*

An individual fighting against threatened losses is in *anger* and manifests predictable aspects of behavior. This is 1.5.

The person who is merely suspicious that loss may take place, or who has become fixed at this level, is resentful. He is in *antagonism,* which is 2.0 on the chart.

Above antagonism, the situation of a person is not good enough for him to be enthusiastic, not bad enough for him to be resentful. He has lost some goals and cannot immediately locate others. He is said to be in *boredom,* or at 2.5 on the Tone Scale chart.

At 3.0 on the chart, a person has a *conservative,* cautious aspect toward life, but is reaching his goals.

At 4.0 the individual is *enthusiastic,* happy and vital.

Very few people are naturally at 4.0 on the Tone Scale. A charitable average is probably around 2.8.

This scale has a chronic or an acute aspect. A person can be brought down the Tone Scale to a low level for ten minutes and then go back up, or he can be brought down for ten years and not go back up.

A man who has suffered too many losses, too much pain, tends to become fixed at some lower level of the scale and, with only slight fluctuations, stays there. Then his general and common behavior will be at that level of the Tone Scale.

The simplest thing to know about this scale is that people find it difficult to respond to communication which is too far above where they are stuck. If you try to help someone in *apathy* by talking to them in *enthusiasm,* you will probably not have much success. The gap between such extremes is not easily bridged unless you understand the Tone Scale.

Using knowledge of the Tone Scale, however, you would recognize the emotion one-half to one full tone above the person, communicate in that tone and thus bring him up to higher tones. By moving up the scale gradiently it is possible to help someone overcome fixed conditions and regain a more happy and vital outlook.

The Tone Scale is of enormous value in life and its relationships. Mr. Hubbard thoroughly researched human behavior and the full body of his work in this area furnishes an accurate description of the attitudes and behavior of others. By knowing where a person falls on the scale, one can precisely predict his actions. Knowledge of the Tone Scale gives one a greater understanding of his fellows than ever before available.

AFFINITY, REALITY AND COMMUNICATION

Another tool of considerable importance in Scientology, and one that greatly assists interpersonal relationships, is the principle of affinity, reality and communication. These three interdependent factors may be expressed in a triangle. The first corner of the triangle is *affinity,* which is the degree of liking or affection or lack of it. It is the feeling of love or liking for something or someone.

The second corner of the ARC triangle is called *reality,* which could be defined as "that which appears to be." Reality is fundamentally agreement. What we agree to be real is real.

The third corner of the triangle is *communication,* defined as the interchange of ideas or objects between two people. In human relationships this is more important than the other two corners of the triangle.

The interrelationship of the triangle becomes apparent at once when one asks, "Have you ever tried to talk to an angry man?" Without a high degree of liking and without some basis of agreement there is no communication. Without communication and some basis of emotional response there can be no reality. Without some basis for agreement and communication there can be no affinity. Thus these three things form a triangle. Unless there are two corners of a triangle, there cannot be a third corner. Desiring any corner of the triangle, one must include the other two.

The ARC triangle is not equilateral. Affinity and reality are much less important than communication. It might be said that the triangle begins with communication, which brings into existence affinity and reality.

Great importance is placed in Scientology on the factor of communication, as Scientologists know that communication is the bridge to higher states of awareness and happiness.

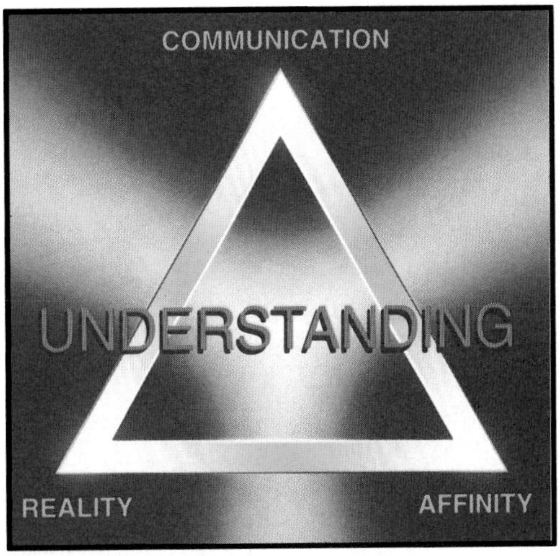

The components of understanding are Affinity, Reality and Communication. Affinity is the degree of liking or affection. Reality is agreement, or that which appears to be, and communication is the interchange of ideas or objects. Together these form an interrelated triangle.

These three terms—affinity, reality and communication—add up to understanding. They are interdependent one upon the other, and when one drops the other two drop also. When one point of the ARC triangle rises, the other two rise also.

The ARC triangle has many uses in life. For example, how do you talk to someone? You establish reality by finding something with which you can both agree. Then you attempt to maintain as high an affinity level as possible by knowing there is something you can like about him. And you are then able to talk with him. If you do not have the first two conditions it is fairly certain that the third condition will not be present, which is to say, you will not be able to talk to him easily. But using the principle that raising any corner of this triangle raises the other two, one can improve his relationship with anyone.

THE SCOPE OF SCIENTOLOGY

Although there are substantially many more ways in which these principles and others may be used to better conditions, one need not spend months studying Scientology before it can be used. People have been led to believe that life is complex and man unknowable, but Scientology holds the opposite view: It is possible for anyone not only to know himself in the fullest sense of the word, but also to gain control over life. Moreover, Scientology is organized so that one may easily employ just a single principle to work remarkable changes.

But quite apart from the immediate bettering of relationships, or sorting out the confusion in one's life, these principles are actually part of the practice of Scientology, and that practice is dedicated to—and has the technology to—consistently raise individuals on the Tone Scale, increase their ARC, and broadly improve their dynamics.

To fully appreciate the depth and scope of the religion, and the actual practice of these principles and others, it is necessary to gain some understanding of the most important applications of Scientology—auditing and training—the subject of the next chapter.

CHAPTER 5

THE PRACTICE OF SCIENTOLOGY

Within the vast amount of data which is the religious *philosophy* of Scientology there are many principles which, when learned, give one a new and broader view of life. Scientology as a philosophical system contains many data one can use to *think with.* Knowing the Tone Scale, for instance, a person can see how best to deal with a grumpy child, mollify an upset friend or get an idea across to a staid employer. These principles amount to a huge area of observation in the humanities. The data exists for a person to think with, to work with, to wonder with, to accept or reject as he wishes. It is a body of knowledge there for the learning. There is nothing authoritarian in it. It is valuable purely as a body of knowledge.

From this body of wisdom the second division of Scientology—the applied philosophy—is derived. And the extraordinary achievement of Dianetics and Scientology has been the development of exact, precise methods to increase man's awareness and capabilities. Other efforts along this line achieved only sporadic or temporary results—if any. Using Scientology, invariable improvements can be obtained when exactly applied.

The importance of application in Scientology comes from the fact that L. Ron Hubbard developed as part of his philosophy an actual *technology* with which his discoveries could be used to effect improvement in people. *Technology* means the *methods of application* of the principles of something, as opposed to mere knowledge of the thing itself. And, using L. Ron Hubbard's technology, applying the methods, one can heighten his perceptions and awareness, increase his abilities and lead a better, more fulfilling life. In short, one can be unhindered by others' ideas that man cannot change and that one can be no better than he was born to be.

Throughout the remainder of this book the term *technology* is used with regard to the application of Scientology principles. Many technologies are extant today, technologies to build bridges and technologies to fire rockets into space. But with the work of L. Ron Hubbard, for the first time there exists a provenly workable technology to improve the functions of the mind and rehabilitate the potentials of the spirit. This is auditing.

A DESCRIPTION OF AUDITING

Although the purely philosophical aspects of L. Ron Hubbard's work are sufficient in themselves to elevate this civilization, only auditing provides a precise path by which any individual may walk an exact route to higher states of awareness.

The goal of auditing is to restore beingness and ability. This is accomplished by (1) helping the individual rid himself of any disabilities and (2) increasing individual abilities. Obviously, both are necessary for an individual to achieve full potential.

Auditing, then, deletes those things which have been added to the person's reactive mind through life's painful experiences and, as well, addresses and improves the person's ability to confront and handle the factors in his life.

Scientology auditing could be described as a very unique form of personal counseling which helps an individual look at his own existence and improves his ability to confront what he is and where he is. There are vast differences between the technology of auditing and other forms of counseling. There is no use of hypnosis, trance techniques or drugs during auditing. The person being audited is completely aware of everything that happens. Auditing is a precise, thoroughly codified activity with exact procedures.

A person trained and qualified in applying auditing to individuals for their betterment is called an *auditor. Auditor* is defined as *one who listens,* from the Latin *audire* meaning to *hear* or *listen.* An auditor is a minister or minister-in-training of the Church of Scientology.

A person *receiving* auditing is called a *preclear*—from pre-Clear, a person not yet Clear. A preclear is a person who, through auditing, is finding out more about himself and life.

The period of time during which an auditor audits a preclear is called an *auditing session.* A session is conducted at an agreed-upon time established by the auditor and preclear.

Auditing uses *processes—exact* sets of questions asked or directions given by an auditor to help a person find out things about himself and improve his condition. There are many, many different auditing processes, and each one improves the individual's ability to confront and handle part of his existence. When the specific objective of any one process is attained, the process is ended and another can then be run to address a different part of the person's life.

An unlimited number of questions *could,* of course, be asked—which might or might not help a person. The accomplishment in Dianetics and Scientology is that L. Ron Hubbard isolated the *exact* questions and directions to invariably bring about improvement.

The questions or directions of the process guide the person to inspect a certain part of his existence and what is found will naturally vary from person to person, since everyone's experiences are different. Regardless of experience or background, however, the individual is assisted in locating not only areas of upset or difficulty in his life, but in locating the source of the upset. By doing this, any person is able to free himself of unwanted barriers that inhibit, stop or blunt his natural abilities and increase these abilities so that he becomes brighter and more able.

There are no variables in the technology of auditing. No random results or haphazard applications. Auditing is not a period of vague free association. Each process is exact in its design and in its application, and attains a definite result when correctly administered.

Scientology auditing can bring any person from a condition of spiritual blindness to the brilliant joy of spiritual existence.

THE IMPORTANCE OF COMMUNICATION

Mr. Hubbard knew from his researches that only by enabling a person to find his own answers to the problems of his life could improvements be attained. As this cannot be forced on a person, auditing relies for its workability upon good communication between the auditor and preclear. The preclear is fully alert during a session and becomes even more alert and brighter as auditing progresses. The auditor and preclear work *together* to help the preclear defeat the preclear's reactive mind. It is not something *done to* the person, but involves his active participation to increase his self-determinism.

Auditing depends utterly on a full knowledge and understanding of the basics of communication. These are thoroughly analyzed in Scientology in many lectures, books and other writings. Several courses of study exist which deal exclusively with the laws and fundamentals of communication and their application.

Communication is vital in auditing and *is* what makes it possible for the process to work.

THE AUDITOR'S CODE

The auditor maintains and practices a code of conduct toward his preclear known as the "Auditor's Code." This is a doctrine of strictly followed rules to ensure a preclear gets the greatest possible gain from auditing, and was evolved over many years of observation. It is the code of ethics which governs an auditor's actions.

Auditing is most successful when the auditor acts toward the preclear according to the Code. The auditor, for example, never tells the preclear what he should think about himself, nor offers his opinion about what is being audited. A goal of auditing is to restore the preclear's certainty in his own viewpoint; evaluation for the preclear only inhibits attainment of this goal. Hence, its prohibition by the Code.

The qualities instilled by the Auditor's Code are essentially those held to be the best in people. An auditor shows his preclear kindness, affinity, patience and other such virtues, to assist the preclear in confronting areas of upset or difficulty.

THE E-METER

Auditing is assisted by use of a specially designed meter which helps the auditor and preclear locate areas of spiritual distress or travail. This instrument is called an *Electropsychometer,* or *E-Meter.* The E-Meter measures the mental state or change of state of a person and thus is of enormous benefit to the auditor in helping the preclear locate areas to be handled. The reactive mind's hidden nature requires utilization of a device capable of registering its effects—a function the E-Meter does accurately.

When the E-Meter is operating and a person holds the meter's electrodes, a very tiny flow of electrical energy (about 1.5 volts—less than a flashlight battery) passes down the wires of the E-Meter leads, through the person's body and back into the E-Meter. The electrical flow is so small, there is no physical sensation when holding the electrodes.

The pictures in the mind contain energy and mass. The energy and force in pictures of experiences painful or upsetting to the person can have a harmful effect upon him. This harmful energy or force is called *charge.*

When the person holding the E-Meter electrodes thinks a thought, looks at a picture, reexperiences an incident or shifts some part of the reactive mind, he is moving and changing actual mental mass and energy. These changes in the mind influence the tiny flow of electrical energy generated by the E-Meter, causing the needle on its dial to move. The needle reactions on the E-Meter tell the auditor where the charge lies, and that it should be addressed by a process.

Different needle movements have exact meanings and the skill of an auditor includes a complete understanding of all meter reactions. Using the meter, the auditor ensures

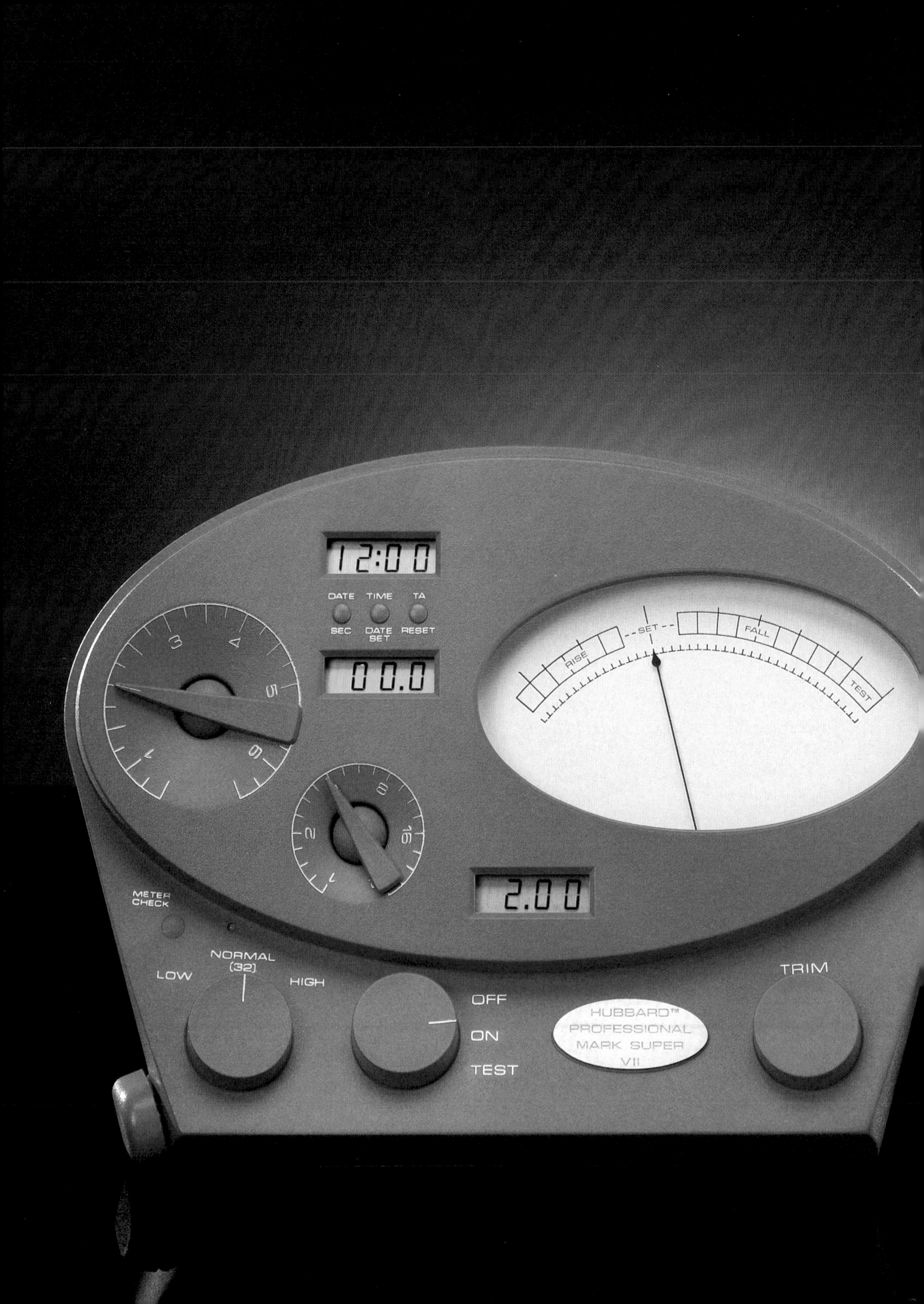
12:00
DATE
TIME
TA
SEC
DATE SET
RESET
00.0
RISE
SET
FALL
TEST
2.00
METER CHECK
LOW
NORMAL (32)
HIGH
OFF
ON
TEST
HUBBARD™ PROFESSIONAL MARK SUPER VII
TRIM

the process covers the correct area in order to discharge the harmful energy connected with that portion of the preclear's reactive mind. When charge lessens, the person heightens his ability to think clearly in the area being addressed and his survival potential increases proportionately. As a result, the preclear discovers things about himself and his life—new realizations about existence, the milestones that mark his gains.

These realizations result in a higher degree of awareness and consequently a greater ability to succeed.

How an Auditing Session Is Conducted

Auditing then consists of certain elements: the preclear, the auditor, the auditing process, communication, the Auditor's Code and the E-Meter. In combination, they address the reactive mind and effect its resolution.

The auditing session takes place in a quiet, comfortable place where it will not be disturbed. Usually the auditor and preclear are seated across a table or desk from one another with an E-Meter set up for the auditor's use.

Before a program of auditing begins, the preclear is familiarized with the elements of auditing during a period of orientation so he knows what to expect in a session. The auditor also ensures the preclear has no distractions or upsets to prevent him from devoting his full attention to the process used in the session.

Different types of auditing are used for the preclear, depending upon his concerns during the session and his earlier auditing. Though auditing addresses the individual, and each individual is different, a precisely delineated gradient of processing steps is used to achieve personal freedom for everyone.

The Electropsychometer, or E-Meter, measures the mental state or change of state of a person, helping the auditor and preclear locate areas of spiritual distress or travail so they can be addressed and handled.

By use of exact questions and the E-Meter, the auditor first locates an area of charge in the preclear's reactive mind to address with the process. When the auditor finds something in the reactive mind, the meter needle surges, indicating that the subject of his questioning contains charge.

Once an area of charge or upset has been located, the auditor then asks the process question or gives the directions needed to assist the preclear in examining it, because he is now inspecting his reactive mind.

The auditor guides the preclear to look at the area more thoroughly. He continues the process and makes notes of the meter reactions and data recovered by the preclear to help chart progress. He maintains the Auditor's Code, never evaluating the data being recovered by the preclear. As the process continues, more and more data from that area of the reactive mind, heretofore hidden from the person's conscious awareness, becomes available in the analytical mind of the preclear.

The process questions and directions help the preclear discharge the harmful energy or force connected with incidents or situations in his past. As the charge lessens, the preclear's awareness of the area increases.

The auditor continues to guide the preclear's attention to the area. Reactions on the E-Meter aid him to direct the preclear to pull more and more data, previously unknown to the preclear, out of the reactive mind and return it to his analytical awareness. Ultimately, the preclear becomes completely aware of the content and is able to view it as it is, without his awareness clouded by reactivity.

During auditing, a preclear has many realizations about life. Such discoveries are called, in Scientology, *cognitions.* A cognition is something a person has come to realize. It is a "What do you know, I just realized why I

This is an auditing session. The auditor is on the left; the preclear is on the right.

always felt that way about . . ." kind of statement. Cognitions result in a higher degree of awareness and consequently greater abilities to succeed in life. When such a realization occurs, that portion of the reactive mind ceases to register on the E-Meter and the needle freely sweeps the dial rhythmically back and forth, a phenomenon plainly visible to the auditor.

The preclear will have gained a higher degree of awareness and rid himself of, perhaps, an irrational fear, psychosomatic illness or disability. The source of what had been bothering him was previously unknown, but, once discovered, its power is nullified. That particular process employed in the auditing session has served its purpose and can be ended. The auditor now proceeds onto additional processes in further auditing the preclear.

As more and more areas of the reactive mind are addressed and alleviated through auditing, its adverse effects continue to lessen and the individual becomes happier and more in control of his life.

With auditing, a person can be more self-confident, effective and successful in his endeavors.

WHY AUDITING WORKS

In a session, the analytical mind of the preclear is assisted by the analytical mind of the auditor in order to vanquish the preclear's reactive mind.

The preclear is victimized by his reactive mind. When this is restimulated, a person is affected by the harmful energy it contains. Since the reactive mind is hidden, the preclear cannot handle it by himself—witness the thousands of years man has philosophized, "soul searched" and tried to understand himself and his motives with no lasting result. In the absence of an auditor, the strength of the preclear's dynamic thrust is *less* than the force capable of being exerted by the reactive mind.

One of the primary reasons auditing works is because the strength of the auditor's dynamic thrust is added to the preclear's dynamic thrust and these two combined are *greater* than the single force of the preclear's reactive mind. Working together and applying L. Ron Hubbard's precise technology, the preclear's reactive mind can be erased.

Each time an area of charge is released from the reactive mind, the preclear's awareness increases. This increase of awareness builds from auditing session to auditing session and the preclear gradually becomes more and more aware of who he is, what has happened to him and what his true potentials and abilities are.

VALIDATION OF RESULTS

Routine testing by Scientology organizations of every preclear has made Dianetics and Scientology the most validated practices in the field of the mind and spirit.

Auditing gains which a person feels subjectively can be shown objectively through testing during the course of an auditing program. Numerous tests are used by technical staff to help gauge a preclear's progress. There are IQ, personality, aptitude, coordination and other tests a preclear takes prior to starting an auditing program. These provide a prediction of how much auditing it may take to achieve a certain result with the preclear. When the preclear is retested afterwards, the improvements he is experiencing personally can be plotted on a graph which validates his gains. The results are used by the auditor to help determine further processes to audit.

Though testing is primarily meant to assist technical staff to deliver a preclear the greatest benefits in his auditing, the consistent results observed have changed man's viewpoint of himself in many regards. Prior to Dianetics, psychiatry and psychology were adamant in their assertion that a person's IQ could not be changed. Their pronouncements were disproven in the face of study after study wherein persons showed dramatic increases in IQ after auditing.

Another routine test is the Oxford Capacity Analysis (OCA). This test accurately measures the preclear's estimation of ten different personality traits. These rise markedly in auditing, reflecting the preclear's gains. Preclears report being calmer, more stable, more energetic and more outgoing as a direct result of auditing and scores on the OCA furnish corroborative data.

Aptitude tests are also a reliable indicator of auditing results. Improvements in aptitude test scores correlate with a decrease in accident-proneness. Many other tests are available which test coordination and different perceptions such as vision, hearing, colorblindness, balance and so on, and these, too, improve as a result of auditing.

Naturally, individual progress is variable since it is largely influenced by the preclear's dedication and the frequency of sessions. Therefore, clearly defined rates of improvement are impossible to establish. The Church makes no claims or guarantees of the gains someone will make in auditing. Church staff, however, have seen so many remarkable improvements in test scores that they expect such as a matter of course.

COMPARISON TO EARLIER THERAPIES

Auditing is quite different, both in terms of approach and result, from other efforts which purport to be therapeutic.

In psychoanalysis, for instance, the analyst does not accept what the person says but interprets it, evaluates his condition for him, reads sexual significance into the person's statements and tells him why he is worried, all of which merely confuse a person further and have no therapeutic effect. In auditing, what the preclear says is never evaluated and his data is never refuted. To do so would totally violate the Auditor's Code. Nor in auditing is the preclear encouraged to ramble on without guidance, ransacking the millions of incidents in his reactive mind and restimulating many, in the hope he might stumble across the right one.

In more brutal practices such as psychiatry, force (physical, chemical or surgical) is used to overwhelm the person's ideas and behavior and render the patient quiet. There is no thought of gain or therapy here but only of making patients more manageable. Auditing bears no resemblance to any part of this field.

Likewise, auditing bears no resemblance to psychology, which is primarily the study of observing responses to stimuli and provides no means of producing actual improvement.

Other practices such as hypnotism consider that a person has to be put into a state of lessened awareness (i.e., a trance) before anything can be done. Auditing is quite the opposite and seeks to wake people up, not put them to sleep.

Some past efforts to help man tried to do so by enforcing moral codes or standards of behavior and conduct but, having no knowledge of the reactive mind or means to relieve its irrational dictates, they effected no lasting improvements.

Auditing is quite different from these past therapies, many of which were impositive and some, like psychiatry, which were actually harmful. In auditing one follows a precisely mapped route which leads to specific gains and it is only the individual being audited who says whether these have been achieved or not. The preclear determines when he has regained an ability or rid himself of a barrier to living, not anyone else. The auditor keeps working with the preclear until the preclear knows of his own volition that he has made it. It is not the auditor or anyone else in Scientology who says the preclear has made a gain. The preclear himself knows.

Given that the goal of auditing is rehabilitation of one's own potentials, the gains can really be determined in no other way.

Auditing is made up of common denominators which apply to all life. There are no variables in auditing; the same procedures apply to all cases. This is a considerable achievement, and is the one which makes auditing Scientology's most important use.

Only auditing restores to the individual his native potentials, enabling him to be the person he knows he really is. Only auditing frees a person from the traps of the reactive mind.

A DESCRIPTION OF SCIENTOLOGY TRAINING

A fundamental idea of Scientology is that increased awareness is the only factor which offers any road to increased survival and happiness.

Through auditing one becomes free. This freedom *must be* augmented by knowledge of how to *stay* free. Scientology contains the anatomy of the reactive mind in its axioms and the discipline and know-how necessary to handle and control the laws of life. The practice of Scientology, then, is composed in equal parts of auditing and training in Scientology principles which includes the technology of their application. Knowing the mechanisms by which spiritual freedom can be lost is itself a freedom and places one outside their influence.

Auditing lets one see *how* something happened, training teaches one *why*.

Therefore, because of the importance of training, one will find Scientologists studying the works of L. Ron Hubbard in any church of Scientology. If one were to look in on them, anywhere in the world, the scene would be the same:

Students seated at tables study the written works of L. Ron Hubbard, dictionaries at hand. Some, wearing headphones, listen to his lectures, while others drill the principles of application—all in the precise sequence as laid out by their materials.

There are no teachers present. Instead, an ambulatory Course Supervisor moves from student to student, monitoring their progress, while a Course Administrator provides any needed materials. Here one sees enthusiastic students, not only assimilating data, but actually learning how to apply it.

This is Scientology training and it is unique in the field of learning.

Training is the way to learn the technology of Scientology. Technology implies *use.* There is a gap between knowledge and the application of that knowledge. By becoming trained, a person becomes able to use the truths found in Scientology to accomplish the purpose of improving conditions in life.

Because Scientology is an applied religious philosophy, the study of Scientology emphasizes application. What exactly does one do to reunite a father and a son, to ease the suffering of a widow or repair a failing marriage? Other practices espouse how one must maintain faith, work out differences or endure with dignity. But does such advice, however well meaning, actually make a difference?

When a student enrolls on a Scientology course aimed at providing him the means to better any relationship, he will actually acquire an understanding of the subject, and equally important, the skill to apply it.

By way of an example, let us suppose that a Scientologist is faced with the prospect of a friend's impending divorce. A trained Scientologist has learned *why* a marriage—any marriage—fails. He understands why good communication ceases between partners and how affinity becomes lowered. Knowing this, he can do something effective to salvage a marriage. He knows methods of reestablishing communication between estranged husbands and bitter wives, and how to rekindle love all but extinguished by marital transgressions. Training in Scientology gives him what nothing else can: a truly workable means of dealing with real-life situations. Someone who has only been audited as a preclear might understand part of a problem in his own marriage but he will not have a complete understanding of it, much less the skills necessary to help others understand theirs.

Any person's involvement with Scientology therefore invariably includes gaining knowledge through education in Scientology principles. By learning the subject, one comes to *own* the knowledge of Scientology for himself and so is able to improve his own life and the lives of others.

HOW ARE SCIENTOLOGISTS TRAINED?

During his research, L. Ron Hubbard made many advances in how best to educate people and these are applied in courses delivered by the Church. He isolated the fundamentals of learning and codified these into a technology of study. Study technology is a separate field in itself, with application to any subject of learning. It is used in all Scientology training but is equally useful in the study of *any* subject.

Among elements unique to Scientology course rooms is the Course Supervisor, an expert in the technology of study, adept at locating and handling any barriers or obstacles to understanding which a student might encounter. The Supervisor does not lecture, nor in any way add his own rendition of the subject. This point is important because the results obtained in Scientology come only from closely following the technology exactly as written by Mr. Hubbard. The subject has already been researched, tested and well proven as workable in application. Verbal renditions passed on from teacher to student would inevitably contain alterations from the original, however unintentional, until Scientology's efficacy would be lost. This is why considerable attention is paid to ensuring a student receives only the pure rendition as written or spoken by Mr. Hubbard himself.

Instead, the Supervisor helps the student grasp the materials, always stressing understanding and application. This method of education has been found to graduate students who understand more and are far better able to use what they have learned than traditional methods of instruction.

Scientology training allows students to learn at their own pace. Each course is organized around what is called a *checksheet.* This is another innovation in the technology of study developed by Mr. Hubbard. A checksheet is a means of arranging and presenting the materials of a subject in a step-by-step manner to facilitate learning. Checksheets lay out the sequence of study and the practical application drills to be followed.

The materials of a Scientology course consist of books, other publications, films and recorded lectures by L. Ron Hubbard. These are laid out in the checksheet and the student studies them in the order listed. The student progresses from one step to the next only when he is ready. There is no "getting left behind," no expecting the student to blindly accept the data, or other such humiliations all too prevalent in the society's educational system. A Scientology course is solely for the benefit of the student; his own advancement in knowledge is the determining factor of progress.

Since the emphasis is on doing, not study for the sake of study, the student soon finds himself working with other students on the practical aspects of his course. Students study together to become proficient in what they have learned, and an atmosphere of mutual assistance pervades the course rooms.

In addition to studying his materials, each Scientology course requires direct application by the student of the data learned. As one progresses through the checksheet, he is required to demonstrate concepts, apply the information to situations in his own life and practice the procedures or techniques being studied until proficient in their use. A balance is struck between study of Scientology principles and practical application of these principles. The product of a Scientology course is someone who not only understands what he has studied but who can demonstrate this understanding through application.

There are course rooms for reading assignments and listening to taped lectures, while other course rooms are reserved for students drilling the application of their materials.

Another feature of Scientology training is the use of films as a tool to teach correct technical application. These films cover specific aspects of Scientology, showing exactly how they are applied in auditing. The films were written by L. Ron Hubbard and many of them were also produced, directed and narrated by him.

When someone completes a course they are awarded a certificate of accomplishment to signify attainment of a particular level of knowledge or skill.

SCOPE OF TRAINING IN SCIENTOLOGY

The broad scope of Scientology is divided into numerous courses, ranging from introductory courses that teach basic principles, to more extensive ones that train professional auditors, to courses which contain knowledge about the ultimate capabilities of the thetan, to those that cover the full philosophic and technical materials of Dianetics and Scientology. There is much to know but all of it is knowable and as one learns more, his view of life becomes clearer and more understandable.

At the heart of all instruction in Scientology are the auditor training courses offered in the Academy of Scientology in any church.

Scientology Academy training gives one an understanding of man, his potentials and the difficulties that confront him, far in excess of anything taught in the humanities or social sciences. Here, one becomes aware of how Scientology principles apply to situations anywhere in life. With this knowledge a person understands why some people are successful while others fail. He understands why one man is happy while another is not. He knows why some relationships are stable and why others fall apart. Life is not a mystery to someone who has studied Scientology. In this respect, training offers every bit as much personal insight as does auditing.

All lives are occasionally beset with trouble. A child falls and gets a scrape, the drinking problem of a neighbor's wife is discovered, a friend's business is failing, a parent becomes ill. The trained Scientologist can bring to bear what he has learned in the Academy to any situation in life and *he can do something about it.*

In a Scientology course room, people study Dianetics and Scientology materials at their own pace with the help of trained Course Supervisors. In addition to reading L. Ron Hubbard's writings and listening to his recorded lectures, students practice the application of those materials to improve their own lives and help others.

FRENCH
ENGLISH
NISH

The skills acquired in training are a discipline in living and a know-how of the parts of life. Training in Scientology is the bridge between one's own learning and experience and livingness, and the truths offered to him in Scientology. It is a bridge from every human being to an understanding of life.

The Academy courses teach different aspects of this understanding as well as methods of their application, a combination which brings about certainty that one does, in fact, *know.* Since life is an *activity,* the emphasis is on *application.* The student, then, learns the actions which constitute their most important application, auditing. This encompasses an understanding of the communication which takes place between auditor and preclear and how to foster good communication.

Once one has learned to do this within the discipline of auditing it becomes simple to do it in life. The student thoroughly studies the theory and mechanics of the E-Meter and then drills with it until he is proficient in its handling and operation. He learns the basic rules of auditing and how to administer a session standardly to a preclear. Each step is studied and then drilled to competence. He watches training films in the Academy film room in order to learn the correct way to perform a particular aspect of auditing. He learns the various codes, laws and axioms that pertain to auditing so that he has a thorough grasp of these basics.

Later steps of his training build upon earlier steps and the student is gradually brought up to actual handling of specific laws by which life operates. The student next learns exact auditing processes and drills them with other students to the point of proficiency.

After two weeks of intensive training the student can complete enough study and drilling to be ready to begin auditing another on elementary processes. His preclear can be a friend, a fellow student, church staff member or anyone. His sessions are carefully supervised by highly trained auditors in the church who help him correctly apply his materials. The student audits his preclear daily and fulfills specific auditing requirements listed on his checksheet. *Application,* whether in life or in auditing, is the prime purpose of his training.

By bringing improvement to another person the student gains the certainty that he in fact does understand his materials. He confirms his competence in handling the elements of life and his certainty in his own abilities rises. This is a factor equally as important to one's spiritual advancement as the personal gains one receives from being audited.

L. Ron Hubbard stressed that half the gains in Scientology come from training in its principles. The truth of this becomes obvious when one considers how much a knowledge of Scientology clarifies a person's view of life. This naturally includes a greater understanding of what goes on in his own auditing sessions and so makes his own progress as a preclear more rapid and certain. Such understanding is gained by training.

In addition, there is considerable pride and personal satisfaction seeing another become more able and happier as a result of one's help. But regardless of whether one chooses to audit professionally, one is alive, and, trained in Scientology, he has new understandings he can use.

After completing the auditing requirements on the checksheet, the student is graduated from his course. An auditor does six major courses in sequence as part of his Academy training. The completion of each signifies a level of skill attained by the auditor and is denoted by a classification, Class 0 through Class V. More advanced classifications, numbering up through Class XII, can be obtained on higher-level training courses available at specific churches around the world. Each course follows the efficient and thorough pattern of instruction described earlier, but adds more advanced theory and procedures. The result is an auditor who becomes more and more knowledgeable in the subject. In this way the different levels of training parallel the levels through which a preclear advances in auditing.

Upon completion of specific training courses, the graduate gains further know-how in applying what he has learned under highly qualified supervision on an internship. Interning turns an auditor into an expert by *doing*. The auditor audits many different preclears on actions in which he has been trained. Such experience imparts the unshakable certainty that comes only from experience of doing something over and over.

Auditing techniques work 100 percent of the time if they are applied correctly. Though the basic principles of auditing are simple in themselves, skill in the application of auditing techniques must be gained by an auditor before he will be able to produce invariable results.

Precision is a requisite for accomplishing many things in life but when one is dealing with life itself, which *is* the preclear, slight variations in application of a procedure can considerably lessen the result obtained. It has long been established that greater gain accrues when the procedure is delivered precisely in all its aspects. The miracles of auditing are the culmination of dozens, even hundreds, of precisely learned, drilled and applied points concerning the wording of procedures, operation of the E-Meter, communication with the preclear and so on. The many steps of an auditing session, correctly taken, result in giant strides of improvement for the preclear.

A highly trained auditor spends thousands of course room hours learning his skills and perfecting them in practice. It is usual for an auditor-in-training to put in forty or more course hours per week. He invests far more time in a study of the mind than does a practitioner in any similar field. At the highest levels of classification, an auditor will have studied a number of course hours comparable to twelve years of classes at a college or university.

Training in Scientology enables one to face and handle existence. The skills of effective communication, of how to really help another, and how to face whatever life may present—all of these attributes have as many applications as there are situations in life requiring a handling.

The need for auditors is great since it is plain that individuals can be salvaged only one at a time. Unlike congregational religions, this salvation ultimately occurs in Scientology in the one-on-one relationship between auditor and preclear. Many Scientologists train to become auditors, and anyone who wishes to help his fellow man can do the same. But of no less importance, one can gain greater skill in handling life than he ever thought possible. There is no more worthwhile purpose than helping one's fellows and no better way to accomplish this purpose than by becoming an auditor. Auditors apply what they have learned to help others with auditing and to change conditions wherever they find that conditions need improving.

This is the mission of the trained Scientologist, and it is in his understanding, his compassion and his skill that the dreams of a better world reside.

THE VALUE OF SCIENTOLOGY

Through auditing and training, Scientologists have come to understand that much in our modern world is transitory and impermanent and based on things not surviving or on things that are in fact being destroyed. They know the practice of Scientology can rehabilitate the individual to his full potentials and that these gains last forever, bringing him to a realization of his own immortality.

Caught on an economic treadmill, hit at every side with the materialism of our age, it is hard for many to grasp that higher states could even exist.

But they do exist.

One sees this for himself when he reaches for them.

Once one starts moving up, there is no wish to stop. The scent of freedom is too strong.

The practice of Scientology is concerned with a better state for man and opens the way with a certain and sure bridge into a future. The way has been dreamed of in ages past. For man it never existed until now.

It exists in Scientology.

Chapter 6

The Bridge to a Better Life

That man could improve and better himself is a traditionally held belief. This idea tended to become obscured by the nineteenth-century theories of psychology which claimed otherwise—that we remain as we were born. More than that, psychology offered the novel—but utterly false—idea that man was only an animal and therefore could not improve his ability, could not improve his behavior and could not improve his intelligence.

Because of this, man in general now finds it rather hard to grasp the older and truer idea that man is a spirit and that he can reach for and attain higher states.

Yet betterment *is* a reality. Many higher states of existence are available to man, and these are attainable through Scientology. L. Ron Hubbard provided a precise delineation of these states, and then clarified how they could be attained by arranging them on a chart which graphically showed each step of the route upward.

Life is improved on a gradient. It is improved a little and then it is improved a little more and then a little more. It does not happen all at once. One cannot expect to be handed a totality of improvement in an instant, like being injected with a syringe that magically cures everything—unless of course one subscribes to the nonsensical idea that a living being has nothing to do with life. What is improved in Scientology is the individual and his awareness. It is not his body, his credit cards, his automobiles or other attendant and appendant machinery surrounding him. The individual himself is improved.

If one had a person with a very serious illness, his mind would be so thoroughly occupied with that condition that he could envision little more than recovery. If in this state someone were to propose the idea he might return to his job and play for the company football team within a week, it is doubtful he would even listen. When the pain subsided and he began to contemplate sitting up, this would be a substantial gain; after which he might even entertain the idea of going downstairs. But if at any point of improvement he were asked to consider the rigors of his job or the company team, it would constitute too big an improvement in too short a time.

Similarly, spiritual advance occurs a bit at a time and one cannot expect someone to immediately leap to the highest levels. The chart Mr. Hubbard devised indicates not only attainable improvements, but also the proper progression, thus avoiding the inevitable setback when attempting to attain too much too soon. An orderly progression, one improvement at a time, as Mr. Hubbard laid out, enables one to ascend at a satisfactory pace to a very high state indeed.

The chart which shows these gradations to betterment is called the *Classification, Gradation and Awareness Chart of Levels and Certificates.* It is divided into two sides—the left-hand side showing training steps one takes in Scientology, and the right-hand side showing the auditing steps.

Classification refers to training in Scientology and the fact that certain actions are required, or skills attained, before an individual is *classified* as an auditor at any particular level and allowed onto the next class.

Gradation refers to the gradual improvement that occurs in Scientology auditing. There are grades to a road and there are grades to steps. There can be shallow or steep steps, or even a vertical ascent, which is not a gradient. The desirable road is a gradual grade upward.

One's *awareness* improves as one progresses in Scientology. By receiving both training and auditing, each equally necessary, one's awareness increases. Different levels of awareness are listed in the center of the chart and correspond precisely to one's progress in training and progress in auditing.

Man, in his religious heritage, has long imagined a bridge spanning the chasm from one's current location to a higher plateau of existence. Unfortunately, many of those attempting to cross that chasm fell into the abyss.

Employing this metaphor, the Classification, Gradation and Awareness Chart, as developed by L. Ron Hubbard, represents, in fact, the bridge which crosses the chasm and brings one to the higher plateau. This is the vision man has cherished for at least ten thousand years, and it is now attainable by following the steps as laid out on the chart. It is an exact route

THE BRIDGE TO TOTAL FREEDOM

SCIENTOLOGY CLASSIFICATION GRADATION AND AWARENESS CHART OF LEVELS AND CERTIFICATES

The following are additional training services that may be done at various points on The Bridge®.

C/S Courses

C/S courses (and C/S internships) exist for the levels of Class IV, Class V, Class V Graduate, Class VA Graduate and each professional auditor training level above that. There is also a C/S course for the solo auditing levels of R6EW to OT III. Additionally, the Purification Rundown, the Clear Certainty Rundown, False Purpose Rundown, Super Power, Cause Resurgence Rundown, New OT VII and New OT VIII each have their own specialized C/S training.

Product: A Case Supervisor who can competently supervise the rundown or action being done to the expected results.

Prerequisites: As designated on the course checksheet for each rundown or action.

Done at Scientology Churches or as designated.

Technical Specialist Courses

Short, fast courses which teach the technology of a specific rundown or technical skill which is not covered on Academy classification courses. Enables an auditor to complete his training in specific rundowns rapidly and conveniently and enables him to co-audit on any rundown on which he is trained.

Scientology Drug Rundown Auditor Course
Scientology Marriage Counseling Auditor Course
Allergy or Asthma Rundown Auditor Course
Ext Repair Auditor Course
Psych Treatment Repair Auditor Course
PTS/SP Auditor Course
South African Rundown Auditor Course
Student Booster Rundown Auditor Course
Vital Information Rundown Auditor Course
Introspection Rundown Auditor Course
PDH Detection and Handling Auditor Course
Handling Fear of People Auditor Course
Purification Rundown In-Charge Course
Fixated Person Rundown Auditor Course*
Knowledge Rundown Auditor Course*
Int by Dynamics Rundown Auditor Course*
New Vitality Rundown Auditor Course*
Cause Resurgence Rundown In-Charge Course*
Dynamic Sort-Out Assessment Auditor Course*
Case Cracker Rundown Auditor Course*
TRs Clay Table Processing Delivery Course
Hubbard Co-Audit Supervisor Course
Hubbard Professional Word Clearer Course
Hubbard Happiness Rundown Auditor Course
Hubbard Senior Security Checker Course
Hubbard False Purpose Rundown Auditor Course

Product: Someone who is capable of delivering the rundown or action or applying the data being taught to the expected result.

Prerequisites: As designated on the course checksheet for each rundown, action or skill.

Done at Scientology Churches.

* Available to contracted Sea Org staff only.

Other Technical Courses

Courses which teach specialized skills for auditors, Course Supervisors or students.

PTS/SP Course (How to Confront and Shatter Suppression)
Clear Certainty Rundown Auditor Course*
Super Power Auditor Course*
Professional Product Debug Course
Cramming Officer Course
Keeping Scientology Working Course
Ministerial Course
Hubbard E-Meter Course
Hubbard Group Auditor Course
Hubbard Mini Course Supervisor Course
Hubbard Professional Course Supervisor Course
Hubbard Key to Life Delivery Course †

Product: Someone who is capable of delivering the rundown or action or applying the data being taught to the expected result.

Prerequisites: As designated on the course checksheet for each rundown, action or skill.

Done at Scientology Churches.

*Available at Flag or authorized orgs only.

† Available at International Training Org only.

Primary Rundown

Product: A superliterate, someone who has the ability to comfortably and quickly take data from a page and be able at once to apply it.

Prerequisites: Method One® Word Clearing, Hubbard Key to Life Course, Hubbard Life Orientation Course (as available).

Done at Scientology Churches.

Hubbard Key to Life Course

Product: A Scientologist® who is in communication because he can express himself easily and clearly both verbally and in writing and can fully understand the communication he receives from others.

Prerequisites: Drug handling as required (as determined by the Case Supervisor).

Done at Scientology Churches.

Hubbard Life Orientation Course

Product: Someone who will be competent in the physical universe.

Prerequisites: Hubbard Key to Life Course (where it is available in the same language in which the student studies).

Done at Scientology Churches.

Third and Fourth Dynamic Administrative Training Courses

Courses in Scientology administrative technology contain the basic laws of organization and the fundamentals vital to any successful activity.

Hubbard Executive Data Series Evaluator's Course*
Flag Executive Briefing Course*
Organization Executive Course
Hubbard Elementary Data Series Evaluator's Course

Product: Someone who is able to competently apply the data studied in order to bring about expansion for his group or activity.

Prerequisites: As designated on the course checksheet for each course.

Done at Scientology Churches.

* Available at Flag only.

T R A I N I N G

Auditor's Class	Certificate	Course	Prerequisites	Teaches About	Where Obtained	End Result
Class XII (Validated)	Class XII (Gold Seal)	Class XII Internship	Class XII (Provisional)	Flubless Class XII Auditing	Flag only	Flubless Class XII Auditor
Class XII Auditor	Hubbard Class XII Auditor (Provisional until interned)	Hubbard Class XII Auditor Course	Class XI Contracted Sea Org staff at Flag	Auditing of L 12, Flag OT Executive Rundown	Flag only	Ability to audit L 12, Flag OT Executive Rundown
Class XI (Validated)	Class XI (Gold Seal)	Class XI Internship	Class XI (Provisional)	Flubless Class XI Auditing	Flag only	Flubless Class XI Auditor
Class XI Auditor	Hubbard Class XI Auditor (Provisional until interned)	Hubbard Class XI Auditor Course	Class X Contracted Sea Org staff at Flag	Auditing of L 11 and L 11 Expanded, New Life Rundown	Flag only	Ability to audit L 11 and L 11 Expanded, New Life Rundown
Class X (Validated)	Class X (Gold Seal)	Class X Internship	Class X (Provisional)	Flubless Class X Auditing	Flag only	Flubless Class X Auditor
Class X Auditor	Hubbard Class X Auditor (Provisional until interned)	Hubbard Class X Auditor Course	OT III Class VIII (Validated) Contracted Sea Org staff at Flag	Auditing of L 10	Flag only	Ability to audit L 10
Class IX (Validated)	HACS (Gold Seal)	Class IX Internship	HACS (Provisional)	Flubless Class IX Auditing	Flag only	Flubless Class IX Auditor
Class IX Auditor	Hubbard Advanced Courses Specialist (HACS, Provisional until interned)	Hubbard Advanced Courses Specialist Course	New OT IV Class VIII (Validated) Contracted Sea Org staff at Flag or Advanced Orgs	The materials of New OT V, "The Second Wall of Fire" (Confidential)	Flag only	Ability to audit others on New OT V, Audited NOTs
Class VIII (Validated)	Class VIII (Gold Seal)	Class VIII Internship	Class VIII (Provisional)	Flubless Class VIII Auditing	Advanced Organizations	Flubless Class VIII Auditor
Class VIII Auditor	Hubbard Specialist of Standard Tech (Provisional until interned)	Hubbard Class VIII Auditor Course	OT III Class VI (Validated)	100% Standard Tech, R6EW – OT III Review Auditing, Special Case Remedies and Class VIII procedures, New OT IV	Advanced Organizations	Exact handling of all cases up to 100% standard results, Class VIII procedures, all processes and corrective actions and ability to audit New OT IV
Class VII Auditor	Hubbard Graduate Auditor (HGA, Gold Seal)	Class VII Internship	Clear Class VI (Validated) Sea Org or 5 year contracted staff	Power Processing	Saint Hills	Ability to flublessly audit Power and Power Plus Processes
Class VI (Validated)	HSS (Gold Seal)	Class VI Internship	HSS (Provisional)	Flubless Class VI Auditing	Saint Hill Colleges of Scientology	Flubless Class VI Auditor
Class VI Auditor	Level P: Hubbard Senior Scientologist, Class VI Auditor (Provisional); Level O: Expanded Lower Grades, NED and Repair Auditor; Level N: Saint Hill Special Briefing Course Theory Graduate; Level M: Basics of Case Repair and Sessions Case Graduate; Levels L–A: [illegible]	Saint Hill® Special Briefing Course	For Level A: Class V or Clear or OT, Pro TR Course, Pro Upper Indoc TR Course, Method One. Each subsequent level then has the previous level as a prerequisite. Class VI consists of 16 separate course checksheets. One completes all 16 to become a Class VI auditor.	Chronological Development of Dianetics and Scientology, their full theory and practice	Saint Hill Colleges of Scientology	Level P: An expert auditor; Levels O–A: [illegible]
Class VA Graduate (Validated)	Hubbard Expanded Dianetics Specialist (Gold Seal)	Class VA Graduate Internship	Hubbard Expanded Dianetics Auditor Course	Flubless Class VA Graduate Auditing	Academies of Scientology as authorized	Flubless Class VA Graduate Auditor
Class VA Graduate Auditor	Hubbard Expanded Dianetics Specialist (Provisional until interned)	Hubbard Expanded Dianetics Auditor Course	Class V Graduate (Provisional) PTS/SP Auditor Course, Hubbard Professional Word Clearer (Provisional)	Expanded Dianetics	Academies of Scientology as authorized	Ability to standardly audit Expanded Dianetics
Class V Graduate (Validated)	HCVGA (Gold Seal)	Class V Graduate Internship	HAA (Validated) & HNEDA (Validated), HCVGA (Provisional)	Flubless Class V Graduate Auditing	Academies of Scientology	Flubless Class V Graduate Auditor
Class V Graduate Auditor	Hubbard Class V Graduate Auditor (HCVGA, Provisional until interned)	Hubbard Class V Graduate Auditor Course	HNEDA (Class V Provisional) HAA (Class IV Provisional)	Scientology and New Era Dianetics Repairs and Case Remedies	Academies of Scientology	Ability to standardly audit Scientology and New Era Dianetics repairs
Class V (Validated)	HNEDA (Gold Seal)	Class V Internship	HNEDA (Provisional) HAA (Validated)	Flubless Class V Auditing	Academies of Scientology	Flubless Class V Auditor
Class V Auditor	Hubbard New Era Dianetics Auditor (HNEDA, Provisional until interned)	Hubbard New Era Dianetics Auditor Course	HAA (Class IV)	NED® (New Era Dianetics®)	Academies of Scientology	Ability to audit NED (New Era Dianetics)
Class IV (Validated)	HAA (Gold Seal)	Class IV Internship	HAA (Provisional)	Flubless Class IV Auditing	Academies of Scientology	Flubless Class IV Auditor
Class IV Auditor	Hubbard Advanced Auditor (HAA, Provisional until interned)	Scientology Academy Level IV	HPA (Class III)	Direct Style Auditing – Dealing with service facsimiles	Academies of Scientology	Ability to audit service facsimiles
Class III Auditor	Hubbard Professional Auditor (HPA, Provisional)	Scientology Academy Level III	HCA (Class II)	Abridged Style Auditing – Dealing with upsets (ARC breaks)	Academies of Scientology	Ability to audit Two-Way Comm, Rehabs, Auditing by Lists, Listing & Nulling
Class II Auditor	Hubbard Certified Auditor (HCA, Provisional)	Scientology Academy Level II	HTS (Class I)	Guiding Style Auditing – Dealing with overt acts and withholds	Academies of Scientology	Ability to audit overts and withholds
Class I Auditor	Hubbard Trained Scientologist (HTS, Provisional)	Scientology Academy Level I	HRS (Class 0)	Muzzled Style Auditing, Objective Processing, Help and Problems	Academies of Scientology	Ability to audit Objectives and Grade I Processes (Help, Problems)
Class 0 Auditor	Hubbard Recognized Scientologist (HRS, Provisional)	Scientology Academy Level 0	Student Hat, Pro TR Course, Pro Upper Indoc TR Course Method One	Listen Style Auditing, Memory and Communication	Academies of Scientology	Ability to audit ARC Straightwire® and Grade 0 Processes (Communication)
Not Classed	Hubbard Professional Upper Indoc TR Course Graduate	Hubbard Professional Upper Indoc TR Course	Pro TR Course	Control	Academies of Scientology	Ability to handle bodies, objects and intention fully
Not Classed	New Hubbard Professional TR Course Graduate	New Hubbard Professional TR Course	Student Hat	Full theory and application of the communication cycle	Academies of Scientology	Ability to confront in session and life and to control communication
Not Classed	Hubbard Graduate of Study Tech	The Student Hat®	None (Method One Word Clearing Recommended)	Study Tech	Scientology Churches and Missions	A student who understands and applies fully the tech of study
Not Classed	Hubbard Method One Co-Audit Course Graduate	Hubbard Method One Co-Audit Course	None (HQS Recommended)	The techniques of Method One Word Clearing	Scientology Churches and Missions	Method One Word Clearing successfully co-audited to completion

Awareness Characteristics

Awareness Characteristics
Total Freedom
Power on all 8 dynamics
21 Source
20 Existence
19 Conditions
18 Realization
17 Clearing
16 Purposes
15 Ability
14 Correction
13 Result
12 Production
11 Activity
10 Prediction
9 Body
8 Adjustment
7 Energy
6 Enlightenment
5 Understandings
4 Orientation
3 Perception
2 Communication
1 Recognition
-1 Help
-2 Hope
-3 Demand for Improvement
-4 Need of Change
-5 Fear of Worsening
-6 Effect
-7 Ruin
-8 Despair
-9 Suffering
-10 Numbness
-11 Introversion
-12 Disaster
-13 Inactuality
-14 Delusion
-15 Hysteria
-16 Shock
-17 Catatonia
-18 Oblivion
-19 Detachment
-20 Duality
-21 Secrecy
-22 Hallucination
-23 Sadism
-24 Masochism
-25 Elation
-26 Glee
-27 Fixidity
-28 Erosion
-29 Dispersal
-30 Dissociation
-31 Criminality
-32 Uncausing
-33 Disconnection
-34 Unexistence

P R O C E S S I N G

PC Grade	Name of State	Subject Audited	Prerequisites	Class of Auditor Required	Where Obtained	Ability Gained
New OT XV	New Section XV OT	The materials of New OT XV (Confidential)	New OT XIV (Mark Super VII E-Meter required)	As given in the materials of New OT XV	Not yet released	As given in the materials of New OT XV
New OT XIV	New Section XIV OT	The materials of New OT XIV (Confidential)	New OT XIII (Mark Super VII E-Meter required)	As given in the materials of New OT XIV	Not yet released	As given in the materials of New OT XIV
New OT XIII	New Section XIII OT	The materials of New OT XIII (Confidential)	New OT XII (Mark Super VII E-Meter required)	As given in the materials of New OT XIII	Not yet released	As given in the materials of New OT XIII
New OT XII	Future	The materials of New OT XII (Confidential)	New OT XI (Mark Super VII E-Meter required)	As given in the materials of New OT XII	Not yet released	As given in the materials of New OT XII
New OT XI	Operating	The materials of New OT XI (Confidential)	New OT X (Mark Super VII E-Meter required)	As given in the materials of New OT XI	Not yet released	As given in the materials of New OT XI
New OT X	Character	The materials of New OT X (Confidential)	New OT IX (Mark Super VII E-Meter required)	As given in the materials of New OT X	Not yet released	As given in the materials of New OT X
New OT IX	Orders of Magnitude	The materials of New OT IX (Confidential)	New OT VIII (Mark Super VII E-Meter required)	As given in the materials of New OT IX	Not yet released	As given in the materials of New OT IX
New OT VIII	Truth Revealed®	The materials of New OT VIII (Confidential)	New OT VII (Mark VI or Mark Super VII E-Meter required)	Solo Auditor (Preferably Class V or higher)	Flag Ship Service Org only	As given in the materials of New OT VIII
New OT VII	Solo New Era Dianetics for OTs (Solo NOTs) Completion	The materials of New OT VII (Confidential)	New OT VI (Mark VI or Mark Super VII E-Meter required)	Hubbard Solo NED for OTs Auditor (Preferably Class V or higher)	Flag only	As given in the materials of New OT VII
New OT VI	Hubbard Solo NOTs® Auditing Course (Confidential)	Solo student auditing on Solo NOTs	New OT IV and New OT V (Preferably Class V or higher) (Mark VI or Mark Super VII E-Meter required)	Solo Auditor (Preferably Class V or higher)	Flag only	As given in the materials of New OT VI
New OT V	Audited New Era Dianetics for OTs (NOTs®)	The materials of New OT V "The Second Wall of Fire" (Confidential)	New OT IV	Class IX (NED for OTs) Auditor	Advanced Organizations	As given in the materials of New OT V
New OT IV	OT Drug Rundown Completion	OT Levels processes for the handling of drugs, medicine and alcohol	OT III Purification Rundown	Class VIII Auditor	Advanced Organizations	As given in the materials of New OT IV
OT III	Section III OT "The Wall of Fire"	The materials of OT III (Confidential)	OT II (Mark VI or Mark Super VII E-Meter required)	Hubbard Solo Auditor (Preferably Class V or higher)	Advanced Organizations	As given in the materials of OT III
OT II	Section II OT	The materials of OT II (Confidential)	New OT I (Mark VI or Mark Super VII E-Meter required)	Hubbard Solo Auditor (Preferably Class V or higher)	Advanced Organizations	As given in the materials of OT II
New OT I	New Section I OT	The materials of New OT I (Confidential)	Clear, valid Eligibility for OT Levels Chit, Hubbard Solo Auditor Course Part Two completed. (Mark VI or Mark Super VII E-Meter required)	Hubbard Solo Auditor (Preferably Class V or higher)	Advanced Organizations	As given in the materials of New OT I
Eligibility for Issue of OT Levels Check	Eligible for OT Levels	Eligibility for Issue of OT Levels Check	Sunshine Rundown (or if didn't go Clear on NED, Power Plus Release)	As C/Sed	Saint Hills	Eligibility for invitation to OT Levels
New Hubbard Solo Auditor Course PART TWO	Hubbard Solo Auditor	Solo student auditing	New Hubbard Solo Auditor Course, Part One and completion of or enrollment on OT Preparations (Mark VI or Mark Super VII E-Meter required)	Preferably Class V or higher	Saint Hills	Ability to Solo audit and case wins from Solo auditing
OT Preparations (advanced religious counseling)	OT Preps Completion	Case preparation for Solo	Sunshine Rundown (or if didn't go Clear on NED, Power Plus Release)	Class V Graduate or above, Clear	Saint Hills	Set up for Solo and OT Levels
New Hubbard Solo Auditor Course PART ONE	Hubbard Solo Auditor Part One	None	Sunshine Rundown (or if didn't go Clear on NED, NED Case Completion). (Mark VI or Mark Super VII E-Meter required)	HQS or Class 0 or above, Student Hat, a TR Course (Preferably Class V or higher)	Scientology Churches	Knowledge of the mind and auditing theory and expert at E-Meter drills
Sunshine Rundown® (pastoral counseling enhancing the state of Clear)	Sunshine Rundown Completion	The materials of the Sunshine Rundown (Confidential)	Clear, Clear Certainty Rundown (or went Clear on the Clearing Course)	None	Scientology Churches	As given in the materials of the Sunshine Rundown
CLEAR	Clear	Clear Certainty Rundown® counseling (to verify and rehabilitate the State of Clear)	Having gone Clear on NED auditing	Clear Certainty Rundown Auditor	Scientology Churches	A being who no longer has his own reactive mind
Clearing Course	Clear	The Reactive Mind	Grade VI Release	Hubbard Solo Auditor (Preferably Class V or higher)	Advanced Organizations	
Grade VI Release	Whole Track Release	The Whole Track	Grade VA Release, Solo Auditor Course Parts One and Two, Solo Setups, Eligibility for OT Levels Chit	Hubbard Solo Auditor (Preferably Class V or higher)	Advanced Organizations	Return of powers to act on own determinism. Freedom from dramatization
Eligibility for OT Levels Check	Eligible for OT Levels	Eligibility for issue of OT Levels check	Power Plus Release	As C/Sed	Saint Hills	Eligibility for invitation to OT Levels
New Hubbard Solo Auditor Course PART TWO	Hubbard Solo Auditor	Solo student auditing	Solo Auditor Course Part One, Enrollment on OT Preparations (Mark VI or Mark Super VII E-Meter required)	Preferably Class V or higher	Saint Hills	Ability to Solo audit and case wins from Solo auditing
OT® Preparations	OT Preps	Case preparation for Solo	Power Plus Release	Class V Graduate or above, Clear	Saint Hills	Set up for Solo and OT Levels
New Hubbard Solo Auditor Course PART ONE	Hubbard Solo Auditor Part One	None	NED Case Completion (Mark VI® or Mark Super VII® E-Meter® required)	HQS® or Class 0 or above, Student Hat, a TR Course	Scientology Churches	Knowledge of the mind and auditing theory and expert at E-Meter drills
Grade VA	Power Plus Release	Power Plus	Grade V Release	Class VII Auditor	Saint Hills	Stabilizes ability to handle power
Grade V	Power Release	Power	NED Case Completion	Class VII Auditor	Saint Hills	Ability to handle power
New Era Dianetics (NED)	New Era Dianetics Case Completion	NED Drug RD, Relief RD, Original Assessment Sheet, Disability RD, Identity RD and other NED RDs and actions	Grade IV Release	Class V – Hubbard NED Auditor	Scientology Churches, Missions, Field Auditors	Clear or a well and happy preclear
Grade IV Expanded	Ability Release	Abilities (service facsimiles)	Grade III Release	Class IV or above	Scientology Churches, Missions, Field Auditors	Moving out of fixed conditions into ability to do new things
Grade III Expanded	Freedom Release	Fixation (past upsets)	Grade II Release	Class III or above	Scientology Churches, Missions, Field Auditors	Freedom from the upsets of the past and ability to face the future
Grade II Expanded	Relief Release	Overts and withholds	Grade I Release	Class II or above	Scientology Churches, Missions, Field Auditors	Relief from the hostilities and sufferings of life
Grade I Expanded	Problems Release	Problems	Grade 0 Release	Class I or above	Scientology Churches, Missions, Field Auditors	Ability to recognize the source of problems and make them vanish
Grade 0 Expanded	Communications Release	Communications	ARC Straightwire Release	Class 0 or above	Scientology Churches, Missions, Field Auditors	Ability to communicate freely with anyone on any subject
ARC Straightwire Expanded	Recall Release	Recall	Purification Rundown and TRs and Objectives as required	Class 0 or above	Scientology Churches, Missions, Field Auditors	Knows he/she won't get any worse
Scientology Drug Rundown	Scientology Drug Rundown Completion	Rehabilitation and Recall Processes addressing drugs	Purification Rundown and TRs and Objectives	Class III or above or Scientology Drug Rundown Co-audit	Scientology Churches, Missions, Field Auditors	Released from harmful effects of drugs, medicine or alcohol
TRs and Objectives	Objectives Completion	TRs 0 – 9 Objective Processes	Purification Rundown (as determined by C/S)	Class I or above or TRs and Objectives Co-audit	Scientology Churches, Missions, Field Auditors	Oriented in the present time of the physical universe
Purification Rundown	Purification Rundown Completion	Biochemical factors	Medical exam and OK to do the Purification Rundown	None	Scientology Churches, Missions, Field Auditors	Freedom from the restimulative effects of drug residuals and other toxins

Alternate Clear Route (For those who did not go Clear on NED): Clearing Course, Grade VI Release, Eligibility for OT Levels Check, New Hubbard Solo Auditor Course Part Two, OT® Preparations, New Hubbard Solo Auditor Course Part One, Grade VA, Grade V.

D I A N E T I C S   A N D   S C I E N T O L O G Y   I N T R O D U C T O R Y   S E R V I C E S

Basic Books and Extension Courses · Public Films · Public Taped Lectures of L. Ron Hubbard · Life Improvement Courses · Hubbard Dianetics Seminar · Success Through Communication Course · Hubbard Qualified Scientologist Course · Anatomy of the Human Mind Course · Scientology Introductory Auditing

The following are additional processing services that may be done at various points on The Bridge.

L 12®, Flag OT Executive Rundown®

Can bring about tremendously increased personal stability, certainty and control of beingness.

Available at Flag only.

L 11®, New Life Rundown®

Addresses the main block or area of irrationality upon which a being introverts and which diminishes one's power; handling this major aberration can bring a new start, a new viewpoint of sanity and rationality.

Available at Flag only.

L 10®

Consists of a series of 23 different actions which address the reasons one withholds oneself or restrains oneself from action; fully handling these factors can increase a person's reach and power and free the individual into a whole new realm of ability and activity.

Any of the L Rundowns may be done after any of the following processing actions: Expanded Grade IV, New Era Dianetics (if pc has not gone Clear on NED), Sunshine Rundown (if the pc went Clear on NED), OT III, New OT IV, New OT VIII, or any individual OT level above New OT VIII.

Available at Flag only.

Cause Resurgence Rundown

A special program that can bring about a tremendous boost to a person's levels of cause and control.

Available at Flag only, when released.

Super Power

Twelve individual rundowns that can put a person into fantastic shape unleashing the super power of a thetan. Can accomplish a wide range of gains, from releasing the person from out-ethics on all flows to restoring impaired or missing perceptics. Super Power can put the person into a new realm of ability. May be delivered at different points on the Grade Chart, as determined by the C/S.

Available at Flag or authorized orgs only, when released.

Flag® Only Rundowns

The following rundowns are available at Flag only. Each addresses a specific aspect of a case which, when fully handled by a particular rundown, can result in an individual who is free from restraints in that area and who is tremendously more causative and able. These actions may be received at different points on The Bridge, as directed by a Case Supervisor. See a Registrar for further information.

Profession Intensive
New Vitality Rundown®
Knowledge Rundown®
Case Cracker Rundown®
Int by Dynamics Rundown
Dynamic Sort Out Assessment
Fixated Person Rundown

Expanded Dianetics™

A specialized branch of Dianetics which directly addresses and handles heavy areas of hidden charge and brings freedom from cruel impulses and chronic unwanted conditions. Delivered, as determined by the C/S, to cases who are not yet Clear but who have completed the Purification Rundown, Objectives and a NED Drug Rundown.

Available at Flag, AOs, Saint Hills, Scientology Churches and Missions as authorized.

False Purpose Rundown®

counseling on considerations and postulates

Cuts straight to the root of false purposes and unwanted intentions and blows them, permitting a resurgence of one's real purposes and certainty of self, with renewed confidence in one's ability to reach.

May be given at any point on the Grade Chart, as determined by the C/S.

Delivered at Scientology Churches and Missions.

Happiness Rundown®

moral precepts pastoral counseling

Puts one on the way to happiness. Best done after Purification Rundown and Objectives, can also be done before or after Grades, after New Era Dianetics, before R6EW (for someone who did not go Clear on NED), after Sunshine Rundown (for those who went Clear on NED) and before any individual OT level above OT III.

Delivered at Scientology Churches and Missions.

PTS Rundown

Handles sources of suppression on a case to bring about new stability and cause level.

Delivered at Scientology Churches and Missions.

Method One Word Clearing

Recovery of one's education.

Delivered at Scientology Churches and Missions.

Rundowns and actions that can be delivered at different points on The Bridge.

The following rundowns and actions address specific aspects of a case which, when fully handled by the applied techniques, can result in an individual who is free from restraints in those areas and tremendously more causative and able. These actions may be received at different points on The Bridge, as directed by a Case Supervisor. Delivered at Scientology Churches and Missions. See a Registrar for further information on these rundowns and actions.

Vital Information Rundown
Repair List for Treatment from Psychiatrists, Psychologists and Psychoanalysts
Allergy or Asthma Rundown
Scientology Marriage Counseling
Student Booster Rundown
Interiorization Rundown
Ext Repair Rundown
Confessionals
South African Rundown
Suppressed Person Rundown
Introspection Rundown
Handling Fear of People Rundown

How to Use this Chart

This chart describes the route to human recovery and ultimate expansion of one's ability and power as a spiritual being. The field of human recovery belongs to Dianetics® technology. Scientology philosophy brings an individual to higher states of being and ability. The chart could be conceived as a map of the expansion of life. It shows at each level the realization of a greater potential with, at the left under *Training*, a new knowledge and skill in handling life, in the center of the chart under *Awareness Characteristics*, an expanded awareness, and at the right under *Processing*, the attainment of a higher state of beingness.

1. In your first reading of the chart you will probably have scanned it over in a general way and become familiar with many parts of it. Be sure, next, to read across the top of the columns to learn what each level describes. You'll see that there are three main areas, *Training*, *Awareness Characteristics* and *Processing*, and all three progress upwards in increasing levels on the chart. Just as each level up to Clear requires an auditor with an added field of knowledge and skill, at each level we find also a preclear ready to be run on the level, having attained all the grades below.

2. Now, look at the various introductory level services at the bottom of the chart under *Introductory Routes*. Note that these introductory level services and activities are not mandatory, but are there to help one begin and become familiar with the fundamentals. One may take any of these routes he chooses – the Registrar at your nearest Church of Scientology can assist you in selecting the one best suited to your needs and interests.

3. Read across each complete level of the chart, only moving up a level when you have satisfied your own understanding of each level as described. You will thereby gain a thorough grasp of the direction and magnitude of Dianetics technology and Scientology philosophy.

4. On the far left and far right of the chart, you will find described various services (training services on the left hand side, processing on the right) that can be done at several different points on one's way up The Bridge. For more information on these, see the Registrar at your nearest Church of Scientology.

5. Read the books of Dianetics technology and Scientology philosophy, available from every Church of Scientology or your local bookstores for continued expansion of your knowledge and use of the subjects.

6. In your study of this chart (and in any study) be sure you do not go past words you do not understand. Use a good dictionary. There is also a *Dianetics and Scientology Technical Dictionary* available from your Church of Scientology.

7. When you have a question about something on this chart, always get it answered. Contact the Registrar of your nearest Church of Scientology who is the expert who will help you to verify your next step.

With this chart in front of you, you have already made the most important step of all – you have contacted truth and the route to freedom. It is hard for man in his present condition to grasp even that higher states of being exist. He had no literature about them, really, or any vocabulary for them. In all of philosophy he had no glimmering at all of Dianetics technology and only a distant hope for spiritual freedom as in Scientology philosophy, but no technology at all.

Factually you've been travelling this universe a very long time without a map.

Now you've got one.

Put this chart on your wall. When you've taken some of the steps, mark them DONE with the date. Find out your next step and mark it TO BE DONE, and WHEN. Then do it. There's plenty of expert help in the Churches and Missions of Scientology; don't hesitate to use it.

Keep track of your progress and keep moving.

You'll make it. All the way.

Definitions

DIANETICS:

Dianetics spiritual healing technology. It addresses and handles the effects of the spirit on the body and can alleviate such things as unwanted sensations and emotions, injuries and psychosomatic illnesses (ones that are caused or aggravated by mental stress). Dianetics means "through the soul" (from Greek *dia*, "through" and *nous*, "soul"). It is further defined as "what the soul is doing to the body."

SCIENTOLOGY:

Scientology philosophy. It is the study and handling of the spirit in relationship to itself, universes and other life. *Scientology* means *scio*, knowing in the fullest sense of the word and *logos*, study. In itself the word means literally *knowing how to know*. Scientology is a "route," a way, rather than a dissertation or an assertive body of knowledge. Through its drills and studies one may find the truth for himself. The technology is therefore not expounded as something to believe, but something to do.

AUDITOR:

a person trained and qualified in applying Dianetics and/or Scientology processes and procedures to individuals for their betterment; called an auditor because *auditor* means *one who listens*.

PRECLEAR:

a person who is on the road to becoming Clear, hence pre-Clear. A Clear is a being who, through Scientology and Dianetics processing is able to form the best possible solutions he can on the data he has and from his viewpoint.

RELEASE:

the term for what occurs when a person separates from his reactive mind or some part of it. The degree and relative permanence of being pulled out of the reactive mind determines the state of Release. There are a number of states or stages of Release and these are called Grades.

CLEAR:

the name of a state achieved through auditing or an individual who has achieved this state. A Clear is a being who no longer has his own reactive mind. A Clear is an unaberrated person and is rational in that he forms the best possible solutions he can on the data he has and from his viewpoint. The Clear has no engrams which can be restimulated to throw out the correctness of computation by entering hidden and false data.

THETAN:

the person himself – not his body or his name, the physical universe, his mind or anything else; that which is aware of being aware; the identity which is the individual. The term was coined to eliminate any possible confusion with older, invalid concepts. It comes from the Greek letter theta (θ), which the Greeks used to represent *thought* or perhaps *spirit*, to which an *n* is added to make a noun in the modern style used to create words in engineering. It is also θ^n, or "theta to the nth degree," meaning unlimited or vast.

OT:

Operating Thetan. It is a state of beingness. It is a being "at cause over matter, energy, space, time, form and life." *Operating* comes from "able to operate without dependency on things," and *Thetan*, the person himself.

Designations and abbreviations such as those found in the body of this chart are to be found in the *Dianetics and Scientology Technical Dictionary*.

with standard procedures providing uniformly predictable gains when correctly applied. The bridge is complete and can be walked with certainty.

Running up the center of the Classification, Gradation and Awareness Chart is a series of awareness levels, which include, for example, *unexistence, disconnection, need of change, demand for improvement, hope* and *ability* to name but a few. These levels represent what the individual person is *aware* of in his or her life. Everyone is *somewhere* on these levels of awareness. The goal of Scientology is to assist the individual to raise his awareness. Each rise in awareness is accompanied by increased ability, intelligence and survival potential.

The chart is a map of what one individual can become aware of. It is, however, important to note that the chart stresses one's personal awareness, not what others may have observed about his behavior. Thus, again, we find that what matters is the individual, for that is what is addressed and improved. Scientology is for the person who sincerely wants change, wants to become better and more able. Scientology thus helps the able to become more able.

As one moves up this bridge, he becomes a trained auditor and learns to help another as well as receive his own auditing. He achieves the state of Clear, advances to the highest levels of auditor training and the highest states of awareness as a spiritual being. The awareness levels are paralleled by the various techniques and activities which approximate them and bring about further improvements as one progresses.

To enjoy the full gains from Scientology, one must move up both sides, training and auditing, if one is to make it all the way. One must learn the axioms of existence by training in Scientology if one is to attain a higher awareness of life. One must experience how these axioms relate to himself through auditing if he is to fully understand himself and his relationship to life. Attempting to walk only one side of the Bridge is like trying to climb a hill by hopping on one leg. But an individual moving up *both* sides of this chart, one step after another, will arrive at the top.

The chart is a guide for the individual from his first awareness of Scientology to each higher state. *Man has never before had such a map.* It is the Bridge to Total Freedom. It *is* the route. It is exact and has a standard progression. One walks it and one becomes free.

THE GOAL OF SCIENTOLOGY

The goal of Scientology is making the individual capable of living a better life in his own estimation and with his fellows.

Although such a statement may seem simple and modest, the ramifications are immense and embody the dream of every religion: the attainment of complete and total rehabilitation of man's native, but long-obscured abilities—abilities that place him at knowing cause over matter, energy, space, time, form, thought and life.

Yet even well before one reaches this state, the changes Scientology can bring are profound. Personal relationships can be repaired or revitalized. Personal goals can be realized and happiness restored. Where once there were doubts and inhibitions, there can be certainty and self-confidence. Where once there had been unhappiness and confusion, there can be joy and clarity.

Those who have seen Scientology at

CHAPTER 7

BASIC BOOKS, EXTENSION COURSES AND LECTURES

Any fundamental of Dianetics and Scientology can be found in L. Ron Hubbard's books and lectures. And any one of his books offers more insight into Dianetics and Scientology than could be gleaned from a thousand magazine articles or interpretations of his work. The best way to find out about something is to go directly to its original materials. In Dianetics and Scientology, these are Mr. Hubbard's books and lectures.

L. Ron Hubbard's books have been read by millions and he is recognized as the most popular author of self-betterment books of all time. His first book on the subject, *Dianetics: The Modern Science of Mental Health,* remains a bestseller more than forty years after its initial publication, a feat unparalleled in publishing history.

All his works are straightforward, exact and written to be understood by anyone. They contain practical knowledge that lends itself to immediate application.

There are many books one can read to find out about Dianetics and Scientology, and so decide for oneself whether the observations and phenomena Mr. Hubbard describes are true. Several of those which contain explanations of the most fundamental principles are described here:

BOOKS ON DIANETICS

The Dynamics of Life

In his introduction to the book, L. Ron Hubbard wrote:

"Dianetics offers the first anatomy of the human mind and techniques for handling the hitherto unknown reactive mind, which causes irrational and psychosomatic behavior. It has successfully removed any compulsions, repressions, neuroses and psychoses to which it has been applied."

This is the first formal record of L. Ron Hubbard's researches on the function of the human mind. It is the original thesis on his work and explains those ideas which formed the basis of his research.

The Dynamics of Life contains the first description of many basic concepts which were later expounded in *Dianetics:* the nature of engrams and their relation to aberration, the earliest description of auditing principles, including the code of conduct followed by the auditor. The book further contains the original discussion of the axioms by which auditing actually works.

Dianetics: The Modern Science of Mental Health

This book marks a turning point in man's knowledge and understanding of himself. In *Dianetics,* L. Ron Hubbard details the dynamic principle of existence (Survive!) and provides the first accurate description of the

The best way to find out about Dianetics is to read the original books on the subject by L. Ron Hubbard.

human mind, what it consists of and how it operates. He describes in great detail the source of all human aberration: the reactive mind and its engrams.

Having discovered this barrier to rationality and survival, L. Ron Hubbard developed a technology to eradicate its harmful effects, resulting in a new state of existence for man, the state of Clear. The auditing techniques for erasing engrams covered in *Dianetics* are more widely used today than in 1950.

As an organized approach to life, *Dianetics: The Modern Science of Mental Health* has brought about great changes predicted by a university professor writing in the *New York Times:*

"As with all great books, the impact of *Dianetics* means the world will never be the same again."

Dianetics: The Evolution of a Science

L. Ron Hubbard traces the exact sequence of events leading to his discoveries about the human mind and his detection of that part of the mind responsible for man's nonsurvival behavior.

The book describes the full potential of the mind and details how Mr. Hubbard was able to isolate an individual's basic personality. He discloses how painful or traumatic events exterior to the individual can become fused with his innermost self, thereby causing fears, insecurities and psychosomatic ills. At a young age, L. Ron Hubbard became greatly intrigued by the mystery of man and his mind. *Dianetics: The Evolution of a Science* is the story of how he came to make the breakthroughs which solve this mystery.

Science of Survival

"While all men are created with equal rights under the law, an examination of the individuals in the society rapidly demonstrates that all men are not created with equal potential value to their fellows," wrote L. Ron Hubbard in *Science of Survival.*

Following a year after *Dianetics: The Modern Science of Mental Health, Science of Survival* is the authoritative work on the subject of human behavior. It is a detailed account of L. Ron Hubbard's observations of man and his discoveries of how man thinks and acts. In the boom following the release of *Dianetics,* much data accumulated on the application of auditing and great advances were made in furthering man's understanding of himself. These advances are contained in *Science of Survival.*

The book is organized around the Hubbard Chart of Human Evaluation which clarifies the seeming confusion of human conduct into definite categories which Mr. Hubbard observed through his research. A chapter of *Science of Survival* is devoted to each column of the chart and explains that column in detail.

One can use *Science of Survival* to accurately predict what another will do in any situation in life, even those with whom one has not had extensive prior experience. By noting the state of another's possessions, for instance, one could predict with keen accuracy his attitude toward children or the state of his health. *Science of Survival* can be used to help one choose employees, friends, those one should avoid and those one can trust and support.

Self Analysis

As L. Ron Hubbard wrote in this book, "Your potentialities are a great deal better than anyone ever permitted you to believe." *Self Analysis* is the first book ever written which provides definite techniques to improve memory, speed reaction time, handle psychosomatic illness and reduce stress.

Self Analysis offers the means to self-discovery through a series of processes designed to give an individual the clearest look he has ever had into his past.

A battery of tests at the beginning of the processing section enables the reader to assess his condition before starting, and provides a gauge of improvements achieved as he continues. The reader then launches into an analysis of his past, guided by specific and easily followed directions. Through the use of a special disk provided with the book, the reader's perception of his past quickly opens. Through the processing contained in *Self Analysis,* a person can discover that he is a much better friend to himself than he ever thought possible.

Dianetics 55!

The quality of one's life is dependent upon his ability to communicate. L. Ron Hubbard's researches into the subject of communication and how to communicate effectively are covered fully in this book.

L. Ron Hubbard carefully analyzes the subject of communication, dissecting it into components and describing the complete cycle of communication between any two people.

A thorough understanding of this book alone could assure success in any endeavor.

Communication is central to the workability of Dianetics and Scientology and this book is Mr. Hubbard's most complete exposition on the subject. In fact, it is *the* manual on communication and thus vital to both living and auditing.

Child Dianetics

Here is a new approach to rearing children utilizing the principles of Dianetics. With the technology provided in this book, one can help a child become calm, happy and self-confident.

There is much practical data in the book, detailing how one can establish a trusting relationship with a child, how much control to exert and how to educate without breaking or discouraging a child. The book also clarifies the reason for childhood revolts, and how best to handle such upsets. A child can be taught honesty and integrity without overwhelming his self-determinism, and this is clearly explained.

A child is a man or woman who has not attained full growth. With this view of children and the practical measures in Mr. Hubbard's book, one can engender a child's love and respect, and help him grow to lead a happy and successful adult life.

BOOKS ON SCIENTOLOGY

Scientology: The Fundamentals of Thought

Mr. Hubbard declared this work to be the first Scientology book. In it, he introduces and explains many of the basic principles of the Scientology religion. This work is a broad summation of his research and contains a complete description of Scientology's most fundamental ideas: the cycle of action, the conditions of existence, the ARC triangle and the parts of man.

The materials described in this book *are* how life works. These data are exact and provide a clear, succinct understanding of the Scientology fundamentals.

A New Slant on Life

This collection of thirty essays by L. Ron Hubbard covers a variety of subjects—including the true story of Scientology, two rules for happy living, the anatomy of failure, professionalism, how to live with children, justice, knowledge and the first usable description of what constitutes true individual greatness.

A New Slant on Life contains both philosophical writings elucidating the Scientology religion, and practical data any reader can use to enhance his life.

The Problems of Work

Work is a large and important part of life for nearly everyone. It is also a major source of many upsets, anxieties and frustrations. L. Ron Hubbard analyzes the subject of work itself in this book and provides pragmatic data to help one succeed at his job and make his working hours calmer, less confusing and more enjoyable.

In *The Problems of Work,* Mr. Hubbard clearly isolates the problems encountered on the job—whether on the assembly line as a shop foreman or even as the CEO. He offers solutions to frayed tempers, exhaustion and the common feeling that one can't possibly accomplish all there is to do. There are ways to handle the confusions that surround any job or activity. There are secrets to efficiency. There are even ways to speed recovery from the burns, bruises or sprains that occur on the job or around the home. Mr. Hubbard covers all this in *The Problems of Work.*

Scientology 0-8: The Book of Basics

Gathered here are the fundamental philosophic and technical data of Scientology. It is essentially a distillation of the entire materials of Scientology. In fact, the title of the book means, "Scientology, zero to infinity," the numeral 8 being the symbol for infinity stood upright.

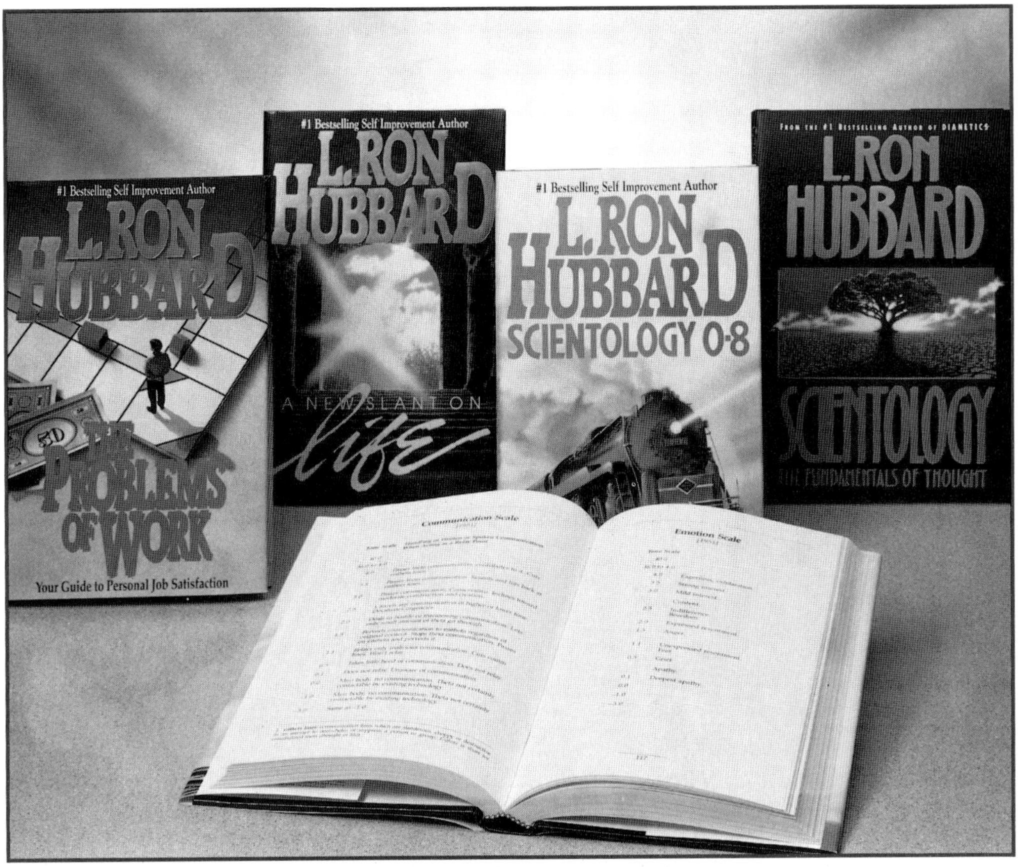

L. Ron Hubbard's books on the fundamentals of Scientology contain practical knowledge that lends itself to immediate application.

Some of the data included are the Axioms of Dianetics and Axioms of Scientology. These are the self-evident agreements upon which the subjects were developed. Included too, are Mr. Hubbard's discoveries of the fundamentals underlying all forms of thought, known as the Logics.

Mr. Hubbard was able to plot many of his observations onto scales of attributes or characteristics of life. The many scales he discovered are included. Use of these scales enables one to understand the extremes and intervening gradients of such things as responsibility, motion, emotion, affinity, time sense, awareness and knowingness itself.

Scientology 0-8 contains the central, senior data of life, concisely stated.

Understanding: The Universal Solvent
Quotations from the works of
L. Ron Hubbard

"The only richness there is is understanding," wrote L. Ron Hubbard. This and hundreds of other quotations have been compiled into a volume of inspirational passages extracted from his millions of published words.

First and foremost, Mr. Hubbard was a writer, and while his enduring legacy stems from his researches, mastery of the language allowed him to convey his discoveries in terms that are often strikingly beautiful. The real strength of his writing however, comes from the truths he conveyed, and this book is filled with his wisdom on such subjects as understanding, communication, survival,

Extension courses can be done at home to promote a more in-depth understanding of the technology contained in L. Ron Hubbard's books.

goals, happiness, leadership, civilization, freedom, art, human relationships, morals and ethics and many more.

Understanding: The Universal Solvent conveys the essence of the Scientology philosophy and at the same time speaks volumes about its author. One could read this work and know at once what L. Ron Hubbard believed and what he strived to achieve.

EXTENSION COURSES

In order to help people better learn the data in Mr. Hubbard's books, the Church provides extension courses which can be done at home. Each extension course covers the entirety of one of Mr. Hubbard's books and is designed to give the reader a full understanding of the subject matter.

One receives an extension course lesson book, which he completes as he reads the book. After reading each section of the book and filling in the corresponding lesson, he then mails it to his local Scientology organization. There, a church staff member grades the lesson, sends a reply and helps with any difficulties. Extension courses can deepen one's understanding of Dianetics and Scientology books, and are an excellent way to acquire the material.

PERSONAL ACHIEVEMENT SERIES LECTURES

To relate his discoveries firsthand, L. Ron Hubbard delivered thousands of lectures to eager audiences all over the world. He lectured extensively throughout the United States, then moved on to London, Melbourne and Johannesburg, to name but a few cities that received him. He lectured to both those only recently acquainted with his works, and to seasoned practitioners.

The selected lectures listed below are particularly apt as introductions to the Scientology philosophy, roughly an hour in length. Each lecture imparts some of the fundamental wisdom of Dianetics and Scientology as well as providing an insight into L. Ron Hubbard himself. Listening to Mr. Hubbard lecture reveals his vitality, humor and enthusiasm as no written work can.

The lectures deal with a wide variety of topics but all communicate something of the flavor of the Scientology religion and its positive view of man's potentials. One can gain real insight into Scientology from hearing L. Ron Hubbard explain the subject. A listing of the titles in the series gives some idea of this:

The Hope of Man

Scientology and Ability

Money

The Story of Dianetics and Scientology

Health and Certainty

Man's Relentless Search

The Machinery of the Mind

Operation Manual for the Mind

The Dynamic Principles of Existence

Miracles

The Dynamics

Scientology and Effective Knowledge

The Road to Truth

Formulas for Success—The Five Conditions

Power of Choice and Self-determinism

The Deterioration of Liberty

Differences Between Scientology and Other Studies

Man: Good or Evil?

The Affinity-Reality-Communication Triangle

Increasing Efficiency

The Road to Perfection—The Goodness of Man

These and other books and lectures by L. Ron Hubbard are available in bookstores, libraries and through Scientology churches, missions and groups.

CHAPTER 8

INTRODUCTORY SERVICES

Though Scientology is immense in scope, one need not familiarize oneself with everything before applying its tenets to life.

The Church offers various introductory services for those who either want help with current problems or simply wish to explore the subject.

Introductory courses and activities provide much insight into the basics of Scientology and furnish data one can immediately apply to improve one's life. Such services are usually short in length and can be done in a few evenings at a church or mission. Their value lies in the instant benefit one gains from practical answers to the problems of life. Several, but by no means all, of these are described in this chapter.

LIFE IMPROVEMENT COURSES

Scientology Life Improvement Courses contain simple basics of Scientology technology which bring immediate improvement in a specific aspect of an individual's life.

The confusions of modern living require solutions. A problem in a relationship, a business or family situation can consume far too much attention. Each Life Improvement Course contains basic Scientology data one can use to rectify problems and improve conditions. There are courses on marriage, interpersonal relations, overcoming the ups and downs in life, personal values and integrity, working more efficiently, raising children, understanding others, and many more.

In every sense of the word, then, these are "how to" courses. Each is illustrated to facilitate understanding, with an emphasis on practical application. One learns the theory of basic Scientology principles, then applies these in course room exercises until one can do so in his life.

Consider, for example, an employee with an unresolving problem with a superior at a job which he otherwise enjoys. Any prospects for advancement are blocked but his current position is better than he would have at another company.

People have solved such situations by quitting, hardening themselves to the disappointment, growing increasingly bitter about management and so on, none of which actually *handle* the problem with the boss.

Rather than such losing propositions, one could take the Life Improvement Course which deals with improving relationships. He would soon discover definite ways, based on Scientology fundamentals, to improve his relationship with others. He would learn the true basis of interpersonal relations and then practice the precise steps needed to improve or repair any relationship. He would learn principles of communication and their application. He would learn

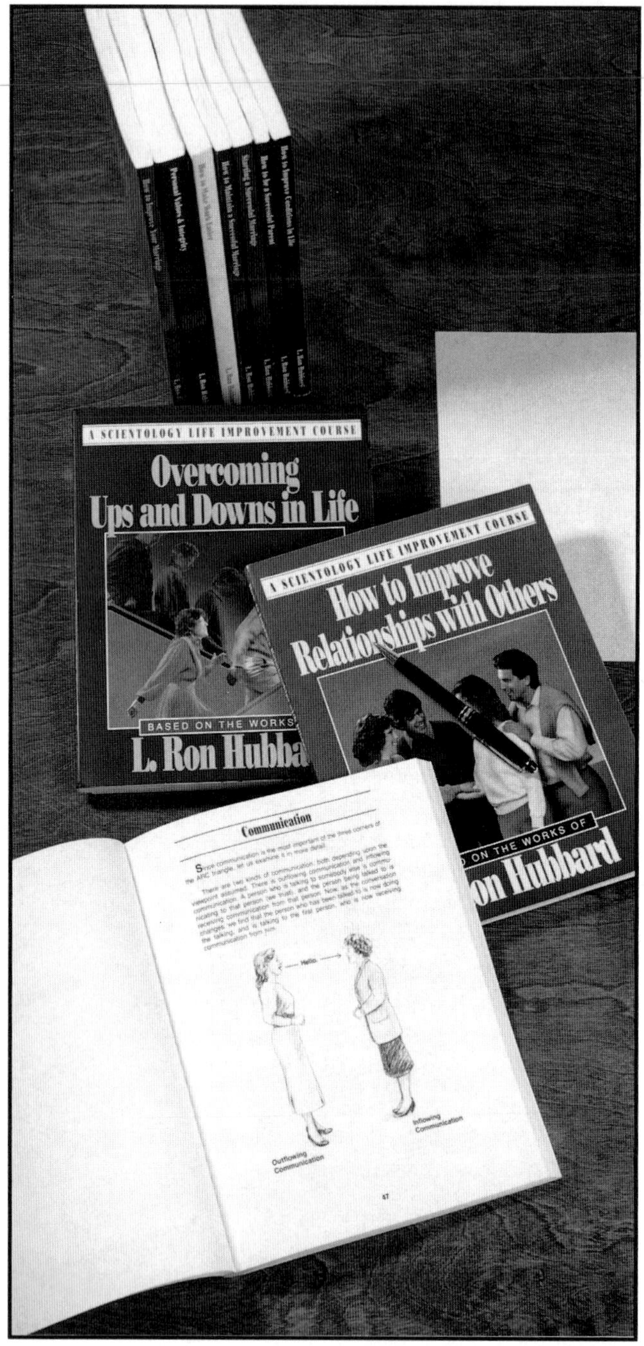

A person can make rapid improvement in a specific area of his life with a Life Improvement Course. These provide Scientology fundamentals directly related to the area for which a person wants immediate help.

the Third Party Law, the discovery made by L. Ron Hubbard concerning the underlying cause of *any* conflict, and how to employ this discovery to resolve strife. Given these and other tools, he could actually *change and improve* the situation with his boss. He would have found things he could actually *do*—not only for his own benefit, but *also* for the benefit of others.

Life Improvement Courses are unique to Scientology. Unlike other movements, with belief systems, Scientology provides practical knowledge. A technology about man leading to higher levels of awareness and ability is something that should be applicable to the everyday concerns of people. These applications exist in Scientology on Life Improvement Courses.

HUBBARD DIANETICS SEMINAR

Over four decades of results demonstrate beyond doubt that Dianetics works. Any person can experience the workability of Dianetics technology for *himself* by attending a Dianetics Seminar and getting Dianetics auditing.

Here, a person is audited on Dianetics and begins to rid himself of the barriers to his confidence, well-being and success.

The seminar begins with the viewing of a video explaining basic Dianetics principles and what happens in an auditing session. The person reads selected portions of *Dianetics: The Modern Science of Mental Health* and is then paired up with another student to practice the auditing procedure. After only a few hours the student is familiar enough with Dianetics technology to begin auditing another person or to receive auditing himself. Students audit each other under the guidance of experienced seminar supervisors, highly trained in Dianetics auditing. Those enrolling on the seminar receive as much Dianetics auditing as they wish, and gain a firsthand understanding of its power.

On the Dianetics Seminar, students pair up and audit each other as much as they want, giving them the firsthand experience of the results of Dianetics and the mutual gain of helping another person.

Through Hubbard Dianetics Seminars, thousands and thousands of people have received Dianetics auditing and started on the road to Clear.

THE SUCCESS THROUGH COMMUNICATION COURSE

Many, many people experience difficulties in communicating. Some have trouble expressing themselves, while others feel uncomfortable in certain social situations. Still others find it difficult to initiate a conversation, while some do not know how to end one. A man cannot get a better job because he does not make an effective sales presentation. A girl cannot keep a boyfriend because she is too shy. An executive does not know how to talk to his employees and so lacks support. Communication difficulties are among the biggest problems people have in everyday living.

One of the greatest discoveries of Scientology is the delineation of the components of communication. All the gains experienced in Scientology stem in one way or another from a knowledge and application of communication. Scientologists have become known around the world as *the* experts on the subject of communication.

The exact technology of how to communicate effectively is taught on the Success Through Communication Course. L. Ron Hubbard developed eighteen separate communication drills to teach a student the basic elements of good communication. The student is paired up with another student and the two work together. Students read a drill and then practice it. Experienced Course Supervisors are always on hand to help with difficulties and ensure smooth progress. Each drill builds on the preceding drill, and as the student moves through these drills he makes the happy discovery that he truly has gained new communication skills. The drills teach one such social and business necessities as how to start talking to anyone, how to get one's point across, how to listen effectively and how to end a conversation.

An ability to communicate well is highly rewarded in life as evidenced by the esteem accorded artists, entertainers, television personalities and the like. But on a more personal scale, one who can truly communicate gets the more desirable job, has the better friends, the deeper relationships and a smoother life than one who cannot communicate.

HUBBARD QUALIFIED SCIENTOLOGIST COURSE

A person is part of life whether he is happy about it or not. There are basic laws to the way life operates and a knowledge of these laws can make life easier to understand and provide tools with which he can improve conditions. This is the subject of the Hubbard Qualified Scientologist Course.

This course offers a broad survey of key Scientology principles. The student studies six of L. Ron Hubbard's basic books and receives a thorough introduction to Scientology. He watches a filmed interview with L. Ron Hubbard in which he discusses how he developed Dianetics and Scientology and explains his philosophy.

There are many practical assignments providing the student with an opportunity to apply what he has studied to real life situations. From such application, he sees for himself how these principles work and so makes them his own, not merely an intellectual pursuit.

The student learns to audit basic Scientology processes and gains experience applying these to others. He drills communication fundamentals and learns how to properly deliver an auditing session. He drills different auditing techniques, then both audits another and receives auditing himself. These techniques include methods to assist those suffering from illness or an accident, how to make an intoxicated person sober, and processes which greatly raise one's awareness of his past—processes, incidentally, that are so powerful they have been known to entirely alleviate neuroses.

On the Hubbard Qualified Scientologist Course a person gets an excellent subjective understanding of what Scientology

These are the course materials and books studied by students on the Hubbard Qualified Scientologist Course. They give one a firm grounding in basic Scientology principles which he can apply to his life, making him a qualified Scientologist.

is all about, sees it working in others and experiences it working in himself.

THE ANATOMY OF THE HUMAN MIND COURSE

The human mind has an exact anatomy. Before Dianetics, however, this anatomy was entirely unknown because those seeking to understand the mind did so from a wholly materialistic standpoint.

The Anatomy of the Human Mind Course contains the precise description of the mind, its components, its workings and its relationship to an individual.

The course consists of twenty lectures, detailing every aspect of the mind. The first period of each course consists of a talk on one portion of the mind. In the second period, students gain actual experience with what was discussed. Demonstrations are performed, examples are found and the students are helped to gain an understanding of such basics as the reactive mind, mental image pictures, engrams, the analytical mind, the body, its nervous system, and aberration.

The Anatomy of the Human Mind Course imparts a real understanding of Dianetics principles and their value to one's life.

SCIENTOLOGY INTRODUCTORY AUDITING

The best way to find out what Scientology auditing can accomplish is to get some.

In mapping the route to higher states, L. Ron Hubbard developed processes which take a person from wherever he is to the next higher level of awareness. There are many processes which do exactly that for the person just beginning auditing. Introductory processes address immediate concerns of an individual and can produce remarkable changes in conditions and his attitudes toward them. That they are introductory in no way lessens their precision or their potential for giving someone insight into a part of his life. Mr. Hubbard designated these processes as particularly applicable for someone with no previous auditing. They give a person his initial auditing gains, which, because they are his first, can be among the most memorable he will ever experience.

Another type of introductory auditing is called "assist auditing." This includes techniques which help a person recover more rapidly from bruises, burns, illnesses, upsets or other mishaps. Assists can actually be done on anyone, no matter how little or how far he has progressed in Scientology. The noticeable improvement that can occur from doing an assist on a burn or bruise makes it a very appropriate introduction to auditing. Someone whose headache has been alleviated by an assist obtains an excellent reality on the workability of auditing.

After a person has received some individual auditing there is another way to continue to receive auditing gains. This is through Group Processing. Mr. Hubbard developed certain auditing processes that are delivered to large numbers of people simultaneously. These techniques are administered by a single auditor to groups gathered in rooms or halls, and provide gains to many in one session. Even Scientologists who are not currently receiving individual auditing attend Group Processing sessions. Group Processing is for everyone, from those who have only experienced a little auditing to those who have had a lot. Though simple, Group Processes sometimes produce startling results and are always enjoyable.

Life does not have to be an unhappy plight. But one would be hard pressed to find a person who has not had his share of knocks or who cannot name an aspect of life he would wish to improve. Like a man dying in a desert for want of water, the world is full of people who lead an unhappy existence for want of answers to vital questions.

Millions have found these answers on introductory services at a Scientology church or mission.

CHAPTER 9

THE PURIFICATION PROGRAM: REHABILITATING A DRUGGED AND POISONED WORLD

Our planet has hit a barrier which prevents any widespread social progress—drugs and other biochemical substances.

The culture was severely harmed by the massive proliferation of drugs which began in the 1960s and today continues unabated. For many years prior to that turbulent decade, psychiatrists had busily endorsed the use of drugs as a solution to a multitude of mental and emotional conditions. LSD, for example (and L. Ron Hubbard warned of its danger to society as early as 1951) was heavily promoted and used by psychiatry during the 1950s and 1960s as a treatment for mental conditions. Subsequently, it was pushed out into the society and billed as a means of attaining enlightenment. In such a wise, the illegal street drug market boomed. Narcotics, stimulants and other substances found wider and wider acceptance in the society. Abuse of such drugs, once confined to a small segment of the population, grew to epidemic proportions in the 1960s among college students and spread from there.

Abetted by giant pharmaceutical firms and much media attention, psychiatry made drug taking an acceptable, mainstream activity for many. In addition to LSD, drug companies unleashed a torrent of drugs into the society—heroin, methadone and countless tranquilizers among others—that have proven to be nightmares for mankind. Added to an increasing use of marijuana, mescaline and other psychedelics, the availability and acceptability of drugs increased enormously.

A common tactic to gain acceptance for a pharmaceutical drug is to release it amid massive public relations campaigns professing the drug's efficacy and safety. But often, cases discrediting the claims of safety and revealing instead harmful side effects soon begin to accumulate. In the mid-1800s, opium addiction begat morphine which was touted by the medical establishment as nonaddictive treatment for opium addiction. But by 1870, morphine was recognized as more addictive than opium. This led to the development of heroin, extolled as a nonaddictive substitute for morphine. Within fifteen years this claim had clearly been shown to be otherwise. Following World War II, psychiatrists began pushing a new drug, methadone, as a cure for heroin addiction, thus foisting a century-old con game on a growing number of victims—all while reaping huge appropriations of public funding for its implementation.

Other prescription drugs such as Valium, Librium, Xanax, Oraflex, Halcion and Prozac were all claimed to be safe, but each has been found to have harmful side effects. Psychiatrists have earned hundreds of millions of dollars prescribing these drugs—and then treating the problems created by their own prescriptions.

The pharmaceutical drug companies reap huge profits, literally tens of billions of dollars a year, from the widespread use of drugs to treat an ever-increasing list of symptoms for new illnesses "discovered" each year by the psychiatric profession. Drugs have, for example, even become entrenched in the educational system. Today, a child labeled "hyperactive" can be given the psychiatric drug Ritalin in the classroom. And hundreds of psychiatric drugs are consumed by millions to "solve" a multitude of modern problems such as sleeplessness, nervousness, stress or just plain boredom.

These illnesses, all of which are given credence with sophisticated names, become official during the American Psychiatric Association's annual convention. Psychiatrists proffer a newly discovered illness and a vote is taken, with a majority consensus creating an official new disease. Why "official"? Official diseases can be treated and paid for by insurance companies, and in that way the psychiatric–drug manufacturer coalition ensures an ever-increasing source of income. Without question this is the greatest fraud of the twentieth century. It remains suppressed through the billions of dollars vested interests have at their disposal for high-tech PR campaigns and expensive marketing strategies, which in turn create the advertising revenues for a media which would be financially crippled if it exposed the scam.

All this is quite in addition to the widespread consumption of illegal drugs (many of which were originally prescription drugs), which are figured to be a 500 billion dollar a year industry in themselves. By some estimates, marijuana is now the biggest cash crop in America. Cocaine and its derivatives became very fashionable in the 1970s and are now widely abused, due in part to false data from psychiatrists who claimed as recently as 1980 in their own texts that cocaine usage was not addictive. They could not have been more wrong. Many medical and psychiatric drugs—heroin, LSD, methadone, Methedrine and tranquilizers, to name a few—were poorly controlled by those professions and allowed to proliferate on the illegal market, further exacerbating the problem. Right now, the most widely prescribed antidepressant, Prozac, is also the hottest kid on the block in the illegal street drug market.

Drug taking seems to be part of being alive in our modern world.

Additionally, technological advances this century have produced many unfavorable byproducts harmful to an individual's well-being. Smog, for instance, was unknown before the rise of manufacturing centers in Britain. Every major city on Earth now advises its inhabitants daily about the quality of air they are breathing. A hundred years ago, the main food preservatives were salt or ice. Today, nearly any packaged food has a list of the artificial ingredients it contains that is longer than the list of natural ingredients. Environmental disasters such as Chernobyl, to say nothing of radiation exposure from widespread nuclear bomb testing, did not exist fifty years ago.

We live in a chemical-oriented society. The Environmental Protection Agency reports that the average American consumes four pounds of pesticides each year and has residues from over 400 toxic substances in his body. More than 3,000 chemical additives are found in the food we eat.

There is no escaping our contaminated civilization and, furthermore, it has been found that these substances can put individuals in a condition which prevents personal improvement.

The drug problem was not of major concern in 1950 when L. Ron Hubbard released *Dianetics*. By the 1960s, however, the frightful specter of drugs had arrived and Mr. Hubbard's research showed that this was a major barrier to a person's spiritual betterment. Drugs, he discovered, affect the mind adversely and block any progress in auditing.

The way a being perceives much of existence is via the sensory channels of the body. The body is a communications center for the being, with the brain acting as a switchboard for translating thought into action. The biochemical actions of drugs alter the normal operations of this pattern, often with harmful or even disastrous consequences.

L. Ron Hubbard researched this barrier to spiritual freedom long before it was recognized by others as the huge social concern it is today. His work yielded a truly effective handling for the adverse biochemical effects of drugs and other toxins.

He made the discovery that residues from drugs and other toxins lodge in the fatty tissues of the body and stay there, even years after they have been ingested. And that these residues can continue to affect the individual adversely long after the effect of the drug has apparently worn off. Such deposits have been known to cause lessened perception, tiredness, confused thinking and a host of other symptoms in people—all of which are counter to what is being achieved through auditing. Cases have been documented where a person reexperienced the effects of LSD years after having taken the drug.

Realizing that this biochemical factor had to be handled before any lasting spiritual gain could be made through auditing, L. Ron Hubbard devised what independent researchers acknowledge as the most effective detoxification program in existence, the Purification program.

Developed solely as a handling for this barrier to spiritual gain caused by drugs, the Purification program is a carefully designed combination of exercise, vitamins, nutrition and sauna use which dislodges drug residues and other toxins from the fatty tissues so that these substances can then be eliminated from the body. A person undergoing the program is closely monitored by specially trained personnel in liaison with medical doctors to ensure that each aspect of the program is administered correctly and the desired benefits are attained.

Once the person has been freed from the harmful effects of these drug residues and other toxins, he is in a far better position to

On the Purification program, running is done to get the blood circulating deeper into the tissues where toxic residuals are lodged and thus act to loosen and release the accumulated harmful deposits and get them moving.

Very important, then, is that the running is immediately followed by sweating in the sauna to flush out the accumulations which have now been dislodged.

Regular nutrition and supplemental nutrition in the form of megavitamin and mineral dosages and extra quantities of oil are a vital factor in helping the body to flush out toxins and to repair and rebuild the areas that have been affected by drugs and other toxic residuals.

A proper schedule with enough rest is mandatory, as the body will be undergoing change and repair throughout the program.

improve as a spiritual being, something many thousands of people have attested to.

After the release of the program in 1980, news of L. Ron Hubbard's breakthrough reached medical circles and the scientific community. Since then, numerous studies of his method of detoxification have been undertaken—studies which validate the tremendous workability of the program.

In 1973, a disaster occurred in the state of Michigan. Cattle feed had mistakenly been contaminated with a toxic fire retardant. The subsequent contamination of milk, meat and other products was widespread, and five years later, 97 percent of the residents of the state had detectable amounts of the fire retardant in their fatty tissues. A group of Michigan residents had been monitored since the initial contamination and the concentration of the toxin had not reduced. The doctors monitoring the study concluded that the toxins were there to stay.

In 1982, a group of these subjects was put through the Purification program. Biopsies of fatty tissue before and after showed a decrease of the fire retardant and other toxins of over 20 percent. A follow-up examination four months later proved even more significant: Levels of toxins continued to decrease after the program had been completed and showed an average decrease of over 40 percent of the toxins.

The deadly chemical dioxin—Agent Orange—was used to defoliate trees during the Vietnam War. Exposure to the chemical resulted in dioxin poisoning of American servicemen. Years later no effective handling had been developed. Then a Florida cardiologist conducting tests on a person who had been exposed to the chemical but who had done the Purification program, found that his patient's level of the chemical had reduced by 29 percent immediately after the program and an astounding 97 percent eight months later—and that all symptoms of dioxin poisoning had disappeared. These and other similarly impressive studies validate the workability of the Purification program.

L. Ron Hubbard's Purification program is the solution to the blight of drugs. Hundreds of thousands of people have been freed from the harmful effects of drugs and other toxins through its use. Many who have completed the program report that, along with eradicating any craving for drugs, they can see or hear better than before, that they are able to learn new subjects much more easily, that they get along better with people, and that they generally feel healthier and happier.

The entire program is explained in detail in the book *Clear Body, Clear Mind: The Effective Purification Program,* including the discoveries which led to its development and an exact description of how and why it works. One can read this book and then, by following the procedures detailed in the text, administer the Purification program to himself to detoxify his own body.

Despite their glorification by drug companies, psychiatrists, the media and the pusher in the streets, one is much better off without drugs.

Until such time as drug companies reform and science can give us advances that are not double-edged swords, the individual will have to contend with these factors.

In the eyes of many legislators, social scientists, educators and others, the drug problem is the most serious threat to our society. Drug companies, psychiatrists and criminal elements make billions in profits while shoving these deleterious and even lethal substances at the peoples of Earth. L. Ron Hubbard's Purification program has proven itself to be the most effective action one can take to free himself from the biochemical devastation caused by drugs.

After more than a decade of successful application and validation by independent researchers, that fact is indisputable.

Over 100,000 people have been freed from the effects of drugs using this technology and thousands more join the roster each month.

These books cover in detail the technology and exact procedures of the Purification program, including a full textbook, an illustrated booklet and a manual to guide one's progress step by step through the program.

MENTAL AND SPIRITUAL FACTORS

The Purification program addresses the biochemical aspect of drugs and toxins. From a personal standpoint however, there are other factors to consider, mental and spiritual ones.

L. Ron Hubbard solved the mental and spiritual harm that drugs do with a series of actions comprising what is called the "Drug Rundown." A rundown designates a series of related actions in Scientology which culminate in a specific end result. In this case, the Drug Rundown consists of the auditing processes and actions necessary to free an individual from the damaging mental and spiritual effects of drugs. The Drug Rundown is delivered in churches and missions by highly trained auditors.

A person who has been on drugs often becomes disassociated from the world around him or even his physical self, as evidenced by the neglect many drug takers show for their hygiene, dress, health, job, friends and family, etc.

The reason is that, among other things, drugs dull a person's communication. This is most directly observed in the action of painkillers which shut off the person's feeling of pain, but it occurs with the use of other drugs as well. Emotions are suppressed with drug use, and perceptions become altered or shut off. A person often becomes less aware of things and people around him and so becomes less considerate and responsible, less active, less capable and less bright. The person factually becomes less conscious of what is happening in the present. One does not have to have been a heavy narcotics addict to experience a lessening of alertness, fogginess or other effects as a result of drug use.

Drugs do something else too: they stick a person's attention at points in his past. Mental image pictures restimulated from the reactive mind appear in the visions of hallucinations a person sees while on certain drugs. Attention often becomes stuck in these pictures after the drug has worn off, with the cumulative effect of the person not feeling "with it" or not feeling in present time.

This can be dangerous to the person himself and to others, as seen in the number of drug-related automobile accidents that occur, to say nothing of less serious accidents or goofs that happen because a person is unaware of what is going on around him. Drug use makes a person less alert mentally, can harm memory and has a host of other effects on attitudes and behavior—all residual consequences of the drugs, which persist indefinitely unless audited.

The spiritual effects of drug use can also be devastating. In the late 1960s, L. Ron Hubbard discovered that a person who had been heavily on drugs was not able to make spiritual gains from auditing. This condition had not been encountered earlier in his researches, as drugs had not yet encroached so deeply into society. But it became more and more prevalent and required a solution, as drugs now represented an increasingly serious block to self-betterment efforts.

The reason drugs are so harmful spiritually is because they can badly scramble the energy contained in the mind, disorienting and confusing the person. His awareness often diminishes and his capabilities of dealing with the energies and masses of reality become less. A person affected by drugs is less able to control the things in his environment and, despite whatever subjective feelings he may have to the contrary, he becomes less powerful and less able.

While on drugs, the pictures in the reactive mind can violently turn on, overwhelming the being and making him afraid to confront anything in the reactive mind thereafter. As a result, the person is stopped dead from any mental or spiritual gain.

Through the different auditing processes and drills of the Drug Rundown, a person is first brought to new awarenesses of his environment and the world around him. This has the effect of unsticking him from points in his past and brings him more into present time.

This is a very important factor in mental and spiritual ability. The more a person can exist in the present without his attention stuck in past incidents, the better able he is to deal with his life. He feels brighter, has increased perception, is better able to control himself and the things in his environment, and becomes more able to deal with others.

Getting the person into present time is not the total answer, however. The actual incidents from his reactive mind associated with drugs must also be addressed in auditing. Drugs scramble the mind to such a degree that freeing the person from these effects requires a precise and thorough approach.

First, experiences the person had while taking drugs are addressed using exact auditing procedures, and the charge in the reactive mind which has accumulated around these incidents is released. Attention that had been fixated by drugs, medicines and alcohol is freed, and the mental masses brought about by drugs are erased.

Drug taking invariably has numerous unwanted physical sensations, emotions, attitudes and other feelings connected with it. So the next stage of a Drug Rundown entails auditing on unwanted feelings connected with specific drugs taken by the person. These are addressed one by one and fully handled, freeing the person from their effects.

L. Ron Hubbard found, though, that people begin taking drugs for a reason: to ease the agony of a physical condition, to numb themselves against certain situations in their lives, to relieve boredom, to feel better; the number of possible reasons is as great as the number of people taking drugs. By taking drugs the person was trying to handle or cure something. At the bottom, then, the drug problem is essentially spiritual. The being in some way hurt and was led into the false solution that drugs could cure this. The solution, as many learned the hard way, turned out to be a trap from which there was no true escape until the drug-handling technology of L. Ron Hubbard.

A vital part of the Drug Rundown, then, includes finding the pains, emotions, sensations, feelings, etc., the person was suffering from—for which drugs became the cure. When these are found, each is addressed in auditing. Unless the reasons a person went onto drugs in the first place are resolved, the person is forever left with the original condition for which drugs were a "solution."

When the original problem has been addressed, the person himself is at last free from any effects of drugs and free from the need to take them. The full solution to the drug problem thus consists of handling all aspects of drug taking.

On Earth today, drugs are very, very big business. We live in a society where human values are routinely shunted aside for the economic concerns connected with drugs, both legal and illegal. The cost in crime, the cost in trying to control the problem, the cost in inefficiency, the cost simply in lives lived under the numbing influence of drugs cannot be calculated. For to do that, one would have to put a price on life itself.

So, what price the headache remedies, the soporifics, the pain relievers, the antidepressants that fill our medicine cabinets? What price the amphetamines given our schoolchildren, turning them into drug-dependent people? What price the narcotics that are used to negate a painful existence? What price the recreational drugs that provide escape from the boredom of affluence? What price these shackles that keep from us the sensations and joys of living itself?

A drug war rages on this planet. L. Ron Hubbard recognized the drug problem long before it became an international concern. And he developed a technology people can use to free themselves from this trap and remain free of it.

His technology is the weapon that can win this war.

CHAPTER 10

STUDY TECHNOLOGY: EFFECTIVE LEARNING AND EDUCATION

The future of our planet will one day rest in the hands of our children. How well equipped will they be to carry society forward? Perhaps the surest gauge is the success with which we are educating them for that role. Sadly, from all indications, this responsibility has not been met. At a time when quality education is more important than during any period in history, our schools are failing at an alarming rate.

Typical of the educational problems faced by most Western countries is the tragedy of the United States student. America once had one of the finest educational systems in the world, yet for nearly three decades that system continues to face a formidable crisis.

Over 25 percent of all students leaving or graduating high school lack the reading and writing skills required by the minimum demands of daily living.

The American high-school dropout rate hovers at around 30 percent to 50 percent in inner city areas.

According to the president of one teachers' association, up to 50 percent of all new teachers quit the profession within the first five years.

SAT (Scholastic Aptitude Test) scores of American students have sunk to levels considerably lower than those achieved by students in the mid-1960s.

The news media regularly report on the continuing decline of standardized test scores, on overcrowding in classrooms, on public disenchantment about pouring more tax dollars into what they perceive to be an increasingly poor investment, and growing teacher disillusionment.

It is indeed a grim picture but is no better in most other parts of the world.

A British survey sponsored by *The Sunday Times* of London, for instance, found 42 percent of those surveyed were unable to add the menu prices of a hamburger, French fries, apple pie and coffee. One out of six British inhabitants could not correctly locate Great Britain on a world map.

From both official and media reports, the pattern of educational decline is evident in almost every Western country—places where excellence in public education was once taken for granted.

These dismal figures translate into an equally depressing economic scene. Internationally, the cost to business in lowered or wasted productivity, unemployment and crime is estimated at $300 billion annually. Businesses are forced to develop their own remedial programs to teach employees the basic reading, writing and computational skills necessary to function on the job.

There seems to be no shortage of ideas and theories on how to accomplish educational reforms. But these programs tend to create as many problems as they solve.

For example, after the crisis in education became headline news, America instituted "get tough" retention policies and

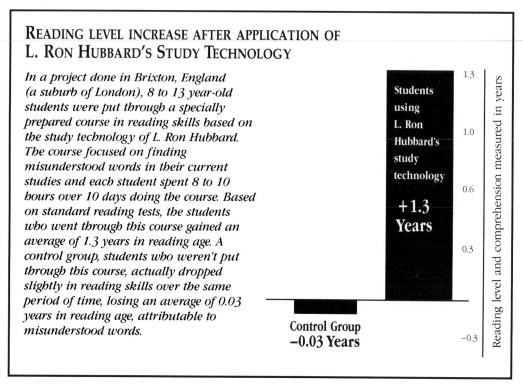

READING LEVEL INCREASE AFTER APPLICATION OF L. RON HUBBARD'S STUDY TECHNOLOGY

In a project done in Brixton, England (a suburb of London), 8 to 13 year-old students were put through a specially prepared course in reading skills based on the study technology of L. Ron Hubbard. The course focused on finding misunderstood words in their current studies and each student spent 8 to 10 hours over 10 days doing the course. Based on standard reading tests, the students who went through this course gained an average of 1.3 years in reading age. A control group, students who weren't put through this course, actually dropped slightly in reading skills over the same period of time, losing an average of 0.03 years in reading age, attributable to misunderstood words.

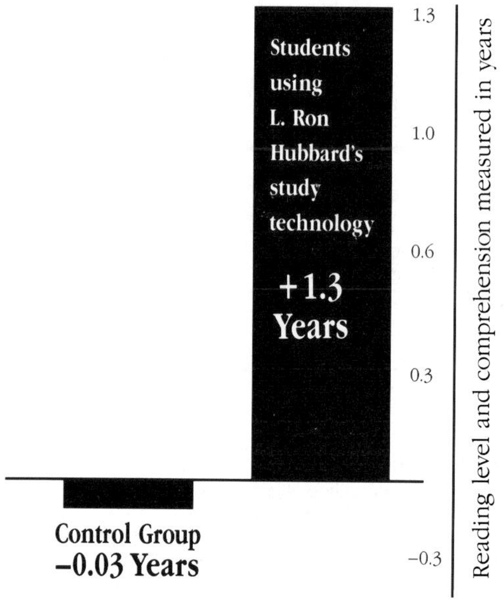

added graduation requirements, on the assumption that a greater challenge for students would improve performance. The opposite occurred. The policies raised rather than lowered the dropout rate in some cities. The president of the American Federation of Teachers argued, "It's ridiculous to raise the hurdle for kids who are unable to jump in the first place."

A WORKABLE ANSWER: STUDY TECHNOLOGY

Failed attempts to improve education in recent decades raise one important question: With so much attention on improving the quality of education, with billions spent each year to remedy the situation, why has there been so little improvement?

There is an answer. Quite simply, these efforts have been directed at solving the wrong problems.

At the root of educational failures lies a fundamental situation that has been almost universally overlooked: *Students have never been taught how to learn.*

Students are thrown into their school years and basic subjects without ever first being taught how to go about learning those subjects. As they grow older they are confronted by more and more complex areas of study, still without ever having learned *how* to learn.

Learning how to learn has been the vital missing ingredient that has hampered all fields of study. It handicaps both children in school and people in life.

Without knowing how to learn what they are studying, a majority of students find education a trying and difficult process. They never master the ability to rapidly learn something with certainty and ease. Others, who apparently have less difficulty studying, find they are unable to apply what they have read.

It is a reality of the modern world that anyone in the work force, whether on the factory floor or in the executive suite, must have an ability to assimilate important information, retain it and then be able to apply it. This process, whether formal or informal, is what is meant by "study."

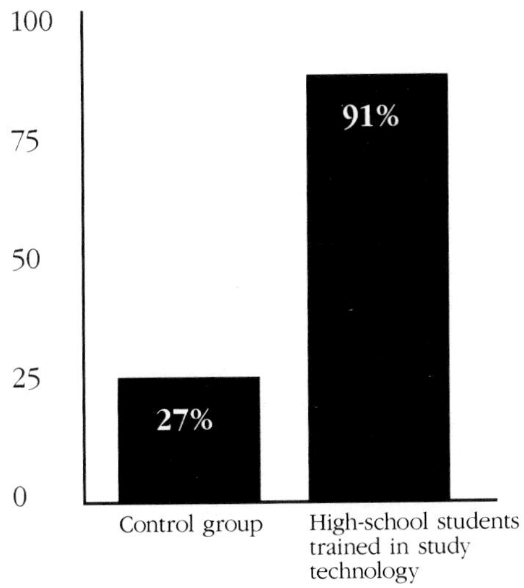

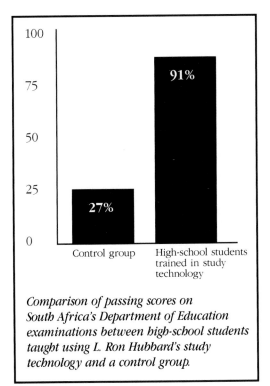

Comparison of passing scores on South Africa's Department of Education examinations between high-school students taught using L. Ron Hubbard's study technology and a control group.

L. Ron Hubbard recognized the failings of modern education and training in 1950, many years before educational horror stories began to make headlines.

His extensive investigation into the problems of teaching others led to a breakthrough—the first comprehensive understanding of the real barriers to effective learning. From this, Mr. Hubbard developed a precise technology on how to learn *any* subject—a technology that ensures a person will not only fully grasp what he is studying, but proficiently apply what he has studied in work or in life.

These breakthroughs came to be known as "study technology," and provide the first fully workable approach to teaching people exactly *how to learn*. Study technology helps anyone learn anything. Used throughout Scientology in all churches, missions and groups, it is also widely used outside the Church in schools and businesses. Study technology opens the door to effective training and makes it possible to raise the general quality of education to new heights.

Study technology is based on laws that underlie all learning. It delineates the barriers which block a person's ability to grasp information and provides precise methodologies to overcome those barriers.

Study technology has been extensively tested and proven to achieve uniform, consistent results wherever it has been applied. Because it is based on fundamentals common to everyone, it cuts across any economic, cultural or racial lines and can be used by all, regardless of age. It is as effective in the executive suites of multinational corporations as it is in elementary school classrooms.

Outstanding improvements have been made by students of all ages in reading level, comprehension, vocabulary and mathematics when they have been instructed in study technology. A Los Angeles study showed an average gain of 1.8 years in vocabulary and comprehension after only 10 hours of tutoring in study technology. One student gained an almost unbelievable 5 years and 9 months in his test scores after 20 hours of instruction. All teachers involved in this study also reported an overall improvement in their students' ability to learn, ability to read and, an unexpected gain, in the general behavior of students as a direct result of study technology.

An Arizona study tested students after the beginning of a school year and then six months later. Teachers ran the classroom using study technology throughout the duration of the study. Standard reading tests were administered and showed an average gain of two years in comprehension and vocabulary. This is four times the expected gain, a remarkable achievement considering individual tutoring was not part of the study.

In South Africa one class of underprivileged high-school students was trained in study technology, and at the end of the school year achieved a 91 percent pass rate on the country's Department of Education examination. A control group, not so trained, had a 27 percent pass rate on the same test.

The numbers collected from these and many similar studies translate, really, into effective education for young people and an assurance they will grow to a confident, self-reliant adulthood with learning skills they will use every day of their lives.

Many principles and procedures make up study technology, but it only takes a brief discussion of a few of the most basic to provide an insight into what it is and what it can accomplish.

THE BARRIERS TO STUDY

L. Ron Hubbard discovered three primary barriers which keep one from successfully studying a subject. Despite all that has been written on the subject, these three barriers, simple as they are, were never isolated as paramount to effective education. For want of this data, the toll in poorly educated students, unfulfilled potential and frustration is incalculable.

The First Barrier—Lack of Mass

Attempting to educate someone without the mass (or object) that he is going to be involved with can make study exceedingly difficult. This is the first barrier to study.

For example, if one is studying tractors, the printed page and the spoken word are no substitute for an actual tractor. Lacking a tractor to associate with the written word, or at least pictures of a tractor, can close off a person's understanding of the subject.

Definite physiological reactions occur when trying to educate a person in a subject without the thing actually present or available. A student who encounters this barrier will tend to feel squashed, bent, sort of spinny, sort of dead, bored and exasperated. He can wind up with his face feeling squashed, with headaches, and with his stomach feeling funny. He can feel dizzy from time to time and very often his eyes can hurt. These reactions are quite common but wrongly attributed to poor lighting, or studying too late at night, or any number of other incorrect reasons. The real cause is a lack of mass on the subject one is studying.

The remedy to this barrier is to supply the thing itself—in the example above, the tractor, or a reasonable substitute for one. Some educators have instinctively known this, but usually it was applied only to younger students and it certainly was never given the importance it warrants at any level of education.

The Second Barrier—Too Steep a Gradient

The next barrier is too steep a study gradient. That is, if a student is forced into undertaking a new action without having understood the previous action, confusion results.

There is a different set of physiological reactions which occur as a result of this barrier. When one hits too steep a gradient, a sort of confusion or reelingness is experienced.

Commonly, the difficulty is ascribed to the new action, when in fact it really stems from the previous action. The person did not fully understand some part earlier and then went into confusion on the new one. This barrier to study is very pronounced in subjects involved with activity.

Take the example of a person learning to drive. He cannot properly coordinate his feet and hands to manually shift the car into another gear while keeping to one lane. The difficulty will be found to lie in some earlier action about shifting gears. Possibly he was not yet comfortable shifting through the gears with the engine off and the car at rest. If this is recognized, the gradient can be cut back, and the person brought up to a point where he can easily shift the gears on a motionless car before performing the same action while in motion.

The Third Barrier—the Misunderstood Word

The third barrier to study is the most important of the three. It is the prime factor involved with stupidity and many other unwanted conditions.

This third barrier is the misunderstood word. A misunderstood definition or a not-comprehended definition or an undefined word can thoroughly block one's understanding of a subject and can even cause one to abandon the subject entirely.

This milestone in the field of education has great application, but it was overlooked by every educator in history.

Going past a word or symbol for which one does not have a proper definition gives one a distinctly blank or washed-out feeling. The person will get a "not there" feeling and will begin to feel a nervous hysteria. These are manifestations distinct from either of the other two barriers.

The barrier of the misunderstood word is far more important than the other two, however. It has much to do with human relations, the mind and different subjects. It establishes aptitude or lack of aptitude and is the key to what psychologists were attempting to test for years without recognizing what it was.

A person might or might not have *brilliance* as a computer programer, but his ability to *do* the motions of computer programing is dependent exclusively and only upon definitions. There is some word in the field of computer programing that the person who is inept did not define or understand and that was followed by an inability to act in the field of computer programing.

This is extremely important because it tells one what happens to doingness and that the restoration of doingness depends only on the location and understanding of any word which has been misunderstood in a subject.

Have you ever come to the bottom of a page only to realize you didn't remember what you had just read? That is the phenomenon of a misunderstood word, and one will always be found just before the material became blank in your mind.

The materials comprising the Student Hat course contain all of L. Ron Hubbard's study technology, as contained in his written works and recorded lectures.

This sweeping discovery is applicable to any sphere of endeavor, and opens wide the gates to education.

These barriers to study and their resolution are contained on a Scientology training course called the Student Hat. "Hat" is a Scientology slang term for a particular job, taken from the fact that in many professions, such as railroading, the type of hat worn is the badge of the job.

The Student Hat course covers the complete technology of how to study *any* subject effectively, providing the student with every needed tool. Much of the study technology is contained in a dozen lectures Mr. Hubbard gave on learning and education, and these are all included, along with many of his pertinent writings.

A full understanding of the barriers to study and how to recognize and fully handle them is gained on the course. The student learns how to clear up a misunderstood word so that he fully understands it and can use it in his speech and writing. One also becomes practiced in a precise method Mr. Hubbard developed to ensure comprehension in what one has studied.

In a technological society, someone who cannot easily assimilate data is in serious danger of being left behind. The Student Hat alone could invigorate the culture.

Study technology is universally applicable and has found wide utilization outside the Church: in schools, universities, businesses and other institutions. To make this technology available to all, the Church offers the following works in addition to the Student Hat materials:

Basic Study Manual

The major breakthroughs of study technology are described for any age or academic level from teenagers on up. All fundamentals are covered, giving a firm grounding to successful learning in any pursuit.

Learning How to Learn

Recommended as the first study book for children, this illustrated work teaches children how to study. Basic to all children's education, it teaches exact skills they need in order to begin learning.

Study Skills for Life

Written specifically for young teenagers, this book enables a person to learn the most basic aspects of study technology in an easy-to-understand format.

Two additional books exist to aid children in study:

How to Use a Dictionary Picture Book for Children

Many children have not been taught to use a dictionary. Thus, when a parent or teacher uses a word beyond their level of comprehension, they have no way to define it. *How to Use a Dictionary Picture Book for Children* teaches children how to find and understand words.

Grammar and Communication for Children

This simple English grammar book was written and illustrated to hold the interest of children. Its purpose is to show the young student the basics of grammar so he can understand and communicate well and does not develop a fear or distaste for the subject.

A TECHNOLOGY TO INCREASE COMPREHENSION

In the years following L. Ron Hubbard's breakthrough on the importance of the misunderstood word, he developed a considerable body of technology which enables one to deal with the misunderstood words or symbols he encounters.

The relay of ideas from one mind to another mind or minds depends upon words, symbols, sounds, pictures, emotions and past associations.

Primary among these, in any developed culture, are words. These can be written or spoken.

While whole subjects exist concerning the development and meaning of words, many of them very learned and worthwhile, practically no work was ever done on the effect of words or the consequences of their misuse or noncomprehension.

What was not studied or known before L. Ron Hubbard's development of study technology is that the flow of ideas in any message or field of learning can be blocked in such a way as to suppress further understanding or comprehension from that point forward. Further, the misunderstood word can even act in such a way as to bring about ignorance, apathy and revolt in the classroom and in the workplace depress productivity.

Not only did these factors remain undiscovered before Scientology, but also, of course, no technology existed to remedy the problem.

To enable a person to handle the effect of misunderstood words, L. Ron Hubbard developed the subject called Word Clearing. Word Clearing is part of the broader field of study technology, but in itself Word Clearing has many uses and applications. Word Clearing can be defined as "the subject and action of clearing away the ignorance, misunderstoods and false definitions of words and barriers to their use."

In his observations of society, Mr. Hubbard had noticed a deterioration in literacy during this century. This conclusion is inescapable if one compares the political speeches and literature of a hundred or even fifty years ago to those of today. He noticed that the public was more and more dependent upon radio, motion pictures and television, all of which contain the spoken word, and he considered the possibility that these messages were not being fully received or understood. His observations were confirmed when an advertising association undertook a survey which showed that television audiences misunderstood between one-quarter and one-third of all the material they watched—findings with alarming implications. Not only are there serious economic consequences, as the study pointed out, wherein up to one-third of advertising expenditures are wasted owing to the fact that the public does not understand the ads; but more importantly, such a gross level of noncomprehension can generate antipathy and even aggression among viewers.

When one speaks or writes, one has the responsibility to others of being understood. Further, one has a responsibility to oneself of ensuring that he understands what he sees and hears.

L. Ron Hubbard developed nine separate methods of Word Clearing and several related technologies for handling the effects of misunderstoods and false data in a person. Each method provides a different way of locating areas of noncomprehension, tracing this back to the misunderstood words underlying the problem and then getting these words fully understood so the person can use them in his own vocabulary.

Thousands of hours of research and hundreds of thousands of cases went into the development of these nine methods.

In the twelve or sixteen years or more that a student spends in school, the unknowing accumulation of undefined words and symbols can present a serious barrier to knowledge and productivity in life. Also, a person contacts words or symbols in everyday activities outside of the classroom which he does not understand and these, too, dull his capabilities.

With the techniques of Word Clearing, whole subjects and educations which were not understood at the time and could not subsequently be applied can be recovered and used. Such is the power of clearing misunderstood words.

Wherever communication is being engaged in, given or received, the technology of Word Clearing will find beneficial use.

Study technology is a complete subject in itself and used by millions of people all over the world, in schools, universities and businesses.

Mr. Hubbard once remarked, "The future is the only frontier without limit and the frontier that we all enter and cross no matter what we do."

Reading news headlines is enough to tell anyone that social problems are escalating in virtually every community and that these portend a bleak future. Drugs, crime, unemployment, poverty and violence are all indicators of how extensive educational failures have become. A great many of those enmeshed in such problems could have been happier, more productive individuals if they had simply learned how to learn. If used, study technology will salvage both our current and future generations.

CHAPTER 11

THE KEY TO LIFE: HANDLING A WORLD OUT OF COMMUNICATION

Communication is one of the key elements of living, a fact that becomes even more apparent as one progresses in Scientology. It is thus not unreasonable to say that a person is as alive as he or she can communicate.

Three cultural changes during the last half-century have combined to lessen this ability in a great majority of people.

After World War II, general education standards were lowered. New systems of education ignored such fundamentals as reading, writing and grammar. School systems adopted a permissive attitude toward education with the inevitable consequence that students learned less and less. The decline was progressive and hastened after 1950 when television became dominant in child care. Mothers plunked their children in front of the TV and let them fixate their attention, the continuous inflow of images serving as both leash and babysitter. The onset of the drug scourge in the 1960s further served to dull the minds of the TV generation.

These three factors have produced generations of people who are bombarded with a large amount of information which they do not comprehend and who have been placed in the role of mere spectators. They are, as a result, out of communication with life.

This has led to lawlessness, inflation, lowered production and many other societal problems, not to mention the individual frustration and unhappiness of wasted potential and wasted years. People ill-equipped for living in a highly technological society get trampled by those who are better equipped; and even the very bright are eventually impeded by those underfoot. Educators in the better private universities routinely find students who cannot read with comprehension, regardless of how well they scored on standardized admission tests.

L. Ron Hubbard recognized these phenomena in the 1950s, as we have seen in the last chapter, and by 1964 he developed the technology of how to study. However, in the late 1970s he saw that even this technology now required a more fundamental handling owing to the general cultural decline. He found that many people, even college educated, were unable to easily assimilate data, including his study technology.

"Functional illiteracy" describes the circumstance wherein an individual appears able to make his way in life, yet is actually so deficient in reading and writing that, for all but menial purposes, he is illiterate. A growing number of students have been little more than baby-sat in the school system for twelve years, then turned loose with almost no chance of contributing to society and with every chance that society will have to support them. The term, *functional illiteracy,* really means simply, "illiteracy" and is a condemnation of an educational system which, entrusted with educating our young people, fails them miserably and fails the rest of us as well.

Over 25 million Americans are illiterate, according to government figures. Another 45 million, at least, are only marginally capable of leading productive lives. These two categories amount to nearly 49 percent of all adult Americans and underscore the general decline in literacy.

Tests made by Mr. Hubbard in the late 1970s revealed that college graduates, when examined on the common materials they would read for pleasure, were found to not understand much of what they read. They could pronounce words but could not define many of the words they pronounced! With respect to these people's ability to comprehend written materials, an *apparency* of understanding masked the actual state of affairs: that these people did not really comprehend what they were reading. Their ability to learn had been stymied.

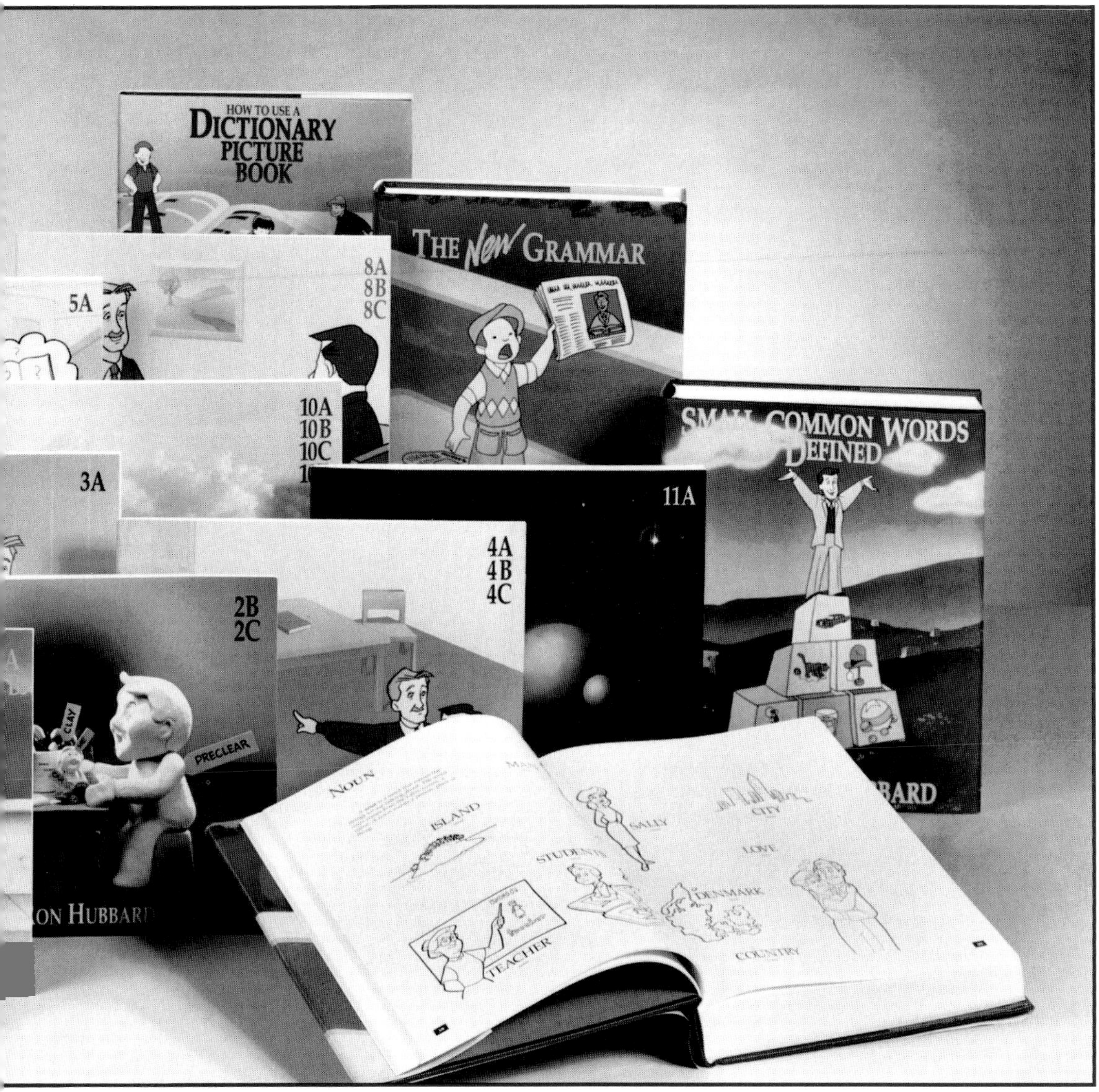

The Hubbard Key to Life Course breaks through the barriers to comprehension and assimilation of data, utilizing thousands of pictures to communicate the fundamental factors of language.

Not everyone suffers from this condition. But it does exist in varying degrees in nearly everyone. For example, in the sentence, "It's as good as gold," most people cannot define the word "as." Yet, "as" is a word used every day. This doesn't classify one as illiterate but it does serve to show that anyone's comprehension could be increased.

If one truly comprehended what he read and heard and if he were able to make himself comprehended by others, all of life would open to him. But to the degree he cannot express himself and make others understand him, and to the degree he cannot understand what others are communicating, life is closed off to him.

In solving the problem of a world out of communication, L. Ron Hubbard developed a thorough handling that not only brings an illiterate up to literacy but increases the ability of *anyone* to comprehend and to be comprehended.

The handling he devised is called the Hubbard Key to Life Course.

Key to Life is a major breakthrough in the field of communication. Step by step, it strips away the reasons why a person cannot clearly comprehend what he reads, writes and hears and why others cannot comprehend him.

In developing the Key to Life, there was a particular problem that cried out for a solution. On a wider sphere, this is a conundrum that has been faced, but not resolved, by every educator in history: How does one teach someone to understand and use the language without assuming that the person under instruction already knows at least some of what one is trying to teach him? How, for example, does one teach the meaning of a word without assuming the person already knows how to read the words being used to teach him? How does one teach the language without assuming the person already knows some of it?

For example, if one opens a dictionary to look up the definition of a word, one can encounter other words that are not understood. If one opens up a book on grammar, one is immediately hit with terminology that is not explained until later. Yet, when one encounters a misunderstood word, he ceases to understand and does not fully grasp or become aware of what follows. Understanding ceases on going past a misunderstood word. This datum is the single most important factor in the whole field of education. How, then, can one teach the language, its construction, its words and its use without laying the person open to misunderstood words?

In cutting this Gordian knot, L. Ron Hubbard solved the problem of literacy itself and of difficulties in comprehension, and so opened the door to a vastly increased understanding of life.

Needed was a way to bypass the possibility of misunderstood words in the student no matter how poor his level of comprehension. Words are used to communicate concepts from one person to another. But other means too can be used. A concept can be communicated by a sign, by a physical gesture, by a noise or by a picture, etc. By drawing a picture of a cat next to the words *felis domesticus,* one can communicate the concept of a house cat, which is what *felis domesticus* means.

The Key to Life Course utilizes thousands of pictures, drawn by top illustrators from Hollywood film studios, to communicate the concepts needed to teach the student the materials on the course. Concepts are defined using pictures as well as words to ensure that comprehension occurs.

In one of the books on the course, each concept in the entire book is illustrated as well as defined and assures comprehension without having to use complex definitions. This is a unique dictionary that fully defines each of the sixty most commonly used words in the language. With the use of pictures, the factor of misunderstood words is circumvented and a student can really learn the words he uses and reads most often, without getting hopelessly tangled up in the complexities of grammar. In this way, a person improves his understanding of what he hears or reads and improves his ability to make himself understood.

The importance of this approach becomes apparent when one realizes that it opens the door to fully learning the most commonly used words in the language, how the language is put together and how to use it. With such knowledge, a person is able to communicate and receive communication with a much higher level of comprehension.

Another breakthrough on Key to Life is a completely innovative approach to the subject of grammar. Mr. Hubbard simplified the language into its basic building blocks and showed people how to use those building blocks to better express their thoughts and understand what they read and hear.

In his book, *The New Grammar,* Mr. Hubbard resolves many of the confusions entered into the language by grammarians and turns grammar into something that one can *use* rather than something one merely *studies.*

THE IMPORTANCE OF *THE NEW GRAMMAR*

"English is now the language of international communication. It is the language used by heads of state. It is the language of international business negotiation. It is the language of the majority of the rapidly growing masses of computerized information.

"Unfortunately, most persons educated by the public education systems in the United States are not competent in understanding and using English. As a teacher in one of the better private universities in the United States I am well aware that many of our students, even though they are among those ranking very high on standardized tests, are unable to read with comprehension. Failing to master the full resources of the English language, students become functionally illiterate.

"This inability to fully understand and use language causes problems in schools and businesses, and these problems affect wider areas of society. In this time of widespread illiteracy L. Ron Hubbard introduces a book that makes grammar understandable and useful to all.

"This book takes grammar and makes it easy. It helps individuals to understand the basic building blocks of the English language and how to use those building blocks to better communicate, express their thoughts and understand what they read.

"L. Ron Hubbard first gained fame as a writer at a time when even the popular magazines of the day expected their readers to appreciate breadth of vocabulary and variety of style.

"Only a professional writer with a writer's sensitivity to language could have written such an innovative approach to grammar. Only such a writer would see grammar not as full of constricting rules, but full of possibilities for rich expressions of thought and action.

"Teaching writers how to write in the 1940s, L. Ron Hubbard has now come full circle with this grammar book and returned to the field of teaching language.

"This is a brilliant book by a brilliant mind. In fact, it is a revolution in thought."

David Rodier, Ph.D.
Associate Professor of Philosophy
American University, Washington, DC

***The New Grammar** focuses not on a study of stultified rules, but on the **use** of grammar to facilitate communication.*

Many people have a distaste for grammar because it has been stultified by grammarians into a maze of complex rules understandable not even to grammarians themselves. Mr. Hubbard showed instead that grammar is really something one *uses* in order to facilitate and enhance meaningful communication, and that grammar really has no other useful purpose. He has put together *the* book that at last clarifies the construction of the language. *The New Grammar* has drastically altered the concept of grammar for the thousands who have completed the Key to Life Course.

The Hubbard Key to Life Course produces a person who is literate and who can express himself easily and clearly, both verbally and in writing, and who can fully understand the communication he receives from others.

In our technological society, which regularly requires a high order of comprehension, the declining level of literacy is disastrous. There are many consequences if one does not understand things in life, and none are good.

The Hubbard Key to Life Course enables an individual to avoid these consequences in himself and opens up to him all of life.

CHAPTER 12

THE LIFE ORIENTATION COURSE: ATTAINING COMPETENCE IN LIFE

It is commonly heard that one can find happiness if he is really doing what he wants to do in life.

But scratching the social veneer finds many whose lives could be happier and just as many who have abandoned earlier dreams. One wanted to be a concert musician, but father fell ill and there was no one to run the store. One dreamed of medical school, but settled for teaching high school when a baby came due and a family had to be supported. One wanted to own a beauty shop, but problems in the marriage prevented it. One was going to be a jet pilot until faced with the seemingly impossible rigors of prerequisite studies.

What fulfillment has faded in the tides and fortunes of living? How many people have settled for a life in which they could get along, rather than the one in which they could flourish? Too many.

If one could conceive of doing what one truly loved, it is not hard to imagine the happiness that would follow. But, to the extent one does not follow his true interests, the factors in his life can be badly misaligned, breeding disharmony and unhappiness.

If all dynamics that constitute a person's life were aligned toward the attainment of a clear and worthwhile purpose, one would be well along a road to success, regardless of any personal advancements he was making spiritually through Scientology auditing or training.

One is often defined, and remembered, by what he does in life. Fundamentally, a thetan is the creator of things. On a day-to-day basis this is represented by his job, what he produces, how he supports himself and so on. Many individuals are not fulfilled in this part of their lives. Their activities are not aligned for optimum productivity, which causes innumerable complications. The man who is unproductive at his job brings his disgruntlement home, making his home life less pleasant. He finds less enjoyment in his leisure time. He may feel anxious about losing his job because the company will not be able to carry him forever if he is not contributing to it. His life would be more worthwhile if he were more productive at work. He certainly would be happier about himself if he could demonstrate a higher level of competence in his activities.

A person's competence can be directly addressed using the technology L. Ron Hubbard developed and made available on the Hubbard Life Orientation Course.

There are many parts to anyone's life—ambitions, friends and associates, a job and social involvements. There are obligations to fulfill, assets to protect, people to look after, a future to make. Just how many factors are there to a life? And what happens if one factor is missing or life is overbalanced in favor of another factor to the neglect of still others?

The Life Orientation Course sorts out every single area of a person's life, utilizing a specific series of steps. Mr. Hubbard observed that the totality of anyone's activities in life can be compartmented into twenty-one separate areas. The first step of the course involves the person's close inspection of each of these twenty-one areas to gain a clear picture of where he stands. He then undertakes a searching study of the eight dynamics, with emphasis on his personal involvement on each dynamic. A special auditing process enables him to closely inspect his dynamics, providing him a clearer view of all life.

Now with a much better vantage point, he can view his life, dynamics, his influence over these dynamics, his decisions along these lines and how these have contributed to where he finds himself. Study alone could not bring about this awareness; the auditing is necessary. This is a more distinct view than ever available before. The individual's existence is being straightened out using the fundamentals on which life operates.

With this sufficiently broad view, he can begin to isolate the actions that promote increased survival from those actions which are nonsurvival. This entails more auditing, developed by Mr. Hubbard especially for the Life Orientation Course. This results in a firm subjective understanding of what happens in life if the dynamics go out of alignment.

The student next learns technology about the consequences of actions harmful to his dynamics and undertakes to locate and view all his transgressions against any part of his life. This tremendous unburdening of past misdeeds and mishaps truly means, for many people, the beginning of a new existence.

With attention unpinned from points in his past, he is ready to learn exact ways to improve his future. He learns the natural laws that govern existence and the tools necessary to arrest the decline that traps so many.

The student now learns how the different activities of his life must each result in something of real use and value. A person who has no real purpose in life or what he does or who produces nothing of value will be miserable. A specific product should result from activity in each part of his life.

His profession, for instance, results in a product which furthers his survival. A person produces something or provides some service for which he is given money on which to live. The establishment and maintenance of his living quarters results in a completely different product, but one which also helps promote a different aspect of his survival. A comfortable, clean home is a pleasant place in which to live, certainly a valuable product in itself. Likewise, each activity in a person's life has a product, and these either aid or inhibit his success and survival depending on how good they are.

On the Life Orientation Course, the person arrives at a clear understanding of where he is heading in life, and what his true purpose really is. Such an awareness makes it possible to straighten out his life because he now sees where he is going. Once this is clear in his mind, he can align all the elements of his life to this purpose and get somewhere—the somewhere he always wanted to be.

The final step of the course gets the person totally oriented to his main product in life, how this fits in with the rest of his dynamics, and brings him to clearly view what he needs to do to viably produce it. This is a major advance because it results in someone who is causative, competent and productive in life.

With this ability gained, the individual's life is truly straightened out and he sees clearly where he is headed, now armed with the tools to make sure he arrives.

It is a great feeling to be oriented in life. Many forces are at work, thrusting one this way and that. People get caught up in them and are carried along, snowed under or left out.

The new alternative, attained on the Hubbard Life Orientation Course, is to get one's life in clear perspective and under control, with a certainty on the laws of life, knowing what one is doing to forward one's *own* purposes.

On the Life Orientation Course purpose, morale, fulfillment and happiness are in the offing.

A frank assessment of the lives of other people usually reveals that many are not leading the lives they would like, but in the manner life "has to be" for one reason or another. L. Ron Hubbard developed the Life Orientation Course to help people better understand where they are going in life and to help them make their lives more fulfilling.

The Life Orientation Course is a route *into* the activity of living. Spiritual gains from the rest of Scientology can be augmented greatly from the knowledge contained on this course.

CHAPTER 13

AUDITING SERVICES

Millions, attesting to the results of auditing, prove beyond doubt that auditing accomplishes far more to better man than any other means ever devised.

Through auditing, a person can rid himself of his reactive mind and the limitations it imposes upon him—limitations which were once thought "natural." Man's full potential, so often speculated about, can be realized. This potential is far, far higher than earlier practices and religions ever thought possible.

Millions of Scientologists have found out more about themselves through auditing and improved their lives as a direct result.

The different processes which comprise auditing technology can be likened to a road—an exact road, with exact steps that anyone can walk. L. Ron Hubbard developed many different auditing processes during his research. He arranged these in a sequence that enables an individual to achieve greater awareness and with this, higher states of existence leading to, ultimately, a recognition of his own immortal nature.

If one thinks about it for a moment, one will recognize that there are many states of existence in life. A man is rich or poor, well or sick, old or young, married or single.

Moreover, in Scientology it is known that there are many states of existence beyond that of so-called normal man. This has been touched on by earlier philosophies but what is new about Scientology is that one can predictably attain these higher states of existence.

Although some savants in the Himalayas have worked in this direction, Gautama Siddhartha (Buddha) spoke of it at length, at least fifteen or twenty years of hard work were required for what was, at best, an uncertain outcome.

With Scientology, there are no such uncertainties. Higher states of existence are attainable through auditing, and these states and how they can be attained are described here.

SCIENTOLOGY EXPANDED GRADES

When they begin auditing, people are usually too beset by problems to immediately face and handle the core of the reactive mind. A person is worried about his mortgage payments. He suffers from job stress. His child needs dental work. His marriage is shaky. His paycheck is shrinking in the face of escalating taxes and inflation, and on and on. The day-to-day pressures of life are simply too consuming; and so one needs increased abilities just to stay abreast of these pressures, much less to surmount and be free of them.

The Scientology Expanded Grades are a series of auditing processes which address and increase specific abilities in order to place the individual in a far better position to survive.

L. Ron Hubbard discovered that there are certain definite barriers to living successfully. If a person is able in these areas he can survive. If he is unable in these areas, he does not survive well and flounders.

The Expanded Grades consist of six separate grades (which are described below) and nearly 150 different processes on which a person is audited. Each grade was designed by Mr. Hubbard to enable the individual to rehabilitate or strengthen specific abilities needed to succeed in life.

When a particular process has been run to its desired result, the person's awareness increases in that area and he becomes more able in that regard. Running more processes on a similar subject returns more ability in the area. When all the processes of a grade have been run the person has become rehabilitated on the whole subject of that grade, at which point the next grade, and another area of ability, can be addressed.

In this way, the Expanded Grades improve the person's abilities gradiently—abilities which were so buried that one has come to believe that his failings were simply a "natural" consequence of life. In fact, however, such failings are not natural at all. Through Scientology Expanded Grades auditing a person's native potentials and characteristics become evident, and flourish.

The six Expanded Grades are:

Expanded ARC Straightwire: "ARC" refers to the components of understanding. "Straightwire" is another term for "straight memory," so called because in the auditing processes on this grade the auditor directs the memory of the preclear and in doing so is stringing wire, much on the order of a telephone line, between the preclear and the standard memory bank in the preclear's mind.

The concept of ARC is one of the most important factors in all of life. If a person can establish ARC for something he can truly understand it. As noted, the subject of Scientology is the person himself, and so it follows that the first grade would involve restoring a preclear's direct and immediate understanding of himself. This is accomplished through the processes of ARC Straightwire.

ARC Straightwire explores the capabilities of one's memory and mind. If a person could increase his ARC for himself, he would realize that he is possibly his own best friend. A person who truly likes himself is an important first milestone to reach on the road to freedom.

Expanded Grade 0: The ability to communicate is one of the most fundamental abilities of a being. This ability too often fades through the course of living. As a consequence, some people grow shy and retiring. Others suffer from knots in their stomachs at the prospect of addressing a crowd. Still others are unable to discuss certain subjects or grow uncomfortable in the presence of the opposite sex or with people not of their age bracket. The number of ways a diminished ability to communicate can manifest itself are really incalculable.

The processes of this grade address a person's ability to communicate and free him, in his *own* estimation, from any blocks in the area, thus restoring the ability to communicate to anyone about any subject. Although some may view such a state as an impossibility, factually thousands and thousands of people have received just such gains with Expanded Grade 0. And with the ability to communicate comes the joy of associating freely with others.

We instinctively revere the great artist, painter or musician and society as a whole looks upon them as not quite ordinary beings.

And they are not. They are a cut above man. He who can truly communicate to others is a higher being who builds new worlds.

Auditing can help an individual achieve this higher state of being—one who can communicate.

Expanded Grade I: This grade deals with the problems a person has in his life. One can be so enmeshed with unwanted situations that any chance for happiness seems remote indeed. The problems of relationships, finances, job, family, one's ambitions, etc., can absorb a tremendous amount of energy.

What distinguishes civilized man as MAN is that he is mired in problems which just get worse the more he tries to "solve" them.

L. Ron Hubbard discovered a precise mechanism common to all problems. Any problem, regardless of how complex or how big, has at its source one intention in opposition to another intention. The conflicts in a person's life all stem from opposing intentions. This mechanism makes a person indecisive, causes his worries and causes situations in his life to "hang up" and not resolve.

The processes on Expanded Grade I bring the preclear up to an ability to recognize the actual source of problems at which point they "vanish"—cease to be problems anymore. A person who can do this is too rare to be easily comprehended. Man *solves* problems. But a being in a higher state looks at them and they vanish.

The mechanisms and phenomena surrounding problems are things which man has never, before Scientology, examined or understood.

Someone with this ability—to make problems vanish with a glance—is certainly in a far better condition in life.

Expanded Grade II: People try as best they can to deal with the hostilities and sufferings of life. Hit with "the slings and arrows of outrageous fortune," one responds in kind, and finds himself in a trap from which there has never been an escape.

The trap is composed of a person's transgressions against the mores of his family, the society and the race. Throughout his life a person has agreed to certain codes of conduct. These are the mores by which he survives in harmony with others. When a person unthinkingly transgresses against the mores to which he has agreed or, with "good cause" knowingly offends them, his misery begins. Having transgressed, the person now feels he must hold back his deed from others, and he begins to withdraw or feel different from the person or group he has harmed. This is the mechanism by which people create misery, bitterness and hatred around themselves. This is the source of the guilty conscience, feelings of vengeance and, actually, all the sufferings and hostilities of life.

Expanded Grade II processes enable a person to take apart this mechanism for himself. It is a tremendous relief to fully view this aspect of one's past in the calm, analytical environment of an auditing session.

The processes of Grade II eradicate these hostilities and sufferings from a person's life and provide relief from the actions that have pinned one to his past.

Expanded Grade III: Man is chained to his prior upsets. He has never understood why he felt so upset about his family or people or situations.

Most people dwell perpetually on troubles they have had. They lead sad lives.

Freedom from upsets of the past, with the resultant ability to openly face the future, is almost an unknown condition to man. But this too can be achieved in auditing.

Times of upheaval can unknowingly pin a person's attention years after the episodes. On Grade III processes one locates specific incidents where upsetting change occurred in life and addresses these. The end result of Expanded Grade III is the freedom to face the future with an enhanced ability to confront, experience and find advantage in the inevitable changes of life.

Expanded Grade IV: The next barrier to ability is addressed on Grade IV. Habit patterns can be nearly impossible to break, yet these fixed conditions hold a person down and rivet his ideas and activities in ways that cloud his potential.

The mechanism by which one falls into such a trap revolves around the concepts of right and wrong. Inborn in everyone is the impulse to be right. A person tries to be right and fights being wrong, no matter how he views these ideas. In the upsets, troubles and failures of life, this impulse to be right and not be wrong can become confused. This results in patterns of conduct that are demonstrably not in the best interests of survival, for they are fixed and repeated over and over in a misguided effort to be right.

The processes of Grade IV enable the preclear to view himself in relation to all life and free himself from any patterns of thought and action which, while seeming to promote one's survival, in reality do everything but. When one makes such a discovery it can dramatically change one's life, and leads to a huge resurgence in the ability to choose, partake in and enjoy new activities.

Countless events over years and years of a lifetime diminish a person's abilities. Many of these events, too insignificant to even notice at the time, yet have telling effects. With auditing, it does not take but a small fraction of one's lifetime to restore abilities and even enhance them beyond what one thought possible. In two or three months of regular auditing a person can make tremendous strides towards a rehabilitation of his native abilities, and experience how good life can be with such barriers out of the way. The gain available from the Scientology Expanded Grades is considerable. It can literally bring one to new states of existence.

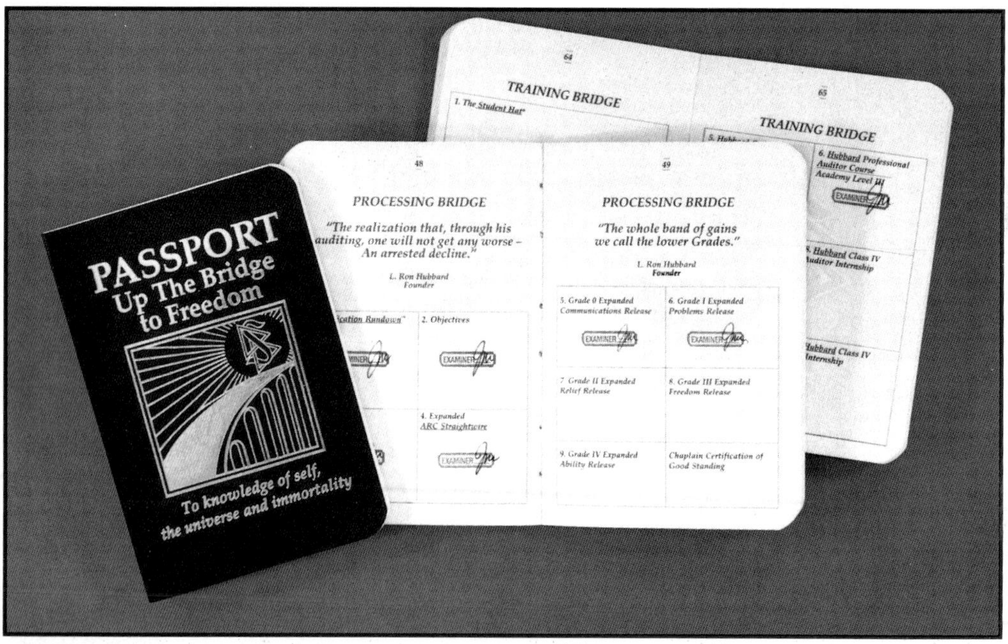

The Scientology Passport to Freedom, used by Scientologists to assist in tracking their orderly progress up the Bridge. As one finishes a grade, the passport is stamped to show completion.

NEW ERA DIANETICS AUDITING

A person able in an area can produce, perform, function and control activity in that area. An able acrobat, for example, performs stunts adroitly. An able chef prepares delicious food. But a person who has attained the abilities from the Scientology Expanded Grades is now able in *living* itself. As such he is more in control, brighter, and enjoys more personal power.

He is also now in a position to rid himself of his reactive mind and its contents. This accomplishment is not possible if a person is too distracted by his environment or cannot overcome the barriers to living the Expanded Grades handle.

Initially, by using the techniques contained in *Dianetics: The Modern Science of Mental Health,* engrams could be contacted and erased, resulting in more gains than were ever before available. The techniques invariably worked, but L. Ron Hubbard continued to research, seeking technology that offered faster and easier-to-attain results.

Refinements, such as the development of the E-Meter, made auditing swifter and more precise, as did development of the Scientology Expanded Grades. Building on the basic principles of Dianetics, Mr. Hubbard undertook further researches and developed more advanced Dianetics techniques. That these later refinements were built on the original axioms and procedures of Dianetics as initially released by him, is a great testimony to the accuracy of his original theories.

To give one an idea of just how effective Mr. Hubbard's new techniques were, consider this: Preclears who might have needed over 2,000 hours of auditing to achieve the highest results obtainable from 1950 technology might now achieve comparable gains in a tenth of that time with modern Dianetics and Scientology.

New Era Dianetics (NED) is the technology which contains L. Ron Hubbard's ultimate refinements of Dianetics auditing. He developed it following discoveries he made in 1978. Using New Era Dianetics technology, preclears can achieve the goals of Dianetics much, much faster than any early Dianeticist might have believed possible.

The reactive mind plagues a person with the unthinking, irrational dictates of its contents and imposes anxieties, fears, unwanted sensations and feelings, strange pains and a host of other undesirable effects. Freeing him from the command value such ills exert over his volition provides new levels of self-determinism.

A person may have suffered the emotional upheaval of losing a loved one. NED auditing addresses these losses and, while it won't replace the affections held for the departed, it can free one from the spiritual trauma of the loss.

Many people are held back by what they consider their flaws or disabilities. NED techniques can erase the sources of these feelings and brighten a person's outlook and feelings about himself remarkably.

New Era Dianetics auditing consists of at least eleven specific rundowns (a series of auditing steps designed to handle a specific aspect of a case) and actions which address the engrams contained in the reactive mind. The different psychosomatic pains, sensations, emotions, feelings and so forth are used to trace back engrams in the reactive mind. Utilizing Dianetics auditing procedure, the preclear erases his engrams and nullifies their harmful energy.

The procedures of New Era Dianetics are precise. Completion of New Era Dianetics can make a well and happy human being with renewed health and his innate sanity recovered.

EXPANDED DIANETICS

This is a branch of Dianetics which uses New Era Dianetics in special ways for specific purposes. Some persons require Dianetics technology specially adapted to their individual requirements and this is delivered on Expanded Dianetics. While New Era Dianetics is very general in application, Expanded Dianetics is specifically tailored to the preclear's needs. It is not the same as New Era Dianetics and requires special training and advanced skills.

Some preclears have particularly heavy histories of drug taking. Others have been victimized by injurious psychiatric treatments or have unresolving psychosomatic complaints. People such as these benefit from the specially adapted technology contained in Expanded Dianetics, which consists of more than a dozen different auditing rundowns designed to address and handle such things as:

- Difficulties the preclear has in his environment
- Experiences of severe emotional stress
- Points of his past from which he cannot free his attention
- Areas of severe personal difficulty stemming from cruel impulses

Expanded Dianetics technology resolves the more difficult aberrations found in the reactive mind. Not every preclear requires Expanded Dianetics but it often brings a spectacular improvement in those receiving it.

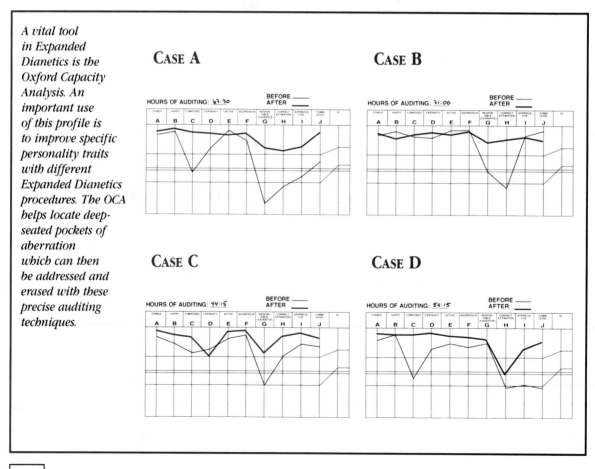

A vital tool in Expanded Dianetics is the Oxford Capacity Analysis. An important use of this profile is to improve specific personality traits with different Expanded Dianetics procedures. The OCA helps locate deep-seated pockets of aberration which can then be addressed and erased with these precise auditing techniques.

CASE A

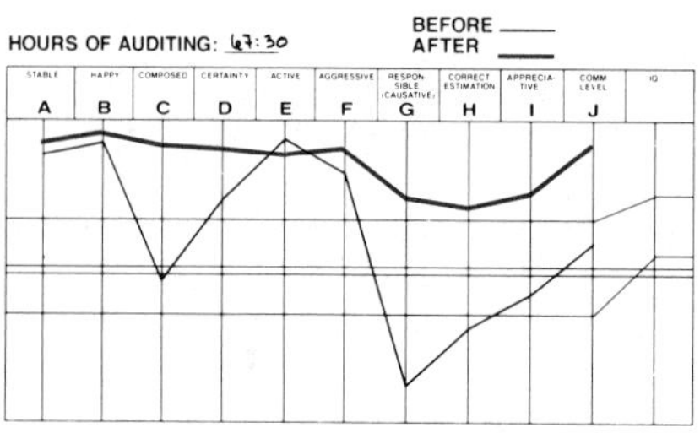

CASE B

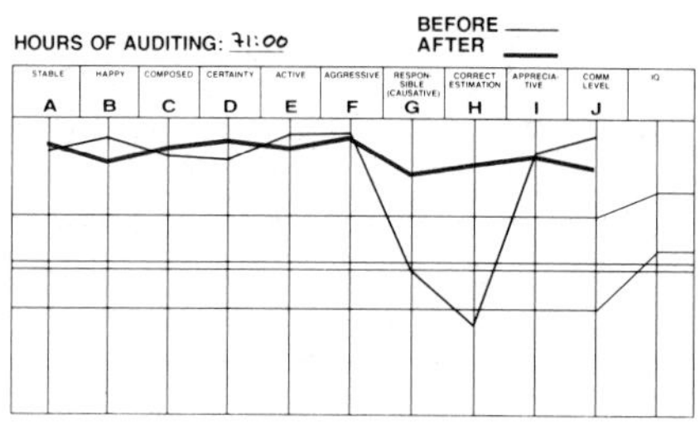

CASE C

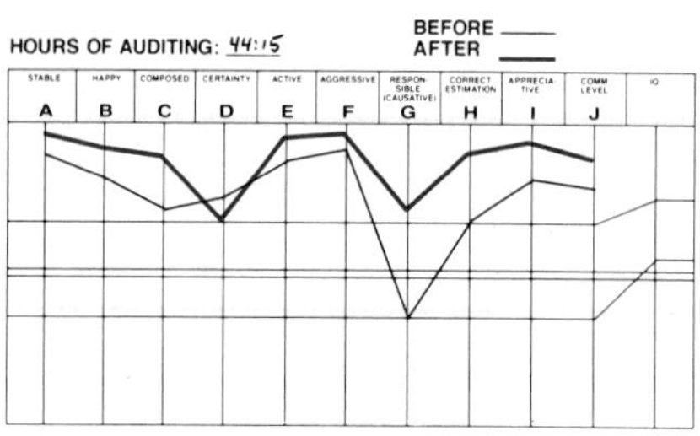

CASE D

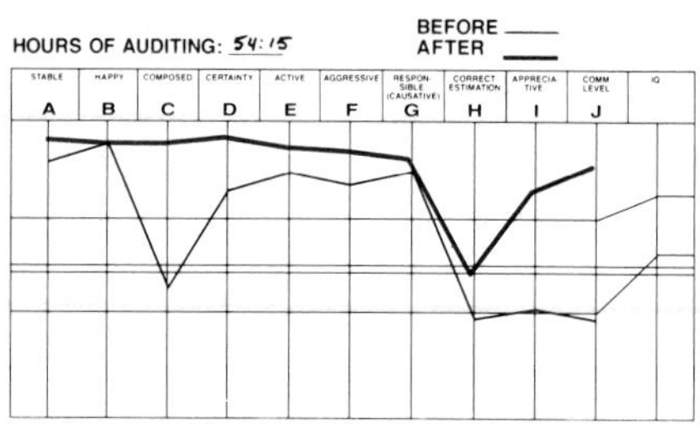

THE STATE OF CLEAR

The goals of Scientology predate all current ideas of "therapy" and are first found in religion and philosophy as long as 10,000 years ago. A Scientologist is trying to make people better and that is a new idea in the field of the human mind.

Clearing someone is erasing his reactive mind. All the misery man experiences is contained in the reactive mind.

There is a definite road out from reactivity, from aberration, from identifying everything with everything else. It leads to increased abilities, increased general performance and other exceptional gains that can be precisely measured and experienced. This road out has certain milestones which must be passed, and these are represented in the Expanded Grades and New Era Dianetics auditing.

The product of traveling the road that runs past these milestones is the erasure of reactivity. When this occurs the person achieves the state of Clear. It is not possible to attain this upper state by ignoring the lower grades.

A Clear is a person who no longer has his own reactive mind. He has vanquished it forever. Without the stimulus-response mechanisms of the reactive mind which can cause a person pain, unwanted sensations and negative emotions, a Clear can act rather than *react*. A Clear has a very high degree of personal integrity and honesty, and is living proof that man is basically good. His own basic beingness returns and his own basic personality flourishes. A person loses all the fears, anxieties and irrational thoughts that were held down by pain in the reactive mind and, in short, regains himself when he goes Clear. A person is much, much more himself without a reactive mind.

Until a person is cleared, no matter how able he becomes by virtue of earlier auditing, it is inevitable, just by the nature of the universe, that he will sooner or later sink back into the reactive mind. That is why clearing is vital. Clear is total erasure of the reactive mind and thus is a stable state, not subject to relapse.

When a person attains the state of Clear he is entitled to wear the Clear bracelet.

Each preclear is different and the type and amount of auditing necessary to erase the reactive mind is unique to each person. The state is therefore reached at either of two different places in a person's auditing. The first place is on New Era Dianetics. If a person does not achieve Clear on NED, he continues with further actions and attains it on the Clearing Course, a later service with a special auditing procedure. Other grades or auditing services do not result in Clear.

The state of Clear has never existed before. No matter how able a being may have been, no matter what powers he possessed, no matter his strengths, the reactive mind was still there, hidden, and eventually dragged him down again.

The full glory of the state of Clear has no comparable description in any literature existing in the culture, religious or otherwise. The state has been long sought but was impossible to achieve until the researches and breakthroughs of L. Ron Hubbard.

But the state does exist and it is attainable and many thousands of Scientologists all over the world are Clear, joined by more each day.

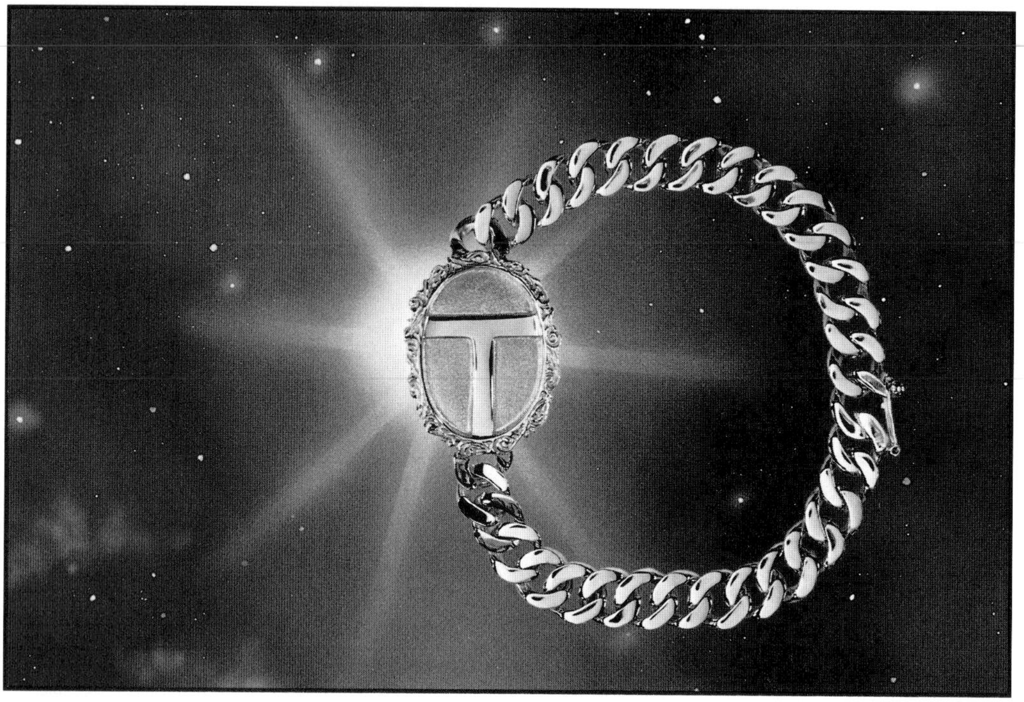

To acknowledge one's attainment of New OT VIII, a Scientologist may wear the OT bracelet.

THE STATE OF OPERATING THETAN

For thousands of years men have sought the state of complete spiritual freedom from the endless cycle of birth and death, a state of full awareness, memory and ability as a spirit independent of the flesh.

By eradicating the reactive mind in clearing we not only achieve an erasure of the seeming evil in man, we also overcome the barriers which made it so difficult to attain total spiritual independence and serenity. Thus, once a person achieves Clear he is now able to become refamiliarized with his native capabilities. As man is basically good, a being who is Clear becomes willing to trust himself with greater and greater abilities.

In Scientology, a state of complete spiritual freedom is attainable. It has been achieved not on a temporary basis but on a stable plane of full awareness and ability, unqualified by accident or deterioration. And it is not limited to a few.

It is called, in Scientology, "Operating Thetan." The definition of the state of Operating Thetan is "knowing and willing cause over life, thought, matter, energy, space and time."

The amount of spiritual gain available to a person is something rarely conceived. In an aberrated state where one's energy is primarily absorbed attempting to straighten out personal problems, a person is unlikely to lift his gaze to the glories that could be his as a fully rehabilitated and able being, not just as *Homo sapiens.*

On the auditing services above the state of Clear, called the "OT levels," one is no longer dealing with a person in relationship to his job, his house payments or his aches and pains. These will have been addressed at lower levels since it is necessary to free a person's attention from these matters in order to address higher aspects of existence. Having been freed of his own reactive mind, the person is able to undertake further steps in auditing by himself, becoming at the same time the auditor and the person being audited. This is "Solo auditing," learned on the Solo Auditor's Course. The Solo auditor uses communication drills, adapted to this level of skill, an E-Meter and exact processes, enabling him to rise into the realm of OT.

At the level of Operating Thetan one deals with the individual's own *immortality* as a spiritual being. One deals with the thetan himself in relationship to eternity; not to the eternity that lies *behind* him, but to the eternity which lies *ahead*.

On the OT levels one is rising to *eternity*. The vastness of time which has existed in the past is matched by at least as much time which lies ahead. *That* is eternity and a being will be in that eternity, and he will be in a good state or a bad state. One can step out of a job or a relationship or a worn-out suit of clothes, but one is not going to step out of life.

Contrary to those who teach that man cannot improve and that some seventy years in a body are all one can expect, there are states higher than that of mortal man. The state of OT does exist and people do attain it. Like any other gain in Scientology it is attained gradiently. Just as it would not be as beneficial to give someone New Era Dianetics auditing before improving his abilities with the Scientology Expanded Grades, so it is fruitless to try and move someone onto the OT levels before he is ready for them. One might as well pull a baby out of its bassinet and demand that he run. He won't make it until he has first learned to crawl and then walk. The reactive mind thoroughly blocks the thetan from regaining and exercising his native powers. But once this block is removed, the person can learn to operate as himself, a spiritual being.

The OT levels contain the very advanced materials of L. Ron Hubbard's researches and it is here the person achieves the ultimate realization of his own nature and his relationship to life and all the dynamics. Abilities return as he advances up through the OT levels and he recovers the entirety of his beingness.

Some of the miracles of life have been exposed to full view for the first time ever on the OT levels. Not the least of these miracles is knowing immortality and freedom from the cycle of birth and death.

The way is true and plainly marked. All one needs to do is to place his feet upon the first rung of the ladder and ascend to Clear and then walk upward to the level of Operating Thetan.

Auditing enables the individual to span the distance from *Homo sapiens*, with his drugs, his pains, his problems, upsets and fears, to higher states and freedom as a spiritual being. Such states are obtainable only through auditing. But they do exist and they are attainable and they fully restore a being to his native potential.

Throughout history man has had many solutions to the problems of existence and has sought far and wide for the answers to himself. Auditing *is* the solution and does provide the answers. Even a small amount of auditing can make this truth abundantly plain.

CHAPTER 14

AUDITOR TRAINING SERVICES

The influence of the reactive mind and its mechanisms present obstacles which destroy man's self-confidence, ruin his ambitions and cause his psychosomatic ills. Real and lasting happiness is difficult to attain if these obstacles remain unseen and unknown.

Training in Scientology principles enables one to unveil the reactive mind, understand its machinations and render them no longer mysterious. By understanding the factors of life and developing skills to handle them, happiness can be achieved.

There is factually no higher ability than the ability to restore life to its native potentials. Thus the value of Scientology technology is found in its actual application to oneself, a preclear or the situations one encounters in life. This chapter describes the primary training services offered in Scientology by which people learn this technology.

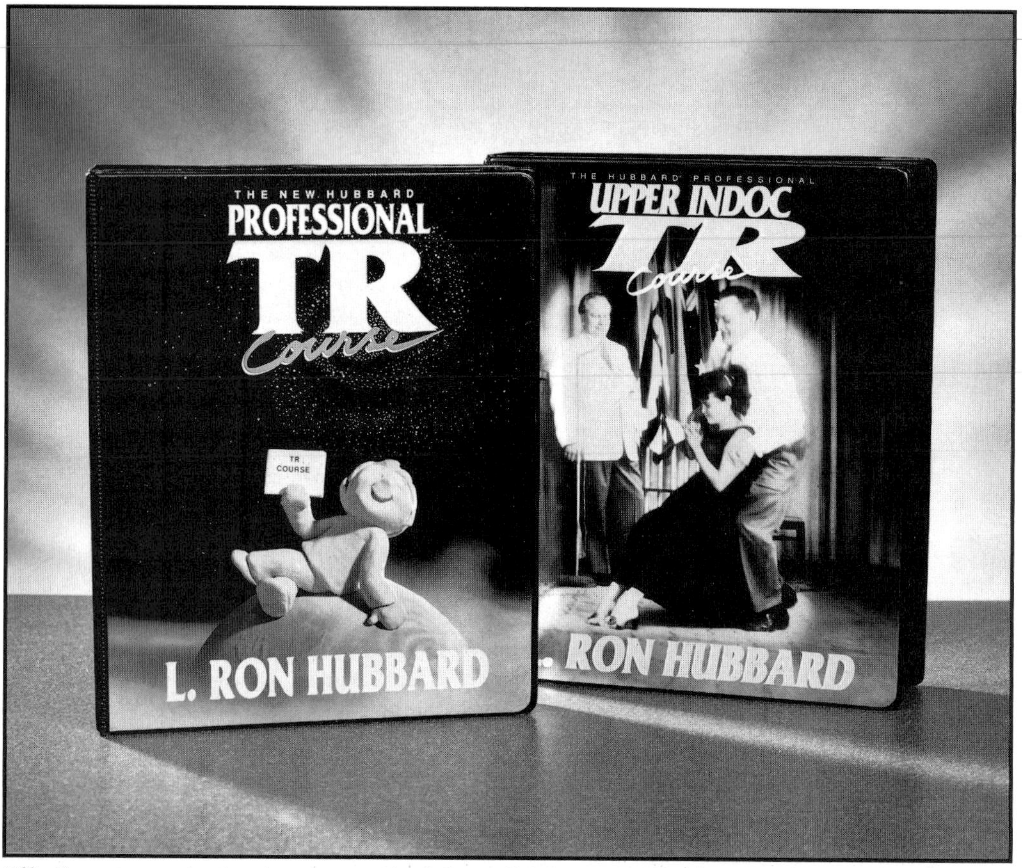

Effective communication is necessary, both in auditing and in life. Thus, Scientology auditor training begins with the Hubbard Professional TR Course and Upper Indoc TR Course. These two courses teach the fundamental factors of communication and give the student extensive practice in using them.

THE FUNDAMENTAL SKILLS OF AUDITING

Hubbard Professional TR Course

"TR" stands for *T*raining *R*outine and on this course a person gains expertise in that very vital ingredient for both successful living and auditing: communication.

As the most important part of the ARC triangle, communication is more important in auditing than the auditing technique used. Communication is what enables the auditor to help the preclear rid himself of his aberrations and regain his abilities. In life, communication is what enables one to perceive and deal with the world around him.

Before L. Ron Hubbard's researches into the subject, no one had isolated what the cycle of communication was, or its relationship to efforts to help man. But it is the essential element in *any* such effort, and so it is little wonder that earlier practices obtained no real or lasting results.

The Hubbard Professional TR Course contains L. Ron Hubbard's discoveries about communication and teaches the skills needed to apply it effectively in life and in auditing. While the Success Through Communication Course gives one skills for handling communication in business or social situations, the Professional TR Course enables one to audit and to handle any situation in life with communication alone. This is a higher-level skill.

On the course, one studies the individual elements of communication and dissects the cycle of communication into each of its components, learning the principles of what communication is and how it is used. Technical training films written, directed and narrated by L. Ron Hubbard facilitate further understanding. The course even contains a set of very special auditing processes that students receive which gives them insight into some of the most basic laws in Scientology and lets them see how these apply to their lives and activities.

Once the student has completed his theory studies and auditing, he begins drilling the Training Routines (TRs), each of which develops skill in a basic part of communication. The drills begin with teaching the student how to face another person comfortably, even with distractions, since one cannot communicate well if one is shy, nervous or unwilling to simply be there to communicate. On subsequent drills, one learns how to deliver a communication so it arrives exactly where one desires, to let another person know that he has been heard and understood, to get one's questions answered (an important skill in living and a vital one in auditing) and to effectively handle what others say in order to maintain good communication with them. Each of these drills builds on the ones before it.

Students pair up and progress through each of the drills, mastering one before going on to the next. In doing the drills, the students become aware of poor communication habits or patterns they may have previously developed and they learn to communicate effectively.

Hubbard Professional Upper Indoc TR Course

The next basic skill needed by an auditor or, for that matter, any successful person, is the ability to control things and to direct people and situations. Control is defined as the ability to start, change and stop something. One is successful in his life to the degree that he can start or change or stop the things and people within his environment.

This skill is learned on the Hubbard Professional Upper Indoc TR Course. "Indoc" is short for "indoctrination" (meaning "to teach") and Upper Indoc TRs, as they are called, are the series of TRs that follow Professional TRs in auditor training. This course teaches adroitness in starting, changing and stopping communication and directing other people. One's abilities in this area are thoroughly drilled until proficiency is attained.

To some, control may have a bad connotation but that is only due to past failures at controlling things or upsets stemming from times when one was poorly controlled.

But if one looks squarely at the subject, one can see that it is not possible to do much of anything in life if one cannot exert control. How, for example, can one drive a car one cannot start, change and stop? Control is a know-how vital to any endeavor, including auditing. Skillful control makes for more positive application of auditing techniques and greater gain for the preclear.

Control is a subject all auditors must master and, factually, is something everyone needs to know. The Professional Upper Indoc TR Course is where such expertise is learned.

ACADEMY AUDITOR TRAINING

The Academy Levels

The Academy Levels are a series of five auditor classification courses where the principles of Scientology and what it achieves become manifest.

Each Academy Level is an intensive two-week course which runs on a schedule of forty hours of course time per week. Students study either on a day schedule of eight hours of course periods five days a week, or on an evening and weekend schedule of three hours per evening and eight hours per day on the weekends. Each course consists

The Academy Levels—auditor training levels 0–IV

of theory study and practical application of a specific aspect of Scientology technology. Each Academy Level corresponds to one of the Scientology Expanded Grades discussed in the last chapter and teaches the underlying principles of that Grade, as well as the auditing techniques.

Because each level deals with a specific aspect of life and the way to improve that aspect, by acquiring the data from these levels one becomes more causative overall. In short, the Academy Levels contain answers to the barriers that hold people back from success in their lives.

Level 0—Class 0 Auditor
(Hubbard Recognized Scientologist)

On Level 0, a person learns the basic actions of auditing, such as proper auditing session form and how to operate an E-Meter. He learns techniques which address communication and how to free another's abilities in this area.

The student reads five of L. Ron Hubbard's basic books and listens to seven selected lectures covering the subjects of communication and auditing fundamentals. He then learns the processes audited on ARC Straightwire and Expanded Grade 0.

Level I—Class I Auditor
(Hubbard Trained Scientologist)

This level teaches a person the anatomy of problems—why people get problems in the first place and the mechanics of eliminating problems.

The student reads two more basic L. Ron Hubbard books, hears eleven lectures on problems and their successful resolution through auditing and learns the auditing skills and processes of Expanded Grade I.

Level II—Class II Auditor
(Hubbard Certified Auditor)

Here, a person learns about the ramifications of harmful acts and how these affect survival. This course contains the technology of bringing relief from such hostilities and returning trust and honesty to life.

The student studies another book, hears fourteen lectures, then learns further techniques and the processes of Expanded Grade II.

Level III—Class III Auditor
(Hubbard Professional Auditor)

Level III covers the technology to free anyone from past upsets. One learns the mechanisms behind personal upheavals and how to alleviate the harmful aftereffects. The student learns more advanced E-Meter drills and more skilled auditing techniques which are used in the processes of Expanded Grade III.

Another book of Mr. Hubbard's and seven more lectures are part of the materials studied on this course.

Level IV—Class IV Auditor
(Hubbard Advanced Auditor)

The final Academy Level teaches the student how to handle fixed conditions in life. The technology of Level IV gives one the ability to change, to accept new ideas and to achieve his goals. Two more books are studied, seven lectures are heard and the Expanded Grade IV processes are taught.

The Academy Levels 0–IV constitute the basic Scientology auditor training. The student not only learns to help preclears in auditing, but also how to better handle his own life and help others deal with theirs.

Class V—Hubbard New Era Dianetics Auditor Course

The next training step upon completing Class IV Auditor training is the Hubbard New Era Dianetics Auditor Course which contains a summary and refinement of Dianetics, based on the decades of experience gained in the subject after its release. New Era Dianetics does not change any of the theories or principles of Dianetics as Mr. Hubbard originally developed them, but later breakthroughs resulted in this ultimate Dianetics technology, New Era Dianetics.

All Dianetics technology is included on this course including three basic books and five lectures on Dianetics and its use. With the procedures and techniques of NED auditing, an auditor can obtain results many times faster than earlier technology.

The student learns auditing procedures that effectively address any psychosomatic complaint a preclear may have. Over ten specific NED rundowns allow the auditor and preclear to erase engrams and often bring him to the state of Clear.

Clearing is within reach of millions and New Era Dianetics technology delivered well by NED Auditors is the primary means by which this will occur.

COMPREHENSIVE TRAINING: CLASS VI THE SAINT HILL SPECIAL BRIEFING COURSE

Auditor training courses in Academies of Scientology teach a person precise theory and techniques to handle the primary factors that complicate life and aberrate a being. In the interests of imparting data to a student that he can apply and get results with rapidly, Academy training courses are, by design, not comprehensive. Application is stressed in the Academy because in this way one can immediately get *results* that are obtainable with auditing and can at once start causing conditions in life to change for the better.

Saint Hill Special Briefing Course students study all materials shown here, including books, films, 12,000 pages of technical volumes and more than 450 recorded lectures.

DIANETICS
THE EVOLUTION OF A SCIENCE
CLASSIFICATION, GRADATION & AWARENESS
FREEDOM CONGRESS
THE FACT OF CLEARING
THE FREEDOMS OF CLEAR
FALSE TONE ARM
E-Meter Instruction Film
Original Screenplay by L. RON
CLEAR PROCEDURE, CREATIVENESS
Assists
Written by L. Ron Hubbard
THE PROFESSIONAL TR COURSE
THE TONE SCALE
UPPER INDOC TRs
THE HISTORY OF THE E-METER
E-METER READS
E-Meter
SAINT HILL SPECIA
BRIEFING COURSE
TRACK ANALYSIS
SAINT HILL SPECIAL BRIEFING COURSE
LECTURES 249 – 264
Saint Hill Special Briefing Course
L. RON HUBBARD

But a full understanding of Scientology and, therefore, of life could only be arrived at in one way: by following the path that L. Ron Hubbard himself took in order to find the way out of the trap. Walking the same road he walked, seeing the same things he saw would give one a total understanding of life, its mysteries and the technology for solving them. The course that traces every step of this path is the Saint Hill Special Briefing Course.

The Saint Hill Special Briefing Course is the largest single course in Scientology. It consists of a comprehensive and chronological study of the entire development of Dianetics and Scientology and contains the largest, broadest body of information on the subject of human behavior, the mind and life that has ever been available.

The course is named after Saint Hill Manor in England, Mr. Hubbard's residence during much of the 1960s, and where he taught the course from March 1961 to December 1966. This covers an intense period of his research, leading to many important discoveries. Auditors came from all over the world to Saint Hill and were present when Mr. Hubbard developed the Bridge to Total Freedom and many of the procedures that today form a large part of any preclear's auditing. The course was hugely popular and auditors who returned to their areas from Saint Hill were regarded with enormous respect. Demand for the training only available on the Briefing Course resulted in it being established in other areas of the world in organizations called "Saint Hills" as a tribute to the original home of the course.

Students study all of L. Ron Hubbard's books and technical bulletins and listen to recordings of more than four hundred of his lectures on the Saint Hill Special Briefing Course.

Due to the scope of the course and the setup necessary to deliver it, only selected Scientology organizations offer the Saint Hill Special Briefing Course. The course consists of sixteen individual checksheets, each requiring an average of three to four weeks of study. Each checksheet covers a specific period of Dianetics and Scientology technology and gives the student a full understanding of the theory and application of the materials of that period.

On the final two checksheets, the student audits extensively and becomes expert in the application of Dianetics and Scientology technology. Special training aids helping the student apply his materials are found only on the Saint Hill Special Briefing Course. All of L. Ron Hubbard's Technical Training Films are seen on the course.

The vast panorama of understanding the human mind and the secrets of life is only attained by an in-sequence study of all the developments one by one as they occurred, a consecutive chain of breakthroughs, each one a milestone in man's understanding of man. Such is available on the Saint Hill Special Briefing Course.

ADVANCED AUDITOR TRAINING

Several more classes of auditor training exist above the Saint Hill Special Briefing Course. These are Classes VII through XII. Each of these auditor classifications teaches advanced auditing techniques and requires that the auditor be very well trained on the lower classifications in order to apply them.

As Mr. Hubbard's research brought to view higher realms of awareness and ability, he codified auditing actions which would allow others to attain these. Of special distinction among the resulting courses is the Class VIII Auditor Course. This stresses an exact, unvarying standard of auditing technology application to all preclears.

Below Class VIII, an auditor learns different styles of auditing, processes, techniques and theory. One has to know all this data before taking the next step; one can then totally align all this knowledge into a simple but wholly effective ability to achieve stellar auditing results on *any* preclear. That is what a Class VIII Auditor can do, and there are no shortcuts to its attainment.

He is trained to administer auditing technology with flawless and invariable precision, a necessity for the advanced techniques and rundowns he learns here. He studies the materials of the course, including nineteen lectures, three times to reach the understanding which underlies a Class VIII Auditor's effortless competence. At Class VIII the highest standards of application are reinforced again and again until the student applies *them* and nothing else. He gains an absolute certainty in the precision of auditing and knows he can get results on any preclear with it. The power in the vast technical data of Scientology becomes concentrated into a relatively few essentials. In the hands of a Class VIII Auditor these essentials produce the high-velocity gains which result from perfect application.

TECHNICAL SPECIALIST COURSES

Factors can arise in a preclear's life which threaten to halt his progress on the Bridge. Different case problems can exist that are best handled by special processes and rundowns not contained in the normal course of auditing actions on the Bridge. So, in addition to the numbered auditor classifications, other training courses teach specialized techniques to help people resolve an array of conditions.

These are classified as Technical Specialist Courses. They comprise a body of post-graduate studies which train an auditor in the technology of a specific rundown or technical skill not covered in Academy classification courses. Each course is only a few days' duration and requires no interning. The procedure learned will resolve an exact condition in the preclear, enabling him to continue to progress up the Bridge.

Technical Specialist Courses are the most direct way for an auditor to learn all the procedures necessary to handle any preclear. (These techniques in addition to the full philosophical theory underlying them are included within the more extensive Saint Hill Special Briefing Course.) On Technical Specialist Courses an auditor learns how, for example, to repair victims of psychiatric abuse, to aid students in resolving study difficulties, to assist people in overcoming specific fears and to help others rid themselves of false purposes. These are all conditions that can slow a preclear's progress, but an auditor trained on Technical Specialist Courses is fully capable of helping any person resolve such barriers so that he may move on up the Bridge to Total Freedom.

PERFECTING SKILLS OF APPLICATION

Auditor Internships

After training, an auditor's skills are developed by experience in auditing others. This is done on internships which come after selected courses.

An internship is a period of serving as an intern under the supervision of technical experts. As in other fields such as medicine where medical school graduates intern under experienced doctors to learn the profession, the recently graduated auditor gets "on-the-job" practical experience working under veteran auditors in the organization. In this way, his skills are honed and polished to a very high level of proficiency.

An intern's auditing skills are carefully reviewed by technical experts. Practical application of actually auditing a preclear brings to light any weakness in the auditor's ability to apply all of his materials. Particular emphasis is then given to these areas until the auditor becomes competent in them. The pattern of auditing, combined with inspection and any needed correction of errors, soon brings about a high level of expertise. Interns audit daily, and work up to an ability to do as much as ten hours of flawless auditing in a single day.

When interns have audited in volume and polished any rough edges so they can think with their materials without hesitation on what to do in an auditing session, they are an internship graduate.

An auditor who completes an internship invariably becomes more accomplished by virtue of the intensive supervision and assistance given by more highly trained and experienced personnel. Internships are rigorous and make a course graduate into a top-flight professional auditor while also raising his general competence in life.

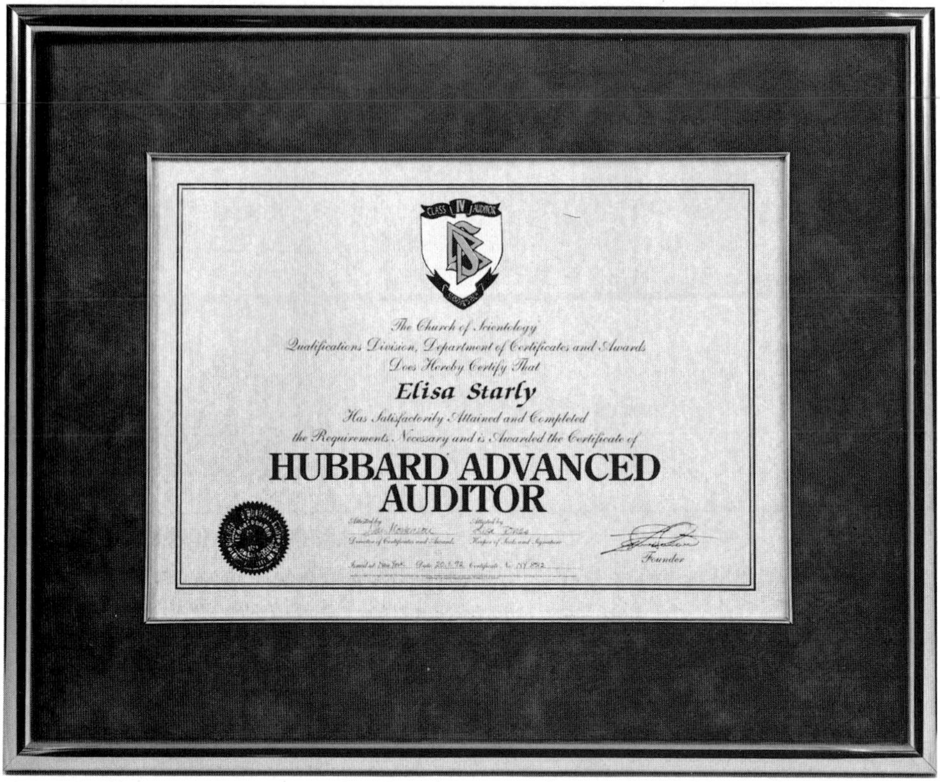

The successful completion of a Scientology training course is validated with certification. When one has passed a thorough period of internship, he earns a gold seal signifying that his certificate is permanent.

AUDITOR SUPERVISION

Successful auditing is a team activity requiring the work of additional people besides the auditor and preclear.

In order to ensure technology is applied correctly in all cases, auditing is overseen by another technically trained person called the Case Supervisor (C/S). The Case Supervisor directs auditing actions for each individual preclear under his care. *Case* is a general term for a person being treated or helped. The Case Supervisor's purpose is to see that the technology is standardly applied for the greatest possible benefit for the preclear. Ultimately, it is the Case Supervisor who is responsible for the technical quality in his area.

The Case Supervisor is a highly trained and interned auditor who does additional training in the technology of supervising auditing. Not every auditor becomes a C/S, but every Case Supervisor is a highly skilled auditor.

The Case Supervisor reviews all auditing sessions done by auditors under his charge. He verifies the auditor's application was standardly done. He directs the auditor on what process to run next on his preclear, based on an overall program of auditing drawn up especially for each individual to ensure his maximum progress. He helps the auditor apply the technology correctly and, if some error in procedure is made, he sees that the auditor is corrected. The C/S, not being directly involved in the session, studies the technical report made by the auditor; this distance often furnishes a clear and valuable view of the preclear's overall progress.

Case Supervisor training consists of courses, followed by internships of their own where the student learns the technology of case supervision and then gains practical experience supervising the auditing of others. There are C/S courses following Class IV, Class V, Class VI, Class VIII, Class IX and Class XII.

AN AUDITOR'S VALUE

Auditor training services gradiently make one more capable in life. Each course and internship builds on the preceding and makes an individual more and more confident and able.

Skills gained by training in the discipline of auditing are the superior skills of handling life. With them one can undo the pain, misery and failures of others and this has never been possible in history. The proficient auditor is valuable beyond compare to his fellows, to the world and to himself. An impulse to help resides in nearly everyone. Auditor training gives one the know-how to provide help of a higher order. An auditor is the only person in the world capable of actually *undoing* unhappiness in another. He is the only one who can help others restore their native powers. No better way to help exists, and no activity is more rewarding.

Chapter 15

Other Ministerial Services

It has long been the function of a church to provide guidance and succor to parishioners in times of need. In fact, beyond strictly spiritual concerns, the church has traditionally seen its mission as easing temporal suffering, helping where help is required and instilling dignity to the pivotal turning points of our lives.

The loss of a loved one, the illness of a relative, marital difficulties, family disputes, and the like—all constitute times when individuals seek guidance, support or solace in their church. Parishioners also turn to their church for weddings, christenings and funeral services. The Scientology Chaplain performs all of the above, but his primary function is to help solve the day-to-day problems that can occasionally keep a Scientologist from moving up the Bridge. Each church has a Chaplain who is well equipped with a variety of means to help resolve such troublesome situations. Whether dealing with someone who experienced the loss of a loved one, the disillusioned husband or wife, or helping Scientologists overcome barriers encountered along their route to freedom, his door is always open.

Helping to Keep People on the Bridge

So great are the pressures of modern life that every once in a while a Scientology student or preclear may find himself drawn off the Bridge by demands from his home, his workplace or neighborhood. While the many services offered by the Church relate to the totality of all life, the person has to be there to take advantage of them. Hence, one of the Scientology Chaplain's duties is to help parishioners stay on the Bridge. Although the particular reasons why someone might have difficulty can vary enormously, the Chaplain is superbly equipped to handle almost anything. He is well trained in Scientology communication principles, and so can help resolve disagreements between preclears, students or members of the staff. He understands the principles of Scientology counseling and can arrange auditing sessions for those who have slipped off the Bridge owing to an upset. He knows how to apply Scientology personality testing to pinpoint difficulties one might encounter in the home or office, or resolve disputes between individuals or marital partners.

Nor are the Chaplain's functions limited to resolving difficulties among the Scientology public. Utilizing the same skills with which he helps the parishioner in the community, he also does much to maintain the high morale of Scientology staff members. He knows that by caring for the morale of each individual, one can raise the morale of all.

Scientology marriage counseling helps create an atmosphere of honesty and open communication between marital partners.

In short, the Scientology Chaplain performs those duties that chaplains have always performed: He helps sort out problems, extends a hand to those who have fallen and works to instill a general well-being, buoyancy and confidence within all members of his group. There are also other ways Scientologists help their fellows through difficult periods.

ASSISTS

L. Ron Hubbard developed many, many techniques to help those suffering from illness or injury—techniques well known to a Scientologist when he enters the hospital or sickroom. These techniques constitute a body of technology classified as "assists," and are undertaken to help the spirit confront physical difficulties. These assists include the *Contact Assist,* designed to help an individual alleviate the mental or spiritual reaction to injuries and so greatly speed the healing process, and the *Touch Assist,* designed to reestablish communication with injured body parts. Both of these assists operate on the principle that if injured, one tends to mentally or spiritually withdraw from the injured area. Although a perfectly understandable reaction to pain, only by restoring communication with the injured area can one bring the spiritual element into the healing process—an element that physicians have long innately recognized but never before had a means to utilize.

HELPING THE FAMILY

The family is the building block of a culture, and when a society loses sight of that fact, it loses its foundations. With that in mind, L. Ron Hubbard did much to isolate the sources of familial problems and provide a means to bring family members back together again.

In the first bloom of love, it seems easy to commit oneself "till death do us part." As the years pass, however, those first sacred vows can too often lose their meaning, and thus marriages can end in divorce. In that the traditional core of the family unit is the relationship between a husband and a wife, Mr. Hubbard set out to discover the *real* reason behind marital failures and how to reignite that first spark of love.

Like the techniques employed to help the ill or injured, Scientology marriage counseling is an assist. It is intended to alleviate marital problems by addressing the root of all such difficulties: transgressions against the previously agreed-upon moral code that now inhibit communication and, in turn, hinder survival. Although forthrightness, honesty and open communication have long been known to form the basis of a healthy marriage, never before has there been a real method to help couples achieve that state.

In the interests of reestablishing open communication, the Scientology Chaplain conducts a marriage counseling session with both partners present—first the Chaplain addresses one spouse while the other looks on, and then their places are reversed.

By way of example, consider the adulterous husband. Quite apart from the health hazards of infidelity, the adulterer carries with him a deep and dark secret. He has broken his marriage vows. To hide his transgression, he lies; and with each new lie he grows more consumed with guilt and further out of communication with his wife. Although adultery may be one failing of a marriage, there are a thousand and more transgressions one might make against the moral code—and with each untold transgression and each new lie to cover it up, the marriage dies a little more.

With these principles firmly understood by both partners, the Chaplain proceeds to help the couple morally cleanse themselves. He very carefully maintains strict impartiality so that by no mannerism, tone of voice or word, does he give the impression that he favors one spouse over the other.

When the husband, for instance, has completed his session, he then looks on while the Chaplain addresses the wife. If the counseling sessions are standardly conducted with strict adherence to the Auditor's Code and other rules of auditing, both partners soon unburden themselves of barriers to marital harmony—the guilt, shame and lies are a thing of the past and communication is restored. Utilizing these procedures Scientology Chaplains have successfully salvaged thousands of marriages from the brink of dissolution.

CHILDREN

In addition to salvaging marriages, and as part of his larger effort to restore family unity, the Scientologist is often called upon to help the child. Children today are not only beset with the problems that have always troubled young people—nightmares, squabbles with friends, difficulties with their studies—but face a whole new host of ills as a consequence of our ailing society. Drugs and sexual abuse steal the happiness of children at an increasingly young age, while gang violence and rampant criminality endanger their lives; and one need only glance at an inner city school to appreciate just how badly our society has served their welfare.

"Save the child," Mr. Hubbard wrote, "and you save the nation." Yet not only has today's society sadly neglected children, but even where efforts are made to help, too often they come to nothing for lack of any real know-how.

Long concerned with the well-being of man's future, L. Ron Hubbard developed dozens of techniques to enhance the welfare of a child. As a basic orientation, Mr. Hubbard points out that the child is not an *enfant terrible* who must be forcefully molded or broken if he is ever to behave as a responsible adult. Rather, the child must be seen for what he is: a fully aware individual in a body that has not attained full growth. And recognizing that what applies to an adult's behavior also applies to the child, the Scientologist may utilize the same means to help children that he employs to help adults.

The ill or injured child, and even infants, may be given Touch Assists. The young student suffering through his studies will find relief through the application of L. Ron Hubbard's study technology. The student who cannot get along with his friends can quickly resolve the matter with communication skills learned on a course specifically designed for him. And even very young children may receive auditing.

Possessing all these tools and more, the Scientologist is well equipped to counsel parents and help their children grow up happy, confident and able. He recognizes that the child is often wonderfully sane, that his values and sense of reality are acutely sharp, and if only adults around him would refrain from attempts to manage and fashion him into their image, he will become a fine, successful human being.

SCIENTOLOGY SERVICES

There are moments in everyone's life when a ceremony lends an appropriate dignity. When getting married, mourning a death or naming our children, most feel that a ceremony is appropriate. Scientology congregations celebrate weddings and christenings with their own formal ceremonies, hold Sunday services and mark the passing of their fellows with funeral rites. The Chaplain or minister conducts these functions with dignity and order, but they are not necessarily solemn. Church services are open to those of any denomination.

Sunday sermons generally revolve around primary points of the Scientology philosophy, including the idea that a person is not a body or mind, but a spiritual being. Other sermons might address any of the eight dynamics, the Axioms or the codes of Scientology. Although such sermons covering the basic truths of Mr. Hubbard's philosophy do much to refresh and revitalize Scientologists, the Chaplain is keenly aware that his sermons will also offer hope to the stranger burdened by life and the workaday world.

That so much of the Scientology minister's work is aimed at helping the infirm, the estranged, the saddened, is traditional. What is not traditional, however, is that he can do more than offer sympathy and compassion that is based upon common sense and faith. With the tools provided by L. Ron Hubbard he can actually better conditions.

A traditional Scientology wedding ceremony

CHAPTER 16

SCIENTOLOGY ETHICS AND JUDICIAL MATTERS

Because it has long been acknowledged that spiritual progress and proper conduct are inextricably linked, all great religious philosophies contain some form of ethical, moral and/or judicial system. Most obviously, one finds the Ten Commandments aimed at outlawing those transgressions deemed most offensive to God and most injurious to the Jewish people. Similarly, the Buddhists developed the concept of Right Livelihood, while Christian notions of sin fill a thousand pages or more. But merely setting down rules has never appreciably led to improvement, and it was not until L. Ron Hubbard defined and codified the subject, that there was any workable technology of ethics and justice for increased happiness, prosperity and survival.

ETHICS

The Scientology system of ethics is based wholly on reason. Whereas morals, Mr. Hubbard pointed out, are essentially laws of conduct laid down from accumulated experience out of ages past and thus may no longer be entirely relevant to survival, ethics consists wholly of rationality toward the highest level of survival for all dynamics. True, in the absence of anything else, a moral code can provide a general yardstick for optimum conduct, and ethical conduct always includes an adherence to society's moral codes. But over time, morals can become outmoded, burdensome, and so invite revolt. Thus, although moral codes are respected, it is the adherence to ethical standards that holds the channels of the Bridge firmly open, enabling Scientologists to progress smoothly and without distraction.

Ethics may be defined as the actions an individual takes on himself to ensure his continued survival across the dynamics. It is a personal thing. When one is ethical, it is something he does himself by his own choice.

The logic of Scientology ethics is inarguable and based upon two key concepts: *good* and *evil.* Like ethics and justice, *good* and *evil* have long been subject to opinion, confusion and obfuscation. But to appreciate what Scientology ethics is all about, it must be understood that *good* can be considered to be a constructive survival action. It is something that, to put it simply, is more beneficial than destructive across the dynamics. True, nothing is completely good, and to build anew often requires a degree of destruction. But if the *constructive* outweighs the *destructive,* i.e., if a greater number of dynamics are helped than harmed, then an action can be considered good. Thus, for example, a new cure which saves a hundred lives but kills only one, is an acceptable cure.

Having thus defined what is good, evil then becomes the opposite of good, and constitutes anything which is destructive more than it is constructive along the dynamics. A thing which does more destruction than construction is evil from the viewpoint of the individual, the future race, group, species, life or physical universe matter that it destroys.

With a firm understanding of these definitions, the Scientologist is well equipped to rationally determine the course of his actions.

The logic behind maintaining high ethical standards is simple. Although modern conceptions of ethics have become hopelessly convoluted with common conflict of interest and gray areas of choice, it cannot be forgotten that greater survival for both individuals and groups comes through abiding by these agreements. Hence, the Scientologist is lawful with regards to his country, fair in his dealings with others and faithful in his relationships. He knows that because every individual is essentially good, he has an innately acute sense of what is ethical and what is not. Thus, when one violates one's personal sense of ethics, he soon loses self-respect and begins to deteriorate from that point forward.

CONDITIONS OF EXISTENCE

With the basic definitions of *ethics, good* and *evil* in place, and the basic *necessity* for ethical conduct established, Mr. Hubbard proceeded to develop a means of allowing one to gradiently raise his ethics level and so increase survival in any area of his life. It is a system of betterment unlike any other, and contains nothing of the "Go-and-sin-no-more" approach that many find so difficult to follow. Rather, it is predicated on the idea that there are degrees of ethical conduct, that things may be surviving more or less well, but can still be greatly improved. Hence, Mr. Hubbard set out to delineate the various ethical states or *conditions* which constitute the degree of success or survival of something, and precisely how to better that condition of survival.

These conditions are not static states, but either improve or worsen, depending upon one's actions. Indeed, it is a fact that nothing remains exactly the same forever, for such a condition is foreign to life and the universe. Things grow or they lessen. They cannot apparently maintain the same equilibrium or stability.

Everything in existence is in one condition or another. A person is in some condition personally, his job is in a condition, his marriage is in a condition and so on. Mr. Hubbard isolated and described these states, then determined what it would actually take to move from any given condition to a higher one. In all, Mr. Hubbard delineates twelve separate conditions. They range from a state of complete confusion where an individual is in no position to produce any product to a condition of stable power wherein very little if anything can imperil his position. Along the way to power, he will pass through such other conditions as normal operation wherein he is gradually taking on more control, producing more and more, but has still not achieved permanent stability. As he continues to properly apply himself, he will eventually move into a condition of affluence—or, failing to take proper steps, may sink into a state of emergency.

Like every fundamental truth in Scientology, the conditions encompass the whole of life. They represent descriptions of actual laws that apply to everything from the growth of trees to the running of an automobile to the raising of a child. Yet discovering these conditions of existence was not all Mr. Hubbard accomplished; he also discovered the exact actions or steps anyone under any circumstances can take to better any condition of existence.

Those steps to improving conditions are aptly called formulas. They are precisely laid out for each condition, and only by following the specific formula for the condition in which one finds oneself can an individual move on to the next higher condition.

To take a very common example, consider the subject of personal relationships between a man and a woman. Obviously, when a couple first begins dating, however strong the attraction, they are not in the same condition as a married couple. Likewise, the marriage beset with strife owing to adultery is not surviving well—and is thus in a lower condition than the entirely harmonious marriage. Yet regardless of how poorly a marriage may be surviving, how bitter the arguments, how seemingly unresolvable the strife, there are *always* steps one can do to better the condition of that marriage. And by continuing to apply those steps, ascending through successively better conditions, one can, with remarkable certainty, always improve that marriage.

The same conditions and their specific formulas can be used to better anything, from personal happiness to the performance of a high-school athletic team to the performance of a multinational corporation. If, to take another example, an employee suddenly finds himself demoted to a lower position in his company, there are specific ways and means by which he can climb back up the corporate ladder. Similarly, if the employee suddenly finds himself promoted to a higher position with a substantial pay increase, a precise application of the Scientology ethics conditions will keep him from falling into the trap of suddenly spending more than he makes or assuming that he is now forever blessed in his boss's eyes.

The important point to recognize here, is that the Scientology conditions formulas are not arbitrary. Yes, they serve to raise a Scientologist's ethics level and so speed his progress on the Bridge. But they also can raise the ethics level, and thus the survival of anyone in any circumstance; for the conditions describe what governs all existence, and if followed, they *do* lead to improvement.

Scientologists use these conditions formulas to handle personal situations, family activities, successes and failures on the job and relationships with other people. The conditions formulas can be applied to *any* situation on *any* dynamic. They *are* the tools by which one makes changes in his life and the world around him.

Spotting one's condition in an area of his life and applying the formula to raise it is the primary activity of ethics. Churches have a staff member, the Ethics Officer, who helps parishioners determine which condition applies to a part of their lives and how, in turn, to apply the right formula. A person may have trouble applying the formulas, as life's complexities can sometimes make it difficult to sort out which formula needs to be applied or how best to proceed with the steps. The Ethics Officer is there to help Scientologists at such times. This is valuable because problems can arise in life that threaten to hinder one's progress up the Bridge. Properly applied, ethics will get one moving again.

Because the conditions formulas follow natural laws that embrace all life's endeavors, they naturally open the door to increased survival on any dynamic and in any course of action. Moreover, the conditions formulas are quickly learned, easily applied and can immediately set one on the road to happiness, success and well-being.

STATISTICS: THE MEASUREMENT OF SURVIVAL

As a further word on the Scientology ethics conditions, mention should be made of how Scientologists use statistical measurement to eliminate the guesswork of applying conditions formulas. Simply put, a statistic is a basic tool for the measurement of survival potential. A statistic is a number or amount compared to an earlier number or amount of the same thing. Statistics refer to the quantity of work done or the value of it and are the only sound measure of any production or any activity. Although one normally thinks of statistics in terms of, say, items sold or payment received, anything can be analyzed in terms of statistics—from gardening to golf. Moreover, only by monitoring statistics can one be certain that he is pinpointing the proper condition, whether bettering or worsening, and not relying on rumor or hearsay. Thus, with an understanding of how to compile, graph and compare statistics, the Scientologist is amply equipped to determine exactly *what* condition an activity is in, and thus exactly what steps he must take in order to better that condition.

THE ANTISOCIAL PERSONALITY

Another key aspect of the Scientology ethics system is the recognition of the antisocial personality. Reflective in man's earliest ethical codes is an innate sense that there are those among us—about 2½ percent of the population—who possess characteristics and mental attitudes that cause them to violently oppose any betterment activity or group. Within this category, one finds the Adolf Hitlers and the Genghis Khans, the unrepentant murderers and the drug lords. Although most blatantly antisocial types may be easy to spot, if only from the bodies they leave in their wake, others are less obviously seen. Enterprises may seem to crumble for no apparent reason, marriages may mysteriously disintegrate and a thousand more ills may affect those associated with the antisocial personality. In fact, all told, 20 percent of the entire population suffers, in one form or another, from a connection with the antisocial personality. For that reason Mr. Hubbard offers very specific guidelines for their detection.

To ensure that these guidelines never perpetuate a witch hunt or an unjust condemnation, he also provides a precise description of the social personality—the category that embraces the great majority of mankind. Moreover, Mr. Hubbard continually stresses that, regardless of apparent traits, all men are basically good—even the most seemingly unrepentant.

The importance of detecting the antisocial personality becomes eminently clear when one considers his effect on the lives of those around him. It has been found that a person connected to an antisocial personality will suffer greatly decreased survival, impeding not only his progress in Dianetics and Scientology but all aspects of his life. Then, too, as his conditions worsen, his ensuing troubles tend to spill over into the lives of others. Hence such a person is designated a "potential trouble source." With the standard application of materials found in Mr. Hubbard's *Introduction to Scientology Ethics,* however, the potential trouble sources can be swiftly helped. Factually, Scientologists use these materials every day to repair marriages, bring parents and children closer together and trade misery for health and happiness.

THE THIRD PARTY LAW

Another key tool that Scientologists regularly use to better their lives, remove barriers that may slow their progress on the Bridge and generally improve conditions is the Third Party Law. This law, defined for the first time by Mr. Hubbard, illuminates the underlying cause of all human conflict—whether in the home, the community or the nation. Precisely stated, the law is this:

"A THIRD PARTY MUST BE PRESENT AND UNKNOWN IN EVERY QUARREL FOR A CONFLICT TO EXIST.

"or

"FOR A QUARREL TO OCCUR, AN UNKNOWN THIRD PARTY MUST BE ACTIVE IN PRODUCING IT BETWEEN TWO POTENTIAL OPPONENTS.

"or

"WHILE IT IS COMMONLY BELIEVED TO TAKE TWO TO MAKE A FIGHT, A THIRD PARTY MUST EXIST AND MUST DEVELOP IT FOR ACTUAL CONFLICT TO OCCUR."

The jealous business associate who continually slanders one to a boss, the spiteful neighbor who slyly belittles a wife to a husband, the disgruntled ex-employee who bad-mouths a company to customers—all may constitute the hidden third parties in a conflict that is severely injurious to survival. Thus, it is not uncommon to find the Third Party Law used in conjunction with the conditions formula steps to, say, salvage a marriage or friendship. As with the detection of the antisocial personality, however, Mr. Hubbard was careful to precisely delineate the application of this tool so that it is not used unjustly.

SCIENTOLOGY JUSTICE

For all the tools that a Scientologist possesses to better his conditions and raise his ethics level, it is occasionally necessary, for the protection of the many, that the group step in and take proper action when the individual fails to take such action himself—hence the Scientology justice system. The basic idea behind Scientology justice is as simple and rational as the underlying theory of Scientology ethics. Justice exists to protect decent people. It is necessary in any successful society. Without it the brute attacks the weak, the good and the productive. The concept and practice of justice as it exists in society today, however, is increasingly ineffective.

That justice system is bogged down in a morass of Latinized grammatical complexities and has become, sadly, a matter of which attorney can present the better argument. Right and wrong, guilt and innocence are relegated to bit players in the show. A lawyer defending a criminal on trial for armed robbery, for instance, is not interested in establishing guilt or innocence; he is looking for a loophole or technicality on which the case can be dismissed and his client set free—whether guilty or not.

Scientology has another system, one unlike any other. Jurisprudence exists within Scientology which is both rapid and fair, and Scientologists utilize this to protect the decent and the productive.

Scientology justice is administered in accordance with a precise set of easily understandable ecclesiastical codes clearly delineated, broadly published and well known by Scientologists. Justice actions are conducted entirely in accordance with these codes, and whether they have been violated or not; suspicion, opinion or caprice play no part. The codes protect the rights of any Scientologist in good standing with the Church.

The sole purpose of justice in Scientology is to establish the truth of a matter and determine guilt or innocence. With this established, proper restitution of wrongs can be made. Scientologists with disputes can use Scientology justice to settle matters amicably. Any Scientologist can avail himself of the justice system to resolve civil disputes, be they with another Scientologist or even a non-Scientologist. And because Scientology justice is fair, economical and occurs without delay, Scientologists find it of great value.

Any justice action in Scientology is completed within a week of being convened, saving the parties involved the unnecessary stress of lengthy delays. Situations are resolved rapidly, with assurance that the outcome will result in the greatest good for the greatest number.

Church justice codes delineate four general classes of crimes and offenses: errors, misdemeanors, crimes and high crimes. These range from minor unintentional errors or omissions in applying Church policy or Scientology technology, to felonies and serious ecclesiastical offenses.

Justice proceedings are effected by bodies formally convened by duly authorized members of the church with the sole purpose of carrying out one particular justice action. These temporary bodies consist of church staff members or other Scientologists who otherwise carry on with their normal duties and activities, but who are given the responsibility of acting on behalf of the group in the matter before them. No attorneys are used and the entire business of a justice action in Scientology is to determine with accuracy the truth of the situation and to see that any wrong is rectified accordingly. There are no legal maneuverings or technicalities which obscure establishing rightness or wrongness, innocence or guilt. One is expected to present the truth, and knowing that the procedures are fair, this is what happens. An accused has access to any reports against him and has the right to face and question his accusers.

Four main types of bodies constitute the Scientology system of justice.

A *Court of Ethics* is convened when known evidence exists of an offense committed against the justice codes by a person. A staff member is appointed as Hearing Officer and adjudicates the facts of the matter and makes a recommendation based on these. The convening authority may direct amends based on the findings commensurate with the offense.

A *Board of Investigation* has the duty to discover the cause of conflicts amongst Scientologists or poor performance in an area in the Church. A three- to five-member board is appointed to conduct an investigation. The board reports on its findings but recommends no disciplinary actions. It may recommend a Committee of Evidence be convened should it uncover serious offenses.

A *Chaplain's Court* exists where grievances may be heard and disputes brought to speedy and equitable resolution. The Chaplain hears all matters, or when requested and allowed by the Chaplain, a body of three people is selected mutually agreeable to both parties. Scientologists use this means of civil justice because it is faster and fairer than what they would receive from any court system.

A *Committee of Evidence* is convened to try more serious matters. This is a fact-finding body composed of between four and seven members. Its duty is to conduct an inquiry into known offenses, hear evidence from witnesses it calls, arrive at a finding and make a full report and recommendation to its convening authority for his action.

Punishment is not a factor in Scientology justice, since it has long been proven in society that punishment more often than not simply hardens the punished person into patterns of destructive behavior. Instead, those guilty of ecclesiastical offenses are instructed to make amends for any damage done by their actions, perform what amounts to community service on behalf of those wronged, and other such actions. In this wise, Scientology justice helps an individual apply ethics to himself and his activities and move up the conditions.

Scientology justice protects the group from the destructive actions of individuals as well. A person who refuses to act ethically and who commits crimes against the group in general may be brought before a justice action in an effort to straighten him out. Depending on the severity of his offenses, a Committee of Evidence may recommend suitable restitution and penalties, taking into consideration any mitigating circumstances. The most extreme penalty that can be leveled at a person is expulsion from the Church. This can occur when blatant actions intended to destroy Scientology or Scientologists are committed, or when the person has clearly proven that he is no longer in agreement with and is actively opposing the Church's goals. Such a person has demonstrated that he opposes what Scientology stands for. By publicly announcing the person's expulsion, Scientologists in good standing are alerted and can avoid being harmed by him until such time as his actions are more in accord with the group.

No further action is taken by the Church or its members as justice has been done by expelling the individual from the group. The exclusion from Scientology is the harshest judgment faced by any Scientologist for it effectively bars any further progress on the Bridge. Once expelled, the person must go his own way and sort out his life without further communication, assistance or guidance from the Church, which is extremely busy giving its help to those who honestly desire it.

With any justice action, even expulsion from the Church, if the individual concerned does not feel justice has been done, he has avenues of recourse to determine the facts and correct matters, if needed. Because Scientology justice is predicated solely on establishing truth, the honest individual is secure in the knowledge that he will receive fair treatment.

The Scientology justice codes align with the mores and legal codes of the society. Acts considered criminal by society are considered criminal by the Church and Scientologists. Scientologists do not tolerate illegal activities of any sort. Experience has taught that those who seriously violate the laws of the land are incapable of maintaining the ethical standards required to accomplish spiritual advancement.

The book *Introduction to Scientology Ethics* contains the full scope of Scientology ethics technology and the Scientology justice system in clearly laid-out terms.

ETHICS, JUSTICE AND MANKIND

Scientology ethics, explained L. Ron Hubbard, are reason. They provide the means by which men conduct themselves toward their long-term survival, the survival of their families, their groups, their planet and more. Implicit within the subject is the recognition that all things are, to one degree or another, interdependent upon all else and that only by constantly considering the survival of the many can the individual ensure his own survival.

With this thinking firmly in mind the Scientologist obeys the law, remains faithful to his spouse, truthful in his business dealings and otherwise conducts himself in accordance with honesty, integrity and decency.

Scientologists understand that rules and laws form the agreements by which a group, society or nation survives, and that high ethical standards, far from inhibiting the enjoyment of life, foster it.

Yet what of the rest of the world?

For want of a workable system of ethics and justice, whole civilizations have gone to ruin, whole forests have been laid to waste and whole sections of our cities have been reduced to racial battlegrounds. Simultaneously, we have witnessed the steady disintegration of the family, a general decay of sexual values, escalating drug abuse, theft, assault and on and on until it seems there is no hope at all—except this: The Scientologist must also live in this society, and he truly does possess the tools to make a difference.

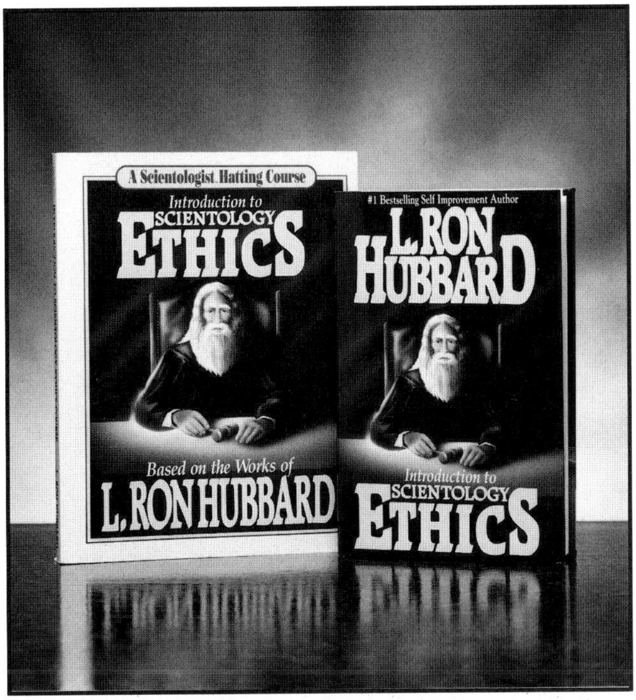

*The **Introduction to Scientology Ethics** book and course provide one with a full understanding of Scientology ethics and justice technology.*

Part Four

The Effectiveness of Scientology

Millions of applications over the course of several decades show Dianetics and Scientology to be workable beyond any methods man ever had before. The point cannot be stressed enough: Answers have been found to the problems of life. They exist in Scientology and people discover this fact for themselves every day.

At a time where many unworkable "solutions" are offered, disappointment can blind people to something which really does work. The effective results of Dianetics and Scientology, then, warrant some comment. The next chapter has been written by individual Scientologists, for their statements are the best testament to its workability.

There is a pathway to full spiritual awareness and an understanding of life. It is clearly mapped and has been traveled with great success by many. The recommended course of progress up this bridge to freedom is described in this part.

Even when progress in Scientology seems balked or when difficulties arise, there are solutions which enable advancement to continue. L. Ron Hubbard isolated reasons for *any* apparent failures in application and thoroughly codified technologies to resolve these, making Scientology, as is covered in Chapter 19, a subject capable of correcting itself. Scientology is an activity where, ultimately, everyone wins.

CHAPTER 17

SUCCESSES OF SCIENTOLOGY

If one honestly avails himself of the technology and sincerely applies himself to gain the benefits offered, there are apparently no limits to what can be achieved.

This chapter is devoted to the stories of individual Scientologists and tells of the gains and results they have experienced. It is in these that the worth of Scientology finds its truest expression.

The opinions of experts or the pronouncements of authorities bear little importance. It is by each individual's reckoning whether or not he arrives at a better place.

People who have benefited come from all over the globe and from all walks of life. L. Ron Hubbard's technology knows no economic, ethnic, racial, political or religious barriers. Wisdom is for any man who chooses to reach for it.

Literally millions of stories are on file in churches and missions in all parts of the world. These are not the stories of the privileged or select. They are the successes of everyday people who were looking for answers and who were bright enough to know when the answers had been found.

The following should not be construed as claims made by the Church concerning personal benefits any individual will experience. The Church provides the services. The results speak for themselves.

The main thing that has really impressed me about Scientology is that there is the most brilliant tech for anything and everything in your life. I've become a more powerful individual with increased abilities. I never even conceived that I could experience these kinds of gains prior to Scientology.

There is a way to handle every part of life with Scientology, and a way to exist that is far beyond any dream that you could ever dream. All of my dreams keep becoming realities and that's very exciting!

Through Scientology, things happen a lot quicker. What used to take weeks or months sometimes happens in days or even minutes!

Life is at my fingertips and with Scientology I've found I can have or be whatever I want.

Kelly Preston
Actress

In January of 1975 I was working on my first film in Durango, Mexico. There I met an actress who gave me the book Dianetics. *During the five weeks we were filming she gave me some auditing sessions and applied some basic principles. That was when I became involved in Dianetics—because it worked.*

When I returned to the United States I began Scientology training and auditing. My career immediately took off and I landed a lead role on the TV show "Welcome Back Kotter" and had a string of successful films. I have been a successful actor for 17 years and Scientology has played a major role in that success.

I have a wonderful child and a great marriage because I apply L. Ron Hubbard's technology to this area of my life.

As a Scientologist I have the technology to handle life's problems and I have used this to help others in life as well.

I would say that Scientology put me into the big time.

John Travolta
Actor

The single greatest thing that studying Scientology has done for me is that it's helped me become freer. Freer to create life as I want to, without being thrown off from my objectives. One of the first simple successes was that I learned to handle and remove my own self-imposed barriers and restraints. Through further study, my ability to handle life around me also increased. This freedom has been hard won, but the rewards are great.

My study of Scientology has also enabled me to write more music. I have become quicker and am able to use all of the musical abilities that I already have. I gained a new understanding of what the proper importances are in the process of creating music.

Scientology has helped me to live better. Using the basic principles of Scientology has become a natural way of life for me. From Scientology I've gotten a freedom to learn whatever I want to learn in life and I'm gaining new abilities all the time.

Chick Corea
Eight-time Grammy Award–winning Jazz Musician & Composer

Being a professional driver dealing with the public and their need to be across town NOW used to be stressful for me. Before Scientology I had no idea about being in control of my vehicle and therefore had my fair share of accidents. After each shift I would be wiped out. Now, I handle my car with certainty and do the impossible as far as my clients are concerned. I'm rarely stressed and when my shift is over I still have plenty of energy to play with my 9-month-old son. Not bad for an old coot of 50, eh?

Henry Baumgard
Taxi Driver

Scientology changed my life because it gave me a direction, it gave me something that I believe in and it gave me truth.

As an artist I have been knocked down I don't know how many times and each time by applying basic principles of Scientology I have been able to bounce back stronger than before.

In a world where nuclear war threatens annihilation and where the earth's natural resources are being destroyed to a point where no one can live on it, I am proud to be a Scientologist and learn the data about happiness, about life and about responsibility.

I thank L. Ron Hubbard for everything he has done for me and for mankind.

Julia Migenes
Opera Star

I sought out other solutions, I tried other philosophies and never found one that really indicated the truth to me.

Scientology presented precepts to me that really made me feel like I had found, at last, the guidelines that I had been searching for.

Before Scientology I had one dream of making a living, doing voice-overs for animation. After I became a Scientologist my abilities have expanded so far and above what I originally dreamed for myself that I've amazed even myself at my enormous increase of abilities.

I've gotten an Emmy, a platinum and a gold album. I've written and starred in a one-woman show and I have a bright future as a producer.

*I've got two beautiful children, an incredibly supportive husband, a staff working with me for the same products, future dreams and goals and **all** of this is because I became a Scientologist.*

Nancy Cartwright
Actress/Writer/Producer & Voice of Bart Simpson

I have been involved in Scientology for 12½ years. Earlier as a student I had felt inadequate in my studies. In Scientology I found out that I had missed basic steps in my education and I was able to resolve my study problems and go on to fulfill my goals to work with children. Now I am a teacher and I use that same technology with my students. Once they learn how to study and apply what they have learned, they have been able to come up 2–3 grades in 8 months. The students are bright, confident and proud of their achievements. It has been a great joy and privilege to share L. Ron Hubbard's study technology with my students.

Carol Loweree
Teacher

As a kid growing up I was very shy, withdrawn, afraid of people and generally unhappy. All these uncomfortable feelings were still there during high school and later in college. The most I could hope for was to make each day as bearable as I could, yet I felt life should be happier.
These ill feelings weren't going to go away all by themselves. I was going to have to DO something about them and what I did was Scientology.
I enrolled on a Scientology communication course and to my surprise and delight my shyness started to disappear and my fear was less and one by one all these uncomfortable feelings started to go away. It was like shedding a skin. And what I found underneath all of this was ME! The more I used what I learned in Scientology the more ME I became. Scientology really works! I became more outgoing, more confident, honest and ethical. I found my integrity. I liked people a lot more, and life became FUN, just like I always thought it should be.

Michael Manoogian
Logo Designer

Scientology gave me and my family a new life. It enabled my kids to survive "teenage madness." Scientology has helped me do a good job of making my marriage survive—I have a really strong relationship with my wife. It has enabled me to understand people so I can cooperate with others. I have increased my ability to help others just by talking and listening to them.

Joe Duncanson
Electrician

I came to America 9 years ago when I was 23 years old. I barely spoke English and couldn't write or read English at all. But I had a dream to make it in this free land. I had no idea how I was going to do that. I was alone here, no friends, my life was just crazy.
Five years ago, I started my first Scientology service. From that point on, my life has improved.
I have become a lady full of confidence. I am now engaged to a wonderful man and I own my own company which is expanding and doing very well. I have learned to read and write English. All of these wins and gains I attribute to Scientology.

Hellen Chen
Business Executive

By the time I got into my late thirties, my life was a mess. Not only did I have a serious problem with alcohol and drugs but I also had been divorced twice. Although I wanted to change things in my life, no matter how hard I tried, nothing worked. Then I found out about Scientology. My life changed. Now I have a wonderful wife and marriage of 14 years, I have great kids and they are doing well. I am happy.

John Taufer
Building Contractor

Scientology makes people free, sane and able. It makes it possible to be more oneself, with the ability to create and change anything being a natural and expected phenomenon. It puts you at cause over your life and makes it easy for you to take responsibility not only for your own life, but for the world. Scientology is sanity and if people who aren't in Scientology knew just how sane their lives could be, they would run to find out about it.

Anne Archer
Actress

With Scientology, I've gained an enormous understanding and love for life and my perceptions have increased. As an artist, that's priceless. My business has skyrocketed and the demand for my work keeps increasing. Scientology gave me the realization of my unlimited potential and the ability to achieve any goal I set for myself. For this I am forever grateful.

James T. Sorensen
Photographer

Before I found Scientology I was a stressed-out executive who was running on tranquilizers and martinis to get through the day. I had ulcers and back problems, and I felt I would burn out before I was forty. I was out of communication with my family and my business associates. Scientology helped me to discover who I really am, which enabled me to pursue my goals in life. I no longer require drugs or alcohol to remain stress free and my body problems have ceased. As the result of Scientology training and counseling I now have a happy marriage, my own successful interior design firm and I have become an accomplished public speaker. Scientology works because it has the technology to change the conditions in life.

Lee Cambigue
Business Executive

I found out about Scientology through a newspaper in Tokyo. I was a very unstable person before Scientology. For example, when I set out to do something, the opinions or influence of others used to have an effect of swaying me off what I was aiming for. I eventually felt I could not trust others, and lost my self-confidence. However, through Scientology I've now found out why and learning this new knowledge gave me back my confidence. I'm working as a translator now, and feel able to do anything I set out to do.

Yoko Suzuki
Japanese Translator

At thirty-five years old, I was not happy and wasn't getting what I wanted from life. I felt if I waited it out or tried harder, things would change. As each failure came my way, whether it be in relationships or career, my world just seemed to get a little smaller. I wondered why the fearlessness and enthusiasm I once had was gone. I did not have the ability to change things so passed time waiting for fleeting moments of happiness. I got interested in Scientology and found that something could be done. I found there is hope and made successes out of my failed purposes and goals. Due to Scientology I have a great marriage, my life is better and I'm able to win again.

Janice Sturgiss
Mother

I have been in Scientology for over 21 years. In those years I have worked hard to make my dreams a reality. Very few dreams have escaped me and I am extremely thankful now for my successes both professionally and personally. The role Scientology has played in my life has been vital. Without it I simply cannot imagine where I would be right now. It has been the source of answers and resolution for every conceivable problem, upset, fear and obstacle life has thrown at me. I have found amazingly that the answers were simple yet totally effective, the resolutions easy and completely workable. Life is not easy. Sometimes life is cruel—even vicious—I've been there, I've felt it. But I've also felt hatred, anger, upset and pain lift off of me and go away forever with Scientology auditing. I've seen the worst possible dilemmas evaporate with the application of Scientology technology—just like magic. But it's not magic—it's Scientology. Easy to understand and apply by anybody, anywhere, anytime. Scientology works.

Billy Sheehan
Internationally Renowned
Rock Bassist

Before Scientology, I found it difficult to communicate with others and make progress towards my goals in life. I was moody and difficult with friends, family and acquaintances. Now, by applying what I have learned through Scientology, I know how to make things go right in my life, I have a wide circle of friends and I am happy beyond any earlier expectations. L. Ron Hubbard was a man of brilliance, and more, he used the brilliance to help better the lives of others.

Doug Walker
Writer

I found that embarking on a career in art had its drawbacks. Drugs seem to be everywhere in the art world. The myth that "artists need to be crazy to be creative" is rampant. It is no wonder that many artists have failed, given up their hopes and are no longer creating. When I discovered Scientology, I learned that you can overcome the critics and the drugs. And the myth? Well, that's all it is—a myth. A sane artist has a much better chance at succeeding and surviving as an artist. Scientology has given me the knowledge, ability and strength to maintain my sanity even when the world gets crazy.

Bobbie Kitchens
Artist

Before Scientology I had my own company that was doing okay, but I didn't have the faintest idea how to get along with people on a professional level. I didn't know how to lead without building up animosity or how to be liked and still have control. It seemed that as a leader one had to continually assert oneself, much like a bull in the field running over a herd of cows. Very macho!

Needless to say, this approach didn't work very well.

Then I found Scientology.

I learned how to handle people effectively while still managing to keep my sense of humor. I learned how to understand people (including myself) and how to get the most out of people and also how to give. I learned how to help other people get along with others. All this has led me to a good, healthy, sane life.

Robert McFarlane
Businessman

Our overall success with Scientology includes terrifically increased stability and significantly fewer upsets in life. In fact, it's even hard for us to get a good fight going now. Using Scientology we make life exciting and worthwhile. It's that simple.

David and Sue Minkoff
Physicians

My life is infinitely better since my first introduction to Scientology. Before Scientology, I was on an emotional "roller coaster." Anytime I'd win at something or gain a moment of happiness, if it was on a Tuesday, you could predict that by Wednesday I'd be down in the dumps again. This "up and down and up and down" was such a point of upset and hopelessness for me that I finally resigned myself to the fact that this was something I was going to have to live with for the rest of my life.

In 1988, as a result of Scientology auditing, this phenomenon ceased for all time. I was shocked. I couldn't believe it. I was no longer on the "helpless" receiving end of life. I am resilient, strong, more self-assured and, most importantly, more able to handle what I encounter.

Physical aches and pains I'd associated with writing my songs have vanished. On stage, I feel much more creative and I am enjoying myself more up there.

My awareness of, interest in and love for other people has risen markedly and the more I study Scientology, the more I feel like I'm coming out of a long, deep sleep. What a relief!

Thank you, L. Ron Hubbard, for this chance to live the full-blown "Technicolor" life I've always dreamed of.

David Pomeranz
Songwriter/Recording Artist

I have studied, for some 20 years now, the various technologies that exist in Scientology. I have firsthand knowledge and experience of the workability of this subject in assisting an individual to dramatically enhance the quality of his life. I can honestly say that I know who I am and that I am much more capable of controlling life (as opposed to life washing me downriver and into the ocean). I am happy. I am successful.

Bill Johonnesson
Management Specialist

Four years ago I was combating depression. Now people ask me if I have always been so cheerful. It makes me think of the times that I didn't want to go on. Scientology has given me the key to knowledge and a way to solve problems so that the answers fall right into place.

With what I learned from Scientology I was able to help my mother who was taking the drug Prozac after surgery. She felt no reason to go on living although she has always been very full of life. I worked with her, using a special Scientology assist to soothe her nerves, and she responded remarkably well. Without Scientology, I would have had to just sit back and do nothing for my mother in her time of need.

Bonnie Jean Damico
Hairdresser

By the time I was 17 years old, I was doing a lot of drugs and was going downhill fast. I had dropped out of high school and left my chances of a good education and successful life behind. I had no real hope or desire to succeed in life. I did L. Ron Hubbard's Purification program and my life was literally saved. I continued in my trade and did volunteer work helping others get off drugs. At the age of 21 I went into business on my own. I now had a strong need for skills at handling life. I turned to Scientology and again found my answers. If not for Scientology technology I am certain I would not be alive today. It truly is a miracle that now, at the age of 31, I own real estate and a million-dollar-a-year business. I am a successful businessman, I have a great marriage and I am happier than ever. I am really winning in life.

Robert Hernandez
Air Conditioning Business Owner

One day I realized that I was not going anywhere. I was broke and unhappy. I lost my driver's license, couldn't work and left Colorado. I moved to LA and then turned to Scientology. The results were instant. Scientology enabled me to completely turn my life around. I am now doing all the things I have ever wanted to do. I can communicate with people, something I could never do before. I can achieve anything I want. I attribute this directly to Scientology.

Jim Blythe
Window Cleaner

Life is much simpler and fun as a Scientologist. Before, I was reeling from a marriage which ended sadly in divorce. I didn't understand the opposite sex. My personal life was practically nonexistent. Constant headaches were handled by taking 8–12 aspirin daily. Employees were often hard to understand and difficult to manage.

When I learned about Scientology and started applying it in my life, here's what happened: I started having fun in life again.

Today I have a lovely wife and five great children.

I successfully made a career change from retail consumer electronics to commercial printing and successfully brought it about. Today, I'm President, CEO and sole shareholder of a multi-million-dollar printing plant in southern California.

Employees are easy to understand and a joy to work with.

Oh, and the headaches? Haven't had one in years, nor even a cold for that matter! Aspirin and drugs are a thing of the past. Scientology has had a tremendous effect on my life, my family, friends and associates. I recommend it to anyone that wants to have a happy and successful life.

Geoffrey Pick
Printing Company Owner

Scientology has enabled me to see clearly what my goals in life are. Before I became a Scientologist I was a professional race car driver but quit. I got involved with Dianetics and Scientology and through my studies and auditing I was able to rekindle my purpose in life and return to my profession. My capabilities increased and I became more certain. As a result, I won the 24 hours of Le Mans. Without Scientology I would never have accomplished this nor found the happiness I now have in life.

Philippe de Henning
Champion Racer &
Winner of the 1987
Le Mans

I didn't know how bad my life was until I did my very first course, a communications course.

Since that time I've been able to apply Scientology to every part of my life. I'm co-founder and executive director of The School of the Natural Voice here in Los Angeles. I have hundreds of singers come to me for voice lessons. Most of my time is spent applying the simplest Scientology technology to their lives, just to help them gain confidence in themselves and their ability. My own singing career has flourished through the use of Scientology. I apply the administrative technology to my business and it's helped me build a business I never knew I had the potential to do. It's one thing for me to sit here and spout off about how great Scientology is and have someone else read what I'm saying and say, "Oh yeah, well you're just saying those things because someone asked you to." All I can say is take ONE PIECE OF DATA and apply it to a part of your life standardly and see what happens. I'm amazed at how it works exactly the way it's supposed to work every time.

Gloria Rusch-Novello
Singer/Writer/Actress

Before Scientology I was extremely shy. I had a big problem even beginning a conversation with someone. I had a lot of trouble making new friends and I was generally an introverted person.

Scientology completely handled this. I have lost my fear of communicating and I found I could talk to people and make friends easily.

I am able to work out problems until all parties are happy. Scientology has made parenting really fun. My daughter grew up in Scientology, she is able to communicate, stays away from drugs and other teen insanities and she and I have a great relationship.

Scientology has given a sense of purpose to my life.

Barbara Pease Stewart
Businesswoman

Scientology has greatly increased my abilities to understand myself and others. The auditing procedures have far exceeded any of my expectations. The difference it has made in my life is so remarkable that I could say life was like trying to walk in a pool of quicksand before Scientology. I think so much more clearly. Problems are easily solved now after the training and auditing I have had.
I've been in Scientology since 1986. I just wish I had found it sooner because it would have made my life so much easier.

Ward Cole
Dentist

I think the most essential thing for an artist, in order to develop and mature, is to get information that he or she can use in terms of communication skills and in terms of affinity and reality with people. The Tone Scale is invaluable wisdom for any artist. I think Scientology is essential. It's been the most practical tool for me to have. I love being a Scientologist. I'm proud to have parents and grandparents who are Scientologists. I love being an individual and expressing myself and Scientology has enabled me to do that.

Kate Ceberano
Australia's Top Female Vocalist

I started in Scientology in 1977 and soon realized the data contained in Scientology would make a huge difference in my life. All the courses and auditing have been extraordinarily enlightening and valuable. My wife and I use Scientology to create a wonderful marriage. In fact, I'm sure there's not a day that I don't apply what I've learned in Scientology dozens (and probably hundreds) of times in a variety of ways.
Scientology is such a key part of my life today that it really constitutes an approach to living that is optimum for me as an individual, as a member of a family, as a member of the groups I belong to, and as a citizen of the world.
Scientology founder L. Ron Hubbard was a great man. We should all be thankful for the insights and knowledge he made available for all people.

Terry Jastrow
Seven-time Emmy Award–winning Producer/Director
ABC Sports

The technology I learned from L. Ron Hubbard's study course has helped me so much that I wish I had it while I was in college and in professional school.

Dr. Steven Lund
Management Consultant

Four years ago I had a beat-up old pickup, my wife had left me and I had no job. It was then that I discovered Scientology and got a renewed attitude toward life. Where things were not possible for me they were now possible. My life has expanded incredibly. I now have my own contracting business, and my wife and I got back together through Scientology Marriage Counseling. We are now very happily married.

Tim Van Pelt
Plumbing Contractor

Before Scientology I never felt confident in my abilities at work, I was introverted and my drive to succeed was getting weaker by the day. With Scientology I've been able to turn this all around. Scientology has increased my ability to handle all areas of my life. I now have a great husband who I love more and more each day and I also have a fantastic career. It is actually hard to think what life would be like without Scientology.

Stephanie Rose
Radio Broadcaster

Well, I didn't have an occupation. At the time, my idea toward life was to see how little I could do and basically how much and how many kinds of drugs I could take. I wasn't doing anything with my life. When I got into Scientology a lot changed right away. For the first time ever, I saw that there was hope and that was very encouraging. When I received Scientology counseling to handle my drug problem, my life started going up and up and up and hasn't stopped since.

Keith Code
Top Motorcycle Instructor

Scientology has changed my whole life for the better. It has given me a better understanding of myself, of others and of life. This makes life much more livable. I would never have the terrific marriage I now have without Scientology. The gains I have had in Scientology enable me to experience events without getting overwhelmed by them, making me a better problem solver and more stable. My ethical and moral standards have risen incredibly, which is a real asset. With Scientology, life is easier, simpler and more fun.

Bill Greenwald
Commercial Real Estate Broker

Before I became a Scientologist, I was hopeless. I came to realize that my life had no real meaning even though I was "doing well." Then I found Scientology. I discovered why I felt so hopeless. I found that I actually had a purpose for life! I met my wife then and we were married. My career boomed. My income shot up 300 percent in less than two years! Now it's been 15 years and I'm doing really well. I enjoy my two wonderful children, and I enjoy my work immensely. Things have come a long way since those hopeless years—thanks to Scientology.

Ed Beckman
Computer Consultant

I came to the United States from Mauritius in 1978. I found out about Scientology and it assisted me in making an easier and more comfortable transition to a new, different country. I learned how to really communicate to others and with L. Ron Hubbard's study technology my command of the English language increased 100 percent.

Françoise Hooks
Legal Secretary

The first thing that struck me about Scientology is that it made sense. I could think with the data. The second was that it actually WORKED and that is why I became a Scientologist. I've been a Scientologist for over 20 years and I'm still awed daily by the things I've learned through Scientology. Not only did my dreams come true but along the way the quality of my life became rich, filled with decency and integrity. Scientology is simply the finest thing I have encountered in my entire existence.

Today I have a magnificent wife, four incredible children and I wake up each morning knowing that I am contributing to the betterment of my family, society and the world around me.

Scientology has made it possible for me to lead a full and productive life.

Jeff Pomerantz
Actor and Founder of
Hollywood Says
No to Drugs

*I went with a friend to the church of Scientology. I didn't believe them, I didn't trust them. I knew nobody could do what they had told me. But I made a deal with the person I saw. "I will read your book [**Dianetics**]. If I like it, I will be back." That was spring, 1975. Over the years Scientology and Dianetics has not failed to work when applied. I see it work every day!*

Roy Brock
Roofer

Twelve years ago, I was successful in the business world but my life was really a mess. I was married to a banker hooked on drugs and had no strength to face the future.

With Scientology, I now live a wonderful life and I truly enjoy what life has to offer. I am in control of my own life now and, best of all, I can help others live better and happier lives, thanks to Scientology.

Lily Guerrero
Sales Manager

I was 37 years old when I first learned about Scientology. I figured I was doing about average for my peer group: My second marriage was in trouble; my business was heading out of control; I was drinking heavily and taking cocaine two to three nights a week on a gradually increasing basis. Now, nine years later, my marriage is happily intact, my business is stably expanding, I take no drugs, have only an occasional beer or glass of wine and I've never been happier, healthier or more prosperous in my life. I can see now what I only dimly suspected back then—that my life was headed down a long, dark chute to nowhere. Only one thing altered that course for me: the truth and wisdom contained in the teachings of L. Ron Hubbard.

Terry Johnston
Farmer

I began taking drugs when I was 14 years old. By the time I was 17 years old I had become an addict. I tried several programs to handle my addiction and none of them worked.

*In 1973 I went to Narconon LA. There, using L. Ron Hubbard's drug rehabilitation technology I was able to successfully come off of drugs. After graduating the Narconon program, I read **Dianetics**, became a trained auditor and received auditing myself. My insecurities, fears and losses in life were handled with Scientology auditing. I can honestly say Scientology saved my life. Today I run a very successful Narconon drug rehabilitation center. I have 3 teenagers that I have raised successfully and most of all I have my life back. I would strongly suggest that anyone out there who is looking for a better life pick up a **Dianetics** book and read it. It will change your life forever!*

Jeannie Trabant
Program Director,
Narconon Los Angeles

Scientology not only revitalized me as an artist, it revitalized me as a person. I had given up on singing and on life before Scientology—and this was after a long, successful singing career of 23 years. You have to realize how far gone I was. I didn't think there was any hope and all my dreams were gone.
The difference in the quality of my life before and after Scientology is quite simply day and night. So many friends tell me that I look ten years younger than I am! Perhaps even more important is that I feel the way I used to in my early 20s. Every person deserves the chance to feel the renewal of life, energy, power and hope.

Maxine Nightingale
Vocalist

If anyone had told me years ago that I would be where I am today I would not have believed them, but here I am! I have an absolutely wonderful marriage. My husband and I have a growing and happy relationship. We can talk to our children about anything and they know they can talk to us. This fact alone is the most valuable thing about Scientology—it helps people get into real communication. Even my parents who are not Scientologists tell me the world would be a wonderful place if all children were as active, helpful and honest as ours are.

Dorda McDaniel
Store Owner

Before Scientology I had no real direction in life and was definitely the effect of it. I had a profession that I was pursuing (being a pilot) but I didn't have the data necessary to learn to do it.
Through studying Scientology I have learned how to communicate and to confront life head-on. I can honestly say that I am no longer the effect of my environment or my future and I'm doing exactly what I want to do in life.

Randy Hepner
Jet Pilot

In my career Scientology is the thing that has made it possible to be in show biz for 21 years. I love the people and I love the work. Scientology has helped me to handle the everyday problems of life, handle confusions and keep my goals focused. It has made my life fulfilling as an actor, father and American citizen and has made it possible for me to fulfill my own American Dream. Being a Scientologist has clarified knowing what freedom really is.

Michael D. Roberts
Actor

Scientology auditing gives you the ability to be as great as you can be. And it takes the stops off the things that prevent you from succeeding.

Floyd Mutrux
Writer/Director/Producer

I have been a Scientologist since 1970, and I have not been the same since the first day I entered the Detroit organization.

I knew at once that Scientology was what I had been looking for all of my life. It is difficult for me to imagine what I was like before I became a Scientologist as it was akin to being totally blind. I am no longer entangled in the confusion of what most people consider daily life. Using Scientology has definitely enhanced my well-being and creates a safer environment for those I come into contact with.

My ability to confront life, handle situations and to take responsibility for myself and others has markedly improved. I can honestly say without the merest shadow of a doubt that had it not been for L. Ron Hubbard and Scientology I would not be as happy nor as successful as I am today.

John W. Frencher
Businessman

Scientology has had a major impact upon both my personal life and my artistic life. It has contributed tremendously to the survival and expansion of both.

As an artist I have had difficulties that were very hard to confront—phenomena such as "stage fright" or "the blank page when writing that first line." The "solutions" to these and other problems, in the form of drugs and alcohol, had plagued me for a long time.

Scientology supplies a technology that assisted me in confronting and handling such situations** very **effectively.

My ability to create impact as an artist has increased tremendously due to Scientology auditing and training.

Marital and familial relationships had long been an unstable area for me. Scientology handled this area of my life and has given me the ability to create a very sane and healthy family and the best possible environment in which to bring up my children.

Applying Scientology technology, for me, has been the smartest decision I could have possibly made toward the betterment of my life and the lives of those around me.

Mark Isham
Grammy Award–winning Musician/Composer

Since becoming a Scientologist I feel very stable and a lot happier than I did before. My understanding of this world was almost nonexistent before Scientology. Now life isn't a mystery to me anymore. I'm not afraid or worried about my past, present or future. I'm now able to handle difficult situations with Scientology technology. I continue to maintain a happy marriage and good relationships with my friends and family. I can't imagine life without Scientology.

Gigi Boratgis
Piano Teacher

A friend of mine had a copy of ***Dianetics*** *on her bookshelf and I had seen it advertised on TV. So I bought the book and started to read it. I came to a part that really made sense to me so I wanted to get some auditing. I called the 1-800 number in the back of the book and was referred to a church of Scientology. My life hasn't been the same since. After a short time I had gotten rid of the need for alcohol and drugs and to this day I haven't felt the need to go back to them.*

Peter Finnegan
Technician

I used to have a fear of crowded places. Every time I'd go to the grocery store or to a movie or almost any place where there were a lot of people, I'd go into a panic; my heart would race, my hands would sweat and I would feel as though I was about to pass out. This problem was completely handled in one hour of Scientology auditing and it has never recurred. If I had gone to a psychiatrist, I am sure it would have cost tens of thousands of dollars and years of therapy and probably still would not be handled.

Dianne Cook
Bookkeeper

Before I was introduced to Scientology, I was moving about in life uncertain of how to create stable success for myself as an artist, in my marriage and for others around me. I just left it to hard work and luck. I now have confidence that I can tackle any venture in life and be able to make it work for the benefit of myself and others around me. This confidence comes from the clarity and workability of a lifetime of research and hard work by L. Ron Hubbard. I am deeply indebted to him.

Pat Frey
Florist

Before Scientology I had no real purpose. I didn't know what I was going to do next week, let alone with my life. I was very unhappy.
My sister started telling me about all these amazing and wonderful things that were happening in her life and I wanted to experience these things myself. I went to the church of Scientology and started the Success Through Communication Course and it was unbelievable. But it didn't end there. I did the Basic Study Manual course. I couldn't believe someone could actually learn how to study. Since then I have done many courses and read several books and apply the things I've learned in life. I thank L. Ron Hubbard for his technology for now I am truly happy.

Paul Girard
Printer

One of the best things that I have gotten from Scientology is a future—a real future. I had what I considered was a good job, but I wasn't going anywhere that interested me. I knew there was something missing in my life. Now I have no doubt about who I am or about the direction I am going. Without Scientology this just would not have happened. My activities are directed now and the goals I made much, much earlier in my life are now defined and real. I recommend Scientology to anyone who wants to put direction into their life and set their goals straight.

Gary Nordfors
Carpenter

I had set high goals in life but was not achieving them, and was backsliding in life. Then I found Scientology and my life turned around. I now have a lot of self-confidence. If it was not for my experiences in Scientology, I would never have had the courage to start my own business.

Jeff Evans
Automotive Machinist

I was a fire fighter in the LA City Fire Service for 26 years. I felt I was failing because I was losing ground in the course of life. In 1977 I read in L. Ron Hubbard's **Dianetics** *about how the reactive mind robs one of his self-determinism, and about the state of Clear. I had to find out for myself. Later, after my Scientology studies, my life turned around. It improved my performance as a fireman and vastly lessened the fear of a job filled with fear.*

Pete Andreasen
Fireman

Man, I was a mess after getting out of college. Drugs, fear, alienation, stagnation; these were the makeup of my existence. By applying Scientology to myself and my environment I was able to pull myself up by the bootstraps. Today I'm married to a wonderful lady who recently gave birth to our first child, Molly, and she is the greatest. I have a new life and love it. I look forward to living it each and every day. Scientology is all about improving and living life with enthusiasm.

Bob Sullivan
Fisherman

I owe my life to Scientology—both literally and figuratively. Prior to getting involved in Scientology I was heavily dependent on drugs. I was killing myself. One day a friend told me about Scientology. It contains so much simple data that is immediately applicable in life. I gained the ability to face life and learned the power of real communication. Scientology technology helped me free myself from drugs and create a new life.

Ron Penner
Caterer

One of the principles of Scientology is "if one knows the technology of something he cannot be the adverse effect of it." In Scientology there is a wealth of know-how on life. I have achieved many goals using the technologies of L. Ron Hubbard. One of the things I have gained through Scientology is to set a target for goals that I want to achieve and then push them through to attainment.

Craig Hooks
Carpet Salesman

Before Scientology, I was using street drugs. It was destroying my life. With Scientology, I have not taken drugs for twenty years. Through the Scientology courses that I have taken, I lead a happy and successful life with a great marriage and two incredible kids. I don't honestly think that I would be alive today had it not been for Scientology and the technology that it has for handling people with drug problems. My life is on the right road now—thanks to Scientology.

Art Stein
Real Estate Manager

Before I was a Scientologist, I was unsure of myself and nervous and shy dealing with men. I got confused and annoyed easily if things did not go my way. Now, after 18 years of being a Scientologist, I cannot believe that I am the same person. I feel so calm. I am self-assured. It's a great feeling.

Carmen Suarez
Manager

Scientology has helped me bring up a teenage boy in a troubled world. We are the best of friends. With Scientology and the precepts of **The Way to Happiness** *by L. Ron Hubbard, I have gotten through the rough years.*

Bob Cook
Painter

Scientology has made it possible for me to change my life and the lives of others. It provided me with tools that I could apply to realize my potential. Not long after I became a Scientologist I got my role as Mary Ellen on the TV show "The Waltons." Through what I have learned in Scientology I am able to confront and handle difficult situations without relying on other people for solutions. I apply what I've learned to other people and have had a positive effect on their lives as well.
Scientology has made me much happier.

Judy Norton
Actress/Singer

From 1972 through 1980, my business merely plodded along. In 1981, I was introduced to L. Ron Hubbard's technology which I quickly applied to my business. In a short period of time, I became the nationally recognized leader of the upscale car detailing industry. I was featured in a number of national news media including ABC, NBC and CBS national news. Scientology works for me—not only in business but in my marriage as well.

Steve Marchese
Automotive Detailer

As a medical professional I am concerned with matters which deal with life. The knowledge about life which I have obtained from Scientology has been an incredible help to me. I have seen so many young doctors become hardened, disillusioned and lose compassion because of the suffering to which they are exposed. Being a Scientologist and knowing Scientology has allowed me to grow in compassion and understanding and has made me more effective in helping my patients, my children and others.

Megan Shields
Physician

We really don't know how we would've kept our marriage together if it wasn't for Scientology. There is so much stress that is placed upon a marriage that it's sometimes difficult to know that you are making the correct decisions. Through Scientology we look forward to each and every day as an adventure, instead of just "getting by." L. Ron Hubbard developed a great deal of technology that has enabled us to face the challenges brought on by day-to-day living. It's really helping our marriage ***work.***

Mr. and Mrs. Sutton
Writers, Illustrators & Publishers of Children's Books

Scientology has been a tremendous asset for my brothers and I as individuals, as a family and in our highly successful firm. The breadth of knowledge available from the subject is hard to conceive. Most notable is the ability to communicate on any subject. That, coupled with L. Ron Hubbard's enormous insights into the mind of man, and the study and administrative technology he has developed, gives one a huge leg up on any endeavor. Being happy with oneself, one's family, one's business activities and life generally is a fantastic accomplishment and the knowledge that one can improve from there still, is incredible; yet we have found it truly achievable with Scientology.

Matt Feshbach
Feshbach Brothers
Investment Managers

Before I found out about Scientology I had no purpose. I worked as a parole officer and because I had very few successes the vast majority of the parolees failed and were reincarcerated. I tended to consider myself a failure.

Since entering Scientology my life has been turned around. My energy level is much better and my outlook on life is very positive.

Rod Randall
Retired Parole Officer

Scientology has had the most profound effect on the raising of our children. By knowing that each of our children are total individuals we have developed an incredible relationship. When I communicate with our children I use everything I learned in Scientology. My husband, Dr. David Singer, and I have a wonderful marriage because we have used Scientology philosophy to create it from the start. Our children, as a result, have grown up in a very safe environment because we have such a happy marriage.

Diana Venegas
Fashion Designer

Scientology helped me as a former Vietnam combat pilot and later as an experimental test pilot, to conquer alcohol abuse which came from my involvement with the Vietnam conflict. I have given numerous interviews around the country on the subject of the Gulf War and its relationship to the Vietnam conflict. Before Scientology I was afraid of talking in front of groups of people. Now I no longer fear getting up and speaking to others. I am much happier now.

Glen Barton
Pilot

After Vietnam I was floundering. The technology of Dianetics and Scientology revitalized my life. I was searching for answers to life and found them. The tools I got from Scientology ethics and administrative technology boosted me to the top of my profession. All of these tools have expanded my awareness and abilities to the point where I can make a difference.

Bill Moon
Research Analyst

When I was first introduced to Scientology, I was doing well in life but I knew there was more. I wanted to know what made people tick and how one could improve his own condition. Now I have the answers to those questions and more. They are contained in the vast wealth of knowledge of Scientology.

Billy Evans
Publisher

As a child I had everything—wonderful parents, a beautiful home, a terrific life. Then my parents moved when I was a teenager and I snapped. We quit communicating and I spent years rebelling against them. We were so out of touch by 1969 it was unbelievable. I was on a quest to find out why I felt the way I did. In 1969 I read the book ***Dianetics*** *by L. Ron Hubbard and that day my life changed. I started the Communications Course and immediately understood how to solve the problem with my parents.*

I went from a rebellious individual trying to hurt my parents to a very happy person. I am now in ***terrific*** *communication with my parents. I have handled the problems that held me down so I don't have to pass them on to my son. I am successful at whatever I do and I find life just gets better and better.*

Tory Bezazian
Mother

Scientology training has changed my life and made me able to function more at cause because I am now able to know that what I am doing is right.

Linda Tucker
Office Manager

I got into Scientology when I was fifteen and at that point I was going downhill pretty fast—with school and family and just about everything. I received Scientology auditing and my life has forever changed. The drowning, "there's-no-hope" feeling has disappeared. I have become cause over more of life and I don't go the effect of others' ideas, opinions or suppression. This has allowed me to expand. I thank L. Ron Hubbard and Scientology for this new life.

David Flate
Office Manager

Before Scientology I knew that I wanted to have a good marriage, happy family and to be successful in life, but it seemed that I kept running into closed doors which I could not open. I got into Scientology in 1972 and knew that I had found a way to achieve my childhood goals and dreams.

Scientology gave me the tools I needed and the understanding which I so lacked, and what was even more important: a way to apply this knowledge to better my life. As I improved and became more capable, it had a definite effect on others as well.

Scientology literally saved my life. I look back on the course of destruction I was on, and had it not been for Mr. Hubbard's technology, I would not have been able to achieve what I have today, a happy family and marriage and success in what I do helping others make their lives more worthwhile.

Jane Allen
National Spokesperson
Citizens Commission on Human Rights

SUCCESSES FROM SPECIFIC SERVICES

Millions of successes are on file in churches of Scientology around the world relating benefits received from Scientology training and auditing services. Here is a representative sampling of gains Scientologists report having experienced from individual services spanning the Bridge to Total Freedom.

Introductory Books and Services

Twenty years ago, although I had a good job and had recently gotten married, I was dissatisfied with life and was seldom really happy. My day-to-day existence seemed futile and had little direction or purpose. I suspected that there must be more to life than what I was experiencing, but it was all a mystery to me.

I picked up a book one day, entitled ***A New Slant on Life****. In this book by L. Ron Hubbard I found answers to my problems. I went to the church of Scientology and got onto a course on communication and suddenly had some tools to change unwanted conditions. My life started to turn around.*

Today, I own my own successful business, the expansion of which I directly attribute to the use of L. Ron Hubbard's principles. I have been happily married for over 23 years and have a teenage daughter who is also happy and doing well in life. Not only am I happier and more successful than I thought possible, but I am now involved in the Church of Scientology's community affairs programs, helping other people to get off drugs and helping to make known the harmful effects of drugs. I am enjoying life and have never looked back!

R.T.

After reading some of L. Ron Hubbard's books in 1976 and taking a course, I found my teaching profession was more enjoyable and productive because now I could understand and therefore handle "problems" that came up.

My children in class were happier, too! My life changed dramatically. Old body aches and pains from an international track and field career vanished with the application of Mr. Hubbard's spiritual technology. With my new awareness and confidence, I stepped into the business world and started my own business. My life is a happy one, filled with new discoveries at every turn. I find it amazing that we are born into this life and are not given an instruction manual on how to live it! I now have one!

I highly recommend the use of L. Ron Hubbard's technology to anyone who wishes he had a "manual" that would better life. You will find, as millions have, that true joy and happiness can be achieved.

I.P.

I wish I had found Scientology 20 years ago when I was first looking for answers to my life. I went to a lot of meetings and read a lot of books and tried a lot of different things but then I just sort of got on with my life. I happened upon ***Fundamentals of Thought*** *one day in a bookstore, stayed up all night reading it and my life has not been the same since. I immediately saw how I had a problem relating to others in many cases, and with the materials L. Ron Hubbard presented in the book I was able to improve the way I deal with other people which has made them and me a lot happier.*

M.T.

Sometimes in life achieving a goal large or small can seem very complex and possibly there are barriers to accomplishment. After having studied the entire book ***Fundamentals of Thought*** *I found I was able to simply play the game of life, knowing with certainty that things would turn out right—and that's exactly what happened! I became more able to make a clear, precise decision about something I wanted to do. And this certainly made the greatest difference in getting it done. I was able to improve my relationship with my husband, my parents and my son through understanding them better. My work became not just easier, but more enjoyable. I was able to enjoy being with people so much more and better deal with even difficult circumstances. Best of all, I am in a much better position to help others. So many times I've had a friend or acquaintance who I could have helped. Before, I would have been sad for them because there was nothing I could have done. But now I have solutions that work.*

T.L.

Before the Success Through Communication Course I was having a rough time talking to people. I wouldn't be able to start a conversation or if I had to leave, I couldn't end one either. But then I did this course and I am now able to talk to people and get my communications across. I can also answer questions easily without being embarrassed and can make friends much more easily and just lead a happier life.

C.E.
Success Through Communication Course

I was dancing ballet and teaching in a university. I had broken a bone in my left foot and was unable really to perform anymore. I'd opted to teach instead of dance. I had had an operation to remove the bone and in fact ended up standing up through my last four months of lectures at the university due to hip pain that started just after the foot operation.

One of my university colleagues told me I should get and read a book called ***Dianetics: The Modern Science of Mental Health.*** *I read the book over three days practically night and day. It made so much sense to me I KNEW it must work.*

I went with a friend to the Dianetics center and received some Dianetics auditing as mentioned in the book. After the second session I was entirely well. The pain in my hip disappeared and to this day has never returned. I resumed dancing and even started performing again.

D.A.
Introductory Auditing

My son died in an accident and in the weeks that followed I was constantly thinking about the moment when my father told me about his death. During all my daily activities I appeared to be functioning properly, but that moment was constantly replaying in my thoughts. I doubt I would have been able to continue to function much longer without it really driving me crazy. After one session of introductory Dianetics auditing, six weeks after his death, that "tape" stopped playing constantly and I was able to proceed with my daily routine and obligations much more easily.

I do not believe I would have been okay without this auditing. My life would probably have completely fallen apart.

S.R.
Introductory Auditing

My success ranks with biblical references to the blind seeing, the lame walking and people being raised from the dead! What the top medical authorities in the fields of internal medicine, orthopedics, radiology and neurology could not handle in 3 years, my auditor with LRH tech handled in one afternoon! I can move my previously debilitated left arm with ease and comfort now. This morning I could not raise it from my side without terrible pain!
The spiritual cause of the problem is resolved and the problem no longer exists.

P.W.
Introductory Auditing

The course has meant regained knowledge, regained awareness, abilities, freedom to speak my mind, listen better, hear more, speak more precisely and clearly and it goes on and on. A miracle has occurred to me!

M.A.
Success Through Communication Course

I was withdrawn, extremely shy and afraid to communicate. Then I did the Success Through Communication Course. As a result, the world became brighter and people were less of a threat to me. I became happier and willing to hold a conversation with anyone. There was a feeling of control in my environment and the sensation of being very big as a spirit. It was the best feeling I had ever experienced.

N.D.
Success Through Communication Course

Purification Program

I did the Purification program and the results were amazing. During the early part I felt for days like I was "stoned." I would get up in the morning in a mental fog. It was definitely reminiscent of the old times when it was miserable to go to work and the future seemed unimportant. My reaction to pressure situations was just to say, "To hell with it" and ignore it. After some time on this program this went away and by the time I was done I felt more bright and awake than I have ever felt. It has been a couple of years since I did the program, and this feeling has persisted. My life has changed.

S.G.
Purification Program

Prior to taking drugs I was full of life, energy and dreams. Life was simple and uncomplicated. I had a very good family life—one in which I loved and trusted my parents. I had good friends that I enjoyed honest relationships with. More than anything I wanted to be happy and have a game to play in which I would win.
But something happened along the way. I got involved with drugs. I was not trying to destroy myself—drugs were the "in" thing—to many people in my generation they were considered part of the "answer." It was too late by the time I realized that drugs were destroying my life. I had become "spaced out" from drugs, and detached from life. Those things that I had held precious in my youth—family, morality and honest friendships—were a thing of the past. Really caring about life and other people were beyond my grasp. What relationships I did have became superficial.
I remember wondering if I could ever really care about someone again. I was scared, as I realized that I was not the same person I had been before drugs. I was not

as sharp , my mind was a fog. I was bitter and untrusting. If there was one part of my life that I wanted to change it was the fact that I had done drugs. There was not a day that went by that I did not worry about this. This only heightened my despair as I knew that I couldn't turn back time. Even after quitting drugs entirely I remained aware of the fact that I was not the same person that I had been before. The guilt, bitterness and sorrow were staggering. Then I did L. Ron Hubbard's Purification program. It handled the effects of the drugs that I had taken. I got my energy back and I am no longer walking around in a fog. I can think clearly and my mind is quick and decisive again. I have my drive back and I'm a part of life. I feel real emotions again that have been shut off for years. I can confront having real and honest relationships with others and I'm restoring those which I lost.

I only hope that everyone else who has been involved with drugs, be they street drugs, medicinal drugs, etc., has the same opportunity as I have had and that they do this program. It will change their lives for the better, and there is an awful lot of good that can be done with one's life to have that ruined by drugs. L. Ron Hubbard's Purification program performed a miracle for me. It gave me back my life and I am living proof of that.

B.D.
Purification Program

I did the Purification program shortly after getting started in Scientology. I was amazed at the changes it produced in me.

It enhanced my perceptions and as a fine artist this is invaluable. It also helped increase my speed in completing my artwork. I was far less moody and much more stable mentally than ever before. These factors allowed me to be more successful in my business relationships and with people in general. It was a great experience.

W.D.
Purification Program

As a Bachelor of Medicine, I found it very interesting to study the Purification program. I found it so interesting that I began the program at the church of Scientology.

After completing the program, I noticed a tremendous upsurge in physical and mental well-being.

Mentally I feel relaxed, my memory has improved a great deal and I feel much less dispersed and freer emotionally. The changes are so vast that I must say that this program has changed my life and my only wish is that these discoveries by L. Ron Hubbard will be broadly implemented to handle our "drug society" which is in so much need of them.

J.M.B.
Purification Program

Study Technology

The technology of L. Ron Hubbard is really incredible—specifically his study technology. I studied for nineteen years. I was in a university and I noticed that I started to feel kind of "stupid." I couldn't grasp the information in my courses as fast as I could before. I started having trouble with my studies. With the study technology of L. Ron Hubbard, everything changed. All my troubles went away and my brightness came back. I was better than ever. Just to give an example: I'm French and I tried to learn English in French schools for eight years. At the end of that time, I knew only ten to twenty words. I started to learn English with L. Ron Hubbard's study technology. Three months later I was able to have a conversation with any English-speaking person. Today, my ability to speak English is impressive. This technology is priceless.

P.M.
Student Hat

This is the most powerful course I have ever done. The wins, gains and changes have been phenomenal. I have changed so much as a student it is hard to believe. I can actually study comfortably now. This material hit into very basic inabilities and has totally changed them around. I have so much more power to operate and I have regained a marvelous sense of who I am and my own ability to communicate.

S.R.
Student Hat

I have been a teacher for nearly twenty years and a student for nearly fifty years. In that time I have seen and experienced much that has been described as "education." Some of it has been good, but an overwhelming amount of it had little or no lasting value.

As a student I found it very difficult to exercise anything other than my memorization skills. I just memorized things without really understanding why I was doing it. The purpose was really just "to get the grade."

My first course in the study technology developed by L. Ron Hubbard completely revitalized me as a student and provided me with the tools to approach study with a purpose and to really learn something for application. It was this technology that gave me my first real interest in teaching. I realized that with the basic tools provided by this exceptional technology, not only was I able to learn anything I set my mind to, but I could help someone else to learn successfully as well.

For nearly twenty years I have been working with students of all ages from around the world, and have found that they all suffer from the same study-related problems and that once in possession of Mr. Hubbard's breakthrough technology they have the tools necessary for successfully learning anything.

I can think of no greater gift than to give a child (or adult) these easily mastered study tools. They last for a lifetime; they open wide the doors of the future and they unlock potential that was always there.

B.W.
Student Hat

I just finished my Student Hat course and I feel great about it. My trouble in school was that I never knew how to study. I was always a kid with cheat sheets in the desk and instead of writing a report by myself, I'd copy the data verbatim from the source.

I now know how to study—and if someone can learn to study then they can learn anything they want to and do it. I never knew before how important proper study technology is, but now I love it. I apply the study technology constantly as it is invaluable. I'd never be without it.

E.B.M.
Student Hat

Key to Life

I have gained ***myself*** *on this course; a certainty of my true beingness and an ability to duplicate others and to be duplicated by others. My confront of life and my willingness and ability to communicate has soared.*

I feel like a new being who has shed tons of confusions and fears and who has tools that will enable me to live life.

T.P.
Key to Life Course

The Key to Life has been the most rewarding course I have done in my life.

"A man is as alive as he can communicate," L. Ron Hubbard wrote. I am ten times more alive than I was when I began this course and have the potential to become many times more so! So much of life's agony is just a failure to understand what was communicated.

R.F.
Key to Life Course

Thoroughly confused and stultified by the educational system, I somehow stumbled through life this far. How, I don't know.

It took this course to undo years of incorrect training and education and then put a foundation there that will stand for the rest of my life. I now feel that I have a chance in life and that I have the ability to go forward and succeed. The course has indeed been aptly named—The Key to Life.

F.A.
Key to Life Course

I have just finished the Key to Life Course. It is indescribable in terms of personal wins and abilities regained or polished up.

If someone had told me that I would experience this much gain, this much revitalization and resurgence from doing the Key to Life, I don't think I would have believed them. The wins are incomparable, that's just how basic and powerful this course is.

S.S.
Key to Life Course

Auditor Training

The Academy Levels were the first courses I did where I learned how to audit and really help another person by handling any difficulties to do with communication. I finished studying the course and then took my first preclear into session. He was a very shy young man who talked with a slight stutter and walked through a room looking at the floor to avoid having to look at and talk to other people. I took him into session and audited him for a few hours. As we walked out of the room after session, he gave me a big grin and said, "Well, let's give this a test." He then walked right up to the first person we met and started chatting, laughing and really enjoying himself, and continued getting into communication in a totally relaxed manner with the people in the room. There were no signs of his stutter. It was like watching a totally different person from the shy person of a few hours earlier, and it left me feeling very, very happy that I had been able to apply what I had learned to produce this incredible result.

H.N.
Academy Level Training

This was possibly the most demanding training I've ever done—and the most rewarding. In learning to audit, I've seen sick people jump out of bed and dance after a session. I've watched psychosis melt away before my eyes. I've seen preclears who felt they had no recall of the past suddenly remember. I've seen major life ruins vanish in one short session, after years of the preclear trying to handle them with other means.

D.M.
Academy Level Training

I just completed training on the Academy Levels and the knowledge contained in them has changed my life in numerous ways. I am now much more at cause and know how things are going to go in my life.

The most rewarding part of the Academy Levels is to sit down in the auditing room with another person and administer the processes and experience the elation when my preclear gets rid of some aberrated pattern he's had all his life.

One has to do it to experience it. The preclear's complexion gets bright, his eyes very bright and clear and a big smile comes across his face and he looks at you with a "what do you know, I thought I would have to live with that for the rest of my life!" expression that tells you what's occurred to him and you know you have made life and livingness a brighter activity for that person. I cannot thank L. Ron Hubbard enough for all the love and caring he put into this work, to ensure that each person who wants to help others change will understand and be able to apply his discoveries.

P.C.
Academy Level Training

I was educated for four years at one of the finest universities in the world but I honestly have to say that there were any number of lectures I heard while doing the Saint Hill Special Briefing Course which taught me more about myself, others and life than any ten courses I took in college. L. Ron Hubbard's depth of understanding of life and the mind was so far beyond anything my professors could teach me that doing the Briefing Course was like a university education several times over. By the time I did the course I was already a trained and experienced auditor but studying all the materials of Dianetics and Scientology in the order that L. Ron Hubbard discovered them gave me a total understanding of his technology and I was able to make it my own because I followed and understood exactly how he did it.

As an auditor I have all the technology under my belt now and I know I can help any person improve. Helping someone else discover more about himself is the most satisfying activity I know and the Briefing Course is the course that teaches you all the technology of how to do this. I have learned in Scientology that there is a technology to life and that once you've learned it, you know it forever. The Saint Hill Special Briefing Course is the most thorough education in life that exists anywhere.

D.K.
Saint Hill Special Briefing Course

My life changed radically from the knowledge gained on the Saint Hill Special Briefing Course, and I will continue to put every part of what I have learned into application.

Without doubt, the Saint Hill Special Briefing Course was the most spectacular adventure of my life. I gained a wealth of knowledge and understanding broad enough and technically perfected to the point where I know with absolute certainty how to set any individual free. I was put in awe many times over at the simplicities and truths presented on the course and I felt myself changing as I have never felt before.

While the course taught me the technology of auditing, what I really learned was the technology of LIFE. I stepped into a new realm of capability and stability and really assumed the beingness of an auditor the way L. Ron Hubbard intended.

I am forever grateful to L. Ron Hubbard for this legacy of technology, for it is a truly amazing body of truths expansive enough to fill the universe, yet maintaining a total simplicity. With it we can free and are freeing beings.

P.A.
Saint Hill Special Briefing Course

What I got out of the Saint Hill Special Briefing Course was an unshakable certainty and an understanding of a tremendous body of truths which left me with the true beingness of a Scientologist and an auditor.

I solved aspects of my own life just by mere knowledge of this data but above and beyond this I gained the know-how of clearing another being of the barriers to his freedom. That is the bottom line and is something that can never be taken away from me—the knowledge of how to free a being.

P.A.
Saint Hill Special Briefing Course

Listening to the Saint Hill Special Briefing Course lectures was the most rewarding training I have ever done as an auditor. Every detail of research that L. Ron Hubbard did at Saint Hill during the 1960s is covered in these tapes and listening to them is really like sitting right next to him and learning how he developed the Bridge to Total Freedom, step by step.

These lectures not only cover all the basic underlying theory of the Bridge but also address just about every facet of life. Mr. Hubbard gives incredible facts about man's past, politics, religion, study, different cultures, music, art and a myriad of other subjects. Once you have heard all these lectures you have a comprehensive understanding of life. What I gained as an auditor from these tapes and this course was a complete certainty on auditing basics.

Auditing became the simplest thing in the world to do because any and all seeming complexities got swiftly eradicated and I just knew that I was able to get any preclear through anything in auditing with ease and with 100 percent results every time.

G.M.
Saint Hill Special Briefing Course

The Class VIII Course has resulted in a quantum leap in my auditing skills. Whereas earlier I felt that I had a mountain of information that I had to remember and use while auditing, now I am just there, relaxed and in communication with the preclear and naturally doing the next correct thing without having to think about it.

Auditing has been reduced to a simplicity where the tech is simply part of me—I own it and can use it with no effort, worry or thought. I can only liken it to an athletic skill. A great athlete is so highly trained that he doesn't think about his next action as that would be much too slow—he simply does it.

I feel honored and privileged to be among the elite of Scientology auditors and being able to help others so effectively in ways that have never before been possible. Auditing is now easy and pure pleasure with every session ending in an excellent result. Thank you, Ron, for this priceless gift—you have made my life truly worthwhile.

L.D.S.
Advanced Auditor Training

Dianetics and Scientology Auditing

I have had many personal successes with Scientology auditing. My ability to let others be, without the need to interfere and unnecessarily interrupt or control them came way up. This was a big win, in the work environment particularly. Also, I found changes in life, often disconcerting in the past, became something I just took in stride. All in all, my ability to confront and handle the pressures and stresses of day-to-day interrelationships increased dramatically and I find myself calmer and enjoying life much, much more.

K.R.
Scientology Auditing

Scientology Expanded Grades have noticeably increased my ability to learn. In my business, I must do extensive reading and research, and I am now able to absorb and understand a much higher volume of material. This ability has been invaluable to me.

Due to Expanded Grades auditing I have become much happier and find my respect for others has increased. My energy level has risen to the point where I've started my own business and have become revitalized as a writer and financial lecturer.

Probably the most amazing thing which has happened to me was the fact of a 20 percent increase in my IQ.

K.G.
Scientology Auditing

After completing Grade II I feel terrific. I feel energetic, enthusiastic and yet at peace with myself. I also sense a new awareness. I can also look back at past hurts, anxieties and frustrations and feel that they will not have any impact on future decisions.

P.N.
Scientology Auditing

I was looking for a way to handle the emotional pain left over from being abused as a child. I went to a psychologist and she said, "I don't know how to help you." Another one said, "All we can do is 'reprogram' you." The third one told me maybe she could do something but that it would take thirty years. Then a friend told me Scientology could handle my problem, like that! It's true. Since I have had Scientology auditing I no longer have to live in the past—I can live in the present and create my future. And it all happened faster than I would have imagined possible!

M.S.
Scientology Auditing

The end result of my Drug Rundown restored me to my teenage years—when I was honest, didn't take drugs or alcohol; when I was so full of life and enthusiasm; when everything was new and wonderful and I could do anything. All I had to do was decide I wanted something or to do something and it happened. That state has been restored to me now. I'm 53.

S.L.D.
Dianetics Auditing

Prior to coming into Scientology I had received a major operation on my nasal passages which were blocked, causing extreme sinusitis. The medical specialist told me that although he could help by removing the blockage, in his experience it would not fully resolve the problems I was having which he felt may be psychosomatic. He was right. Although I experienced relief, I was still crippled by blinding headaches and sinusitis and would literally have to go to bed as it hurt so much. Then came Scientology auditing. One day in my auditing I contacted something which had to do with the extreme pain I was suffering. Suddenly I felt a crunch—I could physically sense the bones in the left part of my face changing. Right afterwards my face felt as if it had woken up after being asleep. It began tingling. The huge pressure build-up from my sinuses had completely disappeared—gone.

I knew that it was over. I no longer felt any sinus pain—I could breathe—I felt alive again.

To this day, twenty years later, it's never returned. What happened to me during that auditing was a miracle.

C.M.
Scientology Auditing

My wife was seven months pregnant when she became very ill and had surgery performed in her abdomen. After the operation the doctor told me she would need to remain in intensive care for several days. He explained that, being pregnant, the pain from the surgery would be very intense and would last for many days. He estimated it would take five days before she could walk.

While she was in intensive care, I audited her and in less than 24 hours she was walking up and down the hall, and in 48 hours she was released from the hospital. The head doctor examined her and told me her recovery was miraculous!

E.E.
Scientology Auditing

I was wearing glasses when I went for my first Dianetics session. I had been wearing them for six years and my vision was steadily deteriorating. During the session I discovered why I had started wearing glasses. All of a sudden I felt a tremendous surge of inner strength and certainty. I took my glasses off and I felt terrific. Things looked really clear. That was over twenty years ago and I haven't worn glasses since. Today my vision is almost perfect. Dianetics really works.

R.B.
Dianetics Auditing

After getting Grade 0 I honestly feel like a new person. It's a wonderful feeling knowing that I can communicate and that I want to communicate. Through this auditing I realized that I have an absolute love for being in communication with people and things. This was a life-changing experience.

A.T.
Scientology Auditing

In the fall of 1990 I developed a physical condition which I had never encountered before. Over three months I visited several doctors to try to determine what it was and to find out how to cure it. Finally after seeing a specialist it was diagnosed as a chronic vascular disease that there was no cure for. I was told by this specialist that I would probably have it for the rest of my life. This news was very upsetting to me. I was 28 years old at the time. Then I got some auditing. After less than one hour I felt much better. Not only that, the physical condition stopped spreading. Within a week of daily auditing, all physical evidence of the condition was gone. It is 1½ years later and the disease has not returned.

J.M.
Dianetics Auditing

New Era Dianetics auditing is absolutely incredible. I never realized really what an engram could do and how solidly fixed they were in one's mind or how insidiously they aberrate you. Then I had a session of New Era Dianetics and I was utterly amazed at what happened. This particular engram was quite severe and I was a little more than nervous to go through it, but with the help of my auditor, I made it through. We ran it several times, each time picking up more of the engram that was hidden beneath unconsciousness and pain. After we had run all the emotional pain out of this engram, I had an incredible realization about my life and why I had been unconsciously behaving in certain ways. That unwanted aspect of myself is gone now, never to return. I couldn't stop smiling for days after that! It was incredible, I felt as if I were floating when I walked. I had never felt so good, and this was just **one** *engram.*

J.J.
Dianetics Auditing

New Era Dianetics auditing has completely changed my life. Things that seemed unresolvable resolved in the first 4–5 hours. Until I experienced it for myself, the reactive mind was not really tangible to me; but let me tell you, when you get in session with an auditor trained on New Era Dianetics and an E-Meter you instantly find and resolve those things that have been haunting you for years. I would never have believed it if someone had told me what had been underlying all my fears and anxieties. Each session ended with me finding out something about myself that I didn't know before and with a new feeling of freedom. I can't say enough about New Era Dianetics auditing—there is no aberration that can hide from its incredible ability to dig out of the reactive mind that which keeps you pinned down in life.

L.D.
Dianetics Auditing

I used to have epilepsy. Through Dianetics auditing, I discovered that the convulsions which traumatized my life for more than 16 years stemmed from a series of electric shocks that my mother underwent when she was pregnant with me.

During the 16 years I suffered attacks of excruciating blinding and stabbing pains through my eyes and head. My body would go rigid and my throat, mouth and arms would go numb. Then I would throw up every twenty minutes for eight hours before the pain would subside.

These attacks occurred from the ages of 11 to 27 years—until I had Dianetics auditing. These attacks vanished after Dianetics auditing at the age of 27. Today, ten years later, I have helped hundreds of people achieve similar results with Dianetics auditing.

J.B.
Dianetics Auditing

Years ago I was burglarized at home. Two guys entered and I was beaten severely and raped. I had 27 fractures in my face and jaw. The doctors said I'd lose my eyes. I was an emotional wreck, unable to face my friends or any part of life. I was terrified by this experience and unable to confront it.

I turned to Scientology auditing. The improvement was so miraculous that one friend who had come with me dropped to her knees and cried. Within two days the emotional trauma was gone. I completely regained my self-confidence and self-respect. This made it possible for my body to heal much faster. Scientology auditing got me over a tragic experience and has enabled me to lead a better life than I ever thought possible.

V.F.
Scientology Auditing

Nearly one year ago my father was struck down by a massive heart attack which left him completely disabled.

We were told by the doctor that he probably would not survive as he was 78 years old and the damage was too great. He was discharged to a convalescent center renowned for its success in stroke rehabilitation.

Two days after he arrived we were told by the director that my father would not benefit from the program as he was too far gone, that it was hopeless and she would not be able to help him.

I gave my father Scientology auditing every day. Day by day he improved until finally six weeks later he walked out of that facility!!!

The same physical therapist who had told us that there was no hope confessed to my sister that in her twenty years' experience with stroke patients she had never seen anyone come back the way my father had.

A.A.
Scientology Auditing

I was very ill for months in the hospital. I was under intensive care for weeks with a bleeding ulcer infection and kidney failure. My heart stopped three times. I was unconscious for over a week, and I did not want to live. The doctors were going to give up on me and stop the treatment. The nurses did not expect me to survive. My wife had a very hard time with it and she couldn't even call to see how I was doing; she had to have someone else call for her. She then received some Dianetics auditing and came to grips with it, at which point she was able to come into my room in the hospital and give me some auditing. She came in every day.

I soon started becoming more aware of my environment and had a determinism to survive. It made life bright enough to live. I am now recovered and would not have lived if it weren't for the technology of L. Ron Hubbard that helped us get through it.

B.G.
Dianetics Auditing

In 1977 I had a serious problem with drugs. I was drinking morning, afternoon and night, as well as using cocaine five to six times a week. Life was gray. I felt hopeless, and there seemed to be no way out. Then I was introduced to the technology of L. Ron Hubbard and believe me, life has not been the same. My drug problem was history after three months. I began to take courses at the church of Scientology on communication, auditing and life. Today, over ten years later, I still have no more urges or cravings for drugs and alcohol.

D.H.
Scientology Auditing

Before I got Expanded Dianetics auditing, I had problems and conflicts with those I worked with and was in trouble all the time.

Expanded Dianetics is very powerful and thorough. I found the very source of my problems with other people and blew this away! It became a pleasure to work with others. I discovered why there were certain locations—cities and even whole countries—I hated or feared. This was fully resolved (prior to my auditing I disliked the city I was in so much that I stayed inside all the time and would only venture out when forced to).

Turmoil and strife disappeared and it was possible for other people to live happily with me for the first time!

A.A.
Dianetics Auditing

In this session, a series of incidents from my childhood that were causing me a tremendous amount of guilt and heartache was completely relieved. This was unconfrontable before. In fact, I'd never been able to talk about it, not in 27 years. My auditor had me return to the moment it happened and go over the incident several times. I was wide awake and fully alert throughout.

As we began, I felt again the same fear and frustration I felt in the incident, but as we continued, the bad feeling was completely discharged and I began to feel much better. By the end of my Dianetics session I was totally free of any effects from this nightmare that had been ruining my life. It's a real miracle—I feel like a 200-pound weight is off my shoulders!

As a Doctor of Dentistry, I'd wholeheartedly recommend Dianetics auditing to anyone. I see now that when you get rid of the upsets, guilt, anger, etc., your whole life changes for the better.

S.C.
Dianetics Auditing

There is so much for me to say about this fantastic auditing. It handled areas of myself and my life that I've wanted handled for so long. I'm incredibly happy. I don't know when I've really ever attained this before.

One of the biggest things that occurred was that I gained self-respect—something I've been without for a very long time. I now have the ability to inspect situations with myself and others and handle accordingly without shame, blame, regret or worry about the future. It's a great life I have and will continue to have. I have a fresh start now!

K.S.
Scientology Auditing

Every two weeks I used to get a migraine headache which literally did not allow me to get up from bed. This was ruining everything I wanted to do in life.

Then I received New Era Dianetics auditing and in the three-hour session I eradicated the source of the migraines. Today, a year and a half later, I've not had another headache. I'm living a new life.

A.P.
Dianetics Auditing

Over 2 years ago I had a severe accident where I smashed both ankles. The bones were in 15 pieces and the surgeon was not positive he could even put them all back together. He said I would never run and may not ever walk. It took all sorts of screws, pins, wire and steel plates just to hold all the pieces together while they healed. I got daily auditing starting the day after the accident, which not only greatly eased excruciating pain both mentally and physically but also produced miracles. My doctors were amazed as they could not believe my speedy recovery. I was walking within months and now I dance, run and play sports which my doctors doubted would ever be possible. There is absolutely no way this would have occurred without L. Ron Hubbard's technology.

G.C.
Dianetics Auditing

State of Clear

Achieving the state of Clear is the most important thing that has happened in my life. Not only because I was relieved of my past unwanted emotions that were affecting my life and making it difficult to be happy, but also because I opened a new door of happiness. I'm now able to help others a great deal more as I can understand them in a way that was not possible before. Abilities that I did not know I had became evident and as a result I could experience and give greater happiness to others.

My dreams and goals are alive and I have certainty that they will happen. My strength and persistence as an individual have been unblocked.

T.L.
State of Clear

Do I feel wonderful! Having recently achieved the state of Clear, everything around me is so calm and my awareness of the environment and life itself has expanded tremendously. I am now able to view life's problems analytically and come up with sound, rational decisions for each and every one of them. My energy level has increased tenfold and I tackle life with an enthusiasm I never had before. Being Clear has enabled me to begin accomplishing all of those things I wanted in life.

J.L.
State of Clear

It's been many years since I went Clear but the feeling of vitality has never faded.

Being Clear, I am able to see things as they are, rather than viewing them through my own reactivity. I notice that though other people might get very upset or frustrated about problems and troubles, I can just view the actual situation and decide on the best solution to handle it rather than automatically REACTING *or losing my temper and saying something I would later regret. With my marriage, being Clear has had a tremendous effect. I feel that communication is the basis of a good marriage. Because I am Clear my ability to communicate is very good and I have a very happy marriage. I have been able to enter a newly chosen career full speed ahead, without veering off onto any side roads or worrying if it was all going to work. It's very easy to do things because I'm definite in my decisions. I know what I can achieve.*

Achieving the state of Clear released me from the barriers of life and left me with a definite sense of freedom.

D.F.
State of Clear

I have just achieved the state of Clear! It is nothing short of miraculous to be rid of one's reactive mind and to have the accompanying freedom, happiness and new-found abilities that I know are lasting. When I first read the Dianetics book and learned for the first time the truth about the mechanics of the mind and how it all works, I wanted to go Clear.

It is an incredible relief to finally understand myself and to know with certainty the cause of man's aberrations, his downfalls, his sorrows and that these can be eradicated to make way for a new life of competence and happiness. The day-to-day problems and obstacles in life no longer pin me down in unwanted conditions. I am able to set and reach any goals that I create and positively affect my relationships with others and family.

Since achieving the state of Clear, I notice that my family and friends are doing far better as well, and I am much more capable of helping them. The doors to my future have blown wide open with potential and possibilities.

G.A.
State of Clear

It is nearly beyond my power of expression to describe the state of Clear—this crystal, shining, effortless state. It is the most basic and the most noble part of **me.** *It is all that I knew I ever was, absolutely unadulterated by past failure, social machinery or false identity. I have the complete freedom of basic personality. Man has perhaps glimpsed this state when witnessing individual acts of mercy, kindness, creativity, courage, truth or any other attribute we commonly personify through art. It isn't a temporary condition or something that will pass, like the happiness we feel during some great moment in our lives. It is lasting and permanent. This is the beginning of something new and great for me and a brand-new vista for mankind as well.*

N.K.N.
State of Clear

Before going Clear I was dissatisfied with life, I felt trapped in some way. I was on a treadmill, and there didn't seem to be any way to get off of it. Going Clear really opened the door to my life and my abilities.

I now see a strong, vibrant future and a way to achieve my goals. It's hard to imagine how I lived at all before I went Clear. My whole concept of what living means has changed and I wouldn't trade it for anything!

C.J.
State of Clear

OT Levels

It seems I've been searching for eons for what I know now. I feel at peace. I am calm and certain. Things that never made sense now make sense. It's so hard sometimes to say enough to really acknowledge the magnitude of what processing is and does. OT levels are the most precious thing in the universe.

R.M.
OT Levels

Moving through the OT levels is like nothing I've ever experienced before. Through them you find the answers to things you never imagined existed. These answers unlock the very truths of life for you. The OT levels are like removing shackles from yourself as a spiritual being—ones you weren't aware you carried with you. I found that I'd been so used to dealing with life in a certain way that I surprised myself when I no longer became upset or acted negatively on my job or in my relationships. My life became calm, it became sane and I became truly cause over each of my dynamics. The OT levels gave me the freedom and understanding of life that has enabled me to accomplish goals I never dreamed were possible.

S.M.
OT Levels

On the OT levels I learned the ultimate truths of man and myself. And the truth does make you free. And with that freedom has come a joy I have never known before. It is a happiness that spills over into the lives of everyone I touch. As if I am so rich in happiness I have plenty left over to give.

I have seen with clarity beyond the cycle of life and death, and risen to an immense vista of freedom where such things as friendships, affections and my personal identity can last beyond one life.

To say my future looks exceedingly bright is an understatement. I am a ***free being!***

S.H.
OT Levels

This was truly the most amazing action I've ever done in Scientology. The power and simplicity of this OT level frequently left me at a loss of words for what had occurred in my universe—the changes were that fast and big. I am now looking forward to an eternal future of new abilities and a new-found insouciance to play the game of life.

M.H.
OT Levels

I can't describe how wonderful I actually feel. Calm, serene—that's it. Also a very deep knowingness. There are things now that I know about why we are like we are (or were, in my case!), about our true nature—and I can testify, MAN IS GOOD. There's no doubt about that. As for myself, I now know that I can be anything I want. It's that easy! I can choose my own path. Many, many additives are gone, leaving more and more and more of just myself. Life is truly beautiful and bright.

The amount of very deep-rooted basic stuff handled is almost unbelievable. The amount of gain is like nothing I've ever experienced in Scientology before. It's a quantum leap.

B.M.
OT Levels

The greatest change for me on this OT level is really finding myself more and more as I always wished to be. I have completely lost all self-invalidation. Things I previously thought as "too hard" or "impossible" or "too exhausting" are now reachable. This level goes deep into the salvation of man. I know I'll never make the same mistakes again.

M.B.
OT Levels

On this OT level I was able to resolve situations that had worried me for an eternity in a matter of minutes. I have become cause over any situation in my life. I can handle, resolve and accomplish what I decide to. Life can be handled totally and solely on a spiritual level. My ability to spot the exact source of a situation and then handle it immediately is unstoppable.

B.R.
OT Levels

The OT levels create such a feeling of freedom you become able to set your own future and go where you want to go. The OT levels take you to an incredible new realm of self-awareness—but the result is the ability to get more done in life!! I am more part of life and I have the ability to join in and make life happen the way I want it.

C.M.
OT Levels

I have regained the power of boundless and limitless persistence. I have regained myself and have no questions as to who I am or why I am. I have regained the spirit of play and the ability to permeate that I had lost and forgotten long ago. This was truly magnificent!

N.B.
OT Levels

My understanding of the human condition has vastly expanded. My care for other people has risen enormously. My life is much calmer now. I am much, much less likely to become upset. The gains I have achieved are greater than anything I have ever experienced. Peace of mind and spirit is priceless.

P.J.B.
OT Levels

On OT II I have gained competence, respect for myself and others, a deeper understanding of life, an amazement with the simplicity of things, and a sense of well-being.

M.P.
OT Levels

Chapter 18

Recommended Course of Progress

The amount of research L. Ron Hubbard conducted on man, the mind and life is towering. He wrote millions of words and delivered many millions more in lectures. By his own creed, wisdom is only worthwhile if it can be shared, and Mr. Hubbard spent years making his materials readily available for anyone with a desire to improve his life. Today, the Church carries on that intention.

Why is there so much information? Dianetics and Scientology contain answers to the broadest field of all, the field of life. And the materials of Dianetics and Scientology are a precisely laid route to higher states of ability and awareness.

However, of greater importance than the sheer quantity and exactitude of material is the fact that one can begin to apply the technology as soon as he has learned any of it. It is not required to sequester oneself away for twenty years on a mountaintop or in a university to see improvement. One is alive now. With L. Ron Hubbard's technology, one can improve now.

With the multitude of services available, the question naturally arises, "Which is the best way to travel up the Bridge?"

There are three general avenues of progress. Each has its advantages. They are: (1) training as an auditor, (2) individual professional auditing as a preclear and (3) a combination of the first two that includes individual professional auditing and auditor training, done concurrently. Below is a discussion of each avenue with recommendations on how to make the most certain progress.

Training as an Auditor

Decades of people moving up the Bridge to Total Freedom have shown that training as an auditor is the most optimum way to progress in Scientology. The value of Scientology training cannot be overstated, since training provides the understanding of life necessary to live successfully.

Before one can succeed in any game he must learn its rules and develop the necessary skills. Without the rules, one upsets the other players; and without the skill, one can hardly play, much less win. Training in Scientology teaches one the rules and develops the needed skills, but here the game is life itself. And with Scientology it is a game where everyone wins.

It is proven that a person who is technically trained in Scientology is much more able to handle work and personnel than an untrained individual. How can people handle life if they have no expert knowledge of how to go about it?

It is not expected for someone who becomes trained as an auditor to then only audit. That is a limited view of Scientology and its applications to life. While the skill of a trained auditor in auditing someone is the most valuable skill of all, a trained Scientologist is more effective in the factories, the offices, the homes and the neighborhoods than someone who is not trained.

Training as a professional auditor has the further advantage of being the most economical course of action to take. As a trained auditor one can receive his own auditing by exchanging with another auditor, and in this fashion get himself up the processing side of the Bridge. He is thus able to move up both sides of the Classification, Gradation and Awareness Chart at the same time and gain both an objective and subjective understanding of the technology.

As an auditor, one can *do* far more to improve people and conditions in life. Foremost amongst things an auditor can do is free another spiritually and no activity is more valuable than that.

Through auditing a person becomes free and only an auditor can make that happen.

By looking at the training side of the Classification, Gradation and Awareness Chart one can see the progression of courses necessary to become an auditor. This sequence usually begins with one or more introductory services, as described earlier, which lead up onto the training side of the Bridge.

After a person has done one or more introductory services, the Student Hat course is a vital first major service. It has been found that the single biggest pitfall in training has been the lack of knowledge of study technology or its proper application. While this is easily remedied once discovered, the student who knows and applies study technology throughout his studies invariably speeds through his courses and becomes an accomplished auditor.

Another indispensable service is the Method One Word Clearing Co-audit Course. Method One is one of the nine methods of Word Clearing. A person can learn to audit this procedure and then co-audit it with another student. Method One Word Clearing is an auditing procedure in which the auditor and preclear search for and clear out of the way any basic word and meaning errors in the preclear's past. The value of doing this can be appreciated when one realizes that with Method One Word Clearing, whole subjects and even entire educations that were not understood at the time can be recovered for the preclear. A person can get hung up at points where he accumulated misunderstoods. Method One frees the person from these points and makes it possible for him to *use* his education.

Either the Student Hat or Method One Word Clearing may be done first, but both are necessary for successful and rapid study.

A student with a long history of drug use may find the effects of drugs severely inhibit his studies. In some cases it is necessary that a student do the Purification program and the Drug Rundown before he can adequately progress. This imposes no economic difficulties on the student, since the needed processes and actions can be done co-audited at any church or mission.

The next key elements to be learned are the communication skills as taught on the Hubbard Professional TR Course and the Hubbard Professional Upper Indoc TR Course. Here, the student masters the communication cycle, which is vitally important in auditing, and the subject of control, which is also indispensable. Many difficulties in the application of auditing can be traced to a faulty understanding of TRs and how to use them.

Once a student has mastered study technology and the TRs, he is ready to learn the theory and techniques of Scientology Expanded Grades auditing. This material is covered in Academy Levels 0–IV, as described in previous chapters. The importance of applying the materials on any training course cannot be overstressed. One does drills to learn how to operate the E-Meter, drills to learn how to properly do each action associated with an auditing session and drills on the techniques used in auditing. All this drilling leads up to an ability to *apply* the technology. It is vital then that students spend adequate time on their drills and learn each one well.

Since definite skills are attained with any training course, it behooves the student to put in as much course time as possible and study outside of course hours as well. In this way course progress is rapid.

After finishing the Academy Levels 0–IV, the auditor should now intern as a Class IV Auditor. An internship gives needed experience as an auditor, polishes the skills learned in the Academy and develops certainty in oneself and one's abilities. Each higher classification attained should be followed by an internship for that class, so experience is gained at each level as one moves up.

Training in Scientology most definitely should include the Saint Hill Special Briefing Course. This course contains all the materials of Dianetics and Scientology necessary for a full understanding of life. By doing the Saint Hill Special Briefing Course, one can also co-audit with another student on any process or action taught on the course, and the student is thus able to receive as much auditing as he desires.

Complete mastery of auditing technology comes with training on the Class VIII Course. The Class VIII Course trains an auditor in the precise standard of application for any case.

By training as an auditor one moves up the entire Bridge in the most economical way possible, gets all the data and all the gains there are to be had. Many Scientologists have advanced far in Scientology by training as auditors. It is the most highly recommended way to progress.

INDIVIDUAL PROFESSIONAL AUDITING

An alternate way to move up the Bridge is to receive individual processing in the Hubbard Guidance Center of a church or mission. This is much faster than training as an auditor in terms of one's own personal progress up the auditing side of the Bridge. It is, however, not as economical because it requires special attention from several staff members to provide the individual service.

Receiving professional auditing in the HGC enables one to receive service in intensive numbers of hours which makes for very rapid progress. The interruptions and upsets of day-to-day living intrude minimally when auditing is done every day for some hours, and a person soon rises above situations which would have dragged him down earlier. More gain is achieved per unit of time when auditing is done this way.

Before beginning auditing, it is wise to become fully familiar with a set of guidelines which, if followed, help ensure that the greatest gains are made in one's sessions. These are supplied by the person in the church who oversees the administration of all auditing, called the Director of Processing. (*Processing* is another word for *auditing*.) These guidelines cover such points as getting sufficient sleep the night before a session, eating properly and refraining from the use of drugs or alcohol for the duration of the auditing, except for medications administered under the care of a physician. Too, the person should keep his personal life as ethical as possible, since problems in one's relationships with others can take up an inordinate amount of auditing time, time that could otherwise be spent on progress up the Bridge.

Any training the person receives before embarking on auditing will be to his advantage. Even a person who has read books on Dianetics and Scientology will be more conversant with what is taking place in his sessions. At some point, in order to make it all the way up the Bridge, one will require auditor training, so the more one knows about the technology early on, the better off he is.

It is important that enough auditing be obtained at the outset to ensure that adequate progress can be attained. An estimate of how many hours will be required to reach a specified point on the Bridge can be ascertained by church technical staff based upon tests and other evaluations made before a preclear starts his auditing. Arrangements to have enough auditing time reserved in advance help ensure that one will reach the level he seeks.

The specific processes that a person receives are determined by the Case Supervisor. Since everyone is different it is impossible to state beforehand exactly how each preclear should progress. The basic route for all persons, however, is laid out on the Classification, Gradation and Awareness Chart and includes, for any case, the Expanded Lower Grades; New Era Dianetics; clearing, either on New Era Dianetics or on the Clearing Course, and each OT level.

Many people who have experienced skilled auditing say it is the most valuable activity there is. Those who move up the Bridge through professional auditing can do so rapidly.

PROFESSIONAL AUDITING AND TRAINING

A third main avenue Scientologists use to progress up the Bridge is by combining professional auditing in the Hubbard Guidance Center with auditor training in the Academy. When the person is not in session as a preclear, he is a student in a course room studying to be an auditor.

This has the advantages of rapidity of progress up both sides of the Grade Chart. One's gains in auditing are augmented by the gains of training, making it an excellent way to progress for those who have the time to do both concurrently.

It should be noted that TRs are not done simultaneously with auditing and so those who wish to study Academy Level training material while receiving auditing in the HGC should do their Professional TR Course and Professional Upper Indoc TR Course beforehand. Experience has taught that apart from teaching auditing skills, the TRs result in vast personal changes and gain as the student's ability to confront and handle communication improves. For this reason, TR training should not be intermixed with auditing.

The above are the three main ways Scientologists progress up the Bridge to Total Freedom. Different people usually find that one way suits them better than the others, but regardless of which route one takes, the adventure of Scientology is a journey of awakening and self-discovery unlike anything else in life.

RECOMMENDED COURSE OF PROGRESS

1

TRAINING AS AN AUDITOR

- Teaches the most valuable skill of all—auditing
- Increases ability to handle life
- Most economical
- Enables one to co-audit up the Bridge

2

INDIVIDUAL PROFESSIONAL AUDITING

- Fastest route up the Bridge
- Intensive auditing makes further progress per hour of auditing
- Full services of the Hubbard Guidance Center to ensure maximum gains

3

PROFESSIONAL AUDITING AND TRAINING

- Enables progress up both sides of the Bridge
- Person can study on course when not in session
- Auditing gains are augmented by gains in training

CHAPTER 19

ANY REASONS FOR DIFFICULTIES AND THEIR CORRECTION

According to the personal accounts of Scientologists in Chapter 17, the gains to be had in Scientology are considerable, even miraculous. By far the largest percentage of people who take part in Scientology training or auditing achieve gains comparable to those. Occasional failures have, however, been reported in Scientology. But, when Scientology appears to go wrong, there is invariably a specific error that has been made in the application of technology which, when remedied, enables it to then work and achieve the expected results. It is a fact that *Scientology works 100 percent of the time when it is properly applied to a person who sincerely desires improvement in his life.*

Such a statement is all the more remarkable when one considers that the general attitude of man toward help or improvement has considerably worsened under the relatively recent influences of psychiatry and psychology. For concurrent with the rise of these two fields came soaring violent crime rates, the creation and rapid proliferation of drug abuse, plummeting educational standards, a weakening of moral standards and a legion of social, economic and other ills. Such a correlation is not coincidental.

These problems of modern living are directly consequential to the massive injection of false psychiatric and psychological solutions into the culture. The steady decay of social institutions in this century followed the ill-considered adoption of psychiatric dogma in the management of our schools, family affairs, child rearing, interpersonal relationships, the arts, criminal justice, politics and other areas.

Furthermore, psychiatric propagandizing against traditional moral values has clouded the concepts of right and wrong and produced generations of people who are confused about themselves, their marriages, their families, their communities and where they are going in life.

Dianetics and Scientology entered a world battered by half a century of this false mental technology and two paramount facts became clear. The abilities of many people to actually perceive, think and reach rational conclusions had noticeably lessened; and many had grown chronically cynical, disabused of the notion that improvement or real help was possible. Dianetics and Scientology, however, *do* produce positive results, spectacular even, if one honestly studies, understands and applies the data. There are methods to produce results even among those who have been victims of this general societal malaise. In fact, the technology of Dianetics and Scientology has proven to be invariably correct. It is therefore of some value to examine why there have been occasional failures and to see exactly how this has been due to incorrect application and not flaws in the existing technology. The fact is, various types of errors can be made, both in training and processing, which could prevent the technology from being exactly applied. The following is a description of these, and how they are easily corrected.

ERRORS IN TRAINING

Wrong Purpose for Studying

Before even starting to study a subject, a person can make a fundamental mistake—trying to study it for some other reason than to really learn, understand and apply it.

Some of the wrong reasons for study include: to earn a certificate or degree, to gain status, to pass an examination, to impress someone or to obey the wishes of a parent or family member.

These reasons might result in a degree, but are no guarantee that a person will be able to *apply* the material he has studied.

If a person studies a Dianetics or Scientology course for the wrong reason, he will only hinder his chances for real improvement.

This could result in a failure to really understand the course and get the full gains possible.

A student should study with the purpose of application in mind. Scientology courses are arranged so that they are easy to get through, step by step. Upon graduation from the course, the student knows the materials he has studied and can apply the data to handle his job, his environment and his life.

The Barriers to Study

In his extensive study of education and learning, L. Ron Hubbard discovered the actual barriers to study which can prevent a person from understanding a subject or from even *wanting* to study. These barriers can get in the way of one's study in a Scientology course room or in life.

The barriers to study have been fully researched and described by Mr. Hubbard; courses exist at churches and missions of Scientology where people can learn what these barriers are and how to easily overcome them.

Past Study Failures

After failures as a student prior to Scientology, a person can become so convinced that he cannot study that he won't even try to study again, or when attempting to study, runs into past failures and doesn't progress. There are various remedies available to students in Scientology to help them overcome such problems and regain the ability to learn quickly and competently.

Past Bad Study Experiences

Past approaches to education have not known the precise causes of study difficulties and, due to this, the methods for handling have not always been effective.

Some of the past handlings for poor study included:

■ Dunce caps on the students while they sat in the corner. This activity has never made any student brighter, but only succeeded in humiliating students, leaving them with less desire to learn.

■ Trick methods of studying and memory systems whereby the student is taught to parrot off facts as a substitute for actual understanding. While a student employing such techniques might look like he has learned something, these methods impart no real knowledge a person can *use.*

■ The use of drugs to quiet a student and make him less active—purportedly to enable him to concentrate and to lengthen attention span. In actual fact, this method makes a student dull and less able to learn for he is less in communication with his physical surroundings. Such drugs also have extremely damaging side effects, which have included instances of suicide.

■ Pain and duress to force a person into obedient study. Examples of this are rapping knuckles with a ruler, spankings and other threats of punishment if a student did not learn as the teacher demanded. Students "taught" in this method often dislike study and have great difficulty with it in future attempts. Pain and duress also stand as a confession from the teacher that he has failed in his job.

It has never been successful to override a person's own determinism to "make" them do something. Consulting someone's understanding and encouraging their sincere willingness and desire to learn has always succeeded. Teaching someone with the idea they are stupid and must be forced to learn destroys the individual's initiative.

In Scientology the actual causes for study difficulties have been isolated. L. Ron Hubbard's study technology can handle reasons why a student would have trouble in study and even more importantly, once a student is taught the technology of study, he can actually prevent difficulties from occurring.

Problems with Earlier Similar Subjects

When a student has developed misconceptions or misunderstandings in subjects studied earlier, it can hinder him in current studies. The later subject can seem complicated or incomprehensible due to confusions stirred up by unwitting association with the earlier subject.

A housewife who has trouble baking may not realize that her botched recipes stem from earlier confusions in her study of arithmetic in school.

An advertising agency copywriter whose clients are unhappy with his ads does not see that his confusions on grammar from high school are ruining his professional life.

A photographer who cannot take a good picture might not connect his difficulties with earlier studies and misconceptions of color harmony in a painting class.

This inability to grasp a current subject is the result of confusions from earlier subjects. The housewife could make better cakes if she understood that half a pint was eight ounces, not four ounces. The ad copywriter could be more successful if he saw that behind his stilted prose lay confusions in grammar. The photographer might take award-winning photos if he knew how to use colors for more pleasing arrangements.

There is a specific handling for such examples as the above—to find the *earlier* subject and clear up the misconceptions and misunderstandings in *it*. The student will then be able to learn the current subject.

This procedure is followed in a Scientology course room, and study failures due to confusion with earlier studies are handled or prevented.

False Ideas or Information

In day-to-day living people often accept ideas without question if they appear to make sense. False ideas and information can come from newspapers, radio, TV or textbooks. They can even come from parents or friends. If a person has been given a lot of false information or concepts in an area, it is difficult to study and apply the subject as it just doesn't make sense.

The subject of religion, for instance, has been seriously muddied up by the mechanistic philosophies of the last century with their false ideas that man is an animal.

Fortunately, there is a very simple procedure developed by L. Ron Hubbard for handling this problem. It helps the person locate the false data he has acquired on a subject, and assists him in stripping it away, thereby freeing up his ability to think in the area where he was formerly confused.

Studying While Tired, Hungry or on Drugs

Trying to study and learn without being well rested and well fed is a student error. It is very hard to understand the information being studied when one's attention is fixed on one's body. It is also a mistake to drink alcohol or to take any kind of drugs while attempting to study.

Taking drugs while studying would defeat the purpose of training, which is to increase a person's awareness and ability. Drugs, whether medical or street drugs or even alcohol, have the opposite effect and impair the senses, the intelligence and the ability to view things clearly. Many medical drugs cause serious side effects, such as hallucinations or mental disturbances. For this reason, taking drugs while on a Scientology course is forbidden.

Even if a person is no longer taking drugs, if he has taken many drugs in the past, he may have trouble studying until the effects of the drugs have been eradicated.

Persons who have taken drugs do the Purification program and receive processing on Objectives and the Drug Rundown. These actions handle the damage caused by drugs and enable one to think clearly and study once again.

Receiving Training While Connected to Someone Who Is Against Spiritual Betterment

A student connected to a person who does not want to see him become better and more self-determined will not be able to get and keep his gains from Scientology training. There is a great amount of information available in Scientology which fully describes this phenomenon and explains how to deal with it.

Suppose a wife is unhappy being a housewife and wants a career of her own where she can use her abilities yet she is too timid to resolve the matter with her husband, who is violently opposed to the idea and believes a wife's place is in the home.

She does a course in Scientology and starts to become stronger and more self-confident. The husband, viewing her progress as a threat to his own plans and comfort, tells his wife that he will divorce her and leave her with no support if she does not stop attending Scientology courses. Or perhaps she comes home after going to course, tells her husband how much she is learning and how great she feels, and he sourly states that he does not see any difference in her. This situation will cause a phenomenon whereby the person feels much better at first and is steadily improving but then loses her gains.

Training must not be continued over such an unhandled situation, as study under this kind of duress will not produce the intended results.

Fortunately, the exact technology to resolve this exists in Scientology and it can be handled quite rapidly. The wife would sit down with a trained Scientologist who would assist her in communicating with her husband. The situation would be resolved in such a way that her own spiritual betterment was not slowed, but also so that her husband's wishes were also respected and accommodated.

In some cases, the cause of this "up-and-down" phenomenon in a person's life cannot be immediately located in the person's environment. If this is the case, there is also special auditing available to help a person discover the real causes and thus become stable in life.

The technology to help people communicate with and deal with others in their environment who are antagonistic to their plans or desires for personal and spiritual betterment is available at Scientology churches and missions.

Schedules

Just as in any well-run organization, Scientology courses are run according to an agreed-upon schedule adhered to by all students. Course periods start and end at an exact time. Each student has the responsibility to arrive on time for course and to follow his course schedule. Students shuffling in at odd hours distract those already studying and contribute to a failure to really understand the material. The remedy is simple: by sticking to the schedule, a minimum of time is wasted and the student can get on with his course.

If a student is having difficulty following the course schedule, he should see his Course Supervisor for assistance.

Illness

It is an error for a person to continue studying in a Scientology course room if he is physically ill. If one is not feeling well while studying on a Scientology course or is unable to attend the course because of illness, he should let the Course Supervisor know right away. The Supervisor can arrange auditing to help handle the emergency if needed, relieve any spiritual or mental trauma and help speed recovery.

Materials

All Scientology courses have course packs and other materials that the student needs to have on hand to study the course. A lack of needed materials obviously would prevent the student from getting on with his studies. Fortunately, the Church makes these easily available

Materials are made available in many languages so parishioners around the world can advance in their study of Scientology.

and, if the student does not speak English, most materials have been translated into the student's language.

Ask the Supervisor, Not a Student

Students in a Scientology course room agree to follow a guide for students which includes simple, common-sense rules that experience has shown make study much easier.

Included in these guidelines is the basic rule that if the student doesn't know something or is confused about course data, he should ask a Supervisor and get his confusion cleared up before continuing. He should not ask another student as this can create progressively worsening misconceptions, since other students don't necessarily know the answers. If the student asks the Supervisor he will be referred to the correct answer contained in his course materials.

Distractions While Studying

If a student has heavy problems in his life these can weigh on him during his time on course and distract his attention from what he is trying to learn. The

Course Supervisor can often be of assistance in such matters and should be consulted, though sometimes auditing is necessary to resolve the situation.

Some students have been in course rooms where the indiscreet "extracurricular" activities of the students and even the teacher or professor have gotten in the way of actual learning. In a Scientology course room it is the right of all students to learn undistracted by unethical interpersonal relationships. The basic rule is, "Do not engage in any sexual activities (or involvements) that could impede or interrupt the processing or training of another Scientologist." When this is violated, one's own self-improvement actions are actually impeded. The correct action is not to engage in such activities.

Dishonesty

Occasionally a student gets through his course dishonestly by falsely signing off items on his checksheet he hasn't done or pretending to have completed a course with full understanding of the material when he *hasn't* fully understood it.

Such a student is only cheating himself. This is easily handled by applying the study technology and owning up to any prior failures to do so. The student will then be able to study honestly and succeed.

Training in Scientology is done on a gradient with more basic courses coming before more advanced materials. If prerequisites to a course are falsified, the student will not grasp the materials or skills taught on the course. Any inclination not to honestly walk each step of the Bridge resolves with the application of auditing and other procedures. In this way the full gains can be attained.

Not Following the Auditor's Code

Even for "student auditors," the Auditor's Code, the code of conduct that must be followed by all auditors, still applies.

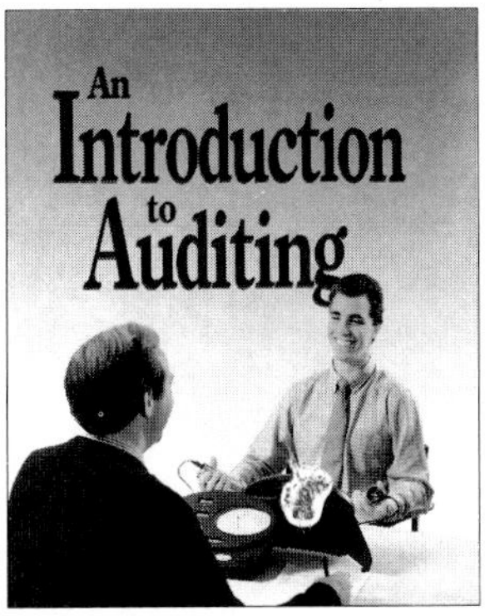

This booklet is provided to all persons newly beginning auditing. It lays out guidelines to follow in order to get maximum gain from one's auditing.

Not following the Code can lead to not getting results on one's preclears. If one feels he can't apply the Code, he should get help from the Supervisor.

Supervisor's Permission

A student should not receive processing from or give processing to anyone under any circumstances without the direct permission of the Director of Training and the Case Supervisor. The exception is if an emergency assist is needed due to injury or illness.

Scientology was not designed to be mixed with other practices; therefore, engaging in any rite, ceremony, practice, mental exercise, meditation, food therapy or any similar occult, mystical or other similar practice while on course without the express permission of the Director of Training is an error.

If a person is involved with any of the above, he should simply inform the Director of Training who will either give him authorization to go ahead with the handling he wishes to do, or otherwise help him remedy the situation he is trying to handle.

It is also an error to give processing to anyone who:

1. Expects to be cured of any terminal illness.
2. Has an extensive institutional or psychiatric history which includes heavy drugs, shocks of various kinds and/or so-called psychiatric brain operations.

By "institutional history" is meant having been knowingly or unknowingly given such treatment in a public or private institution for the insane, a psychiatric ward in a hospital, a psychiatrist's, psychologist's or other mental practitioner's clinic or office or a mental health center. It is not that such individuals cannot, in many instances, be helped. But they require many more hours of auditing than someone who has not been so harmed and often, too, due to the damage received in such "treatment" are so unstable as to require more attention and facilities than the church could possibly provide. Therefore, in order to do the greatest good for the greatest number, it is more survival to use Scientology to bring about improved conditions in the individuals in society who are already capable and who would progress fastest. These people, made even more capable, will increase their spheres of influence. The society will then support constructive reform measures such as eliminating the unworkable and even debilitating practices of psychiatry and psychology. And the Church spearheads and supports such efforts so as to prevent further harm by these professions.

Moreover, in that their condition was not brought about by the Church, but rather by psychiatrists, they fall outside the zone of responsibility of Scientology.

3. It is also an error to process a third category of individual, which includes members of organizations who by their conduct show themselves to be hostile to the best interests of mankind. This includes members of police spy organizations, government spy organizations such as the CIA or FBI, or other such federal agencies in any country. This category would include also those who have publicly attacked Scientology in the media or who have attacked or harmed other self-betterment groups.

   It has been found that all such attacks on Scientology were instigated by those who either knew full well that their allegations were false or had no information on the subject in the first place. Such persons constitute a minor percentage of the population and work against any self-betterment group or activity, for they perceive the improvement of others as a threat to their power.

ERRORS IN AUDITING

Just as there are guidelines for a student on training, there are also guidelines which the preclear should follow to get the most out of his auditing. Some of the errors that a student can make in a course room are also applicable to preclears. The most common errors made by preclears and how these can be easily remedied are as follows:

Not Getting Sufficient Food or Sleep

Just as being well fed and well rested are requirements for a student, so they are for a preclear.

Not getting enough sleep while getting audited can slow one's progress and keep one's attention on the body. The preclear should get seven or eight hours of sleep a night (or more if he needs it) to ensure he is well rested.

Snacking on soft drinks and chips instead of nutritious meals with plenty of vegetables and protein is also a mistake. If the preclear feels run-down or has attention on his body, he will have less attention to give to the processes in session. To get the most gains, one's concentration has to be on the process.

If one's diet is not providing adequate nutrients, many preclears have found vitamin and mineral supplements helpful.

Vitamins B_1 and E taken during auditing have been found especially beneficial. L. Ron Hubbard discovered in his research that preclears require a certain amount of mental energy to carry through with processing. Vitamins B_1 and E can be helpful in generating that energy.

Misunderstood Words

As mentioned in a previous chapter, one of the barriers to study is a phenomenon that occurs when words one reads or hears are not fully understood. This applies in processing as well. If a person who is being audited does not really understand what the auditor is saying or asking, he might well be trying to do something totally different from what the auditor and the process intend. He might experience a lack of gains, become puzzled, and possibly would not want to receive any further auditing.

To prevent this situation from occurring, a person about to receive auditing is given a thorough understanding of the basic terms and concepts used in processing. The exact procedures to be followed are reviewed until the person feels confident that he understands them.

If later during processing a question or uncertainty comes up, the person should tell the auditor immediately. The auditor will assist him in clearing up any misunderstood words and getting any questions answered.

Having Attention on Something Else

Sometimes a person tries to receive auditing while having his attention on something else. Perhaps he knows that the money he put in the parking meter will run out in half an hour, or he knows that if he has not completed his session at a certain time, no one is going to pick up his children from the babysitter.

Situations like this must be handled *before* processing takes place. The preclear simply works to find a solution, such as parking in another spot or getting someone else to pick up the children.

Not Following Instructions

An auditor knows what he is doing and in working with people his goal is to *free* the individual, not suppress him. No matter if it seems difficult at times to do as he says, it will be to the preclear's advantage to do so. Following instructions to the best of one's ability is the keystone of fast progress. The auditor will be the most understanding person the preclear knows; cooperation with him will save many hours.

Not Staying in Communication with the Auditor

The preclear should remain in communication with his auditor. If he feels an unusual or new sensation, he should inform the auditor; he can help to the degree that communication with him is maintained. If the auditor does something that the preclear doesn't like, the preclear should inform the auditor immediately. The communication should not be kept to oneself or saved for the neighbors. Failure to maintain good communication can stop auditing progress entirely. If the preclear feels something is wrong, he should say so. Auditors are usually perceptive but few are psychic.

To receive help as a preclear, a person has to be honest with his auditor. If he doesn't tell his auditor what is really going on—even things he's done that he is ashamed of or for which he thinks he'll be thought less of—he will simply block his own progress up the Bridge. A preclear should also take responsibility for his own case. As he consciously works toward his own improvement he will enhance his progress. He should follow instructions, but help the auditor by remaining in communication with him and by telling him whenever he feels there is something he would like to talk about or work on.

Not Understanding the Auditor's Code

The Auditor's Code (see Chapter 33) is the governing set of rules for the general activity of auditing. The preclear should understand that the auditor is guided in his conduct as an auditor by the Auditor's Code. One point of the Code states that he is not allowed to sympathize with the preclear, but instead must be effective in helping the preclear. He also is trained not to evaluate for a preclear or to tell him what to think about his case in session.

Confusions about the E-Meter

The E-Meter is a very accurate instrument and the full gains in auditing are impossible without its use. Confusions about what the E-Meter does or how it works can get in the way of auditing.

The meter does not diagnose or cure anything. Its value is in helping the auditor locate areas of spiritual travail and charge in the preclear's reactive mind, and in this capacity it is invaluable.

At the beginning of auditing the preclear is shown how to hold the meter electrodes, and has the meter's use in auditing explained to him. The meter electrodes and other conditions need to be adjusted to fit the preclear for comfort or else false readings can be obtained which can mislead the auditor in session. For instance, if the preclear's hands are excessively dry and calloused, a hand cream may need to be applied in order to ensure proper skin contact. Such things as an uncomfortably cool auditing room or wearing shoes that are too tight can also affect the operation of the meter. The auditor is trained to check for and handle this kind of thing before session.

Self-Auditing

Sometimes a person engages in what is called "self-auditing." This consists of going around running concepts or processes on oneself. It is out-of-session wondering and chewing on one's reactive mind.

This is an error, as the person himself does *not* know how to resolve the problem. Most people have been trying to figure out what is wrong with themselves all their lives without success, so the self-auditing approach does not work.

Auditing is a team activity, with the auditor and the preclear working together. The auditor gives the auditing command, the preclear looks to his reactive mind, gets the answer to the question, tells the auditor, and then the auditor acknowledges the answer. In this way the preclear and auditor work together to handle the preclear's reactive mind.

(Self-auditing is not to be confused with *Self Analysis* auditing. *Self Analysis* auditing is done using the exact commands in the book *Self Analysis* by L. Ron Hubbard and actually amounts to being processed by the author. Neither is it the same thing as Solo auditing which is a precise technology developed by Mr. Hubbard to enable one to attain various of the OT levels.)

Discussing One's Case

Case has an exact technical definition in Scientology. It means the entire accumulation of upsets, pain, failures, etc., residing in the preclear's reactive mind. This is what is handled with auditing.

Discussing one's case with anyone else besides an auditor in session is forbidden as this can cause problems in session. If a preclear has done this he should let his auditor or Case Supervisor know. The Case Supervisor is the staff member who directs the auditor and guides him in what auditing actions are done for each individual preclear under his care.

If one does wish to say something about his case before going into session or in between sessions, there is a staff member one can visit, called the Examiner. The preclear can tell the Examiner anything he wishes the Case Supervisor to know, and it is part of the Examiner's duty to make sure the Case Supervisor receives the communication.

Actions Unknown to Case Supervisor

Sometimes people get into situations where they are being audited by an auditor, and at the same time are given other Scientology actions by someone else, such as another auditor or staff member or maybe a friend or family member. This should be avoided, as such other actions, unknown to the Case Supervisor, could foul up the person's case. If this situation arises, it should be immediately communicated, so the auditor can ensure that any needed handling is done.

Fooling Around with Processes

Another error consists of fooling around with nonstandard processes outside of session, without a meter; it is sometimes done by students, stirring up cases. Such activity is forbidden. Standard auditing occurs in session with a trained auditor using proper procedures developed by L. Ron Hubbard.

Taking Drugs or Medicine

Taking drugs while receiving processing is an error just as it is while receiving training, and for the same reasons. Drugs, whether medical or street drugs or even alcohol, should not be consumed while a person is receiving processing.

Illness

It is important if a person becomes ill or has an injury while receiving auditing, even if it is just a cold, to let his auditor know. It is a mistake to not mention an illness or injury, as this will only slow progress. By informing his auditor right away, the auditor can work out the correct auditing steps and suggest medical attention if needed.

If one needs to get an assist on an emergency basis, this is fine, but make sure that the person who gives the assist writes down what occurred in the session and gets it into the auditing folder (the folder which holds all the records of auditing sessions and other vital data on a preclear's case). In this way the Case Supervisor will be fully informed of all actions taken.

Receiving Processing While Connected to Someone Who Is Against Spiritual Betterment

Just as with training, it occasionally happens that a person receiving auditing is associated with someone who does not care for the fact the person is trying to improve himself. For reasons of their own, a friend or family member sometimes feels threatened if anyone in their vicinity seeks to become brighter or more able. In such instances the person being audited sometimes has to suffer another person's displeasure at his becoming better. Those being audited while connected to people antagonistic to their hopes for improvement may have trouble keeping their gains from auditing. The stress they are subjected to between sessions from the antagonistic person can pose too much of a distraction to the auditing. If the preclear feels this is occurring he should make the situation known. He can then receive assistance from staff in the organization to resolve the source of the antagonism and restore enough harmony so that auditing may progress as expected.

Breaking Auditing Appointments

An auditor's time is very valuable. If an auditing appointment is made, it is a mistake not to keep it. No matter what "emergencies" or other factors arise. If the preclear doesn't show up for session one too many times, he shouldn't be surprised to find that his auditor has been assigned to somebody else! There is a great demand for auditing and people who can keep their auditing appointments naturally get first preference.

If a session absolutely has to be missed or one has to go out of town, he should be sure to let his auditor know with plenty of advance warning.

Not Getting Enough Auditing

Auditing should be given and received intensively, and in sufficient quantity to ensure a stable improvement can be achieved.

Life tends to knock a person about somewhat, and can prevent one from making steady gains if too much time passes between individual sessions. Additionally, it can be predicted based on a person's current case state that it will take a certain amount of hours of auditing to achieve a specific result. The preclear should ensure he has secured enough hours of processing to attain the end result.

Denying One's Integrity

One of the most basic truths of Scientology is that something is not true if it is not true for the individual himself. No one but the individual himself can determine that he has benefited from auditing. If one claims to have benefited for specious reasons such as to be better thought of by one's friends or to have the status of having attained a higher level on the Bridge, this inevitably causes problems sooner or later. Each level of auditing builds on the earlier levels below it and if one skips through lower levels in a desire to get to a higher level, this eventually shows up and needs to be corrected. What happens is that the gains from the higher levels are unobtainable when the lower levels have not been honestly achieved. This is corrected by going back and honestly doing the missed levels, which then enables the full gains to be reached.

Getting Discouraged Easily

Do *not* be discouraged easily. Give the processes a fair chance to work. A preclear will often experience different emotions or attitudes during the course of processing, and discouragement can be one of them.

The only way out is the way through. Sometimes a preclear has to have the courage to persist through a difficult spot in auditing to emerge with the full gains that can be had.

But *do* persist. If the auditor and the preclear work together as a team, results will occur every time. Man has spent countless years sinking into his present state. Processing will not handle every problem a person might have in a day or a week. But the technology is available to greatly increase a person's ability and to restore his health, self-confidence and happiness. Man *can* pull himself up.

Scientology does not claim to be a perfect system. It is a *workable* system, and *does* produce definite, predictable and positive results, far in excess of any other practice.

It is the responsibility of the individual student and preclear to apply Scientology exactly, just as it is the auditor's and Course Supervisor's. When applied exactly, it gives 100 percent success.

Remedying Case Difficulties

Scientology's workability is enhanced by the unique aspect of being able to correct itself. Problems that arise or errors made in its application can be rectified and L. Ron Hubbard developed a corrective technology to accomplish this.

He devised auditing techniques to remedy any error that can occur during the course of an auditing session. These locate the error and get it out of the way. He developed these over the course of more than twenty years' research into the application of auditing techniques and thorough study of auditing done by other auditors. The result is a standard corrective technology that keeps the bumps on the road as incidental as can be expected when one is handling something as tumultuous as life.

Everybody is different. In moving up the Classification, Gradation and Awareness Chart, aspects of a person's life may need to be addressed that are not a part of the general run of processing delivered on the chart. Case conditions can exist which, while not requiring attention in the majority of persons being audited, nevertheless could stall the progress of some people.

L. Ron Hubbard's intention was to provide a technology that brought freedom to *all*, not just to many or to most. To this end, he was constantly alert to phenomena showing up in people's progress in auditing which indicated conditions that might require special procedures in order to completely resolve them.

As a result, a large amount of auxiliary auditing actions were developed so a person's progress up the Bridge could be made smoother. These help a person sort out a specific problem he may be having in his life, such as problems with his marriage. Other actions can address past therapies the person has been engaged in which had adverse effects. One may have trouble with his profession which could be resolved more rapidly by a concentrated address to that specific situation rather than in the general course of auditing. Difficulties one has as a student might be the subject for another auditing action that concentrates on that area.

Life can present different situations that stall a person's progress. Sometimes these can knock the person off the Bridge entirely, but L. Ron Hubbard devised handlings even for that. People who have stumbled on the Bridge have gotten patched up and gotten going again, often at an improved rate of advance.

The idea of a corrective technology to repair any errors in application is, in the field of the humanities, unique to Dianetics and Scientology. L. Ron Hubbard developed this technology in order that failures would be minimized and that any error would be remediable. This is routinely accomplished whenever misapplications of Dianetics and Scientology occur. This is the reason why one finds so many successes in Scientology. L. Ron Hubbard did his researches with an eye toward anyone being able to improve and indeed has made Scientology the game where everyone wins.

Part Five

Churches of Scientology and Their Activities

Parishioners study Scientology technology and receive auditing in Scientology churches around the world. Yet whether in London, Sydney, San Francisco or any of hundreds of other locations on every continent, a church of Scientology has the same basic organizational structure and pattern of operation and performs the same functions. Each church has a common purpose to make the technology of L. Ron Hubbard available and to ensure it is properly learned and applied to the improvement of its parishioners and those in its local community. For these reasons, a church of Scientology is unique among churches—busy, bustling and geared to efficiency.

In order to minister to the spiritual needs of expanding congregations and to ensure uniform application of Dianetics and Scientology, the worldwide churches of Scientology are organized in a hierarchical structure which includes the many public and special service organizations. This section provides an explanation of that hierarchy and how it functions to keep Scientology expanding. The Church has done much to improve society with its betterment and reform efforts and these programs too, are covered, demonstrating that spiritual gains achieved in Scientology translate into effective action to change our troubled world.

Chapter 20

What Occurs in a Church of Scientology

A church of Scientology is a special place, quite different from the popular conception of a church. The church is not only open on Sundays. The Scientology community around a church come and go at different times during the week, and it is an integral part of their lives. It is where they come to study Scientology technology, receive auditing, coordinate community activities or simply to meet friends. Through its doors, they walk a road that can be walked nowhere else, a road to personal discovery, awareness and truth.

The atmosphere in a church of Scientology is what one would expect to find in a place where people are doing well, where they are learning about things, where they are actively pursuing their goals and succeeding. It is *alive,* cheerful and the hope of a better world seems to imbue every activity. The church is a friendly place and anyone is welcome.

Churches are staffed by dedicated Scientologists who leave their homes each morning knowing that when they return in the evening they will have spent the day helping their fellows become happier and freer. In a thoroughly materialistic and often cold world, there are not many who can say the same.

The church is open seven days a week. Delivery of service to church members usually begins at 9:00 A.M. and continues throughout the day. Many churches have two sets of staff, one for weekdays and another to service parishioners on evenings and on the weekends. The Day staff work from 9:00 to 6:00. The second staff (called the Foundation staff) take over from the Day staff at dinner time and keep the church open until 10:30 at night during the week and from 9:00 to 6:00 on weekends. When not working, both Day and Foundation staff tend to the rest of their lives which includes their families, other obligations and, of course, their own progress in Scientology.

The church is always there, literally as well as figuratively, and Scientologists count on it as a stable reference point in their lives. Scientologists tend to be very active in life and are, of course, not always at the church, but they know when they need something, someone will be there to help them.

THE PRECLEAR

Most parishioners come to the church for two primary services: to receive auditing or to study on a training course. The church is organized around the administration of these activities and all staff, in one way or another, help ensure that these services are standardly delivered. To understand how the church operates, consider the progress of a typical parishioner arriving there for auditing services. He has, for instance, progressed part of the way to Clear and is returning after an absence to continue further auditing. The church Registrar helps enroll him for his next services. Processing is best done in closely spaced blocks of auditing, at least 2½ hours per day for five consecutive days in a week. This 12½-hour block is called an "intensive." Auditing progress is faster and smoother when delivered on an intensive basis, for life's distractions intrude less. The preclear might enroll for 75 hours of auditing, planning to complete this over the next six weeks.

Auditing is delivered in that part of the organization called the Hubbard Guidance Center (HGC). The HGC is staffed with professional auditors and numerous other personnel necessary for efficient delivery of auditing. After enrolling with the Registrar, the parishioner meets with the Director of Technical Services in the HGC, who sets the schedule for his auditing. Some parishioners find it more conducive to receive their auditing in the mornings, some in the afternoons, some in the evenings. These preferences are taken into account. What matters is that the parishioner receives his auditing predictably and regularly.

When the schedule has been arranged, the person next sees the Director of Processing, the administrator over all auditing delivered to church members. The Director of Processing selects an auditor for the parishioner, and arranges for a battery of tests to be taken. These tests serve to monitor the preclear's progress as he continues up the Bridge. The test results and records from his previous auditing are passed to the Case Supervisor, who then writes a program of auditing actions to ensure the greatest and swiftest gain.

The next day the person returns to the church to commence his auditing. His first stop is the HGC lounge, which exists so auditors can locate their preclears readily. He arrives a little early, and while waiting, meets fellow Scientologists also receiving service, giving him the opportunity to rekindle old friendships or make new ones.

At the appointed hour, the preclear's auditor meets him in the lounge and takes him to the auditing room where the next 2½ hours will be spent making further progress up the Bridge to Clear. Other auditors and preclears come and go throughout the day as the HGC conducts its activities.

When the session is over the auditor takes the preclear to a staff member called the Examiner. The preclear says anything he wishes about the auditing he has just received or anything he would like his Case Supervisor to know. The Examiner's purpose is to ensure that auditing technology has been applied standardly. The information from the Examiner assists the Case Supervisor to ensure all auditing progresses smoothly for the benefit of the preclear. After seeing the Examiner, the preclear is complete until the next day, when the same basic routine occurs again. Rapid gains in awareness and ability happen when auditing is delivered in this way. At the end of the day, all the auditors turn in reports of their sessions and administrative staff route these to the Case Supervisor, who further checks that the auditing was standardly delivered and directs the next day's auditing.

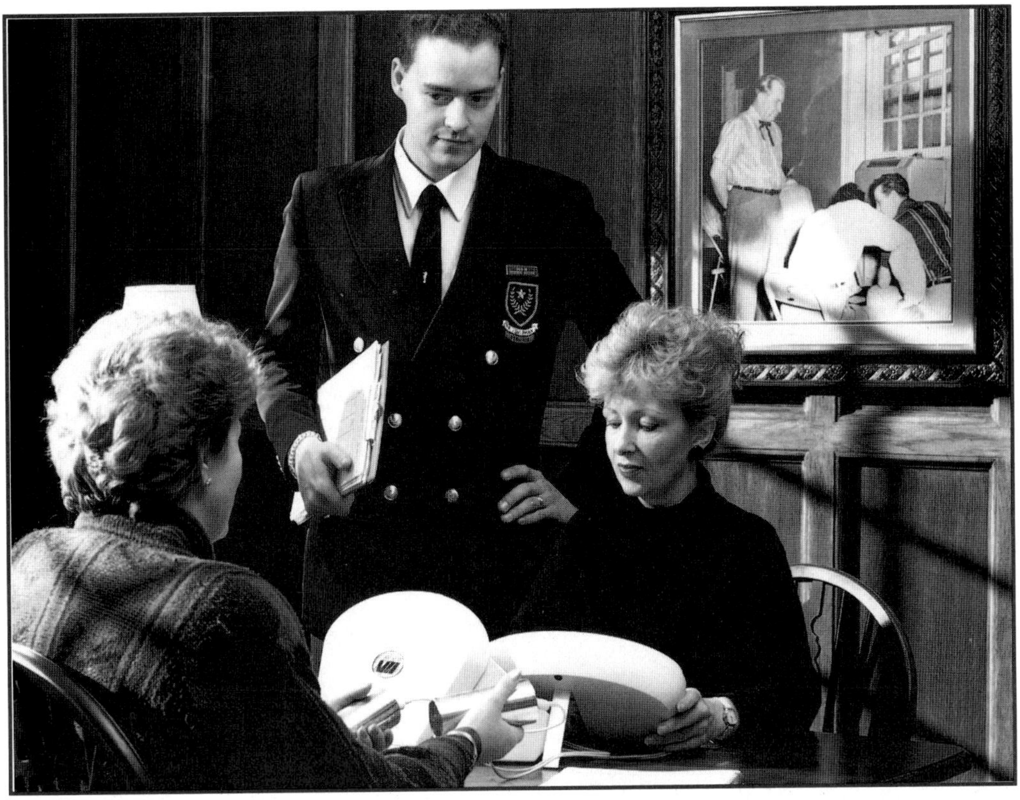

The Course Supervisor ensures students understand and can apply what they are studying.

THE STUDENT

Students arriving at the church for training also see the Registrar to enroll. Following this, the student visits the church bookstore and obtains the materials needed for his studies. Depending on the course, he will require Scientology books, taped lectures, a pack of technical materials (called bulletins), an E-Meter and accessories, or a combination of these. The bookstore is fully stocked and supplies all Scientologists and the public at large with these items.

The student then goes to the Academy, where all auditor training courses are delivered. Like any course room, Academy courses run on set schedules. Course starts at 9:00, runs until lunch and resumes in the afternoon until dinner, with a midafternoon break. A full-time student can put in 40 hours of course time per week on such a schedule and make very rapid progress through his training. On the Foundation schedule, courses run from 7:00 to 10:30 so Scientologists with day jobs can train. On weekends, course runs from 9:00 to 6:00, similar to the weekday schedule.

The Director of Training is in charge of all training activities and is assisted by the Director of Technical Services, who, as in the case of preclears, also works out student schedules. The Church recognizes the vital necessity for anyone to train in Scientology regardless of other activities in their life. For example, a working mother whose job and family demands do not permit the standard five-night-a-week and weekend schedule, may have allowances made and special schedules arranged. So as not to disrupt those on standard schedules, these part-time students have their own course room. Full-time students study a minimum of 40 hours per week and in practice it is expected that part-time students study at least 12½ hours a week. Less than this has been found to disproportionately extend the amount of time it takes a student to graduate.

Once a course schedule is set, the Course Administrator is seen. He is in charge of all materiel in the course room—its tables and chairs, tape playback machines, films, dictionaries and reference books, etc. After giving the student his course checksheet, he logs him in the course roll book. The Course Supervisor then greets the student and orients him to the Academy, its layout, schedule and rules. He works closely with the student throughout his training, answers questions, helps him with any problems and ensures he understands his materials.

The Course Supervisor begins each course period with a roll call and then study begins. He personally sees each student and together they work out how much progress the student can make that day. This is the student's goal for the day and the Supervisor and his other personnel assist the student as needed to reach the target he has set for himself.

The course room has a staff member who is expert in locating and clearing student misunderstoods. He is called the "Word Clearer" and is someone the student can go to if difficulties arise in study. The Word Clearer uses study technology and Word Clearing to resolve any inability to understand or apply what is being learned so the student may continue smoothly. The course period ends at its scheduled time, students put away their materials and leave for the day. The next day, course begins again with roll call and the routine is repeated.

When a student completes his course requirements he sees the Examiner who verifies the student's checksheet is complete and that he knows and can apply his materials. In some cases a written examination is administered.

Once a week, usually on Friday, students, preclears and other Scientologists gather for graduation. This is a time for parishioners to acknowledge those students and preclears who have completed a course or level of auditing during the week. Completions have a chance to share their gains with the assembly, which encourages everyone's progress up the Bridge. Graduation also provides an informal setting in which Scientologists may socialize.

While most people recognize the need for a stronger emphasis on religion in their lives, as a general rule, none are as actively committed to the practice of their religion as Scientologists. Whereas many members of congregational religions meet only on Sundays, Scientologists in addition to their career and family commitments, may spend several hours each day, five days a week for a period of several weeks at their church while receiving auditing or training. Many are also highly committed to church-sponsored community betterment programs. Such dedication to moving up the Bridge and forwarding the aims of the Church, is indicative of the fact that Scientologists have experienced, firsthand, the benefits of Mr. Hubbard's technology. They know they have become brighter, more aware and more able—all to the benefit of their careers, their families and their lives in general—and know, too, that such gains can be had by others. As they see it, practice of the religion itself—auditing and training—is truly bettering the world, and this world very much needs improving.

To assist those not currently enrolled on training or auditing, the church offers "home-study" extension courses based on L. Ron Hubbard's books. Many Scientologists also find it helpful and enjoyable to read L. Ron Hubbard's books or listen to his taped lectures on their own, as these works in themselves provide valuable insight into the everyday events of life.

OTHER CHURCH ACTIVITIES

When parishioners are not currently on a service at the church, they still want to remain in touch and the church is organized to encourage this. Each church publishes its own magazine which keeps parishioners abreast of news, recent course and auditing completions, upcoming events such as seminars or celebrations and the like. Church staff maintain contact with parishioners by mail and help arrange their return for further service.

Scientologists celebrate several meaningful occasions throughout the year, among them L. Ron Hubbard's birthday, the New Year, the anniversary of Dianetics and Auditor's Day. Parishioners are briefed on important church affairs and activities and updated on the overall expansion of Scientology. In addition to the thousands attending at the central location (which varies from event to event in cities around the world), events are also telecast to all Scientology churches across the globe, such as Los Angeles, New York, Toronto, London, Paris, Berlin, Barcelona, Sydney, Milan, Johannesburg, Copenhagen, Clearwater and scores of other cities in numerous countries. These events draw parishioners by the thousands to their local churches or public auditoriums to enjoy the event telecast. As well as being informative briefings, these occasions instill a sense of unity among Scientologists everywhere.

Individual churches also regularly host smaller events for local parishioners, including tape plays of L. Ron Hubbard's lectures, Sunday church services, briefings from top auditors and open houses for those new to Scientology and members of the local community.

The church makes every effort to let a person find out for himself what Scientology has to offer in accordance with Mr. Hubbard's principle that, in Scientology, it is only what you find true for yourself that is true. Regular introductory lectures are conducted on basic Dianetics and Scientology principles. Free personality testing is offered to help people isolate the exact areas in their lives they can improve upon and gives them direction as to how this might be accomplished. Films are shown which explain different Dianetics and Scientology concepts. Church staff are always more than happy to answer questions. In particular, the church Registrar is an expert regarding church services and assists individuals in selecting those services which best help them to advance on the Bridge.

Churches offer an array of services designed for a new person. These are delivered in a part of the organization separate from the HGC and the Academy, catering mostly to beginning students. Here, a person just finding out about Dianetics and Scientology can receive services at an introductory level.

Although many Scientologists live some distance from their churches, the church continues to remain a focal point in their lives even when they are not actively involved in an auditing or training service. A Scientologist who has completed professional auditor training and established a practice in the field, for instance, can receive case supervision services and materials from the church.

If a parishioner has difficulty moving up the Bridge or hindrances in any part of his life, the church Ethics Officer helps him apply ethics technology to improve his condition. And when traumatic or personally upsetting situations arise—perhaps a marital quarrel or a dispute with another Scientologist—the Chaplain is always available.

Each Sunday, the Chaplain conducts services open to anyone of any denomination who shares the hope of a better and happier future for man. For the person new to Scientology, this is an opportunity to gain a better understanding of the religion. For the Scientologist, it provides the chance to gain further insight into familiar concepts.

The Chaplain also performs Scientology weddings, christenings and funerals for parishioners and their family members.

Scientologists form numerous groups to aid local programs, particularly in the areas of social reform, education, drug abuse and neighborhood betterment. The church also lends its support to many community-sponsored organizations, and often provides facilities to those who work toward similar goals.

All Scientology activities in the local area fall under the Executive Director and his Executive Council. He is in charge of the church and sees to the well-being of church members, his staff and the expansion of Dianetics and Scientology in his city or area.

But there is even more to a church than what goes on inside. As a central point from which dedicated Scientologists come and go, applying what they have learned to help those around them, the church, in turn, becomes a central point of betterment for the whole community. Thus as the church itself flourishes, so too do those around it.

Scientology events, celebrations and briefings are held several times a year and are attended by thousands of parishioners. Events held at a central location, such as this New Year's gathering, are telecast to churches around the globe. Here, Church leaders have an opportunity to talk to other Scientologists and brief them on Church activities and expansion news from different parts of the world.

SYSTEM OF DONATIONS

Some churches have a system of tithes, others require their members to pay for pew rentals, religious ceremonies and services. In the Church of Scientology, parishioners make donations for auditing or training they wish to take. These contributions by Scientologists are the primary source of financial support for the church and fund all the community programs and social betterment activities of Scientology. Scientologists are not required to tithe or make other donations.

The church also has a "Free Scientology Center" where parishioners may receive auditing without donation, from ministers-in-training. Auditor training is encouraged by making it very economical and by also offering scholarships to deserving Scientologists. This has a dual benefit, creating valuable auditors who can help their fellows, and who can also co-audit their way up the Bridge with another student without charge.

Ideally, Dianetics and Scientology services would be free, and all Scientologists wish they were. But those are not the realities of life. When one considers the cost of delivering even one hour of auditing, requiring extensively trained specialists, and the overhead costs of maintaining church premises, the necessity of donations becomes clear.

The donation system in Scientology is the most equitable as those who use the facilities of the church are the ones who most directly contribute to its upkeep and continued existence. Naturally, no donation is expected from those not receiving auditing or training. And church doors are always open to those who wish to learn more about the philosophy of Scientology, be they parishioners or not. There are tape plays of L. Ron Hubbard's lectures, introductory lectures, books available, people to discuss questions with, and of course the more traditional church activities—Sunday services, sermons, weddings, christenings, funerals—all of which are provided without any donation necessary.

Scientology does not have hundreds of years of accumulated wealth and property like other religions—it must make its way in the world according to the economics of today's society.

Scientologists' donations keep the church alive and functioning, fund its widespread social reform programs, make Scientology known to people who may otherwise never have the opportunity to avail themselves of it and help create a safe and pleasant environment for everyone.

SCIENTOLOGY ADMINISTRATIVE TECHNOLOGY

Scientology is an entirely new activity, and cannot be organized along general religious or secular lines. Unlike other churches, it provides services for parishioners seven days a week, not merely on Saturdays or Sundays. Its primary services, however, are not congregational, where one minister serves the needs of hundreds or a thousand parishioners at once. Nor is it a social or commercial activity, for its province is strictly spiritual, providing freedom to man through the exact application of a precise technology administered like no other.

Recognizing this, L. Ron Hubbard spent many years developing a wholly new system of organization designed specifically for the purpose of making auditing and training broadly available and accessible. This system contains all functions an organization must perform in order to efficiently provide for its parishioners and is based upon what is called an "organizing board."

The Scientology organizing board has been used in all Dianetics and Scientology

These volumes contain the codification of the administrative technology required to successfully operate Scientology organizations.

ORGANIZATION EXECUTIVE COURSE BASIC STAFF HAT L. RON HUBBARD 0
ORGANIZATION EXECUTIVE COURSE HCO DIVISION L. RON HUBBARD 1
ORGANIZATION EXECUTIVE COURSE DISSEMINATION DIVISION L. RON HUBBARD 2
ORGANIZATION EXECUTIVE COURSE TREASURY DIVISION L. RON HUBBARD 3
ORGANIZATION EXECUTIVE COURSE TECHNICAL DIVISION L. RON HUBBARD 4
ORGANIZATION EXECUTIVE COURSE QUALIFICATIONS DIVISION L. RON HUBBARD 5
ORGANIZATION EXECUTIVE COURSE PUBLIC DIVISION L. RON HUBBARD 6
ORGANIZATION EXECUTIVE COURSE EXECUTIVE DIVISION L. RON HUBBARD 7
MANAGEMENT SERIES L. RON HUBBARD VOLUME 1
MANAGEMENT SERIES L. RON HUBBARD VOLUME 2
MANAGEMENT SERIES L. RON HUBBARD VOLUME 3
OEC AND MANAGEMENT SERIES POLICY INDEX L. RON HUBBARD INDEX

organizations since it was developed in 1965. It is an arrangement of functions necessary to obtain a product. The church's product is not a manufactured item, it is totally freed beings.

This pattern contains seven divisions which describe all the actions encompassed by the organization. Each division is subdivided into three departments. In these seven divisions and their twenty-one departments one finds all the functions, duties, positions, sequences of action and command channels of the organization.

The Divisions 1 through 7 of the organizing board are laid out in a sequence known as the *cycle of production.* L. Ron Hubbard discovered that for any cycle of action to complete successfully, it must go through these seven main stages. That is, to produce something of value, an organization must have all seven divisions operating.

The organizing board works as follows: The first division of the organization is the Hubbard Communications Office—so named because its main functions were originally part of L. Ron Hubbard's office in the early days of Scientology. This division establishes and keeps the church running. The functions include hiring personnel, answering the phones, handling the mail, delivering internal communications, filing reports on the church's operations and administering its ethics and justice system.

The next division, Division 2, is the Dissemination Division. *Dissemination* means to spread or scatter broadly. In a Scientology church, this division makes Scientology services and materials widely known. It produces mailings and publications, such as the church's magazine, which are sent to all parishioners, and operates the church bookstore. The staff in this division inform individuals about Scientology. Church members often write to request information or to arrange for services. Those letters are answered within this division.

Division 3 is the Treasury Division. All corporations, even religious ones, are required to keep proper financial records. Donations from parishioners provide the wherewithal for the church to disseminate Scientology, carry on its work in the community and continue to make auditing and training available. Division 3 invoices donations, pays the bills, disburses other monies and keeps financial records. It also provides for the upkeep and ensures the continued value of the organization's premises and equipment.

The Technical or Production Division of the organization, Division 4, provides the major training and auditing services of the Bridge. It gives excellent and fast service, schedules people for auditing, and provides high-volume, high-quality Scientology training and processing. The Technical Division is the central activity of the organization. It produces the product by which the organization expands and survives. The Technical Division contains more staff than other divisions, as these are needed to assist parishioners with arrangements for service, provide course supervision and other course room services, and deliver auditing. The other divisions in the organization factually exist to facilitate the Technical Division's production of its product.

The next division, Division 5, is the Qualifications Division. The functions of this division are unique to Scientology churches. Whereas many organizations maintain quality control over products, this division does much more: It sees to the enhancement, correction and care of those who actually *produce* the product. If a staff member in any way has difficulties performing his duties, he receives immediate attention and help from Division 5. Without such concern for its members, an organization may eventually fail. In addition to its routine correction duties,

Division 5 trains and audits the staff. It also corrects students and auditors on any inability to apply what they have learned and runs the internship to make auditor training course graduates into top-flight professionals. And it verifies that the full gains of all auditing have been received by church parishioners.

Division 6 is called the Public Division. In a Scientology church, Division 6 introduces new people to Scientology through lectures and films, open houses, Sunday church services and tape plays. It also offers introductory courses. This division reaches into the community to provide needed assistance and contribution to local social programs. Through the Public Division, the church performs many goodwill actions which benefit the community. Additionally, Scientologists often form "field groups" which offer basic Dianetics and Scientology services to the public. Division 6 assists setup of field groups and missions in new areas so more people can benefit from Dianetics and Scientology.

The last division is the Executive Division, Division 7, which keeps the overall activity viable and expanding through careful planning and supervision. The Executive Director is located here. Division 7 is responsible for legal affairs and government relations. Another important executive in each church is the L. Ron Hubbard (LRH) Communicator—a position established when Mr. Hubbard served as Executive Director of the Church and maintained a local representative in each church to facilitate his communication channels. Today, the LRH Communicator sees that the church adheres to Mr. Hubbard's writings. The LRH Communicator also preserves the L. Ron Hubbard office maintained in all churches as a mark of respect for the Founder of the religion. The LRH Communicator's duties are especially key because it is the standard application of L. Ron Hubbard's technology which makes the gains and accomplishments of Dianetics and Scientology possible.

This pattern of organization also serves as a "philosophical system" by which any organization or even one's own life can be analyzed. Each division contains three smaller departments, making twenty-one departments in all. The departments correspond to levels of awareness as found on the Classification, Gradation and Awareness Chart. The design of the organization, then, follows the progression of a person up the Bridge itself. A person comes into the church through Reception in Division 1, is routed to Division 2 where he enrolls on his service, makes his donation in Division 3, receives his service in Division 4, is verified as having achieved the full result in Division 5 and stays connected up with the organization through its field activities in Division 6, all of which is coordinated and directed by Division 7.

The organizational pattern, then, is actually an upward spiral with Division 7 adjacent to but higher than Division 1. When parishioners reenter the organization for further services, they are on a higher plane. Through this pattern and system people receive the knowledge and abilities of Scientology.

Each division produces a specific product which contributes to the overall cycle of production of the organization. Each department within a division produces its own product, which in turn contributes to the product of the division.

The organization corrects itself through the Qualifications Division, under the authority of the Executive Division.

These principles of organization apply to an individual's own life as thoroughly as they do to a large corporation composed of many thousands. The functions and activities contained in the divisions and departments exist in a person's life. For instance, a person produces a product on his job; that is his Division 4,

Technical. He handles his finances; that is his Division 3, Treasury, and so on. A person can look over the divisions and departments and see what is missing in his own life.

An organization, or a life, fails because it is lacking one or another of these divisions. But, by knowing and applying this pattern and its principles, organizations and individuals can expand and prosper.

All Scientology churches or groups are covered by the organizing board. The divisions are manned in such a way that the maximum amount of service can be delivered to parishioners. A ratio exists between number of staff needed to deliver training and auditing services to number of staff needed to administer and support delivery. The Technical and Qualifications Divisions (Divisions 4 and 5) are the primary portions of the organization which deliver auditing and training services to public and staff. These require many staff to supervise students, audit preclears, train staff, run an internship and so on. The organization is manned in a ratio of one staff member in Technical or Qualifications Divisions to one staff member in all the other divisions. This has been found to satisfy demand for auditing and training and administrative support services.

The staff in Division 4 (Technical Division), for instance, need to be supplied with a building, furniture, utilities and so forth. They need somebody to sign up new preclears for service, somebody to pay the electric bill, somebody to keep the premises clean and other actions which can be efficiently done by others, leaving the technical staff free to deliver services.

Man has a tendency to fill all the boxes on an organization chart. This is extremely inefficient and hinders expansion. Allotting personnel to every post regardless of need leaves some posts overloaded and others underworked. The formula of one administrative staff member for every technical staff member handles this. Thus, the Technical and Qualifications Divisions are heavy with personnel, containing five times as many as each of the other divisions.

In expanding the organization, each department acquires five subsections, every subsection acquires five units.

Such a pattern of organization is remarkable in its effectiveness. Application of it in churches of Scientology has provided a stable, constantly expanding structure which has contributed greatly to the Church flourishing around the world. It was designed not to make money or to make Scientologists. Its whole purpose is to forward the "Ability to Better Conditions," which is the mission of Scientology. A simplified version of the organizing board is contained at the end of this chapter.

THE TECHNOLOGY OF ADMINISTRATION

Having described the basic organizational form, one can now begin to understand the specific policies upon which that framework functions. These precise and workable administrative policies were also developed by Mr. Hubbard through years of research and experience, and constitute a tremendous body of material relating to the survival of a group.

As with everything Mr. Hubbard accomplished, his discoveries came from hard-won experience. He isolated administrative fundamentals for every level of organization from top to bottom. When Executive Director of Scientology organizations internationally, he worked in virtually every position and function, ironing out difficulties and forming the policy for smooth and efficient operation. He wrote policies covering the theory and particulars of every working facet in a Scientology organization. In total, these spell out the basic laws of the third dynamic (group survival) and constitute a body of knowledge as important to administration of groups as his writings on Dianetics and Scientology are to rehabilitation of the spirit.

Staff members therefore study this administrative technology avidly. In applying auditing technology they have learned that an exact procedure results in the improvement of a specific condition in the preclear. Likewise, it is apparent that by following and maintaining exact administrative procedures, one can remedy, handle or reinforce situations relating to the group.

All of this administrative technology has been arranged into a twelve-volume set of reference texts. Volume 0, the *Basic Staff Hat,* contains all policies pertinent to any church staff member and provides a thorough orientation to the organization for new staff members. Seven of the remaining volumes, numbered one through seven, correspond to the same numbered divisions of the organizing board. Volume One, for example, covers Division 1; Volume Two, Division 2; and so on. Each divisional volume contains all the policies pertaining to the purpose and functions of that division. Organized in this way, any person in the organization can easily find the policies which describe his own functions within the group. Or he can refer to other volumes and gain an understanding of any duty in the organization and thus work more efficiently and harmoniously as a group member. The remaining volumes encompass Mr. Hubbard's writings on the subject of management and executive know-how.

These books contain a codification of all the ingredients required to successfully operate Dianetics and Scientology organizations. When any necessary functions are found to be missing, the organization is, to that degree, unsuccessful. And to the degree that each function is present and operating, the organization thrives.

Mr. Hubbard also devised the means to monitor the production of any post in the organization, using statistics to ensure that no individual is lost in the group. By staticizing activities, church executives can direct the activities of the organization more efficiently. This single principle allows for the exact isolation of areas or functions which require attention, and its application alone has dramatically enhanced the success of many organizations. The entire body of technology concerning statistics is intimately related to application of the principles of the conditions of existence—statistics are a guide to the application of the correct condition. As each staff position contributes to the overall well-being of the group, it follows that one can use these principles to enhance the survival of the entire organization.

In his policies, L. Ron Hubbard further delineated the purposes, functions and products of every post and, in turn, every department, so organization members could work as a team and achieve their overall product. In so doing, he codified a workplace technology applied all over the world today by Scientology churches, missions and groups.

Church executives train on courses which cover the totality of these volumes and learn to apply them in their day-to-day running of the organization.

Although Mr. Hubbard developed this technology to help administer Dianetics and Scientology, parishioners who worked outside the organization began to apply these principles to other groups as well. L. Ron Hubbard discovered and delineated the basics on which *any* group operated and, as such, these breakthroughs are broadly applicable. Since then his administrative principles have been used by many other organizations around the world with extraordinary success.

ORGANIZING BOARD

(Simplified version, showing the organizational pattern used in all churches of Scientology)

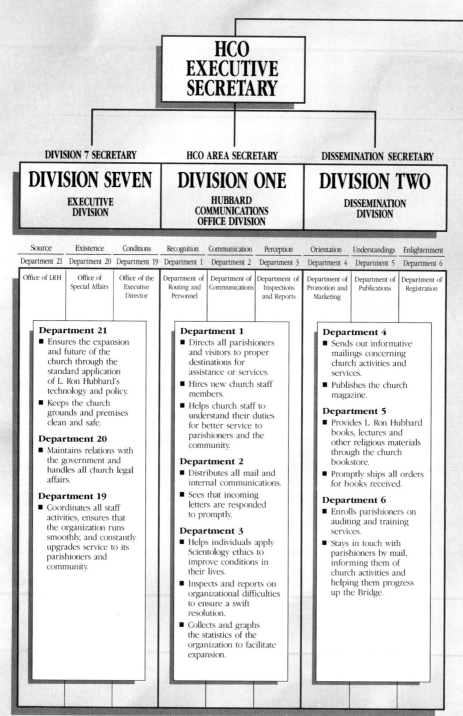

HCO EXECUTIVE SECRETARY

DIVISION 7 SECRETARY	HCO AREA SECRETARY	DISSEMINATION SECRETARY
DIVISION SEVEN EXECUTIVE DIVISION	**DIVISION ONE** HUBBARD COMMUNICATIONS OFFICE DIVISION	**DIVISION TWO** DISSEMINATION DIVISION

Source	Existence	Conditions	Recognition	Communication	Perception	Orientation	Understandings	Enlightenment
Department 21	Department 20	Department 19	Department 1	Department 2	Department 3	Department 4	Department 5	Department 6
Office of LRH	Office of Special Affairs	Office of the Executive Director	Department of Routing and Personnel	Department of Communications	Department of Inspections and Reports	Department of Promotion and Marketing	Department of Publications	Department of Registration

Department 21
- Ensures the expansion and future of the church through the standard application of L. Ron Hubbard's technology and policy.
- Keeps the church grounds and premises clean and safe.

Department 20
- Maintains relations with the government and handles all church legal affairs.

Department 19
- Coordinates all staff activities, ensures that the organization runs smoothly, and constantly upgrades service to its parishioners and community.

Department 1
- Directs all parishioners and visitors to proper destinations for assistance or services.
- Hires new church staff members.
- Helps church staff to understand their duties for better service to parishioners and the community.

Department 2
- Distributes all mail and internal communications.
- Sees that incoming letters are responded to promptly.

Department 3
- Helps individuals apply Scientology ethics to improve conditions in their lives.
- Inspects and reports on organizational difficulties to ensure a swift resolution.
- Collects and graphs the statistics of the organization to facilitate expansion.

Department 4
- Sends out informative mailings concerning church activities and services.
- Publishes the church magazine.

Department 5
- Provides L. Ron Hubbard books, lectures and other religious materials through the church bookstore.
- Promptly ships all orders for books received.

Department 6
- Enrolls parishioners on auditing and training services.
- Stays in touch with parishioners by mail, informing them of church activities and helping them progress up the Bridge.

EXECUTIVE DIRECTOR

ORGANIZATION EXECUTIVE SECRETARY

TREASURY SECRETARY	TECHNICAL SECRETARY	QUALIFICATIONS SECRETARY	DISTRIBUTION SECRETARY
DIVISION THREE	**DIVISION FOUR**	**DIVISION FIVE**	**DIVISION SIX**
TREASURY DIVISION	TECHNICAL DIVISION	QUALIFICATIONS DIVISION	PUBLIC DIVISION

Energy	Adjustment	Body	Prediction	Activity	Production	Result	Correction	Ability	Purposes	Clearing	Realization
Department 7	Department 8	Department 9	Department 10	Department 11	Department 12	Department 13	Department 14	Department 15	Department 16	Department 17	Department 18
Department of Income	Department of Disbursements	Department of Records, Assets and Materiel	Department of Technical Services	Department of Activity	Department of Production	Department of Examinations	Department of Review	Department of Certifications and Awards	Department of Public Information	Department of Clearing	Department of Success

Department 7
- Invoices parishioner donations and maintains records of donations received.

Department 8
- Sees to the material needs of the church and its staff by purchasing all items required to keep the church functioning.
- Pays any bills incurred by the church.

Department 9
- Cares for all church furniture, equipment and the like, ensuring such property is well maintained and properly functioning.
- Keeps records of church accounts.

Department 10
- Sees that parishioners are well cared for and receive rapid service.
- Helps arrange housing for out-of-town parishioners.
- Provides technical staff with needed supplies and materials to deliver auditing and training.

Department 11
- Standardly delivers Scientology training services to all parishioners.
- Graduates auditors who can help others move up the Bridge.

Department 12
- Standardly delivers auditing to church parishioners with excellent results.

Department 13
- Verifies that students and preclears have received the full results of their services.

Department 14
- Locates and corrects failures to standardly apply the technology.
- Cares for church staff by providing them with auditing and training.

Department 15
- Issues certificates to those who complete church services.

Department 16
- Makes Dianetics and Scientology more broadly known and delivers introductory lectures to inform people about the subjects.

Department 17
- Provides introductory training, auditing and seminars.
- Delivers chaplain services including marriage counseling.
- Performs ministerial services including weddings, naming ceremonies and Sunday services.

Department 18
- Appoints and assists volunteer ministers to perform their functions in the community.
- Helps open new Dianetics and Scientology groups in the area.
- Assists the local community with church goodwill programs.

CHAPTER 21

SCIENTOLOGY AROUND THE WORLD

The rapid expansion of Scientology has been due, in large part, to the scores of churches of Scientology. These now exist in most major cities throughout the world and provide auditing and training services to individuals who want to advance up the Bridge.

Although each church is usually incorporated separately, with its own board of directors and executives responsible for its activities, these churches together form the stable building blocks of an international network which spans the globe.

To clarify this further, however, it should also be understood that these churches are part of a hierarchical structure arranged in a pattern which matches the Classification, Gradation and Awareness Chart of Scientology. In other words, at the lower level of this hierarchy individuals and organizations provide beginning-level auditing and training; and, at the upper level, church organizations deliver the highest levels of auditing and training. It is a logical sequence of organization, one that reflects the progress of Scientology parishioners up the Bridge.

Below the local churches are individual Scientologists and various groups that support them; above them are higher-level churches which deliver more advanced levels of auditing and training. Generally, the higher-level organizations deliver all services of the organizations beneath them. Spanning everything is an ecclesiastical management structure that supports, coordinates and assists the activities of each and every organization, in order for Scientology as a whole to achieve its aims.

This ecclesiastical hierarchy is paralleled by a corporate structure, as is the case in many religions. Religious non-profit corporations provide the Church with a legal identity that allows it to interact with society; open bank accounts; purchase goods and services; and enter into contractual relationships with other corporations and individuals. These separate corporations are each fully independent and responsible for their own activities and well-being, though they receive ecclesiastical guidance and assistance from others and form part of the larger picture which is the religion of Scientology.

From top to bottom, in this ecclesiastical hierarchy, Scientologists are united in action by common purposes.

FIELD AUDITORS AND DIANETICS COUNSELING GROUPS

At the lowest level of the Scientology hierarchy are field auditors and Dianetics Counseling Groups. Any properly qualified individual Scientologist may become a "field auditor" and deliver auditing and introductory services. People often find that when they become trained in Scientology they want to help others with what they have learned, and this is frequently how field auditors get started—auditing friends and family.

Field auditors operate either alone or as part of a Dianetics Counseling Group with other auditors who work together to contact new people, get them started on the Bridge and then refer them to a church of Scientology where they continue their auditing and training. In either case, they offer auditing services up to the classification training levels of the auditors involved. This is an outreach activity that is an important aspect of the religion's expansion.

Field auditors and Dianetics Counseling Groups are assisted by the International Hubbard Ecclesiastical League of Pastors (I HELP). I HELP, located in Los Angeles, California, was created to provide auditors who deliver services outside organized churches and missions with the guidance they need to operate successfully. It aids auditors in the field to minister to the public by providing them with materials, publications and consultation services. It also offers assistance with any administrative or technical difficulties they may encounter. I HELP ensures field auditors maintain high standards of application and discipline.

Field auditors and Dianetics Counseling Groups provide the following religious services:

- INTRODUCTORY LECTURES
- TAPE PLAYS OF L. RON HUBBARD'S LECTURES
- HUBBARD DIANETICS SEMINAR
- SUCCESS THROUGH COMMUNICATION COURSE
- OTHER INTRODUCTORY SERVICES FOR PEOPLE NEW TO SCIENTOLOGY
- PURIFICATION PROGRAM
- DIANETICS AND SCIENTOLOGY AUDITING THROUGH NEW ERA DIANETICS AND EXPANDED DIANETICS

I HELP

SCIENTOLOGY MISSIONS

Scientology missions comprise the next level of the ecclesiastical hierarchy. A mission is a religious nonprofit corporation granted the right to provide elementary Dianetics and Scientology services. Missions are a front-line dissemination activity of Scientology that reach out to those who have not previously come in contact with the religion. Missions do not have full church status, nor do they have the authority to train or ordain Scientology ministers. They are often started in areas of the world not previously introduced to Scientology. There are hundreds of missions located on every continent on Earth.

Missions offer all the introductory and beginning services of Dianetics and Scientology, including extension courses, Life Improvement Courses, Dianetics Seminars, the Success Through Communication Course, the Student Hat course, Hubbard Qualified Scientologist Course and certain co-auditing courses where students learn to audit each other on specific actions. Missions may also deliver all auditing actions up through New Era Dianetics, including introductory auditing, Expanded Lower Grades and Expanded Dianetics.

Scientology Missions International (SMI) is the mother church for all missions. SMI provides guidance and help for existing missions, keeps the far-flung network of missions in communication with each other, and assists Scientologists to open new missions, encouraging them particularly in countries and cities where no missions already exist. Any qualified Scientologist may open a mission and contribute to the advancement of Scientology into society.

After a mission or group expands, it can eventually become a Scientology church. There are many more missions than there are Scientology churches, each reaching out into the society and bringing Dianetics and Scientology to mankind through beginning services.

There are hundreds of missions located in scores of countries around the world. They deliver the following religious services:

- INTRODUCTORY LECTURES, FILMS AND TAPES
- EXTENSION COURSES
- LIFE IMPROVEMENT COURSES
- HUBBARD DIANETICS SEMINAR
- SUCCESS THROUGH COMMUNICATION COURSE
- OTHER INTRODUCTORY SERVICES FOR PEOPLE NEW TO SCIENTOLOGY
- SCIENTOLOGIST HATTING COURSES
- THE STUDENT HAT
- PURIFICATION PROGRAM
- AUDITING THROUGH NEW ERA DIANETICS AND EXPANDED DIANETICS

SMI

CLASS V ORGANIZATIONS

Above missions in the Scientology hierarchy come the churches of Scientology. The first echelon of churches provide beginning and intermediate Dianetics and Scientology training and auditing. This includes all religious services that missions may deliver, and they additionally train auditors to the level of Class V Graduate Auditor. For this reason they are known within Scientology as Class V organizations.

Scientology Class V churches are located around the world with more opening all the time.

They deliver the following religious services:

- ALL INTRODUCTORY SERVICES PROVIDED BY MISSIONS
- ALL AUDITING THROUGH NEW ERA DIANETICS AND EXPANDED DIANETICS
- AUDITOR TRAINING TO THE LEVEL OF CLASS V GRADUATE
- THE MINISTER'S COURSE AND ORDAINING MINISTERS
- TECHNICAL SPECIALIST COURSES
- THE HUBBARD KEY TO LIFE COURSE
- THE HUBBARD LIFE ORIENTATION COURSE
- SOLO AUDITOR COURSE PART ONE
- CLEAR
- SUNSHINE RUNDOWN

Class V organizations can also provide other services such as training on Technical Specialist Courses, the Hubbard Key to Life Course and Hubbard Life Orientation Course. Only churches have the authority to train and ordain Scientology ministers.

Many Class V organizations establish smaller offices in nearby areas and towns to provide introductory services, after which public then go to the central church for further training and auditing.

Each church in each city is the center of Scientology activity in that area and functions as the source and dissemination point of the technology. It is the core of Scientology in its district, playing a major role in helping individuals and groups provide Dianetics and Scientology services to the public.

Class V organizations make Dianetics and Scientology broadly known to people in their area, and also assist Scientologists to set up groups and missions which in turn contact and service their local public and in this way expansion continues to keep up with the increased demand for L. Ron Hubbard's technology.

Class V organizations are concerned with the quality of technical delivery in local missions and groups and among field auditors, ensuring that the technologies of Dianetics and Scientology are standardly applied so parishioners receive the expected gains.

The church is the central point for numerous community activities. Blood drives, antidrug rallies, toy drives, entertaining the elderly, cleaning up local parks, crime watches and the like are often spearheaded by the church.

Scientology Class V organizations provide a safe and stable point for all the Scientology activities in an area to help parishioners move up the Bridge to Total Freedom.

Celebrity Centres

L. Ron Hubbard once wrote, "A culture is only as great as its dreams, and its dreams are dreamed by artists." Artists supply the spark of creativity and the vision of what could be leading us into tomorrow.

Artists wield enormous influence over society, setting cultural trends and forwarding new ideas, both good and bad. In the sixties, musicians promoted drugs, and helped lead an entire generation into the drug culture. On the other hand, many artists work to raise public awareness of environmental concerns. By example, and through their art, they influence millions. By improving the lives of artists, great progress can be achieved to better the condition of society—for any artist with an increased ability to communicate, who is drug free and has high moral standards imparts a positive influence to many others.

To forward their dreams and help artists elevate the culture, L. Ron Hubbard established Celebrity Centres. They are located in cities around the world and assist artists to achieve their goals through the application of Dianetics and Scientology. They offer services to artists and professionals in such fields as the performing arts, fine arts, sports and business. Church of Scientology Celebrity Centres deliver the same services as Class V organizations and missions but additionally provide special services which help artists apply Scientology principles to their chosen fields. A training service exists, for instance, which covers L. Ron Hubbard's codification of the field of art.

The availability and types of services offered accommodate the unique needs and aspirations of these individuals. Apart from providing a location where Scientology artists are able to meet each other, Celebrity Centres also offer a distraction-free environment where they can concentrate on their auditing and training.

There are thirteen Church of Scientology Celebrity Centres which provide the following religious services:

- All services provided by Class V churches
- Specialized Scientology courses for artists

Celebrity Centre International

SAINT HILL ORGANIZATIONS

The original Saint Hill church organization was located at Mr. Hubbard's home, Saint Hill Manor, in East Grinstead, Sussex, England. It was there that Mr. Hubbard delivered the Saint Hill Special Briefing Course (SHSBC), the most extensive auditor course in all of Scientology.

When other organizations were formed in Copenhagen and Los Angeles to meet the demand for SHSBC training, they were named "Saint Hill" organizations, as they specialize in delivering the Saint Hill Special Briefing Course.

Saint Hill Organizations are centralized church colleges for advanced auditor training. They provide extensive training facilities to parishioners from both local areas and remote locations. Most Saint Hill students arrange their schedules so they can devote themselves to an intensive period of training—several months to a year—on the Briefing Course. Thus, Saint Hills have a high concentration of full-time students, who study in an environment uniquely suited to auditor training.

Saint Hills play an important role in the religion of Scientology as they train expert auditors who gain a comprehensive understanding of life. A chronological study of the development of the Scientology philosophy from its beginning to the present gives graduates of the Briefing Course a wide-ranging ability to benefit society and their fellow man.

In 1983, the newest Church of Scientology Saint Hill Organization opened in Sydney, Australia.

There are Church of Scientology Saint Hill Organizations located in four cities around the world.

They deliver the following religious services:

- ALL AUDITING AND TRAINING SERVICES PROVIDED BY SCIENTOLOGY CLASS V CHURCHES
- POWER PROCESSING
- THE SAINT HILL SPECIAL BRIEFING COURSE
- CLASS VII AUDITOR TRAINING
- AUDITING SERVICES ON THE GRADE CHART THROUGH ELIGIBILITY FOR OT LEVELS AUDITING
- SOLO AUDITOR COURSE PART TWO

ADVANCED ORGANIZATIONS

Advanced Organizations (AOs) are located in Los Angeles, East Grinstead in England, Copenhagen and Sydney. They offer advanced auditing and training, with an emphasis on auditing. This is where a person progresses through the OT levels, to the completion of OT Section V. Advanced Organizations also train auditors on the Class VIII Auditor and C/S Courses.

The Advanced Org churches service parishioners from a wide area who move up the Bridge from missions and Class V orgs. In the case of the Advanced Organization Los Angeles for instance, parishioners from all over the United States, Canada, Mexico and South America travel to Los Angeles to progress up the OT levels or do Class VIII Auditor training.

The staff at these higher-level churches require a higher level of training in Scientology in order to administer these advanced levels of the Bridge.

There are four Church of Scientology Advanced Organizations.

They deliver the following religious services:

- ALL AUDITING AND TRAINING SERVICES PROVIDED BY CLASS V CHURCHES
- ALL PROCESSING SERVICES FROM GRADE VI RELEASE THROUGH NEW OT V NEW ERA DIANETICS FOR OTs
- DOCTORATE SERIES COURSE FOR OTs
- CLASS VIII AUDITOR AND C/S TRAINING

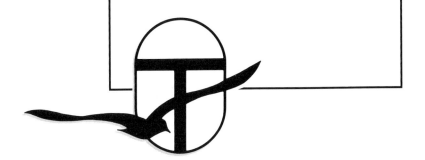

FLAG SERVICE ORGANIZATION

The Flag Service Organization (FSO) is a religious retreat for Scientologists of every nationality. It provides the highest levels of religious services. (The term *Flag* denotes that this organization was first established on a ship, the *Apollo.* Beginning in 1967, Mr. Hubbard conducted his research into the upper levels of Scientology with a group of dedicated Scientologists aboard three ships. These advanced services were then delivered aboard the *Apollo,* flagship of the flotilla, until land-based organizations were established for greater accessibility. This is more fully described later in this chapter.)

The FSO, in Clearwater, Florida, is the largest single Scientology church in the world, with well over 750 staff members. As people travel there from all over the world to receive auditing and training, staying for several weeks or even months at a time before returning home, the FSO also provides accommodations for its parishioners in a distraction-free environment so they can make the most progress on the Bridge during their stay, without the turbulence of the day-to-day world.

Here, auditors train to the level of Class XII, which is the highest auditor classification in Scientology. The FSO also delivers Dianetics and Scientology services from the bottom of the Bridge through to New OT VII, plus certain specialized auditing services only available there.

Auditor training above Class VIII is exclusive to the FSO. Included among its staff are the most experienced and highly trained auditors, case supervisors, course supervisors and other training specialists on the planet. The FSO sets the technical standard in Scientology and enjoys a reputation for the highest standards of technical perfection. Churches and missions from around the world send their technical staff to be trained to Flag standards.

The Flag Service Organization is unique. It delivers all religious services available in all lower organizations. Additionally, it delivers:

- NEW OT VI AND NEW OT VII
  (SOLO NEW ERA DIANETICS FOR OTS)
- AUDITOR TRAINING THROUGH CLASS XII
- SPECIALIZED AUDITING AVAILABLE ONLY AT THE FSO INCLUDING:

L10 Rundown

L11 New Life Rundown

L12 Flag OT Executive Rundown

New Vitality Rundown

Profession Intensive

Knowledge Rundown

Case Cracker Rundown

Interiorization by Dynamics Rundown

Dynamic Sort Out Assessment

Fixated Person Rundown

FLAG SHIP SERVICE ORGANIZATION

Whereas the FSO offers the highest level of auditor training and auditing from the bottom of the Bridge up through OT VII, the delivery of OT VIII, the most advanced OT level available, is entrusted to the Flag Ship Service Organization (FSSO). This church is located aboard a ship, the 450-foot motor vessel *Freewinds.* This ship forms an ideal religious retreat off the crossroads of society where full attention can be devoted to spiritual advancement. Parishioners normally stay for several weeks to receive OT VIII and also to take special training courses which help a person enhance his abilities as an OT. This setting makes an ideal environment, far from everyday distractions, for the delivery of these advanced spiritual services.

The Church of Scientology Flag Ship Service Organization only delivers specialized religious services to advanced Scientologists.

- NEW OT VIII, THE HIGHEST AUDITING LEVEL AVAILABLE IN SCIENTOLOGY
- THE HUBBARD KEY TO LIFE COURSE
- THE HUBBARD LIFE ORIENTATION COURSE
- THE NEW HUBBARD PROFESSIONAL TR COURSE
- SPECIAL TRAINING COURSES TO ENHANCE ABILITIES AS AN OT

THE CHURCH OF SCIENTOLOGY INTERNATIONAL

The system of ecclesiastical management used in the Church was developed to individually care for the large number of Scientology churches, missions and groups which exist, while at the same time providing the broad planning and direction needed to advance the propagation of Scientology in the world.

Individual churches of Scientology are governed by their own council of executives from that local church. The executive council is fully responsible for the application of Scientology policy and technology to ensure the expansion of Dianetics and Scientology in that area.

However, to assist individual churches, and ensure the overall expansion of Scientology, there is a mother church for all Scientology—the Church of Scientology International (CSI), located in Los Angeles.

Through CSI's ecclesiastical management activities, individual Scientology churches receive guidance in applying the scriptures both technically and administratively.

CSI broadly plans and coordinates Scientology expansion overall; providing programs to be carried out by the individual organizations and groups, and then helping with their implementation toward expansion.

CSI provides specialized training programs for church executives on the entirety of Scientology administrative technology which allows them to better serve their parishioners. This training is conducted at CSI's headquarters in the Hollywood Guaranty Building in Los Angeles.

In addition to coordinating the overall expansion of Scientology, CSI sees to the distribution of Scientology scriptures, both in written and audiovisual form. Golden Era Productions produces all the E-Meters, religious training films, slide shows and videos of Scientology and the recorded lectures of Mr. Hubbard.

Translations of L. Ron Hubbard's books, courses, lectures and films into many languages is also a function of Golden Era.

Church management provides ecclesiastical guidance to each of the Scientology organizations, coordinates the activities and expansion of Scientology internationally and in doing so makes it possible for Dianetics and Scientology to meet the demand for its services from people around the world.

RELIGIOUS TECHNOLOGY CENTER

Utmost importance is given to the precise application of Dianetics and Scientology, because, when standardly applied, with the honest cooperation of one who is seeking spiritual betterment, it works 100 percent of the time. Such a technology has never before existed. Millions of people around the world regard this technology as valuable beyond comparison, and it is of great interest to Scientologists everywhere that it be maintained in a pure state, exactly as L. Ron Hubbard developed it.

In the past—in fact, since the beginning of Dianetics in 1950—some unscrupulous individuals have attempted to misuse the technology of Dianetics and Scientology for their own personal profit. Mr. Hubbard's intention from the beginning was that the benefits of Dianetics and Scientology be available to all, and Scientologists work hard to keep it so. Scientology was developed to rehabilitate the spirit—not to make money.

Within the Church itself, numerous staff see to proper application and protection of the technology and these responsibilities permeate the ecclesiastical hierarchy.

To help maintain the purity of the technology both inside and outside the Church, many of the words and symbols of the Scientology religion have been registered as trademarks with appropriate government agencies in countries all over the world.

This ensures nobody can deliver some offbeat version of Dianetics and Scientology and represent it as real Scientology.

The enforcement of the trademarks of the Scientology religion guarantees its integrity and prevents corruption or perversion.

Until 1982, all the trademarks and service marks were owned by L. Ron Hubbard. In May of that year he gave the marks of the Scientology religion to a newly formed church, Religious Technology Center (RTC).

RTC possesses ultimate ecclesiastical authority over the international hierarchy concerning the maintenance and standard application of L. Ron Hubbard's technology. RTC owns all the Scientology trademarks and service marks and controls their licensing and use. RTC is not part of the management structure of the Church. Its purpose is to safeguard the proper use of trademarks, to protect the public, and to make sure that the technologies of Dianetics and Scientology remain in good hands. It sees to the pure and ethical ministration of Scientology religious services.

This provides protection for the parishioner. It means that a person knows when he goes to a Scientology organization to receive a specific service, he will get exactly that service. It protects unsuspecting persons, should unscrupulous individuals outside the Church try to pervert and use L. Ron Hubbard's technology to further their own ends. Thus, the technology is kept pure. This is the intention of all Scientologists and RTC receives their wholehearted support in maintaining it.

Scientology Staff Members

Scientology missions and Class V churches are administered by staff members who contract to work for the Church for either two-and-a-half or five years at a time, in order to make Scientology and Dianetics available to all who reach for it.

Some staff positions are technical, requiring auditor or other specialized training; others are administrative and help keep the church functioning and provide the support so auditing and training can be delivered. In order to accomplish these duties, staff members work at the organization from morning to evening, with a period set aside for Scientology training and auditing. As with any other job, they return to their homes and families at the end of the day.

Every position in a church is different, but there are exact duties for each and staff members study policies which delineate these specific functions. Each job or position is called a hat, taken from the fact that in many professions such as railroading, the type of hat worn is the badge of the job. Staff engage in 2½ hours of study or auditing each day and, when they have completed the hatting courses and know how to do their jobs, many proceed on to other training, perhaps as an auditor, or use this time to move up the Bridge as a preclear.

Those staff who have signed a five-year contract may be sent for full-time training at a higher organization—either technical training at Saint Hill or the FSO, or administrative training at the mother church. This training can last up to a year, but in any event results in a highly trained church administrator, auditor or case supervisor.

There is also an entirely different category of staff in Scientology: members of the Sea Organization.

Entrusted with delivery of the most advanced levels of Scientology, the Sea Organization had its beginnings in 1967 when, after resigning all corporate and administrative responsibilities, L. Ron Hubbard set to sea with a handful of veteran Scientologists to research and develop the OT levels. For many years, the Sea Org operated from a fleet of ships, headed by its flagship, the *Apollo*. Sea Org members, in keeping with the tradition of these beginnings still wear maritime uniforms and have ratings and ranks, though the majority of Sea Org members are located on land today.

This group is a religious order within the hierarchical structure of Scientology and spans various churches and corporations. Sea Org members are responsible to the board of the church corporation they work in. Today there are almost 5,000 Sea Org members, the dedicated core of the religion, each of whom has signed a pledge of eternal service to Scientology and its goals.

All Church organizations above the level of Class V are manned by Sea Org members. This includes the Saint Hills, Advanced Orgs, FSO, FSSO and all of CSI and RTC.

Sea Org members continue the tradition of competent and professional teamwork that was the hallmark of the years at sea. New Sea Org members undergo rigorous basic training designed to raise their ability to confront and deal with their environment, their competence and their ethics level.

Sea Org members, having devoted their lives to their religion, work long hours for little pay and live a communal existence with housing, meals, uniforms, medical and dental care provided by the Church. They receive training and auditing during a portion of each day, but otherwise dedicate themselves to whatever their assigned task may be in the furtherance of the objectives of Scientology. Sea Org members achieve a great deal and have a high esprit de corps and sense of accomplishment.

The Sea Organization is dedicated to achieving the objective of a cleared planet through the standard application of the technologies of Dianetics and Scientology. It is a challenge met with determination and dedication.

Cooperation and Expansion

Each echelon in the Scientology hierarchy has a distinctly different responsibility. Together, they form a global network that has contributed to the rapid growth of the Church over nearly four decades.

Over the past thirty years, the growth factor of the Church has dramatically increased. In the past decade, Scientology has opened new organizations in more than fifty countries. In one recent six-month period alone, more than two hundred new Scientology groups became active. In less than four decades, Scientology has grown from a handful of organizations to a worldwide network.

Every duty in every organization—from the highest levels of Church management, down to the churches, missions, groups and auditors which offer services directly to those new to the subject—exists to help get the technology of Dianetics and Scientology known and used. Scientology continues to expand because it gets results: bringing people happiness, self-confidence, freedom from drugs, freedom from psychosomatic pain and fear, the ability to learn, stable relationships and a host of other priceless gains achieved every day in churches around the world. There is no more valuable activity on Earth, and thus the horizons for Scientology are bright and unbounded.

Whether a person wishes to attend a lecture on basic principles of Scientology, or receive auditing and training at the highest levels of the Bridge, there is a Scientology organization to provide him the services he needs. The object of any of these organizations is totally freed beings, a goal they help achieve daily.

Chapter 22

The International Association of Scientologists

The International Association of Scientologists (IAS) was formed at a convention held at Saint Hill Manor in East Grinstead, Sussex, England, in 1984. Delegates from around the world representing the Scientologists in their areas gathered in recognition of the need to unite all Scientologists as one international body. Its purpose is to assure the survival of the religion and guarantee that Scientology will be practiced for all time through a strong group that is composed of those who believe in the rights of man and freedom of religion.

The IAS is today a membership organization open to all Scientologists from all nations. It unifies the members and provides a forum to keep them informed of important developments and sharing the successes of the religion around the world. It is the strength of the individual members of the team, briefed and coordinated one with another that gives strength to the group. All great movements have succeeded based on the personal conviction and dedication of their members to overcoming any barriers to achieving their objectives.

Regrettably, history has seen many attempts to suppress religious freedom and human rights. From the persecution of early Christians in Rome, to the nineteenth-century assault on Mormons in the United States, to the slaughter of Jews in Nazi concentration camps, many faiths have suffered dearly. The International Association of Scientologists also serves the purpose of protecting Scientology from similar attempted persecution.

For this reason, in the 1984 convention at Saint Hill Manor, in addition to forming the IAS and adopting a constitution and electing a board, the delegates also formulated and signed the Pledge to Mankind to rededicate themselves to the aims of Scientology.

The IAS was enthusiastically embraced by Scientologists all over the world and, through their financial support and membership activities, rapidly became a major force, both protecting the religion and supporting the Church and individual Scientologists in their actions for social reform.

Each year, delegates representing Association members from all areas of the world gather at an Annual Convention of Delegates to review the accomplishments of the previous year, plan for the next and elect the board members of the Association as necessary. The Annual Convention of Delegates is held in different locations around the world, together with a large anniversary celebration. Significant accomplishments and progress toward the aims of Scientology are acknowledged and the event is broadcast to members in many countries.

MEMBERSHIP IN THE ASSOCIATION

Members of the International Association are entitled to certain rights and privileges. Churches of Scientology have adopted membership in the International Association of Scientologists as their membership system and grant special privileges and benefits to Association members designed to help them move more quickly up the Bridge.

Membership in the Association is open to any Scientologist. There are three categories of membership in the Association:

1. Introductory Membership

An introductory free membership is offered to new Scientologists. It is valid for a period of six months and is not renewable. Beginning members receive magazines and promotional materials from the IAS.

2. Annual Membership

Annual membership is valid for one year. It entitles the holder to benefits of the Association including a membership card and copies of *IMPACT,* the Association's magazine.

Also included are written briefings to keep members abreast of events and occurrences in Scientology, invitations to Association briefings and events, and the right to participate in IAS award programs and projects.

3. Lifetime Membership

Lifetime membership is valid for the lifetime of the holder and entitles him to all benefits and privileges of the Association.

In addition to the three categories of membership, there are special honor statuses awarded for extraordinary contributions toward achieving the goals of the Association. These honor statuses are valid for the duration of the membership of the holder. There are several categories awarded according to the level of support: "Sponsor of the Association," "Member of the Honor Roll," "Patron of the Association," "Patron with Honors," "Patron Meritorious," "Gold Meritorious" and "Member of the Senior Honor Roll." These statuses are acknowledged through publication to all members of the names of the individuals so awarded, presentation of special pins and plaques and award dinners held to honor the recipients.

Also, anyone who is in agreement with the Pledge to Mankind and the Aims of Scientology, even if he does not attend a church of Scientology or participate in its religious services may, upon contribution to the Association, be accorded the status of Associate. Associate status does not entitle the holder to the benefits and privileges of membership.

ASSOCIATION SUPPORT

The Association provides support to members engaged in activities which greatly assist the expansion of Scientology or directly contribute to the eradication of threats to the well-being of mankind. The Association makes monetary grants and calls upon its members to support such worthy projects, which results in many Scientologists volunteering their time and effort. In this way, the Association helps individual members gain valuable support from their fellow Scientologists to carry out worthwhile projects.

IMPACT MAGAZINE

All members receive *IMPACT* magazine which contains news and information relating to every Scientologist, including official news of the Association, major actions undertaken by the Association and its members, and announcements of services for its members.

IMPACT reports particularly on notable activities of Association members around the world who forward the aims of Scientology. IAS members contribute in many ways: They make Scientology more widely known, get it more widely used and help make the truth about the practices and value of the Scientology religion broadly understood.

FREEDOM MEDAL WINNERS

Each year the Association recognizes individuals who have defended the cause of religious and personal freedom. They are awarded the Freedom Medal by the Association at its anniversary celebration in October. There are no higher honors accorded the contributions of a Scientology parishioner than an IAS Freedom Medal.

The International Association of Scientologists works ceaselessly to forward the aims of Scientology and welcomes the membership of all who would aid in bringing hope to mankind.

The International Association of Scientologists Freedom Medal awarded annually to Scientologists in recognition of outstanding achievements

CHAPTER 23

A VITAL FORCE IN THE COMMUNITY

That a church would involve itself in charitable works and community betterment is both natural and traditional. For if it can be said that all great religions sprang from what is decent and beneficent in man, then it follows that charity and social responsibility are logical extensions of spiritual values. Prior to government welfare programs, for example, only the church could be counted upon to provide for the needy and the destitute, and through much of the world it is still only the church that provides.

Recognizing this tradition, and inspired by the many works of Mr. Hubbard, the Church of Scientology has become a notably vital force in the community.

Social betterment programs are fully supported by Church management, and every local church has a department devoted to carrying out these activities. It is from here that local Scientologists are coordinated and directed in programs which address the specific needs of their communities. Local Scientologists volunteer their services for these programs and, consequently, many individual Scientologists are leaders in community improvements.

In particular, the Church of Scientology has focused on four areas of concern: drug abuse, community betterment, criminal reform and charitable contribution. The Church and its members' motives are simple: Keenly conscious of his place in the world, the Scientologist knows that the only optimum solution is that which brings the greatest benefit to the greatest number of dynamics. To that end, his guidelines are rationality and an acute awareness that all dynamics are inextricably linked so that one man's well-being cannot be divorced from the well-being of all.

It is with this broad view in mind, then, that the Church and Scientologists are committed to social betterment—in the local neighborhood, the nation or in the world as a whole. The tools employed are those acquired from study of L. Ron Hubbard's works, including Mr. Hubbard's drug rehabilitation technology, his literacy programs, his essays on safeguarding the environment and, perhaps most important, the immense compassion for others that pervades everything he wrote.

The Church's areas of concern tend to center on those that each community regards as most pressing. Church environmental projects, for example, were prompted by a recognition that whole cities have quietly and sadly given up hope for a better future in the face of urban disintegration. That entire sectors of the population have emerged from schools without basic skills to survive has prompted Church educational programs. And the fact that even fundamental concepts of human decency are now under assault, has motivated Scientology's community cleanup campaigns

Scientologists are at the forefront of the fight against drugs, spearheading programs in cities around the world to provide effective solutions to reducing drug abuse.

world over. Then too, Scientologists tend to help where they themselves feel help is most needed, which is why their efforts are so diverse.

Utilizing L. Ron Hubbard's technology, Scientology churches are often catalysts for constructive change and provide rallying points for those who seek to improve conditions in their communities.

ANTIDRUG PROJECTS

Drug abuse is arguably the greatest problem society faces, directly and indirectly pushing crime to previously unimagined proportions. Quite apart from the individual tragedies involved, drug abuse has turned inner cities into battlegrounds and led to dwindling moral values and a general disregard for even the most basic ethical conduct. Moreover, and this is of special concern to Scientologists, drug abuse of all kinds lessens individual awareness, which when spread across whole sectors of society, does much to undermine the culture. With the world's most effective and statistically successful drug rehabilitation program, Scientologists have helped thousands of hard-core users free themselves from addiction and the lasting effects of substance abuse. But treating the victim of drug abuse on an individual basis is only one way Scientology meets the problem.

Uniting concerned community groups, staging public awareness forums, antidrug rallies and educational conferences, the Church of Scientology is at the forefront of the international grass-roots fight against drugs.

Using programs developed and supervised by their local churches as a focal point, Scientologists then reach out effectively into society.

In the United States, for instance, the Church-sponsored "Lead the Way to a Drug-Free USA" national campaign has helped millions of people by fighting further drug proliferation.

It has done this by raising funds for youth groups such as "Teen Canteen," an organization that helps runaway teens solve their problems; by enlisting the aid of celebrities for concerts with antidrug themes; and by hosting conferences of community leaders and antidrug activities, such as the one in Washington, DC which led city commissioner Bob King to present the Church's local "Lead the Way" program with a proclamation lauding its efforts in the war against drugs.

Nor was he by any means the only one to recognize the Church's efforts. Not long after the establishment of "Lead the Way" in the District of Columbia (DC), the director of the Office for Substance Abuse Prevention of the US Department of Health commended the Church for its drug-fighting initiative, writing, "It is because of the participation of dedicated groups like yours that we are making progress in the reduction of alcohol and other drug problems."

In 1991, "Lead the Way" began to broaden its influence with the inception of its first national conference in Washington, DC in the Sam Rayburn Congressional Office Building. More than 100 leaders in the antidrug field from around the country attended, including members of drug rehabilitation and social betterment groups, congressional aides, government official and media representatives. By bringing community leaders together, the conference helped expand antidrug programs to a truly concerted national level.

The Church has also enlisted the direct support of government officials. In Philadelphia, for example, it received a special recognition from the city's drug czar, who heads the Mayor's Office on Drug Control. But then, he went a step further and, in order to assist the Church's "active and cooperative participation in the war on drugs," as he put it, he became a national advisor to the "Lead the Way to a Drug-Free USA" campaign.

Dr. Hans Janitschek, author and consultant to the United Nations, neatly summed up the activities of "Lead the Way":

"In a world where serious problems such as drug abuse receive much attention, much talk and little in the way of effective action, 'Lead the Way to a Drug-Free USA' is a breath of fresh air.

"It has pooled together action-oriented individuals and groups from throughout the world in a shoulder-to-shoulder effort to bring to our communities REAL help for drug addicts, REAL preventative actions that keep our kids off drugs, and a REAL network of like-minded leaders who seek a drug-free USA."

Drug abuse knows no international boundaries, however, and Scientologists are active in many other nations. A glimpse of these activities reveals how pervasive and effective this work is.

In Canada, members of the Church of Scientology founded the national "Say No to Drugs, Say Yes to Life" campaign, which serves as a key force in turning youth away from drugs before they start.

Aimed at gaining the support of entertainment and sports figures because of their appeal to youth, the "Say No to Drugs, Say Yes to Life" campaign enlisted the Toronto Maple Leafs hockey team, the Toronto Blue Jays baseball team, the Toronto Argonauts and the Saskatchewan Roughriders football teams, all of whom have signed the "Say No to Drugs, Say Yes to Life" Honor Roll.

Members of the Church additionally gained the support of Canadian city officials to endorse the campaign. In eleven cities in the province of Ontario, for instance, mayors have proclaimed March 13—L. Ron Hubbard's birthday—"Say No to Drugs, Say Yes to Life" Day in their cities. Each proclamation has credited the Church, and one of them, from the mayor of Brampton, Ontario, specifically commended the Church for "helping educate communities toward an understanding that to achieve their goals, they must be drug free."

Canadian law enforcement officials, who regularly deal with drug-destroyed lives, also support the Church. Police welcome the enthusiasm that Scientologists bring to activities against this tragic scourge. In fact, to encourage others, the police force of Mercier, near Quebec, celebrated its 21st anniversary by publishing a booklet which included a long description of the Church's antidrug work.

AROUND THE WORLD

European members of the Church feel the desire to help no less than their fellow Scientologists in North America. Consequently they have joined in the fight against the truly pandemic drug problem.

Scientologists in Germany, France, Switzerland, Denmark, Belgium, Holland, Austria, Sweden, Norway, Italy and the United Kingdom lead successful and popular "Say No to Drugs, Say Yes to Life" campaigns.

The Italians, who also have a "Say No to Drugs" Honor Roll, enlisted the support of Philips, Italy's most famous volleyball team. While touring Italy, members of the legendary Spanish football team, Real Madrid, each signed the honor roll. And, further maintaining a high profile in the field of sports, the Church antidrug campaign sponsors major sporting events to heighten public awareness of the problem and its solution.

Other avenues are also utilized. In particular, the Church conducts regular drug-free musical concerts throughout Italy, enlisting the support of popular musicians.

But arguably no other program has such a direct practical impact as the Church's response to the widely acknowledged health menace of used hypodermic syringes discarded in public parks by addicts.

Groups of church volunteers and celebrities lead regular citywide drives to round up and safely dispose of these potentially lethal hazards. Rome, Verona, Padova, Torino, Brescia, Pordenone, Novara, Monza, Florence and Milan have all benefited from such cleanup drives.

The achievements of Scientology's Italian volunteers have earned recognition from not only those local Italian mayors and city officials who witness the goodwill firsthand, but from members of the Italian Parliament as well.

Scientologists in Scandinavia are no less active. In Sweden, parishioners of all ages, carrying banners and placards, regularly conduct "Say No to Drugs, Say Yes to Life" marches down major thoroughfares to raise public awareness of the issue.

In Denmark, the "Say No to Drugs, Say Yes to Life" association has taken a more adversarial position. There, they have been educating members of Parliament, city officials, police chiefs and other community leaders on the dangers of drug use—particularly the liabilities of methadone. Originally billed as a solution to heroin addicts, methadone ultimately proved to be just as addictive. Acutely aware that substituting one drug for another is no solution at all, Danish Scientologists have loudly decried this psychiatric "quick fix," with thousands of signatures on the "Say No to Drugs, Say Yes to Life" Honor Roll. Danish Scientologists also run a radio station which broadcasts effective life improvement tips—including advice on saying no to drugs.

Germany also faces a methadone problem of frightening proportions, and Scientologists in Hamburg published a brochure describing the destructiveness of methadone "therapy," and distributed more than 50,000 copies of it throughout the city. This led to a long-overdue national exposé of the abuses occurring in Hamburg's "Needle Park."

As elsewhere, concerts and rallies effectively mobilized public concern for Germany's drug crisis and helped many among Germany's youth understand that one does not have to take drugs to be happy and successful in life.

In Switzerland, where antidrug events are regularly held in Lucerne, Basel, Bern, Lausanne and other cities, Scientologists also take an activist role. Working with other local organizations, the church in Zurich launched a petition drive that closed an infamous park to drug addicts and pushers, amid widespread media coverage.

Support for the Church's antidrug activities has come from both federal and state members of Parliament. In Geneva, the mayor signed the "Say No to Drugs, Say Yes to Life" Honor Roll and became an honorary member of the association.

Here too, Swiss Scientologist sports celebrities give many antidrug lectures to schoolchildren and raise public awareness of the drug problem by answering questions about drugs at "Say No to Drugs" public information stands.

French Scientologists, including well-known and popular celebrities have organized marches, concerts and street events promoting the Church's antidrug message, reaching hundreds of thousands of Parisians. Contacting still more through the media, celebrities regularly discuss the workability of L. Ron Hubbard's drug rehabilitation technology. A set of radio cassettes produced on the Church's "Say No to Drugs, Say Yes to Life" campaign is played on radio stations throughout France.

In Spain, where drug trafficking has earned the nation the title "drug crossroads of Europe," local Scientologists formed a "Freedom Without Drugs" association and conducted a series of antidrug events in Madrid.

Utilizing public events with just as much efficiency, Mexican Scientologists run a "Say No to Drugs" campaign, with well-known entertainers in cities such as Torreón, Guadalajara and Mexico City.

Similarly, South African Scientologists inaugurated a "Say No to Drugs, Say Yes to Life" Honor Roll, with events at schools, clubs and other organizations. To date, tens of thousands of South Africans have signed the honor roll, including the mayors from Port Elizabeth, Cape Town and Soweto.

In both Australia and New Zealand, Scientologists campaign against drug abuse with a "Say No to Drugs, Say Yes to Life" Honor Roll, receiving support from a wide range of sports celebrities, including the legendary New Zealand All Blacks rugby team, and many famous automobile and motorcycle racing stars.

The work of Scientologists on the antidrug front has been widely recognized. Scores of cities throughout the world have issued commendations to the Church for its antidrug work. From Perth to Adelaide in Australia, from Madrid to Stockholm to Milan in Europe, from Cape Town to Pretoria in South Africa, from more than forty cities in the United States and fifty in Canada, city governments have recognized the value of the efforts of Scientologists in this area. In fact, whenever one finds a church of Scientology, one will find a coordinated and concerted effort to turn youth away from drugs and rehabilitate the addict.

Throughout the world, members of the Church are spreading the word that a drug-free life is a better, more productive and happier one. Literally hundreds of hours of public service announcements and radio or television programs provided by the Church are broadcast every week. These programs often contain readings from the works of L. Ron Hubbard on such subjects as helping others overcome difficulties, how to improve home and community conditions and—as an underlying message—that no problem, not even epidemic drug use, is too large to surmount so long as people care enough and are determined enough to persevere.

REDUCING CRIMINALITY

Inexorably linked with both drug abuse and urban decay is crime. To the degree that a man perceives his environment as a threat, Mr. Hubbard wrote, he will not thrive. With that in mind, Scientologists have dedicated themselves to the reduction of criminality in an effort to further safeguard their environment. Of course, they believe the ultimate solution to crime is the eradication in individuals of criminal impulses, made possible with Scientology auditing technology. Witness the case of a Melbourne, Australia resident who, after receiving Scientology auditing, turned himself in to local authorities and confessed to having stolen eight hundred dollars years earlier. His reason: He decided that he could not achieve spiritual gain until he had taken full responsibility for past transgressions and repaid the money, which he did. The judge said this action was unheard of and reduced the penalty to a suspended sentence, describing the man's behavior as exceptional and stating that it clearly showed he had been rehabilitated.

At the same time, Scientologists have also joined law enforcement officers around the world in their fight to reduce senseless criminal violence.

In San Francisco, California, for example, Scientologists spearheaded the creation of a Neighborhood Crime Watch program designed to protect those who live in the community near the church.

In Montreal, Canada, the church of Scientology sponsors a contest inviting the public to write essays regarding crime reduction as a means of raising public awareness of, and appreciation for, the daily task of law enforcement officials.

In an effort to ease police–public tensions in Mexico City, Scientologists conducted seminars to teach police officers better human relations techniques. Members of the Mexican Federation of Dianetics delivered seminars to 250 policewomen from the central police headquarters in Mexico City.

When the 1992 Los Angeles riots shook the city, *The Times* of London reported, "Further east, at the fabled intersection of Hollywood and Vine, 300 members of the Church of Scientology ignored the citywide curfew and surrounded an entire block to protect their building. By midnight it was one of the very few blocks on Hollywood Boulevard where no business had been torched or looted."

With an all too obvious need to rebuild their city in the wake of the Los Angeles riots, community leaders gathered in a spirit of cooperative endeavor to heal the city's wounds, among them the president of the Church of Scientology International. Invited to serve on the board of a newly formed group called Los Angeles Model Plan, he soon took an active part in the "healing" process. The group, which also includes Los Angeles City Council members, a California state senator, the president of the Los Angeles United Way and other leaders, was specially formed to address the problems of education, a matter of great concern to Scientologists.

Scientologists also spearheaded the formation of East Hollywood People Against Crime, which brought that community together in an effective campaign to reduce local crime. Under the Church's leadership, events were held to wipe out graffiti covering twenty-eight gang-ridden city blocks, and funds were raised to purchase equipment for neighborhood foot patrols.

Acknowledging the difficult task performed by law enforcement officials, Scientologists encourage citizen support for their work. Churches regularly present special awards to police officers in recognition of the value of police work in their local communities. The Church supports the efforts of police forces to help create an environment where citizens can safely walk the streets and raise their children.

While crime has become an increasing factor in the lives of people throughout the world, in these and many other ways Scientologists are contributing to the creation of a safe environment.

Environmental Revitalization Projects

Because individual churches and their parishioners are involved in their communities, environmental efforts naturally tend to reflect community needs. Thus in one city, Scientologists can be found heading recycling projects, public park cleanups and the removal of graffiti; while in another they can be found planting trees or protecting wildlife.

In Los Angeles, for instance, a murals project sponsored by the Church's Community Outreach Group and the Church's Visual Artists Association beautifies the environment. Through the years, scores of large murals have been provided to Dependency Courts and related facilities for children throughout Los Angeles County. The Community Outreach Group has received city, county and state recognition as a result, in fact, being named the community group of the year in Los Angeles.

Equally energetic is the Tustin, California "Scientologists for a Better Community" who enhance their city's image with graffiti cleanups and by painting murals. While in Orlando, Florida, Scientology received the city's 1990 "Church Volunteer of the Year" award for its contributions to the cleanup and restoration of the local historic train station and surrounding streets.

In Santa Barbara, California, the church is a participant in California's "Adopt a Highway" program, taking responsibility for maintaining the cleanliness of a portion of a major highway.

Ecologically minded South African Scientologists celebrate Earth Day each year with educational campaigns to stress the importance of safeguarding and improving their environment. They have also helped with clean-up events at local parks and beaches. A church-organized antilitter campaign in Durban, South Africa, involving hundreds of volunteers from both the church and the community, received special recognition and a warm letter of thanks from the Durban City Council.

In Australia, the "Clean Up Australia Day" organization recognized the Church of Scientology's community clean-up events with a proclamation acknowledging the Church's "outstanding contribution." Scientologists run a constant educational campaign in Melbourne and other Australian cities to reduce pollution in the environment.

Scientologists are constantly engaged in smaller, unreported projects—discouraging neighborhood youth from defouling property with spray cans, or encouraging those around them to use litter baskets. These activities are all part of Scientology's larger world view that no dynamic can thrive unless all thrive, and that each man is not only vitally linked to all other men but also to the world in which he lives.

ETHNIC AFFAIRS AND CIVIL RIGHTS

By the Creed of the Church, "All men of whatever race, color or creed were created with equal rights." In its efforts to secure freedom and human rights for all individuals, the Church of Scientology has provided effective assistance for members of minority groups who have suffered hardship because of race or belief.

In the United States, the Church of Scientology maintains an Office of Ethnic and Cultural Affairs, to coordinate Church efforts on behalf of all minorities.

Churches have continuously affirmed the truth that although one man's skin may be white and another's black, red or yellow, the spirit has no color.

One of the services of the Church's Office of Ethnic and Cultural Affairs for many years has been to publish a popular column, syndicated in newspapers around the country, providing positive guidelines on educational reform, self-esteem and other applications of L. Ron Hubbard's technology. The column has exposed government abuses against minorities and championed the cause of equal rights and equal opportunity for all.

In fact, the Church provided the first national exposure of widespread racial discrimination against IRS employees by IRS officials. In 1990 Scientologists investigated and exposed voluminous reports received on the IRS's discriminatory policies and practices in Chicago; New York; Los Angeles; Indianapolis; Kansas City; Jackson, Mississippi and Norfolk, Virginia.

Scientologists have also investigated and challenged racially motivated police brutality on the streets of Los Angeles. The Church helped initiate reforms of the Los Angeles Police Department.

In Washington, DC, Scientologists established an award-winning program which has assisted hundreds of African-American inner-city children to raise their scholastic competence and self-esteem. Many Scientologists volunteer their time every weekend to help these underprivileged children and, as a result, have received community awards for their hard work, dedication and results.

To increase understanding and tolerance between diverse groups, to ensure justice for all regardless of color or creed—these are not merely words to the Scientologist, but deeply felt convictions, seen as a true cornerstone for survival.

SUPPORTING GOODWILL AND COMMUNITY ORGANIZATIONS

In cities on every continent, members of the Church donate thousands of hours in community work and provide assistance to a wide range of other goodwill and community groups.

The Church supports and contributes to other established community programs such as the Red Cross, the Cystic Fibrosis Foundation and local community groups in cities around the world. Church members' support of and contribution to these programs range from broad participation

The good works of the Church are covered in the media around the world, with hundreds of articles every week.

SOUTHERN
Los Angeles TODAY
Daily News
The Anchorage Times
The Portland Observer
Schools, clubs sign petition against drugs
BOSTON HERALD
THE TORONTO STAR
The Vancouver Sun
BRITISH COLUMBIA'S NEWSPAPER
Deutsche Presse
DENVER HERALD-DIS
THE FOOTHILL LEADER
Daily Camera
THE Sunday NEWS
Scientologists Say no
Dianetics Foundation recognizing drug-free businesses
New Haven Register
The City
SAN FRANCISCO POST
Church Supports Toy Drive
Church launches an anti-drug campaign
stampa SERA
La Gazzetta
Raccol in parc
STAR-NEWS
Hollywood Independent
FREE COPY
CALIFORNIA EXAMINER
roubled kids
HAROLD N. HUBBARD
Free Pr
The Bakersfield News Observer
WEDNESDAY, JULY 11, 1990
Church Of Scientology And Neighborhood Watch Hold Fundraiser To Fight Crime
Church of Scientology blood drive
Churc
THE ORANGE COUNTY Register
THURSDAY, DECEMBER 19, 1991
Scientology aids homeless vets
Religion
Scientologists crusade for rights
Los Angeles Times
JUNE 24, 1990
Scientologists Lead Way in Crime Fight
Gangs: Neighbors have joined members of the Church of Scientology in an East Hollywood crime watch group and anti-graffiti brigade.
By JOSH MEYER
mally like to keep a low profile. But members began passing out 5,000 flyers to area residents asking them to meet and plan for the defense of their community—a mix of noisy commercial boulevards and quiet residential streets—and they began lobbying for a greater police presence in the area.
As many as 200 church members and neighborhood residents showed up at the first meeting, held three weeks ago in the church's auditorium on Berendo Street, and there have been weekly meetings since.
The East Hollywood People Against Crime was formed as
dents block by block, and has begun graffiti eradication measures. The first "paint-out" in early June drew more than 150 people, who covered up graffiti over a 28-block area, and more than 100 area residents attended a cookout and organizational meeting last Sunday, according to a Scientology spokeswoman.
Officer Richard Ledesma of LAPD's Northeast Division said the crime watch group is already making its mark by cleaning up graffiti-ridden alleyways and by urging neighbors to report suspicious activities to police.
"They have a big problem
Spokes
mber 15, 1990
cientology & food drive
food contributions is Nov. 21st at which time the food will be given to the Emergency Foodshelf Network Inc. The food drive will end with an Open House on Nov. 21st from 10:00am until 4:00pm. There will be continuous showings of the film Dynamics of Life and refreshments will be served.
TAMPA TRIB
Thursday, September 17, 1992
CLEARWATER
Scientologists collecting for Andrew victims

in drug-free blood drives, to citywide collection of holiday toys for needy children, to donations of food and clothing for underprivileged families.

For years, the church of Scientology in Portland has provided assistance to the Northeast Emergency Food Program, sponsored by Ecumenical Ministries of Oregon. The Portland church displays the award certificate received for "outstanding contribution" to the program's fundraising efforts.

In Orange County, California, Scientologists helped form a local chapter of the "Food for All" program with Lutheran Social Services and Presbyterian and Catholic groups in the area which provides food for the homeless.

The Church of Scientology of St. Louis raises funds for the US Marine Corps "Toys for Tots" program, while also carrying out a successful education program aimed at safeguarding children from crime. Both the Marine Corps and *The Police News* of Missouri have recognized the church for its community service activities.

In Dallas, Scientologists raised thousands of dollars on behalf of Bryan's House, a facility that helps children suffering from AIDS.

Church members in Sacramento head a project called "Operation Caring"—a community outreach program providing support and companionship for the elderly.

In Arizona, church volunteers participated in a pledge drive to support public television, raising $25,000—more than double the target set by the local public television station.

In Australia, the Church of Scientology of Sydney works hand in hand with the Salvation Army, running the local drive for food, clothes and toys. Church volunteers in Australia also conduct clothing drives for underprivileged families and provide musical entertainment for the elderly.

In Germany, church volunteers also provide musical entertainment for the elderly at old-age homes, while in nearby Belgium, local Scientologists supported an annual 24-hour bicycle race, raising funds for cancer research.

Honoring a long tradition of helping the needy, and particularly children, over the Christmas holidays, Scientologists help spread Christmas goodwill in cities around the world. From California to New York, Scientologists in the United States collect food and gifts to cheer the holidays of those in need.

For many years the church in Los Angeles has worked with the Department of Children's Services of Los Angeles County to provide toys and holiday entertainment for foster children under the department's care. These children are, most commonly, from broken families or victims of abuse. Over the years, the various contributions made by Scientologists have resulted in many commendations from the department.

In 1991 the department asked the church to provide gifts and entertainment for more children than ever before. Responding to the call, church staff and volunteers organized a massive toy drive that resulted in more than 5,500 gifts for these children, who otherwise would have gone without.

Scientologists also provided entertainment at nine separate parties throughout Los Angeles County, some of them attended by several hundred children. These holiday events culminated in an enormous party for more than 3,000 children.

In addition to these activities in the Los Angeles area, for years the church has sponsored the popular "Winter Wonderland" in Hollywood, complete with the film capital's largest Christmas tree and many tons of snow. Santa lights the tree during the annual Christmas parade and the setting plays host to thousands of children and their parents. Winter Wonderland is a tradition begun by L. Ron Hubbard's gift of a Christmas tree donated to the city each year, and carried on by the church as a goodwill activity in the Hollywood area.

Clearwater, Florida Scientologists are active in the Women's Auxiliary, providing hundreds of Christmas presents to underprivileged children via the local Marine Corps Reserve. Also through the Women's Auxiliary, gifts were provided to the Future Homemakers of America for children of Florida migrant workers. A choir comprised of children of church staff makes numerous holiday season appearances each year at retirement homes and other care facilities in the Clearwater area. Scientologists also participate in such community events as the annual Clearwater Christmas Parade. Each year, Scientologists organize a toy drive and party for Clearwater's foster children.

Also in Florida, the Miami church annually supports the Salvation Army's toy drive for tens of thousands of local children; across the country in Seattle, the church donates a large Christmas tree to the community every year. Scientologists there help organize events in celebration of the tree's arrival and to foster holiday spirit. Seattle Scientologists also collect toys for the Seattle Police drive for underprivileged children.

The Children's Choir of the Church of Scientology of St. Louis specializes in bringing holiday season joy to the elderly. As the manager of a local home for seniors wrote, "In today's world of so busy lives, the seniors are too often forgotten. Your visit put a smile on their faces as well as in their hearts."

In the United Kingdom, as elsewhere around the world, Scientology performers visit homes for disadvantaged children and the elderly, providing music and other entertainment.

In Australia, Scientologists also collect food, clothing and toys each year and distribute them to the needy, and Christmas carolers visit local nursing homes.

In Vancouver, the church's participation in the city's toy drive has received widespread appreciation from community officials and press coverage. The church has, as well, been instrumental in the success of the Vancouver Christmas Cruise, enlisting the participation of yacht owners who offer children free excursions and toys.

The Toronto church is the site of a Christmas street festival, where toys are passed out by Santa to hundreds of area children. Toronto Scientologists also sponsor a special Christmas distribution of gifts to underprivileged children.

Canadian Scientologists team up with local law enforcement officers and firefighters in Ottawa and Montreal for annual toy drives and caroling for underprivileged youth and residents of care centers.

Nor does Scientology charity in Canada stop with Christmas. Year around Canadian church members greet and care for arriving immigrants and refugees and their families—and round-the-clock as necessary. The Church of Scientology of British Columbia was acknowledged with a certificate of appreciation for "generous contribution" from the Immigrant Services Society of British Columbia for helping newly arrived refugee families.

In Montreal, the church is an active fund-raiser, joining forces with the Canadian National Hockey Team for various charities. Scientologists in Montreal support the Cerebral Palsy Association, led by a Scientologist who serves as vice-president of the association's fund-raising committee.

In addition to these charitable activities and programs, the Church supports one other community effort—the Volunteer Minister program.

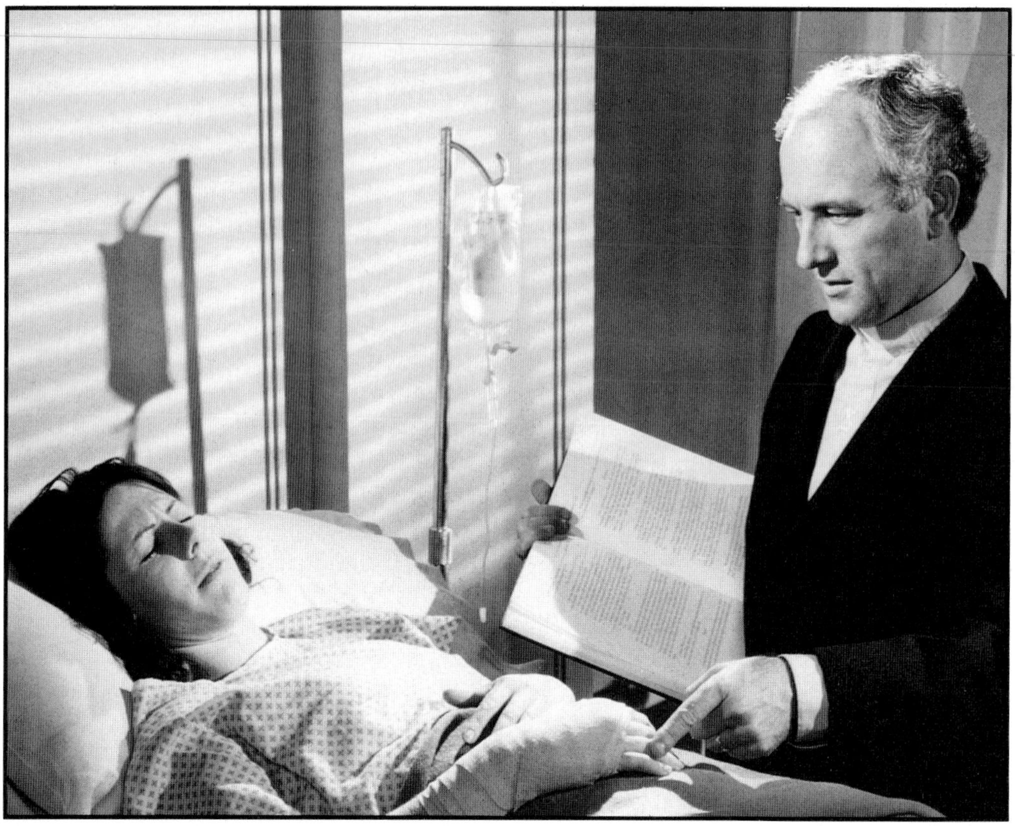

***The Volunteer Minister's Handbook** provides Scientologists and non-Scientologists alike with fundamental Scientology technology to aid the injured, handle troubled marriages and rescue drug addicts from their addiction.*

VOLUNTEER MINISTERS

In the mid-1970s, L. Ron Hubbard concluded that criminal activities were rising in proportion to the decline in religious influence. He further noted that many had no place to turn when they needed solutions to life's problems. Yet Scientology contains data that anyone can use in any part of their lives, data people can use to help each other. When Scientology is used, conditions do improve. The way to a better society is to make it available as broadly as possible. One of the key ways the Church fosters this idea is through the Volunteer Minister program.

The program makes help broadly available by providing fundamental aspects of Scientology technology to *anyone,* Scientologist and non-Scientologist alike. To supply this technology *The Volunteer Minister's Handbook,* by L. Ron Hubbard, was published in 1976. Since then, thousands of individuals have performed a vital role as Volunteer Ministers in their communities.

The Church takes an active role to help them by distributing the handbook, offering training and certification on its materials, putting Volunteer Ministers in contact with each other and assisting them to start in their ministry. The Volunteer Minister program is nonsectarian and, in addition to training lay people, also trains ministers of other denominations to render more effective assistance to those around them.

There are no restrictions on who may become a Volunteer Minister or what he may do to assist others. Anything a minister would do, a Volunteer Minister does. And any area of life can benefit from his help.

The Volunteer Minister's Handbook is the result of hundreds of thousands of hours of research and application. It teaches many of the helpful fundamentals of Scientology in a series of simple and swiftly learned lessons. After studying these lessons, one can immediately begin ministering to the needs of the community in a volunteer capacity. Volunteer Ministers need not belong to any association or congregation. All one requires is knowledge of the handbook and the desire to help.

Those following any faith may become a Volunteer Minister. But he *is* a minister and he helps his fellow man. He does not shut his eyes to the pain, evil and injustice in the world. Rather, he is trained to handle such misery and help others achieve the relief that comes from the application of Scientology technology to conditions in life. People in all areas can do something for their fellow man through the Volunteer Minister program.

A Volunteer Minister eases the tribulations of people. He saves troubled marriages, helps failing students, resolves conflicts between individuals and groups, rescues drug addicts from the agony of withdrawal convulsions, eases physical discomfort and assists the injured. Such are just some of the miracles Volunteer Ministers accomplish every day. He supplies services which are lacking in the society, and there is a tremendous amount he can do.

Each section of *The Volunteer Minister's Handbook* teaches a body of basic Scientology technology on a different subject. With each lesson learned, the Volunteer Minister becomes more able to effectively deal with situations he sees in life:

A person smashes his hand in a car door. The Volunteer Minister is taught assist technology and so can help alleviate the pain and help the injury heal more rapidly. He applies similar techniques to ease illnesses as well. A married couple has constant arguments. The Volunteer Minister knows the mechanisms which underlie marital conflicts and can counsel them, restore harmony and save the marriage. Two shop owners in the neighborhood are in conflict. With what he is taught, the Volunteer Minister can locate the real source of the conflict and resolve it. A friend has fallen on hard times and is using drugs. The Volunteer Minister has studied how to get him off drugs and can help him straighten out his life. A restaurant owner's business has taken a downturn. The Volunteer Minister can isolate the reason for this and help the owner right his business. These are not unusual circumstances; they happen all the time. Ordinarily, people are helpless in such situations, even if they want to help; a Volunteer Minister, on the other hand, has been trained to render effective assistance. And so he does something about it.

If the person desires to do it, an optional course is offered at his church or mission. Such training at the church, by virtue of assistance from experienced personnel, can better equip a Volunteer Minister to perform his duties.

Volunteer Ministers frequently form groups with each other which enable them to better serve the community. Such groups allow newer ministers to gain experience by working with more practiced ones. Some even have congregations, holding Sunday services or seminars with topics relevant to their communities and individual interests.

Volunteer Ministers also work with and assist ministers of other denominations.

All churches are involved in helping their fellow man and can work together to accomplish these goals. Upon invitation, Volunteer Ministers deliver sermons at other churches.

By mutual cooperation and assistance, ministers of all denominations strengthen the force of religion in the world. In so doing they help reverse the cultural decay stemming from the rampant materialism plaguing modern society.

The good works of Volunteer Ministers are noticed by the society at large. A perfect example came from a South African Volunteer Minister, the Reverend William Mesilane. This sixty-nine-year-old minister of the Christ Assembly Church utilized Scientology technology to help people in his community.

"He eased someone's pain using the Touch Assist on the train from Maclear to Sterkstroom," the newspaper reported. "He saw a woman crying, who jumped with terror if anyone spoke to her. He asked her what was wrong and she did not know. He offered to do a Touch Assist, which took twenty minutes. During that time, the train conductor came and watched him at work, as well as curious passengers. At the end of the Touch Assist the woman was laughing and calm.

"William claims he took on a new lease in life when he began to study the handbook. He eagerly plans to use all he learns to help his people further."

As more and more people see the value of bringing true help to another, the Volunteer Minister program spreads further throughout the society. By freely offering his assistance to those who need it, the effective contributions of the Volunteer Minister are making the world a better place.

LONG-RANGE GOAL

Although it may be reiterated that the Church has received thousands of awards and commendations for its work within communities, these are incidental to both the intention and the deed. Scientologists help because help is part of the fabric of their religion, and L. Ron Hubbard has always stressed the importance of taking responsibility for one's fellows.

It should also be pointed out that, in addition to these listed activities, a legion of unheralded Scientologists in countries all over the world engage in a host of unreported activities. Whether they are organized by the Church, or simply the actions of individual Scientologists who willingly accept responsibility for their fellows and their neighborhoods, it is part and parcel of the broader view that there is no finer satisfaction than that which comes from helping. Thus, wherever one finds a church of Scientology, one also finds a steady, if unpublicized, effort to help where help is needed.

Reducing criminality and drug abuse, community cleanup and charitable contributions—when one considers the larger purpose of Scientology, it is no accident that members of the Church have chosen to focus their social betterment programs on these areas. For although the primary emphasis of Scientology remains on bettering the individual, on bringing him to greater heights of spiritual awareness, the long-range aim has always been the same—a civilization without insanity, without criminals and without war, where the able can prosper and honest beings can have rights, and where man is free to rise to greater heights. And so, as the numbers of Scientologists continue to grow, so, too, is their presence increasingly felt as a vital force in the community.

Some of the numerous recognitions the Church has received for its community activities

Office of the Mayor
Tullahoma, Tennessee
Proclamation
County of Los Angeles
Church of Scientology
Community Outreach Program
City of Hartford
Connecticut
PROCLAMATION
By
The Honorable CARRIE SAXON PERRY, Mayor
City of Los Angeles
Certificate of Appreciation
In Recognition of outstanding citizenship and activities enhancing community betterment
Proclamation
Office of the Mayor
Camden, New Jersey
Proclamation
City of Bridgeport, Co
Proclamation
City of Vancouver
Proclamation
County of Los Angeles
Lead the Way to a Drug Free LA Day
City of Helena
Proclamation
City of Westwego
Proclamation
Office of the Mayor
Proclamation
Proclamation
Office of The Mayor
Harrisburg, Pennsylvania
Proclamation
Los Angeles
Community Outreach Group of the Church of Scientology
Office of the Mayor
City of Holyoke
Proclamation
City of Durham
North Carolina
Proclamation
County of Los Angeles
The Community Outreach Group of the Church of Scientology
The Office of the Mayor
City of Boise,
State of Idaho
Proclamation
Certificate of Appreciation
May it be known that
California Legislature Assembly
Certificate Of Recognition
Senate
California Legislature
July 13, 1989
Proclamation
Proclamation
Elkhart
Louisiana
Proclamation
Saginaw
Proclamation
City of Tucson Office of the Mayor
Proclamation
L. Ron Hubbard Day
State of California
Senate
Rules Committee
Resolution
The Community Outreach Group of the Church of Scientology
The City of Reading, Pennsylvania
Proclamation
City of W
Williamsb
The Mayor's Office on Drug Control
City of Philadelphia, PA
The Church of Scientology of Pennsylvania
and its volunteers
are hereby awarded this
For active and cooperative participation in
The "War on Drugs"
in the
City of Philadelphia
March, 1991
Robert Armst
Drug Czar, Philad
City of Los Angeles
State of California
Resolution
Whereas, the Outreach Group of the Church of Scientology
has devoted thousands of hours to assist the Department of Children's Services provide better care for and respond to the needs of children and their families, and
Proclamation
By the Mayor

CHAPTER 24

SPEARHEADING SOCIAL REFORM

While religious leaders have long recognized that man's spiritual well-being cannot be entirely divorced from temporal concerns, few churches have dedicated themselves so thoroughly to the cause of social reform as the Church of Scientology. Through its diligent and aggressive activities, it is recognized by many as a leading champion of human rights, one that involves itself in arenas wherever injustice has been perceived.

For a church to actively involve itself—as the Church of Scientology has done—in the exposure of psychiatric abuses around the world, Internal Revenue Service (IRS) illegalities in the United States, international law enforcement corruption and a host of other ills that plague society, may seem unusual, but the fact is Scientologists care as much about the here and now as the hereafter. The Creed of the Church specifically addresses the inalienable rights of all men, regardless of race, color or creed, and the actions of Scientologists everywhere have given these words true substance.

These endeavors by Scientologists who care enough to investigate, to overcome the resistance of powerful vested interests, and even to place themselves at risk, have also resulted in remarkable achievements. Laws have been passed, lives saved, victims rescued, restitution paid, criminals arrested and life-threatening activities halted. In a word, they have resulted in justice, a sometimes rare commodity in today's world.

Scientologists have, in a very real sense, drawn the line. They have raised their voices in the collective cry: "Enough!" Enough butchery of innocents, enough enslavement of the weak, enough intolerance, enough abuse of power by those who hold it. Enough. While such statements may sound inflammatory, verging on drama and exaggeration, they are not—except to those too timid to see, those who huddle in the security of their homes and jobs, or those who, when they witness evil on the evening news or upon the streets of their cities say, "This has nothing to do with us."

That the presence of evil is as real as the shadows that dog our footsteps will be shown in this chapter. It is man's burden and will continue to be so for as long as it has nothing to do with us. No matter how technologically advanced our age, no matter how "enlightened" the opinions on talk shows or the advice so liberally handed out in magazines, it is not enough. As repugnant as the thought may be, there are those among us on a mission of destruction, and it will take more than talk to abort such missions.

Scientologists are acutely aware of this. And thus they have taken the task of man's freedom upon themselves. For as has been implied and discussed and stated in this book, the mission of Scientology involves spiritual freedom. But just as there can be no soaring flight while anchored to the ground, so there can be no true and lasting spiritual freedom while tyranny and injustice govern any man among us.

The Code of Honor of a Scientologist states quite plainly: "Your integrity to yourself is more important than your body." And while no ethical code can be enforced, it is a beacon that stands as an ideal. To many Scientologists it is even more—it is a reality to live by. Which is why they are willing to draw that line, to persist against unfriendly fire, and to show by deeds that enough is indeed enough.

To carry these battles forward, the Church and concerned Scientologists have founded a number of nonprofit organizations such as the Citizens Commission on Human Rights (CCHR) and the National Commission on Law Enforcement and Social Justice (NCLE) which seek social reform in the areas of psychiatric excess and corruption in law enforcement, respectively. And, to quickly and broadly bring the results of its research in these areas and others into the light of day, the Church publishes an international journal.

FREEDOM MAGAZINE

With its main editorial offices in Los Angeles, *Freedom* magazine is published in nine countries and five languages. In addition to breaking stories on the enforced drugging of schoolchildren, psychiatric brutalities and more, *Freedom* has, since founded in 1968, become widely recognized as one of the foremost voices for taxpayer rights and tax agency reform.

A forum for hard-hitting, investigative journalism, *Freedom* has taken on stories that other media have been reluctant to investigate or publish. And as its readership has grown, so has public awareness of areas in need of social reform.

CITIZENS COMMISSION ON HUMAN RIGHTS

From the United States to Australia, South Africa to Germany, the Church has relentlessly exposed psychiatric criminality and oppression—all in pursuit of a civilization "where man is free to rise to greater heights," as Scientology states in its aims.

In 1969, the Church established the Citizens Commission on Human Rights. Since then it has expanded around the world. Today, CCHR International, located in Los Angeles, supervises offices in most major cities in more than two dozen countries including the United States, United Kingdom, France, Germany, Norway, Switzerland, Denmark, Sweden, South Africa, Canada, Italy, Spain, Mexico, Netherlands, Israel, Australia, New Zealand and others.

Psychiatry Unmasked

During investigations into basic human rights abuses, one of the more fertile fields trod by the Church of Scientology, interestingly enough, has been the practice of psychiatry—interesting because it is a field which claims both humanitarian motive and leadership in the treatment of "mental health." It is a positioning that for many years has filled its trough with lucrative government appropriations and given it no small measure of societal power.

Based upon the realities, however, a more apt analogy might be that it has been looting the coffers for many years, for if, as is true for most of us in society, payment is received in return for a valuable service or product, psychiatry has been pulling the wool over government eyes for a very long time. Having taken the high ground much earlier this century simply due to the fact that nothing much had been done as far as studies of the mind were concerned, psychiatry stepped into the void and declared its leadership position. There were no competitors to speak of, for medicine had its hands full with advances in physical treatment and virtually no interest in the mind. And so, initially at least, in a society newly infatuated with the claims of science, there was little opposition to these new theories that claimed for themselves the same scientific status. Funded by governments interested in the control of populations, psychiatrists donned white cloaks in their laboratories, ran their tests on mice and monkeys and dogs and issued scholarly papers, written in a rapidly developed lexicon virtually incomprehensible to the layman—or the politician.

In truth, and as time finally proved, it was simply another case of an emperor with no clothes. The problem was not minor, however; it lay in the basic premise. Any researcher faces many choices in virtually limitless directions. And more than a century ago, psychiatry and its cousin, psychology, chose a certain path which has since, with minor exceptions, been slavishly followed. The premise was that man was an animal (thus the experiments on animals), that all mental activity originated in the brain (thus physical treatment of this physical organ was a primary solution), and that he responded to environmental stimuli (thus his behavior could be manipulated by such stimuli). Psychiatry has done little to diverge from this premise.

Unfortunately, the path has led only to a dead end. The fact of the matter is that these self-appointed experts have never discovered and do not know to this day that the mind is composed of mental image pictures, that the brain is simply a conduit, and that man is a spiritual being. Such oversights would be ludicrous and even amusing if the consequences were not so disastrous.

For today, as psychiatry still stumbles in circles around that cul-de-sac into which they were led, they have had to step over the bodies of the victims lying in their wake. Even a car mechanic learns about engines—what they are, what motivates them, how they work—before diving in with a wrench. Psychiatry has not only missed this basic premise, but its tools are dangerous. In lieu of understanding, their only instruments are a vast cornucopia of mind-altering pharmaceuticals, electroshock machines and surgeons' knives. And as the basic premise is inaccurate, and they actually have no idea *what* they are treating (other than easily observed symptoms), the results are naturally dismal.

The obvious question that arises is what does one do in such circumstances? They have claimed a leadership position by virtue of the fact there were no other candidates, and now they are expected to deliver. Unfortunately, they have virtually no idea what they are doing. It is a difficult position to be in. And so we have the undeniably applicable maxim: Desperate men do desperate things.

L. Ron Hubbard was one of the first to notice the nakedness of this emperor—and the desperation of his acts. From his earliest contact with the field in the late 1940s, he saw that something was very wrong: an arrogance, a venality, a disconcern for the individual and a serious incompetence. He noted with due outrage that for all the talk of enlightened psychiatric care, unmanageable patients were still routinely warehoused in dreadful conditions, drugged into vegetative states that left them permanently impaired, and punitively electroshocked. He also noted that, beyond food, clothing and a padded cell, psychiatry possessed no tools at all for dealing with the mentally ill.

To sum up, Mr. Hubbard wrote, psychiatry stood for ineffectiveness, lies and inhuman brutality. Its basic assumption revolved around the idea that with enough punishment, anyone could be restored to sanity; and if all else failed, one could always sever the patient's prefrontal lobes. With this and more in mind, Mr. Hubbard declared it to be the Scientologist's duty "to expose and help abolish any and all physically damaging practices in the field of mental health." Thus came about the formation of CCHR—the Citizens Commission on Human Rights.

Chelmsford—The Endless Sleep

Chelmsford is a name that Australian members of CCHR will probably never forget. For many, it was their first contact with unmitigated evil. And for all of them, it tested both their courage and their ability to persist in the face of derision, disbelief and an uncaring bureaucracy.

For Australians as a whole, the name of Chelmsford is today synonymous with madness, barbarism and horror; of psychiatry run amok, of bizarre experiments that, one magazine claimed, "rival those performed by Dr. Josef Mengele in Nazi Germany." New South Wales Health Minister, Peter Collins, called it "the darkest episode of the history of psychiatry in this country." And in mute witness, at least forty-nine crematoriums and cemeteries around Sydney hold Chelmsford's victims.

The Chelmsford Private Hospital in Sydney's northwest Pennant Hills was headed up by Dr. Harry Bailey who by 1963 had started to administer what is called deep sedation therapy, or more commonly, deep sleep therapy. As a later story by the *Sydney Morning Herald* described it, the title was a misnomer.

"First of all it isn't a therapy," having shown no therapeutic benefits. "Nor is it sleep. It is a coma induced by large doses of barbiturates."

Bailey's technique for handling mentally disturbed Chelmsford patients who were sent to him for help and care was essentially simple, if heavy-handed. He would place them in a coma for up to two weeks, during which period he would administer daily doses of electroshock therapy and/or psychosurgery, often without the consent or knowledge of the "sleeping" patient.

The Church's exposure of the atrocities at Chelmsford resulted in an international scandal and much needed psychiatric reform.

From mid-1963 to 1979, during his autocratic reign at Chelmsford, the deaths from this "treatment" mounted. Then there were the suicides by patients who were able to make it out of the facility alive, although the number of these was difficult to verify.

In the mid-1970s, CCHR began to receive reports of what was happening at Chelmsford. And by 1978, after investigating, it had collected hard evidence of six deaths related to deep sedation therapy. At that point, CCHR went public.

What followed was a significant demonstration of the unwillingness of authorities to view emperors in their nakedness—and failure of the psychiatric establishment to police itself. It was, in fact, a tedious merry-go-round of letter writing and lobbying. The Royal Australian and New Zealand College of Psychiatrists was given the evidence, and did nothing. The state of New South Wales Attorney General Department was given the evidence, and did nothing. The Minister of Health was given the evidence, and did nothing. The Health Commission and the Medical Board were given the evidence, but they each referred CCHR to the other. Meanwhile, public relations attacks were mounted against CCHR.

It took CCHR ten years of persistent investigation and bulldog-like determination before the New South Wales government appointed a Royal Commission in 1988 to look into deep sleep therapy in Chelmsford and throughout the state. Finally, after the two-year inquiry was completed and the full litany of horrors was uncovered—which included the possibility of 183 patient deaths, either at Chelmsford or within a year of discharge—a thorough shake-up of mental health care in New South Wales was recommended, along with a mental health patient bill of rights.

And what of psychiatry's stance after CCHR first uncovered what was happening at Chelmsford? It was ignored for as long as possible. However, this comment by a leading international figure provides an apt summation of psychiatric concerns. On January 6, 1981, Sir Martin Roth, Professor of Psychiatry at Cambridge University, wrote to another psychiatrist, who was calling for an inquiry, that the "Scientologists and other organizations will have obtained ammunition for years or decades to come. There is, therefore, a pressing need for maintaining strict confidentiality at this stage until one can set these barbarities in the context of contemporary practice in psychiatry in a carefully prepared statement that comes from colleges and other bodies concerned."

Scientology's remorseless work to uncover the truth was not without compensation. Deep sleep therapy was banned in New South Wales. Chelmsford was closed. And, of even more significance, many of the surviving victims who received electroshock therapy took their cases to the Crime Victims Compensation Board. So far, the board's tribunal has recognized in more than thirty of these cases that the patients were indeed subjected to acts of violence, and has accordingly awarded them compensation. Two of the psychiatrists who worked at Chelmsford finally faced criminal charges in 1992. And CCHR continued its work, exposing psychiatric abuses at Townsville Hospital in the northern state of Queensland. In practices frighteningly similar to Bailey's deep sleep treatments, sixty-five deaths were attributed to "unlawful and negligent treatment" after CCHR triggered a government investigation.

Finally, what of Bailey himself? He was never prosecuted. In September, 1985 he killed himself with the same drugs he had been feeding to his own patients. In his suicide note he blamed Scientologists, saying, "They have finally won."

Psychiatric Slave Camps

In the 1970s, a traveling windowpane salesman lost his way in the semirural countryside outside of Johannesburg, South Africa. Stopping to ask directions at what seemed to be a desolate mining compound, he happened upon a troubling sight: a naked and obviously terrified native woman was attempting to flee a uniformed guard.

The salesman happened to be a Scientologist and mentioned what he had seen to the Church. As the South African edition of *Freedom* began to investigate, what emerged was a story that would long stand as a dark symbol of psychiatric greed and inhumanity.

That apparently abandoned mining compound was one of thirteen psychiatric facilities owned and operated by the Smith-Mitchell Holding Company, a group that by the mid-70s was absorbing about one-third of the South African mental health budget. Nine of these facilities were for black patients; four for whites.

What CCHR uncovered was shocking. In 1976, more than 70 percent of all black certified mental patients in South Africa were in the hands of this group. The Smith-Mitchell hospitals had a patient population of more than 10,000. And the blacks were treated little better than animals, providing twelve-hour-a-day forced labor to line the pockets of their keepers. Nutrition was minimal, patients slept on mats on bare concrete floors, and in some institutions there was only one nurse on duty for anywhere from 300 to 1,000 patients. Nor were there equipped medical facilities, and at least one patient died a day. Accurately described by media as "hidden slave camps" and "human warehouses," most of these Draconian camps were hidden from view, and surrounded by spiked fences.

Troublesome patients were made tractable with a trip to the nearest state hospital where electroshock therapy was administered—without anesthetic.

The exposure of these grim revelations in Church publications brought an understandable wave of public outrage, both in South Africa and overseas. The World Health Organization and the United Nations Commission on Human Rights investigated and confirmed the atrocities uncovered by CCHR. Of even greater significance, and as a direct result of CCHR's work, in 1991 the United Nations unanimously issued for the first time a body of principles to protect persons with mental illness and improve mental health care—a mental health bill of rights.

CCHR and US Psychiatric Institutions

Since the late 1960s CCHR has investigated a virtually endless array of psychiatric abuses in the United States. In 1976, for instance, it provided California lawmakers with evidence and witnesses documenting the unexplained deaths of more than 100 people at the Camarillo and Metropolitan State psychiatric institutions. These exposés led to an investigation by the California state legislature and resulted in substantial administrative changes in both institutions.

In 1990 a similar pattern of abuse was discovered at the Patton state psychiatric institution in San Bernardino, California. CCHR discovered that the death rate at Patton had increased five times since the head of the institution had assumed office. Again, the California legislature investigated and the executive director was forced to resign.

CCHR was also instrumental in 1976 for laws passed in California to restrict the use of electric shock and lobotomies. The measures prohibited the use of these brutal practices on children and required that psychiatrists fully inform adult patients of the damaging effects and helpful alternatives before either procedure could be consented to.

Psychiatrists and Sexual Abuse

Although the Chelmsford atrocities and the disgraceful South African mental health camps are broad and telling examples of psychiatric desperation, there is a less dramatic yet extremely pervasive form of abuse which, mainly through the efforts of CCHR, has made headlines throughout the United States: psychiatric sexual abuse.

A growing problem among psychiatrists and psychologists, the sexual exploitation of patients—men, women and children—had long gone unreported owing to the unique and powerful control mental health professionals hold over their patients. Less than 5 percent of patients sexually assaulted by their therapists ever take action against them. And there are even cases on record wherein psychiatrists have actually used their instruments of trade—electroshock and heavy sedation—to silence patients they have sexually abused.

While there have been widespread reports of these abuses in institutions, CCHR investigations and the appearance of more and more newspaper accounts show the problem is not limited to those who have been committed to psychiatric care. It ranges from one-man practitioners in small towns and cities, to high officials. Early in 1992, for instance, John Hamilton, deputy medical director of the American Psychiatric Association, stepped down from office and had his license suspended for a year—after having sexual relations with a patient who was courageous enough to file a complaint. Ironically, Hamilton wrote and edited the APA peer review manual.

However, this type of rap on the knuckles is all too common—and, more unfortunately, all too rare. In the last ten years, the APA has suspended or expelled only 113 psychiatrists for exploiting patients. These are mild actions when one considers findings of the California task force that about 66 percent of those who are sexually exploited by mental health practitioners experience serious emotional repercussions, and 1 percent even commit suicide.

The intrinsic problem here, of course, is that like doctors and lawyers, psychiatrists righteously and loudly claim that a peer review system is firmly in place to handle member malfeasance. Outsiders, particularly those involved in enforcement of laws, are not needed, thank you. However, the reality demonstrated in all these professions shows serious flaws. Two factors come into play: A peer is after all an equal and a member of the same group and, unless one is motivated by deeply rooted ideals, it is, to say the least, uncomfortable to reprimand one's equals; and, perhaps of more pertinence, if judgments are too harsh they are invariably publicized, thus airing the profession's dirty linen. Bad publicity is anathema to a profession already standing on shaky ground. And faced with this disturbing threat, ranks tend to close rather quickly.

Therefore, knowing full well that the psychiatric community has consistently demonstrated an inability to police its own actions, CCHR has long felt it only just that the perpetrators of actions that break the law of the land should face criminal prosecution. And so, it has taken it upon itself to see that they do. Victims of psychiatric abuse have little other recourse. Virtually nobody else is willing to stand up for their rights, perhaps because of the societal stigma attached to mental difficulties. More and more, however, they turn to CCHR as the word goes out that Scientologists care.

Thus, in 1991 and 1992, CCHR has been responsible for the prosecution of scores of criminal psychiatrists, psychologists, psychiatric workers and psychiatric facilities. In the first nine months of 1992 thirty-six of these people were put behind bars, a clear sign of increasing activity since the twenty-one who were sentenced in 1991.

While exploitation of women patients is common, CCHR's investigations have revealed that the majority of these cases involve even more distasteful acts against children.

- One of the first cases CCHR investigated was that of Orange County psychiatrist, James Harrison White, who had sexually assaulted a fifteen-year-old boy. White was sentenced in 1990 to six years and eight months in prison. The Senior Deputy District Attorney, Dennis D. Bauer wrote to CCHR:

"I commend you and your staff for the tireless energy and unselfish commitment to solving one of society's neglected and secret problems . . . 'experimental psychiatry.' "

- That same year, another case involved the Children's Farm Home, a residential center for children with behavioral and emotional problems, in Oregon. Three men, William Henry Dufort, psychiatrist and director, another psychiatrist and a case worker, were all charged with sexual assault and/or sodomy of young boys under their care. Dufort was charged with forty-three counts and sentenced to forty-eight years in prison.

- On July 27, 1992, Alan J. Horowitz of Schenectady, New York was sentenced to ten to twenty years in prison for sodomizing a nine-year-old psychiatric patient the previous year. Allegedly, he has assaulted a string of children from California to Israel to New York in the past twenty years.

The problem is widespread. Each year, CCHR investigates scores of crimes such as these and ceaselessly lobbies for stronger laws against psychiatric rapists, in particular to make sexual relations with patients by psychotherapists and/or other mental health practitioners illegal. After many years of CCHR efforts, such a law was passed in California in 1989. By 1992 ten states had these laws and the Church was actively working with other states to enact similar legislation.

Psychiatric Drugs

When LSD was accidentally discovered, it was not put on the shelf, but actively developed by its maker and subsequently heavily promoted by noted psychiatrists and psychologists from the 1950s on. By the mid-60s it started to become a campus fad.

Around the same time, however, as *Freedom* exposed, it was also being given to unknowing US soldiers by their government. The results of these experiments included death, birth defects in offspring and lifelong psychotic reactions for some of the victims.

Due to the work of the Church, which located a number of these unfortunate veterans, the Army conducted a program to locate and notify all who had been tricked into participating in these covert psychiatric mind-control programs.

Psychiatric drugs have long been a CCHR target. Mind-altering, with immensely powerful and dangerous side effects, they have been used extensively by psychiatrists who lack real answers to problems they don't understand. From Valium, which was the psychiatric "wonder drug" of the 60s—until it was found to cause violent rages and to be highly addictive—to today's destructive drugging of more than a million US schoolchildren with Ritalin, psychiatric drugs have done nothing but further destabilize individuals in our society.

Ritalin, a powerful amphetamine-like drug prescribed by psychiatrists for so-called hyperactive children of all ages, has turned essentially normal, healthy children into depressed, listless, and sometimes violent or suicidal addicts. In fact, Ritalin is bought on the street by heroin addicts. Through an educational program directed at parents, to information campaigns aimed at banning the drug, CCHR is enlightening society to its dangers.

The latest wonder drug, Prozac, which is linked with violence, permanent mental instability and death, has been consistently exposed by CCHR. The Food and Drug Administration has received more adverse reaction reports on this drug since it was introduced in 1987 than any drug in history. Yet it is still being prescribed to millions of people around the world. CCHR has conducted a massive public awareness campaign to make the facts known, demanding its removal from the market.

No battle is one-sided, however, and Scientology has been subjected to predictably intense and unrelenting attacks by the enormously wealthy psychiatric drug companies. Small wonder, when one considers that Prozac is the single largest worldwide moneymaker in Eli Lilly & Co.'s arsenal of drugs. Utilizing a malleable media, they have strafed Scientology from every possible angle. Still, as noted, these assaults were predictable and the Church has refused to be intimidated. Principle is a far more substantive and defensible stance than greed.

Psychiatric Fraud

Greed is, of course, what motivates the fraudulent—a category of criminal that has been no stranger to the ranks of psychiatry. According to investigations by CCHR, the mental health system is riddled with them.

In 1992 a hearing before the US House of Representatives Select Committee on Children, Youth and Families heard numerous cases of such abuse provided to the committee by CCHR and others. These incidents ranged from adolescents and children subjected to psychiatric practices they never needed in the first place, to institutions that hired "bounty hunters" to kidnap patients they could hold against their will—all for the insurance money.

Insurance has, in fact, been a major area of psychiatric fraud, particularly among private hospitals. The giant psychiatric hospital chain National Medical Enterprises (NME), and its subsidiary organization, Psychiatric Institutes of America, has, for example, been under investigation in Texas, Florida and New Jersey by officials ranging from attorneys general to state insurance commissioners—investigations helped by information from CCHR. In 1992 ten insurance companies filed suit against NME for defrauding them and trampling on the rights of mental health patients.

But NME is no lone offender. Other organizations, including Community Psychiatric Centers, Charter Medical Corp., and Hospital Corp. of America have also been investigated.

The widespread industry abuses discovered by CCHR and other investigators include: sending patients back into the street as soon as insurance ran out after the thirty days most companies were willing to pay for inpatient care; paying social workers, school counselors, crisis hot-line workers and even ministers to refer patients; abusing children with violent therapy; diagnosing without sufficient detail; and, multiple unnecessary treatments. Preying on the young and/or helpless is a common theme.

Fraud, however, wears as many faces as its participants can dream up schemes. In 1989 CCHR uncovered and exposed documents to show that two psychiatric facilities in Los Angeles that had been paid hundreds of thousands of dollars in government funding, did not even exist—except on paper.

Whether involving fraud, physical and mental abuse, unethical behavior or the poisoning of our children with drugs, CCHR's tireless work against psychiatric wrongdoing has been lauded by law enforcement, politicians, human rights groups and those victims who had been unable to stand alone against these brutal practices.

In 1986 the United Nations recognized CCHR's work in a report stating, "The main task of CCHR has been to achieve reform in the field of mental health and the preservation of the rights of individuals under the Universal Declaration of Human Rights.

"CCHR has been responsible for many great reforms. At least thirty bills throughout the world, which would otherwise have inhibited even more the rights of

*Some of the many issues of **Freedom** magazine published and distributed by the Church to educate the public on important social issues*

ETHIQUE & LIBERTÉ
FREEDOM
AG and Crown Office Not Above the Law
PARENTS CLAIM PSYCHIATRIST DESTROYED SON'S LIFE
Psychiatric Victims Expose Horrors of Deep Sleep "Therapy"
New Documents Confirm CIA Links to "Deep Sleep" Psychs
PSYCHIATRIC DRUG RUINS CHILDREN FOR LIFE
Chelmsford Investigations Continue:
"Deep Sleep" – The International Links
Chelmsford: The Nightmare Continues
INTERPOL
The Drug Scandal
MOTHER CHARGES:
National Inquiry Demanded
GETTING TOUGH ON TOXIC WASTE
JIM BREWER
IRS Workers Lied to By Senior IRS Officials
IN THE FOOTSTEPS OF THE GREATEST
Subverting Religious Freedom
THE ULTIMATE COVER-UP
13-Year-Old Ritalin Pusher:
'We Accuse!'
Ritalin in the Streets
Xanax: A Psychiatric Chemical Nightmare
Taxpayers' Bill of Rights
The Greenspanning of America
Speaking Out Against IRS ABUSES
Pilots on Speed
KIDS ON RITALIN
Holier Than Thou
Rescuing the U.S. Economy
A National Sales Tax
Exposing IRS Crimes
Racism Rampant In IRS
PROZAC CRASH!
Investors Abandon Killer Drug

mental patients, or would have given psychiatry the power to commit minority groups and individuals against their will, have been defeated by CCHR actions."

Psychiatry too has recognized CCHR's work, although not necessarily with such admiration. In fact, with CCHR's revelations in South Africa, Australia, the United States, Germany, Canada, Italy, France, Switzerland and other countries, psychiatry had no choice but to realize that in Scientology it faced its worst enemy.

How to Start a CCHR

Forming a CCHR does not demand prior expertise or research. The primary prerequisite is a willingness and desire to do something to eliminate psychiatric abuse and restore human rights. Anyone wishing to start a CCHR chapter should merely contact their nearest CCHR office.

CCHR members have already compiled the successful actions needed to set up a local chapter, how to document abuses, what to look for when touring a psychiatric institution and numerous other helpful pointers. These are included in the information packets needed to start a CCHR chapter.

NATIONAL COMMISSION ON LAW ENFORCEMENT AND SOCIAL JUSTICE

Information is one of the most valuable commodities in this technological age. From the exchange of demographics to the sale of names for mailing lists, there are a thousand seemingly innocuous business activities that deal in information. But there is a more sinister aspect to consider. For instance, false and inaccurate reports in computer data banks have been known to ruin innocent lives. The man who has an incorrect credit report entered and can suddenly no longer get credit; the law-abiding citizen who has the same name as a criminal and unexpectedly finds himself under arrest; these situations are not that uncommon. And even more dangerous are files that have the authority of national governments behind them.

The problem of false reports in government agency files has, for many years, been of primary concern to the Church of Scientology, and in 1974 it formed the National Commission on Law Enforcement and Social Justice (NCLE) to reform the entire system of secret government dossiers.

The Church found that the basic rights and freedoms of citizens in all countries could be seriously jeopardized by uncorrected information, particularly in government files. And the potential for harm and abuse was compounded by the fact that many agencies shared their information data bases—an act that knows no international boundaries.

In today's computer age, false information can spread more quickly than germs—and become just as destructive. Data, accurate or not, filed by an authorized agency in one country, can spread throughout the world in the form of secret government dossiers that are simply assumed to be accurate. The potential for abuse is obvious. Government files can, and have, been deliberately poisoned by interested sources.

NCLE's early investigations of the origins of false information in government files—particularly those in foreign countries—led to a murky source about whom little was then known: the International Criminal Police Organization (Interpol). Originally formed to track international criminals, Interpol is a private organization—a fact unknown to the public before NCLE exposed it—and not subject to the direction, review or authority of any government.

__Freedom__ magazine and the Church-sponsored National Commission on Law Enforcement and Social Justice investigated and exposed widespread criminal activities on the part of Interpol, including drug trafficking and money laundering. The Church uncovered and released the photograph above showing the Interpol Secretary General presenting then Panamanian dictator, Manuel Noriega, an award for his "anti-drug activities" in 1987, just before Noriega was indicted as a major international drug trafficker. The results of the Church's research are summarized in the widely distributed publication, "Private Group, Public Menace—Interpol: A Police Organization Involved in Criminal Activities."

Documents obtained by NCLE proved conclusively that Interpol was feeding false reports from law enforcement groups to government agencies in countries around the world. Numerous cases were documented of individuals jailed, harassed and even physically abused by police officials because of these reports.

And investigation into the history and activities of Interpol exposed for the first time that it had a long and close relationship with Nazi Germany. In fact, NCLE revealed in 1974 that the relationship had not completely ended with the Second World War: The president of this private organization between 1968 and 1972 had actually been a Nazi SS officer during the war.

Not surprisingly with such a background, evidence was also uncovered and widely exposed connecting Interpol with drug trafficking and other criminal activities on an international scale.

Government Investigations Confirm Church Findings

In 1976 NCLE researchers testified before the US Senate hearings on Interpol and presented information they had thus far gathered on the agency.

Following on the heels of this report, NCLE helped formulate questions for a US General Accounting Office (GAO) investigation into Interpol's activities. The GAO's report contained the following conclusions which confirmed NCLE's exposés:

- No government or state body monitors the activities of Interpol and there is no control over the distribution of information disseminated through Interpol.
- There were no guidelines from Interpol's headquarters governing exchange of unverified accusations, raw intelligence or other data, potentially regarding innocent citizens.
- Although a private organization, Interpol could carry out police, diplomatic, intelligence, law enforcement and other functions without effective oversight by any US government agency.
- None of the cases inspected by GAO investigators showed that Interpol was engaged in the combating of crime syndicates or major criminals.

A further GAO investigation into Interpol in 1986 recommended that the organization be required to verify the accuracy of reports it receives and disseminates. This and two subsequent investigations in 1990 were initiated by the GAO as a result of new information uncovered by NCLE and the Church's *Freedom* magazine and turned over to congressional offices.

Interpol: Promoting Drugs?

Although Interpol has publicly claimed since 1972 that the "war on drugs" has been its "number one priority" and that it has had the major drug trafficking routes "under investigation," researchers for NCLE and *Freedom* magazine found and exposed evidence that Interpol officials have in fact been involved in drug trafficking themselves:

- In April 1970, two members of the US State Department's Agency for International Development (AID) investigated drug law enforcement in Bolivia and reported that two former Interpol chiefs had been dismissed for corruption and suspected involvement in drug dealing.
- During the 1970s and into the 1980s, Interpol chiefs from the following countries were arrested, charged and convicted of drug trafficking: Mexico, Panama, Peru, Ecuador, Bolivia and Colombia.
- Incredibly, in a 1987 ceremony, Interpol Secretary General Raymond Kendall awarded the organization's highest honor, a bronze medal for "international effectiveness in combating drug trafficking," to former Panamanian dictator Manuel Noriega who, at the time, was under investigation in the United States for drug trafficking and money laundering. Furthermore, information from former high-ranking Panamanian officials had just been made public which implicated Noriega in a multibillion-dollar drug smuggling ring. Noriega was subsequently tried and found guilty in the United States on drug trafficking charges and sentenced to forty years in prison.

Over the years, investigations of Interpol by NCLE and *Freedom* have disclosed more and more criminal activities involving violations of the basic rights of individuals. The results of these investigations have been presented to government officials across the world, and have led to long-needed curtailment of Interpol corruption. These have included the Council of Europe, the European Parliament, the US Congress and federal parliaments and congresses of many other countries.

Material relating to Interpol corruption and its violations of individual rights was so extensive, the Church published a handbook, *Interpol: Private Group, Public Menace,* which clearly exposed the public danger inherent in Interpol.

When the executive director of the US National Association of Chiefs of Police received a copy of *Interpol: Private Group, Public Menace,* he felt the information was so important that he contacted the Church to arrange a mailing to over 15,000 chiefs of police across the country.

In the United States, state governments, now aware of the liability, enacted laws to keep their files out of Interpol hands. Various national police agencies in Europe also no longer trust or use Interpol, and an organization of five European countries (Germany, France, Belgium, the Netherlands and Luxembourg) signed a treaty which prohibits Interpol from accessing their police data bases.

Throughout the world, NCLE is alerting government and law enforcement officials to the abuses and dangers of Interpol. And the reform measures enacted continue to spread, little by little, ensuring greater protection of individual rights for all.

How to Start an NCLE Chapter

If you care about individual rights, privacy and freedom, you can start an NCLE chapter by contacting NCLE's main office in Los Angeles, California.

FREEDOM OF INFORMATION

In 1822 James Madison, fourth president of the United States and a primary creator of the democratic principles which form the American system of government, wrote a letter putting forward a basic proposition concerning democracy:

"A popular government, without popular information, or the means of acquiring it, is but a Prologue to a farce or a Tragedy; or, perhaps, both. Knowledge will forever govern ignorance; and a people who mean to be their own Governors must arm themselves with the power which knowledge gives."

Passed into law in 1966 and greatly strengthened in 1974, the US Freedom of Information Act is a worthy effort by Congress to breathe life into Madison's words.

Under this act, a citizen can request access to any records of the executive branch of the federal government. The act provides that those records *must* be released to the requester unless they are shielded from disclosure by some provision of the Freedom of Information Act itself, or by some other federal law.

As Madison implied, a knowledgeable and informed citizenry is able to make intelligent decisions regarding its own future. And the Freedom of Information Act is one of the most valuable tools allowing people to learn exactly what their government is doing—and if government agencies have files about them. When one considers that Martin Luther King, Jr., was the subject of tens of thousands of government documents peppered throughout FBI and IRS files, one can see why this is sometimes worth knowing. However, King had no access to a workable Freedom of Information Act at that time.

The concept of freedom of information has not been without opposition. More than a few government agencies have waged pitched court battles to preserve their secrecy.

To help counter these and other attempts to circumvent the law, the Church of Scientology submitted an open letter to Congress on July 4, 1981, signed by 146 organizations opposing an effort at that time to limit the effectiveness of the act.

Widely recognized among public interest groups as a leading expert on freedom of information legislation, the Church of Scientology has also earned a substantial reputation for its role in informing US citizens of their rights under the Freedom of Information Act. Nor have Scientologists limited their energies in these matters to the United States. When freedom of information legislation was passed in France (1978), Canada (1982), Australia (1982), New Zealand (1983), Italy (1991) and Belgium (1991), members of the Church played a decisive role to bring these laws about.

In 1991 Scientologists also assisted passage of a new law in France providing individuals greater access to the files of *Renseignements Généraux* (General Information), the French intelligence police, known as the "RG."

In 1992 an international conference on freedom of information, organized by a Scientologist, was held in Hungary with speakers from the United States, Canada, Sweden, Portugal, Scotland and Germany, and delegates from Czechoslovakia, Yugoslavia, Romania, Albania, Bulgaria, the Ukraine, Latvia and Poland. This three-day international meeting, attended by 120 people and cosponsored by the Hungarian Ministry of the Interior and Ministry of Justice, under the auspices of the Council of Europe, brought a vital message on the subject for all those emerging from former political repression.

Broad public education concerning freedom of information is essential if people are to understand their rights. In the mid-1970s the Church of Scientology published the first of its informative booklets on freedom of information—a layman's guide for filing requests and overcoming arbitrary refusals to provide valid information.

A revised and updated edition was published in 1989 and distributed as a public service to more than 60,000 individuals and groups. Entitled *How to Use the Freedom of Information Act: Holding the Government Accountable for Its Actions,* the revised handbook received countless accolades by letter and in the media.

Fighting for Freedom of Information

Ever willing to fight unwarranted government secrecy in the courts, the Church of Scientology's litigation with various US government agencies has established legal precedents further empowering the citizen with his right to monitor his government.

In May 1991, for example, a federal court in the United States credited the Church, in a case it brought against the Internal Revenue Service, for helping bring about significant reform. "Furthermore," the court stated, "communications between the IRS and the Church indicate that this litigation contributed to the IRS' decision to review its procedures and that resulting improvements in these procedures will enable better handling of over 1,000 cases involving identical legal issues."

In another precedent-setting case that will be of value to everyone, because it sets a standard to be obeyed by government in the future, the US Court of Appeals for the District of Columbia ruled that the National Security Agency could not simply assert that it was unable to locate records in response to a Church FOIA request. The court ordered the agency to conduct new searches, stating, in part, "If the agency can lightly avoid its responsibilities by laxity in identification or retrieval of desired materials, the majestic goals of the act will soon pass beyond reach."

In yet another case, a federal judge in Los Angeles granted *Freedom* magazine's motion to require the IRS to produce a detailed and specific index of records being withheld by the agency, rather than merely listing them out by general category.

And with each success through and for the Freedom of Information Act comes not just another victory for Scientology, but a victory for all those who might one day suffer from government secrecy.

It was in acknowledgment of such unprecedented efforts that noted author and expert on US intelligence matters, Victor Marchetti, declared:

"I would like to commend the Church of Scientology for its faith in itself and its determination to work within the constitutional democratic system of our nation. It has fought the good fight against great odds openly and legally . . . and it has survived . . . which is more of a tribute to its membership than it is to our own government. By its tenacity and determination, the Church of Scientology has forced that government to adhere to the Constitution . . . something that will benefit all Americans in the long run."

This handbook, printed and distributed by the Church to hundreds of thousands of citizens, has made individual rights known and has provided individuals with simple directions for using the Freedom of Information Act and informed them of their rights under this law.

RELIGIOUS FREEDOM

According to the Creed of the Church of Scientology, Scientologists believe that all men have inalienable rights to their own religious practices and their performance, and that no agency less than God has the power to suspend or set aside these rights.

However, like all of man's treasured freedoms, freedom of religion is maintained only through vigilance and refusal to succumb to those who seek to enslave and suppress.

Over the years, the Church of Scientology has been a leader in championing the cause of religious freedom for all. It strongly believes that as the United States was founded on this principle, separation of church and state forms an essential base for all other freedoms. And that continuous attempts by government to encroach upon this right must be strenuously fought, for this is the sign of an oppressive government.

During the 1970s one of the methods used by vested interests to undermine religious freedom in the United States was a broad-scale propaganda and lobbying campaign directed at both state and federal legislatures. Efforts were made to introduce bills which would have legalized the activities of antireligious hate groups, restricted the legitimate dissemination activities of churches and given state agencies the green light to take control of day-to-day church operations.

Through the dedicated work of Scientologists and friends in other religious groups, antireligious legislation of this type met defeat in Alabama, California, Connecticut, Delaware, Florida, Illinois, Kansas, Massachusetts, Michigan, Minnesota, New Jersey, New York, Nevada, North Carolina, Ohio, Oregon, Pennsylvania and Texas.

Milestone Victories

A landmark California case, which began in 1979 as an attempt to subjugate religion under a psychiatric yoke, ended with passage of a law that protects churches from punitive damage claims by antireligious interests.

The case, involving a frivolous lawsuit filed against a Christian church over the suicide of a parishioner, progressed through a series of rulings and appeals in California state courts over a period of ten years. The Church of Scientology worked with more than 1,500 religious organizations in opposing the suit and making its ramifications known to other religions and the public.

In the eventual 1989 decision, the US Supreme Court endorsed a California Supreme Court decision which held that the state's laws forbid the filing of such cases against churches. The right to free practice of religion was upheld, and this attempt to position psychiatrists as overseers of religion was dismissed.

In another milestone victory, the Church of Scientology mustered interfaith support for a bill prohibiting claims for punitive or exemplary damages against religions, with strictly defined exceptions.

Many religious groups joined the Church in support of the bill, including the California Catholic Conference, the California Council of Churches, the Church of Jesus Christ of Latter-day Saints and the National Congress for Religious Liberty.

Two years of concerted efforts culminated on September 27, 1988, when California Senate Bill No. 1 was signed into law by the California governor.

Establishing an Important Precedent

Churches have traditionally been guardians of freedom, protecting citizens against government attempts to dilute or eradicate their rights, and therefore they have often come under attack. To help protect churches from unwarranted government intrusion the 1984 Church Audits Procedures Act was passed by Congress "to give churches a special audit procedure to require the IRS to take greater care in the examination of churches."

This law is a step intended to help close the door on IRS intimidation and attempts to silence religions and subvert their role in society.

The Church of Scientology has blocked efforts by the Internal Revenue Service (IRS) to undermine this act, and in the course of doing so has preserved the rights of all religions in the United States.

The Church of Scientology has long been a vocal critic of government abuses, and some IRS officials saw the law as an obstacle to their habitual circumvention of constitutional safeguards. The IRS commissioner from 1981 to 1986 called the law's regulations "little more than a series of mechanistic tests and hoops for the Service to jump through."

The Church of Scientology established the first major court precedent strengthening the Church Audit Procedures Act in 1990 when the US District Court in Boston ruled against the IRS' request to rummage through 200,000 pages of church documents.

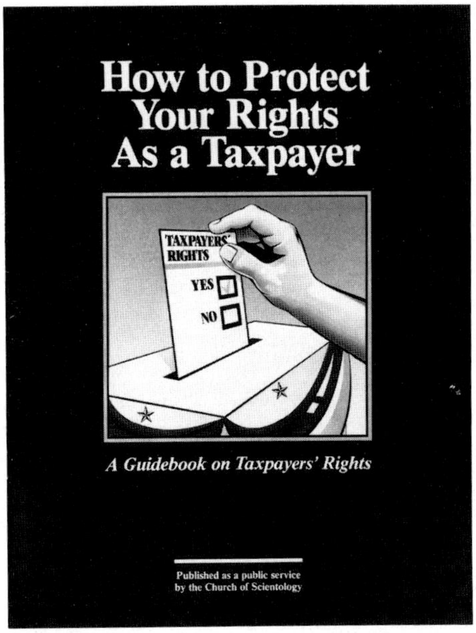

How to Protect
Your Rights
As a Taxpayer
TAXPAYERS' RIGHTS
YES
NO
A Guidebook on Taxpayers' Rights
Published as a public service
by the Church of Scientology

Another publication provided by the Church as a public service to all citizens

This Church of Scientology case was observed widely by many religious leaders as the first major test of the law—with an outcome that would be significant for all churches in the United States.

After the Church's courtroom triumph, the *Legal Times* reported, "Other church groups are hailing the decision as a victory for religious freedom, and warn that the IRS had better think twice before sticking its nose in religious organizations' business again."

Establishing Religious Freedom Week

With the groundswell of public support for religious freedom generated by Church of Scientology initiatives, leaders of other mainstream religions joined in petitioning the US Congress to enact an annual national Religious Freedom Week.

The original Religious Freedom Week resolution was signed into law by the president of the United States on September 20, 1988 and has now become an annual national tradition.

The Religious Freedom Week celebrations, in which churches of nearly every faith participate, have brought about a renewed awareness throughout the country of the importance of defending the right for all citizens to practice their faith according to their own conscience.

Crusades for Religious Freedom

Throughout Europe, Religious Freedom Crusades organized by the Church of Scientology have been conducted in response to threats from antireligious influences.

In France, 2,500 Scientologists assembled in Strasbourg to proclaim a "Declaration of Religious Freedom" which was subsequently accepted by the Council of Europe.

In Germany, the Church of Scientology played a key role in establishing the ecumenical "European Council of Religious Movements" whose members represent their respective churches and religions in dealing with issues of religious freedom.

In its battles against attempts to violate or negate religious freedom, the Church of Scientology and its members have maintained a firm stance that religious freedom must be preserved for all faiths.

The work of Scientologists on behalf of religious freedom is nondenominational; it is carried out with the view that liberty of religious belief and practice is the cornerstone of freedom itself, and that when one religion is infringed upon, the rights of all men are endangered.

Keep
Say NO to Psychiatric Drugs!

Psychiatrie tötet !
Psychiatrie ! Hände weg von unseren Kindern !

An Ongoing Crusade Against Injustice

These are just some of the highlights of the Church of Scientology's ongoing work to eradicate injustice, abuse of the weak and betrayals of public trust. It is no easy task; social reform requires constant vigilance and a willingness to confront those ugly facts most of us would like to ignore.

A just and enlightened civilization does not tolerate brutalities toward the helpless among its citizens. Nor does a true civilization allow monolithic governments to subvert the rights of its most honest and productive people. It is often said that power corrupts. And so it has been in many civilizations that have come and gone in ages past. When citizens feel they can no longer do something about injustice, they have taken a giant step toward abdicating their rights to freedom.

Scientologists have the courage and determination to do something about it. They have, indeed, drawn the line, not just for themselves, but for all men of goodwill. While some of the dreadful things that happen in this world may seem far distant from the life you live, you should know this: that what Scientologists are doing, they are doing for you. And in doing so, they are bringing all mankind closer to a higher and better civilization.

Scientologists care enough to speak out against the injustice, brutality and abuse found in our society.

PART SIX

THE ASSOCIATION FOR BETTER LIVING AND EDUCATION (ABLE)

It is impossible to ignore the signs of decay in modern society—drug abuse, criminality, failing education and moral decline. They are issues discussed at every political convention, in every civic group and nearly every home. They are also issues of pressing concern to Scientologists, for they, too, must live in this world—thus, the formation of ABLE, the Association for Better Living and Education.

Coordinating the efforts of Scientologists to eradicate these problems through the use of L. Ron Hubbard's technology, ABLE has proven itself to be the most successful organization of its kind in the world. This chapter describes the various activities of ABLE and how it is making a difference.

CHAPTER 25

ABLE: SOLUTIONS TO A TROUBLED SOCIETY

Since its earliest days, the Church of Scientology has been concerned about the decline in society at large, well knowing that Mr. Hubbard's technology had wide applications that would be of inestimable benefit beyond the religious arena. Beginning in the 1960s, Scientologists became involved in a number of social betterment activities to reverse this decline.

As the aims of Scientology seek evolution to higher states of being for both the individual and society, these activities have grown increasingly important to the Church and, in 1988, it formed the Association for Better Living and Education (ABLE) to support, promote and expand the social betterment organizations that use Mr. Hubbard's technologies in society.

Today, under the umbrella of ABLE, thousands of Scientologists and non-Scientologists alike are extensively involved in many community groups and programs which apply the discoveries and technology of L. Ron Hubbard toward the resolution of society's most devastating problems: rampant drug and alcohol abuse, widespread illiteracy, escalating crime and the dramatic decline in personal integrity, ethics and moral values.

Located in Los Angeles in the Hollywood Guaranty Building, ABLE's activities are supported at the Church's highest ecclesiastical levels. There is also substantial direct financial sponsorship by the Church and donations by its members, all of which amount to many millions of dollars a year to help these programs carry out their activities.

The function of ABLE is to assist social betterment groups to accomplish their purposes through advisory and fund-raising services, as well as to carry out promotional and public relations campaigns. These campaigns address individuals and groups (such as corporations, clubs, institutions, departments of local and national governments, etc.) to inform them that the solutions to the problems of today's society can be found in ABLE's social betterment groups.

To assist these groups, ABLE has offices around the world covering all continents, and regional offices where they are needed. In addition to providing books and materials, ABLE also sends administrative and technical experts to outer areas to help resolve any difficulties they might be having and ensure that Mr. Hubbard's technology is being correctly applied so that the full results are attained.

ABLE supports groups which apply the technology of L. Ron Hubbard to handle four of the most severe blights in society:

Drug and alcohol abuse: Narconon International, which oversees a global network of drug rehabilitation and drug education centers, is dedicated to restoring drug-free lives to drug-dependent people, and also delivers educational programs to help people avoid the trap of drugs.

The offices of Association for Better Living and Education in Los Angeles

Crime: Criminon International is aimed at restoring a sense of responsibility to criminals so they can become productive members of society and at bringing about reform so that prisons actually rehabilitate.

Education: Applied Scholastics International assists students, parents, teachers, educational organizations and businesses around the world to eradicate illiteracy with Mr. Hubbard's study technology.

Morals: The Way to Happiness Foundation is creating a groundswell of international support for moral reform utilizing Mr. Hubbard's nonreligious moral code, *The Way to Happiness.*

These organizations have succeeded in salvaging many lives through the application of L. Ron Hubbard's technology. Each has made vital contributions to improving life in a troubled world.

ABLE exists to bring about genuine betterment of conditions on a planetwide scale, a goal shared by all Scientologists. ABLE and its programs are supported by thousands of Scientologists around the world, volunteering their time and providing donations. Neither the Church nor its parishioners receive monetary remuneration for this charitable activity. Those involved, however, are rewarded with a great deal of personal satisfaction.

The staff of ABLE and the groups they support are applying L. Ron Hubbard's technology to bring sanity to a troubled and dying society. They are on the front lines, creating a new civilization here on Earth, one in which drugs, illiteracy and crime are things of the past. And, fortunately for the future well-being of mankind, their activities continue to grow.

NARCONON:

DRUG REHABILITATION

Narconon (meaning *no drugs*) began in 1966 through the efforts of Arizona State Prison inmate William Benitez. A hard-core addict from the age of thirteen, then serving his fourth prison term, Benitez had unsuccessfully tried numerous ways to kick his drug habit.

In Mr. Benitez's words:

"My failure to come off drugs wasn't due to not wanting to. Believe me, I really tried. I read and read . . . Freud, Jung, Menninger—and studied one philosophy after another, everything I could get my hands on to find out about myself. I underwent psychiatric aid and participated in all sorts of programs and as time went on, I knew less about myself instead of more. The only thing that kept me from putting a gun to my head was that I knew someday I would make it. I felt so sorry for my friends who were constantly trying to get off drugs. I wanted to help them and yet I couldn't even help myself. . . . I was so tired of the life of addiction, thieving, prostitution and all that goes with it. On my fourth and last trip to Arizona State Penitentiary, I was tried as a habitual criminal which sentence carried a mandatory fifteen years to life, of which I received fifteen to sixteen years. It was at this point that I began to go into agreement with the idea that once you were an addict, you remained an addict."

His search for solutions led him to L. Ron Hubbard's *Scientology: The Fundamentals of Thought,* and with the principles in this book, he was at last able to kick his addiction.

As Mr. Benitez continued his studies, he soon realized that L. Ron Hubbard's mental and spiritual discoveries offered the first real hope for addicts, and began applying that material to help other inmates.

"When first applied to a pilot group at Arizona State Penitentiary in 1966," Mr. Benitez reported, "it consisted only of the basic communication exercises. Yet, seven out of ten of the first group in their own words, 'made it.' Their success spread at grass-roots level to other prisons, and drawing on further research by L. Ron Hubbard, the program was expanded."

An initial group of ten grew to one hundred inmates within the first year. And, although originally organized to help heroin addicts, Narconon's usefulness and workability led to enormous interest from the general prison population. In 1967 prison officials granted permission for any inmate to join the group, and thereafter Narconon was opened to all who wished to improve their lives.

Mr. Benitez wrote to L. Ron Hubbard, who encouraged him to expand the program. The church of Scientology in Phoenix also assisted by donating materials, and the most effective drug rehabilitation program in the world had been born.

By 1970, Mr. Benitez had been released from prison and traveled to Los Angeles to assist in opening the national office of Narconon. This bureau became known as Narconon US, and commenced a program of expansion throughout the United States.

Initial Narconon programs in California institutions such as California's Rehabilitation Center in Norco, the California Men's Colony in San Luis Obispo and the Youth Training School in Ontario were well received and highly successful.

An official evaluation of the ten-month program at the Youth Training School showed that disciplinary offenses among the control group increased 10 percent during the second five-month period, while those of the Narconon group decreased by 81 percent. The grade average of the control group increased from C to C+, while that of the Narconon group increased from C– to B–.

Narconon successes continued to mount. In May 1972, a program was started at the Ventura School for Boys and Girls in Ventura, California. After considerable expansion it later received funding from the California Youth Authority.

That same year, Narconon opened its first residential programs, making it possible to take an addict through the Narconon withdrawal program and other Narconon courses. This expansion was an important step for Narconon as it brought all stages of rehabilitation into the safety of a residential environment.

The Narconon Program: Producing New Lives Without Drugs

The need for effective drug rehabilitation technology is today greater than ever before, for the scope of the problem is vast. Internationally, the illegal narcotics industry has estimated annual revenues of between $500 billion and $1 trillion.

This astonishing statistic is only one indicator of the many social repercussions of drug abuse. Criminals on drugs, for example, are responsible for the vast majority of all crimes committed. According to US Justice Department studies, three out of four suspects arrested for crimes of violence test positive for illegal drugs.

To meet this crucial need for effective drug rehabilitation, Narconon has expanded greatly in the years since its founding. As the program moved into other countries, Narconon International was formed to direct the drug education and rehabilitation activities of Narconon and provide assistance and support to Narconon centers and their staffs throughout the world. Narconon International has a goal to achieve a drug-free Earth. It provides effective and complete drug rehabilitation for those enslaved by drugs and works to prevent our future generations from ever becoming addicted. Located in Los Angeles, Narconon International today supervises worldwide drug education and drug rehabilitation programs.

Narconon centers are located throughout the world, with more opening every year. Currently, Narconons operate in Canada, Denmark, France, Germany, Italy, the Netherlands, Spain, Sweden, Switzerland, the United Kingdom and the United States. Today there are 34 Narconon organizations in 11 countries, and more than 25,000 people had availed themselves of Narconon services by 1992.

Narconon also operates the largest training and rehabilitation facility of its kind in the world, the Narconon Chilocco New Life Center near Newkirk, Oklahoma. Set on 167 acres of lush Great Plains landscape, it was formerly the site of the Chilocco Indian Agricultural School, and was developed with the agreement of leaders from five Native American tribes.

This peaceful campus brings a new life to many in need of rehabilitation with the highest quality and most effective drug rehabilitation program available in the world. It is also here that Narconon personnel come from many countries for training to administer this Narconon program to others. Narconon Chilocco is the international training center, turning out highly qualified and competent staff trained in L. Ron Hubbard's technology so that it can be delivered in all nations. These dedicated Narconon staff return to their cities and countries to bring a new life to drug and alcohol abusers there.

Narconon's efficacy comes entirely from the technology developed by L. Ron Hubbard who, years before the drug crisis became headline news internationally, had extensively researched the antisocial side effects of drugs.

He discovered the insidious effects not only of illegal or "street" drugs but also of alcohol and psychiatric drugs—the latter often far more devastating and injurious than the original condition they were intended to "cure."

Narconon utilizes a completely *drug-free* rehabilitation program to restore life to drug and alcohol abusers and give them back control of their lives.

Compared to other programs in the drug rehabilitation field Narconon's results are exceptional. While most programs have a 15 percent success rate, two independent studies of Narconon showed that 84.6 percent of graduates from a 1981 Swedish program no longer used drugs, and in Spain, a 1985 study found 78.37 percent were still drug free a year later.

In a field loaded with drug programs that substitute addictions with yet more drugs, L. Ron Hubbard developed exact techniques to deal with the physical *and* mental damage brought about by substance abuse. None of these techniques involve the use of methadone or any other substitute drug.

The Narconon program today consists of a series of exercises, drills and study steps done in a precise sequence. The techniques and learning programs help the individual withdraw from current drug use; get into communication with others and the environment; remove the residual drugs from his body; gain control of himself and his environment and reach the point where he can take responsibility, not only for himself, but also for others. The Narconon program consists of the following:

1. Drug-Free Withdrawal—The first step of the Narconon program helps the individual cease current drug use rapidly and with minimal discomfort through proper nutrition, vitamins and care from experienced Narconon staff. Various assists help the person come off the drugs with minimal discomfort.

2. Therapeutic TR Course—Once withdrawal is complete, a series of communication drills (called training routines, or "TRs") are used to extrovert the person and get him in touch with others and with the environment. Each TR increases the person's ability to face life and communicate with others.

3. The Narconon New Life Detoxification Procedure—Next, the person cleanses his body of drug residues and other toxic substances through a regimen of exercise, sauna and nutritional supplements as described in the book *Clear Body, Clear Mind: The Effective Purification Program* by L. Ron Hubbard. Drug residues remain locked in the fatty tissues of the body and can be released into the bloodstream years after the person has stopped taking drugs, thus rekindling old cravings for drugs. This step purges the body of these residues and other toxins.

4. The Learning Improvement Course—Here, the student gains the ability to study and retain knowledge, along with the ability to recognize and overcome the barriers to study. He can now proceed with further educational steps to prepare him to lead a productive and ethical life.

5. The Communication and Perception Course—On this step, the student repeats the TRs, plus additional exercises which get him into full communication with others and his environment. The exercises pull the person's attention off himself, where it has been fixed by drugs, and out to the world around him. The student also helps another student do the exercises, which not only gives him increased responsibility, but a tremendous sense of pride and satisfaction because of this newly gained ability to help others.

6. The Ups and Downs in Life Course—Now the student gains the knowledge to spot and handle those influences in his environment that would cause him to lose any gains he has made. He learns the characteristics of the antisocial personality and the social personality so he can recognize the two, spot the differences between them and better choose his friends and associates. Completing this course makes a person less susceptible to those who would influence a reversion to drugs.

The Narconon program consists of a series of exercises, drills and study steps done in a precise sequence. The study materials and workbooks shown here guide the individual through the program.

7. The Personal Values and Integrity Course—The student gains the data he needs to improve his survival potential. The course teaches the student about the eight dynamics, ethics, honesty and integrity, showing him how to correct contra-survival behavior by ridding himself of the effects of past harmful deeds.

8. The Narconon Changing Conditions in Life Course—This course covers the ethics technology of L. Ron Hubbard and shows the student exactly how to apply it to improve conditions in his life, something the student needs if he is to reassert his self-determinism.

9. The Narconon "The Way to Happiness" Course—Based on a nonsectarian moral code called *The Way to Happiness,* this course gives the student a guide to living a life where real happiness is attainable.

This comprehensive program addresses and handles the reason why the individual started using drugs in the first place and arms him with the knowledge and certainty he needs to lead a happy, drug-free life. Vocational training programs are also available to develop needed job skills so graduates can better support themselves.

Narconon programs are delivered by dedicated individuals who choose to work with Narconon because it has proven itself in the drug rehabilitation field. In some cases these staff are Scientologists. In many other cases, they are those who have progressed themselves from addict to ex-addict to contributing Narconon staff member.

Effective Drug Education Lectures

Prevention is also an important part of the Narconon program.

The international spokesperson for Narconon is actress Kirstie Alley. She tirelessly promotes the benefits of a drug-free life attainable through Narconon, with numerous radio and television interviews and public appearances at fund-raising events.

Other Narconon spokespersons delivered nearly ten thousand lectures on drug abuse to approximately three-quarters of a million students in the 1980s and early 1990s.

These "Truth About Drugs" lectures result in a dramatic change in attitude toward drugs. A 1989 study by the Foundation for Advancements in Science and Education measured the attitude change of students from the second grade to twelfth grade in high school and concluded:

"Narconon's drug education program is effective in teaching students about the adverse consequences of drug abuse and has a very positive influence on the attitudes of students toward drugs. The most dramatic effect on attitude [was] observed in the borderline group of students—those indicating that they might use drugs in the future."

Of the students in this category, 86 percent indicated that they were less likely to use drugs following the presentation.

Film and television actress, Kirstie Alley, is Narconon's international spokesperson.

Scientologists Support Narconon

While talk of drug and alcohol abuse is endless, solutions do not come as easily. Nearly 80 percent of the American public, for instance, believe that drug abuse is a concern that the US government must deal with immediately, yet 70 percent feel their government's "war on drugs" is ineffective.

Scientologists strongly believe that both drug education and real rehabilitation are vital. Based on results, Mr. Hubbard's technology provides the most effective solutions to drug and alcohol abuse.

In nearly three decades of service in the war against drugs, Narconon has shown itself to be the most effective rehabilitation program there is. It is something that the peoples of Earth urgently need.

Thus, Scientologists support Narconon. Many contribute time and energy to help Narconon staff, serving as part-time volunteers in Narconon's community and prison programs.

Administrative staff in Narconon's worldwide network help acquire donations for new premises or materials, and assist to recruit staff for these programs. Scientology churches, through ABLE, have donated millions of dollars, as well as materials, furniture and supplies to Narconon programs. And individual Scientologists have also enthusiastically contributed financially to support Narconon.

This combination of dedicated staff and L. Ron Hubbard's technology has served Narconon for over twenty-five years as the acknowledged pacesetter in the field of drug and alcohol prevention, education and rehabilitation.

Expansion Because of One Reason: Results

From the simple beginnings and single L. Ron Hubbard book, to the full lineup of today's Narconon program, the fact of workability lies at the core of Narconon's success. Professionals in the field of drug rehabilitation from many countries have attested to Narconon's results.

For instance, one leading researcher in the field of public health, well known for his work with professional football players in America, Dr. Forest Tennant, remarked on the excellence of the Narconon program:

"Narconon has emerged during the past decade as one of the premier residential treatment centers for persons who have severe drug dependence. I have referred patients to Narconon centers in recent years and I have seen the tremendous results."

He further stated, "Of particular note is that, although the use of vitamins, minerals and amino acids is now standard treatment, I thought it was false in 1974 when I first heard of Narconon's belief in the use of megavitamins. Further, Narconon was also one of the first to reveal that drugs are retained in the body, a belief which I also believed false in 1974 when I first heard it. There is now unquestionable scientific evidence that, when drugs such as marijuana, cocaine, PCP or methamphetamines are taken, the drugs do go into body fat and remain for weeks or months. Accordingly, it is entirely possible that Narconon was simply twenty years ahead of its time. . . ."

Kent McGregor, a nationally respected American drug abuse consultant whose career in drug prevention began with then-president Richard Nixon's "war on drugs," said this about Narconon:

"I have been to some of the high-powered programs in the nation and I can say, unequivocally, that what you are doing here is better than anything I have seen anywhere else. Even to the point that if [my sons] . . . had a drug problem, I would bring them here. And that's over the other programs I talked about."

Narconon is accredited by the prestigious Commission for Accreditation of Rehabilitation Facilities (CARF), widely recognized as the foremost authority on drug rehabilitation programs in the United States. CARF's standards are the highest in the nation and have been adopted by many states and federal agencies as the benchmark for all rehabilitation programs to measure up to.

Narconon is also recognized by numerous governments as a safe and highly effective program.

In Sweden, Denmark, Italy, the Netherlands and Switzerland, governments provide funding for Narconon's drug education efforts and support delivery of the drug rehabilitation program.

The Parliamentary Assembly of the Council of Europe recognized the success of L. Ron Hubbard's drug rehabilitation technology and Narconon in a resolution passed in January 1988.

More and more, judges and government agencies today refer drug addicts to Narconon for rehabilitation, rather than to jail or prison. Such an option is given by courts in Denmark, Germany, Italy, the Netherlands, Spain, Sweden and the United States.

Two decades of success prove that the Narconon program gets *real* results, far better than any other drug rehabilitation program in the world. Narconon has documented many, many cases of successful release from drugs and resultant drug-free lives.

A parole agent from the California Department of Youth Authority commented on the effectiveness of Narconon:

"I am very impressed by some of the gains I have seen in wards placed in Narconon. One of the most dramatic changes I ever noted was produced in a ward who had failed to show improvement in other local drug treatment programs. At Narconon he made rapid and outstanding improvement. The improvement was due to the Narconon program alone since all other factors remained constant."

Another California Youth Authority representative had this to say about Narconon's approach to drug abuse prevention and rehabilitation:

"As one of our more congenial community resources, Narconon has produced results with some of our wards, where other programs have failed. It is reassuring to have an organization such as Narconon that meets the needs of our parolees and goes a little beyond—they care."

Like many others, a New London, Connecticut attorney who studied the results of Narconon's residential program responded to the Narconon program with great admiration:

"Without equivocation, of all the social agencies with which I have had contact over the past two years, Narconon is the one to which I turn when all other possibilities have vanished. It is staffed with youthful, outgoing, knowledgeable and dedicated men and women who can communicate properly with their 'clients.' Let me offer my highest possible commendation: that this is the number one social agency serving the community in the reduction of crime and drug abuse."

An official with the Canadian Penitentiary Service wrote:

"The Narconon program is the only program I have observed to produce quick and stable results in assisting addicts to give up their dependency on drugs. I have been employed in Corrections since 1964 and have had the opportunity to participate in and observe varied treatment programs for addicts, but this is the first program that I have observed to achieve what it claims to achieve."

A former Los Angeles public health official who witnessed results in the early years of Narconon's residential program said this:

"It is one of the few programs which has enabled drug/alcohol abusers to evolve a rational, humanistic approach to social and personal tensions. Narconon has proven its success inside institutions and on the streets. It is well staffed and well organized; people associated with its programs are dedicated and cooperative. I therefore highly recommend Narconon."

The head of a Russian delegation from the Ministry of the Interior, which seeks solutions to the drug problem in Russia, concluded after his study of several Narconon facilities:

"The only place in the world where I have seen with my own eyes drug addicts fully cured from heroin and cocaine is Narconon. This technology is not only taking the person off the addiction, it also . . . keeps them cured and ethical and in a high moral state.

". . . I see these methods as the future hope for all those unfortunate addicts in Russia and the other republics."

How a Narconon Program Is Started

Anyone interested in pioneering a Narconon program should contact the nearest Narconon center or Narconon International or an ABLE representative who will provide the needed assistance. (See the list of centers and offices in the back of this book.)

The first step to opening a Narconon is recruiting others interested in working in the field of drug rehabilitation. A willing and able staff is the nucleus of any successful Narconon. These individuals are then trained to deliver the program. Staff training facilities exist to make this as easy as possible.

Narconon International helps obtain suitable premises and ensures that all local regulations and requirements are met.

Manuals and other materials are available from Narconon offices to set up and operate one's own Narconon center and to contact and help those in need of Narconon's services.

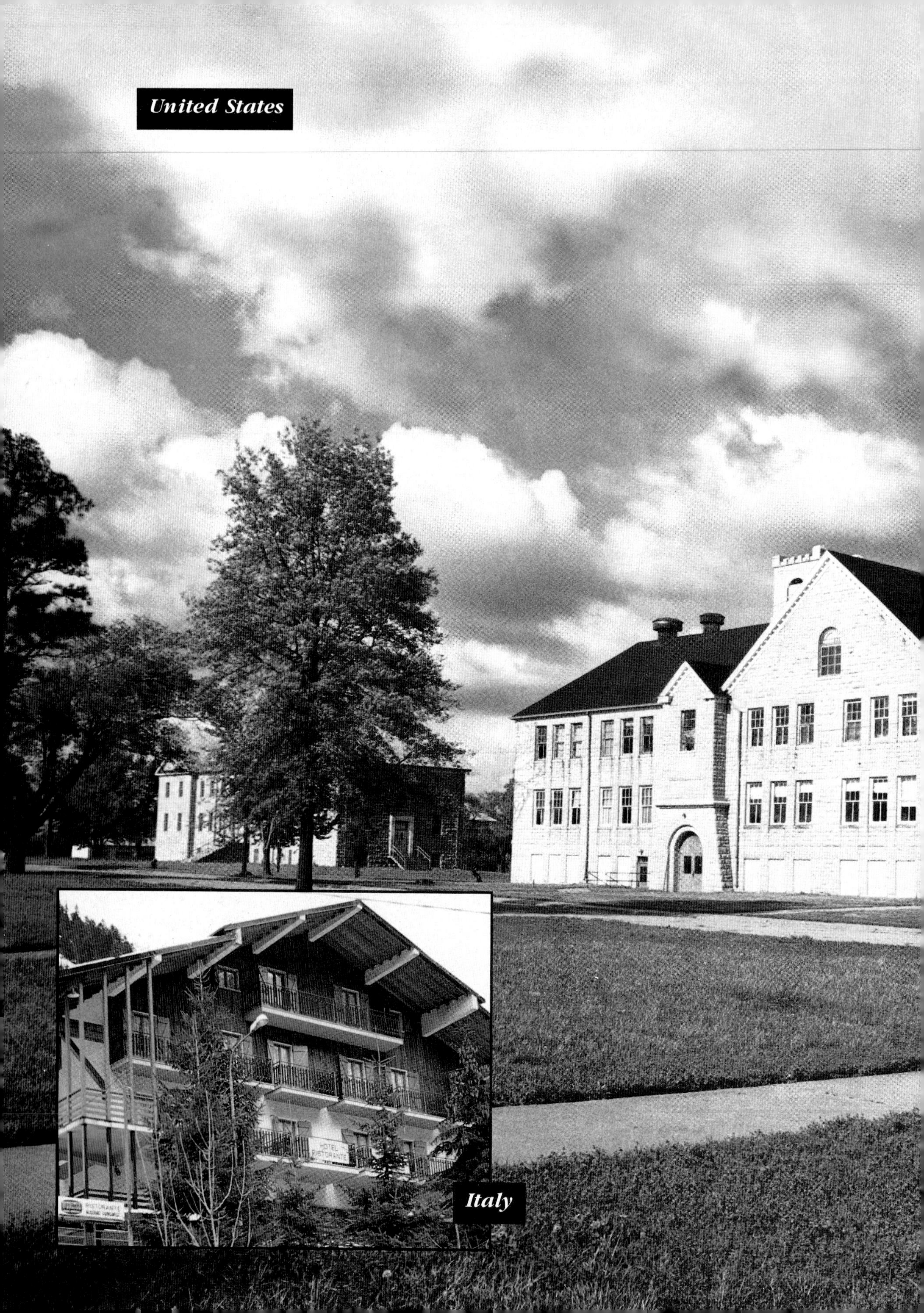

United States

Italy

Spain

Sweden

Switzerland

Narconon centers are located in eleven countries around the world, several of which are pictured here. Narconon's international training facility (center) is in Chilocco, Oklahoma.

Representatives from Narconon International and Narconon's regional offices assist in all aspects of getting the new center set up and running successfully. They place one in contact with referral agencies that lead to people in need of the program, help locate local sources of funding and provide organizational advice and direction.

Donations may be needed for beginning expenses and course materials. In many cases the local community has assisted in donating furnishings, bedding, food and sometimes money to new Narconon programs. The Narconon consultant advises how to go about obtaining donations for these important prerequisites.

The drug problem ranks high among the vital concerns of society. Untold numbers of lives have been ruined. But there is a viable solution, one that restores self-respect and a willingness to be a part of life once more. L. Ron Hubbard's technology, applied throughout the world by Narconon, is the road back. Each time a person is rehabilitated through Narconon, the scourge of drugs disappears a little more from the world. Narconon offers hope that drug abuse will one day be a thing of the past.

SUCCESSES OF NARCONON GRADUATES

The drug problem ranks high among the vital concerns of society. Untold numbers of lives have been ruined. But there is a viable solution, one that restores self-respect and a willingness to be a part of life once more. L. Ron Hubbard's technology, applied throughout the world by Narconon, is the road back. Each time a person is rehabilitated through Narconon, the scourge of drugs disappears a little more from the world. Narconon offers hope that drug abuse will one day be a thing of the past.

I came here already destroyed. I had lost about twenty kilos in the streets. I was gaunt, pale and could not physically move as a result of daily drug abuse. This was occurring physically, but it was not all [of it], as morally I arrived with no hope of anything and full of doubts as to whether or not I would ever want to make it in life Nothing mattered in life.

I had been in two [other rehabilitation] centers, but I got nothing from being in these centers. I started the [Narconon] program and bit by bit I became freer of drugs. I started to regain my lost hopes and desire to live again. But not only that, I am now happy without having to live with drugs—to wake up in the morning with a desire to smile and with the thought that I start a new beautiful day and that the road for better days will continue.

M.B.

I was a drug addict for four years. During this time I used every drug there is. For two years I was very, very heavily addicted to heroin. I almost died from this. Since joining Narconon my whole life has changed. I am now able to communicate much easier with anybody. I have learned to control myself and my environment much better. I now have responsibility (which I couldn't face up to before). I don't need drugs anymore because I am now higher than I have ever been on drugs. I thank you L. Ron Hubbard and everyone helping people with Narconon.

D.K.

The first time I walked in the Narconon office I was desperate. My son had not spent more than a few months out of jail at any given time period for over five years and all of his incarcerations had been directly related to drug and alcohol offenses. Counseling, and even hospitalization, had not helped. You were my last hope. As I read the letters on the wall in the waiting room I remember my eyes stinging with tears. I wondered if I would ever be able to write a letter thanking Narconon for the successful treatment of my son. There were a lot of rocky moments for all of us during the instruction stage; phone calls, home visits, even a few disappointments. When he finished the program I don't think any of us knew for sure what the final outcome would be. That was almost two years ago and with a happy, grateful heart I am writing you and your dedicated, wonderful, committed staff to let you know that the program proved successful. The nightmare of drug and alcohol abuse is finally in the past. My son has become a happy and confident individual, with your assistance. The program established itself to be the best investment we could have ever made. Would I recommend Narconon to anyone? In a heartbeat! May God bless each and every one of you. Keep up the great work.

N.N.

For a while, I thought drugs were fun. But then they almost killed me the way they have so many other musicians. I did the Narconon program and it literally saved my life. I have lived drug free for a number of years now and continue to reach new levels of creativity and satisfaction with life. Now it's life that's fun. I would have hated to have missed it!

N.H.

From this day on I will be all I can be in this world thanks to Narconon. The staff are very brave people here at Narconon. They are good people and without them and their kindness I would never have made it. I feel great today, and I will feel great tomorrow too, because I am a drug-free person.

S.B.

I came here beaten up by the use of drugs. I was at the point where I wanted to die, my attitude and perception of life was all screwed up. I am now a new person. This program has saved my life. I have had so many wins and realizations. I do know that I have the ability, the technology and the courage to lead a drug-free life. I would really encourage others to do this program and get the gains I have got.

D.K.

Narconon saved my life. For years, seventeen to be exact, I battled with drugs and alcohol. This program was the only one that showed me how to stay off drugs and how to live my life honestly, and work toward happiness.

L.V.

Having now completed this program I can say without any reservation whatsoever, I feel I am living proof that there is certainly more to life than three bottles of wine or the equivalent consumption each evening. Without the Narconon program and the compassion of the staff who deliver it, I would not be as alive as I am today and I would certainly not be looking forward to life as I am. So a big, big thank you and my eternal affinity and love for saving my life.

M.B.

I am a fully recovered drug addict. My life was in total ruin before I entered the Narconon program in 1989.

Today I have a happy and productive life. After I completed my program at Narconon, I wanted to give others what was given me. Narconon gave me my life back and I have seen and helped countless others to achieve what I have.

Drugs only bring about insanity and health problems that put us all at risk. L. Ron Hubbard has given us the technology so that we all can be free. I am more than happy to help make this happen.

K.D.

I am a staff member here at Narconon Los Angeles. Working here is the best thing I have ever done. I am a former drug user who was addicted to drugs for twenty years. It wasn't until I came to Narconon that I came to a total understanding of why I did drugs. I not only learned why I did drugs, but I also learned how to confront difficult situations, how to communicate with people and how to control my life. I now can handle situations logically and analytically rather than running for a syringe or a pill.

Working at Narconon I have seen people walk in the door messed up on drugs and alcohol. They're in bad shape mentally and physically.

To see these people turn their lives around and become happy, confident and productive is the most rewarding feeling a person can ever feel. To really help people and see the results of the Narconon program is nothing short of a miracle.

P.J.

CRIMINON:

CRIMINAL REFORM

Each day in the United States, more than 31,000 petty and hard-core criminals are released back into their communities. Within one year, up to 80 percent, or more than 25,000 of these men and women a day, will have committed ten or twenty more crimes before being arrested again and sent back to prison.

The figures speak for themselves. The 80 percent recidivism rate makes a mockery of current psychiatric-oriented rehabilitation methods, demonstrating that, for all intents and purposes, there is in fact no such thing as criminal rehabilitation. A report published recently by the National Council on Crime and Delinquency in America concurred, stating that there was "little evidence that either institutional programs or noninstitutional efforts to rehabilitate offenders make any appreciable difference."

And so go the revolving doors of the US penal system.

L. Ron Hubbard once quite accurately pointed out that although the percentage of criminals is relatively small, the amount of grief and turmoil they create in the world is out of all proportion to their numbers. "Thus," he concluded, "the criminal mind is a subject one cannot avoid in research as it is a major factor in the distortion of a culture."

From the need to remedy this glaringly destructive societal flaw—and through the fruits of L. Ron Hubbard's research—Criminon (which means "without crime") was born in New Zealand in 1970. A branch of Narconon, it is an organization that operates within the penal system to rehabilitate criminals and restore their sense of worth so that they can become productive members of society.

Criminon actually grew out of the very successful Narconon prison programs. By the 1980s, with increased drug usage in all sectors of society, the Narconon program shifted its emphasis to community-based activities. At that point, Criminon expanded into the correctional facilities to fill a need.

Criminon program results have been astoundingly successful. A Butler County, Alabama study among juvenile offenders who were exposed to a part of the program, for instance, showed that only 2 percent of the pilot group were recidivist; of a comparable control group not on the program, the usual 80 percent were recidivist.

Rehabilitating a Sense of Responsibility

Headquartered in Los Angeles, Criminon today runs programs in 203 prisons and penal institutions in 39 states. So far, in the last five years, more than 3,200 inmates have successfully participated in the programs. This success naturally raises basic questions: What makes Criminon different? What does it do? Perhaps the best place to start is with what Criminon does not do:

Criminon does not drug inmates. It does not use punitive restraints. It does not use aimless conversation for lack of a better tool. It is not psychiatry or psychology.

From psychiatry's ineptitude within the penal system—in spite of the immense funding and power bestowed upon it—the uncharitable conclusion could be drawn that rehabilitation is not necessarily what it intends to accomplish. However, the more obvious and arguable point is that it is unable to rehabilitate criminals because it has no knowledge of what makes a criminal. Unproven theories are easy to come by, and psychiatry/psychology has no lack of them. Criminality is blamed on everything from poor environmental conditions, inherited drives, biological imbalances in the brain, to "sluggish nervous systems."

Criminon's success, on the other hand, is due to the fact that in order to devise *workable* rehabilitation methods, Mr. Hubbard extensively researched criminality until he found the actual source of what makes a criminal. And from this point of truth, he was able to develop workable methods.

"Do you know that there is not a criminal anywhere in any prison who is not a criminal because he was degraded and lost his personal pride?" Mr. Hubbard asked in one of his lectures. "I have done a very thorough cross-check of this—what they call 'bad women,' 'criminal men.' Their badness and criminality is immediately traceable to a loss of their powers and personal pride, and after that they were 'bad'; they were 'dangerous.'

"If you want to rehabilitate a criminal, just go back and find out when he did lose his personal pride. Rehabilitate that one point and you don't have a criminal anymore."

By addressing this point of rehabilitation, Scientologists through their support of Criminon are taking effective action to end this repeating cycle of criminality and reform the prison system.

The Program

The key element of the Criminon program is The Way to Happiness Extension Course, based on a booklet of the same name. As the first step toward rehabilitation, this correspondence course is designed to give students knowledge of right and wrong conduct. A nonreligious moral code, *The Way to Happiness* is practical and incisive, and provides fundamental guides to behavior—a vital step, often overlooked in the family life and education of the criminal.

Students do practical exercises on this course and mail them in to Criminon staff and volunteer groups of Scientologists around the country who grade the exercises. They maintain communication with the inmate and encourage him. When the course is completed, Criminon issues a certificate.

Other elements in the Criminon course, some of which are delivered in prisons by staff and volunteers to the inmates, are similar to those used in Narconon drug rehabilitation programs. They include the following:

■ The Learning Improvement Course. As many inmates suffer literacy problems, this course in study skills is invaluable as a tool both during incarceration and upon release. As it provides the ability to learn any subject, it is a fundamental that will help in vocational and other training.

■ The Communication and Perception Course. These communication exercises increase the inmate's ability to face life and not withdraw from it—the very act that exacerbated the criminal condition.

■ The Ups and Downs in Life Course. As recidivism is often due to the return of an inmate to his previous environment, this invaluable course helps him learn the social and antisocial characteristics of his friends and associates. The person is thus less susceptible to bad influences.

■ The Personal Values and Integrity Course. This study of the eight dynamics, ethics and integrity, helps the inmate take responsibility for, and rid himself of, his past misdeeds.

And as with the Narconon program, other courses address subjects such as how to change conditions in life, how to contribute effectively and other basics vital to successful living.

All in all, the Criminon program totally replaces the unworkable rehabilitation methods that only exacerbate crime. It directly and effectively rehabilitates individuals so that criminal behavior becomes a thing of the past and remains that way.

Because of its workability, word of Criminon is spreading rapidly from prison to prison. And of the thousands of prisoners released every day, more and more will be truly rehabilitated. In time, the revolving door will be closed.

PRISONERS SPEAK OF RESULTS

Thousands of letters and testimonials from prisoners describe how Criminon helped them cope with prison life, increased their self-worth and happiness, and began to change their outlook and behavior for the better.

This course has taught me the many changes that life can take and it has polished my ability to deal with those changes. It has taught me the importance of trust and the importance of fulfilling my obligations. I have to be an industrious individual in society. I have a four-year-old son and I am a single parent and it is very important to remember that setting good examples enhances your child's chances of becoming a more successful and industrious member in this society. It has also taught me a little of what my religion teaches me and that is knowledge of self and discipline, which are the main ingredients that 75 percent of this nation lacks.

Q.W.B.
Detroit

I am so thankful to you for The Way to Happiness Course. I had lost all my self-respect and personal pride. I didn't care for myself or anyone else. However, through this course I have gotten all my pride back and my self-respect as well. I didn't think I could ever face my family or the world again. But thanks to The Way to Happiness Course I can hold my head up again. I also know for sure that I will never again commit another crime or come back to prison.

C.P.
Western United States

The Way to Happiness Course has been a large part of my getting back my self-respect. The time I spent working the lessons, and then putting the lessons to work, were a big part of my feeling human again. I believe so strongly in this program that I have told many others about the course and will continue to do so in the future. Thank you Criminon for making these programs available to me and others in my position.

J.C.
El Reno
Correctional Facility
Oklahoma

Before entering this program [Criminon] I didn't know what success was. I didn't even know the tremendous feeling of self-assurance you adopt from this program. I can now honestly say that the works of L. Ron Hubbard are very inspiring. They have taught me the value of hard work and self-awareness. Others around me have noticed the change in my whole being. My attitude, my patience, my ability to deal with hostile situations with calm assurances, this is something I never had or was able to do. But with what I have learned on this program I have attained those characteristics and more.

I feel in control of my life, and although I am presently a guest of the state (prisoner) in a correction facility, I never felt more free in my life!!

I know when I am released I can truly be happy and prosper in society because I no longer have a destructive nature. Rather I have come to learn of a productive and positive way to go about life thus making my survival and those around me safe with room to grow.

T.W.
Delaware State Prison

We are very grateful and appreciative of the books and tapes that you [Library Donation Service] donated. Your books were very beautiful and from the moment we received them they became very much in demand because they relate to us as people in a way we never have seen before. There is great truth in this philosophy you gave us, and we are very much in your debt.

The tape lectures of Mr. Hubbard's have changed the lives of a lot of people here. We started a night class and over fifty inmates have attended. Some of the men said that if they heard this tape before they got in trouble with the law, they would have never wound up in jail.

How can we make it available to more people? This stuff really can prevent crime.

S.P.
Federal Correctional Institution
Florida, USA

For many years I seemed to be living in a very dark room. When I completed the [Criminon] course it was like someone had switched the light on in this dark room and I beheld some pretty good things in there. I saw kindness, love, respect, self-control, honesty and many, many more beautiful things. What's amazing in all of this, it was myself that I saw. I realized for the first time in my life I had sincerely and truly found myself. The other amazing thing is, I didn't hate myself anymore because I understood.

R.P.
Kingston Penitentiary
Ontario, Canada

Since I've been doing this course, I have gone seven months major ticket free [without major disciplinary action], which I have never done and I'm involved in a trade called food tech and I'm steadily bettering myself. I would like everyone to know that this course has done a great deal for me and I'm very thankful for it. 'Cause now I feel ready for the real world and ready for the people around me. Thank you!

J.W.
Lakeland Correctional Facility
Michigan, USA

After thirty-eight years trying to understand life, I became very confused and wound up serving three years in a penitentiary and at the end of my rope.

Mentally battered and exhausted, I came across a book called ***Dianetics: The Modern Science of Mental Health.*** *At this point a change had occurred within. I started to think clearly, my life suddenly had meaning. I understand myself and others better, I feel freedom within and I have become a very happy individual because of these books and courses by L. Ron Hubbard.*

I'm afraid to think what could have happened to me, had I not come across this data. However, I have come across this data, I have used it and studied it and I am truly free and happy because of it.

Now, you have also come across this same data. What are you going to do with it? Do you want happiness and freedom in your life? Do you want to be a winner? Well! It's your move!

R.V.P.
Canada

While taking The Way to Happiness Course I felt a renewed sense of pride in who I really am and my capabilities to do good. I have regained certainty that I am not a bad person. I made a mistake and I have paid my debt to society. Now this course has re-lighted in me to be good and do good, because only that will ensure my happiness and the happiness of others.

T.A.C.
Indiana Reformatory USA

APPLIED SCHOLASTICS:

SOLUTIONS IN EDUCATION

As early as 1950, L. Ron Hubbard expressed his deep concern over the poor quality of so-called "modern" education.

"Today's children will become tomorrow's civilization," he wrote. "The end and goal of any society as it addresses the problem of education is to raise the ability, the initiative and the cultural level, and with all these the survival level of that society. And when a society forgets any one of these things it is destroying itself by its own educational mediums."

Decades later, Mr. Hubbard's observation has proven accurate and the continued disintegration of many of our institutions can be predicted unless the deterioration of society's educational systems is arrested.

There is hope, however, because Mr. Hubbard developed breakthrough educational technology capable of turning schools into institutions of unprecedented learning excellence.

Improving Education with L. Ron Hubbard's Study Technology

The ability to understand and retain data, the ability to actually learn, is vital for virtually everyone in today's world, be they adult or child. New technologies, the constant avalanche of information, even something as simple as reading the directions of household electronic equipment requires comprehension.

L. Ron Hubbard's study technology is thus an advance of gigantic significance in a world where educational standards have steadily declined, where education has abdicated its responsibility to the extent that it does not even teach our students to learn how to learn.

Study technology is a vast body of knowledge that not only consistently teaches people to learn how to learn, but delineates the three major barriers to effective study. Armed with these and the other tools provided, anyone can successfully study. It amounts to nothing less than a revolution in the field of education.

It is the job of Applied Scholastics to get this technology into the hands of a world that sorely needs it and revitalize our abilities to study.

Applied Scholastics International is a nonprofit, public benefit corporation whose purpose is to improve education worldwide. Located in Los Angeles, it has affiliated offices in Canada, Mexico, the United Kingdom, South Africa, Denmark, Sweden, Germany, Austria, France, Italy, Australia, Malaysia, China, Russia and Venezuela. Its materials are translated into many different languages.

In the 1960s, public school teachers who knew of L. Ron Hubbard's study technology used it in their public school classes and reported great improvement in learning abilities among their students.

In 1971, the first educational organization specializing in the use of study technology was started in California by a Scientologist teacher.

Then, in 1972, Applied Scholastics was founded to advance the application of Mr. Hubbard's study technology outside the churches of Scientology and thus broadly remedy learning difficulties for people of all ages and intellects.

Formed by a team of educators and teachers from a number of American schools and universities, Applied Scholastics today coordinates the many programs throughout the world which utilize study technology. Through ABLE, the Church and its members support and sponsor Applied Scholastics because it has a proven solution to the debacle in education today.

More than 3 million people have participated in Applied Scholastics programs

L. Ron Hubbard's study technology is delivered throughout the world by 183 groups in 30 countries on 6 continents. Shown here are just some of the fully illustrated educational study materials which can be applied to a wide range of academic levels.

throughout the world. L. Ron Hubbard's study technology is delivered by 183 groups in 30 countries in all 6 continents.

Working at the grass-roots level and with educational authorities, Applied Scholastics addresses six main areas of education: teacher training; schools; English as a second language; tutoring individuals; training business staff to apply the study technology; and, training human resource professionals so that they, in turn, can train their staff. This involves, of course, both adults and children.

Among the Applied Scholastics International affiliates throughout most of Europe, there is the Association for Effective Basic Education in Denmark; Centers of Individual and Effective Learning in Switzerland; Modern Instruction Centers in Italy; Studema in Sweden; the Effective Education Association and Basic Education and Supplementary Teaching Association in the United Kingdom; and the list goes on, with new organizations and affiliates opening each year.

In the growing number of schools and colleges affiliated with Applied Scholastics, students who are taught study technology from an early age are routinely eager, bright and interested in life around them.

Among the many schools in the United States which use study technology are:

Oregon's Delphian School, which occupies an 800-acre campus near Portland, enrolling students from around the world in a full-time academic program. It also operates training and apprenticeship programs for teachers, educators, school administrators and parents.

Ability Plus School, located in southern California, teaches students of all ages from toddlers through high school. The school also offers apprenticeships for teacher trainees in their state-licensed preschool and supplementary teacher training based on the study technology.

Florida's True School, where students are also enrolled on a full curriculum, is noted for its community outreach program called "Operation: Educate America." The school provides speakers to other community groups to publicize the urgency of improving American education.

These and other schools throughout the world routinely graduate eager, literate students who can make their way in life.

Increasing Productivity in the Workplace

One of the major concerns of business, particularly in the United States, lies in the dismal statistic that 27 million, or 20 percent of America's adults, are functionally illiterate, with basic skills below a fifth-grade level. Another 45 million adults are marginally literate.

This failure of our educational system costs American business and industry billions of dollars a year. Companies have thus found it necessary to introduce extensive, and expensive, training programs. In fact, US business spends about $45 billion annually to train from the top of the corporate ladder to the bottom. This does not include the staggering amount the government spends to train workers—with little result.

L. Ron Hubbard's study technology, furnished by Applied Scholastics, provides vitally necessary educational programs to a wide variety of businesses to increase employee efficiency, initiative and performance. It is currently used by thousands of businesses around the world.

Businesses that utilize study technology range from General Motors and Mobil Oil to Electronic Data Systems and Perrier, phone companies, computer software and hardware manufacturers, retail chains, clothing manufacturers, beverage companies, restaurants and more.

General Motors, for instance, spent millions of dollars on a computer system that nobody could use. For years they tried to train new operators, and failed. Their intensive lecture seminars resulted only in sleeping students, or those who begged for a break. They were almost ready to scrap the system.

Consultants trained in the application of the study technology, came into the company and rewrote a 1,000-page manual with graphics, a checksheet and a full glossary. They also put students through a study course prior to the computer course. The result was a meteoric reduction in ramp-up time—the time it takes graduates to apply what they have learned on the job. Normally six to twelve months, it was cut down to an unheard-of three weeks.

Programs tailored for executives raise the ability to assimilate, evaluate and retain large amounts of information—skills important for any executive.

Employees unable to read company manuals or follow written instructions are also put through Applied Scholastics courses, resulting not only in greater efficiency, but in enhancement of their entire lives.

Applied Scholastics has trained thousands of company executives and employees on L. Ron Hubbard's study technology. These innovative study materials, provided by ABLE and used internationally by Applied Scholastics groups, teach students of all ages.

Teacher Training Programs

Applied Scholastics also trains teachers to apply study technology and runs successful programs in many countries which accomplish this. These programs supply needed teaching skills based on L. Ron Hubbard's methods and rekindle the infectious enthusiasm for learning that every good teacher brings to his classroom.

Teachers throughout the world are today giving new meaning to what they do. Education Alive, for instance, the Applied Scholastics affiliate which delivers L. Ron Hubbard's study technology in South Africa and other parts of the continent, was established in 1975 and since then has trained more than 2 million students. Greatly helping to improve the deplorable educational standards for Blacks in that troubled land, Education Alive has also trained literally tens of thousands of teachers since its inception. In one teachers' college, for instance, the dropout rate for teacher trainees fell dramatically to only 2 percent after Education Alive services.

When Mr. Hubbard visited South Africa in the early 1960s, he predicted a series of massive social upheavals and a severe rift between Black and White communities there. To avert disaster, he advised measures and provided the technology that would enable the country's large Black population to become literate.

The appreciation and increased hope and human dignity resulting from Education Alive's programs is clear from this teacher's remarks:

"I stand like a warrior to conquer all difficulties I have come across with much ease. The entire world has become a phenomenon that needs restudy and to be observed with a different perspective. . . ."

Encouraged by Education Alive's results, major corporations have provided financial support for its vital work.

As one teacher wrote, "Education Alive has rescued me, and saved the lives of many pupils, students and teachers, as well as employees. I honor L. Ron Hubbard and his successors for the work they have done for the African child. Everybody who has heard these lectures is thirsty for further lessons and, at the same time, in a hurry to go out and experiment with these wonderful methods of teaching."

The following are some of the many organizations that have used L. Ron Hubbard's study technology:

ALLSTATE INSURANCE

EXECUTIVE SOFTWARE

GENERAL MOTORS

LANCÔME

REALWORLD CORPORATION

STERLING MANAGEMENT SYSTEMS

SURVIVAL INSURANCE

TIGRE LIS ENTERPRISES

U-MAN INTERNATIONAL

EPSON AMERICA

BUICK

OHIO INSTITUTE OF TECHNOLOGY

TRANSWESTERN INSTITUTE

INTERFACE COMPUTERS

VOLKSWAGEN/AUDI

PERRIER

ELIZABETH ARDEN

NATIONAL CASH REGISTER

CITROËN

CYANAMID

MOBIL OIL

TRUST BANK OF SOUTH AFRICA

In the People's Republic of China, a country with many millions of illiterate people, Applied Scholastics International has been active since 1984. Since then, more than 5,000 teachers and industrial managers have been trained in study technology.

In the Yunnan provincial capital city of Kunming, junior high school English teachers are now required by the City Education Bureau to use the Chinese translation of Mr. Hubbard's study materials for their teacher training.

The Shandong Education Commission cosponsored a correspondence course for teachers to allow L. Ron Hubbard's study technology to reach the population more quickly. And the major textbook publisher in China, in preparation for more extensive use of the study technology throughout the country, trained its editorial staff in Applied Scholastics courses.

In Costa Rica, extensive teacher training on study technology has resulted in a more rapid and thorough application of English as a second language for teachers. In recognition of the role Mr. Hubbard's study technology has played in raising the standard of education there, a representative of the Costa Rican Ministry of Education presented a plaque to Applied Scholastics at its twentieth anniversary celebration in Los Angeles in 1992.

"On behalf of Costa Rica, we are pleased to present this token of our appreciation to Applied Scholastics for its support in the teaching of English to Costa Rica's teachers," said Dr. Humberto Perez.

"We congratulate Applied Scholastics on this anniversary and hope that its relationship with Costa Rican education will grow and strengthen in the future."

A long-term professor of English at a California university had this to say about the results of study technology:

"I have never felt so good about my work nor achieved such consistent academic successes as I have since I incorporated the study technology of L. Ron Hubbard into my classes. No teacher should enter a classroom without this knowledge. No student should exit a school without this knowledge. This is what we all should have known long ago and didn't. Thank you, L. Ron Hubbard, for your gift to humanity."

These are only some of the many thousand testimonials from teachers around the world.

Spectacular Results of Study Technology

Even among gang members in the riot-torn Los Angeles city of Compton, California, L. Ron Hubbard's study technology has been winning endorsements. Introduced to community leaders and educators, in a grass-roots program coordinated by the Church, L. Ron Hubbard study technology has been described by youth counselors as "heaven sent." For not only have younger children markedly increased their reading and communication skills with the application of Mr. Hubbard's study materials, but even gang members, normally disdainful of any remedial education program, are willingly attending study classes. "These study materials," commented a community minister who is helping institute the program, "will set people free."

Additionally, working with African-American churches, Applied Scholastics initiated a program to train parents to be tutors so that they can pass the study technology on to families and other members of the community. Since then, the program expanded to south central Los Angeles, another area plagued by illiteracy.

Because of its enormous value and wide application, this study technology has been widely used with spectacular results.

■ In New Zealand, students in a girls' school showed an increase of twelve IQ points on the Otis Lennon Mental Ability Test after completing a course based on Mr. Hubbard's learning methods.

■ College students at the East Los Angeles College in California received twenty

In South Africa, L. Ron Hubbard's study technology has been taught to 2 million underprivileged children.

hours of instruction in the study technology. Tested before and after the course in vocabulary, reading comprehension, arithmetic reasoning, arithmetic fundamentals, language mechanics and spelling, the students improved an equivalent of approximately one grade level in each area tested.

■ Another study conducted in England showed that students shot ahead 1.29 years in their reading levels after just ten hours of study using Mr. Hubbard's study technology. Comparatively, no gain in reading levels was found in a control group of students not instructed in study technology.

■ In a separate project in Los Angeles, high-school students tested after a forty-hour period of classroom instruction in study technology showed a remarkable average gain of over two years per student. In a similar project in South Africa, the average gain in reading age was two years and three months.

■ In Mexico City, the study technology was introduced into a private school. High-school students in one class had failed 95 percent of their materials. After application of L. Ron Hubbard's study technology, the class passed 90 percent of the materials the following year.

Applied Scholastics International and its associated groups are bringing the study technology of L. Ron Hubbard to people from all walks of life—technology that is not only successful beyond any other approach to education, but fully capable of generating a renaissance in learning.

Every day, in businesses, schools and learning centers all over the world, more and more individuals are having the door of opportunity opened to them through the study technology of L. Ron Hubbard.

Delphi, Oregon, USA

Ability School, New Jersey, USA

Ability School, Virginia, USA

Several schools from around the world which exclusively use L. Ron Hubbard's study technology

Greenfields School, Sussex, England

SUCCESSES IN APPLICATION

Every day, in businesses, schools and learning centers all over the world, more and more individuals are having the door of opportunity opened to them through the study technology of L. Ron Hubbard.

I am a teacher by profession. I have taught boys and girls who are now teachers, graduates, clergymen, doctors, etc. But after I took up studies of L. Ron Hubbard's study technology . . .

I felt ashamed of myself when I started to look back at all the long period of my teaching career. I thought the dropouts who left school were permanently stupid and dull. I am now able to carry on even with retarded children. Hats off to those who have sown this seed until it reached me!

E.G.

As a teacher of English as a second language in a large inner city high school in Manhattan, I have successfully used the study technology to help my students become more able people and acquire a greater understanding of the lessons they were taught.

Other teachers and administrators in my school have noticed the change and improvements in my students' test scores and speaking ability, as well as the atmosphere in my classroom.

Their praise has validated my application of Mr. Hubbard's study technology and its goals: that being a good teacher produces students who can apply what they have learned.

L.K.

I had to send my daughter to a state school in Holland. After one year at school she had to wear glasses, started to stutter and had a lot of trouble with her math. Even though I was helping her at home, the problems became worse and she became very unhappy.

My son also went to the same school and he became very introverted and quiet. His teacher told me he was deaf (reason for being quiet) and he had an underlying psychological problem. Well, he had been a very lively child up until then and not deaf—I can assure you of that!

We decided to move and bring our children to Greenfields School which uses L. Ron Hubbard's study technology in all its classes. Even though there was a language barrier they both felt much happier at their new school.

Within no time my son was a happy, very lively boy again and all the signs of his "problems" were gone, and he could still hear very well.

My daughter's problem with math came down to not knowing the three barriers to study and how to handle them. She actually loves math now and her stuttering completely disappeared. The use of study technology has saved my children's school life without a doubt!

I.M.H.

I've finally gotten the data that's been denied to me for so long! I've wanted to know how to study so earnestly throughout my so-called education. It is safe to say that I've learned more on this course than the entirety of my previous schooling.

J.D.

I have been in a school without the study technology and I know that L. Ron Hubbard's study technology that I use is much better. When I study I learn much faster and I love what I learn about. When I use this, I stay at a nice steady pace. I also know now what I am learning, I can use, because I really understand what I am learning.

C.B.

I am a teacher at the Ohio Institute of Technology. This is an electronics technical school and we have students from all social backgrounds and educational levels. I used the methodology as laid out in the ***Basic Study Manual*** *for two quarters at the Institute and met with tremendous success. The school administration was so impressed with my results that they have given me three months' leave of absence to get more training in the technology developed by Mr. Hubbard.*

C.K.

Using L. Ron Hubbard's basic study techniques, we found profound jumps in productivity among staff. Employees stopped making costly mistakes.

R.H.

At the time I was first introduced to Mr. Hubbard's theories and methods, I was very discouraged about what was happening to student literacy and motivation. I was even considering tendering my resignation. However, after learning about the basic barriers to study and what could be done about them, I began using more and more of the data with students. Eventually, I created an entire study skills course and also taught my grammar and writing course fully utilizing the study technology. The result has been one rehabilitated English teacher and hundreds of enthusiastic, rejuvenated students.

B.E.P.

I can think of no more valuable and necessary element of any course of study, practical or theoretic, than study technology courses.

R.V.D.

Some people try to say common things with uncommon words instead of saying uncommon things with common words. But this course taught me to understand simple words which turn out to be the ones we often don't understand. I have changed a great deal in just two days of this course. Yesterday I spent my day practicing what I learned and it became great fun. I no longer worry about how I am going to study. L. Ron Hubbard's study technology is amazing.

P.R.N.

Our company is one of the leading software manufacturers for micro and personal computers. This is a highly competitive, high-technology business and demands top standards of excellence in communication and education.

All of our executives and staff apply the study technology developed by L. Ron Hubbard and this fact has been very instrumental in our success. This technology is fundamental not only to our high-technology business but any activity where individuals must learn skills in order to survive; in other words, all of life.

D.Y.

It helped me on my report card. It helped me in math, social studies, science, health, listening and following directions, finishing work on time, keeping materials in order and it helped me be more dependable. It helped me so I wouldn't be held back. I improved in eight different subjects.

C.A.

THE WAY TO HAPPINESS FOUNDATION:

IMPROVING MORALS IN TODAY'S WORLD

Every culture in every age has relied upon a moral code to provide broad guidelines for conduct that is conducive to survival. Although much in these past moral codes may not seem particularly relevant to the late twentieth century, when those codes were written they were entirely relevant. They helped ensure the perpetuation of the family, the group and nation. They provided the means by which people upheld the basic tenets of honesty and mutual trust. In short, the moral code supplied the overriding principles by which men could live peaceably, prosperously and in harmony with one another.

Today's declining moral standards have long been a point of grave concern. If art and entertainment are any reflection of our culture, then we live in genuinely frightening times. It is an era of gratuitous violence wherein we have the potential for immense destruction, but no corresponding moral standards to check that destruction. It is an age of senseless killing, unrestrained greed and such profoundly deep cynicism that even the concept of morals often brings sneers.

But just as all ancient cultures required a moral code for their survival, so too does our own culture desperately need such a code by which we may live. Judging by modern crime rates, divorce rates, substance abuse and falling confidence in government, one could predict that the seeds have been sown for a serious social upheaval unless countered by a commensurate effort to restore traditional values.

L. Ron Hubbard was keenly aware of this situation in 1980 when he observed that our modern world lacked a code of morals befitting our faster, high-tech and highly pragmatic society. Old values had been broken but not replaced by new ones, and many were left to flounder on rapidly shifting sands of societal change. Moreover, the moral codes of ages past were religiously based and demanded a faith that many could not muster in this era of waning church attendance. Thus, Mr. Hubbard set out to write a new moral code, one that was based not on faith, but on common sense; one that appealed purely to man's reason and his natural inclination to better survival.

That moral code is *The Way to Happiness.* It is the first moral code based wholly on common sense, and the only one that is entirely nonreligious in nature. It carries no other appeal than to the good sense of the individual man or woman, boy or girl who reads it. Beneath the many differences of national, political, racial, religious or other hue, each of us as individuals must make our way through life. Such a way, *The Way to Happiness* teaches, can be made better if the precepts it presents are known and followed, and if one gets others to know and follow them as well.

Life in an immoral society can be much worse than simply difficult. One's own survival is constantly under threat as even the most basic human values are held up to ridicule. To counter such declining moral trends, *The Way to Happiness* contains twenty-one separate precepts—each constituting a rule for living and has relevance for anyone in our global village. "Safeguard and Improve Your Environment" it advises. "Be Worthy of Trust." "Fulfill Your Obligations." These and the other precepts are fully explained with examples of how each should be applied in one's life and how one can make it known by others. Regardless of the course of any person's life, the precepts can be likened to the edges of the road: Violating them, one is like the motorist who plunges onto the verge—the result can be wreckage of the moment, the relationship, the life. Abiding by the precepts gives one a chance to attain true and lasting happiness.

Mr. Hubbard offered *The Way to Happiness* to others as something they would find useful in their efforts to live more successfully. People read it. They understood its sensible argument for adopting values which foster greater survival for all. Realizing the code's intrinsic value, Scientologists were among the first to use it in their daily lives. The code began to spread through the society from hand to hand, city to city, country to country. To date, many tens of millions of copies of the booklet have been passed out in more than forty countries and translated into sixteen languages.

A Better Life for Millions

The Way to Happiness Foundation, based in Los Angeles, was organized to meet the grass-roots demand for *The Way to Happiness* and to provide copies to the many millions of interested people.

By promoting the booklet's distribution and use, The Way to Happiness Foundation is changing the lives of the many people reached with it—and thereby improving conditions in communities around the world.

The booklet enjoys widespread popularity because it is effective in reestablishing moral values wherever its message is heard. It has received four US Congressional recognitions and has been enthusiastically endorsed by police, civic leaders, businessmen, educators and other groups who have distributed it broadly. Hundreds of groups and officials have used the booklet to bring about greater harmony in their communities.

Distribution occurs through sponsorships; any individual or group may donate copies to youth groups, schools, clubs, social service agencies, military organizations or any of a multitude of other groups. These then distribute the booklets to their members or people with whom they are in contact.

Thousands of schools and millions of students participate in the broad promotion of *The Way to Happiness* precepts. With the help of sponsoring groups, local schools and youth organizations initiate projects that range from cleaning up the environment to setting good examples for peers and helping rid schools of drugs.

MORAL PRECEPTS FROM THE WAY TO HAPPINESS

1. *Take Care of Yourself*
2. *Be Temperate*
3. *Don't Be Promiscuous*
4. *Love and Help Children*
5. *Honor and Help Your Parents*
6. *Set a Good Example*
7. *Seek to Live with the Truth*
8. *Do Not Murder*
9. *Don't Do Anything Illegal*
10. *Support a Government Designed and Run for All the People*
11. *Do Not Harm a Person of Good Will*
12. *Safeguard and Improve Your Environment*
13. *Do Not Steal*
14. *Be Worthy of Trust*
15. *Fulfill Your Obligations*
16. *Be Industrious*
17. *Be Competent*
18. *Respect the Religious Beliefs of Others*
19. *Try Not to Do Things to Others that You Would Not Like Them to Do to You*
20. *Try to Treat Others As You Would Want Them to Treat You*
21. *Flourish and Prosper*

One of the many sponsoring groups is the Concerned Businessmen's Association of America (CBAA), a nonprofit, charitable educational organization founded in 1981. Through its efforts, many young people are no longer involved in drug abuse, crime and gang violence. Since CBAA began, more than six million copies of *The Way to Happiness* booklet have been distributed throughout the school system, with over five million students participating in its programs—involving more than seven thousand elementary, junior high and high schools.

CBAA has conducted two very successful nationwide campaigns based on *The Way to Happiness*: "Set a Good Example" and "Get Drugs off School Grounds."

These consist of two contests, one for individual students who demonstrate how they use the precept "Set a Good Example" in their lives, and one for schools, promoting their efforts to keep drugs off their campuses. More than thirty state governors, along with directors of state alcohol and drug-abuse programs and departments of education in hundreds of communities, have endorsed the "Set a Good Example" contest using *The Way to Happiness.*

One Ohio school, prior to becoming involved with one of these contests, had routine violence, crime and drug abuse among its students and tested well below the average national reading level. After participating in the program for two years, the school was declared drug-free and reading levels had risen well above the national level.

The Way to Happiness is reaching into the hearts of our cities, where gang violence and street warfare have become a way of life. The simple reading of this book to hundreds of gang members has actually brought reform. In Los Angeles, for example, after hard-core gang members read (or were read to, in some cases) *The Way to Happiness,* they voluntarily removed graffiti from 130 buildings in their neighborhood, while passing out hundreds of copies of the booklets to neighbors.

Many concerned citizens use *The Way to Happiness* to bring their communities together. Such was the case during and after the 1992 Los Angeles riots. The Way to Happiness Foundation volunteers passed out hundreds of thousands of copies throughout the city while assisting on food drives and cleanup actions.

Said one south central Los Angeles community leader who heads an organization called Parents of Watts: "We've been giving out this book now for about two or three months. Nothing different has come into the community except this particular book—and we do see a change and we have to relate it to *The Way to Happiness.*"

Many other campaigns have been sponsored around the world. In the South African township of Soweto, a campaign based on the precept "Safeguard and Improve Your Environment" was supported by the largest food chain in the country and two major labor unions. Still another campaign in the South African city of Pietermaritzburg was highly successful in easing racial tensions.

Also in South Africa, in 1992, the South African police requested 114,000 copies of *The Way to Happiness* booklet—one for every policeman in the country.

Children and teenagers all over the world regularly participate in community cleanups based on the precept, "Safeguard and Improve Your Environment."

The Youth Service Bureau, a national organization founded to prevent delinquency and divert youth from the criminal justice system, is one of many groups that distributes *The Way to Happiness.* Its executive director, who uses the book with the bureau's youth counselors, reported: "Our youthful clients lack a set of principles by which they can live a successful, happy life. *The Way to Happiness* certainly focuses on 21 positive principles which, if applied, would lead to a happy and successful life, rather than a life of drugs, crime and welfare."

On a similar note, a Girl Scout official wrote, "Thank you for sending the booklets and thank Mr. Hubbard for writing it. I only wish it could be distributed to every family in the country. The positive impact it could have (if ideally everyone *used* it) is mind-boggling. You can be sure that the people we distribute it to will put it to wise and frequent use!"

Throughout the United States, tens of thousands of corporate executives, professionals and travelers read copies of *The Way to Happiness,* compliments of hotels that provide the booklet in their guest rooms.

Upon ordering a stock of books for his guests, one Hilton Hotel manager remarked, "It is obvious that the morals and integrity of a large portion of our population are lacking today. Your book says it simply, as it should be, and hopefully will play on the conscience of many people to realize the need to adjust their lifestyles for a more healthy and vital environment, not only for themselves but for everyone around them."

Worldwide Recognition

In one year alone, 324 major recognitions were received by the Foundation, 131 of them from government officials worldwide acknowledging *The Way to Happiness* for its role in fostering greater social responsibility and tolerance.

One former Toledo, Ohio, police officer remarked, "After having read *The Way to Happiness,* I've never felt so uplifted. In a world so wrought with destruction these days, it's a blessing to have such a publication available to help instill strong moral values in our youth today."

In Moscow, the chief of the city's police force—one of the largest in the world—ordered 5,000 copies of the Russian edition of the book for his officers noting: "This book is recommended to you by the Moscow City Police Department in hopes that it will help you lead a better and happier life."

Even the drug-torn nation of Colombia has felt the impact. The country's largest and most influential newspaper, *El Tiempo,* distributed copies of the booklet to all subscribers and printed a series of quotes from the booklet in its editions. Referring to the violence that had shaken the nation, the newspaper president stated, "The root of this illness is not in politics but in the soul of our people. When I read *The Way to Happiness,* I realized that this is our solution for social and personal illness."

One Colombian army general was so taken with the work that he had 30,000 copies distributed to soldiers fighting the drug war. Yet another general urged judges in Colombia's demoralized justice system to follow *The Way to Happiness* to restore justice in the country.

Colombia's Minister of Education endorsed the booklet, announced a "Set a Good Example" contest, and suggested all teachers, alumni, directors of education and parents organize classrooms where *The Way to Happiness* would be available to help people discuss and handle their problems.

The president of Olympian International (and a world-renowned trainer and sports physician) helped get copies of *The Way to Happiness* to many Olympic athletes, explaining: "It's a wonderful way to educate the people on the harmful effects of drugs and to build their self-esteem for better understanding right and wrong by using their common sense."

And the Minister of Foreign Affairs in Austria said: "After reading about your international campaign based on tolerance, trust and understanding I must say that the values expressed in your activities should be the basis of human life on this Earth."

In *The Way to Happiness,* L. Ron Hubbard has given everyone a guide by which they can chart a course to a world where violence is not a solution to the bumps in the road and where mutual respect and trust make the way smoother for all. Like gentle oil spread upon the raging sea, the calm generated by *The Way to Happiness* will flow outward and outward. The Way to Happiness Foundation helps the revitalization of moral values in our world by assisting in every way possible the spreading of this common-sense guide to better living.

WINNING WITH *THE WAY TO HAPPINESS*

Moral values have been heavily assaulted in this century. Many people have recognized the decline within their own lifetimes and avidly support the concepts expressed in ***The Way to Happiness.*** *It has been used by tens of millions around the world, helping spread a common-sense approach to living in our turbulent world.*

I am writing this letter in reference to one of the greatest self-esteem/self-help books I have come across in quite a while, ***The Way to Happiness.*** *As a police officer, many situations that I see along with other officers, are often sad ones. So many people seem to be unable to pull within themselves to find good.*

The Way to Happiness *book encourages people to search for the goodness within themselves and spread that goodness to others.*

Officer F.P.
Hartford Police Department

We think that the publication of the book in Lithuanian would be useful and beneficial. Our community, having experienced a long and severe period of communist oppression, is in great demand of spiritual values such as honesty, conscientiousness, sincerity and tolerance. These qualities will help us to overcome the severe inheritance and to advance on the road of freedom and independence to the European community of nations.

Professor L.A.
Ministry of Energy, Lithuania

We like ***The Way to Happiness*** *booklet because the way we work with children around here is to recognize that they seem to be in the dark about how to handle life. They need real direction, so we try to provide the lantern that lights up the road for them.*

The Way to Happiness *booklet has the true ingredients for this. It provides moral support, common sense, the real basic things these children need to know to avoid trouble and it is not so lengthy that they can't get through it.*

The mother I gave the booklet to told me it helped her to phrase what she had always wanted to tell her children but couldn't find the words for. She said this booklet refreshes the things I have always known. Things I felt I myself or someone ought to write a book on so our children could know them. That won't be necessary now that we have ***The Way to Happiness*** *booklets.*

Everyone we give booklets to expresses their appreciation. Teachers, parents, clergy and the citizens here have all wanted extra copies for their friends so they have joined us in efforts to get the booklet into the hands of every parent in the area. We already have requests for over 25,000 copies.

A.H.
Director, Parents of Watts

Participating with ***The Way to Happiness*** *has been most rewarding to me. I have thoroughly enjoyed hearing my patients' favorable responses. Many have personally thanked me for* ***The Way to Happiness*** *booklet and were pleased to get another to pass it on to friends.*

I encourage anyone considering participating in The Way to Happiness program to do so. The more people who have access to this booklet, the better our society will be.

M.S.
D.D.S.

*Thank you so much for the beautiful book, **The Way to Happiness**. It is beautifully bound and has a beautiful message. It is a wonderful and insightful guide to living a more peaceful life on a personal and world-wide basis.*

T.L.
United States Senate
Washington, DC

Reading the book was very interesting and helpful. I have no doubt that reading and using this guide can help people think and behave in a more positive way. Allow me to express to you my sincere appreciation of the blessed activity of The Way to Happiness Foundation and my best wishes to your success in disseminating the message of peace and harmony.

R.A.
Knesset Member
Jerusalem, Israel

*We love your **Way to Happiness** booklet. The **values**, moral and ethical, are exactly what we believe schools should emphasize. Maybe, if we start them young, they will have the foundation for happiness. Our students find it easy to understand, and direct and to the point.*

L.H.
Principal
Board of Education
City of New York

*After having read **The Way to Happiness,** I've never felt so uplifted. We here at ADD LOVE Productions, have provided our children's performing group, The Positive Force Performers, each with their own copy to study. To date, we've distributed over 1,500 copies throughout Toledo, Ohio and Detroit, Michigan during our special presentations. Everyone who has received a copy only had the highest praise for its positive message.*

In a world so wrought with destruction these days, it's a blessing to have such a publication available to help instill strong moral values in our youth today.

D.A.
Executive Producer
ADD LOVE Productions

*Thanks for sending copies of **The Way to Happiness!** We love the whole concept, and it goes hand-in-hand with our mission—which is to inspire girls in the highest ideals of character, conduct and patriotism in order to help them reach their full potential. The book will be invaluable for use in troop meetings, service unit gatherings, and as inspiration to many of our volunteers.*

M.C.
West Texas Girl Scout Council, Inc.

*Please accept my thanks for the wonderful book, **The Way to Happiness.** It is filled with gems, and it certainly gives some interesting pointers on happiness.*

G.P.
US Congressman
Washington, DC

BURBANK
Proclamation
CITY OF PHILADELPHIA
Proclamation
Proclamation
Proclamation
For the City of Pawtucket by His Honor
Mayor Brian J. Sarault
PROCLAMATION
WHEREAS, the future of succeeding generations and, therefore, the progress of the United States and communities therein depends upon the education of our children
Proclamation
Office of the Governor
PROCLAMATION
State of Tennessee
THE SENATE
A RESOLUTION
Resolution
The Delphi Academy
WHEREAS, The Delphi Academy of Palo Alto achieved first place national honors in the junior high school competition this year from among more than 5,000 schools which entered the American Set A Good Example Contest, and upon this occasion, the Delphi Academy is deserving of special public recognition and the highest commendations; and
The City of Inglewood
California Legislature
Resolution
City of PORTLAND, OREGON
Proclamation
WHEREAS, the future of succeeding generations and therefore the progress of the United States, and communities therein, depends upon the education of our children and workforce; and
State of Rhode Island and Providence Plantations
OFFICE of the GOVERNOR
The Governor of the State of Rhode Island
PROCLAMATION
WHEREAS, founded on the inspiration of William Benitez inside the walls of Arizona State Prison twenty-five years ago, the Narconon Program treats thousands of individuals throughout the world who suffer from drug and alcohol addiction; and
WHEREAS, aiming to make our society drug-free, Narconon is fighting the war through prevention and education in our schools, juvenile facilities, and community organizations, as well as offers rehabilitation to those already addicted; and
WHEREAS, we honor not only the staff at the Narconon Centers for their outstanding leadership, but the volunteers who carry the message of
Resolution of Commendation
WHEREAS, today's youth are tomorrow's civilization and the youth of Santa Clara County California and America are the hope of the future; and
WHEREAS, drugs are a serious threat to the future of today's youth which undercuts the objectives of our schools, whose purpose is to prepare youth for life in our society; and
WHEREAS, the Concerned Businessmen's Association of America out of a concern for our youth and their future, created the American Set A Good Example Contest and Campaign To Get Drugs Off School Grounds and out of our communities; and
WHEREAS, this campaign encourages young people across the United States to set a good example, to educate themselves and their peers in common sense standards of right and wrong conduct as contained in the book The Way To Happiness; and
WHEREAS, Students of Delphi Academy in Palo Alto, California achieved first place national honors in the 1989-1990 junior high school competition from among more than 5000 schools enrolled in the nationwide Set A Good Example Contest; and
"SET A GOOD EXAMPLE" MONTH

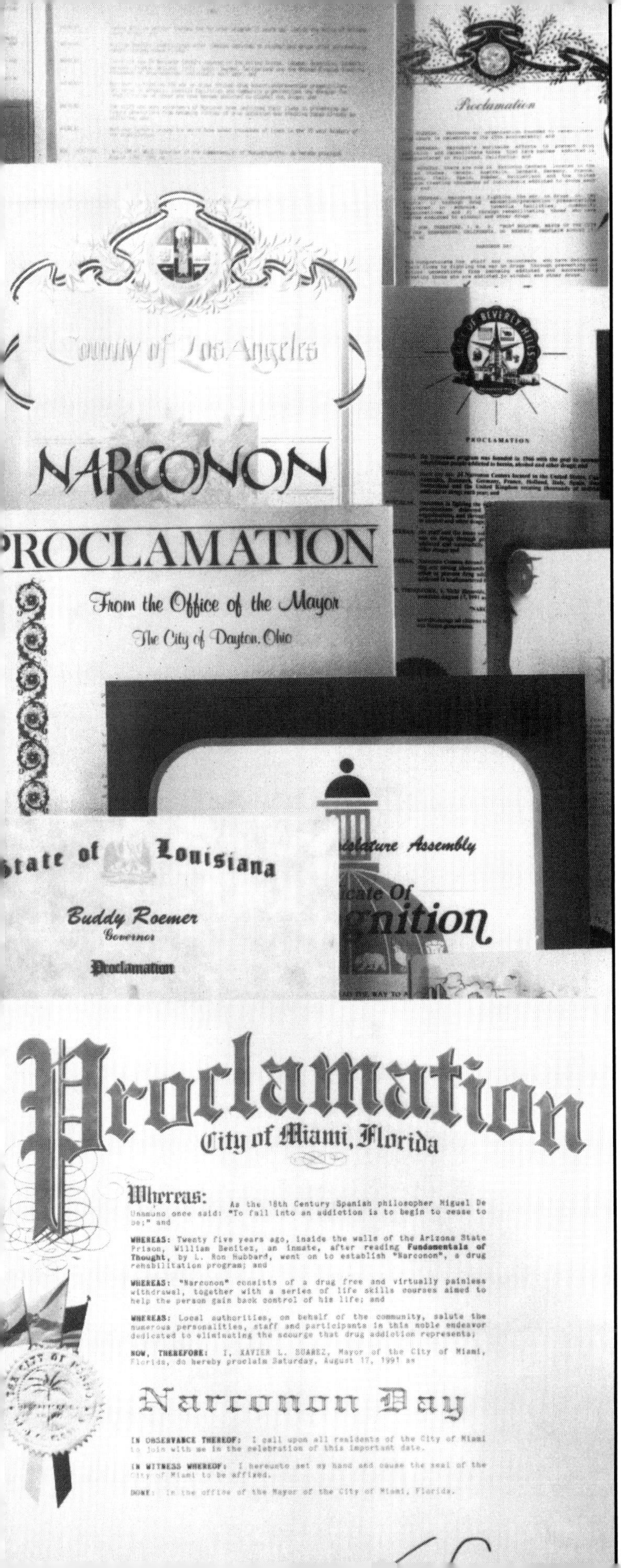

A BETTER WORLD THROUGH ABLE

ABLE's support and promotion of invaluable social betterment programs today offers new hope for millions of individuals on six continents. From the addicted who find new meaning in drug-free lives, to the illiterate who learn to read and suddenly find a future, from criminals who once again find pride in who they are and their potentials, to children who discover the value of morals, ABLE is helping and changing lives.

And to understand why the Church of Scientology supports all the programs of ABLE, one need only look again at some of the many success stories presented in this chapter.

While ABLE's mission is to reverse the decline of our civilization—to once again make learning a joy, our streets safe, our people able to face life sanely and rationally—the satisfaction gained by the staff of ABLE and its Scientology supporters and volunteers comes from helping individuals, those basic building blocks of our society so often ignored and overlooked. There is no greater fulfillment in any act than there is in safeguarding life, in restoring to an individual hope and pride and competence.

The successes of ABLE are successes for all. And the Church of Scientology and its members will continue to do all they can to bring about a better world through the application of the technology of L. Ron Hubbard.

These are some of the thousands of recognitions and proclamations saluting community betterment programs that are supported by ABLE.

Part Seven

World Institute of Scientology Enterprises (WISE)

If Scientologists are to survive in this world, L. Ron Hubbard explained, they must see to the survival of all men. They must dedicate themselves to the eradication of injustice, constantly work to raise levels of ethics and restore sanity in all sectors of society.

Although members of the World Institute of Scientology Enterprises represent a diverse group—from presidents of advertising companies to owners of repair shops—each has discovered a vital fact: that the same administrative policies used to expand Scientology organizations may also be used to expand any organization. And, as this chapter details, because expansion goes hand-in-hand with ethics, they are making the entire business community a better place in which to work.

CHAPTER 26

WISE: ENABLING GROUPS TO FLOURISH AND PROSPER

Until Dianetics and Scientology, no one knew the principles of a successful group any more than they knew the principles of the human mind.

Recognizing that what all too often passes for life in the modern workplace is endless drudgery, inefficiency, insecurity and bureaucratic entanglements, individuals began to utilize the same administrative principles L. Ron Hubbard developed for use in Scientology churches to improve their own businesses, organizations, groups and even their personal lives.

Their reasoning was simple: If Mr. Hubbard's administrative policies could bring sanity, stability and expansion to a Scientology organization, surely the application of those policies could do the same outside the Church. Why, for example, must a businessman suffer sleepless nights through uncertain economic times when Mr. Hubbard's policies so plainly outlined the means of survival in any economic climate? Why, too, must one suffer from continual infighting, backbiting and day-to-day duress when Mr. Hubbard so precisely laid out rules for group harmony? Moreover, many had long been utilizing principles from such Scientology books as *Problems of Work* to help resolve problems in group situations. Some even compiled their own manuals using some of Mr. Hubbard's material for use in training their employees, while others used what they knew to assist colleagues.

Thus it was that the World Institute of Scientology Enterprises (WISE) was born in 1979. A religious fellowship organization, WISE is made up of businessmen and professionals in numerous fields, who share a common certainty that only through the application of Mr. Hubbard's administrative technology can one do for the third (group) dynamic what Scientology does for the individual: eliminate confusions, replace hardship with happiness, and generally better survival.

Their tools are the extensive writings on the subject of administrative technology which resulted from Mr. Hubbard's research and codification of the Scientology religion. Originally written for church administration, these works address the subject of life in a group with the same thoroughness and attention to fundamental truths as Mr. Hubbard's writings on Scientology address the life of an individual. Thus, just as Dianetics and Scientology opened the way to an understanding of the mind and the spirit, the administrative technology leads to an understanding of just what comprises a successful group. Be it a local Boy Scout troop or the largest government agency, with these principles, one can turn any group into a productive, smooth-running and expanding concern.

These writings contain practical knowledge in all areas of administration and organization. With their principles, one can solve problems ranging from the hiring of a secretary to the implementation of multinational corporate plans. Similarly, by employing the

The offices of WISE International, located in Los Angeles

principles contained in the Scientology organizing board, one can remarkably streamline all aspects of operation. And because the fundamentals of the organizing board apply equally well to one or one thousand, even the individual can greatly improve his life by simply aligning his activities according to the Scientology organizing board. In fact, with the application of even a small part of this data, any group or personal activity can be immediately bettered.

Because every group, from a softball team to a steel mill work force, seeks to achieve some goal, the material on the use of statistics to monitor progress toward that goal is particularly valuable. Utilizing Mr. Hubbard's principles, one can even better define goals and employ a precise system for laying out the steps to achieve them. The entire subject of logic is described—how to think and how to make logical decisions about any aspect of living. Ethics technology, including the correct application of the conditions of existence, is covered in detail, and there is a series of policies on the subject of establishing any organization and the personnel within it. In fact, there is no sphere of organizational knowledge not covered by L. Ron Hubbard's administrative technology.

Simply put, this technology encompasses the basic laws needed to succeed in any endeavor in any zone of application. No wonder then that individuals regularly use this technology in not only their careers but *also* their personal lives. With such knowledge so readily available, it was only natural that businessmen and professionals would begin implementing these discoveries to better relationships within their fields of practice and with their friends and families. Today, this technology is utilized with excellent results by thousands of individuals, groups and organizations. Its use results in increased survival and well-being, allowing any group to flourish and prosper.

The WISE membership is administered by WISE International, a religious nonprofit corporation located in Los Angeles. WISE members forward a basic principle of honesty and fairness to create a sane and productive working environment where everyone can flourish and prosper. If a WISE member violates these agreements, WISE International does everything possible to correct the member through proper training in ethics and justice codes before revoking his membership.

THE BENEFITS OF MEMBERSHIP

WISE members share a commonality of interest. They conduct business with one another, provide referrals and gain access to other like-minded individuals which may not otherwise be available.

The administrative functions of WISE also include supplying different members' benefits. These include issue authority (for use of copyrighted L. Ron Hubbard materials in publications), newsletters, membership directories, seminars, conventions and arbitrations for business disputes.

Some members employ the administrative principles solely within the framework of their own business or profession. Others study Mr. Hubbard's administrative breakthroughs and become consultants. A WISE consultant is a skilled expert in administration, who is trained on the technology and has learned how to help others apply it. WISE itself does no consulting. But the WISE members who are professional consultants routinely produce spectacular results when called in to help. WISE consultants have rightly earned the reputation of resolving situations that others, lacking their know-how, have been unable to crack. For the technology they have at their fingertips undercuts and corrects even the most difficult organizational problems.

In order to ensure proper and standard use of copyrighted materials, consultants are licensed by WISE. This acts as a safeguard against offbeat activities or the publication of altered versions held out to be the technology of L. Ron Hubbard. Being a WISE member in good standing is an assurance to others that one is maintaining the high level of ethical standards and conduct contemplated in Mr. Hubbard's writings.

A membership card for WISE International

WISE also furnishes arbitration services to its members. These are conducted in accordance with the ethics and justice codes of Scientology. As such they are swift, fair and determine, based on facts, restitution for any wrongs that may have been committed. This is an extremely valuable service, saving WISE members a great deal of the time, money and uncertainty that is part and parcel of the legal system.

For these reasons, WISE membership has grown since its inception in 1979, to more than 2,700 individuals, groups and companies (many with hundreds of employees). WISE members are found in more than 30 countries and many sectors of society. They are sought after for their high ethical standards and knowledge of administration and management principles and procedures. Recently, WISE members have been called upon to assist in the organization and management of newly privatized businesses and industries in Russia and other countries formerly under communist rule.

THE WISE CHARTER COMMITTEE

To ensure that high ethical standards are maintained by its members, WISE has established local Charter Committees, composed of the most ethical and trusted WISE members (called Charter members). The purpose of the Charter Committee is to use the Scientology system of ethics and justice to create a more ethical business environment.

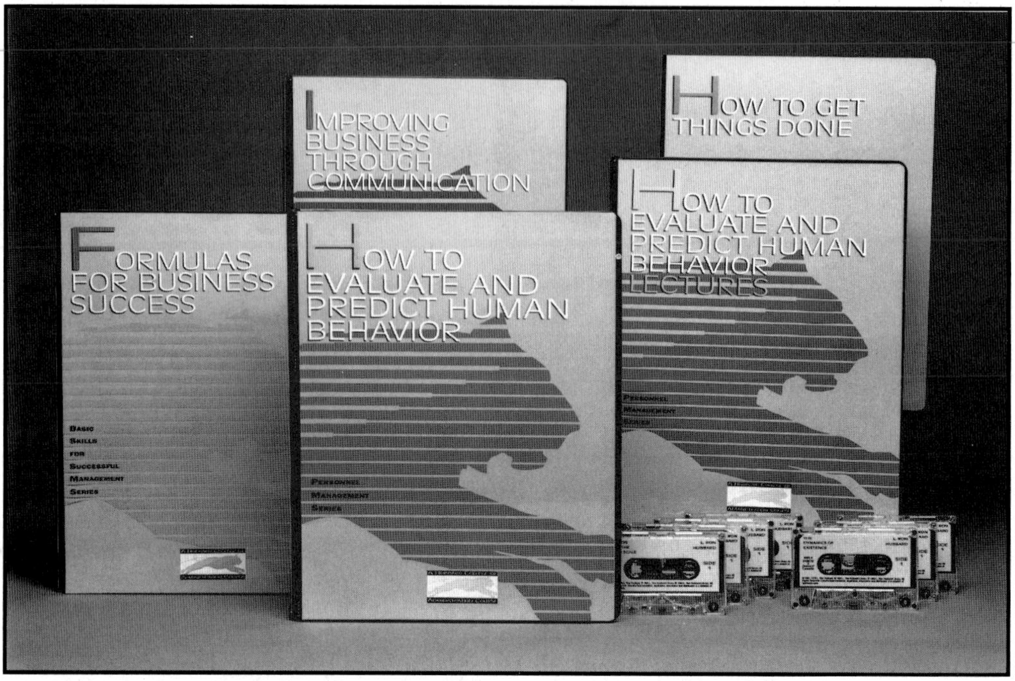

Organizational skills are learned and perfected on courses covering L. Ron Hubbard's administrative technology.

Charter Committees are self-governing entities that regulate their own territories and members in achieving WISE's objective: the productive and standard use of L. Ron Hubbard's administrative technology to improve third dynamic conditions.

Through the administration of standard Scientology ethics and justice procedures to their members, Charter Committees arbitrate and rapidly and fairly resolve business disputes.

THE HUBBARD COLLEGE OF ADMINISTRATION

Because so many businesses and industries now use Mr. Hubbard's technology, WISE has established the Hubbard College of Administration to expand the business professional's ability to tackle the challenges of administering and running a group, company or organization. The Hubbard College provides training in L. Ron Hubbard's management technology.

Whether one is learning specific tools to apply to his or her own business or studying to become a consultant to help others, the Hubbard College provides the highest caliber of L. Ron Hubbard's administrative technology.

The curriculum is laid out in such a way that even the novice can rapidly grasp the basics and move on to more advanced training within a very short period of time. Hubbard College courses are available on either a full- or part-time basis.

A businessman or woman who studies at the Hubbard College first spends some time with an adviser to clarify the purpose of their study. Then an individualized program is developed with the focus on applying the technology to their area. Some of the aspects in which graduates have directly and positively affected the well-being of their companies are: increased production, reduced stress, streamlined organization, improved management/staff relations and heightened ethical levels amongst employees.

One of the most comprehensive courses for resolving undesirable third dynamic situations teaches the student to apply Mr. Hubbard's discoveries in the field of logic. Through this course, the business professional or consultant becomes expert in perceiving *through* the "apparent" reasons for a problem and zeroing in on the true underlying source of the decline or difficulty.

The Hubbard College also delivers specialist courses covering such subjects as:

- the application of ethics to business
- executive essentials and leadership
- management by statistics
- communication lines
- public relations
- the use of surveys
- how to increase personnel and company efficiency
- effective communication
- how to put planning into implementation
- hiring of personnel
- the use of testing in personnel hiring and placement
- troubleshooting, and
- computers

SUCCESSFUL APPLICATIONS

By the early nineties, 35,000 of these courses had been delivered. Successes reach far more broadly than business and professional application, however. Many of the College's course graduates report that, as a result of the organizational know-how they have gained, other areas of life improve as well—a better overall outlook, marriages salvaged, happier family life, achievement of personal goals, etc.

Evidence from one chiropractor who had received assistance from a WISE member applying the administrative technology:

"My practice had a lot of disorder and inefficiencies before you came in. Thanks to the Hubbard data and your help, I am now achieving the success I have worked so hard for.

"But more important for me, I also have the quality of life and am enjoying my success thanks to your program. Even though production and income [are] higher, I actually am able to spend more time with my family. My personal life has improved along with the practice."

And from another: "Seven weeks ago I was unsure as to whether or not I would continue practicing chiropractic. I had lost my sense of purpose and felt overwhelmed with confusion and sadness at the condition of the world, where I found myself and in life. Not a pretty picture. As a last resort I attended [a WISE] introductory seminar.

"On December 30, 1991, I took myself to the introductory seminar. On December 31st I decided to sign up for a complete management package. I immediately noticed a dramatic change in one of my chiropractic assistants, and for myself the decision to begin the management program signified a clear commitment to my belief in myself. All was not lost after all.

"Now only seven weeks later, my original failing practice has almost doubled and . . . I know my purpose and willingly accept the responsibility that goes along with it. I am filled with energy and find true happiness in my work. I feel like this is my first year in practice instead of my seventh."

An Allstate insurance industry executive wrote this testimonial concerning the implementation of Mr. Hubbard's administrative procedures in his office by another WISE member:

"I'm convinced that the training provided by you and your firm had a good deal to do with the positive results we experienced during the last year.

"Our production results were above goal; we have a better partnership atmosphere in the region; our managers feel they are in better control of their destiny rather than letting the environment control them."

The manager of a famous Hollywood restaurant reported: "Using the organizational technology of L. Ron Hubbard has done more in the last 11 months than the 20 years before to make the restaurant an efficient, effective and profitable organization. In my opinion, no other investment could have come close to that performance."

A technology consultant who worked as a staff scientist at Massachusetts Institute of Technology, wrote: "I highly recommend that any serious student in the business would observe for himself the practical method that Mr. Hubbard has developed."

A marketing executive reported: "L. Ron Hubbard has developed extremely workable procedures for predicting and handling the problems that accompany periods of rapid growth. As a result of knowing and applying these procedures we now find ourselves well organized to deal with our current high level of production, and we are prepared to expand further without undue strain on our resources.

"We consider Hubbard administrative technology to be a fundamental key to our continued success."

A major corporation executive said: "As president of my company, it has been my good fortune to be connected with the WISE organization, receiving business consultation. I have tried many other business technologies, especially in the areas of marketing and management leadership, and was very discouraged at the results. In a very short time working with a WISE consultant, using the administrative technology of Mr. Hubbard, I found I could easily apply the information and raise the production level of my company. I have also noticed a marked increase in the morale of my staff due to the material they learned through WISE courses."

A chartered accountant stated: "With the direction from the WISE membership I was able to find the exact L. Ron Hubbard administrative technology which I needed to handle a major problem with my company. By training my staff on courses at the Hubbard College, I have easily doubled my production. Without WISE membership assistance and L. Ron Hubbard's administrative technology made available, I would not have been able to locate or handle this problem at all."

According to a highly successful investment counselor: "L. Ron Hubbard's management technology is world-class. It is an innovative and remarkably workable method of improving conditions. Being a WISE member and using this technology has allowed me to improve my business and to face head-on the challenges of work and life with a smile and with enthusiasm.

"This is priceless data. It's also simple and basic. Results are immediate. If you are having any business difficulties this stuff can turn your entire career or business around in a matter of days. It's that powerful."

And, from an insurance adjustment company senior executive: "L. Ron Hubbard administrative technology has been the management technology that I have followed since I started our insurance adjusting company in 1979. This technology has taken my company from a one-man operation out of a rented house to the fastest growing insurance adjusting company in southern California with over 140 employees.

"Prior to studying and applying this technology, I studied business administration throughout my more than six years in college. I had been attempting to get answers in the areas of personnel, client relationships, finance, production, quality of work product and marketing. Somehow the answers I got were vague and not data that could be readily applied.

"I came upon Hubbard Management Technology in the early 70s and decided it was worth looking into. And that it was. I have taken courses in this technology and apply it to my company on a daily basis. Almost all of our employees have graduated from the more advanced programs.

"Through WISE membership this technology has been made available. I urge all businessmen to become WISE members and take advantage of its services and benefits."

And one member reports the outcome of a WISE arbitration: "The thought of an arbitration used to cause me to sweat cold bullets . . .

"Then I got an arbitration from WISE. The results were amazing. And yes, I felt much better afterwards. But the real bonus was the end result—fairness. Both parties had to confront their own responsibility in the matter and the ethics of the situation was taken into account, not just the technicalities of some obscure law . . . I thoroughly recommend it. Really for the first time, it is possible to resolve disputes sanely, without paying exorbitant sums on legal fees."

WHY IS WISE IMPORTANT?

Inflation, recession, lowered productivity, imbalance of trade, bankruptcy, soaring national debts, strikes, unemployment, poverty and want—these well-known symptoms of economic decline and instability on this planet are actually indicators of a much deeper problem—a crippling lack of administrative know-how. If today's businesses and governments could grasp and competently apply the basic principles of organization and administration, they would be able to enact workable solutions to end economic chaos rather than perpetuate it. Increased survival on the third dynamic would ensue.

WISE offers the hope of improvement in this sphere of society. WISE members bring sanity and order into their environment. Every WISE member is a point of stability that reduces confusion in this uncertain world. Businesses can prosper, governments can rule wisely and populations can live without economic duress. With L. Ron Hubbard's administrative technology, the goals that have evaded society for so long are within reach.

THE WORKABILITY OF L. RON HUBBARD'S ADMINISTRATIVE TECHNOLOGY

Robert Goldscheider, a management technology consultant for thirty-three years, has been special counsel to multinational corporations, the UN Industrial Development and the World Intellectual Property Organizations. He observed the application of Mr. Hubbard's administrative technology in the business world.

"Having had a firsthand opportunity to delve rather deeply into the administrative writings of L. Ron Hubbard, I am impressed. The technology is infused with common sense and practicality.

"Particular aspects, proven to be successful at all levels of the corporations I visited and analyzed, include:

"AVAILABILITY—The entire body of his administrative technology is carefully recorded in bound volumes, indexed and cross-referenced by title, subject and date. This affords a stability at all levels where corporate executives and staff alike can become acquainted with policy and cooperate as a group.

"THE ORG BOARD—The organizing board pattern is an innovative discovery which can be adapted to accommodate a large multipurpose corporation or customized to the needs, purposes and strategies of a particular organization.

"MANAGEMENT BY STATISTICS—A carefully organized reporting system, broken down to quantify and qualify virtually every aspect of operations relevant for sensitive management control. The ability to react very promptly to developments is one of the attributes of LRH administrative technologies, and is perhaps the key reason they have been successfully applied so consistently.

"INDIVIDUALITY—The techniques and systems developed to choose the correct personnel for a job, and how to train and stabilize them to perform their functions, has never before been so well described or completely delineated.

"In my opinion, the management technologies of L. Ron Hubbard superbly take into account long-run policies and daily needs of modern business and administrative operations. If the MBA products of our most eminent business schools had measured up to these standards in the past decade, I doubt that the American and world economies would be in their current disarray.

"I know of no other body of administrative laws and methods which is as complete, as workable and as broadly applicable as Mr. Hubbard's. His philosophy of organizational know-how and his lucid explanations for its application deserve wide use in industry, commercial enterprises, and government."

Robert Goldscheider, Chairman
The International Licensing Network, Ltd.,
Technology Management Consultants

PART EIGHT

THE STATISTICS AND GROWTH OF SCIENTOLOGY

No religion in history has spread as fast or as far in as short a time as Scientology. Today it is practiced in more than 30 languages in 74 countries on every continent.

This part details the expansion of Scientology from its birth in the United States in the early 1950s to its scope today. The next five chapters cover a wide variety of data on Scientology and Scientologists, the "firsts" which have spurred its ascendancy, the history of its expansion, documentation of the sources who have opposed it and the predictions about Scientology by sociologists, religionists and others.

Here is a look at the phenomenon of a new religion emerging and flourishing in a time of generally declining religious influence.

CHAPTER 27

DEMOGRAPHIC AND STATISTICAL FACTS ABOUT SCIENTOLOGY

This chapter presents facts and figures about Scientology which detail its rapid dissemination and growth around the world. These include results of an extensive demographic survey of Scientologists from every continent which provide a picture of who they are, what they are like, their attitudes, lifestyles and more.

Scientologists represent a tremendously varied cross section of society, and include Kenyan farmers, Norwegian fishermen, Brazilian soccer players, Japanese businessmen, Italian educators and on and on. To typify a Scientologist, one must disregard age, race, occupation, nationality or political allegiance, for Scientologists cover the entire spectrum.

Scientologists are healthy (over half do not miss a single day of work in any given year), active (a majority are involved in some form of church, human rights, environmental or charitable activity) and successful in their work (¾ in the US earn more than the national average wage). Scientologists are also drug free (none at all use illegal street drugs).

Such figures run counter to many current trends in society and underscore the fact that Scientology helps people lead better lives. More people are discovering and embracing Scientology every day. Its expansion increases because it continues to offer meaningful solutions to universal problems.

WORLD EXPANSION OF DIANETICS AND SCIENTOLOGY

NUMBER OF COUNTRIES

WHERE DIANETICS AND SCIENTOLOGY TECHNOLOGIES ARE AVAILABLE AND IN USE

Since the establishment of the first Dianetics and Scientology organizations in the early 1950s, the number of countries where Dianetics and Scientology technologies are available and in use has grown by almost 20 times. At the current rate of expansion, Scientology churches will be found in every country in the world within 15 years.

(Statistics shown below are cumulative.)

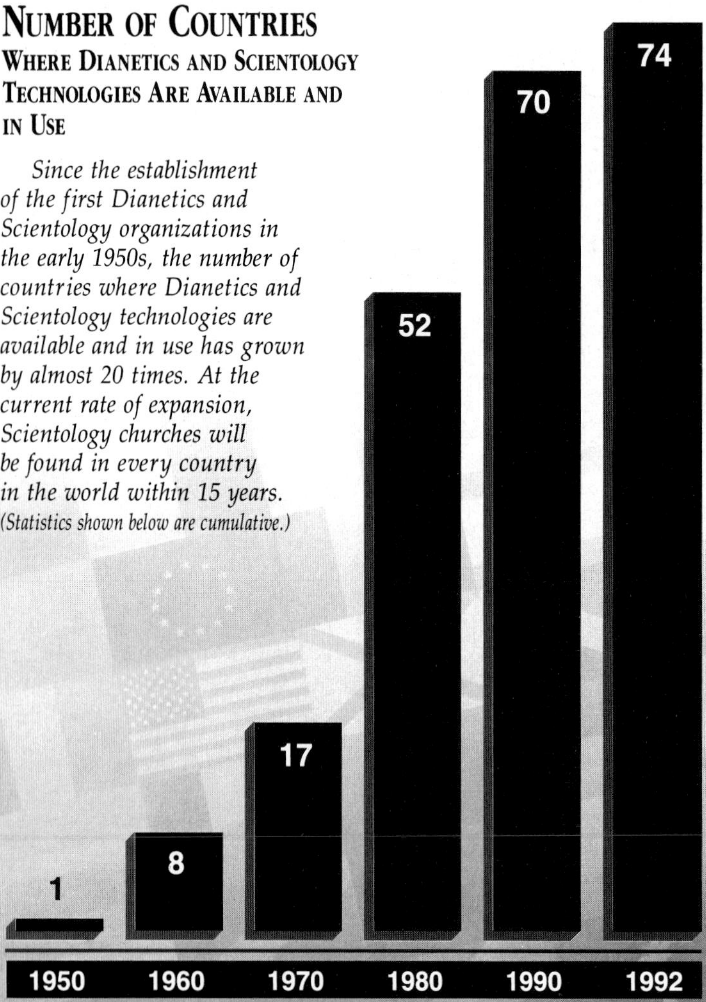

COUNTRIES

IN WHICH DIANETICS AND SCIENTOLOGY SERVICES ARE DELIVERED

1. ALBANIA
2. ALGERIA
3. ARGENTINA
4. AUSTRALIA
5. AUSTRIA
6. BELGIUM
7. BRAZIL
8. BULGARIA
9. CANADA
10. CHILE
11. CHINA
12. COLOMBIA
13. COSTA RICA
14. CROATIA
15. CUBA
16. CZECH REPUBLIC
17. DENMARK (INCLUDING GREENLAND)
18. DOMINICAN REPUBLIC
19. ECUADOR
20. EL SALVADOR
21. ESTONIA
22. ETHIOPIA
23. FINLAND
24. FRANCE
25. GERMANY
26. GHANA
27. GREECE
28. GUATEMALA
29. HONDURAS
30. HUNGARY
31. INDIA
32. INDONESIA
33. IRELAND
34. ISRAEL
35. ITALY
36. IVORY COAST
37. JAPAN
38. KENYA
39. LUXEMBOURG
40. MALTA
41. MALAYSIA
42. MEXICO
43. NEPAL
44. NETHERLANDS
45. NETHERLANDS ANTILLES
46. NICARAGUA
47. NIGERIA
48. NORWAY
49. NEW ZEALAND
50. PAKISTAN
51. PERU
52. PHILIPPINES
53. POLAND
54. PORTUGAL
55. PUERTO RICO
56. ROMANIA
57. RUSSIA
58. SAUDI ARABIA
59. SIERRA LEONE
60. SINGAPORE
61. SLOVENIA
62. SOUTH AFRICA
63. SOUTH KOREA
64. SPAIN
65. SWEDEN
66. SWITZERLAND
67. TAIWAN
68. TANZANIA
69. TURKEY
70. URUGUAY
71. UNITED KINGDOM
72. UNITED STATES
73. VENEZUELA
74. ZAIRE
75. ZIMBABWE

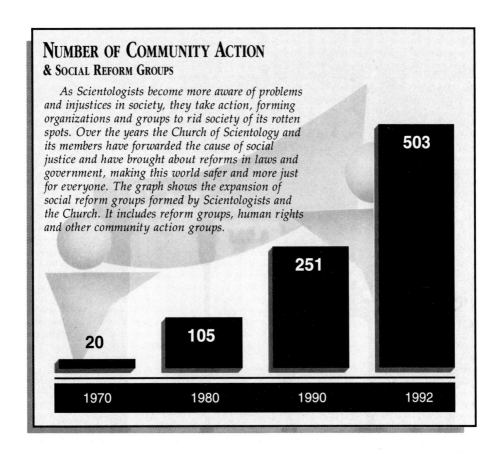

NUMBER OF COMMUNITY ACTION
& SOCIAL REFORM GROUPS

As Scientologists become more aware of problems and injustices in society, they take action, forming organizations and groups to rid society of its rotten spots. Over the years the Church of Scientology and its members have forwarded the cause of social justice and have brought about reforms in laws and government, making this world safer and more just for everyone. The graph shows the expansion of social reform groups formed by Scientologists and the Church. It includes reform groups, human rights and other community action groups.

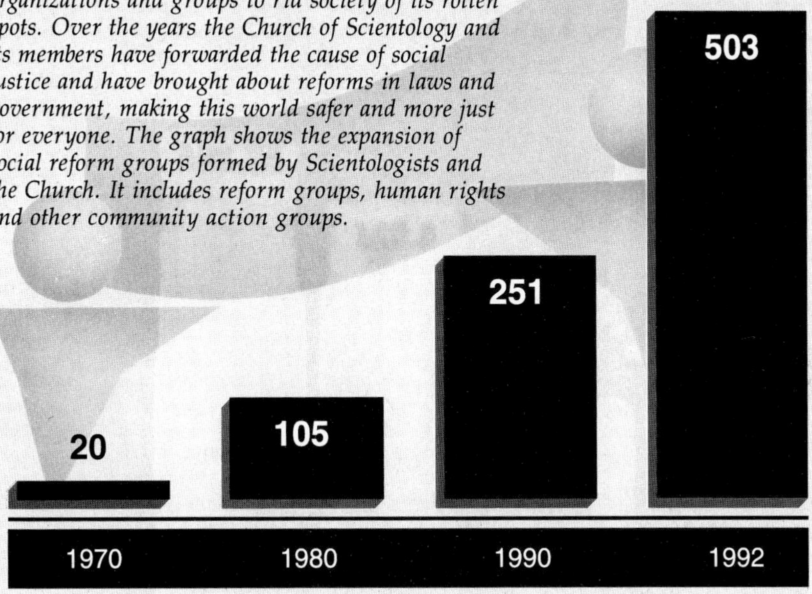

CHURCHES, MISSIONS AND ORGANIZATIONS:
OVER 40 YEARS OF GROWTH

L. Ron Hubbard's technology is made available to individuals through a growing number of organizations around the world that provide a broad range of services from education and drug rehabilitation to Scientology auditing and training.

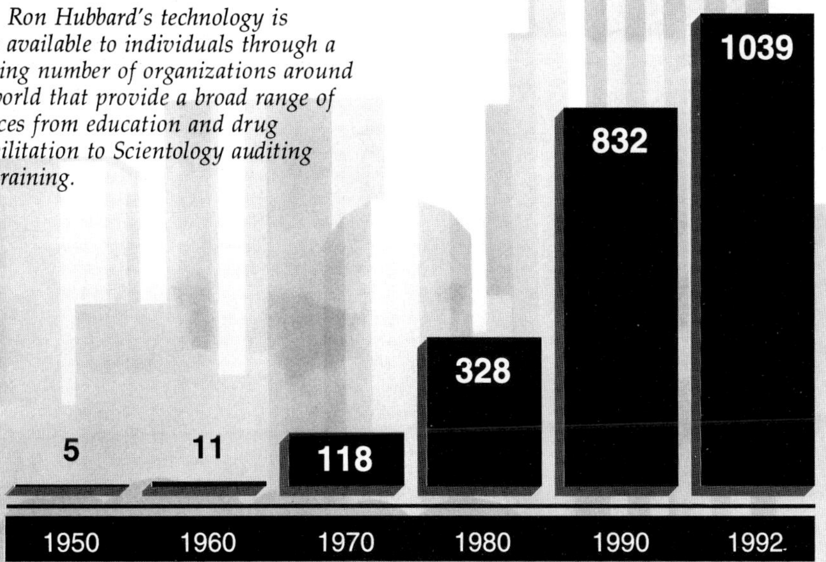

CHURCH OF SCIENTOLOGY STAFF

CONTRACTED SCIENTOLOGY STAFF IN CHURCHES AND MISSIONS INTERNATIONALLY

With the expansion of Dianetics and Scientology, the need for staff to train and audit members of the Church has increased commensurately. In the last two decades the number of contracted Scientology staff in churches and missions around the world has grown by more than 4 times. This reflects more organizations and the growth of existing ones.

(1970 is the first year that accurate records for contracted staff internationally are available.)

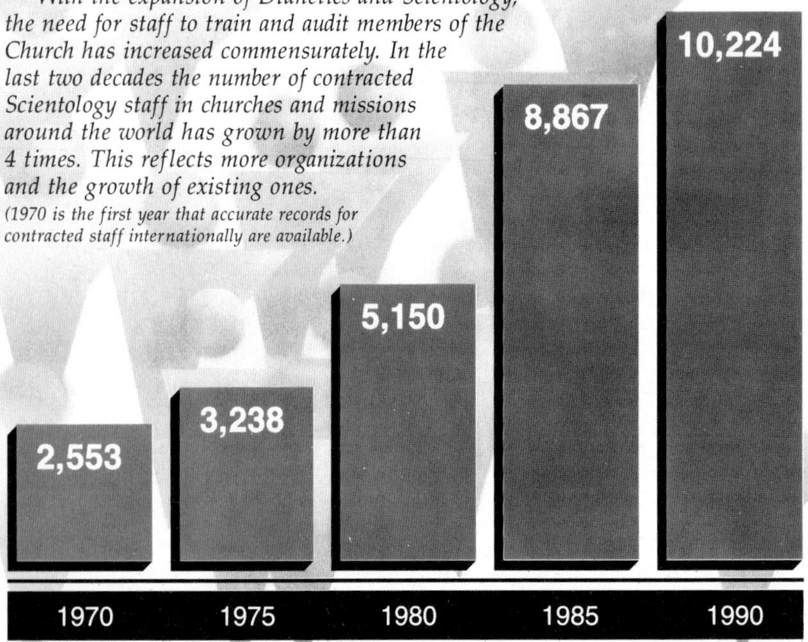

PERCENTAGE DISTRIBUTION OF CHURCH AND MISSION STAFF

The graphic below shows the global distribution of Scientology staff.

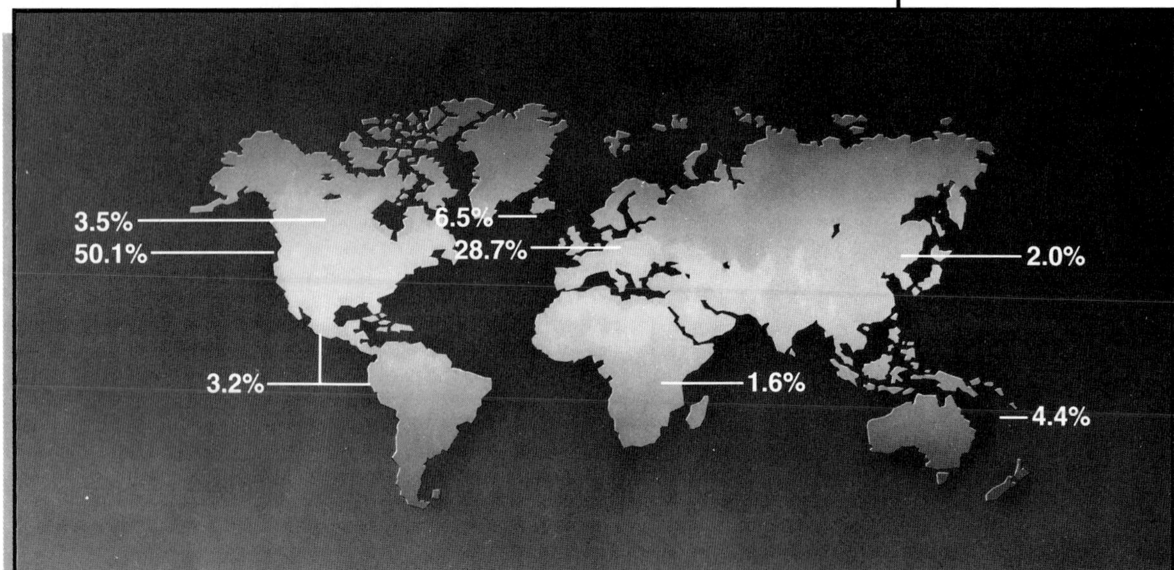

SERVICES OF THE CHURCH OF SCIENTOLOGY

NUMBER OF PEOPLE
PARTICIPATING IN SCIENTOLOGY FOR THE FIRST TIME (PER YEAR)

A fair gauge of just how many people are interested in Scientology can be seen in the following graph, which reflects the annual number of individuals entering a church or mission for the first time, obtaining a service, book or lecture. The volume each year has increased by over 5½ times since 1970—to almost half a million new people a year in 1990.

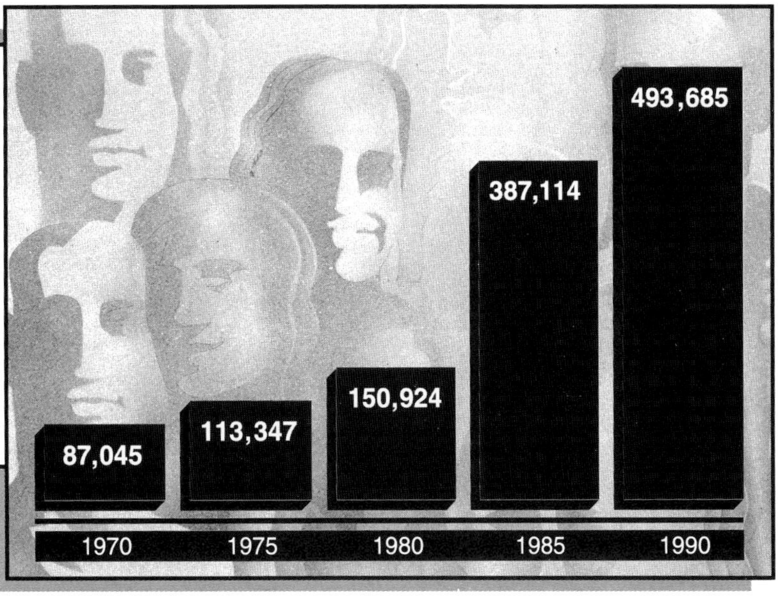

NUMBER OF AUDITING HOURS
DELIVERED YEARLY IN CHURCHES AND MISSIONS (NOT CUMULATIVE)

The number of yearly auditing hours delivered in church organizations is seen in the graph below. In just the last decade, auditing hours have almost doubled and the 10-year total is over 10 million hours. There are countless hours of auditing delivered outside churches and missions around the world every day which are not included in the figures below.

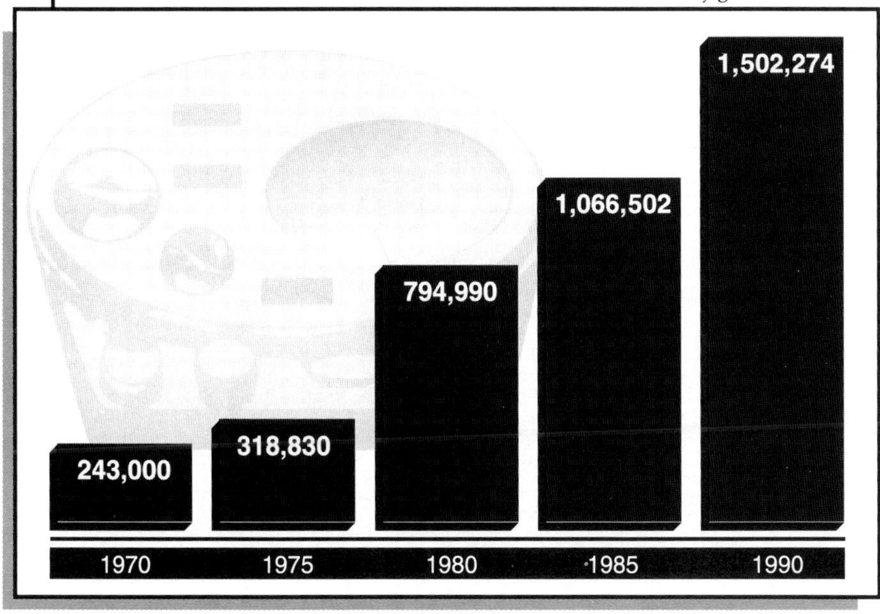

SCIENTOLOGY MAGAZINE DISTRIBUTION

GROWING IN CIRCULATION

Churches and missions produce their own periodicals which are regularly mailed to their members.

*Three of the Church's more important publications are **The Auditor,** the magazine of all Saint Hill Organizations, **Source** magazine, the publication of the Flag Service Organization and **Advance!** which is the magazine of the Advanced Organizations. Their increasing circulation reflects the constant growth of these organizations.*

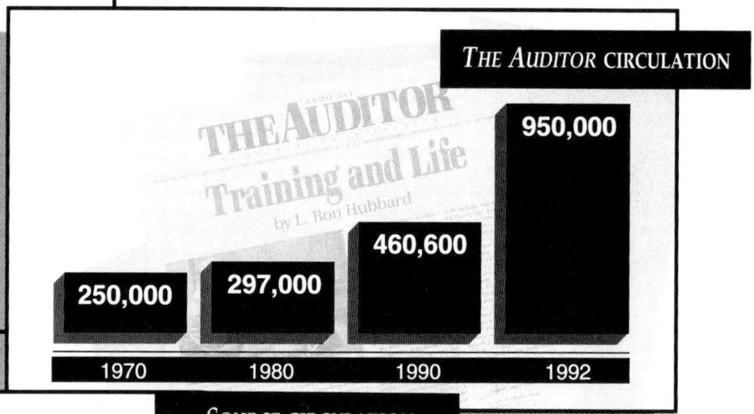

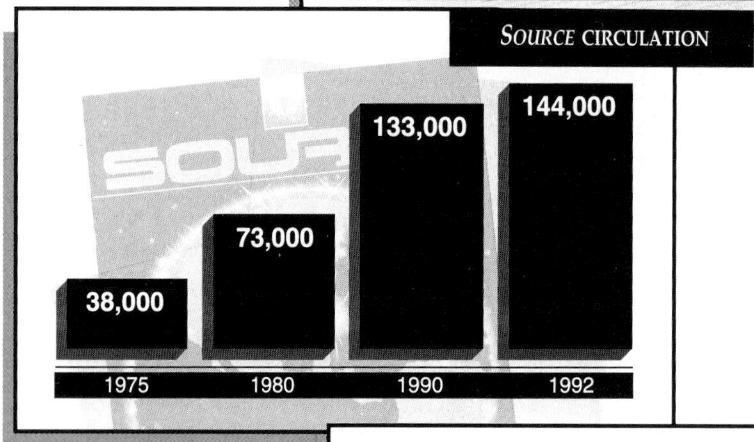

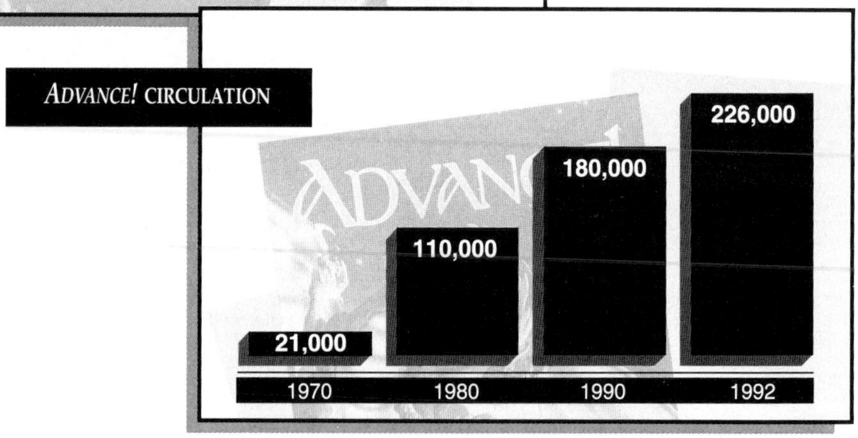

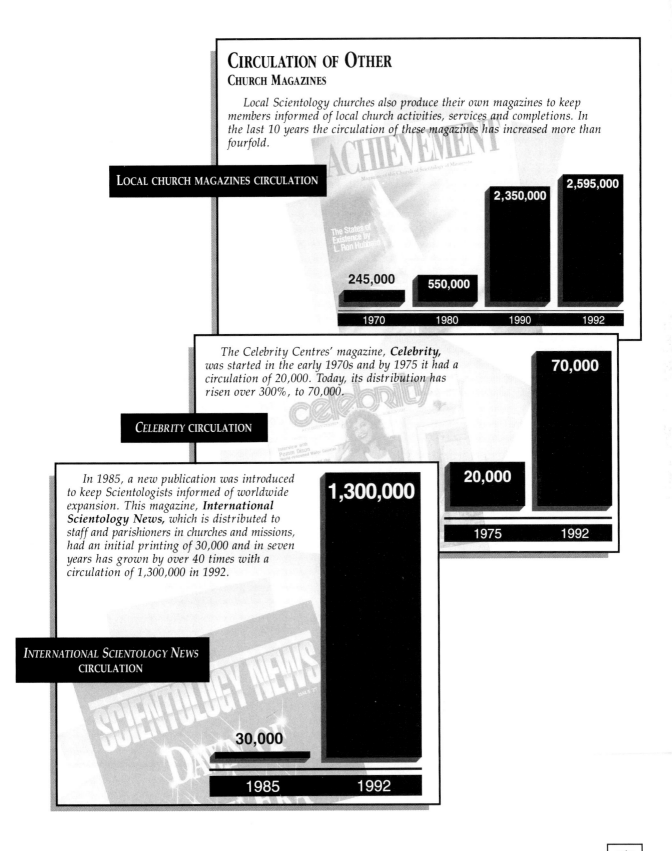

CIRCULATION OF OTHER CHURCH MAGAZINES

Local Scientology churches also produce their own magazines to keep members informed of local church activities, services and completions. In the last 10 years the circulation of these magazines has increased more than fourfold.

LOCAL CHURCH MAGAZINES CIRCULATION

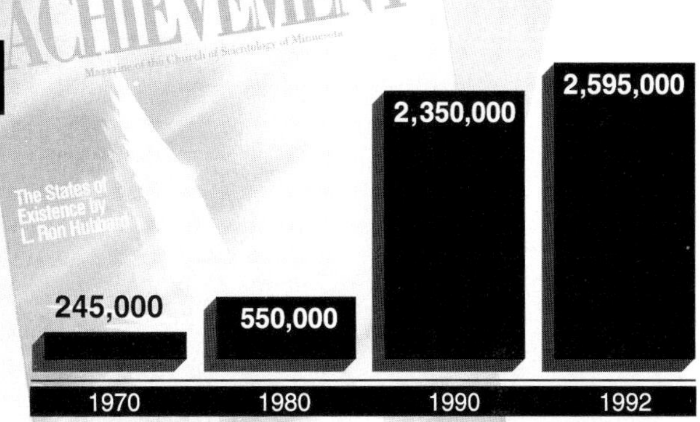

The Celebrity Centres' magazine, ***Celebrity,*** *was started in the early 1970s and by 1975 it had a circulation of 20,000. Today, its distribution has risen over 300%, to 70,000.*

CELEBRITY CIRCULATION

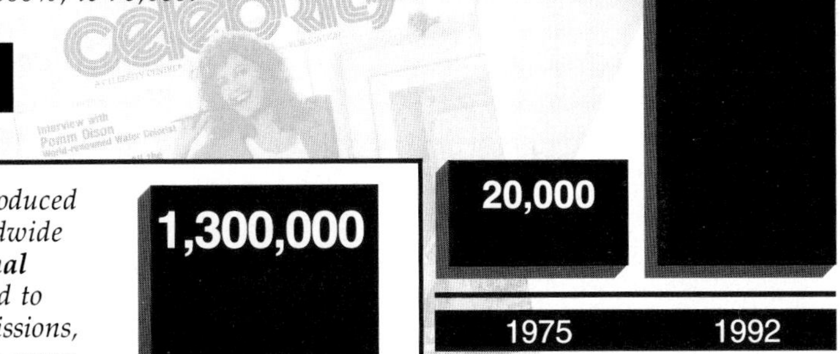

In 1985, a new publication was introduced to keep Scientologists informed of worldwide expansion. This magazine, ***International Scientology News,*** *which is distributed to staff and parishioners in churches and missions, had an initial printing of 30,000 and in seven years has grown by over 40 times with a circulation of 1,300,000 in 1992.*

INTERNATIONAL SCIENTOLOGY NEWS CIRCULATION

POSITIVE RESPONSE TO DIANETICS AND SCIENTOLOGY

In 1988, the Church of Scientology hired an independent national research company to conduct two public opinion surveys: one among those who had purchased copies of ***Dianetics: The Modern Science of Mental Health*** *and the other among members of the Church.*

An extraordinarily high consensus of opinion was revealed. In fact, the research company admitted that it had never seen responses so uniformly favorable.

DIANETICS IMPROVES LIVES

When ***Dianetics*** *bookbuyers were asked, "Would you say that applying the techniques in* ***Dianetics*** *has changed your life?" 79% responded affirmatively. 90% felt that* ***Dianetics*** *was successful in "helping man to improve his potential," while 84% felt that the book "helped people become more successful" and "taught people how to be happier."*

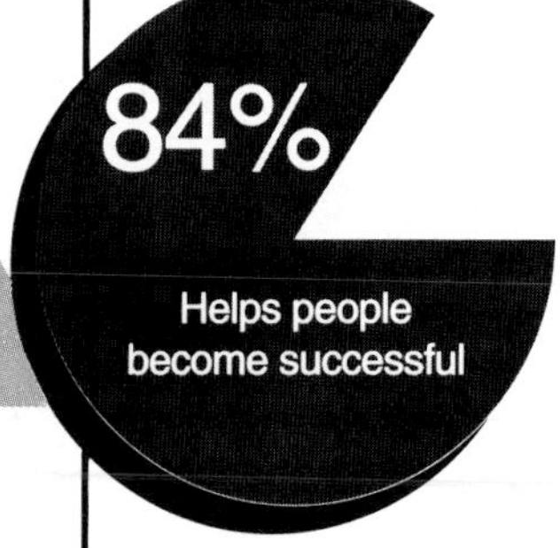

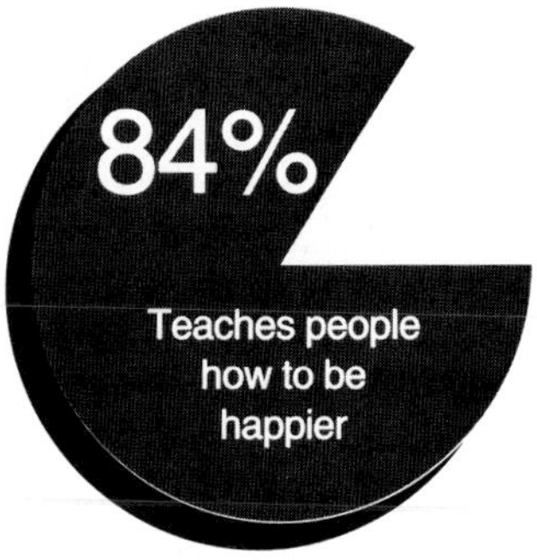

SCIENTOLOGY MAKES A DIFFERENCE

In a survey among Church of Scientology members, 97% responded that Scientology has made "a great deal" of difference in their lives, with the remaining 3% responding that it had made some difference. 91% stated that Scientology had either "exceeded" or "met" their expectations.

Ninety-six percent of Church members reported that they had received auditing, with 97% of those who had been audited saying it was helpful and 95% stating they wanted more.

Eighty-eight percent of the Scientologists said that the idea of becoming an auditor themselves was appealing. 100% of those surveyed agreed that Scientology successfully "teaches people to think more clearly."

These responses are testimony to the workability of Dianetics and Scientology.

L. RON HUBBARD'S BOOKS

PUBLIC POPULARITY

The popularity of Scientology can be measured by the number of Dianetics and Scientology books in public hands. The total number of L. Ron Hubbard's nonfiction titles sold since 1950 is 60,447,625. The rate of increase in public demand is possibly best seen in the number of ***Dianetics: The Modern Science of Mental Health*** *books sold since its release in 1950. The graph below shows the cumulative* ***Dianetics*** *sales over the last 22 years.*

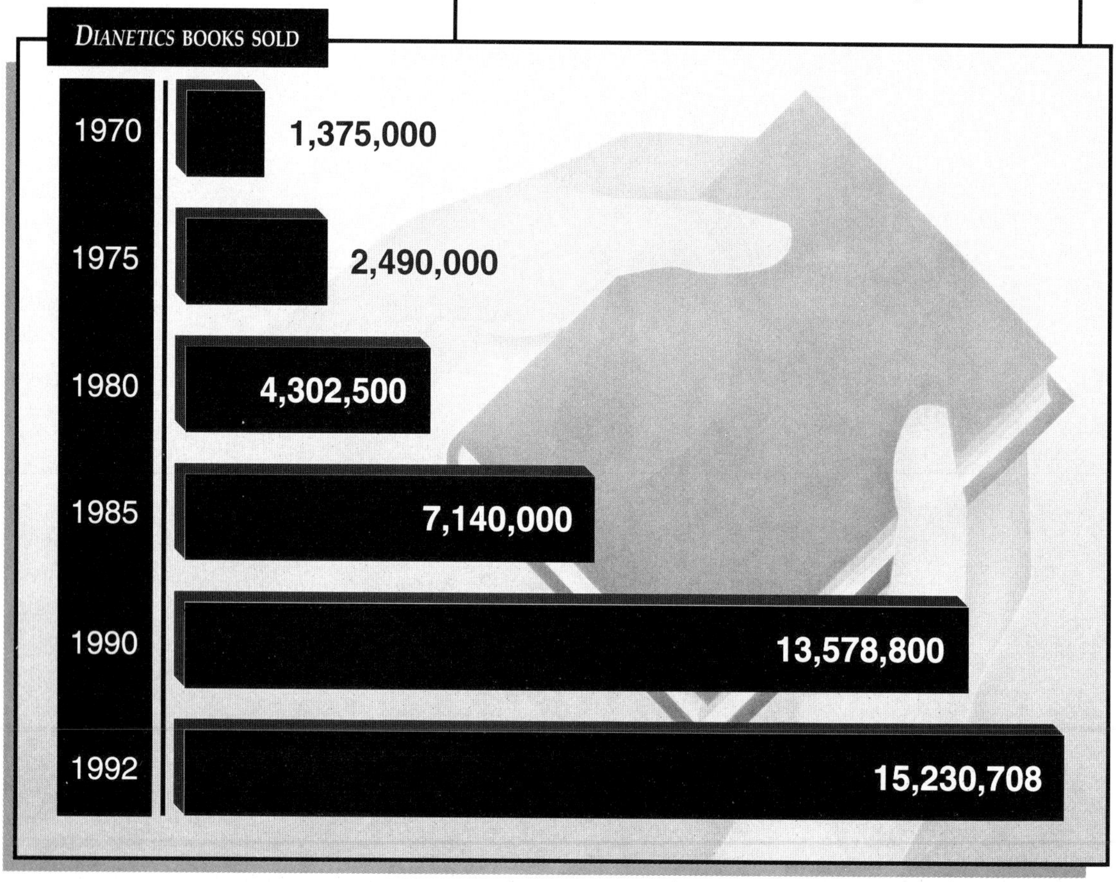

L. Ron Hubbard's works are in such huge demand around the world that they are distributed in the 104 countries shown below.

1. *Albania*
2. *Algeria*
3. *Argentina*
4. *Australia*
5. *Austria*
6. *Bahamas*
7. *Belgium*
8. *Belorussia*
9. *Bolivia*
10. *Brazil*
11. *Bulgaria*
12. *Cameroon*
13. *Canada*
14. *Chile*
15. *China*
16. *Colombia*
17. *Congo*
18. *Costa Rica*
19. *Croatia*
20. *Cuba*
21. *Cyprus*
22. *Czech Republic*
23. *Denmark (includes Greenland)*
24. *Dominican Republic*
25. *Ecuador*
26. *Egypt*
27. *El Salvador*
28. *Estonia*
29. *Ethiopia*
30. *Finland*
31. *France (includes Reunion Island, Polynesian Islands [Tahiti], St. Pierre & Miquelon)*
32. *French Guiana*
33. *French Polynesia*
34. *Germany*
35. *Ghana*
36. *Greece*
37. *Guadeloupe*
38. *Guatemala*
39. *Guyana*
40. *Haiti*
41. *Honduras*
42. *Hungary*
43. *Iceland*
44. *India*
45. *Indonesia*
46. *Ireland*
47. *Israel*
48. *Italy*
49. *Ivory Coast*
50. *Jamaica*
51. *Japan*
52. *Jordan*
53. *Kenya*
54. *Korea*
55. *Kuwait*
56. *Latvia*
57. *Lebanon*
58. *Lithuania*
59. *Luxembourg*
60. *Madagascar*
61. *Mali*
62. *Malta*
63. *Malaysia*
64. *Mauritius*
65. *Mexico*
66. *Monaco*
67. *Morocco*
68. *Netherlands*
69. *Netherlands Antilles*
70. *Nepal*
71. *New Zealand*
72. *Nicaragua*
73. *Nigeria*
74. *Norway*
75. *Pakistan*
76. *Peru*
77. *Philippines*
78. *Poland*
79. *Portugal*
80. *Romania*
81. *Russia*
82. *Senegal*
83. *Singapore*
84. *Slovenia*
85. *South Africa*
86. *Spain*
87. *Sri Lanka*
88. *Sudan*
89. *Sweden*
90. *Switzerland*
91. *Taiwan (Formosa)*
92. *Tanzania*
93. *Thailand*
94. *Trinidad*
95. *Tunisia*
96. *Turkey*
97. *Ukraine*
98. *United Arab Emirates*
99. *United Kingdom (includes Bermuda, Gibraltar, Hong Kong & Montserrat)*
100. *United States (includes Puerto Rico)*
101. *Uruguay*
102. *Venezuela*
103. *Zaire*
104. *Zimbabwe*

To meet the worldwide demand for L. Ron Hubbard's works, his books have been published in the 31 languages listed below.

1. *Afrikaans*
2. *Arabic*
3. *Bahasa Indonesia*
4. *Chinese*
5. *Czechoslovakian*
6. *Danish*
7. *Dutch*
8. *English*
9. *Finnish*
10. *French*
11. *German*
12. *Greek*
13. *Hebrew*
14. *Hungarian*
15. *Italian*
16. *Japanese*
17. *Korean*
18. *Norwegian*
19. *Polish*
20. *Portuguese*
21. *Punjabi*
22. *Russian*
23. *Serbo-Croatian*
24. *Sotho*
25. *Spanish*
26. *Swahili*
27. *Swedish*
28. *Taiwanese*
29. *Urdu*
30. *Xhosa*
31. *Zulu*

SOCIAL BETTERMENT AND REFORM ACTIVITIES

NUMBER OF
SOCIAL BETTERMENT GROUPS

The Church of Scientology and its members actively participate in bettering society by establishing nonchurch groups and organizations around the world. Using L. Ron Hubbard's technology, Scientologists help children with school and study problems; work to rehabilitate drug addicts and criminals and bring about a safer environment through programs to increase moral values. The graph below shows the number of officially established and recognized groups using L. Ron Hubbard's technology to better social problems. There are many thousands of others less formally organized, but no less dedicated or effective—however, there are no accurate records of them available.

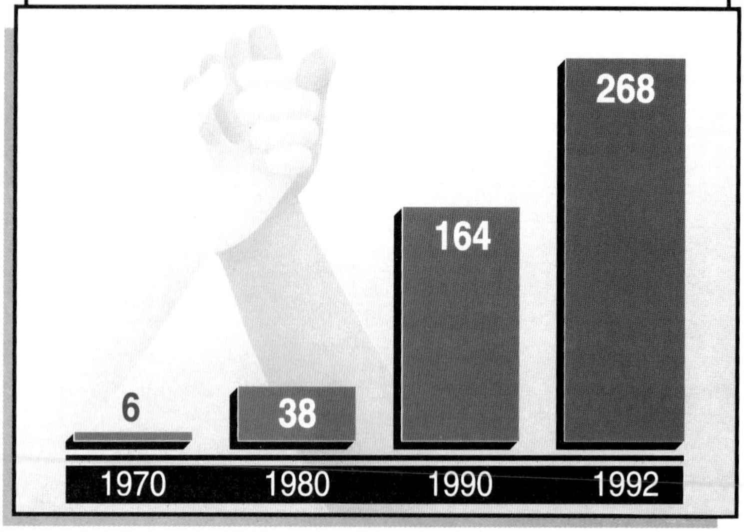

NARCONON
DRUG EDUCATION

Narconon (the drug rehabilitation program that uses L. Ron Hubbard's technology in this field) not only gets people off drugs, but also delivers drug education lectures and seminars to schools and community groups.

Starting their educational program in the early 1980s, in response to the onslaught of cocaine and crack addiction among Western youth, Narconon has delivered an average of more than 2 lectures per day reaching over 66,000 people a year.

Through its actions, Narconon has helped hundreds of thousands of students and adults avoid the horrors of drug use. The figures below are cumulative for each area.

NARCONON CENTER	NUMBER OF LECTURES	NUMBER OF ATTENDEES
Greater Los Angeles	5,327	203,576
Boston	1,704	168,143
Italy	1,500	300,000
Chilocco	534	24,750
Malmö	90	5,348
Huddinge	400	12,000
Spain	31	2,280
Switzerland	2	80
Denmark	137	4,176
Canada	98	7,806
Cumulative Total:	9,823	728,159

EFFECTIVENESS OF NARCONON
DEMONSTRATED BY GOVERNMENT STUDY

In 1987, a study was completed and released by an independent sociological research group in Spain on the success of Narconon. The research group, often used by the Spanish government, confirmed the remarkable results of Narconon.

Of the students surveyed, 69.2% were still off drugs two years later. Over two-thirds of those who had received other types of rehabilitation treatment stated that the effects from these treatments had been negative and unsuccessful, while 86.5% rated Narconon as very positive and 89.2% stated that the Narconon staff were very qualified.

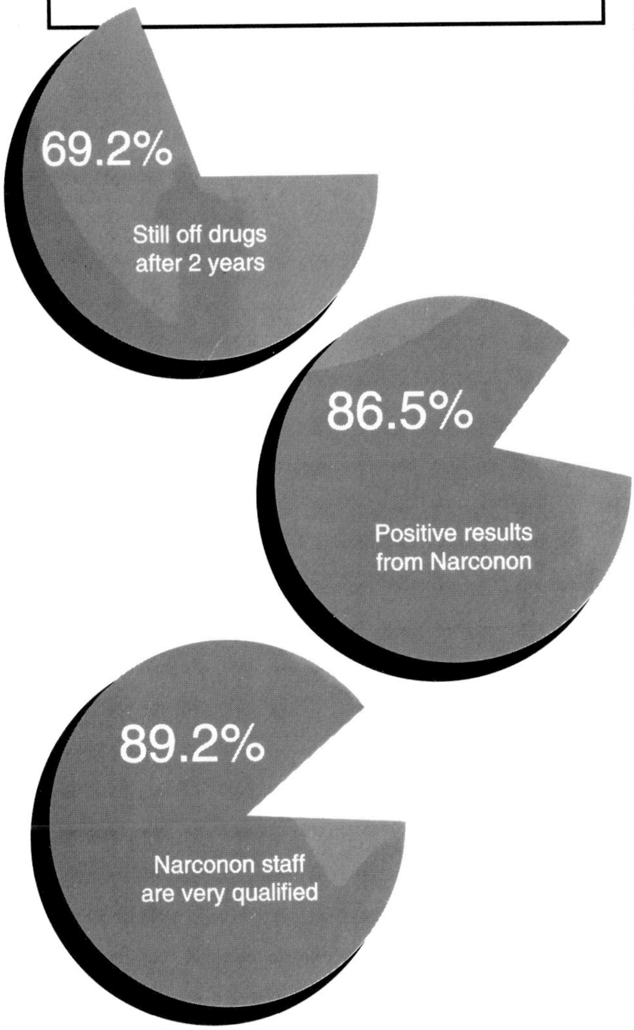

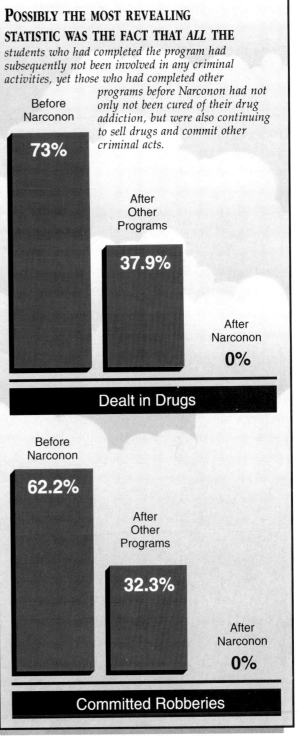

POSSIBLY THE MOST REVEALING STATISTIC WAS THE FACT THAT *ALL* THE *students who had completed the program had subsequently not been involved in any criminal activities, yet those who had completed other programs before Narconon had not only not been cured of their drug addiction, but were also continuing to sell drugs and commit other criminal acts.*

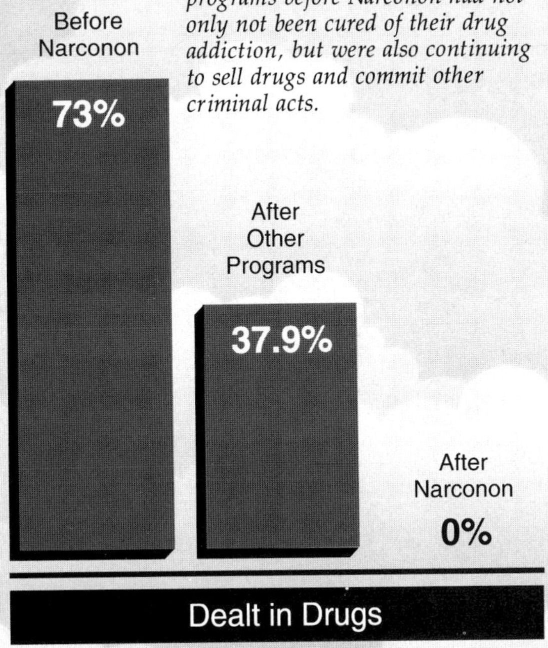

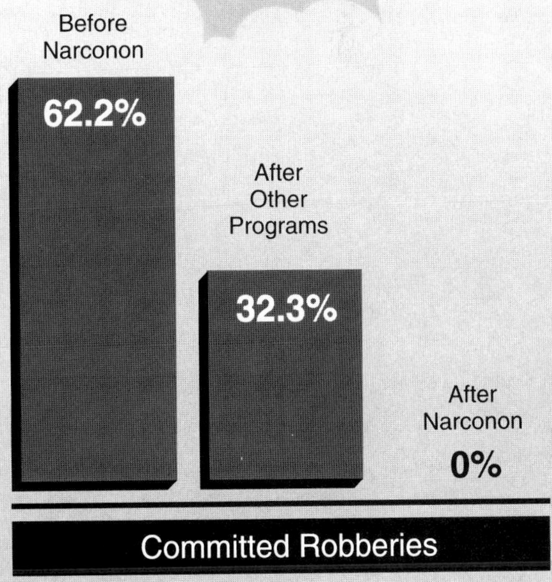

VITAL STATISTICS OF SCIENTOLOGISTS ACROSS THE WORLD

WHAT ARE SCIENTOLOGISTS LIKE?

What are their backgrounds and how do they live? What is important to them and what are their habits and interests? To answer these questions, surveys were mailed to Scientologists around the world. The statistics and graphs on the following pages reflect the results—showing attitudes, lifestyles and backgrounds of Scientologists. (A margin of ±3% is allowed to cover both statistical and sampling errors.)

HOW WERE YOU INTRODUCED TO SCIENTOLOGY?

Scientologists want their friends to know about what they find helpful. It is no surprise then that well over half of today's Church members were first introduced to Scientology through a friend or relative.

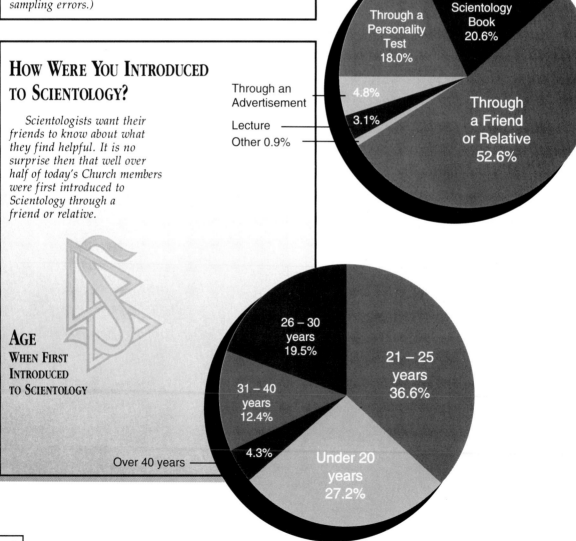

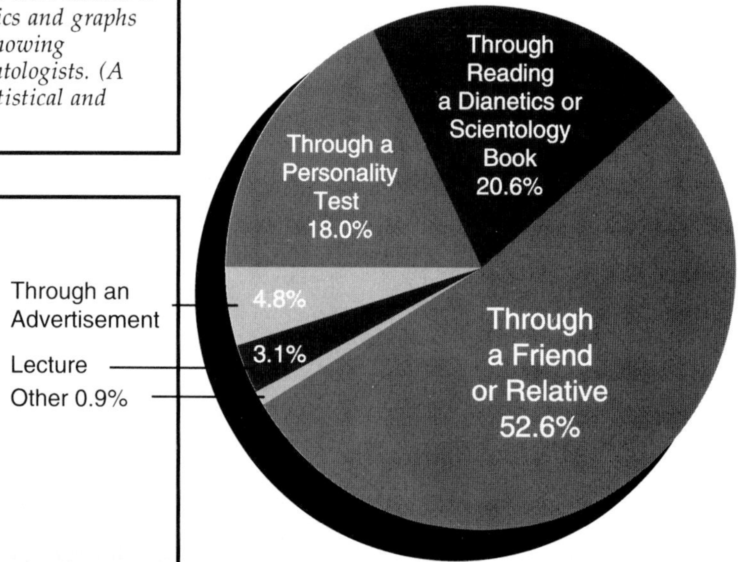

AGE
WHEN FIRST INTRODUCED TO SCIENTOLOGY

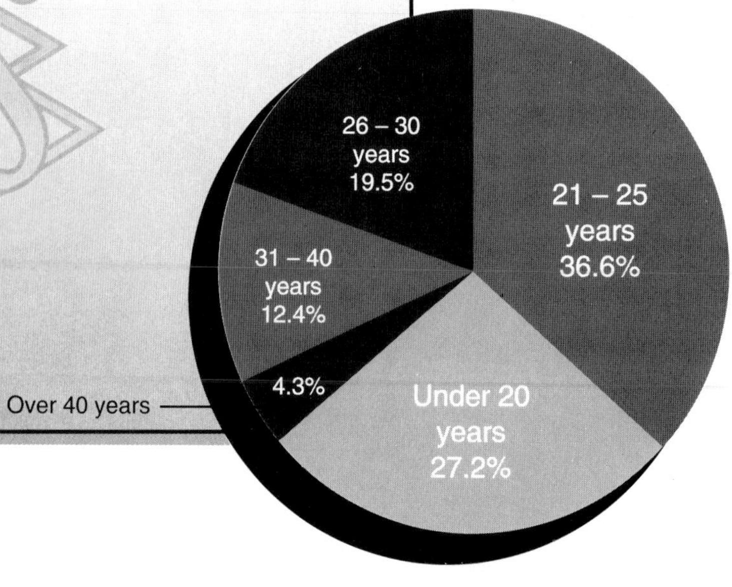

LENGTH OF TIME IN SCIENTOLOGY

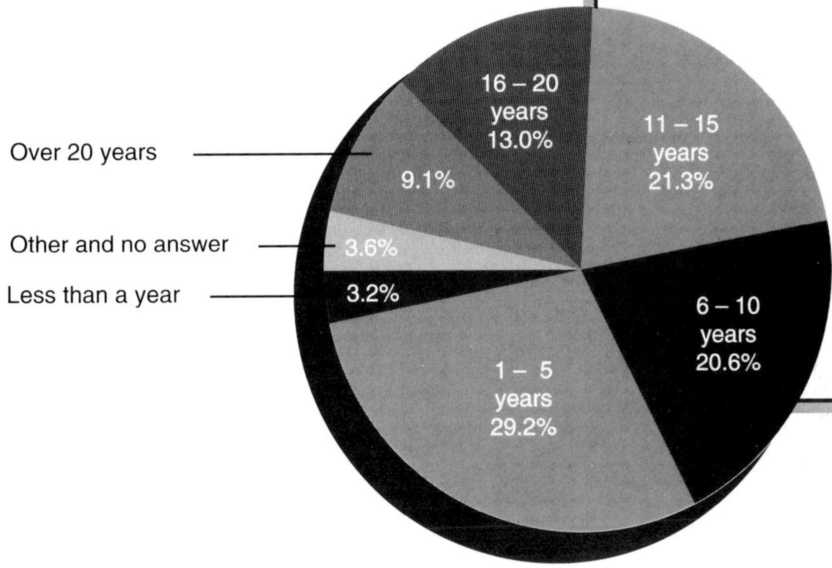

RELIGIOUS BACKGROUND

Scientologists have diverse ethnic and religious backgrounds.

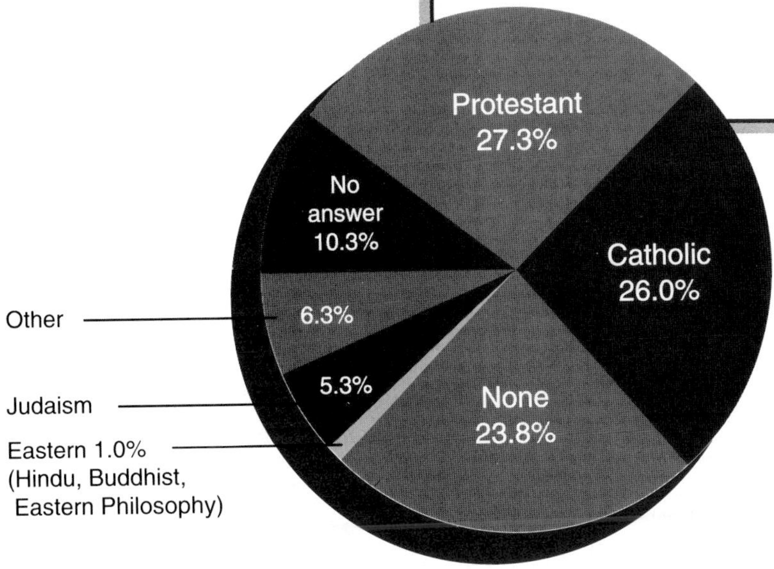

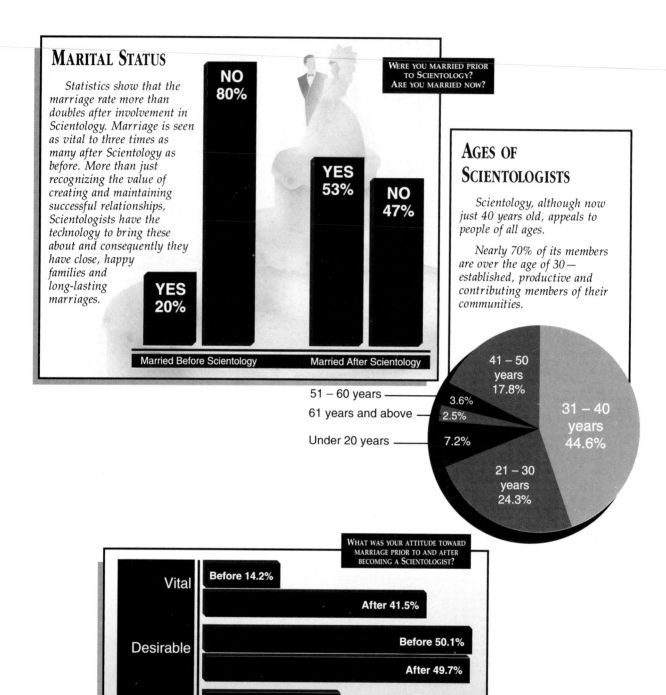

MARITAL STATUS

Statistics show that the marriage rate more than doubles after involvement in Scientology. Marriage is seen as vital to three times as many after Scientology as before. More than just recognizing the value of creating and maintaining successful relationships, Scientologists have the technology to bring these about and consequently they have close, happy families and long-lasting marriages.

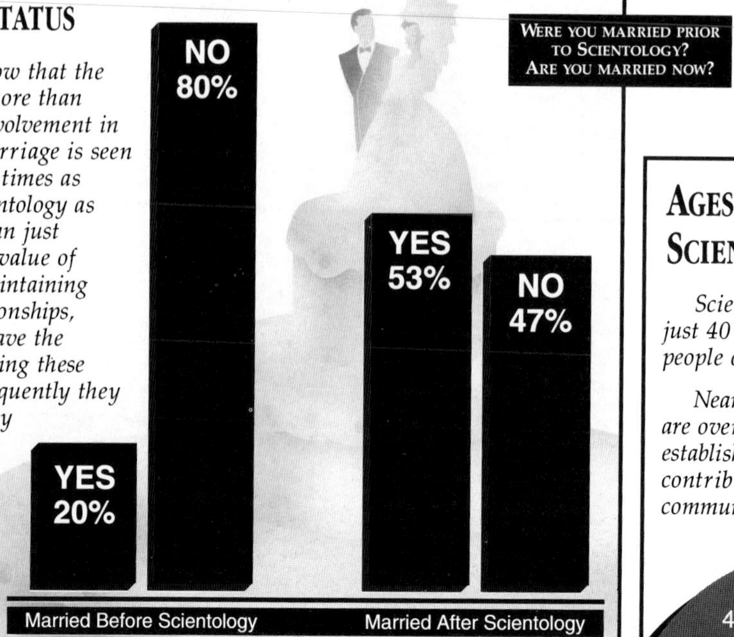

AGES OF SCIENTOLOGISTS

Scientology, although now just 40 years old, appeals to people of all ages.

Nearly 70% of its members are over the age of 30—established, productive and contributing members of their communities.

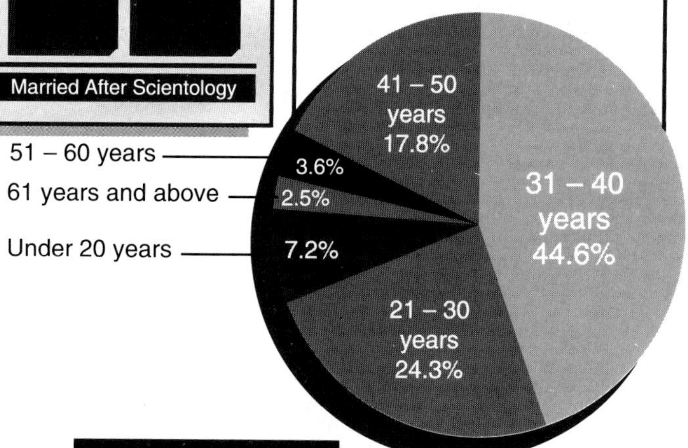

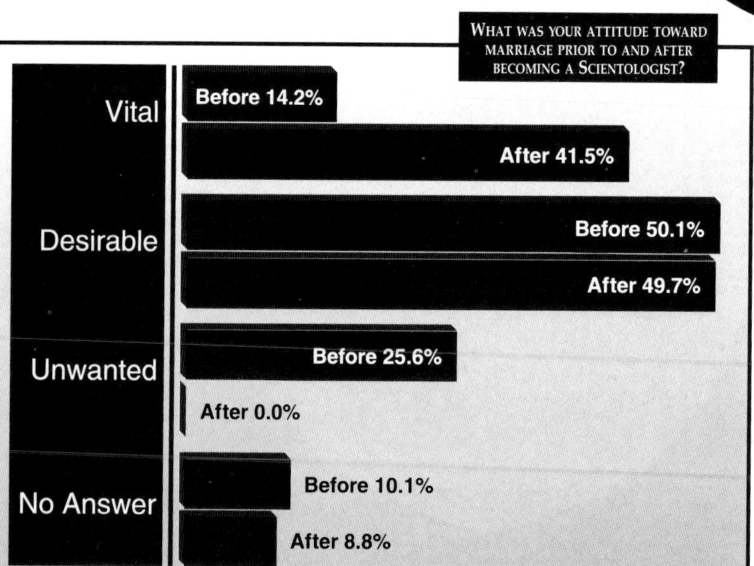

SCIENTOLOGISTS
AND THEIR FAMILIES

Over 97% of Scientology's married couples have children. They enjoy raising children, as do many other parents, and ensure that their children are involved in community and school projects, sports and other activities to give them a well-rounded upbringing.

(As a comparative, US census statistics show that 51% of America's married couples do not have children.)

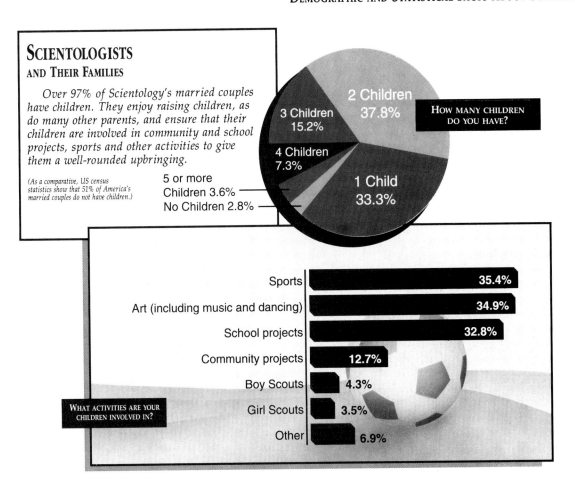

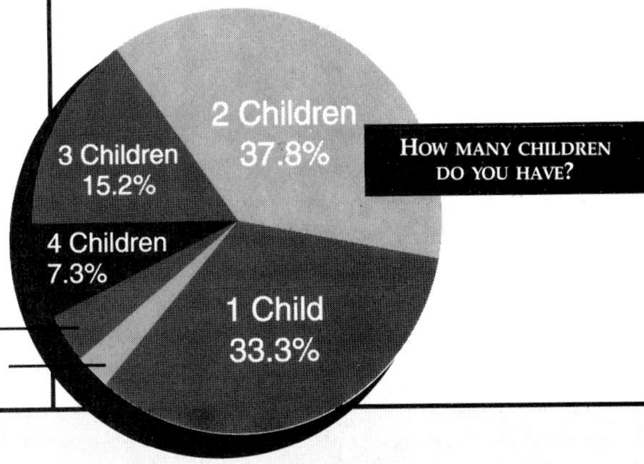

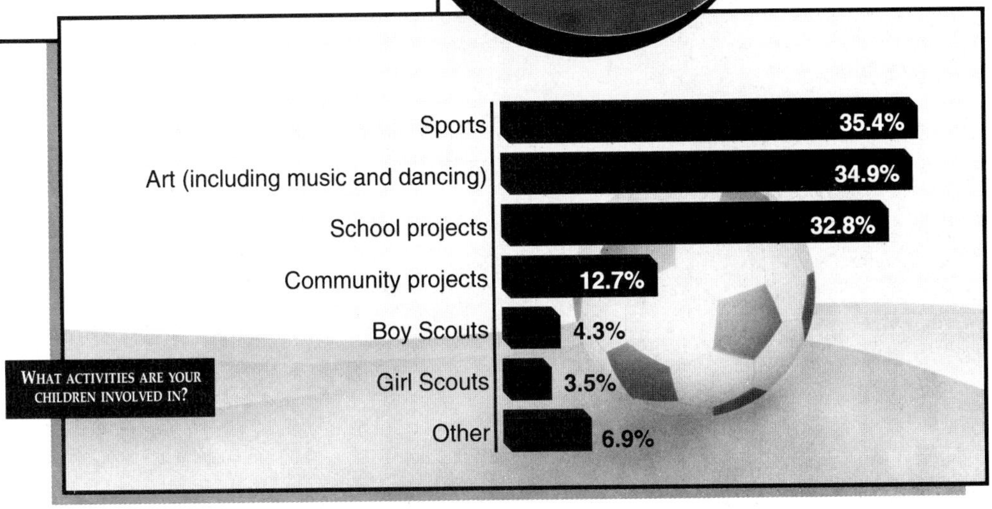

SCIENTOLOGISTS'
RESIDENCES

With over 50% of Scientologists married with children, corresponding numbers live in houses rather than apartments.

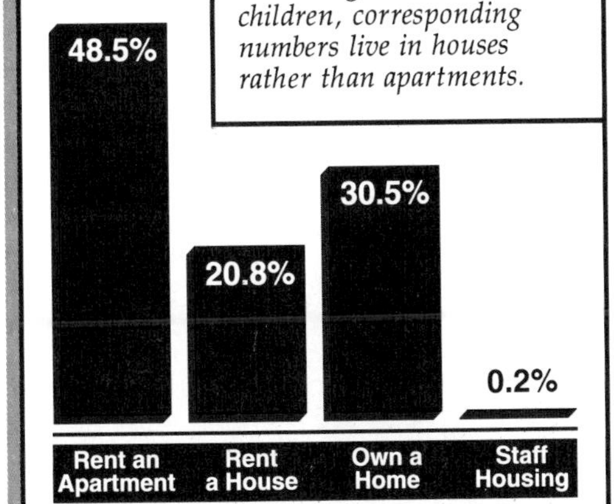

BOOKS READ
PER YEAR

Many individuals find Scientology improves their literacy. With this improvement comes a more avid interest in literature, with two-thirds of Scientologists reading 5 or more books per year.

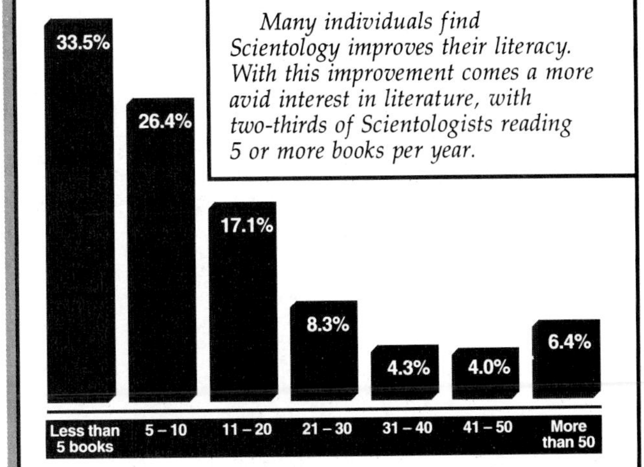

SCIENTOLOGISTS
& THEIR EDUCATION

Scientologists are well educated, with over 80% graduating high school and 23% graduating college including postgraduate work. Compared to the average educational levels found in the United States, the percentage of Scientologists graduating high school is more than 8% higher and those graduating college is more than 30% higher than the norm.

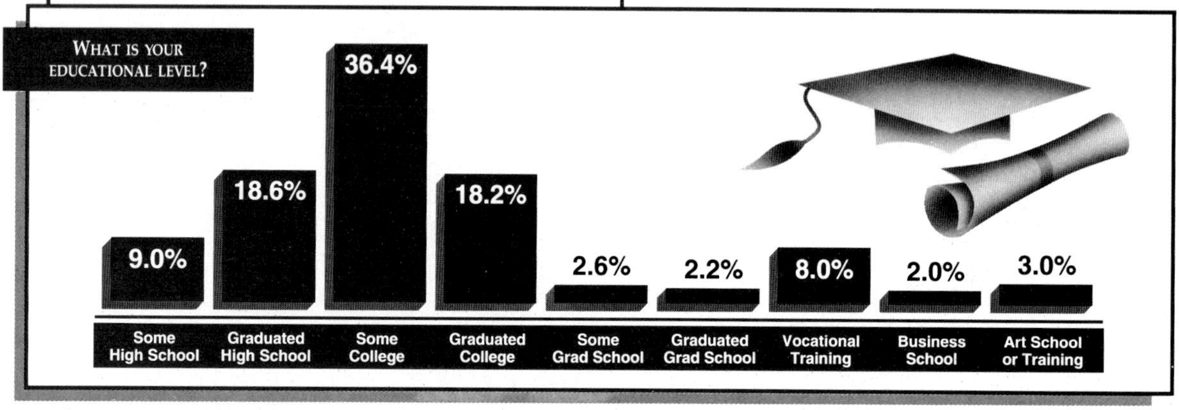

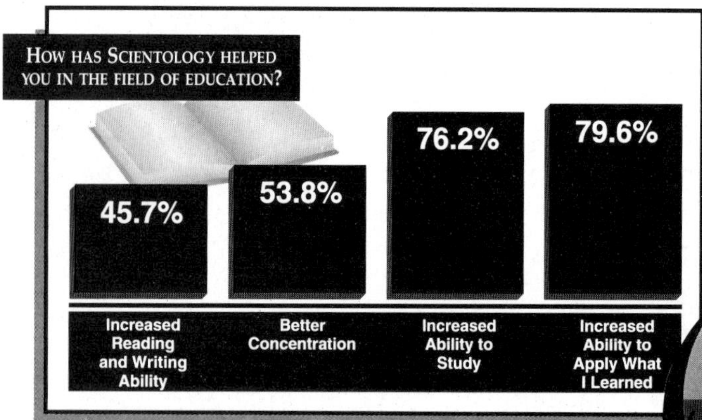

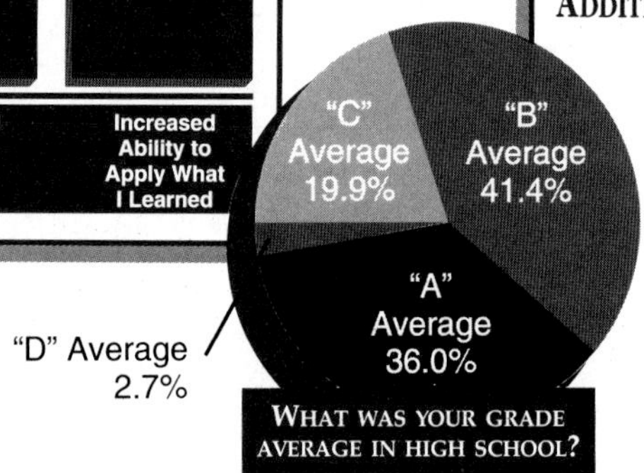

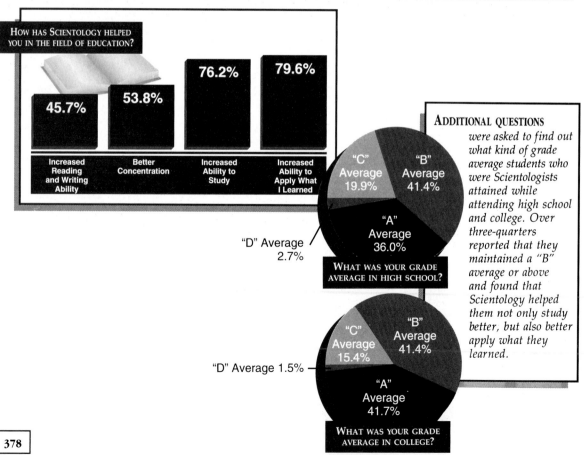

ADDITIONAL QUESTIONS *were asked to find out what kind of grade average students who were Scientologists attained while attending high school and college. Over three-quarters reported that they maintained a "B" average or above and found that Scientology helped them not only study better, but also better apply what they learned.*

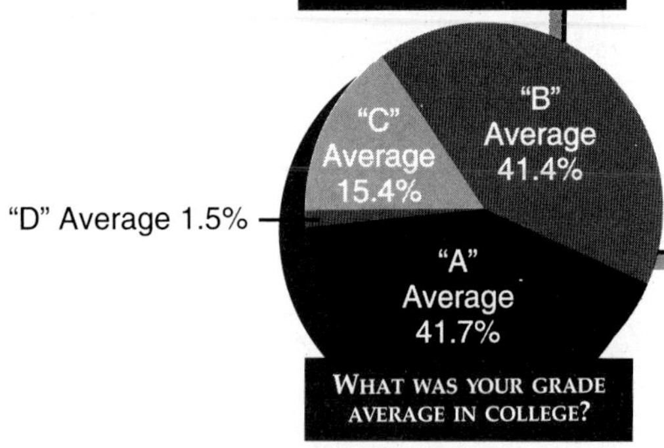

SCIENTOLOGISTS & WORK

Scientologists find that no matter what their occupation, Scientology helps them improve their competence. As a result they are more productive and valuable to their profession.

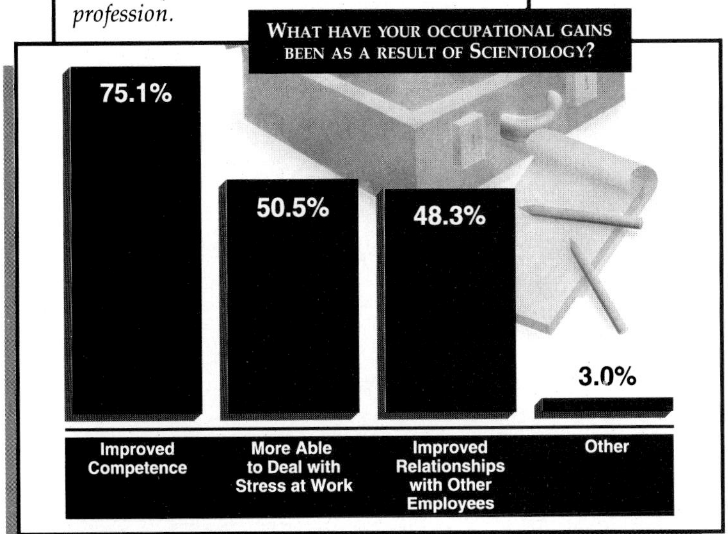

WHAT IS YOUR CURRENT OCCUPATION?

Managerial Position	16.5%	*Student*	4.8%
Arts, Technical & Engineering	15.6%	*Marketing & Advertising*	4.6%
Owner or Part-owner of Company	14.0%	*Clerical*	4.5%
Sales	10.2%	*Secretarial*	4.0%
Computers	8.1%	*Communications*	2.7%
Teaching	6.2%	*Law*	1.3%
Medical (including Nursing, Dental, etc.)	5.8%	*Sports*	0.9%
		Civil Service	0.8%
Construction	5.5%	*Armed Forces*	0.5%

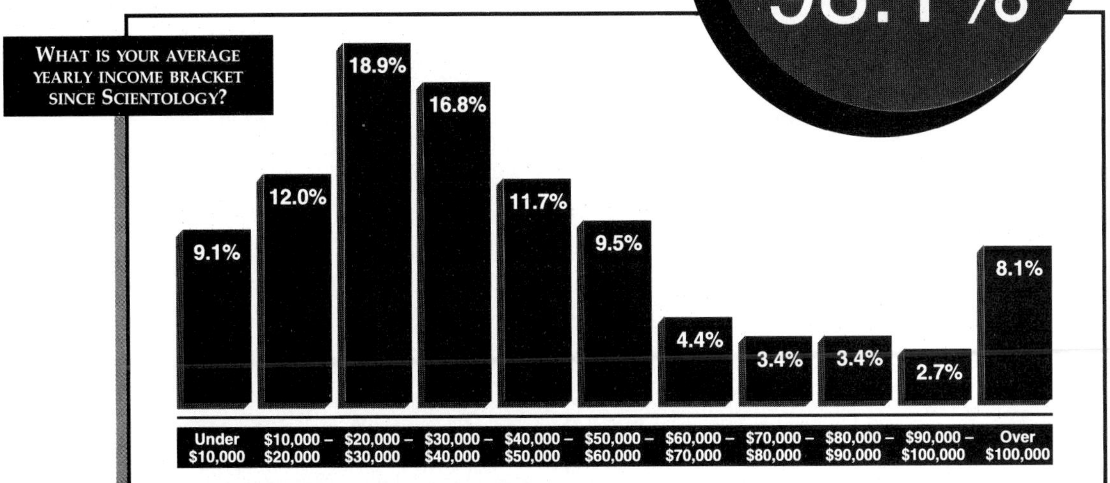

INCOME INFORMATION

*Per an independent national research group study of individuals who have purchased and read the book **Dianetics,** 84% of **Dianetics** book readers felt that Dianetics helped people become more successful. One measurement of success is the amount of income one makes.*

Today's average annual wage in the United States is $22,563: Of Scientologists surveyed 60% make in excess of $30,000 annually, and almost 80% exceed $20,000. Clearly the overwhelming majority of Scientologists have achieved greater success.

Scientologists do not look toward others to help them survive. They work hard to support themselves and their families. The percentage of Scientologists on welfare (which includes Scientologists in such countries as Sweden, Denmark and the United Kingdom where public assistance is even more prevalent than in the United States) is less than half of the average in the United States, which today is estimated at 4%.

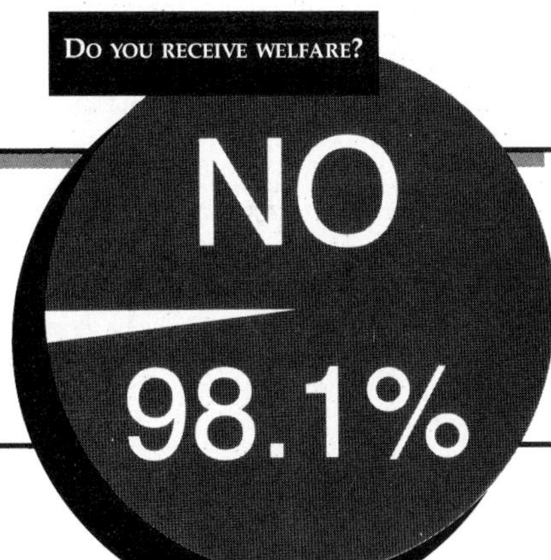

SCIENTOLOGISTS' HEALTH

Scientologists make productive employees. Almost 75% report they are ill less often than they were before Scientology. More than half report that, in the last year, they did not miss any days of work due to illness, and over 85% fall under the United States absenteeism average of almost 5 days missed a year due to illness.

A health-and-employee-benefits insurance expert reviewed the medical expenses for the 1,200 staff of the Church of Scientology International. He stated that its per capita medical costs ran between 10% and 20% of the national average.

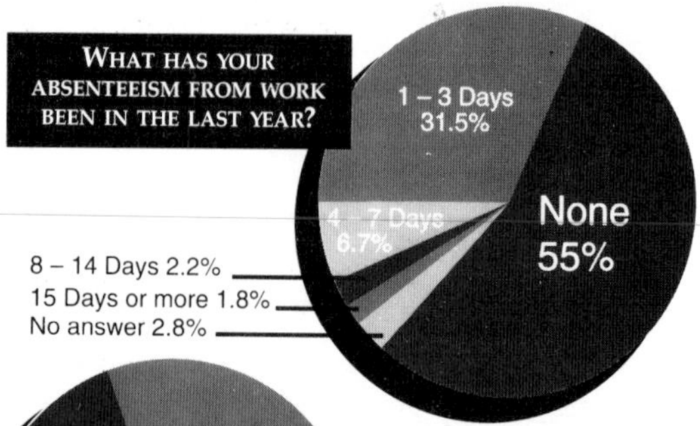

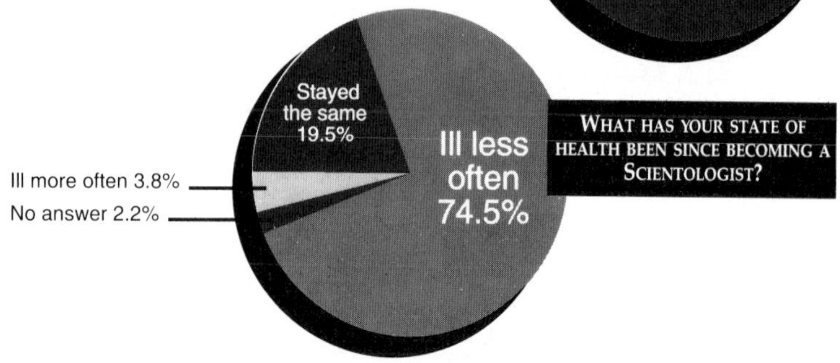

SCIENTOLOGISTS ARE LESS ACCIDENT-PRONE

Scientologists find that auditing and training greatly improve awareness of surroundings. In being more aware of one's environment, Scientologists tend to be less accident-prone than others. The following statistic shows that after Scientology the number of individuals involved in accidents is dramatically decreased.

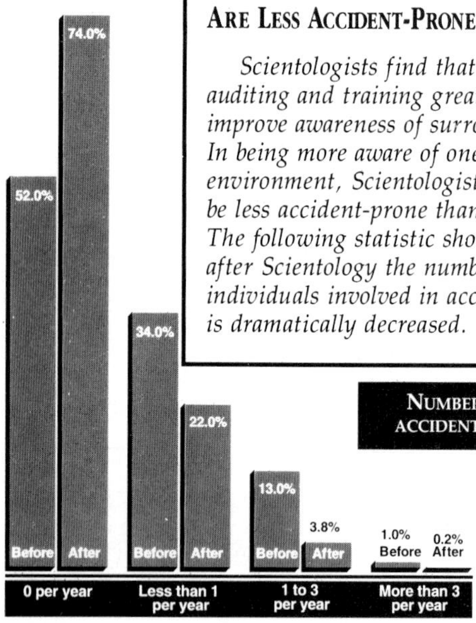

EXERCISE HABITS OF SCIENTOLOGISTS

Scientologists are active and extroverted—over 75% exercise at least once a week.

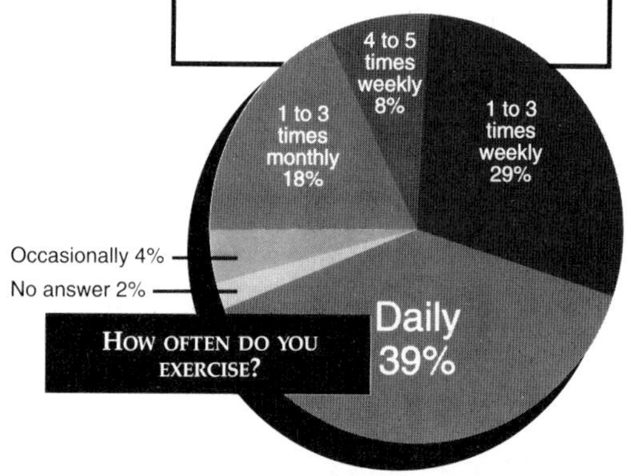

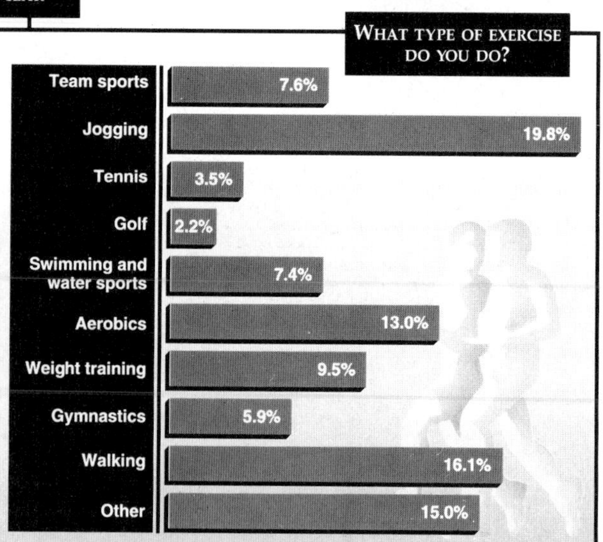

ALCOHOL USE
BY SCIENTOLOGISTS

Recent alcohol-use surveys done in the United States revealed that 7% drank alcohol daily, 56% sometimes and 37% never. In comparison, Scientologists' use of alcohol is lower than averages for the US and no Scientologist surveyed drinks on a daily basis.

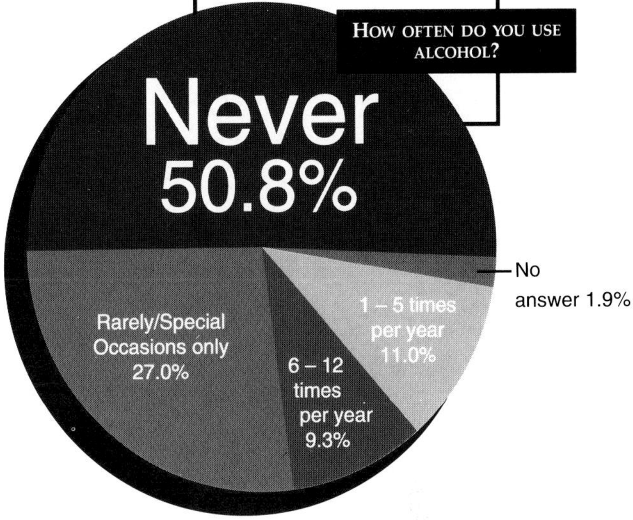

DRUG INTAKE
OF SCIENTOLOGISTS

In a drug-ridden culture, it is a fact that all Scientologists are drug free. 100% say they take no street drugs at all. This statistic is even more dramatic when compared to the 1990 US government figures showing that over 50% of those between the ages of 18 to 25 use drugs.

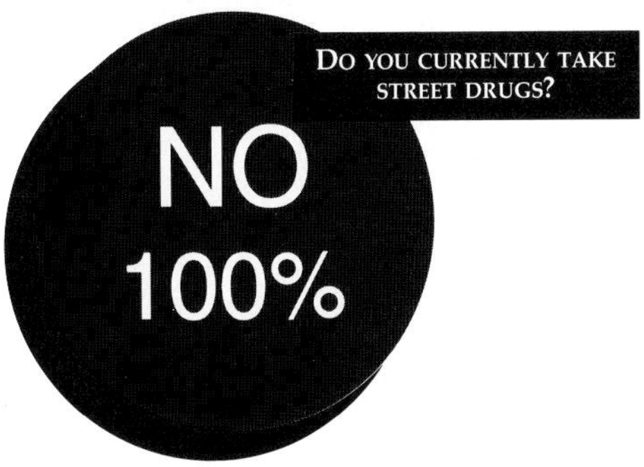

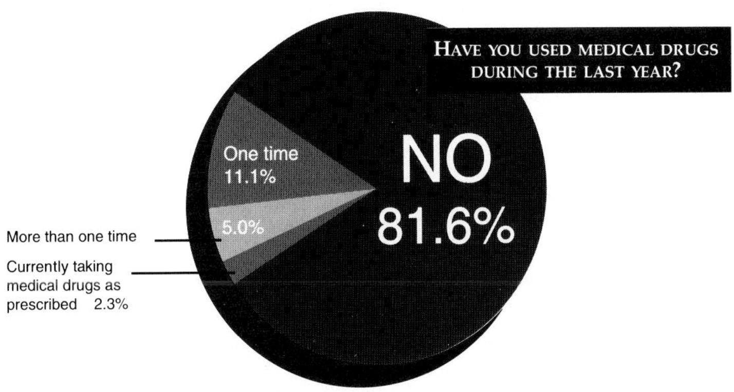

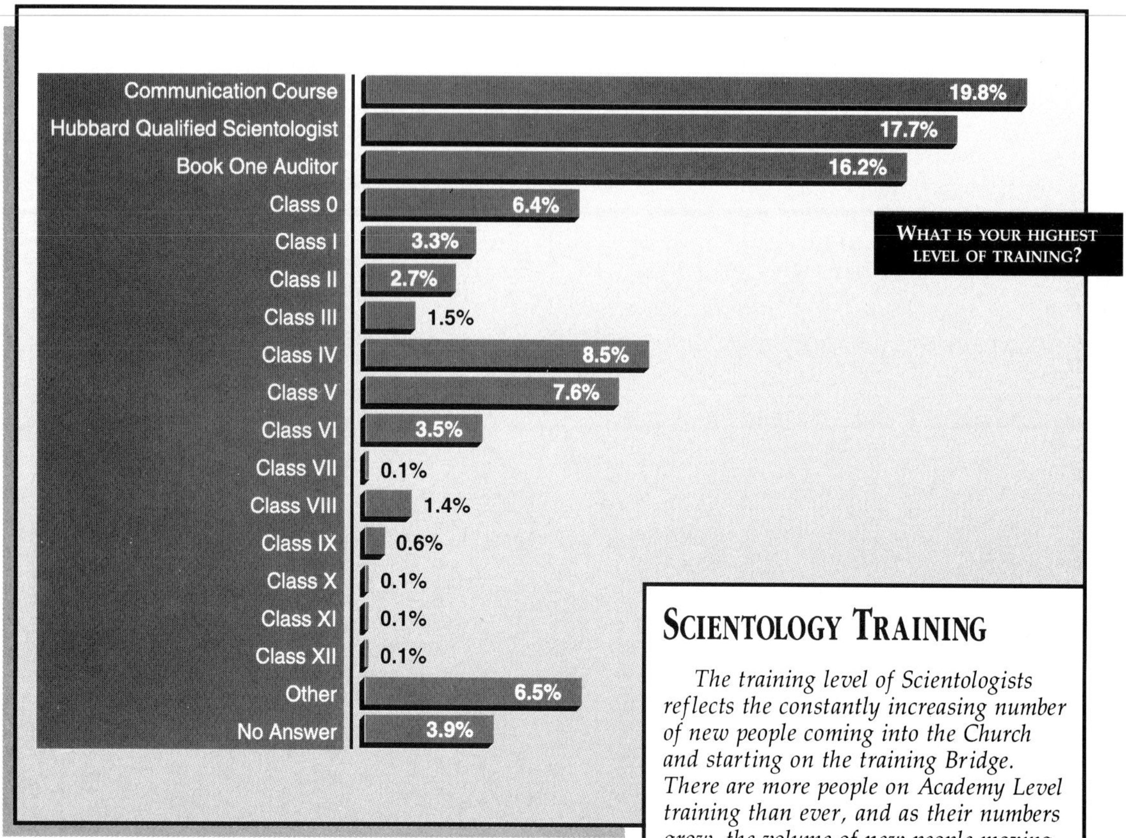

SCIENTOLOGY TRAINING

The training level of Scientologists reflects the constantly increasing number of new people coming into the Church and starting on the training Bridge. There are more people on Academy Level training than ever, and as their numbers grow, the volume of new people moving onto the beginning of the Bridge grows even faster.

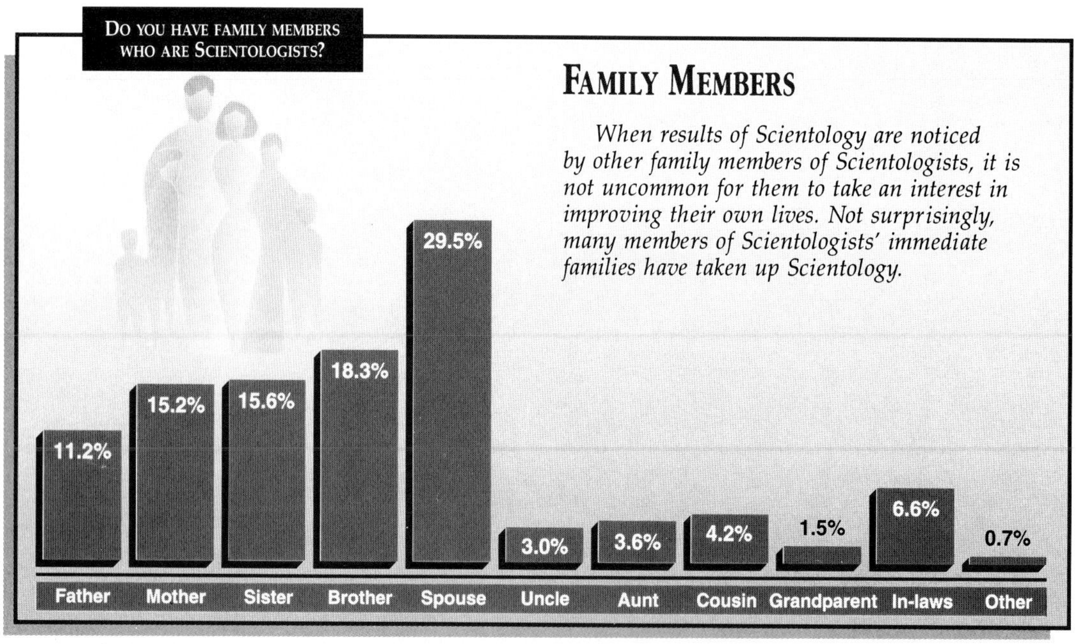

FAMILY MEMBERS

When results of Scientology are noticed by other family members of Scientologists, it is not uncommon for them to take an interest in improving their own lives. Not surprisingly, many members of Scientologists' immediate families have taken up Scientology.

SCIENTOLOGISTS' INVOLVEMENT IN COMMUNITY ACTIVITIES

As seen in the preceding pages, Scientology helps improve and better one's own life. But for Scientologists it is just as important to become involved in activities to better the quality of life around them. As seen in this graph, Scientologists are involved in diverse activities to better the community and society.

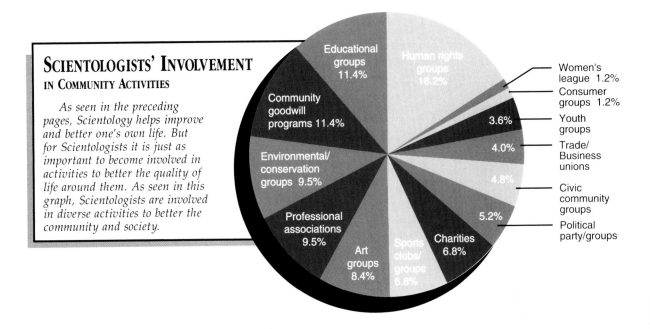

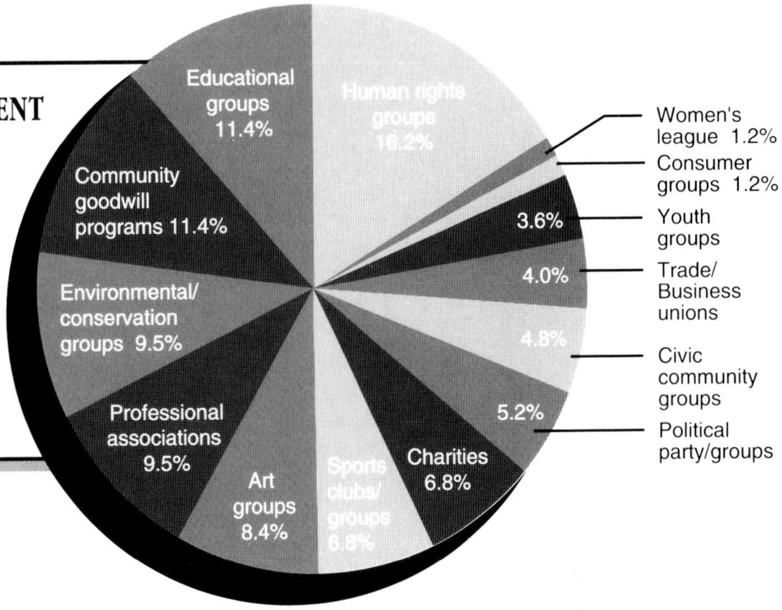

SCIENTOLOGISTS' ATTITUDES TOWARD LIFE

Scientologists live honest and ethical lives. They are interested in the well-being of others while achieving their own potentials. They have a positive outlook on life.

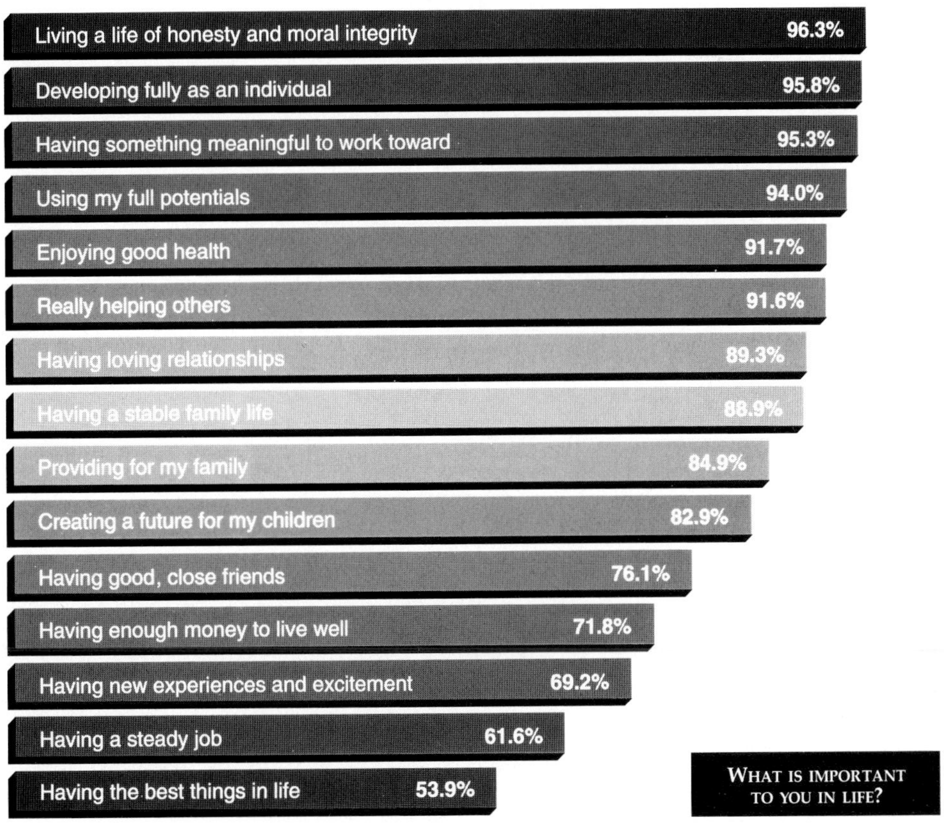

SCIENTOLOGY WORKS

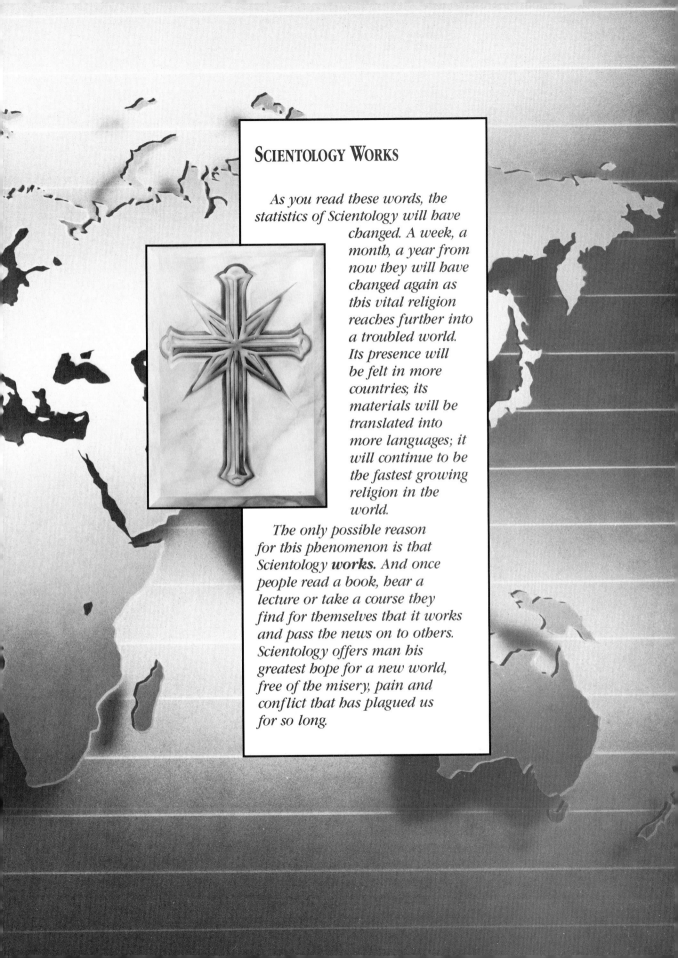

As you read these words, the statistics of Scientology will have changed. A week, a month, a year from now they will have changed again as this vital religion reaches further into a troubled world. Its presence will be felt in more countries; its materials will be translated into more languages; it will continue to be the fastest growing religion in the world.

The only possible reason for this phenomenon is that Scientology ***works.*** *And once people read a book, hear a lecture or take a course they find for themselves that it works and pass the news on to others. Scientology offers man his greatest hope for a new world, free of the misery, pain and conflict that has plagued us for so long.*

CHAPTER 28

THE FIRSTS OF DIANETICS AND SCIENTOLOGY

Once upon a time, L. Ron Hubbard wrote, some remote ancestor discovered the secrets of controlling fire, and from that unsung first came a whole host of firsts upon which every succeeding culture was founded. Previously inedible foodstuffs could be made palatable. Inclement weather could be borne, metals could be forged. Civilization began. And although that mythical pyrotechnician has long been forgotten, the fruits of his invention still form the backbone of our culture today.

Similarly, with L. Ron Hubbard's discovery of Dianetics and Scientology came a whole host of firsts that will continue to reshape our culture. For when one has made a truly basic and fundamental discovery in any field, many lesser discoveries proceed thereafter and many "firsts" occur. This has been the case with Dianetics and Scientology.

To begin with, Dianetics and Scientology offer the first axiomatic construction of the basic laws of thought and behavior in man. These axioms predict and explain all questions relating to human behavior and so constitute an achievement that many had previously attempted to no avail. It was also through the course of his initial research that Mr. Hubbard discovered the dynamic principle of all existence: Survive.

With Dianetics and Scientology came the first description and classification of all parts of the human mind, thus correcting decades-old fallacies found in Freudian theory and the work of Pavlov, including the false notion that man cannot remember before the age of three.

And with this delineation of the mind, comes the first workable description of the so-called unconscious mind—which, in fact, was shown not to be unconscious, but merely hidden. Following this discovery, Mr. Hubbard provided the man in the street with the first means whereby anyone could apply simple techniques to better themselves and their fellows—Dianetics.

Of no less importance, particularly when considering future generations, is Mr. Hubbard's discovery that regardless of all earlier claims to the contrary, the human fetus is acutely aware of his environment—what is said in the mother's presence, what she ingests and any injuries she may suffer. So, too, is the child acutely aware of his environment at birth. And only by safeguarding these very formative periods, can one safeguard his future.

From the utilization of Scientology and Dianetics principles comes the first effective guidelines for the raising of children, the resolution of marital difficulties and maintaining the well-being of the family. Previously, theories on family life were derived primarily from psychology, and proved not only useless but, in many instances, destructive.

Although psychology and psychiatry have long held that one's IQ is inherent and fixed, the application of Dianetics and Scientology auditing has proved this not to be true. Intelligence can be raised, as thousands of case histories show.

Dianetics and Scientology are the first technologies of the mind and spirit subjected to validation tests, which confirm Mr. Hubbard's projections. And, in consequence, Scientology and Dianetics became the first to offer man truly new states of existence far in excess of anything previously imagined possible.

Scientology was the first to isolate the basic life unit, i.e., that which perceives and generates energy, but is distinct from either the mind or body. This discovery resolves long-outstanding questions and has enormous impact on the lives of millions around the world.

From the revelations of Scientology came the first complete understanding of the phenomenon of death, the first real definition of man's spiritual potential and a truly eternal view of his destiny.

Moreover, Scientology offered man the first means of determining for himself what it means to be a spirit, delineating his potentials, the ways in which he operates and his relationship to the universe.

Dianetics was the first subject to determine the *exact* cause of psychosomatic illness, offering a provenly workable resolution to such. Correlative to this, Dianetics proved to be the earliest field to establish that function monitors structure, despite widespread medical beliefs to the contrary. Thus it was determined that the mind could indeed change the body and, that by addressing mental problems, one could radically enhance the body's ability to heal itself. Similarly, the tenets of Scientology defined, for the first time, the mechanistic limits of medicine.

Dianetics was the first to not only define the sources of psychosomatic illness but also the *extent* of the mind's impingement on the body. Freud and Breuer had vaguely known that psychic trauma led to hysterical paralysis, digestive dysfunctions and other ailments. Before Dianetics the severity and scope of psychosomatic illness was not known.

The Scientology E-Meter is the first device to accurately measure thought.

As Mr. Hubbard continued his research into mental phenomena, he soon made another revolutionary discovery: the Emotional Tone Scale, whereby human emotions are plotted in exact ascending sequence to enable the prediction and analysis of human behavior.

Mr. Hubbard's emergency assists provide the first delineation of how an injury affects the communication channels of the body—how a knowledge of nerve and energy flows can lead to truly lifesaving results through a restoration of communication to injured body parts.

Mr. Hubbard was also the first to determine the effects of aspirin and other pain depressants and soporifics on the mind and nervous system, and how to eliminate those effects.

Equally dramatic are Mr. Hubbard's discoveries relating to psychosis, or the obsessive desire to destroy. In 1970, the true cause of psychosis was isolated, and subsequently, Mr. Hubbard offered the first and only remedy for the condition. This, quite naturally, eliminates the need for earlier barbaric treatments and makes possible an alleviation of insanity throughout the society.

Scientology offers man the first system of bettering individuals through the improvement of their communication skills, with techniques that greatly increase one's ability to relate to his fellows. Mr. Hubbard's discoveries on the subject, which included defining the component parts of communication and led to the communication formula, represent an entirely new approach to communication.

Part and parcel of the above, Scientology is the first to precisely isolate barriers to study and provide the means to remove those barriers. From this discovery came a technology whereby anyone could successfully study any subject and, just as importantly, could successfully *apply* the fruits of his study. With this breakthrough came also solutions to the mutinous and rebellious conduct which had become the order of the day in modern schools. In short, then, Scientology provided the first effective resolution of all problems relating to learning.

Also in the field of learning, Mr. Hubbard was the first to develop a speedy and permanent handling for both illiteracy and "hidden illiteracy," thus stripping away the reasons why one cannot clearly comprehend what he reads, writes and hears and why others cannot comprehend his communication. Inclusive in these discoveries, Mr. Hubbard offers a revolutionary approach to English grammar, which constitutes the last word on this long-misunderstood subject.

Scientology is also the first to make whole classes of backward children averagely bright using drills which the teacher can do for a few minutes a day. Never before had something like this been accomplished.

Because one cannot address the problems of modern society without also addressing the problems of substance abuse, Mr. Hubbard also became the first to develop an entirely workable means of handling drug and alcohol addiction. Contained within his revolutionary solution to substance abuse is a technology for not only eradicating the craving for drugs and alcohol, but also the reason why one began taking such substances in the first place.

Mr. Hubbard was also the first to discover that, even long after one has ceased taking drugs, residual amounts of those drugs still remain in the body's fatty tissues. Mr. Hubbard's *Purification program* is the first means of ridding the body of environmental toxins picked up through the normal course of living in a highly polluted world.

Mr. Hubbard examined the questions of management—a subject that, like the mind, man previously had no real conception of and certainly no means of resolving. From this examination came the first precise tools of management, including the first effective methods of monitoring production by statistics, and of reversing the downward trend of any organization. In a related study, Mr. Hubbard further determined the first means of resolving all difficulties in the workplace, while offering principles to handle exhaustion, reduce injuries and vastly increase efficiency.

Mr. Hubbard addressed the question of ethics, and from that investigation came the world's first wholly rational ethics system whereby anyone can better his condition in any area of his existence. Also as part of this research, he determined the root cause of criminality, the precise mechanism whereby transgressions lead to increasing disability and unhappiness, and exactly how to restore one's happiness.

Mr. Hubbard may be further credited with the first breakthrough in centuries on the subject of logic, which had previously lacked any applicable use. Mr. Hubbard's discoveries on the subject offer man a truly workable breakdown of the subject, define its terms and offer methods to facilitate the perception, isolation and resolution of any problem.

Scientology offers the first real answer to that age-old question, "What causes war?" For although it was commonly held that "It takes two to make a fight," Mr. Hubbard found that behind every conflict is a hidden third party. With the application of this principle, any conflict may be resolved.

Just as questions of ethics and logic had baffled men for centuries, so, too, had the subject of aesthetics. Addressing the subject as a matter of "pure research," he devised the first workable definition of *art* and the first codification of the subject—which has led to a full revitalization of talents for many of the world's most respected figures of literature, music, drama and other arts. Mr. Hubbard was first to answer the question, "How good does a work of art have to be?"

These, then, are some of the firsts of Dianetics and Scientology. More important, however, are what can be accomplished with them. If one honestly avails himself of the technology and if one sincerely applies himself to gaining the benefits offered, there are apparently no limits to what can be achieved in Scientology.

Many, many people, millions in fact, have partaken of the services of Dianetics and Scientology over the last four decades. Their experiences point to the indisputable fact that Scientology, when properly applied to a person who is honestly seeking to improve and who is willing to communicate, produces results which match or exceed anyone's expectations.

A wide, wide range of benefits have been reported by Scientologists from their participation in Scientology. The conditions that can be improved by wholehearted application of the technology have been thoroughly documented since the 1940s. Following is a long and varied enumeration of what individuals have reported that Scientology achieves and the conditions it handles. None of these benefits are claims made by the Church; they are simply statements made by individuals about what they have achieved.

Although we shall never forget the name of L. Ron Hubbard, as we have forgotten that first bold experimenter with fire, the end results are quite similar: With fire came the means to establish civilization; with Dianetics and Scientology come the means to make a civilization of which we can be proud.

WHAT INDIVIDUALS SAY THEY HAVE ACHIEVED FROM SCIENTOLOGY

- Increased efficiency
- Increased energy and vitality
- Increased self-confidence
- Increased intelligence quotient
- Alleviation of neuroses
- Alleviation of psychoses
- Relief from mental trauma of injury or illness
- Faster recovery from broken bones, bruises, burns and injuries
- Alleviation of illness symptoms, colds, fevers, coughs and the like
- Salvaged marriages
- Happier relationships
- Ability to study any subject and be able to understand and apply it
- Improved school grades
- Better work habits
- Recovery from bereavement over loss
- Alleviation of psychosomatic illness
- Alleviation of painful memories
- Alleviation of postpartum depression
- Better communication skills
- Certainty of oneself as a spiritual being able to exist separate from the body
- Better performance in athletics
- Increased ability in artistic endeavors
- Increased literacy and ability to express oneself easily and clearly, both verbally and in writing
- Increased ability to understand others
- Ability to communicate freely with anyone on any subject
- Ability to recognize the source of problems and make them vanish

- Greater affinity for others
- Better relations at work
- Fewer problems in life
- Fewer colds and illnesses
- Fewer days absent from work
- Relief from the hostilities and sufferings of life
- Freedom from the upsets of the past and ability to face the future
- Freedom from fixed conditions and increased ability to do new things
- Increased well-being
- Ability to handle sources of personal suppression
- Certainty of one's immortality
- Increased self-determinism
- Freedom from the restimulative effects of drug residuals and other toxins
- More enjoyment from work
- Relief from the harmful effects of drugs, medicine or alcohol
- Better organization in one's life
- More and better friendships
- Increased competence
- Alleviation of cruel impulses and chronic unwanted conditions
- Increased personal stability
- Improved memory
- Raised ethical standards
- Ability to think clearly and rationally
- Improved relationships with others
- Improved family relations
- Rehabilitation of criminals
- Better rearing of children
- Improved reaction time
- Improved perceptions (sight, hearing, taste, etc.)
- Fewer physical ailments
- Improved concentration
- Rehabilitation of drug addicts and habitual drug users
- Restoration of sense of self-worth
- Alleviation of guilt feelings
- Increased creativity
- Increased productivity at work
- Increased happiness

Chapter 29

The History of Scientology's Expansion

The story of Dianetics and Scientology expansion is a simple one. Having developed the world's first workable technology of the mind and an applied religious philosophy that struck a vital chord in so many people, L. Ron Hubbard found that word of his discoveries began to spread. And as he continued researching, his further milestone discoveries created greater and greater interest.

In order to make these discoveries available, training centers, missions and churches were founded; and as more and more people discovered that Dianetics and Scientology worked, the cycle perpetuated itself.

This is the broad view. For a real sense of the story, however, one must return to early January 1950, when word of the forthcoming *Dianetics: The Modern Science of Mental Health* generated so many advanced orders that the publisher literally had to force his way past a mound of envelopes that had been dropped through the mail slot of his office door.

Dianetics Bursts on the Scene

Published on May 9, 1950, *Dianetics: The Modern Science of Mental Health* quickly led to a national movement. Bookstores, unable to keep copies on the shelves, slipped them beneath the counters for favored customers. Campus discussion groups and Dianetics clubs sprang up from coast to coast. Having grasped the essentials of Dianetics from their reading, thousands were either auditing or receiving auditing, while a number of hospitals adopted Mr. Hubbard's technology as the *only* effective means of helping those suffering from psychosomatic ills. As for the author, by late summer 1950, readers were actually camping on his lawn in the hopes that he might consent to offer personal instruction.

To meet this demand, the Hubbard Dianetic Research Foundation opened in Elizabeth, New Jersey in June 1950. There, Mr. Hubbard delivered the first Professional Auditors Course to students arriving from across the nation. With sales of the book approaching the 100,000 mark, five more branch offices soon opened in Chicago; New York; Washington, DC; Los Angeles and Hawaii.

Concurrent with the establishment of the Dianetics offices, those first hectic months after publication saw Mr. Hubbard on the lecture circuit—first to Los Angeles where, with little promotion, more than 6,000 people welcomed him to the Shrine Auditorium; then on to the San Francisco Bay area for a series of lectures in Oakland. Returning to Los Angeles, Mr. Hubbard continued lecturing and instructing students. When these students returned to their home towns to audit friends, family members and associates—the word continued to spread.

Having spent the spring of 1951 in pre-communist Havana, Cuba, where relative anonymity afforded him the opportunity to complete his second major work on Dianetics, *Science of Survival*, Mr. Hubbard accepted an offer to pursue his research and instruction at a newly opened Dianetics Foundation in Wichita, Kansas.

Here Mr. Hubbard formed the first organization that he himself actually administered, the Hubbard College. This organization trained auditors under his personal supervision, and only when those auditors could competently demonstrate auditing skills and results were they certified.

As news of Mr. Hubbard's return to the United States circulated, scores of students appeared, so that by June 1951 the First Annual Conference of Hubbard Dianetic Auditors brought 114 leading auditors to Wichita. Thereafter, Mr. Hubbard continued to lecture and oversee auditor training, while delivering a series of evening talks to the Wichita Chamber of Commerce on how his discoveries might be employed to expand their community.

Scientology Is Announced

With the continuation of his research through the autumn and early winter of 1951, Dianetics auditors were invited to study a new subject, one which would place them squarely in the spiritual realm—Scientology. By early spring 1952, some 15,000 persons were utilizing Scientology principles toward the betterment of their lives.

In order to train and audit these founding Scientologists, a Scientology center was established at 1407 North Central Avenue, Phoenix, Arizona. There, the recently formed Hubbard Association of Scientologists International (HASI) offered two classes of membership, one technical and one general. To keep HASI members informed of technical breakthroughs and Association news, the first *Journal of Scientology* was published in August 1952—a typewritten mimeograph, partially funded with paid notices from HASI members offering instruction and auditing in such cities as Boston; Detroit; Philadelphia; Chicago; Honolulu; and Little Rock, Arkansas.

As news of Scientology moved east across the Atlantic and interest took root in England, Mr. Hubbard was asked to lecture in London. Arriving in September 1952, he found a surprisingly substantial Scientology community. Under his supervision, England soon had nine certified Scientology auditors and many more students in training at the London center. And to help ensure the growth rate continued, introductory lectures were given in London's Hyde Park.

Back in the United States, Scientologists were equally enthusiastic, touring the length and breadth of California to offer free auditing demonstrations and Group Processing—all, as the *Journal* reported, "in a very spirited fashion."

The Philadelphia Doctorate Course

After delivering a series of lectures to the newly formed Hubbard Association of Scientologists in London and completing his landmark work, *Scientology 8-8008*, Mr. Hubbard returned to the United States for a celebrated series of December 1952 lectures in Philadelphia. Known as the *Philadelphia Doctorate Course*, these lectures described the full range of man's spiritual potential as well as a wide analysis of human behavior. As recordings of these lectures began to circulate throughout the Scientology field, and a third printing of *Scientology 8-8008* rolled off the press, the ranks of Scientology kept increasing on both sides of the Atlantic.

By early 1953, Mr. Hubbard resumed his instruction of auditors at the Hubbard Association of Scientologists International center in Marlborough Place, London. The organization now boasted many more auditors in training and a burgeoning field of preclears. Concurrently, American Scientologists opened new centers in

Houston, Texas; Hollywood and El Cerrito, California. In order to apprise them of the latest technical breakthroughs, the Hubbard Communications Office in London opened and the first *Professional Auditor's Bulletins* were published.

The Church Is Born

"After a very careful examination of a poll," declared Scientologists in a 1954 *Journal of Scientology,* "one would say very bluntly: Scientology fills the need for a religion." Consequently, and independently of Mr. Hubbard, the first Church of Scientology was founded by parishioners in Los Angeles.

At about the same time in Phoenix, a major Scientology and Dianetics congress was soon underway. Featuring L. Ron Hubbard's lectures, seminars and auditing demonstrations, the congress attracted 450 Scientologists from across the United States.

Also indicative of expansion through this period: news that Scientology had taken root in Australia; word from South Africa where 35 Scientologists had enrolled on a course taught in Durban; a notice from New Zealand (which now had a church in Auckland) that a Phoenix-trained auditor opened a course for 24 new Scientologists; and letters from Tel Aviv and Cairo where Scientologists were desperately hungry for more books. All told, by the summer of 1955 there were eight buildings in Mr. Hubbard's Phoenix center, and 22 full-time staff members.

Although still lagging in comparison, Great Britain now boasted nearly 500 auditors offering services in such towns as Farnham, West Croydon and Liverpool. As the worldwide Scientology network grew, Mr. Hubbard moved to more centrally located Washington, DC where, in July 1955, the Founding Church of Scientology and the first Academy of Scientology were formed. Here also, the first Scientology distribution center was established to oversee the printing and dissemination of material around the world. To ease the administration of this now sizable organization, Mr. Hubbard drafted the first of what would ultimately be volumes of administrative policies laying out the functions, actions and duties of the organization.

Books Create Worldwide Growth

Dissemination, L. Ron Hubbard advised in January of 1957, was a matter of getting Scientology books into the hands of the public. The prolific Mr. Hubbard had by now written *The Fundamentals of Thought, The Problems of Work, Scientology: A History of Man, Self Analysis in Scientology* and *How to Live Though an Executive.* Inspired by his words, Scientologists distributed books at an unprecedented rate. As a result of the growth that followed, the Hubbard Association of Scientologists International gathered in Washington, DC to appoint a new secretary for Great Britain to help oversee the broadening activities throughout the British Isles. Also resolved at that Washington conference: the establishment of offices in the then Union of South Africa, where the Church of Scientology of Johannesburg had also been founded. Nor was South Africa the only far-flung land where Scientology was taking root, for as of June 1958 *Scientology: The Fundamentals of Thought* had been translated into Greek.

Returning to London in the fall of 1958, after lectures in Washington, Mr. Hubbard found plans in place for a new London educational center. The center was to utilize Scientology techniques for the advancement of British schoolchildren. The project sparked so much interest among Londoners that a number of those who turned up for the first public lecture had to be turned away for want of available seating.

The hall was also crowded in New Delhi when a sister project initiated a course to train ranking members of the Indian government (including the Minister of Labor) on how Scientology principles might be utilized in the educational realm.

A few thousand miles to the southeast, excitement continued to build in Auckland, New Zealand where the book campaign was in full swing and demand was so high that the local Scientology bookstore regularly sold out its stock. Keeping books in stock also proved a problem in Australia, South Africa, France and outlying areas of England and the United States—continents now dotted with Scientology churches and missions. The largest concentration, however, still remained in the United States, where some 500 turned up at Washington, DC's Shoreham Hotel in July 1959 for 9 hours of lectures by L. Ron Hubbard on new clearing procedures. Eight weeks later another 400 met at London's Royal Empire Society Hall in Trafalgar Square, while dozens of advanced students attended the First Melbourne Advanced Clinical Course.

The Move to Saint Hill

To establish a central training, management and dissemination point, Mr. Hubbard and his family moved to Saint Hill Manor in East Grinstead, Sussex, England. Here, in July 1959, the Hubbard Communications Office Worldwide was established. In keeping with his advice from two years earlier, one of the first departments to be established was a shipping office for books—and orders poured in so quickly that they could not be filled fast enough. To help staff members cope with the demand for books and services, 1959 saw such administrative policy letters as "How to Handle Work" and "How to Get Approval of Actions and Projects."

"Hubbard Communications Office is now safely and securely established at Saint Hill Manor, East Grinstead, Sussex," Mr. Hubbard had written in the closing days of 1959, and by early 1960 the half-hundred acres at Saint Hill were the scene of much activity. Cables and telegrams arrived at all hours of the day and night with requests for more books, advice and reports of expansion in 11 different countries.

To ensure orderly growth, Mr. Hubbard continued his study of administrative procedure, codifying the basic principles and drafting appropriate policy letters. Meanwhile, the call went out for staff to help with everything from delivering messages and typing, to training and auditing, to executive functions.

With the firm establishment of these worldwide organizational basics at Saint Hill the previous summer, Scientology entered into an accelerated period of expansion through 1960. After yet more lectures at his home, Mr. Hubbard set off to South Africa in September. There, he standardized the administration of a steadily building organization before moving on to Washington for another series of lectures. Returning to Saint Hill in early January 1961, he found letters from such frontiers as Cuba, where a resident doctor was attempting to organize a correspondence course; Thailand, where pioneer Scientologists offered an introductory Scientology course to the monks of a Bangkok monastery; and Israel, where a number of teachers were reading *Dianetics.* There were also letters from Bombay where educators were utilizing Scientology principles, and more orders for books from Peoria, Illinois to Auckland, New Zealand.

The Saint Hill Special Briefing Course

Following another trip to South Africa in late January of 1961, when another church was founded in Cape Town, Mr. Hubbard returned to Saint Hill and initiated the famed Saint Hill Special Briefing Course. In a matter of months, study space was at such a premium that students were regularly found auditing on the tennis court and lawns—prompting Mr. Hubbard to initiate plans for the conversion of buildings. And as those Briefing Course graduates returned to their home towns telling of their successes, new pioneer groups were soon established.

Armed with the fruits of new technical breakthroughs, Scientologists continued to reach into society—into Mexico where a Spanish translation of *Scientology: The Fundamentals of Thought* had sparked a small movement in Mexico City; and into France where a pair of Scientologists had recently founded a Parisian church of Scientology and now needed French translations of Scientology materials.

Once again, to guarantee a steady but orderly rate of expansion, Mr. Hubbard drafted further administrative policy letters in 1963 to outline such organizational fundamentals as the delineation of duties for a staff member and the importance of administration. Through the implementation of these and other policy letters, as well as steady dissemination in the field, the mid-60s saw 4 newly founded Scientology churches around the world, including Port Elizabeth and Durban, South Africa; Detroit, Michigan; and Honolulu, Hawaii. With these churches in place, the total number of Scientology churches had reached 13 by the end of 1964.

Meanwhile, as Scientologists had continued to arrive at Saint Hill for training and auditing, the organizational staff likewise increased. Mr. Hubbard, continuing his technical research and breakthroughs, presented 7 lectures on the field of education in 1964, which formed the basis of study technology.

By 1965, more than 200 staff provided services to Scientologists and, all told, some 1,000 hours of auditing were delivered every week. To impress upon them just how vital it was to maintain standard application of Dianetics and Scientology through each and every one of those hours, and, in fact, for all time, Mr. Hubbard issued 2 more administrative policy letters: the very critical issues "Keeping Scientology Working" and "Safeguarding Technology." Additionally, the first Foundation (at Saint Hill) was founded in June to meet the increasing demand of the local population for services during evenings and weekends.

The Bridge to Freedom

With the release of the Classification and Gradation Chart in September 1965, delineating the exact steps of auditing and training on the Bridge to Total Freedom, Scientologists now had an exact route to follow to achieve the state of Clear. This included the release of the Scientology Grades 0–IV to establish a firm foundation at the beginning of the Bridge.

Concurrent with his technical research, Mr. Hubbard had been examining the very basics of organization as part of his continuing efforts to make his technology readily available and standardly delivered. As a result, in November Mr. Hubbard announced the Seven-Division Organizing Board—immediately implemented at Saint Hill, sent out to organizations around the world, and becoming the standard pattern of operation still in use today.

In consequence, Scientology continued to reach new areas in Australia where more Scientology lectures and demonstrations were organized; in South Africa where a Cape Town Scientologist launched a course for businessmen; and in New Zealand where Scientologists wrote in their thanks for the new international *Auditor* magazine telling of technical advances and success. And with every issue of *The Auditor* came news from other corners of the world, instilling a sense of unity among Scientologists, be they in Alberta, Canada; Port Elizabeth, South Africa; Puerto Rico; or Glenrock, Illinois.

The State of Clear and Beyond

Continuing his technical research through the early months of 1966, L. Ron Hubbard announced a breakthrough of supreme importance: The state of Clear was now attained with certainty by any well-trained auditor. A few months later, Mr. Hubbard released the first two OT levels beyond the state of Clear, and with these new levels now available Scientologists flocked to Saint Hill from around the world.

By mid-May 1966, the first Clears were attesting at Saint Hill, and the routine attainment of this long-dreamed-of state was particularly meaningful to Scientologists. Clears were often featured on the cover of *The Auditor,* and returning to their homelands, were regularly called upon to speak. Their success, in turn, inspired others to move out into the world—auditing, setting up introductory courses and generally spreading the word. To that end, two enterprising Scientologists began translating Scientology materials into Danish, while others were either opening or expanding Scientology centers in Austin, Texas; Buffalo, New York; Manchester, England; Guadalajara, Mexico and The Hague, Netherlands.

With the pattern of organizations now in place and the field continuing to expand at a healthy rate, Mr. Hubbard took another critical step for the future. He resigned Scientology directorship to devote himself fully to further research. In September 1966, all his administrative duties were turned over to Executive Council Worldwide and 100 staff charged with the responsibility of administering the existing Scientology network and ensuring its further expansion.

The Sea Organization Begins

To support L. Ron Hubbard's ensuing research and the delivery of soon-to-be-released OT Levels III, IV, V and VI, the Sea Organization was formed on August 12, 1967. Its first operational vessels were the *Enchanter* (later rechristened the *Diana*) and the *Avon River* (rechristened the *Athena*). Within a few months the *Royal Scotman* (rechristened the *Apollo*), became the third vessel. With these research vessels operating and a dedicated team for support, Mr. Hubbard continued to provide Scientology with technical breakthrough after technical breakthrough.

OT III Released

On September 9, 1967, in a particularly important recorded message, Mr. Hubbard announced that he had discovered the means to eradicate those mental factors which stand in the way of peace and tolerance for mankind. This new level of the Scientology Bridge was OT III.

Further growth followed, with 104 organizations, missions and field groups in 12 countries around the world. All told, Scientologists were now delivering some 50,000 auditing hours per year. By the end of 1967 there were also over 500 Clears.

To provide Scientologists with the fruits of Mr. Hubbard's upper-level research, 1968 saw Sea Organization teams establish Advanced Organizations in Edinburgh, Scotland and Los Angeles, as well as an American Saint Hill Organization in Los Angeles.

The year 1968 additionally signaled a significant boom in churches around the world. For instance, hundreds of students could be found in the Academy during any given course period. Likewise, San Francisco's newly formed church of Scientology, with 23 staff members, reported large numbers of students on course, as did Detroit, Toronto and London. More than 400 Scientologists convened at a Saint Hill graduation to hear those who had recently completed the OT levels and the one-thousandth Clear attested in March. A broader look at statistics revealed 15,000 professional auditors, and by this time, some 3,000,000 people had purchased Scientology books or services from 37 official Scientology churches worldwide.

As Scientologists continued to reach deeper and deeper into society, however, they increasingly came face to face with society's problems—in particular, drug abuse which had risen to epidemic proportions by 1968. To help reverse the trend, Mr. Hubbard began a comprehensive research program to search out a means to alleviate not only the effects of drug abuse but also the causes. This work led to the first Drug Rundown in 1968, allowing still more to ascend the Bridge.

The First Class VIII Auditors

To ensure that each and every organization standardly delivered auditing services, Mr. Hubbard launched a new advanced training course in August 1968 to emphasize standard technical application. This was the Class VIII Auditor Course conducted aboard the

Apollo and attended by top auditors from churches around the world.

With the release in 1969 of the Hubbard Standard Dianetics Course to simplify and standardize Dianetics procedures, and the earlier arrival of the first Class VIII graduates to ensure standardized application of all auditing, Scientology course rooms were soon packed, from New York to New South Wales. As more and more students continued up the Bridge, a third Advanced Organization and Saint Hill was opened in Denmark.

"By rehabilitating the artist," Mr. Hubbard had said, "one does much for rehabilitating the culture." With this incentive, the first Scientology Celebrity Centre was established in 1969. Aimed at assisting the now numerous artists and celebrities who had found Scientology technology indispensable to their creative well-being, the course rooms of the Los Angeles Celebrity Centre were soon also filled with students. In addition to regular Scientology services, Celebrity Centre provided a forum for poets, playwrights, actors, painters and musicians—all part of the effort to help revitalize the arts.

Meanwhile, by August 1970, as demand for advanced levels continued to increase, the Edinburgh Advanced Organization was forced to move to larger quarters at Saint Hill.

Flag Management Is Formed

In the interest of further expansion, L. Ron Hubbard developed a completely new system of management and established the Flag Bureaux aboard the *Apollo* in 1970 to carry out this function for all of Scientology. To relay and implement the Flag Bureaux's orders, liaison offices were opened in Los Angeles for the United States, Saint Hill for the United Kingdom and Copenhagen for Europe.

In April 1970, Mr. Hubbard invited executives from all churches to attend his Flag Executive Briefing Course on the flagship *Apollo*. The end result placed true administrative experts in all local churches. And with the later publication of the *Organization Executive Course* and *Management Series* volumes, all policy was now readily available to the 2,553 staff of the 118 churches and missions in 20 nations.

As of early 1971, 250 professional auditors had joined the Los Angeles Auditors Association to deliver the newly expanded Scientology Lower Grades. Later this same year, Mr. Hubbard released three new auditing rundowns: L10, L11 (the New Life Rundown) and L12 (the Flag OT Executive Rundown). These rundowns were delivered only by the first, specially trained Class XII Auditors aboard the *Apollo*. At the same time, fellow auditors were busy at newly formed churches in Las Vegas, Nevada; Pretoria, South Africa; Göteborg and Stockholm, Sweden; Copenhagen, Denmark; Munich, Germany; Plymouth, England; Buffalo, New York and Boston, Massachusetts.

Employing new technical releases containing refinements of study techniques to greatly speed students through their courses, 1972 saw Scientology increase in size under Sea Organization guidance. All told, these breakthroughs helped push the number of Clears to the 4,000 mark by early 1974; while future Clears stepped onto the Bridge at newly opened Scientology churches in Sacramento, California; Ottawa, Ontario; Manchester, England; Malmö, Sweden; Vancouver, British Columbia; Portland, Oregon and Vienna, Austria.

After months of research and compilation, the *Dianetics and Scientology Technical Dictionary* was completed in early 1975. This long-awaited work defined all Dianetics and Scientology words and abbreviations used in connection with auditing and training, and thus greatly aided study.

The Flag Land Base Established

Another milestone for 1975 was the landing of the Sea Organization, and the establishment of the Flag Land Base in Clearwater, Florida. Located in the 11-story Fort Harrison Hotel and the nearby

Clearwater Bank Building, the Flag Land Base constituted the largest single Scientology organization in history. As the spiritual headquarters of the Church and the only place where preclears could receive the special L Rundowns, it was soon drawing Scientologists from all over the world.

Nineteen seventy-five also saw the opening of Chicago's church of Scientology, another church in Philadelphia and the first Canadian pocket book edition of *Dianetics.*

A new Spanish translation of *Dianetics* was released in Mexico in 1976, and some 12 million television viewers watched as Hispanic celebrities told of its benefits.

In August, 10,000 Scientologists convened for a convention in Anaheim, California. And all the while, Scientology and Dianetics continued to repair lives around the world: in the Philippines where business leaders discovered L. Ron Hubbard's technology, and in the slums of London where his study technology was put to good use helping impoverished children.

Approximately one hundred miles east of Los Angeles, at the desert community of La Quinta, Mr. Hubbard established a Scientology training film studio (Source Productions) in 1977. Under his personal direction, in an 8-month period, Source Productions produced a public Scientology information film and 7 technical instruction films to preserve the standard training and application of Scientology long into the future.

The same year, to accommodate the flood of Scientologists arriving for services, the 520,000 square foot Cedars of Lebanon complex in Hollywood was purchased—soon to be the new home of the Church of Scientology Los Angeles, the American Saint Hill Organization, the Advanced Organization and various administrative offices. This was also a big year for the Flag Land Base with the release of two L. Ron Hubbard written and directed public information films, *The Secret of Flag Results* and *The Case He Couldn't Crack.* And to help keep all running smoothly, L. Ron Hubbard's dictionary of Scientology management terms was released.

The Year of Technical Breakthroughs

Christened "The Year of Technical Breakthroughs," 1978 was another landmark with the release of New Era Dianetics, providing lightning-fast gains for those who were not yet Clear. In cities across the world—now including Oslo, Norway; Bern, Switzerland; and Milano, Italy—students entered course rooms to learn the techniques of NED.

Later that year, New Era Dianetics for OTs (New OT V) was introduced. As word of the truly extraordinary gains this level offered circulated, Scientologists began pouring into the Flag Land Base.

Still more technical releases were celebrated in 1979, most notably the Purification program to rid the body of harmful residuals of drugs and environmental pollutants.

In order to handle the subsequent flood of Scientologists arriving at Flag, the 100-room Sandcastle Hotel, half a mile from the Fort Harrison Hotel, was purchased and renovated.

By the end of June 1980, more than twenty new churches had been founded in locations as diverse as Brussels, Belgium and Bogotá, Colombia.

New OT VI and VII Released

The most significant achievement of 1980 was the release in September of another two OT levels, New OT VI and VII. Expanding the scope of gains available for the individual beyond any commonly envisioned state, these levels were soon bringing still more Scientologists to the Flag Land Base.

Mr. Hubbard issued several new bulletins on how best to make Scientology known in the early 1980s; and cities where demand was so great that new Scientology churches were opened included: Phoenix, Arizona; Edmonton, Canada; Albuquerque, New Mexico; Berlin, Germany; Geneva, Switzerland; Tel Aviv, Israel;

Canberra, Australia; Cincinnati, Ohio; Quebec, Canada and four in Mexico City.

The first L. Ron Hubbard lecture series on cassette was released in 1980 by Golden Era Productions—formerly Source Productions at La Quinta and now relocated to a nearby 500-acre property to facilitate not only film production, but also audio and technical compilations for speeding Scientologists up the Bridge. And for an indication of just how big Scientology had grown by 1980: Dianetics and Scientology were now available in 52 countries at 328 organizations, missions and auditor groups, serviced by 5,150 staff who helped deliver 794,990 auditing hours that year.

With liaison offices now established for Canada and Latin America, a total of 8 such offices were ensuring steady expansion under Sea Organization direction. As of 1981, twelve of Mr. Hubbard's technical training films were completed and released to help standardize Scientology training. Mr. Hubbard also released the Sunshine Rundown to heighten one's awareness of new abilities as a Clear.

New Directions in Management

Nineteen eighty-one additionally saw several key administrative changes, initiated in response to a problem that many organizations suffer through rapid expansionary periods. In 1981, after a series of Sea Organization inspections of the Guardian's Office (GO), it was found that the GO—a small unit of the Church established in 1966 to protect the Church from external threats—had become entirely autonomous, operating without regard to Mr. Hubbard's policies and was, in fact, attempting to usurp control of the Church.

Further investigation by Sea Org executives revealed that the GO's corruption was so extensive it had been hindering Church expansion internationally—inhibiting both public and staff from advancing up the Bridge. As a result of these investigations, Sea Org officials disbanded the Guardian's Office entirely.

To safeguard these administrative changes, the corporate structure of the Church was updated and the Church of Scientology International was formed as the international mother church.

With all Church organizations now fully aligned with Mr. Hubbard's policies, preclears began moving far more speedily and confidently to Clear and beyond. As a result, there was a surge in the total number of Clears and OTs produced at the Flag Land Base and Advanced Organizations.

Nineteen eighty-two brought the formation of the Religious Technology Center, a corporation to which L. Ron Hubbard donated all trademarks of Dianetics and Scientology. Its purpose: To safeguard the proper use of trademarks, to protect the public and to make sure that the powerful technology of Dianetics and Scientology remains in good hands and is properly used.

To cope with the new administrative load, July of 1982 saw the establishment of the International Network of Computer Organized Management (INCOMM). Utilizing computer systems, based upon Mr. Hubbard's developments in the field, INCOMM fully computerized international church management to facilitate efficiency of operations and the huge rate of Scientology expansion.

As just one more indication of how quickly Scientology was now expanding through the early 1980s, a new Advanced Organization opened in Sydney, Australia.

Dianetics: *Perennial Bestseller*

To spread word of technical breakthroughs and generally inform the world of just what Scientology has to offer, the Planetary Dissemination Organization was founded in 1983. One of the organization's first tasks: to make *Dianetics* even more widely available. And the result a few months later: *Dianetics* once again reached the bestseller lists with the 7 millionth copy sold.

Concurrently, new churches were founded in Hamburg, Bern, Zurich and Verona, soon followed in the US with churches in Long

Island, New York and Orange County, California. And to serve the artistic community in New York, a Celebrity Centre organization was opened there.

Two more German churches opened in 1984 and, by then, scores of Scientology churches and missions spanned the globe. It seemed only appropriate then, that on October 7, 1984 the International Association of Scientologists was formed at Saint Hill in England, to unite Scientologists from all nations.

Man has long suffered from inability to consistently pursue his true purposes, and in 1984 Mr. Hubbard released the solution to such problems: the False Purpose Rundown. As with all earlier technical releases, Scientology course rooms from Sydney to St. Louis were soon filled with auditors learning how to remove those factors which obscure a being's real purposes. So great were the numbers of students and preclears at the Flag Land Base that the Flag Bureaux, previously located in Clearwater, was moved to Los Angeles in order to make more room for more delivery to parishioners and consolidate management. As an added bonus, Scientologists were soon to be listening to the first of Mr. Hubbard's lectures in Clearsound—a revolutionary development in tape restoration making possible the release of all of Mr. Hubbard's lectures from 1950 forward.

Nineteen eighty-five saw the 150th church open in Monza, Italy. To fill the demand around the world for taped lectures (over 90,000 students and preclears completed services in 1985) a full production and recording studio was established at Golden Era Productions. And, looking to the future, for a glimpse of what was to come: Sea Organization teams began scouting for a new motor vessel for the delivery of Scientology's most advanced auditing level.

While the Sea Organization was ensuring the availability of the OT levels, other Scientologists were making L. Ron Hubbard's work better known to those who had not yet stepped onto the Bridge. As a result of these efforts: copies of *Dianetics* selling in Gdańsk, Poland for the first time; a Peruvian mission established in Lima; a team of three Scientologists distributing Scientology materials in Hong Kong; and, a Celebrity Centre in Nashville, Tennessee opening its doors in 1987. New Scientology missions also opened in Puerto Rico, North Carolina, Palm Springs and Zaire and—fulfilling the long-laid seeds—Ambala, India. And lest one had any doubts as to just how many were now reaching for L. Ron Hubbard's works; *Dianetics* reached the number one position on the *New York Times* bestseller list. Concurrently, *Dianetics* was released, and became instantly popular in a new quarter—mainland China—with the first printing selling out in less than 2 weeks.

Painstakingly researched, the new fully up-to-date Scientology Academy Levels were released in the first days of 1988. Also in 1988, the greatly improved Mark Super VII E-Meter was released. Further plans to make L. Ron Hubbard technology available to larger numbers led to the formation of the Association for Better Living and Education (ABLE). Among other projects ABLE would soon help initiate—bringing L. Ron Hubbard study technology to classrooms in China where 190,000 copies of *Dianetics* had sold by this point. In order to handle equally impressive North American sales of L. Ron Hubbard books, Bridge Publications (formerly the Publications Organization, United States) moved into new and larger quarters in Los Angeles.

New OT VIII—Truth Revealed

After four years of intensive work locating, purchasing and refitting, the Sea Organization motor vessel was christened the *Freewinds.* Setting sail on June 6, 1988, she was not only the first Sea Organization vessel to see service in 13 years, but she is the only place where Scientologists can take the highest available step on the Bridge: New OT VIII, Truth Revealed.

The unveiling of two new facilities was cause for celebration among Scientologists in 1989. The first was the 12-story, 110,000-square-foot Hollywood Guaranty Building, which was to serve as the home of international church management. The second was the Saint Hill Castle, a building modeled after a medieval English castle, that Mr. Hubbard originally conceived and designed in 1965. It now offered advanced Scientology services and the Saint Hill Special Briefing Course. Three more new churches opened in 1989: one in Atlanta, Georgia; another in Hanover, Germany and the third in Stuttgart.

These three churches brought the total number of Scientology organizations, missions and field groups up to 830, with some 10,000 staff members delivering services to over 200,000 students and preclears for a grand total of 1.4 million auditing hours per year. That same year also saw Scientologists moving into society with 251 social reform groups and 164 social betterment groups.

While the demand for Dianetics and Scientology in China was growing, another Asian nation was responding in a significant way to Mr. Hubbard's technology: Japan. In a matter of months, the first Scientology church in Tokyo was delivering courses and auditing to scores of Japanese citizens.

Into the Nineties

With the full implementation of L. Ron Hubbard's policies, advices, directives and technical material, the early 1990s presaged a new era of unprecedented expansion.

Among the highlights: Thousands of Scientologists poured into their churches to enroll on the Hubbard Key to Life Course, first made available on May 9, 1990; the March 13, 1991 release of the complete *Organization Executive Course* and *Management Series* volumes containing all of L. Ron Hubbard's organizational policies; soon followed by the 18-volume collection of Mr. Hubbard's technical writings.

More than 700 invited guests—including leaders of the business community, the arts and political dignitaries—were on hand for the 1991 opening of the L. Ron Hubbard Life Exhibition in Hollywood.

Auditor's Day, 1991, celebrated the completion of a 5-year program to compile, verify as totally accurate, and make available all of L. Ron Hubbard's auditing and training technology on the Bridge to Total Freedom. And with this, the final Classification, Gradation and Awareness Chart was released at an event at Saint Hill in England.

In July 1992, the newly restored Celebrity Centre International was officially opened to service the many artists in Scientology.

And with the iron curtain down, such formerly inaccessible nations as Russia, Hungary and what had been East Germany, were soon reaching for L. Ron Hubbard's technology. To meet their needs, a Sea Org liaison office opened in Russia, while teams flew in to deliver Mr. Hubbard's educational and administrative technologies. And with those formerly Eastern-bloc nations now enjoying Mr. Hubbard's materials—bringing the total number of countries offering Scientology up to 74—new translations of his work followed. In all, there were now 422 translated titles available in 31 languages.

Finally, and for another view of just how broad Scientology had become—now that there were 1,039 Scientology organizations, missions and groups around the world—the yearly number of Scientology book sales of 1967 were currently exceeded every day. There were also over 1.5 million auditing hours delivered in 1991—or more auditing in just 12 days than in the whole of 1967, and a 1991 survey revealed that Dianetics and Scientology had become so widely known they were household words.

But however great the numbers become—the new preclears and auditors sitting down for their first session, the new readers picking up their first copies of *Dianetics*—the story of Scientology expansion is still a simple one: Having discovered that L. Ron Hubbard's technology works, people make it known to others.

CHAPTER 30

FUTURE PREDICTION OF SCIENTOLOGY

If a founding Scientologist had been asked in 1952 to predict the impact of Scientology on the world forty years later, would he have been able to imagine the extent to which it has grown today? Would he have been able to envision from a stucco building in Phoenix, Arizona, the more than one thousand churches, missions and groups that exist today? Would he have been able to envision the hundreds of thousands who have been helped to rid themselves of the curse of drugs, or the millions who have been placed on the road to literacy through the use of L. Ron Hubbard's technologies?

Surely, these pioneer Scientologists had some idea of what potential L. Ron Hubbard's discoveries held for mankind, just as today Scientologists envision even greater expansion in the future.

Today, Scientology is the fastest growing religion on the planet—and so long as Mr. Hubbard's technologies are available to all who wish to reach for them, and so long as they are applied standardly, Scientology will continue to grow.

To understand what this growth might mean to a troubled world, religious leaders, professionals, educators and others have offered the following predictions on the future of the Scientology religion.

"The movement founded by L. Ron Hubbard will engage itself increasingly in the design of a new world following the collapse of the Soviet Union and Communism. A new awakening of spiritual powers is taking place and his vision will help shape events."

Hans Janitschek
President
Society of Writers
United Nations

"Scientology has come a long way, and has grown in numbers.

"There are so many people of different types—and into different activities—art, human rights, rehabilitation and more.

"Obviously, it will last. It can be geared to individual interests, and even if the interests change, people can use the basic technology to adapt to new ones."

Loretta Needle, B.A.
University of Toronto

"Scientology is a practical religious theology which embodies the technology of helping people discover themselves and at the same time to become aware of the evils that plague our society, such as the prevalent use of dangerous psychiatric drugs.

"The pastoral counseling program of Scientology puts man in touch with reality and enhances and strengthens his relationship with God and his fellow man.

"The beauty of Scientology is you don't have to give up your religious upbringing to become a Scientologist. You can still remain in your original church.

"Scientology has a great future because it helps those who are in frustration and despair to shift their position to a helpful and useful one."

Rev. Dr. Leo Champion
Pastor
Fellowship Missionary
Baptist Church
Milwaukee, Wisconsin

"In looking at the future of Scientology, as a sociologist I am cautious about predicting long-range futures. But I may say this, if it is a futile undertaking it will not last, but if it has a providential function this will manifest itself in time. So it would be wise for us to let it be lest we be opposing providence in the age of religious freedom. This was Gamaliel's advice on the Christians to his fellow Jews. If it had continued to be taken (as it was by his immediate listeners) thousands of years of conflict between the great religions of the Book might have been saved. (Acts 5:34–39)"

Noel Ryan
Sociologist
Australia

"Like so many relatively new religions, the Church of Scientology has been forced to spend much of its time and resources fighting religious prejudice and prosecution. Despite those pressures, the Church has been a real force for good in the lives of many of its adherents and a champion of religious freedom."

Robin Johansen
Attorney and Religious
Freedom Fighter

"Your Church's noble principles of high ideals and ethical living along with the beliefs of accepting so many aspects of knowledge meets very close to the ideals of the American Institute of Islamic Studies. I find it a pleasure and privilege to reach out for common thoughts. The future looks so optimistic that we shall convey our common principles to the world side by side."

Amir Gillani
President
American Institute of
Islamic Studies
Toronto, Canada

"There are many Bible-believing Evangelicals and others in the established Christian community who have not yet accepted the Church of Scientology. Nevertheless, they should thank the Lord for them, because the Scientologists have fought a lot of battles that have helped protect and safeguard freedom for us all.

"Because of these efforts, Scientology is continuing to gain more and more acceptability among leaders in the religious community, and the Church has won most of its battles. However, while they are enjoying a breathing period, be assured there are a lot more battles to be fought, and won, down the road."

Rev. Jim Nicholls
Producer of "Voice of America" Radio and TV Show

"I have traveled far and wide throughout my professional life and see the peoples of Earth as incredibly diverse in character as well as needs. Oftentimes our efforts to understand and help them have been too narrow. In the many years I have worked with the Church of Scientology the one thing which has impressed me the most and which will characterize the Church far into future centuries is its ability to deal with humankind as a whole.

"At the heart of Scientology's activities is the betterment of all people no matter what creed, what race, what socioeconomic status to develop themselves spiritually and mentally so that each individual can improve his own life. Scientology's far-reaching goals are designed to tend to each individual uniquely with compassionate concern and commitment. These rare attributes are essential in these times of trouble and uncertainty and most assuredly provide the Church with a platform for growth and strength in the years to come."

L. Fletcher Prouty
Col. US Air Force (Ret.)

"As American society becomes more diverse in the years ahead, we will be looking for leadership from those organizations that represent the moral tenets which united us as a country: personal responsibility, compassion, tolerance, respect and a commitment to community. The Church of Scientology is one of those organizations—as its commitment to the Hollywood community so clearly demonstrates."

Mark A. Robbins
1992 Republican Candidate for Congress 29th District of California

"The Church of Scientology is an important force in our society seeking to enhance the people's ability to know what our government is doing, is not doing and why, and otherwise striving to enable citizens to make the government more accountable for its actions. I believe that in the future, when the need for such efforts will be more necessary, the Church's role will be even stronger and more effective."

Quinlan J. Shea, Jr.
Former Senior Justice Department Official
Director Center for Citizen Access to Government Information

"For many years an international organization has been masquerading as a legitimate defender of the citizens of the world. This agency, INTERPOL, while claiming to work against criminals has protected terrorists like George Habash, drug dealers such as Manuel Noriega, crooked banks like BCCI and others. For many years Nazis and former Nazis led INTERPOL.

"It has been the Church of Scientology that has taken the leadership to unmask this canard. By doing so, it is helping get rid of drug dealers, crooks and terrorists from the planet. This is the type of social action that all religious organizations should emulate."

Steve Frank
Public Affairs
Consultant

"It is notable that while the major denominations in Canada are careless about religious rights (and, therefore, careless about the ultimate welfare of our people), Scientologists have courageously and at great cost struggled against state abuses of these and other rights. If they hold out and succeed, all of us will one day have to bring our proper thanks that through their endurance we enjoy our freedom."

The Right Reverend
Juris Calitis, D.D.
Evangelical Lutheran
Church in Canada

"Drugs are the scourge of mankind, and they are the problem we must solve as we exit the twentieth century. The twenty-first century promises hope because Scientology is here and has the solutions to drugs."

Bob King
Advisory Neighborhood
Commissioner
Washington, DC

"The mind is a magnificent thing, and Scientologists rightfully are against mind-altering drugs. We cannot continue to destroy the minds of people with drugs. This goes against nature. Scientology is on the right track, giving the mind a chance to work on its own."

Lillian Ray
Assistant Deputy Mayor
for Drug Control Policy
Philadelphia, Pennsylvania

"Scientology has a background of benefiting its members as well as the general public through a number of social betterment programs in areas like drug rehabilitation, education and government reform. This broad spectrum of beneficial activities is a tribute to the Church as well as its members and is something I believe guarantees the Church of Scientology a bright future."

Dr. Isaac N. Brooks, Jr. Ph.D.
Executive Chairman
National Task Force on
Religious Freedom
Legislation and Litigation
Washington, DC

"Scientology provides technology for improving a person's ability to study and educate himself. They also are accomplishing much in fighting crime and keeping people from returning to drugs. Provided they can make this more known in the society, it can be very helpful in changing the direction of the society. Scientology will be very helpful in improving everyday life."

William Orozco
Former Representative for
California State Senator
Diane Watson

"It's the largest growing religious movement in the entire world. I see the future for Scientology just being bigger and bigger."

Richard Allatorre
Former State Assemblyman
California

"It's a new religion, and it will meet many difficulties. But Scientology stands on fine ground, and all resistance will be broken down."

Harry Widemyr
Social Inspector
Sweden

"I think the Church's involvement in such issues as religious freedom and ending psychiatric abuses within the field of mental health demonstrate the Church is interested in more than just spirituality, but in enabling all people to enjoy their human rights. The support for these efforts can only grow."

Cedric Hendricks
Congressional Aide
Washington, DC

"There is and will be a more positive view of Scientology through the actions of community work and the various community outreach programs that the Church presents.

"It has been a fulfilling experience working with Community Outreach staff for over ten years.

"I look forward to a long relationship utilizing the talent, the time, and dedication to helping young people which has been our source of contact over the years."

Carole J. Simpson
County of Los Angeles
Department of Children Services

"On the threshold of the twenty-first century Scientology will continue to grow and be very strong and effective in its impact around the world. They will continue to be admired for putting hands and feet to their beliefs. Their example in fighting for religious freedom will continue to inspire all other faith groups in the ongoing struggles for religious freedom. Keep on keeping on."

Rev. Wm. Solomon
Executive Minister
Metro Toronto Black Clergy Association

"Scientology relies on the energy of each and every one of its members. As a result, as the energy and enthusiasm of its members grow so will Scientology and its many programs designed to help society."

Carlos A. Rodriguez
Political Consultant

"It is inevitable that Scientology will expand because from my experience, the types of people I have met are walking advertisements for it. I think more and more people are looking for a practical philosophy."

The Hon. Herbert Graham
Former Member of West Australian Parliament

"As the Church of Scientology is a well-arranged organization, I see very good survival chances for its future. This is because the survival of a religion depends very much on its organization."

Dr. Rainer Flasche
Philipps University
Marburg, Germany

"Observers of the Church [of Scientology] seem to be predominantly of the opinion that as a phenomenon it will develop and become larger due to the symptoms shown by unsolved problems and conflicts in our technical-scientific world."

Rudolf Grimm
Reporter
Berlin, Germany

"Special attention belongs to Scientology however . . . It is the forerunner of coming religions and philosophical movements with absolutely separate ethics, no longer bound to Western ethical ideas."

Pfarrer Haack
Evangelical Expert
Germany

"Scientology is likely to be engaged more and more in public affairs. The main problem will be abuse and false information peddled by its opponents and those in public affairs who wish the public to be kept in ignorance. It is my view that the public generally who have little knowledge of the Church of Scientology will learn more—particularly through the media, who I believe will be paying more positive attention to its activities."

Arthur Lewis, MP
United Kingdom

"It's far better known than it was a few years ago. People are more aware now. As society becomes more complex, people will want to associate with something to get a handle on life. I see this as a religious movement with all churches."

Michael Franchetti
Former Deputy Attorney General
California

"I feel [Scientology's] future is good, given the conditions in society today—and the need for people to find themselves. It's a good future, but a rough one, as long as organizations with strong religious prejudices exist and want to create problems for others. It's unfortunate, but inevitable."

Professor J. Stillson Judah
The Graduate Theological Union
San Francisco

"It is axiomatic in the history of religion that when a new religious movement publishes, it is here to stay. Scientology surely has *published,* a lot, in its quest to help man help himself. The eight million adherents of the Church are here to stay—with increasing benefit of the human family.

"The Scientologists we are privileged to know are sincere, dedicated human beings who are striving hard for the betterment of all."

Marvin Bordelon
President
American Conference on
Religious Movements

"I expect the Church of Scientology increasingly to contribute positively to interfaith understanding in a true spirit of dialogue. This will be a valuable and welcome development. Such cooperation and dialogue will, in itself, help to break down barriers and increase trust, and will produce a broad stream of people of faith and ethics seeking and working for world peace."

Rev. Brian Cooper
Chairman
Christian Peace Conference
England

"I am confident that the Church of Scientology will continue to be on the cutting edge of government reform simply because the Church has been doing it for years and doing it well. Scientology does this type of work better than any other organization in the country."

Wayne C. Bentson
FOIA Specialist
Western Information Network

"The Church is expanding more and more rapidly from what I see on the TV and on the radio. The Church will move into the mainstream of society. Scientology will be the focus point in the 1990s and will set the direction in which this country will go.

"Scientology will be known as the place to go where people really care."

Bill Hoston
Political Activist
Los Angeles

"Scientology offers a true bridge between the East and the West and Scientologists can effectively help solve the great problems that plague both cultures.

"Scientology will become a major religion in the Western world before the end of the century."

Loek Hopstaken
Postal Manager
Amsterdam, Netherlands

"As an attorney, concerned resident of Hollywood and former Chairman of the Board of Directors of the Hollywood Chamber of Commerce I wanted you to know that we are proud of Scientology's accomplishments here in 'Tinsel Town.' Please, continue to let your 'light shine' and share your success with others.

"The Church has been active in the Hollywood area for over a decade and continue to be 'excellent' citizens, good neighbors and a positive influence in the community."

John O. Adams, Esq.
Honorary Director
Hollywood Chamber of Commerce

"I see the Church of Scientology becoming a very strong community structure. What I see happening is [a] continued reach out to assist those who are not members and the formation of a working unit with the Church made up of people of all religions."

Lester Smith, Jr.
Founder and President of
The Natural High
Entertainment Group, California

"I would see the Church of Scientology being a part of all the other churches who recognize that there must be a new direction and a coming together of all churches for the betterment of mankind.

"Each Church has its unique role. Basically I see the role of the Church of Scientology as cleaning man's thinking, redirecting man's thinking, because obviously the old thought process has gotten us in the mess that we have. We must look at old values, old ways of doing things and not be afraid to question. And if we find that these values are incorrect in view of new enlightenment, then be willing to change—not feel threatened by new ideas, but embrace them and give them a chance to be proved or disproved."

Rev. E.L. Woods
Pastor of Ebony Missionary
Baptist Church
Los Angeles, California

"The laws of our land are often administered in an unfair and unequal manner. In the future, however, I see the technology of the Church of Scientology assisting those in the judicial system inequitably administering these laws. In this manner, the judicial system can effectively contribute to bringing about the aims of Scientology as outlined by L. Ron Hubbard."

Reginia Rogers Jackson
Attorney
Washington, DC

"Scientology's Citizens Commission on Human Rights is fighting a cause, the abuses of psychiatry and the devastation of their drugs to which the general public is beginning to awaken. They are creating a safer world for us all."

Ann Tracy
Prozac Survivors Support
Group Director
Utah Branch

"It is obvious that the Church of Scientology feels a moral responsibility to attack serious social problems and improve conditions. I see the Church building on this background and expanding its activities into the practical hard-nosed field of education where it can play a major role in resolving some of the bitter conflicts which are preventing the proper education of our children. We need our children to be literate to have real-world skills. I see the Church of Scientology playing a major role in making this happen."

Patrick Groff, Ed.D.
Professor Emeritus
San Diego State University

"Based on the time I've been in Hollywood and seen what the Church of Scientology has accomplished, all indications appear that the Church in the next five years will continue to make progress in the community, specifically as it relates to handling gang violence, graffiti, etc.

"The outreach achieved is significant and I think it is very positive. The Church continues to have faith and continues to help those in need of direction, upgrade their properties, and contribute to community development."

Frank L. Buckley
Board Member
Hollywood Chamber of Commerce

"We, at the Bible Holiness Movement, have—over the years—been gratefully aware that the Church of Scientology has actively endeavored to express its committal to the God-given rights and liberties, including religious freedom, that are essential to society, and this with them has not been an abstract ideal but an essential practical effort along with other religious and concerned bodies of people.

"It is also good to have known personally of many instances when these Scientologists have acted on behalf of others who would differ with them, simply on the basis of principle and human compassion. Two instances come to mind, one where an Evangelical youth was under illegal effort to force a denial of faith in Christ, and the other of compassionate and effective effort in improving the lot of South African Black mental patients who were suffering vicious abuse in a form of virtual slavery.

"What of the future? It would be our hope and expectation that the Scientologists will continue in their social conscience and concern for human liberty."

Wesley H. Wakefield
Bishop General of the
Bible Holiness Movement

"The trend today is for people to go back to conservatism.

"As long as the Church of Scientology provides a visible alternative it's going to grow and expand.

"We are through the permissive age and people are questioning values. You will get larger if you continue to provide an active social side to the Church.

"If you continue to reassure people that it isn't all hopeless and the world isn't coming to an end you'll continue to do well."

Robert Carr
Journalist
Ontario Parliament
Press Gallery

"Scientology will endure. It will be accepted more and more into normality as with other religious associations."

Svante Nycander
Writer
Sweden

"The delightfully informative L. Ron Hubbard Life Exhibition, combined with Celebrity Centre's magnificently restored Manor Hotel, have created for the citizenry of Hollywood two brilliant examples of the Church's commitment to improve not only the cultural scene, but also to add vision and financial resources to the increasingly important community revitalization program. Add to that the Herculean 'neighbor safety' efforts of staff and membership during the recent civil unrest in Los Angeles, and you have created a blueprint for a successful future throughout the community."

Michael Teilmann
Teilmann International Productions
Hollywood, California

"I feel that the Church has been a great help to many people. It has brought enlightenment—I hope you continue in your strides."

Lilyann Mitchell
Argus *Newspaper*
England

"Scientology has shown its valuable place in society not only in its stand against religious suppression but by providing education and study technology for people of all races. This ensures the most fundamental of all human rights, the right to literacy. The Church of Scientology will be here as a guiding light for future generations."

Ron Segal
Education Committee
United Nations Association of Australia

"Because the Church of Scientology has a legitimate philosophy on the human situation, it will endure. I see it outliving and speeding the demise of its main antagonist, the state-sponsored religion of psychiatry. Despite the current financial power of psychiatry and its ability to spread its dark message that man is but an animal, I believe the day will come when the Church of Scientology will be joined by other churches dancing on psychiatry's coffin."

Seth Farber, Ph.D.
Executive Director
Network Against Coercive Psychiatry

Although these views greatly vary, all have common denominators; that Scientology has workability, has produced results and is a growing authority in the humanities and spiritual nature of man.

The future, L. Ron Hubbard said some twenty years ago, would tell more than he ever could about the value of his work.

Thus far it has told an extraordinary story—a story of millions who have found a way to better themselves and their fellows through the use of this technology, of new rights for the mentally ill, of new lives for drug abusers and of new hope for the illiterate.

But what does the future hold from this point forward? Many of those who have attempted to halt Scientology in the past are still with us, and it is not unreasonable to assume that there may be future battles to fight. But in the final analysis, authority belongs to those who can DO the task in any given field. Authority sustained by pompousness, the laws passed and "we who know" cannot endure.

Scientology has the answers. Authority belongs to those who can do the job. And Scientology will inherit tomorrow as surely as the sun will rise.

Chapter 31

Those Who Oppose Scientology

Dianetics did not come quietly into the world. Even before publication of L. Ron Hubbard's *Dianetics: The Modern Science of Mental Health,* excitement had been created on a relatively small scale—small, in hindsight of what was to come later. It had begun with a mimeographed copy of his earlier work *Dianetics: The Original Thesis,* which was passed hand to hand around the country, and soon followed by an article in the *Explorers Club Journal.*

Then, on May 9, 1950 *The Modern Science of Mental Health* reached the bookstores. Almost immediately, a groundswell of public enthusiasm vaulted the book onto national bestseller lists. Stores simply could not keep copies in stock as hundreds of thousands across the nation formed themselves into auditing groups, and Mr. Hubbard's discoveries even began to take root on distant shores. To meet the astonishing response from all sectors of society—the fashionable, the academic and, most importantly, the man on the street—the publisher instantly ordered further printings. Yet still supply could barely keep pace with demand. By the end of six weeks, Dianetics was not merely a phenomena; it was the beginning of the global movement that continues to grow today.

There were, however, a scant few among society's ranks who were not quite so enthusiastic, i.e., certain key members of the American medical/psychiatric establishment. That their numbers were pitifully small—literally measured in the dozens—did not necessarily concern them. They were well entrenched and well connected; and when they decided that Dianetics must be stopped to preserve their kingdom, they were fully prepared to make use of every one of those connections.

Thus it was that two diametrically opposed forces were unleashed on May 9, 1950. On the one hand stood the hundred thousand and more everyday men and women who eagerly read and applied *Dianetics* with extraordinary success. On the other stood a small clique of medical and psychiatric practitioners, who knew nothing of the human mind, and had not even read *Dianetics.* Nonetheless, they were certain that a handbook, which made self-improvement possible to anyone, would constitute a severe financial loss to the healthcare establishment. After all, they reasoned, how can psychiatrists expect to command large salaries if the man on the street knew more about the mind than they did? Seen within this context then, May 9, 1950 not only saw the birth of Dianetics, but also psychiatry's first shot that began a war.

The Real Issues

To understand the forces ranged against L. Ron Hubbard, in this war he never started, it is necessary to gain a cursory glimpse of the old and venerable science of psychiatry—which was actually none of the aforementioned. As an institution, it dates back to shortly before the turn of the century; it is certainly not worthy of respect by reason of age or dignity; and it does not meet any known definition of a science, what with its hodgepodge of unproven theories that have never produced any result—except an ability to make the unmanageable and mutinous more docile and quiet, and turn the troubled into apathetic souls beyond the point of caring.

That it promotes itself as a healing profession is a misrepresentation, to say the least. Its mission is to control.

Psychiatry as we know it today is more priesthood than science. Its conglomeration of half-baked theories is handed down by an arbitrary elite—authorities who have attained such status through who they know and who can sweet-talk the government into parting with yet more grant money.

While as for what they actually *do,* there are only three primary methods of "treatment"—electroshock, psychosurgery and psychotropic drugs.

To illustrate the unscientific basis of this "science," in Fascist Italy in the 1930s, Professor Ugo Cerletti noted that back in A.D. 43 or so, Roman citizens would sometimes try to rid themselves of headaches by putting a torpedo fish on their heads. A torpedo fish generates about 25 volts of electricity. Perhaps it was just coincidence that the Empire fell soon after that, but be that as it may, Cerletti was undeterred by this observation and set off on a new path. He began his experiments by killing dogs with huge jolts of electricity. However, before he could significantly reduce Rome's canine population, inspiration came in the form of a visit to a pig slaughterhouse. There, much to his delight, he found that pigs were not killed by the electricity administered, but only sent into epileptic convulsions, whereupon their throats could conveniently be cut by the butchers. After experimenting further—and losing a great many pigs—to discover how much electricity it would take to kill one of the porcine creatures, he was ready for man. The unfortunate vagrant he chose (generously supplied by the police) received 70 volts to the head, fell, then shouted, "Not a second [one]. It will kill!" Later, it was discovered that human beings could withstand between 140 and 150 volts to the brain. Thus electroconvulsive shock therapy (ECT) was born.

Psychosurgery had equally shabby beginnings, according to the medical historians. In 1848, Phineas Gage of Vermont was peering into a blasting hole when a charge detonated and blew a metal tamping rod through his brain—an unfortunate accident that he managed to survive. But, his astute physician noted with amazement, Gage had changed! A most noticeable change—from efficient and capable, to self-indulgent and profane. Thus Gage made his place in history as the first person to survive a lobotomy. The man who actually established himself as the father of the lobotomy (a procedure conducted on intractable patients to make them more manageable) was Dr. Egas Moniz. He operated on about one hundred patients. However, in at least one case, the operation might have been a success but the doctor died: he was shot by one of his lobotomized patients. That in 1949 he was given the Nobel prize for this questionable advancement is one of the saddest ironies of medical history. Nonetheless, it assured that many followed his path.

As for drugs, witch doctors have used the natural variety for centuries. Today's pharmaceutical psychotropic drugs began their development with attempts to brainwash recalcitrant citizens and political prisoners. Virtually all of the original research—in Russia, Germany and the United States—was funded by intelligence agencies. Once again, the aim was to make individuals more tractable and malleable. And, in the United States, at least, most of it was illegal, conducted on unknowing servicemen and citizens. Except, of course, in the oft-cited instance of CIA psychiatrist, Dr. Louis Jolyon West, who was the only man known to have killed an elephant with LSD.

That all of this experimentation—drugs, psychosurgery, ECT—has never cured anyone of anything but, on the contrary, has either made people more manageable or damaged them beyond recognition, has never stopped the psychiatric community from continuing these practices. After all, these are the only tools they have. Without them, they would have nothing to sell.

Which brings up a crucial point: to whom do they sell their services? Not to the broad public (and only sometimes even to their own patients), for the majority have no faith in this parody of science and would never even entertain the idea of actually visiting a psychiatrist. Then, of course, there is also the shame and embarrassment associated with going to a psychiatrist—which is largely due to the way psychiatrists themselves have characterized mental illness in a sales campaign that backfired. The only customers they have, the only ones willing to pay for their services (and very generously) are governments, particularly the clandestine arms of the government, or those that desire to control people, be they prisoners, children or society's unwanted.

These, then, constitute the force that tried to stop Dianetics and Scientology.

And this is the world Dianetics entered. A world where psychiatry was entrenched among the US intelligence services, living off the fat of government grants, and experimenting—with the help of ex-Nazi scientists—on an oblivious public. A world where their critics were simply labeled insane and "in need of psychiatric help."

Thus the battle lines were drawn. Dianetics offered a means to happiness, stability and success. It provided a solution to psychosomatic illnesses. It created an interest in the workings of the mind among people of all classes and ages. And it gave the man in the street a method that, for the first time, he himself could utilize to improve his own condition. Additionally, it should be kept in mind that L. Ron Hubbard achieved something that psychiatrists have long been attempting to achieve: to write a book about the mind that was genuinely popular, that people actually wanted to read, that was both understandable and applicable.

But Dianetics did more. It labeled the latest and greatest psychiatric drugs as dangerous. And it directly exposed the inhuman crimes of psychiatrists and the harm they caused with ECT and lobotomies, clearly substantiating the irreparable damage these treatments caused to healthy brain tissue.

That mental health professionals were incensed by Mr. Hubbard's not-so-gentle upbraiding is understandable, particularly as he was not a member of their elitist clique. But when all was said and done, the issue was clearly financial: How long could one continue to convince the American taxpayer to foot the bill for multimillion-dollar psychiatric appropriations in the face of what Dianetics could accomplish for the price of a book?

THE MARSHALING OF FORCES

Among the many, many positive reviews and articles on Dianetics were a few strategically placed "hits" specifically designed to dampen public enthusiasm.

These first negative "reviews" on Dianetics came through the American Medical Association—a group instinctively opposed to any unregulated or nonmember means to better health and living. But it was not as it appeared; more the result of a ventriloquism act. The actual link to the AMA was made by the American Psychiatric Association (APA) medical director, Dr. Daniel Blain, who well knew that psychiatry enjoyed nothing close to the credibility of its medical colleagues, and none of the clout. The voice of the AMA was essentially that of he and his colleagues.

But using the AMA to take potshots was only the first round. The full APA plan was far more elaborate. First, false propaganda was to be published in "authoritative" journals; then, once the "experts" had passed judgment, these opinions would be given to mainstream media sources. Dossiers would be created to contain all this unflattering "information" and passed still further afield including, of course, to appropriate government agencies.

Although simple in both design and execution, the consequences would be far-reaching. Indeed, to one degree or another, the subsequent attacks on Dianetics and Scientology were but a result of this original scheme to fabricate dossiers and then spread them far and wide.

Mind Control Exposed

During the continual process of Dianetics research, both as an auditor and as an observer of other auditors, Mr. Hubbard naturally came into contact with a wide variety of cases. And, it was inevitable that these would include those who had been in the hands of psychiatrists closely allied to the intelligence community.

Thus it came about, fully twenty-five years before the facts were made public by Congress, that Mr. Hubbard was the first to announce and decry government mind manipulation programs. Eventually, of course, these and other revelations of Central Intelligence Agency criminality would entirely reshape public perception of this group of spies from a patriotic and somewhat glamorous image to that of a rogue agency of dirty tricksters, with its own citizens as victims.

The vehicle was his 1951 book *Science of Survival,* and in it he described in no uncertain terms the combined use of pain, drugs and hypnosis as a behavioral modification technique of the worst kind. It was, he said, so extensively used in espionage work, it was long past the time people should have become alarmed about it. It had taken Dianetic auditing to discover the widespread existence of these brainwashing techniques, and, he added, the only saving grace was that Dianetics could undo their effects.

With such covert government activity so openly addressed by Mr. Hubbard and Dianeticists, he had compounded his "crime": In his first book, he offended psychiatrists; in his second, the intelligence community. That the two, already closely connected, should now draw even closer in the common effort to stop him, was not surprising. What was surprising was the velocity and frequency of subsequent attacks. By the mid-1950s, as we shall see, at least half a dozen Federal agencies were brought into the effort to suppress Dianetics and its assault on the mental health field, including the Federal Bureau of Investigation (FBI), the Internal Revenue Service (IRS) and the Food and Drug Administration (FDA).

"You would have thought that at the very least I was inciting whole populations to revolt and governments to fall," a slightly bemused Mr. Hubbard later wrote of these events. "All I really was doing was trying to tell man he could be happy, that there was a road out of suffering and that he could attain his goals."

The Battle Mounts

Yet even while Mr. Hubbard successfully told man he could be happy and the numbers of Scientologists mounted, psychiatry was attempting to strengthen its grasp on society.

The plan involved what came to be known as the Siberia Bill, actually named the Alaska Mental Health Bill. The more popular title came from the fact that the proposed outcome of this cherished psychiatric plan was likened to a Siberia-type camp for mental health patients in the frozen wastelands of Alaska. Presumably, this was far enough away from the well-traveled roads of the world to allow psychiatrists to conduct their mind control and other experiments on a captive population, unhindered by the glare of publicity. To ensure a captive population, the measure incorporated a "simplified commitment procedure," so simple, in fact, that it eradicated such wasteful and costly activities as jury trials and legal defenses and allowed any peace officer, friend, medical doctor and, of course, psychiatrist, to institute commitment proceedings.

But just after January 1956, and the bill's unanimous, yet barely noticeable, passage through Congress, a coalition of members of the Church of Scientology and civil rights groups launched a campaign to inform the American public just what this bill held in store for them. Under the rallying cry, "Siberia, USA!" a massive letter-writing campaign inspired political opposition.

When it was over, the commitment section of the bill was deservedly dead, leaving merely an act to authorize mental health funding to the territory of Alaska.

A wounded psychiatry struck back, this time utilizing the FDA as its main battering ram. Thanks to the Freedom of Information Act, Scientologists later uncovered a mountain of documents which well demonstrated the activities of the participants—egged on by members of both the AMA and APA. A veritable beehive of activity took place, with letters and meetings between interested psychiatric parties, the Department of Justice, the Washington, DC police department, the United States Post Office, the IRS, the AMA, of course, and even the US Army's Criminal Investigation Command—all continuously linked and regularly prodded by a now extremely nervous psychiatry.

The upshot of all these schemes? The first action was a ludicrous failure, the second a waste of time, the third an embarrassment.

The first, based on a psychiatrist's "tip" that the Church was using illegal drugs, led to a "raid" on the Washington, DC church by a US deputy marshal who seized a few bottles of said drug. When it turned out to be a compound of the commonly available vitamin B_1, vitamin C, niacinamide and calcium, that case obviously went nowhere.

Drug dealing proving an unworkable premise, the FDA and other interested agencies decided that Scientology practicing medicine without a license would prove fertile ground for exploration. On March 19, 1959, FDA agent Taylor Quinn infiltrated the church, taped a religious service, and passed the information on to the US Attorney's Office. Unfortunately, as he reported to the FDA, the church had required him to sign a contract that he was not to learn to cure anyone. Nor was there any evidence of fraud.

With both drugs and illegal healing dead-ended, the only avenue remaining to the FDA was the E-Meter. Perhaps, they theorized, it was used to "diagnose" or "cure illness." So, on January 4, 1963, US marshals, deputized longshoremen and armed police barged their way into the Founding Church of Scientology in Washington, threatened the staff, and left with two vans of not only E-Meters, but books, scriptures and other materials.

Still, as outrageous as it was, it didn't match the sheer audacity of what happened in Seattle where the FDA's fingerprints were figuratively all over the handgun that was used to murder the head of the church there.

A local resident, Russell Johnson, who had heard about the FDA's actions in Washington, DC, thought they would provide a sympathetic ear to his current problem. He called them to complain about "the practices of a Dr. William Fisk who operates as the Church of Scientology" and claimed Fisk was attempting to seduce his wife.

The enterprising FDA official he spoke to immediately suggested that Johnson join forces with the FDA as an "undercover agent" and infiltrate the church. Johnson dutifully did this, reported in, and was instructed to return and get further information.

Johnson carried his duties as an intelligence agent into tragic and bloody extremes. On September 10, 1963, he walked into the Seattle church and shot and killed the Executive Director before a roomful of horrified congregation members.

The FDA then carried the concept of expediency to new and distasteful heights. Instead of confessing that one of its "agents" had just committed murder, it contacted the Seattle police department and arranged to send its own people illegally into church premises with the homicide team, to further gather information for its "investigation." As usual, however, the FDA discovered nothing illegal in the church.

Altogether, for more than a decade the FDA would remain obsessed with the E-Meter. With other government agencies, it would repeatedly infiltrate the Church with agents and informants, employ bugging devices, place a "cover" on Church mail, and obtain confidential Church bank account information.

It would get nowhere. In 1969, the Washington, DC Federal Appeals Court ruled the Church a bona fide religion protected by the US Constitution, and that the E-Meter had not been improperly labeled or used.

Still, it was not until 1973 that a reluctant FDA finally returned those stolen church materials: 5,000 books, 2,900 booklets, and the E-Meters.

MEDIA–GOVERNMENT COLLUSION

There remains one illuminating point to the FDA fiasco. It involves the enlistment by the FDA of *The Saturday Evening Post* and their star feature writer, James Phelan.

After being approached by the AMA to do a story on Scientology, the *Post* assigned the piece to Phelan, who traveled to England to interview Mr. Hubbard. He was warmly welcomed and assisted in every manner possible, as befits a seemingly interested and unbiased journalist, which is how he represented himself.

That Phelan was anything but that was borne out by two facts: Immediately upon his return to Washington and *before* the story was published, he gave his story to the FDA for coordination purposes; and, the resulting story was a hatchet job of the first order—an unrestrained attempt to smear both Mr. Hubbard and Scientology, obviously a flanking action to the FDA's attempted case against use of the E-Meter.

Phelan was followed by many others—a long string of stories through the years, concocted to create a climate conducive to governmental harassment. It was a similar pattern to that which occurred in Germany in the 1930s—the very successful media actions to create public "indignation" that would legitimize not only the most blatant violations of civil rights, but, indeed, the Holocaust.

THE IRS CAMPAIGN

The FDA had conclusively proven its incompetence, not only by botching its mandate to destroy Scientology, but by taking so long to do it—thus allowing Scientology to grow meteorically, both in the United States and around the world. Thus, the FDA was dismissed to do what it does best: harass vitamin salesmen, and give carte blanche to powerful drug companies well before completion of the product safety tests.

The weight of the mission now fell on IRS shoulders. Actually, the IRS had been part of the same program, harassing the Church since the early 1950s, denying tax-exempt status to various Scientology churches, and issuing Federal tax liens against others. It also provided information to the post office to "support a charge of misrepresentation," and later sent a host of other government agencies blatantly ludicrous falsehoods on the order of: "LSD and perhaps other drugs are widely used by the members while assembled" and that the Church used "electric shock" on its parishioners in an "initiation ceremony"—fabrications that would have been laughable, if not for the consequences.

IRS illegalities were the subject of 1976 Congressional hearings that found the IRS had been engaged in "intelligence gathering" and had been used as a political weapon disrelated to tax concerns. Thus among the materials turned up through the Freedom of Information Act was a St. Louis IRS file labeling the Church as politically subversive to justify further harassment. This charge, it should be mentioned, is particularly outrageous in view of the fact that Scientology is one of the most politically nonpartisan religions on Earth—fighting discrimination and injustice on the left, the right and all points in between.

The whole tedious history of IRS attacks would fill a book. In fact, it fills scores of filing cabinets of documents obtained under the Freedom of Information Act, revealing not merely a genuinely shocking parade of IRS dirty tricks, but also a mad agency scramble to fabricate a case—any kind of case—against the Church of Scientology.

Specifically, these documents tell of IRS attempts to redefine the term *church,* expressly to disqualify Scientology from tax-exempt status. And when that didn't work, an even more unbelievable story unfolded: In an attempt to circumvent the fact that the Church committed no crimes, the IRS engaged in a truly Machiavellian scheme which they pursued for several years.

The plan called for nothing short of complete destruction of the Church. As part of the agenda: infiltration of the Church with a network of undercover agents and the manufacture of evidence. Forged documents were to be seeded into Church files where, through the course of a planned IRS raid, they would be conveniently found and used as evidence for prosecution. The infiltrators were not only to be rewarded financially when Church assets were looted, but they were also to be installed as IRS puppets running a fully tax-exempt church that would use the name but bear no resemblance to Scientology.

Yet, even as the IRS was implementing its plans—attempting to infiltrate church premises, working out how to forge and plant documents—Church attorneys exposed all. In addition to concerns over ensuing public outrage at this exposure, the IRS now had to contend with another problem; one doesn't spend several years investigating a church at enormous cost to the taxpayer only to report that no crimes were found.

In a last-ditch effort to save face, not to mention careers, the IRS tried to persuade the Department of Justice to bring some kind, any kind, of prosecution as a justification for what they had done. Justice may be blind, but it's not stupid, and Justice Department attorneys rebuked the IRS and refused to entertain any prosecution or even further investigation. After all, anyone could see that no crimes had been committed beyond those of the IRS themselves.

This did not stop the IRS, however. Their assault only intensified, and literally thousands of agents—entire task forces—were thrown into the fray to work on the "Scientology problem."

The Church, with an abundance of evidence, responded by filing a $120 million damages suit in Federal Court in August 1991. That suit named seventeen Washington, DC and Los Angeles-based Internal Revenue Service officials. It charged agency officials with waging a thirty-three-year campaign of illegal acts, violating the constitutional rights of the Church and large numbers of its parishioners.

Furthermore, the Church took its case to the public, unleashing a massive media campaign to expose IRS crimes and abuses, with daily advertisements in the American national newspaper, *USA Today.*

Finally, however, even this war came to an end. After subjecting the churches of Scientology to the most intensive scrutiny any organization ever faced—including a meticulous review of its operations and financial records—the IRS came to the only possible conclusion from such an examination: Scientology churches and their related entities were organized and operated exclusively for charitable purposes.

Thus, on October 1, 1993, the Internal Revenue Service issued letters recognizing this fact to churches of Scientology and their affiliated organizations across the US and in other parts of the world. The mother church and all Scientology churches, missions, social betterment and social reform groups in the United States, as well as several major Scientology organizations abroad, were granted full tax-exempt recognition by the IRS—a formal acknowledgment of Scientology's religious bona fides and its benefit to society as a whole.

But what of those blatant false reports that had originated in the 1950s and continued to spew forth in later decades? They had traveled far and wide—to the major European countries, to Australia, to South Africa, there to be used as ammunition against Scientology.

To counter these, the IRS agreed to apprise government agencies around the world of its decision to recognize the Church, and to send them all a full, *accurate* briefing on the Scientology religion and its activities.

A major campaign in the war against Scientology had truly ended.

Behind the Worldwide Campaign

Although the forty-year assault against Scientology assumed large proportions, the source must be remembered—that small but influential circle of psychiatrists and their government stooges. Nor did the means change over the years: false allegations selectively planted in the media, then seeded into even more federal files as background "fact."

It is a method, with small adjustments, that also served to cause trouble overseas. The international pipeline left the US, primarily through IRS and FBI links, and discharged among the voluminous dossiers of Interpol, a private organization which worked closely with the Nazis during World War II, and had as its president an ex-SS officer as late as 1972—as the Church was the first to expose.

Interpol (originally designed to coordinate criminal apprehension between countries) was convenient on three counts: First, because as a private organization, it is above the laws of any country, free to amass secret dossiers and spread them far and wide; second, files bearing the authoritative Interpol stamp are assumed to be true; and, third, it had a decades-old relationship with the IRS and the FBI, the main repositories of false reports on Scientology in the US. In fact, IRS and FBI files contained virtually every rumor ever disseminated about Scientology, further substantiating Congressional findings that these agencies were often used to launch politically motivated attacks against targets that had committed no crimes at all.

What happened was fairly predictable: attacks against Scientology by government agencies in England, France, Germany, Italy, Spain and Australia—all with fervent media support involving the most outrageous allegations. Still, as usual, in every instance, Scientology prevailed.

So it goes. Key psychiatric figures, their US government allies and psychiatric colleagues overseas—together they have spent untold millions of dollars around the world to stop Scientology.

And they never have.

The End of the Fight

While psychiatry had US government agencies infiltrating, raiding and investigating the Church in the early and mid-1960s, and inquiries in Australia and Great Britain underway during the same decade, the technologies of Scientology and Dianetics were widely available in five countries. Despite unabated attacks, these technologies became available in five more countries by the mid-1970s, in fifty-six countries in the late 1980s, and in seventy-four countries by the turn of the 1990s. All of which demonstrates that psychiatry has been about as effective in stopping Scientology as it has been in treating mental illness.

It has, in fact, become increasingly evident that psychiatry offers no valuable contribution to society whatsoever. Electric shock, brain operations, and indiscriminate drugging of patients in nineteenth-century-like horror chambers passed off as mental hospitals, have killed and maimed people on a daily basis. And during the period psychiatry has held its position of authority, the most dramatic era of social unrest, civil disobedience, drug proliferation and criminality in the history of the Western world has gained momentum.

Today, there are 500 Dianeticists and Scientologists to every psychiatrist, and while Scientology expands, enrollment in psychiatric university curriculums has slid to a drastic low since a peak in the 1960s. Without government appropriations, even these few psychiatrists would not be able to economically survive, for they have nothing to offer worth a cent of the public's money. Hence, while Scientology is more visible than ever, with churches dotting every continent on Earth and millions of parishioners around the world, one is hard pressed to find even a single psychiatrist with a shingle on his door. True, one can still find them in scuffed-linoleum offices of state and county hospitals, and lodged in the federal bureaucracy. But when was the last time anyone saw a sign advertising lobotomies, electric shock and seriously incapacitating drugs?

In short, then, while psychiatry, which lives off government handouts, is shrinking, Scientology, which receives only public donations from people who know it works, is growing faster than any religion in the world. And if Scientology had anything to hide, it would not have survived the relentless attacks detailed in this chapter.

Thus the story of the attacks against Scientology is basically very simple. Dianetics and Scientology cut across vested interests which then ruthlessly attempted to destroy it. The issue was never any wrongdoing by the Church, merely encroachment on turf claimed by a mental health industry who would stop at nothing to preserve their stake.

Still, while psychiatry's offensive against Scientology has been all but defeated, the battle is not over. True, their allies among US government agencies have retired from the conflict. And finally their staunchest battering ram, the IRS, has also recognized the Church and its benefit to society. But psychiatry's traditional allies and symbiotic partners have always been the drug companies. Psychiatry invents the "disease"—the pharmaceutical companies invent the "cure." The side effects of the drugs ensure that the patient stays with the psychiatrist and, based upon these symptoms, a new disease is created. Which is the tail and which the dog in this vicious circle is debatable, but in any event, the drug companies jumped on the bandwagon. They stand to lose literally billions of dollars *a year* when people fully discover that ills and addictions can be resolved without mind-bending and mood-altering chemicals.

It would be well to remember, then, that when alarming reports are heard about Dianetics and Scientology, they stem from those who would prefer to manhandle problems with mind-altering drugs or enough electricity to throw a pig into convulsions—and as any fool knows, sticking one's finger in a light socket or clamping electrodes to one's skull cures nothing. (Even psychiatrists are not that stupid. When widely offered $10,000 to undergo their own "treatment," not one has ever agreed to subject himself to electroconvulsive therapy.)

The lessons of history provide the best context within which to consider such attacks. Every great movement which has opened new vistas and shaken the strongholds of archaic thought has been attacked by those who profit from the persistence of outmoded ideas. Thus, as Scientologists continue their work toward a new civilization without insanity, criminality or war, those with billion-dollar vested interests in just those ills will continue to lash out.

Yet it is ironic to view these attacks in the context of time. Scientology did not choose to fight this battle with psychiatry and, indeed, was not the one to fire the opening salvos. Mr. Hubbard was simply the one to come up with real answers to problems of the mind. Perhaps sensing that implicit in a solution to the mind lay their own demise, psychiatrists decided to destroy him and his technology. And just as they feared, Scientology has become their nemesis, exposing their brutality and their crimes.

Recognition of the Church by the IRS in 1993 has been welcomed as a major turn in this tide. Truth has once again demonstrated its power by prevailing against odds that would have overwhelmed any lesser cause.

What remains of the old guard stands increasingly alone and the shrill voices of their heirs grow fainter and fainter. For try as they might to maintain their privileged positions and spread their falsehoods, the ears and eyes of the world have changed. Truth, after all, sheds light. The dark shadows in which they have hidden have grown ever more insubstantial.

But even as their tirades drone on, there is another point they should consider: The world which they helped create, a world where the wasted insane wander aimlessly through our inner cities, where senseless criminality claims a new life every few minutes, and entire generations sag under the double onslaught of drug dependency and illiteracy, this is a world in which they too must live.

And so, in the end, even those who attempted to stop Scientology will ultimately benefit from its victory.

THE TRUE STORY OF SCIENTOLOGY BY L. RON HUBBARD

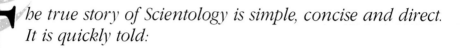

The true story of Scientology is simple, concise and direct. It is quickly told:

1. A philosopher develops a philosophy about life and death.

2. People find it interesting.

3. People find it works.

4. People pass it along to others.

5. It grows.

When we examine this extremely accurate and very brief account, we see that there must be in our civilization some very disturbing elements for anything else to be believed about Scientology.

These disturbing elements are the Merchants of Chaos. They deal in confusion and upset. Their daily bread is made by creating chaos. If chaos were to lessen, so would their incomes.

The politician, the reporter, the medico, the drug manufacturer, the militarist and arms manufacturer, the police and the undertaker, to name the leaders of the list, fatten only upon "the dangerous environment." Even individuals and family members can be Merchants of Chaos.

It is to their interest to make the environment seem as threatening as possible, for only then can they profit. Their incomes, force and power rise in direct ratio to the amount of threat they can inject into the surroundings of the people. With that threat they can extort revenue, appropriations, heightened circulations and recompense without question. These are the Merchants of Chaos. If they did not generate it and buy and sell it, they would, they suppose, be poor.

For instance, we speak loosely of "good press." Is there any such thing today? Look over a newspaper. Is there anything **good** *on the front page? Rather, there is murder and sudden death, disagreement and catastrophe. And even that, bad as it is, is sensationalized to make it seem worse.*

This is the coldblooded manufacture of "a dangerous environment." People do not need this news; and if they did, they need the facts, not the upset. But if you hit a person hard enough, he can be made to give up money. That's the basic formula of extortion. That's the way papers are sold. The impact makes them stick.

A paper has to have chaos and confusion. A "news story" has to have "conflict," they say. So there is no good press. There is only **bad** *press about everything. To yearn for "good press" is foolhardy in a society where the Merchants of Chaos reign.*

Look what has to be done to the true story of Scientology in order to "make it a news story" by modern press standards. Conflict must be injected where there is none. Therefore the press has to dream up upset and conflict.

Let us take the first line. How does one make conflict out of it? No. 1, **A philosopher develops a philosophy about life and death.**

The Chaos Merchant **has** *to inject one of several possible conflicts here: He is not a doctor of philosophy, they have to assert. They are never quite bold enough to say it is not a philosophy. But they can and do go on endlessly, as their purpose compels them, in an effort to invalidate the identity of the person developing it.*

In actual fact, the developer of the philosophy was very well grounded in academic subjects and the humanities, probably better grounded in formal philosophy alone than teachers of philosophy in universities.

The one-man effort is incredible in terms of study and research hours and is a record never approached in living memory, but this would not be considered newsworthy. To write the simple fact that a philosopher had developed a philosophy is not newspaper-type news and it would not disturb the environment. Hence, the elaborate news fictions about No. 1 above.

Then take the second part of the true story: ***People find it interesting.*** *It would be very odd if they didn't, as everyone asks these questions of himself and looks for the answers to his own beingness, and the basic truth of the answers is observable in the conclusions of Scientology.*

However, to make this "news" it has to be made disturbing. People are painted as kidnapped or hypnotized and dragged as unwilling victims up to read the books or listen.

The Chaos Merchant leaves No. 3 very thoroughly alone. It is dangerous ground for him. ***People find it works.*** *No hint of workability would ever be attached to Scientology by the press, although there is no doubt in the press mind that* ***it*** *does work. That's why it's dangerous. It calms the environment. So any time spent trying to convince press that Scientology works is time spent upsetting a reporter.*

On No. 4, ***People pass it along to others,*** *the press feels betrayed. "Nobody should believe anything they don't read in the papers. How dare word of mouth exist!" So, to try to stop people from listening, the Chaos Merchant has to use words like* ***cult.*** *That's "a closed group," whereas Scientology is the most open group on Earth to* *anyone. And they have to attack organizations and their people to try to keep people out of Scientology.*

Now, as for No. 5, **It grows,** *we have the true objection.*

As truth goes forward, lies die. The slaughter of lies is an act that takes bread from the mouth of a Chaos Merchant. Unless he can lie with wild abandon about how bad it all is, he thinks he will starve.

The world simply must **not** *be a better place according to the Chaos Merchant. If people were less disturbed, less beaten down by their environments, there would be no new appropriations for police and armies and big rockets and there'd be not even pennies for a screaming sensational press.*

So long as politicians move upward on scandal, police get more pay for more crime, medicos get fatter on more sickness, there will be Merchants of Chaos. They're paid for it.

And their threat is the simple story of Scientology. For that is the true story. And behind its progress there is a calmer environment in which a man can live and feel better. If you don't believe it, just stop reading newspapers for two weeks, and see if you feel better. Suppose you had all such disturbances handled?

The pity of it is, of course, that even the Merchant of Chaos needs us, not to get fatter, but just to live himself as a being.

So the true story of Scientology is a simple story.

And too true to be turned aside.

Part Nine

A Scientology Catechism

Throughout history, religions have traditionally published summaries of their basic principles in catechism form. The following chapter will answer some of the most commonly asked questions people have about the fundamentals of Dianetics and Scientology.

When individuals first hear about the subject, their questions are usually quite diverse. They range from "Why is Scientology called a religion?" and "What is the difference between Dianetics and Scientology?" to "Who was L. Ron Hubbard?" to "What is the E-Meter and how does it work?"

These questions, and many others, are answered in the following pages.

Chapter 32

Answers to Common Questions

What does the word* Scientology *mean?

The word *Scientology* means "the study of knowledge" or "knowing about knowing" from the Latin word *scio* which means "know" or "distinguish," and from the Greek word *logos* which means "reason itself" or "inward thought." So it means the study of wisdom or knowledge, or "knowing how to know." *Scientology* is further defined as the study and handling of the spirit in relationship to itself, universes and other life. The word was coined by L. Ron Hubbard.

What is Scientology about?

Developed by L. Ron Hubbard, Scientology provides *exact* principles and practical technology for improving self-confidence, intelligence and ability. Scientology does not require faith or belief—one can apply the principles and see for oneself if they work and are true.

Scientology addresses the spirit—not simply the body or mind—and is therefore completely apart from materialistic philosophies which hold that man is a product of his environment—or his genes.

Scientology is a religion by its basic tenets, practice, historical background and by the definition of the word *religion* itself. It is recognized as such by courts in country after country around the world, including the highest courts in the United States, Australia, Germany, Sweden, Italy and many others.

All denominations are welcome in Scientology.

Scientology is a *route,* a way, rather than a dissertation or an assertive body of knowledge.

Through its drills and studies one may find the truth for oneself. It is the only thing that can show you who *you* really are.

The technology is therefore not expounded as something to believe but something to *do.*

How did Scientology start?

L. Ron Hubbard began his studies of the mind in 1923. In 1947 he wrote a manuscript detailing some of his discoveries. It was not published at that time, but circulated among friends, who copied it and passed it on to others. (This manuscript was formally published in 1951 as *Dianetics: The Original Thesis* and later republished as *The Dynamics of Life.*)

As copies of the manuscript circulated, Mr. Hubbard began to receive an increasing flow of letters requesting further information and more applications of his new subject. He soon found himself spending all his time answering letters and decided to write a comprehensive text on the subject.

His first published article on the subject, "Terra Incognita: The Mind," appeared in the Winter/Spring 1950 issue of the *Explorers Club Journal*, followed by the book *Dianetics: The Modern Science of Mental Health*, which was published in May 1950. It became a nationwide bestseller almost overnight. By late summer, people across the country were not only reading the book, but were also organizing their own groups for the purpose of applying Dianetics techniques. The book has remained a bestseller ever since, again becoming number one on the *New York Times* bestseller list, almost four decades after its initial publication. It continues to appear on bestseller lists around the world.

During the course of thousands of hours of Dianetics counseling on thousands of individuals all over the country, incontrovertible evidence was amassed about the fundamentally spiritual nature of man. L. Ron Hubbard himself had discovered early in his research that man was a spiritual being, inhabiting a body and using a mind. These discoveries led him to realize that he had entered the realm of religion.

In 1954, the first church of Scientology was formed in Los Angeles by a group of Scientologists. Within a few years churches had been formed across the country and around the world.

In the years that followed, L. Ron Hubbard completed his research into the spiritual nature of man. Today, all his writings on the subject are available to anyone who wishes to study Scientology. Although Mr. Hubbard departed his body in 1986, he is still with us in spirit and the legacy of his work continues to help people around the world.

How come it's all based on one man's work?

In the early 1950s, L. Ron Hubbard wrote: "Acknowledgment is made to fifty thousand years of thinking men without whose speculations and observations the creation and construction of Dianetics would not have been possible. Credit in particular is due to:

Anaxagoras, Thomas Paine, Aristotle, Thomas Jefferson, Socrates, René Descartes, Plato, James Clerk Maxwell, Euclid, Charcôt, Lucretius, Herbert Spencer, Roger Bacon, William James, Francis Bacon, Sigmund Freud, Isaac Newton, van Leeuwenhoek, Cmdr. Joseph Thompson (MC) USN, William A. White, Voltaire, Will Durant, Count Alfred Korzybski, and my instructors in atomic and molecular phenomena, mathematics and the humanities at George Washington University and at Princeton."

Why is Scientology called a religion?

Religion is defined as "Any specific system of belief and worship, often involving a code of ethics and a philosophy. . . ." *(Webster's New World Dictionary, Third College Edition)*

Religious philosophy implies study of spiritual manifestations, research on the nature of the spirit and study of the relationship of the spirit to the body; exercises devoted to the rehabilitation of abilities in a spirit.

Scientology is a religion in the most traditional sense. It deals with man as a spirit and is distinguishable from material and nonreligious philosophies which hold man to be a product of material circumstances. Scientology does not demand blind faith, but endeavors to help the individual discover past experiences and shed the trauma and guilt (sin) which encumber him.

The Church of Scientology also conducts basic services such as sermons at church meetings, christenings, weddings and funerals.

Why is Scientology a church?

The word *church* comes from the Greek word *kurios* meaning "lord" and the Indo-European base *kewe,* "to be strong." Current meanings of the word include "a congregation," "ecclesiastical power as distinguished from the secular" and "the clerical profession; clergy."

The word *church* is not only used by Christian organizations. There were churches ten thousand years before there were Christians, and Christianity itself was a revolt against the established church. In modern usage, people speak of the Buddhist or Moslem church, referring in general to the whole body of believers in a particular religious teaching.

A church is simply a congregation of people who participate in common religious activities; *church* is also used to refer to the building where members of a religious group gather to practice their religion and attain greater spiritual awareness and well-being.

Scientology helps man become more aware of God, more aware of his own spiritual nature and that of those around him. Scientology scriptures recognize that there is an entire dynamic (urge or motivation in life) devoted to the Supreme Being (the eighth dynamic), and another dynamic that deals solely with one's urge toward existence as a spirit (the seventh dynamic). Acknowledgment of these aspects of life is a typical characteristic of religions. Thus, Scientology is a religion and the use of the word *church* when referring to Scientology is correct.

In the 1950s, Scientologists recognized that L. Ron Hubbard's technology and its results dealt directly with the freeing of the human spirit, and that greater spiritual awareness was routinely being achieved. There was no question in their minds that what they were dealing with was a religious practice; thus, in the early 1950s, they voted that a church be formed to better serve the needs of Scientologists. The first church of Scientology was incorporated in 1954. Since that time, dozens of court rulings in many different countries have upheld the fact that Scientology is a religion.

WHAT SCIENTOLOGY DOES FOR THE INDIVIDUAL

How does Scientology work?

Scientology philosophy provides answers to many questions about life and death; it encompasses an exact, precisely mapped-out path. Through application of Scientology technology in an auditing session, a person is able to remove barriers and unwanted conditions and so become more himself. As a person progresses, he often reaches out to help others in the ways he has been helped.

In developing Scientology, L. Ron Hubbard found the means to develop a technology to free the human spirit and thereby allow man to really know himself. He thoroughly tested all of his procedures and recorded for future use those that proved most workable in bringing about uniformly predictable results. These comprise standard Scientology technology.

That which is real to the person himself is all one is asked to accept of Scientology. No beliefs are forced upon him. By training and processing, he finds out for himself the answers he is looking for in life.

What does Scientology accomplish?

Since Scientology is an *applied religious philosophy,* the stress is on application and workability. It addresses the individual and brings about self-improvement by increasing a person's awareness and ability to handle life. It differs from other religious philosophies in that it supplies the means through which a person can increase his ability to effectively handle the problems and situations he and others face in life.

What claims are made for Scientology?

Scientology can increase a person's awareness and its application can help one to achieve greater happiness, self-confidence and ability.

Man has often been attracted to philosophies that sound plausible but which have no technology that can be applied to bring about desirable changes in one's life. Scientology and Dianetics, on the other hand, supply the tools with which an individual can improve his own life and the lives of those around him.

Scientology philosophy is based on the premise that man is basically good and that man can improve conditions in his life. However, Scientology cannot promise to do anything by itself. Only the individual can bring about his own improvement by applying Scientology tenets to himself, his life and others in his environment.

How do people get into Scientology?

Usually by word of mouth, often by reading a book or seeing promotional materials or taking a personality test at a church of Scientology. Sometimes by meeting a Scientologist and seeing that he has "something"—a positive attitude toward life, certainty, self-confidence and happiness—which they too would like. Fundamentally, people get into Scientology because they want to improve something in their lives or because they wish to help others improve themselves and thus make a better civilization.

SCIENTOLOGY AND OTHER PRACTICES

Is Scientology like hypnotism, meditation, psychotherapy or other mental therapies?

There is no resemblance. In fact, it was as a result of L. Ron Hubbard's investigation of hypnotism and many other mental practices that he saw the need for practical answers to man's problems. In his book, *Dianetics: The Modern Science of Mental Health,* he wrote that he had found hypnotism and psychotherapy to be dangerous and impractical. Nearly all other methods of alleged mental science are based on principles that are quite the opposite of those used in Scientology. They treat man as a "thing" to be conditioned, not as a spiritual being who can find answers to life's problems and who can improve enormously.

Is Scientology a secret society?

Not at all. Scientology churches are open—you can go in at any time. Scientology literature is freely available to anyone. There is no demand for the individual to withdraw from society; on the contrary, Scientologists become *more* involved in life around them, as they want to take responsibility for improving conditions.

In what way does Scientology differ from other religions and religious philosophies?

Nearly all religious philosophies share a belief in helping man live a better life. In Scientology, this concept is expressed as one of the aims of the Church, which is to achieve a world without insanity, war and crime.

While Scientology religious philosophy has much in common with other religions in this regard and in terms of its basic religious concepts and its outreach into the community with social reform programs, the most valuable asset that Scientology has to offer is a wealth of technology which brings about greater spiritual awareness.

In Scientology there is no attempt to change a person's beliefs or to persuade him away from any religion to which he already belongs. Scientology helps people to achieve their goals: (1) through reading the materials contained in the books and publications; (2) through the unique counseling technology called auditing; (3) through training courses which utilize L. Ron Hubbard's discoveries in the field of education. Scientology makes it possible for *any* religion to attain its goals and is therefore a religion of religions.

Does Scientology interfere with other religions?

Scientology is all-denominational in that it opens its membership to people of all faiths. Part of the Church's Creed states that "all men have inalienable rights to their own religious practices and their performance."

Membership in Scientology does not mean that there is any necessity to leave your current church, synagogue, temple or mosque.

What does Scientology think of other religions?

Scientology respects all religions.

Scientology does not conflict with other religions or other religious practices. Quite often Scientology church members rekindle a greater interest than ever in the subject of religions—including the one of their birth.

What does Scientology have to say about Christianity?

Scientologists hold the Bible as a holy work and have no argument with the Christian belief that Jesus Christ was the Savior of Mankind and the Son of God. We share Christ's goals for man's achievement of wisdom, good health and immortality. Christianity is among the faiths studied by Scientology ministerial students.

There are probably many types of redemption. That of Christ was to heaven.

SCIENTOLOGY BELIEFS

Is man a spirit?

Yes. Here's a short exercise you can do to find out for yourself.

Close your eyes and get a picture of a cat.

Done?

That which is looking at that cat is you, a spirit.

How does one know man is a spirit?

It is a matter that each individual must examine for himself. Scientologists believe man is more than a mind and body and that it is he, himself, the spirit, who can control his mind and body.

Do you think your body would *do* anything by itself if it were not guided by you, the being?

What is the Scientology concept of God?

The Church has no dogma concerning God, and each person's concept is probably different. As a person becomes more aware of himself, others, the environment and God, each person attains his own certainty as to who God is and exactly what God means to him. The author of the universe exists. How God is symbolized or manifested is up to each individual to find for himself.

In his book *Science of Survival,* L. Ron Hubbard writes: "No culture in the history of the world, save the thoroughly depraved and expiring ones, has failed to affirm the existence of a Supreme Being. It is an empirical observation that men without a strong and lasting faith in a Supreme Being are less capable, less ethical and less valuable to themselves and society. . . . A man without an abiding faith is, by observation alone, more of a thing than a man."

Can't God be the only one to help man?

Scientologists take the maxim quite to heart that God helps those who help themselves. They believe that each person has the answers to the mysteries of life; all he requires is awareness of these answers, and this is what Scientology helps a person achieve. Man is accustomed to asking for pat answers. Scientology requires that the person think for himself and thus help himself become more intelligent, happy and healthy.

Does Scientology believe in brotherly love?

Yes, and perhaps goes a step further. L. Ron Hubbard wrote that "To love is the road to strength. To love in spite of all is the secret of greatness. And may very well be the greatest secret in this universe."

Why do Scientologists want to help people?

For several reasons. First, because Scientologists themselves have been helped enormously—and they want others to share the same successes. Second, Scientologists understand that life is not lived alone. An individual has more than just one dynamic (the urge to survive as self). He wants to help his family, his groups, mankind itself and living things survive better.

Does Scientology recognize good and evil?

Yes, in Scientology, a very clear distinction is made between good and evil. Those actions which enhance survival on the majority of the eight aspects or dynamics of life are good, and those which destroy or deny these aspects of life are evil. Decisions are then based on enhancing the majority of these dynamics of life.

Good may be defined as constructive. *Evil* may be defined as destructive.

Does Scientology believe man is sinful?

It is a basic tenet of Scientology that man is basically good, but that he is aberrated (capable of erring or departing from rational thought or behavior) and therefore commits harmful acts or sins, thus reducing his awareness and potential power.

Through Scientology he can confront his actions, erase the ignorance and aberration which surrounds them and know and experience truth again.

All religions seek truth. Freedom of the spirit is only to be found on the road to truth.

Sin is composed, according to Scientology, of lies and hidden actions and is therefore untruth.

Will Scientology put one in control of his mind?

Yes. As you are a spiritual being, quite separate from your mind and your body, Scientology will help *you* achieve a far better command over your mind, just as it helps you to intelligently control all aspects of your life.

Is Scientology about the mind?

No. Scientology is about the individual himself as separate and distinct from the mind. Dianetics concerns the mind and contains the most advanced technology of the mind man has.

Does Scientology believe in mind over matter?

Scientology addresses you—not your mind, not your body, but you.

Scientologists have found that the spirit is *potentially* superior to material things, and that the spirit, i.e., you, if cleansed of past traumas, transgressions and aberrations, can make miraculous changes in the physical universe that would not otherwise be possible.

Does Scientology believe one can exist outside of the body?

Before entering Scientology many people experience the feeling of looking down on one's body, and by achieving greater spiritual awareness through Scientology, this experience becomes nothing out of the ordinary. Scientology believes that man is not his body, his mind or his brain. He, a spiritual force, energizes the physical body and his life.

Scientology proved, for the first time, that man was a spiritual being, not an animal.

Does Scientology believe in reincarnation or past lives?

Reincarnation is a definite system and is not part of Scientology. It is a fact that unless one begins to handle aberrations built up in past lives, he doesn't progress.

The definition of the term *reincarnation* has been altered from its original meaning. The word has come to mean "to be born again in different life forms," whereas its actual definition is "to be born again into the flesh or into another body."

Today in Scientology, many people have certainty that they have lived lives prior to their current one. These are referred to as past lives, not as reincarnation.

Individuals are free to believe this or not; past lives are not a dogma in Scientology, but generally Scientologists, during their auditing, experience a past life and then *know* for themselves that they have lived before.

To believe one had a physical or other existence prior to the identity of the current body is not a new concept—but it is an exciting one.

In Scientology, you are given the tools to handle upsets and aberrations from past lives that adversely affect you in present time, thus freeing you to live a much happier life.

Does Scientology believe in charity and welfare?

It does. However, Scientologists also believe in the principle that exchange is necessary. If a person only receives and never gives, he will not be a happy person and will lose his own self-respect. Therefore, any Scientology-sponsored charity programs also encourage those receiving the charity to make some form of contribution by helping others so that self-respect can be maintained.

Does Scientology hold any political views?

Scientology is nonpolitical. By its Creed, "All men have inalienable rights to conceive, choose, assist or support their own organizations, churches and governments." Scientologists are free to hold their own political views, vote for the candidates of their choice, etc., and are not given direction from the Church as to what position to take on political issues or candidates. The Church believes there should be separation of church and state.

Can children participate in Scientology? How?

Yes, there are many children who participate in Scientology. There are no age restrictions as to who can take Scientology courses or receive auditing. Some churches also deliver special courses and study programs specifically designed for young people. If the person is below the legal age, he must first get written consent from his parents or guardian to take Scientology services. Scientologists generally want their children to have Scientology available to them so are quite agreeable to have their children take Scientology services.

What does Scientology say about the raising of children?

L. Ron Hubbard has written a great deal about raising children. In Scientology, children are recognized as people who should be given all the respect and love granted adults.

Scientologists believe children should be encouraged to contribute to family life, not just be "seen and not heard" as the old saying goes. Children are spiritual beings, and as such they need to exchange with those around them in order to thrive and live productive, happy lives. For more information on handling children, the book *Child Dianetics* and the course "How to Be a Successful Parent" are recommended.

Most children raised in good Scientology homes are above average in ability and quickly begin to understand how and why people act as they do. Life thus becomes a lot safer and happier for them.

Can one make up his own mind about Scientology?

One can and indeed one should. Scientology enables you to think for yourself. There is no purpose served in studying Scientology because someone else wants you to. But if you've taken a good look at your life and have decided that you want to make it better, the best thing is to start and find out for yourself what Scientology can do for you. One should read one of the basic books by L. Ron Hubbard, such as *Dianetics: The Modern Science of Mental Health* or *Scientology: The Fundamentals of Thought.*

What is real in Scientology for you is what you find in it that is real for you.

What is the Scientology cross?

It is an eight-pointed cross representing the eight parts or dynamics of life through which each individual is striving to survive. These parts are: the urge toward existence as self, as an individual; the urge to survive through creativity, including the family unit and the rearing of children; the urge to survive through a group of individuals or as a group; the urge toward survival through all mankind and as all mankind; the urge to survive as life forms and with the help of life forms such as animals, birds, insects, fish and vegetation; the urge to survive of the physical universe, by the physical universe itself and with the help of the physical universe and each one of its component parts; the urge to survive as spiritual beings or the urge for life itself to survive; the urge toward existence as infinity. To be able to live happily with respect to each of these spheres of existence is symbolized by the Scientology cross.

As a matter of interest, the cross as a symbol predates Christianity.

What religious holidays do Scientologists celebrate?

Scientologists celebrate several major holidays annually. These include the birthday of L. Ron Hubbard (March 13); the date marking the initial publication of *Dianetics* (May 9); Auditor's Day, in honor of all auditors (second Sunday in September); and the International Association of Scientologists Anniversary, to mark the founding of this organization which unites, supports and protects the Scientology religion and Scientologists in all parts of the world (October 7).

Additionally, each local country or area may observe its own significant dates, such as the founding of the church in its area or the opening of the first Dianetics or Scientology organization in that country. Members of the Church also observe traditional religious holidays such as Christmas.

SCIENTOLOGY'S FOUNDER

Is L. Ron Hubbard still alive?

No. L. Ron Hubbard passed away on January 24, 1986, but he remains with us in spirit and through the legacy of his technology and its continual application around the globe.

Who was L. Ron Hubbard?

L. Ron Hubbard is the Founder of Dianetics and Scientology and the author of its scriptures. His research on the mind and life is recorded in the tens of millions of words on the subject of the human spirit which comprise Dianetics and Scientology philosophy. His works cover subjects as diverse as drug rehabilitation, education, marriage and family, success at work, administration, art and many other aspects of life.

His best-selling self-help book *Dianetics: The Modern Science of Mental Health* alone has sold millions and millions of copies and has continued to appear on the *New York Times* and other bestseller lists around the world over four decades after its original publication.

Testimony to the applicability and workability of his discoveries are the millions of happy and successful people and the hundreds of Dianetics and Scientology churches, missions and groups internationally.

L. Ron Hubbard dedicated his life to helping others. He saw that times needed to change, and he created a workable technology so that needed changes could occur for millions of people. He departed his body on January 24, 1986 leaving with us his life's work which is continued today through the application of his discoveries which help millions around the world.

What was L. Ron Hubbard's role in the Church?

L. Ron Hubbard founded the Scientology philosophy. A group of Scientologists then formed the first church of Scientology in Los Angeles in 1954.

Mr. Hubbard ran the early Dianetics and Scientology organizations until 1966, when he retired from running them on a day-to-day basis and turned this function over to Scientology Church executives. He continued to take an interest in the Church's expansion and advised on administrative matters when specifically asked for advice, but he mainly spent his time researching the upper levels of Scientology and codifying the technology.

Has L. Ron Hubbard's death affected the Church?

L. Ron Hubbard recorded the results of all his research in writing, on film or in taped lectures so that the technology would be preserved. As a result, Scientology has continued to expand, and its future survival is assured.

All great religious leaders of the past have died. Their work flourishes. Men die. Wisdom and ideas do not.

How did L. Ron Hubbard rise above the reactive mind when others didn't?

He applied to himself the principles he had found.

Did L. Ron Hubbard make a lot of money out of Scientology?

No. He received no royalties from the fees paid to Scientology organizations for training and processing. In fact, L. Ron Hubbard forgave Scientology churches a thirteen-million-dollar debt in 1966 when he retired as Executive Director.

He made his money from the royalties on his books. One book alone, *Dianetics,* has sold *millions* of copies, and his total book sales of both fiction and nonfiction are in excess of one hundred million copies around the world, including more than twenty national bestsellers in the 1980s.

In fact, Mr. Hubbard's books still sell by the millions each year and the royalties from the sale of these books and his life's fortune were willed to the Church to help ensure the future application of his technology to the betterment of mankind.

Was L. Ron Hubbard a millionaire?

L. Ron Hubbard was one of those fortunate people who never made problems over money. He inherited some wealth at an early age, but in the early 1930s became one of the highest paid writers in America long before *Dianetics.*

He was a millionaire several times over from his book royalties. His public book sales continue to be astronomical.

How is it that one man could discover so much information?

He simply cared enough to want it and had the intelligence and persistence to research and find it.

Few men have been trained in all the Eastern philosophies and in the highest levels of Western science as well.

Knowing that his research was only as valuable as it provided workable solutions to man's problems, he tested all of his discoveries and found the most effective methods for applying the results of his research. His workable methods enabled him to continue research into higher and higher realms of spiritual awareness.

Do Scientologists believe that L. Ron Hubbard was Jesus Christ?

No. L. Ron Hubbard personally stated he was a man as others are men. He was a much-loved friend and teacher and continues to be respected and loved.

Did L. Ron Hubbard go Clear?

Yes. In order to map the route for others he had to make it himself.

Scientology Attitudes and Practices

How do Scientologists view life?

As a game—a game in which everyone can win. Scientologists are optimistic about life and believe there is hope for a saner world and better civilization and are actively doing all they can to achieve this.

What moral codes do Scientologists live by?

There are four main codes that Scientologists apply in life. One is the Auditor's Code which gives the basic rules an auditor must abide by to ensure excellent auditing results.

Another is the Code of a Scientologist, guidelines which Scientologists agree to follow in order to achieve the aims of Scientology.

There is an ethical code, called the Code of Honor, that Scientologists use in dealing with their fellow men.

L. Ron Hubbard has also written a nonreligious moral code called "The Way to Happiness" which gives basic precepts for a happy life. This moral code is used by Scientologists and non-Scientologists alike, with tens of millions of copies distributed in communities all around the world.

What is Scientology's view on drugs?

Scientologists consider that drugs cause damaging effects on a person—physically, mentally and spiritually. They decrease awareness and hinder abilities. They are a "solution" to some other problem, which themselves become a problem.

Scientologists do not take street drugs or mind-altering psychiatric drugs.

Scientologists do use prescribed drugs as part of medical programs from competent physicians, but have found that as a result of auditing, they need to take medical drugs much less frequently and also that medications such as antibiotics seem to work more rapidly when being audited.

For more information about drugs and what can be done about them, the book *Clear Body, Clear Mind: The Effective Purification Program* is recommended.

Why are there so many young people on staff in Scientology?

Many Scientologists are under thirty-five. We find that young Scientologists enjoy the lifestyle working in the Church. It may be that due to the expansion of Scientology they find that there are many opportunities to achieve responsible positions quite rapidly. Many families have three generations working in Scientology. There are also a great many older people in Scientology.

Do you have any special dietary laws or rules against smoking or drinking in Scientology?

No. There are no dietary laws whatsoever and no general prohibitions against smoking or drinking. The only guidelines in Scientology are that no alcohol is allowed twenty-four hours prior to or during auditing sessions, and that no drinking is allowed twenty-four hours prior to or during study. The effects of the alcohol would make it impossible to get the gains one can get from auditing and training.

Smoking is forbidden in course rooms or during auditing sessions, as such would distract oneself and others. Rules for student behavior are laid out in a Church policy called the "Student's Guide to Acceptable Behavior."

Do Scientologists use medical doctors?

Yes. The Church of Scientology has always had the firm policy of sending sick parishioners to medical doctors to handle the physical aspect of any illness or injury. A Scientologist with a physical condition is instructed to get the needed medical examination and treatment. He then resumes his auditing so as to handle any spiritual trauma connected with the physical condition. There are also many medical doctors who are Scientologists.

In Scientology does one have to sacrifice one's individuality?

No. People are unique, even though they have in common certain problems and aberrations. As they become disentangled from the stimulus-response part of their mind, they become more themselves, more unique, more individual and learn to believe in themselves. In fact, becoming more aware of and able to express one's own unique beingness is encouraged in Scientology. Scientology teaches one to maintain his personal integrity and to develop fully as an individual.

What benefits can one get from Scientology?

In reviewing success stories written by Scientologists, there are a few common themes that stand out. One is that many people have attained the ability to communicate in relationships, whether with family members and spouses, friends, or even mere acquaintances; another is that they are freed from stress at work and in other areas of their lives; another common one is that they can expand their potential and do things they never thought possible.

What is Scientology's system of ethics?

L. Ron Hubbard has defined *ethics* as "reason and the contemplation of optimum survival."

In Scientology, ethics is a rational system based on a number of codes of practice.

L. Ron Hubbard has pointed out: "Dishonest conduct is nonsurvival. Anything is unreasonable or evil which brings about the destruction of individuals, groups, or inhibits the future of the race."

Man has long postulated a means by which he could put himself on the right path. As long ago as 500 B.C., religions recognized that confession frees a person spiritually from the burden of sin.

In Scientology, it has been found that a Confessional (a type of auditing) assists the person who has transgressed against his own and his group's moral code to unburden himself and again feel good about himself and be a contributing member of the group.

L. Ron Hubbard has written: "No man who is not himself honest can be free—he is his own trap. When his own deeds cannot be disclosed, then he is a prisoner; he must withhold himself from his fellows and is a slave to his own conscience."

In addition to the Confessional, Scientology's ethics system includes a body of technology called conditions formulas. Mr. Hubbard discovered that there are various states of existence in which an individual operates (called "conditions") and that there are exact formulas connected with these operating states. Each formula has a number of exact steps.

A person can determine what condition or operating state any area of his life is in and apply the conditions formulas to move it into a higher condition.

While very simple, such actions are quite powerful and have enabled millions of individuals to improve conditions in their lives in ways they never thought possible.

These are just two of the tools from the wealth of ethics technology that exists in Scientology. Complete information on this subject is contained in the book *Introduction to Scientology Ethics* by L. Ron Hubbard.

What does "clear the planet" mean?

It means that Scientologists want to clear the planet of insanity, war and crime, and in its place create a civilization in which sanity and peace exist. In order to do this, they must help individuals become clear of their own individual insanities and regain awareness that they are basically good.

What does "suppressive person" mean?

According to L. Ron Hubbard, a suppressive person is "a person who seeks to *suppress,* or squash, any betterment activity or group. A suppressive person suppresses other people in his vicinity. This is the person whose behavior is calculated to be disastrous." Well-known examples of such a personality are Napoleon and Hitler.

Mr. Hubbard found that a suppressive person, also called an antisocial personality, has definite antisocial attributes.

The basic reason the antisocial personality behaves as he or she does lies in a hidden terror of others.

To such a person every other being is an enemy, an enemy to be covertly or overtly destroyed.

The fixation is that survival itself depends on "keeping others down" or "keeping people ignorant."

If anyone were to promise to make others stronger or brighter, the antisocial personality suffers the utmost agony of personal danger.

Because of this, the suppressive person seeks to upset, continuously undermine, spread bad news about and denigrate Scientology and Scientologists. The antisocial personality is against what Scientology is about—helping people become more able and improving conditions in society.

For the good of the Church and the individuals in it, such a person is officially labeled a suppressive person so that others will know not to associate with him.

For more understanding of suppressive persons and how to handle them, the book *Introduction to Scientology Ethics* is recommended.

What is disconnection?

A Scientologist can have trouble making spiritual progress in his auditing or training if he is connected to someone who is suppressive or who is antagonistic to Scientology or its tenets. He will get better from Scientology, but then may lose his gains because he is being invalidated by the antagonistic person. In order to resolve this, he either handles the other person's antagonism with true data about the Church, or as a last resort when all attempts to handle have failed, he disconnects from the person.

In 1983, L. Ron Hubbard clearly defined the two terms, "disconnect" and "handle," as related to this subject:

"The term *handle* most commonly means to smooth out a situation with another person by applying the technology of communication.

"The term *disconnection* is defined as a self-determined decision made by an individual that he is not going to be connected to another. It is a severing of a communication line.

"The basic principle of handle or disconnect exists in any group and ours is no different.

"It is much like trying to deal with a criminal. If he will not handle, the society resorts to the only other solution: It 'disconnects' the criminal from the society. In other words, they remove the guy from society and put him in a prison because he won't *handle* his problem or otherwise cease to commit criminal acts against others."

A person who disconnects is simply exercising his right to communicate or not to communicate with a particular person. This is one of the most fundamental rights of man. "Communication, however, is a two-way flow," Mr. Hubbard pointed out. "If one has the right to communicate, then one must also have the right to not receive communication from another. It is this latter corollary of the right to communicate that gives us our right to privacy."

Another example is marriage. In a monogamous society, the agreement is that one will be married to only one person at a time. If one partner, say the husband, starts to have second dynamic relations with a person other than his partner, the wife has the right to insist either that this communication cease or that the marriage itself ends.

In this example, the optimum solution would be for the wife to resolve the situation through communication so that her husband, who is violating the agreements, is handled. But if this is not possible, then the wife has no choice other than to disconnect (sever the marriage communication lines if only by separation). To do otherwise will only bring disaster, as the wife is connected to someone antagonistic to the original agreements on which the marriage is based.

With the technology of handle or disconnect, Scientologists are, in actual fact, doing nothing different than any society, group or marriage down through thousands of years.

Is Scientology a cult?

Assuming that modern usage of the word *cult* implies an elite secrecy and unthinking zealotry, then consider this: Scientology is the fastest growing religion in the world today. The materials that comprise Scientology scriptures are fully codified, broadly published and available to anyone. Churches and missions are open to the public seven days a week. Anyone can come in for a tour and see for himself what the Church is all about.

Scientology is unique in that it contains no dogma and its adherents are not told or forced to "believe" anything. In Scientology, what is true for the individual is only what he has observed and knows is true for him. Scientology is a technology one can use and through its use discover its workability for oneself.

Scientologists come from all walks of life, ranging from teachers to businessmen, physicians, housewives, artists, engineers, nurses, construction workers, celebrities, marketing and administrative personnel, secretaries, athletes, civil servants and many others.

The Church and its actions are far from secretive; there is nothing mystical about Scientology or its members or practices. The Church's leaders are in close touch with the membership; they hold a number of briefing events each year which are attended by tens of thousands.

Scientologists actively improve their communities; they are out there, involved, visible and effective.

The fact of the matter is there isn't a religion today that hasn't been called a cult at some point in its history by antagonistic interests. Nazis thought Jews and Eastern European religious sects to be cults. In the sixteenth century Catholics considered reform churches cults. Earlier than that Roman rulers considered the Christian community a cult. History has taught us to beware of those who would label *any* religious group a cult. It is traditionally the first step before wholesale persecution, and is always the statement of an unenlightened and uninformed individual, usually with ill motives as the Nazi history makes so clear.

Does Scientology engage in brainwashing or mind control?

No. In fact, what we do is exactly the opposite. We free people and enable them to think for themselves.

Millions of Church members from literally all walks of life have attested to the positive benefits received from Scientology. A common theme to their personal success stories is that they are now more in control of their lives than they ever have been.

In fact, Mr. Hubbard was one of the first to discover and expose *actual* mind control and brainwashing experimentation conducted by United States military and intelligence agencies during and after World War II. He called these techniques "pain-drug-hypnosis" or PDH.

In his 1951 book, *Science of Survival*, Mr. Hubbard wrote:

"There is another form of hypnotism . . . This form of hypnotism has been a carefully guarded secret of certain military and intelligence organizations. It is a vicious war weapon and may be of considerably more use in conquering a society than the atomic bomb. This is no exaggeration. The extensiveness of the use of this form of hypnotism in espionage work is so wide today that it is long past the time when people should have become alarmed about it. It required Dianetic processing to uncover pain-drug-hypnosis. Otherwise, pain-drug-hypnosis was out of sight, unsuspected and unknown."

Not only did he uncover such blatantly destructive experimentation, but the technology he developed, Dianetics, could *undo* the effects of PDH and free a person from the grip of mind control.

Years after Mr. Hubbard learned about these government-sponsored psychiatric mind control experiments, documents released under the Freedom of Information Act detailed the extent to which these techniques were being used.

Over the years, the Church of Scientology has exposed numerous instances of brainwashing or mind control practices, such as those involved in so-called "deprograming." In this case, individuals are taken captive and forced to renounce their chosen religious or political group, generally using some form of coercion, food or sleep deprivation and sometimes drugs.

Such practices are diametrically opposed to the aims of Scientology, which are to free man and return to him his ability to control his own life.

Does Scientology actively promote for new members?

Yes. Scientologists make the technology broadly available to others because they want others to receive the same gains they have experienced. The Church wants more people to know and apply the works of L. Ron Hubbard and actively and vigorously promotes this.

Does one really need Scientology to do well in life?

That is a question you will have to answer for yourself. A Scientologist's viewpoint is that while some people might be surviving quite well without Scientology, they can always do better and expand their potentials even further. In fact, Scientology was developed to help the able become more able and one usually finds the people doing best in life are the first ones to embrace Scientology.

If you are interested in self-improvement, Scientology provides a tested route by which you can obtain tremendous benefits and learn to use your mind, talents and abilities to the fullest.

If you know people who are doing well but have never heard of Scientology, the question is: "Could they be doing better?"

Does one have to believe in Scientology?

No. One is not expected to believe in Scientology. One is only expected to study and apply the data and see for himself if it works for him. To quote L. Ron Hubbard, "Anything that isn't true for you when you study it carefully isn't true."

Why do Scientologists sometimes seem so intent on what they are doing?

If you had a chance to change yourself and civilization so greatly, you would be interested as well.

What do the terms preclear, student *and* auditor *mean?*

A *preclear* is someone who is receiving Scientology or Dianetics auditing on his way to becoming Clear. Through auditing he is finding out more about himself and life.

A *student* is one who reads in detail in order to learn and then apply the materials he has studied. One studies Scientology for itself and uses it exactly as stated, then forms his own conclusions as to whether or not the tenets he has assimilated are correct and workable.

An *auditor* is a Dianetics or Scientology practitioner trained in the technology of auditing. *Auditor* means "one who listens" (from the Latin word *audire*). An auditor listens and computes, applying standard technology to preclears to help them achieve the abilities as stated on the Classification, Gradation and Awareness Chart. An auditor's job is to ask the preclear to look, and get him to do so.

What is the E-Meter and how does it work?

E-Meter is a shortened term for *electropsychometer.* It is a religious artifact used as a spiritual guide in auditing. It is for use only by a Scientology minister or a Scientology minister-in-training to help the preclear locate and confront areas of spiritual upset.

In itself, the E-Meter does nothing. It is an electronic instrument that measures mental state and change of state in individuals and assists the precision and speed of auditing. The E-Meter is not intended or effective for the diagnosis, treatment or prevention of any disease.

The book *Understanding the E-Meter* offers a simple explanation of how the E-Meter works and what it actually measures. In order to understand what the E-Meter does, it is necessary to understand some basic Scientology concepts.

There are three basic parts of man—mind, body and thetan. The thetan is an immortal spiritual being—the individual himself. He (the thetan) inhabits a body, which is a carbon-oxygen machine. He has a mind, which is a collection of mental image pictures he has created.

These pictures have weight and mass and can impinge on the person when he is emotionally upset.

This is what makes the E-Meter read—the impingement of such pictures against the body.

The E-Meter puts a very small electrical current (approximately one and a half volts) through the body. This is about the same amount of current as in the average battery-powered wristwatch.

When a person thinks a thought, looks at a picture, reexperiences an incident or when he shifts some part of the pictures in his mind, he is moving and changing actual mental mass and energy. These changes in the person's mind affect the tiny flow of electrical energy generated by the E-Meter, which causes the needle on its dial to move.

The E-Meter thus measures changes that are caused by the spiritual being in his own mind (i.e., the movement of mental masses around him) and in this capacity, it is a religious artifact.

The E-Meter is used to help the individual who is being audited uncover truth. By locating areas of mental or spiritual trauma, the E-Meter helps both the auditor and the preclear locate exactly what to address in auditing.

THE ORGANIZATIONS OF SCIENTOLOGY

Scientology is a philosophy. Why does it need to be organized?

Scientology is an *applied* religious philosophy. Therefore organization is needed to make the technology available and teach people to apply it.

How many people work in a Scientology church?

The number of staff varies from church to church. Small churches may have 20 and large ones over 500.

How is Scientology organized?

There is a "mother church" which is the Church of Scientology International. It is headquartered in Los Angeles. It is responsible for the ecclesiastical supervision of the rest of the Scientology churches around the world, which are organized in a hierarchical structure not dissimilar to that of the Catholic Church. (For more information about the structure of the Church, see Part 5.)

Where are Scientology churches located?

Scientology churches and missions exist all over the world. There are a great many churches and far more missions in various countries.

What does a Scientology church or mission actually do?

The main activities of Scientology churches and missions are training Scientology ministers and providing auditing. The church also conducts Sunday services, weddings, funerals and christenings and delivers other chaplain services. The church helps the individual become more able to help himself and to help others. This is done by training and auditing.

What is the Office of Special Affairs?

The Office of Special Affairs (OSA) deals with legal affairs for the Church. It also publishes the facts about the social betterment works of Scientology, informing the government, the media, other religions and other groups with interests similar to those of the Church. OSA also oversees the social reform programs of the Church, among which are those that expose and effectively handle violations of individual and human rights.

What is the Flag Service Organization?

The Flag Service Organization (FSO), often referred to as "Flag," is located in Clearwater, Florida. It delivers advanced spiritual training and auditing. It retains its name from the days when it used to operate from the flagship *Apollo.* ("Flag" in nautical terms means "the flagship" or the vessel which gives orders to others.)

What is the Flag Ship Service Organization?

The Flag Ship Service Organization is located aboard the 450-foot ship called the *Freewinds,* and is an advanced religious retreat that delivers the level of auditing called New OT VIII and specialized training to Scientologists.

What is the Sea Organization?

The Sea Organization (commonly referred to as the Sea Org) is a confraternal organization existing within the formalized structure of the Church. It is composed of the most dedicated Scientology staff who have decided to devote their lives to the delivery and expansion of Scientology.

The Sea Organization has no separate corporate structure or identity and its members work for various different churches of Scientology and are subject, as are all other employees of that church, to the orders and directions of the board of directors.

The Sea Org was established in 1967 and once operated from a number of ships. It was set up to help L. Ron Hubbard with research of earlier civilizations and to carry out supervision of Church organizations around the world to keep Scientology expanding. It is also entrusted to deliver the advanced services of Scientology.

The Sea Organization retains its name in celebration of the fact that the Founder's life was majorly connected with the sea. It exists to help keep Scientology working.

Is it true that people in the Sea Org sign a billion-year contract?

Yes, they do. It is a symbolic document which, similar to vows of dedication in other faiths and orders, serves to signify an individual's eternal commitment to the goals, purposes and principles of the Scientology religion. Sea Org members have dedicated their lives to working toward these ends and toward a world without war, drugs, crime and illiteracy.

Why does Scientology have ministers? Are all Scientologists ministers?

The Church of Scientology has ministers to deliver Scientology religious services to church parishioners. Only those who specifically enroll in and graduate from the Scientology Minister's Course and its prerequisites, and fulfill the requirements for ordination are Scientology ministers. All Scientology auditors are required to become ordained ministers; however, they are allowed to audit as ministerial students while fulfilling their ordination requirements.

What are field staff members?

Field staff members are individual Scientologists who disseminate Scientology, provide books to interested friends, family members and associates and introduce (or select) people to the Church. They are appointed by their nearest Scientology organization. Because they have had gains from Dianetics and Scientology themselves, they naturally want to share it with others.

Why is everything copyrighted and trademarked in Scientology?

Scientology and Dianetics are technologies that work if applied exactly. If they are altered, the results will not be uniform.

For this reason, the technology is copyrighted and the words and symbols which represent the technology are trademarked. This way, nobody can misrepresent something as standard Scientology or Dianetics that really isn't.

In fact many persons have tried to rip off and profit from the technologies of Dianetics and Scientology. The subjects were developed for spiritual salvation, not for anyone's personal enrichment. Through ownership of the trademarks and copyrights, such ill-intentioned actions are prevented by the Church.

Church Funding

Why do Scientologists make donations?

Some churches have a system of tithes, others require their members to pay for pew rentals, religious ceremonies and services. In the Church of Scientology, parishioners make donations for auditing or training they wish to take. These contributions by Scientologists are the primary source of financial support for the Church and fund all the community programs and social betterment activities of Scientology. Scientologists are not required to tithe or make other donations.

Ideally, Dianetics and Scientology services would be free, and all Scientologists wish they were. But those are not the realities of life. When one considers the cost of delivering even one hour of auditing, requiring extensively trained specialists, and the overhead costs of maintaining church premises, the necessity of donations becomes clear.

The donation system in Scientology is the most equitable as those who use the facilities of the Church are the ones who most directly contribute to its upkeep and continued existence. Naturally, no donation is expected from those not receiving auditing or training. And church doors are always open to those who wish to learn more about the philosophy of Scientology, be they parishioners or not. There are tape plays of L. Ron Hubbard's lectures, introductory lectures, books available, people to discuss questions with, and of course the more traditional church activities—Sunday service, sermons, weddings, christenings, funerals—all of which are provided without any donation necessary.

Scientology does not have hundreds of years of accumulated wealth and property like other religions—it must make its way in the world according to the economics of today's society.

Scientologists' donations keep the Church alive and functioning, fund its widespread social reform programs, make Scientology known to people who may otherwise never have the opportunity to avail themselves of it, and help create a safe and pleasant environment for everyone.

Why does one have to make donations to separate organizations for their services?

Scientology churches and missions are separate corporations and have separate financial records. The donations that go to each church for services delivered by that church must be separately banked and accurate records kept in alignment with the accounting procedures and laws in each country.

What about those who cannot afford to make donations for services?

There is a Free Scientology Center in churches of Scientology where those who cannot afford the donations can receive free auditing from ministerial students.

Many Scientology services are free and the knowledge is free to all men. There are also books, books, books and free public lectures, Sunday services and other religious services for which there is no cost. Books can be obtained in the local area either by going to a church of Scientology, a public bookstore or local library.

But it's interesting that once a person becomes more causative through the application of Scientology technology in his life, he does not usually need or want free services for very long. He becomes capable of holding a good job and thereby able to exchange for the services he wants.

Ministers-in-training can receive free auditing from other students while they are doing their training.

Is the Church profit making?

No. Scientology churches are nonprofit organizations, as the donations all go back into the support and expansion of the religion.

In fact, the Internal Revenue Service has expressly ruled that churches and missions of Scientology in the United States operate *exclusively* for religious purposes and that no part of the earnings of any Scientology organization benefits any private individual or private interest.

Is the Church of Scientology tax exempt?

Yes, the mother church and all Scientology churches, missions and related charitable and educational institutions in the United States, as well as several important Scientology organizations outside the US, have been recognized by the Internal Revenue Service as tax-exempt organizations. Parishioners' donations thus qualify as charitable contributions and are tax deductible in the US.

Tax laws in countries outside the US vary, but many individual churches in other countries are also tax exempt.

How much does it cost to go Clear?

The cost varies from individual to individual depending on which route to Clear one takes.

One route is to pay for professional auditing and get audited all the way up to Clear. The preferred route, however, is to get trained as an auditor and co-audit with another Scientology student. The co-auditing route to Clear requires far less donations than professional auditing plus one helps another to progress. As professional auditing is much more expensive for the organization to deliver (requiring several staff to service one parishioner) the donations are necessarily higher. Training donation rates are much more economical and an incentive for persons to train while they co-audit without cost to the state of Clear.

No matter which route one chooses to achieve the state of Clear, all who have attained it express the pricelessness of the increased spiritual freedom they have achieved.

How well paid are Scientology staff?

The pay varies from church to church and from time to time. Staff are paid in proportion to the amount of donations received by their individual organizations. Thus, staff members are in control of how much they make by virtue of how well they perform individually on their own jobs.

In any event, Scientology staff aren't motivated by money and in no instance anywhere in the church structure is pay exorbitant. Scientology staff are motivated by a desire to help, not get rich.

SCIENTOLOGY BOOKS

What is the best book for a beginning Scientologist to read?

Dianetics: The Modern Science of Mental Health, which is the best-selling self-help book of all time, is the book recommended for beginners who are interested in the mind and how it works. This book has been a bestseller for over forty years.

In 1977, *Publishers Weekly* called *Dianetics: The Modern Science of Mental Health* "perhaps the best-selling non-Christian book of all time in the West." In 1988, *Publishers Weekly* awarded *Dianetics* its prestigious "Century Award" for more than 100 weeks on its bestseller list, officially designating it the No. 1 best-selling self-help book of all time.

If a person is more interested in starting with a broad summary of L. Ron Hubbard's research and findings about man as a spiritual being and basic principles of life, the first recommended book is *Scientology: The Fundamentals of Thought.* (Chapter 37 gives a more detailed explanation of the books available and suggested course of reading.)

Are the books difficult to understand?

Not at all. The books are quite easy to understand. Depending on what aspect of Scientology and Dianetics you are most interested in, any church Bookstore Officer can recommend the best sequence in which the books should be read.

Where can L. Ron Hubbard's books be purchased?

All of his books are available at missions and churches of Scientology. Many of his books are also available in popular bookstores and in libraries in cities all over the world.

What books should one read to get information about:

1. Dianetics:
   The Basic Dianetics Picture Book
   Dianetics: The Modern Science of Mental Health
   The Dynamics of Life
   Dianetics: The Evolution of a Science
   Child Dianetics

2. Basic Scientology principles:
   The Basic Scientology Picture Book
   Scientology: The Fundamentals of Thought
   A New Slant on Life
   Scientology 0-8: The Book of Basics

3. Self-help, tests and processes:
   Self Analysis

4. Handling the residual effects of drugs and toxins:
   Purification: An Illustrated Answer to Drugs
   Clear Body, Clear Mind: The Effective Purification Program

5. Basic principles of communication:
   Dianetics 55!

6. Predicting human behavior and understanding people:
   Science of Survival

7. How to increase success on the job:
   The Problems of Work
   How to Live Though An Executive

8. Basic principles of organization:
   The Organization Executive Course volumes 0–7

9. Basic principles of management:
   Management Series volumes 1, 2 and 3

10. The principles of ethics and how to use them to live a more productive life:
    Introduction to Scientology Ethics

11. Study methods:
    Basic Study Manual
    Learning How to Learn
    Study Skills for Life
    How to Use a Dictionary Picture Book for Children

12. Procedures to increase one's spiritual awareness and abilities:
    The Creation of Human Ability
    Advanced Procedure and Axioms
    Scientology 8-8008
    Scientology 8-80

13. Past lives and how they relate to this life:
    Have You Lived Before This Life?
    Scientology: A History of Man

14. The application of basic Scientology technology to help others improve their lives:
    The Volunteer Minister's Handbook

These books were all written by L. Ron Hubbard or compiled from his works, and are just a few of the dozens and dozens of Scientology and Dianetics books available at churches of Scientology.

How can one get happiness out of a book?

The key to happiness is knowledge. Scientology and Dianetics books contain knowledge one can actually apply in life.

Being able to accomplish these improvements definitely makes people happier.

Dianetics

What is Dianetics?

L. Ron Hubbard discovered the single source of stress, worry, self-doubt and psychosomatic illness—the reactive mind. In his book *Dianetics: The Modern Science of Mental Health* he described the reactive mind in detail and laid out a simple, practical, easily taught technology to overcome it and reach the state of Clear. Dianetics (which means "through soul") is that technology.

What is the mind? Where is the mind?

The mind is basically a communication and control system between the thetan—the spiritual being that is the person himself—and his environment. It is composed of mental image pictures which are recordings of past experiences.

The individual uses his mind to pose and resolve problems related to survival and to direct his efforts according to these solutions.

What is the difference between the analytical mind and the reactive mind?

The analytical mind is the conscious, aware mind which thinks, observes data, remembers it and resolves problems. The reactive mind is the portion of a person's mind which works on a totally stimulus-response basis, which is not under his volitional control, and which exerts force and the power of command over his awareness, purposes, thoughts, body and actions.

What is the difference between Scientology and Dianetics?

Dianetics is a technology which uncovers the source of unwanted sensations and emotions, accidents, injuries and psychosomatic illnesses, and which sets forth effective handlings for these conditions.

Dianetics comes from the Greek *dia* meaning "through" and *nous,* "soul." It is further defined as "what the soul is doing to the body."

Scientology is the study and handling of the spirit in relationship to itself, universes and other life. It is used to increase spiritual freedom, intelligence and ability and to enable a person to realize his own immortality.

Dianetics and Scientology are *separate* subjects, but the delivery of each has in common certain tools like the E-Meter and the basic rules of auditing.

SCIENTOLOGY AND DIANETICS COURSES

What training should a person take first?

The first action a person should take in his Scientology training is to read a book, such as *Dianetics: The Modern Science of Mental Health* or *Scientology: The Fundamentals of Thought.* He can study these on an extension course which is designed to help people understand the basic fundamentals of L. Ron Hubbard's books and find out about Scientology for themselves. The lessons in the course are completed and mailed in to the Extension Course Supervisor who grades them and informs the student by return mail what his grade is and any parts of the book he may have misunderstood.

After completing a book or extension course, he should go into a church and see one of the Public Division Registrars who can help him decide which course he should do next. There are many different services available. For instance, many Life Improvement Courses exist, on such subjects as marriage, children, work, relationships with others and personal integrity. These help a person move from effect to cause in a specific area of life. Or there is the Hubbard Dianetics Seminar which utilizes Dianetics auditing techniques based on *Dianetics: The Modern Science of Mental Health,* providing as much Dianetics auditing to a person as he wants and giving him experience applying Dianetics to another. There is also the Success Through Communication Course which teaches the basic communication skills one needs to succeed in social or other situations.

Factually, it is best to talk to someone to find out which of the many courses available is addressed most directly to what one wants to handle or improve in life.

What does one get out of Scientology and Dianetics courses?

Training gives a person the knowledge and tools to handle life. A basic datum in Scientology is that what one learns is only as valuable as it can be applied, and as it helps one do better in life. This is why Scientology is correctly called an *applied* religious philosophy. The information and technology a person learns is not just to increase his understanding (although it will definitely do that as well), but it is for USE.

Although many Scientologists become practicing Scientology ministers, many others simply use the data in their everyday lives, on the job, and with their friends and family members. They report that life becomes more confrontable, their abilities increase and they are happier because they are winning in the game of life.

How are Scientology and Dianetics training different from studying philosophy or other religions?

The major difference is that Scientology and Dianetics training give one *tools* to use in life. Whereas studying other philosophies or religions may provide information that is interesting, only in Scientology does the individual get the exact tools he needs to change and improve conditions in his life.

Should I get my auditing before I get trained?

L. Ron Hubbard has written many times about the fact that 50 percent of one's gains are from training and 50 percent are from auditing. It is actually impossible to successfully make it through the upper processing levels of Scientology without also being trained. Therefore, to get the most from Scientology, one progresses in his training simultaneously with or at a comparable rate to his progress in auditing.

When can I take Scientology courses?

Most churches of Scientology are open from 9:00 in the morning until 10:30 at night weekdays and 9:00 A.M. to 6:00 P.M. on weekends. Several different course schedules are offered within these hours.

How are Scientology courses run?

Scientology training is unique. Each course is done by following a checksheet. A checksheet is a list of materials, divided into sections, that lay out the theory and practical steps which, when completed, lead one to a study completion. The items contained on the checksheet, such as books, recorded lectures and other written materials, add up to the required knowledge of the subject. Each student moves through his checksheet at his own rate. This ensures nobody is ever held back by slower students, and no one is under pressure from faster students. A trained Course Supervisor is always available to help the student, to refer him to the exact materials, to answer his questions and to ensure he is applying standard study technology to gain the full benefits from his studies.

When do I actually gain experience in auditing others?

Every major training course in Scientology is followed by an internship. This is a period of auditing others under the supervision of technical experts. In this way, an auditor's skills are honed and polished to a very high level of proficiency.

When can I take the Minister's Course?

This course can be studied by any Scientologist who is training in Scientology or Dianetics. The course provides an appreciation of the world's great religions, the religious background and philosophy of Scientology, the ethical codes of Scientology and the ceremonies of the Church. One also learns to deliver services and carry out basic ministerial duties.

How long do courses take?

Each course takes as long as it takes—since the student goes through each course at his own pace, he regulates his own progress. How long it takes depends on how diligently he applies study technology and how honestly he completes each item on his checksheet before proceeding to the next. The length of each course will also depend on how many hours he studies per week. On the average, Scientology courses take anywhere from a few days (for most introductory courses) to several months (for more advanced training).

Introductory services are designed to take one week at 2½ hours a day. Academy training to become an auditor is generally two weeks, at forty hours a week, for each individual level.

The required time to complete the more advanced courses is quite extensive. The Saint Hill Special Briefing Course, which is a chronological study of Scientology and Dianetics from 1948 to the present, takes approximately one year, at forty hours a week. This course gives the Scientologist the entire philosophic and technical development of the subject, and is the most extensive training course in Scientology.

Church staff ensure that auditors are professionally and thoroughly trained so that they can achieve the best results with their preclears.

Are Scientology Course Supervisors university trained?

According to demographic studies, a high proportion of Scientologists have graduated from college or university studies. However, this is not a prerequisite for becoming a Scientology Course Supervisor.

In Scientology, there is a very precise technology of how to supervise and successfully help students through their courses. All Scientology Course Supervisors are trained in this technology to ensure that students get the most from their training.

SCIENTOLOGY AND DIANETICS AUDITING

What is the difference between the auditing and training routes in Scientology?

The reference that best explains the difference between these two routes is the Classification, Gradation and Awareness Chart.

On the right side of the chart there are various steps a person moves through as he receives auditing. Each grade listed has a column for "Ability Gained" that describes the increasing levels of awareness and ability achieved at each stage. In auditing, one is working toward improving himself and regaining recognition of and rehabilitating his spiritual nature and abilities. This is done on a gradient (a gradual approach to something, taken step by step), so those states of being which are seemingly "too high above one" can be achieved with relative ease.

The left-hand side of the chart describes the gradient steps of training on which one gains the knowledge and abilities necessary to audit another on each level. Each course listed includes a description of the subject matter that is taught at that level. In training, one is learning about the various facets of life with a view to helping others.

These two different paths parallel each other. Optimally, a person follows both paths.

The chart is a guide for the individual from the point he first enters Scientology, and shows him the basic sequence in which he will receive his auditing and training.

Do all the people on staff in Scientology receive auditing as well as training?

Yes, auditing and training of staff members is part of the exchange for their work in Scientology organizations.

Why does one have to wait six weeks for auditing if one has been habitually using drugs?

Research has shown that it takes at least that long for the effect of drugs to wear off. Quite simply, auditing is not as effective while drugs are in the system because a person on drugs is less alert and may even be rendered stupid, blank, forgetful, delusive or irresponsible.

Will antibiotics prevent me from getting auditing?

No. Antibiotics work differently than drugs. If the preclear has a doctor's prescription for antibiotics and is taking these to handle an infection, he should be sure to let his Director of Processing know, but this will not prevent him from receiving auditing. Many people claim that antibiotics work more rapidly and effectively if one is receiving auditing at the same time.

Is it okay to take any sort of drugs when you are in Scientology?

Except for antibiotics or prescribed medical drugs by a medical doctor, no.

If one has a medical or dental condition requiring treatment and wishes to take some medical drug other than antibiotics, he should inform his Director of Processing. A medical or dental consultation will be advised and a handling worked out in liaison with the Director of Processing to best accommodate one's progress in Scientology.

Any other drug use, such as the use of street drugs or psychiatric mind-altering drugs, is forbidden.

Drugs are usually taken to escape from unwanted emotions, pains or sensations. In Scientology, the real reasons for these unwanted conditions get handled and people have no need or desire for drugs. Drugs dull people and make them less aware. Scientology's aim is to make people brighter and more aware.

Drugs are essentially poisons. Small amounts may act as a stimulant or as a sedative, but larger amounts act as poisons and can kill one.

Drugs dull one's senses and affect the reactive mind so that the person becomes less in control and more the effect of his reactive mind, a very undesirable state.

Despite the claims of psychiatrists that drugs are a "cure-all," at best they cover up what is really wrong, and at worst, actually harm one. The real answer is to handle the source of one's troubles—and that is done with Scientology.

How many hours of auditing a day do people receive?

This depends upon one's particular auditing program. Some receive longer or shorter hours of auditing than others, but an average would be 2½ hours a day. Auditing is best done intensively, at least 12½ hours a week. The more intensively one is audited, the more rapid progress he makes as he is not bogged down by current life upsets. Therefore it is best to arrange for many hours of consecutive auditing, i.e., 50 to 100 hours at 12½ hours a week minimum.

Of course, one is not always receiving auditing so when one is, his best chance of making rapid progress is intensively.

Has the technology of auditing changed since the early days of Scientology?

The basics of auditing have not changed, but there have been considerable advances and refinements in auditing processes over the years. L. Ron Hubbard continued his research and development of Scientology auditing technology throughout his life, and completed it before he passed away. All of his technology is now available and laid out in an exact sequence of gradient steps in which it should be used.

What will I get out of auditing?

Scientology auditing is delivered in a specific sequence which handles the major barriers people encounter when trying to achieve their goals. After receiving auditing, you will start to recognize for yourself that you are changing, that your outlook on life is improving and that you are becoming more able. In Scientology, you will not be told when you have completed an auditing level—you will know for yourself, as only you can know exactly what you are experiencing. This gives you the certainty that you have attained what you want to attain from each level.

There will also no doubt be some outwardly demonstrable or visible changes that occur: Your IQ may increase, you might look healthier and happier, and may well have people comment on how calm or cheerful you look or, for instance, how you are doing better on your job.

Results like these are the products of auditing. Each person knows when he has achieved them.

Does auditing really work in all cases?

Dianetics and Scientology technologies are very exact and well-tested procedures that work in 100 percent of the cases in which they are applied standardly.

The only proviso is that the preclear must be there on his own determinism and must abide by the rules for preclears during his auditing to ensure optimum results. The Church makes no guarantee of results as auditing is something which requires the active participation of the individual. Auditing is not something done *to* an individual—it is something done in which he is the active participant.

What auditing handles physical pains or discomfort?

Dianetics auditing is used to help handle physical pains or discomfort stemming from the reactive mind.

What can auditing cure?

Scientology is not in the business of curing things in the traditional sense of the word. Auditing is not done to fix the body or to heal anything physical, and the E-Meter cures nothing. However, in the process of becoming happier, more able and more aware as a spiritual being through auditing, illnesses that are psychosomatic in origin (meaning the mind making the body ill) often disappear.

Can one go exterior (be separate from the body) in auditing?

Exteriorization is the state of the thetan, the individual himself, being outside his body with or without full perception, but still able to control and handle the body.

Exteriorization is a personal matter for each individual. Many Scientologists have been known to go exterior, so it would not be at all surprising if you do too at some point during your auditing.

This can happen at any time in auditing. When a person goes exterior, he achieves a certainty that he is himself and not his body.

THE STATE OF CLEAR

What is Clear?

Clear is the name of a specific state achieved through auditing, or a person who has achieved this state. A Clear is a being who no longer has his own reactive mind, and therefore suffers none of the ill effects the reactive mind can cause.

How does one go Clear?

Simply by taking one's first step in Scientology, or by taking the next step as shown on the Classification, Gradation and Awareness Chart and then continuing up the levels as laid out on this chart.

How long does it take to go Clear?

It varies from person to person, but it takes an average of anywhere from one year to two years to go from the bottom of the Grade Chart through Clear, depending on how much time one spends each week on his auditing. Those who get intensive auditing and do not stop along the way progress the fastest.

If one goes Clear, will he lose his emotions?

No, on the contrary, a Clear is able to use and experience any emotion. Only the painful, reactive, uncontrolled emotions are gone from his life. Clears are very responsive beings. When one is Clear, he is more himself. The only loss is a negative—the reactive mind—which was preventing the individual from being himself.

What can you do when you are Clear?

A Clear is able to deal causatively with life rather than react to it. A Clear is rational in that he forms the best possible solutions he can with the data he has and from his own viewpoint. A Clear gets things done and accomplishes more than he could before he became Clear.

Whatever your level of ability before you go Clear, it will be greatly increased after you go Clear.

Are Clears perfect?

No, they are not perfect.

Being a Clear does not mean a person who has had no education, for example, suddenly becomes educated. It does mean that all the abilities of the individual can be brought to bear on the problems he encounters and that all the data in his analytical memory banks is available for solution to those problems.

A Clear has become the basic individual through auditing. The basic individual is not a buried, unknown or a different person, but an intensity of all that is best and most able in the person.

Do Clears eat food and sleep?

Most definitely.

Do Clears get colds and get sick?

A Clear can still get sick, but this occurs much less often than before he became Clear. In other words, a Clear still has a body, and bodies are susceptible at times to various illnesses. However, no longer having his reactive mind, he is much more at cause and is not adversely affected by many of the things that would have caused psychosomatic illnesses before he went Clear.

To measure a Clear only by his health, however, would be a mistake because this state has to do with the individual himself, not his body.

If Clears no longer have a reactive mind, why do they still need to get auditing?

There are many more states of awareness and ability that can be achieved above the state of Clear as he is only Clear on the first dynamic. Once Clear, an individual wants to continue his auditing to achieve these higher states.

THE STATE OF OPERATING THETAN

What is meant by Operating Thetan (OT)?

Operating Thetan is a state of beingness above Clear. *Thetan* refers to the spiritual being, and *operating* means here "able to operate without dependency on things." An Operating Thetan (OT) is able to control matter, energy, space and time rather than being controlled by these things. As a result, an OT is able to be at cause over life.

There are numerous auditing steps on the Bridge called OT levels. People on these levels are progressing to the state of full OT and becoming more and more OT along the way.

How would you describe the state of Operating Thetan?

OT (Operating Thetan) is a state of spiritual awareness in which an individual is able to control himself and his environment. An OT is someone who knows that he knows and can create positive and prosurvival effects on all of his dynamics. He has been fully refamiliarized with his capabilities as a thetan and can willingly and knowingly be at cause over life, thought, matter, energy, space and time.

As a being becomes more and more OT, he becomes more powerful, stable and responsible.

Why are the OT materials confidential?

Because understanding of and ability to apply the OT materials are dependent upon having fully attained the earlier states of awareness and abilities per the Classification, Gradation and Awareness Chart. Thus, these materials are released on a gradient, only to those who have honestly attained all earlier states.

A SCIENTOLOGY CAREER

Can one audit as a career?

Yes. There are many Scientology ministers who audit full time as their life's work. Auditing provides a rewarding career as it is one in which you are always helping people and constantly seeing miraculous results on your preclears. It is very satisfying to know that you are making people's lives happier and saner.

Auditors are very valuable and in great demand.

L. Ron Hubbard's opinion of auditors is well known: "I think of an auditor as a person with enough guts to *do something about it.* This quality is rare and this quality is courageous in the extreme. It is my opinion and knowledge that auditors are amongst the upper tenth of the upper twentieth of intelligent human beings. Their will to do, their motives, their ability to grasp and to use are superior to that of any other profession."

Of what value would it be to have my child trained as an auditor?

First of all, it would provide a young person with certainty and knowledge in dealing with every possible type of human problem, be it interpersonal, familial, organizational, ethical, moral or religious. Secondly, it would provide a career of fulfillment in aiding people from all walks of life to gain greater awareness and respect for themselves and others.

Auditors are in demand in every church of Scientology and mission throughout the world. Therefore, your child would be fulfilling a great demand and contributing greatly to making this world a saner place by getting trained as an auditor.

Can one make Scientology a career in some other way than by being a minister?

Yes, there are thousands of professional Scientologists who work full time in churches and missions throughout the world as executives or administrative staff. There are also those who further the dissemination of Scientology on a one-to-one basis or through the dissemination of Scientology materials and books, those who hold jobs in the Church's social reform groups and those who work in the Office of Special Affairs involved in community betterment or legal work. All of these provide rewarding careers as each forwards the expansion of Scientology and thereby makes it possible for more and more people to benefit from its technology.

SCIENTOLOGY IN SOCIETY

I've heard that Scientologists are doing good things for society. What are some specific examples?

These activities would fill a book in themselves, and are covered in more detail in Part 5 of this book, but here are just a few examples that are typical of the things that Scientologists are doing around the world.

Scientologists regularly hold blood drives to get donations of blood for hospitals, the Red Cross and other similar organizations. As Scientologists do not use harmful drugs, these donations of drug-free blood are welcomed by those in charge of health care.

Scientologists regularly hold drives to get donations of toys, food and clothing to make life happier for those in need.

During the annual holiday season, Scientologists are particularly active in this sphere. In downtown Hollywood, California, for example, Scientologists build a "Winter Wonderland" scene each Christmas, complete with a large Christmas tree, Santa Claus and even "snow," creating a traditional Christmas setting for children who otherwise might never see one.

In Canada, a group of Scientologists spends many weeks each year raising funds to sponsor visits to summer camps by underprivileged children.

Church members utilize their artistic talents to bring new experiences and joy to children by performing puppet shows in orphanages, schools and shopping malls, and magic shows for children in foster homes.

Scientologists can also be found in many communities contributing to the care of the elderly. They visit old-age homes and provide entertainment, draw sketches or just drop by and talk with senior citizens.

You will find Scientologists helping with "community cleanup" campaigns and assistance to the injured at Veteran's Administration hospitals.

Scientologists have taken a leading role fighting drug abuse, actively educating community officials and groups on the dangers of drugs and solutions to the problems. There are many groups utilizing L. Ron Hubbard's technology and freeing people from the detrimental effects of drugs.

L. Ron Hubbard's technology on how to study has been used by Scientologists around the world to help students and teachers alike. One place where this technology has made major inroads combating illiteracy is in South Africa, where well over a million native Africans have improved their ability to study.

Another important area of activity for Scientologists is raising moral standards in society. Scientologists all around the world have distributed tens of millions of copies of the nonreligious moral code called "The Way to Happiness," now available in more than fifteen different languages. Its use has led to a revitalization of purpose for people of all ages who apply its simple truths to their lives and to the environment around them.

The Church and many of its members are also engaged in interfaith activities, the main thrust of which has been to work with leaders of other faiths in the areas of interreligious dialogue, religious freedom, constitutional law and "religion in society" issues—all aimed toward protecting and forwarding the freedom of religion for everyone.

Another prevalent activity for Scientologists is to expose and eradicate the violations of human rights perpetrated by psychiatry. Many Scientologists do this as members of the Citizens Commission on Human Rights (CCHR), a reform group which was established by the Church in 1969.

They actively investigate psychiatric abuses and bring these to the attention of the media, legislators and other groups concerned with protecting people from brutal psychiatric techniques. Such practices as psychosurgery, electroshock treatment and the administration of dangerous psychiatric drugs have destroyed the minds and lives of millions of individuals. Through the efforts of Scientologists working for CCHR, public awareness of the disastrous results of psychiatric methods has been raised and major steps taken to outlaw such practices.

Is Scientology active in Black communities and countries?

Definitely. By the Creed of the Church, "All men of whatever race, color or creed were created with equal rights." Thus, there are no limitations placed on who can receive and benefit from Scientology services.

There are Scientologists of all races, colors and religious backgrounds.

For example, there are Dianetics and/or Scientology organizations in Ghana, Zaire, Zimbabwe, Ethiopia and Sierra Leone, among other countries, and Black Scientologists are applying Scientology technology in their communities wherever possible. The Church maintains a Department of Ethnic Affairs specifically to interact and work with minorities.

Do doctors, schools, social workers, businessmen and other professional people use Scientology?

Yes, they do. There are members of all of these professions who use Scientology technology to improve the results being obtained in their fields of endeavor.

Schools and universities in many countries apply L. Ron Hubbard's study methods to improve literacy and teaching success, drug rehabilitation groups use his drug rehabilitation technology to successfully get people off drugs, doctors observe basic Dianetics principles to speed up the recovery of their patients, businessmen apply L. Ron Hubbard's administrative procedures to create thriving businesses.

Scientology applies to all spheres of life and uniformly gets results when standardly used. Therefore, there is hardly an area of social or community concern where you will not find people using some aspect of L. Ron Hubbard's technology.

Why has Scientology sometimes been considered controversial?

Like all new ideas, Scientology has come under attack by the uninformed and those who feel their vested interests are threatened.

As Scientologists have openly and effectively advocated social reform causes, they have become the target of attacks.

For those vested interests who cling to a status quo that is decimating society, Scientology's technology of making the able more able poses a serious threat. Attacks follow as an attempt to stop application of Scientology technology.

When the Church steps in to handle the attack, the conflict grabs the attention of the press, which lives on controversy. Regardless of the unfounded nature of the attackers' claims, reporters freely promote the controversy. Those seeking to stop Scientology then join the media in regurgitating and regenerating the created controversy.

Scientology has always flourished and prospered in the face of attacks. In every case where public disputes have been manufactured, intentional and blatant false reports about Scientology and its founder have been discovered to be the common denominator. As the falsehoods are proven lies, the controversy quickly fades, and the truth about Scientology, what the Church really is and what its members do replaces it. The source of these attacks and the controversy they have generated is detailed in Chapter 31 of this book.

Why has Scientology been to court a lot of times?

The Church has gone to court in many countries to uphold the right to freedom of religion. In Australia, as one example, legal actions by the Church brought about a landmark victory which greatly expanded religious freedom throughout that country.

In the United States, the Church's use of the Freedom of Information Act, taking government agencies to court and holding them accountable to release vital documents to the public on a variety of subjects, has been heralded as a vital action to ensure honesty in government.

In certain cases, the Church has used the courts to protect its copyrighted materials, or to ensure its rights and the rights of its members are safeguarded.

During the history of the Church, a few unscrupulous individuals, lusting for money, have observed how Scientology is prospering and rapidly expanding, and have abused the legal system to try to line their own pockets. In the handful of cases where such attempts have occurred, they have uniformly failed.

Are there any laws against the practice of Scientology? Has it been banned?

Of course not.

In fact, the Church has received numerous recognitions, citations and validations from various governments for contributions to society in the fields of education, drug and alcohol rehabilitation, crime reduction, human rights, raising moral values and a host of other fields.

How does Scientology view deprogramers and groups that attempt to force people to denounce their chosen religion?

These so-called "deprogramers," better described as psychiatric depersonalizers, are money-motivated individuals who kidnap others for profit. Their methods include brainwashing, imprisonment, food and sleep deprivation and various forms of torture.

Such activities are clearly against the principles held by Scientologists—and have been proven to be against the law as well. Psychiatric depersonalizers in many countries have gone to jail for their violent and illegal practices.

Situations in which families have expressed concern over family members' involvement in various religions can generally be handled with communication. No one need resort to violence and mercenaries to resolve the upset.

The Church does not condone the use of violence and advocates that each person has an inalienable right to their own beliefs.

Why is Scientology opposed to psychiatry?

As the stepchildren of the German dictator Bismarck and later Hitler and the Nazis, psychiatry and psychology formed the philosophical basis for the wholesale slaughter of human beings in World Wars I and II. Psychiatry uses electric shock, brain-mutilating psychosurgery, and mind-damaging drugs to destroy a person and make him "docile and quiet" in the name of "treatment."

Psychiatric methods involving the butchering of human beings and their sanity are condemned by the Church. Scientologists are trying to create a world without war, insanity and criminality. Psychiatry is seeking to create a world where man is reduced to a robotized or drugged, vegetable-like state so that he can be controlled.

A primary difference between Scientology and psychiatry is that psychiatrists routinely tell their patients what they think is wrong with them. This interjects lies or ideas which are not true for the individual himself, and thus psychiatric "therapy" violates the basic integrity of the individual.

On the other hand, Scientology technology enables a person to find out for himself the source of his troubles and gives him the ability to improve conditions in his own life and environment.

The underlying difference is the fact that Scientology recognizes that man is a spiritual being, while psychiatrists view man as an animal. Scientology is a religion. Psychiatry is strongly opposed to all religions as it does not even recognize that man is a spiritual being.

Scientologists strongly disagree with the enforced and harmful psychiatric methods of involuntary commitment, forced and heavy drugging, electroconvulsive shock treatment, lobotomy and other psychosurgical operations.

By the Creed of the Church of Scientology, the healing of mentally caused ills should not be condoned in nonreligious fields. The reason for this is that violent psychiatric therapies cause spiritual traumas. At best, psychiatry suppresses life's problems; at worst, it causes severe damage, irreversible setbacks in a person's life and even death.

Why do some people oppose Scientology?

There are certain characteristics and mental attitudes that cause a percentage of the population to oppose violently any betterment activity or group. This small percentage of society (roughly 2½ percent) cannot stand the fact that Scientology is successful at improving conditions around the world. This same 2½ percent is opposed to any self-betterment activity. The reason they so rabidly oppose Scientology is because it is doing more to help society than any other group.

Those who are upset by seeing man get better are small in number compared to the millions who have embraced Scientology and its efforts to create a sane civilization and more freedom for the individual.

Is Scientology trying to rule the world?

No. Scientology's aim, as expressed by L. Ron Hubbard, is that of creating "a civilization without insanity, without criminals and without war, where the able can prosper and honest beings can have rights, and where man is free to rise to greater heights. . . ."

"We seek no revolution. We seek only evolution to higher states of being for the individual and for society."

Scientology does want to improve and reform societal ills, and Scientologists believe there can be a better world by doing so.

It is not Scientology's mission to save the world. It is Scientology's mission to free *you*.

Can Scientology do anything to improve the world situation?

Yes, and it does so every single day.

By making the able individual in society more able and more certain of his abilities, and by continuing the Church's expansion and social reform programs throughout the world, the world can become a better place.

It is possible to bring people to higher levels of communication with the environment and those around them. And as one raises the level of communication, one raises also the ability to observe and change conditions and thereby create a better world and a better civilization.

The Aims of Scientology by L. Ron Hubbard

A civilization without insanity, without criminals and without war, where the able can prosper and honest beings can have rights, and where man is free to rise to greater heights, are the aims of Scientology.

First announced to an enturbulated world in 1950, these aims are well within the grasp of our technology.

Nonpolitical in nature, Scientology welcomes any individual of any creed, race or nation.

We seek no revolution. We seek only evolution to higher states of being for the individual and for society.

We are achieving our aims.

After endless millennia of ignorance about himself, his mind and the universe, a breakthrough has been made for man.

Other efforts man has made have been surpassed.

The combined truths of fifty thousand years of thinking men, distilled and amplified by new discoveries about man, have made for this success.

We welcome you to Scientology. We only expect of you your help in achieving our aims and helping others. We expect you to be helped.

Scientology is the most vital movement on Earth today.

In a turbulent world, the job is not easy. But then, if it were, we wouldn't have to be doing it.

We respect man and believe he is worthy of help. We respect you and believe you, too, can help.

Scientology does not owe its help. We have done nothing to cause us to propitiate. Had we done so, we would not now be bright enough to do what we are doing.

Man suspects all offers of help. He has often been betrayed, his confidence shattered. Too frequently he has given his trust and been betrayed. We may err, for we build a world with broken straws. But we will never betray your faith in us so long as you are one of us.

The sun never sets on Scientology.

And may a new day dawn for you, for those you love and for man.

Our aims are simple, if great.

And we will succeed, and are succeeding at each new revolution of the Earth.

Your help is acceptable to us.

Our help is yours.

PART TEN

REFERENCES

Chapter 33

The Creeds and Codes of Scientology

The parishioners of every religion are bound together by creeds and codes.

These serve to state their aspirations, their duties, their mores and their beliefs. They further align purposes and reinforce the basic tenets of the religion.

The codes and creeds of Scientology were written by L. Ron Hubbard in the 1950s during the formative years of the religion. These set the guidelines for conduct and expansion and still serve those ends today.

Included are codes for the auditor, the supervisor, the manager and additional codes by which all Scientologists strive to live. Like all Scientology, the usefulness of these principles determines their worth. Scientologists follow them in their application of Scientology technology, their dealings with others, the administration of their groups and the practice of their religion.

THE CREED OF THE CHURCH OF SCIENTOLOGY

The Creed of the Church of Scientology was written by L. Ron Hubbard shortly after the Church was formed in Los Angeles on February 18, 1954. After he issued this creed from his office in Phoenix, Arizona, the Church of Scientology adopted it as official because it succinctly states what Scientologists believe.

We of the Church believe:

That all men of whatever race, color or creed were created with equal rights;

That all men have inalienable rights to their own religious practices and their performance;

That all men have inalienable rights to their own lives;

That all men have inalienable rights to their sanity;

That all men have inalienable rights to their own defense;

That all men have inalienable rights to conceive, choose, assist or support their own organizations, churches and governments;

That all men have inalienable rights to think freely, to talk freely, to write freely their own opinions and to counter or utter or write upon the opinions of others;

That all men have inalienable rights to the creation of their own kind;

That the souls of men have the rights of men;

That the study of the mind and the healing of mentally caused ills should not be alienated from religion or condoned in nonreligious fields;

And that no agency less than God has the power to suspend or set aside these rights, overtly or covertly.

And we of the Church believe:

That man is basically good;

That he is seeking to survive;

That his survival depends upon himself and upon his fellows and his attainment of brotherhood with the universe.

And we of the Church believe that the laws of God forbid man:

To destroy his own kind;

To destroy the sanity of another;

To destroy or enslave another's soul;

To destroy or reduce the survival of one's companions or one's group.

And we of the Church believe that the spirit can be saved and that the spirit alone may save or heal the body.

THE AUDITOR'S CODE

This code first appeared as a chapter in the book *Dianetics: The Original Thesis* (later retitled *The Dynamics of Life*) written by L. Ron Hubbard in 1947 and eventually published in 1951.

The ensuing years saw a great deal of auditing done by auditors other than Mr. Hubbard and from these experiences he was able to refine the Code and thus improve the discipline of auditing.

The Auditor's Code was revised in 1954, appearing in Professional Auditor's Bulletins 38 and 39.

Over the next four years, several additions were made to the 1954 Code, one of which appeared in the book *Dianetics 55!* Another was released in Hubbard Communications Office Bulletin of 1 July 1957, ADDITION TO THE AUDITOR'S CODE, and two more items were added when the Auditor's Code of 1958 was published.

The Auditor's Code 1968, released in October of that year, was issued as a Hubbard Communications Office Policy Letter. It was released in celebration of the 100 percent gains attainable by standard tech.

Hubbard Communications Office Policy Letter 2 November 1968, AUDITOR'S CODE, added three more clauses to the Code.

The final version of the Code was published by Mr. Hubbard on 19 June 1980.

The Auditor's Code is a fundamental tool of not only auditing but of life. As L. Ron Hubbard wrote in *Dianetics,* "The Auditor's Code outlines the *survival conduct pattern* of man. The Clear operates more or less automatically on this code." Because the basic axioms of Dianetics and Scientology comprise the fundamentals of thought itself, what works in auditing also works in life.

I hereby promise as an auditor to follow the Auditor's Code.

1 I promise not to evaluate for the preclear or tell him what he should think about his case in session.

2 I promise not to invalidate the preclear's case or gains in or out of session.

3 I promise to administer only standard tech to a preclear in the standard way.

4 I promise to keep all auditing appointments once made.

5 I promise not to process a preclear who has not had sufficient rest and who is physically tired.

6 I promise not to process a preclear who is improperly fed or hungry.

7 I promise not to permit a frequent change of auditors.

8 I promise not to sympathize with a preclear but to be effective.

9 I promise not to let the preclear end session on his own determinism but to finish off those cycles I have begun.

10 I promise never to walk off from a preclear in session.

11 I promise never to get angry with a preclear in session.

12 I promise to run every major case action to a floating needle.

13 I promise never to run any one action beyond its floating needle.

14 I promise to grant beingness to the preclear in session.

15 I promise not to mix the processes of Scientology with other practices except when the preclear is physically ill and only medical means will serve.

16 I promise to maintain communication with the preclear and not to cut his communication or permit him to overrun in session.

17 I promise not to enter comments, expressions or enturbulence into a session that distract a preclear from his case.

18 I promise to continue to give the preclear the process or auditing command when needed in the session.

19 I promise not to let a preclear run a wrongly understood command.

20 I promise not to explain, justify or make excuses in session for any auditor mistakes whether real or imagined.

21 I promise to estimate the current case state of a preclear only by standard case supervision data and not to diverge because of some imagined difference in the case.

22 I promise never to use the secrets of a preclear divulged in session for punishment or personal gain.

23 I promise to never falsify worksheets of sessions.

24 I promise to see that any fee received for processing is refunded, following the policies of the Claims Verification Board, if the preclear is dissatisfied and demands it within three months after the processing, the only condition being that he may not again be processed or trained.

25 I promise not to advocate Dianetics or Scientology only to cure illness or only to treat the insane, knowing well they were intended for spiritual gain.

26 I promise to cooperate fully with the authorized organizations of Dianetics and Scientology in safeguarding the ethical use and practice of those subjects.

27 I promise to refuse to permit any being to be physically injured, violently damaged, operated on or killed in the name of "mental treatment."

28 I promise not to permit sexual liberties or violations of patients.

29 I promise to refuse to admit to the ranks of practitioners any being who is insane.

THE CODE OF HONOR

The Code of Honor first appeared in Professional Auditor's Bulletin 40 on 26 November 1954. As Mr. Hubbard himself explained:

"No one expects the Code of Honor to be closely and tightly followed.

"An ethical code cannot be enforced. Any effort to enforce the Code of Honor would bring it into the level of a moral code. It cannot be enforced simply because it is a way of life which can exist as a way of life only as long as it is not enforced. Any other use but self-determined use of the Code of Honor would, as any Scientologist could quickly see, produce a considerable deterioration in a person. Therefore its use is a luxury use, and which is done solely on self-determined action, providing one sees eye to eye with the Code of Honor.

"If you believed man was worthy enough to be granted by you sufficient stature so as to permit you to exercise gladly the Code of Honor, I can guarantee that you would be a happy person. And if you found an occasional miscreant falling away from the best standards you have developed, you yet did not turn away from the rest of man, and if you discovered yourself betrayed by those you were seeking to defend and yet did not then experience a complete reversal of opinion about all your fellow men, there would be no dwindling spiral for you."

"The only difference between paradise on Earth and hell on Earth is whether or not you believe your fellow man worthy of receiving from you the friendship and devotion called for in this Code of Honor."

1 Never desert a comrade in need, in danger or in trouble.

2 Never withdraw allegiance once granted.

3 Never desert a group to which you owe your support.

4 Never disparage yourself or minimize your strength or power.

5 Never need praise, approval or sympathy.

6 Never compromise with your own reality.

7 Never permit your affinity to be alloyed.

8 Do not give or receive communication unless you yourself desire it.

9 Your self-determinism and your honor are more important than your immediate life.

10 Your integrity to yourself is more important than your body.

11 Never regret yesterday. Life is in you today, and you make your tomorrow.

12 Never fear to hurt another in a just cause.

13 Don't desire to be liked or admired.

14 Be your own adviser, keep your own counsel and select your own decisions.

15 Be true to your own goals.

CODE OF A SCIENTOLOGIST

The Code of a Scientologist was first issued as Professional Auditor's Bulletin 41 in 1954. In it, L. Ron Hubbard provides a Scientologist with guidelines in dealing with the press and in fighting for human rights and justice through social reform. It is a vital code for any Scientologist active in the community. The code was reissued in 1956 in the book, *Creation of Human Ability.* Revised in 1969 and again in 1973, the code is given here in its final version.

As a Scientologist, I pledge myself to the Code of Scientology for the good of all.

1 To keep Scientologists, the public and the press accurately informed concerning Scientology, the world of mental health and society.

2 To use the best I know of Scientology to the best of my ability to help my family, friends, groups and the world.

3 To refuse to accept for processing and to refuse to accept money from any preclear or group I feel I cannot honestly help.

4 To decry and do all I can to abolish any and all abuses against life and mankind.

5 To expose and help abolish any and all physically damaging practices in the field of mental health.

6 To help clean up and keep clean the field of mental health.

7 To bring about an atmosphere of safety and security in the field of mental health by eradicating its abuses and brutality.

8 To support true humanitarian endeavors in the fields of human rights.

9 To embrace the policy of equal justice for all.

10 To work for freedom of speech in the world.

11 To actively decry the suppression of knowledge, wisdom, philosophy or data which would help mankind.

12 To support the freedom of religion.

13 To help Scientology orgs and groups ally themselves with public groups.

14 To teach Scientology at a level it can be understood and used by the recipients.

15 To stress the freedom to use Scientology as a philosophy in all its applications and variations in the humanities.

16 To insist upon standard and unvaried Scientology as an applied activity in ethics, processing and administration in Scientology organizations.

17 To take my share of responsibility for the impact of Scientology upon the world.

18 To increase the numbers and strength of Scientology over the world.

19 To set an example of the effectiveness and wisdom of Scientology.

20 To make this world a saner, better place.

THE SUPERVISOR'S CODE

Just as auditors must follow a code of conduct, so too does the Supervisor in a Scientology course room. Unlike teachers in many traditional classrooms, Course Supervisors do not set themselves up as "authorities" who tell their students what to think, or espouse their opinions on the subject. Instead, students are guided to find the answers for themselves in Dianetics and Scientology materials.

In the following code, Mr. Hubbard sets forth the key guidelines that ensure instruction in a Scientology course room is standard and professional, with maximum benefit to the students. This code is followed by Supervisors in churches of Scientology throughout the world, guaranteeing a high level of training in the technology. It was first published in 1957.

1 The Supervisor must never neglect an opportunity to direct a student to the actual source of Scientology data.

2 The Supervisor should invalidate a student's mistake ruthlessly and use good ARC while doing it.

3 The Supervisor should remain in good ARC with his students at all times while they are performing training activities.

4 The Supervisor at all times must have a high tolerance of stupidity in his students and must be willing to repeat any datum not understood as many times as necessary for the student to understand and acquire reality on the datum.

5 The Supervisor does not have a "case" in his relationship with his students, nor discuss or talk about his personal problems to the students.

6 The Supervisor will, at all times, be a source-point of good control and direction to his students.

7 The Supervisor will be able to correlate any part of Scientology to any other part and to livingness over the eight dynamics.

8 The Supervisor should be able to answer any questions concerning Scientology by directing the student to the actual source of the data. If a Supervisor cannot answer a particular question, he should always say so, and the Supervisor should always find the answer to the question from the source and tell the student where the answer is to be found.

9 The Supervisor should never lie to, deceive or misdirect a student concerning Scientology. He shall be honest at all times about it with a student.

10 The Supervisor must be an accomplished auditor.

11 The Supervisor should always set a good example to his students: such as giving good demonstrations, being on time and dressing neatly.

12 The Supervisor should at all times be perfectly willing and able to do anything he tells his students to do.

13 The Supervisor must not become emotionally involved with students of either sex while they are under his or her training.

14 When a Supervisor makes any mistake, he is to inform the student that he has made one and rectify it immediately. This datum embraces all phases in training, demonstrations, lectures and processing, etc. He is never to hide the fact that he made the mistake.

15 The Supervisor should never neglect to give praise to his students when due.

16 The Supervisor to some degree should be pan-determined about the Supervisor–student relationship.

17 When a Supervisor lets a student control, give orders to or handle the Supervisor in any way, for the purpose of demonstration or other training purposes, the Supervisor should always put the student back under his control.

18 The Supervisor will at all times observe the Auditor's Code during sessions and the Code of a Scientologist at all times.

19 The Supervisor will never give a student opinions about Scientology without labeling them thoroughly as such; otherwise, he is to direct only to tested and proven data concerning Scientology.

20 The Supervisor shall never use a student for his own personal gain.

21 The Supervisor will be a stable terminal, point the way to stable data, be certain, but not dogmatic or dictatorial, toward his students.

22 The Supervisor will keep himself at all times informed of the most recent Scientology data and procedures and communicate this information to his students.

THE CREDO OF A TRUE GROUP MEMBER

In our bureaucratic age, members of a group are often left feeling hopeless and ineffective in the face of seemingly insurmountable difficulties. Some even come to feel they might be better off without allegiance to any group. But inevitably, no one can survive alone, and denying oneself membership in a group is denying oneself that certain pride and satisfaction which can only come through teamwork.

In his research into the technology of groups, L. Ron Hubbard codified the key principles which members of any group should follow to attain its goals. These are offered in the following code, written in January 1951.

With these guidelines, a person can greatly increase his contribution to a group, while at the same time maintaining his own self-determinism.

1 The successful participant of a group is that participant who closely approximates in his own activities the ideal, ethic and rationale of the overall group.

2 The responsibility of the individual for the group as a whole should not be less than the responsibility of the group for the individual.

3 The group member has, as part of his responsibility, the smooth operation of the entire group.

4 A group member must exert and insist upon his rights and prerogatives as a group member and insist upon the rights and prerogatives of the group as a group and let not these rights be diminished in any way or degree for any excuse or claimed expeditiousness.

5 The member of a true group must exert and practice his right to contribute to the group. And he must insist upon the right of the group to contribute to him. He should recognize that a myriad of group failures will result when either of these contributions is denied as a right. (A welfare state being that state in which the member is not permitted to contribute to the state but must take contribution from the state.)

6 Enturbulence of the affairs of the group by sudden shifts of plans unjustified by circumstances, breakdown of recognized channels or cessation of useful operations in a group must be refused and blocked by the member of a group. He should take care not to enturbulate a manager and thus lower ARC.

7 Failure in planning or failure to recognize goals must be corrected by the group member for the group by calling the matter to conference or acting upon his own initiative.

8 A group member must coordinate his initiative with the goals and rationale of the entire group and with other individual members, well publishing his activities and intentions so that all conflicts may be brought forth in advance.

9 A group member must insist upon his right to have initiative.

10 A group member must study and understand and work with the goals, rationale and executions of the group.

11 A group member must work toward becoming as expert as possible in his specialized technology and skill in the group and must assist other individuals of the group to an understanding of that technology and skill and its place in the organizational necessities of the group.

12 A group member should have a working knowledge of all technologies and skills in the group in order to understand them and their place in the organizational necessities of the group.

13 On the group member depends the height of the ARC of the group. He must insist upon high-level communication lines and clarity in affinity and reality and know the consequence of not having such conditions. *And he must work continually and actively to maintain high ARC in the organization.*

14 A group member has the right of pride in his tasks and a right of judgment and handling in those tasks.

15 A group member must recognize that he is himself a manager of some section of the group and/or its tasks and that he himself must have both the knowledge and right of management in that sphere for which he is responsible.

16 The group member should not permit laws to be passed which limit or proscribe the activities of all the members of the group because of the failure of some of the members of the group.

17 The group member should insist on flexible planning and unerring execution of plans.

18 The performance of duty at optimum by every member of the group should be understood by the group member to be the best safeguard of his own and the group survival. It is the pertinent business of any member of the group that optimum performance be achieved by any other member of the group whether chain of command or similarity of activity sphere warrants such supervision or not.

THE CREDO OF A GOOD AND SKILLED MANAGER

Leadership is considered a rare commodity, a gift possessed by a few uncommon individuals. And after a few years in a high executive position, whether in the private or the public sector, many individuals wonder whether this gift is in fact illusory.

In his management technology, L. Ron Hubbard developed a large body of guidelines that enable executives and managers not only to apply their powers with intelligence but to exercise sane leadership that will enable their groups to flourish and prosper. Following this code can greatly increase one's success as a manager in any group, from a business to a commonwealth of nations. This code was also written by Mr. Hubbard in 1951.

To be effective and successful a manager must:

1 Understand as fully as possible the goals and aims of the group he manages. He must be able to see and embrace the *ideal* attainment of the goal as envisioned by a goal maker. He must be able to tolerate and better the *practical* attainments and advances of which his group and its members may be capable. He must strive to narrow, always, the ever-existing gulf between the *ideal* and the *practical.*

2 He must realize that a primary mission is the full and honest interpretation by himself of the ideal and ethic and their goals and aims to his subordinates and the group itself. He must lead creatively and persuasively toward these goals his subordinates, the group itself and the individuals of the group.

3 He must embrace the organization and act solely for the entire organization and never form or favor cliques. His judgment of individuals of the group should be solely in the light of their worth to the entire group.

4 He must never falter in sacrificing individuals to the good of the group both in planning and execution and in his justice.

5 He must protect all established communication lines and complement them where necessary.

6 He must protect all affinity in his charge and have himself an affinity for the group itself.

7 He must attain always to the highest creative reality.

8 His planning must accomplish, in the light of goals and aims, the activity of the entire group. He must never let organizations grow and sprawl but, learning by pilots, must keep organizational planning fresh and flexible.

9 He must recognize in himself the rationale of the group and receive and evaluate the data out of which he makes his solutions with the highest attention to the truth of that data.

10 He must constitute himself on the orders of service to the group.

11 He must permit himself to be served well as to his individual requirements, practicing an economy of his own efforts and enjoying certain comforts to the wealth of keeping high his rationale.

12 He should require of his subordinates that they relay into their own spheres of management the whole and entire of his true feelings and the reasons for his decisions as clearly as they can be relayed and expanded and interpreted only for the greater understanding of the individuals governed by those subordinates.

13 He must never permit himself to pervert or mask any portion of the ideal and ethic on which the group operates nor must he permit the ideal and ethic to grow old and outmoded and unworkable. He must never permit his planning to be perverted or censored by subordinates. He must never permit the ideal and ethic of the group's individual members to deteriorate, using always reason to interrupt such a deterioration.

14 He must have faith in the goals, faith in himself and faith in the group.

15 He must lead by demonstrating always creative and constructive subgoals. He must not drive by threat and fear.

16 He must realize that every individual in the group is engaged in some degree in the managing of other men, life and MEST and that a liberty of management within this code should be allowed to every such submanager.

Thus conducting himself, a manager can win empire for his group, whatever that empire may be.

CHAPTER 34

THE VICTORIES OF SCIENTOLOGY

For more than forty years, those who perceive Scientology as a threat to their vested interests have attempted to curb its expansion. Today, Scientology has expanded to the point where it cannot be stopped, and a summation of battles fought and won demonstrates the persistence of Scientologists and their active involvement to preserve religious freedom and the rights of man, not just for Scientology, but for everyone.

Witness Australia in 1965. In the state of Victoria, after a kangaroo court inquiry in which Scientologists were not even allowed to appear, the Church was banned. Naturally, such legislation was unenforceable, but it took eighteen years of sustained actions in the courts before Scientology not only won, but received full recognition in a landmark decision from the High Court of Australia that established the legal definition of religion in Australia.

So it has been in every country where Scientologists and their church have met with resistance from vested interests opposed to human betterment. For example, members of the British Parliament, urged on by psychiatric interests and the notorious yellow journalism of the British press, enacted a ban on foreign students entering the country to study Scientology. Exposure of the vested interests behind the ban, and a legal suit eventually forced a reversal of the decision twelve years later. Today, foreigners have free access to the many churches and missions that now dot the British Isles.

Many battles have been fought over the last three decades. And, as the following summary substantiates, all have been won. Scores of court decisions now affirm the religious bona fides of Scientology throughout the world. In every instance, those who would seek to destroy Scientology eventually disappear, while the Church continues to grow across the world.

Indeed, in every instance where Scientology has met resistance, the Church has emerged stronger, larger and with ever greater impact on society, testament to its validity and legitimacy. Any other movement subject to the magnitude of attacks sustained and overcome by Scientology would have long since ceased to exist.

LATE 1956

The so-called "Siberia Bill" was defeated by a coalition of citizen groups and Scientologists. If the measure, introduced in the US Congress in 1954, had passed, it would have allowed any peace officer or medical doctor to institute commitment proceedings against any US citizen. Legislation in Alaska would have made it possible for those dubbed "mentally ill" to be transferred to the territory of Alaska. After the serious human rights dangers of the bill were brought to public attention, it was killed.

JULY 16, 1957

The Church of Scientology of New York was recognized as tax exempt by the Internal Revenue Service as a religious organization.

JANUARY 4, 1963

The Founding Church of Scientology in Washington, DC was desecrated and looted by United States marshals and deputized longshoremen with drawn guns, acting for the US Food and Drug Administration (FDA). Five thousand volumes of Church scriptures, 20,000 pages of literature and 100 E-Meters were seized. It took 8 years of courtroom battle to finally obtain the return of the materials and victory for the Church. [See July 30, 1971 entry]

FEBRUARY 1, 1965

A Federal District Judge in Washington, DC ruled that Scientology ministers may refuse to violate confidences divulged to them by parishioners in pastoral counseling sessions.

FEBRUARY 5, 1969

In a landmark legal decision, the US Court of Appeals in Washington, DC ruled that Scientology was a bona fide religion and that auditing was an integral part of Scientology's religious doctrines and practices. The case had begun dramatically with the armed FDA raid on the Founding Church and seizure of E-Meters and Church literature. [See January 4, 1963 entry] Later all E-Meters and books were ordered returned to the church. [See July 30, 1971 entry]

JUNE 15, 1969

In a Scientology minister's draft exemption case, the US Court of Appeals ruled that the Church of Scientology was recognized as a church.

NOVEMBER 18, 1969

A court in Western Australia dismissed a case brought against the Hubbard Association of Scientologists International (HASI) for "practicing Scientology." (This case negated an unconstitutional law that had attempted to prohibit the practice of Scientology, following an "inquiry" held in the state of Victoria in 1965.) [See May 25, 1973 entry]

MAY 20, 1970

Narconon Los Angeles was recognized by the state of California as a nonprofit corporation.

OCTOBER 27, 1970

The Church of Scientology of Adelaide, Australia was granted exemption from payment of property tax on the basis that the property occupied by the church was used for religious purposes in the advancement of a religion.

DECEMBER 2, 1970

The Perth, Australia Court of Petty Sessions recognized Scientology as a religion and exempted a minister of the church from military service.

JULY 30, 1971

The US District Court for the District of Columbia ordered the Food and Drug Administration to return to the Church the E-Meters and books that had been seized from the Founding Church 8 years earlier. In its decision, the court recognized the Church's constitutional right to protection from the government's excessive entanglement with religion. [See February 5, 1969 entry]

JUNE 19, 1972

In an immigration case concerning a foreign Scientology minister who sought permanent residence in St. Louis, Missouri, the court acknowledged the religious nature of the Church, recognized the applicant's status as a minister of the Scientology religion and granted her permanent residence in the United States on the basis of her status as a minister.

DECEMBER 22, 1972

Applied Scholastics Los Angeles was granted tax-exempt status by the Internal Revenue Service.

FEBRUARY 7, 1973

The attorney general of Australia wrote to the president of the Church announcing that the Church was now officially a recognized denomination. This letter provided federal recognition of the Church of Scientology in Australia.

MARCH 1, 1973

The IRS acknowledged the tax-exempt status of the Church of Scientology, Mission of Davis, California.

MAY 25, 1973

The Western Australia legislation aimed at restricting the activities of the Church of Scientology was formally repealed. [See November 18, 1969 entry]

JULY 27, 1973

The church in New South Wales, Australia was granted exemption from the payment of payroll tax.

NOVEMBER 2, 1973

The church of Scientology in Calgary, Alberta, Canada was exempted from paying business tax on the basis of being a nonprofit organization.

NOVEMBER 21, 1973

The Church of Scientology of Toronto was granted exemption from payment of business tax on the basis of being a religion.

NOVEMBER 22, 1973

The Church of Scientology was recognized as a bona fide religion by the Bavarian Ministry of Education and Culture.

MARCH 4, 1974

The Church of Scientology, Mission of Fort Lauderdale, Florida was recognized as a religious organization and granted exemption from sales and use tax by the Florida Department of Revenue.

MARCH 15, 1974

The Church of Scientology of Minnesota was granted exemption from paying income tax and employer's excise tax by the state Department of Revenue.

APRIL 11, 1974

The "Scientology Prohibition Act" of 1968, which had unsuccessfully attempted to prevent the practice of Scientology in South Australia, was repealed by the South Australian Parliament.

APRIL 18, 1974

A minister of the Church of Scientology of New Zealand was officially registered under the Marriage Act to perform marriage ceremonies.

APRIL 23, 1974

The minister for immigration in Australia lifted all previous restrictions on foreign Scientologists immigrating to Australia.

JULY 3, 1974

On March 11, 1970 the World Federation for Mental Health, Incorporated (WFMH), issued a Writ of Summons for defamation against the Church for statements made in *Freedom* magazine in the United Kingdom, characterizing the WFMH as a vast psychiatric conspiracy aiming to dominate and control governments by the use of degrading psychiatric treatment and misleading advice. On July 3, 1974, by order of Master Waldman, the action was dismissed with costs of £4,804.86 (approximately $10,000) and interest awarded against the WFMH. The WFMH subsequently retreated to Canada and reincorporated there to avoid payment.

OCTOBER 17, 1974

A decree was received from the Finance Management Department of the City of

Zurich, Switzerland recognizing the Church of Scientology as a religious organization and exempting the Church from state and general municipal taxes.

DECEMBER 30, 1974

The US Department of State officially recognized the Church of Scientology as a religious denomination having a bona fide organization in the United States.

JANUARY 20, 1975

Narconon Los Angeles was officially recognized by the Internal Revenue Service as a nonprofit, tax-exempt organization.

APRIL 7, 1975

The church of Scientology in Las Vegas, Nevada was granted exemption from payment of city business-license tax based on its status as a nonprofit religious organization.

JUNE 4, 1975

The church of Scientology in Hawaii was granted tax-exempt status after the deposition testimony of an IRS agent revealed that the IRS' grounds for attempting to revoke the church's exemption had no basis in fact.

JUNE 16, 1975

The church of Scientology in Portland, Oregon was granted tax-exempt status by the Internal Revenue Service as a nonprofit religious organization.

JUNE 19, 1975

The church of Scientology in Seattle, Washington was granted tax-exempt status as a nonprofit religious organization by the Internal Revenue Service.

JULY 14, 1975

The Church of Scientology of Miami was granted tax-exempt status as a nonprofit religious organization by the Internal Revenue Service.

JULY 18, 1975

The churches of Scientology in Detroit and Buffalo were granted tax-exempt status by the Internal Revenue Service as nonprofit religious organizations.

JULY 22, 1975

The church of Scientology in Boston was granted tax-exempt status by the Internal Revenue Service as a nonprofit religious organization.

JULY 30, 1975

The church of Scientology in Nevada was granted tax-exempt status by the Internal Revenue Service as a nonprofit religious organization.

JULY 31, 1975

The church of Scientology in Minnesota was granted tax-exempt status by the Internal Revenue Service as a nonprofit religious organization.

AUGUST 4, 1975

The church of Scientology in Missouri was granted tax-exempt status by the Internal Revenue Service as a nonprofit religious organization.

AUGUST 28, 1975

The church of Scientology in Buffalo, New York was granted exemption from payment of property tax.

SEPTEMBER 5, 1975

The church of Scientology in Texas was granted tax-exempt status by the Internal Revenue Service as a nonprofit religious organization.

SEPTEMBER 18, 1975

The church of Scientology in Sacramento, California was granted tax-exempt status by the Internal Revenue Service as a nonprofit religious organization.

SEPTEMBER 26, 1975

The Church of Scientology of Florida was confirmed by the Department of Revenue as being exempt from Florida corporation income tax as a nonprofit organization.

AUGUST 1976

Mr. Herbert Graham, Deputy Premier of Western Australia, formally apologized for the passing of earlier legislation which had banned Scientology in his state, describing it as "the blackest day in the political history of Western Australia."

DECEMBER 8, 1976

In a decision in a case before the Stuttgart District Court, the Church of Scientology was recognized as a religious community.

MARCH 28, 1977

The Church of Scientology of New York's status as a tax-exempt, nonprofit religious organization, first recognized in 1957, was reconfirmed by the Internal Revenue Service.

JUNE 23, 1978

Based on its status as a religion, the Church of Scientology of Sydney, Australia was granted exemption from sales tax by the Australian Taxation Office.

DECEMBER 19, 1978

The Australian Taxation Office granted the Church of Scientology of Western Australia exemption from income tax based on its religious status.

FEBRUARY 9, 1979

In a judgment in a Church of Scientology tax case in Munich, Germany the court stated: "Scientology is not only a religion in the oldest sense of the word but also a religion in the common linguistic usage of the word."

MARCH 13, 1979

The church of Scientology in Melbourne, Australia was granted exemption from payment of income tax on the basis of being a religion.

FEBRUARY 12, 1980

In a tax case involving the Church of Scientology of California, the IRS stipulated that "Scientology is and at all relevant times was a religion within the purview of the First Amendment to the Constitution of the United States."

FEBRUARY 20, 1980

The Church of Scientology of St. Louis, Missouri was granted property tax exemption by the City of St. Louis on the basis that the church was a bona fide religion and used its property exclusively for religious purposes.

FEBRUARY 29, 1980

An appeals court acquitted a former executive of the church of Scientology in Paris of fraud charges, and at the same time recognized the Church as a religion. The appeals court decision overturned a lower court decision from 1978 when this executive had been investigated and tried in absentia. Two other former church executives who were similarly tried in 1978 were fully acquitted by the appeals court on December 21, 1981 and July 13, 1982.

JULY 16, 1980

A 1968 ban on the entry of foreign Church of Scientology students into the United Kingdom to study or work was lifted by the secretary of state for the Home Office.

AUGUST 29, 1980

The Church of Scientology of San Diego, California was granted tax-exempt status by the Internal Revenue Service as a nonprofit religious organization.

FEBRUARY 26, 1981

The Church of Scientology, Mission of Salt Lake City, Utah was acknowledged as tax exempt by the Internal Revenue Service as a nonprofit religious organization.

AUGUST 14, 1981

The Church of Scientology of San Francisco was granted exemption from California state taxes by the California Franchise Tax Board as a nonprofit religious organization.

OCTOBER 23, 1981

In a suit brought by a Scientologist, the DC Court of Appeals ruled for the first time that Interpol was not immune to suit in the United States for wrongs committed against US citizens.

NOVEMBER 1, 1981

The Church of Scientology International was founded, signaling a new era of Scientology management. A strong standardized corporate structure was required to facilitate the rapid expansion of Scientology and maintain high ethical standards in a widespread international network of churches. This followed a series of Sea Org inspections that discovered that the Guardian's Office (which had been established in 1966 to protect the Church from external attacks and care for its legal matters) had become entirely autonomous and corrupt. The Guardian's Office had been infiltrated by individuals antithetical to Scientology and had become an organization that operated completely apart from the day-to-day activities of the Church. Their secret actions in violation of Church policy had resulted in eleven members being jailed for obstruction of justice. Sea Organization executives overthrew the Guardian's Office and disbanded it. Part of the measures taken to ensure a similar situation could never recur was the formation of the Religious Technology Center on 1 January 1982. L. Ron Hubbard bestowed the trademarks of Scientology to RTC, whose purpose is to safeguard the proper use of the marks and ensure they remain in good hands and are properly used.

MAY 3, 1982

The Oregon State Court of Appeals threw out a 1979 verdict from an earlier trial against the church of Scientology in Portland and ordered a new trial for a woman who sued the church after being deprogramed and forced to renounce her religion. In its ruling, the Court of Appeals officially recognized Scientology as a bona fide religion. [See July 16, 1985 entry]

MAY 6, 1982

The church of Scientology in Montreal, Quebec, Canada obtained property tax exemption because it was recognized that the church building was owned by a religious institution.

JUNE 29, 1982

In a joint meeting of commonwealth and state attorneys general in Victoria, Australia, long-unenforced legislation against the practice of Scientology, which had been in place in Victoria since the 60s, was repealed.

AUGUST 19, 1982

The Church of Scientology of Toronto, Ontario, Canada was granted unconditional exemption by the Customs and Excise Department from payment of federal sales tax on the sale of books written by L. Ron Hubbard.

JANUARY 7, 1983

The Regional Court in Munich, Germany validated the Church's policy on refunds, saying that the plaintiff had no valid claim to receive more money than the amount worked out as refundable in accordance with Church policy.

JANUARY 19, 1983

In a case brought by the Church to force the FBI and other US agencies to cease their unconstitutional conduct against the Church, the US District Court in Washington, DC found that the FBI had been improperly withholding documents concerning the Church and ordered the documents released. The court ruled the Church of Scientology was to be treated like all other mainstream denominations.

JUNE 18, 1983

A bogus probate case alleging, incredibly, that L. Ron Hubbard had passed away, filed in Riverside, California was dismissed. The judge found that L. Ron Hubbard was doing very well, that his personal affairs were in good order and that he was entitled to his privacy.

JUNE 28, 1983

A Massachusetts Superior Court judge ruled that the Church of Scientology "satisfies the criteria of a religion" as "the teachings involve a theory of the spiritual nature of man." The ruling also stated that the practice of auditing is central to the practice of Scientology, and that the organization of the Church has many resemblances to recognized hierarchical religious institutions.

OCTOBER 27, 1983

The Church of Scientology won a case against the high commissioner for payroll tax in Australia. In a 5–0 decision issued by the High Court of Australia, the judges stated: "The conclusion that it is a religious institution entitled to the tax exemption is irresistible." During this case, the Church established the legal definition of religion for the Australian Constitution for the first time in history.

JANUARY 23, 1984

The church of Scientology in Sydney, Australia was granted exemption from the payment of land tax, based on the fact that Scientology is a religion.

FEBRUARY 27, 1984

In four consolidated cases in Los Angeles, California, the US District Court of the Central District of California ruled: "This court finds that the Church of Scientology is a religion within the meaning of the First Amendment. The beliefs and ideas of Scientology address ultimate concerns—the nature of the person and the individual's relationship to the universe."

MARCH 27, 1984

An appeals court upheld a November 1982 decision that found the Vancouver church of Scientology exempt from property tax as a religious organization.

MAY 11, 1984

A judge in Boston, Massachusetts ruled: "As far as I am concerned, Scientology is a religion. I don't think there should be any serious doubt about that. I will take judicial notice that it is a religion, period."

JANUARY 28, 1985

In a defamation case brought by a Scientologist against the International Criminal Police Organization (Interpol), Interpol was ordered to pay $55,681 in costs and attorney fees and also retracted the document containing false information on the Scientologist, which it had circulated to 125 countries.

JANUARY 30, 1985

The Stuttgart District Court reversed an earlier negative lower court ruling concerning church proselytizing because: "The conduct of the concerned served a direct religious purpose."

APRIL 30, 1985

The US Department of Justice was ordered to pay $17,097.72 to the Church of Scientology for improperly withholding documents which the Church had a right to receive, and for noncompliance with court orders.

MAY 15, 1985

The Social Security Agency of Angers, France ruled that a staff member of the Church of Scientology of Angers was not required to make Social Security payments because his commitment to the Church was of a purely spiritual nature and his work could not be compared to that of a normal wage earner.

MAY 20, 1985

A case was won in the District Court of Stuttgart acknowledging the Church's dissemination activities as part of the pursuit of its religion.

JUNE 5, 1985

In the case of the Church vs. the City of Munich, the appeals court announced that the court accepts (a) that auditing is an essential part of the teachings of Scientology according to the self-understanding of the Church; (b) that based on this, the term "commercial enterprise" cannot be applied to the Church.

JUNE 11, 1985

The Social Security Agency in Pau, France issued a decision granting exemption from making Social Security payments, due to the religious nature of the Scientologists' work.

JULY 16, 1985

A judge in Multnomah County, Oregon declared a mistrial in a second case involving a former parishioner of the church who had been kidnapped by deprogramers and then forced to renounce her religion. The judge's decision threw out a 39-million-dollar verdict against the church and declared that the court had not properly protected the rights of the church as a religion during the trial. This reversal came about after tens of thousands of Scientologists from around the world traveled to Portland for the first Religious Freedom Crusade and stood, shoulder to shoulder for 60 days, until justice was done. [See May 3, 1982 entry]

OCTOBER 28, 1985

The Church of Scientology of Melbourne, Australia was exempted from paying city taxes on the basis of being a religion.

NOVEMBER 20, 1985

A proceeding in the Padova Court in Italy for alleged labor law violations was dismissed because no violations were found; the church pursued religious aims; and church staff did not fall within the purview of the labor law.

1986

Education Alive South Africa was granted official tax-exempt status from the Commissioner of Inland Tax Revenue.

MARCH 26, 1986

In the United Kingdom, a permanent injunction was obtained against a group of individuals using copyrighted Church scriptures without permission. The group was also ordered to pay the costs of the case and £5,000 in damages.

MAY 5, 1986

The Bologna Court in Italy dismissed a baseless prosecution against Scientology staff on the basis that no crime was committed, also finding the Church to be a religion.

JUNE 5, 1986

A case involving the incorporation of the Scientology Mission of Ulm, Germany was decided in the Church's favor, validating the mission as a religious organization.

JUNE 23, 1986

In a court case involving an individual using copyrighted Church scriptures without permission, the United States Court of Appeals for the Second Circuit upheld the Religious Technology Center's ownership of the trademarks of Dianetics and Scientology and the right of the Church of Scientology International to enforce the proper use of the marks.

JULY 16, 1986

Five Seattle "deprogramers" pleaded guilty to charges that they had attempted to force a Scientologist to give up her chosen religious beliefs. The deprogramers were sentenced to one year's probation and fined $5,000.

AUGUST 11, 1986

A court in Denmark ordered three individuals to pay $175,000 in damages for theft of confidential Scientology scriptures from the Church of Scientology.

SEPTEMBER 4, 1986

All Scientology churches and missions in California were exempted from California State Unemployment Insurance Taxes, retroactive to January 1, 1984.

DECEMBER 8, 1986

The Immigration and Naturalization Service (INS) National Office issued an official ruling to regional and local INS offices, stating that the Church of Scientology is a bona fide religion and is to be treated as any other religion.

1987–1988

All Canadian churches of Scientology received official recognition from the Revenue Department of the federal government, validating staff members of those churches as religious workers and exempting the churches from unemployment insurance and pension plan payments for their staff.

JUNE 29, 1987

An injunction was granted by the Court of Appeal in Bern, Switzerland against the illegal duplication of copyrighted taped lectures on Scientology by L. Ron Hubbard.

NOVEMBER 19, 1987

Deprogramer Ted Patrick was ordered by a US District Court judge in Los Angeles to pay $184,900 in attorney fees and sanctions to a member of the Church of Scientology who had been kidnapped by

Patrick in 1981 and held against her will for 38 days.

DECEMBER 29, 1987

Two deprogramers from England were convicted in Germany on charges of kidnapping a 32-year-old Scientologist. They spent six weeks in jail, were tried, sentenced and deported to England.

DECEMBER 31, 1987

The Tax Office in Pau, France issued a decision concerning the Pau mission, stating that donations for Scientology courses and auditing were tax exempt.

FEBRUARY 17, 1988

The Regional Court in Hamburg, Germany recognized Scientology as a bona fide religion and granted incorporation as a religious organization to the Church of Scientology's Hamburg Celebrity Centre.

MARCH 17, 1988

A German court cancelled proceedings against the Frankfurt mission, reaffirming the mission's incorporation as a charitable organization.

APRIL 7, 1988

The church of Scientology in Portugal was recognized and registered as a religious organization.

JUNE 10, 1988

The Inspector of Corporate Taxes in Amsterdam, Holland granted exemption from value added tax (VAT) and corporate tax to the Church of Scientology Amsterdam and cancelled assessments for corporate taxes for prior years.

JUNE 16, 1988

The Utah State Tax Commission found the Church of Scientology, Mission of Salt Lake City to be a religious institution and granted exemption from state sales and use tax.

JULY 11, 1988

Narconon in Germany was recognized as a nonprofit organization.

JULY 20, 1988

A Los Angeles Superior Court judge dismissed a billion-dollar lawsuit filed "on behalf of all disaffected Scientologists in the world." This was a total of 6 people—out of 8 million adherents around the world. Although the plaintiff's allegations were carried widely in the media, the judge dismissed the suit as entirely unsubstantiated. The judge ordered the plaintiffs on 7 separate occasions to provide evidence in support of their claims. They were unable to do so—he dismissed the suit as groundless. The dismissal was upheld on appeal in 1990 and costs of conducting this litigation were awarded to the Church.

SEPTEMBER 20, 1988

The week of 25 September was proclaimed by Congress and President Ronald Reagan as National Religious Freedom Week, due in large part to the work of members of the Church of Scientology in the US.

SEPTEMBER 28, 1988

The California governor signed into law a bill that protects churches and religious organizations from unfounded punitive damages claims. The law, first conceived by Scientologists, requires stringent proof of actual damages before such a claim is accepted for trial.

OCTOBER 12, 1988

In a Berlin, Germany decision, the court recognized the Church as a religion.

DECEMBER 30, 1988

The Tax Commission of the City of New York granted full property tax exemption to the church as a religious organization.

JANUARY 23, 1989

In Bolzano, Italy the court threw out charges against 11 Scientologists involved in the Bolzano church's delivery of the Purification Rundown. The charges, all based on false information supplied by a psychiatrist, were ruled as "unfounded" and the Scientologists were fully acquitted.

MARCH 1989

The District of Schöneberg in Berlin, recognized the church as a religious organization.

JUNE 7, 1989

The Frankfurt, Germany court ruled that auditing was the central religious practice of the Church and was covered under Freedom of Religion. The court further ruled that the religious services of the Church cannot be measured in monetary terms, and serve to forward the overall activity of the Church.

JUNE 21, 1989

The Church of Scientology was victorious in a United States Supreme Court ruling that upheld the right of Federal courts to place legal restraints on the IRS when there is reason to suspect that the tax agency is likely to violate the law and abuse its powers.

JULY 19, 1989

The City of Munich, Germany dropped a case against the church and affirmed its religious status.

OCTOBER 10, 1989

A Munich court ruled that the church should have no restrictions placed on its dissemination activities on city streets.

FEBRUARY 1990

The Federal Finance Office in Germany exempted Scientology Missions International, the mother church for Scientology missions, from paying tax on the tithes paid to them by German missions, and made the decision retroactive to 1982.

FEBRUARY 15, 1990

The Church of Scientology, Mission of Anchorage, Alaska was granted property tax exemption based on religious status.

FEBRUARY 15, 1990

Following 13 years of Trademark Office rejections of Church applications for trademark registration, the German Patent Court ruled that the term "Scientology" could be registered as a trademark.

MARCH 27, 1990

The Monza Tax Commission in Italy ruled that the Church of Scientology was a tax-exempt organization and should not be subject to taxation because it is a religion.

APRIL 4, 1990

The National Commission on Law Enforcement and Social Justice of San Francisco received tax-exempt status from the IRS.

MAY 23, 1990

The Citizens Commission on Human Rights was granted tax-exempt status by the IRS.

JUNE 18, 1990

A judge ruled in favor of the Church of Scientology of Boston and denied the IRS access to church records in the IRS's attempt to repeal the tax-exempt status of the Boston church, which was granted in 1975. The judge also reprimanded the IRS for intrusive and abusive practices. The IRS appealed the decision but lost again in the higher court. The church set a nationwide precedent that protects all religions from IRS meddling in church affairs.

SEPTEMBER 4, 1990

A Frankfurt, Germany court affirmed the religiosity of Scientology and its right to set up information stands and distribute information about Scientology throughout the city.

SEPTEMBER 18, 1990

A Valencia court ruled that Narconon is noncommercial and exempt from the payment of social security tax.

SEPTEMBER 20, 1990

A tax assessment against the church of Scientology in Torino, Italy was withdrawn because Scientology was a religion.

OCTOBER 31, 1990

In Hanover, Germany a court upheld the Church's constitutional right to disseminate its religion. The decision recognized the religiosity of the Church of Scientology.

JANUARY 16, 1991

In a lawsuit filed against two trademark infringers in Brisbane, Australia, a decision was obtained in favor of New Era Publications against all unauthorized use of the copyrighted materials of L. Ron Hubbard.

FEBRUARY 21, 1991
The local tax commission confirmed that the Scientology mission in Lecco, Italy did not have to pay value added tax because it is a church and delivering religious services.

MARCH 18, 1991
The United States Supreme Court issued a ruling that vacated an earlier $2.5 million judgment against the Church in a case involving a former member and sent the case to the California Court of Appeals with instructions to review its procedures against the US Constitution.

MAY 24, 1991
A US District Court judge in Los Angeles ruled that a Freedom of Information case brought by the Church against the Internal Revenue Service clearly served public benefit and caused the IRS to review its procedures which led to the resolution of nearly 1,000 similarly situated cases brought by other US citizens against the agency. The judge awarded monetary compensation to the Church of Scientology for the expenses it incurred in this suit against the IRS.

JUNE 3, 1991
A magistrate ordered the IRS to pay attorney fees for unnecessarily prolonging the litigation of a Freedom of Information Act suit filed by the Church of Scientology of Boston.

JUNE 21, 1991
A US District Court judge ordered monetary penalties against the IRS, who filed a motion solely to "harass, cause unnecessary delay, or needlessly increase the cost of litigation" in two Freedom of Information Act suits filed by the Church.

JULY 2, 1991
The Milan court in Italy after a two-year-long trial, acquitted all Scientologists charged with any crime; fully affirmed the religious nature of the Church; acknowledged the goal of Scientology as spiritual freedom; recognized the E-Meter as a religious artifact; and cited the technology of Scientology as effective in drug rehabilitation. This ended psychiatric-backed government attacks in Italy.

SEPTEMBER 1991
The Dresden mission in Germany became the first officially registered Scientology association in what had been East Germany, handing a defeat to the local anti-religious movement who opposed the registration.

OCTOBER 18, 1991
The Federal Constitutional Court of Germany, the highest court in the land, overturned a decree by the City of Hamburg forbidding the Citizens Commission on Human Rights, a Church-supported group, to distribute fliers in the streets.

NOVEMBER 4, 1991
After three years of investigation by Spanish authorities, the national court in Spain dropped all charges that were an attempted direct attack against the religion of Scientology, and had earlier resulted in the unwarranted arrest of several members of the church based on false information.

DECEMBER 2, 1991
In Toronto, the court ruled that the Ontario Provincial Police 1983 raid of the church, the largest raid in Canadian history, was illegal and that all 2 million documents seized in the raid had to be returned. The church is suing the Ontario Provincial Police (OPP) and the Ministry of the Attorney General for $19 million. The complaint is based on the grave and unwarranted intrusion into church affairs and seeks to recover the costs of legal proceedings required to gain return of the materials.

JANUARY 23, 1992
The Hamburg Administrative Court recognized the local church's right to freely disseminate its religion and lifted all bans on promotion that had been placed by the city of Hamburg.

JUNE 17, 1992
The Superior Court in Germany accepted the religious and philosophical nature of

the Church and concluded that the insinuations of a newspaper in Stuttgart were false facts and a violation of personal rights.

AUGUST 4, 1992

The Scientology Center of St. Petersburg became the first center in Russia to be incorporated.

AUGUST 14, 1992

The Oklahoma Board of Mental Health and Substance Abuse Services granted Narconon Chilocco an exemption from their certification process on the basis of Narconon's accreditation by the prestigious Commission on Accreditation of Rehabilitation Facilities.

AUGUST 17, 1992

In the first ruling of its kind, the US Ninth Circuit Court of Appeals ruled that the public have the right to sue the IRS to remove false information from their files. The case was brought to court by two Scientologists who had discovered a false and damaging report in their IRS files.

AUGUST 17, 1992

A United States District Court judge in Los Angeles ordered the IRS to pay $16,881.56 in attorney fees and costs to the Church of Scientology Western United States. The church prevailed in a Freedom of Information Act suit against the IRS and caused the IRS to release records that it had improperly withheld.

AUGUST 19, 1992

In cases involving the Church of Scientology International and the Church of Scientology Western United States, the US Court of Appeals for the Ninth Circuit held that the IRS must be held to a higher standard of proof when seeking records from churches.

OCTOBER 26, 1992

The Oklahoma State Department of Health granted Narconon Chilocco its license—the final administrative step that officially allows Narconon Chilocco to operate as a drug rehabilitation facility.

NOVEMBER 16, 1992

In a case brought against the IRS, the Church of Scientology of California won a unanimous decision by the US Supreme Court which protects the constitutional right to privacy of all US citizens. The precedent-setting ruling by nine judges held that "A person's interest in maintaining the privacy of his 'papers and effects' is of sufficient importance to merit constitutional protection."

NOVEMBER 19, 1992

The Italian Constitutional Court, the highest court in the country, upheld the Church's interpretation of the nation's tax law as correct, quashing a Torino prosecutor's attempt to declare this longstanding law unconstitutional. On the same day, the Church in Novara emerged victorious in another tax case when the judge dismissed charges ruling that the Church was to be recognized as a religion not merely pursuant to its statutes, "but also for the nature and the ends of the activities actually brought about."

DECEMBER 9, 1992

The Church's religious practices and policies were upheld by the Stuttgart State Court in Germany when it ruled against a claimant suing for a refund more than a year after he had received service. The court, in its ruling, affirmed that Scientology is religious in nature, that auditing addresses the spirit and any physical benefit is incidental, not the main objective, and that the ninety-day rule for requesting a refund was legally binding and applicable in the case.

DECEMBER 10, 1992

In Los Angeles, California, the United States District Court ordered the IRS to release to a Scientologist documents concerning him that they were holding. The judge ruled that the IRS had failed to demonstrate any legitimate law enforcement purpose relating to those documents.

JANUARY 8, 1993

The US District Court in Los Angeles issued a permanent injunction against a hypnotherapist who was infringing on a Church trademark, forbidding him further use of the mark. The court ordered that the infringer turn over to Religious Technology Center (for destruction) any and all labels, signs, prints, packages, wrappers, merchandise and advertisements bearing that mark or any confusingly similar symbol. Religious Technology Center and Church of Scientology International were also awarded damages and all legal fees totaling more than a quarter of a million dollars.

JANUARY 19, 1993

In Los Angeles, California, the IRS was ordered by a US District Court judge to turn over to the Church documents they had collected during two trumped-up investigations. Surrendering these documents was hotly contested by the IRS, because they proved that there was no wrongdoing by the Church. However, the magistrate's order was upheld by both a district judge and the Court of Appeals, and the documents were released.

MARCH 15, 1993

A judge of the US District Court in Los Angeles, California, required the IRS to release documents on the Church which they had previously withheld by claiming that the materials were part of an ongoing investigation. When it was proven by the Church that the investigation being referred to actually *ended* in May 1985, the court ruled that all reports in the files after May 1985 were not legitimately part of that investigation and thus must be released to the Church.

APRIL 5, 1993

A judge in Atlanta, Georgia gave full religious recognition to the Church of Scientology and dismissed a suit brought against the Atlanta church on the basis that the suit violated the Church's religious freedoms under the United States Constitution.

SEPTEMBER 28, 1993

A federal judge in San Diego, California awarded the Church of Scientology International a permanent injunction against a trademark infringer. The ruling upholds the Church's rights to use the copyright and trade secret laws to protect the tech against unlawful copying and use. The same judge later ordered the infringer to pay $52,000 in damages to the Church.

SEPTEMBER 30, 1993

The United States Court of Appeals for the Eleventh Circuit gave full religious recognition to the Flag Service Organization, invalidating a Clearwater, Florida ordinance designed to harass the Church by requiring it register all of its fundraising activities; disclose its budget, staff salaries and bank connections; give the names of FSMs, the amounts and nature of parishioner donations as well as the intended use of these funds. The court described the objective of the city in passing the ordinance as "patently offensive to the First Amendment [of the United States Constitution]." The court also awarded the Church its costs in defeating an earlier version of this ordinance.

1 OCTOBER 1993

The IRS issued a series of rulings expressly recognizing that the Church of Scientology and all of its subordinate churches and related charitable and educational institutions (such as ABLE, Narconon and Applied Scholastics) in the United States are tax-exempt organizations. The ruling also specifically designates the International Association of Scientologists as a tax-exempt religious entity. This action, which encompassed not only every Scientology church in the US but also several important Scientology organizations outside the US (including Flag Ship Service Org and New Era Publications), signified that the IRS—and the US government—had formally recognized that the Church operates exclusively for religious purposes and that Scientology, as a *bona fide* religion, is beneficial to society as a whole. Another consequence of this action was that donations to the Church in the US, including those for auditing and training, qualify as charitable contributions and could be claimed as deductions on contributors' federal and state income tax returns.

Chapter 35

The Holidays of Scientology

To commemorate memorable dates in its history, the Church of Scientology observes holidays in all parts of the world through the course of the year. The most significant are celebrated with internationally telecast events to link all Scientology churches. Regular church services are suspended for events, and in those cities where the local church simply cannot accommodate the thousands of parishioners attending the event, suitable auditoriums are rented. Major events are important to every Scientologist, be they in Africa, America, Asia, Australia or Europe as they provide a special sense of unity.

The major Scientology events feature briefings by senior church members on such subjects as the introduction of L. Ron Hubbard's works into new nations or sectors of society, the outstanding accomplishments of individual Scientologists and reviews of worldwide growth. Events further feature releases of new Scientology books, materials, courses and society betterment programs—all cause for celebration. Although highly dignified affairs, they are also joyous.

Other occasions, such as the founding of the church in a particular country or a city, may be locally observed. Traditional holidays, such as Christmas, Easter, the United States Independence Day and French Bastille Day are not listed, although Scientologists celebrate these occasions in their own countries according to custom. The following calendar lists major holidays around the world.

JANUARY

16 Recognition Day Africa, to celebrate recognition in 1975 of the church of Scientology in South Africa.

25 Criminon Day, to celebrate the 1970 founding of Criminon, the prison rehabilitation program.

28 National Founding Day New Zealand, to celebrate the founding of the first church in New Zealand, the Church of Scientology Auckland in 1955.

FEBRUARY

7 Recognition Day Australia, to celebrate the recognition in 1973 of the Church of Scientology across Australia, by the then Federal Attorney General, Senator Lionel Murphy. Scientology was recognized under Section 26 of the Commonwealth Marriage Act, 1961–1966.

18 National Founding Day United States, to celebrate the founding of the first church in the US, the Church of Scientology Los Angeles in 1954.

19 Narconon Day. On this day in 1966, an Arizona State Prison inmate initiated the Narconon drug rehabilitation program, which utilizes the technology of L. Ron Hubbard. Narconon has expanded to a network of more than thirty programs in countries throughout the world.

22 Celebrity Day, to celebrate the opening of the Celebrity Centre International in Los Angeles in 1970, dedicated to the rehabilitation of the culture through art.

MARCH

5 CCHR Day, to mark the formation in 1969 of the Citizens Commission on Human Rights. First formed in England, the commission is now a worldwide organization which has achieved major reforms internationally against psychiatric abuses.

13 MARCH

L. Ron Hubbard's Birthday

The birthday of the Founder of Dianetics and Scientology, March 13, 1911, is commemorated each year with a major celebration honoring L. Ron Hubbard's achievements and his continuing contributions to mankind. Outstanding churches and missions are recognized for service to their parishioners and communities during the previous year.

13 National Founding Day Belgium, to celebrate the founding of the first church in Belgium, the Church of Scientology Brussels in 1980.

13 National Founding Day Holland, to celebrate the founding of the first church in Holland, the Church of Scientology Amsterdam in 1972.

16 National Founding Day Italy, to celebrate the founding of the first church in Italy, the Church of Scientology Milano in 1978.

19 National Founding Day Venezuela, to celebrate the founding of the first Dianetics center in Venezuela, the Asociación Cultural Dianética de Venezuela, A.C., in 1981.

24 Student Day, to celebrate the commencement of the Saint Hill Special Briefing Course in 1961. The course was begun at Saint Hill Manor, East Grinstead, Sussex and in 1968 was expanded to the American Saint Hill Organization in Los Angeles. Today, the Saint Hill Special Briefing Course is also available in Copenhagen, Denmark; Sydney, Australia and at the Flag Land Base. This course, the largest in Scientology, covers the chronological development of Dianetics and Scientology.

31 National Founding Day Austria, to celebrate the founding of the first church in Austria, the Church of Scientology Vienna in 1971.

APRIL

4 Recognition Day Germany, to celebrate the recognition in 1974 of the church of Scientology in Munich.

16 National Founding Day Sweden, to celebrate the founding of the first church in Sweden, the Church of Scientology Göteborg in 1969.

20 L. Ron Hubbard Exhibition Day, to celebrate the opening in 1991 of the L. Ron Hubbard Life Exhibition in Hollywood, California. Featuring impressive audiovisual displays on the life and accomplishments of L. Ron Hubbard, the exhibition is visited by thousands of Scientologists and non-Scientologists annually.

25 Recognition Day New Zealand, to celebrate recognition of the Church in 1974 with Scientology ministers licensed to perform marriages.

MAY

9 MAY

Anniversary of Dianetics

The annual international celebration on this day salutes the publication of *Dianetics: The Modern Science of Mental Health* on May 9, 1950. It is the occasion when Scientologists and community leaders from around the world acknowledge the contributions Dianetics has made to the betterment of individuals and society at large and the daily miracles that occur through its widespread application.

15 National Founding Day Colombia, to celebrate the founding in 1980 of the first Dianetics center in Colombia, the Centro Cultural de Dianética in Bogotá.

22 National Founding Day Switzerland, to celebrate the founding of the first church in Switzerland, the Church of Scientology Basel in 1974.

25 Integrity Day, to mark the 1965 release by L. Ron Hubbard of his studies on ethics—the reason and contemplation of optimum survival.

JUNE

5 National Founding Day Denmark, to celebrate the founding of the first church in Denmark, the Church of Scientology Denmark in 1968.

6 JUNE

Maiden Voyage Anniversary

On this date in 1988, the Sea Org Motor Vessel *Freewinds* began her maiden voyage, during which

New OT VIII was released publicly. In memory of that day, OT VIII completions convene aboard the *Freewinds* for a week of special briefings and acknowledgments to New OT VIII completions for their work in disseminating and expanding Scientology.

12 National Founding Day Scotland, to celebrate the founding of the Hubbard Academy of Personal Independence in Edinburgh, Scotland in 1968.

17 National Founding Day Portugal, to celebrate the founding in 1982 of the first Dianetics institute in Portugal, the Instituto de Dianética in Lisbon.

18 Academy Day, in celebration of the 1964 release of L. Ron Hubbard's study technology.

26 National Founding Day Norway, to celebrate the founding of the first church in Norway, the Church of Scientology Oslo in 1980.

JULY

2 Advanced Organization Founding Day Australia-New Zealand-Oceania, to celebrate the opening in 1983 of the Advanced Organization and Saint Hill in Sydney.

7 Advanced Organization Founding Day Europe, to celebrate the opening of the Advanced Organization Denmark in 1969.

21 Founding Day Washington, DC, to celebrate the incorporation in 1955 of the Founding Church of Scientology and the opening of the first Academy of Scientology.

AUGUST

12 Sea Org Day, commemorating the establishment of the Sea Organization in 1967, is celebrated by all Sea Organization members throughout the world. Rank and rating promotion ceremonies are held, and speeches are delivered by leading Sea Organization members.

13 Advanced Organization Founding Day Los Angeles, to celebrate the opening of the American Saint Hill Organization and the Advanced Organization Los Angeles in 1968.

17 Advanced Organization Founding Day United Kingdom, to celebrate the opening of Advanced Organization United Kingdom at Saint Hill, Sussex, England in 1970.

SEPTEMBER

4 Clear Day, to mark the inauguration of the Clearing Course in 1965. First released at Saint Hill Manor, the course is now available to Scientologists at Advanced Organizations in the United Kingdom, the United States, Denmark and Australia as well as at the Flag Service Organization in Florida.

8 National Founding Day Canada, to celebrate the founding of the first church in Canada, the Church of Scientology Toronto in 1967.

SECOND SUNDAY IN SEPTEMBER

Auditor's Day

On this day auditors are acknowledged for their dedication in bringing man up the Bridge to Total Freedom. Top auditors from around the world are recognized for their efforts in helping their fellow man.

18 National Founding Day Zimbabwe, to celebrate the founding of the first church in Zimbabwe, the Church of Scientology Bulawayo in 1967.

20 National Founding Day Mexico, to celebrate the founding of the first Dianetics institute in Mexico, the Instituto de Filosofía Aplicada, A.C., in 1979.

21 National Founding Day England, to celebrate the beginning of Scientology in England, marking the opening of the London branch of the Hubbard Association of Scientologists International in 1952.

25 National Founding Day Israel, to celebrate the beginning of the first Scientology and Dianetics college in Tel Aviv, Israel in 1980.

OCTOBER

7 OCTOBER

International Association of Scientologists (IAS) Anniversary

Held at a different host city each year, members of the IAS gather to commemorate the founding of the IAS and to rededicate themselves to its aims. The annual IAS freedom awards are presented. This event coincides with the annual convention of IAS delegates.

15 National Founding Day Germany, to celebrate the founding of the first church in Germany, the Church of Scientology Munich in 1970.

26 National Founding Day France, to celebrate the founding of the first church in France, the Church of Scientology Paris in 1959.

NOVEMBER

11 National Founding Day South Africa, to celebrate the founding of the first church in South Africa, the Church of Scientology Johannesburg in 1957.

27 Publications Day, to celebrate the opening of the first publications organization, Publications Worldwide, at Saint Hill Manor in 1967.

DECEMBER

6 Flag Land Base Day, to celebrate the opening of the Flag Land Base in Clearwater, Florida in 1975.

30 Freedom Day US, to celebrate the official recognition in 1974 of the Church of Scientology in the United States.

31 National Founding Day Spain, to celebrate the founding of the first church in Spain, the Church of Scientology Barcelona in 1981.

31 National Founding Day Japan, to celebrate the beginning of Scientology in Japan, which marks the opening of the Scientology Organization Tokyo in 1988.

31 DECEMBER

New Year's Eve

This event welcomes in the new year with a review of accomplishments over the previous year and a look forward to the upcoming year and plans for further reach into new areas of society with L. Ron Hubbard's technology. Stellar accomplishments of Scientology parishioners helping new people to move up the Bridge to Total Freedom are acknowledged.

CHAPTER 36

THE COMPLETE SERVICES OF SCIENTOLOGY

Services are offered in Scientology which cover its full range of philosophic and technical data. Courses and auditing services exist which address any aspect of existence. No matter a person's condition in life, Scientology has services which can help improve it.

The listings in this chapter categorize and provide useful information about Dianetics and Scientology courses and auditing services. These are laid out in a sequence usually followed by Scientologists in obtaining them. The approximate length of time a particular service takes is noted, in addition to where one would normally obtain that service.

There are different levels of Scientology organizations, from those that primarily deliver the most basic services to those that provide increasingly advanced levels of training and auditing.

The vast majority of Scientology services are available in most cities around the world. They are delivered by field auditors, field groups, missions and Scientology Class V organizations.

The advanced training and auditing services are available only at higher-level organizations, due to the degree of skill and experience required of the delivery staff, yet are still very accessible. These services are delivered at Saint Hills, Advanced Organizations, the Flag Service Organization and the Flag Ship Service Organization.

Higher-level organizations have the capability to deliver all services including lower-level courses and auditing services, though they do not specialize in them.

For more information on any Dianetics or Scientology services, contact the Scientology church or mission nearest you. A list of Scientology organizations is included at the back of this book.

INTRODUCTORY SERVICES

There is an introductory service available for any person depending on his personal interest or immediate concerns. Introductory services provide information to a person who has had no or little prior contact with Scientology, answer his questions and help him begin to understand himself better.

There is no definite sequence in which the introductory services described below need be done, or how many must be done. Often a person will do one or a few before enrolling onto training in an Academy of Scientology or auditing in the Hubbard Guidance Center.

Introductory services are most frequently obtained from field auditors, field groups, missions and Class V organizations, which specialize in delivering such services.

- ***Personality Testing and Evaluation***

Includes Oxford Capacity Analysis (personality profile which measures 10 different personality traits), IQ and aptitude tests. Trained staff evaluate the tests to help a person estimate his condition and make correct choices about his future.
1–2 hours

- ***Introductory Lectures***

Lectures by church staff help a person gain an elementary understanding of Scientology and answer his questions.
1 hour

- ***Introductory Tape Plays***

Selected lectures by L. Ron Hubbard convey basic principles of Dianetics and Scientology for people new to the subject.
1 hour

- ***Introductory Films and Videos***

There are many films or videos which show how Scientology helps people improve their lives and what it offers to anyone. These cover a variety of different subjects and one even features an interview with Mr. Hubbard discussing Scientology principles. Running time for these is approximately 30 minutes each.

BOOKS AND EXTENSION COURSES

L. Ron Hubbard's books open the route to improvement and a better life. Extension courses are designed to accompany them and help the reader gain a deeper understanding through home study of the knowledge they contain. Each extension course consists of 20 lessons which take the reader through a particular book. Lessons help the student greatly increase his comprehension of what he is reading. The student answers lesson questions and mails them in to the organization, where staff grade and return them. At least one lesson per week is the minimum rate of progress, though most courses can be entirely completed in 2 or 3 weeks.

Extension courses exist for nearly all Mr. Hubbard's books. They are useful for the beginner in gaining an understanding of the subject and for the veteran Scientologist in filling out his knowledge of the subject while not on major church services. For this reason, extension courses are regularly delivered by all churches of Scientology including higher organizations.
For additional data, see Chapter 7.

BASIC DIANETICS SERVICES

Those interested in Dianetics receive a thorough familiarity with the subject through the services listed here. Course lengths are figured on a part-time schedule of 3 hours per day, 5 days per week.
For additional data, see Chapter 8.

- ***Hubbard Dianetics Seminar***

Teaches basic auditing skills used in Dianetics and then gets students co-auditing with each other. Lets a person find out for himself that something can be done about the reactive mind. Students may co-audit as much as they want.
Seminars can be completed in 2 days full time (over a weekend) or during a week of evening classes, meeting each night for 3 hours. Naturally, this can take longer depending on how much co-auditing students want to do.

- ***Hubbard Dianetics Auditor Course***

The purpose of this course is to make a person into a Hubbard Dianetics Auditor and to see that the person receives Dianetics auditing himself. It contains further auditing techniques and a series of L. Ron Hubbard's lectures on Dianetics. Students co-audit as much as they want and make further progress toward Clear.
Course normally takes 3 weeks.

- ***Professional Dianetics Auditing***

This is auditing as taught on the Hubbard Dianetics Auditor Course but delivered by professionally trained staff in intensives of 12½ hours. A person receiving it does not train on Dianetics or audit another in return. Instead, professional Dianetics auditing is a rapid way to learn subjectively about Dianetics and experience its gains.

BASIC SCIENTOLOGY SERVICES

People interested in Scientology can do the following services. Each contains basic data and techniques of application. Course lengths are figured on a part-time schedule of 3 hours per day, 5 days per week.
For additional data, see Chapter 8.

- ***Life Improvement Courses***

These courses offer solutions to immediate concerns of the student. He learns specific things he can *do* about the condition he needs to change. Rapid improvement in a person's life is possible with these services in such areas as relationships, marriage, parenting, the workplace, personal values and others.
Most can be completed in 1 week.

- ***Success Through Communication Course***

Teaches communication skills for use in social or business situations. There are 18 separate drills learned, each one dealing with a different aspect of good communication.
1½ weeks

- ***Hubbard Qualified Scientologist Course***

Contains a broad survey of many Scientology basics and gives a student numerous techniques he can use to assist others. Students study from six of Mr. Hubbard's books, learn to audit and then give and receive as much co-auditing as they want. This course equips someone with a good working knowledge of fundamental Scientology data.
4 weeks

- ***Anatomy of the Human Mind Course***

Twenty lessons cover the makeup and mechanisms of the mind, man, life and the universe. Each course

period consists of a lecture on a different subject followed by demonstrations and practical application. Imparts a basic understanding of key principles of Dianetics and Scientology.
4 weeks—one lesson per evening for 20 evenings

- ***Basic Scientology Auditing Services***

One of the ways that people find out about Scientology is by receiving a session from an auditor.
For additional data, see Chapter 8.

- ***Introductory and Demonstration Auditing***

These auditing processes are ones designed for a person with no previous auditing experience and are delivered by professionally trained auditors. These processes result in a personal awareness that Scientology really works.
Individual sessions vary in length depending on the process being audited but may last an hour or more.

- ***Assist Auditing***

Scientology techniques can alleviate physical and mental trauma stemming from injuries or illnesses. These are used by Scientologists to help someone with burns, bruises, aches, pains, upsets and other such situations which occur in the course of living. Assists are rendered whenever the need for them arises, and are delivered by anyone qualified to do them.
Individual assist sessions vary in length depending on the assist process used.

- ***Group Processing***

Auditing procedures which can be delivered to a group of people simultaneously. Group Processing is delivered by any auditor who has been trained to audit groups. This type of auditing is not introductory as such; it is for persons who have previously received at least some individual auditing. Group Processing is regularly taken by Scientologists as it is an ideal service to receive when they are between major grades or levels of the Bridge. For this reason it is often also delivered in higher-level organizations.
Sessions last about 1 hour.

TRAINING SERVICES

Scientology organizations offer a wide range of training courses, for learning how to deliver auditing and gaining an understanding of the mechanics of life.

Most of the training services in Scientology are available at Class V organizations. More advanced training is available only at higher-level churches, which are Saint Hills, Advanced Organizations and the Flag Service Organization. Where delivery of a particular service is restricted to only certain organizations, this is designated below.

The average course lengths are estimated on the basis of a full-time study schedule of 8 hours per day, 5 days per week.
For additional data, see Chapter 14.

STUDY TECHNOLOGY SERVICES

■ *Basic Study Manual Course*

Consists of the fundamentals of study technology, fully illustrated to facilitate comprehension. Designed for teenagers or older. Due to its broad application, this course is also delivered by field auditors, groups and missions.
1 week

■ *Student Hat*

This is the course covering all aspects of study technology. It is a prerequisite course for all Academy training, enabling a student to fully understand his later studies or any subject in life. Also delivered by missions.
2 weeks

■ *Hubbard Method One Co-audit Course*

Rapidly trains two people to co-audit Method One Word Clearing, a technique which locates and clears away misunderstood words and symbols from one's past. Completion of Method One greatly speeds progress on further courses, in addition to recovering a person's earlier education. Student learns enough basics to enable him to successfully co-audit with another. Also delivered by missions.
Course takes 4 days up to the auditing part of the course, which varies but ordinarily lasts another 2 or 3 weeks.

■ *Primary Rundown*

A full course in study technology and augmented with thorough word clearing of all course materials. It results in the state of *superliteracy*, in which a person can comfortably and quickly take data from a page and be able at once to apply it.
4 weeks

KEY TO LIFE AND LIFE ORIENTATION COURSES

These are companion courses which boost any person to a much higher potential of ability and activity. Key to Life opens up all life to a person and puts him in communication. Directly following Key to Life, the Life Orientation Course enables him to use his new abilities to become competent in life.
For more information, see Chapters 11 and 12.
5 weeks for the Hubbard Key to Life Course; 4 weeks for the Hubbard Life Orientation Course

TR COURSES

TR courses contain drills in the cycle of communication, essential to auditing and any activity in life. *See Chapter 14 for more information.*

- ***New Hubbard Professional TR Course***

A prerequisite to all auditor training, this course teaches the skills needed to be successful in auditing. Drills in communication (called "TRs" and numbered from 0–4) are studied and thoroughly drilled to mastery. The course also contains special auditing processes, available on this course only, to enhance the student's understanding of his materials.
3 weeks

- ***Hubbard Professional Upper Indoc TR Course***

Teaches further TRs needed to become wholly effective in all areas of auditing. These drills build on TRs 0–4 and bring a student to proficiency in handling people and communication while greatly increasing the student's ability to get his intention across. This is also a prerequisite to classed auditor training.
1½ weeks

- ***Therapeutic TR Course***

While TRs are the backbone of auditor training, they also result in remarkable case gains. This course is designed primarily for those taking the individual auditing route up the Bridge. Students do the TRs and experience the personal benefits these give, which also aids them in their further auditing. As this course is delivered as part of a person's case handling, it is also available at missions.
1½ weeks

AUDITOR TRAINING COURSES

- ***Auditor Classification Courses***

Auditor training teaches an understanding of life and know-how to handle it. Each auditor classification covers different aspects of Scientology principles and skills of application. It results in a certificate authorizing one to audit corresponding to the level on the processing side of the Bridge (i.e., Academy Level 0 teaches one to audit Grade 0 processes).
See Chapter 14 for further information.

Academy Level 0 *Hubbard Recognized Scientologist*	2	wks
Academy Level I *Hubbard Trained Scientologist*	2	wks
Academy Level II *Hubbard Certified Auditor*	2	wks
Academy Level III *Hubbard Professional Auditor*	2	wks
Academy Level IV *Hubbard Advanced Auditor*	2	wks
Class IV Internship	3	wks
Class V *Hubbard New Era Dianetics Auditor Course*	3	wks
Class V Internship	3	wks
Class V Graduate *Hubbard Class V Graduate Auditor Course*	3½	wks
Class V Graduate Internship	3	wks
Class VA Graduate *Hubbard Expanded Dianetics Auditor Course*	1½	wks
Class VA Graduate Internship	3	wks

■ *Technical Specialist Courses*

These teach a classed auditor skills to deliver a specific rundown or action. Technical Specialist Courses round out an auditor's training by giving him technology to handle a wide variety of conditions.
See Chapter 14 for more information.

Scientology Drug Rundown	2½ days
Scientology Marriage Counseling	3 days
Hubbard Happiness Rundown	2 wks
Allergy or Asthma Rundown	2 days
Est Repair	2 days
Psych Treatment Repair	2 days
PTS/SP	10 days
South African Rundown	10 days
Student Booster Rundown	2 days
Vital Information Rundown	2 days
Introspection Rundown	2 days
PDH Detection and Handling	5 days
Handling Fear of People	2 days
Hubbard Senior Security Checker	2 wks
Hubbard False Purpose Rundown	2 wks
Fixated Person Rundown	2 days
Knowledge Rundown	2 days
New Vitality Rundown	10 days
Dynamic Sort Out Assessment	2 days
Int by Dynamics Rundown	1 day
Profession Intensive	1 day
Case Cracker Rundown	2 days
Clear Certainty Rundown *Delivered at the Flag Service Organization or Advanced Organizations only*	1 wk

■ *Saint Hill Special Briefing Course (Hubbard Senior Scientologist, Class VI Auditor)*

This is the most comprehensive course in Scientology. The 16 separate checksheets listed below cover a complete chronological study of Dianetics and Scientology. The student acquires all auditing skills taught below this level in addition to a full command of the philosophical aspects of the subject.
See Chapter 14 for more information.
Delivered only at Saint Hill organizations and the Flag Service Organization.

Level A:	*The Fundamentals of Dianetics*	3 wks
Level B:	*The Fundamentals of Scientology*	3½ wks
Level C:	*The Fundamentals of Havingness and Objectives Processing*	3½ wks
Level D:	*The Basics of Metering*	3 wks
Level E:	*The Principles of Auditing*	3 wks
Level F:	*The Handling of Problems*	2 wks
Level G:	*The Fundamentals of Confessionals*	4 wks
Level H:	*The Basics of Listing*	3 wks
Level I:	*The Basics of Listing and Nulling*	3½ wks
Level J:	*The Handling of ARC Breaks and Service Facsimiles*	3½ wks
Level K:	*The Recognition of Pc Indicators*	3 wks
Level L:	*The Fundamentals of the Grade Chart*	3 wks
Level M:	*The Basics of Case Repair and Resistive Cases*	3 wks
Level N:	*The Developments and Techniques of Modern Auditing*	3½ wks
Level O:	*Auditing the Expanded Lower Grades, New Era Dianetics and Repair Actions*	4 wks
Level P:	*Auditing Expanded Dianetics and the Specialist Rundowns*	4 wks
Class VI Internship		4 wks

■ ***Advanced Auditor Training***

These classifications teach highly advanced auditing rundowns and skills. The level of Class VIII stresses complete mastery of all auditing fundamentals and makes an auditor who achieves spectacular gains on any preclear through totally standard delivery of the technology.
See Chapter 14 for more information.

With the exception of Class VIII, delivery of advanced auditor training is only to contracted staff members of Scientology organizations. These are delivered by Saint Hills (Class VII), Advanced Organizations (Class VIII) and the Flag Service Organization (Class VII to XII).

Hubbard Class VII Auditor Course *Hubbard Graduate Auditor*	1	wk
Hubbard Class VII Internship	3	wks
Hubbard Class VIII Auditor Course *Hubbard Specialist of Standard Tech*	6	wks
Class VIII Internship	3	wks
Hubbard Class IX Auditor Course *Hubbard Advanced Courses Specialist*	1	wk
Class IX Internship	3	wks
Hubbard Class X Auditor Course	1½	wks
Class X Internship	3	wks
Hubbard Class XI Auditor Course	1	wk
Class XI Internship	3	wks
Hubbard Class XII Auditor Course	1	wk
Class XII Internship	3	wks

MINISTERIAL COURSE

Required for ordination as a minister of the Church of Scientology and for permanent certification as an auditor. Provides a survey of religious studies throughout history and a study of the religious ceremonies and traditional religious services of Scientology.

OTHER SCIENTOLOGY COURSES

These provide data and teach a variety of technical skills of a non-auditor nature, such as supervising the Purification program or a course room.

Keeping Scientology Working Course	1	wk
PTS/SP Course How to Confront and Shatter Suppression	2	wks
Purification Rundown In-Charge Course	1	wk
Professional Product Debug Course	4	days
Cramming Officer Course	5	days
Cramming Officer Internship	3	wks
Hubbard Mini Course Supervisor Course	5	days
Hubbard Professional Course Supervisor Course	3	wks
Hubbard Professional Course Supervisor Internship	2	wks
Hubbard Co-audit Supervisor Course	4	days
Hubbard Professional Word Clearer Course	2	wks
Hubbard Professional Word Clearer Internship	2	wks
Hubbard Basic Art Course *Delivered only by Celebrity Centre organizations and higher-level churches*	4	days

CASE SUPERVISOR TRAINING

■ *C/S Classification Courses*

Beyond auditor training come skills needed to supervise auditing done by others. Each course teaches a different level of case supervision skills, building on what is learned on lower classifications. (See Chapter 14 for more information.) C/S courses are delivered by the same organizations that deliver the corresponding auditor classification levels.

Class IV C/S Course	2½	wks
Class IV C/S Internship	3	wks
Class V C/S Course	1	wk
Class V C/S Internship	3	wks
Class V Graduate C/S Course	1	wk
Class V Graduate C/S Internship	3	wks
Class VA Graduate C/S Course	1	wk
Class VA Graduate C/S Internship	3	wks
Class VI C/S Course	2	wks
Class VI C/S Internship	2	wks
Class VII C/S Course	3	days
Class VII C/S Internship	1	wk
Class VIII C/S Course	4	wks
Class VIII C/S Internship	3	wks
Class IX C/S Course	1	wk
Class IX C/S Internship	2½	wks
Class XII C/S Course	1	wk
Class XII C/S Internship	2	wks

■ *C/S Specialist Courses*

These teach skills to case supervise specialized auditing actions. Delivery of the Solo C/S, Clear Certainty Rundown C/S and Solo New Era Dianetics for OTs C/S Courses is restricted to higher-level organizations.

Purification Rundown C/S Course	4	days
Purification Rundown C/S Internship	1	wk
False Purpose Rundown C/S Course	4	days
False Purpose Rundown C/S Internship	1	wk
Solo C/S Course	3	wks
Solo C/S Internship	3	wks
Clear Certainty Rundown C/S Course	2	wks
Solo New Era Dianetics for OTs C/S Course	1	wk
Solo New Era Dianetics for OTs C/S Internship	3	wks

ADMINISTRATIVE TRAINING

These teach administrative technology necessary for group survival. These courses mainly exist to train Church staff members but Scientologists can train on this third dynamic technology as well.

Staff Status I	2	days
Staff Status II	5	days
Executive Status I	2	days
Hubbard Causative Leadership Course *Not including auditing actions that are part of course*	2	days
Hubbard Elementary Data Series Evaluator's Course	2	wks
Organization Executive Course *Includes study of OEC Volumes 0–7*	16	wks
Basic Staff Hat (Organization Executive Course Volume 0)	2	wks
Organization Executive Course, Volume 1	3	wks
Organization Executive Course, Volume 2	2	wks
Organization Executive Course, Volume 3	1	wk
Organization Executive Course, Volume 4	3	wks
Organization Executive Course, Volume 5	2	wks
Organization Executive Course, Volume 6	3	wks
Organization Executive Course, Volume 7	3½	wks
Flag Executive Briefing Course *Delivered at the Flag Service Organization only*	6	wks
Hubbard Executive Data Series Evaluator's Course *Delivered at the Flag Service Organization only*	4	wks

OT HATTING COURSES

These are special courses comprised of L. Ron Hubbard's lecture series that are particularly relevant to Scientologists on OT levels. Each course covers a different body of knowledge about the thetan's potentials and capabilities. These are delivered at the Flag Ship Service Organization for the purpose of providing Scientologists with training on the state of Operating Thetan.

The Time Track of Theta	3	days
The Route to Infinity	3	days
Secrets of the MEST Universe	5	days
The Perception of Truth	3	days
Universes and the War Between Theta and MEST	16	days
The Phoenix Lectures	9	days
The Creation of Human Ability	12	days
The Power of Simplicity	12	days
The Anatomy of Cause	9	days
The Whole Track	3	days
The Solution to Entrapment	10	days
The Ability Congress	5	days
State of Man Congress	4	days
The Doctorate Series Course for OTs *Also delivered by Celebrity Centres, Advanced Organizations and the Flag Service Organization*	4	wks

SCIENTOLOGIST HATTING COURSES

Designed for experienced Scientologists, Scientologist Hatting Courses provide extensive data on a single aspect of Dianetics and Scientology technology, such as ethics, the Tone Scale and dissemination, which greatly increase a Scientologist's knowledge of these areas. These services are also available from missions.

Introduction to Scientology Ethics Course	5 days
Special Course in Human Evaluation	1 wk
Field Staff Member Specialist Course	2–3 days
Hubbard Dissemination Course	1½ wks

CHILDREN'S COURSES

Designed for children ages 8 through 12. Each is fully illustrated and teaches important skills for succeeding in school and with people. They cover a range of Scientology fundamentals but are presented at a level for young readers. Subjects dealt with include ARC, the eight dynamics, the parts of man, the Tone Scale and others. There are also children's courses which teach L. Ron Hubbard's study technology.

These courses are also delivered by field auditors, groups and missions.

They generally require 1 to 3 weeks of part-time study to complete.

AUDITING SERVICES

These are the main steps taken to advance a person all the way up to the highest states of awareness and ability. The services listed below are given in the basic sequence of progress, though individual progress may vary.
See Chapter 13 for more information.

Lower-level auditing services are most frequently delivered by field auditors, groups, missions and Class V organizations. Upper levels of auditing are delivered only in Saint Hills, Advanced Organizations, the Flag Service Organization or Flag Ship Service Organization, as designated below.

Note: When the length of time to complete a given series of actions or grades is given, these are only approximations and should be used as guidelines only. Each preclear varies in how long he takes to attain the designated result. An auditing process can take as little as minutes or as long as many, many hours over a number of sessions to achieve the end result.

- ***Purification Rundown***

This rundown (also called Purification program) enables someone to attain freedom from the restimulative effects of drug residuals and other toxic substances.
See Chapter 9 for more information.
20 to 30 days at 5 hours per day

- ***TRs and Objectives***

This service may be done on a co-audit basis on the TRs and Objectives Co-audit Course. Students learn auditing skills and then co-audit on processes which get the person into present time and oriented to his environment and the physical universe.
Co-audit course study is 4 days; length of auditing is two 12½-hour intensives.

- ***Scientology Drug Rundown***

Students may co-audit this rundown by doing the Scientology Drug Rundown Co-audit Course, where they learn the technique of auditing out the harmful mental effects of drugs and then do so.
Co-audit course study is 3 days; length of auditing is one 12½-hour intensive.

- ***Scientology Expanded Grades***

These are a series of six auditing levels which address and increase a preclear's abilities in a part of his life. The gains exceed by far anything man has had available to him previously. The amount of time it takes a preclear to move up through the Grades may vary depending on the case, but on the average is approximately a dozen 12½-hour intensives of auditing, delivered over a period of a few months. It is quite common for students training in the Academy to co-audit each other through all the Grades.

ARC Straightwire Expanded
Recall Release
Grade 0 Expanded
Communications Release
Grade I Expanded
Problems Release
Grade II Expanded
Relief Release
Grade III Expanded
Freedom Release
Grade IV Expanded
Ability Release

■ ***New Era Dianetics Auditing (NED)***

New Era Dianetics consists of over a dozen specific rundowns (a series of auditing steps designed to handle a specific aspect of a case) and actions which address the engrams contained in the reactive mind. Among these are actions which:

- Resolve any situation causing "ups and downs" in the preclear's life
- Increase the preclear's perception of and ability to control his environment
- Locate and handle any reasons the preclear began taking drugs
- Relieve trauma from losses suffered in life
- Audit out fixed computations which limit abilities and activity in life
- Resolve any difficulties with learning and education
- Alleviate a wide range of psychosomatic complaints
- Handle any disability the preclear considers he suffers from
- Enable the preclear to shed undesirable personality traits unknowingly adopted from others

These New Era Dianetics rundowns and actions are aimed at making a well and happy preclear. It can take approximately eight intensives of auditing to accomplish this, but the gains are tremendous—New Era Dianetics auditing can result in attainment of the state of Clear.
See Chapter 13 for more information.

■ ***Expanded Dianetics Auditing***

This is a specialized branch of Dianetics which directly addresses and handles heavy areas of hidden charge on a preclear's case and brings freedom from cruel impulses and chronic unwanted conditions. A person who did not attain Clear on New Era Dianetics would receive this auditing. An Expanded Dianetics program is tailored to each individual preclear's case and can take approximately six intensives of auditing.
See Chapter 13 for more information.

UPPER-LEVEL AUDITING

These are auditing levels which move a person into the highest levels of ability and freedom. Each has its own precise subject and techniques of delivery. Lengths of time to deliver any service can vary from person to person. Where any service is delivered is noted below.

■ ***Grade V***
Power Release

Grade VA
Power Plus Release

Grade VI
Whole Track Release

Clearing Course

These four services comprise an alternate route to Clear. A preclear who, upon completing New Era Dianetics and Expanded Dianetics, has not yet attained Clear, would receive auditing on Grades V and VA at a Saint Hill or higher-level organization. He would then train as a Solo auditor and do Grade VI and the Clearing Course at an Advanced Organization or the Flag Service Organization. The full alternate route to Clear takes, on an average, several months to travel.

■ ***Sunshine Rundown***

A short action done immediately after achieving the state of Clear, whether one goes Clear on New Era Dianetics or the Clearing Course. Delivered at Class V organizations or higher-level churches.

■ ***Solo Auditor Course***

This teaches full theory and practical skills of Solo auditing, necessary for anyone doing advanced auditing levels on the Bridge. This course consists of two parts: Part One, which covers all theory of Solo auditing, is delivered in Class V organizations. Part Two, which covers practical application of Solo auditing skills, is delivered only at Saint Hills, Advanced Organizations and the Flag Service Organization.

Hubbard Solo Auditor Course Part One	4	wks
Hubbard Solo Auditor Course Part Two	3	days

■ ***OT Preparations Auditing Eligibility for Issue of OT Levels Check***

Auditing actions which prepare a person to move smoothly onto the OT levels. Delivered at Saint Hills or higher-level organizations.

■ ***New OT I***
OT II
OT III—"The Wall of Fire"

After Clear, one arranges the time to Solo audit on New OT I through OT III without interruption. These services are available at an Advanced Organization or the Flag Service Organization. These three levels altogether can require several months' daily Solo auditing to complete.

■ ***New OT IV, OT Drug Rundown***

An audited level requiring 12½ to 25 hours to complete. Delivered at Advanced Organizations and the Flag Service Organization.

■ ***New OT V,***
Audited New Era Dianetics for OTs—"The Second Wall of Fire"

New OT VI,
Hubbard Solo New Era Dianetics for OTs Auditing Course

New OT VII,
Hubbard Solo New Era Dianetics for OTs Auditing

These three levels comprise the band of New Era Dianetics for OTs auditing. The first rundowns are done as an audited level, at an Advanced Organization or the Flag Service Organization. One then trains to audit New Era Dianetics for OTs Solo. New OT VII is a lengthy level, requiring a considerable amount of time to complete. One Solo audits at home daily, returning every 6 months to the Flag Service Organization for a check on one's progress. Though time in auditing stretches out quite a bit at these levels, the gains achieved are proportionately greater than those attained at lower levels.

■ ***New OT VIII, Truth Revealed***

This is the highest OT level now available. It is a Solo audited action, requiring about one month to complete. Delivered at the Flag Ship Service Organization only.

Further OT Levels to New OT XV to be released.

OTHER AUDITING SERVICES

These are specialized auditing actions addressing specific aspects of the reactive mind or a person's spiritual abilities, received by preclears as directed by the Case Supervisor. Many of the actions below require about one 12½-hour intensive to complete. These services are delivered by auditors certified to deliver them.

Happiness Rundown
PTS Rundown
Method One Word Clearing
Vital Information Rundown
Repair List for Treatment from Psychiatrists, Psychologists and Psychoanalysts
Allergy or Asthma Rundown
Scientology Marriage Counseling
Student Booster Rundown
Interiorization Rundown
Est Repair Rundown
Confessionals
South African Rundown
Suppressed Person Rundown
Introspection Rundown
Handling Fear of People List
Hubbard Consultant Outpoint-Pluspoint Lists
False Purpose Rundown

FLAG SERVICE ORGANIZATION-ONLY AUDITING

These are advanced auditing rundowns requiring the most highly trained auditors. They address particular aspects of aberration or ability and people come from all over the world for the case benefits these actions bring.

The L Rundowns, as they are called, unlock some of a thetan's most powerful abilities, enabling him to operate much more effectively in any area of life. Each L Rundown requires approximately 25 hours to complete.

On the other rundowns listed below, the time estimate depends on the individual's case.

L10
L11, New Life Rundown
L12, Flag OT Executive Rundown
Cause Resurgence Rundown
Super Power
Profession Intensive
New Vitality Rundown
Knowledge Rundown
Case Cracker Rundown
Int by Dynamics Rundown
Dynamic Sort Out Assessment
Fixated Person Rundown

OTHER CHURCH SERVICES

Traditional functions delivered by churches are covered here, as well as non-audited services to help church members with specific needs. These services are delivered by all Scientology ministers.

See Chapter 15 for more information.

Sunday Church Services
Weddings
Funerals
Christenings
Chaplain's Assistance
Ethics Consultations
Word Clearing
Qual Consultation
Cramming

Chapter 37

Suggested Books, Lectures and Videos

The best source of information on Dianetics and Scientology technology is the books and lectures of L. Ron Hubbard. This list of materials offers a path of discovery, from basic materials on the subjects to the more advanced or specialized. Some of the materials are available in public bookstores and libraries; the rest can be obtained at any of the Scientology organizations listed in Chapter 38. Many of these works have been translated into a number of different languages.

BOOKS

■ Basic information on Dianetics and its procedures

The Basic Dianetics Picture Book

Gives essential information to the new reader in abbreviated form with each principle clearly illustrated. Shows mechanisms of the reactive mind and how Dianetics auditing works.

Dianetics: The Modern Science of Mental Health

Basic text of Dianetics and the first accurate description of the human mind and Dianetics therapy. This handbook contains instructions one can apply, with no other training, and audit another on Dianetics.

The Dynamics of Life

L. Ron Hubbard's first book on his research into the mind and life. Contains several case histories of early auditing results.

Self Analysis

Over twenty auditing lists a person can use by himself to gain tremendous insight into his past. Contains a version of the Hubbard Chart of Human Evaluation and tests for reader to plot himself on the chart before and after auditing.

Dianetics: The Evolution of a Science

Traces the track of discovery which led to Dianetics breakthroughs. Details each milestone L. Ron Hubbard passed to chart the mind and develop technology to nullify engrams.

■ Books covering advanced Dianetics principles and procedures

Science of Survival

Most complete description of human behavior ever written. Built around the Hubbard Chart of Human Evaluation. Makes possible thorough prediction and understanding of human behavior.

Dianetics 55!

Full description of communication and its applications to life and auditing. L. Ron Hubbard's most complete exposition of the subject.

Notes on the Lectures of L. Ron Hubbard

Compiled from L. Ron Hubbard's lectures shortly after the publication of *Dianetics: The Modern Science of Mental Health*. Contains first descriptions of the Tone Scale and ARC triangle.

Advanced Procedure and Axioms

Advanced Dianetics principles and auditing techniques. Provides descriptions of mental phenomena discovered after publication of *Dianetics*. Appendix contains Tone Scale, Logics and Dianetics Axioms.

Handbook for Preclears

Written as an advanced personal workbook. A companion text to *Advanced Procedure and Axioms*. Contains auditing lists a person can do on his own or in conjunction with an auditor.

■ Dianetics principles and procedures to be applied to children

Child Dianetics

Explains a new approach to child rearing using Dianetics principles and technology. Contains many techniques for use with children of all ages.

■ Basic information on Scientology; the philosophy and practice of Scientology principles

The Basic Scientology Picture Book

An illustrated explanation of fundamental data of Scientology and their application to the individual in auditing. Includes the eight dynamics, the parts of man, ARC, the E-Meter, how auditing works and other basic principles.

Scientology: The Fundamentals of Thought

Basic text of Scientology. Describes many key philosophic principles and covers specific processes essential to increased ability.

A New Slant on Life
Collection of insightful writings on a wide variety of subjects including the two rules for happy living, justice, professionalism, marriage, what is greatness and over twenty others. Excellent as a broad survey of Scientology data.

Scientology 0-8: The Book of Basics
Compilation of the key knowledge of Scientology. Contains the Factors, Axioms, Logics, scales and codes of Dianetics and Scientology. Extremely useful reference work of fundamental data.

■ Advanced Scientology books, covering advanced information on Scientology principles and procedures

Scientology 8-80
Details Technique 8-80, a specialized form of Scientology, specifically, the electronics of human thought and beingness. Provides basic answers to goals of life in the physical universe.

Scientology 8-8008
Advanced explanation of techniques to rehabilitate abilities, ethics and goals. Was textbook for famous Philadelphia Doctorate Course lecture series given in late 1952. Book gives basic description of native potentials and abilities of the thetan.

The Creation of Human Ability
A manual containing over 100 auditing procedures aimed at restoring the thetan's determinism over his thoughts, decisions and actions.

■ Information on the subject of past lives

Scientology: A History of Man
Unique description of the principal events that have shaped man as he exists today. Describes common thetan experiences on the time track, explaining relationship between a thetan and his body and how electronics affect the thetan.

Have You Lived Before This Life?
First thorough account of the exploration of past lives. Dozens of case histories accurately reported which detail people's experiences with this phenomenon.

■ Books containing the full philosophic and technical data of Dianetics and Scientology

The Technical Bulletins of Dianetics and Scientology
Eighteen volumes containing all of L. Ron Hubbard's technical bulletins, articles and essays from 1950 to the present. Fully indexed. The broadest, most complete written record on the spirit, the mind and life in existence.

The Research and Discovery Series
A massive (over 100 volumes when complete) transcription and publication of all L. Ron Hubbard's recorded technical lectures and demonstrations. The only complete running record of all Mr. Hubbard's research into the mind and life. Supplemental material contained in each volume illuminates track of research and development.

■ Books covering the handling of drugs and toxins; how to rid one's body of unwanted toxins, drug residues and other harmful substances

Clear Body, Clear Mind: The Effective Purification Program
Comprehensive explanation of L. Ron Hubbard's breakthrough methodology for detoxifying the body of harmful drug residuals and other toxins. Contains all necessary data and technology to enable a person to do the entire program.

Purification: An Illustrated Answer to Drugs
Describes in picture form the harmful effects of drugs and other toxins on the body and how the Purification program eliminates these.

All About Radiation

Written in conjunction with a medical doctor, L. Ron Hubbard describes his research in the field of radiation. Explains the nature of radiation's effects on life. Provides means of preventing and counteracting these.

■ Books to improve job satisfaction and increase one's success in the workplace

The Problems of Work

Contains the fundamentals of workplace technology, such as how to handle confusions and be effective on the job. Applicable to any working environment or job.

How to Live Though an Executive

Advanced principles of administration such as how to efficiently run a company and how to handle employees, for executive use.

Organization Executive Course Volumes

Eight volumes plus an index volume which contain all L. Ron Hubbard's administrative policy. Contains the technology of groups and how to make them survive.

Management Series Volumes 1, 2 and 3

Full collection of third dynamic management technology. Contains all tools needed for successful management at any level: personnel, organizing, finance, data, targeting out group goals, management by computer, marketing, public relations and others.

■ Information on remedying difficulties with students and preclears

The Book of Case Remedies

Dozens of techniques applied to assist someone having difficulty as a student or preclear. The remedies resolve the problem and enable the person to progress again on the Bridge. Particularly valuable book for auditors, Case Supervisors or Course Supervisors.

■ Information on the subject of ethics, justice and morals

Introduction to Scientology Ethics

All fundamentals of Scientology ethics and justice systems. Includes all conditions formulas, ethics and justice codes of Scientology, application of ethics to others, and a fold-out copy of the organizing board; these are many tools to raise one's condition in life.

The Way to Happiness

A common-sense guide to better living. Written as a nonreligious moral code, it contains twenty-one precepts for successful living in a modern world. Over 40 million copies of the book have been distributed throughout the world.

■ Books of quotations from L. Ron Hubbard's writings

Understanding: The Universal Solvent

Hundreds of quotations on myriad subjects which convey the essence of Scientology.

Knowingness

A companion volume filled with hundreds of profound quotations from L. Ron Hubbard's writings.

■ E-Meter books, giving the full theory and use of the E-Meter

Understanding the E-Meter

Fully illustrated explanation of the principles and mechanics of the E-Meter. Includes photographs of every meter model ever developed.

Introducing the E-Meter

Basic book on E-Meter setup and operation. First book on E-Meter studied in Academy training.

E-Meter Essentials

Explains basics of recognition and interpretation of E-Meter reactions. Vital for correct use of the meter.

The Book of E-Meter Drills
The complete set of all drills developed by L. Ron Hubbard to train someone in proper use of the E-Meter. E-Meter training manual for auditors.

■ Books on study technology—for both children and adults

Basic Study Manual
Fundamentals of study technology for teenagers on up. Fully illustrated presentation of how to study to ensure comprehension and understanding and the ability to apply anything one studies.

Learning How to Learn
Introduction to learning for young students aged 8 to 12. Presents most basic data of study technology in fully illustrated format.

Study Skills for Life
Contains basics of study technology for young teenagers. Fully illustrated.

How to Use a Dictionary Picture Book for Children
Gives young students skills needed to use a dictionary, a vital necessity for learning. Fully illustrated.

Grammar and Communication for Children
Contains L. Ron Hubbard's breakthrough in the subject of grammar. Fully illustrated and presented for young students. Makes grammar understandable and something a person can *use* in his life.

■ Handbooks for auditors

Assists Processing Handbook
The basic Scientology assists which allow anyone to help ease suffering from illness and injuries and greatly speed recovery.

Introductory and Demonstration Processes Handbook
Contains over 200 processes specifically designed to give those new to Scientology a subjective glimpse of how it can improve their lives.

Group Auditor's Handbook
Group processing is formal auditing delivered to a group of people at the same time. This handbook offers thirty-three processes and full instructions on how a group auditor delivers these processes.

The Volunteer Minister's Handbook
Full body of basic Scientology technology which anyone can read and apply to change conditions. Dozens of techniques and principles thoroughly explained to provide effective ways one can bring real help to others.

■ Ceremonial information

Ceremonies of the Church of Scientology
Contains the inspiring and beautiful church services, sermons and ceremonies.

■ Technology and know-how of art

Art
Contains all of L. Ron Hubbard's essays on art, used by artists to achieve their goals. Codifies for the first time artistic endeavors in any art form.

LECTURES

■ Lectures on personal achievement: The Personal Achievement Series

There are nearly 3,000 recorded lectures by L. Ron Hubbard on the subjects of Dianetics and Scientology. The following list presents a sampling of some of these lectures; each one is an excellent introduction to Dianetics and Scientology principles.

The Story of Dianetics and Scientology
L. Ron Hubbard shares his earliest insights into human nature and gives a compelling account of his experiences in developing Dianetics and Scientology.

The Road to Truth
Explains man's attempts to find truth and the traps and half-truths that he has fallen into on the way. Mr. Hubbard tells

why this has occurred and how the road to truth can be traveled.

Scientology and Effective Knowledge

Describes why man has remained for so long at a loss for workable answers to life. Explains the relationship of observation to knowledge and reveals the key to truly knowing and understanding a subject.

The Deterioration of Liberty

Discusses three subjects—freedom, liberty, justice—important to man's survival. Analyzes how man loses his freedom and outlines the actions one can take to regain it, for himself and his fellows.

Power of Choice and Self-determinism

Man's ability to determine the course of his life depends on his ability to exercise power of choice. L. Ron Hubbard describes how one can increase the power of decision for himself and for others.

Scientology and Ability

Tells how a person becomes unable to cause things in his environment and explains workable methods which can be used to restore a person's ability and success in life.

The Hope of Man

Various men in history brought forth the idea that there was hope of improvement, but L. Ron Hubbard's discoveries in Dianetics and Scientology have made that hope a reality. Explains how Scientology has become man's one true hope for freedom.

The Dynamics

Data on the eight dynamics is covered here, including how man creates on them, what happens when a person gets stuck in just one dynamic, and how wars relate to the third dynamic.

Money

Explains what money really is and how a money system operates. Provides an understanding of how one can gain greater control over his own income and finances.

Formulas for Success—The Five Conditions

Natural laws govern the conditions of life, with exact steps to take in handling each of these conditions. Invaluable technology to help one succeed in *any* endeavor.

Health and Certainty

Explains how one's health is related to his certainty or lack of it, how false certainties can be forced on him. Shows the way to achieve certainty and improve one's condition in life.

Operation Manual for the Mind

Difficulties of trying to get along in life without knowing how the mind works are explored. Describes why man existed for thousands of years without any understanding of how his mind was supposed to operate, and how this problem has been solved in Scientology.

Miracles

Defines what a miracle is and sheds light on why they are so apparently lacking in the world today. Miracles are usually thought of as only having happened centuries ago in some distant place but this is not the case.

The Road to Perfection—The Goodness of Man

Unlike earlier practices that sought to "improve" man because he was "bad," Scientology assumes that man has good qualities that simply need to be increased. Shows how workable this assumption really is, and how one can begin to use his mind, talents and abilities to the fullest.

The Dynamic Principles of Existence

Some people seem more interested and involved in life than others, and generally have more fulfilling lives as a result. Discusses the importance of being a knowing part of and participant in any and all of the functions of life.

Man: Good or Evil?

Gives usable definitions of *good* and *evil,* and powerfully illustrates what man's basic nature really is. Man has struggled with the concepts of good and evil throughout his history. This lecture greatly illuminates them.

Differences Between Scientology and Other Studies

Oftentimes the important questions in life are the ones a person asks himself; and unlike other studies which try to force a person to accept beliefs, Scientology enables one to find his own answers. It points the way to true understanding of and belief in oneself.

The Machinery of the Mind

Gives an understanding of different mental phenomena, how these can cause a person to lose control and how one can regain power of decision and control of his life.

The Affinity-Reality-Communication Triangle

Explains how the ARC triangle works and how it can be used to resolve problems and improve personal relationships.

Increasing Efficiency

Inefficiency is a major barrier to success, but there are ways to increase one's efficiency. Provides data on how to increase one's effectiveness in life.

Man's Relentless Search

Describes what man is really searching for in life and how he can find it. His quest to find himself has repeatedly ended in failure and disappointment. With Scientology one's search no longer has to end this way.

VIDEOS

How to Use Dianetics

A succinct explanation of Dianetics principles and step-by-step instructions of how to do Dianetics auditing as taught in *Dianetics: The Modern Science of Mental Health*. The soundness of L. Ron Hubbard's theories and workability of his techniques are clearly demonstrated.

Introduction to Scientology

An hour-long interview with L. Ron Hubbard, who provides candid answers to many commonly asked questions about Scientology. The source of Scientology relates his researches into life and the development of Scientology, its fundamentals, procedures and organizations.

Scientology Missions

International Office

Scientology Missions International
6331 Hollywood Boulevard, Suite 501
Los Angeles, California 90028

Western United States

▲ **Scientology Missions International Western United States Office**
1307 N. New Hampshire
Los Angeles, California 90027

Missions and Dianetics Centers

Mission of Anchorage
440 W. 5th Avenue
Anchorage, Alaska 99501

Mission of Fairbanks
401 West 5th Avenue
Fairbanks, Alaska 99701

Mission of Phoenix
2213 East Campbell
Phoenix, Arizona 85014

Mission of Beverly Hills
109 N. La Cienega Boulevard
Beverly Hills, California 90211

Mission of Capitol
7637 Fair Oaks Boulevard, #2
Carmichael, California 95608

Mission of Sacramento
5738 Marconi Avenue, Suite 12
Carmichael, California 95608

Mission of Butte County
5 Williamsburg Lane
Chico, California 95926

Mission of Escondido
324 S. Kalmia Street
Escondido, California 92025

Mission of Brand Boulevard
144 S. Brand Boulevard
Glendale, California 91204

Mission of South Bay
3940 Marine Avenue No. B
Lawndale, California 90260

Mission of Long Beach
5951 Cherry Avenue
Long Beach, California 90805

Mission of Westwood
3200 Santa Monica Boulevard
Suite 200
Los Angeles, California 90404

Mission of Los Gatos
475 Alberto Way, Suite 110
Los Gatos, California 95032

Mission of San Bernardino
22458 Barton Rd.
Grand Terrace, California 92324

Mission of Glendale
2254 Honolulu Avenue
Montrose, California 91020

Mission of Monterey
546-D Hartnell Street
Monterey, California 93940

Mission of Berkeley
466 Santa Clara, Suite 310
Oakland, California 94610

Mission of Antelope Valley
PO Box 90071
Palmdale, California 93590

Mission of Palm Springs
44-855 Las Palmas Avenue, Suite C
Palm Desert, California 92260

Mission of Concord
3313 Vincent Road, Suite 207
Pleasant Hills, California 94523

Mission of Redwood City
617 Veterans Boulevard, #205
Redwood City, California 94063

Mission of River Park
1485 River Park Drive, Suite 100
Sacramento, California 95815

Mission of Salinas
908 Riker Street
Salinas, California 93901

Mission of San Diego Coast
3288 El Cajon Boulevard, #3
San Diego, California 92104

Mission of San Francisco
406 Sutter Street
San Francisco, California 94108

Mission of San Jose
826 N. Winchester
San Jose, California 95128

Mission of Marin
1930 4th Street
San Rafael, California 94901

Mission of Sonora
20100 Barnwood Court
Sonora, California 95370

Mission of South Pasadena
915 Fremont Avenue
South Pasadena, California 91030

Mission of Buenaventura
180 N. Ashwood Avenue
Ventura, California 93003

Mission of West Valley
20315 Ventura Boulevard, Suite A
Woodland Hills, California 91364

Mission of Alamosa
511 Main Street
Alamosa, Colorado 81101

Mission of Boulder
1320 Pearl Street, Suite B-50
Boulder, Colorado 80302

Mission of South Denver
6565 S. Dayton, Suite 1000
Englewood, Colorado 80111

Mission of Denver
6739 W. 44th Avenue
Wheat Ridge, Colorado 80033

Mission of Honolulu
941 Kam Highway, #207
Pearl City, Hawaii 96782

Mission of Golden Valley
5707 Highway 7, #140
St. Louis Park, Minnesota 55416

Mission of Espanola
401 N. Riverside Drive, Suite M
Espanola, New Mexico 87532

Mission of Casa Linda
10204 Garland Road
Dallas, Texas 75218

Mission of Houston
2727 Fondren, Suite 1-A
Houston, Texas 77063

Mission of the Woodlands
℅ 2727 Fondren, Suite 1-A
Houston, Texas 77063

Mission of San Antonio
10609 IH 10 W., Suite 208
San Antonio, Texas 78230

Mission of Bellevue
1545 134th Avenue N.E.
Bellevue, Washington 98005

Mission of Seattle
2124 3rd Avenue
Seattle, Washington 98121

Mission of Burien
15216 2nd Avenue S.W.
Seattle, Washington 98166

EASTERN UNITED STATES

▲ **Scientology Missions International**
Eastern United States Office
349 W. 48th Street
New York, New York 10036

Missions and Dianetics Centers

Mission of Clearwater
100 N. Belcher Road
Clearwater, Florida 34625

Mission of Fort Lauderdale
371 E. Commercial Boulevard
Fort Lauderdale, Florida 33334

Mission of Champaign-Urbana
312 W. John Street
Champaign, Illinois 61820

Mission of Peoria
2020 N. Wisconsin
Peoria, Illinois 61603

Mission of Indianapolis
109 E. 9th
Anderson, Indiana 46012

Mission of Baton Rouge
7855 Jefferson Highway
Baton Rouge, Louisiana 70809

Mission of Albany
57 Wilshire Drive
Cheshire, Massachusetts 01225

Mission of Merrimack Valley
PO Box 6231
Haverhill, Massachusetts 01831

Cape Cod Dianetics Center
PO Box 2017
Orleans, Massachusetts 02653

Mission of Baltimore
410 Ingleside Avenue
Baltimore, Maryland 21228

Mission of Genesee County
PO Box 407
Davisburg, Michigan 48503

Mission of Omaha
PO Box 670
Bellevue, Nebraska 68005

Mission of Greater Concord
228 London Road, Suite 5
Concord, New Hampshire 03301

Mission of Collingswood
Greentree Executive Campus
Lincoln Drive W. Route 73, 5001-G
Marlton, New Jersey 08053

Mission of New Jersey
810 Main Street
Hackensack, New Jersey 07601

Dianetics Center of Rochester
6 Bickford Street
Macedon, New York 14502

Mission of Rockland
7 Panoramic Drive
Valley Cottage, New York 10989

Mission of Cleveland
18118 Harland Avenue
Cleveland, Ohio 44119

Mission of Northeast Ohio
PO Box 2002
Streetsboro, Ohio 44241

Mission of Lake Erie
℅ 460 E. 10th Street
Erie, Pennsylvania 16503

Mission of Harrisburg
112 Baltimore Street
Hanover, Pennsylvania 17331

Mission of Pittsburgh
RD #2 Box 379
Charleroi, Pennsylvania 15022

Mission of Charleston
1519-A Harbourview Road
Charleston, South Carolina 29412

Mission of St. Albans
103 6th Avenue
St. Albans, West Virginia 25177

Mission of Fairfax
7409-H Little River Turnpike
Annandale, Virginia 22003

Mission of Southwest Virginia
PO Box 205
Troutville, Virginia 24175

Mission of Milwaukee
710 E. Silver Spring Drive
Suite E
Whitefish Bay, Wisconsin 53217

UNITED KINGDOM

▲ **Scientology Missions International**
United Kingdom Office
Saint Hill Manor
East Grinstead, West Sussex
England RH19 4JY

Missions and Dianetics Centers

Mission of Wirral
Woodcroft Eleanor Road
Bidston Birkenhead Merseyside
England L43 7QW

Mission of Cambridge
21 Park Road
Cambridge
England CB5 8AR

Dianetics Information Center of Carlisle
37 Grey Street
Carlisle, Cumbria
England CA1 2HJ

Chichester Dianetics Center
Globe House, Station Approach
Southgate Chichester
England PO19 2DN

Dianetics Information Center of East Grinstead
19 Portland Road
East Grinstead, West Sussex
England PO20 GRN

Dianetics Information Center of Leicester
29 Albert Street
Leicestershire
England

Dianetics Information Center of Hove
170 Sackville Road
Hove, East Sussex
England BN3 7AG

Mission of Kendal
Ashleigh Ashmount Road
Grange-Over-Sands
Cumbria
England LA11 6BX

Dianetics Information Center of Leighton Buzzards
Shenstone Acres
Stewkley Road, Soulbury
Leighton Buzzards
England

Dianetics Information Center of North London
61 Lincoln Road
London
England N2 9DJ

Dianetics Center Camberwell
146 Frien Road
London SE 22
England

Dianetics Information Center of Norwich
11 Fir Tree Road
Norwich, Norfolk
England NR7 9LG

Dianetics Information Center of Bournemouth
East Wing Jolliffe House
32 West Street
Poole, Dorset
England BH15 1LA

Dianetics Information Center of Southampton
43 Butts Road
Sholing, Southampton
Soton 449077
England

Dianetics Information Center of Torpoint
9 Adela Road
Torpoint, Cornwall
England

Dianetics Information Center of Tottenham
98 Dowsett Road
Tottenham, London
England N17 9DH

Dianetics Information Center of York
9 Don Avenue
York, Yorkshire
England Y02 2PT

Cardiff Dianetics Center
12 Clare Road Grangetown
Cardiff, Wales

India

Dianetics Center of Patiala
Talwar House, 1st Floor
Opp. Bengali Garage
Phowara Chowk, The Mall
Patiala 147001
India

Dianetics Center of Ambala Cantt
6352 Punjabi Mohalla
Ambala Cantt 133001
India

School of Punjabi Studies
Punjab University
Chandigarh 160014
India

Ireland

Dianetics Information Center of Dublin
62/63 Middle Abbey Street
Dublin
Ireland

Pakistan

Dianetics Information Center of Hyderabad
306–307/ A Latifabad, Unit No. 11
Hyderabad (Sind)
Pakistan 71800

Nazimabad Dianetics Center
5 3, 23/13 Nazimabad
Karachi
Pakistan

Dianetics Center for Personal Excellence
7/213 Sirajuddaula Road
DMMCHS
Karachi
Pakistan

Ability Center of Rawalpindi
53-C Satellite Town
Opp. Wapda Office Chandni Chowk
Rawalpindi
Pakistan

EUROPE

▲ **Scientology Missions International European Office**
Sankt Nikolajvej 4–6
Frederiksberg C
1953 Copenhagen
Denmark

Missions and Dianetics Centers

Austria

Dianetik-Zentrum Salzburg
Rupertgasse 21
5020 Salzburg
Austria

Dianetik Wolfsberg
Wienerstrasse 8
9400 Wolfsberg
Austria

Belgium

Dianetics Center of Antwerpen
Lange Gasthuisstr. 13, Baite 9
2000 Antwerpen
Belgium

Mission of Brugge
Groene Poortdreef 15A
8200 Brugge
Belgium

Mission of Brussels
Jean d'Ardennstraat, 16/4
1050 Brussels
Belgium

Bulgaria

Dianetic Center Bulgaria
L. Karave Lov 67
1000 Sofia
Bulgaria

Dianetic Counseling Group Bulgaria
Akazia #2
1421 Sofia
Bulgaria

Czech Republic

Mission of Prague
Hastalka 4
11000 Praha 1
Czech Republic

Denmark

Dianetik Kursus Center of Aalborg
Boulevarden 39 KL
9000 Aalborg
Denmark

Mission of Copenhagen City
Bülowsvej 20
1870 Frederiksberg C
Denmark

Hubbard Kursus Center of Kolding
Ejlersvej 24 1 Sal
6000 Kolding
Denmark

Dianetik Lyngby
Sorgenfrivej 3
2800 Lyngby
Denmark

Mission of Fyn
Absalonsgade 42
5000 Odense C
Denmark

Hubbard Kursus Center of Silkeborg
Virklundvej 5
8600 Silkeborg
Denmark

Finland

Scientology Mission of Helsinki
Alkukuja 2-6K
PL 8
00711 Helsinki
Finland

France

Centre de Dianétique de Bordeaux
4, cour de la Somme
33800 Bordeaux
France

Centre de Dianétique de Brunoy
2, rue Traversière
91800 Brunoy
France

Mission de Scientologie Les Gobelins
26, avenue Pasteur
94250 Gentilly
France

Centre de Dianétique de Lyon
3, rue du Dr. Augros
69005 Lyon
France

Centre de Dianétique de Marseille
6, cours Joseph Thierry
13001 Marseille
France

Centre de Dianétique de Missillac
Le Croissant
44780 Missillac
France

Centre de Dianétique de Montpellier
9, rue Fontaine St. Berthomieux
34000 Montpellier
France

Centre de Dianétique de Mulhouse
13, rue du Sauvage
68100 Mulhouse
France

Centre de Dianétique de Vence
1, rue Maurice Jaubert
06000 Nice
France

Centre de Dianétique de Paris
25, rue Levis
75017 Paris
France

Centre de Dianétique de Reims
36, rue Libergier
51100 Reims
France

Centre de Dianétique de Toulouse
31, rue Bernard Mule
31400 Toulouse
France

Germany

Dianetik-Zentrum Bremen
Osterdeich 27
2800 Bremen 1
Germany

Mission of Villingen
Schramberger Strasse 14
7211 Eschbronn 2
Germany

Dianetik-Zentrum Esslingen
Sulzgrieserssteige 20
7300 Esslingen
Germany

Scientology Dresden e.V.
Bischofsweg 46
D–0–8060 Dresden
Germany

Dianetik Göppingen
Geislingerstrasse 21
7320 Göppingen
Germany

Dianetik und Scientology Heilbronn
Frankfurterstrasse 47
7100 Heilbronn
Germany

Dianetik-Zentrum Karlsruhe
Kaiserstrasse 163
7500 Karlsruhe
Germany

Zentrum für angewandte Philosophie
Kaiserallee 36
7500 Karlsruhe
Germany

Dianetik Mannheim
Schwabenheimerstrasse 13
6800 Mannheim 10
Germany

Dianetik-Zentrum Münster
Bernhard-Ernst-Strasse 7
4000 Münster
Germany

Scientology Mission Munchen Süd
Müllerstrasse 33
8000 Munich 5
Germany

Scientology Mission Nymphenburg
Nymphenburgerstrasse 186
8000 Munich 19
Germany

Scientology-Kirche Bayern e.V.
Nuremberg Mission
Farberstrasse 5, Postfach 4804
8500 Nuremberg 1
Germany

Dianetik Reutlingen
Heinestrasse 9
7410 Reutlingen
Germany

Scientology Mission Ulm
Eythstrasse 2
7900 Ulm
Germany

Dianetik Wiesbaden
Kaiser-Friedrich-Ring 70
6200 Wiesbaden
Germany

Greece

Applied Philosophy Center of Athens
Patision 200
11256 Athens
Greece

Applied Philosophy Center of Kolonos
Ioanninon 6
Kolonos
Greece

Hungary

Dianetika Egyesylet
Letet 215
1299 Budapest, PF: 701
Hungary

Netherlands

Dianetics Centrum of Oostakapelle
Vronesteyn 27
4356 Ac Oostakapelle
Netherlands

Dianetics Studiecentrum Den Haag
Laan Van Meedervoort 542B
2563 BL 's Gravenhage
Netherlands

Romania

Dianetic Center Romania
NR 4, SC A
ET III, Apt 15
Iasi, Cod 6600
Romania

Russia

Mission of St. Petersburg
Bldg 17, Kor 1, Apt 14
195279 St. Petersburg
Russia

St. Petersburg Dianetics Group
Bldg 22, Apt 13
Kovalevskaya St
195043 St. Petersburg
Russia

Slovenia

Dianetic Center of Koper
Zupanciceva 39
Koper
Slovenia

Spain

Centro de Mejoramiento Personal
Cambrils 19
28034 Madrid
Spain

Centro de Mejoramiento Personal
Urb. los Milanos Primera Fase 14
41007 Seville
Spain

Centro de Mejoramiento Personal
c/o Hermanos Rivas 22 1°
46018 Valencia
Spain

Sweden

Mission of Hässeholm
Stobygatan 16
281 39 Hässeholm
Sweden

Mission of Norrköping
Vattengatan 13
602 20 Norrköping
Sweden

Dianetikhuset
Grev Turegatan 55, ö.g.
114 38 Stockholm
Sweden

Switzerland

Mission de Scientologie Geneva
Rue de Genève 88
1225 Chêne-Bourg
Switzerland

Scientology Mission Luzern-Haldenstrasse
Haldenstrasse 37
6006 Luzern
Switzerland

Scientology Luzern
Sentimattstrasse 7
6003 Luzern
Switzerland

Dianétique Fribourg
Route de Moncor, 14
1752 Villars-sur-Glâne
Switzerland

Dianetik-Zentrum Zurich
Regensbergstrasse 89
8050 Zurich
Switzerland

Italy

▲ **Scientology Missions International Italian Office**
Via Torino, 51
20063 Cernusco sul Naviglio
Milan
Italy

Missions and Dianetics Centers

Chiesa di Scientology Missione di Aosta
Avenue du Conseil des Comis, 8
11100 Aosta
Italy

Chiesa di Scientology Missione di Avellino
Via Derna, 3
83100 Avellino
Italy

Chiesa di Scientology Missione di Barletta
Via N. Piccinini, 5
70051 Barletta
Italy

Chiesa di Scientology della Bergamasca
Via Camozzi, 77
24100 Bergamo
Italy

Dianetik und Scientology
Beda Weber Strasse 19
39031 Bruneck
Italy

Chiesa di Scientology Missione di Cagliari
Via Einauidi, 12
09127 Cagliari
Italy

Chiesa di Scientology Missione di Cantù
Via Magenta, 4
20038 Seregno (Milano)
Italy

Chiesa di Scientology Missione di Castelfranco
Via Borgo Piave, 35
Castelfranco Veneto
Italy

Chiesa di Scientology Missione di Clusone
Via Carpinoni, 11
Clusone
Italy

Chiesa di Scientology Missione di Codigoro
Via Riviera Cavallotti, 15
44021, Codigoro (FE)
Italy

Chiesa di Scientology Missione di Como
Via Borgovico, 155
Como
Italy

Chiesa di Scientology Missione di Cosenza
Via Piave, 95 H
87100 Cosenza
Italy

Chiesa di Scientology Missione di Enna
Via Franco Longo, 16
Enna
Italy

Chiesa di Scientology Missione di Firenze
Via Borgo S. Lorenzo, 4
50100 Florence
Italy

Chiesa di Scientology Missione di Lecco
Via Madonnina, 2
220404 Garbagnate Monastero
Lecco
Italy

Chiesa di Scientology Missione di Livorno
Via della Madonna, 41
57123 Livorno
Italy

Chiesa di Scientology Missione di Lucca
Via Tofanelli, 24
55100 Lucca
Italy

Chiesa di Scientology Missione di Macerata
Via Roma, 13
62100 Macerata
Italy

Chiesa di Scientology Missione di Milano
Viale Caldara, 27
20122, Milan
Italy

Chiesa di Scientology Missione di Modena
Via Modonella, 21
41100 Modena
Italy

Chiesa di Scientology Missione di Palermo
Via M. Toselli, 36/I
90100 Palermo
Italy

Chiesa di Scientology Missione di Gaggino
V. Fornaci, 12
22027 Ronago (CO)
Italy

Chiesa di Scientology
Missione di Siracusa
Via Filisto Ronco II No. 21
Siracusa
Italy

Chiesa di Scientology
Missione di Varese
Via Piave 30
Azzate (Varese)
Italy

AFRICA

▲ **Scientology Missions International**
African Office
Security Building, 2nd Floor
95 Commissioner Street
Johannesburg 2001
South Africa

Missions and Dianetics Centers

Ethiopia

Dianetics Information Center of Addis Ababa
PO Box 2852
Addis Ababa
Ethiopia

Mission of Ethiopia
PO Box 100505
Addis Ababa
Ethiopia

Ghana

Mission of Accra
PO Box 11584
Accra-North
Ghana 71800

Mission of Tema
PO Box 403
Tema
Ghana

Ivory Coast

Dianetics Center of Abidjan
01BP5003 Abidjan 01
Ivory Coast

Kenya

Dianetics Technology Center of Kenya
PO Box 1682
Thika
Kenya

Nigeria

Mission of Ibadan
PO Box 9943
University Post Office
Ibadan, Oyo State
Nigeria

Mission of Lagos
190/192 Ikorodu Road Palm Grove
PO Box 70745 Victoria Island
Lagos
Nigeria

Sierra Leone

Mission of Sierra Leone
PO Box 1396
Freetown
Sierra Leone

South Africa

Mission of East London
9 Salisbury Road
East London 53749
South Africa

Mission of Hillbrow
PO Box 18913
Hillbrow, Johannesburg 2038
South Africa

Mission of Soweto
893 Moletsane
PO Box 496
Kwa Xuma-Soweto
South Africa

Mission of Norwood
18 Trilby Street
Oaklands, Johannesburg 2192
South Africa

Tanzania

Dar Es Salaam Dianetics Group
PO Box 9563
Dar Es Salaam
Tanzania

Zaire

Mission de Kinshasa
BP 1444 Fele No. 7
Kinshasa/Limete
Zaire
Africa

AUSTRALIA, NEW ZEALAND AND OCEANIA

▲ **Scientology Missions International**
Australian, New Zealand and Oceanian Office
201 Castlereagh Street
Sydney, New South Wales 2000
Australia

Missions and Dianetics Centers

Australia

Mission of Camberwell
235 Camberwell Road, 2nd Floor
Camberwell, Victoria 3124
Australia

Mission of Perth
PO Box 1049
West Perth 6872
Australia

Japan

Mission of Tokyo
Park Heights Ikebukuro 1102
1-17-11 Higashi Ikebukuro
Toshima-ku 171
Tokyo
Japan

New Zealand

Mission of Christchurch
PO Box 1843
Christchurch
New Zealand

Philippines

Dianetics Center of Manila
PO Box 1182 MCC
Makati 1299
Metro Manila
Philippines

Taiwan

Mission of Taichung
51 Da Long Road
Taichung
Taiwan

LATIN AMERICA

▲ **Scientology Missions International**
Latin American Office
Federación Mexicana de Dianética
Avenida Montevideo 486
Colonia Linda Vista
C.P. 07300
Mexico, D.F.

Missions and Dianetics Centers

Argentina

Asociación Hubbard de Filosofía Aplicada
Neuquen 793-San Isidro
Buenos Aires
Argentina

Misión de Santa Fe
Prov de Santa Fe
La Rioja 3922
Argentina

Misión de Parana
Panama 911
Parana
Argentina

Brazil

Misión do Brasil
Rua Pedro Paulo Koerig 444
85670 Salto do Lontra
Estado do Parana
Brazil

Chile

Misión de Chile
Nuncio Laghi 6558
La Reina
Santiago
Chile

Colombia

Misión de Medellín
EL 32 No. 69B-33
Medellín
Colombia

Costa Rica

Instituto Tecnológico de Dianética
Frente Oficinas Centrales Invu Calles
5-3 Avenida 9
Apdo 8099-1000
San José
Costa Rica

Cuba

Dianetic Counseling Group of Cuba
Calle 100 #3909
Apto. 1, Entre 39 y 41
Marianao 14, Havana
Cuba

Ecuador

Centro de Dianética y Cienciología
Elizalde 119 Y Pichincha
4 Piso, Oficina 2
Guayaquil
Ecuador

Guatemala

Misión de Escuintla
Ira Ave. 1-25
Zona 4
Colonia Los Naranjales
Escuintla
Guatemala

Dianética de Guatemala
Vía 1 4-51 Zona 4
01004 Guatemala Ca
Guatemala

Mexico

Dianetics Center of Aguascalientes
308 D-301
Triana
C.P. 20270 Aguascalientes

Instituto de Filosofía Aplicada Bajio
Juárez No. 224
Leon GTO 37000
Mexico

Mission of Monterrey
Simón Bolívar No. 1335 NTE
Colonia Mitras Centro
Monterrey NL
Mexico

Mission of Mexicali
Av Nicaragua 807
Frac. Sonora
C.P. 21210 Mexicali
Baja California

Dominican Republic

Misión de Santo Domingo
Condominio Ambar Plaza II
Edificio II, Apto. 302
Avenida Saratosa Esq. Núñez de Cáceres
Bella Vista, Santo Domingo
Dominican Republic

CANADA

▲ **Scientology Missions International Canadian Office**
696 Yonge Street
Toronto, Ontario
Canada M4Y 2A7

Missions and Dianetics Centers

Mission of Calgary
824 C Edmonton Train North East
Calgary, Alberta
Canada T2E 3J6

Mission of Halifax
1574 Argyle Street, Suite 11
Halifax, Nova Scotia
Canada B3J 2B3

Mission of St. Georges
130 125E rue St. Georges Est
Beauce, Quebec
Canada G5Y 2X9

Mission of North York
227 Beverley Street
Toronto, Ontario
Canada M5T 1Z4

Mission of Vancouver
1892 Kings Way
Vancouver, British Columbia
Canada V5N 2S7

I HELP

(INTERNATIONAL HUBBARD ECCLESIASTICAL LEAGUE OF PASTORS)

INTERNATIONAL HUBBARD ECCLESIASTICAL LEAGUE OF PASTORS

1340 N. Berendo Street
Los Angeles, California 90027

FREEDOM MAGAZINE OFFICES

INTERNATIONAL OFFICE

Church of Scientology International
Freedom Magazine
6331 Hollywood Boulevard, Suite 1200
Los Angeles, California 90028

EUROPE

Church of Scientology of Belgium
Freedom Magazine
61, rue du Prince Royal
1050 Brussels
Belgium

Church of Scientology of Denmark
Freedom Magazine
Vesterbrogade 66B
1620 Copenhagen V
Denmark

Church of Scientology of Paris
Freedom Magazine
65, rue de Dunkerque
75009 Paris
France

Church of Scientology of Hamburg
Freedom Magazine
Steindamm 63
2000 Hamburg 1
Germany

Church of Scientology of Amsterdam
Freedom Magazine
Nieuwe Zijds Voorburgwal 271
1012 RL Amsterdam
Netherlands

Church of Scientology of Norway
Freedom Magazine
Storgata 9
0155 Oslo 1
Norway

Asociación Civil de Dianética de Madrid
Freedom Magazine
Montera 20, Piso 1° dcha.
28013 Madrid
Spain

Church of Scientology of Stockholm
Freedom Magazine
St. Eriksgatan 56
112 34 Stockholm
Sweden

Church of Scientology of Zurich
Freedom Magazine
Badenerstrasse 141
8004 Zurich
Switzerland

ITALY

Church of Scientology of Milan
Freedom Magazine
Via Abetone, 10
20137 Milan
Italy

AFRICA

Church of Scientology of Johannesburg
Freedom Magazine
Security Building, 2nd Floor
95 Commissioner Street
Johannesburg 2001
South Africa

UNITED KINGDOM

Church of Scientology United Kingdom
Freedom Magazine
Saint Hill Manor
East Grinstead, West Sussex
England RH19 4JY

CANADA

Church of Scientology Canada
Freedom Magazine
696 Yonge Street
Toronto, Ontario
Canada M4Y 2A7

LATIN AMERICA

Federación Mexicana de Dianética
Freedom Magazine
Avenida Montevideo 486
Colonia Linda Vista
C.P. 07300
Mexico, D.F.

AUSTRALIA, NEW ZEALAND AND OCEANIA

Church of Scientology of Sydney
Freedom Magazine
201 Castlereagh Street
Sydney, New South Wales 2000
Australia

Church of Scientology New Zealand
Freedom Magazine
32 Lorne Street
Auckland 1
New Zealand

CITIZENS COMMISSION ON HUMAN RIGHTS GROUPS

INTERNATIONAL OFFICE

Citizens Commission on Human Rights International
6362 Hollywood Boulevard, Suite B
Los Angeles, California 90028

UNITED STATES

Citizens Commission on Human Rights Phoenix
PO Box 16723
Phoenix, Arizona 85011

Citizens Commission on Human Rights Mountain View
483 Alicia Way
Los Altos, California 94022

Citizens Commission on Human Rights Los Angeles
6362 Hollywood Boulevard, Suite B
Los Angeles, California 90028

Citizens Commission on Human Rights Santa Barbara
1111 B Coast Village Road
Montecito, California 93108

Citizens Commission on Human Rights Riverside
17305 Santa Rosa Mine Road
Perris, California 92570

Citizens Commission on Human Rights San Francisco
PO Box 422696
San Francisco, California 94142

Citizens Commission on Human Rights San Luis Obispo
PO Box 4134
San Luis Obispo, California 93403

Citizens Commission on Human Rights Orange County
16581 Jib Circle #2
Huntington Beach, California 92649

Citizens Commission on Human Rights Colorado
PO Box 21401
Denver, Colorado 80221

Citizens Commission on Human Rights New Haven
909 Whalley Avenue
New Haven, Connecticut 06515

Citizens Commission on Human Rights Clearwater
639 Cleveland Street, Suite 325
Clearwater, Florida 34615

Citizens Commission on Human Rights South Florida
1400 S. Dixie Highway #2W
Pompano Beach, Florida 33060

Citizens Commission on Human Rights Atlanta
2362 Piedmont Road N.E.
Atlanta, Georgia 30324

Citizens Commission on Human Rights Chicago
PO Box 4243
Arlington Heights, Illinois 60006

Citizens Commission on Human Rights Boston
448 Beacon Street
Boston, Massachusetts 02115

Citizens Commission on Human Rights St. Louis
342 Tally Ho
St. Charles, Missouri 63301

Citizens Commission on Human Rights Buffalo
47 W. Huron Street
Buffalo, New York 14202

Citizens Commission on Human Rights Ohio
483 Fleming Road
Cincinnati, Ohio 45231

Citizens Commission on Human Rights Portland
PO Box 1922
Portland, Oregon 97207

Citizens Commission on Human Rights Philadelphia
PO Box 171
Philadelphia, Pennsylvania 19105

Citizens Commission on Human Rights Austin
403 E. Ben White #A
Austin, Texas 78704

Citizens Commission on Human Rights Dallas
PO Box 742-826
Dallas, Texas 75374

Citizens Commission on Human Rights Houston
PO Box 22088
Houston, Texas 77277

Citizens Commission on Human Rights Seattle
300 Lenora Street #B-252
Seattle, Washington 98121

Citizens Commission on Human Rights Washington, DC
2125 "S" Street N.W.
Washington, DC 20008

Citizens Commission on Human Rights Governmental Affairs Office
301 4th Street N.E.
Washington, DC 20002

Citizens Commission on Human Rights Alaska
3707 Spenard
Anchorage, Alaska 99503

Citizens Commission on Human Rights Louisiana
6489 Goodwood Ave.
Baton Rouge, Louisiana 70806

Citizens Commission on Human Rights Nevada
PO Box 91941
Henderson, Nevada 89009

Citizens Commission on Human Rights New Mexico
10124 Norman N.E.
Albuquerque, New Mexico 87112

Citizens Commission on Human Rights Utah
PO Box 1746
Sandy, Utah 84070

UNITED KINGDOM

Citizens Commission on Human Rights United Kingdom National Office
Saint Hill Manor
East Grinstead, West Sussex
England RH19 4JY

Citizens Commission on Human Rights Brighton
PO Box 529
Brighton
England BN2 2XX

Citizens Commission on Human Rights Bournemouth
PO Box 1546
Poole, Dorset
England BH15 1ZE

Citizens Commission on Human Rights London
28 Byron Court
Byron Road, Harrow
England HA1 1JT

Citizens Commission on Human Rights Northwest Office
3 Dorchester Avenue
Prestwich, Manchester
England M25 8LH

EUROPE

Citizens Commission on Human Rights Denmark
Lundegaardsvej 19
2900 Hellerup
Denmark

Finland

Citizens Commission on Human Rights Finland
PL 67
02771 Espoo
Finland

France

Citizens Commission on Human Rights France (CCDH France)
54, rue Custine
75018 Paris
France

Citizens Commission on Human Rights Angers (CCDH d'Angers)
42, rue Fulton
49000 Angers
France

Germany

Commission for Psychiatric Abuse Against Human Rights Germany
Postfach 620241
2000 Hamburg 62
Germany

Commission for Psychiatric Abuse Against Human Rights Düsseldorf
Beethovenstrasse 36
4000 Düsseldorf 1
Germany

Commission for Psychiatric Abuse Against Human Rights Frankfurt
Diersbachtal 13
6273 Waldems 3
Germany

Commission for Psychiatric Abuse Against Human Rights Göppingen
Geislinger Strasse 21
7320 Göppingen
Germany

Commission for Psychiatric Abuse Against Human Rights Karlsruhe
Am Wetterbach 100
7500 Karlsruhe 41
Germany

Commission for Psychiatric Abuse Against Human Rights Munich
Frankfurter Ring 105
8000 Munich 45
Germany

Commission for Psychiatric Abuse Against Human Rights Rodgau
Obere Markt Strasse 7
6054 Rodgau 3
Germany

Commission for Psychiatric Abuse Against Human Rights Stuttgart
Gaishämmer Strasse 12
7000 Stuttgart 1
Germany

Commission for Psychiatric Abuse Against Human Rights Wiesbaden
Mainzer Strasse 46
6200 Wiesbaden
Germany

Israel

Citizens Commission on Human Rights Israel
Suskin 9
Nahariya 22404
Israel

Netherlands

Citizens Commission on Human Rights Holland
Postbus 11354
1001 GJ Amsterdam
Netherlands

Norway

Citizens Commission on Human Rights Norway
Post Boks 237
1322 Hoevik
Norway

Spain

Citizens Commission on Human Rights Barcelona (CCDH Cataluña)
Apartado de Correos 30241
C.P. 08080 Barcelona
Spain

Citizens Commission on Human Rights Madrid (CCDH Spain)
Apartado de Correos 14.696
Madrid
Spain

Sweden

Citizens Commission on Human Rights Sweden
Hammarvägen 6
136 73 Haninge
Sweden

Citizens Commission on Human Rights Göteborg
Box 17100
402 61 Göteborg
Sweden

Switzerland

Citizens Commission on Human Rights Basel
Augsterheglistrasse 36
4133 Pratteln
Switzerland

Citizens Commission on Human Rights Bern
Postfach 338
3000 Bern 7
Switzerland

Citizens Commission on Human Rights Biel
Bei Baettig
Jurastrasse 53
2503 Biel
Switzerland

Citizens Commission on Human Rights Burgdorf
Hohengasse 3
3400 Burgdorf
Switzerland

Citizens Commission on Human Rights Geneva
Grand-Pré 2
1202 Geneva
Switzerland

Citizens Commission on Human Rights Lausanne
Boîte Postale 231
1000 Lausanne-7
Switzerland

Citizens Commission on Human Rights Thun
Bodmerstrasse 3
3645 Gwatt
Switzerland

Citizens Commission on Human Rights Zurich
Badenerstrasse 141
8004 Zurich
Switzerland

ITALY

Citizens Commission on Human Rights Italy National Office
Via Val di Porto, 19
20056 Trezzo sull'Adda (MI)
Italy

Citizens Commission on Human Rights Brescia
Viale Piave, 50/B
25125 Brescia
Italy

Citizens Commission on Human Rights Catania
Via San Camillo
95100 Catania
Sicily

Citizens Commission on Human Rights Monza
Via Nazario Sauro, 17
20049 Concorezzo (MI)
Italy

Citizens Commission on Human Rights Cantù
Via Fattori, 1
22063 Cucciago (CO)
Italy

Citizens Commission on Human Rights Como
Via Napoleone, 16
Como
Italy

Citizens Commission on Human Rights Milan
Fermo Posta Cordusio
20100 Milan
Italy

Citizens Commission on Human Rights Novara
Via della Riotta, 13
28100 Novara
Italy

Citizens Commission on Human Rights Padua
Via Buonarroti, 65
35100 Padua
Italy

Citizens Commission on Human Rights Pordenone
Casella Postale, 45
33170 Pordenone
Italy

Citizens Commission on Human Rights Turin
Via Luserna di Rora, 29
10100 Turin
Italy

Citizens Commission on Human Rights Vicenza
Casella Postale, 29
Montecchio Maggiore
36075 Vicenza
Italy

AFRICA

Citizens Commission on Human Rights South Africa National Office
PO Box 710
Johannesburg 2000
South Africa

Citizens Commission on Human Rights Cape Town
PO Box 374
Milnerton
7435 Cape Town
South Africa

Citizens Commission on Human Rights Durban
PO Box 24054
Hillary
4024 Durban
South Africa

Citizens Commission on Human Rights Pretoria
PO Box 11053
Brooklyn
Pretoria 0001
South Africa

AUSTRALIA, NEW ZEALAND AND OCEANIA

Citizens Commission on Human Rights Australia National Office
201 Castlereagh Street
Sydney 2000
Australia

Citizens Commission on Human Rights Adelaide
28 Waymouth Street
Adelaide 5000
Australia

Citizens Commission on Human Rights Brisbane
106 Edward Street
Brisbane 4000
Australia

Citizens Commission on Human Rights Canberra
15 Blythe Close
A.C.T. 2617
Australia

Citizens Commission on Human Rights Melbourne
44 Russell Street
Melbourne 3000
Australia

Citizens Commission on Human Rights Perth
39 King Street
Perth 7000
Australia

Citizens Commission on Human Rights New Zealand
32 Lorne Street, 4th Floor
Auckland 1
New Zealand

LATIN AMERICA

Citizens Commission on Human Rights Mexico
Tuxpan 68
Colonia Roma Sur
Mexico City
Mexico

CANADA

Citizens Commission on Human Rights Canada National Office
696 Yonge Street, Suite 802
Toronto, Ontario
Canada M4Y 2A7

Citizens Commission on Human Rights Edmonton
10187, 112 Street
Edmonton, Alberta
Canada T5K 1M1

Citizens Commission on Human Rights Montreal
4489 Papineau Street
Montreal, Quebec
Canada H2H 1T7

Citizens Commission on Human Rights Toronto
696 Yonge Street, Suite 601
Toronto, Ontario
Canada M4Y 2A7

Citizens Commission on Human Rights Vancouver
401 W. Hastings
Vancouver, British Columbia
Canada V6B 1L5

NATIONAL COMMISSION ON LAW ENFORCEMENT AND SOCIAL JUSTICE

National Commission on Law Enforcement and Social Justice
3917 Riverside Drive
Toluca Lake, California 91505

ASSOCIATION FOR BETTER LIVING AND EDUCATION

INTERNATIONAL OFFICE

Association for Better Living and Education
6331 Hollywood Boulevard, Suite 700
Los Angeles, California 90028

WESTERN UNITED STATES

Association for Better Living and Education Western United States Office
1307 N. New Hampshire
Los Angeles, California 90027

EASTERN UNITED STATES

Association for Better Living and Education Eastern United States Office
349 W. 48th Street
New York, New York 10036

UNITED KINGDOM

Association for Better Living and Education United Kingdom Office
Saint Hill Manor
East Grinstead, West Sussex
England RH19 4JY

EUROPE

Association for Better Living and Education European Office
Sankt Nikolajvej 4–6
Frederiksberg C
1953 Copenhagen
Denmark

Russia

Association for Better Living and Education Russian Office
48 Vavilova Street
Building 4, Suite 169
Moscow 117333
Russia

ITALY

Association for Better Living and Education Italian Office
Via Nerino, 8
20213 Milan
Italy

AFRICA

Association for Better Living and Education African Office
Security Building, 4th Floor
95 Commissioner Street
Johannesburg 2001
South Africa

AUSTRALIA, NEW ZEALAND AND OCEANIA

Association for Better Living and Education Australian, New Zealand and Oceanian Office
201 Castlereagh Street
Sydney, New South Wales 2000
Australia

LATIN AMERICA

Instituto de Tecnología Para La Educación, A.C.
Tetla #6 Colonia Ruiz Cortines
Delegación Coyoacán
C.P. 64630
Mexico D.F.

CANADA

Association for Better Living and Education Canadian Office
696 Yonge Street
Toronto, Ontario
Canada M4Y 2A7

APPLIED SCHOLASTICS

INTERNATIONAL OFFICE

Applied Scholastics International
7060 Hollywood Boulevard, Suite 200
Los Angeles, California 90028

WESTERN UNITED STATES

Applied Scholastics Los Angeles
503 Central Avenue
Glendale, California 91203

EUROPE

Applied Scholastics
F.F. Ulriksgade 13
2100 Copenhagen O
Denmark

AFRICA

Education Alive
CDH House, 3rd Floor
217 Jeppe Street
Johannesburg 2001
South Africa

AUSTRALIA, NEW ZEALAND AND OCEANIA

Applied Scholastics
319 Canterbury Road
Ringwood Victoria 3134
Australia

CANADA

Applied Scholastics
840 Pape Avenue, Suite 201
Toronto, Ontario
Canada M4K 3T6

CRIMINON

INTERNATIONAL OFFICE

Criminon International
6381 Hollywood Boulevard, Suite 420
Los Angeles, California 90028

WESTERN UNITED STATES

Criminon Western United States
PO Box 9091
Glendale, California 91226

EASTERN UNITED STATES

Criminon Eastern United States
PO Box 6
Demarest, New Jersey 07627

Criminon Florida
639 Cleveland Street, Suite 210
Clearwater, Florida 34615

Criminon New Hampshire
282 Loudon Road
Concord, New Hampshire 03301

Criminon Minnesota
PO Box 82
Newport, Minnesota 55055

Children's Commission
Butler County Courthouse
700 Court Square
Greenville, Alabama 36037

EUROPE

Criminon Brussels
Rue Père Be Beken 6
1040 Brussels 4
Belgium

ITALY

**Criminon Italy
Associazione Criminon**
Via Nerino, 8
20123 Milan
Italy

AFRICA

Criminon Africa
82 St. Georges Road
Belleulle 2198
South Africa

NARCONON

INTERNATIONAL OFFICE

Narconon International
6381 Hollywood Boulevard, Suite 420
Los Angeles, California 90028

WESTERN UNITED STATES

Narconon Los Angeles
3429 W. Olympic Boulevard
Los Angeles, California 90019

Narconon Professional Center
4421 Lankershim Boulevard
North Hollywood, California 91602

Narconon Northern California
2718 Homestead Road
Santa Clara, California 95051

Narconon Chilocco
Route 2, Box 400
Newkirk, Oklahoma 74647

EASTERN UNITED STATES

Narconon Boston
1500 Main Street, Suite 4
Weymouth, Massachusetts 02190

UNITED KINGDOM

**Narconon United Kingdom
Delivery Center Rannoch**
Rannoch Road Crowborough
East Sussex
England TN6 1RF

EUROPE

Narconon Europe
Ny Carlsbergvej 37
1760 Copenhagen V
Denmark

Denmark

Narconon Denmark
Åmosevej 73
Skellingsted
4440 Mørkøv
Denmark

France

Narconon France
Rue de la Commande
Carrefour de la Croix de Dague
64290 Lasseube
France

Narconon Aquitaine
Rue de la Commande
Carrefour de la Croix de Dague
64290 Lasseube
France

Germany

Narconon Itzehoe
An der B 877
2210 Itzehoe
Germany

Narconon Schliersee
Neuhauserstrasse 1
8162 Schliersee 2
Germany

Netherlands

Narconon Holland (National)
℅ Gasthuissingel 16
2012 Dn Haarlem
Netherlands

Narconon Zutphen
Deventerweg 93
7203 Ad Zutphen
Netherlands

Spain

Asociación Narconon Los Molinos
C/San Nicolás S/N
Chalet Mari Solea
28460 Los Molinos de Guadarrama
Madrid
Spain

Asociación Española de Mejoras Sociales
Avenida de la Constitución No. 1
Primero B
41500 Alcalá de Guadaira
Seville
Spain

Asociación Narconon Retiro
Chalet Herrera
41500 Alcalá de Guadaira
Seville
Spain

Asociación Narconon Mediterraneo
Ctra. Alcalá–Dos Hermanas Km 2,5
Chalet San Luis
41500 Alcalá de Guadaira
Seville
Spain

Sweden

Narconon Sweden
Box 3081
143 00 Vårby
Sweden

Narconon Huddinge
Vårbackavägen 1
143 00 Vårby gård
Stockholm
Sweden

Narconon Knutby
Gränsta
740 12 Knutby
Sweden

Narconon Malmö/Eslöv
Södergård-Skarhult
241 00 Eslöv
Sweden

Spain

Narconon La Paloma
Tocon, Granada
Spain

Switzerland

Narconon Romandie
Les Plans-sur-Bex 1888
Switzerland

Narconon Innerschweiz
6 Eichzelg
Grosswangen
Switzerland

Italy

Associazione Narconon Airone
% Villaggio Ionio
Via S. Francesco Larena, Fondo 5
95100 Catania
Italy

Associazione Narconon Pellicano
Via Coppa Montaltino, 41
70051 Barletta (Bari)
Italy

Associazione Narconon Il Falco
Contrada Monti
Altilia
87040 Cosenza
Italy

Associazione Narconon Delfino
Via San Francesco Larena
Villaggio Ippocampo, Via delle Rose 40
Catania
Italy

Associazione Narconon Cormorano
Via San Francesco Larena
Villaggio Ippocampo, Via delle Rose 40
Catania
Italy

Narconon Il Gabbiano
% Hotel Punta Dell'est
Strada Statale per Taranto
Zona 172/C
Taranto
Italy

Associazione Narconon per un Futuro Migliore
Via Cadamosto, 8
20124 Milan
Italy

Comunità Narconon Albatros
Strada Statale
18 Campora San Giovanni
87032 Amantea
Cosenza
Italy

Narconon La Fenice
% Hotel Holiday
Via Amalfi, 35
Villarosa di Martinsicuro
Teramo
Italy

Narconon Tucano
% Hotel Concorde — Val Canale
24020 Ardesio
Bergamo
Italy

Narconon Condor
Via E. Giusti, 68 BIS
21019 Somma Lombardo
Varese
Italy

Narconon Grifone
Via Parafera, 29
Ficarezzi
Acicastello
95100 (Catania)
Italy

Narconon Life
% Hotel Maya
66010 Palombaro
Chieti
Italy

CANADA

Narconon Vancouver
204–4609 Kingsway
Burnaby, British Columbia
Canada V5H 4L3

Narconon Toronto
840 Pape Avenue, Suite 201
Toronto, Ontario
Canada M4K 3T6

THE WAY TO HAPPINESS

INTERNATIONAL OFFICE

The Way to Happiness Foundation International
6324 Sunset Boulevard
PO Box 2930
Hollywood, California 90028

AFRICA

The Way to Happiness Foundation Africa
CDH House, 3rd Floor
217 Jeppe Street
Johannesburg 2001
South Africa

AUSTRALIA, NEW ZEALAND AND OCEANIA

The Way to Happiness Foundation Australia, New Zealand, Oceania
PO Box A1044
Sydney South, New South Wales 2001
Australia

LATIN AMERICA

The Way to Happiness Foundation Latin America
Tetla #6 Colonia Ruiz Cortines
Delegación Coyoacán
Mexico 04630 D.F.

Colombia

The Way to Happiness Foundation Colombia
Carrera 10 A, No. 27-71
Res Tequendama (Sur)
Bogotá
Colombia

EUROPE

The Way to Happiness Foundation Russia
Stoliarny Per 7-2
Moscow
Russia

WORLD INSTITUTE OF SCIENTOLOGY ENTERPRISES

INTERNATIONAL OFFICE

World Institute of Scientology Enterprises International
6331 Hollywood Boulevard, Suite 701
Los Angeles, California 90028

WESTERN UNITED STATES

World Institute of Scientology Enterprises Western United States Office
1308 N. Berendo Street
Los Angeles, California 90027

WISE Charter Committee Los Angeles
100 N. Brand Boulevard, Suite 501
Glendale, California 91203

WISE Charter Committee Orange County
701 W. 17th Street
Santa Ana, California 92706

WISE Charter Committee San Francisco
100 Old County Road, Suite 100–B
Brisbane, California 94005

WISE Charter Committee San Diego
6055 Estelle Street #6
San Diego, California 92115

Hubbard College of Administration International
3540 Wilshire Boulevard, Suite 811
Los Angeles, California 90010

Hubbard College of Administration
Santa Clara Valley
901 Campisi Way, Suite 140
Campbell, California 95008

EASTERN UNITED STATES

World Institute of Scientology Enterprises Eastern United States Office
349 W. 48th Street
New York, New York 10036

WISE Charter Committee Clearwater
1221 Rogers Street, Suite A
Clearwater, Florida 34616

WISE Charter Committee Atlanta
33 Ponce de Leon, Suite 214
Atlanta, Georgia 30308

WISE Charter Committee Chicago
710-C E. Silver Springs Dr.
Whitefish Bay, Wisconsin 53217

WISE Charter Committee New England
91 Halls Mill Road
PO Box 938
New Fields, New Hampshire 03856

WISE Charter Committee New York
20 W. 20th Street, Suite 801
New York, New York 10011

WISE Charter Committee DC
5622 Columbia Pike, #105
Falls Church, Virginia 22041

WISE Charter Committee Miami
8303 Bird Road
Miami, Florida 33155

WISE Charter Committee Philadelphia
11085 Woodbourne Road
Levittown, Pennsylvania 19056

WISE Charter Committee Buffalo
3910 Maple Road
Amherst, New York 14226

Hubbard College of Administration Clearwater
1221 Rogers Street, Suite A
Clearwater, Florida 34616

Hubbard College of Administration Atlanta
1640 Powers Ferry Road
Marietta, Georgia 30067

Hubbard College of Administration Buffalo
1135 Maple Road
Williamsville, New York 14221

UNITED KINGDOM

World Institute of Scientology Enterprises United Kingdom Office
Saint Hill Manor
East Grinstead, West Sussex
England RH19 4JY

WISE Charter Committee United Kingdom
18–24 Chequer Road
East Grinstead, West Sussex
England RH19 3BY

EUROPE

World Institute of Scientology Enterprises European Office
Sankt Nikolajvej 4–6
1953 Frederiksberg C
Copenhagen
Denmark

Austria

WISE Charter Committee Vienna
Obere Donaustrasse 59
1020 Vienna
Austria

Hubbard College of Administration Vienna
Erlachplatz 2–4
1100 Vienna
Austria

Denmark

WISE Charter Committee Denmark
Svanemollevej 77
2900 Hellerup
Denmark

France

WISE Charter Committee Paris
6, Place D'Estienne D'Orves
75009 Paris
France

Germany

WISE Charter Committee Düsseldorf
Am Rottchen 32
4000 Düsseldorf 30
Germany

WISE Charter Committee Hamburg
Mittelweg 118
2000 Hamburg 13
Germany

WISE Charter Committee Stuttgart
Ludwig-Richter Str. 4
7024 Filderstadt 4
Germany

Hubbard College of Administration Heidelberg
Hohenaspen 20
6914 Rauenberg
Germany

Netherlands

WISE Charter Committee Holland
Stadhoudersgkade 159
1074 BC Amsterdam
Netherlands

Hubbard College of Administration Holland
Stadhoudersgkade 159
1074 BC Amsterdam
Netherlands

Russia

World Institute of Scientology Enterprises Russian Office
48 Vavilova Street
Building 4, Suite 169
Moscow 117333
Russia

Hubbard College of Administration Moscow
B. Pereyaslavskaya, 52
Moscow 129041
Russia

Hubbard College of Administration Siberia
Usolye-Sibirskoye
Chemical-Pharmaceutical-Combine
665470 Usolye-Sibirskoye
Irkutsk Region
Russia

Spain

WISE Charter Committee Madrid
Federico Morreno Torroba 1–10C
28031 Madrid
Spain

Switzerland

Hubbard College of Administration Lausanne
Mot-de-Faux 6
1023 Crissier
Switzerland

WISE Charter Committee Zurich
Bachstrasse 39
8912 Obfelden
Switzerland

ITALY

World Institute of Scientology Enterprises Italian Office
Via Torino, 51
20063 Cernusco sul Naviglio
Milan
Italy

WISE Charter Committee Milan
Via Boito, 115
20052 Monza
Italy

AFRICA

World Institute of Scientology Enterprises African Office
Security Building, 4th Floor
95 Commissioner Street
Johannesburg 2001
South Africa

Hubbard College of Administration South Africa
403 Highland Road
Kensington 2094
South Africa

WISE Charter Committee South Africa
403 Highland Road
Kensingston 2094
South Africa

AUSTRALIA, NEW ZEALAND AND OCEANIA

World Institute of Scientology Enterprises Australian, New Zealand and Oceanian Office
201 Castlereagh Street
Sydney, New South Wales 2000
Australia

WISE Charter Committee Melbourne
274 High Street
Windsor, Victoria 3181
Australia

Hubbard College of Administration Brisbane
2nd Floor, Suite 2
119 Leichhardt Street
Spring Hill, Queensland 4000
Australia

LATIN AMERICA

World Institute of Scientology Enterprises Latin American Office Federación Mexicana de Dianética
Avenida Montevideo No. 488
Colonia Linda Vista
C.P. 07300
Mexico, D.F.

Hubbard College of Administration Caracas
Parque Central
Edificio Tacagua
Piso 5, Apto 5–H
Caracas, Venezuela

CANADA

World Institute of Scientology Enterprises Canadian Office
696 Yonge Street
Toronto, Ontario
Canada M4Y 2A7

WISE Charter Committee Toronto
873 Broadview Avenue, Lower Level
Toronto, Ontario
Canada M4K 2P9

WISE Charter Committee Vancouver
5731 Mayview Circle
Burnaby, British Columbia
Canada V5E 4B7

WISE Charter Committee Montreal
2300 Bourbonniere, Suite 2
Montreal, Quebec
Canada H1W 3P3

PUBLICATIONS ORGANIZATIONS

BRIDGE PUBLICATIONS, INC.
4751 Fountain Avenue
Los Angeles, California 90029

NEW ERA PUBLICATIONS INTERNATIONAL APS
Store Kongensgade 55
1264 Copenhagen K
Denmark

United Kingdom
NEW ERA Publications, Ltd.
78 Holmethorpe Avenue
Redhill, Surrey
England RH1 2NL

France
NEW ERA Publications France
111, boulevard de Magenta
75010 Paris
France

Germany
NEW ERA Publications Germany GmbH
Bahnhofstrasse 40
2153 Neu Wulmstorf
Germany

Russia
NEW ERA Publications Russia
B. Pereyaslavskaya 50, Suite 511
Moscow 129041
Russia

Spain
NEW ERA Publications España, SA
C/de la Paz, 4, entpta dcha.
28012 Madrid
Spain

Italy
NEW ERA Publications Italia Srl
Via L.G. Columella, 12
20128 Milan
Italy

Africa
Continental Publications Pty Ltd.
6th Floor
Security Building
95 Commissioner Street
Johannesburg, 2001
South Africa

Australia
NEW ERA Publications Australia Pty Ltd.
Level 3 Ballarat House
68–72 Wentworth Avenue
Surry Hills, New South Wales 2000
Australia

Japan
NEW ERA Publications Japan, Inc.
5-4-5-803 Nishi Gotanda
Shinagawa-ku
Tokyo
Japan 141

Latin America
ERA DINÁMICA EDITORES, S.A. de C.V.
Nicolás San Juan No. 208
Colonia Narvarte
C.P. 03020
Mexico, D.F.

Canada
Continental Publications Liaison Office
696 Yonge Street
Toronto, Ontario
Canada M4Y 2A7

All books on Dianetics and Scientology may be obtained directly from the organizations listed above.

GLOSSARY OF TERMS

Philosophy has always had the liability of gathering to itself a great many new words and labels. The reason for this is that the philosopher finds phenomena in the physical universe or in the mind or humanities which have not hitherto been observed or properly identified. Each one of these tends to require a new word for its description. In actual fact this cycle of new observations requiring new labels is probably the growth of language itself. Language is obviously the product of unsung observers who then popularized a word to describe what had been observed.

The system which has been followed in Dianetics and Scientology in labeling phenomena or observed things was originally to make verbs into nouns or vice versa. The practice of developing new nomenclature was actually held to a minimum. However, it was found that many old words in the field of philosophy, when used, conveyed to people an entirely new idea. The exactness of Dianetics and Scientology required a more precise approach. This approach was achieved by special naming with an eye to minimal confusion with already supposed or known phenomena. The Dianetics and Scientology vocabulary is nevertheless not large.

In the search which brought about Dianetics and Scientology many new phenomena were encountered which resulted, for the first time, in a workable, predictable technology of the spirit. The introduction of a few words of new meaning to make this possible seems to be a small price to pay.

This glossary contains the Dianetics and Scientology terms appearing in *What Is Scientology?*

aberration: a departure from rational thought or behavior. It means basically to err, to make mistakes, or more specifically to have fixed ideas which are not true. The word is also used in its scientific sense. It means departure from a straight line. If a line should go from A to B, then if it is *aberrated* it would go from A to some other point, to some other point, to some other point, to some other point, to some other point, and finally arrive at B. Taken in this sense, it would also mean the lack of straightness or to see crookedly as, for example, a man sees a horse but thinks he sees an elephant. Aberrated conduct would be wrong conduct, or conduct not supported by reason. When a person has engrams, these tend to deflect what would be his normal ability to perceive truth and bring about an aberrated view of situations which then would cause an aberrated reaction to them. *Aberration* is opposed to sanity, which would be its opposite. From the Latin, *aberrare,* to wander from; Latin, *ab,* away, *errare,* to wander.

ABLE: an acronym for *A*ssociation for *B*etter *L*iving and *E*ducation International. See Chapter 25.

action phrases: word phrases contained as part of the content of engrams which dictate some type of "action" in the mind.

affinity: the degree of liking or affection or lack of it. It is the feeling of love or liking for something or someone.

affinity-reality-communication (ARC) triangle: a triangle which is a symbol of the fact that *a*ffinity, *r*eality and *c*ommunication act together to bring about understanding. No point of the triangle can be raised without also raising the other two points, and no point of it can be lowered without also lowering the other two points. See Chapter 4.

analytical mind: that part of the mind which one consciously uses and is aware of. It is the portion of the mind which thinks, observes data, remembers it and resolves problems. See Chapter 4.

antisocial personality: a person who possesses a distinct set of characteristics and mental attitudes that cause him to suppress other people in his vicinity. This is the person whose behavior is calculated to be disastrous. Also called *suppressive person.* See Chapter 16.

AO: abbreviation for *A*dvanced *O*rganization. See Chapter 21.

apparency: something that seems to be, that appears to be a certain way; something that *appears* to be but is different from the way it looks. In Dianetics and Scientology *apparency* is used to mean something that looks one way but is, in actual fact, something else. For example, a person "gives an *apparency* of health," whereas he is actually sick. From the Latin, *apparere,* to appear.

ARC: a word coined from the initial letters of *a*ffinity, *r*eality and *c*ommunication. See Chapter 4.

ARC break: a sudden drop or cutting of *a*ffinity, *r*eality or *c*ommunication with someone or something. Upsets with people or things (ARC breaks) come about because of a lessening or sundering of affinity, reality or communication or understanding. Scientologists usually use the term *ARC break* instead of *upset,* because if one discovers which of the three points of understanding have been cut, one can bring about a rapid recovery in the person's state of mind.

assessment: an auditing technique which helps to isolate specific areas or subjects on which a preclear has charge so that they can be addressed in auditing.

auditing: Scientology counseling, taken from the Latin word *audire* which means "to hear or listen." Auditing is a very unique form of personal counseling which helps an individual look at his own existence and improves his ability to confront what he is and where he is. See Chapter 5.

Auditing by List: a technique used in certain auditing procedures.

auditor: a minister or minister-in-training of the Church of Scientology. *Auditor* means one who listens, from the Latin *audire* meaning "to hear or listen." An auditor is a person trained and qualified in applying auditing to individuals for their betterment. An auditor does not do anything *to* a preclear, he works together with the preclear to help the preclear defeat his reactive mind. See Chapter 5.

beingness: the assumption or choosing of a category of identity. Beingness can be assumed by oneself or given to oneself or attained. Examples of beingness would be one's own name, one's profession, one's physical characteristics, one's role in a game—each or all of these could be called one's beingness.

Book One: a colloquial term for the first book published on the subject of Dianetics, *Dianetics: The Modern Science of Mental Health.* A *Book One Auditor* is someone who knows the data in this book and uses it to audit others.

case: a general term for a person being treated or helped. It is also used to mean the entire accumulation of upsets, pain, failures, etc., residing in a preclear's reactive mind.

case gains: the improvements and resurgences a person experiences from auditing; any case betterment according to the preclear.

Case Supervisor: a highly trained auditor who is also trained in the technology of supervising auditing. The Case Supervisor reviews all auditing sessions done by auditors under his charge. His purpose is to see that the technology is standardly applied for the greatest possible benefit for the preclear. See Chapter 14.

CCHR: abbreviation for Citizens Commission on Human Rights. See Chapter 24.

charge: harmful energy or force contained in mental image pictures of experiences painful or upsetting to the person, which is handled in auditing. See Chapter 5.

Claims Verification Board: an official group within the Church of Scientology which facilitates refund requests.

Clay Table Processing: a particular process used in certain types of auditing.

Clear: a highly desirable state for the individual, achieved through auditing, which was never attainable before Dianetics. A Clear is a person who no longer has his own reactive mind and therefore suffers none of the ill effects that the reactive mind can cause. The Clear has no engrams which, when restimulated, throw out the correctness of his computations by entering hidden and false data. See Chapter 13.

control: the ability to start, change and stop something. One is successful in his life to the degree that he can start or change or stop the things and people within his environment. For example, a driver who cannot exert control over a car by making it start move about and stop when he wants it to is quite likely to have accidents. A person who *can* control a car, on the other hand, will be able to arrive where he intends to.

counter-effort: an effort of something or someone in a person's environment against that person.

C/S: abbreviation for Case Supervisor. Also used to designate a Case Supervisor direction of what to audit on a preclear (as in "he was given a new C/S"), or the giving of such a direction by the Case Supervisor (as in "the preclear was C/Sed for his next action"). *See also* **Case Supervisor** in this glossary.

CSI: abbreviation for Church of Scientology International. See Chapter 21.

Data Series: a series of policy letters written by L. Ron Hubbard which deal with logic, illogic, proper evaluation of data and how to detect and handle the causes of good and bad situations within groups and organizations.

determinism: power of choice; power of decision; ability to decide or determine the course of one's own or others' actions.

Dianetics: comes from the Greek words *dia,* meaning "through" and *nous,* meaning "soul." Dianetics is a methodology developed by L. Ron Hubbard which can help alleviate such ailments as unwanted sensations and emotions, irrational fears and psychosomatic illnesses. It is most accurately described as *what the soul is doing to the body through the mind.* See Chapter 4.

dramatization: the acting out of an engram in its entirety or in part by an aberrated person in his current environment. Aberrated conduct is entirely dramatization. For example, a woman receives an engram in which she is kicked in the side and told that she is no good, that she is always changing her mind. At some time in the future, this engram could be reactivated and the woman might experience a pain in her side, feel that she is no good or get the idea that she is always changing her mind. This would be a dramatization of the engram.

dwindling spiral: a condition characterized by continuous worsening, decreasing or shrinking.

dynamics: the eight urges, drives or impulses of life. See Chapter 4.

E-Meter: short for *Electropsychometer,* a specially designed instrument which helps the auditor and preclear locate areas of spiritual distress or travail. The E-Meter is a religious artifact and can only be used by Scientology ministers or ministers-in-training. It does not diagnose or cure anything. It measures the mental state or change of state of a person and thus is of benefit to the auditor in helping the preclear locate areas to be handled. See Chapter 5.

engram: a recording made by the reactive mind when a person is "unconscious." An engram is not a memory—it is a particular type of mental image picture which is a complete recording, down to the last accurate detail, of every perception present in a moment of partial or full "unconsciousness." See Chapter 4.

enturbulence: turbulence or agitation and disturbance.

Est Repair Rundown: an auditing action designed to repair the damage done to a person mentally and spiritually by the practice of est (Erhard Seminars Training). Est was an offbeat group which used destructive techniques, and some people new to Scientology are found to have been previously involved with est. It is necessary to undo the harmful effects of est before such persons can make adequate progress in Scientology auditing.

exteriorization: the state of the thetan being outside his body with or without full perception, but still able to control and handle the body. When a person goes exterior, he achieves a certainty that he is himself and not his body. See Chapter 4.

floating needle: a rhythmic sweep of the needle on an E-Meter dial at a slow, even pace, back and forth, back and forth. A floating needle means that the charge on a subject being audited has dissipated, and is one of the indications of a process being complete.

FSO: abbreviation for *F*lag *S*ervice *O*rganization. See Chapter 21.

FSSO: abbreviation for *F*lag *S*hip *S*ervice *O*rganization. See Chapter 21.

genetic entity: a term coined in early Dianetics research to denote that part of a human being which takes care of the automatic mechanisms of the body, such as heartbeat, respiration, etc.

gradient: a gradual approach to something, taken step by step, so that, finally, quite complicated and difficult activities or concepts can be achieved with relative ease.

grant beingness: to let someone else be what he is. Listening to what someone has to say and taking care to understand them, being courteous, refraining from needless criticism, expressing admiration or affinity are examples of the actions of someone who can grant others beingness.

HASI: an acronym for *H*ubbard *A*ssociation of *S*cientologists *I*nternational. See Chapter 29.

hat: a Scientology slang term for a particular job, taken from the fact that in many professions, such as railroading, the type of hat worn is the badge of the job. The term *hat* is also used to describe the write-ups, checksheets and packs that outline the purposes, know-how and duties of a job in a Scientology organization.

hatting: the training given to a person so that he or she can successfully perform the functions and produce the products of a specific job, duty or activity. *See also* **hat** in this glossary.

havingness: the concept of being able to reach. By *havingness* we mean owning, possessing, being capable of commanding, taking charge of objects, energies and spaces. Specific processes exist in Scientology to help a preclear increase his havingness, and these are appropriately called Havingness Processes.

HCO: abbreviation for *H*ubbard *C*ommunications *O*ffice. See Chapter 20.

HGC: abbreviation for *H*ubbard *G*uidance *C*enter. See Chapter 20.

Hubbard Consultant Outpoint-Pluspoint List: a list of illogics (outpoints) and logics (pluspoints) used in an auditing process to help the preclear locate and handle illogical thinking in the area being addressed.

IAS: abbreviation for *I*nternational *A*ssociation of *S*cientologists. See Chapter 22.

I HELP: an acronym for *I*nternational *H*ubbard *E*cclesiastical *L*eague of *P*astors. See Chapter 21.

INCOMM: an acronym for *I*nternational *N*etwork of *C*omputer *O*rganized *M*anage*m*ent. See Chapter 29.

int: short for *interiorization,* the action of going into something too fixedly and becoming part of it too fixedly. *Int* is also used to refer to the auditing procedure which handles the adverse mental and spiritual effects of interiorization.

invalidate: refute, degrade, discredit or deny something someone else considers to be fact.

knowledge-responsibility-control (KRC) triangle: a triangle which is a symbol of the fact that *k*nowledge, *r*esponsibility and *c*ontrol act together as a whole entity. In order to handle any area of one's life, it is necessary to *know* something about it, take some *responsibility* for it and *control* it to the degree necessary to achieve the desired result. This triangle interacts best when used with high ARC, thus it interlocks with the ARC triangle. *See also* **affinity-reality-communication (ARC) triangle** and **control** in this glossary.

Listing and Nulling: a specialized technique used in certain auditing processes.

lock: a mental image picture of an experience where one was knowingly or unknowingly reminded of an engram. It does not itself contain a blow or a burn or impact and is not any major cause of upset. It does not contain unconsciousness. It may contain a feeling of pain or illness, etc., but is not itself the source of it. For example, a person sees a cake and feels sick. This is a lock on an engram of being made sick by eating cake. The picture of seeing a cake and feeling sick is a lock on (is locked to) the incident (unseen at the moment) of getting sick eating cake.

mental image pictures: three-dimensional pictures which are continuously made by the mind, moment by moment, containing color, sound and smell, as well as other perceptions. They also include the conclusions or speculations of the individual. Mental image pictures are composed of energy, have mass, exist in space and follow definite routines of behavior, the most interesting of which is the fact that they appear when somebody thinks of something. See Chapter 4.

MEST: a word coined from the initial letters of *m*atter, *e*nergy, *s*pace and *t*ime, which are the component parts (elements) of the physical universe.

meter: short for *E-Meter. See* **E-Meter** in this glossary.

missed withhold: a withhold which has *almost* been found out by another, that leaves the person who has the withhold in a state of wondering whether or not his hidden deed is known. *See also* **withhold** in this glossary.

NCLE: abbreviation for *N*ational *C*ommission on *L*aw *E*nforcement and Social Justice. See Chapter 24.

NED: an acronym for *N*ew *E*ra *D*ianetics. See Chapter 13.

New Era Dianetics for OTs (NOTs): a series of auditing actions, delivered as part of the OT levels, developed by L. Ron Hubbard during his research into New Era Dianetics in the late 1970s.

NOTs: an acronym for *N*ew Era Dianetics for *OTs. See* **New Era Dianetics for OTs** in this glossary.

Objectives: short for *Objective Processing,* an auditing action which helps a person to look or place his attention outward from himself.

OCA: abbreviation for *O*xford *C*apacity *A*nalysis. See Chapter 5.

Operating Thetan: a state of being above Clear, in which the Clear has become refamiliarized with his native capabilities. An Operating Thetan is knowing and willing cause over life, thought, matter, energy, space and time. See Chapter 13.

organizing board: a system of organizing that contains all functions a Scientology organization must perform in order to efficiently provide for its parishioners. See Chapter 20.

OSA: an acronym for *O*ffice of *S*pecial *A*ffairs. See Chapter 32.

OT: abbreviation for *O*perating *T*hetan. *See* **Operating Thetan** in this glossary.

overrun: continue an auditing process or a series of processes past the point of completion.

overt: a harmful act or a transgression against the moral code of a group. When a person does something that is contrary to the moral code he has agreed to, or when he omits to do something that he should have done per that moral code, he has committed an overt. An overt violates what was agreed upon. An overt can be intentional or unintentional.

pan-determined: able to view both sides. Pan-determinism is *across* determinism or determinism of two sides. If a person were playing both sides of a chess game, he would be exercising pan-determinism. *See also* **determinism** in this glossary.

PDH: abbreviation for *p*ain *d*rug *h*ypnosis, a behavioral modification technique used by military and intelligence services in which pain, drugs or hypnosis, or any combination of these, are administered to drive an individual into a state whereby he can be given suggestions or commands subconsciously. Dianetics auditing can undo the effects of PDH. For more information, see Chapter 31.

perceptic: any sense message such as sight, sound, smell, etc.

postulate: a conclusion, decision or resolution made by the individual himself to resolve a problem or to set a pattern for the future or to nullify a pattern of the past. For example, a person says, "I like Model-T Fords. I am never going to drive another car." Years later, no longer consciously aware of this postulate, he will wonder why he is having so much trouble with his Buick; it's because he has made an earlier promise to himself. In order to change he has to change that postulate.

potential trouble source: a person who is in some way connected to and being adversely affected by a suppressive person. Such a person is called a *potential* trouble source because he can be a lot of trouble to himself and to others. *See also* **suppressive person** in this glossary.

preclear: a person who is receiving Scientology or Dianetics auditing on his way to becoming Clear, hence pre-Clear. Through auditing he is finding out more about himself and life. See Chapter 5.

process: an exact set of questions asked or directions given by an auditor to help a person find out things about himself and improve his condition. See Chapter 5.

processing: another word for *auditing. See* **auditing** in this glossary.

PTS: abbreviation for *p*otential *t*rouble *s*ource. *See* **potential trouble source** in this glossary.

Qual: short for *Qualifications Division*. See Chapter 20.

RD: abbreviation for *r*un*d*own. *See* **rundown** in this glossary.

reactive mind: that part of the mind which works on a totally stimulus-response basis, which is not under a person's volitional control, and which exerts force and the power of command over his awareness, purposes, thoughts, body and actions. See Chapter 4.

reality: that which appears to be. Reality is fundamentally agreement—what we agree to be real is real.

rehab: short for *rehabilitation,* an auditing action which is used to help a person regain a former ability, state of being or more optimum condition which has been discredited, denied or suppressed.

restimulation: the "awakening" of an old engram, which occurs when a person's present environment contains enough similarities to the elements found in the engram to cause a reactivation of it. When an engram is restimulated, a person can experience similar pains and emotions to those contained in the original incident.

R6EW: the designation for the auditing process used on Grade VI. See Chapter 36.

RTC: abbreviation for *R*eligious *T*echnology *C*enter. See Chapter 21.

rundown: a series of related actions in Scientology which culminate in a specific end result. For example, the Drug Rundown consists of several different auditing processes and actions which, done fully and in sequence, result in the freeing of a person from the mental and spiritual effects of drugs.

Scientology: comes from the Latin *scio,* which means "know" and the Greek word *logos,* meaning "the word or outward form by which the inward thought is expressed and made known." Thus, Scientology means knowing about knowing. Scientology is an applied religious philosophy developed by L. Ron Hubbard. It is the study and handling of the spirit in relationship to itself, universes and other life. See Chapter 4.

Sea Org: short for *Sea Organization.* See Chapter 21.

self-determinism: the condition of determining the actions of self; the ability to direct oneself. *See also* **determinism** in this glossary.

service facsimile: a consideration that one must be consistently in a certain state in order to survive. This consideration will cause the individual to deliberately hold in restimulation selected parts of his reactive mind to explain his failures in life. For example, a person may keep an old injury in restimulation so that his family has to look after him.

SHSBC: abbreviation for *S*aint *H*ill *S*pecial *B*riefing *C*ourse. See Chapter 14.

SMI: an acronym for *S*cientology *M*issions *I*nternational. See Chapter 21.

SP: abbreviation for *s*uppressive *p*erson. *See* **suppressive person** in this glossary.

stable terminal: someone who is reliable, responsible and who can be depended upon to competently perform the duties of his job.

standard memory banks: recordings in the analytical mind of everything perceived throughout the lifetime up to the present by the individual except physical pain, which is recorded in the reactive mind. See Chapter 4.

suppressive person: a person who possesses a distinct set of characteristics and mental attitudes that cause him to suppress other people in his vicinity. This is the person whose behavior is calculated to be disastrous. Also called *antisocial personality.* See Chapter 16.

theta: energy peculiar to life which acts upon material in the physical universe and animates it, mobilizes it and changes it; natural creative energy of a being which he is free to direct toward survival goals. The term comes from the Greek letter *theta* (θ), which the Greeks used to represent *thought.*

thetan: an immortal spiritual being; the human soul. The term *soul* is not used because it has developed so many other meanings from use in other religions and practices that it doesn't describe precisely what was discovered in Scientology. We use the term *thetan* instead, from the Greek letter *theta, (θ),* the traditional symbol for thought or life. One does not *have* a thetan, something one keeps somewhere apart from oneself; one *is* a thetan. The thetan is the person himself, not his body or his name or the physical universe, his mind or anything else. It is that which is aware of being aware; the identity which IS the individual. See Chapter 4.

time track: the consecutive record of mental image pictures which accumulates through a person's life. It is a very accurate record of a person's past. As a rough analogy, the time track could be likened to a motion-picture film—if that film were three-dimensional, had fifty-two perceptions and could fully react upon the observer. See Chapter 4.

TRs: abbreviation for *t*raining *r*outines, practical drills which can greatly increase a student's ability in essential auditing skills, such as communication. See Chapter 14.

unmock: become nothing, disappear, cease to exist.

whole track: the whole span of the time track. *See also* **time track** in this glossary.

WISE: an acronym for *W*orld *I*nstitute of *S*cientology *E*nterprises International. See Chapter 26.

withhold: an overt a person has committed but is not talking about; an unspoken, unannounced transgression against a moral code by which a person was bound. Any withhold comes *after* an overt. *See also* **overt** in this glossary.

WW: abbreviation for *W*orld*w*ide—the worldwide headquarters of the Church of Scientology at Saint Hill, where management was located until the early 1970s.

INDEX

A

E

F

G

H

I

L

M

N

O

P

Q

R

S

T

U

V

W–Z

Preface

As the sequencing phase of the human and other genome projects nears completion, we are faced with the task of understanding how the vast strings of Cs, As, Ts, and Gs encode a being. With the recent advent of microarrays and other high throughput biologic technologies, we have moved from trying to understand single molecules and pathways to that of integrative systems. We are only beginning to grasp the questions we can ask as we are now challenged to understand these large in silico, in vitro, and in vivo data sets. The new field of Bioinformatics was born of a series of meetings among "wet-bench" scientists, in the early 1980s, to meet this challenge. With the recruitment of mathematicians, computer scientists, statisticians, and astrophysicists to this field, we have now begun to design and implement some of the basic tools that will enable data integration and multidimensional analyses of these varied but unified data sets. For those new to Bioinformatics, this cross pollenization of the Life, Physical, and Theoretical sciences wants for a common language. With this in mind, *Introduction to Bioinformatics: A Theoretical and Practical Approach* was written as an introductory text for the undergraduate, graduate, or professional.

At once, this text provides the physical scientist, whether mathematician, computer scientist, statistician or astrophysicist, with a biological framework to understand the questions a life scientist would pose in the context of the computational issues and currently available tools. At the same time, it provides the life scientist with a source for the various computational tools now available, along with an introduction to their underlying mathematical foundations. As such, this book can be used as a bridge toward homologation of these fields. By bringing these disciplines together we may begin our journey toward understanding the nuances of the genetic code.

Introduction to Bioinformatics: A Theoretical and Practical Approach is divided into four main sections. The first two sections are well suited to the physical scientist who is new to studying biological systems. They provide the biological vocabulary, i.e., an overview of the various biological processes that govern an organism and impact health. The first section, *Biochemistry, Cell, and Molecular Biology*, describes basic cellular structure and the biological decoding of the genome. *In silico* detection of the promoter elements that modulate genome decoding is also explained. The second section, *Molecular Genetics*, will lead the reader through a discussion of the long range regulation of genomes, the *in silico* detection of the elements that impact long range control, and the molecular genetic basis of disease as a consequence of replication. Clinical human genetics and the various clinical databases are reviewed, followed by a discussion of the various issues within population genetics that can be used to address the question: "How do we evolve as we respond to our environment?"

The third section, *The UNIX Operating System*, was written for the life scientist, to demystify the UNIX operating system that is commonly used to support advanced computational tools. Along with understanding the installation and management of UNIX-based software tools, examples of command line sequence analyses are presented. These chapters should enable the life scientist to become as comfortable in a command line environment as in the Graphical-User Interface environment.

The *Computer Applications* section provides a common area for the physical and life scientist to meet. The management and analysis of DNA sequencing projects is presented, along with a review of how DNA can be modeled as a statistical series of patterns. The latter forms the basis of most protein and nucleic acid sequence analysis routines. These considerations are followed by a discussion of the various genome databases, the representation of genomes, and methods for their large scale analyses. This culminates in addressing the question: "Can I learn about my sequence from what is known about a similar sequence?" To directly answer this question a discussion of the various methods of pattern discovery follows, including basic multiple sequence alignment to identify both functionally and structurally related components. The accompanying protein visualization chapter outlines how these tools can aid in predicting structures that often represent homologous segments from evolutionarily conserved gene families. This final section concludes with a review of how multiple sequence alignment can be used to infer both functional and structural biological relationships. In closing, the final chapters of the book review the new field of Transcription Profiling, examining the current state of analysis software for systems biology. We conclude our journey with a discussion of the *in silico* analysis and prediction of patterns of gene expression that will ultimately guide our understanding of living systems.

Though the text provides a detailed description and examples, the CD supplement also contains a complete set of illustrations from each chapter, many of which are present in color. This provides a visual resource for both the student and the teacher that should prove invaluable for those of us preparing our next Bioinformatics lecture or seminar. In addition, several full version and limited trial versions of the programs that are discussed in the text are included. These encompass a broad spectrum, from DNA sequencing project management to microarray analysis, offering the reader the opportunity to easily access some of the software tools that are discussed. It is our hope that the current and next generation of physical and life scientists will use these resources as a springboard to help us move forward in the important quest for an integrated understanding of our physical being.

Stephen A. Krawetz
David D. Womble

Introduction to Bioinformatics

A Theoretical and Practical Approach

Edited by

Stephen A. Krawetz, PhD

Wayne State University School of Medicine, Detroit, MI

and

David D. Womble, PhD

Wayne State University School of Medicine, Detroit, MI

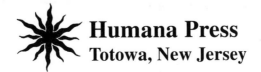

Humana Press
Totowa, New Jersey

999 Riverview Drive, Suite 208
Totowa, New Jersey 07512

humanapress.com

This publication is printed on acid-free paper. ∞
ANSI Z39.48-1984 (American Standards Institute) Permanence of Paper for Printed Library Materials.

Production Editor: Mark J. Breaugh.

Cover design by Patricia F. Cleary and Paul A. Thiessen.

Cover illustration by Paul A. Thiessen, chemicalgraphics.com.

For additional copies, pricing for bulk purchases, and/or information about other Humana titles, contact Humana at the above address or at any of the following numbers: Tel.: 973-256-1699; Fax: 973-256-8341; E-mail: humana@humanapr.com, Website: humanapress.com

Printed in the United States of America. 10 9 8 7 6 5 4 3 2 1

Library of Congress Cataloging in Publication Data

Introduction to bioinformatics : a theoretical and practical approach / edited by Stephen A. Krawetz and David D. Womble.
p. ; cm.
Includes bibliographical references and index.
ISBN 1-58829-064-6 (alk. paper) (HC); 1-58829-241-X (PB); 1-59259-335-6 (e-book)
1. Bioinformatics. I. Krawetz, Stephen A. II. Womble, David D.
[DNLM: 1. Computational Biology--methods. 2. Computer Systems. 3. Databases, Genetic. 4. Genomics. 5. Sequence Analysis, DNA. 6. Software. QH 506 I646 2002]
QH 507 .I575 2002
570'.285--dc21 2002190207

Introduction to Bioinformatics

Contents

Contributors

JILL S. BARNHOLTZ-SLOAN • *Wayne State University School of Medicine and Barbara Ann Karmanos Cancer Institute, Detroit, MI*

LINDA B. BLOOM • *Department of Biochemistry and Molecular Biology, University of Florida, Gainesville, FL*

JAMES K. BONFIELD • *Laboratory of Molecular Biology, Medical Research Council, Cambridge, UK*

BROŇA BREJOVÁ • *Department of Computer Science, University of Waterloo, Waterloo, ON, Canada*

PETER J. BRIDGE • *Department of Medical Genetics, Alberta Children's Hospital, Calgary, AB, Canada*

BRYON CAMPBELL • *Van Andel Institute, Grand Rapids, MI*

ANTHONY V. COX • *The Sanger Centre, Wellcome Trust Genome Campus, Cambridge, UK*

PAROMITA DEB-RINKER • *Department of Genetics, The Hospital for Sick Children, Toronto, ON, Canada*

SORIN DRAGHICI • *Department of Computer Science, Wayne State University, Detroit, MI*

BRIAN FRISTENSKY • *Department of Plant Science, University of Manitoba, Winnepeg, MB, Canada*

DAVID J. HEARD • *Department of Bioinformatics, ExonHit Therapeutics SA, Paris, France*

TERUYOSHI HISHIKI • *Biological Information Research Center, National Institute of Advanced Industrial Science and Technology, Tokyo, Japan*

JON HOLY • *Department of Anatomy and Cell Biology, University of Minnesota School of Medicine, Duluth, MN*

BRADLEY C. HYMAN • *Department of Biology, University of California at Riverside, Riverside, CA*

DAVID P. JUDGE • *Department of Biochemistry, University of Cambridge, Cambridge, UK*

JERZY JURKA • *Genetic Information Research Institute, Mountain View, CA*

BEN F. KOOP • *Department of Biology, Center for the Environment, University of Victoria, Victoria, BC, Canada*

JEFFREY A. KRAMER • *Monsanto Life Sciences, St. Louis, MO*

STEPHEN A. KRAWETZ • *Wayne State University School of Medicine, Detroit, MI*

MING LI • *Department of Computer Science, University of California at Santa Barbara, Santa Barbara, CA*

ERIC MARTZ • *Department of Microbiology, University of Massachusetts at Amherst, Amherst, MA*

JOHN R. MCCARREY • *Department of Biology, University of Texas at San Antonio, San Antonio, TX*

THOMAS W. O'BRIEN • *Department of Biochemistry and Molecular Biology, University of Florida, Gainesville, FL*

JOHN D. OFFERMAN • *Life Sciences Software Inc., Long Lake, MN*

KOUSAKU OKUBO • *Medical Institute of Bioregulation, Kyushu University, Fukuoka, Japan*

DANIEL A. RAPPOLEE • *Department of Obstetrics/Gynecology, Wayne State University, Detroit, MI*

C. A. RUPAR • *Biochemical Genetics Laboratory, Division of Clinical Biochemistry, CPRI, London, ON, Canada*

WOJCIECH RYCHLIK • *Life Sciences Software Inc., Long Lake, MN*

SITTICHOKE SAISANIT • *Department of Bioinformatics, Genetics, and Genomics, Hoffman-La Roche Inc., Nutley, NJ*

STEPHEN W. SCHERER • *Department of Genetics, The Hospital for Sick Children, Toronto, ON, Canada*

GAUTAM B. SINGH • *Department of Computer Science and Engineering, Oakland University, Rochester, MI*

RODGER STADEN • *Laboratory of Molecular Biology, Medical Research Council, Cambridge, UK*

JAMES W. STALKER • *The Sanger Centre, Wellcome Trust Genome Campus, Cambridge, UK*

STEVEN M. THOMPSON • *School of Computational Science and Information Technology, Florida State University, Tallahassee, FL*

TOMÁŠ VINAR • *Department of Computer Science, University of Waterloo, Waterloo, ON, Canada*

THOMAS WERNER • *GSF-National Research Center for Environment and Health, Neuherberg, Germany*

DAVID S. WISHART • *Faculty of Pharmacy and Pharmaceutical Sciences, University of Alberta, Edmonton, AB, Canada*

DAVID D. WOMBLE • *Center for Molecular Medicine and Genetics, Wayne State University, Detroit, MI*

CATHY H. WU • *Department of Biochemistry and Molecular Biology, Georgetown University Medical Center, Washington, DC*

THOMAS P. YANG • *Department of Biochemistry and Molecular Biology, University of Florida, Gainesville, FL*

Part I

Biochemistry, Cell, and Molecular Biology

A. The Cell

1. Nucleic Acids and Proteins: *Modern Linguistics for the Genomics and Bioinformatics Era*
2. Structure and Function of Cell Organelles
3. Cell Signaling

1 Nucleic Acids and Proteins

Modern Linguistics for the Genomics and Bioinformatics Era

Bradley C. Hyman

Introduction

Genomics and Bioinformatics have the power to transform all facets of society. From anthropology to agriculture, medicine to manufacturing, virtually all disciplines undeniably will be changed by these promising fields. The goal of genomics is to mine the genomes of all relevant organisms to identify genes and their encoded products that govern the biological reactions that provide fuels, food, fiber, and other materials essential for our health. In addition to feeding the burgeoning world population, genomics/bioinformatics-based discovery will lead us to safer and more nutritious foods; self-resistant crops; disease-resistant animals; foods with prolonged shelf life; an understanding of why pathogens are virulent; and novel bio-based "smart molecules"such as alternative fuels, pharmaceuticals, and environmental sensors. Access to the genetic codes of microbes, plants, and animals will enable a clearer understanding of how life evolved on our planet.

Training in genomics/bioinformatics requires a unique amalgam of skills in statistics, computer science (including algorithm development and database management), engineering, analytical chemistry, and of course, genetics and molecular biology. This chapter introduces venerable, fundamental concepts in molecular biology from a contemporary genomics/bioinformatics perspective using a language-based approach.

Building Definitions in the Genomic Era

What is Meant by Molecular Biology?

Many different kinds of molecules are components of living cells: carbohydrates, lipids, proteins, nucleic acids. All can be studied at the molecular level, including biosynthesis and assembly, atomic and molecular architecture, physiochemical properties, cellular targeting, and function. The common denominator among these avenues of investigation is the genes aligned along lengthy DNA strands. Stretched end-to-end, the genome would extend 2 to 3 meters in a normal human cell. Genes encode information for synthesizing molecules and their assembly into cellular structures. Molecular biology focuses on the structure and activity of these genes, which can be defined in two broad, fundamental ways:

1) The flow of information within a cell. One very famous descriptor of this activity is the *Central Dogma of Molecular Biology*. In its original concept, the *Dogma* was stated as seen in Scheme 1:

➥ transcription ➥ translation

DNA $\rightleftarrows$ RNA $\rightarrow$ PROTEIN [Scheme 1]

reverse transcription

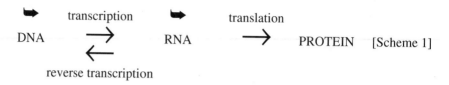

By this scheme, DNA was considered to be self-replicating (➥), providing information in the form of a template for the precise duplication of one DNA molecule, the double helix, into two copies; the intracellular flow of information would continue to follow a strict path by *transcription* of a gene copy in the form of RNA, followed by interpreting the language of nucleic acids (nucleotides) into the language of proteins (amino acids) via *translation* of the RNA into a polypeptide chain. As seminal advances were made in the 1970s and 1980s, modifications were added to the central dogma that involved *reverse transcription* of RNA into DNA (typical of many dangerous retroviruses such as HIV-1, the AIDS virus), and self-replication of RNA molecules.

2) Heredity, or the flow of information between cells (as during cell division; binary fission in bacteria and mitosis in higher cells) and through the generations of an organism (typically mediated by eggs and sperm, produced through meiosis). The chromosomal basis of inheritance is founded on the process of DNA replication, and requires an intimate understanding of the functional architecture of the DNA molecule.

How Does Molecular Biology Help Us Define, in Contemporary Terms, Genomics and Bioinformatics?

The term *genome*, coined in the 1930s, refers to the complete set of genetic information found within an individual organism. Our understanding of molecular biology has enabled the establishment of a simple organizational hierarchy (*see* Fig. 1) that provides a useful scaffold for this discussion. We see that the genome is the all encompassing term for hereditary instructions, whereas the *nucleotide* is the fundamental chemical building block for the genetic material. Therefore, the genome is composed of the entire collection of nucleotides polymerized into long DNA strands. In the human genome, approx 3×10^9 nucleotides comprise one copy of our genome, condensed into each egg and sperm cell. This hierarchy can be annotated for humans by adding additional numerical values (*see* Fig. 2) to illustrate the interrelationship between the genome and other molecular units that collectively define our genetic material.

In Fig. 2, we find that each copy of the human genome is subdivided into 23 chromosomes. (When an egg and sperm unite during fertilization, the newly formed zygote contains 46 chromosomes, or two genome copies; most cells in our body are in this *diploid* state; eggs and sperm in the offspring remain *haploid* with one genomic copy). Individual chromosomes contain one DNA double helix, so each haploid genome is composed of 23 individual DNA duplexes. Distributed among these 23 helicies are an estimated 30,000 genes (although human gene approximations have ranged from 30,000–100,000). Nucleotides are bonded together to create the 23 indi-

GENOME
◊
CHROMOSOME
◊
GENE
◊
DNA
◊
NUCLEOTIDE

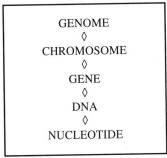

Fig. 1. Simple organizational hierarchy of genetic material.

GENOME (1)
◊
CHROMOSOME (23)
◊
DNA (23)
◊
GENE (~30,000)
◊
NUCLEOTIDE (3×10^9)

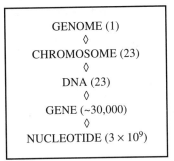

Fig. 2. Numerically annotated hierarchy of genetic material.

vidual DNA chains. Sizes of the 23 chromosomes range from 50×10^6 to greater than 250×10^6 nucleotides.

This hierarchy now allows us to define a "completely sequenced genome." Using high-throughput molecular technology and robotics in concert with sophisticated computer algorithms, it is now possible to assemble the precise order of the four nucleotide building blocks that comprise the single DNA helix within each chromosome. When such sequences are available for all chromosomes in an organism, the genome has been sequenced. Genome sizes range from about 2 million nucleotides for single bacterial chromosomes to $100{,}000 \times 10^6$ for some amphibians and plants. Each report of a completely sequenced genome represents an explosion of data that adds to the rapidly expanding international databases.

How Can All This Data be Stored, Accessed, Manipulated, Managed, and Analyzed?

Here, computer science and molecular biology partner into the new and rapidly emergent field of *Bioinformatics*. It is the goal of Bioinformatics to make sense of nucleotide sequence data (and for proteins, or *Proteomics*, amino acid sequence data). Assume that as we read this sentence, there are no spaces between words nor punctuation marks delimiting the boundaries of written thought. This same sentence might appear as:

assumethataswereadthissentencetherearenospacesbetweenwordsnorpunctuationmarks delimitingtheboundariesofwrittenthought

If this were a DNA sequence written in the language of the four nucleotide building blocks, or a protein sequence inscribed in the language of the 20 amino acids, informatic methodologies would be employed to extract and make sense of information encrypted in what superficially appears as a nonsense string. Bioinformatics as applied to DNA sequences would be exploited to find individual genes in the form of protein coding sequences (exons), expanses of nucleotides that might interrupt gene regions (introns), domains within the DNA that might control the expression of individual genes (e.g., promoters, enhancers, silencers, splice sites), repeated elements (insertion sequences and transposons in prokaryotes; micro- and mini-satellites in eukaryotic genomes), and other elements important for chromosome and gene maintenance. For proteins, identifying important domains within polypeptides, such as catalytic active sites, substrate binding sites, regions of protein-protein interaction, and the prediction of protein-folding pathways are important applications of bioinformatics. Exhuming this information is often conducted by aligning unknown nucleotide (or amino acid) strings with well-understood expanses of DNA or protein sequences to assist in the identification and determination of functional architecture. One popular avenue of research within Bioinformatics is the development and implementation of sophisticated alignment algorithms for the purpose of mining information from DNA and protein sequences.

The Language of DNA in the Genomics Era: Nucleotides and the Primary Structure of Nucleic Acid

This chapter is written in the English language that is composed of a 26-letter alphabet. Users of the language string letters into words, words into sentences, sentences into paragraphs, and so forth. The precise order of the letters conveys definition and meaning. Similarly, chains of DNA (and RNA) are polymers of four different chemical letters, or *nucleotide bases*; the precise order of polymerization is called the *primary structure* of nucleic acid and embedded within the primary structure is the definition of gene content.

The molecular structure of nucleotides also dictates important chemical properties of DNA. Nucleotides are composed of three chemically distinct precincts that confer functionality (*see* Fig. 3). These include a deoxyribose (DNA) or ribose (RNA) sugar, phosphate groups bonded to the 5' carbon in the deoxyribose (or ribose) sugar, and one of four nitrogenous bases (B; Fig. 3) that are attached to the 1' carbon. For DNA, the bases are: the purines, adenine (A) and guanine (G); the pyrimidines, cytosine (C) and thymine (T). Uracil (U), a pyrimidine that replaces T in RNA. When the complete DNA sequence of a genome is reported, it is actually the primary structure, or precise polymerization order, of the nitrogenous bases that are published as a simple string of As, Gs, Cs, and Ts. Sugars and phosphate groups remain invariant in the DNA chain (*see* Fig. 4).

See companion CD for color Fig. 4

The phosphate groups and deoxyribose (or ribose) sugars are highly polar and confer upon DNA (and RNA) the property of solubility in aqueous environments such as the interior of cells. At physiological pH, the phosphate group is ionized (deprotonated) conferring a net negative charge onto the nucleic acid polymer (*see* Fig. 4). In contrast, the nitrogenous bases are nonpolar entities that are "driven" into seclusion, away from aqueous environments. The interior of a DNA *double helix* provides such an environment; it is these hydrophobic forces, along with the additive Van der Waals interactions (0.1–0.2 kcal/mole) among the bases now stacked in the interior of the helix, that help stabilize the double helical structure. However, it is the unique arrangement of atoms within the nitrogenous bases that provides most of the stability to the double helix. When A is juxtaposed with T, and G is adjacent to C, the opportunity now exists for hydrogen bonding between hydrogen atoms of lower electronegativity resulting in a partially positive character, and oxygen atoms of high electronegativity with a partially negative character (*see* Fig. 5). This pairing behavior is often referred to as complementarity between bases (A and T, G and C). Hydrogen bonds (1–10 kcal/mole) formed precisely between the two *complementary* base pairs (A and T; G and C) stabilize the association between the two DNA chains resulting in the double helix.

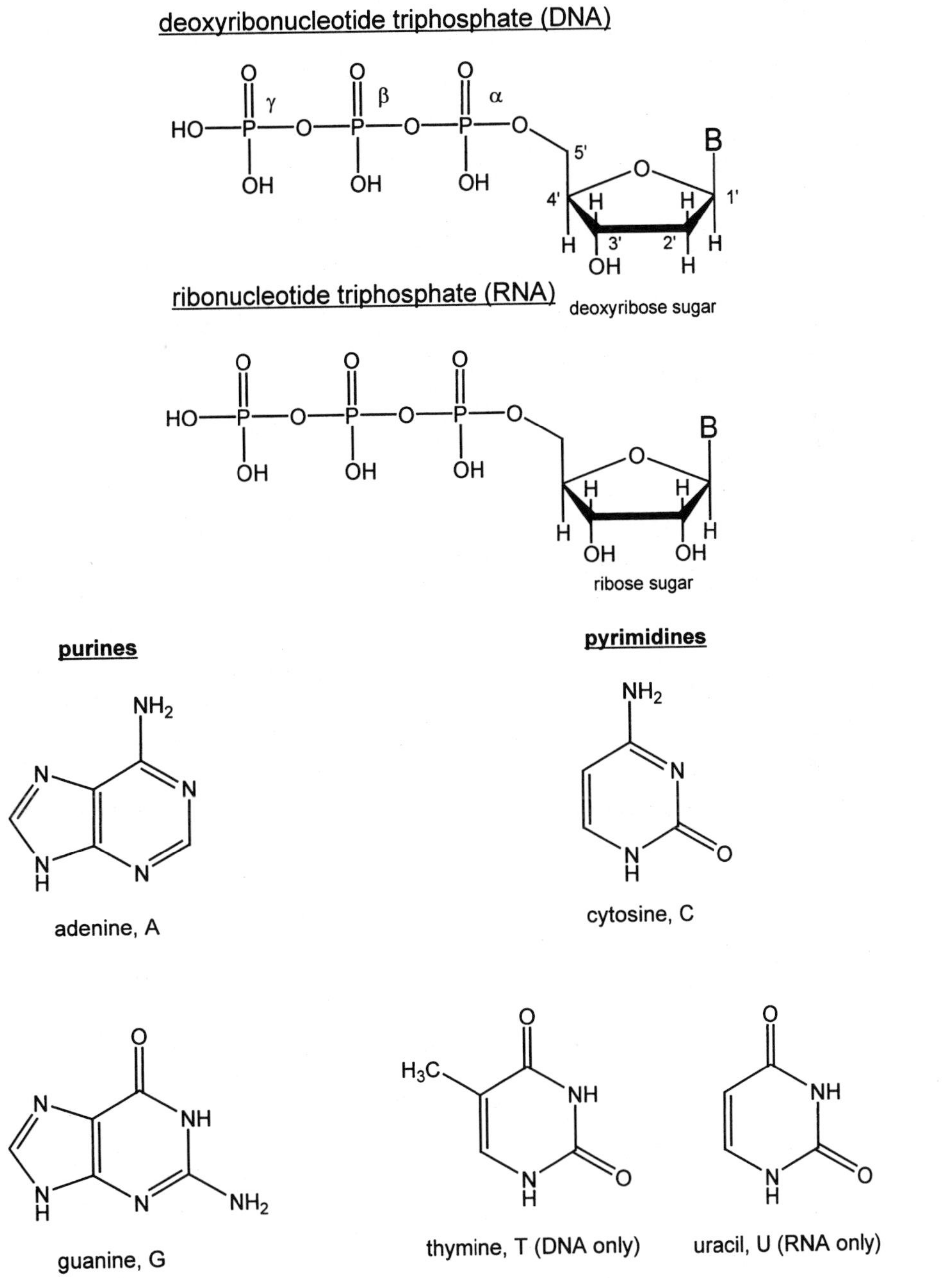

Fig. 3. Molecular structure of nucleotides, the building blocks of DNA and RNA. The 1' → 5' numbering convention used to designate carbons in the deoxyribose and ribose sugars is annotated only on the deoxyribose sugar. "B" extending from the 1' carbon of deoxyribo- and ribonucleotides represent the purine and pyrimidine nitrogenous bases. Designation of the different phosphate groups (α, β, γ) are depicted on the deoxyribose nucleotide.

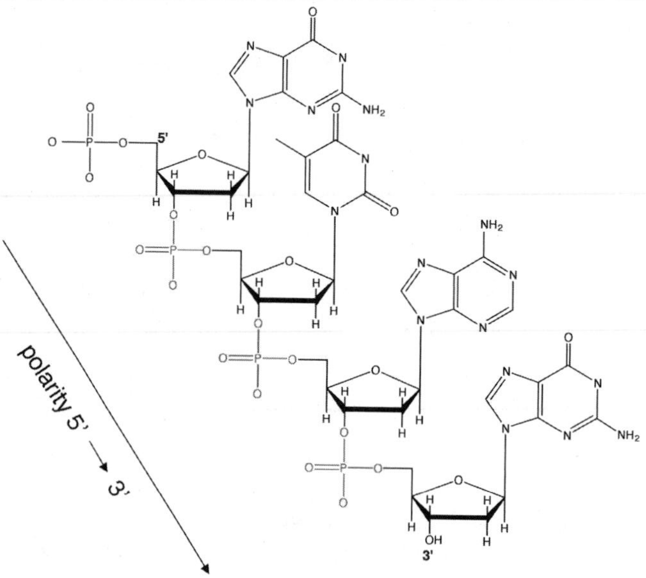

Fig. 4. Molecular structure of the tetranucleotide GTAG. The H present at 2' carbon of each sugar indicates that this is a DNA chain composed of deoxynucleotides. Phosphates involved in cementing adjacent nucleotides together with a phosphodiester bond are shown in red (on CD). A single free, 5' phosphate is pictured in blue. A free 3'-OH group at the opposite end of the chain is also depicted in blue.

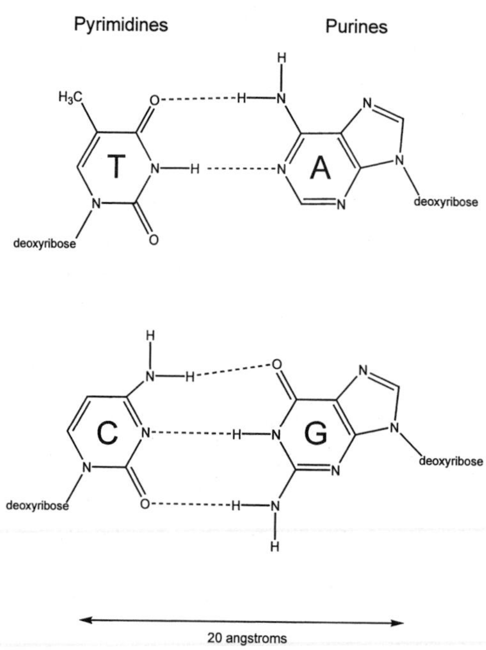

Fig. 5. Complementarity between specific nitrogenous bases. Pictured are the A-T and G-C base pairs present in a DNA double helix. (- - - -) represent hydrogen bonds between participating atoms. A purine juxtaposed with a pyrimidine after hydrogen bond formation generates a dimension of 20 angstroms, the width of a DNA double helix.

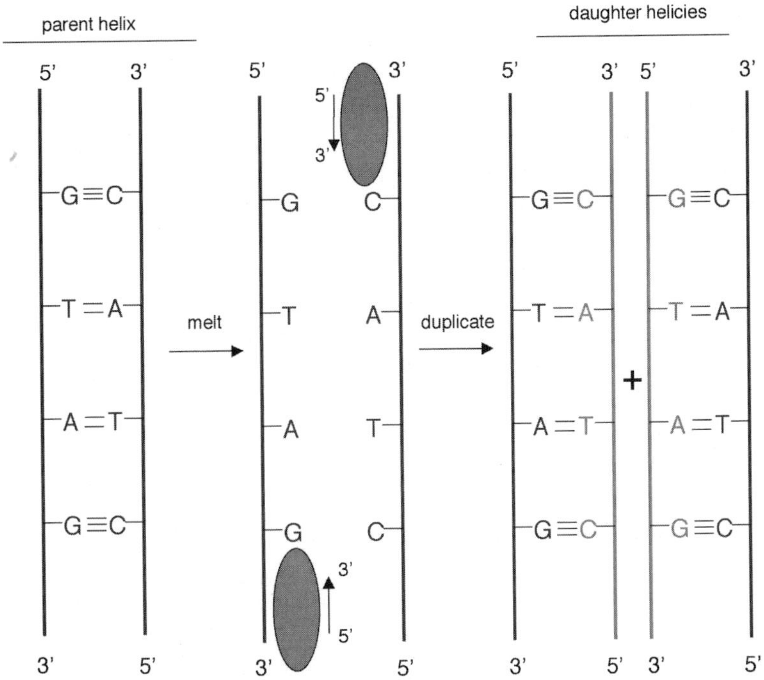

Fig. 6. Base pair complementarity is the basis for faithful duplication of the double helix. Chains of a DNA helix are pictured in an antiparallel configuration. Horizontal lines between the complementing bases denote hydrogen bonds (*see* Fig. 4). DNA polymerase (oval) polymerizes DNA in a 5' to 3' in an antiparallel direction on each strand. Each new daughter helix is composed of an original stand and a newly synthesized chain, indicative of semi-conservative replication.

As immediately recognized in their classic 1953 paper that first described the double-helical nature of the genetic material (*see* Suggested Reading), Watson and Crick explained

> "...the specific pairing we have postulated immediately suggests a possible copying mechanism for the genetic material."

See companion CD for color Fig. 6

What this statement was intended to convey is that each of the two strands in a DNA duplex, by virtue of their complementary, can act as an informational template to specify the primary structure of the second strand in a double helix (*see* Fig. 6). It is the principle of complementarity that provides the foundation for the faithful duplication of DNA, requisite to transmitting the genetic material at cell division and across generations. Semi-conservative DNA replication, in which the new daughter helices each contain one parental and one newly synthesized strand *(see* Fig. 6) is the initial step in the Central Dogma of Molecular Biology and at the mechanistic level provides the foundation for many procedures involved in genome sequencing This is discussed further in Chapter 4.

Nucleotides represent the basic chemical building blocks of the DNA or RNA chain. However, chromosomes are extremely long polymers of nucleotides cemented together. The glue between adjacent nucleotides in a nucleic acid chain is the *phosphodiester bond* (*see* Fig. 4). Formation of the phosphodiester bond in nature is catalyzed by the enzyme DNA polymerase (Figure 6, oval). Amazingly, the enzyme recognizes three substrates in a simultaneous fashion: 1) a free 3'-OH group of the nucleotide representing the growing end of a DNA chain (*see* Fig. 4, -OH); 2) the template DNA (the "opposite strand in a double helix) that provides instructions for the next nucleotide to be added in the form of complementary information (*see* Fig. 6, DNA strands); and 3) the appropriate nucleotide to be added to the growing end of the chain. The nucleotide to be added next into the polymer is in the form of a high energy *deoxynucleotide triphosphate* (dNTP; *see* Fig. 3). Note that the phospho-diester bond cementing two adjacent nucleotides together in the DNA chain contains but a single phosphate group (*see* Fig. 4, red). The energy released by the excision of two phosphate groups from the dNTP during polymerization is recruited by DNA polymerase to catalyze the formation of a a new covalent bond between the 3'-OH of the preceding nucleotide and the α-phosphate of the nucleotide that will be added (*see* Fig. 3). The overall chemical reaction for the polymerization of DNA can be written as shown in Equation 1:

$$(\mathrm{dNMP})_n + \mathrm{dNTP} \rightarrow (\mathrm{dNMP})_{n+1} + \mathrm{PP_i} \qquad \text{[Eq. 1]}$$

In Equation 1, n represents the number of nucleotides already polymerized in the DNA chain, dNMP represents any nucleotide polymerized into a DNA chain (note only one phosphate, a Monophosphate defines the precise structure of a phosphodiester bond), and PP_i is inorganic phosphate, the two phosphates released from the deoxynucleotide triphosphate during addition of a nucleotide to a growing DNA chain.

DNA strands have a chemical directionality, or *polarity*. Specifically, the functional groups that make up the two ends of a DNA chain are different. We noted that a phosphate group resides at the 5' end nucleotide (*see* Fig. 4, phosphate group). That means that one end of the chain terminates in a phosphate group that is not otherwise occupied in a phosphodiester bond holding two adjacent nucleotides together. There will also be one 3'-OH group (*see* Fig. 4, -OH group) not engaged in cementing two nucleotides together in the polymer. This unoccupied -OH group will be found at the opposite end of the chain. Thus, the polarity of a DNA chain is arbitrarily defined as 5' → 3' and DNA sequences are recorded and read in this fashion. Hence, the sequence $^{5'}$P-GTAG-OH$^{3'}$ (shown in Fig. 4) would offer very different informational content than $^{5'}$P-GATG-OH$^{3'}$, the simple reversal of the above sequence. Importantly, the two extended chains in a double helix reveal an opposite, or *antiparallel* polarity (*see* Fig. 6). If we again take the tetranucleotide sequence: $^{5'}$P-GTAG-OH$^{3'}$ and now write this molecule in the form of a double helix, obeying all the rules of base pair complementarity, the correct depiction would be:

```
5'P –GTAG–O H3'
      | | | |
3'HO–CATC–P5'
```

where the vertical lines denote hydrogen bonds between the complementing nucleotide bases in each strand.

Complementarity provides an important check for the precision of sequencing in the laboratory. When a nucleotide sequence is determined for one strand of a DNA duplex, the sequence of the opposite strand is easily predicted. Sequencing both strands of a gene region permits an infallible determination of a DNA sequence because of the cross-check provided by base pairing within the double helix. You may see the term "single pass" in some reports of genomic sequencing efforts, meaning that only one strand of the DNA was sequenced, but a single time. There is some inherent error as the sequence is not experimentally validated by its complement, but single-pass sequencing is useful for rapidly deducing the information content of a genomic region.

Transcription: Converting the Informatics of DNA into a Working RNA Copy

Transcription, or *gene expression* is the second step in the Central Dogma. Controlling gene expression at the level of transcriptional regulation is the subject of more papers published in Molecular Biology than any other topic. The process of transcription involves duplicating a gene sequence encoded in the DNA into an RNA copy. RNA, like DNA, is written in the language of nucleotides, although uracil (U) is substituted for thymine (T) in RNA molecules. The structural similarities between T and U (*see* Fig. 3) allow for either base to hydrogen bond with A. Chemical languages are not changed for RNA synthesis because both DNA and RNA are polymerized nucleotide chains. Information in DNA is simply copied, and this process is referred to as *transcription*. If the gene encodes a protein, the RNA draft is called *messenger*, or *mRNA*. The end-products of some genes are simply RNA copies, not protein. Typically, these are genes that encode *transfer RNAs (tRNAs)* and *ribosomal RNAs (rRNAs)*, both components of the translation apparatus.

Transcription, in biochemical terms, proceeds much like replication. The process can be described by the familiar Equation 2:

$$(\text{rNMP})_n + \text{rNTP} \rightarrow (\text{rNMP})_{n+1} + \text{PP}_i \qquad \text{[Eq. 2]}$$

The deoxyribonucleotides building blocks of DNA have been replaced with *ribonucleotides*, one of which carries the nitrogenous base uracil (U; *see* Fig. 3). The ribonucleotides contain a ribose sugar (*see* Fig. 3). When ribonucleotides are polymerized into RNA, the resulting chain is chemically unstable relative to its close DNA relative. Hydroxyl group (-OH) on the 2' carbon of the ribose sugar (*see* Fig. 3) in RNA can undergo a nucleophilic attack upon an adjacent phosphodiester bond in an RNA polymer and break the bond, fragmenting the RNA polymer. In contrast, deoxyribose sugars, the constituent of the DNA backbone, contain a chemically benign hydrogen at the 2' position (*see* Fig. 3). Although RNA is thought to be the Earth's first informational macromolecule, DNA has likely replaced RNA as the primary source of heritable genetic material because of its chemical stability.

See companion CD for color Fig. 7

RNA, like DNA, can assume various secondary structures. Whereas DNA is usually found as a rigid rod-like double helix as a consequence of hydrogen bonding between chains, RNA polymers typically exhibit intra-strand base pairing, G to C (as in DNA) and A to U (remember U replaces T in RNA). The result is a highly folded RNA chain. A classic example of RNA secondary structure is that assumed by tRNA, which folds into the well-recognized cloverleaf conformation (depicted in Fig. 7). RNA secondary structures provide important architectural features that influence function. Many RNA molecules, for example, are catalytic *ribozymes*, including the *peptidyltransferase* activity of the ribosome (which catalyzes the formation of peptide bonds). Its precise folding is required for this activity. Secondary structure at the 5' end of an mRNA molecule often influences the ability of the ribosome to engage the initiation of protein synthesis and provides a check point for controlling gene expression at the post-transcriptional level.

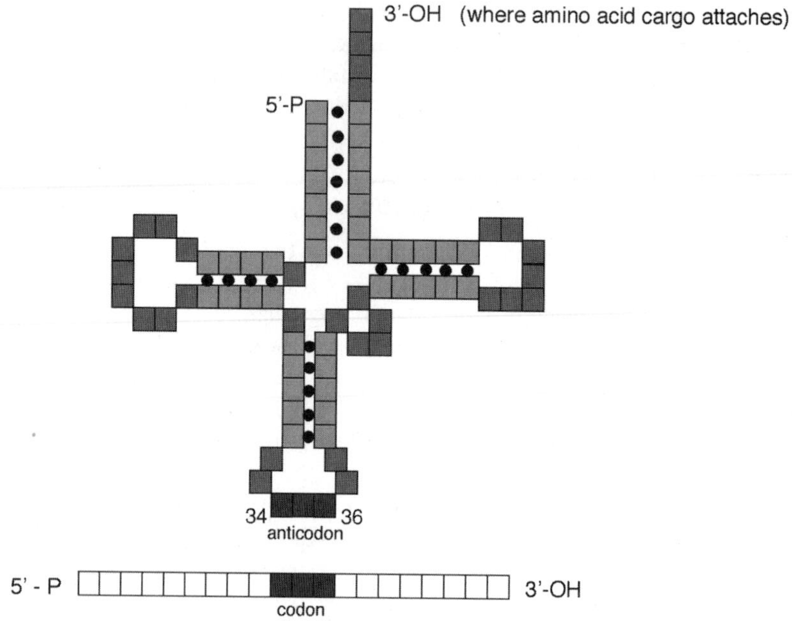

Fig. 7. A transfer RNA (tRNA) molecule acting as an interpreter between the language of nucleic acids (DNA and RNA) and the language of amino acids (proteins). A tRNA, pictured as a polymer of 76 individual ribonucleotides (individual squares), is folded into the universal cloverleaf structure by virtue of intra-molecular hydrogen bonding between complementing bases. The black dots denote base-pairing by hydrogen bonds to form *stems*. Gray squares are unpaired nucleotides, forming loops. The triplet anticodon nucleotides (34–36) are shown recognizing and interacting via hydrogen bonding with the appropriate triplet codon within an mRNA molecule.

Embedded within the primary sequence of DNA are sequences that control the initiation or termination of transcription. In effect, these are the primary regulators of gene expression. These signals are *promoters*, *enhancers*, *silencers*, *terminators*, and other sites along the DNA chains that are targets for DNA binding proteins. For example, promoters may be targets for RNA polymerases and other *general transcription factors* (TFs); enhancers provide docking sites for the proteins that are also needed to activate transcription, called *transcriptional activation factors* (TAFs); silencers bind proteins that inhibit or suppress transcription. One goal of genomics and bioinformatics initiatives is to identify these elements within genomic sequences, and address questions regarding commonalities among controlling elements for different genes. These strategies are helpful in providing a means to understand how genes residing at great distances along the DNA chain, or on different chromosomes, may be co-regulated in response to environmental cues.

The Language of Protein in the Genomics Era: Amino Acids and the Functional Architechure of Proteins

The central goal of genomics and bioinformatics is to understand the complete set of information encoded in a genome. Most of this information will reside in the ensemble of genes that dictates cellular functionality and the "assembly" of an organism. The end-product of most expressed genes is a protein, and the entire set of proteins elaborated by a specific cell type or by an organism is defined as the *proteome.*

The language of proteins is composed of an elaborate, 20 amino acid chemical alphabet. As with nucleic acids, the primary structure of a protein (the precise order of its amino acids) helps dictate the structure of a polypeptide. By analogy with nucleotides, we can dissect the chemical anatomy of amino acids to understand their role in directing protein structure. The typical structure of an amino acid is:

$$\begin{array}{c} \mathrm{R} \\ | \\ \mathrm{NH_2\text{-}CH\text{-}COOH} \end{array}$$

There are two important chemical features characteristic of this simple structure that are important for understanding the conformation of proteins. First, we note a chemical polarity to amino acids, with an *N-* or *amino- terminal* end (the NH_2 - amino group) and a *C-* or *carboxy-terminal* end (the -COOH or carboxylic acid group). Here we can draw an analogy with the chemical polarity of nucleotides defined by the 5' phosphate and 3'-OH groups. The NH_2-CH-COOH "backbone" is common among all 20 amino acids. Just as nucleotide bases are distinguished by one of four nitrogenous bases, amino acids differ from each other by the presence of one of 20 *side chains*, or *R-groups*. These R-groups are the information content of amino acids when polymerized into proteins, just as the nitrogenous bases are the informational component of nucleic acid chains.

The 20 side chains can be catalogued into three major groups depending on whether the R-group is nonpolar, polar, or charged at physiological pH (+ charge = basic; - charge = acidic). Figure 8 catalogues all 20 amino acids in these groups. When polymerized into proteins, amino acids will dictate whether a portion of the polypeptide is soluble in an aqueous environment (hydrophilic) usually if the protein region is rich in polar or charged amino acids, or is repelled by a water-like environment (hydrophobic) if the protein chain is locally rich in nonpolar R-groups. By sequestering nonpolar amino acids within the interior of a globular protein, and exposing polar and charged amino acids to the exterior, proteins in an aqueous environment are forced to assume a three dimensional, or "tertiary" conformation.

See companion CD for color Fig. 9

Proteins involved in membrane function provide an excellent example of how the precise distribution of amino acids within a polypeptide polymer govern structure/function relationships within a biological system (*see* Fig. 9). Membranes are composed of lipids, nonpolar hydrocarbons that present a hydrophobic environment. Proteins embedded in membranes serve many functions, including communicating with the environment and providing channels for transit of essential metabolites into and out of cells. A typical membrane protein (*see* Fig. 9) contains a series of trans-membrane domains composed almost exclusively of nonpolar, uncharged amino acids (small darker dots) that seek a hydrophobic environment within the interior of a membrane, as well as segments that interact with the aqueous interior and exterior of cells comprised by runs of polar and charged amino acids (small lighter dots).

Amino acids represent the building blocks of proteins. Adjacent amino acids are glued together via a peptide bond (*see* Scheme 2 on page 17). Two adjacent amino acids would exhibit the following structure shown in Scheme 2:

As with the synthesis of DNA, polymerization of amino acids into proteins involves a condensation/dehydration reaction that results in a peptide bond. R1 and R2

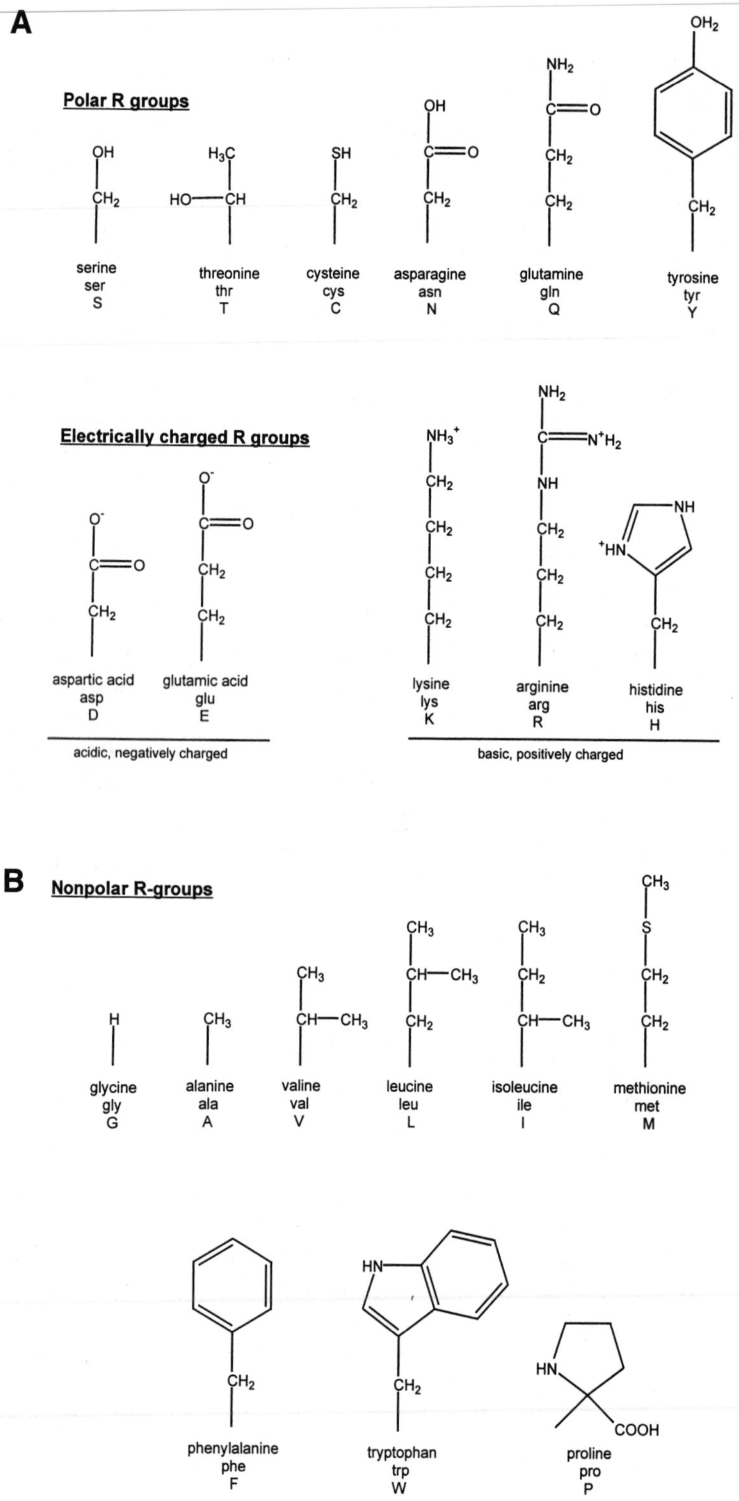
A
Polar R groups
serine
ser
S
threonine
thr
T
cysteine
cys
C
asparagine
asn
N
glutamine
gln
Q
tyrosine
tyr
Y
Electrically charged R groups
aspartic acid
asp
D
glutamic acid
glu
E
acidic, negatively charged
lysine
lys
K
arginine
arg
R
histidine
his
H
basic, positively charged
B
Nonpolar R-groups
glycine
gly
G
alanine
ala
A
valine
val
V
leucine
leu
L
isoleucine
ile
I
methionine
met
M
phenylalanine
phe
F
tryptophan
trp
W
proline
pro
P

Fig. 8. *(opposite page)* Molecular structure of the 20 amino acid side-chains (R-groups), listed according to chemical character (**A**, polar or **B**, charged). Beneath each structure is the name of the R-group, is three-letter designation, and its single letter designation. In an amino acid, the individual side-chain is attached to by a covalent bond to the common backbone NH_2 -CH-COOH, where C indicates the position of attachment.

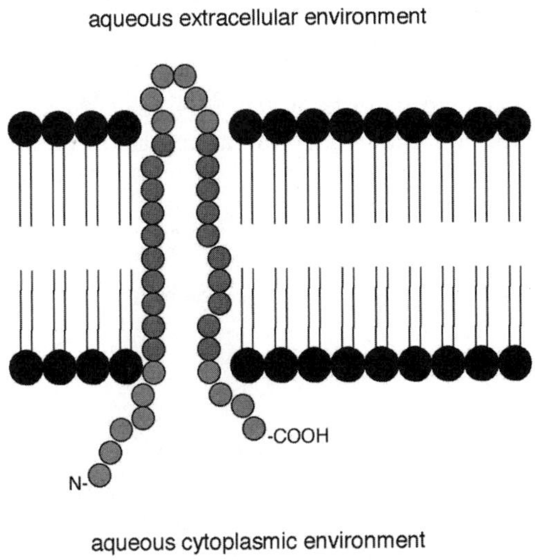

Fig. 9. Membrane proteins: An example of how amino acid distribution dictates structure and function. Pictured in black are phospholipids that create the hydrophobic interior of a lipid bi-layer membrane. Small darker dots indicate nonpolar, hydrophobic amino acid constituents of a polypeptide chain. Small lighter dots represent polar, charged, amino acid residues that are capable of interacting with the aqueous, hydrophilic environments on either side of the cell membrane. Such trans-membrane protein domains typify proteins that serve as channels and as receptors to perceive external stimuli.

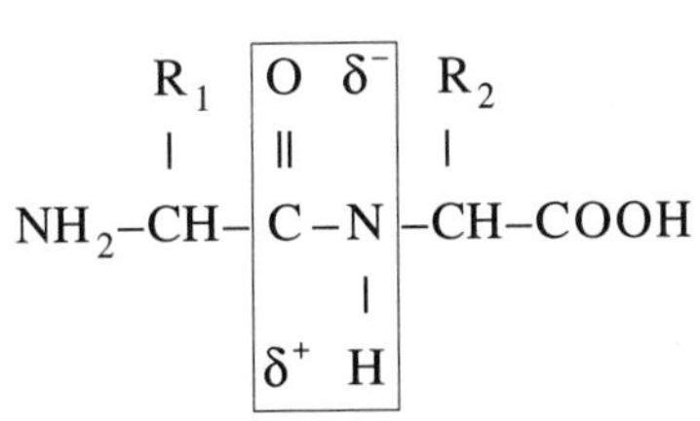

[Scheme 2]

represent two different side chains. Each amino acid with their unique side-chain is typically given a three letter or a single letter designation (*see* Fig. 8). If the dipeptide depicted above is composed of the amino acids glycine and phenylalanine, the peptide would be written NH_2 -GLY-PHE-COOH or NH_2 - GP-COOH, or most often "GP." Note that proteins also have a chemical polarity, arbitrarily written from the N-terminal → C-terminal direction. Thus the dipeptide "GP" would be a very different from "PG." Chemical polarity serves an important role in the informational content of nucleic acids and proteins, as well as in how we annotate the primary structure of both macromolecules.

The oxygen and nitrogen atoms present in the peptide bond are electronegative. As such, the oxygen takes on a partial negative charge (δ^-) and the hydrogen covalently bonded to nitrogen a partial positive charge (δ^+). In a protein with hundreds of peptide bonds, this charge distribution is a recurrent theme, and hydrogen bonding (as in nucleic acids) between the partially charged H and O atoms occurs resulting in important secondary structures known as the α-*helix* and the β-*pleated sheet*. The α-helix is a coil, much like the a telephone handset cord; the β-pleated sheet adds a flattened, sheet-like topology to specific domains of the folded protein, much like a tightly routed "switchback" on a hiking trail.

One additional contributor to protein folding is offered by the chemical composition of the side-chain featured by the amino acid cysteine. The R-group for CYS (or C) is:

```
  H
  |
 -C-S-H
  |
  H
```

When two CYS residues in different regions of a folded protein chain find themselves in the vicinity of each other as a consequence of protein folding, oxidation allows a convalent bond (below) to form between the S atoms in each participating side chain, resulting in a disulfide bridge:

```
  H       H
  |       |
 -C-S—S-C-
  |       |
  H       H
```

We observe that folded protein chains can become stabilized by the formation of disulfide bridges, contributing to the overall topography of the polypeptide. Unlike DNA, every individual protein assumes a unique three-dimensional, tertiary conformation that is necessary for catalytic activity (in the case for enzymes) or to play structural roles within the cell. Tertiary structure, then, is determined by a combination of factors that include the precise order of amino acids (the primary structure), formation of secondary structures in the form of α- helicies or β-pleated sheets and folding due to the generation of disulfide bridges, then driven by hydrophobic and hydrophilic interactions between amino acids and their environment. An even higher level of structure is achieved because many active proteins are not monomers (one properly-folded polypeptide chain), but subunits that must interact with other properly folded proteins to form an active *quarternary structure*. One popular example is the protein hemoglobin, the oxygen carrier protein in our red blood cells. Active hemoglobin is a tetramer comprised of two α and two β subunits in erythrocytes of adult humans. In isolation, these individual protein subunits are inactive, but when they come together they bind and carry oxygen.

Translation: Converting the Language of Nucleic Acids into the Language of Proteins

Proteins are composed of amino acids; however, the information for directing the precise order of amino acids within a peptide (the primary structure) is encoded within DNA and its constituent nucleotides. Conversion between any two languages requires a translator, and no less is true in the cell. The molecular interpreter is the *ribosome*, the cellular site where polymerization of amino acids into protein occurs. *Translation* is the final step in the Central Dogma.

The primary sequence of the nucleotides within DNA, and its RNA copies, can be considered a code that requires deciphering. Proteins are composed of 20 different amino acids, and the first question regarding the code is "How many nucleotides are required to specify one amino acid in a protein sequence?" This question led to the concept of the *coding ratio*: number of nucleotides required to encode one amino acid, or the number of nucleotides/amino acid.

There are four nucleotides (A,G, C, T). Thus if one nucleotide encoded one amino acid (coding ratio = 1), the genetic code could only accommodate 4 amino acids. This is not suffient to encode 20 amino acids. If the coding ratio were two, there are $4^2 = 16$ possible dinucleotide combinations, and 16 amino acids could be encoded. The requirement to encode 20 amino acid is not quite achieved with a doublet code. A coding potential of 64 amino acids (4^3) is achieved with a coding ratio of three, and hence the *triplet codon* (three contiguous nucleotides along the DNA or RNA chain) encodes the information for a single amino acid (*see* Table 1). The 64 codon carrying capacity of this code far exceeds the necessary requirement to encode 20 amino acids. However, the code is redundant; i.e., the same amino acid is often encoded by several different nucleotide codons that are synonyms. For example, the amino acid leucine (LEU) is encoded by six different triplets (*see* Table 1).

Three codons do not encode any amino acid. They are *termination* or *stop codons* that delimit the C-terminal end of the protein, where translation stops. Continuing with our analogy of languages, termination codons serve as the period to end a sentence.

The mRNA copy of the information encoded in DNA is translated into a protein in groups of three nucleotides. Translation typically commences at an AUG (methionine, MET) codon that also signals the initiation of translation. This sets the *reading frame*, one of three possible ways any mRNA molecule can be read in groups of triplets. To illustrate the concept of a reading frame, let us create an mRNA molecule as a sentence in the English language that consists of words with only three letters: "<u>The</u> <u>fat</u> <u>cat</u> <u>ate</u> <u>the</u> <u>big</u> <u>rat</u>." When read as triplets, this rendition makes sense to us. But read in triplets from a different start point, the sentence could also be read "..T <u>hef</u> <u>atc</u> <u>ata</u> <u>tet</u> <u>heb</u> <u>igr</u> at.." or even in a third frame as "..Th <u>efa</u> <u>tca</u> <u>tat</u> <u>eth</u> <u>ebi</u> <u>gra</u> t.." A triplet code implies there are three possible reading frames within a mRNA molecule. The AUG *start codon* establishes the correct reading frame, the one that makes sense. This is defined as an *open reading frame* that typically begins with a start codon (AUG) and ends with one of three termination codons (UAG, UGA, UAA). Gene discovery within genomic sequences, annotating genes, and using sequence information for alignments relies on these features of the nearly universal genetic code (*see* Table 1).

Clearly, a molecular adaptor is required to decipher each triplet codon and deliver the correct amino acid into the growing protein chain. This adaptor is a specific tRNA molecule of about 76–80 nucleotides in length (*see* Fig. 7). Typically residing at nucleotides 34–36 is a set of three continguous nucleotides, a triplet anticodon with base

Table 1
Universal Genetic Code

First	*Second*				*Third*
5'	*U*	*C*	*A*	*G*	*3'*
U	Phe	Ser	Tyr	Cys	U
	Phe	Ser	Tyr	Cys	C
	Leu	Ser	Tyr	Stop	A
	Leu	Ser	Tyr	Trp	G
C	Leu	Pro	His	Arg	U
	Leu	Pro	His	Arg	C
	Leu	Pro	Gln	Arg	A
	Leu	Pro	Gln	Arg	G
A	Ile	Thr	Asn	Ser	U
	Ile	Thr	Asn	Ser	C
	Ile	Thr	Lys	Arg	A
	Met	Thr	Lys	Arg	G
G	Val	Ala	Asp	Gly	U
	Val	Ala	Asp	Gly	C
	Val	Ala	Glu	Gly	A
	Val	Ala	Glu	Gly	G

pair complementarity to a codon along the mRNA chain (*see* Fig. 7). At the 3' end of this molecule the corresponding amino acid cargo is carried (*see* Fig. 7, Table 1). The mRNA and tRNAs congregate at the ribosome, a complex cellular organelle with multiple functions that include: 1) transiting along the mRNA chain in three nucleotide (codon) intervals; 2) capturing the tRNA dictated by the appropriate anticodon/tRNA combination; 3) catalyzing the hydrolytic removal of the amino acid from the tRNA adaptor and 4) condensing the same amino acid to the growing peptide by formation of a peptide bond. This same series of reactions occurs in a sequential fashion, three nucleotides at a time, for each codon found in the mRNA. Translation is an energetically expensive and complex process; three high energy molecules at ATP or GTP are invested to add each amino acid to a growing protein chain as further discussed in Chapter 5.

A Perspective

Modern genomics and bioinformatics is really a new kind of linguistics. Nature, through dynamic evolutionary forces, inscribes genetic information in the form of long nucleotide chains, or genomes. Deciphered by the cell using steps in the Central Dogma, the end-products of sensible nucleotide strings (the genes) are highly versatile proteins whose three-dimensional structure dictates function. The universal genetic code was *cracked* over four decades ago. Yet, how genomes encode traits that make each organism and species different from each other and each individual within a species unique, remained encrypted information until now. With the advent of DNA and protein methodologies, genomes no longer present themselves as molecular hieroglyphics.

Glossary and Abbreviations

Amino Acids Building blocks of protein chains.

Amino Terminal End The end of a protein chain with a free amino group; sometimes called the N-terminal end.

Antiparallel DNA chains in a double helix polymerized in the opposite polarity.

β-Pleated Sheet One of two major secondary strcuture conformations assumed by protein chains.

Bioinformatics Analysis of nucleic acid or protein sequence data.

Coding Ratio Number of nucleotides required to encode a single amino acid .

Complementary Describes the precise base pairing of A with T and G with C by hydrogen bonding.

Cracked Decoded.

Diploid A cell containing two complete sets of chromosomes or genetic information, as found in most body cells.

dNTP Deoxynucleotide triphosphate, the building block of DNA chains.

dNMP deoxynucleotide monophosphate, the form of the building block that eventually becomes incorporated into DNA chains.

DNA Deoxyribonucleic acid.

DNA Replication The act of duplicating DNA from one double helix to two new helicies.

Double Helix The famous two stranded secondary structure of DNA.

Enhancer Binding site in DNA, upstream or downstream from a promoter, for transcription factors that enhance gene expression.

Gene Expression Converting a segment of DNA (gene) into a RNA copy.

General Transcription Proteins necessary to turn on transcription of gene factors.

Genome The complete set of genetic information found in an organism.

Haploid A cell containing one complete set of chromosomes or genetic information, as found in sperm and eggs.

α-Helix One of two major secondary structure conformations assumed by protein chains.

Messenger RNA RNA copy of the gene that encodes a protein.

MRNA Messenger RNA.

N-Terminal End The end of a protein chain with a free amino group; also called the amino terminal end.

Nucleotide The monomer building block of nucleic acid chains.

Nucleotide Bases One of five ring structures, A, G, C, T, U that provides information content to nucleic acid chains.

Open Reading Frame A nucleotide sequence beginning at AUG (the start codon), then read for many consecutive triplets, and ending with one of three stop codons.

Petidyltransferase Catalytic activity of ribosomes that create peptide bonds when amino acids are polymerized into proteins.

Phosphodiester Bond The bond that cements two adjacent nucleotides together in a DNA or RNA chain.

Polarity The chemical directionality of a nucleic acid or protein chain.

Primary Structure The precise order of nucleotide bases or amino acids in a nucleic acid or protein chain, respectively.

Promoter Binding site in the DNA for transcription factors and RNA polymerase; The on/off switch for gene expression.

Proteome Entire collection of proteins in a cell or organism.

Proteomics The study of the entire ensemble of proteins in a cell or organism.

Quarternary Structure Level of structural organization when two or more individual protein chains (subunits) interact to form an active complex.

R-Group One of 20 amino acid side chains that specify chemical properties to each amino acid.

Reading Frame Lengthy contiguous stretches within a gene that specify consecutive triplet codons without encountering a stop codon; this specifies the coding region of a gene; also known as an open reading frame.

Reverse Transcription Synthesizing DNA from an RNA template, as is the case for the AIDS virus.

Ribosomal RNA RNA that forms the structural and catalytic cores of ribosomes.

Ribosome Multisubunit organelle in all cells that is the site of protein synthesis.

Ribozymes RNA molecules that exhibit a catalytic activity.

RNA Ribonucleic acid.

rNTP Ribonucleotide triphosphate, the building block of DNA chains.

rNMP Ribonucleotide monophosphate, the form of the building block that eventually becomes incorporated into DNA chains.

rRNA Ribosomal RNA.

Side Chain One of 20 different chemical groups that confer properties to different amino acids.

Silencer Binding site in DNA for proteins that suppress transcription (gene expression).

Start Codon The triplet AUG that specifies where protein synthesis begins and sets the reading frame.

Stop Codon One of three triplet codons, UAG, UAA, UGA that specify where an mRNA is to stop being translated into protein.

TAF Transcription activation factor.

Terminator Segment of DNA where transcription ends.

Termination Codon One of three triplet codons, UAG, UAA, UGA that specify where an mRNA is to stop being translated into protein.

TF Transcription factor.

Transcription Synthesizing RNA from a DNA template using RNA polymerase transcription activation factor accessory proteins needed for gene expression.

Translation Synthesizing a protein (polypeptide) from mRNA instructions with the ribosome.

Transfer RNA Small RNA molecule that adapts the language of nucleic acids to the language of proteins.

Triplet Codon A string of 3 consecutive nucleotides in an mRNA molecule that specifies one of the 20 amino acids.

TRNA Transfer RNA.

Suggested Readings

Basic Texts

Brown, T. A. (1999) Genomes, John Wiley and Sons, New York, NY, p. 472.
Lewin, B. (2000) Genes VII, Oxford University Press, Oxford, UK, p. 990.
Mount, D. W. (2001) Bioinformatics: Sequence and Genome Analysis, Cold Spring Harbor Laboratory Press, Cold Spring Harbor, NY, p. 564.
Russell, P. J. (2001) iGenetics, Benjamin Cummings, San Francisco, CA, p. 828.
Weaver, R. F. (1999) Molecular Biology, WCB/McGraw-Hill, Boston, MA, p. 788.

Some Primary Literature

(2001) The Human Genome Issue, Nature 409, 745–764.
(2001) The Human Genome Issue, Science 291, 1145–1434.
(2000) Breakthrough of the Year: Sequenced Genomes, Science 290, 2201–2372.
Watson, J. D. and Crick, F. H. C. (1953) Nature 171, 737–738.

2 Structure and Function of Cell Organelles

Jon Holy

Introduction

The myriad biochemical reactions that comprise life processes are too numerous and complex to be carried out entirely by simple diffusion-mediated interactions between enzymes and substrates. Instead, sequences of biochemical reactions must be efficiently organized and integrated with other sets of reactions by the cell. Two fundamental structural elements are used by eukaryotic cells to organize and integrate these reactions: membranes and a cytoskeletal system. An elaborate system of cellular membranes, in the form of the plasma membrane, membrane-bound organelles, and the nuclear envelope, has evolved to provide reaction surfaces and to organize and compartmentalize molecules involved in specific metabolic pathways. Other cytosolic biochemical reactions, as well as the organization of membranous organelles within the cell, are regulated by interactions with the cytoskeletal system. Consequently, enzymes and proteins involved in biochemical reactions can be located in the cytosol, within membranes, on the surfaces of membranes, within the interior of membrane-bound compartments, or in association with the cytoskeleton. The elaboration of these structural elements has allowed for the sophisticated level of biochemical integration that exists in living eukaryotic cells.

Over two hundred different types of cells are found in higher animals, including humans, and the interaction of these diverse cell types is responsible for the formation and functioning of tissues and organs. Different types of cells carry out specialized functions, but all cells face similar sets of challenges to exist. In general, cells must maintain a barrier against, and sensing mechanisms to interact with, their external environment; synthesize and recycle their structural and enzymatic components; repair physical or chemical damage; grow and reproduce; and generate energy for all of these activities. These generalized functions, as well as the more specialized functions of individual cell types, are all performed by cell organelles. Cell organelles perform the basic functions that allow cells to survive and replicate, and are dynamic entities that become modified to help specialized cells carry out specific functions. For example, all cells contain a cytoskeletal filamentous system that functions in maintenance of cell shape and allows for some degree of movement, but muscle cells contain far greater numbers of these filaments to carry out the contractile activity that comprises muscle activity.

Classically, the phrase *cell organelle* has been used to denote distinct membrane-bound structures that are readily visible by light or electron microscopy and possess characteristic morphological features that make them readily identifiable in essentially all eukaryotic cells. Such structures include the plasma membrane, ER, Golgi apparatus, lysosomes, peroxisomes, and mitochondria (Fig. 1). The structure and function of these organelles, as well as the cytoskeleton and nucleus, are described in this chapter. Because membrane structure plays fundamental roles in organelle function, the basic features of membrane organization will be considered first.

Membrane Structure

Cell membranes are composed of lipid and protein, which are assembled into two opposing layers called the lipid bilayer. Four major types of phospholipids and cholesterol comprise most of the lipid portion of the bilayer. The phospholipids include the choline-containing lipids phosphatidylcholine and sphingomyelin, and the amine-containing lipids phosphatidylethanolamine and phosphatidylserine. All of these phospholipids possess hydrophilic polar heads, and two hydrophobic fatty acid tails. The membrane bilayer represents an energetically favorable conformation of these lipids in that the tails associate with each other to form a hydrophobic environment in the center of the bilayer, with the polar heads facing outward to interact with the charged aqueous environment of the cytoplasm, organelle lumen, or extracellular space. The hydrophobic region resulting from the association of lipid tails creates a barrier to the passage of charged molecules, and only small uncharged molecules, or lipid-soluble molecules, can freely penetrate the lipid bilayer. Cholesterol, which is shorter and stiffer than phospholipids, can comprise up to about 50% of the total membrane lipid. The hydroxyl end of cholesterol interacts with the polar heads of phospholipid molecules, with the rest of the molecule in the same plane as the fatty acid tails of phospholipids. Its presence in membranes is thought to help prevent phase transitions by stiffening membranes at higher temperatures, while also maintaining membrane fluidity at lower temperatures. Although cholesterol is prevalent and equally represented

---

Fig. 1. *(opposite page)* Overview of cell organization. **(A)** Diagram of the major cell organelles, including the cytoskeleton and nucleus. This drawing depicts a single idealized cell, and so does not include the cell-cell and cell-ECM junctions elaborated by cells in tissues. **(B–D)** Examples of low-power electron micrographs of thin sections of rat tissues showing how cell organization reflects cell function. **(B)** Shows intestinal epithelial cells, which are modified to aid in the digestion and absorption of food. The apical membranes of these cells develop highly organized microvilli (MV), which are supported by bundles of microfilaments, to increase the surface area of these cells. The epithelial cells are bound to each other by junctional complexes (JC) consisting of a cluster of tight junctions, zonulae adherens junctions, and desmosomes. The tight junctions prevent material in the intestinal lumen from diffusing between cells into the body cavity, and the adherens and desmosomal junctions firmly anchor cells to each other. A migrating immune cell (LYM, lymphocyte) is also present in this section. **(C)** Shows salivary gland cells, which are specialized to produce and release large amounts of secretory glycoproteins. These cells contain extensive arrays of rough endoplasmic reticulum (RER), and become filled with secretory vesicles (SV). Two nuclei are present in this section, and both display prominent nucleoli (NU). **(D)** Shows cells of the esophageal epithelium, which are specialized to accomodate and resist mechanical stresses. These cells are constantly renewed by the mitotic activity of a basal layer of cells (MC, mitotic cell). As cells are produced and differentiate, they move toward the lumen of the esophagus, become flattened, and form extensive desmosomal connections (D) with neighboring cells.

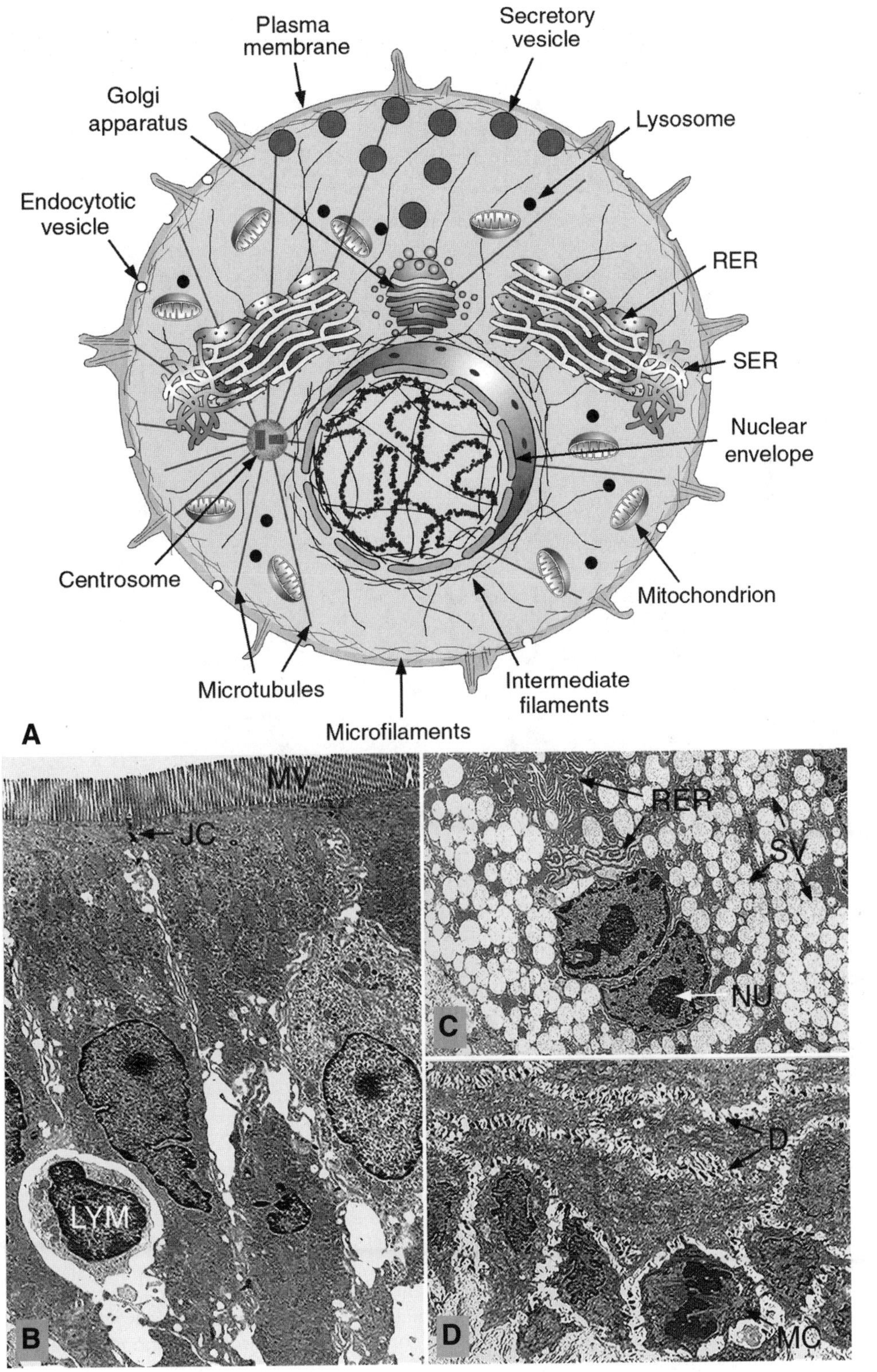
Plasma membrane
Secretory vesicle
Golgi apparatus
Lysosome
Endocytotic vesicle
RER
SER
Nuclear envelope
Centrosome
Mitochondrion
Microtubules
Intermediate filaments
Microfilaments
A
MV
JC
LYM
B
RER
SV
NU
C
D
MC
D

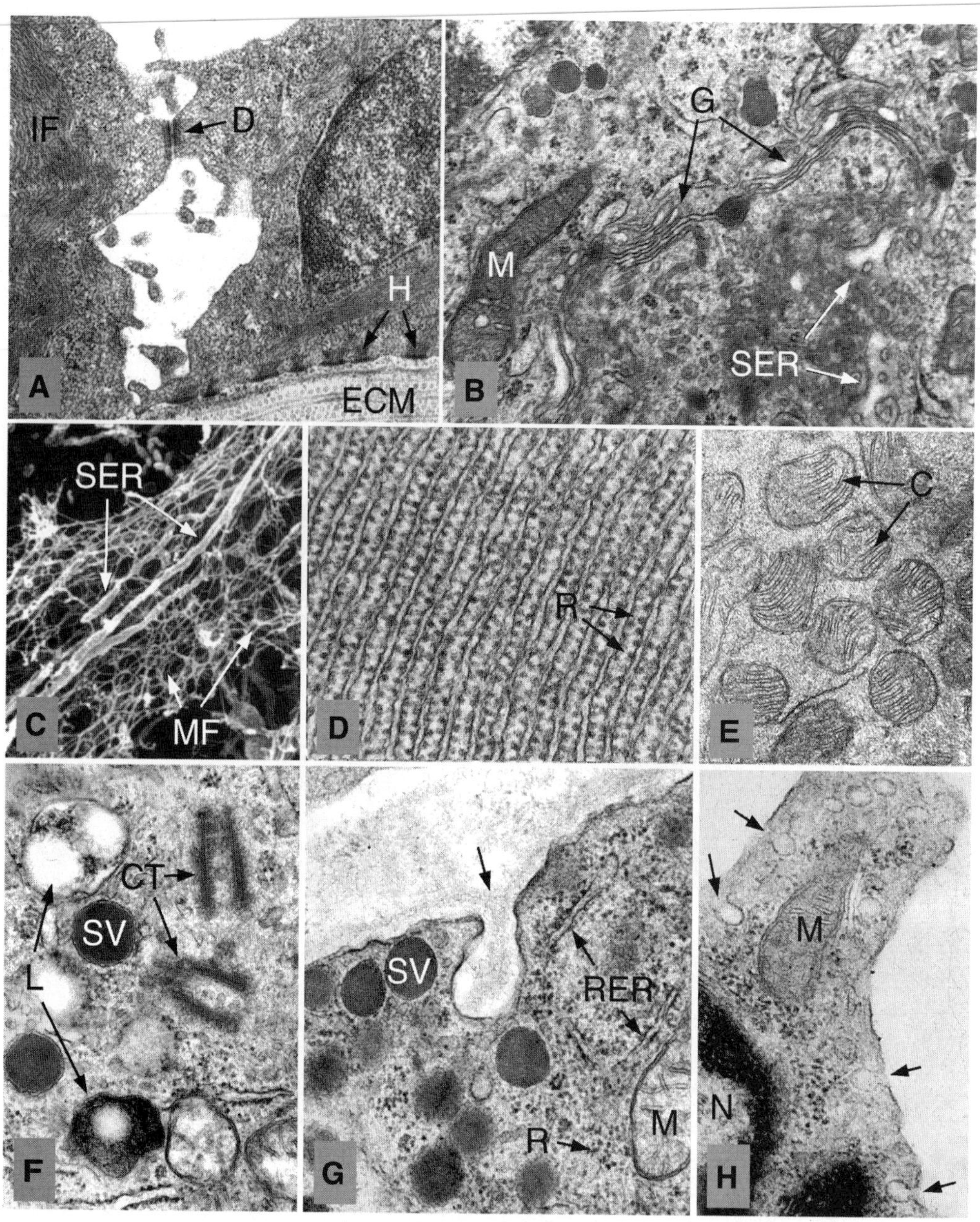

Fig. 2. Electron micrographs illustrating the structural features of various cell organelles. **(A)** Epithelial cells from a tadpole (*Rana pipiens*) tail; **(B)**, **(F)**, **(G)**, and **(H)** show endocrine cells from a rat pituitary gland; **(C)** sea urchin coelomocyte; **(D)** and **(E)** secretory cells from digenetic trematodes (*Halipegus eccentricus* and *Quinqueserialis quinqueserialis*). **(A)** Low-power electron micrograph of an epidermal cell, showing a number of cell-cell and cell-extracellular matrix junctions. These cells elaborate numerous desmosomes (D) and hemidesmosomes (H), and the cytoplasm is filled with prominent bundles of intermediate filaments (IF), which interconnect these junctions. ECM, extracellular matrix. **(B)** Cytoplasm of an endocrine cell, showing a mitochondrion (M), smooth endoplasmic reticulum (SER), and flattened cisternae of the Golgi apparatus (G). Also present are small clusters of

in both bilayers of a membrane, the major phospholipids are asymmetrically distributed, with higher concentrations of choline-containing phospholipids present in the noncytoplasmic layer (i.e., the layer facing organelle lumens and the layer of the plasma membrane facing the extracellular matrix), and higher concentrations of amine-containing phospholipids in the layer facing the cytoplasm.

In addition to lipid, membranes are also composed of protein. Membrane proteins are either classified as integral membrane proteins if they penetrate or are anchored in the bilayer, or as peripheral membrane proteins if they are just associated with the surfaces of the bilayer. Integral membrane proteins are difficult to remove from membranes, usually requiring disruption of the lipid bilayer (e.g., with detergents) to be released. Peripheral proteins are easier to remove from membranes, as they are generally held in place by protein-protein interactions. Integral membrane proteins can penetrate the bilayer completely a single time (single-pass proteins) or multiple times (multi-pass proteins). They can also be anchored in the membrane through covalent attachments to lipid molecules in the bilayer.

A number of membrane lipids and proteins are glycosylated. Glycosylation of membrane components takes place in the ER and Golgi apparatus. Because glycosylation occurs exclusively within the interior (or lumen) of these organelles, the sugar groups of glycoproteins and glycolipids all face toward the lumenal surface of membranes of organelles, and the extracellular matrix (ECM) side of the plasma membrane. Glycosylation of membrane lipids and proteins is thought to help protect membranes, and in the case of the plasma membrane, to help identify the cell and to assist in the adhesion of cells to the ECM.

Membrane lipids and proteins carry out a number of functions. In addition to serving as the structural framework of the membrane, they mediate the functions of all membranes of the cell. Membrane lipids can form specialized subdomains composed of specific lipid populations (lipid rafts) that appear to facilitate localized membrane function, and some membrane lipids are intimately involved in signal transduction events. Membrane proteins carry out a wide variety of functions, including serving as membrane channels, carriers, and pumps; transducing cytoplasmic and extracellular signals; targeting membranes to specific locations; and adhering membranes to each other and to the ECM.

Fig. 2—*(continued)*

free ribosomes, secretory vesicles, and part of the nucleus (upper left corner). **(C)** Low-voltage scanning electron micrograph of an extracted cell (the plasma membrane and soluble cytoplasmic proteins were removed by detergent), showing a few tubular extensions of SER embedded in a network of microfilaments (MF). This type of microscopy shows the surface features of organelles. **(D)** A dense array of RER from a secretory cell; note the high level of organization in the parallel alignment of cisternae. Attached ribosomes (R) appear as small granular bodies. **(E)** Section of cytoplasm containing a number of mitochondria. Their striped appearance is due to the invagination of the inner mitochondrial membrane, which forms cristae (C). **(F)** Endocrine cell cytoplasm, showing two small lysosomes (L), secretory vesicles (SV), and a centriole pair of a centrosome. In this section, pericentriolar material and attached microtubules are not clearly displayed. **(G)** Exocytosis in an endocrine cell. This micrograph shows the periphery of the cell, and the deep invagination of the plasma membrane indicates the site where a secretory vesicle has undergone exocytosis (arrow). A mitochondrion (M), some strands of RER, and clusters of free ribosomes (R) are also shown. **(H)** Pinocytosis in an endocrine cell. The plasma membrane of this cell displays numerous small, smooth invaginations (arrows), characteristic of non-clathrin mediated internalization of material.

The Plasma Membrane

The plasma membrane encloses the cytoplasm of a cell and carries out multiple functions. It forms both a barrier to, and an interface with, the cellular environment. The plasma membrane is a selectively permeable barrier that, by regulating what enters and exits a cell, is a primary determinant of the composition of the cytoplasm. The plasma membrane is associated with sensing mechanisms that transduce environmental information into a cytoplasmic or nuclear response. The plasma membrane is involved in cell-cell and cell-ECM attachments, and also contains cell-specific molecules that help identify cells, thereby helping to establish the appropriate position and arrangement of each cell in the body.

Barrier Functions

The hydrophobic nature of the central region of the lipid bilayer serves as a barrier to charged or large hydrophilic molecules; thus, the lipid bilayer is impermeable to small ions (e.g., Na^+, K^+, Cl^-) and proteins. Only small, uncharged molecules (e.g., CO_2, H_2O), or molecules freely soluble in lipid (e.g., steroid hormones, dioxin) are able to pass directly through the lipid bilayer. In this way, the plasma membrane is selectively permeable. However, materials can be transported into and out of the cell by specific transport mechanisms carried out by the plasma membrane (*see* Transport Functions). The carbohydrate moieties of glycolipids and glycoproteins also serve as barriers by impeding the access of molecules to the surface of the plasma membrane, which can also serve to protect plasma membranes exposed to harsh environments (e.g., the stomach and intestinal lumen).

Transport Functions

Because the lipid bilayer is impermeable to most types of organic molecules, the cell must possess mechanisms to move materials between the cytoplasm and the external environment. Two approaches are used by the cell to move material into and out of the cytoplasm: 1) transport through the membrane, and 2) transport involving membrane flow.

Transport Through the Plasma Membrane

Transport through membranes is mediated by integral membrane proteins, which help conduct material past the hydrophobic lipid bilayer in a number of ways. Integral membrane proteins can form channels by associating to form pore-like structures in the membrane. Such channels allow for diffusion of molecules small enough to fit through them. This type of transport allows for the flow of molecules down their concentration gradient and an expenditure of energy is not needed if the channel is open. Thus, molecules can move through protein channels by passive diffusion. Examples include ion channels that allow for the passage of ions such as Na^+ and K^+, and the connexons in gap junctions, which allow for the passage of molecules <1000 daltons through the plasma membrane. Whether these channels are open or closed is tightly regulated in order to prevent the constant leakage of small molecules into or out of the cell.

Integral membrane proteins can also act as carriers that bind specific molecules and help them traverse the lipid bilayer. Binding of the appropriate molecule to carrier proteins results in a conformational change in carrier protein structure such that the ligand is conveyed across the membrane. This type of transport is also driven by the concentration gradient of the ligand, and does not require the expenditure of energy by the cell. An example of transport by this method of facilitated diffusion includes glucose transporters in the basolateral membranes of intestinal epithelial cells.

Cells must also transport molecules against their concentration gradients, and this type of transport is carried out by integral membrane proteins that act as pumps and requires the expenditure of energy. This is referred to as active transport and is an essential process in living cells. Examples include a number of different ion pumps, which keep the cytoplasm relatively low in Na^+ and high in K^+. Ion pumps are vital elements of the plasma membrane and it has been estimated that as much as one-third or more of the energy consumed by a living cell is used to actively transport Na^+ out of the cell. The concentration gradient of certain ions established by these membrane pumps can itself serve as a motive force for other transport mechanisms. For example, in addition to moving out of a cell by facilitated diffusion, glucose is actively transported into cells by integral membrane proteins that bind both glucose and Na^+. Because these transporters bind both Na^+ and glucose, the high concentration of Na^+ outside the cell relative to the cytoplasm drives the movement of both Na^+ and glucose into the cell, against the concentration gradient of glucose.

Acquisition of glucose from the small intestine is an elegant example of how active transport can be coupled with facilitated diffusion to move molecules past epithelia. The apical membrane of intestinal epithelial cells contain Na^+-coupled active transporters that move glucose against its concentration gradient to accumulate in the cytoplasm. Consequently, the concentration of glucose is higher in the cytoplasm of these cells than in the extracellular spaces underlying them, and carrier proteins in the basolateral membranes of these cells allow for the facilitated diffusion of glucose out of the cell (down its concentration gradient) and into the circulation. It can be seen from this example that directional transport of molecules past epithelial cells requires that integral membrane transport proteins occupy specific locations within the plasma membrane (i.e., either the apical or basolateral membrane). How transporters are organized within the plasma membrane is determined by specific targeting mechanisms acting in conjunction with cell junctions and the cytoskeleton.

Transport Involving Membrane Flow

In addition to movement of materials through membrane channels, carriers, and pumps, the plasma membrane mediates the transport of material into and out of cells by membrane flow. Internalization of extracellular material can occur by entrapment in membrane-bound vesicles that pinch off from the plasma membrane and are transported into the cytoplasm for processing. This process, called endocytosis, can be subdivided into a number of different categories based on the mechanics of how the formation of vesicles occurs at the plasma membrane, and includes the formation of clathrin-coated vesicles from coated pits, and the formation of nonclathrin-coated vesicles derived from structures called caveolae.

Clathrin-coated vesicles comprise a major pathway in which specific extracellular molecules are recognized and bound to the plasma membrane prior to internalization. This process involves membrane receptors, which are integral membrane proteins of the plasma membrane that recognize specific ligands. The best understood example of this process involves how cholesterol is taken up by cells. In the circulation, cholesterol is packaged in low-density lipoprotein (LDL) particles, which are small particles composed of protein and cholesterol esters. Specific LDL receptors are present in the plasma membrane that bind and anchor LDL particles to the surface of the cell. Occupied LDL receptors form clusters in the membrane that recruit adapter proteins and the cytoplasmic protein clathrin. Clathrin molecules assemble beneath receptor clusters to form a basketwork that deforms the plasma membrane into an invagination referred to as a coated pit. Continued assembly of the clathrin coating results in the continued invagination, pinching off and release of a membrane-bound coated vesicle containing LDL receptor and LDL cargo into the cytoplasm. Once the vesicle is formed, the clathrin coating is disassembled and the clathrin recycled to the plasma membrane to assist in the formation of more coated pits. The clathrin-free vesicle then fuses with a membrane-bound compartment called an endosome, which, in addition to receiving vesicles from the plasma membrane, also receives lysosomal vesicles filled with hydrolytic enzymes packaged by the Golgi apparatus. Membrane-bound structures containing a mixture of LDL particles and acid hydrolases then arise from the endosome to form mature lysosomes. During this process, LDL dissociates from the LDL receptor in the acidic endosomal environment, and vesicles enriched in LDL receptor pinch off from the endosome to be recycled back to the plasma membrane. Digestion of LDL particles occurs in the lysosome, followed by the release of cholesterol from the lysosome into the cytoplasm of the cell. This process of receptor-mediated endocytosis is used to concentrate and internalize a number of extracellular molecules. Other common features of receptor-mediated endocytosis include the recycling of both clathrin and the receptor; the fusion of internalized vesicles with endosomes; and the formation of lysosomes (digestive organelles) for material internalized by this route.

A second endocytotic pathway exists that does not involve clathrin, and may bypass delivery of internalized material to lysosomes. In this pathway, which appears to involve both receptor-mediated endocytosis as well as the nonspecific internalization of extracellular fluid, vesicles are created from clathrin-free invaginated membrane regions called caveolae. Caveolae are associated with specialized membrane domains with distinct phospholipid contents called lipid rafts. Invagination and formation of vesicles in these areas does not require clathrin, and the vesicles formed may be transported directly to the Golgi apparatus or endoplasmic reticulum instead of the endosomes and lysosomes. Presumably this route is used for material that would be damaged or degraded by exposure to lysosomal enzymes. Many cells display a constitutive formation and internalization of these vesicles in a process sometimes referred to as pinocytosis, or *cell drinking*.

Signaling Functions

The plasma membrane serves as the interface with the cell environment and possesses a number of mechanisms to detect and transduce specific extracellular signals. Integral membrane proteins that serve as signal receptors can be categorized into three broad classes: ion channel-linked receptors, G-protein-linked receptors and enzyme-linked receptors.

Ion channel-linked receptors undergo conformational changes upon ligand binding, opening a membrane channel permeable to small ions. Examples of this type of receptor include some types of neurotransmitter receptors. G-protein-linked receptors are integral membrane proteins that, upon ligand binding, activate small GTP-binding proteins (G-proteins), which in turn activate other effector molecules, including ion channel-linked receptors and various enzymes (e.g., adenylate cyclase). Thus, G-protein-linked receptor activity can lead to ion transients across the plasma membrane, or the generation of second messengers such as cAMP. Examples of G-protein-linked receptors include polypeptide hormone receptors. The third class of membrane-associated signaling molecules are enzyme-linked receptors, which upon ligand binding activate an enzyme activity, which is usually a protein kinase or a guanylyl cyclase. Examples of enzyme-linked receptors are growth factor receptors, whose tyrosine kinase activity is an important regulator of the cell cycle.

In addition to membrane receptors involved in signal transduction events, cells possess other types of receptors not associated with the plasma membrane. For example, steroid hormones (e.g., estrogen and testosterone) are lipid soluble and pass directly through the lipid bilayer without the need to bind to proteins exposed on the external face of the plasma membrane. Receptors for these types of signaling molecules are found in the cytoplasm and nucleus.

Cell Junctions

Specializations of the plasma membrane also help cells adhere to each other and to the ECM. They form barriers against the diffusion of material between cells of an epithelium, and form channels between adjacent cells. All of these functions are carried out by cell junctions.

Cell-Cell Barrier Junctions

It is important for the body to prevent the passage of material between epithelial cells. For example, a major function of intestinal and bladder epithelia is to prevent the direct passage of the contents of the intestine and bladder into the body cavity. The ability of epithelia to form effective barriers between different compartments is owing to the presence of special cell-cell junctions called occluding, or tight, junctions. Tight junctions are composed of linear arrays of the integral membrane proteins occludin and claudin; forming a barrier between cells as strands of occludin encircling the apical part of adjacent epithelial cells line up and bind to each other. Epithelia that form strong barriers to intercellular leakage contain many tight junction strands, whereas more leaky epithelia generally display fewer strands. Occludin and claudin molecules are associated with other cytoplasmic proteins that appear to furnish some linkages with the cytoskeleton. Extensive cytoskeletal interactions, such as those associated with adhesive-type cell junctions, are not readily apparent in tight junctions.

Cell-Cell Adhesive Junctions

These specializations of the plasma membrane allow cells in an epithelium to bind tightly to each other, and can be subdivided into two categories: adherens junctions and desmosomes. Adherens-type cell-cell junctions form belt-like arrays encircling the apical part of epithelial cells and are associated with a thick band of microfilaments. Zonulae adherens are comprised of integral membrane proteins belonging to the cadherin family of proteins, a number of the linking proteins that interconnect cadherins to microfilaments, including vinculin and catenin, and associated microfilaments. Cadherins from adjacent cells bind tightly to each other in the presence of Ca^{2+}, and the chelate of Ca^{2+} promotes cell dissociation. Interestingly, β-catenin functions not only as an adherens plaque protein, but also as a transcription factor in the nucleus.

Thus, β-catenin may serve as a sensing device that translates changes in cell-cell adhesion into changes in gene activity.

Desmosomes are punctate cell-cell adhesive junctions that are associated with the intermediate filament cytoskeleton. Like adherens junctions, they are also composed of cadherin integral membrane proteins and proteins that interlink cadherins and the associated cytoskeletal filament system. One type of desmosomal cadherin is a protein called desmoglein, and the major linking protein of desmosomes is a member of the plakin family of proteins called desmoplakin. Desmosomal intermediate filaments form dense bundles that interconnect desmosomal plaques, thus strengthening cell-cell attachments that contribute to the mechanical integrity the epithelium.

Cell-Cell Communicating Junctions

Two types of cell-cell junctions, gap junctions and synapses, constitute specializations of the plasma membrane that allow cells to communicate with each other. Gap junctions are punctate structures that electrically couple cells through channels that provide for direct cytoplasmic communication between adjacent cells. Gap junctions are composed of clusters of pore-like structures, called connexons, that span the lipid bilayer and allow passage of molecules smaller than 1000 daltons. Connexons, made up of hexameric arrays of the integral membrane protein connexin, line up between adjacent cells to form continuous, tightly sealed channels from cell to cell. These connections maintain a barrier against leakage of material to, or from the extracellular compartment, but ions and small molecules can diffuse from cell-to-cell to permit electrical coupling. The electrical coupling of gap junctions perform vital functions in propagating the contraction of cardiac muscle. The conformation of connexons is regulated by Ca^{2+} such that they remain open in low concentrations of Ca^{2+}, but close in the presence of higher concentrations Ca^{2+}.

In addition to the direct coupling of cells at gap junctions, neurons also communicate with each other at synapses. At synapses, cells release neurotransmitters in quantal fashion by the regulated exocytosis of membrane-bound vesicles. Neurotransmitters rapidly diffuse across a narrow extracellular space to bind to specific receptors on the plasma membrane of the adjacent cell. These receptors are either ion channels, or, in some cases, G-protein-linked receptors. When stimulated by a neurotransmitter, ion channels open, allowing Na^+ to enter the cell by diffusing down its concentration gradient, thereby depolarizing the plasma membrane. G-protein-linked receptors that bind neurotransmitter release activated G-proteins that may subsequently activate and open other ion channels. Depolarization of the plasma membrane is conducted down the body of the stimulated cell, and can trigger the release of the neurotransmitter at synaptic junctions between the stimulated cell and other adjacent cells. In this way, signaling activity is propagated between cells interconnected by synapses.

Cell-ECM Adhesive Junctions

Cells elaborate two types of cell-ECM junctions that assist in their adherence to the ECM. Hemidesmosomes anchor epithelial cells to underlying connective tissue and are associated with intermediate filament cytoskeletal fibers, whereas focal contacts can be formed by many types of cells and involve microfilament-associated linkages with the extracellular matrix. Hemidesmosomes resemble half-desmosomes where proteins called integrins form the integral membrane component, linked to intermediate filaments by members of the plakin family of proteins. Integrins are also the integral membrane proteins of focal contacts, and are connected to bundles of microfilaments by vinculin, talin, and other linking proteins. Focal contacts are associated with protein kinases, called focal adhesion kinases (FAKs). FAKs are thought to help transmit the status of cell-ECM linkage at focal contacts to the cytoplasm and nucleus. Normal (noncancerous) cells must usually be in contact with a substrate to divide, and FAKs may be involved in relaying contact information to regulatory elements of the cell cycle.

Cell Protection and Cell Identity

Many proteins and lipids of the plasma membrane possess covalently-linked sugar groups. These sugar groups are asymmetrically distributed, and are presented exclusively on the ECM side of the membrane. Plasma membrane glycoproteins and glycolipids serve important roles in both protecting the membrane, and in identifying specific cell types. Epithelial cells lining the small intestine elaborate a thick glycocalyx that helps to protect them against the harsh digestive conditions of the intestinal lumen. Examples of cell recognition processes involving glycoproteins and glycolipids include the patterns of antigens on red blood cells responsible for blood groupings. Another example involves the initial adhesion of neutrophils to capillary endothelium in areas of inflammation. During inflammation, endothelial cells express the integral membrane protein P-selectin, which contains a lectin domain that recognizes a four sugar group (N-acetylglucosamine, galactose, fucose, and sialic acid) present on glycoproteins and glycolipids of neutrophils. Neutrophils adhere to endothelial cells expressing P-selectin. This facilitates their subsequent migration past the capillary bed to reach the sites of inflammation.

Endoplasmic Reticulum

The ER is a prominent organelle in most cells, and its total membrane area can constitute more than half of all the membrane of a cell. ER membranes delimit enclosed spaces that vary in shape from flattened sheets, or cisternae, to branching tubules, to distended sacs; the total enclosed lumenal space can occupy 10% or more of the cell volume. A number of distinct functions are carried out by the ER. The ER is the primary site of synthesis of membrane lipids and integral membrane proteins for all membranous organelles (ER, Golgi, lysosomes, endosomes, secretory vesicles, and plasma membrane) except mitochondria and peroxisomes. It is also the site of production of secreted proteins and lumenal proteins of ER, Golgi, and lysosomes. In addition, the ER functions in lipid synthesis, detoxification reactions, and Ca^{2+} regulation.

ER can be categorized as either rough (RER) or smooth (SER). RER is so designated owing to the presence of numerous ribosomes bound to the cytoplasmic surface of the cisternal membranes, whereas SER lacks associated ribosomes. These different forms of ER are specialized for different functions; RER is the site where integral, lumenal, and secretory proteins are synthesized, whereas SER is the major site of detoxification and lipid synthesis.

Protein Synthesis

Protein synthesis takes place on ribosomes, which are either located free in the cytoplasm, or attached to membranes of the ER (forming RER). Cytoplasmic proteins (e.g., cytoskeletal proteins) are synthesized by free ribosomes, whereas proteins associated with membranes (including the plasma membrane) or the lumenal compartments of membrane-bound organelles, as well as proteins destined for secretion, are synthesized by RER. The lipid components of membranes are also made by the ER, and both protein and lipid are delivered to the plasma membrane and most organelles by membrane flow. This involves the transport and fusion of membrane-bound vesicles between ER, the Golgi apparatus, and other target organelles. Exceptions to this pattern of membrane biogenesis and renewal include mitochondria and peroxisomes. Interestingly, most proteins of mitochondria, and all peroxisome proteins, are made by free ribosomes and subsequently delivered to these organelles via transport mechanisms that move individual proteins into or past their membranes. Membrane lipids are delivered to these organelles by transport proteins that extract lipid from ER membranes and insert them in the membranes of mitochondria and peroxisomes.

Whether ribosomes remain free in the cytoplasm or are bound to ER is determined by the amino acid sequence of the polypeptide chain as it emerges from the ribosome. ER-associated proteins possess a signal sequence that functions in docking the polypeptide to the membranes of the ER. The signal sequence is recognized and bound by a signal recognition particle, or SRP. The SRP in turn binds to a SRP receptor in the membrane of the ER. A protein translocator apparatus forms a pore in the ER membrane through which growing polypeptide chains can pass. It also associates with the SRP and SRP receptor, and receives the protein as translation proceeds. Thus, proteins with signal sequences are injected directly into the membrane of the ER as they are synthesized. The signal sequence, which is hydrophobic, remains inserted into the lipid bilayer while the rest of the protein spools past as it elongates. The relative orientation of the signal sequence influences whether the N- or C-terminus of the polypeptide is threaded into the ER lumen. Soluble lumenal proteins spool all the way through the bilayer, and a signal peptidase then clips the protein at the signal sequence, liberating the protein into the lumen. Single- and multi-pass membrane proteins are thought to achieve their conformations by internal stop-transfer and start-transfer sequences, which interact with the bilayer to either promote the passage of the growing polypeptide chain through the bilayer (start-transfer sequences), or halt the transmembrane passage (stop-transfer sequences). Multiple start- and stop-transfer sequences therefore can result in a polypeptide chain that doubles back and forth to penetrate the bilayer at multiple points, forming loops in both the cytoplasm and ER lumen.

A number of post-translational modifications of proteins occur in the ER, as well as in the Golgi apparatus. Chaperone proteins that help direct the correct folding of newly synthesized protein are present in the ER cisternae; disulfide bonds form and many proteins are glycosylated, or may have glycolipid anchors added. Glycosylation is carried out by the initial assembly of sugars into polymeric structures attached to the membrane lipid dolichol. The assembled carbohydrate group is then transferred from dolichol to the protein. The glycoprotein may be processed in the ER by trimming some sugars, and addition of others. Further processing of glycoproteins, and the formation of glycolipids, are major functions of the Golgi apparatus.

Lipid Synthesis

In addition to synthesis of proteins for membranes, lysosomes, and secretory vesicles, the ER is also responsible for the synthesis of most membrane lipid for all organelles (including mitochondria and peroxisomes). Enzymes involved in lipid synthesis are embedded in the membrane of the ER, with their active sites facing the cytoplasm. Fatty acids are added to glycerol phosphate to form phosphatidic acid, which then receives various head groups. Phosphatidylcholine, phosphatidylserine, and phosphatidylethanolamine are formed in this way and initially added to the cytoplasmic leaflet of the ER lipid bilayer. Phospholipid translocators (*flippases*) are present in the membrane that transfer choline-containing phospholipids from the cytoplasmic half to the lumenal half of the bilayer. These translocators keep the total numbers of phospholipid molecules approximately equal between the two layers, but give rise to membrane asymmetry in the distribution of these lipids. Sphingomyelin synthesis is more complex; serine is first attached to fatty acids to form ceramide, which is exported to the Golgi apparatus, where phosphocholine head groups are added. Mitochondria and peroxisomes appear to receive their membrane lipid from the ER through the activity of phospholipid exchange proteins, which transfer phospholipids between membrane systems by extraction and insertion of individual lipid molecules. In addition to membrane lipid synthesis, the ER plays important roles in other aspects of lipid metabolism. For example, steroid hormones are synthesized from cholesterol in the SER.

Detoxification

Harmful substances that are relatively insoluble are difficult to clear from the cell. Such substances can occur as either environmental contaminants or as products of metabolism. SER contain a variety of enzymes that are able to process insoluble toxicants to make them more water-soluble and amenable for excretion. The best studied detoxification enzymes are members of the cytochrome P450 family of enzymes. Liver hepatocytes are among the most active cells involved in detoxification reactions, and contain large amounts of SER that house the P450 enzymes. The quantity of SER within a cell can fluctuate in response to different levels of exposure to toxic compounds.

Ca^{2+} Regulation

The ER membrane contains Ca^{2+}-ATPases that actively transport cytoplasmic Ca^{2+} into the ER lumen. This activity keeps cytoplasmic Ca^{2+} levels very low, which is necessary to allow Ca^{2+} to effectively function as a signaling molecule. In electrically excitable cells, depolarization of the plasma membrane promotes influx of Ca^{2+} from outside the cell; in nonexcitable cells, however, most of the Ca^{2+} released into the cytoplasm comes from the ER. ER membranes contain Ca^{2+} release channels that are activated by inositol triphosphate (IP3), a signaling molecule released by the activation of certain G-protein-linked receptor proteins at the plasma membrane. The contraction of muscle cells is triggered by Ca^{2+}, and these cells possess an extensive and specialized SER system, the sarcoplasmic reticulum, that contains a second type of Ca^{2+}-release channel in the SER membrane. After release from the ER, Ca^{2+} concentrations are lowered in the cytoplasm by the activity of plasma membrane and ER pumps.

Golgi Apparatus

The Golgi apparatus functions as the post office of a cell, packaging and directing different types of cargo from the ER to different organelles and the plasma membrane. In addition to packaging and targeting membrane-associated protein and lipid, as well as secreted protein, to their appropriate destinations, the Golgi apparatus modifies certain proteins and lipid received from the ER. Glycolipids are formed in the Golgi by the addition of oligosaccharide chains to ceramide; in addition, further processing of glycoproteins continues in the Golgi.

The Golgi apparatus is made up of a set of flattened, membrane-bound cisternae and associated tubulovesicular elements and membrane-bound vesicles in the process of being transported between ER, Golgi, and other locations. The stacks of Golgi cisternae are biochemically distinct, and the entire stack is polarized, so that a *cis*, or entry face, and a *trans*, or exit face, exist. The *cis* face lies adjacent to ER, and is the site of vesicular traffic back and forth between the ER and Golgi. The *trans* face is the site of formation of a number of types of vesicles that convey material to the plasma membrane, produce secretory vesicles, and form lysosomes. Integral membrane proteins, membrane lipids and soluble cisternal protein formed by the ER traverse the Golgi and are targeted to their appropriate destinations by this organelle. Three major routes of export from the Golgi occur: 1) constitutive delivery of membrane-bound vesicles to the plasma membrane; 2) formation of secretory vesicles whose exocytosis is regulated; and 3) formation of lysosomes. Specific targeting signals are associated with the formation of lysosomal vesicles and secretory vesicles; however, the pathway from the Golgi apparatus to the plasma membrane appears to be largely constitutive and unregulated, forming a default pathway.

Proteins destined to be secreted in a regulated manner (e.g. release of hormones from endocrine cells) are concentrated and packaged in membrane-bound vesicles formed by the *trans* Golgi. These secretory vesicles are stored in the cytoplasm until signals to fuse with the plasma membrane are received, resulting in the liberation of their contents outside the cell. Targeting mechanisms exist that direct secretory vesicles to the appropriate cellular location for release. For example, some secretory vesicles are released from the apical plasma membranes of epithelial cells, whereas others fuse with basolateral membranes.

Proteins destined for lysosomes are tagged with mannose-6-phosphate (M6P) groups in the Golgi. M6P receptors are present in Golgi membranes, and vesicles containing lysosomal proteins bound to M6P receptors bud off from the Golgi and fuse with endosomes to form mature lysosomes. During this process, M6P receptors are recycled for repeated use by vesicular trafficking from endosome to Golgi apparatus.

Lysosomes

Lysosomes are the digestive organelles of the cell, and are filled with acid hydrolases that are most active at a pH of about 5.0. Lysosomal vesicles from the Golgi apparatus fuse with endosomes that have received material from endocytotic vesicles. Endosomes have a moderately acidic pH of about 6.0 that promotes dissociation of ligand from internalized plasma membrane receptors as well as dissociation of lysosomal hydrolases from M6P receptors. Both types of receptors are recycled by being routed back toward the plasma membrane and the Golgi apparatus in membranous vesicles that are pinched off from endosomes. The endosome then matures to form a lysosome by condensing into a spherical or irregular membrane-bound structure. Proton pumps in the membrane of the maturing lysosome lower the pH inside the organelle to maximally activate the acid hydrolases to digest the internalized material. Other transporters exist in the lysosomal membrane to allow digested organic molecules to enter the cytoplasm for use by the cell.

In addition to the confluence of lysosomal and endocytotic vesicles at endosomes, material can be targeted for lysosomal degradation by at least two other mechanisms. Neutrophils and macrophages are cells specialized for the engulfment of bacteria and other large particulate material, which are internalized by phagocytosis. Lysosomes fuse with these large phagocytotic vesicles to deliver their hydrolases, resulting in the formation of phagosomes. Lysosomes also contribute to the breakdown of cellular material that is not needed or should be turned over. Excess, old, or malfunctioning organelles can be targeted for destruction by becoming enveloped by cisternae of ER, which then fuse with lysosomal vesicles to form autophagosomes. Recently, evidence has been gathered suggesting that a fourth route to lysosomes may exist that involves the transport of single cytoplasmic molecules through the lysosomal membrane by specific transport proteins.

Membrane Flow

It is apparent that there is a complex, but effective and elegant, flow of membranes and molecules between the various organelles and cytoplasmic compartments of eukaryotic cells. With the exception of mitochondria and peroxisomes, the membranes of all organelles, vesicles, and the plasma membrane are initially produced by the ER, modified and packaged by the ER and Golgi, then targeted and delivered via the trafficking of membrane-bound vesicles. A number of different types of signals and targeting mechanisms are used to regulate this flow of the membrane. Between the ER and Golgi, vesicles are coated with coat proteins (COPs), that either direct vesicles from the ER to the Golgi (COPII), or direct vesicles from the Golgi to the ER (COPI). Although no mechanisms appear to exist that restrict the flow of material from the ER to the Golgi, the amino acid sequences KDEL and KKXX (where X is any amino acid) mark lumenal and integral membrane proteins, respectively, for return transport from the Golgi to the ER. Thus, proteins with these sequences are essentially restricted to the ER by being rapidly returned from the Golgi apparatus. The exact mechanism of membrane flow through the Golgi apparatus has been a matter of some debate, but at least part of the flow appears to be carried out by membrane-bound vesicles. The flow of membrane from the Golgi to plasma membrane includes a constitutive, default pathway that operates in the absence of specific targeting signals. However, delivery of material to secretory vesicles and lysosomes requires defined targeting information. Interestingly, clathrin is involved in the formation of lysosomal and secretory vesicles from the *trans* Golgi, but not in the constitutive formation of vesicles destined for the plasma membrane. In addition to the ER and Golgi apparatus, bi-directional membrane flow also occurs between plasma membrane and endosome, and plasma membrane and Golgi. Clathrin-coated endocytotic vesicles from the plasma membrane travel inward to fuse with endosomes, and the receptors subsequently return to the plasma membrane via small vesicles formed from endosomal membranes. Endocytotic vesicles formed from caveolae may bypass lysosomes and fuse directly with Golgi or ER. Although the details of vesicular targeting are not well understood, it has been proposed that SNARE (soluble N-ethylmaleimide-sensitive-factor attachment protein receptors) proteins on the surfaces of membrane-bound vesicles (v-SNAREs) and target organelles (t-SNAREs) mediate the correct patterns of docking between vesicles and organelles.

Mitochondria

The primary function of mitochondria is to convert energy sources into forms that can be used to drive cellular reactions. Not surprisingly, they comprise a significant volume of the cell—normally, about 20% of the total cell mass. Mitochondria replicate by a process involving growth and fission of pre-existing mitochondria. Interestingly, mitochondria contain their own DNA that resembles the genome of prokaryotes. Based on this and other lines of evidence, it appears that mitochondria (and plastids in plant cells) arose by the colonization of eukaryotic cells by prokaryotes early in their evolution. Although mitochondria contain DNA and are able to carry out transcription and translation, they only produce about 5% of their protein, the rest being encoded by nuclear genes and synthesized by cytoplasmic ribosomes. They also appear to obtain most of their membrane lipid from the ER, mediated by of phospholipid transfer proteins that shuttle these molecules from the ER to the various organelles, including mitochondria.

Cells use ATP as their primary energy source, and the main function of mitochondria is the production of ATP from food sources. Energy is obtained from the oxidation of food by the sequential transfer of high energy electrons to lower energy states; the released energy is used to drive membrane-bound proton pumps, thus establishing an electrochemical gradient. Protons are then allowed to flow back across the membrane down their concentration gradient, and the released energy is used to drive the synthesis of ATP from ADP and Pi. The electrons are ultimately transferred to O_2, and the entire process is therefore referred to as oxidative phosphorylation.

Mitochondrial Structure

Mitochondria are composed of two membranes, that enclose distinct compartments. The outer mitochondrial membrane is somewhat permeable to small molecular weight compounds (<5000 daltons); conversely, the inner membrane contains a very high ratio of protein to lipid, and movement of material past this membrane is tightly regulated. The space between the two membranes is called the *intermembrane space*, and the compartment delimited by the inner membrane is called the mitochondrial matrix. The inner membrane is folded into sheet- or tube-like invaginations within the matrix, thus increasing its surface area. The increased surface area of this membrane allows mitochondria to house greater numbers of electron transport enzyme systems and ATP synthase complexes. The intermembrane space resembles the cytoplasm, but the internal matrix is biochemically distinct. The matrix is the site of conversion of pyruvate and fatty acids to acetyl CoA and is the location of the citric acid cycle, where acetyl CoA is oxidized.

Chemiosmotic Generation of ATP

With respect to energy production, the pathways of carbohydrate and lipid metabolism converge in the generation of acetyl CoA in the mitochondrial matrix. Carbohydrate is converted to glucose-6-phosphate, which, as a substrate for glycolysis, gives rise to two pyruvate molecules. Pyruvate is transported to the mitochondrial matrix were it is converted to acetyl CoA by the pyruvate dehydrogenase complex. Fatty acids are oxidized in the mitochondrial matrix, releasing acetyl groups that are then linked to CoA. Acetyl CoA derived from carbohydrate and fatty acid metabolism is fed into the citric acid cycle, resulting in the production of CO_2 and NADH. NADH conveys high energy electrons to the electron transport chain, which is located on inner mitochondrial membrane. The electron transport chain is a complex composed of at least 40 different proteins. The actual transfer of electrons is carried out by a number of different heme groups linked to various cytochromes, iron-sulfur center-containing proteins, ubiquinone, copper atoms, and a flavin. These are organized into three large enzyme complexes, with ubiquinone and cytochrome C serving as carriers of electrons between the complexes. The three complexes are the NADH dehydrogenase complex, the cytochrome B-C1 complex, and the cytochrome oxidase complex. Electrons shuttled across these complexes move from high to low energy states, with the released energy used to pump H^+ from the matrix to the intermembrane space. Then, H^+ is allowed to flow down its concentration gradient (from the intermembrane space to the matrix) through the ATP synthase complex. This is a large transmembrane complex of about 500,000 daltons that contains multiple proteins, and constitutes about 15% of the total inner membrane protein. The energy that is released is used to couple Pi to ADP to make ATP. Finally, the electrons used to drive the H^+ pumps are combined with O_2 and H^+. Thus, the generation of ATP from high energy electrons by this chemiosmotic mechanism consumes O_2 and produces water.

Other Mitochondrial Functions

In addition to converting food energy into ATP, mitochondria also are involved in a number of other functions, including Ca^{2+} regulation and apoptotic signaling. Like the ER, mitochondria sequester Ca^{2+} to help keep cytoplasmic levels low. In addition to producing ATP, the H^+ gradient can be used to import Ca^{2+} into the mitochondrial matrix, where it is used in part to help regulate the activity of certain mitochondrial enzymes. Deposits of calcium can be formed in mitochondria in response to high cytoplasmic levels of Ca^{2+}. Mitochondria are also involved in the regulation of programmed cell death, or apoptosis. A central mechanism by which apoptosis is carried out involves activation of the caspase family of proteases. Release of cytochrome C by mitochondria facilitates caspase activation by forming a complex with other molecules (e.g., APAF-1) and pro-caspases to activate the caspase cascade. Release of cytochrome C from mitochondria can occur in response to specific membrane signaling events, as well as from cytoplasmic, mitochondrial, or nuclear damage.

Peroxisomes

Peroxisomes are membrane-bound vesicular organelles that are involved in various oxidative reactions. They contain high concentrations of enzymes that are able to form H_2O_2 by the transfer of hydrogen atoms from substrates to molecular oxygen. In addition, peroxisomes contain catalase, which breaks down H_2O_2 to oxidize various substrates, including some types of toxins. Like mitochondria, peroxisomes replicate by fission and growth of pre-existing organelles. All protein and lipid of the peroxisome is synthesized in the cytoplasm, and subsequently imported into the peroxisomal membrane and lumen.

The Cytoskeleton

The cytoskeleton of eukaryotic cells is composed of a complex system of proteinaceous filaments that are present in both cytoplasm and nucleus. The three major cytoskeletal systems elaborated by cells are microfilaments, microtubules, and intermediate filaments. These different cytoskeletal systems are biochemically and functionally distinct.

Microfilaments

Microfilaments are small solid filaments about 6 nm in diameter, composed of the 45 kDa globular protein actin. Actin is one of the most abundant proteins in cells, composing up to 5% or more of the total cell protein. Microfilaments help support and organize the plasma membrane and are involved in cell motility and the maintenance of cell shape, serving as the *muscle* of the cell.

A large number of actin-associated proteins mediate the functions of microfilaments, including regulating actin polymerization (e.g., profilin, WASp, and ARP), cross-linking microfilaments to form organized arrays (e.g., filamin, fimbrin, and villin), interacting with membrane proteins to establish and maintain distinct membrane domains (e.g., vinculin, catenins, and Z0-1 of tight junctions), and functioning as motor proteins (e.g., type I and II myosins) to carry out motility events. Much of the actin in cells is present as soluble monomers (g-actin) bound to profilin. This interaction inhibits the polymerization actin monomers into filaments (f-actin). Signals from the plasma membrane, mediated in large part by small GTP-binding proteins (e.g., rac and rho), activate WASp and ARP proteins, to promote the dissociation of profilin from g-actin and seed the growth of new microfilaments from the sides of pre-existing microfilaments. Microfilament polymerization is controlled by the addition of capping proteins to the end of growing filaments, and turnover of filaments occurs by the actions of microfilament cutting proteins such as gelsolin, followed by depolymerization of f-actin to g-actin and association of the latter with profilin.

Although some cell movements and membrane activities appear to be driven by the polymerization and depolymerization of actin, many other types of actin-associated motility require the interaction of microfilaments with myosin motor molecules. Myosin functions as an actin-activated ATPase, undergoing cycles of microfilament attachment and detachment, with associated conformational changes, resulting in *power strokes*. These events are linked to the binding, hydrolysis, and release of ATP, Pi, and ADP. Myosin activity can slide microfilaments past each other, transport vesicles and other cargo down microfilaments and deform membranes that are attached to microfilaments.

A number of mutations are known that interfere with microfilament functioning. WASp protein was discovered as the protein mutated in Wiscott-Aldrich syndrome, which results from deficits in the ability of actin to polymerize. Dystrophin is a large linking molecule that interconnects submembrane arrays of microfilaments to integral membrane proteins and ECM proteins in skeletal muscle cells. Mutations in dystrophin that interfere with its ability to link microfilaments with the plasma membrane weaken the plasma membrane, causing the eventual death of the muscle cell and giving rise to some forms of muscular dystrophy.

Microtubules

Microtubules are small hollow proteinaceous tubes about 25 nm in diameter, composed of the protein tubulin. Microtubules function to organize the cytoplasm and mediate intracellular motility events. They are associated with motor proteins that interact with membrane-bound organelles and vesicles to help determine their location and organization within the cytoplasm. They also carry out crucial functions in cell division, forming the spindle apparatus that segregates replicated chromosomes among the daughter cells. Microtubules also support and power cilia and flagella, which are highly motile appendages produced by ciliated epithelial cells and sperm.

Unlike microfilaments and intermediate filaments discussed below, microtubules are associated with a distinct organizing center, called the centrosome (or MTOC, for microtubule-organizing center). The centrosome is composed of a pair of centrioles surrounded by an amorphous mass of pericentriolar material. Centrioles themselves are short, barrel-like arrays of microtubules and are associated with the ability of the centrosome to replicate. Pericentriolar material is a biochemically complex layer of amorphous material that surrounds the centrioles, which both nucleates microtubule growth and anchors the ends of microtubules. Three types of tubulin genes are expressed in eukaryotic cells, including α-, β-, and γ-tubulin. Microtubules are composed of heterodimers of α- and β-tubulin; γ -tubulin is a component of the pericentriolar material. Microtubules possess an intrinsic polarity and are all oriented so one end (the *minus* end) is anchored in the pericentriolar material, with the free end (the *plus* end) extending into the cytoplasm. Microtubule polymerization and depolymerization occurs at the plus end and involves the addition or removal of α-β heterodimers. Heterodimers of α- and β-tubulin are associated with GTP or GDP. GTP-containing heterodimers readily polymerize, whereas GDP-containing heterodimers bind much more weakly to each other and tend to dissociate. GTPases that hydrolyze microtubule-bound GTP to GDP are present in the cytoplasm; however, because heterodimer addition and removal occur at just the plus end, as long as the terminal tubulin subunits are associated with GTP, the microtubule will grow by the addition of GTP-containing heterodimers. Occasionally, the GTPase activity catches up with a growing end of the microtubule, hydrolyzing GTP to GDP in the terminal subunits. At this point, the microtubule rapidly disassembles, shrinking in size back toward the centrosome. Depolymerizing microtubules can be *rescued* and re-grown if sufficiently high concentrations of GTP-containing tubulin heterodimers are present so that the GTP *cap* can be re-established. Because of these events, most microtubules in the cell continuously oscillate between slow growth and rapid depolymerization, a feature that has been called *dynamic instability*.

Like the microfilament cytoskeleton, the organization and functions of microtubules are regulated and carried out by associated proteins. Microtubule-associated proteins are generally categorized as either structural proteins or motor proteins. Structural proteins include higher molecular weight proteins called MAPs (for microtubule-associated protein), and lower molecular weight tau proteins. Structural MAPs and tau are thought to help organize microtubule arrays in the cytoplasm. Microtubule-associated motor proteins include dynein and kinesin, both of which, like myosin, undergo cycles of binding, conformational changes, and dissociation in an ATP-dependent manner to move microtubules past each other, or to move cargo along microtubules. Microtubule-mediated intracellular transport is carried out by multiple members of both the dynein and kinesin families of protein, but ciliary and flagellar motility selectively utilize dynein. The microtubule bundle, or axoneme, supporting a cilium is anchored in a specialized centrosome called a basal body. Unlike regular centrosomes, axoneme microtubules originate as direct extensions from one of the centrioles in a basal body, and not from associated peri-centriolar material. Axoneme microtubules form circular arrays of doublets surrounding a central pair of microtubules. The outer microtubule doublets are associated with dynein, which spans adjacent microtubule pairs. Dynein motor activity attempts to slide microtubule pairs past each other, which is converted into a bending of the cilium because the bases of the microtubule pairs are attached to the basal body and are not free to slide. In this way, hydrolysis of ATP by dynein powers the rapid, whip-like movements of cilia and flagellae in a microtubule-dependent manner. Other forms of microtubule-mediated motility occur in the cytoplasm, where membrane-bound vesicles, organelles, and other cargo associated with dynein or kinesin move along microtubules. Motor proteins exhibit a directionality which allows for vectorial transport of material within the cell. Dyneins move cargo toward the minus ends of microtubules and kinesins generally move cargo toward the plus ends of microtubules (although minus end-directed members of the kinesin family are known).

In dividing cells, centrosomes replicate along with DNA in S-phase and subsequently participate in the formation of the mitotic spindle. Daughter centrosomes move apart and promote the complete reorganization of the microtubular cytoskeleton prior to, and during, nuclear envelope breakdown. The plus ends of microtubules radiating from the centrosomes, now called spindle poles, bind and become stabilized by the kinetochores of chromosomes, forming distinct bundles of kinetochore microtubules. Microtubule-mediated motility events at the kinetochore line chromosomes up on the metaphase plate and are subsequently responsible for the separation of daughter chromosomes in anaphase of mitosis. Pinching the cell into two daughter cells (mediated by bundles of microfilaments in association with the plasma membrane at the cleavage furrow) leads to the inheritance of the correct number of chromosomes and a single centrosome by each daughter cell. Interestingly, other organelles such as mitochondria and peroxisomes appear to be randomly apportioned to each daughter cell by virtue of the fact that they are distributed throughout the cytoplasm, whereas the ER and Golgi apparatus vesiculate and disperse throughout the cytoplasm early in mitosis to be inherited in the same way.

A number of drugs interfere with microtubule dynamics; examples include colchicine, which actively promotes tubulin depolymerization; and taxol, which stabilizes microtubules and inhibits depolymerization. Both of these drugs are toxic to cells, indicating that the oscillation between polymerization and depolymerization is crucial to microtubule function. A number of taxol-based compounds have been developed for use in the chemotherapeutic treatment of cancer, highlighting the importance of microtubule dynamics in cell division.

Intermediate Filaments

Intermediate filaments (IF) are solid filaments about 10 nm in diameter, made up of one or more of a large family of intermediate filament proteins. Intermediate filaments are found in both the cytoplasm and the nucleus. They function in strengthening the cytoplasm of cells, as well as in mechanically integrating cells of a tissue by interconnecting desmosomes and hemidesmosomes.

The IF family of proteins is the most complex family of cytoskeletal proteins, with over 50 different IF gene products elaborated by cells of higher vertebrates. IF proteins can be divided into five groups: 1) acidic keratins, 2) neutral/basic keratins, 3) vimentin-like proteins, 4) neurofilament proteins, and 5) lamins. Intermediate filament proteins are expressed in tissue-specific patterns, with epithelial cells containing keratins, cells of mesenchymal origin expressing vimentin-like IF proteins, and neuronal cells expressing neurofilament IF proteins. Lamins are present in essentially all nucleated cells and form a filamentous network underlying and supporting the inner membrane of the nuclear envelope. There is evidence that lamins help organize chromatin and are involved in some aspects of DNA synthesis, as well.

IF proteins are long, rod-like molecules that contain a central domain rich in α-helices. The rod domain of IF proteins coil around each other to form coiled-coil dimers, which then associate into higher order structures, much like weaving together individual strands to form a rope. The polymerization state of IF proteins is mediated by phosphorylation, and it has been suggested that hyperphosphorylation of IF proteins leads to dissociation of IFs by repulsion of subunits bearing multiple negative phosphate charges. One of the best studied examples is the depolymerization and repolymerization of nuclear lamina filaments during cell division. At the onset of mitosis, lamins are hyperphosphorylated and the nuclear lamina depolymerizes, facilitating nuclear envelope breakdown. At the end of mitosis, lamins are dephosphorylated and the nuclear lamina and nuclear envelope re-forms around the daughter nuclei.

Only a relatively few IF-associated proteins are known, and these appear to help organize intermediate filaments and mediate interactions with other cytoskeletal proteins and organelles. Intermediate filaments frequently form a dense basketwork around the nucleus; thus, the nucleus of many cells is supported both by an internal IF lamina, as well as protected by a cytoplasmic network of IF fibers.

Nuclear Organization

The largest and most prominent structure in most cells is the nucleus. It serves as the repository and organizing center for the genome. In humans, chromosomal DNA—of a total length of about two meters when fully extended—is packaged into an average nuclear size of about 10 μM (1/100 of a millimeter) in diameter. The DNA must be packaged in such a way as to allow access to transcriptional and replication machinery, and extensive nuclear-cytoplasmic transport must occur. These functions are mediated by the organization of DNA within the nucleus, and the organization of the nuclear envelope.

The nucleus is bounded by the nuclear envelope, which is comprised of two membranes (the inner and outer nuclear membranes), the nuclear lamina, and numerous nuclear pores that span the inner and outer membranes. Nuclear pores are multimolecular arrays exhibiting eight-fold symmetry that are involved in the exchange of material between cytoplasm and nucleus. Material moves through nuclear pores by both passive diffusion and by active transport; molecules smaller than 5000 daltons are freely permeable between nucleus and cytoplasm, but those larger than about 60,000 daltons must be actively transported. Molecules between these sizes can move between nucleus and cytoplasm without being actively transported, but take longer to equilibrate with increasing size. Proteins actively transported into the nucleus contain nuclear localization sequences that are recognized by the pore complexes. Nuclear localization signals vary in amino acid sequence, but usually contain a number of lysines and are positively charged.

The first step in DNA packaging involves the winding of DNA around octamers of histone proteins, which are positively charged proteins that closely interact with the negatively charged DNA. This first order of DNA packing gives rise to a *beads on a string* appearance, with the beads, or nucleosomes, composed of about 200 base pairs of DNA wrapped almost twice around a histone octamer core. Nucleosomes are further coiled to form a 30 nm diameter solenoid fiber, which loops out to form euchromatin (loosely compacted and generally active DNA), or becomes more tightly compacted to form heterochromatin (tightly compacted and relatively inactive DNA). Each chromosome usually consists of a mixture of heterochromatin and euchromatin, and occupies a more-or-less defined region within the nucleus. Portions of a number of chromosomes that contain amplified sequences encoding ribosomal RNA and ribosomal protein mRNAs cluster together and associate with a number of other protein elements in the nucleus to form the *nucleolus*. This is a specialized area where transcription of ribosomal genes and assembly of ribosomal subunits occurs.

Mounting evidence suggests that chromosomes may be organized on a protein or protein-RNA based scaffolding. This scaffolding, or nuclear matrix, is biochemically ill-defined, but appears to be composed of filaments that form a three-dimensional meshwork within the nucleus, which is surrounded by the denser filamentous mat of lamin IFs underlying the nuclear envelope. Although the composition of the nuclear matrix is not well-understood, it is possible that lamin IFs are not restricted to the nuclear periphery, but contribute to at least some of the matrix fibers. Certain DNA sequences bind to the nuclear matrix much more tightly than others, leading to the proposal that distinct matrix attachment regions, or MARs, periodically link chromosomes to the matrix. These linkages result in the formation of large (20–200 kilobase) loops of DNA tethered to the matrix at MAR domains. MAR DNA sequences do not display a rigid consensus sequence, but have a number of distinguishing features, including being relatively AT-rich, histone-poor, and possessing multiple topoisomerase II binding sequences. MAR domain DNA also may confer position independent expression of exogenous DNA incorporated into random sites within the genome. Thus, it has been proposed that MAR domains form long-range regulatory elements helping to control gene expression.

The high concentrations of DNA, RNA and protein in the nucleus make it challenging to study nuclear structure. However, some structural aspects of gene expression and mRNA processing can be visualized by electron microscopy in the form of perichromatin fibers and interchromatin granules. These structures represent sites of RNA processing, and include mRNA as well as associated ribonucleoproteins and RNAs that form elements of the splicing machinery, including spliceosomes and splicing islands.

Conclusion

Living eukaryotic cells must carry out and coordinate an enormous number of biochemical reactions in order to obtain and convert energy to usable forms, break down and interconvert organic molecules to synthesize needed components, sense and respond to environmental and internal stimuli, regulate gene activity, sense and repair damage to structural and genomic elements, grow and reproduce. This level of complexity requires that biochemical reactions be highly organized and compartmentalized, and this is the major function of cell organelles and the cytoskeleton. Cells have elaborated an elegant cytoplasmic membrane system composed of the nuclear envelope, endoplasmic reticulum (ER), Golgi apparatus, and associated endocytotic, endosomal, lysosomal, and secretory vesicles. These membrane systems serve to both organize and compartmentalize biochemical reactions involved in protein and lipid synthesis, targeting, and secretion. The cytoskeleton facilitates not only cytosolic molecular interactions, but also serves to organize the entire cytoplasmic membrane system. The key to cellular life is organization, and eukaryotic cells display a remarkably rich and elegant architecture to carry out the demands of life.

Glossary and Abbreviations

Actin The protein used to form microfilaments. Actin can be either soluble (g-actin) or polymerize to form microfilaments (f-actin).

Adherens Junction A type of cell-cell adhesive junction in which bundles of microfilaments are connected to the plasma membrane via linking proteins (e.g., catenin). The linking proteins connect microfilaments to integral membrane proteins called cadherins, which bind to each other in the presence of Ca^{2+} to adhere cells together.

ADP Adenosine 5'-diphosphate. A nucleotide associated with cellular energy regulation. The release of one of the three high-energy phosphate groups of ATP yields usable energy and ADP (which contains two phosphate groups and is at a lower energy state). ATP can be regenerated from ADP with the input of energy to attach a third high-energy phosphate group.

Apoptosis The process by which cells actively destroy themselves. Specific biochemical pathways exist, that, when activated, result in the destruction of key cytoplasmic and nuclear proteins.

ATP Adenosine 5'-triphosphate. High energy molecule, most of which is normally generated by oxidative phosphorylation in mitochondria. ATP is the primary source of cellular energy used to power enzymatic reactions.

Basal body A specialized type of centrosome (or MTOC) that gives rise to a cilium or flagellum.

Cadherin An integral membrane protein found in desmosomes and adherens junctions. In the presence of Ca^{2+} , cadherins from adjacent cells bind, adhering cells to each other. Cadherins are connected to microfilaments at adherens junctions via linking proteins such as catenin, and to the intermediate filament cytoskeleton at desmosomes via linking proteins such as desmoplakin.

Caspases Proteases that are activated during apoptosis. Caspases destroy key cellular components, as well as activate nucleases, thus promoting nuclear disassembly and cell death.

Catenin A type of linking protein found in adherens-type cell-cell junctions. Catenins are particularly interesting in that they can translocate to the nucleus and function as transcription factors, thus transducing events at the cell surface into changes in nuclear activity.

Caveolae Invaginations of the plasma membrane involved in endocytosis. Caveolae are not associated with clathrin, but possess a distinct lipid makeup, and may constitute a specialized type of lipid raft.

Cell Junction Specializations of the plasma membrane that allow for anchorage and communication between cells, and between cells and the extracellular matrix.

Centriole A short, barrel-like structure composed of a cylindrical array of microtubule triplets. Centrioles are associated with centrosomes, basal bodies, and spindle poles, and function in the replication of these microtubule organizing centers.

Centrosome The organizing center for the microtubular cytoskeleton. Centrosomes are composed of centrioles and pericentriolar material. Three forms of centrosomes are found in cells, including the single centrosome of non-dividing cells, the two spindle poles of dividing cells, and the basal bodies of ciliated cells.

Cilia Motile, whip-like extensions of the cell, supported by a bundle of microtubules that are connected to basal bodies. Cilia actively beat back and forth as a result of interactions between microtubules and the motor protein dynein, in an ATP-requiring process.

cis-Golgi The portion of the Golgi apparatus that receives membrane-bound vesicles from the ER.

Clathrin A protein involved in receptor-mediated endocytosis. Clathrin forms a coat around invaginations of the plasma membrane, forming coated pits, which subsequently pinch off into the cytoplasm to form coated vesicles.

Claudin An integral membrane protein associated with tight junctions that helps form a transcellular barrier between cells.

Coated Pit *see* **Clathrin**

Coated Vesicle *see* **Clathrin**

COPs Proteins involved in directing membrane-bound vesicles between the ER and the Golgi apparatus.

Cytochrome P-450 A group of proteins involved in detoxification reactions.

Cytoskeleton A system of filaments and tubules in the cytoplasm and nucleus that perform numerous functions, including maintaining cell shape, driving cell motility and cell division, and organizing the cytoplasm. Three major types of fibers comprise the cytoskeleton: microfilaments, microtubules, and intermediate filaments.

Dalton A measure of the mass of a molecule; one dalton is about the mass of a hydrogen atom. Small proteins are a few thousand daltons in size, medium and large proteins range from tens of thousands to few hundred thousand daltons, respectively.

Desmosome A type of cell-cell adhesive junction in which bundles of intermediate filaments are connected to the plasma membrane via linking proteins (e.g., desmoplakin). The linking proteins connect intermediate filaments to integral membrane proteins called cadherins, which bind to each other in the presence of Ca^{2+} to adhere cells together. Numerous desmosomes are found in tissues subjected to mechanical stress, such as epidermis and heart muscle.

DNA Deoxyribonucleic acid.

ECM Extracellular matrix.

Endocytosis A process by which cells internalize material via the formation of depressions in the plasma membrane which pinch off in the cytoplasm to form membrane-bound vesicles containing the engulfed material. Specific extracellular molecules can be concentrated and internalized by this method in a process called receptor-mediated endocytosis.

Endoplasmic Reticulum An extensive, membrane-bound cytoplasmic organelle involved in protein and lipid synthesis, as well as in detoxification reactions and Ca^{2+} regulation. Membranes of the ER form an enclosed compartment that range in morphology from flattened sheets to an interconnected tubular network. Protein and lipid products made by the ER can be delivered to other parts of the cell or secreted, via membrane-bound vesicles that traffic between the ER, Golgi apparatus, and plasma membrane. Protein synthesis occurs in ER that possesses attached ribosomes (RER), and lipid synthesis is primarily associated with ER lacking ribosomes (SER).

Endosome A membrane-bound structure formed by the coalescence of endocytotic vesicles and vesicles containing lysosomal enzymes from the Golgi apparatus. Endosomes can give rise to lysosomes, organelles that efficiently digest internalized material.

ER Endoplasmic reticulum.

Exocytosis A process by which cells secrete material via fusion of membrane-bound secretory vesicles with the plasma membrane.

Extracellular Matrix An elaborate system of proteins and polysaccharides that surrounds cells and tissues. Composed of structural elements, as well as soluble factors that influence cell growth, differentiation, and function.

FAK Focal adhesion kinase.

Flippase A membrane-associated enzyme that is able to transfer phospholipids between each layer of the lipid bilayer.

Focal Adhesion Kinase A protein kinase associated with focal contacts involved in transducing contact information at the cell surface into a cellular response.

G-Protein Small proteins involved in signaling functions that are able to bind GTP or GDP. G-proteins cycle between active and inactive states, depending on whether they are associated with GTP or GDP.

Gap Junction A type of cell-cell communicating junction that allows for the direct passage of small molecules between cells. Gap junctions are formed by the alignment of membrane-spanning pores, or connexons, between cells.

GDP Guanosine 5' diphosphate. A nucleoside formed by the hydrolytic removal of a phosphate group from GTP.

Golgi Apparatus The organelle associated with targeting protein and lipid synthesized by the ER to their appropriate locations. Material is transported between ER and Golgi, and between Golgi, lysosomes, and the plasma membrane by small membrane-bound vesicles. Modification of proteins and lipids (e.g., glycosylation) also occurs in the Golgi apparatus.

GTP Guanosine 5' triphosphate. A nucleoside associated with cell signaling and the regulation of cytoskeletal organization.

Hemidesmosome A type of adhesive junction that attaches epithelial cells to extracellular matrix. Bundles of intermediate filaments are connected to integral membrane proteins called integrins via linking proteins. Hemidesmosomal integrins bind to proteinaceous elements of the ECM, thereby providing mechanical linkage between IFs and the ECM.

IF Intermediate filament.

Inositol Triphosphate A type of membrane-associated phospholipid molecule involved in cell signaling.

Integral Membrane Protein A protein that passes through a lipid bilayer one or more times. Integral membrane proteins are strongly attached to membranes, and usually require disruption of membrane structure to be released.

Intermediate Filament One of the three major cytoskeletal groups of proteinaceous fibers found in cells. Associated with desmosomes and hemidesmosomes, they function in strengthening the cytoplasm of cells, as well as in mechanically linking cells of an epithelium with each other and with the ECM.

IP3 Inositol triphosphate.

LDL Low density lipoprotein.

Lipid Bilayer The structure phospholipid molecules adopt to form a membrane. Composed of two layers of phospholipid molecules, where the hydrophobic tails face each other and the polar heads face outward, creating a hydrophobic central region sandwiched between charged surfaces.

Lipid Raft A region of the plasma membrane exhibiting a specialized phospholipid makeup. Associated with specific functions, including formation of caveolae and signal transduction.

Lumen An enclosed space, or chamber. Usually refers to the compartment enclosed by a membranous organelle.

Lysosome A digestive organelle formed by the ER and Golgi apparatus. Hydrolytic enzymes synthesized by the ER are concentrated and packaged by the Golgi apparatus into lysosomal vesicles. Lysosomal vesicles fuse with either endosomes or with old cell organelles to digest internalized material, or cellular material to be recycled, respectively.

M6P Mannose-6-phosphate.

MRNA Messenger RNA; the type of RNA that encodes the sequence of amino acids to be assembled into a specific protein in association with a ribosome.

Mannose-6-Phosphate A polysaccharide "tag" attached to hydrolytic enzymes that marks them for packaging into lysosomal vesicles by the Golgi apparatus.

MAR Matrix attachment region.

Matrix Attachment Region A specialized sequence of DNA that is bound to the nuclear matrix.

Microfilament One of the three major cytoskeletal groups of proteinaceous fibers found in cells. Microfilaments are concentrated underneath the plasma membrane, which they support and help organize. They are also associated with adherens junctions, microvilli, and cleavage furrows. Microfilaments are involved with maintaining cell shape and powering cell motility.

Microvilli Finger-like extensions of the plasma membrane supported by core bundles of microfilaments. Microvilli serve to increase the absorptive area of epithelial cells.

Microtubule One of the three major cytoskeletal groups of proteinaceous fibers found in cells. Microtubules help organize the cytoplasm, participate in intracellular transport, allow for ciliary and flagellar motility, and organize and segregate chromosomes during mitosis.

Microtubule Organizing Center (MTOC) *see* **Centrosome**.

Mitochondria Double-membraned organelles primarily involved in converting the energy from food molecules into a form usable by the cell. This is largely accomplished by using food energy to create a proton gradient across the inner mitochondrial membrane, which in turn is used to drive the synthesis of ATP. Mitochondria also function in calcium homeostasis and in the regulation of programmed cell death, or apoptosis.

Mitosis The segregation of chromosomes during cell division. Cell division includes mitosis, followed by cytokinesis, or the division of the parental cell into two daughter cells.

MTOC Microtubule organizing center.

Nuclear Envelope A double-membraned structure enclosing the nucleus that establishes and maintains a distinct nuclear environment. The nuclear envelope is perforated by nuclear pores, which allow for the regulated transport of material between nucleus and cytoplasm.

Nuclear Matrix A protein (and possibly RNA) based scaffolding within the nucleus that is thought to help organize chromatin. The molecular makeup of the nuclear matrix is not well understood, but it appears to play important roles in DNA synthesis and the regulation of gene activity.

Nucleolus A specialized structure within the nucleus involved in ribosomal RNA synthesis and ribosome assembly.

Occludin An integral membrane protein associated with tight junctions that helps form a transcellular barrier between cells.

Occluding Junction Another term for tight junction (*see* **Tight Junction**).

Organelle Readily identifiable cellular inclusions that possess a characteristic morphology and function. The term is usually used to refer to the major membrane-bound structures within cells, including the nucleus, endoplasmic reticulum, Golgi apparatus, lysosomes, peroxisomes, and mitochondria.

Pericentriolar Material The amorphous material surrounding centrioles in a centrosome. Microtubules associated with centrosomes and spindle poles arise from the pericentriolar material.

Peripheral Membrane Protein A membrane-associated protein that is not embedded in the lipid bilayer. Peripheral proteins can be associated with the phospholipid heads of the bilayer, or with the portions of integral membrane proteins that extend beyond the bilayer.

Peroxisome Organelle involved in oxidation reactions, including the generation and destruction of H_2O_2.

Phagocytosis A type of endocytosis where very large particulate matter is taken up by a cell (e.g., the engulfment of bacteria by macrophages).

Pinocytosis A type of endocytosis where small vesicles internalize extracellular fluid for uptake by a cell.

Plasma Membrane The membrane surrounding a cell. The plasma membrane, sometimes called the plasmalemma, encloses the cytoplasm and protects the cell contents from the environment. It carries out vital functions in protection, transport of material into and out of the cell, sensing and responding to the environment, and in cell identification.

RER Rough endoplasmic reticulum.

Rough Endoplasmic Reticulum Endoplasmic reticulum that possesses ribosomes (thus presenting a "rough" surface). RER is primarily involved in protein synthesis.

Ribosome A multimeric array of protein and ribonucleic acid that is involved in protein synthesis. Ribosomes assemble individual amino acids into a polymer, or polypeptide, in a specific sequence determined by an associated messenger RNA molecule. Ribosomes can exist either "free" in the cytoplasm, or attached to the ER. In the former case, the proteins they produce are released into the cytoplasm; in the latter case, the proteins are either inserted into the membrane of the ER, or released into the lumen of the ER.

RNA Ribonucleic acid. Includes a number of subtypes, including messenger RNA (mRNA), ribosomal RNA (rRNA), and transfer RNA (tRNA).

SER Smooth endoplasmic reticulum.

Signal Recognition Particle An assembly of proteins that help dock ribosomes to ER (forming RER).

Smooth Endoplasmic Reticulum Endoplasmic reticulum that lacks ribosomes (thus presenting a "smooth" surface). SER is involved in lipid synthesis, calcium transport, and detoxification reactions.

SNAREs Proteins that help regulate the trafficking of membrane bound vesicles between different organelles.

S-Phase The stage of the cell cycle where DNA synthesis occurs.

Spindle Pole A microtubule organizing center that assembles the microtubule spindle during cell division. When cells divide, their centrosome duplicates and moves apart to form a bipolar spindle.

Spliceosome An assembly of protein and RNA molecules that processes newly-made mRNA into mature mRNA.

SRP Signal recognition particle.

Start-Transfer Sequence A specific sequence of amino acids that initiates the penetration of a growing polypeptide chain into the lipid bilayer of RER.

Stop-Transfer Sequence A specific sequence of amino acids that stops the insertion of a polypeptide chain into the lipid bilayer of RER.

Synapse A type of communicating cell-cell junction found between neurons in nervous tissue.

Tight Junction A type of cell-cell junction that establishes a transcellular barrier. Also referred to as an occluding junction. The barrier is established by the integral membrane proteins occludin and claudin, which are arranged in strands that adhere to each other, and form an apical network around epithelial cells.

***trans*-Golgi** The portion of the Golgi apparatus that releases membrane-bound vesicles after their contents have been processed by the Golgi.

Tubulin The protein used to form microtubules. Most microtubules continually oscillate between growth and disassembly by the addition or removal of soluble tubulin dimers at the tubule termini.

WASp The protein mutated in Wiscott-Aldrich syndrome patients. This protein plays important roles in regulating actin polymerization.

Zonula Adherens A large, belt-like adherens junction usually found encircling the apical regions of epithelial cells.

Suggested Reading

Plasma Membrane

Fielding, C. J. and Fielding, P. E. (2000) Cholesterol and caveolae: structural and functional relationships, Biochim. Biophys. Acta. 1529, 210–222.

Fleming, T. P., Ghassemifar, M. R., and Sheth, B. (2000) Junctional complexes in the early mammalian embryo, Semin. Reprod. Med. 18, 185–193.
Gagescu, R., Gruenberg, J., and Smythe, E. (2000) Membrane dynamics in endocytosis: structure—function relationship, Traffic 1, 84–88.
Ikonen, E. (2001) Roles of lipid rafts in membrane transport, Curr. Opin. Cell. Biol. 13, 470–477.
Lee, A. G. (2000) Membrane lipids: it's only a phase, Curr. Biol. 10, R377–380.
Mukherjee, S. and Maxfield, F. R. (2000) Role of membrane organization and membrane domains in endocytic lipid trafficking, Traffic 1, 203–211.
Simons, K. and Toomre, D. (2000) Lipid rafts and signal transduction, Nat. Rev. Mol. Cell. Biol. 1, 31–39.
Telo, P., Lostaglio, S., and Dejana, E. (1997) Structure of intercellular junctions in the endothelium, Therapie. 52, 395–398
von Heijne, G. (1999) Recent advances in the understanding of membrane protein assembly and structure, Q. Rev. Biophys. 32, 285–307.

Endoplasmic Reticulum; Golgi Apparatus; Lysosomes

Agarraberes, F. A. and Dice, J. F. (2001) Protein translocation across membranes, Biochim. Biophys. Acta. 1513, 1–24.
Baumann, O. and Walz, B. (2001) Endoplasmic reticulum of animal cells and its organization into structural and functional domains, Int. Rev. Cytol. 205, 149–214.
East, J. M. (2000) Sarco(endo)plasmic reticulum calcium pumps: recent advances in our understanding of structure/function and biology, Mol. Membr. Biol. 17, 189–200.
Ellgaard, L. and Helenius, A. (2001) ER quality control: towards an understanding at the molecular level, Curr. Opin. Cell. Biol. 13, 431–437.
Glick, B. S. (2000) Organization of the Golgi apparatus, Curr. Opin. Cell. Biol. 12, 450–456.
Griffiths, G. (2000) Gut thoughts on the Golgi complex, Traffic. 1, 738–1745.
Lafontaine, D. L. and Tollervey, D. (2001) The function and synthesis of ribosomes, Nat. Rev. Mol. Cell. Biol. 2, 514–2520.
Lippincott-Schwartz, J. and Zaal, K. J. (2000) Cell cycle maintenance and biogenesis of the Golgi complex, Histochem. Cell. Biol. 114, 93–103.
Pshezhetsky, A. V. and Ashmarina, M. (2001) Lysosomal multienzyme complex: biochemistry, genetics, and molecular pathophysiology, Prog. Nucleic Acid Res. Mol. Biol. 69, 81–114.
Yew, N. S. and Cheng, S. H. (2001) Gene therapy for lysosomal storage disorders, Curr. Opin. Mol. Ther. 3, 399–406.

Mitochondria

Frey, T. G. and Mannella, C. A. (2000) The internal structure of mitochondria, Trends Biochem. Sci. 25, 319–324.
Gottlieb, R. A. (2001) Mitochondria and apoptosis, Biol. Signals Recept. 10, 147–161.
Martinou, J. C. and Green, D. R. (2001) Breaking the mitochondrial barrier, Nat. Rev. Mol. Cell. Biol. 2, 63–67.
Rassow, J. and Pfanner, N. (2000) The protein import machinery of the mitochondrial membranes, Traffic 1, 457–464.
Szibor, M., Richter, C., and Ghafourifar, P. (2001) Redox control of mitochondrial functions, Antioxid. Redox. Signal. 3, 515–523.

Peroxisomes

Hayashi, S., Fujiwara, S., and Noguchi, T. (2000) Evolution of urate-degrading enzymes in animal peroxisomes, Cell. Biochem. Biophys. 32, 123–129.

Wanders, R. J., Vreken, P., Ferdinandusse, S., Jansen, G. A., Waterham, H. R., van Roermund, C. W., and Van Grunsven, E. G. (2001) Peroxisomal fatty acid alpha- and beta-oxidation in humans: enzymology, peroxisomal metabolite transporters and peroxisomal diseases, Biochem. Soc. Trans. 29, 250–267.

Cytoskeleton

Banwell, B. L. (2001) Intermediate filament-related myopathies, Pediatr. Neurol. 24, 257–263.

Feng, Y. and Walsh, C. A. (2001) Protein-protein interactions, cytoskeletal regulation and neuronal migration, Nat. Rev. Neurosci. 2, 408–416.

Morgan, K. G. (2001) Nonmuscle motility/cytoskeleton, Am. J. Physiol. Cell. Physiol. 280, C1634–C1635.

Nogales, E. (2001) Structural insight into microtubule function, Annu. Rev. Biophys. Biomol. Struct. 30, 397–420.

Powledge, T. M. (2001) Tensegrity lives, J. Cell. Biol. 154(2), 254.

Reilein, A. R., Rogers, S. L., Tuma, M. C., and Gelfand, V. I. (2001) Regulation of molecular motor proteins, Int. Rev. Cytol. 204, 179–238.

Scholey, J. M., Rogers, G. C., and Sharp, D. J. (2001) Mitosis, microtubules, and the matrix, J. Cell. Biol. 154, 261–266.

Stidwill, R. P. and Greber, U. F. (2000) Intracellular virus trafficking reveals physiological characteristics of the cytoskeleton, News. Physiol. Sci. 15, 67–71.

Nucleus

DePamphilis, M. L. (2000) Review: nuclear structure and DNA replication, J. Struct. Biol. 129, 186–197.

Houtsmuller, A. B. and Vermeulen, W. (2001) Macromolecular dynamics in living cell nuclei revealed by fluorescence redistribution after photobleaching, Histochem. Cell. Biol. 115, 13–21.

Imamoto, N. (2000) Diversity in nucleocytoplasmic transport pathways, Cell. Struct. Funct. 25, 207–216.

Jackson, D. A. (2000) Features of nuclear architecture that influence gene expression in higher eukaryotes: confronting the enigma of epigenetics, J. Cell. Biochem. 35, 69–77.

Kiseleva, E., Goldberg, M. W., Cronshaw, J., and Allen, T. D. (2000) The nuclear pore complex: structure, function, and dynamics, Crit. Rev. Eukaryot. Gene. Expr. 10, 101–112.

Sotolongo, B. and Ward, W. S. (2000) DNA loop domain organization: the three-dimensional genomic code, J. Cell. Biochem. 35, 23–26.

Textbooks

Alberts, B., Bray, D., Lewis, J., Raff, M., Roberts, K., and Watson, J. D. (1994) Molecular Biology of the Cell, 3rd. ed., Garland Publishing, Inc., New York, NY.

Cooper, G. M. (2000) The Cell, A Molecular Approach, 2nd. ed., Sinauer Associates, Inc., Sunderland, MA.

3 Cell Signaling

Daniel A. Rappolee

Introduction

Intercellular communication is essential for development and homeostatic function in multicellular organisms. The language of intercellular communication takes many different forms. These include protein growth factors e.g., local paracrine, like Fibroblast growth factor (FGF), blood-borne endocrine growth hormone; hydrophobic steroids, e.g., estrogen; lipid mediators, prostaglandins, leukotrienes; modified amino acids, e.g., neurotransmitters such as adrenaline and other metabolites, e.g., nitric oxide. This chapter will focus largely on small protein growth factors that modulate growth, differentiation, apoptosis and steady state function during development and in the adult.

An essential role of signal-transduction is to coordinate functions of diverse cell types and sets of identical cells within an organ that require close and synchronous activity in the multicellular organism. The speed of intercellular communication is dependent on distance and the mode of delivery of the intercellular signal. Local or paracrine intercellular communication acts within milliseconds over distances less than 10–20 cell diameters (approx 200 microns), but endocrine or blood-borne signaling that occurs over a distance of meters requires minutes. Specialized short distance signaling, like that mediated by gap junctions, allows linked cells to share small intracellular signal-transduction intermediates downstream of receiving cell-surface receptors. Specialized long distance signaling, over a distance of meters, can be expedited to the millisecond range, by increasing the conductance speed. This is accomplished by saltatory movement of signals in neurons coupled with the fast action of neurotransmitters at post-synaptic membranes.

Once the interactor, i.e., the ligand, has bound to its receptor, intracellular signal-transduction is initiated. After the receptor is activated by phosphorylation, receptor binding of nonenzymatic docking molecules like IRS-1 (insulin-receptor substrate) peaks within 1 min. At the end of this signal transcription pathway, phosphorylation of transcription AP-1 factor initiates transcription of c-fos within 1 min which peaks within 15 min. Other hormones, such as estrogen activate transcription over slower time periods, approaching 1 h. In some signal-transduction processes, such as vision, the complete process of photons activating rhodopsin is computed in one second.

The Receptor

If the ligands are the words of intercellular language, the receptors are the *ears*. Trans-membrane plasmalemma receptors are of several types:

1. Receptor tyrosine kinases such as the FGF receptor;
2. Serine-threonine kinase receptors such as the TGF-β receptor;
3. Nonenzymatic transmembrane receptors (e.g., integrins) that are linked to intracellular tyrosine kinases (e.g., focal adhesion kinase [FAK] and proline rich tyrosine kinase tyrosine kinases [PYK2]);
4. Seven transmembrane spanners receptors linked to G-proteins (e.g., Wnt ligand-wingless and int oncogene- and its receptor; frizzled);
5. Non-enzymatic receptors that are linked to signaling pathways which are derepressed by allosteric-conformational changes (e.g., smoothened receptor for hedgehog ligand);
6. Receptors which are proteolytically converted to ligand (e.g., the Notch intracellular C terminal domain).

Another class of signaling receptors is located in the cytoplasm. They bind hydrophobic hormones such as steroids (e.g., estrogen), thyroid hormones, and retinoic acid ligands. They are then translocated to the nucleus; where they act as transcription factors.

The Signal Cascade

Signaling cascades within the cell start as allosteric changes in the receptor or non-enzymatic docking proteins (e.g., the IRS-1 family and FRS2). These convey the signal by conformational change and by becoming targets for phosphorylation by receptor kinases. In either case, the function of the signal-transduction pathway is to quickly amplify, and directionally conduct information reaching the cell by transmitting it through a series of tyrosine and serine-threonine kinases.

The majority of the transmembrane receptors are in the *off* state until induced by an extracellular ligand. At this point receptors act like allosteric enzymes with the enzyme in the cytoplasmic domain. Many of the tyrosine kinases require multimer formation as there is not sufficient flexibility in the transmembrane alpha-helix to mechanically transduce the ligand-induced conformational change. Multimerization brings together cytoplasmic enzyme domains that cross-activate and then signal downstream docking and enzymatic signal-transduction proteins.

The receptor is activated for a period of time before it is destroyed (internalized and degraded), desensitized (by phosphorylation by a receptor induced kinase such as β-adrenergic receptor kinase), or dephosphorylated. During the activation period, a single activation event can lead to a highly amplified signal-transduction event. For example, a single quantum of light activating the photoreceptor rhodopsin leads to the hydrolysis of one hundred thousand cGMP signaling molecules for the duration of 1 s. The activated receptor has multiple possible phosphorylation sites on the cytoplasmic domains. These are capable of interacting with large numbers of signaling intermediates that *see* the activated receptor through the *src* homology domain-2 (SH2) that bind phosphorylated tyrosines (*see* Fig. 1).

This branching of pathway choices immediately downstream of the FGF receptor is summarized in Figs. 1 and 2. The array of these docking proteins distinguishes different cell types that may each express the same receptor and facilitates different

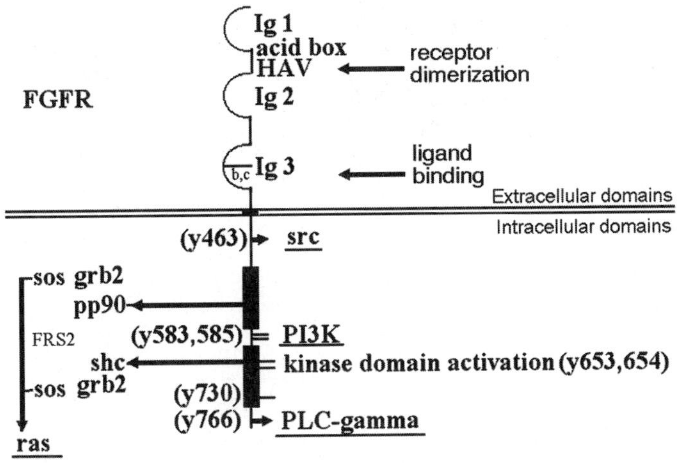

Fig. 1. The FGF receptor. The FGF receptor is an allosteric enzyme with the allosteric sites in the ectodomain and the enzymatic tyrosine kinase in the cytoplasm. Many mapped potentially functional and functionally active tyrosine activation sites are known.

signal types in cells with the same receptor. If the activated receptor is the hub of activity, the docking proteins provide the spokes that radiate out to multiple downstream targets. Docking proteins such as IRS-1 and FRS-2 (insulin and FGF receptor substrate) are receptor-binding proteins that can initiate many branches of the signal-transduction pathway. The importance of the additive effect of branched pathways is indicated by recent studies analyzing the effects of mutating the phosphorylation/docking sites of the PDGF receptor on the activation of sets of newly transcribed genes (Hill and Treisman, 1999). Sets of newly transcribed genes have been analyzed for quality and magnitude of the induction using cDNA-based microarrays. The results suggest that more than one phosphorylation/docking site on the PDGF receptor is needed for the full and proper magnitude and breadth of the transcriptional response.

There are three MAPK families (*see* Figs. 2 and 3, Table 1), each having its own nonenzymatic signal-transduction intermediate before the G protein/*ras* signal-transduction intermediate that is itself a GTPase. Thus, *ras* is a key component in mitogenic signal-transduction. There are 4 sequential vertical tiers of serine-threonine kinases (*see* Table 1); each can have different *horizontal* interacting components. In the three MAPK signal-transduction pathways, the first two serine-threonine kinases have only cytoplasmic targets, whereas the last two tiers have both cytoplasmic targets and nuclear targets. Therefore, the activation of these last two tiers of serine-threonine kinases (MAPKs and MAPKAPS) can lead to nuclear localization, transcription factor phosphorylation (e.g., Elk1 and ATF2 for ERK1,2) and gene transcription. Other nontyrosine kinase initiated pathways also have homologous cytoplasmic signal transducers. For example, although it is thought that Raf-1 mediates the effects of the FGF receptor (*see* Fig. 2, Table 1), Raf-1 homologs in the TGF-β pathway (TAK-1; Fig. 3, Table 1), and seven-spanner G-protein pathway (RafB; Fig. 3, Table 1) also act as cytoplasmic signal transducers. Branching of the pathway can occur at any tier of the vertical cascade (*see* Table 1). Regulation of branching also distinguishes cell types and experience of the cell.

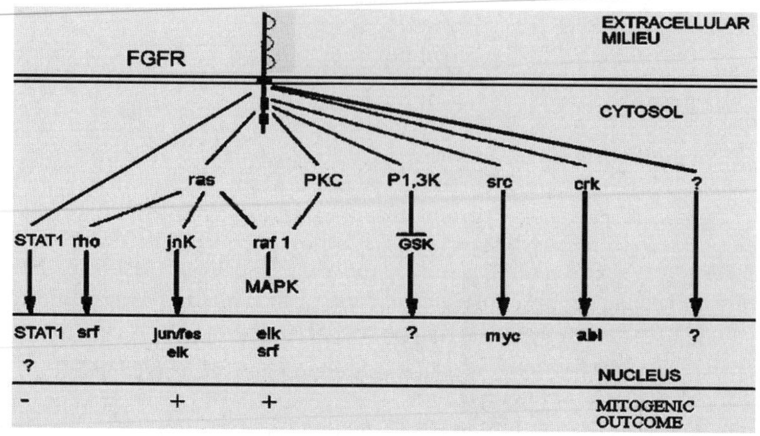

Fig. 2. Mitogenic and transcription activating signal-transduction pathways downstream of FGFR. A preponderance of evidence in cell lines suggests that the *ras*-MAP kinase pathway mediates the mitogenic signal of FGFR. Note that the *src*, crk are only indirectly implicated in FGFR signal-transduction due to sequence homology with other receptors and possible binding sites in the cytosolic domain. Jun kinase and P1,3 kinase can be mitogenic in certain circumstances, but mutation of the P1,3 kinase activating site in an FGFR in vitro did not prevent a mitogenic response to FGF. The STAT1 pathway has recently been shown to be anti-mitogenic in FGFR-3 mediated chondrocyte cell division cessation. The + indicate the most likely pathways for FGFR cell-division control.

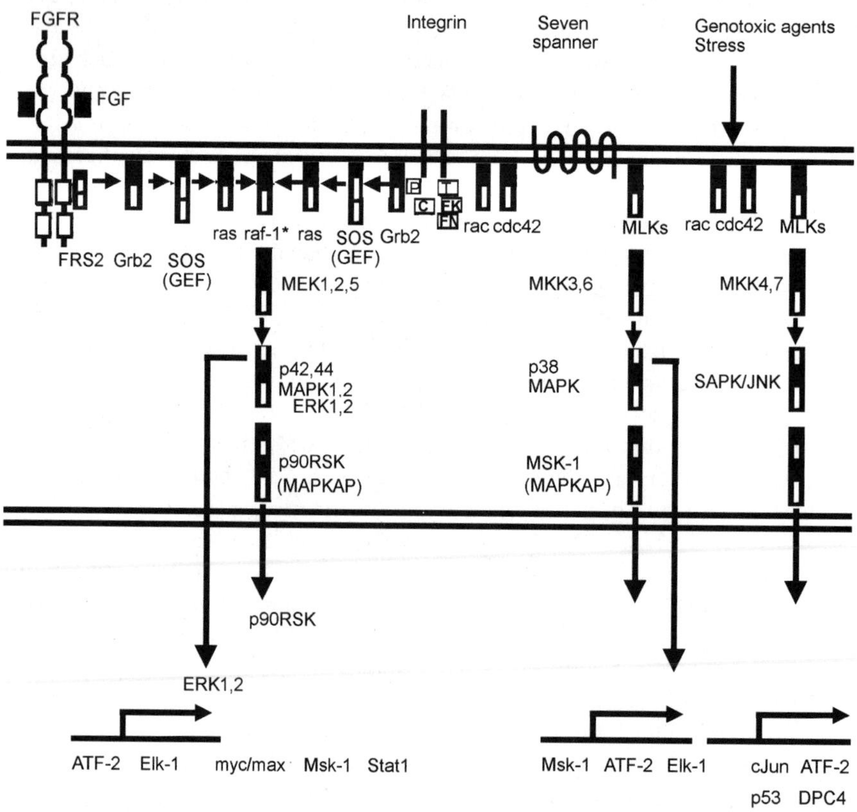

Turning Off the Response

Signaling requires expeditious and tight control to maintain homeostasis and to ensure proper development. Control is exerted at all tiers of the pathway and at various levels of production and activation of the signal-transduction proteins. The receptor is activated for a period of time before it is destroyed, desensitized, or dephosphorylated. Other tiers of the pathway are regulated in similar ways. Ras is inactivated by GTPase activating proteins (GAPs), MEK family members are dephosphorylated and inactivated by protein phosphatase (PP)-1 and PP2A, ERK family members are dephosphorylated and inactivated by MAP kinase phosphatases MKP-3 and MKP6, and JNK is inactivated by M3/6. The mRNA transcripts for many of the signal-transduction genes have a consensus destruction sequence in the 3'- untranslated region that confers a short half-life. Rapid regulation is achieved at the levels of protein and mRNA stability, protein activation, and signal-transduction.

Signal Transduction Pathways

A list of signal-transduction pathway websites is presented in Table 2. Information can be obtained on the activation of PKA and PKC, the mechanism of Calcium-calmodulin signaling, prostaglandins and leukotrienes, and nitric oxide. Other cytostatic pathways mediated by JAK-STAT receptors for the interferon-γ (IFN-γ) receptor, and apoptosis pathways through tumor necrosis factor-α (TNF-α) are also included. Noncanonical pathways mediated by serine-threonine receptor kinases (TGF-β receptor), and novel pathways for signaling by derepressing seven spanner receptors (Hedgehog-ligand derepression of patched receptor by smoothened) are also included. A novel signaling mechanism important in development, signaling by proteolytically cleaved ligand-activated receptor (Delta ligand activation of the Notch protein that cleaves and translocates the protein to the nucleus), is at the Science website for Signal Transduction Knowledge environment (*see* Website: http://www.stke.sciencemag.org). The Wnt-frizzled-GSK3-β-catenin pathways interaction with E-Cadherin-β-catenin are not discussed in this chapter. FGF receptor, integrin, and G protein- activating receptors and their activation of the three MAPK families (*see* Figs. 2 and 3) can be used to illustrate the basic principles of signal-transduction pathways.

Fig. 3. *(opposite page)* The MAPK family. Each member is embedded in enzymatic cascades of intracellular serine-threonine kinases regulated by tyrosine kinases and allosteric docking proteins. The pathways initiate at the plasmalemma by receptor tyrosine kinases, ECM-binding integrins, and G-protein binding receptors. ATF-2- Activating transcription factor 2, CRE-BP1, CREB2; Cas Crk-associated substrate, p130CAS (**C in integrin signaling complex); c-Raf Raf proto-oncogene S/T protein kinase; DPC-4- Deleted in pancreatic cancer locus 4, SMAD4; ELK1-Ets domain transcription factor, ERK-Extracellular signal-regulated kinase, MAPK; FAK- Focal adhesion kinase (**FK in integrin signaling complex); FGF-fibroblast growth factor; FGFR-fibroblast growth factor receptor; FRS2- FGF receptor stimulated, lipid-anchored Grb2 binding protein; Fyn- src family tyrosine kinase (**Fn in integrin signaling complex); GEF Guanine nucleotide exchange factor (example is SOS son-of-sevenless); GRB2-Growth factor receptor-bound protein 2; JNK-Jun N-terminal kinase; Jun-transcription factor; MAPK-Mitogen-activated protein kinase; MAPKAP- MAP kinase-activated protein kinase 2; MEK-MAPK/ERK kinase, MAPKK; MKK MEK kinase; MLK-Mixed lineage kinase; MSK-1- Mitogen and stress-activated kinase 1; p53 Tumour suppressor protein that protects from DNA damage; Paxilin (P in integrin signaling complex); PYK2-Proline-rich tyrosine kinase-2 (**P in integrin signaling complex); rac-G-protein; ras-G-protein; RSK- Ribosomal S6 kinase; SAPK- Stress-activated protein kinase; STAT- Signal transducer and activator of transcription; Talin (**T in integrin signaling complex).

Table 1
Extracellular to Intracellular Signal-Transduction for Three MAPK Families: Levels of Signal-Transduction in the Cascades of the Three MAPK Families[a]

Ligand ↓	FGF1-23	Other ligands		
Receptor ↓	FGFR1-4	Other receptors		
Nonenzymatic Docking molecule 1 RTK binding ↓	FRS2	GAB1,2	IRS1-4	
Nonenzymatic Docking molecule 2 RTK binding Docking molecule 1 binding ↓	Grb2	shc	shb	
Ras superfamily Regulatory molecules ↓	SOS (GEF family)	GRF family Rate limiting	GAP family	vav
Ras superfamily G protein family Enzyme ↓	*ras*	Rac Rho	dc42	Rap1
Kinase 1 (MEKK) Enzyme ↓	Raf-1	RafB KSR	Tak1	
Kinase 2 ↓	MEK1, 2, 5	MEK3,6	MEK4,7	
Enzyme ↓	MAPK family One	MAPK family Two		MAPK family Three
Kinase 3 ↓	p42, 44 ERK1,2 MAPK1,2, MAPK5	p38MAPK	SAPK/JUNK enzyme	
Kinase 4 Enzyme ↓	p90RSK	MAPKAP	MNK1,2	MSK1
Resident or Translocated nuclear Factors	Elk1 myc/max pRSK90 MAPK family ATF-2 STAT1 Jun			

[a]FGF signaling is used as an example. *See* Fig. 3 caption for abbreviations.

Table 2
Signal Transduction Websites:
Electronic Resources for Signal-Transduction Reagents and Information

Website: http://stke.sciencemag.org/
Signal-transduction knowledge environment (STKE). Excellent resource for broad and focused signal-transduction electronic and archival published literature. PDFs and full text articles with JPG figures are available. Requires AAAS membership and an STKE users fee.

Website: http://kinase.oci.utoronto.ca/signallingmap.html
Very good focus with map of the 3 MAPK families and clickable short to long descriptions of molecules on the map.

Website: http://www-personal.umich.edu/%7Eino/List/
Good outline of signal-transduction pathways with links to PubMed discovery articles.

Website: http://www.grt.kyushu-u.ac.jp/spad/index.html
Good, clickable diagrams, but not recently updated.

Website: http://vlib.org/Science/Cell_Biology/signal_transduction.shtml
Good cross-referenced site for information about function and sequence references for signal-transduction genes.

Website: http://www.cellsignal.com/
Company site. Short description of signaling intermediates in the literature and available antibodies. Also, check sections under pathway diagrams for other web resources .

Website: http://www.clontech.com/gfp/
Company site for signal-transduction expression transgenes.

Website: http://www.scbt.com/
Company site. Short description of signaling intermediates in the literature and available antibodies. Also, check sections under pathway diagrams for other web resources.

Receptor Tyrosine Kinases (FGF Receptor) and Mitogenesis

Ligand-dependent autophosphorylation and activation of the FGFRs signals into four pathways leading to new transcription in cell lines (*see* Figs. 1 and 2). Two of these, p38MAPK and Jun kinase, are generally not mitogenic in cell lines. The major FGFR mitogenic signaling pathway is the *ras*-Raf-1-MAPK pathway, also known as the *universal cassette* because of the weight of evidence for its mitogenic role in diverse cell lines. FGF activation of MAPK (ERK-1, ERK-2) is necessary and sufficient to activate transcription factors elk and SRF, leading to new transcription and a strong mitogenic response in cell lines.

A second pathway that mediates mitogenesis through the FGFRs leads to binding of phospholipase C (PLC)-γ and Ca^{2+}-dependent PI-3-kinase through phosphorylation of other unique tyrosine residues and the subsequent activation of phosphoinositol turnover, generation of diacylglycerol and the activation of PKC. There are three groups of PKC; conventional (α,β,γ), novel (η, ν, θ), and ξ) atypical (λ). The ξ and atypical families are not mitogenic and are brain-specific. Activation of PKC-α,β, and γ leads to an increased mitogenic response, primarily through Raf-1 and MAPK, although this appears to be less important than the *ras*-dependent MAPK pathway. Substitution of the tyrosine on FGFR-1 responsible for PLC-γ binding and activation of PKC does not diminish FGF-dependent mitogenesis, suggesting that PKC is not necessary for mitogenesis. However, in studies with a related PDGF receptor, mutations causing inactivity in all tyrosine sites for mitogenic effects were rescued by the inclusion of the the tyrosine that activates the PLC-PKC pathway. This suggested that the PKC pathway can be sufficient for mitogenesis. It is important to note that PKC and *ras* activate Raf-1 by a separate mechanism and that Raf-1 activates mitogenesis via MAPK activity. Therefore, the FGF receptor can activate Raf-1 through either pathway, although *ras* is most powerful. Recent analysis of the *raf-1* null mutant has suggested that *ras* is the most important, but that the Raf-B, not Raf-1 is necessary for growth factor mediated mitogenesis.

As observed in cell lines, activation of *src* is a third possible pathway of FGFR cell cycle activation. The FGFR activation of *src* (*see* Fig. 1) has not been found to be mitogenic for FGF, but is mitogenic in other cell lines and mediates functions like cell scattering and activation of nuclear transcription during PC-12 differentiation.

A fourth pathway where FGF activity suppresses cell division through STAT1 has been identified. In the gain-of-function mutation leading to sporadic nonfamilial dwarfism, a single change in a transmembrane amino acid in FGFR-3 results in a gain-of-function enzymatic activity that leads to cessation of the cell cycle in chon-drocytes. Recently, suppression of chondrocyte division was shown to require STAT1 activity, but the mode of activation of STAT1 is not understood. The expression of the STAT1 pathway has not been tested in preimplantation embryos. However, STAT1 should be considered when interpreting results after perturbing FGF receptors.

MAPK Families

The structure of the cascading biochemical pathway of the three MAPK family pathways docking proteins and kinases, are very similar (*see* Table 1, Fig. 3). However, functionally, the MAPK/ERK pathways are more mitogenic and the p38MAPK and SAPK/JNK pathways are cytostatic. The mechanistic basis of the separation of function is not clear, but is based more on the quantity of each type of transcription factor activated than the quality. Each MAPK family activates a large overlapping group of transcription factors (*see* Fig. 3), but overexpression of receptors (increasing pathway strength), can change the outcome of mitogenesis to one of differentiation within a single cell type. Early studies examined functionally similar receptors (mitogenic FGF and PDGF) and did not compare receptors that mediate more diverse biological outcomes. In comparison, recent studies using cDNA microarrays have suggested that different factors result in transcriptional activation of similar sets of genes. Differences in strength of transcription is an important difference. The use of cDNA microarrays to analyze intermediate transcriptional outcomes (primary and secondary waves of induced transcription) with respect to upstream receptor signaling capacity and downstream biological outcome, will yield significant insights into the function of signaling pathways.

As described in the section "The Signal Cascade", the three MAPK family pathways go through similar tiers of nonenzymatic docking proteins and serine threonine kinases. Each of these tiers branch to affect cytoplasmic targets, but only the last two tiers of proteins migrate to the nucleus and directly affect transcription factors (*see* Table 1; Fig. 3).

A long initial phase of research in signal-transduction has focused upon identifying novel signaling intermediates and their roles in the various pathways. The three MAPK families illustrate common features of related and interacting signal-transduction pathways: speed of transduction, amplification via cascading enzymatic activity, branching and interaction with other pathways, and distinct and shared biologic function mediated through shared and distinct and shared transcription factors. The next phases of research will focus on the function of all members within a family of signal-transduction genes as the human and mouse genome projects provide complete sets of family members. Large-scale approaches paint a broader picture of the responses of cells to ligands that induce distinct biological outcomes, such as cell death, mitosis, or motility. In this case, microarrays will be utilized to detect broad changes in signaling quantity and quality of the sets of transcription factors between normal cells and null mutants or cells with receptor mutants with differential signal-transduction capacities. For example, differences in transcriptional quantity and quality of functionally different receptors that activate mitogenesis through FGF receptor-ERK signaling, that block mitogenesis through TGF-β receptor-SMAD (contraction of Sma and Mad [Mothers against decapentaplegic] genes) signaling or induce apoptosis through TNF-α receptor- Fas-associated protein with death domain (FADD) signaling, are sure to be studied.

Glossary and Abbreviations

ATF A family of activating transcription factors (ATF) binding both AP-1 and CRE response elements in promoters and using leucine zipper protein interaction domains. These transcription factors are targets of stress, UV, and viral infection (*see* Fig. 2 and Suggested Reading).

ERK (MAPK family) One of three families of serine threonine kinases designated extracellular-signal regulated kinases (ERK) that mediate the largely mitogenic signals of extracellular growth factors/hormones and neurotransmitters. There are currently five members of the family; ERK1, ERK2 (aka MAPK1 or p42, and MAPK2 or p44), ERK3, ERK5, and ERK 6. Phosphorylation of threonine and tyrosine residues by upstream MEK1, 2, and 5 is required for activation. Activation by phosphorylation is followed by nuclear translocation and phosphorylation of transcription factors such as Elk-1 (*see* Fig. 2 and Suggested Reading).

Grbs SHc SHb Docking proteins with SH2-phospho-tyrosine binding domains that directly bind activated receptors or receptor activated docking proteins like IRS and FRS family docking intermediates. These proteins then interact with GRFs, GEFs, and GAPs to modulate downstream *ras* family activity. Grb2 is essential for survival of very early mammalian development.

GTPase releasing factors (GRF), SOS enhancing factors (GEF), and activating factors (GAP) A large family of molecules that enhance the activity of *ras* by facilitating its existence in the GTP bound state. These activating factors act by ridding inactive *ras* of bound GDP (GDP-release factors or GRFs), and by promoting binding of GTP to *ras* to activate it (GTP exchange factors or GEFs). The inactivating factors activate *ras* inherent GTPase activity, converting *ras*-GTP into inactive *ras*-GDP (GTPase activating protein- GAPs).

IRS1-4, FRS-2 Nonenzymatic, docking molecule families that directly bind the phosphorylated and activated insulin receptor and FGF receptors. Upon binding of tyrosine phosphorylated receptors through SH2 or PBZ domains, each receptor substrate has multiple tyrosines that can be phosphorlated and provide docking sites for downstream SH2 or PBZ domain expressing signal-transduction proteins.

MAPKAP MAPK Activated Protein Kinases that are activated by the three MAPKs subsequently have cytoplasmic targets or migrate to the nucleus. The family includes MSK-1, Mnk, and RSK family members.

MEK A family of homologous mixed-function kinases downstream of the Raf1 family of serine threonine kinases and upstream of the three MAP-ERK kinase families. There are currently seven members of the family. The prototype, MEK1, specifically phosphorylates MAPK/ERK1,2 on both regulatory threonine and tyrosine residues. MEK 2-7 phosphorylate and activate all three MAPK family serine threonine kinases in the following interactions; MEK2:ERK1,2, MEK3:p38MAPK (aka MKK3), MEK4:p38MAP or MEK:JNKMAPK (aka MKK-4), MEK5:ERK5, MEK6:p38MAPK, and MEK7:JNKMAPK (*see* Fig. 2 and Suggested Reading).

MSK-1 Mitogen activated S6 kinases (MSK) are MAPKAPs (MAPK-activated protein kinase) that is activated by ERK as well as p38 MAPK in response to growth factors and cellular stress. There are currently three members of the family. MSK protein is similar to MAPKAP RSK in having two kinase domains on either side of a regulatory domain (*see* Figs. 2 and 3 and Suggested Reading).

p38 (MAPK family) One of three families of related MAPKs designated p38 MAPK. p38 is more similar to SAPK/JNK in its activation by stress, UV, and cytokines/inflammation more than growth factors. Related proteins include SAPK4 and yeast HOG1. Targets include max transcription factor, ATF-2 and MAPKAP-2.

Raf family (aka MAPKKK) A family of serine threonine kinases that are activated on separate domains downstream to *ras* and PKC (protein kinase C). There are three family members Raf-1, RafA, and RafB and two related proteins (below). Raf-1 is stimulated downstream to receptor tyrosine kinases and *src*. Raf activates MEKs and is required for activation of the ERK/MAPK pathway. TAK-1 (TGF-β activated kinase) and KSR (kinase suppressor of *ras*) are related serine threonine kinases.

Ras-G proteins (*ras*-Rac-Rho-Rap1,2-Ral) GTPase enzymes that activate Raf and other downstream cytoplasmic signaling kinases while in their GTP bound state. Cellular localization is essential to function and *ras* family proteins are localized to plasmalemma, cytoskeleton, and vesicular membranes. Currently includes three *ras* family members, three Rap1 and Rap2 family members, two Ral family members; six Rac, Rho, and cdc42 family members, and three Rho family members.

RSK Ribosomal S6 kinase (RSK) are MAPKAPs (MAPK activated protein kinase) that are activated by mitogens and stress. There are currently three family members Rsk-1 (aka p90RSK), Rsk-2, and Rsk-3. RSKs were initially thought to have ribosomal S6 protein as a target, but now nuclear transcription factors and proteins such as histone H3 are thought to be the physiologic targets (*see* Figs. 2 and 3, Suggested Reading).

SAPK/JNK (MAPK family) One of three families of related MAPKs designated stress activated protein kinase (SAPK)/cJun kinase (JNK). They are related to ERK/MAPK in requiring activation by phosphorylation of nearby tyrosine and threonine residues by upstream MEKs. They are activated by stresses such as UV and viral infection, not mitogens. There are currently three family members; JNK-1-3. (*see* Fig. 2 and Suggested Reading).

STAT STATs are a family of 6 currently known transcription factors that bind growth factor receptor tyrosine kinases (e.g., STAT1 binds directly FGF receptor) and cytokine activated IFN-γ receptors that activate STATs through the JAK intracellular non-receptor tyrosine kinases.

Suggested Reading

Introduction; Background and Reviews

Alberts, B., Bray, D., Lewis, J., Raff, M., Roberts, K., Watson, J. D. (eds.) (1994) Molecular Biology of the Cell, 3rd ed. Garland Publishing, NY, p. 755.

Angel, P. and Karin, M. (1991) The role of Jun, Fos and the AP-1 complex in cell-proliferation and transformation, Biochem. Biophys. Acta. 1072, 129–157.

Cherfils, J. and Chardon, P. (1999) GEFs: Structural basis for their activation of GTP-binding proteins, Trends Biochem. Sci. 24, 306–311.

Heim, M. H. (1999) The Jak-STAT pathway: cytokine signalling from the receptor to the nucleus, J. Recept. Signal. Transduct. Res. 19, 75–120.

Murakami, M. and Morrison, D. K. (2001) Raf-1 Without MEK? Science STKE, 1–3.

Myers, M. G., Wang, L.-M., Sun, X. J., Zhang, Y., Yenush, L., Schlessinger, J., et al. (1994) Role of IRS-1-GRB-2 complexes in insulin signaling, Mol. Cell. Biol. 14, 3577–3587.

Nishida, E. and Gotoh, Y. (1993) The MAP kinase cascade is essential for diverse signal transduction pathways, Trends Biochem. Sci. 18, 128–131.

Perrimon, N. and Perkins, L. (1997) There must be 50 ways to rule the signal: The case of the Drosophila EGF receptor, Cell 89, 13–16.

Rappolee, D. A. and Werb, Z. (1994) The Role of Growth Factors in Early Mammalian development, Advances in Developmental Biology 3, 41–71.

Rappolee, D. A. (1998) Growth factors and hormones in mammalian development. Growth factors in the mammalian pre- and post-implantation embryo, in: Hormones and Growth Factors in Development and Neoplasia, (Dickson, R. and Salomon, D., eds.) John Wiley and Sons, New York, NY, pp. 93–115.

Robinson, M. J. and Cobb, M. H. (1997) Mitogen-activated protein kinase pathways, Curr. Op. Cell. Biol. 9, 180–186.

The Receptor

Alberts, B., Bray, D., Lewis, J., Raff, M., Roberts, K., Watson, J. D. (eds.) (1994) Molecular Biology of the Cell, 3rd ed. Garland Publishing, NY, p. 755.

Amaya, E., Musci, T. J., and Kirschner, M. W. (1991) Expression of a dominant negative mutant of the FGF receptor disrupts mesoderm formation in Xenopus embryos, Cell 66, 257–270.

Chai, N, Patel, Y., Jacobson, K, McMahon, J., and Rappolee, D. A., (1998) FGF is an essential positive regulator of the fifth cell division in all stem cells of the preimplantation mouse embryo, Devel. Biol. 198, 105–115.

Clyman, R. I., Peters, K. G., Chen, Y. Q., Escobedo, J., Williams, L. T., Ives, H. E., and Wilson, E. (1994) Phospholipase C gamma activation, phosphotidylinositol hydrolysis, and calcium mobilization are not required for FGF receptor-mediated chemotaxis, Cell Adhes. Commun. 4, 333–342.

Feldman, B., Poueymirou, W., Papaioannou, V. E., DeChiara, T. M., and Goldfarb, M. (1995) Requirement of FGF-4 for postimplantation mouse development, Science 267, 246–249.

MacNicol, A. M., Muslin, A. J., and Williams, L. T. (1993) Raf-1 kinase is essential for early Xenopus development and mediates the induction of mesoderm by FGF, Cell 73, 571–583

Ornitz, D. M., Xu, J., Colvin, J. S., McEwen, D. G., MacArthur, C. A., Coulier, F., Gao, G., and Goldarb, M. (1996) Receptor specificity of the fibroblast growth factor family, J. Biol. Chem. 271, 15,292–15,297.

Rappolee, D. A. (1998) Growth factors and hormones in mammalian development. Growth factors in the mammalian pre- and post-implantation embryo, In: Hormones and Growth Factors in Development and Neoplasia, (Dickson, R. and Salomon, D., eds.) John Wiley and Sons, New York, NY, pp. 93–115.

Sorokin, A., Mohammadi, M., Huang, J., and Schlessinger, J. (1994). Internalization of fibroblast growth factor receptor is inhibited by a point mutation at tyrosine 766, J. Biol. Chem. 269, 17,056–17,061.

Ueno, H., Gunn, M., Dell, K., Tseng, Jr., A., and Williams, L. (1992) A truncated form of fibroblast growth factor receptor 1 inhibits signal-transduction by multiple types of fibroblast growth factor receptor, J. Biol. Chem. 267, 1470–1476.

The Signal Cascade

Alberts, B., Bray, D., Lewis, J., Raff, M., Roberts, K., Watson, J. D. (eds.) (1994) Molecular Biology of the Cell, 3rd ed., Garland Publishing, NY, p. 755.

Hill, C. S. and Treisman, R. (1999) Growth Factors and Gene Expression: Fresh Insights from Arrays, Science STKE 3, 1–6.

Feramisco, J. R., Clark, R., Wong, G., Arnheim, N., Milley, R., and McCormick, F. (1985) Transient reversion of *ras* oncogene-induced cell transformation by antibodies specific for amino acid 12 of *ras* protein, Nature 314, 639–642.

Jun, T., Gjoerup, O., and Roberts, T. M. (1999) Tangled Webs: Evidence of Cross-Talk Between c-Raf-1 and Akt, Science STKE 13, 1–3.

Turning Off the Response

Shaw, G. and Kamen, R. (1986) A conserved AU sequence from the 3' untranslated region of GM-CSF mRNA mediates selective mRNA degradation, Cell 46, 659–667.

Sun, H., Charles, C. H., Lau, L. F., and Tonks, N. K. (1993) MKP-1 (3CH134), an immediate early gene product is a dual specificity phosphatase that dephosphorylates MAP kinase in vivo, Cell 75, 487–493.

Receptor Tyrosine Kinases (FGF Receptor) and Mitogenesis

Dekker, L. V. and Parker, P. J. (1994) Protein kinase C-a question of specificity, Trends Biosci. 19, 73–77.

Deng, C., Wynshaw-Boris, A., Zhou, F., Kuo, A., and Leder, P. (1996) Fibroblast growth factor receptor 3 is a negative regulator of bone growth, Cell 84, 911–921.

Huang, J., Mohammadi, M., Rodrigues, G. A., and Schlessinger, J. (1995) Reduced activation of RAF-1 and MAP kinase by a fibroblast growth factor receptor mutant deficient in stimulation of phosphatidylinositol hydrolysis, J. Biol. Chem. 270, 5065–5072.

Landgren, E., Blume-Jensen, P., Courtneidge, S. A., and Claesson-Welsh, L. (1995) Fibroblast growth factor receptor-1 regulation of Src family kinases. Oncogene 10, 2027–2035.

LaVoie, J. N., L'Alemain, G., Brunet, A., Muller, R., and Pouyssegur, J. (1996) Cyclin D1 expression is regulated positively by the p42/p44 MAPK and negatively regulated by the p38/HOGMAPK pathway, J. Biol. Chem. 271, 20,608–20,616.

Mohammadi, M., Dionne, C. A., Li, W., Li, N., Spivak, T., Honegger, A. M., Jaye, M., and Schlessinger, J. (1992) Point mutation in FGF receptor eliminates phosphatidylinositol hydrolysis without affecting mitogenesis, Nature 358, 681–684.

Mohammadi, M., Dikic, I., Sorokin, A., Burgess, W., Jaye, M., and Schlessinger, J. (1996) Identification of six novel autophosporylation sites on fibroblast growth factor receptor-1 and elucidation of their importance in receptor activation and signal-transduction, Mol. Cell. Biol. 16, 977–989.

Newton, A. C. (1997) Regulation of protein kinase C, Curr. Opin. Cell. Biol. 9, 161–169.

Partanen, J., Vainikka, S., Korhonen, J., Armstrong, E., and Alitalo, K. (1992) Diverse receptors for FGFs, Prog. Growth Factor Res. 4, 69–83.

Peters, K. G., Marie, J., Wilson, E., Ives, H. E., Escobedo, J., Del Rosario, M., Mirda, D., and Williams, L. T. (1992) Point mutation of an FGF receptor abolishes phosphatidylinositol turnover and Ca2+ flux but not mitogenesis, Nature 358, 678–681.

Sahni, M., Ambrosetti, D. C., Mansukhani, A., Gertner, R., Levy, D., and Basilico, C. (1999) FGF signaling inhibits chondrocyte proliferation and regulates bone development through the STAT-1 pathway, Genes Dev. 13, 1361–1366.

Spivak-Kroizman, T., Mohammadi, M., Hu, P., Jaye, M., Schlessinger, J., and Lax, I. (1994) Point mutation in the fibroblast growth factor receptor eliminates phosphatidylinositol hydrolysis without affecting neuronal differentiation of PC12 cells, J. Biol. Chem. 269, 14,419–14,423.

Transcription Factors

Amati, B., Dalton, S., Brooks, M. W., Littlewood, T. D., Evan, G. I., and Land, H. (1992) Transcriptional activation by the human c-Myc oncoprotein in yeast requires interaction with Max, Nature 359, 423–426.

Binétruy, B., Smeal, T., and Karin, M. (1991) Ha-Ras augments c-jun activity and stimulates phosphorylation of its activation domain, Nature 351, 122–127.

Franza, B. R., Rauscher, F. J., Josephs, S. F., and Curran, T. (1988). The Fos complex and Fos related antigens recognize sequence elements that contain AP-1 binding sites, Science 239, 1150–1153.

Pulverer, B. J., Kyriakis, J. M., Avruch, J., Nikolakaki, E., and Woodgett, J. R. (1991) Phosphorylation of c-Jun mediated by MAP kinases, Nature 353, 670–674.

ATF

Gupta, S., Campbell, D., Derijard, B., and Davis, R. J. (1995) Transcription factor ATF2 regulation by the JNK signal transduction pathway, Science 267, 389–393.

Livingstone, C., Patel, G., and Jones, N. (1995) ATF-2 contains a phosphorylation-dependent transcriptional activation domain. EMBO J. 14, 1785–1797.

Montminy, M. R., Sevarino, K. A., Wagner, J. A., Mandel, G., and Goodman, R. H. (1986) Identification of a cyclic-AMP-responsive element within the rat somatostatin gene, Proc. Natl. Acad. Sci. USA 83, 6682–6686.

ERK (MAPK Family)

Bar-Sagi, D. and Feramisco, J. R. (1986) Induction of membrane ruffling and fluid-phase pinocytosis in quiescent fibroblasts by *ras* proteins, Science 233, 1061–1068.

Boulton, T. G., Nye, S. H., Robbins, D. J., Ip, N. Y., Radziejewska, E., Morgenbesser, S. D., et al. (1991) ERKs: a family of protein-serine/threonine kinases that are activated and tyrosine phosphorylated in response to insulin and NGF, Cell 65, 663–675.

Cheng, A. M., Saxton, T. M., Sakai, R., Kulkarni, S., Mbalmalu, G., Vogel, W., et al. (1998) Mammalian Grb2 regulates multiple steps in embryonic development and malignant transformation, Cell 95, 793–803.

Crews, C. M., Alessandrini, A., and Erikson, R. L. (1992) The primary structure of MEK, a protein kinase that phosphorylates the ERK gene product, Science 258, 478–480.

Dérijard, B., Raingeaud, J., Barrett, T., Wu, I.-H., Han, J., Ulevitch, R. J., and Davis, R. J. (1995) Independent human MAP-kinase signal-transduction pathways defined by MEK and MKK isoforms, Science 267, 682–685.

Diaz-Meco, M. T., Berra, E., Municio, M. M., Sanz, L., Lozano, J., Dominguez, I., et al. (1993) A dominant negative protein kinase C β subspecies blocks NF-kappa B activation, Mol. Cell. Biol. 13, 4770–4775.

Kouhara, H., Hadari, Y. R., Spivak-Kroizman, T., Schilling, J., Bar-Sagi, D., Lax, I., and Schlessinger, J. (1997) A lipid-anchored Grb2-binding protein that links FGF-receptor activation to the Ras/MAPK signaling pathway, Cell 89, 693–702.

LaMorte, V. J., Kennedy, E. D., Collins, L. R., Goldstein, D., Harootunian, A. T., Brown, J. H., and Feramisco, J. R. (1993) A requirement for Ras protein function in thrombin-stimulated mitogenesis in astrocytoma cells, J. Biol. Chem. 268, 19,411–19,415.

Lechner, C., Zahalka, M. A., Giot, J. F., Moller, N. P., and Ullrich, A. (1996) ERK6, a mitogen-activated protein kinase involved in C2C12 myoblast differentiation, Proc. Natl. Acad. Sci. USA 93, 4355–4359.

Morrison, D. K., Kaplan, D. R., Rapp, U., and Roberts, T. M. (1988) Signal transduction from membrane to cytoplasm: growth factors and membrane-bound oncogene products increase Raf-1 phosphorylation and associated protein kinase activity, Proc. Natl. Acad. Sci. USA 85, 8855–8859.

Payne, D. M., Rossomando, A. J., Martino, P., Erickson, A. K., Her, J. H., Shabanowitz, J., et al. (1991) Identification of the regulatory phosphorylation sites in pp42/mitogen-activated protein kinase (MAP kinase), EMBO J. 10, 885–892.

Sahai, E., Olson, M. F., and Marshall, C. J. (2001) Cross-talk between *ras* and Rho signaling pathways in transformation favours proliferation and increased motility, EMBO J. 20, 755–766.

Williams, N. G., Roberts, T. M., and Li, P. (1992) Both p21 *ras* and pp60 v-*src* are required, but neither alone is sufficient, to activate the Raf-1 kinase. Proc. Natl. Acad. Sci. USA 89, 2922–2926.

Zhou, G., Bao, Z. Q., and Dixon, J. E. (1995) Components of a new human protein kinase signal transduction pathway, J. Biol. Chem. 270, 12,665–12,669.

Grbs SHc SHb

Cheng, A. M., Saxton, T. M., Sakai, R., Kulkarni, S., Mbalmalu, G., Vogel, W., et al. (1998) Mammalian Grb2 regulates multiple steps in embryonic development and malignant transformation, Cell 95, 793–803.

GTPase Releasing Factors (GRF), SOS Enhancing Factors (GEF), and Activating Factors (GAP)

Cherfils, J. and Chardon, P. (1999) GEFs: Structural basis for their activation of GTP-binding proteins, Trends Biochem. Sci. 24, 306–311.

IRS1-4, FRS-2

Myers, M. G., Wang, L.-M., Sun, X. J., Zhang, Y., Yenush, L., Schlessinger, J., Pierce, J. H., and White, M. F. (1994) Role of IRS-1-GRB-2 complexes in insulin signaling, Mol. Cell. Biol. 14, 3577–3587.

MAPKAP

Waskiewicz, A. J., Flynn, A., Proud, C. G., and Cooper, J. A. (1997) Mitogen-activated protein kinases activate the serine/threonine kinases Mnk1 and Mnk2, EMBO J. 16, 1090–1920.

MEK

Crews, C. M., Alessandrini, A., and Erikson, R. L. (1992) The primary structure of MEK, a protein kinase that phosphorylates the ERK gene product, Science 258, 478–480.

Holland, P. M., Suzanne, M., Campbell, J. S., Noselli, S., and Cooper, J. A. (1997) MKK7 is a stress-activated mitogen-activated protein kinase kinase functionally related to hemipterous, J. Biol. Chem. 272:24,994–24,998.

Tournier, C., Whitmarsh, A. J., Cavanagh, J., Barrett, T., and Davis, R. J. (1997) Mitogen-activated protein kinase kinase 7 is an activator of the c-Jun NH2-terminal kinase, Proc. Natl. Acad. Sci. USA 94, 7337–7342.

Wu, J., Harrison, J. K., Dent, P., Lynch, K. R., Weber, M. J., and Sturgill, T.W. (1997) Identification and characterization of a new mammalian mitogen-activated protein kinase kinase, MKK2, Mol. Cell. Biol. 13, 4539–4548.

MSK-1

Kozma, S. C., Ferrari, S., Bassand, P., Siegmann, M., Totty, N., and Thomas, G. (1990) Cloning of the mitogen-activated S6 kinase from rat liver reveals an enzyme of the second messenger subfamily, Proc. Natl. Acad. Sci. USA 87, 7365–7369.

Moller, D. E., Xia, C. H., Tang, W., Zhu, A.X., and Jakubowski, M. (1994) Human rsk isoforms: cloning and characterization of tissue-specific expression, Am. J. Physiol. 266, C351–C359.

Zhao, Y., Bjorbaek, C., Weremowicz, S., Morton, C. C., and Moller, D. E. (1995) RSK3 encodes a novel pp90rsk isoform with a unique N-terminal sequence: growth factor-stimulated kinase function and nuclear translocation, Mol. Cell. Biol. 15, 4353–4363.

p38 (MAPK Family)

Alam, J., Wicks, C., Stewart, D., Gong, P., Touchard, C., Otterbein, S., et al. (2000) Mechanism of heme oxygenase-1 gene activation by cadmium in MCF-7 mammary epithelial cells. Role of p38 kinase and Nrf2 transcription factor, J. Biol. Chem. 275, 27,694–27,702.

Brewster, J. L., de Valoir, T., Dwyer, N. D., Winter, E., and Gustin, M. C. (1993) An osmosensing signal transduction pathway in yeast, Science 259, 1760–1763.

Goedert, M., Cuenda, A., Craxton, M., Jakes, R., and Cohen, P. (1997) Activation of the novel stress-activated protein kinase SAPK4 by cytokines and cellular stresses is mediated by SKK3 (MKK6); comparison of its substrate specificity with that of other SAP kinases, EMBO J. 16, 3563–3571.

Han, J., Lee, J.-D., Bibbs, L., and Ulevitch, R. J. (1994) A MAP kinase targeted by endotoxin and hyperosmolarity in mammalian cells, Science 265, 808–811.

Jiang, Y., Chen, C., Li, Z., Guo, W., Gegner, J. A, Lin, S., and Han, J. (1996) Characterization of the structure and function of a new mitogen-activated protein kinase (p38beta), J. Biol. Chem. 271, 17,920–17,926.

Nishida, E. and Gotoh, Y. (1993) The MAP kinase cascade is essential for diverse signal transduction pathways, Trends Biochem. Sci. 18, 128–131.

Olofsson, B., Chardin, P., Toudrot, N., Zahraoni, A., and Tavitian, A. (1988) Expression of the *ras*-related ral A rho 12 and rab genes in adult mouse tissues, Oncogene 3, 231–234.

Raingeaud, J., Gupta, S., Rogers, J. S., Dickens, M., Han, J., Ulevitch, R. J., and Davis, R. J. (1995) Pro-inflammatory cytokines and environmental stress cause p38 mitogen-activated protein kinase activation by dual phosphorylation on tyrosine and threonine, J. Biol. Chem. 270, 7420–7426.

Schonwasser, D. C., Marais, R. M., Marshall, C. J., and Parker, P. J. (1998) Activation of the mitogen-activated protein kinase/extracellular signa-regulated kinase pathway by conventional, novel, and atypical protein kinase C isotypes, Mol. Cell Biol. 18, 790–798.

Stacey, D. W., Feig, L. A., and Gibbs, J. B. (1991) Dominant inhibitory Ras mutants selectively inhibit the activity of either cellular or oncogenic Ras, Mol. Cell. Biol. 11, 4053–64.

Ueda, Y. Hirsi, S., Osada, S., Atsushi, S., Mizuno, K., and Ohno, S. (1996) Protein kinase C activates the MEK-ERK pathway in a manner independent of *ras* and dependent on raf, J. Biol. Chem. 271, 23,512–23,519.

Wang, X. S., Diener, K., Manthey, C. L., Wang, S. W., Rosenweig, B., Bray, J., et al. (1997) Molecular cloning and characterization of a novel p38 mitogen activated protein kinase, J. Biol. Chem. 272, 23668–23674.

Zervos, A. S., Faccio, L., Gatto, J. P., Kyriakis, J. M., and Brent, R. (1995) Mxi2, a mitogen-activated protein kinase that recognizes and phosphorylates Max protein. Proc. Natl. Acad. Sci. USA 92, 10,531–10,534.

Raf Family (aka MAPKKK)

Avruch, J., Zhang, X. F., and Kyriakis, J. M. (1994) Raf meets Ras: completing the framework of a signal transduction pathway, Trends Biochem. Sci. 19, 279–283.

Downward, J. (1995) KSR: a novel player in the RAS pathway, Cell. 83, 831–834.

Heidecker, G., Huleihel, M., Cleveland, J. L., Kolch, W., Beck, T. W., Lloyd, P., et al. (1990) Mutational activation of c-raf-1 and definition of the minimal transforming sequence, Mol. Cell. Biol. 10, 2503–2512.

Morrison, D. K., Kaplan, D. R., Rapp, U., and Roberts, T. M. (1988). Signal transduction from membrane to cytoplasm: growth factors and membrane-bound oncogene products increase Raf-1 phosphorylation and associated protein kinase activity, Proc. Natl. Acad. Sci. USA 85, 8855–8859.

Turner, B., Rapp, U., App, H., Greene, M., Dobashi, K., and Reed, J. (1997) Interleukin 2 induces tyrosine phosphorylation and activation of p72-74 Raf-1 kinase in a T-cell line, Proc. Natl. Acad. Sci. USA 88, 1227–1231.

Williams, N. G., Roberts, T. M., and Li, P. (1992) Both p21ras and pp60v-src are required, but neither alone is sufficient, to activate the Raf-1 kinase, Proc. Natl. Acad. Sci. USA 89, 2922–2926.

Yamaguchi, K., Shirakabe, K., Shibuya, H., Irie, K., Oishi, I., Ueno, N., et al. (1995) Identification of a member of the MAPKKK family as a potential mediator of TGF-β signal transduction, Science 270, 2008–2011.

Ras-G Proteins (ras-Rac-Rho-Rap1,2-Ral)

Olofsson, B. (1997) Rho guanine dissociation inhibitors: pivotal molecules in cellular signalling, Cell Signal. 11, 545–554.

Sahai, E., Olson, M. F., and Marshall, C. J. (2001) Cross-talk between *ras* and Rho signaling pathways in transformation favours proliferation and increased motility, EMBO J. 20, 755–766.

RSK

Bjorbaek, C., Zhao, Y., and Moller, D. E. (1995) Divergent functional roles for p90rsk kinase domains, J. Biol. Chem. 270, 18,848–18,852.

Jensen, C. J., Buch, M. B., Krag, T.O., Hemmings, B. A., Gammeltoft, S., and Frodin, M. (1999) 90-kDa ribosomal S6 kinase is phosphorylated and activated by 3-phosphoinositide-dependent protein kinase-1, J. Biol. Chem. 274, 27,168–27,176.

Kozma, S. C., Ferrari, S., Bassand, P., Siegmann, M., Totty, N., and Thomas, G. (1990) Cloning of the mitogen-activated S6 kinase from rat liver reveals an enzyme of the second messenger subfamily, Proc. Natl. Acad. Sci. USA 87, 7365–7369.

Moller, D. E., Xia, C.H., Tang, W., Zhu, A. X., and Jakubowski, M. (1994) Human rsk isoforms: cloning and characterization of tissue-specific expression, Am. J. Physiol. 266, C351–C359.

Zhao, Y., Bjorbaek, C., Weremowicz, S., Morton, C. C., and Moller, D. E. (1995) RSK3 encodes a novel pp90rsk isoform with a unique N-terminal sequence: growth factor-stimulated kinase function and nuclear translocation, Mol. Cell Biol. 15, 4353–4363.

SAPK/JNK (MAPK Family)

Derijard, B., Hibi, M., Wu, I.-H., Barrett, T., Su, B., Deng, T., Karin, M., and Davis, R. J. (1994) JNK1: a protein kinase stimulated by UV light and Ha-Ras that binds and phosphorylates the c-Jun activation domain, Cell 76, 1025–1037.

Devary, Y., Rosette, C., DiDonato, J. A., and Karin, M. (1993). NF-κ B activation by ultraviolet light not dependent on a nuclear signal, Science 261, 1442–1445.

Waskiewicz, A. J., Flynn, A., Proud, C. G., and Cooper, J. A. (1997) Mitogen-actiated protein kinases activate the serine/threonine kinases Mnk1 and Mnk2, EMBO J. 16, 1090–1920.

Yamaguchi, K., Shirakabe, K., Shibuya, H., Irie, K., Oishi, I., Ueno, N., et al. (1995) Identification of a member of the MAPKKK family as a potential mediator of TGF-β signal-transduction, Science 270, 2008–2011.

STAT

Sahni, M., Ambrosetti, D. C., Mansukhani, A., Gertner, R., Levy, D., and Basilico, C. (1999) FGF signaling inhibits chondrocyte proliferation and regulates bone development through the STAT-1 pathway. Genes Dev. 13, 1361–1366.

B. Transcription and Translation

4 DNA Replication, Repair, and Recombination

Linda B. Bloom

Introduction

DNA contains the instructions needed to produce and regulate the components of a cell. This information is encoded in the order, or sequence, of the four possible nucleotide bases contained in the DNA polymer. Hydrogen bonding interactions between complementary base pairs bring two linear DNA polymers together to form a double helix. James Watson and Francis Crick not only deduced the double helical structure of DNA but also recognized that hydrogen bonding between complementary DNA bases would provide a mechanism for DNA duplication. Watson-Crick base pairing allows one strand of DNA to serve as a template for synthesis of a new strand by directing the incorporation of adenine opposite thymine and guanine opposite cytosine (*see* Fig. 1). This complementary base pairing also provides a mechanism for preserving the code. If one strand of DNA is damaged, the other can be used as a template to regenerate the damaged strand and recover information encoded in its sequence.

DNA Replication

Overview of DNA Replication

Every time a cell divides, its DNA must be duplicated so that each daughter cell receives an identical copy of instructions. The size of a DNA molecule alone makes replication an amazing undertaking. For example, human cells contain 3 billion base pairs of DNA divided into chromosomes ranging in size from about 50–250 million base pairs. If they were completely stretched out, these DNA molecules would range in length from about 1.7–8.5 cm. Many enzymes and proteins are required to physically manipulate these large polymers and to catalyze the synthesis of new DNA. These enzymes and the process of DNA replication are regulated by the cell so that replication is complete and genomes are duplicated only once every cell division.

See companion CD for color Fig. 2

DNA replication begins at a specific time in the cell cycle and at specific sites, *origins of replication*, in the genome. The DNA duplex is unwound at these replication origins to allow the enzymes that synthesize DNA access to the individual DNA strands (*see* Fig. 2). Each strand of parental DNA serves as a template for a *DNA polymerase* to make a new strand of DNA. Single nucleotide monomers that form Watson-Crick pairs with template bases are incorporated into a new DNA polymer by

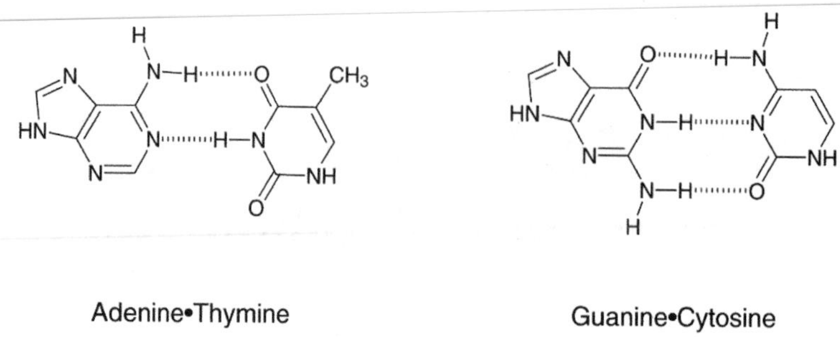

Fig. 1. Watson-Crick A•T and G•C base pairs.

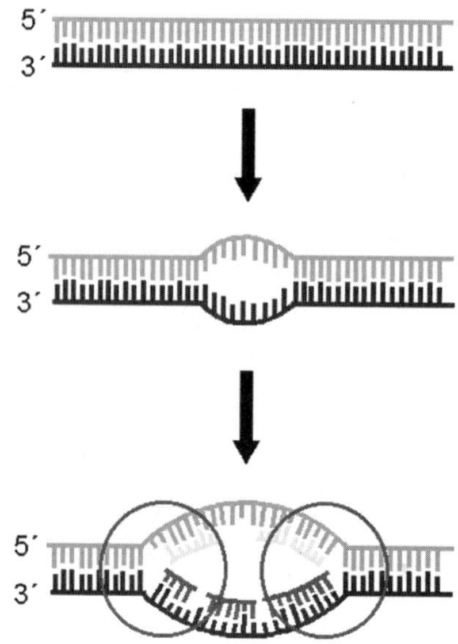

Fig. 2. Unwinding DNA at the origin of replication and the formation of replication forks. DNA replication begins at specific sites known as origins of replication. Origin binding proteins recognize these sites and initiate unwinding of the DNA duplex so that replication proteins can access the individual strands of DNA. Initially a small bubble is formed that is opened further by the activity of a DNA helicase. Replication complexes assemble on both sides of the bubble and these replication forks (circled) move away from the origin in both directions so that replication is bidirectional. At each fork, two new copies of DNA are synthesized using the parental strands as a templates.

DNA polymerases. As the new DNA grows, the parental duplex is progressively unwound forming *replication forks* that move away from the origin. DNA replication is *semi-conservative*, ultimately forming two DNA double helices that contain one strand of parental DNA and one strand of new DNA. In bacteria, replication forks move at a rate of about 500 nucleotides per second while in eukaryotes they move somewhat slower. Because genomes of eukaryotes are in general larger than bacteria and replication fork movement is slower, replication in eukaryotes is initiated at several origins instead of a single origin so that DNA duplication can be accomplished in a reasonable amount of time.

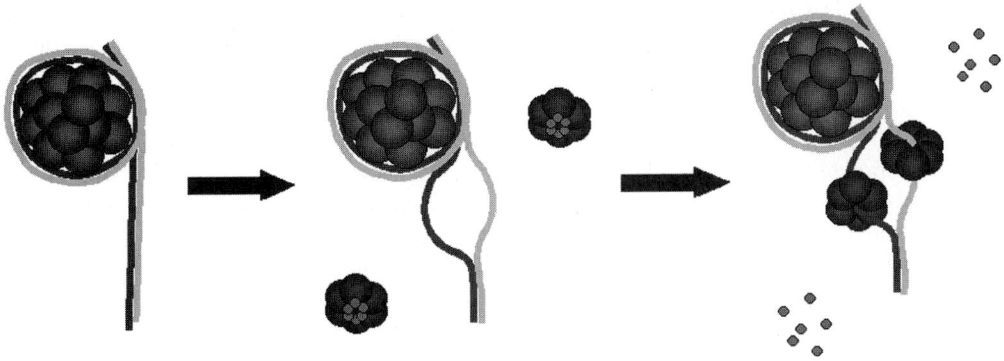

Fig. 3. Initiation of DNA replication at *oriC* in *E. coli*. DnaA protein binds to *oriC* to form a protein-DNA complex where the DNA is wrapped around several molecules of DnaA protein. DnaA binding induces unwinding of the DNA duplex at the A•T rich segments. DnaC protein binds the ring-shaped hexameric DnaB helicase and assembles the helicase onto the origin. One helicase complex is assembled at each fork of the replication bubble. After assembling the helicase, DnaC is released.

Much of what we know about DNA replication is based on studies in bacteria and viruses. However, more recent investigations of eukaryotic systems are revealing that many of the features of the bacterial replication machinery are also common to eukaryotes. Because replication in bacteria has been studied in greater detail to date, the *Escherichia coli* replication machinery will be presented for illustrative purposes and compared to eukaryotic systems.

Initiation of DNA Replication

Origins of DNA replication contain two general DNA sequence elements, an element that is relatively easy to unwind, and an element that is recognized by initiation proteins. The genome of *E. coli* exists as a single circular DNA molecule of about 4.5 million base pairs and contains a single 245 base pair (bp) origin of replication, *oriC*. Within *oriC* are three 13-bp AT-rich regions of DNA that are relatively easy to unwind and four 9-bp regions that are recognized by the *E. coli* initiator protein, DnaA. A complex containing several DnaA molecules binds to *oriC* in the region containing the 9-bp repeats and bends the DNA. This bending helps to unwind the DNA helix at the 13-bp AT-rich sequences (*see* Fig. 3). Many of the steps in DNA replication and repair, such as the unwinding of the origin, require energy to manipulate the structures of macromolecules and disrupt noncovalent interactions such as hydrogen bonding. The enzymes catalyzing these changes utilize the chemical energy stored in the phosphate bonds of adenosine-5'-triphosphate (ATP) to do the mechanical work. The DnaA protein utilizes the energy gained from ATP hydrolysis to power the unwinding of DNA at the origin. An origin recognition complex also exists in eukaryotes but its mechanism of action has not yet been completely defined.

See companion CD for color Fig. 3

Once the DNA duplex is opened, a *DNA helicase* can be loaded onto the single-stranded DNA to continue the unwinding process. DNA helicases are enzymes that utilize the energy from hydrolysis of ribonucleoside 5-triphosphates, most commonly ATP, to break hydrogen bonding interactions between complementary DNA strands and unwind nucleic acid duplexes. In *E. coli*, six molecules of the DnaB protein form a ring-shaped hexamer that encircles single-stranded DNA and functions as a helicase. This hexameric helicase structure is common to other organisms including eukaryotes where the MCM (Mini-Chromosome Maintenance) proteins are believed to perform the function of replicative DNA helicase. In *E. coli*, the DnaB hexamer is assembled around DNA by the ATP-dependent activity of DnaC (*see* Fig. 3).

Before DNA synthesis can begin, RNA primers must be made. DNA polymerases are unable to synthesize DNA *de novo* and can only extend RNA (or DNA) primers that are already paired with the template to be copied. *Primases* synthesize these primers using ribonucleoside 5'-triphosphates as building blocks to form a short strand of RNA complementary to the DNA template. The *E. coli* primase interacts with the DnaB helicase and begins synthesis of RNA primers shortly after DnaB has begun to unwind DNA. In eukaryotes, a hybrid RNA-DNA primer is synthesized by an enzyme complex containing both primase and DNA polymerase α. Once primers are formed, they can be extended by a DNA polymerase.

Enzymes at the Replication Fork

See companion CD for color Fig. 4

Assembly of a *replisome* is complete when the replicative DNA polymerase and its accessory proteins join the helicase and primase at the replication fork (*see* Fig. 4). The replisome will then continue to synthesize new DNA, unwinding the parental duplex as it goes. The actual synthesis of new DNA is catalyzed by a DNA polymerase contained within the replisome. Cells contain many different DNA polymerases that have different functions in DNA replication and repair. There are 5 known DNA polymerases in *E. coli* and at least a dozen in humans. In *E. coli*, DNA polymerase III catalyzes the bulk of DNA synthesis during replication and DNA polymerase δ does so in eukaryotes.

See companion CD for color Fig. 5

All DNA polymerases use 2'-deoxyribonucleoside–5'-triphosphates (dNTPs) as monomeric building blocks for making DNA. They catalyze the attack of the 3' hydroxyl group of the nucleotide at the primer end on the α-phosphoryl group of an incoming dNTP displacing pyrophosphate (*see* Fig. 5, upper panel). Thus, DNA polymerases extend DNA polymers in the 5' to 3' direction by incorporation of 2'-deoxyribonucleoside monophosphates. Watson-Crick base pairing interactions between the incoming dNTP and the next unpaired template base direct incorporation of correct nucleotides. Frequencies of adding incorrect nucleotides can be as low as one in a million, but even with this low error frequency mistakes will be made. To further reduce error frequencies, the DNA polymerases that function in replication contain a 3' to 5' exonuclease activity that allows them to *proofread* nucleotides that have been incorporated. This exonuclease activity catalyzes the hydrolysis of phosphodiester bonds to remove the last nucleotide added to the 3' primer end (*see* Fig. 5, lower panel). Thus, a nucleotide that has been added incorrectly can be removed.

See companion CD for color Fig. 6

The overall efficiency of synthesis by DNA polymerases is enhanced by accessory proteins which increase DNA polymerase *processivity*, or the number of nucleotides incorporated per DNA binding event. These accessory proteins consist of a ring-shaped sliding clamp that binds both DNA and the DNA polymerase and a clamp loader that assembles the clamp on DNA. Sliding clamps, made of identical protein subunits, encircle DNA and are capable of sliding along a DNA duplex (*see* Fig. 6).

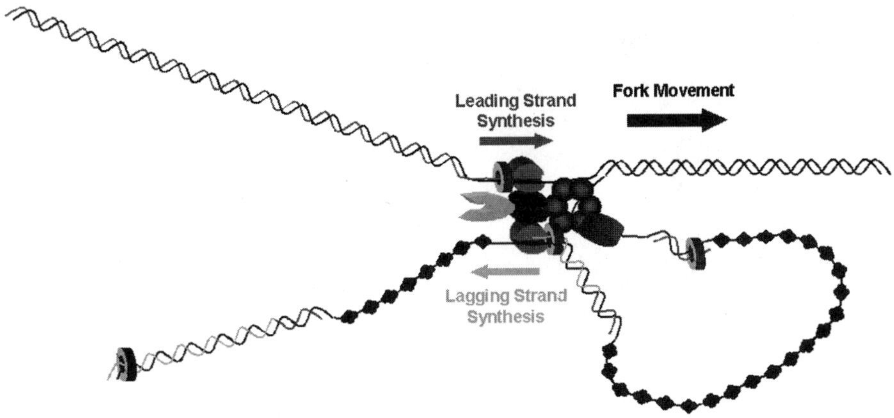

Fig. 4. Proteins at the *E. coli* replication fork.The dimeric polymerase complex is capable coordinated DNA synthesis on the leading and lagging strands. The leading strand polymerase synthesizes new DNA in the direction of fork movement and the lagging strand polymerase synthesizes DNA in the opposite direction. The hexameric helicase (light blue) unwinds DNA ahead of the polymerase and primase (red) makes RNA primers (red lines) on the lagging strand. Single-stranded DNA that forms as the helix unwinds is coated with single-stranded binding protein to prevent reannealing of strands and to remove secondary structure that may form within a single-strand. Sliding clamps (green) are assembled on each primer on the lagging strand by the clamp loading complex (yellow and dark blue). *See* companion CD for color.

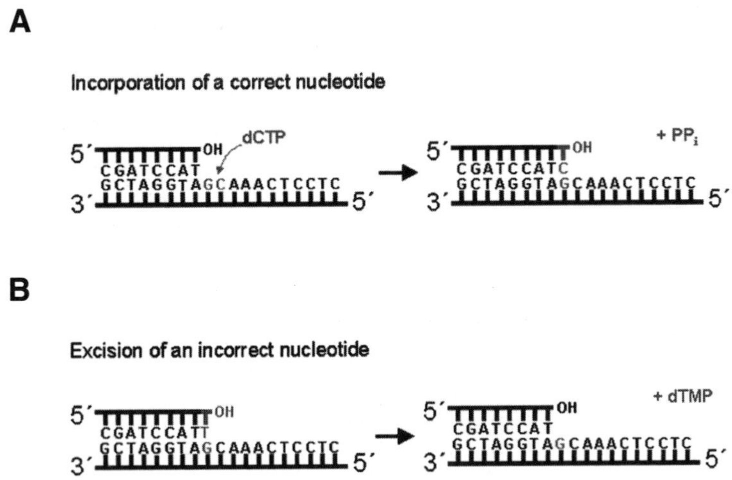

Fig. 5. Reactions catalyzed by DNA polymerases. **(A)** 2'-Deoxyribonucleoside 5'-triphosphates are used as substrates by DNA polymerases to extend a primer in template-directed reactions. The net reaction is incorporation of 2'-deoxyribonucleoside monophosphates onto the 3' hydroxyl of a primer with loss of pyrophosphate. **(B)** DNA polymerases can proofread newly incorporated nucleotides and excise incorrect nucleotides. The excision reaction removes the last nucleoside monophosphate that was incorporated.

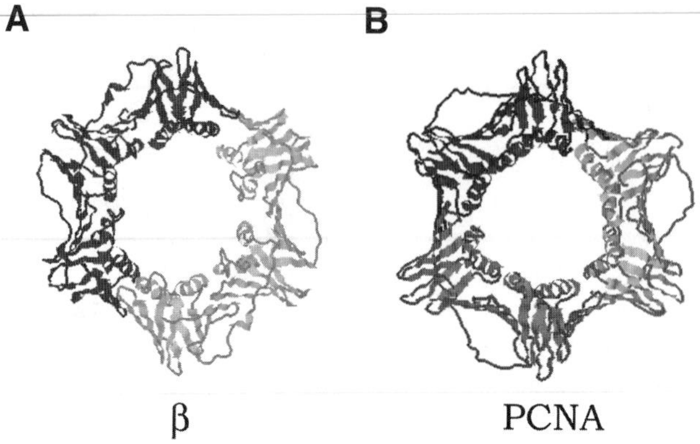

Fig. 6. Structures of sliding clamps from *E. coli* and humans. **(A)** The *E. coli* β sliding clamp is a head-to-tail dimer of identical monomer subunits. **(B)** The human PCNA sliding clamp is similar in overall structure to the β clamp but is composed of identical trimers. Each ring has a central hole that is large enough to encircle B-DNA.

By binding a sliding clamp, a DNA polymerase is effectively tethered to a DNA template so that it is capable of incorporating thousands of nucleotides without dissociating. In the absence of a sliding clamp, DNA synthesis is less efficient because DNA polymerases frequently dissociate from the template and must rebind to continue. Sliding clamps are assembled around DNA by the ATP-dependent activity of clamp loaders.

Leading and Lagging Strand Synthesis

In *E. coli*, a complex containing a dimeric DNA polymerase and accessory proteins interacts with the helicase and primase to form a replisome. This interaction stimulates the activity of the helicase and increases the rate of fork movement. The replisome, which contains two copies of DNA polymerase III, is capable of simultaneously copying both strands of parental DNA at the replication fork. But the two DNA polymerases must work in opposite directions to do this because DNA strands in a duplex are antiparallel and DNA polymerases can only synthesize DNA in the 5' to 3' direction. To accomplish this, one DNA polymerase working on the *leading strand*, synthesizes DNA in a single continuous piece moving in the direction of the replication fork. The other DNA polymerase working on the opposite or *lagging strand*, synthesizes DNA in shorter fragments named *Okazaki fragments* after Reiji Okazaki whose work led to their discovery (*see* Fig. 4). In *E. coli*, Okazaki fragments are 1000–2000 nt in length and in eukaryotes they are 100–200 nt. As the fork progresses, a loop of single-stranded DNA is created on the lagging strand and an RNA primer is synthesized by an enzyme called primase to begin each Okazaki fragment. The lagging strand polymerase extends these primers in the direction opposite to fork movement until it encounters a completed Okazaki fragment. Then, the polymerase dissociates and rebinds a new primer closer to the fork and extends it. Thus, the lagging strand polymerase must repeatedly dissociate from completed Okazaki fragments and rebind to new primers to continue DNA synthesis in a discontinuous manner. Overall, DNA synthesis is *semi-discontinuous* because it is made in one continuous strand on the leading strand and in discontinous fragments on the lagging strand.

To complete DNA replication, RNA primers must be replaced by DNA and Okazaki fragments must be joined together to form a continuous strand. In *E. coli*, removal of RNA primers and synthesis of DNA can be accomplished by a single enzyme, DNA polymerase I. The 5' to 3' exonuclease activity of DNA polymerase I degrades RNA primers while the 5' to 3' polymerase activity simultaneously synthesizes DNA to replace the RNA. In eukaryotes, separate enzymes are responsible for degrading the RNA and replacing it with DNA. Finally, DNA fragments on the lagging strand are joined by a *DNA ligase* to form one continuous polymer. DNA ligase catalyzes the formation of a phosphodiester bond between the 3' hydroxyl group at the end of one Okazaki fragment and the 5' phosphate at the beginning of the next. Any *nick* in one strand of a DNA duplex that has a 3' hydroxyl on one side and 5' phosphate on the other can be sealed by the activity of a DNA ligase.

Fidelity of DNA Replication and Mismatch Repair

DNA replication can be accomplished with as few as one mistake in a billion nucleotides incorporated. This amazing accuracy or *fidelity* of synthesis is achieved for the most part by the DNA polymerase but is enhanced by a group of mismatch repair enzymes that function to detect and correct replication errors. One main feature of a DNA polymerase that contributes to its fidelity is the geometry of the active site, which is optimized for binding Watson-Crick base pairs where the overall shape of both A•T and G•C pairs are the same (*see* Fig. 1). Mismatches such as G•T deviate from this ideal geometry so that incorrect nucleotides are incorporated much less efficiently. Frequencies of adding an incorrect nucleotide range from 1 in 1000 to 1 in 1,000,000 nucleotides depending on the nucleotide added. In the rare instant when a mistake is made, DNA polymerases have the ability to remove the incorrect nucleotide using the 3' to 5' exonuclease activity contained in the enzymes. This proofreading capability is further enhanced by a reduced efficiency of adding the next correct nucleotide onto a primer that ends with an incorrect nucleotide. Thus, when a mistake is made, the rate of adding more nucleotides is greatly reduced which allows the exonuclease time to remove the incorrect nucleotide. Once an incorrect nucleotide is removed, rapid incorporation of correct nucleotides by the DNA polymerase activity resumes. This proofreading activity increases the accuracy of DNA synthesis by a factor of about 10–100.

See companion CD for color Fig. 7

Mismatches that escape proofreading by the DNA polymerase can be corrected by the postreplicative mismatch repair process (*see* Fig. 7). The net result is the removal of a segment of DNA containing the incorrect nucleotide and resynthesis of DNA to replace the segment that was excised. The key enzymes responsible for mismatch repair in *E. coli* are MutS, MutL, MutH, and MutU. Mismatches are detected in double-stranded DNA by MutS which then interacts with the MutL protein. Together MutS and MutL signal where the mismatch is located to MutH and MutU. MutH is an endonuclease that is stimulated by MutL to cut the DNA strand containing the incorrect nucleotide. MutU is a DNA helicase that unwinds the duplex displacing the strand containing the incorrect nucleotide which is then degraded by an exonuclease. New DNA is synthesized to replace the segment that was removed. Homologs to MutS and MutL exist in eukaryotic cells and the overall repair process is similar.

How do the mismatch repair enzymes recognize which nucleotide of the mismatch is incorrect? In *E. coli*, the methylation status of the DNA allows the mismatch repair enzymes to distinguish between the newly synthesized DNA strand and the parental

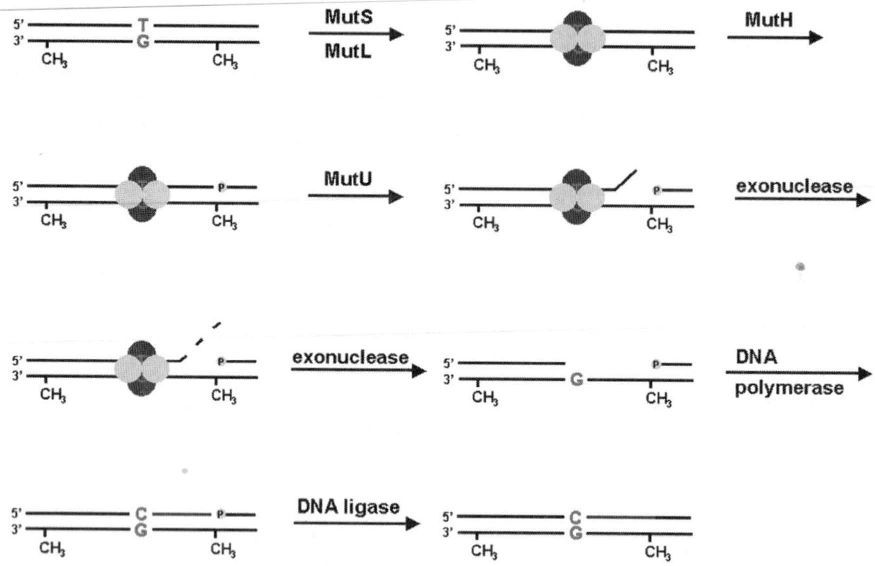

Fig. 7. Methyl-directed mismatch repair in *E. coli*. MutS protein recognizes and binds mismatches such as G•T in DNA and is joined by the MutL protein. MutL within the MutS-MutL-mismatched DNA complex stimulates the endonuclease activity of MutH to cleave the unmethylated DNA strand at the GATC sequence closest to the protein-mismatched DNA complex. The cut DNA strand is unwound by the activity of MutU helicase and then degraded by an exonuclease until the mismatch is removed. The missing segment of DNA is replaced by a DNA polymerase and the DNA strands are joined together by the activity of a DNA ligase. The letter P indicates a 5' phosphate group.

strand. Adenine is methylated in the *E. coli* genome when it appears in the sequence 5'GATC. This methylation of the genome occurs shortly after replication, so for a short time, the daughter strand is unmethylated while the parent strand is methylated. These 5'GATC sequences are also recognized by MutH which cuts the unmethylated daughter strand. These cut sites can be up to 1000–2000 nt away from the mismatch so a fairly large segment of DNA may be removed and replaced. While the overall process of mismatched repair is similar in eukaryotes, it is not yet clear how the eukaryotic enzymes distinguish between the newly synthesized strand and the parental strand.

DNA Recombination

Through the process of recombination, two DNA duplexes can exchange information to create hybrid molecules containing sequences from each of the original molecules. Recombination provides mechanisms for generating genetic diversity and for repairing DNA strand breaks. Recombination pathways can be grouped into two major classes, homologous and site-specific. Homologous recombination is the most general mechanism for recombination and plays a central role in both the generation of genetic diversity and repairing DNA. Homologous recombination occurs between two regions of DNA with similar or homologous sequences. Crosses between these two regions produce two new molecules that are hybrids of the original sequences.

See companion CD for color Fig. 8

During meiosis (process of cell division that ultimately produces germ cells containing a single copy of each chromosome), these crosses allow alleles (alternate forms of the same gene) to be exchanged between homologous chromosomes so that chromosomes passed onto haploid daughter cells are a hybrid of their progenitors (*see* Fig. 8A). This process allows a child to inherit traits from each of its grandparents even though the child only receives a single chromosome from each of its parents. Recombination between homologous duplexes also provides a mechanism for repairing a double-stranded break in one duplex or a damaged segment of DNA.

Site-specific recombination does not require homologous sequences between two DNA duplexes. As its name implies, site-specific recombination occurs when one DNA sequence is inserted into a specific site in another DNA duplex. This type of recombination produces a new DNA duplex where information from one is *spliced* into the other duplex. Some viruses use site-specific recombination to integrate their genomes into the genome of a host. Bacteriophage λ integrates its viral genome into the genome of its *E. coli* host and retroviruses such as HIV integrate a double-stranded DNA copy of their viral RNA genome into the host genome. Transposition is an example of site-specific recombination where a genetic element, transposon, moves from one location in a genome to another. This repositioning requires a specific nuclease, a transposase, encoded within the transposon. Site-specific recombination also provides a mechanism for immune cells to rearrange genetic elements to generate the diversity necessary to produce many different antibodies. By assembling different combinations of genetic elements through the process of V(D)J recombination immune cells are capable of producing genes encoding a multitude of different immunoglobulins that recognize different antigens.

Homologous Recombination

Homologous recombination is the most general pathway of recombination and is fairly well-defined. Homology or significant complementarity in DNA sequences is a prerequisite for homologous recombination between two duplexes. In addition, the physical exchange of information requires breaking and rejoining of the DNA molecules. Modern models of homologous recombination propose that recombination is initiated by the formation of a double-stranded break in one of the two duplexes. These breaks can be created by specific enzymes or can result from DNA damage. The broken duplex will serve as a substrate to initiate recombination after it is partially degraded by an exonuclease to generate free single-stranded ends. One of the single-stranded ends will invade the intact duplex and pair with the homologous region to produce a heteroduplex containing strands from two separate DNA duplexes (*see* Fig. 8B). The *strand invasion* and homologous pairing reactions are not spontaneous but require the activity of an enzyme, RecA protein in *E. coli* and its homolog, Rad51, in eukaryotes, to catalyze the reactions.

See companion CD for color Fig. 8

The strand invasion reaction generates a D-loop structure formed by the complementary strand from the intact duplex that was displaced. The invading strand can be extended by a DNA polymerase, which increases the size of the single-stranded region in the D-loop. This opens up a region of DNA homologous to the other single-stranded end of the broken DNA which then pairs with the D-loop. This end can also be extended by a DNA polymerase. Extension of both ends effectively replaces the segments that were removed by the exonuclease to generate single-stranded ends that initiate recombination.

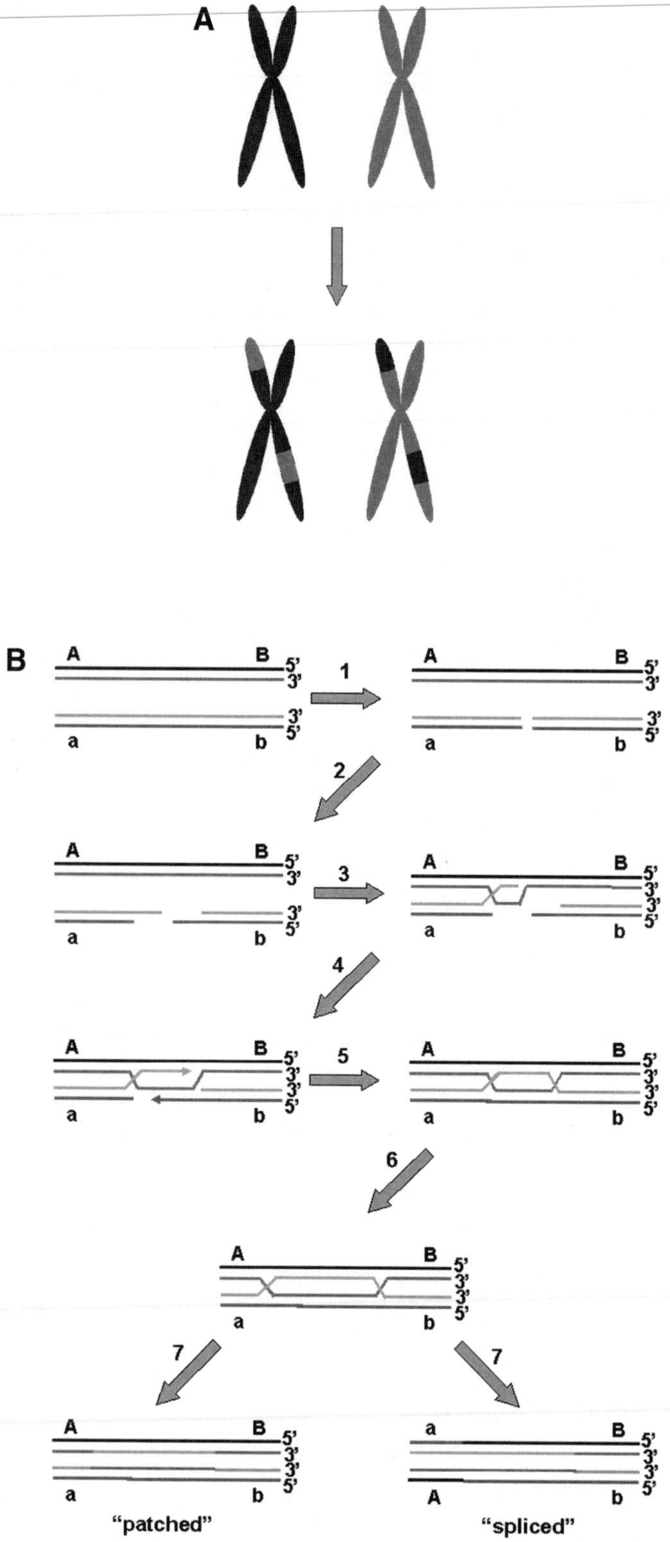
A
B
A
B
5'
3'
3'
5'
a
b
1
2
3
4
5
6
7
7
"patched"
"spliced"

Two crossover points between the two homologous duplexes are created following strand invasion by one half of the broken duplex and pairing between the displaced D-loop and the other half of the broken duplex. These crossed strands are named *Holliday junctions* after Robyn Holliday, who first proposed their occurrence in homologous recombination. Holliday junctions can migrate down the DNA duplexes *unzipping* the original duplexes while simultaneously *zipping* these strands together with new partners to extend heteroduplex regions of DNA. This process of *branch migration* can continue as long as homology between the regions of DNA is high.

Following branch migration, the two DNA duplexes are separated by cleaving the DNA strands at the Holliday junctions. This cleavage is catalyzed by a nuclease or resolvase that is specific for DNA in Holliday structures. Depending on which strands of the junctions are cleaved, two distinct products can be formed that contain different segments of DNA from the original duplex (*see* Fig. 8B). A spliced product can be formed where each end of the hybrid duplex is derived from one of the original duplexes. Alternatively, a patched product can be formed where the hybrid duplex contains a single-stranded segment from one duplex within a duplex derived from the other original duplex.

DNA Repair

DNA, like any other molecule, can spontaneously decompose with time, react with other chemicals (naturally present in a cell), or be damaged by UV or ionizing radiation. Damage to DNA can have many deleterious effects on the cell. Some types of damage alter DNA structure so that the sequence is misread by DNA polymerases causing it to incorporate erroneous bases and generate mutations. Others are so severe that DNA synthesis is blocked at the site of damage. DNA damage occurs with a frequency high enough that it would be lethal to a cell if it were not repaired. Recombination, as discussed earlier, provides a mechanism for repairing DNA strand breaks.

There are two general strategies that can be taken by a cell to fix DNA damage, direct reversal of the damage, and removal of a segment of DNA containing damage. Direct reversal of DNA damage relies on different enzymes capable of catalyzing different chemical reactions to undo the damage. There are two known examples of enzymes that repair DNA by direct reversal of damage. The majority of DNA damage is repaired using an excision/resynthesis strategy where a group of enzymes removes a

---

Fig. 8. *(opposite page)* Homologous recombination. **(A)** Recombination between sister chromatids during meosis results in exchange of information to generate two new chromatids that are hybrids of the originals. **(B)** Double-strand break model for homologous recombination. In this model, recombination is initiated by forming a double-stranded break (step 1) in one of the homologous duplexes. The broken DNA is then processed by partial degradation by an exonuclease to generate single-stranded DNA on the 3' ends (step 2). One 3' single-stranded end invades the homologous duplex forming a D-loop in the intact duplex (step 3). The invading 3' end is extended by a DNA polymerase enlarging the D-loop which can then pair with the remaining 3' single-stranded end (step 4). As the D-loop expands, it can displace the 5' end of the broken duplex which is then free to pair with the intact duplex (step 5). Branch migration enlarges the regions of heteroduplex DNA by unzipping the regions that were originally paired and zipping them onto the homologous duplex (step 6). Finally, the cross-over points or Holliday junctions are resolved by cleavage of the crossing strands (step 7). Two different products, patched and spliced, are formed depending on which of the crossed strands are cleaved.

thymine cylcobutane dimer O^6-methylguanine

Fig. 9. Structures of a thymine cyclobutane dimer and O^6-methylguanine.

segment of DNA containing damage and replaces it with new DNA. For this type of process, the same basic set of enzymes can remove many types of DNA damage.

Direct Reversal of DNA Damage

DNA Photolyase Catalyzed Splitting of Thymine Cyclobutane Dimers

When exposed to UV light, two neighboring pyrimidine bases, C or T, in DNA can react with each other to become covalently joined. One reaction that occurs is the formation of thymine cyclobutane dimers (*see* Fig. 9). When these thymine dimers are formed, they distort the local structure of DNA and are no longer recognized as a pair of T's by DNA polymerases. In bacteria, the enzyme, DNA photolyase, reverses the formation of thymine dimers. Enzyme-bound cofactors absorb light and initiate an electron transfer reaction that catalyzes the splitting of the thymine dimer to regenerate two intact thymine bases.

Removal of Methyl Groups by O^6-Methylguanine Methyltransferase

Chemicals that are naturally present in the cell, as well as chemicals in the environment, can react with DNA to methylate bases. One product of this reaction, O^6-methylguanine (O^6-MeG), induces the incorporation of an incorrect base by a DNA polymerase (*see* Fig. 9). O^6-MeG is repaired by O^6-methylguanine methyltransferase (MGMT) by directly removing the methyl group to regenerate a normal guanine residue. MGMT is not an enzyme in the true sense of the word because it does not act catalytically; instead it is a suicide enzyme. The methyl group is transferred from guanine to a cysteine residue on the protein where a covalent bond is formed. Because MGMT cannot be demethylated, it is incapable of catalyzing the removal of other methyl groups and becomes inactive. MGMT is found in both bacteria and eukaryotes.

Repair by Excision/Resynthesis

The process of excision of a section of damaged DNA followed by resynthesis allows cells to use the same basic chemical reaction and a common set of enzymes to repair many different types of DNA damage. The two main pathways responsible for excision repair are *base excision repair* that usually replaces a single damaged base and *nucleotide excision repair* that replaces a short segment of DNA containing the damaged nucleotide.

Base Excision Repair

The base excision repair pathway primarily repairs damage to DNA bases much of which occurs spontaneously in the cell without the influence of environmental hazards. Examples include oxidation, deamination, and alkylation of DNA bases. These damaged bases are recognized by damage-specific *DNA glycosylases* that initiate the base excision repair pathway. DNA glycosylases bind to damaged bases and cleave the C1'-N glycosylic bond between the base and sugar. This leaves a baseless sugar, or *AP site* (for apurinic or apyrimidinic), in DNA that is removed by other enzymes in the pathway (*see* Fig. 10A). Several different DNA glycosylases are present in cells and each recognizes a specific damaged base or a class of damaged bases. For example, uracil DNA glycosylase recognizes and excises only uracil which can be formed in DNA by deamination of cytosine. Formamidopyrimidine (FaPy) DNA glycosylase recognizes several different bases damaged by oxidation.

See companion CD for color Fig. 10

Once a DNA glycosylase has removed a damaged base, the AP site that it leaves must be repaired. An *AP endonuclease* starts this process by cleaving the phosphodiester bond on the 5' side of the AP site to generate a 3'hydroxyl and a deoxyribose phosphate. A deoxyribophosphodiesterase then cleaves the 3' phosphate of the baseless sugar to remove it and leave a one nucleotide gap in the DNA. A polymerase subsequently adds the missing nucleotide and the nick is sealed by the activity of a DNA ligase. In *E. coli*, separate enzymes catalyze the removal of the baseless sugar and the incorporation of the missing nucleotide. In humans, DNA polymerase β contains contains two enzymatic activities and is capable of both incorporating the missing nucleotide and removing the baseless sugar.

Nucleotide Excision Repair

The nucleotide excision repair pathway recognizes and repairs damage that generates larger more bulky lesions and local distortions in the DNA structure. In the nucleotide excision repair pathway, damage is recognized by a protein complex capable of identifying many different types of damage. It is believed that this complex recognizes distortions in the overall DNA structure at sites of damage or an increase in the ease of unwinding the duplex in the region of the damage. Regardless of the mechanism, this complex identifies sites of damage and helps recruit the rest of the repair machinery (*see* Fig. 10B). This repair complex unwinds the DNA duplex at the damaged site. Endonuclease activities within the complex cleave the DNA backbone both 5' and 3' to the site of damage. This creates a short oligonucleotide segment, 12–13 nt long in bacteria and 24–32 nt long in eukaryotes, that is displaced by a DNA helicase. The resulting gap in DNA can be filled in by a DNA polymerase to leave a nick that is sealed by DNA ligase.

Conclusion

The instructions needed for producing all the components of a cell and for regulating their functions are encoded in the sequence of DNA. Accurate transmission of this information to progeny and protecting of the genome from chemical degradation are essential to life. Complementary base pairing in duplex DNA provides an elegant means for accurate replication of DNA and repair of DNA damage. Each strand of the duplex provides a template for generating the other strand and in essence acts as a "back-up copy" of the information. The many different proteins and enzymes

A. Base Excision Repair

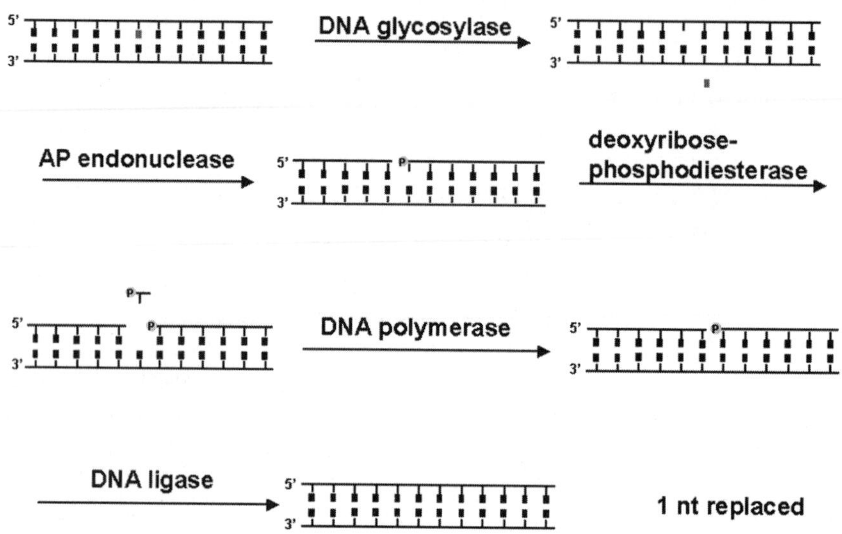

B. Nucleotide Excision Repair

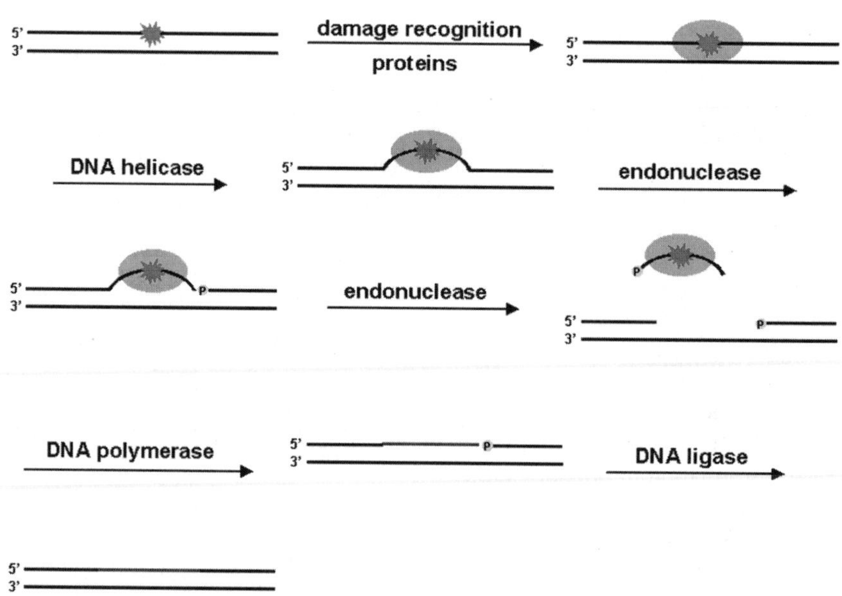

required to physically manipulate large DNA polymers in replication, recombination, and repair, all take advantage of the complementary base pairing between strands to accomplish their tasks. These enzymes are capable of a sufficient level of accuracy to maintain genetic integrity, yet also allow a low level of mutations to generate genetic diversity ultimately allowing a population to adapt to changing conditions. Understanding how the cellular machinery functions to replicate, recombine, and repair the genome is central to understanding evolution of species and the origin of genetic diseases.

Glossary and Abbreviations

AP Endonuclease An enzyme that cleaves the DNA backbone on the 5' side of an AP site to create a 3' hydroxyl and 5' phosphate.

AP Site A baseless sugar in DNA. AP is an abbreviation for apurinic or apyrimidinic.

Base Excision Repair A pathway that repairs damage to DNA bases by excising the damaged base and replacing it with an undamaged nucleotide.

Branch Migration Movement of a Holliday junction that unwinds DNA strands ahead of the junction and pairs them with homologous strands behind the junction.

DNA Glycosylase An enzyme that catalyzes the excision of damaged bases by cleaving the C1'-N glycosylic bond between the damaged base and the sugar.

DNA Helicase An enzyme that catalyzes the unwinding of duplex DNA.

DNA Ligase An enzyme that joins two strands of DNA at a nick by ligating a 3' hydroxyl end to a 5' phosphate end.

DNA Polymerase An enzyme that catalyzes the extension of a DNA polymer by incorporating 2'-deoxynucleoside monophosphates in a template directed reaction.

Exonuclease An enzyme that catalyzes the excision or removal of nucleotides from a DNA strand.

Fidelity Refers to the accuracy of synthesis by DNA polymerases.

Holliday Junction A four-way DNA junction formed when strands from homologous duplexes crossover during recombination.

Fig. 10. *(opposite page)* Repair of DNA by excision of the damage and resynthesis of DNA. **(A)** The base excision repair pathway begins with the removal of a damaged base by a DNA glycosylase. In this scheme undamaged DNA bases are indicated by black squares and the damaged base is indicated by a light square. The C1'-N glycosylic bond between the base and the sugar is cleaved leaving a baseless sugar residue (AP site) in DNA. The DNA strand is cut 5' to the AP site creating a 3' hydroxyl on one side of the cut and a 5'phosphate ("P") on the other. Deoxyribophosphodiesterase activity is required to excise the sugar-phosphate residue to create a one nucleotide gap that can be filled in by a DNA polymerase. Repair is complete when the strands are ligated by a DNA ligase. **(B)** The nucleotide excision repair pathway removes a short segment of DNA containing a damaged base (red starburst). The damaged base is recognized and bound by a protein complex. This protein complex serves to direct the other proteins to the site of damage so that it can be repaired. A DNA helicase separates the DNA strands on either side of the damaged nucleotide. Specific endonucleases recognize the forked single-stranded/double-stranded DNA junctions at these sites and cleave the DNA at the junctions. The DNA strand is cleaved 3' to the damaged nucleotide followed by cleavage on the 5' side. The gap created by excision of the damaged DNA segment is filled in by a DNA polymerase and the two strands are joined by a DNA ligase.

Lagging Strand The strand synthesized in discontinuous segments called Okazaki fragments.

Leading Strand The strand of DNA synthesized in one continuous piece in the direction of replication fork progression.

Nick A single-stranded break in a DNA duplex.

Nucleotide Excision Repair A pathway that repairs DNA damage by removing a short segment of DNA containing the damage and resynthesizing that segment.

Okazaki fragments Discontinuous segments of DNA that are synthesized on the lagging strand.

Origin of replication A site in the genome where DNA synthesis is initiated during replication.

Primase An enzyme that synthesizes short segments of RNA to prime synthesis by DNA polymerases.

Processivity Refers to the number of nucleotides that a DNA polymerase can incorporate in a single DNA binding event.

Proofreading The process of removing incorrectly paired nucleotides catalyzed by the 3' to 5' exonuclease activity of DNA polymerases.

Replication fork The branched DNA structure formed when a DNA helicase separates the two complementary strands of DNA during replication.

Replisome The ensemble of enzymes that function at the replication fork to duplicate DNA.

Semi-Conservative Refers to replication of DNA that produces duplexes composed of one newly synthesized and one original strand.

Semi-discontinuous Refers to DNA synthesis that produces one continuous strand on the leading strand and Okazaki fragments or discontinuous strands on the lagging strand.

Strand invasion Pairing of a single-stranded DNA with a homologous region of duplex DNA to form a D-loop.

Suggested Reading

DNA Replication

Davey, M. J. and O'Donnell, M. (2000) Mechanisms of DNA replication, Curr. Opin. Chem. Biol. 4, 581–586.

Goodman, M. F. (2000) Coping with replication "train wrecks" in *Escherichia coli* using Pol V, Pol II, and RecA proteins, Trends Biochem. Sci. 25, 189–195.

Gulbis, J. M., Kelman, Z., Hurwitz, J., O'Donnell, M., and Kuriyan, J. (1996) Structure of the C-terminal region of p21WAF1/CIP1 complexed with human PCNA, Cell 87, 297–306.

Kelly, T. J. and Brown, G. W. (2000) Regulation of chromosome replication, Annu. Rev. Biochem. 69, 829–880.

Kong, X.-P., Onrust, R., O'Donnell, M., and Kuriyan, J. (1992) Three-dimensional structure of the β subunit of *E. coli* DNA polymerase III holoenzyme: A sliding DNA clamp, Cell 69, 425–437.

Kunkel, T. A. and Bebenek, K. (2000) DNA replication fidelity, Annu. Rev. Biochem. 69, 497–529.

Waga, S. and Stillman, B. (1998) The DNA replication fork in eukaryotic cells. Annu. Rev. Biochem. 67, 721–751.

DNA Recombination

Haber, J. E. (2000) Partners and pathways repairing a double-strand break, Trends Genet. 6, 259–264.

Kowalczykowski, S. C. (2000) Initiation of genetic recombination and recombination-dependent replication, Trends Biochem. Sci. 25, 156–165.

West, S. (1997) Processing of recombination intermediates by RuvABC proteins, Annu. Rev. Genet. 31, 213–244.

DNA Repair

Batty, D. P. and Wood, R. D. (2000) Damage recognition in nucleotide excision repair of DNA, Gene 241, 193–204.

de Laat, W. L., Jaspers, N. G. J., and Hoeijmakers, J. H. J. (1999) Molecular mechanism of nucleotide excision repair, Genes Dev. 13, 768–785.

Lindahl, T. (1993) Instability and decay of the primary structure of DNA. Nature 362, 709–715.

Lindahl, T. (2000) Suppression of spontaneous mutagenesis in human cells by DNA base excision-repair, Mutation Res. 462, 129–135.

5 Transcription, RNA Processing, and Translation

Thomas P. Yang and Thomas W. O'Brien

Introduction

The processes of transcription, RNA processing (in eukaryotes), and translation constitute the pathway that leads to the conversion of genetic information in the linear sequence of bases in genomic DNA into the linear amino acid sequences of functional proteins. Thus, DNA undergoes *transcription* to synthesize a primary RNA transcript, which in eukaryotes undergoes *RNA processing* to produce a mature messenger RNA (mRNA), then mRNAs are *translated* into functional polypeptides. Each of these cellular processes will be described below.

Transcription

The process of transcription involves the sequential and enzyme-catalyzed polymerization of ribonucleotide triphosphates into a single-stranded linear RNA molecule that is complementary to, and encoded by, one strand of a DNA template. This process in eukaryotes occurs in the nucleus. The growth of the nascent RNA chain proceeds from the 5' end to the 3' end of the chain, elongating by adding nucleotides to the –OH group at the 3' end of the RNA. As depicted in Fig. 1, polymerization occurs by formation of a phosphodiester bond between the –OH group of the ribose moiety at the 3' end of the elongating RNA and the 5' phosphate of the ribonucleotide triphosphate (rNTP) precursor to be added to the growing RNA chain. Thus, unidirectional growth of the RNA chain occurs in the 5' to 3' direction. The phosphodiester bond is synthesized by a condensation reaction involving the 3' –OH group of the sugar and the α phosphate group of the rNTP, with release of pyrophosphate (PPi). As shown in Fig. 1, the nucleotide sequence of the elongating RNA chain is specified by the nucleotide sequence of one strand of the duplex DNA template. Following the rules of Watson-Crick base pairing, adenine, cytosine, guanine, and thymine in the template DNA sequence direct the addition of uracil, guanine, cytosine, and adenine, respectively, to the RNA sequence. In most cases, only one strand of a given region of double-stranded DNA is transcribed into RNA, though a small but increasing number of eukaryotic genes show transcription from both strands over all or a portion of the gene. In several cases, a gene encodes a functional *sense* transcript as well as a so-called *anti-sense* transcript (often of unknown function) that extends over the entire region encoding the

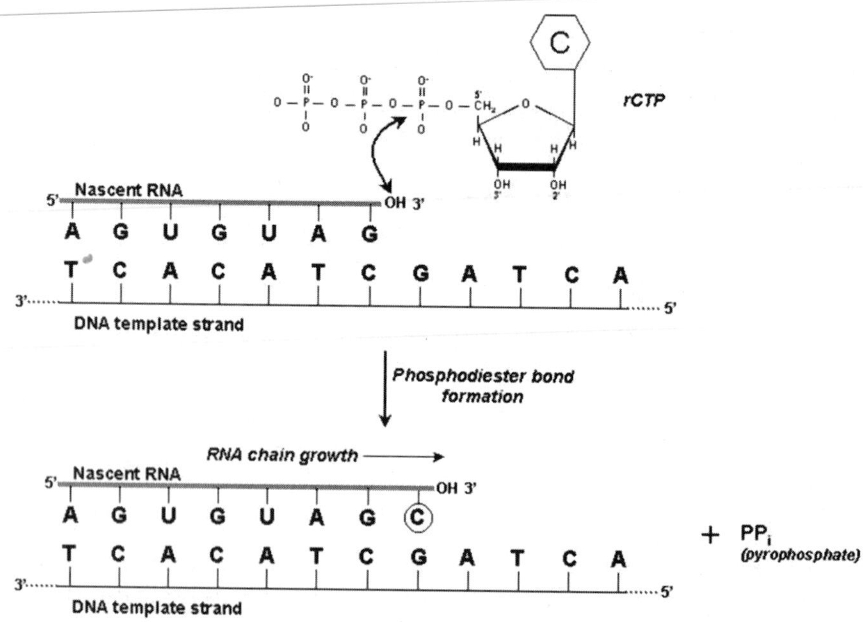

Fig. 1. DNA-dependent synthesis of RNA. In this example, a cytidine triphosphate (rCTP) precursor is added to the 3' end of an elongating RNA chain by forming a phosphodiester bond between the 5' phosphate of the rCTP precursor and the 3' OH of the previously added nucleotide. The nucleotide sequence of the nascent RNA is specified by the complementary nucleotide sequence of the DNA template strand according to Watson-Crick base pairing. The circled C residue indicates the position of the newly added nucleotide.

sense transcript. Some of these anti-sense transcripts have been postulated to regulate the expression of the sense transcript.

The synthesis of RNA from a DNA template is catalyzed by the enzyme RNA polymerase. Most, if not all, RNA synthesis in prokaryotes is directed by a single RNA polymerase, while RNA synthesis in eukaryotes is catalyzed by three different RNA polymerases, pol I, pol II, and pol III, each of which transcribes a different class of genes. The high-resolution structure of both bacterial RNA polymerase and eukaryotic RNA polymerase II has recently been determined by X-ray crystallography. The amino acid homology of certain subunits in the prokaryotic and eukaryotic polymerases and their many shared structural features are notable though not unexpected due to their similar functions.

The macromolecular complex formed during the process of transcription consists of RNA polymerase, the DNA template, and the nascent RNA (*see* Fig. 2). The double-stranded DNA template is melted to form a transcription *bubble* (of approx 12 base pairs) within the bubble the elongating nascent RNA forms an approx 9 bp RNA:DNA duplex with the template strand of the DNA at its 3' end. As the polymerase moves downstream along the DNA template, the double-stranded DNA helix is unwound at the front of the bubble and rewound behind the bubble. Growth of the nascent RNA occurs by the addition of nucleotides at the 3' end of the nascent RNA within the bubble, with nucleotide triphosphate precursors presumably translocated to the active site of the enzyme via a pore and channel within the structure of the polymerase.

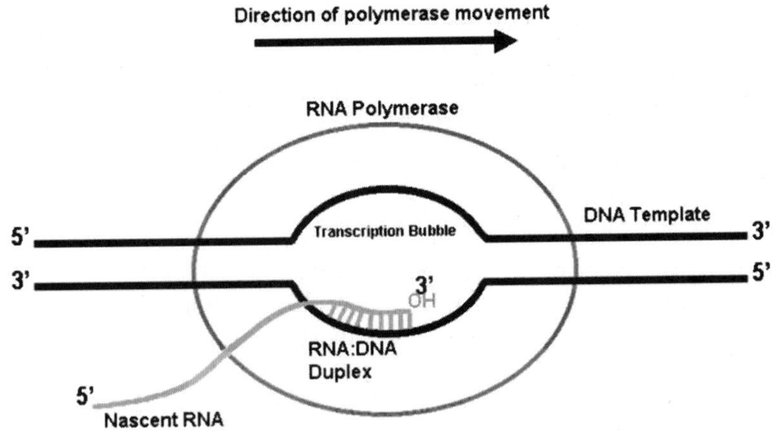

Fig. 2. Schematic of the transcription elongation complex.

Regulation of transcription, particularly regulation of transcription initiation, is a major mechanism that regulates macromolecular biosynthesis in the cell. However, the processes by which transcription is initiated and regulated in prokaryotes and eukaryotes are notably different. Therefore, a description of each of these processes in prokaryotes and eukaryotes is presented.

Transcription in Prokaryotes

Transcription of prokaryotic genes is accomplished by a single RNA polymerase. The prototype of the prokaryotic RNA polymerase is the polymerase of *Escherichia coli*. It is composed of four different polypeptide subunits, α, β, β', and σ. The RNA polymerase core enzyme, which functions in transcription elongation, is composed of two α subunits, and one each of the β and β' subunits. The RNA polymerase holoenzyme, which initiates transcription, is organized as the core enzyme plus one copy of the σ subunit.

To initiate transcription, RNA polymerase holoenzyme first binds to DNA sequences immediately upstream of a gene. This region upstream of the gene, termed *the promoter*, contains DNA sequences specifically recognized and bound by the RNA polymerase holoenzyme. The σ subunit confers upon the holoenzyme the ability to recognize and bind to the promoter in a DNA sequence-specific manner, and to initiate transcription at a site specifically from the template strand of the DNA. Different σ subunits, such as σ^{54} and σ^{70}, recognize and bind different subsets of prokaryotic promoter sequences. For example, σ^{70}-containing holoenzyme recognizes and contacts (via the σ subunit) specific promoter sequences surrounding positions –10 and –35 (upstream of the transcription initiation site).

Initial binding of the polymerase to the promoter leads to formation of a *closed* binary complex where the polymerase-bound DNA duplex remains double-stranded. This closed complex is then converted to a more stable *open* complex where melting of the DNA duplex occurs and the two strands of the promoter DNA undergo separation. The DNA duplex is melted over ~12 bp, from the –10 region to just downstream of the transcription initiation site (i.e., the deoxynucleotide in the DNA, encoding the first ribonucleotide in the RNA transcript). Both the closed and open promoter complexes are composed of multiple intermediate forms, with formation of an open complex accompanied by a major conformation change in the RNA polymerase. Conversion to an open promoter complex is followed by entry of ribonucleotide triphosphates (rNTPs) and binding of the initial (rNTP) to form a ternary complex. For σ^{70} promoters, conversion and stability of the open promoter complex does not require rNTP hydrolysis, though for some promoters (e.g., certain σ^{54} promoters) this conversion from a closed to open complex requires interaction with activator proteins bound to the DNA upstream of the promoter as well as hydrolysis of ATP. After forming the open ternary complex, active transcription begins with the synthesis of a series of abortive transcripts. These are short transcripts <10 nucleotides in length that are repetitively synthesized and released without release of the polymerase from the promoter. Once a nascent transcript reaches a length of 8–10 nucleotides, σ factor is released from the holoenzyme and RNA polymerase escapes and clears the promoter to begin committed elongation of the transcript. The transcription elongation complex (TEC) is a stable association of the core polymerase with the DNA template and nascent RNA. Elongation proceeds by movement of the TEC down the linear DNA template, with sequential and continuous addition of nucleotides to the 3' end of the nascent transcript. The exact ribonucleotide added to the elongating RNA chain is specified by the next base in the DNA template sequence according to Watson-Crick base pairing (i.e., A:U, C:G, G:C, T:A for DNA:RNA base pairs). Misincorporation of a nucleotide in the nascent RNA, or pausing of the polymerase along the DNA template during elongation, leads the polymerase to backtrack along a short stretch of the DNA, cleavage of the newly synthesized portion of the nascent RNA at the 3' end, and continuation of elongation from the newly truncated nascent RNA (including resynthesis of the cleaved portion of the RNA).

Termination of transcription in prokaryotes occurs at specific sites downstream of the coding region of genes and is accomplished by either of two possible mechanisms. One, termed *rho-dependent termination*, is mediated by the action of the rho termination protein and requires the hydrolysis of ATP. The second mechanism is rho-independent termination and occurs via formation of specific hairpin structures in the nascent RNA that destabilizes the ternary complex immediately downstream of the hairpin and leads to dissociation of the ternary complex and transcription termination. Rho-independent termination can also occur via terminators formed by an RNA:DNA hybrid between the nascent RNA and the DNA template just upstream of the elongation complex.

Following termination of transcription and release of the RNA polymerase from the DNA template and the RNA transcript, the free core polymerase is able to rebind another σ factor and re-initiate another round of transcription.

Regulation of transcription in prokaryotes occurs by a wealth of different mechanisms that often involve activator and repressor proteins. Descriptions of the diverse mechanisms of prokaryotic transcriptional regulation are beyond the scope of this chapter.

Initiation and Regulation of Transcription in Eukaryotes

The three eukaryotic RNA polymerases all synthesize RNA transcripts encoded by a DNA template, but transcribe different subsets of genes. RNA pol I synthesizes the precursor of ribosomal RNAs (rRNAs) which is eventually processed into the mature 5.8S, 18S, and 28S rRNAs. The bulk of RNA synthesis in a cell is carried out by pol I. RNA pol II primarily transcribes the mRNA encoding genes, and therefore is responsible for transcription of the largest and most diverse subset of genes in the cell. RNA pol III catalyzes synthesis of an assortment of small RNAs including tRNAs and 5S rRNA. Unlike the prokaryotic RNA polymerase, highly purified eukaryotic RNA polymerases do not recognize promoter sequences by themselves or initiate transcription by binding directly to specific DNA sequences in eukaryotic promoters. Rather eukaryotic polymerases are recruited to promoter regions via protein-protein interactions by both proteins that bind to specific DNA sequences in promoter and other regulatory regions as well as additional proteins that interact with these DNA-binding proteins.

The following description of eukaryotic transcription and regulation will focus on mechanisms of pol II transcription because of the diversity of genes it transcribes and the current intensive efforts to elucidate mechanisms of pol II transcription and regulation.

RNA Polymerase II and Pol II Core Promoters

Eukaryotic RNA polymerase II (pol II) consists of 12 subunits totaling greater than 500 kD in size, with all subunits very similar between yeast and humans. Most human subunits can function in place of their yeast homolgues, and 9 pol II subunits are highly conserved among the three different eukaryotic RNA polymerases. Furthermore, the two largest pol II subunits, Rpb1 and Rpb2, show significant similarity to the β' and β subunits of bacterial RNA polymerase, respectively, while two other pol II subunits show lesser similarity to the α subunit of the bacterial enzyme. The structure of yeast pol II has recently been determined by X-ray crystallography at 2.8 angstrom resolution. The largest pol II subunit, Rpb1, contains a conserved tandem repeat heptapeptide sequence at the C-terminus termed the *C-terminal domain* (CTD). The CTD and its phosphorylation state play a critical role in both transcription and RNA processing. An unphosphorylated CTD is associated with the pol II initiation complex, whereas a phosphorylated CTD is correlated with the elongation phase of transcription and association of the pol II complex with RNA processing factors.

Promoters transcribed by pol II exhibit a diverse structure. Most consist of a core promoter (sometimes referred to as the basal promoter) located in the immediate vicinity of the transcription initiation site, as well as nearby regulatory sequences that activate or repress activity of the core promoter, usually in response to e.g., cellular conditions, extracellular signals and environment, cell type, and stage of development. In addition, the function of many eukaryotic promoters, particularly in higher eukaryotes, is positively and/or negatively modulated by regulatory DNA sequences that can be located within the gene, upstream of the gene and/or downstream of the gene at distances exceeding 50 kb of DNA.

The core promoter contains cis-acting elements (i.e., DNA sequences) that can act as a nucleation site for the formation of the pre-initiation complex (PIC) and recruitment of pol II. Core promoter elements in association with the PIC also determine the site(s) where transcription of each gene is initiated. These core elements frequently include the so-called TATA box; however, other core DNA elements can either replace the function of the TATA box in TATA-less promoters, or can act in conjunction with the TATA box to facilitate transcription initiation. These other cis-acting elements in the basal promoter include initiator (Inr) elements, a downstream promoter element (DPE), and a TFIIB recognition element (BRE). These cis-acting elements function by interacting with sequence-specific DNA-binding proteins that initiate and/or mediate PIC assembly.

Formation of the Pre-Initiation Complex

A multi-protein complex, termed the *pre-initiation complex* (PIC) and consisting of a series of general transcription factors (GTFs) as well as pol II, is assembled at the core promoter as the first step of transcription initiation. These GTFs include the transcription factors TFIIA, TFIIB, TFIID, TFIIE, TFIIF, and TFIIH, though not all promoters require all of these factors. In vitro studies suggest that the PIC is assembled at core promoters in a sequential fashion (*see* Fig. 3). For genes with a canonical TATA box in the core promoter, this sequential assembly is initiated by the sequence recognition and binding of the multi-subunit GTF TFIID to the TATA box; TFIID consists of a DNA-binding subunit termed the *TATA box-binding protein* (TBP) that recognizes and binds the TATA sequence, plus a variety of TBP-associated factors (TAFs). TBP appears to be a common component of the PIC formed at pol I, pol II, and pol III promoters. Binding of TFIID to the core promoter DNA of pol II genes is followed by binding of TFIIA and TFIIB to the TFIID-TATA box complex, then recruitment of a pre-formed complex of pol II, TFIIF and TFIIE, and finally binding of TFIIH. TFIIA appears to stabilize the binding of TBP to DNA, and TFIIB may function in selecting the position of the transcription initiation site. TFIIF bound to pol II suppresses non-specific binding of the polymerase to DNA and stabilizes the PIC. TFIIE may be involved in recruiting TFIIH and melting the DNA duplex when forming the open promoter complex. The multi-subunit complex that comprises TFIIH contains an ATP-dependent helicase activity, a DNA-dependent ATPase, and CTD kinase activity. Thus, TFIIH appears to be involved in forming the open promoter complex via its helicase activity, and also may be required for the conversion of abortive transcription to committed elongation. The kinase activity of TFIIH phosphorylates the CTD of pol II and, therefore, may be involved in triggering the functions associated with a phosphorylated CTD. In addition, the observed coupling of transcription and DNA repair appears to be due to the common subunits shared by TFIIH in the transcription complex and the nucleotide excision repair complex.

However, a significant percentage of eukaryotic promoters lack a canonical TATA box and/or contain other core promoter elements such as an Inr (initiator element), DPE (downstream promoter element), and BRE (TFIIB recognition element). This leads to a diversity of mechanisms for forming the PIC at different promoters and for the activation of basal transcription from the core promoter. TATA-less promoters often contain an Inr element that serves as the nucleation site for assembly of PIC. The Inr is a short conserved DNA sequence spanning the transcription initiation site that acts as the binding site for several different DNA-binding initiator proteins such as YY1, TFIII, USF, $TAF_{II}250$, and $TAF_{II}150$. The Inr (bound by its transcription factors) can function alone in TATA-less promoters, or in combination with a TATA box or DPE (if these elements are present) to nucleate assembly of the PIC at core promoters. If present in a core promoter, the DPE is typically located approx 30 bp downstream of the transcription initiation site and is recognized and bound by subunits of the general transcription factor TFIID. The BRE element is located immediately upstream of the TATA box in certain core promoters with TATA boxes and facilitates the interaction and binding of TFIIB to the core promoter. In addition, a

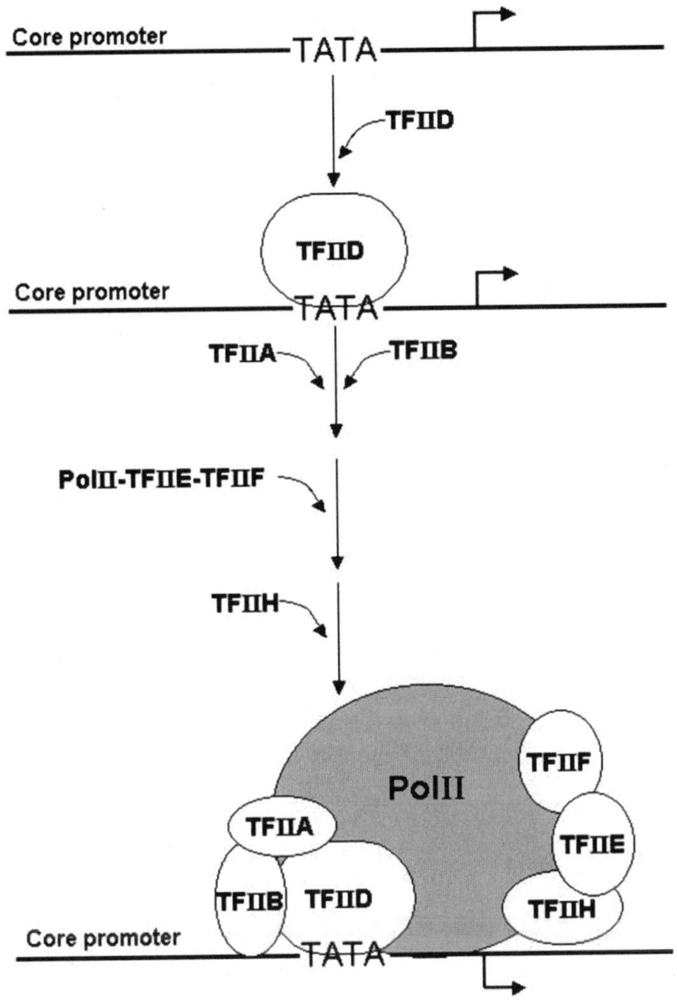

Fig. 3. Model for sequential assembly of the general transcription factors (GTFs) and pol II into the pre-initiation complex (PIC). The right angled arrow indicates the position and direction of transcription initiation.

subset of promoters, commonly those that lack TATA boxes, do not initiate transcription at a discrete nucleotide, but initiate transcription at multiple sites within the core promoter.

Overall, assembly of the PIC on the various forms of the core promoter serves to recruit and stabilize binding of pol II to the promoter, positioning pol II at the correct site on the gene for initiating transcription. It helps form an open transcription initiation complex by melting of the DNA duplex, and in the conversion of the PIC from transcription initiation to the transcription elongation complex. The open transcription initiation complex formed at the core promoter is associated with a melted DNA duplex of 12–15 bp that extends halfway from the transcription initiation site to the TATA box.

Activators, Co-Activators, Enhancers

Transcription from the core promoter is usually augmented by the action of additional transcriptional activator proteins that bind regulatory DNA sequences outside (upstream and/or downstream) of the core promoter. These activator (or repressor) elements serve to increase (or decrease) levels of transcription above the basal activity of the core promoter. They often act in the context of cell type, e.g., cellular conditions, stage of development, and response to stimuli such as hormones and growth factors. The combinatorial action of multiple activators and repressors on a given gene under a given set of cellular conditions determines the transcriptional status of the gene and governs its level of expression.

Activator proteins bound to their cis-acting regulatory sites appear to function by at least two mechanisms. Some activators bind their cognate site in the vicinity of the core promoter and appear to facilitate recruitment of certain GTFs to the core promoter and assist in formation of the PIC. These activators are presumed to assist PIC formation via protein-protein interactions between the activator and its target component(s) of the PIC. Alternatively, some activators may function by stimulating activity of the PIC and facilitating release of the PIC from the core promoter and/or facilitating transcription elongation. Some activators also appear to act by participating in the recruitment of chromatin modifying and remodeling complexes. In many cases of activator function, contact between the DNA-bound activator protein and the PIC requires bending or looping of the intervening DNA. Thus, some classes of activator proteins function by facilitating the bending of the DNA between the bound activator and the core promoter.

However, not all DNA-binding activator proteins that act on assembly or functions of the PIC can operate by direct contact with components of the PIC. Some activators require the action of an intermediary protein or protein complex between the activator and the PIC. These co-called co-activators act through protein-protein interactions as a bridge between the DNA-bound activator protein and the PIC at the basal promoter. Thus, the function of many activator proteins are carried out via association with co-activator proteins or protein complexes. A protein complex (of ~20 subunits in yeast) that appears to play an important role in activated transcription is the *mediator* complex. It functions as a general co-activator of transcription and appears to mediate the action of a variety of activator proteins. The mediator complex is bound to the unphosphorylated form of the CTD of pol II and has been found to be a component of the pol II holoenzyme complex.

In addition to cis-acting activator sequences that bind activator proteins in the vicinity of the core promoter, other cis-acting activator sequences are found at larger distances from the core promoter (up to tens of thousands of kb) both upstream, downstream and within genes. Some of these distal activator sequences are thought to function by looping the intervening DNA to contact the transcriptional machinery in the vicinity of the core promoter. A subset of these long-range activators, termed *enhancers*, have been found to act regardless of their distance from the promoter, location relative to the promoter (i.e., upstream and downstream) and either in the forward or reverse orientation of the cis-acting activator element. These enhancer sequences have been shown to contain a variety of binding sites for a constellation of DNA-binding transcription factors that are presumed to form large DNA-protein complexes that activate transcription.

A large enhancer-like region spanning several thousand bps in mammals, termed a *locus control region* (LCR), also activates transcription at a distance, and can regulate activation of multiple co-regulated genes within a gene cluster such as the β-globin gene family. The characteristic feature of LCRs is their ability to allow ectopically integrated transgenes to be regulated independent of the effects from the flanking DNA and chromatin at their new integration sites. LCRs also have been postulated to be involved in opening of chromatin structure across entire loci or domains; however, this role for LCRs is currently unclear.

Pol II Holoenzyme

Recently, holoenzyme complexes containing pol II have been purified intact from eukaryotic cells. These heterogeneous pol II holoenzyme complexes include pol II, a subset of the GTFs and the mediator complex which is believed to be bound to the CTD of pol II. This finding of a pol II holoenzyme complex suggests that formation of the PIC in vivo may not always involve step-wise and sequential assembly of the GTFs and pol II and that much of the PIC, as well as co-activators required for activation of the basal promoter, may be preassembled in vivo and brought to the core promoter intact. Nonetheless, the lack of TBP in these pol II holoenzyme complexes suggest that, in part, formation of the PIC with these holoenzyme complexes may still be initiated by TBP binding to the TATA box followed by recruitment of the holoenzyme.

The Role of Chromatin Structure

A major mode of transcriptional regulation in eukaryotes involves altering the chromatin structure of genes and regulatory regions to repress and/or activate transcription. DNA is packaged with basic histone proteins within the eukaryotic nucleus to form chromatin. The basic unit of packaging genomic DNA into chromatin is the nucleosome, a discrete nucleoprotein complex composed of ~200 bp DNA wrapped around a highly structured core of the histone proteins H2A, H2B, H3, and H4. Linear arrays of nucleosomes resembling "beads on a string" form the first level of packaging DNA in the nucleus; organization of the linear nucleosomal array into higher-order configurations continue the packaging of genomic DNA into the chromatin found in eukarotic nuclei. The structures of these higher-order organizations of nucleosomal arrays are still not well-defined.

The formation of nucleosomes over promoters and other regulatory regions generally has a repressive effect on the transcription of genes by blocking or otherwise inhibiting the binding of specific transcription factors to their cognate regulatory DNA sequences. Furthermore, in higher eukaryotes, the higher-order packing of nucleosomal arrays also appears to regulate transcription by governing the general access of an entire locus (with its regulatory regions) to components of the transcriptional machinery. Thus, modulating the higher-order chromatin structure of an entire gene or *domain*, as well as altering the position and structure of individual nucleosomes over regulatory DNA sequences, constitute critical mechanisms regulating transcription of eukaryotic genes. A number of transcriptional activators (and repressors) appear to act by recruiting and regulating the function of chromatin modifying and remodeling complexes within specific genes.

The position and structure of individual nucleosomes associated with critical regulatory regions of genes has recently been shown to be regulated by ATP-dependent, multi-subunit complexes that remodel or modify nucleosomes or localized nucleosomal arrays (e.g., Swi/Snf, NURD, CHRAC, RSC). Some of these nucleosome remodeling complexes appear to act by repositioning (e.g., sliding, and/or transferring) intact nucleosomes from regulatory regions or sites, and presumably *uncover* previously obstructed binding sites in DNA for sequence-specific DNA-binding transcription factors. Furthermore, a number of remodeling complexes also appear capable of subtly altering the structure of individual intact nucleosomes by changing the interactions of the DNA with the histone core. This allows transcription factors access to their otherwise obstructed DNA binding sites within native nucleosomes.

Nucleosome structure is also altered by the activity of various nucleosome modifying complexes. These complexes covalently modify the side chains of amino acids (particularly lysines) in the N-terminal region of histones, thereby altering the structure of the associated nucleosomes and/or nucleosomal arrays. Examples of these nucleosome modifying complexes include histone acetylation and deacetylation complexes, as well as histone methylases. Acetylation of histone H4 has been associated with actively transcribed chromatin, while underacetylation of histone H4 has been associated with transcriptionally repressed chromatin. Presumably, these histone modifiying activities alter chromatin structure and either facilitate or preclude the access of transcription factors to their sites of action. Regulation of higher chromatin structure (i.e., the organization of nucleosomal arrays into higher-order structure) across entire genes or domains is not well-understood, and mechanisms and regulatory elements that carry out these structural alterations of chromatin have not been definitively identified. This is further discussed in Chapter 6.

In summary, the opening of higher-order chromatin structure, the modification and/or positioning of nucleosomes to allow transcription factors to bind their cognate DNA binding sites, and the action of activators, enhancers, etc. all facilitate formation of a stable and functional PIC. Assembly of the transcriptional machinery at the promoter is associated with formation of a stable open promoter complex, leading to clearance of the pol II complex from the promoter and elongation of the nascent RNA.

Elongation

As with prokaryotic transcription elongation, the initial phase of RNA chain elongation is associated with abortive transcription, the repetitive synthesis of very short RNA molecules that are synthesized, released, and re-initiated. After the polymerization of four or more nucleotides into a nascent RNA, the transcript becomes stabilized in the complex. In part, this permits a transition from transcription initiation to promoter release (or clearance) and productive elongation. Conversion of the pol II complex from transcription initiation to elongation is accompanied by phosphorylation of the CTD of pol II, release of certain general transcription factors GTFs and the mediator complex, and association of TFIIS and other elongation factors as well as certain RNA processing factors. However, details of the process that converts the initation complex to transcription elongation are not well-understood.

Specific factors have been identified that facilitate promoter clearance (e.g., P-TEFb) while other factors act negatively to repress promoter clearance (e.g., NELF, DSIF). Positive elongation factors that facilitate promoter clearance also include the GTFs TFIIF and TFIIH. Other factors facilitate the processivity of elongation by the pol II complex such as TFIIS, elongin, and CSB. The elongation complex appears to contain 9 bp of RNA:DNA hybrid within the transcription bubble, with the front of the bubble positioned 3 nucleotides before the beginning of the RNA:DNA hybrid. As with prokaryotic transcription, the pol II elongation complex catalyzes the sequential addition of ribonucleotides to the 3' end of the elongating mRNA. The exact linear sequence of ribonucleotides in the mRNA is dictated by the nucleotide sequence of the template DNA strand based upon Watson-Crick base pairing.

Termination

Termination of eukaryotic gene transcription differs significantly from termination in prokaryotes. Rather than terminating transcription at discrete sites as seen in prokaryotes, termination in eukaryotes does not appear to occur at specific sites, but appears to occur by loss of processivity or stability of the elongation complex downstream of the gene. Thus, 3' end formation of eukaryotic mRNAs does not occur as a direct result of transcription termination at a specific site, but occurs by post-transcriptional processing of the RNA transcript where sequence-specific cleavage of the transcript at a specific site in the RNA is followed by post-transcriptional polyadenylation of the 3' end of the cleaved transcript. Evidence suggests that the polyadenylation signal and/or the site-specific cleavage of the nascent RNA may be involved in signaling or facilitating transcription termination downstream.

RNA Processing

Generating a mature eukaryotic mRNA molecule from the primary transcript produced by transcription requires a series of post-transcriptional RNA processing steps that include 5' mRNA capping, 3' polyadenylation, RNA splicing, and RNA editing. Alternative sites for polyadenylation and RNA splicing within the same gene also play a significant role in post-transcriptional regulation of gene expression. As discussed in the following, several of these processes appear to be directly coupled to transcription via association with the elongating pol II complex.

5' Capping

After the nascent RNA transcript has reached the ~25–30 nucleotides, the 5' end of the transcript is covalently modified by enzymatic addition of a guanine triphosphate moiety via an unusual 5'–5' covalent linkage (*see* Fig. 4A). This novel bond structure between the first and second nucleotides at the 5' end of the mature mRNA protects the mRNA from degradation by a 5'→ 3' exonuclease activity in the cell. Formation of this 5' cap structure is catalyzed, in part, by guanylyltransferase, an enzyme that is bound to the phosphorylated form of the CTD of pol II. Subsequent to the capping reaction, methytransferases add methyl groups to the N7 position of the newly added guanine to generate the 7-methylguanosine cap, and a methyl group to the 2' hydroxl group of the first and second (in vertebrates) ribose moieties of the nascent transcript.

Polyadenylation

Formation of the 3' end of eukaryotic mRNAs is accomplished by enzymatic cleavage of the nascent RNA transcript followed by the post-transcriptional enzymatic addition of 100–250 adenosine residues to the 3' end of the mRNA (*see* Fig. 4B). Cleavage and polyadenylation is initiated by recognition of the polyadenylation signal sequence AAUAAA in the RNA transcript, followed by cleavage of the transcript at a discrete site 10–25 nucleotides downstream of the sequence, and polyadenylation of

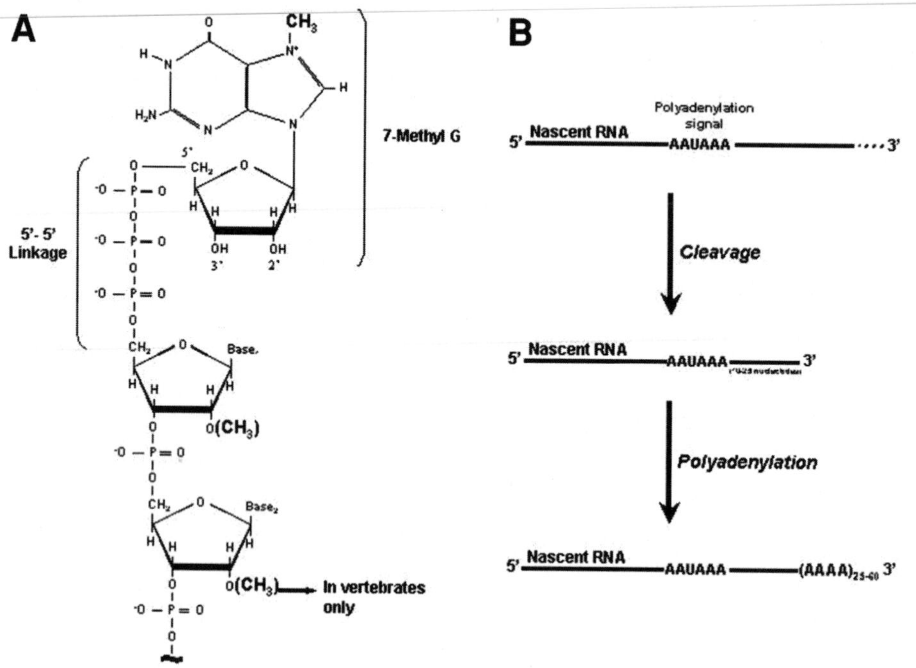

Fig. 4. Capping and polyadenylation. **(A)** The 5' mRNA cap structure. **(B)** 3' polyadenylation of mRNA.

the 3' end of the upstream fragment generated by the cleavage reaction. The downstream RNA fragment generated by transcript cleavage is rapidly degraded. Transcript cleavage and polyadenylation is accomplished by a well-characterized, multi-subunit complex that assembles over the polyadenylation signal sequence of the RNA transcript. Addition of A residues to the 3' end of the cleaved transcript is performed by poly(A) polymerase, a component of the complex. In addition to the apparent coupling of transcription termination with polyadenylation, polyadenylation is also coupled to transcription elongation by binding of polyadenylation factors (e.g., the cleavage stimulatory factor CStF) to the CTD of pol II. In fact, some factors involved in polyadenylation appear to associate with the CTD at the time of transcription initiation at the promoter. As a mechanism of post-transcriptional gene regulation, alternative sites of polyadenylation within the same gene can generate different protein products, e.g., in different cell types, different stages of development, or in response to extracellular signals.

RNA Splicing

Many eukaryotic genes, particularly in higher eukaryotes, contain DNA sequences that interrupt the nucleotide sequence that encodes the mRNA produced from the gene. These intervening sequences, termed *introns*, are transcribed and included in the primary RNA transcript generated by the process of transcription. These introns are then precisely removed post-transcriptionally and the coding portions of the mRNA, termed *exons*, are rejoined by the process of RNA splicing. A single gene can contain multiple introns, some extending for tens of thousands of bases between exons. RNA splicing is carried out in the nucleus on the nascent RNA by a large ribonucleoprotein complex termed the *spliceosome*. The spliceosome, in turn, is composed of proteins and a variety of small nuclear ribonucleoprotein particles (snRNP's), each containing a small nuclear RNA (and associated proteins) that participate in the splicing reaction. The sequence of reactions leading to the removal of an intron and covalent joining of two exons is carried out during the sequential assembly and disassembly of the spliceosome.

Nucleotide sequences in the nascent primary RNA transcript are recognized by components of the spliceosome and mediate the splicing reaction. As shown in Fig. 5A, these sites in the nascent RNA include: 1) the GU and AG sequences found at the 5' and 3' ends, respectively, of most introns; 2) the A residue located in the intron (20–50 nucleotides upstream of the 3' end of the intron) that will participate in formation of the lariat intermediate; 3) a pyrimidine-rich region just upstream of the 3' splice site; and 4) the splicing enhancer sequences in the RNA transcript that facilitate the splicing reaction.

As depicted in Fig. 5B, the removal of an intron between two coding region exons is initiated by a transesterification reaction that breaks the ester bond between the last nucleotide of exon 1 (i.e., the upstream exon) and the first nucleotide at the 5' end of the intron, and forms a new ester bond between the 2' oxygen of the branchpoint A residue and the 5' end of the intron. This reaction forms the lariat structure characteristic of the splicing reaction. Then a second transesterification reaction breaks the phosphodiester bond between the last nucleotide of the intron and the first nucleotide of exon 2 (the downstream exon) and forms a new phosphodiester linkage between the 3' end of exon 1 and the 5' end of exon 2. This results in covalent joining of the two exons into a contiguous uninterrupted sequence in the mature mRNA and release of the intron-containing lariat structure which is then degraded.

The process of RNA splicing is highly precise; any deviation from single-nucleotide accuracy would introduce mutations into the final mRNA leading to the synthesis of defective proteins. The accuracy of the splicing reactions is mediated in part by the SR proteins, a family of structurally related serine- and arginine-rich RNA-binding proteins. The SR proteins are required for accurate recognition of exons and splice sites during assembly of the spliceosome and during the splicing reactions. Specific sequences in the nascent RNA, termed *splicing enhancers*, also are involved in *exon definition* (i.e., recognition of exons by the spliceosome) and recognition of splice sites, as well as facilitating the splicing reactions. These splicing enhancers do not appear to share an identifiable consensus nucleotide sequence, but are recognized and bound by SR proteins.

Like capping and polyadenylation, several lines of evidence indicate that RNA splicing also appears to be coupled to transcription. This evidence includes the co-localization of splicing factors in the nucleus to discrete sites of active transcription and the association of SR-like proteins to the CTD of pol II.

Alternative pathways of splicing exons within the same gene can lead to the formation of different mature mRNAs from the same gene, each of which carries a different subset of exons from the same primary transcript (*see* Fig. 5C) Thus, from the same nascent transcript, some spliced mRNAs can skip specific exons that are present in other mRNAs from the same primary transcript, or have additional exons that are absent in other mRNAs. This alternative splicing of exons from a single primary RNA transcript is highly regulated (mediated by SR proteins) and often

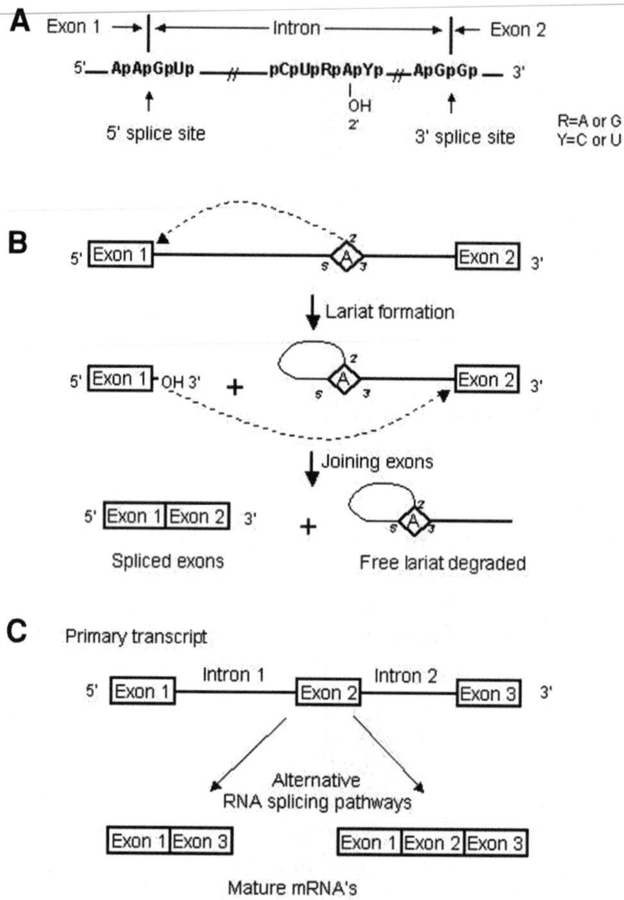

Fig. 5. Schematic of RNA splicing. **(A)** Location of conserved elements involved in RNA splicing. **(B)** Sequence of reactions in RNA splicing. **(C)** Alternative RNA splicing; a gene with three transcribed exons produces two different mRNAs via alternative splicing pathways.

leads to synthesis of different proteins with different functions from the same gene. This process constitutes a major mechanism of post-transcriptional regulation of gene expression in mammals.

RNA Editing

The final post-transcriptional processing of the RNA transcript in eukaryotes is the alteration of the transcribed nucleotide sequence in the RNA molecule to a different nucleotide sequence independent of the DNA template and transcription, thus potentially changing the amino acid coding of the mature mRNA. This RNA editing process involves changing the sequence of nucleotides in the newly synthesized RNA to a new nucleotide sequence that is not encoded in the DNA template from which the RNA was originally transcribed. This post-transcriptional modification has been identified for a relatively small number of genes in species as diverse as trypanosomes and humans. These changes in the RNA sequence can occur by inserting or deleting specific nucleotides at specific positions in the RNA transcript, or by modification of specific bases at specific sites in the RNA nucleotide sequence, thereby converting one base to another (e.g., C → U via deamination of C). RNA editing is carried out by macromolecular complexes termed the *editosome*.

Transcription of genomic DNA and the subsequent post-transcriptional processing of the primary RNA transcript generate a mature mRNA whose linear sequence of nucleotides encodes a linear sequence of amino acids. The synthesis of a functional polypeptide from a mRNA template is accomplished by the process of translation.

Translation

Overview of Protein Synthesis

The ordered interaction of well over 100 different macromolecules is required to make a single protein. The entire process takes place in a huge enzymatic machine, the *ribosome*, which in all life forms consists of two ribonucleoprotein subunits (subribosomal particles). The ribosome provides a large, dynamic platform for the sequential polymerization of amino acids according to the sequence of triplet codons in a bound messenger RNA (mRNA) molecule. Ribosomes are necessarily large, in excess of 2.5 MDa, because their substrates are large. The enzymatic substrates for protein synthesis are amino acyl-tRNAs, activated forms of the amino acids carried in ester linkage on the 3' terminal nucleotide of the various tRNAs (transfer RNAs). Each amino acyl-tRNA synthetase enzyme is specific for one of the 20 different amino acids and for all of the tRNAs having anticodons corresponding to the particular amino acid. The amino acyl-tRNAs are escorted to the ribosome as ternary complexes with initiation (IF-2) or elongation factors (EF-Tu) and GTP. The selection of particular amino acyl-tRNAs on the ribosome is made on the basis of tRNA anticodon base-pairing interactions with triplet codons that are exposed in a limited region of mRNA within the decoding center on the small ribosomal subunit. The peptidyl transferase activity of the large subunit catalyzes peptide bond formation between amino acids carried by amino acyl-tRNAs (or peptidyl-tRNAs) that are juxtaposed at specific sites (A, *amino acyl*; and P, *peptidyl*) in the intersubunit space. After each peptidyl transferase reaction, the peptidyl-tRNA and the *uncharged* tRNA which has donated an amino acid to the growing peptide chain are moved (translocated) with the aid of elongation factor EF-G, along with the mRNA, to maintain the reading frame and present the next codon in the A site of the decoding center. Next an amino acyl-tRNA having an anticodon complementary to the A site codon enters the A site and this process is repeated until a termination codon is encountered in the decoding center. Then, with the aid of protein termination factors, the protein is released from peptidyl tRNA, and another protein, RRF, *ribosome-recycling factor*, promotes disassembly of the translation complex.

Given the wealth of information about protein synthesis in bacterial systems and the recent advances in bacterial ribosome structure, it is appropriate to review protein synthesis in prokaryotes.

Elements of Translation in Prokaryotes

The Genetic Code

The 20 natural amino acids are each specified by one or more triplet codons in the mRNA. Four bases in mRNA, taken three at a time, results in 64 different triplet com-

	U	C	A	G
U	UUU Phe UUC Phe UUA Leu UUG Leu	UCU Ser UCC Ser UCA Ser UCG Ser	UAU Tyr UAC Tyr UAA **End** UAG **End**	UGU Cys UGC Cys UGA **End** UGG Trp
C	CUU Leu CUC Leu CUA Leu CUG Leu	CCU Pro CCC Pro CCA Pro CCG Pro	CAU His CAC His CAA Gln CAG Gln	CGU Arg CGC Arg CGA Arg CGG Arg
A	AUU Ile AUC Ile AUA Ile **AUG** Met	ACU Thr ACC Thr ACA Thr ACG Thr	AAU Asn AAC Asn AAA Lys AAG Lys	AGU Ser AGC Ser AGA Arg AGG Arg
G	GUU Val GUC Val GUA Val GUG Val	GCU Ala GCC Ala GCA Ala GCG Ala	GAU Asp GAC Asp GAA Glu GAG Glu	GGU Gly GGC Gly GGA Gly GGG Gly

Fig. 6. The genetic code, as used by most organisms. The first base of the codon (5' end) is shown in the first column, and the second base is shown in the top row. AUG (and sometimes GUG and UUG) usually serves as the initiation codon, when it occurs at the beginning of the open reading frame. The three termination codons (end) are recognized by termination factors.

binations (*see* Fig. 6). Some of the amino acids (identified here by their three letter abbreviations) are specified by single codons (AUG, for Methionine), while others are specified by as many as six different codons (Leucine, for example).

The mRNA

Messenger RNAs may contain one open reading frame (monoscistronic), bounded by initiation and termination codons, or several (polycistronic). The mRNAs often have a nontranslated leader sequence at their 5' end preceding the initiation codon. Some mRNAs have short regions of four to six bases, which are complementary to sequences in the 3' end of 16S RNA exposed on the platform of the small ribosomal subunit. These sequences, called Shine-Dalgarno sequences, lie 10 or so bases upstream of the initiation codon, serving to bind and orient the mRNA, placing the initiation codon within the decoding center on the small subunit. The greater the region of complementarity, the stronger the binding and consequently the particular mRNA will be translated more frequently, relative to those with weaker Shine-Dalgarno interactions.

The Transfer RNAs (tRNAs)

All organisms use tRNAs as so called *adaptor* molecules to convert the sequence of nucleic acid codons into a sequence of amino acids. These are a family of small RNA molecules, 70–80 nucleotides long, which fold into a series of stem-loop structures, usually depicted as a characteristic cloverleaf structure (*see* Fig. 7). They typically contain unusual or modified bases, such as dihydrouracil (prominent in the D loop, so named because of the dihydrouracil content), pseudo uracil, and ribothymidine. The sequences of the various tRNAs are different, but they contain an invari-

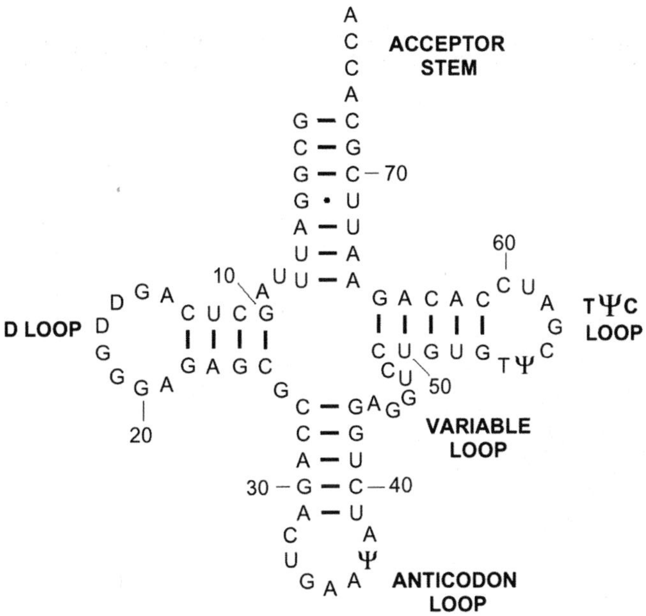

Fig. 7. Transfer RNA structure. Shown here is the secondary structure of phenylalanyl-tRNA (Phe-tRNA), in the familiar *cloverleaf* diagram characteristic of most tRNAs. The anticodon, 5'GAA, is complementary to one of the two codons for Phe (5'UUC) in Fig. 6. D, dihydrouridine; Ψ, pseudouridine; T, ribothymidine.

ant CCA, added postranscriptionaly at the 3' end of the amino acid acceptor stem, as well as a sequence, TΨCG, in the TΨC loop. As its name suggests, the variable loop is highly variable, both in sequence, as well as size. The anticodon and the amino acid that it specifies are separated by about 70 Angstroms, at opposite ends of the L-shaped molecule (*see* Fig. 8A) which forms when the D loop and TΨC loop fold further, stabilized by additional, tertiary base pair interactions.

The Aminoacyl-tRNA Synthetases

Amino acids are *activated* through coupling in ATP-dependent reactions to the appropriate tRNAs by amino acyl-tRNA synthetases specific for each amino acid and for the corresponding tRNAs. There are two general classes of synthetase enzymes, I and II, which tend to function as monomers or dimers, respectively. The enzymes recognize key identity elements at various locations in the cognate tRNAs.

The Ribosome

The small subunit (30S) of prokaryotic ribosomes contains one 16S RNA molecule and about 21 proteins. The RNA molecules are generally characterized by their sedimentation coefficient (S) as an indication of their size or mass. The larger and more compact the RNA molecule is, the higher the sedimentation coefficient. The 16S rRNA (ribosomal RNA) of *E. coli* is1542 nucleotides long (*see* Fig. 9), and the molecule is folded into a rather compact shape (*see* Fig. 10A). Adjacent complementary regions along the molecule result in the formation of a series of stem-loop structures. This has the effect of bringing together distant complementary regions to form additional stems,

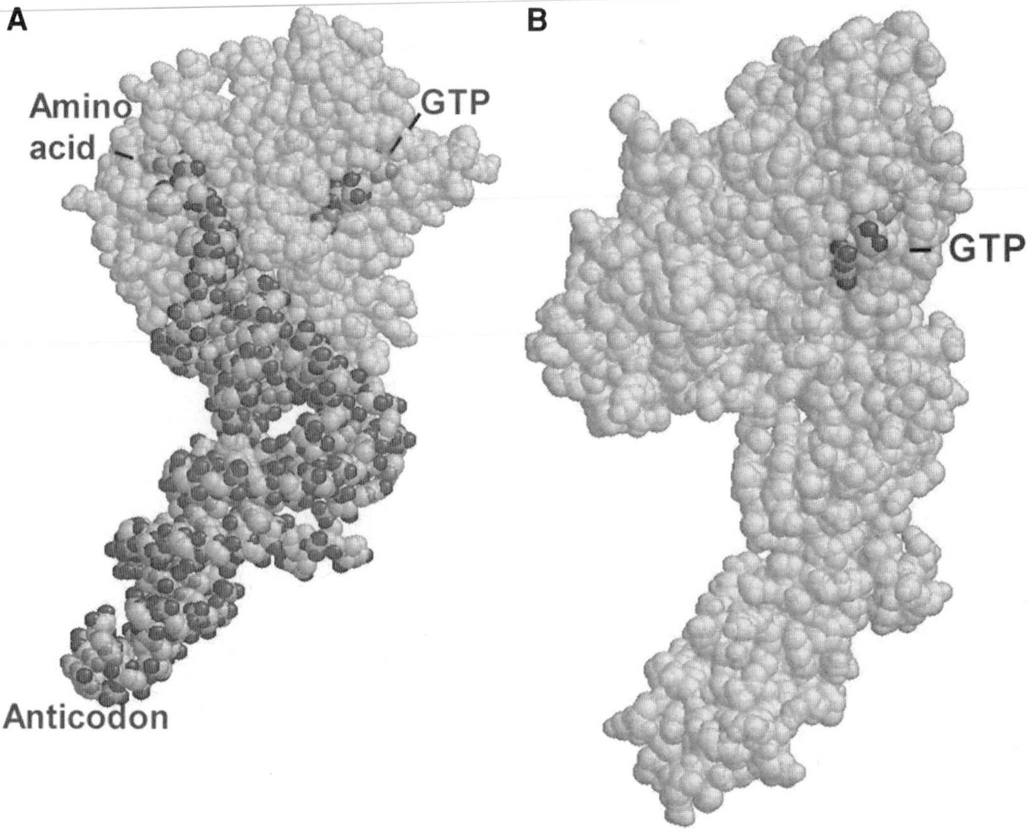

Fig. 8. Elongation factors EF-Tu and EF-G. **(A)** EF-Tu (lighter gray) is shown as a ternary complex with bound amino acyl-tRNA and GTP. **(B)** EF-G resembles the complex of the protein EF-Tu and amino acyl-tRNA. This is an example of macromolecular mimicry where similar binding sites accommodate the different species.

resulting in the formation of distinct domains through these long distance interactions (*see* Fig. 9). The 5' domain, extending from nucleotides 1 through 556 and the penultimate stem (positions 1400–1500) comprise the RNA structure of the *body* (*see* Fig. 10A). The 5' central domain (positions 567 to 883) forms the *platform*, and the *head* contains nucleotides 920–1372. The 21 proteins are distributed around the periphery, mainly on the back or solvent side. Only one protein, S12, is located on the interfacial side, near the decoding center.

The large subunit (50) contains two rRNA molecules, a 5S RNA, forming the central crown structure (*see* Fig. 10F), and a larger 23S RNA, forming the body of the subunit. The 33 proteins of the large subunit are located mainly on the periphery and the backside of the subunit. One of the ribosomal proteins, L12, is present in four copies. These proteins form two L12-dimer structures (*see* Fig. 10F). The L12 dimer stalk is the site where the elongation factors (EF-Tu and EF-G) first engage the ribosome. The 30S and 50S subunits associate during the initiation phase of protein synthesis to form a roughly spherical 70S ribosome.

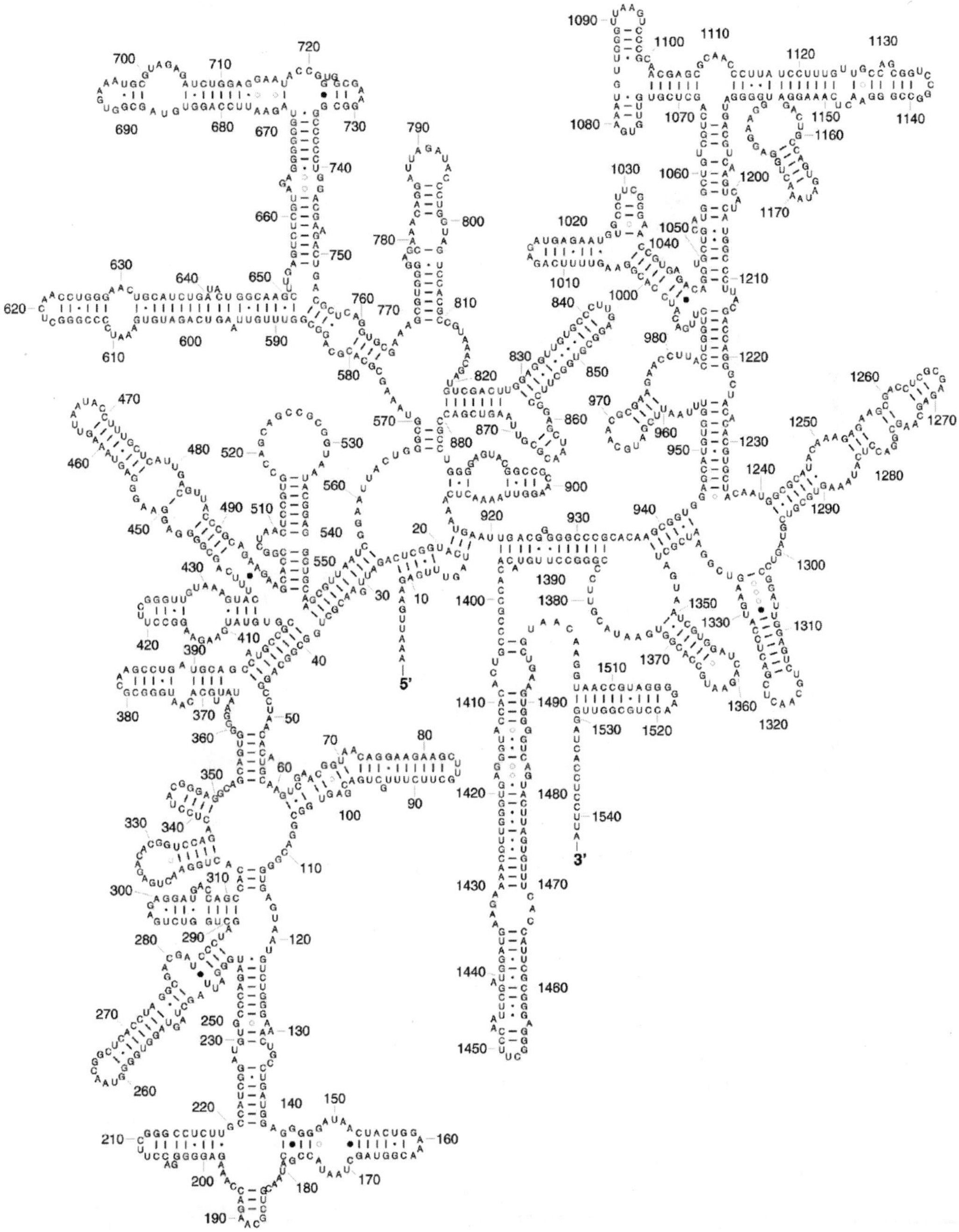

Fig. 9. Secondary structure of *E. coli* 16S rRNA. Several non-canonical base pairs are evident in the molecule, including A-G, G-G, U-G and U-U base pairs. The 16S RNA folds into a compact structure which defines the overall shape of the 30S subunit (*see* Fig. 10).

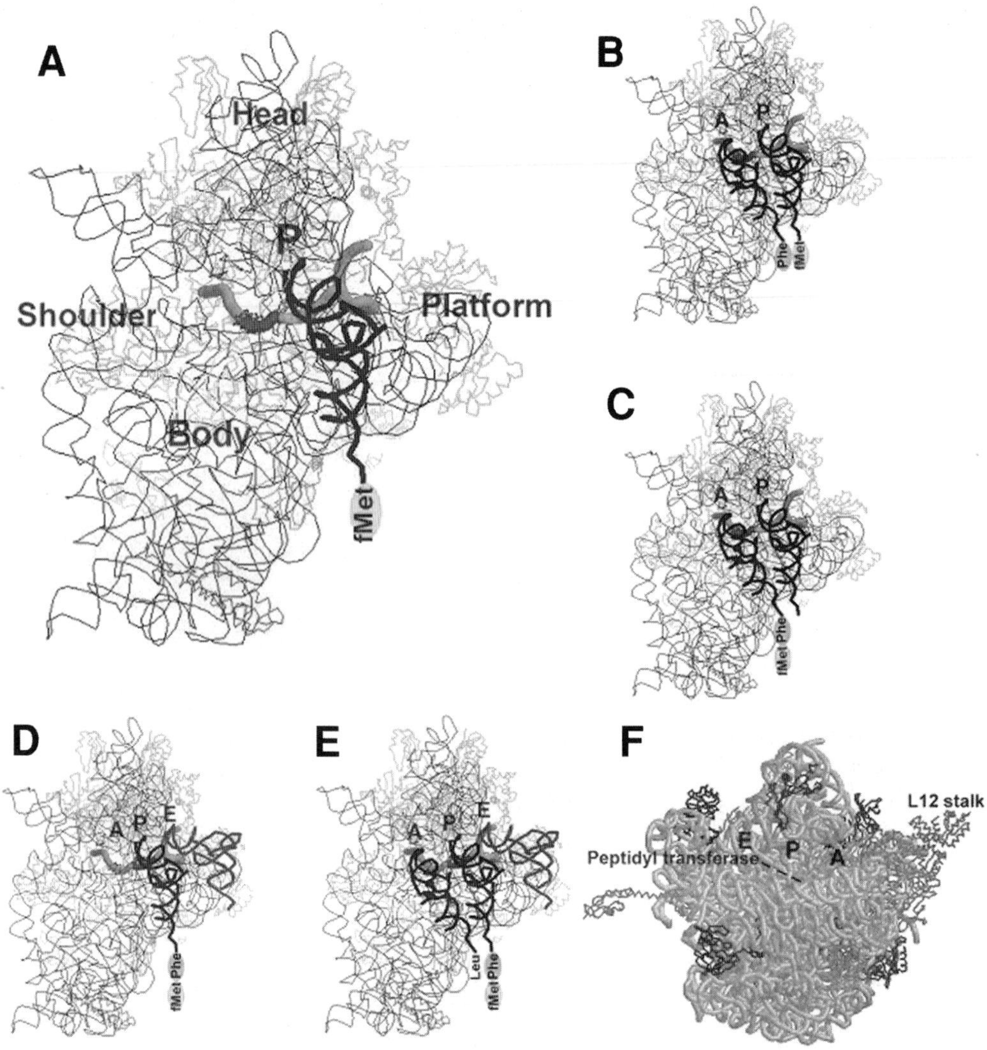

Fig. 10. Structure of the small and large subunits of the bacterial ribosome. **(A)** Interfacial aspect of the 30S subunit, showing the 16S RNA backbone (thin dark tracing) and associated proteins (alternatively shaded). A section of bound mRNA (thick bright backbone) includes the Shine-Dalgarno region (5' helical structure on the right), the initiation codon and an adjacent Phe codon. The anticodon of the initiator tRNA, fMet-tRNA (thick dark backbone) is base paired with the initiation codon in the P site. **(B)** Same as (A) with the addition of Phe-tRNA at the adjacent codon in the A site. **(C)** Peptidyl transferase catalyzed transfer of the fMet to the Phe-tRNA, resulting in a dipeptidyl-tRNA in the A site. **(D)** Post translocation state of the ribosomal small subunit. Through the action of EF-G with bound GTP, the uncharged initiator tRNA, fMet-Phe-tRNA and the mRNA are moved, in register, into the E and P sites. **(E)** Entry of the third amino acyl-tRNA into the A site, in advance of the ejection of the E site tRNA and peptide transfer (peptidyl transferase reaction). **(F)** Interfacial aspect of the 50S subunit, showing the 5S and 23S RNA (thick backbone) and associated proteins (variously shaded). The peptidyl transferase activity lies deep within a cleft in the 23S RNA, an area entirely devoid of protein. The coordinates for the 30S subunit, mRNA fragment, A, P, and E site tRNAs are available at the RCSB data base with PDB accession numbers 1GIX and 1JGO.

Initiation of Protein Synthesis

Initiation of protein synthesis takes place on the small subunit. The mRNA binds in the region between the head and the body, tracking from the platform through a downstream entrance channel formed between the head and the shoulder of the subunit (*see* Fig. 10A). If the mRNA has a Shine-Dalgarno sequence, it binds more efficiently, stabilized by base pairing with the complementary region of 16S rRNA exposed on the platform. This interaction places the initiation codon in the vicinity of the decoding center, where it can base pair with the anticodon of the initiator tRNA. The initiator tRNA in prokaryotic systems is fMet-tRNA, a special tRNA that carries a methionine modified by formylation on its amino group. This fMet-tRNA is escorted to the small subunit in a ternary complex with initation factor 2 (IF-2) and GTP. The fMet-tRNA is the only amino acyl-tRNA to bind directly and initially to the P site, where the initation codon will be able to form base pairs with the anticodon (*see* Fig. 10A). This interaction is facilitated by two other initiation factors, IF-1 and IF-3. IF-1 is a protein mimic of tRNA and it binds to the A site on the small subunit, forcing the IF-2 ternary complex to enter at the adjacent P site. IF-3 binds between the head and the platform, where it serves a dual role. It acts as an anti-association factor, ensuring a supply of free 30S subunits for initiation complex formation and it promotes the fidelity of initiation complex formation by favoring the dissociation of noncanonical complexes, such as base pair interactions between elongator tRNAs and the initiation codon. Upon proper recognition of fMet-tRNA by the initiation codon in the P site, the IF-2-bound GTP is hydrolyzed to GDP, causing a conformational change allowing IF-2-GDP to leave after depositing the initiator tRNA in the P site. The 50S subunit then joins the 30S initiation complex to form the 70S initiation complex, setting the stage for the elongation phase.

Elongation Phase of Protein Synthesis

The elongation factor EF-Tu (*see* Fig. 8A) escorts the various amino acyl-tRNAs to the ribosomal A site as ternary complexes with GTP. They engage the ribosome first at the L12 stalk and if the codon exposed in the A site (UUC, in Fig. 10B, for example) is complementary to their anticodon, the amino acyl-tRNA is deposited and the EF-Tu-bound GTP is hydrolyzed, favoring the exit of EF-Tu-GDP. Note that the mRNA is *kinked* between the adjacent codons in the decoding center. This kinking allows the A and P site tRNAs to read adjacent codons. In this manner the amino acyl ends of the A and P site tRNAs are placed within 5 Angstroms of each other (*see* Fig. 10B), in the peptidyl transferase center of the 50S subunit (*see* Fig. 10F) where they await peptide bond formation. Peptidyl transferase activity of the 50S RNA catalyzes the transfer of the fMet to the Phe-tRNA in the A site (*see* Fig. 10C). At this point in the elongation cycle the peptidyl-tRNA (fMet-Phe-tRNA, in the example of Fig. 10C) and the P site tRNA must be moved to open the A site for entry of the next amino acyl-tRNA able to base pair with the third codon brought into the A site. Elongation factor G, EF-G with bound GTP (*see* Fig. 8B) engages the L12 stalk on the large subunit and proceeds to carry out this translocation event, while maintaining the mRNA reading frame fixed by the A and P (E) site tRNAs. During translocation, the uncharged tRNA is moved into the E site while the A site peptidyl-tRNA moves into the P site (*see* Fig. 10D). EF-G is a striking example of tRNA mimicry by protein. Note the structural resemblance of EF-G (*see* Fig. 8B) and EF-Tu-amino acyl-tRNA (*see* Fig. 8A) which bind to similar sites on the ribosome. After hydrolysis of the bound GTP, EF-G leaves to make the A site available for entry of the next amino acyl-tRNA (*see* Fig. 10E). The growing peptide chain will emerge through a tunnel traversing the body of the 50S subunit. Upon entry of the next cognate amino acyl-tRNA the affinity of the E site for the uncharged tRNA is lowered, allowing for release of the E site tRNA. This cycle is repeated until a termination codon appears in the A site, setting the stage for the termination of protein synthesis.

Termination of Protein Synthesis

Termination codons exposed in the A site are recognized by protein release factors. RF1 recognizes UAA and UAG, and RF2 recognizes UAA and UGA. After binding of either release factor in the A site, peptidyl transferase activity transfers the C-terminal residue of the polypeptide to a water molecule, resulting in release of the protein. The departure of RF1 and RF2 is facilitated by a third release factor, RF3, which is another example of mimicry in translation systems. RF3 is a GTP binding protein that resembles EF-G.

Translation in Eukaryotes

The fundamental process of protein synthesis in eukaryotes resembles that of prokaryotes, with the introduction of additional complexity and regulatory features. The ribosomes are larger and the initiation factors are more numerous. Eukaryotes do not employ a Shine-Dalgarno-like mechanism to promote mRNA binding, but rather use a collection of initiation factors that recognize a uniquely eukaryotic decoration of the 5' end of mRNAs, the 5'-methyl-G cap structures. In addition, most of the mRNAs are further decorated by a poly(A) tail at their 3' end, which recruits poly(A)-binding proteins (PABPs). The 40S ribosome small subunit contains 18S RNA. The large subunit contains three molecules of RNA, a large, 28S RNA, 5S RNA and a species unique to eukaryotes, a 5.8S RNA. The 80S ribosome contains about 80 different proteins, some of which are homologues of bacterial ribosomal proteins, but many of them unique to eukaryotes.

The initiation phase of protein synthesis employs at least 12 initiation factors, containing as many as 28 protein subunits. These protein factors interact with the initiator Met-tRNAi, the mRNA, the 40S and 60S subunits to promote formation of the 80S initiation complex. The factor names are preceded by "e" to denote their eukaryotic nature. The factor eIF1A is homlogous to the bacterial IF1 and it aids in positioning the initiation codon in the decoding center. The homolog of IF2, eIF2 escorts Met-tRNAi to the P site of the ribosomal 40S subunit. The large factor eIF3, which contains 11 protein subunits, binds to the platform region of the 40S subunit. The eIF4F factor is a heterotrimeric factor; in addition to its central component, eIF4G, its eIF4A component is an ATP-dependent RNA helicase, and its eIF4E subunit binds to the 5'cap structure on the mRNA. The versatile factor eIF4G serves as a *bridging* factor that binds to eIF4E, as well as the PABPs (on the poly(A) tail), which has the effect of bringing the 5' and 3' ends of the message together. The message is then brought to the 40S subunit when the *loaded* eIF4G binds to eIF3 already on the subunit. The initiation AUG codon is as many as 100 or more nucleotides downstream of the 5'cap structure. This necessitates an ATP-dependent scanning search for the downstream initiation codon, recognizable by its ability to base pair with the waiting anticodon of Met-tRNAi. After selection of the initiation codon, eIF5 is recruited to aid in the dissociation of eIF2-GDP, eIF3, and eIF4 factors in preparation for the joining of the 60S subunit to form the 80S initiation complex. Some mRNAs, such as the polycistronic genomic RNA of the poliovirus, have no 5'-methyl-G cap structures, but contain internal ribosome entry sites (IRES) where initiation of protein synthesis can take place without the need for the initiation factors required for most cellular mRNAs.

Acknowledgments

We thank Christine Mione, Sara Rodriguez-Jato, Wesley Brooks, and Paul Wright for generating all of the figures on transcription and RNA processing for this chapter.

Glossary and Abbreviations

Transcription

Activator Proteins that augment and/or stabilize formation of the PIC, often by binding to activator DNA sequences.

Anti-sense RNA RNA transcript that is complementary to a known coding RNA; transcribed from the non-template strand of DNA.

BRE TFIIB recognition element.

Closed binary complex The DNA-protein complex consisting of RNA polymerase (or the PIC in eukaryotes) and double-stranded DNA of the promoter where the double helix of DNA is not melted.

Coactivator A protein or protein complex that act as an intermediate or bridge for interactions between activators and the PIC.

Core enzyme Form of prokaryotic RNA polymerase that functions during transcription elongation; consists of two α subunits, one β subunit, and one β' subunit.

Core promoter *(also referred to as the basal promoter)* In eukaryotes, the minimal promoter region that is required to form the PIC and initiate transcription.

CTD C-terminal domain of the largest subunit of RNA polymerase II.

DNA template strand Strand of the DNA double helix that encodes an RNA.

DPE Downstream promoter element.

GTFs General transcription factors.

Hairpin A region of an RNA or single-stranded DNA, that folds back upon itself and forms intramolecular Watson-Crick base pairing.

Holoenzyme In prokaryotes, the core RNA polymerase enzyme plus sigma factor; in eukaryotes, a complex of RNA polymerase II, several general transcription factors (usually not including TBP), and the mediator co-activator complex.

Inr Initiator element; the DNA sequence spanning the transcription initiation site that is bound by initiator proteins that mediate formation of the PIC in TATA-containing or TATA-less promoters.

Mediator complex Co-activator complex that is bound to the CTD of RNA polymerase II.

Nucleosomal array A stretch of DNA organized into a series of nucleosomes forming a beads-on-a-string structure.

Nucleosome Basic unit of DNA compaction in eukaryotic nuclei; consists of ~200 bp of DNA wrapped around an octamer core of histone proteins.

Open binary complex The DNA protein complex of double-stranded DNA and RNA polymerase (or the PIC in eukaryotes) where the DNA duplex bound by the polymerase is melted into single-stranded regions.

PIC Pre-initiation complex.

Pol I, pol II, pol III RNA polymerase I, II, and III, respectively.

Promoter clearance *(also referred to as promoter release)* Release of the PIC from the promoter and conversion of the PIC to the transcription elongation complex.

Rho protein Protein that mediates rho-dependent transcription termination in prokaryotes.

RNA:DNA duplex A region in which one strand of DNA is base paired with its complementary sequence of RNA.

rNTP Ribonucleotide triphosphate.

rRNAs Ribosomal RNAs.

TAFs TBP-associated factors; subunits of TFIID.

TATA box A short region ~30 bp upstream of the transcription initiation site that contains the DNA sequence TATA and is bound by TBP.

TBP TATA-binding protein; the subunit of transcription factor TFIID that binds to the TATA box.

TFIIA, B, D, E, F, H General transcription factors that are components of the pre-initiation complex of genes transcribed by RNA polymerase II.

Transcription elongation complex RNA polymerase and its associated components and factors that forms after promoter clearance and elongates a nascent RNA.

Watson-Crick base pairing Pairing of complementary bases; A:T, A:U, G:C.

RNA Processing

Capping Addition of a 7-methyl G residue to the 5'end of mRNAs via a 5'→5' linkage.

Deamination Removal of an amine group from a base; deamination of cytosine yields uracil.

Editosome Macromolecular complex that carries out RNA editing.

Exon Portion of a gene (and RNA) that is included in the final fully-processed mature mRNA molecule.

Exon definition The process in RNA splicing that allows the spliceosome to accurately recognize and splice exons within an unspliced primary RNA transcript.

Intron DNA (and RNA) sequences located between exons that interrupt the mRNA-coding portion of a gene (and RNA transcript).

Polyadenylation Addition of a string of A residues to the 3' end of mRNAs in eukaryotes.

Polyadenylation signal sequence The AAUAA sequence that dictates downstream cleavage of the primary RNA transcript, thereby forming the 3' end of the mRNA and the site for polyadenylation.

Post-transcriptional Molecular processes (such as RNA processing) that occur after an RNA has been transcribed.

RNA editing The non-templated addition, deletion, or modification of nucleotides within a mature mRNA that occurs after transcription.

RNA splicing Removal of introns from the primary RNA transcript to form the mature mRNA.

Spliceosome Large RNA-protein complex that carries out RNA splicing reactions.

SR proteins Family of serine- and arginine-rich proteins that play central roles in RNA splicing.

Transesterification reaction Chemical reaction occurring during splicing that involves breakage or exchange of one ester bond for the formation of a new ester bond.

Translation

A site Ribosomal site where aminoacyl-tRNAs enter and bind during the elongation phase of protein synthesis.

Anticodon A series of three nucleotides in the base loop of tRNA that are complementary to a codon specifying the amino acid attached to a particular amino acyl-tRNA.

Codon A series of three bases (A, G, C or T) in the mRNA open reading frame that specify a particular amino acid.

E site Exit site, where uncharged tRNAs are bound after translocation, from which they exit the ribosome.

EF-G Prokaryotic Elongation factor G, the translocation factor for prokaryotic ribosomes.

EF-Tu Prokaryotic Elongation Factor T, forms ternary (three component) complex with amino acyl-tRNA and GTP; carries aminoacyl-tRNA to ribosomal A site.

IF2 Prokaryotic Initiation factor 2, the factor that binds, along with GTP, to initiator tRNA, and carries the initiator tRNA to the ribosomal P site.

IRES Internal Ribosome Entry Site; eukaryotic ribosomes can initiate protein synthesis at these sites in mRNAs that lack the 5' cap decoration.

P site Ribosomal site where initiator tRNA enters and binds.

Peptidyl-tRNA tRNA with the growing peptide attached at its 3' end.

Shine-Dalgarno sequence A short four-to-seven base sequence in the 3' end of bacterial small ribosomal subunit RNA (16S RNA) that is complementary to a short sequence of bases upstream of the initiation codon in some mRNAs.

Translocation EF-G catalyzed movement of tRNAs and mRNA in the ribosome following peptidyl transfer to the aminoacyl-tRNA in the A site. During translocation the uncharged tRNA in the P site and the peptidyl-tRNA in the A site, are moved, along with the mRNA, into the E and P sites, respectively.

Suggested Reading

Transcription and RNA Processing

Cramer, P., Bushnell, D. A, Fu, J., Gnatt, A. L., et al. (2000) Architecture of RNA polymerase II and implications for the transcription mechanism, Science 288, 640–649.

Cramer, P., Bushnell, D. A., and Kornberg, R. D. (2001) Structural basis of transcription: RNA polymerase II at 2.8 angstrom resolution, Science 292, 1863–1876.

deHaseth, P. L., Zupancic, M. L., Record, M. T. (1998) RNA polymerase-promoter interactions: The comings and goings of RNA polymerase, J. Bacteriol. 180, 3019–3025.

Hirose, H. and Manley, J. L. (2000) RNA polymerase II and the integration of nuclear events, Genes Dev. 14, 1415–1429.

Lee, T. I. and Young, R. A. (2000) Transcription of eukaryotic protein-coding genes, Annu. Rev. Genet. 34, 77–137.

Mooney, R. A., Artsimovitch, I., and Landick, R. (1998) Information processing by RNA polymerase: Recognition of regulatory signals during RNA chain elongation, J. Bacteriol. 180, 3265–3275.

Translation

Garret, R. A., Douthwaite,S. R., Liljas, A., Matheson, A. T., Moore, P. B., and Noller, H. F. (2000) The Ribosome: structure, function, antibiotics and cellular interactions, ASM Press, Washington, DC.

Gutell R. R. (1996) Comparative Sequence Analysis and the Structure of 16S and 23S rRNA, in: Ribosomal RNA. Structure, Evolution, Processing, and Function in Protein Biosynthesis, (Dahlberg, A. and Zimmerman, B. eds.) CRC Press, Boca Raton, FL, pp. 111–128.

Yusupova, G. Z., Yusupov, M. M., Cate, J. H., and Noller, H. F. (2001) The path of messenger RNA through the ribosome, Cell 106, 233–241.

Yusupov, M. M., Yusupova, G. Z., Baucom, A., Lieberman, K., Earnest, T. N., Cate, J. H., and Noller, H. F. (2001) Crystal structure of the ribosome at 5.5 A resolution, Science 292, 883–896.

Part II Molecular Genetics

A. Genomics

6 Epigenetic Mechanisms Regulating Gene Expression

John R. McCarrey

Epigenetics:

"The study of mitotically and/or meiotically heritable changes in gene function that cannot be explained by changes in primary DNA sequence."

A. D. Riggs, 1996

Introduction

Epigenetic mechanisms regulate gene function in a heritable manner, but do so without modulating the DNA sequence of the affected gene. Many different genetic functions are influenced by epigenetic mechanisms in various species. These include regulation of gene expression, DNA modification and restriction, genomic imprinting, X-chromosome inactivation, paramutation, position effect variegation, mating type, cell determination, transposable elements, and mutator and suppressor genes. This chapter will focus on epigenetic mechanisms that regulate gene expression and the manner in which they accomplish this in mammalian species.

Nuclear DNA acts as the repository of genetic information in eukaryotic cells. In mammals, and many other animal species, a complete representation of the genome is maintained in essentially every nucleated cell. However, only a subset of this collection of genes is expressed in any particular cell type. Thus, it is not the presence of specific genes, but rather the expression of specific genes, that leads to the unique identity and function of any particular cell.

For over 25 years, the mechanisms that regulate gene expression have been the focus of extensive investigation. For protein-encoding genes, two primary steps are involved in gene expression: transcription of DNA into RNA, and translation of that RNA into a polypeptide. This affords two levels of regulation of gene expression: transcriptional regulation and translational (or post-transcriptional) regulation. For tissue-specific genes (those expressed in only a subset of tissues or in a single tissue or cell type), regulation is primarily manifest at the transcriptional level. Extensive studies of this process have revealed a consensus mechanism whereby the promoter region, typically located at the 5'-end of the gene, acts to bind specific proteins called transcription factors which, in turn, attract (or prevent) binding of the RNA polymerase that is required to initiate transcription.

Binding of transcription factors to specific gene promoters and to specific sites within those promoters is regulated by the ability of a DNA binding domain within each protein factor to recognize a unique three-dimensional structure of double-stranded DNA. This unique structure is imparted by a specific nucleotide sequence, typically 5–15 base pairs (bp) in length. Thus, this mechanism does rely on the DNA sequence and is therefore not a truly epigenetic mechanism. However, because these transcription factors can be either ubiquitous or tissue-specific, and can either promote or inhibit transcription, this mechanism can modulate tissue-, cell-type, or developmental-stage specificity of transcription, as well as controlling the relative level (or frequency) of transcription. Nevertheless, protein-DNA interactions between transcription factors and promoter sequences, respectively, are not the only mechanism by which gene expression is regulated in eukaryotic cells.

In mammals there are several examples in which genes are regulated by mechanisms other than transcription factors. For example, in female somatic cells, genes on the active X chromosome are transcribed, whereas homologous genes on the inactive X chromosome remain transcriptionally silenced. This is despite the fact that both the active and inactive copies of these genes share identical nucleotide sequences and reside within the same nucleus. Thus the presence of identical promoter sequences and cognate transcription factors alone does not ensure identical regulation of genes. Similarly, in mammals, the phenomenon of genomic imprinting results in the expression of only one of the two copies of a particular gene within a single diploid cell. In this case the choice of which allele is expressed is dictated by the parental origin of that allele. However, the mechanism that regulates such monoallelic expression cannot be based solely on transcription factors and promoter sequences, because the former are present throughout the nucleus in which both alleles reside, and the latter are often identical on both alleles.

The unavoidable conclusion from these observations is that there must be additional mechanisms by which gene expression is regulated in eukaryotic cells, and these mechanisms must function in a manner that does not depend on differences in nucleotide sequence or the cell-type specific presence or absence of transcription factors. Yet, as exemplified by the examples noted earlier for X-chromosome inactivation and genomic imprinting, these mechanisms must function in a heritable manner, such that the same alleles remain expressed or silenced, even after replication of the DNA and division of one cell to produce two daughter cells.

We now know that there are multiple mechanisms that meet the criteria of epigenetic mechanisms in that they regulate gene expression in a heritable manner that does not rely on differences in DNA sequence. Examples of mechanisms that either have been shown to operate in this manner or have the potential to operate in this manner include: DNA methylation, chromatin structure and/or composition, DNA loop domains and association with the nuclear matrix, and DNA replication timing.

DNA Methylation

See companion CD for color Fig. 1

In mammals, methylation of DNA is found only on cytosines present in a 5'-CpG-3' dinucleotide sequence. Because cytosine and guanine are complementary bases, wherever there is a CpG dinucleotide in one DNA strand, there will be a complementary CpG on the opposite strand. This double-stranded structure can exist in three different states with respect to methylation (*see* Fig. 1). It can be *fully methylated*,

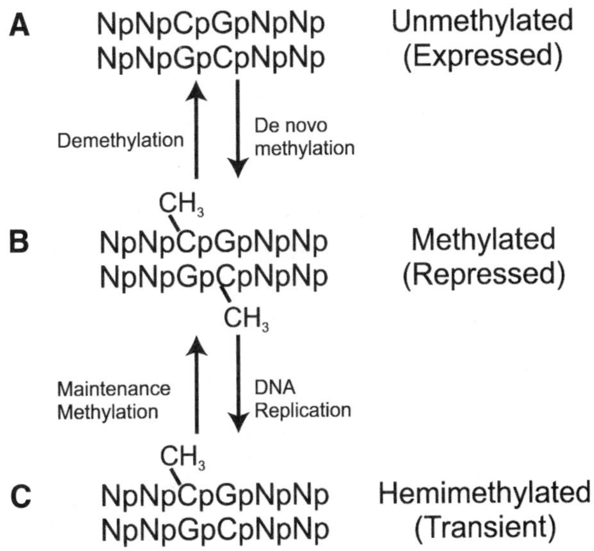

Fig. 1. Alternate states of DNA methylation in mammalian DNA. Methylation occurs only on cytosines present in CpG dinucleotides in mammalian DNA. A CpG dinucleotide sequence in one DNA strand mandates the presence of a complementary CpG dinucleotide in the other strand of double-stranded DNA. **(A)** If both cytosines in such a site are unmethylated, the site is said to be completely unmethylated. This structure is often found in actively expressed or potentiated genes, especially in the 5' regulatory region. **(B)** An unmethylated site can undergo *de novo* methylation to form a fully methylated site in which both cytosines are methylated. This structure is often found associated with repressed genes. Conversely a demethylase activity can convert a fully methylated site to a fully unmethylated site in the absence of DNA replication. **(C)** Upon semi-conservative replication of a fully methylated site, a hemimethylated site is formed. This structure is typically transient as a maintenance DNA methyl transferase rapidly recognizes a hemimethylated site and returns it to a fully methylated state. The function of the maintenance methylase provides a mechanism to heritably maintain DNA methylation patterns. C, cytosine; G, guanine; N, any base; p, phosphate bond; CH_3, methyl group.

meaning that both cytosines are methylated (*see* Fig. 1B), or it can be completely unmethylated if neither cytosine is methylated (*see* Fig. 1A). When a fully methylated site is replicated by semi-conservative replication, the resulting structure is hemimethylated (*see* Fig. 1C). This is typically a transient state because it forms a template for a ubiquitously functioning DNA maintenance methyl transferase that recognizes the hemimethylated structure and returns it to a fully methylated state. Thus, fully methylated and unmethylated sites are maintained (and/or re-established) throughout replication of DNA and cellular division. In this way methylated and unmethylated states of DNA are heritable.

It is possible for an unmethylated site to be directly converted to a fully methylated site, and vice versa. Methylation of an unmethylated site is achieved by a *de novo* methylase, whereas a direct transition from a fully methylated to an unmethylated structure in the absence of DNA replication is accomplished by a demethylase activity. The function of these enzymatic activities and the manner in which they are regulated are not as well-characterized as that of the maintenance methylase activity.

However, there is ample evidence that such activities do indeed exist. Shortly after fertilization in the mouse, nearly all of the methylation that is brought into the zygote by the gametic genomes is lost, such that the blastocyst genome is nearly devoid of DNA methylation except for that at a few imprinted sites. This may occur either by dilution of methylated strands as replication proceeds in the absence of maintenance methylase activity or by direct demethylation, or by some combination of these two mechanisms. Subsequently, at about the time of gastrulation, there is a *de novo* methylation event at numerous different sites throughout the genome. This must be accomplished by a *de novo* methylase because completely unmethylated sites become fully methylated. Following gastrulation, many different cell lineages become allocated and begin to develop and differentiate. Coincident with this, selective demethylation of many tissue-specific genes is often observed within the cell lineage in which these genes will ultimately be expressed. In most cases this appears to occur via a demethylase activity, because in at least some cases demethylation occurs in the complete absence of DNA replication or cellular division.

In addition to tissue-specific genes that are expressed in a limited tissue-, cell-type, or developmental-stage specific pattern, another set of *housekeeping* genes is widely expressed in a ubiquitous and constitutive manner. These genes, which do not require as complicated transcriptional regulation as that needed for tissue-specific genes, often bear a *CpG island*, most commonly in the 5'-portion of the gene. A CpG island has been defined as a region in the mammalian genome of >100 bp with a GC content of >50% that lacks the typical underrepresentation of CpG dinucleotides seen in other regions of the genome. Generally, CpG islands remain constitutively unmethylated throughout development and differentiation of cells. Exceptions to this rule include CpG islands associated with genes on the inactive X chromosome or with nonexpressed, inactive alleles of imprinted genes, as well as those associated with certain genes in cancerous tumors (e.g., tumor-suppressor genes). In these cases, the island associated with the nonexpressed allele or gene is typically methylated.

For both individual CpG dinucleotides located in non-CpG island regions, and CpG dinucleotides within CpG islands, a general correlation has been observed between the presence of DNA methylation and inhibition of expression, and between the absence of DNA methylation and active transcription. This is especially true for sites in the 5'-flanking region or in the 5'-half of transcribed portions of genes. At least two types of mechanisms have been proposed by which DNA methylation, or the lack thereof, might contribute to regulation of transcription. In one case, the presence or absence of methylation on key cytosines within a particular transcription factor binding site may modulate the ability of the factor to bind to that site. In a second scenario, the presence or absence of methylation at sites either within factor binding sites or in regions adjacent to factor binding sites may inhibit factor binding indirectly by affecting chromatin structure.

A direct mechanistic connection has now been established between DNA methylation and chromatin structure (*see* "Interactions Among Epigenetic Mechanisms"). In this case, it is suggested that the presence of methylation stabilizes a condensed (*closed*) chromatin structure that is, in turn, refractory to binding by transcription factors and/or RNA polymerase. Conversely, an absence of methylation leads to a less condensed (*open*) chromatin structure that is accessible to transcription factors and RNA polymerase. Effects of DNA methylation on chromatin structure appear to be mediated by methylated DNA-binding proteins that bind to methylated DNA on the basis of the presence or absence of methylation, rather than on the basis of a particular binding sequence as is the case for transcription factors.

Two methylated-DNA binding proteins were originally identified, MeCP1 and MeCP2. MeCP1 is a large protein complex that binds best to regions of DNA containing >10 methyl-CpGs, and has been shown to be involved in repression of transcription from densely methylated promoters. It also binds to, and represses transcription from, more sparsely methylated promoters, although this is a much weaker interaction. MeCP2 is a single polypeptide that can bind to as few as a single fully methylated CpG site. In vivo it appears to bind predominantly to highly methylated satellite DNAs adjacent to centromeres in the mouse genome, but shows a more dispersed binding pattern in the genomes of humans and rats, which do not contain highly methylated satellite DNA.

Recently, screens for cDNAs encoding methyl-CpG binding domains (MBDs) have revealed at least four such genes, *MBD1-4*. The MBD1 protein is a component of the MeCP1 protein complex. MBD2-*4* encode methylated DNA binding proteins that are distinct from those associated with either MeCP1 or MeCP2, but bear a striking similarity to the MBD of MeCP2. The products of *MBD2* and *MBD4* bind to methylated CpGs both *in vitro* and *in vivo*, and are thus considered to be additional candidates for mediators of mechanisms associated with methylated DNA.

The manner in which tissue-, cell-type and/or gene-specific patterns of DNA methylation are established or modulated remains to be fully elucidated. However there appears to be a combination of general and specific mechanisms that contribute to this process. The general mechanisms include those that result in genome-wide loss or gain of methylation, especially during early embryogenesis, along with the maintenance methylase activity that re-establishes full methylation at hemimethylated sites following replication of DNA. Cell-type, developmental-stage, and gene-specific demethylation have been shown to be regulated by signal sequences within the promoter region of at least one tissue-specific gene. Regulation of CpG island methylation has also been shown to be dependent on signal sequences within certain imprinted genes. However, it appears that different methylases and demethylases may be responsible for *de novo* methylation/demethylation of CpG dinucleotides within or exclusive of CpG islands, respectively.

Chromatin Structure and Composition

Although DNA exists in a double helix structure within eukaryotic cells, this structure alone, otherwise known as *naked DNA*, is rarely found in cells in vivo. Rather the nuclear DNA is typically complexed with proteins to form chromatin. At a primary level, chromatin structure commonly involves double-stranded DNA wrapped periodically around protein structures called nucleosomes (*see* Fig. 2A). Approximately 150 bp of double-stranded DNA are wrapped in two superhelical turns around each nucleosome, and nucleosomes are typically separated by approx 10 bp of double-stranded DNA. This forms what has been termed a *beads on a string* structure that is approx 10 nm in diameter. This is also known as an *open* or *potentiated* chromatin structure, and is the structure most commonly found in genes that are undergoing active transcription. In this structure the nucleosomes are typically evenly spaced at regular intervals of approx 10 bp, however, as necessary, nucleosomes can be displaced, eliminated, or newly formed to facilitate initiation of transcription from a

See companion CD for color Fig. 2

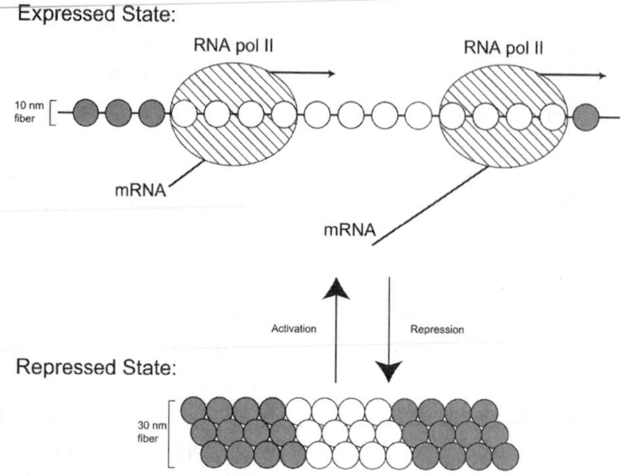

Fig. 2. Alternate states of chromatin structure. **(A)** In eukaryotic cells double-stranded DNA is typically complexed with clusters of histones called nucleosomes to form a *beads on a string* structure. This structure, which forms a fiber of approx 10 nm in diameter, is typically found in genes that are undergoing active transcription as shown in the Expressed State in this figure. The RNA polymerase II complex is able to traverse and transcribe portion of this structure to produce mRNA transcripts. **(B)** Long-term repression of gene transcription is accomplished by condensation of chromatin to form a 30 nm fiber as shown in the Repressed State in this figure. This condensed structure is refractory to binding by transcription factors and/or RNA polymerase II inhibiting initiation of transcription. Open circles, nucleosomes within the transcribed portion of the gene; filled circles, nucleosomes between genes; hatched oval, the RNA II polymerase complex.

promoter region. Such modifications may be required to permit or even promote access to specific factor binding sites in the double-stranded DNA.

Changes in chromatin structure at the level of nucleosome positioning can be modulated by ATP-dependent chromatin remodeling complexes. The SWI2/SNF2 complex originally discovered in *Drosophila*, is the best characterized of these. It is also conserved in mammals where it functions in a similar manner. The primary function of chromatin remodeling machinery is to remodel nucleosomal arrays to enhance accessibility to transcription factors. Once the necessary transcription factors and then the RNA polymerase complex have become bound to the gene promoter, transcription can proceed through the entire gene as it exists in the 10 nm diameter chromatin structure.

An alternate chromatin structure is achieved when the 10 nm chromatin fiber becomes supercoiled to form a 30 nm structure sometimes referred to as a *solenoid* (*see* Fig. 2B). This structure is typically found in transcriptionally repressed genes. This highly condensed structure is refractory to nucleosome displacement and/or factor binding. Thus, if transcription factors cannot gain direct access to their cognate binding sites in the double-stranded DNA, they will not bind and hence will not promote initiation of transcription. The option to exist in this repressive chromatin structure reconciles how a gene that contains all necessary factor-binding sites can reside in a nucleus in which all the necessary transcription factors are present, and still not be transcribed.

The composition of chromatin has been shown to vary in a manner that correlates with the different structures described earlier. A primary component of nucleosomes are histones. Each nucleosome consists of an octamer of two molecules each of histones H2A, H2B, H3 and H4, plus one linker histone H1 or H5. When chromatin is present in the 10-nm open or potentiated configuration most often associated with active transcription, the histone H4 in that region is often hyperacetylated. Conversely, when chromatin is present in the 30 nm repressed structure, histone H4 is typically hypoacetylated. Acetylation of histone H4 is believed to inhibit condensation of the 10 nm chromatin fiber and thus contribute to the maintenance of an open or potentiated chromatin structure, whereas the absence of acetylation on histone H4 contributes to chromatin condensation to form the repressive 30 nm structure. The acetylation of histones is regulated by a dynamic balance of histone acetyl transferases (HATs) and deacetylases (HDACs). The recruitment of these enzymes to specific loci can be regulated by transcription factors located by specific protein-DNA interactions, or by the methylated DNA-binding proteins. The latter are particularly associated with histone deacetylases. This provides a mechanistic basis for the frequently observed correlation between hypermethylation of DNA and a condensed, repressed chromatin structure (*see* "Interactions Among Epigenetic Mechanisms").

DNA Loop Domains and Association with the Nuclear Matrix

Regulation of chromatin structure and transcriptional activity can occur over relatively large distances within the mammalian genome. While this affords significant advantages for coordinate regulation of gene expression, it also poses potential disadvantages in that it raises the possibility that controlling influences targeted to one locus could inadvertently affect other loci, resulting in ectopic and/or inappropriate gene expression or suppression. This potential problem is mitigated in mammals by an additional level of regulation that results in segregation of chromatin into essentially independent loop domains (*see* Fig. 3). Delineation of these domains is believed to be achieved by the presence of *boundary elements* and/or by anchorage of the boundaries of each loop to a three-dimensional proteinaceous structure in the nucleus called the *nuclear matrix*. This arrangement affords multiple additional opportunities for control of gene expression. First, each loop is essentially insulated from adjacent loops and can thus be regulated independently. Second, it has been proposed that many factors and enzymes that regulate DNA replication, transcription, and post-transcriptional processes may be embedded in the nuclear matrix, so that proximity of individual genes to the matrix may influence the rate at which these processes occur in a gene-specific manner.

See companion CD for color Fig. 3

Specific sequences in chromosomal DNA have been shown to have nuclear matrix-binding capacity. These regions are known as *matrix attachment regions* or *MARs* (the nuclear matrix is also known as the *nuclear scaffold* and so these attachment regions are also known as *scaffold attachment regions* or *SARs*). MARs/SARs can be A/T-rich sequences that are often found at the boundaries of transcription units or in the vicinity of transcriptional enhancers. There appear to be at least two classes of MARs, constitutive and facultative. Constitutive MARs are believed to remain bound to the matrix in all cell types at all developmental stages. Thus, constitutive MARs would define a primary loop domain structure. Facultative MARs are believed to be differentially associated with, or disassociated with the matrix in a gene-, cell-type, and developmental-stage specific manner. Thus, facultative MARs

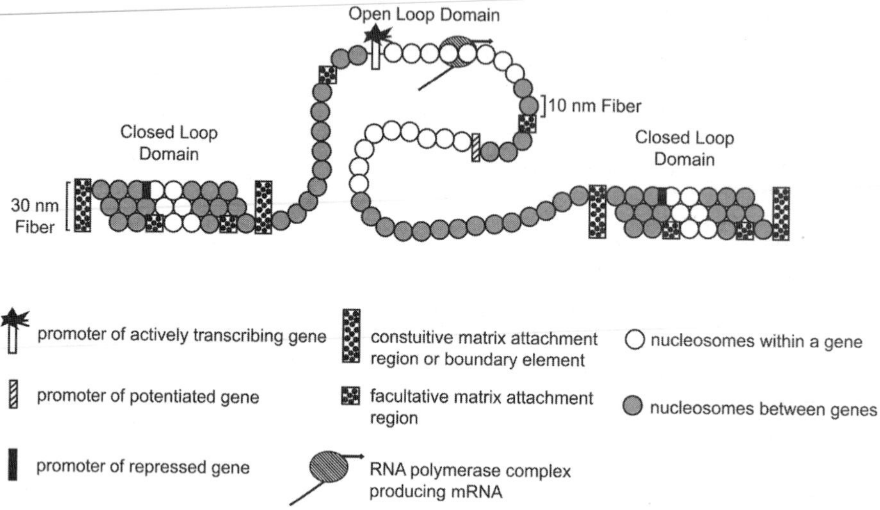

Fig. 3. Organization of DNA loop domains. Adjacent chromatin loop domains can exist in alternate states of condensed (closed) or decondensed (open) structure. Genes within closed domains are typically repressed. Genes within open domains are potentiated for transcriptional activation. Activation of transcription requires transcription factor binding and initiation of RNA synthesis by RNA polymerase II. (Modified with permission from Krawetz, et al. [1999]).

would have the potential to form a secondary loop structure, and/or to regulate tissue- or stage-specific associations between individual genes and the nuclear matrix. The extent to which boundary elements and MARs represent identical or distinct structures remains to be clearly elucidated.

Chromosome loop domains show both developmental-stage and tissue-specificity. These loops are generally small in nuclei of sperm and early embryonic cells, but become larger in differentiating somatic cells. Although the germ cells also undergo significant differentiation during gametogenesis, the loop sizes appear to remain generally smaller than in somatic cells. This difference in loop size could be produced by differential activity of facultative MARs, such that more of these are functional in germ cells and early embryonic cells leading to an increased incidence of DNA-matrix interactions in these cells and hence, delineated loops of smaller average size. It is tempting to suggest that small loop size is characteristic of a state of genetic/developmental pluripotency. This is consistent with the observation that genes that are actively transcribed, or in a state of readiness or *potentiated* for transcriptional activation and are typically found more closely associated with the nuclear matrix than are transcriptionally repressed genes. Thus, in the gametes and early embryonic cells, maximum use of facultative MARs could maintain a maximum number of genes in a potentially expressible state. However, as specific cell lineages become committed to a particular differentiated phenotype, many unneeded genes could become terminally repressed by selective disassociation of facultative MARs from the matrix to sequester the repressed genes away from transcription factors and RNA polymerase complexes associated with the matrix.

Replication Timing

The entire genome is duplicated during S phase of the cell cycle. However, the order in which gene loci are replicated varies among cell types and at different developmental stages. Typically, genes that are actively expressed in a particular cell type are replicated relatively early during S phase, whereas repressed genes are replicated later. For example, the same tissue-specific gene that is replicated early in the expressing cell type may be replicated later in nonexpressing cell types.

For most genes, both alleles are replicated simultaneously during S phase. However, in cases of monoallelic expression as seen for imprinted genes or genes on the active and inactive X chromosomes, the two alleles replicate asynchronously. In the case of X-linked genes, expressed alleles on the active X chromosome tend to be replicated earlier than their nonexpressed homologues on the inactive X. Interestingly, while imprinted genes also show asynchronous replication, the paternal allele is always replicated earlier than the maternal allele, regardless of which allele is expressed and which is repressed.

Differential replication timing has been demonstrated by direct fluorescence *in situ* hybridization (FISH) and by DNA hybridization using cells separated according to DNA content by fluorescence-activated cell sorting (FACS). It is not clear whether this is a cause or effect of related epigenetic mechanisms. It has been suggested that key chromatin remodeling and/or transcription factors may be limiting within individual nuclei and that following disassociation of these factors from the DNA during replication, early replicating genes or alleles might be afforded a preferential opportunity to reassociate with these factors immediately following replication (*see* Fig. 4). If so, this could then contribute to subsequent differential transcriptional activity of these genes or alleles. However, this theory is not supported by the observation that for certain imprinted genes, the maternal allele is preferentially expressed even though the paternal allele is replicated early. An alternative hypothesis is that early replication might simply be a reflection of the presence of DNA replication enzymes associated with, and/or embedded in the matrix, since actively expressed or potentiated genes tend to be more closely associated with the nuclear matrix. In either case, replication timing is indicative of epigenetic differences among gene loci and/or between alleles of the same gene.

See companion CD for color Fig. 4

Interactions Among Epigenetic Mechanisms

The epigenetic mechanisms discussed earlier represent additional levels of gene regulation that are available to mammalian cells beyond that afforded by direct protein-DNA interactions between transcription factors, the RNA polymerase complex, and gene promoters. An important question is how these multiple levels of gene regulation are orchestrated by the cell to achieve proper patterns of expression of batteries of housekeeping and tissue-specific genes. Clearly a variety of strategies are employed depending on the particular regulated gene and/or the particular cell type in which the regulation takes place. An example cascade of epigenetic and genetic mechanisms is presented below to demonstrate how these different mechanisms could interact to facilitate transcriptional activation of a tissue-specific gene.

See companion CD for color Fig. 5

Activation of transcription of a tissue-specific gene requires a derepression process that takes the gene from a transcriptionally repressed state first to a potentiated state, and subsequently to a transcriptionally active state (*see* Fig. 5). The transcriptionally

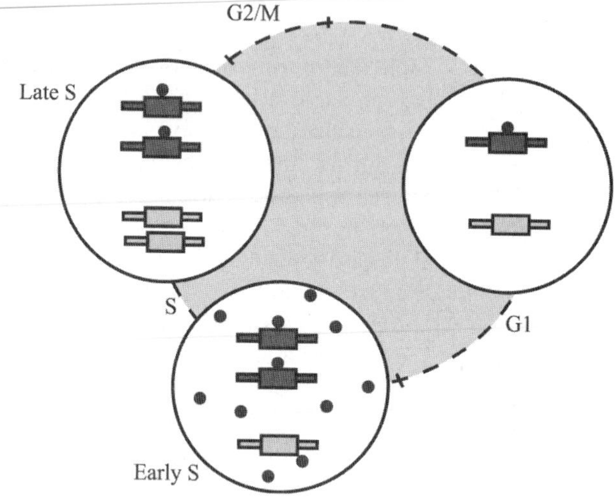

Fig. 4. Distinction of genes or alleles based on differential replication timing. The potential for differential timing of replication during S phase to maintain an epigenetic distinction between different genes or between different alleles of the same gene is depicted in this figure. The model is based on the concept that protein-DNA interactions become disrupted during DNA replication. These interactions must be re-established following replication. If certain proteins are present in limiting quantities, those genes or alleles that replicate earliest during S phase will gain preferential access to bind these proteins. In this way one gene or allele will bind a disproportionate quantity of a specific protein(s) and become distinguished from another gene or allele, even if both genes or alleles share similar protein-binding sequences. (Reproduced with permission from Simon, et al. [1999]).

repressed state of a gene is typically characterized by a condensed chromatin structure in which histones are deacetylated, DNA is hypermethylated and complexed with methylated DNA-binding proteins, and the gene is disassociated from the nuclear matrix and replicates relatively late during S phase. In the scheme depicted in Fig. 5, an initial tissue- and gene-specific demethylation event leads to a loss of binding of methylated DNA-binding proteins and their associated histone deacyetylase activity (*see* Fig. 5A,B). The histones then become acetylated and this facilitates a transition from the condensed, 30-nm chromatin structure to the decondensed, 10 nm structure, a process that has been termed *gene potentiation* (*see* Fig. 5B,C). Once the gene is in this open configuration, chromatin remodeling complexes can rearrange or displace nucleosomes to provide direct access for interaction between transcription factors and their cognate binding sites in the promoter region (*see* Fig. 5C–E). The bound transcription factors then attract the RNA polymerase complex to the proper transcriptional start site to initiate synthesis of RNA (*see* Fig. 5E–G).

It is possible that the initial demethylation event also facilitates, and/or is coincident with, enhanced association of the gene with the nuclear matrix. This could, in turn, provide enhanced proximity to replication machinery so that the gene would be subsequently replicated earlier during S phase. This could also provide more direct access to histone acetylases, chromatin remodeling complexes, transcription factors and RNA polymerase that may be embedded in, or associated with the matrix.

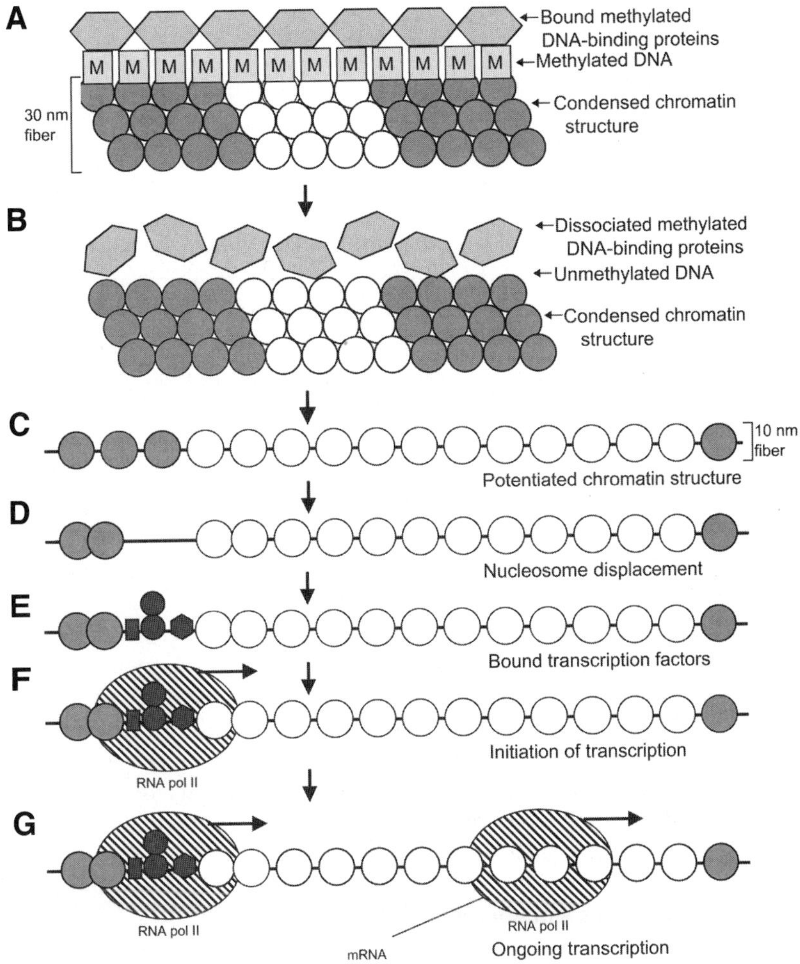

Fig. 5. Interactions among epigenetic mechanisms to regulate gene expression. Multiple epigenetic mechanisms contribute to regulation of transcriptional activity in mammals. An example of how this may occur is presented in this figure. **(A)** A fully repressed gene is often found to be hypermethylated, complexed with methylated-DNA binding proteins, comprised of deacetylated histones, and in a condensed chromatin structure characterized by a 30-nm structure that inhibits binding of transcription factors or RNA polymerase. **(B)** Derepression leading to transcriptional activation begins with demethylation of the gene, which in turn leads to dissociation of methylated-DNA binding proteins and acetylation of histones. **(C)** Potentiation of chromatin structure is marked by decondensation of the chromatin fiber from the 30 nm structure to the 10 nm *beads on a string* structure. **(D)** Displacement of nucleosomes creates an assayable DNase I hypersensitive site which marks the presence of naked DNA that is available for binding by transcription factors. **(E)** Binding of ubiquitous transcription factors to the core promoter region and tissue-specific transcription factors to enhancer regions attract the RNA polymerase II complex to the gene promoter. **(F)** Binding of the RNA polymerase II complex initiates transcription. **(G)** Ongoing transcription is characterized by sequential binding of multiple RNA polymerase II complexes to facilitate synthesis of multiple RNA transcripts. Open circles, nucleosomes within the transcribed portion of the gene; filled circles, nucleosomes between genes; squares containing Ms, DNA methylation; hexagons, methylated-DNA binding proteins; small filled hexagons, circles and rectangles, bound transcription factors; large, hatched oval, RNA polymerase II complex.

Epigenetics and Cloning

The critical role of epigenetic mechanisms governing gene regulation for normal mammalian development has recently come under particular scrutiny with the application of cloning of individuals by nuclear transplantation. In species that reproduce sexually, the union of male and female gametes at fertilization is the initial step in the development of a new offspring. Fusion of the haploid gametic genomes forms the diploid zygotic nucleus from which the genetic information required to direct the development of all subsequent cells of the embryo and fetus is derived. In both male and female mammals, gametogenesis is a complex process that includes epigenetic reprogramming processes that are unique to germ cells, and appear to contribute to preparing the gametic genomes to direct development of the ensuing embryo. When cloned mice are produced by transplantation of a somatic cell nucleus into an enucleated egg, the resulting zygotic nucleus is diploid, but it consists of two haploid genomes that have not undergone the reprogramming processes unique to gametogenesis. Presumably, reprogramming queues emanating from the ooplasm of the enulceated oocyte into which the somatic donor nucleus is transplanted are able to signal sufficient, rapid epigenetic reprogramming in the newly formed zygote.

Only a small proportion of embryos produced by *nuclear transplantation* (NT) develop to birth, and only a subset of these grow into fertile adults. Recent evidence has indicated that certain processes including X-chromosome inactivation and adjustment of telomere length appear to become properly reset in cloned mice. However, other epigenetic programs such as those affecting methylation patterns and expression of imprinted genes are often not properly reset and result in aberrant gene expression. Thus, proper epigenetic programming, which is typically manifest during gametogenesis, is indispensably required for normal mammalian development.

Interestingly, epigenetic reprogramming appears incomplete and/or unstable in cloned mice. If these mice are able to subsequently participate in natural breeding they produce offspring that appear relatively normal. Thus it appears that genetic and epigenetic programming is largely restored in the gametes of cloned mice by mechanisms that function uniquely in the germline. Inasmuch as the oocyte is a product of gametogenesis in the female, it is not surprising that it contains signaling factors that can potentially contribute to reprogramming of a transplanted somatic cell nucleus. However, those epigenetic mechanisms that normally function uniquely during spermatogenesis are not represented in a zygote produced by NT, and this deficiency may contribute to the very low success rate of full-term development of clones produced by NT.

Conclusions

As the human genome project nears its completion, the estimated number of genes in the mammalian genome has been reduced from an original concept of approx 100,000 genes to a revised estimate of approx 35,000 genes. However, even with this reduction, the challenge to each mammalian cell of correctly orchestrating the expression of these genes to facilitate the proper development and function of numerous different cell types remains a daunting task. It is therefore not surprising that mammals and other eukaryotes have evolved multiple mechanisms of gene regulation and that these mechanisms afford the cell multiple levels of control over gene expression. When considering the process of differential gene expression and the mechanisms which regulate this, it is important to bear in mind that there are various levels of control and that these are based on a combination of genetic and epigenetic mechanisms. A great deal of emphasis has been placed on the genetic mechanism of protein-DNA interactions between transcription factors and promoter binding sites for regulating gene expression. Although this mechanism is indeed critical to transcriptional regulation, it can only function if it is preceded by the proper functioning of the epigenetic mechanisms described in this chapter.

Glossary and Abbreviations

General

Cloning by Nuclear Transplantation (NT) The process of producing a genetically identical individual by transferring a diploid somatic nucleus into an enucleated egg.

Epigenetics The study of mitotically and/or meiotically heritable changes in gene function that cannot be explained by changes in primary DNA sequence.

Epigenetic Reprogramming The process by which epigenetic modifications are reversed or modified, especially during reproduction.

Gametogenesis The process by which germ cells differentiate to form the mature gametes, spermatozoa in males and ova in females.

Gene Expression Transcription and/or translation of a gene or gene product.

Genome One haploid complement of chromosomes.

Genomic Imprinting An epigenetic distinction of alleles in a parent-of-origin specific manner.

Germ Cells Those cells that give rise to the gametes and from which the genetic contribution to the subsequent generation is derived.

Housekeeping Gene A gene that is expressed in all or a significant majority of tissues or cell types.

Monoallelic Expression Expression of only one copy of a gene in a cell carrying two or more copies of the gene.

Replication Timing The time during S phase of the cell cycle at which a particular gene is replicated.

Semi-Conservative Replication of DNA The mechanism by which double-stranded DNA is replicated such that each new double helix includes one previously existing strand and one newly synthesized strand.

Tissue-Specific Gene A gene that is expressed in only a single tissue or cell type, or in only a subset of tissues or cell types.

X-Chromosome Inactivation Transcriptional silencing of an entire X chromosome used to compensate for differences in dosage of X-linked genes in XX and XY individuals.

Gene Expression

Coordinate Regulation The coordinated regulation of expression of more than one gene simultaneously.

Ectopic Gene Expression Expression of a tissue-specific gene in a tissue or cell type in which it is not normally expressed.

Promoter The region of a gene that regulates initiation of transcription.

Protein-DNA Interactions Binding of specific proteins (e.g. transcription factors) to specific sites in DNA.

RNA Polymerase The enzyme complex responsible for transcribing DNA to produce RNA.

Transcriptional Activation Initiation of transcription of a regulated gene.

Transcription Factors Proteins that bind to specific sequences in the gene promoter and regulate initiation of transcription.

DNA Methylation

CpG Island A region in mammalian DNA in which the representation of CpG dinucleotides is significantly greater than that found in the genome as a whole. Specifically, a region of > 100 base pairs in which the GC content is > 50% and the occurrence of CpG dinucleotides is > 60% of that predicted by random statistical occurrence.

De Novo Methylase An enzyme capable of adding methyl groups to both cytosines in a previously unmethylated CpG dinucleotide site in double-stranded DNA.

Demethylase Activity The active loss of methylation from both cytosines in a previously fully methylated CpG dinucleotide site in double-stranded DNA.

DNA Methylation A covalent modification of DNA produced by the addition of a methyl group to a cytosine base in mammalian DNA.

Fully Methylated DNA The presence of a methyl group on both cytosines in a CpG dinucleotide site in double-stranded DNA.

Hemimethylated DNA The presence of a methyl group on only one cytosines in a CpG dinucleotide site in double-stranded DNA.

Maintenance Methylase An enzyme capable of adding a methyl group to a cytosine in a hemimethylated CpG dinucleotide site in double-stranded DNA.

Methylated-DNA Binding Protein A protein that binds to DNA on the basis of the presence of methyl groups rather than on the basis of a specific base sequence.

Unmethylated DNA The absence of a methyl group on either cytosine in a CpG dinucleotide site in double-stranded DNA.

Chromatin

'Beads On A String' Structure The structure produced by the periodic presence of nucleosomes separated by a stretch of naked DNA in chromatin.

Boundary Elements Specific sequences in DNA that function to delimit DNA loop domains and/or to insulate one domain of DNA from a neighboring domain.

Chromatin DNA plus associated proteins.

Chromatin Composition The chemical status of chromatin that can be modified to include or exclude specific proteins or specific modifications to proteins (e.g. phosphorylation, acetylation, methylation).

Chromatin Structure The configuration of DNA plus associated proteins that can be relatively condensed to preclude transcription or relatively decondensed to facilitate transcription.

DNA or Chromosome Loop Domains Organization of genomic DNA into domains anchored at each end to the nuclear matrix.

Hyperacetylated Histones Histones, especially H4, that are predominantly acetylated.

Hypoacetylated Histones Histones that are predominantly unacetylated.

Histone Acetlyl Transferases (HATs) Enzymes responsible for acetylating histones.

Histone Deacetylases (HDACs) Enzymes responsible for deacetylating histones.

Matrix Attachment Regions (MARs) or Scaffold Attachment Regions (SARs) Specific sequences in DNA that bind to the nuclear matrix or scaffold either constitutively or facultatively.

Naked DNA DNA devoid of any associated proteins.

Nuclear Matrix A three-dimensional proteinaceous structure within the nucleus (aka the nuclear scaffold).

Nucleosomes Histone octamers found in chromatin.

Open or Potentiated Chromatin Chromatin that is decondensed such that it is accessible for transcription by RNA polymerase.

Suggested Readings

Introduction

Russo, E., Martienssen, R., and Riggs, A.D. (eds.) (1996) Epigenetic Mechanisms of Gene Regulation, Cold Spring Harbor Laboratory Press, Cold Spring Harbor, NY.

DNA Methylation

Ariel, M., Cedar, H., and McCarrey, J. R. (1994) Developmental changes in *Pgk-2* gene methylation during spermatogenesis in the mouse: Reprogramming occurs in epididymal spermatozoa, Nat. Genet. 7, 59–63.

Ben-Porath, I. and Cedar, H. (2000) Imprinting: focusing on the center, Curr. Op. Genet. Dev. 10, 550–554.

Bestor, T. H. (2000) The DNA methyltransferases of mammals, Hum. Mol. Genet. 9, 2395–2402.

Brandeis, M., Kafri, T., Ariel, M., Chaillet, J. R., McCarrey, J. R., Razin, A., and Cedar, H. (1993) The ontogeny of allele-specific methylation associated with imprinted genes in the mouse, EMBO J. 12, 3669–3677.

Gardiner-Garden, M. and Frommer, M. (1987) CpG islands in vertebrate genomes, J. Mol. Biol. 196, 261–282.

Hendrich, B. and Bird, A. (1998) Identification and characterization of a family of mammalian methyl-CpG binding proteins, Mol. Cell. Biol. 18, 6538–6547.

Jones, P. L., Veenstra, G. J., Wade, P. A., Vermaak, D., Kass, S. U., Landsberger, N., Strouboulis, J., and Wolffe, A. P. (1998) Methylated DNA and MeCP2 recruit histone deacetylase to repress transcription, Nat. Genet. 19, 187–189.

Kafri, T., Ariel, M., Shemer, R., Urven, L., McCarrey, J. R., Cedar, H., and Razin, A. (1992) Dynamics of gene specific DNA methylation in the mouse embryo and germ line, Genes Dev. 6, 705–714.

Nan, X., Tate, P., Li, E., and Bird, A. P. (1996) DNA methylation specifies chromosomal localization of MeCP2, Mol. Cell. Biol. 16, 414–421.

Ng, H-.H. and Bird, A. (1999) DNA methylation and chromatin modification, Curr. Op. Genet. Dev. 9, 158–163.

Ramsahoye, B. H., Biniszkiewicz, D., Lyko, F., Clarck, V., Bird, A. P., and Jaenisch, R. (2000) Non-CpG methylation is prevalent in embryonic stem cells and may be mediated by DNA methyltransferase 3a., Proc. Natl. Acad. Sci. USA 97, 5237–5242.

Riggs, A. D. and Porter, T. N. (1996) X-chromosome inactivation and epigenetic mechanisms, in: Epigenetic Mechanisms of Gene Regulation, (Russo, E., Martienssen, R., and Riggs, A.D., eds.) Cold Spring Harbor Laboratory Press, Cold Spring Harbor, NY, pp. 231–248.

Shemer, R. and Razin, A. (1996) Establishment of imprinted methylation patterns during development, in: Epigenetic Mechanisms of Gene Regulation, (Russo, E., Martienssen, R., and Riggs, A.D., eds.) Cold Spring Harbor Laboratory Press, Cold Spring Harbor, NY, pp. 215–230.

Tilghman, S. M. (1999) The sins of the fathers and mothers: genomic imprinting in mammalian development, Cell 96, 185–193.

Zhang, L. P., Stroud, J. C., Walter, C. A., Adrian, G. S., and McCarrey, J. R. (1998) A gene-specific promoter in transgenic mice directs testis-specific demethylation prior to transcriptional activation *in vivo*, Biol. Reprod. 59, 284–292.

Chromatin Structure and Composition

Carey, M. and Smale, S. T. (2000) Transcriptional regulation in eukaryotes, Cold Spring Harbor Laboratory Press, Cold Spring Harbor, NY, p. 640

Kramer, J. A., McCarrey, J. R., Djakiew, D., and Krawetz, S. A. (1998) Differentiation: The selective potentiation of chromatin domains, Development 9, 4749–4755.

Urnov, F. D. and Wolffe, A. P. (2001) Chromatin remodeling and transcriptional activation: the cast (in order of appearance), Oncogene 20, 2991–3006.

Varga-Weisz, P. D. and Becker, P. B. (1998) Chromatin-remodeling factors: machines that regulate? Curr. Op. Cell. Biol. 10, 346–353.

Wolffe, A. P. (1992) Chromatin, Academic Press, San Diego, CA, p. 213.

DNA Loop Domains and Association with the Nuclear Matrix

Bell, A. C., West, A. G., and Felsenfeld, G. (2001) Insulators and boundaries: versatile regulatory elements in the eukaryotic genome, Science 291, 447–450.

Klaus, A., McCarrey, J. R., Farkas, A., and Ward, W. S. (2001) Changes in DNA loop domain structure during spermatogenesis and embryogenesis, Biology of Reproduction 64, 1297–1306.

Mirkovitch, J., Mirault, M. E., and Laemmli, U. (1984) Organization of the higher-order chromatin loop: specific DNA attachment sites on nuclear scaffold, Cell 39, 223–232.

Sotolongo, B. and Ward, W. S. (2000) DNA loop domain organization: the three-dimensional genomic code, J. Cell. Biochem. Suppl. 35, 23–26.

Stein, G. S. and Berezney, R. (2000) 25 years of contributions to characterizing gene expression and replication within the three-dimensional context of nuclear architecture, Crit. Rev. Eukaryot. Gene. Expr. 10, v–vi.

Replication Timing

Goldman, M. A., Holmquist, G. P., Gray, M. C., Caston, L. A., and Nag, A. (1984) Replication timing of genes and middle repetitive sequences, Science 224, 686–692.

Hansen, R. S., Canfield, T. K., Lamb, M. M., Gartler, S. M., and Laird, C. D. (1993) Association of fragile X syndrome with delayed replication of the FMR1 gene, Cell 73, 1403–1409.

Kitsberg, D., Selig, S., Brandeis, M., Simon, I., Keshet, I., Driscoll, D. J., Nichols, R. D., and Cedar, H. (1993) Allele-specific replication timing of imprinted gene regions, Nature 364, 459–463.

Simon, I., Tanzen, T., Rubinoff, B., McCarrey, J., and Cedar, H. (1999) Asynchronous replication of imprinted genes is established in the gametes and maintained during development, Nature 401, 929–932.

Epigenetics and Cloning

Eggan, K., Akutsu, H., Hochedlinger, K., Rideout, III, W., Yanagimachi, R., and Jaenisch, R. (2000) X-chromosome inactivation in cloned mouse embryos, Science 290, 1578–1581.

Humpherys, D., Eggan, K., Akutsu, H., Hochedlinger, K., Rideout, 3rd, W. M., Biniszkiewicz, D., et al. (2001) Epigenetic instability in ES cells and cloned mice, Science 293, 95–97.

Krawetz, S. A., Kramer, J. A., and McCarrey, J. R. (1999) Reprogramming the male gamete genome: a window to successful gene therapy, Gene 234, 1–9.

Lanza, R. P., Cibelli, J. B., Blackwell, C., Cristofalo, V. J., Francis, M. K., Baerlocher, G. M., et al. (2000) Extension of cell life-span and telomere length in animals cloned from senescent somatic cells. Science. 28, 665–669.

Rideout, III, W. M., Eggan, K., and Jaenisch, R. (2001) Nuclear cloning and epigenetic reprogramming of the genome, Science 293, 1093–1098.

Wakayama, T., Perry, A. C. F., Zuccotti, M., Johnson, K. R., and Yanagimachi, R. (1998) Full-term development of mice from enucleated oocytes injected with cumulus cell nuclei, Nature 394, 369–374.

7 Gene Families and Evolution

Ben F. Koop

Introduction

Gene families refer to two or more genes that come from a common ancestral gene in which the individual members of the gene family may or may not have a similar function. The idea of gene families implicitly invokes a process in which an original gene exists, is duplicated and the resulting gene products evolve. The most common result of gene duplication is that mutation renders one of the products nonfunctional and in the absence of conserving natural selection, one of the members becomes no longer recognizable. Gene families may be clustered or dispersed and may exchange with each other through the mechanisms of gene conversion or unequal crossover. Therefore understanding the processes of molecular evolution are essential to understanding what gene families are, where they came from and what their function might be. In a sense, duplicate genes allow for more evolutionary potential. At first glance this could be beneficial; if one gene incurred a lethal mutation the other gene simply takes over, there is some protection from mutation based on redundancy. Having two identical genes could result in twice as much product; this may or may not be beneficial in a cell where the integration of thousands of gene products must be coordinated and slight concentration differences can alter biochemical pathways.

Antiquity of Gene Families

Almost all genes belong to gene families. Evidence from sequence or structural similarity indicates that all or at least large parts of genes came from ancestral genes. Analysis of the human genome has shown that over half of the human genome is comprised of clearly identifiable repeated sequences. Although much of this is owing to self-replicating transposons, i.e., mobile genetic elements, over 5 % of the genome has been involved in large segmental duplications in the past 30 million years. If we look further into the past using evidence from protein similarity of three or more genes that occur in close proximity on two different chromosomes, we find over 10,310 gene pairs in 1,077 duplicated blocks contain 3,522 distinct genes. Because our observations are based on genes that retain similarity, only a small fraction of the ancient duplications can be detected by current means. What is clearly evident is that a very large part of the human genome has come from duplications and that duplication is a very frequent event.

With the evidence showing that gene duplication plays a major role in modern genomes, the question is where did it all begin? How many genes did life start with? Various estimates of the minimal gene set suggest that as few as 250 genes could provide the minimal number of components necessary to sustain independent life. The number of genes in mycoplasms ranges from 500–1500 genes and in bacteria from 1000–4000 genes. Yeast (*S. cervisiae*) has ~ 6000 genes, worms (*C. elegans*) have ~ 18,000 genes, the fruit fly (*D. melangaster*) has ~13,000 genes, a plant, *Arabidopsis*, has 26,000 genes, and humans have at least 30,000 genes. The difference between 250 or 1000 genes and 30,000–40,000 genes is only two orders of magnitude yet the difference in the complexity of life forms seems far greater than could be explained by a simple gene count. Certainly with the increased number of genes comes the opportunity for more complexity in terms of gene interaction. But can synergy alone explain the differences in morphological complexity? Partial explanations invoke more complex differential splicing to account for a higher proportional number of protein products stemming from only 30,000 genes, but one wonders if this observation is merely an artifact of the few numbers of whole genomes available to us.

Origins

Gene duplications can come from a variety of sources including whole or partial genome duplication. Polyploidy results from a failure of chromosome segregation during the cell division of gametes. The most distinguishing feature of polyploidy is that it effects all of the genes simultaneously so that the relative proportion of genes within cells remains the same. Among plants and invertebrates, polyploidy is quite common and in many species it has little effect on phenotype. Ohno has argued that whole genome duplications are the most important events in evolution yet others have suggested that polyploidy has no effect on phenotype. More recent discussions acknowledge the potential that polypoidy brings to gene family evolution but also appreciate the role of complexity of gene interactions in determining the impact of whole genome duplications.

In vertebrates, polyploidy is quite rare. Most of the 188 examples of genome duplication have been found in amphibians, reptiles and some fish (salmon). In these instances, polyploid species have undergone dramatic changes to reestablish diploidy through chromosome loss, mutation, and rearrangement. Tetraploid genomes have no trouble going through cell division as long as chromosomes remain very similar. But as mutations arise and duplicated chromosomes begin to differ, cell division can no longer insure equal division of genetic material to germ cells and severe imbalances can occur during chromosomal segregation. The initial transition phase from tetraploid to diploid results in huge losses of gametes and developing young. In salmon it is estimated that approx 50 million years after a polypoid change, only 53% of duplicate genes remain. The result of duplication by whole or partial genomes can result in large changes in gene number but there are major difficulties in cell replication that must be overcome.

The rapid increase in genome size through polyploid events has been used to explain the increased size of mammalian genomes. Ohno suggested that two rounds of genome duplication occurred early in vertebrate history. This may explain the Cambrian explosion in which vertebrates appeared in paleontological records quite rapidly. Evidence for two rounds of genome duplication comes from vertebrates having four times the number of developmental regulator genes (*Hox*, *Cdx*, *MyoD*,

60A, Notch, elav, btd/SP...) as *Drosophila*. While this concept has become very popular in the literature, recent studies examining expected phylogenetic relationships among genes have called into question whether the number of genes was a result of two genome-wide duplications or simply a result of ongoing, frequent genome segment duplications. While the primary support for quadruplicated genomes comes primarily from chromosomes 2, 7, 12, and 17, which contain the *Hox* gene clusters, a more extensive examination of the number of homologous genes within humans as compared to genes within *Drosophila* was unable to resolve the question of whether two whole genome duplications gave rise to modern vertebrate genomes.

Mechanisms

Duplication of large blocks of DNA can not be explained by chromosomal segregation errors. Mechanisms of large segmental duplication are varied and the role of transposable elements in gene duplication is often cited as a primary cause. Transposable elements and in particular retrotransposable elements are highly repetitive dispersed sequences that can replicate independent of nuclear division. In humans they comprise over 45% of the genome. While there are a number of instances where retroposons have been found at the junctions of duplicated segments, there are also a number instances where they have not. To understand why gene segment duplications appear common, it is perhaps important to look at the DNA molecule itself. DNA is composed of duplex strands held together by hydrogen bonds whose strength varies. In a fluid environment, various local salt concentrations, temperatures, physical torsion forces and local nucleotide compositions (e.g., levels of G + C, simple repeats) can result in temporary separation of strands of duplex DNA. If similar sequences are found in the same physical location, unstable heterologous duplexes can form. Heterologous pairing or single-strand conditions are prone to stress and breakage. These situations are repaired correctly in the vast majority of cases but occasionally mistakes are made that result in new gene neighbors. The possibility of error is particularly high during cell division when DNA is being replicated and when similar sequences are in close proximity. The potential impact of highly repeated transposable elements as a destabilizing factor and a potential focal point for rearrangement becomes clear in our genome. It is therefore somewhat surprising to find that many of the duplications are not flanked by repeat elements. What is clear is that duplication involves local chromosome instability that results in breakage and aberrant repair of the ends.

Factors that promote segmental duplication include close proximity and high sequence similarity. It then follows that duplications resulting in adjacent genes would be more susceptible to further changes than duplications resulting in dispersed genes. Furthermore, adjacent duplications create far fewer chromosomal segregation problems during cell division and therefore should be found more often in the genome. What is observed is that large segmental duplications involving multiple genes are dispersed throughout the genome whereas duplications involving single gene segments are both dispersed and in close proximity. There are many instances of clustered gene families (globins, *Hox*, Ig, Tcr, Mhc, and rRNA).

Among tandemly duplicated gene segments there is the possibility of extensive gene conversion and unequal crossing over (*see* Fig. 1). The later is the predominant mode of change. Unequal crossing over between dispersed genes results in extreme difficulties in chromosomal segregation in cell division but gene conversion does not.

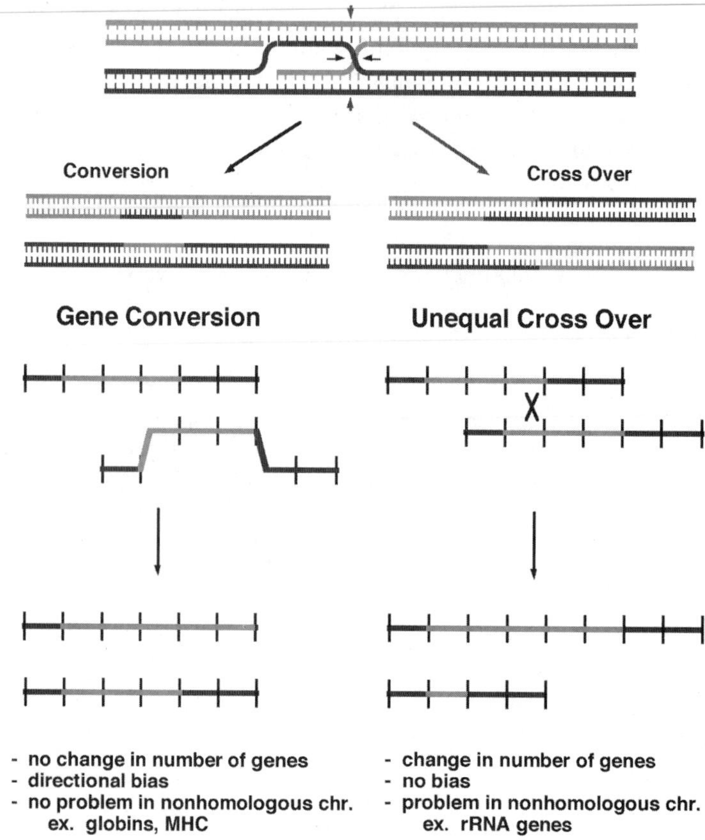

Fig. 1. Gene conversion and unequal crossing over mechanisms of communication among gene family members. The arrows indicate possible break points that would result in either conversion or crossover results.

Gene conversion replaces the sequence of one family member with the sequences of another close (>90% similarity) member but it does not effect the total number of genes. Gene conversion requires DNA strand breakage followed by strand migration to a similar gene and the formation of a heteroduplex. DNA repair mechanisms then repair differences in the heteroduplex often using one strand corresponding to the unaffected homologous chromosome as a template. The heteroduplex then resolves and may go back to its original location carrying with it DNA changes. Heteroduplex formation is often temporary and most often occurs between alleles of the same gene though occasionally it may affect paralogous genes in which more than 100 bases are greater than 95% similar. Depending on the resolution of the heteroduplex and biases in mismatch repair, adjacent base differences may both reflect one or the other parental strand, or they may reflect a combination of parental strands. The end result is that the total genetic variation is reduced but a particular gene may increase its number of alleles. Genetic variation at one gene can increase over a single conversion event, but over multiple conversion events variation is reduced.

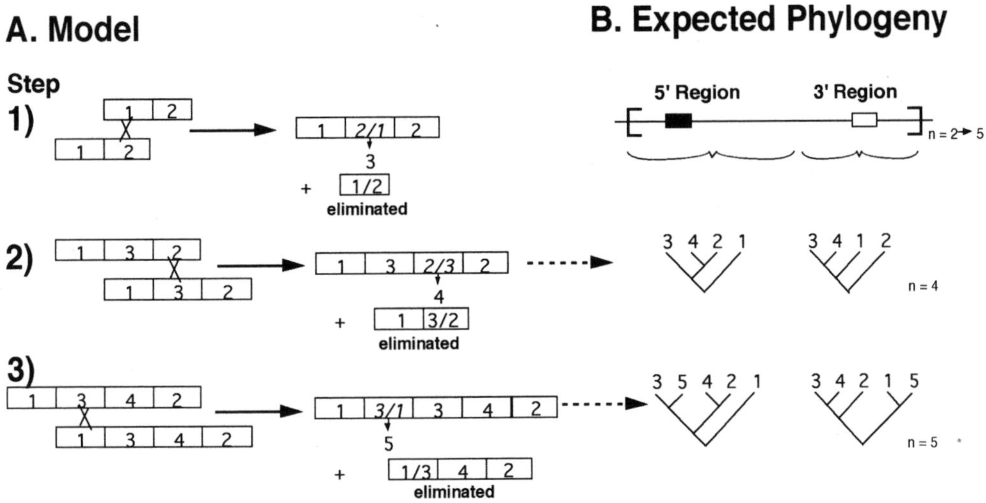

Fig. 2. Unequal crossing over between tandemly arrayed gene family members. This model **(A)** assumes a break point near the middle of the duplicated segments. The expected phylogeny **(B)** represent sequence relationships between the 5' and 3' regions of the duplicated gene segments.

The resolution of heterduplexes formed from the invasion of a DNA strand from one gene segment into the duplex of a similar, adjacent duplicate can also result in unequal crossing over. Unequal crossing over changes the number of genes. For example, in a tandem arrangement, unequal crossing over results in one chromosome with one duplicate and the other chromosome with three duplicates where the front and the back parts of the single duplicate and the middle duplicate of the triplicated segment reflect different origins. Figure 2, shows three successive unequal crossing-over events and shows the expected phylogenetic relationships of the front (5') and back (3') parts of the gene. It is evident from the final trees for the 5' and 3' parts of a tandemly arrayed gene segment that it is possible to describe some of the major, more recent evolutionary events that have occurred. Because information is lost due to the fixation of one of the cross over products in each population, it may never be possible to obtain a complete historical picture. But we can see in examples from the literature that unequal crossing over is the major factor in clustered gene families.

Variation

Genetic variation increases when the number of duplicates increases but it is decreased when the number of duplicates decreases. It is important to remember several tenets of unequal crossing over. First, the ultimate fate of duplicates undergoing multiple unequal crossing overs is to return to a single copy unless selection maintains multiple copies. Second, while the overall variation may increase over a single event, the result over multiple expansions and deletions is homogenization of duplicates (example rRNA genes). Third, unequal crossing over between dispersed gene segments often results in fatal problems in cell division. Lastly, unequal crossing over is the predominant mechanism that increases or decreases the number of gene family members in clusters. It appears that the factors that promote duplication include proximity, high similarity, larger numbers of existing duplicates and internal sequences that are prone to breakage. Given these factors, it is perhaps surprising that we do not see more evidence of repetitive elements playing a larger role in gene duplication. At the same time it becomes easy to see the complex evolution and interactions among both dispersed and clustered gene families.

Genes and Domains

Duplication can involve very large stretches of DNA, whole genes or even parts of genes. Of 1077 duplication blocks containing three or more genes in the human genome, 159 contained 3 genes, 137 contained 4 genes, and 781 contained five or more genes. At the same time we often see clusters of gene family members. This indicates that duplications often involve one gene or even parts of genes. Clearly the mechanisms of duplication outlined earlier play a major role at all levels of gene family evolution. However, it is important to remember that the events that are most evident are those that are fairly recent or those that involve conserved genes. Sequence similarity for older duplications of noncoding DNA rapidly fades. It is our focus on function that draws us to study genes. As mentioned, several genes within larger segments can be duplicated but perhaps just as interesting, parts of genes (introns and groups of introns) can be duplicated. This is particularly interesting because genes are composed of functional domains. Remarkably, there may be fewer than 1000 classifications in existence. Domains can be mixed, matched, duplicated and modified to provide novel functions within genes as well as between genes. Only 94 of the 1278 protein families in our genome appear to be specific to vertebrates. That may be an overestimate resulting from our inability to recognize similarity. It appears that the 30,000-plus genes in the human genome are not novel but simply products of duplications and mixing and matching of existing genes and domains to create new genes and new functions.

Species Evolution and Gene Evolution

The study of gene evolution is incomplete without the study of species evolution. Gene evolution and species evolution is not the same but knowledge of one greatly benefits our knowledge of the other. Modern species are the result of a dense network of transient species that occasionally give rise to other species. Using paleontological records as well as morphological, physiological, and developmental studies of extant and extinct life forms we are able to trace some of the origins of modern species. But numerous gaps in our understanding remain. Gene evolution can occur within a species but when a speciation event occurs, gene evolution within each new lineage is independent of gene evolution in other lineages. For example, gene evolution within humans is independent of gene evolution within chimpanzees. To illustrate this point, Fig. 3A shows a gene duplication in a common ancestor of species A and B followed by a speciation event and separate A and B lineages. Below Fig. 3A is the corresponding gene phylogenetic tree. Note that the timing of speciation events can be used to time major events in gene evolution. In Fig. 3A, gene duplication occurred before the speciation event. In Fig. 3B, a more complex gene evolution is shown. Within each species one of the genes has been eliminated and the other has been duplicated so that each species has two genes, which appear to have arisen after the speciation event.

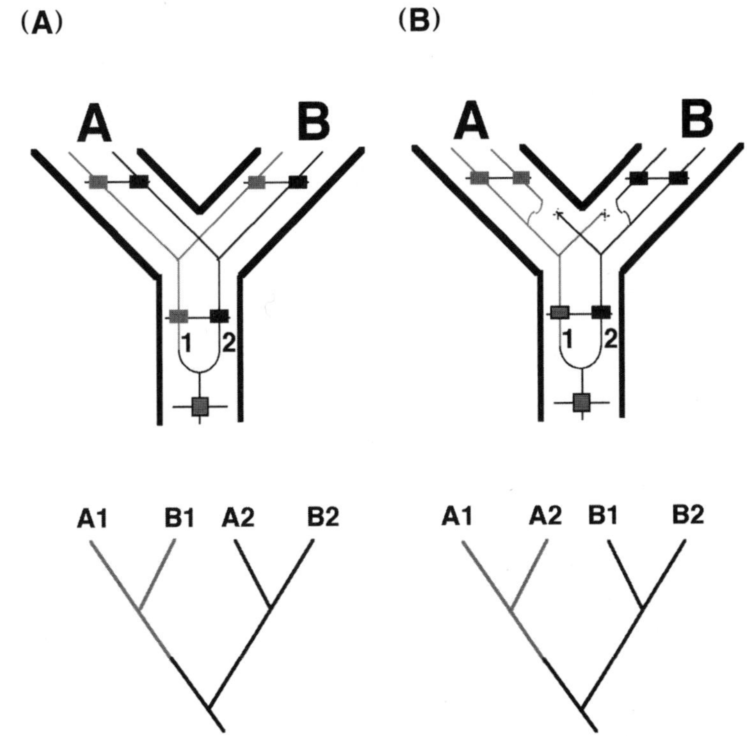

Fig. 3. Species evolution (in bold outline) and gene evolution (light lines). **(A)** Shows a gene duplication in a common ancestor of species A and B followed by a speciation event and separate A and B lineages. **(B)** A more complex gene evolution is shown. Within each species one of the genes has been eliminated and the other has been duplicated so that each species has two genes, which appear to have arisen after the speciation event.

While many other scenarios can occur, these two illustrations show how even in relatively simple cases, one must be cautious when interpreting gene trees. A number of studies have used these methods to identify new gene family members (Goodman et al., 1975). Slightom et al. (1987) was one of the first to use combined gene and species studies to examine genetic mechanisms of change. What is clear is that the use of both gene trees and species trees can be a very powerful method of studying species evolution and gene evolution.

Examples

The globin gene family offers one of the most studied and widely discussed examples of gene family evolution. Globin proteins function to transport oxygen and are found in bacterial, plant and animal kingdoms. In vertebrates, a series of gene duplications (*see* Fig. 4) correspond to major events in the evolution of man. A monomeric globin gene duplicated 600–800 million years ago to give rise to myoglobin (functional in muscle) and hemoglobin (functional in blood). 450–500 million years ago another duplication gave rise to an α form and a $\alpha\beta$ form. About this same time hemoglobin changed from a monomeric form to a tetrameric form (2α subunits and 2β subunits),

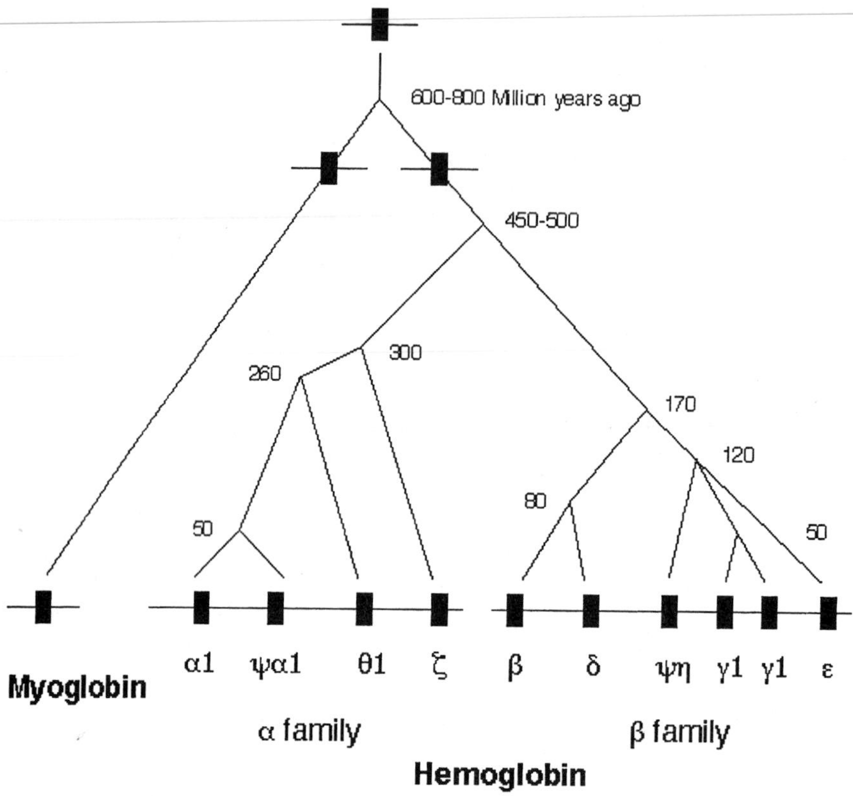

Fig. 4. Vertebrate globin evolution.

which Permitted oxygen transport in a much broader range of physiological conditions. The time frame for this event is supported by molecular clock estimates and by the fact that fish, amphibians, birds, and mammals all have a tetrameric hemoglobin with 2α and 2 β subunits. Over the next several hundred million years homeothermy evolved. Prior to the separation of mammals and marsupials (~150 million years ago), the β gene duplicated and gave rise to a form (ε) that is only found expressed in embryo's and a form (β) that is expressed in adults. Subsequent to the separation of marsupials and true mammals (eutherians), the embryonic form again duplicated into three separate genes. At this same time, major changes in the placenta made it possible to *hatch* eggs inside the body and allow for prolonged development prior to birth. In most eutherians there are also two adult forms (δ and β). In primates as well as cows (artiodactyls) the γ gene is found expressed in juveniles. In the α lineage, a similar chain of events occurred giving rise to embryonically expressed genes and genes expressed in the adult. What is clear from the study of globin gene evolution is that duplication allowed subsequent specialization, which in turn allowed for greater physiological complexity within species. The study of globin gene evolution within and between species also provided evidence for mechanisms of change which helps us to understand several globin-related diseases (thalasemia).

Over the past three decades, many other gene families have been studied and in each case these studies have provided important information about the numbers of gene family members, distribution, and functional specialization as well as information about the rates, modes, and mechanisms of change within each family. There is a tremendously diverse array of gene families with their own story. Some of the gene families such as the immunoglobulin super gene family incorporate evolutionary mechanisms of change into their function. In T-cell receptor genes, recombination, and alternative splicing of up to a hundred different gene family members results in the production of up to 10^{15} different receptors. This capability greatly facilitates the ability of T-cell receptors to recognize foreign proteins in the body and is a critical component in the overall function of the immune system. The rRNA genes also incorporate mechanisms of change into their overall functionality. In humans ~ 300 tandemly arrayed rRNA genes undergo extensive unequal crossing over to maintain several hundred nearly identical genes. In most cases, duplication of genes results in new and better control of physiology, growth, and development.

Significance

Evolutionary biologists have suggested that gene duplication followed by modification is the most important mechanism for generating new genes and biochemical processes. This has made it possible to evolve complex organisms from primitive ones. Based on traditional models, once duplications occur, one of the two genes is redundant and thus freed from functional constraints. All mutations, even missense or nonsense mutations, occurring in a redundant gene will be neutral unless by chance a mutation or combination of mutations results in a modified gene with some novel function. There are problems with this model because both gene products may still be subject to selection. Altered gene duplicates often result in products that can compete with each other for limited cis-acting promoter/enhancer molecules, or can produce altered products that can interfer with biochemical processes and molecular interactions. Furthermore there are examples (primates, opsins) where alternative alleles code for different functions and when gene duplication occurs, both functions are separated and free to be independently expressed (e.g., primate opsin genes resulting in bicolor versus tricolor vision). While there are a number of cases where bifunctionality precedes gene duplication, the duplication process itself is more dependent on factors such as the number of existing gene family members, proximity, similarity, and internal sequence fragile sites. Since duplications can involve many different genes or no genes at all, it is unlikely that bifunctionality precedes most duplications but it certainly affects the rate at which duplications survive and are fixed in populations. Duplication, rearrangement, and mutation of genes and domains are the critical forces in the evolution of gene families. The diverse affects of gene duplications offers a tremendous opportunity for diversification of gene function and is essential when evolving from a more generalized function to more specialized functions. Gene families have made it possible to evolve complex organisms from primitive organisms.

Suggested Readings

Baltimore, D. (2001) Our genome unveiled, Nature 409, 814–816.

Claverie, J.-M. (2001) What if there are only 30,000 human genes?, Science 291, 1255–1257.

Graur, D. and Li, W.-H. (2000) Fundamentals of Molecular Evolution, 2nd ed., Sinauer Associates, Inc., Sunderland, MA.

Goodman, M., Moore, G. W., Matsuda, G. (1975) Darwinian evolution in the genealogy of hemoglobin, Nature 253, 603–608.

Hughes, A. L. (1999) Adaptive Evolution of Genes and Genomes, Oxford University Press, New York, NY.

International Human Genome Sequencing Consortium (2001) Initial sequencing and analysis of the human genome, Nature 409, 890–921.

Lewin, B. (2000) Genes VII, Oxford University Press, New York, NY.

Otto, S. P., Whitton, J. (2000) Polyploid incidence and evolution, Annu. Rev. Genet. 34, 401–437.

Sankoff, D. and Nadeau, J. H. (eds.) (2000) Comparative Genomics, Kluwer Academic Press, Dordrecht, The Netherlands.

Slightom, J. L., Theissen, T., Koop, B. F., and Goodman, M. (1987) Orangutan fetal globin genes: nucleotide sequences reveal multiple gene conversions during hominid phylogeny, J. Biol. Chem. 262, 7472–7483.

Venter, J. C., Adams, M. D., Myers, E. W., Li, P. W., Mural, R. J, Sutton, G. G., et. al. (2001) The sequence of the human genome, Science 291, 1304–1351.

8 Repetitive DNA
Detection, Annotation, and Analysis

Jerzy Jurka

Introduction

Eukaryotic genomes are composed primarily of nonprotein-coding DNA. The most actively studied portion of this DNA is called *repetitive DNA*, which is produced in multiple copies by a variety of mechanisms. Repetitive DNA represents the most recent addition to nonprotein coding DNA and is expected to hold important clues to the origin and evolution of genomic DNA. There are good reasons to believe that contemporary mechanisms underlying the origin and evolution of repetitive DNA are essentially the same as mechanisms that generated other nonprotein-coding sequences in the distant past.

Repetitive DNA began surfacing in unprecedented detail as soon as critical mass of human sequence data permitted comparative analyses. This set the stage for a new era of repeat studies dominated by computer-assisted sequence comparisons. Currently, 42% of the human genome is recognizable as being derived from repetitive DNA. This proportion may vary from species to species in a seemingly arbitrary manner and the exact reasons why some eukaryotic species preserve more DNA than others are not well understood.

Studies of repetitive DNA are important not only per se, but also in the context of genome biology, including its structure, stability, and evolution. Repeats often obscure proteins and other regions of biological significance and for this reason they need to be identified and filtered out of the sequence data to facilitate such studies. Identification of repeats is also necessary for probe and primer design in DNA-DNA hybridization and polymerase chain reaction (PCR) studies, respectively. Inevitably, they are increasingly being studied in various biological contexts including but not limited to phylogenetic analysis, population studies, gene polymorphism, and chromosomal organization.

Simple Sequence Repeats (SSRs)

There are two basic classes of repetitive DNA sequences: 1) those expanded spontaneously on-site; and 2) those transposed from somewhere else as copies of transposable elements (TEs). These two classes are not totally independent because TEs can initiate or stimulate on-site expansion of repetitive DNA. The most common repeats generated on site are tandem repeats, often referred to as simple sequence repeats or

SSRs. Typically, tandem repeats with a unit size of 10 bp or less are referred to as *microsatellites*. Tandem repeats with a unit size over 10 bp are called *minisatellites*. There is a significant *twilight zone* between micro- and minisatellites, usually applicable to repeats with unit size 7–14 bp, which is listed in either category in the scientific literature.

The number of units, i.e., overall length of micro- and minisatellites, can vary from generation to generation and this property makes them very useful in studies of sequence polymorphism in eukaryotic populations. Growing evidence indicates that micro- and minisatellite expansion occurs by different mechanisms: the former mostly due to *polymerase slippage*, and the latter due to an illegitimate recombination process stimulated by double-stranded breaks. Tandem repeats are often transformed to a cryptically simple DNA composed of various sequence motifs rearranged and often obscured by mutations. Tandemly repeated sequences include satellite DNA. Satellites are primarily located in centromeres, whereas other tandem repeats tend to be interspersed within genomic DNA. Like other tandem repeats, satellites are quite variable and even closely related species may carry completely unrelated satellites. Satellite variability may be fueled by mechanisms similar to those involved in minisatellite variability.

Transposable Elements (TEs)

The major source of *interspersed repetitive DNA* are transposable elements (TEs). There are two major classes of TEs in the eukaryotic organisms: class 1, retro-elements; class 2, DNA transposons; including *rolling-circle* transposons, which was recently discovered in plants and nematodes (*see* Fig. 1).

Retroelements include long interspersed nuclear elements (LINEs) and elements related to retroviruses, including some *domesticated* endogenous retroviruses. All retroelements use reverse transcriptase to copy their RNA to DNA as a part of their reproduction process. LINEs generate a variety of retropseudogenes including SINE elements.

In the case of mammalian LINE1 (L1) element, reverse transcription is initiated (primed) by a reverse trancriptase-generated nick in host DNA. A second nick is generated on the opposite strand leading to target site duplication (TSD) where the duplicated target is represented by a short, ~15 bp long DNA fragment delimited by the nicks. The final integration is probably completed by the host replication system. Unlike LINEs, retroviruses appear to be inserted in a separate step after they are reverse transcribed to DNA. There is no specific mechanism for excision of retroelements although integrated retroviruses can be deleted due to homologous recombination between long terminal repeats (LTRs), leaving behind a single (solo) LTR repeat.

DNA transposons (class 2) encode transposase, which is involved in insertion and excision of these elements to and from host DNA. The transposase recognizes terminal inverted repeats (TIRs). Replication of a DNA transposon is accomplished by the host replication system. If excision does not occur, the transposon becomes permanently integrated usually as an inactive repetitive element.

The third class of eukaryotic TEs is represented by complex rolling-circle (RC) transposons. In addition to a cleavage and replication transposase, RC transposons use enzymes such as helicases and the single-strand DNA-binding protein, probably adopted from the host. RC transposons integrate at AT dinucleotides without target site duplication.

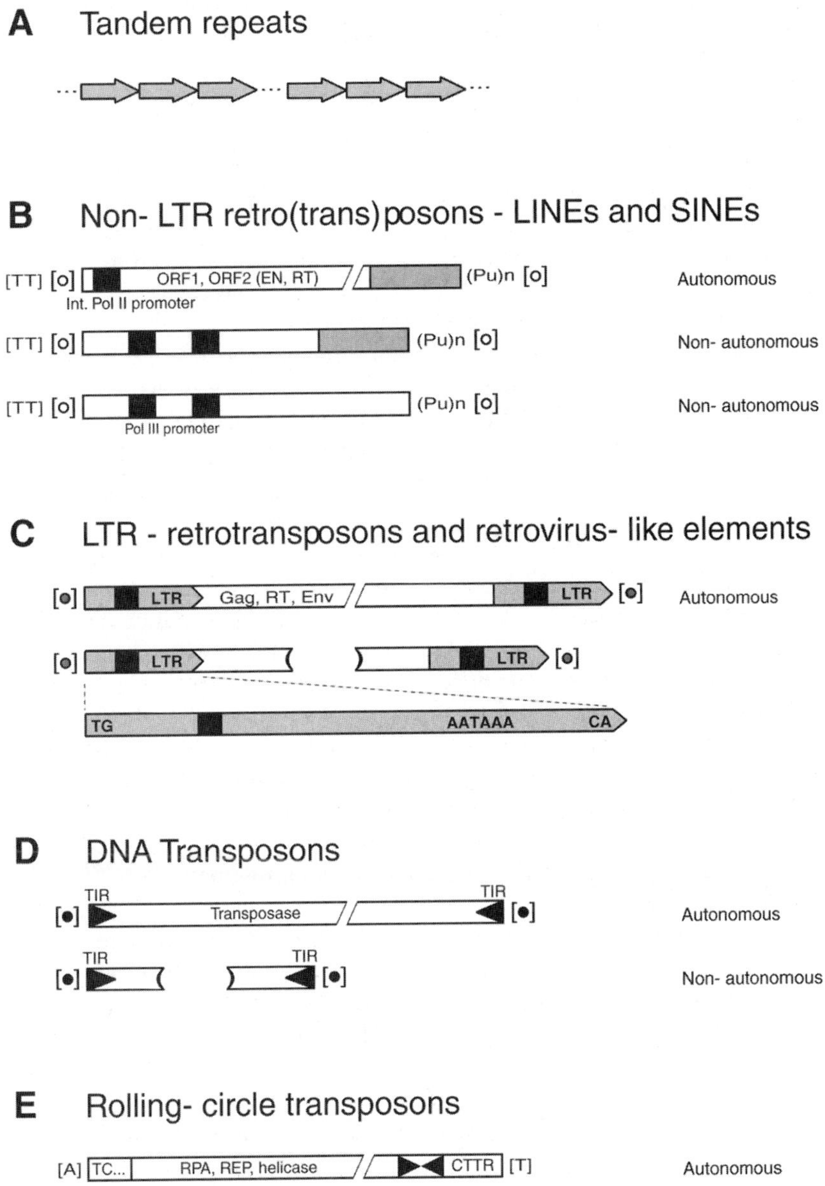

Fig. 1. Basic categories and biological characteristics of repetitive elements. **(A)** Tandem repeats including minisatellites, microsatellites, and satellites. **(B)** Structure of LINE (autonomous) and SINE (nonautonomous) retroelements; black boxes show transcription promoters and (Pu)n indicate purine (A or G) tails. Target site duplications (TSDs) and other target components throughout the figure are indicated by brackets [ ]. **(C)** LTR-retrotransposons and retrovirus-like elements. Characteristic sequence features of LTRs: 5′ TG, 3′ CA, and polyadenylation signal AATAAA are indicated in the enlarged long terminal repeat. **(D)** Autonomous and nonautonomous DNA transposons. Black triangles at both ends indicate terminal inverted repeats (TIRs). **(E)** Autonomous and nonautonomous rolling-circle transposons. Characteristic 5′ TC, 3′ CTTR and hairpin-like structures (inverted black triangles) are indicated.

All classes of autonomous TEs in eukaryotes are associated with nonautonomous elements that do not encode any active enzymes. They depend on their autonomus relatives for reproduction and insertion into the genome. In this context, autonomous TEs can play a role of *mutator genes* that must be restricted or tightly controlled by the host. In general, only few active TEs at a time appear to find favorable circumstances for proliferation in any given population. They produce a discrete *genomic fossil record* of repetitive families/subfamilies derived from a limited number of actively expressed source genes or active TEs. Both autonomous and nonautonomous elements have their actively expressed source genes. Source genes can be active for millions of years but are eventually replaced by their variants or become extinct. Interestingly, copies of nonautonomous elements, particularly short ones, tend to predominate over the autonomous ones.

It appears that all eukaryotic genomes integrated a patchwork of TEs inserted at different times from the beginning of their evolutionary history. As indicated earlier, the human genome is among the best repositories of repetitive DNA going back over 200 million years. Unlike humans, all repetitive elements in plants and insects appear to be relatively young. This may indicate a rapid turnover of TEs in plant and insect genomes.

Reference Collections of Repeats

A practical approach to identifying and masking repetitive DNA began with creating comprehensive reference collections of repeats that could be compared against newly sequenced DNA. Prior to whole-genome sequencing projects, only human sequences were available in sufficient quantities to reveal a significant variety of human repeat families. These studies laid the foundation for the first collection of 53 representative human repeats. It was followed by collections of other mammalian repeats and placed in a database named *Repbase*. Since 1997, Repbase was succeeded by *Repbase Update* and over time it included repeats from other eukaryotic species as they became available. Originally, Repbase Update (RU) played the role of a database and an electronic journal releasing newly discovered repetitive families that were not published elsewhere. As of September 2001, all previously unreported families are first published in a peer-reviewed electronic journal entitled Repbase Reports (*see* Website: http://www.girinst.org), and subsequently released to RU. This arrangement is designed to facilitate proper referencing and documentation of the original data deposited in RU.

Current Content of Repbase Update

The current release of RU contains around 2400 unique entries from all sequenced eukaryotic species. The primary release of RU is in the EMBL format. A sample entry is shown in Fig. 2. Simultaneously, RU is also released in fasta format (without annotations) as well as in preprocessed, software-specific RepeatMasker format. The major files in the current release include repeats from humans (humrep.ref), rodents (rodrep.ref), other mammals (mamrep.ref), Zebrafish (zebrep.ref), other vertebrates (vrtrep.ref), *Caenorhabditis elegans* (celrep.ref), *Drosophila melanogaster* (drorep.ref), other animals (invrep.ref), *Arabidopsis thaliana* (athrep.ref), other plants and fungi (plnrep.ref), and simple repeats (simple.ref). Some sections can be merged together, pending specific needs. For example, the reference collection of plant repeats used by CENSOR server (*see* Website: http://www.girinst.org) includes two RU files: athrep.ref and plnrep.ref.

```
ID   LOOPER    repbase; DNA; HUM; 1460 BP.
CC   LOOPER DNA
XX
AC   ;
XX
DT   01-APR-1998 (Rel. 6.4, Created)
DT   13-MAY-1999 (Rel. 6.9, Last updated, Version 2)
XX
DE   Molecular fossils of autonomous DNA transposon - a consensus sequence.
XX
KW   Putative autonomous DNA transposon; TTAA-superfamily; LOOPER.
XX
OS   Homo sapiens (consensus)
CC   consensus
OC   Eukaryota; Animalia; Metazoa; Chordata; Vertebrata; Mammalia;
OC   Theria; Eutheria; Primates; Haplorhini; Catarrhini; Hominidae.
XX
RN   [ 1]
RP   1-1460
RC   [ 1]  (bases 1 to 1460)
RA   Kapitonov V.V., Jurka J.
RT   ;
RL   Direct submission (March 31, 1998)
XX
RN   [ 2]
RP   1-1460
RC   [ 2]  (bases 1 to 1460)
RA   Kapitonov V.V., Jurka J.
RT   ;
RL   Direct submission (May 12, 1999)
XX
CC   LOOPER encodes 278 aa-long  protein (position 480-1313) similar
CC   to the transposase-like protein encoded by ORF1 in IFP2
CC   (PiggyBac) DNA transposon from cabbage looper (see IFP2 transposon
CC   in the invrep.ref section of Repbase).
CC   There are about 200-500 copies of LOOPER preserved in the human
CC   genome. Most of them are severely damaged by mutations since LOOPER
CC   is relatively old element. There is 80% average nucleotide identity
CC   between LOOPER's copies and the consensus sequence.
CC   LOOPER belongs to the TTAA superfamily of DNA transposons in mammals.
CC   Hallmarks of this superfamily are TTAA target site duplication and
CC   short terminal inverted repeats, including 5'- and 3'-terminal
CC   CCY and GGG, respectively.
CC   Activity of the protein encoded by the LOOPER-like elements could be
CC   related to multiple transpositions of non-autonomous elements MER75
CC   and MER85 identified recently in the human genome.
CC   The consensus sequence may be incomplete.
XX
CC   [ 2] (Consensus)
XX
SQ   Sequence 1460 BP; 521 A; 199 C; 240 G; 465 T; 35 other;
     ccttyagaay aycatcaggt cttgnannnn nttttatttt tgagttttta httgtaacta        60
     ...
//
```

Fig. 2. This is a sample entry from RU that describes a new class of human DNA transposons, related to *PiggyBac* transposon in cabbage looper. Its sequence has been reconstructed from the genomic fossil record (*see* subheading "Identification, Reconstruction and Classification of New TEs"). The entry includes: a uniqe sequence identification name (ID); definition (DE), date of creation and of the latest update (DT), keywords (KW), biological classification of the species in which it was found (OC), reference (RN, RA, RL), basic commentary (CC), source of the sequence data (DR), and base composition of the consensus sequence (SQ). This particular consensus sequence led to identification of a PiggyBac-like gene in the human genome.

Sequences deposited in RU continue to be updated over time and the record of modified entries is preserved in appendix files accompanying the active files. For example, changes in the active file of human/primate repeats *humrep.ref* are documented in *humapp.ref*; changes in *rodrep.ref* are documented in *rodapp.ref*. Appendix files are for documentation purposes only, and they should not be used for annotation. Most repetitive elements deposited in RU have been assigned to general biological categories discussed earlier. For practical reasons, some of these categories are expanded within the framework of the original classification. For instance, mammalian retroviruses include *true* retrovirus-like elements and a distinct category of retroelements called *MaLRs*, distantly related to retroviruses. Moreover, long terminal repeats (LTRs) are listed separately from internal protein-coding retrovirus sequences. LTRs often represent the only known fragments of retroviruses in RU because they are by far more abundant and more readily identifiable than the internal sequences. Finally, except in the case of LINEs and SINEs, separation between autonomous and nonautonomous elements is not always possible because many elements in RU are reconstructed from inactive genomic copies. Therefore, nonautonomous and autonomous LTR-retroelements and DNA transposons are listed together.

Nomenclature

Each repetitive element listed in RU carries a unique name. Originally, standard names such as *medium reiteration frequency repeats* or *MERs* were assigned to unclassified sequence fragments discovered at the time. As more sequence information became available the nomenclature has evolved. For example, MER37 was later classified as a DNA transposon and became *Tigger*, MER115 and MER118 led to identification of *Zaphod* (*see* Repbase Update). The evolving nomenclature has been preserved in the keyword *KW* sections of RU entries (*see* Fig. 2), and in the appendix files. Unfortunately, new names usually are not any more informative than the old ones, as there are no standards that would systematically relate particular names to biological classification. Entire genomes have been sequenced and annotated based on Repbase Update. The value of such annotation depends to a large extent on the ability of non-specialists to rapidly classify particular repeats based on their names. This requires comprehensive indexes linking individual names, or groups of names from RU to the corresponding classes of repeats. Because repeat annotation in the human genome is based exclusively on RU and the reference collection of repeats is among most complete in RU, the first such index was prepared for human TEs. This index is expanded here (*see* Table 1 on pages 157 and 158) to include the nomenclature of other mammalian repeats from RU. Table 1 includes three columns. Column 3 summarizes individual and group names of repetitive families/subfamilies as used in RU. Column 1 lists major biological categories discussed in the previous section. Column 2 reflects further subdivision of TEs based on biological attributes as well as on their occurrence in different mammalian species. It must be noted here that many repetitive elements are shared among different mammals (e.g., MIR, MIR3) or are closely related (e.g., L1 elements). For practical purposes, the shared elements are listed only once in Table 1. For example, MIR, MIR3, and L3 present in all mammals, are listed only under *human/shared* category. This category also contains human-specific sequences such as Alu, SVA, and SVA2.

The current release of RU contains 835 mammalian repeat families and subfamilies, many of which share variants of the same name (e.g., MT2A, MT2B, MT2C).

Table 1
Major Categories of Mammalian Repetitive Families from Repbase Update and Their Family/Subfamily Loci Names

Major categories	*Subcategories*	*Family/Subfamily loci names*
LINEs	Human/shared	IN25, L1*, L2A, KER2, L3, CR1_HS
	Rodent/shared	LINE3_RN (L1_RN), LX*, LLME
	Other mammalian	ARMER1, ART2*, BDDF*, BOV2, BTALU2, LINE1E_OC, LINE_C, THER2
SINEs	Human/shared	Alu*, FLA*, HAL1*, L2B, MIR, MIR3, SVA, SVA2
	Rodent/shared	B1*, B2*, B3*, BC1, FAM, ID_B1, MUSID* (ID1-6), PB1*, RDRE1_RN (ID_RN), RNALUIII, RSINE1, RSINE2*(B4*), SQR2_MM
	Other mammalian	BCS, BOVA2, BOVTA, BTALU1, BTCS, C_OC, CHR-1, CHR-2, D_CH, DRE1, MAR1, MON1, MVB2, NLA, PRE1_SS, SINEC*, THER1
Retroviruses and retrovirus-like elements *(internal sequences)*	MaLRs- human/shared	MLT1R, MLT1AR (MLT-int), MLT1CR (MLT1-int), MLT1FR (MLT1F-int), MSTAR (MST-int), THE1BR
	MaLRs- rodent/shared	MTAI (MT-int), ORR1AI (ORR1-int), ORR1BI (ORR1B-int).
	Other human/shared retroviruses	ERVL, HARLEQUIN, HERV*, HRES1, HUERS-P*, LOR1I, MER4I, MER4BI, MER21I, MER31I, MER41I, MER50I, MER51I, MER52AI, MER57I, MER57A_I, MER61I, MER65I, MER66I, MER70I, MER83AI, MER83BI, MER84I, MER89I, MER110I, PABL_AI, PABL_BI, PRIMA4_I, PRIMA41
	Other rodent/shared retroviruses	ETNERV, IAPA_MM, IAPEYI, IAPEZI, MERVL, MMETN, MMLV30, MULV, MYS1_PL (MYSPL), MYSERV
Long terminal repeats (LTRs) *a*	MaLR LTRs- human/shared	MLT1*, MST*, THE1*
	MaLR LTRs- rodent/shared	MTA, MTB, MTC, MTD, MTE, MT2*, ORR1A*, ORR1B*, ORR1C, ORR1D
	Other human/shared retrovirus LTRs	HARLEQUINLTR, LTR*, LOR1, MLT2*, MER4*, MER9, MER11*, MER21*, MER31*, MER34*, MER39*, MER41*, MER48, MER49, MER50*, MER51*, MER52*, MER54*, MER57*, MER61*, MER65*, MER66*, MER67*, MER68*, MER70*, MER72*, MER73, MER74*, MER76, MER77, MER83*, MER84, MER87, MER88, MER89, MER90, MER92*, MER93*, MER95, MER101*, MER110*, PABL_A, PABL_B, PRIMA4_LTR, PTR5

(continued on next page)

Table 1 *(continued)*

Major categories	*Subcategories*	*Family/Subfamily loci names*
	Other rodent/shared retrovirus LTRs	BGLII, LTRIAPEY, LTRIS, MERVL_LTR, MYS1_LTR, NICER_RN, PMR89, RAL, RLTR*, RMER2,RMER3, RMER4, RMER5, RMER6*, RMER10, RMER12, RMER13*, RMER15, RMER16, RMER17*, RMER19,RMER20
	Other mammalian retrovirus LTRs	ALTR2, BTLTR1, ECE1LTR, FCLTR1, MTV9LTR1_SM
DNA Transposons	Human/shared	BLACKJACK, CHARLIE*, CHESHIRE*, GOLEM*, HSMAR*, HSTC2, LOOPER, MADE1, MARNA, MER1*, MER2*, MER3, MER5*, MER6*, MER8, MER20*, MER28, MER30*, MER33, MER44*, MER45*, MER46, MER53, MER63*, MER69*, MER75, MER80, MER81, MER82, MER85, MER91*, MER94, MER96*, MER97*, MER99, MER103, MER104*, MER105, MER106*, MER107, MER113, MER115, MER116, MER117, MER119, ORSL, PMER1, RICKSHA*, TIGGER*, ZAPHOD, ZOMBI*
	Rodent/shared	URR1
Minisatellites Satellites	Human	IVR, R66
	Human/shared	ALR*, BSR, CER, (GGAAT)n, GSAT*, HSATI*, LSAU, MER22, MER122, MSR1, REP522, SAR, SATR*, SN5, TAR1
	Rodent/shared	CENSAT, GSAT_MM, ISAT_RN, R91ES8_RN, SATI_RN, SATMIN, ZP3AR_MM
	Other mammalian	BMSAT1, BTSAT*, FASAT(?), OOREP1(L1?), OSSAT*, SSRS2, RTREP1, SATIA_MM
Composite/simple	Human	MER120
	Rodent	SQR1_MM
	Other mammalian	MRSAT1, SSRS1
Unclassified/ incomplete	Human	HIR, MER35, MER109, MER112, MER121
	Rodent	ALSAT_RN (L1?), C573, CYRA11_MM, DRB_RN, LPKR_RN, MREP_MC, PMR89 (HERVL?), RMER1*, SQR4_MM, YREP
	Other mammalian	LMER1

a This list does not include the internal sequence names listed above.

* Indicates multiple names starting with the same theme name. For example, RMER1* represents three subfamilies named RMER1, RMER1A, and RMER1B. The theme name *RMER1* is shared among the three.

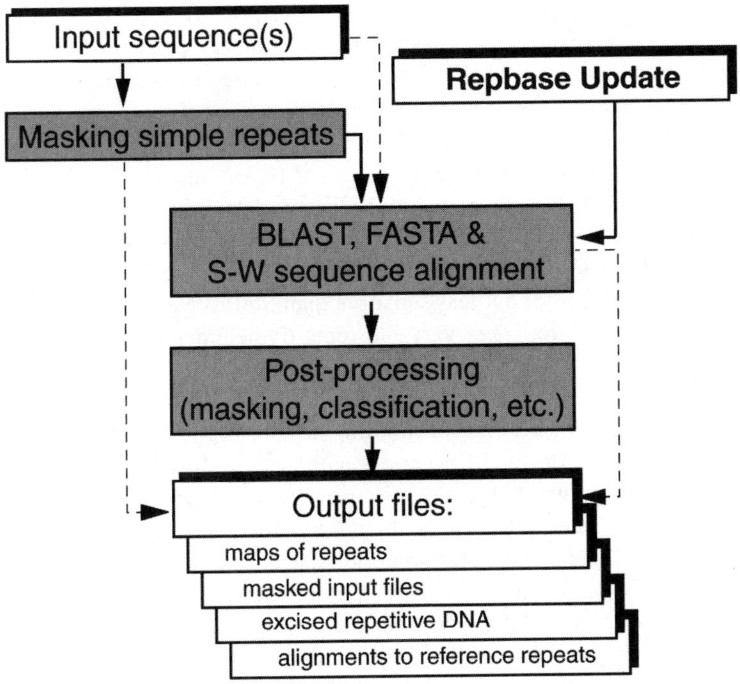

Fig. 3. A scheme for automated identification and annotation of repetitive DNA. Continuous arrows indicate critical steps, whereas broken arrows show major variants of the process. Typical output files include: maps of repeats (*see* Fig. 4), masked query file(s), a list of masked sequences and alignments against the reference sequences as described in the text.

Such variants are grouped together and the variations are indicated by asterisks (MT2*, *see* column 3). For example, RLTR* stands for 27 different long terminal repeats (LTRs). For historical reasons LTRs also carry other unassuming names such as BGLII, PMR89, and RMER. The corresponding internal retroviral sequences, if available, are listed in a separate section above the LTR section in Table 1. The application of Table 1 to the interpretation of repeat annotation is discussed in the next section.

Analysis of Repetitive DNA

Identification and Annotation of Known Repeats

The basic routine underlying identification and annotation of repetitive DNA remains essentially unchanged since it was first implemented in the Pythia server, and re-implemented in XBLAST and CENSOR. Since 1996, major progress has been achieved in terms of speed and sensitivity of repeat detection based on dedicated hardware used in CENSOR server (*see* Website: http://www.girinst.org/Censor_Server.html), and an efficient implementation of Smith-Waterman algorithm used in RepeatMasker (*see* Website: http://repeatmasker.genome.washington.edu).

Detection and annotation of repetitive DNA is based on comparing a query sequence against representative collections of repeats as schematically shown in Fig. 3.

To avoid nonspecific matches, it is first advisable to filter out simple repeats from the query or reference sequences prior to the analysis by replacing sequence letters with neutral characters such as "N" or "X." There are several ways to identify simple repeats based on their similarity to a reference set, or on their non-random base composition. Another program, particularly useful for analyzing cryptically simple repeats, has been implemented as a part of repeat analysis on the CENSOR server (*see* Website: http://www.girinst.org/Censor_Server.html). After simple repeats are masked, *complex* repeats can be detected by sequence comparisons using the FASTA (1988), BLAST (1990), or Smith-Waterman (1981) algorithms. FASTA and BLAST are significantly faster but less sensitive than Smith-Waterman-based programs. The latter are essential to detect very old repetitive elements such as the extinct human MIR3 and LINE3 elements that are related to CR1 elements from birds. Conversely, relatively young repeats such as most Alu subfamilies can be detected using a less sensitive approach. Therefore, dividing repeats into detectable categories and the selective application of different algorithms may facilitate the detection process. Apart from these knowledge-based improvements, there are algorithm-based attempts to accelerate repeat detection without sacrificing the sensitivity of the process. It must be noted, the major determinant of speed, sensitivity, and accuracy is the quality of reference collections as discussed in the next section.

There are several types of output files generated by repeat annotation programs (examples are listed in Fig. 3). They include *maps of repeats* summarizing location and basic characteristics of individual elements, query file (s) with masked repeats, sequences and coordinates of the identified repeats and alignment to reference sequences for detailed inspection. A sample of repeat maps generated by CENSOR (*see* Website: http://www.girinst.org/Censor_Server.html) is shown in Fig. 4. The top part of the figure (Fig. 4A), illustrates a human endogenous retrovirus HERV3 flanked at both ends by long terminal repeats (LTR61). It also contains a MER11A element inserted in opposite orientation. All MER11 elements are classified as LTRs different from LTR61 (*see* Table 1). Therefore, MER11A most likely represents a remnant from a different retrovirus inserted at that spot. The internal portion of the retrovirus (HERV3) and the 5' LTR are chopped by the program into smaller fragments separated by *blank regions* without any identified repeats. Because the blank regions are relatively short (<50 bp), the fragments can be combined into a single LTR (see the bottom part of the figure). If the bank regions are much longer in relative terms, additional testing may be required. For example the first two 5' fragments of the internal sequence HERV3 are separated by 457 bp. A corresponding gap of similar size can be seen in the reference sequence from RU (*see* columns 4–6). This suggests that the nucleotide sequence at positions 54,059–54,515 represents another homologous fragment of the same retrovirus not detected by the algorithm. In such cases a separate test may be needed to verify whether or not such a spot does not represent any unknown element (s) inserted in the retrovirus. In this case, additional alignment has shown that this region is most similar to HERV3 and, therefore, it can be incorporated in the internal portion of the retrovirus pictured below the map.

The bottom example (Fig. 4B), shows a more complicated pattern of insertion into another endogenous retrovirus (HERVK22I), flanked by LTR22. This retrovirus contains two independent L1 elements (L1PA2 and L1PA3) inserted in its internal sequence. L1PA2 appears to be complete or nearly complete whereas L1PA3 is repre-

A

GB Acc.	Beg.	End	RU Locus	Beg.	End	O	S
AC007379	53088	53232	LTR61	74	233	d	0.74
AC007379	53260	53333	LTR61	234	311	d	0.76
AC007379	53368	53661	LTR61	299	595	d	0.77
AC007379	53671	54058	HERV3	10	393	d	0.74
AC007379	54515	54846	HERV3	794	1126	d	0.69
AC007379	55021	55802	HERV3	1302	2081	d	0.73
AC007379	55925	56582	HERV3	2161	2826	d	0.71
AC007379	56638	57091	HERV3	2863	3305	d	0.72
AC007379	57108	57996	HERV3	3334	4221	d	0.77
AC007379	58043	58767	HERV3	4268	5005	d	0.73
AC007379	58861	59905	MER11A	1126	1	c	0.86
AC007379	60087	61081	HERV3	5278	6313	d	0.72
AC007379	61173	61305	HERV3	8287	8418	d	0.74
AC007379	61316	61829	LTR61	72	595	d	0.74

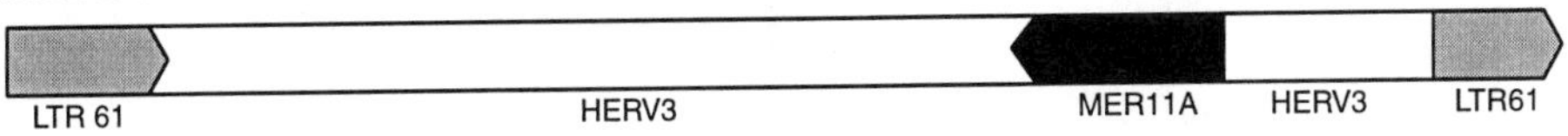

B

GB Acc.	Beg.	End	RU Locus	Beg.	End	O	S
AB045363	38248	38745	LTR22	1	580	c	0.70
AB045363	38748	40067	HERVK22I	5514	6835	c	0.89
AB045363	40075	40494	L1PA3	483	902	c	0.98
AB045363	40495	42621	HERVK22I	5527	2327	c	0.86
AB045363	43041	43432	HERVK22I	339	741	c	0.85
AB045363	43434	48611	L1	1	5303	d	0.95
AB045363	48612	49463	L1PA2	51	902	d	0.97
AB045363	49492	49842	HERVK22I	3	350	c	0.88
AB045363	49845	50338	LTR22	1	580	c	0.69

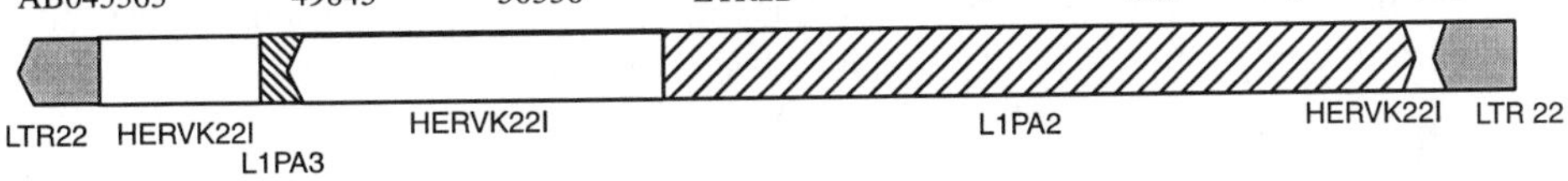

Fig. 4. Sample maps of repetitive elements generated by CENSOR (*see* Website: http://www.girinst.org), and their graphic interpretation. Column 1 lists the GenBank accession numbers of the query sequences, followed by coordinates of the repeats. Column 4 lists repeat names and coordinates relative to RU sequences. Column 7 shows the orientation of the repeats (direct or complementary), and the last column shows similarities to sequences from RU. Graphic interpretations are given below the maps. **(A)** HERV3 flanked by LTR61. **(B)** HERVK221 flanked by LTR22.

sented only by a short 419 bp 3' fragment and its orientation is opposite to L1PA3. Due to this opposite orientation, and typical 5' truncation, it is likely that L1PA3 represents a separate integration event of an incomplete L1 element.

Identification, Reconstruction and Classification of New TEs

Interspersed repetitive DNA seldom contains complete copies of TEs. It is believed that from the start many retro (trans)posons generate 5' truncated copies of themselves (e.g., L1PA3 in Fig. 4B). Even if the inserted copies are originally complete, over time they can undergo genetic rearrangements or partial to complete deletion. Furthermore, copies of TEs undergo base-substitution mutations, accelerated by methylation of CpG dinucleotides, due to conversion of the 5-methylcytosine to thymine by spontaneous deamination. As a result methylated CpG doublets mutate to CpA or TpG at a rate about a factor of magnitude higher than the average mutation rate. Thus, fragmented and mutated copies usually represent the only source of information about complete and active TEs. For this reason most TEs deposited in RU represent consensus sequences reconstructed from scattered partial sequence information. Consensus sequences are not only more complete, but also more similar to individual repeats than individual repeats to each other. The relationship between similarity to the consensus (y) and average pairwise similarity between individual repeats (x) is given by the Equation 1:

$$y = \frac{1 + \sqrt{12x - 3}}{4} \qquad \text{[Eq. 1]}$$

For example, individual repeats that are on average 50% similar to each other will be 68% similar to their quality consensus sequence (i.e., for x = 0.5, y = 0.68). This significantly facilitates the identification of highly diverged repeats.

The reconstruction process is usually, but not necessarily, associated with discovering new repetitive elements. There are many different ways in which previously unknown repetitive elements can be identified. For example, the coordinates of potential new repeat sequences can be determined from *blank spots* in the maps similar to those described above. A routine approach, presented in Fig. 5, takes advantage of the same computer software as used in annotating known repeats. It starts with masking the existing repeats from a Genbank file or other large data set. The masked sequence data is then compared against itself, preferably in opposite orientation to minimize obvious matches from known multi-copy genes. The resulting output file will contain homologous sequence fragments including repeats. These repeats need to be tested to exclude matches between duplicated genes or other obvious similarities not related to repetitive DNA. The next critical step is the generation of a multiple alignment as a basis for developing a consensus as summarized in Fig. 5. Multiple alignment of partial sequences can be carried out using CLUSTALX program (*see* Chapter 31), but it usually requires refinement using sequence editors. A partial consensus sequence may be used to realign sequence fragments in order to verify and improve the original alignment. This iterative approach is particularly useful in the case of highly diverged sequences.

Prior to consensus building it is important to subdivide repetitive elements into meaningful subfamilies if the number of repeat sequences is sufficient. In most cases it can be done using a standard phylogenetic analysis package (e.g., PHYLIP; *see* Website: http://evolution.genetics.washington.edu/phylip.html). In the past, constructing phylogenetic trees proved to be unsuccessful in determining Alu classification, and alternative approaches were necessary. Retrospectively, most difficulties encountered using tree-based classification for repeats were due to interference between rapidly mutating CpG doublets and other sequence positions containing critical information. Therefore, in the case of at least CpG-rich repeats, it may be important to exclude CpG doublets and their common derivatives (TpG, CpA) when constructing phylogenetic trees.

Initial reconstruction almost always leads to partial consensus sequences. To determine exact boundaries, it is important to obtain maps of repeats that would include the newly built consensus sequence. The best way to determine exact ends of the new

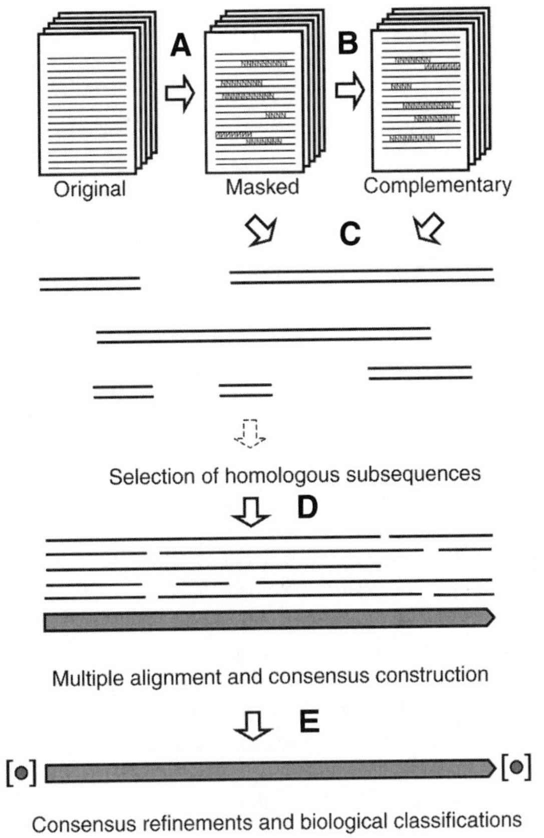

Fig. 5. Identification and reconstruction of TEs. The steps involved are: **(A)** masking known repeats in the query database; **(B)** generation of a complementary database; **(C)** comparison of direct and complementary databases in search of homologous regions, followed by selection of potential repeats; **(D)** multiple alignment and consensus building; **(E)** evaluation of consensus and determination of target sites as detailed in the text.

repeat is to study its insertions into other repetitive elements. This is also the best way to determine target site duplications that are often essential for proper classification of the repeat.

Systematic analysis of sequence data during the last decade has revealed a large variety of transposable elements in eukaryotic genomes. This has led to the creation of specialized databases and tools essential for eukaryotic genome analysis during the sequencing era. Some approaches outlined in this chapter are relatively straightforward. However, much of the analysis still relies heavily on human judgement and creativity that have not yet been encoded in computer software. Transposable elements are intrinsically involved in biological processes that still remain to be understood. Therefore, repetitive DNA is no longer viewed as a troublesome *junkyard* but rather as a gold mine of information underlying biology of eukaryotic genomes.

Acknowledgment

I thank Jolanta Walichiewicz, Violaine Genot, and Michael Jurka for help with editing the manuscript.

Suggested Readings

Introduction

Andersson, G., Svensson, A. C., Setterblad, N., and Rask, L. (1998) Retroelements in the human MHC class II region, Trends Genet. 14, 109–114.

Hartl, D. L. (2000) Molecular melodies in high and low C, Nature Genet. Rev. 1, 145–149.

Jabbari, K. and Bernardi, G. (1998) CpG doublets, CpG islands and Alu repeats in long human DNA sequences from different isochore families, Gene 224, 123–128.

Jurka, J. (1990) Novel families of interspersed repetitive DNA sequences from the human genome, Nucleic Acids Res. 18, 137–141.

Jurka, J. (1998) Repeats in genomic DNA: mining and meaning, Curr. Opin. Struct. Biol. 8, 333–337.

Lander, E. S., Linton, L. M., Birren, B., et al. (2001) Initial sequencing and analysis of the human genome, Nature 409, 860–921.

Sherry, S. T., Harpending, H. C., Batzer, M. A., and Stoneking, M. (1997) Alu evolution in human populations: using the coalescent to estimate effective population size, Genetics 147, 1977–1982.

Shimamura, M., Yasue, H., Ohshima, K., Abe, H., Kato, H., Kishiro, T., et al. (1997) Molecular evidence from retroposons that whales form a clade within even-toed ungulates, Nature 388, 666–670.

Surzycki, S. A. and Belknap, W. R. (1999) Characterization of repetitive DNA elements in Arabidopsis, J. Mol. Evol. 48, 684–691.

Simple Sequence Repeats (SSRs)

Hancock, J. M. (1995) The contribution of slippage-like processes to genome evolution, J. Mol. Evol. 41, 1038–1047.

Jeffreys, A. J., Barber, R., Bois, P., Buard, J., Dubrova, Y. E., Grant, G., et al. (1999) Human minisatellites, repeat DNA instability and meiotic recombination, Electrophoresis 20, 1665–1675.

Jurka, J. (1995a) Human Repetitive Elements, in: Molecular Biology and Biotechnology. A Comprehensive Desk Reference, (Meyers, R. A., ed.), VCH Publishers Inc., New York, NY, pp. 438–441.

Jurka, J. (1998) Repeats in genomic DNA: mining and meaning, Curr. Opin. Struct. Biol. 8, 333–337.

Kashi, Y., King, D., and Soller, M. (1997) Simple sequence repeats as a source of quantitative genetic variation, Trends Genet. 13, 74–78.

Kidwell, M. G. and Lisch, D. R. (2001) Perspective: transposable elements, parasitic DNA, and genome evolution, Evolution Int. J. Org. Evolution 55, 1–24.

Toth, G., Gaspari, Z., and Jurka, J. (2000) Microsatellites in different eukaryotic genomes: survey and analysis, Genome Res. 10, 967–981.

Weber, J. L. and May, P. E. (1989) Abundant class of human DNA polymorphisms which can be typed using the polymerase chain reaction, Am. J. Hum. Genet. 44, 388–396.

Transposable Elements (TEs)

Jurka, J. (1995a) Human Repetitive Elements, in: Molecular Biology and Biotechnology. A Comprehensive Desk Reference, (Meyers, R. A., ed.), VCH Publishers Inc., New York, NY, pp. 438–441.

Jurka, J. (1995b) Origin and evolution of Alu repetitive elements, in: The Impact of Short Interspersed Elements (SINEs) on the Host Genome, (Maraia, R. J., ed.), R. G. Landes Company, Austin, TX, pp. 25–41.

Jurka, J. (1997) Sequence patterns indicate an enzymatic involvement in integration of mammalian retroposons, Proc. Natl. Acad. Sci. USA 94, 1872–1877.

Jurka, J. and Kapitonov, V. V. (1999) Sectorial mutagenesis by transposable elements, Genetica 107, 239–248.

Reference Collections of Repeats

Jurka, J. (1990) Novel families of interspersed repetitive DNA sequences from the human genome, Nucleic Acids Res. 18, 137–141.

Jurka, J., Walichiewicz, J., and Milosavljevic, A. (1992) Prototypic sequences for human repetitive DNA, J. Mol. Evol. 35, 286–291.

Jurka, J., Kaplan, D. J., Duncan, C. H., Walichiewicz, J., Milosavljevic, A., Murali, G., and Solus, J. F. (1993) Identification and characterization of new human medium reiteration frequency repeats, Nucleic Acids Res. 21, 1273–1279.

Jurka, J. (2000) Repbase Update: a database and an electronic journal of repetitive elements, Trends Genet. 16, 418–420.

Kaplan, D. J. and Duncan, C. H. (1990) Novel short interspersed repeat in human DNA, Nucleic Acids Res. 18, 192.

Kaplan, D. J., Jurka, J., Solus, S. F., and Duncan, C. H. (1991) Medium reiteration frequency repetitive sequences in the human genome, Nucleic Acids Res. 19, 4731–4738.

Smit, A. F. (1993) Identification of a new, abundant superfamily of mammalian LTR-transposons, Nucleic Acids Res. 21, 1863–1872.

Smit, A. F., Toth, G., Riggs, A. D., and Jurka, J. (1995) Ancestral, mammalian-wide subfamilies of LINE-1 repetitive sequences, J. Mol. Biol. 246, 401–417.

Annotations Based on Repbase Update

Lander, E. S., Linton, L. M., Birren, B., Nusbaum, C., Zody, M. C., Baldwin, J., et al. (2001) Initial sequencing and analysis of the human genome, Nature 409, 860–921.

Nomenclature

Iris, F., Bougueleret, L., Prieur, S., Caterina, D., Primas, G., Perrot, V., et al. (1993) Dense Alu clustering and a potential new member of the NFkappaB family within a 90 kilobase HLA class III segment, Nature Genet. 3, 137–145.

Jurka, J. (1990) Novel families of interspersed repetitive DNA sequences from the human genome, Nucleic Acids Res. 18, 137–141.

Jurka, J., Kaplan, D. J., Duncan, C. H., Walichiewicz, J., Milosavljevic, A., Murali, G., and Solus, J. F. (1993) Identification and characterization of new human medium reiteration frequency repeats, Nucleic Acids Res. 21, 1273–1279.

Jurka, J., Kapitonov, V. V., and Smit, A. F. A. (2003) Repetitive DNA, detection of, in: Encyclopedia of the Human Genome, (Cooper, D. N., ed.) Nature Publishing Group, New York, NY.

Kaplan, D. J. and Duncan, C. H. (1990) Novel short interspersed repeat in human DNA, Nucleic Acids Res. 18, 192.

Kaplan, D. J., Jurka, J., Solus, S. F., and Duncan, C. H. (1991) Medium reiteration frequency repetitive sequences in the human genome, Nucleic Acids Res. 19, 4731–4738.

Lander, E. S., Linton, L. M., Birren, B., Nusbaum, C., Zody, M. C., Baldwin, J., et al. (2001) Initial sequencing and analysis of the human genome, Nature 409, 860–921.

Smit, A. F. A. and Riggs, A. D. (1996) *Tiggers* and other DNA transposon fossils in the human genome, Proc. Natl. Acad. Sci. USA 93, 1443–1448.

Analysis of Repetitive DNA

Identification and Annotation of Known Repeats

Bedell, J. A., Korf, I., and Gish, W. (2000) MaskerAid: a performance enhancement to RepeatMasker, Bioinformatics 16, 1040–1041.

Claverie, J. M. (1994) Large scale sequence analysis, in: Automated DNA Sequencing and Analysis, (Adams, M. D., Fields, C., and Venter, J. C., eds.), Academic Press, San Diego, CA, pp. 267–279.

Karlin, S. and Altschul, S. F. (1990) Methods for assessing the statistical significance of molecular sequence features by using general scoring schemes, Proc. Natl. Acad. Sci. USA 87, 2264–2268.

Jurka, J. and Milosavljevic, A. (1991) Reconstruction and analysis of human Alu genes, J. Mol. Evol. 32, 105–121.

Jurka, J., Walichiewicz, J., and Milosavljevic, A. (1992) Prototypic sequences for human repetitive DNA, J. Mol. Evol. 35, 286–291.

Jurka, J. (1994) Approaches to identification and analysis of interspersed repetitive DNA sequences, in: Automated DNA Sequencing and Analysis (Adams, M. D., Fields, C., and Venter, J. C., eds.), Academic Press, San Diego, CA, pp. 294–298.

Jurka, J. and Pethiyagoda, C. (1995) Simple repetitive DNA sequences from primates: compilation and analysis, J. Mol.Evol. 40, 120–126.

Jurka, J., Klonowski, P., Dagman, V., and Pelton, P. (1996) CENSOR-a program for identification and elimination of repetitive elements from DNA sequences, Comput. Chem. 20, 119–121.

Milosavljevic, A. and Jurka, J. (1993) Discovering simple DNA sequences by the algorithmic significance method, Comput. Applic. Biosci. 9, 407–411.

Milosavljevic, A. (1998) Repeat analysis, in: ICRF Handbook of Genome Analysis, vol. 2, (Spurr, N. K., Young, B. D., and Bryant, S. P., eds.), Blackwell Science Inc., Malden, MA, pp. 617–628.

Pearson, W. R. and Lipman, D. J. (1988) Improved tools for biological sequence comparison, Proc. Natl.Acad. Sci. USA 85, 2444–2448.

Silva, R. and Burch, J. B. (1987) Evidence that chicken CR1 elements represent a novel family of retroposons, Mol. Cell. Biol. 9, 3563–3566.

Smith, T. F. and Waterman, M. S. (1981) Identification of common molecular subsequences, J. Mol. Biol. 147, 195–197.

Wootton, J. C. and Federhen, S. (1996) Analysis of compositionally biased regions in sequence databases, Meth. Enzymol. 266, 554–571.

Identification, Reconstruction and Classification of New TEs

Bao, Z. and Eddy, S. R. (2002) Automated de novo identification of repeat sequence families in sequenced genomes, Genome Res. 12, 1269–1276.

Faulkner, D. V. and Jurka, J. (1988) Multiple Aligned Sequence Editor (MASE), Trends Biochem. Sci 13, 321–322.

Galtier, N., Gouy, M., and Gautier, C. (1996) SeaView and Phylo_win, two graphic tools for sequence alignment and molecular phylogeny, Comp. Appl. Biosci. 12, 543–548.

Ivics, Z., Hackett, P. B., Plasterk, R. H., and Izsvak, Z. (1997) Molecular reconstruction of Sleeping Beauty, a Tc1-like transposon from fish, and its transposition in human cells, Cell 91, 501–510.

Jurka, J. and Milosavljevic, A. (1991) Reconstruction and analysis of human *Alu* genes, J. Mol. Evol. 32, 105–121.

Jurka, J. (1994) Approaches to identification and analysis of interspersed repetitive DNA sequences, in: Automated DNA Sequencing and Analysis (Adams, M. D., Fields, C. and Venter, J. C., eds.), Academic Press, San Diego, CA, pp. 294–298.

Jurka, J. (1998) Repeats in genomic DNA: mining and meaning, Curr. Opin. Struct. Biol. 8, 333–337.

Jurka, J. and Smith, T. (1988) A fundamental division in the *Alu* family of repeated sequences, Proc. Natl. Acad. Sci. USA 85, 4775–4778.

Kapitonov, V. V. and Jurka, J. (2001) Rolling-circle transposons in eukaryotes, Proc. Natl. Acad. Sci. USA 98, 8714–8719.

Thompson, J. D., Higgins, D. G., and Gibson, T. J. (1994) CLUSTAL W: improving the sensitivity of progressive multiple sequence alignment through sequence weighting, position-specific gap penalties and weight matrix choice, Nucleic Acids Res. 22, 4673–4680.

9 Molecular Genetics of Disease and the Human Genome Project

Paromita Deb-Rinker and Stephen W. Scherer

Introduction

The haploid (n) human genome contains approx 3 billion nucleotides (or bases) of DNA strung amongst 23 chromosomes (*see* Fig. 1). The diploid (2n) complement, which consists of a haploid genome inherited from each parent, therefore comprises 46 chromosomes of 6 billion nucleotides of DNA, all contained within the cell nucleus. The same complement of DNA is found in every cell (except red blood cells) in the body. Mitochondrial DNA, which is a circular molecule of genetic material, 16,000 nucleotides long, is also part of the human genome. It is located outside the nucleus in the cytoplasm of the cell and encodes a small but important subset of human genes. Mitochondrial DNA is only transmitted from mothers to their offspring. On average, the human genome is 99.9% identical between any two individuals, with nucleotide differences existing only about 1 in every 1000 bases. Less than 5% of the genome contains genes or protein-coding regions. The remaining 95% (noncoding part) contains repetitive elements (*see* Chapter 8) and other sequences whose functions are not completely understood and is often referred to as junk DNA. These regions may play a role in maintaining the structural integrity of chromosomes. There at least 30,000–40,000 genes in the human genome, ranging in size less than 1 to 200 kilobases (kb), with the average size of a gene being 50 kb. General information on the human genome is provided in Table 1.

Genes are comprised of exons—regions that code for mature mRNA—and introns—intervening segments of DNA that are transcribed, but then cut out from the transcript during mRNA processing (*see* Fig. 2). There is no uniformity to the number or size of introns; this is the main reason why there is a vast range of gene sizes. Genes contain promoter sequences at their start (5' end). Typical promoters contain several DNA sequence motifs that bind regulatory proteins and control the level of transcription and the start position of the mRNA. Expression of tissue-specific genes are unique to individual or sets of tissues (muscle, brain, liver, etc.) in our bodies. There are also housekeeping genes that are expressed in all cell types because their products provide basic functions (*see* Table 2).

Simple and Complex Patterns of Inheritance

Every individual has two copies of each gene, one on'each of the chromosomes. Owing to DNA sequence variation, there can be two or more alternative forms of a gene

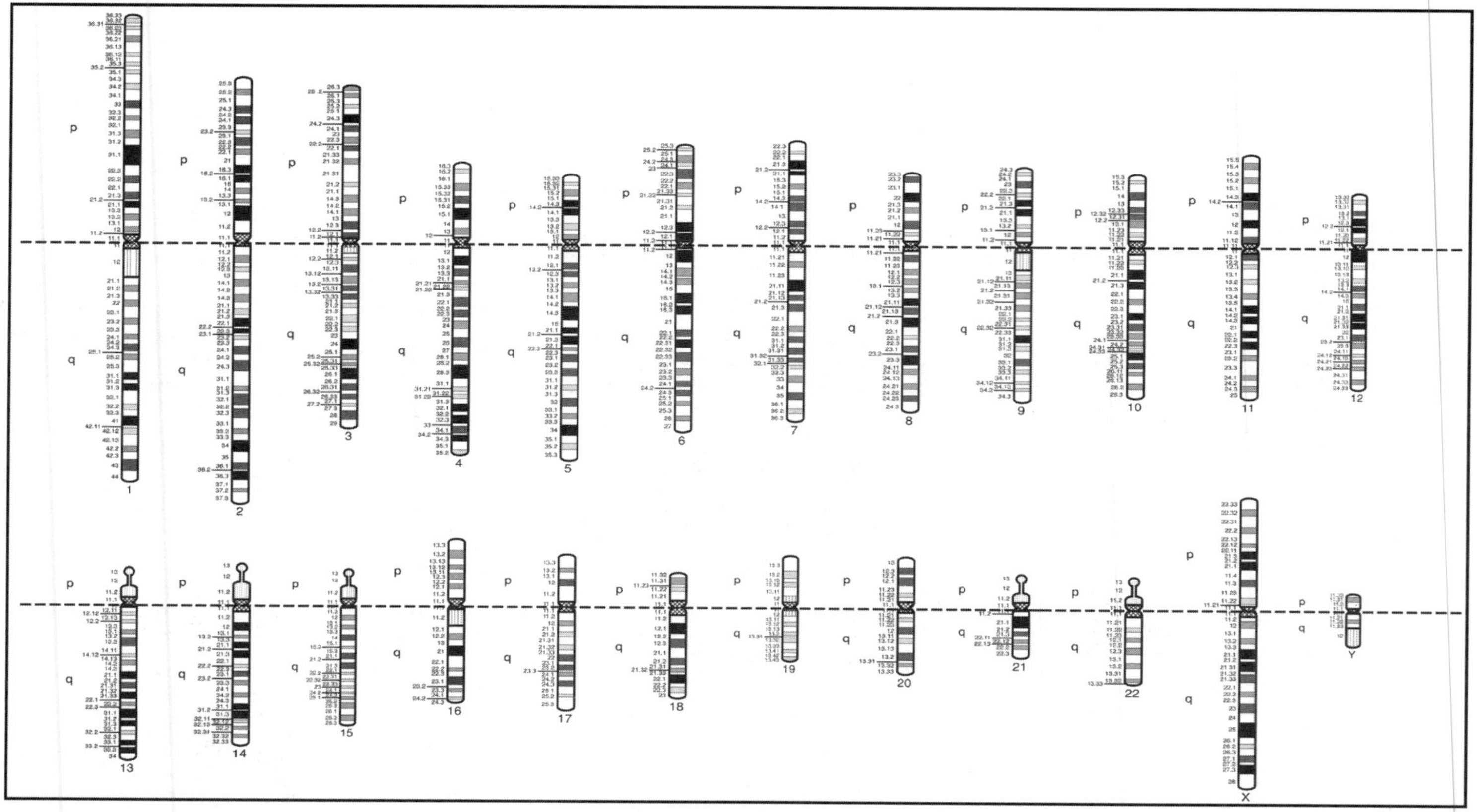

Fig. 1. The 23 chromosomes in the human genome. There are 22 autosomes (chromosomes 1 to 22) and two sex chromosomes (X and Y). Females inherit 22 autosomes and one X chromosome from each parent (46;XX). Males inherit 22 autosomes from each parent, an X chromosome from the mother and a Y chromosome from the father (46;XY). Metacentric chromosomes have a centromere (where spindle fiber binds during cell division) in the middle. Acrocentric chromosomes (chromosomes 13, 14, 15, 21, and 22) have their centromere near the end. The lighter bands of the chromosomes represent regions that have a higher GC-nucleotide content and more genes than the darker bands. Housekeeping genes tend to be located within the light bands and tissue-specific genes in the dark bands. The distribution of genes between chromosomes is also not uniform. For example, chromosome 21 is relatively gene-poor, while chromosome 19 is extremely gene-rich.

Table 1
Components of the Human Genome

- The genome is the total genetic material in a cell.
- The nuclear genome is comprised of 46 chromosomes, which come as 23 pairs; one of each pair comes from either parent.
- Mitochondrial DNA is also part of the genome. It is always inherited from the mother and is found in the cytoplasm.
- Chromosomes are made of deoxyribonucleic acid (DNA).
- DNA is made of four chemical units (nucleotides) called adenine (A), guanine (G), cytosine (C), and thymine (T).
- The genome is comprised of about 3 billion A, C, G, and Ts.
- Genes are the portions of DNA that encode functional RNA molecules or proteins.
- There are approx 30,000–40,000 genes in the genome.
- Proteins provide the structure for the cell and are involved in biochemical reactions (enzymes).

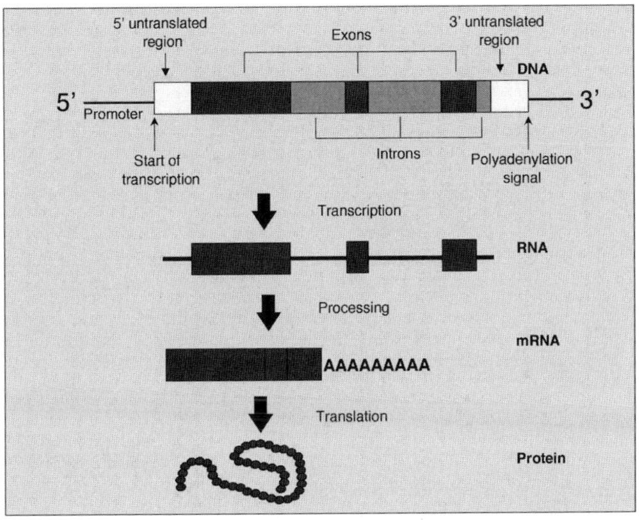

Fig. 2. Anatomy of a gene. Information flows from DNA to RNA (transcription) to protein (translation).

(called alleles), that result in different gene products. This variation contributes to the uniqueness of individuals. The term genotype is defined as the complete heritable genetic composition of an individual. Phenotype is the physical or biochemical manifestation of that genotype, and in some instances this can be associated with disease. However, in most cases, different alleles contribute to physical characteristics such as height, hair color, and other nondisease related cellular functions. The dominant and recessive forms of a trait in any given person are governed by which alleles (dominant or recessive) are inherited from the parents (*see* Fig. 3). Only individuals with two recessive alleles will show the recessive form of a trait (e.g., blue eyes). However, in the presence of a dominant allele (e.g., brown eyes), the trait associated with the recessive allele is not expressed phenotypically. Recessive alleles are not lost in a population; they can be passed on to subsequent generations where in the presence of another copy of the allele, the recessive trait reveals itself again.

See companion CD for color Fig. 3

Table 2
Gene Expression

Transcription	The synthesis of a single-strand RNA molecule from a DNA template in the cell nucleus. This process is controlled by the interactions between proteins and DNA sequences near each gene.
RNA processing	
Capping	Addition of a modified nucleotide chain to the 5' end of a growing mRNA chain. This is required for the normal processing, stability, and translation of mRNA.
Splicing	The process of removing introns and joining exons into a mature mRNA molecule.
Polyadenylation	Addition of 20–200 adenosine residues (poly A tail) to the 3' end of the RNA transcript.
Transport	The fully processed RNA is taken to the cytoplasm where translation takes place.
Translation	The synthesis of a protein from its mRNA template.
Housekeeping genes	Expressed in all cell types because their products provide basic functions in cells.
Tissue-specific genes	Expressed in only certain cell-types because their products have specific functions.

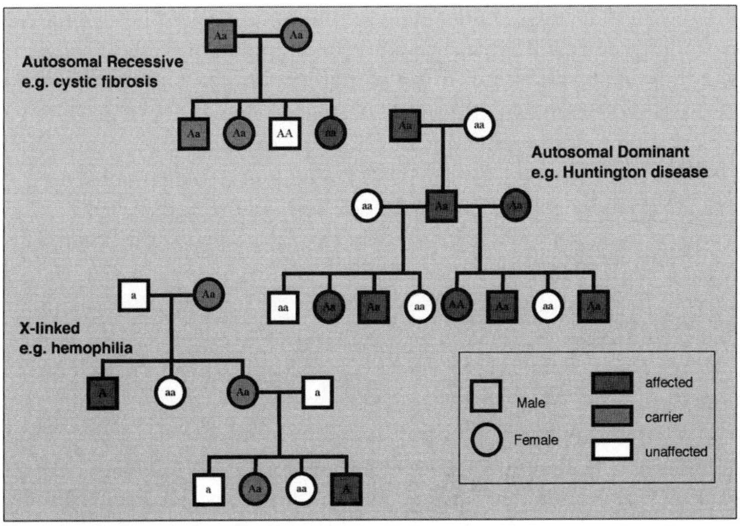

Fig. 3. Patterns of inheritance for autosomal recessive, autosomal dominant and X-linked disorders. Recessive alleles are indicated by 'a' and dominant alleles by 'A'. Males only have one X chromosome, therefore only one allele is shown for X-linked inheritance.

There are a number of diseases that are manifested owing to this simple dominant/recessive pattern of expression. Sickle cell anemia and cystic fibrosis are common examples of when the disease (termed autosomal recessive) develops owing to the presence of two copies of the recessive gene. A person with only one copy of the recessive allele does not develop the disease, but remains a carrier, because the normal copy of the gene predominates. Autosomal dominant disorders like Huntington's disease are produced when a single mutated dominant allele is present even if the other copy of the allele is normal. Diseases resulting from mutations in genes on the X chromosome are known as X-linked disorders. Since males only have one X chromosome, these diseases (e.g., hemophilia) act like dominant mutations in males. Females on the other hand, act as carriers and in the next generation their male offspring may or may not be affected (*see* Fig. 3).

Not all disorders and traits follow a simple pattern of inheritance as described earlier. One gene can influence more than one trait (pleiotropy) and several genes can affect only one trait (polygenic disorders). Although genes may determine whether or not a person will have heart disease or be predisposed to cancer, many traits can be triggered or influenced by the environment as well, as in the case of complex multifactorial diseases such as schizophrenia and alcoholism.

DNA Sequence Variations and Gene Mutations

The human genome is predominantly stable and does not vary significantly between individuals. As described earlier, the genome of two individuals is only 0.1% different. Some parts of the genome are more prone to variations than others, based on properties inherent to the DNA sequence. Most of these variations are found outside the coding regions of genes and are thus not harmful. These variations include mutations and polymorphisms.

A mutation is any permanent, heritable change in the DNA sequence that in some cases can result in disease. There are different kinds of genetic mutations. Gene mutations can be inherited from a parent or acquired during an individual's lifetime. The former, known as germline mutations, exists in the reproductive cells and can be passed on to later generations. This type of mutation is present in every cell that descended from the zygote to which the mutant gamete contributed. Somatic mutations are changes that occur in non-sex cells in the body (e.g., bone marrow or pancreatic cell), and are not passed on to the next generation. Whatever the effect, the ultimate fate of that somatic mutation is to disappear when the cell in which it occurred, or the individual, dies. On average, approx 200 somatic mutations accumulate within the genome during each of our lifetimes.

Genes can be altered in many ways (*see* Table 3). An incorrect base may be incorporated into the DNA sequence (point mutations) or a nucleotide or more may be left out (deletions) or added (insertions). In some diseases like cystic fibrosis, different mutations in the same gene can produce different effects in different individuals (*see* Fig. 4), but mutations in several different genes can also lead to the same clinical consequence, as in some forms of Alzheimer's disease. In some cases, the effects of mutational changes may not be critical to the proper functioning of proteins and these are called silent mutations. Other mutations can affect the structure and function of proteins. The outcome is related to the degree of change in the protein and the role a particular protein might play in the body. At times, longer stretches of DNA, millions of nucleotides long, can also be deleted or inserted. Occasionally, longer segments of DNA are doubled (duplications) or interchanged between chromosomes (translocations). The gain or loss of entire chromosomes or chromosomal segments can also occur. Common disorders associated with these kinds of chromosomal changes include Down's syndrome, trisomy 18 and trisomy 13. Patients with these diseases carry an extra chromosome 21, 18, or 13, respectively, in their cells.

Polymorphisms are differences in the genetic make-up of individuals that can be observed at the chromosomal, gene or even single base-pair level. They were originally considered to be genome variations that were neither harmful nor beneficial. However, there is evidence that polymorphisms can sometimes influence an individual's risk to disease. A single nucleotide polymorphism (SNP), which is a DNA point mutation, comes from variations in single nucleotides where any four of the bases may be substituted at a particular position. Most SNPs tend to have only two alleles instead of four. Considering that the human genome contains more than 3 million SNPs that make up 90% of polymorphisms and most of the genome variations, the trend towards genome-wide screening for insights into disease mechanisms is increasing.

Microsatellites (also called short tandem repeats, STRs) represent another class of genetic polymorphism. These are tandemly repeated sequences, where the repeating unit is 1–4 nucleotides long. The number of times the unit is repeated in a given STR can be highly variable, a characteristic that makes them useful as genetic markers. The majority of microsatellites occur in gene introns or other noncoding regions of the genome. Generally, the microsatellite itself does not cause disease; rather it is used as a marker to identify a specific chromosome or locus. When being used as a marker, the specific number of repeats in a given STR is not critical, but the difference in the number of repeats is of importance. There are other genetic markers that vary in length from 2–60 nucleotides; these are called variable number tandem repeats (VNTRs).

Table 3
Types of Mutations and Their Effects

Missense mutations	Single-nucleotide changes resulting in the substition of an amino acid in the protein.
Nonsense mutations	Single-nucleotide changes that create one of the three termination codons (TAA, TGA, or TAG) resulting in a shortened, dysfunctional protein.
Silent mutations	Have no detectable phenotypic effect.
Splice-site mutations	Altered sequences at the ends of introns (5' donor or 3' acceptor) during RNA processing, that affect gene splicing and function.
Insertions	Addition of extra DNA sequences of varying sizes.
Duplications	Doubling of DNA sequences.
Translocations	Interchange of segments of DNA between two different chromosomes.
Inversions	Occur when a region of DNA inverts its orientation with respect to the rest of the chromosome.
Trinucleotide repeats	Expansion of triplet repeat sequences.
Deletions	Loss of part of a DNA sequence (could be loss of a single nucleotide or millions of nucleotides).

Deletion of:	Effects:
A gene	No protein product
An exon	Truncated protein
An intron	Usually no phenotypic change
Promoter	Gene nonfunctional
Splice-site	Protein nonfunctional
Many genes	Chromosomal abnormalities and usually a heterogeneous phenotype

The Human Genome Project and DNA Sequencing

The Human Genome Project (HGP) was formally initiated in the early 1990s, as an international effort to determine the complete DNA sequence of the human genome and all of the genes it encodes. The most immediate benefit of this information was to facilitate disease gene research.

DNA sequencing is the process of determining the specific order and identity of the three billion base pairs in the genome, with the ultimate goal of identifying all of the genes. Mapping is the process of identifying discrete DNA molecules of known position on a chromosome, which are then used for sequencing. Mapping is a crucial step for proper reconstruction of the genome. It usually precedes sequencing but is also necessary at the postsequencing stage.

Sequencing is now carried out through a process called fluorescence-based dideoxy sequencing. Fragments of DNA are first cloned in bacteria; they are then put into a polymerase catalyzed reaction with free nucleotides, some of which are tagged with fluorescent dyes. Nucleotides attach themselves to the DNA fragments in a particular order. Similarly, dyed nucleotides can attach themselves to the DNA fragments, but

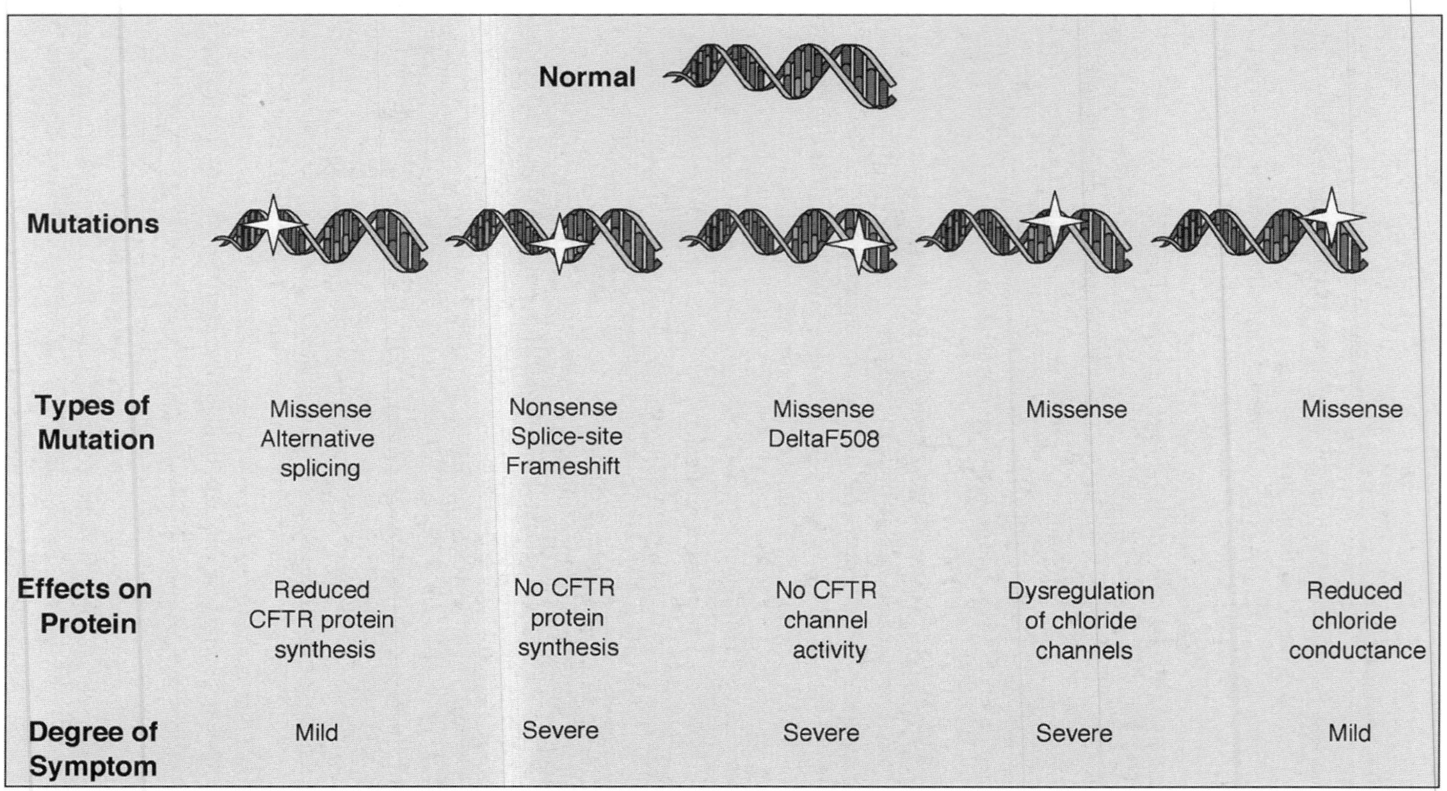

Fig. 4. Different mutations in the same gene (e.g., CFTR in cystic fibrosis) can produce different clinical outcomes. The clinical symptoms (severe/mild) correlate to the pancreatic function of the patients. Adapted from Zielenski and Tsui (1995).

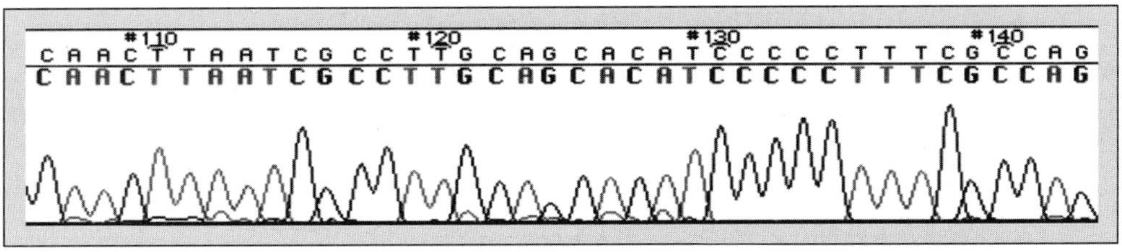

Fig. 5. DNA sequencing. Four different fluorescently tagged dyes (red for thymines, green for adenines, blue for cytosines, and black for guanines) represent the four nucleotides.

See companion CD for color Fig. 5

other nucleotides will not adhere to the dyed nucleotides. Thus the enzymatic reaction generates DNA fragments of varying lengths that terminate at fluourescently labeled A, T, C, or G nucleotides. An automated sequencing machine then determines the underlying sequence for the range of DNA fragments created in the chemical reaction (*see* Fig. 5). The fluorescently tagged bases at the ends of the fragments are detected with a laser and a computer collects the resulting information. The order in which the particular tagged nucleotides are read reflects their order on the stretch of DNA that has been replicated. Each reaction reveals the sequence of at least 500 letters (G, A, T, C) of DNA before the process runs its course.

Once these relatively tiny sequences are obtained, their place in the overall genome DNA sequence must be determined. To achieve a working DNA sequence draft of the genome, two approaches were followed. The HGP began by creating detailed genetic and physical maps, to provide a framework for ordering the generated DNA sequences. Using this approach, the HGP divided the genome into about 30,000 segments (a technique called physical mapping), each containing an average of 100,000–200,000 base pairs. Each of these sections was then broken down into even smaller fragments, of about 2000 base pairs and sequenced. Initially, the plan was to put the fragments in order and systematically determine the sequence of each fragment so that the entire human DNA sequence would be revealed. This method produces a highly accurate sequence with few gaps. However, the up-front process of building the sequence maps is costly, time-consuming, and therefore, determines the speed at which the project is completed.

A second approach used by the HGP to generate a draft sequence of the human genome is what is called the whole genome shotgun or WGS (an approach that bypasses the need to construct physical maps). In WGS, sufficient DNA sequencing is performed at random so that each nucleotide of DNA in the genome is covered numerous times, in fragments of about 500 base pairs. Determining where those individual fragments fit in the overall DNA is accomplished through the use of powerful computers that analyze the raw data to find overlaps. A working draft of DNA sequence usually covers 95% of the genome (maintaining 99% accuracy) but it is divided into many unordered gapped segments. Additional sequencing is required to generate the finished DNA sequence, such that there are no gaps or ambiguities. The final sequence has an accuracy of greater than 99.99%. Only partial data was collected from each DNA fragment. This was then assembled to generate a working or rough draft. This change of strategy was partly due to the launching of a privately funded company, Celera Corporation.

Positional Cloning

Positional cloning is the process by which disease-causing genes are identified on the basis of their chromosomal location, with limited or no prior knowledge of the gene's function (*see* Fig. 6). Positional cloning can be divided into the following three steps.

Step 1: Family Studies

The first step in the positional cloning process is the collection of information on families who have the disease. Family trees (pedigrees) are established and DNA from blood is used for genetic analyses. Critical to this step is the diagnosis and assignment of proper phenotypic features to family members affected by the disease. Finding suitable families can be rate-limiting, particularly when the disease is rare, or for disorders in which affected individuals die at a young age. Two general approaches are used when collecting families for studies. A small number of very large families can be studied, where all affected members of the pedigree are known to have the same genetic disease, presumably caused by a mutation in a single gene. The alternative approach is to collect a large number of smaller families. This is easier to do for relatively common diseases, but it carries the risk that not all families may have the genetically identical disorder. However, with proper epidemiological studies, the mode of inheritance of the disease (X-linked, autosomal recessive, autosomal dominant or multifactorial) can often be determined.

Step 2: Mapping and Sequencing

The next step in positional cloning is to identify informative chromosomal rearrangements or genetic markers that are always found in family members affected by the disease. In the simplest case, the disease gene might be closely associated with a chromosomal anomaly, which helps define the position of the causative gene on the chromosome. Unfortunately this is a rare event and not the case for most genetic disorders. In the remainder of cases, genetic mapping is performed to determine the chromosomal region containing the disease gene being sought. This is accomplished by examining genetic markers that have already been mapped to particular chromosomes across the genome, to determine which ones are linked to the disease. If each family member that has the disease also has a particular DNA marker, it is likely that the gene responsible for the disease is in close proximity to that marker, thus defining where the gene search should be focussed.

Step 3: Candidate Gene Isolation and Mutation Analysis

The last step in positional cloning is to identify the genes within the candidate region. Historically, mapping the disease gene was followed by the construction of physical maps by ordering overlapping fragments of DNA along the region of interest and determining the nucleotide composition of the clones. Now that most of the human genome has been sequenced, candidate genes from the chromosomal region of interest are usually available for further study. However, a complete gene catalogue is not yet established. Therefore, at times, one must scan the DNA sequence to look for features characteristic of genes. Since the coding sequence of genes is usually not continuous, this is not always simple. Looking for exon-intron boundaries of coding and noncoding regions, amino acid encoding DNA sequences

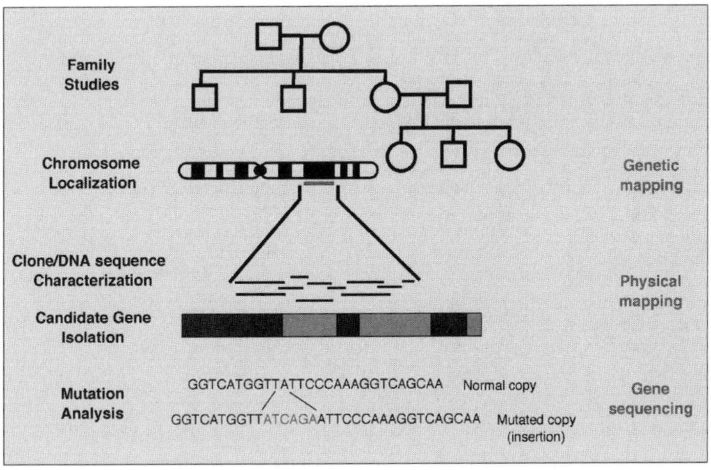

Fig. 6. Disease gene identification by positional cloning using mapping and DNA sequencing techniques.

to determine the start and end of the gene, or evolutionarily conserved DNA segments, all help to focus this search. The confirmation that a candidate gene is causative in the disease requires a direct association between a mutation in that gene and expression of the disease phenotype. The identified mutation should be present only in affected individuals and not in unaffected relatives or controls. However, in some individuals the mutation may not cause the disease, a phenomenon known as incomplete penetrance. The mutation could also cause a variation of the disease, a phenomenon known as reduced penetrance. In the case of a late-onset disorder like Huntington's disease, the mutation may not have had time to manifest itself. A key issue while looking for mutations in a disease gene is the ability to discriminate between nondisease-causing sequence polymorphisms that may just be linked to the disease gene and the actual disease-causing mutations. Various bioassays can be designed to show that a particular gene defect (correlated to an altered amino acid in the protein) can cause the phenotype in question. For example, the abnormal gene can be introduced in an animal model to see if it causes the disease. Alternatively, the normal form of the gene can be introduced and tested to determine if it can replace the abnormal copy of the gene.

The HGP is rapidly identifying all of the genes in the human genome. The goal of this effort is to find the location and pinpoint the function of the at least 30,000–40,000 human genes by the year 2005 (*see* Fig. 7). Positional cloning has thus far been used to identify hundreds of disease genes, including the gene for cystic fibrosis, Huntington's disease, some types of Alzheimer's disease, and early-onset breast cancer. The identification of a gene prior to the HGP is described in the following.

Identification of the Gene Causing Cystic Fibrosis

The gene for cystic fibrosis (CF) was identified in 1989, providing a paradigm for dozens of future disease gene discoveries using HGP data. CF is the most common fatal, autosomal recessive disorder in the Caucasian population. It is characterized by chronic

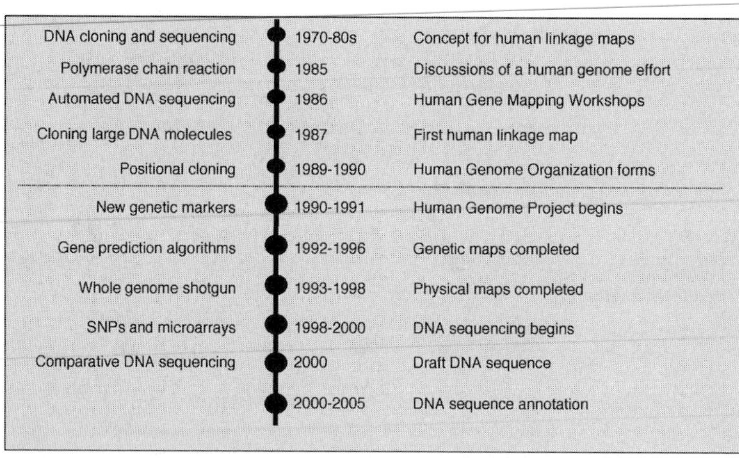

Fig. 7. Timeline of the Human Genome Project (HGP). A historical summary of some of the enabling technologies (on the left) and the achievements (on the right) leading up to and including the HGP are shown. The formal international HGP began in 1990. Other aspects of the HGP are the study of model organisms, analysis of genome variation, and the development of bioinformatics. Establishing training and public education programs, as well as the study of the ethical, legal, and social issues of genetics research in society, are also important priorities.

lung disease and pancreatic insufficiency, and affects 1 in 2500 individuals. The severity of the disease can often be correlated with the mutations present (*see* Fig. 4).

In order to locate the CF gene, researchers tested DNA from CF families with a large number of genetic markers. A total of 211 families were pooled and analyzed and eventually two markers located on chromosome 7 were found to flank the gene. This key finding, published in 1985, indicated that the CF gene must be inherited along with the markers on chromosome 7. Next, a combination of genetic techniques, including chromosome *walking* and *jumping*, was used. In walking to either direction of a known marker, an initial clone containing the marker gene is used to isolate another clone that contains overlapping information from the genome. The DNA segments can then be placed in an order corresponding to that on the chromosome and the process is repeated. A complimentary approach to this technique, called chromosome jumping, utilizes only the ends of cloned segments, making jumps over uninformative or repetitive regions of DNA. In the search for the CF gene, each DNA fragment isolated was compared to DNA from animal species in order to determine whether any of these fragments were conserved during evolution. A match was found with a sequence from chicken, mouse, and cow, suggesting that this gene was also encoded in these animals. This fragment of DNA represented the start of the CF gene and was used to identify the remainder of the gene. Since no chromosomal abnormality was evident in the patients, researchers then began searching for a difference between DNA from normal and CF patients. In 1989, a small deletion was found in a particular DNA fragment that appeared in 70% of the chromosomes from CF patients, but was absent from normal chromosomes. The gene was found to be 250 kb long, comprised of 24 exons, encoding a trans-membrane protein, 1480 aa long. This gene located on chromosome 7 was called CFTR (cystic fibrosis trans-membrane conductance regulator), which encodes a chloride channel protein. In the majority of patients, the error that causes CF is minute, only three of the base pairs are missing. This principal mutation, DeltaF508 (deletion of phenylalanine amino acid at position 508 in the protein), is found in approx 70% of carriers of European ancestry, and is enough to radically disrupt the function of patients' lungs, sweat glands, and pancreas. The CF gene is also associated with mutational heterogeneity. Over 550 other mutations have been identified. Many of these are extremely rare, but a few reach frequencies of 1–3 % in CF carriers.

The Human Genome Project and Disease Gene Identification

With the development of new mapping resources and technologies, and massive amounts of DNA sequence generated by the HGP, the ability to clone rearrangement breakpoints and map disease genes has been greatly simplified. This has also accelerated the pace of discovery of new disease loci and the underlying mutational mechanisms. For example, the gene for Parkinson's disease (alpha synuclein) on chromosome 4q21-q23 and the gene for speech and language disorder (FOXP2) on chromosome 7q31, were identified within only a few months of determining their chromosomal location.

After a decade of experience in positional cloning, and with the HGP DNA sequence now well-advanced, it has become possible to dissect the molecular genetics of multifactorial diseases such as cancer and cardiovascular disease. These involve multiple combinations of genes and strong environmental components. Scientists will continue to work on the HGP with an emphasis on annotating the DNA sequence to find new genes, determine the function of the gene products (functional genomics), and apply all of this information to the study of common diseases.

Glossary and Abbreviations

Acrocentric Human chromosomes (13, 14, 15, 21 and 22) with the centromere near one end.

Allele One of the alternative versions of a gene that may occupy a given locus.

Autosome The nuclear chromosomes other than the sex chromosomes.

Base pair (bp) A pair of complementary nucleotide bases in double stranded DNA.

CF Cystic fibrosis.

CFTR Cystic fibrosis trans-membrane conductance regulator.

Chromosome The threadlike structures in the cell nucleus consisting of chromatin that carries the genetic information (DNA).

Deletion A loss of a sequence of DNA from a chromosome.

DNA Deoxyribonucleic acid. The molecule that encodes the genes responsible for the structure and function of living organisms and allows the transmission of genetic information from parents to offspring.

Dominant A trait is dominant if it is phenotypically expressed in heterozygotes.

Exon A transcribed region of a gene that is present in mature messenger RNA.

Gamete A reproductive cell (ovum or sperm) with the haploid chromosome number.

Gene A hereditary unit, a sequence of chromosomal DNA that is required for the production of a functional product.

Genetic disorder A defect caused by genes.

Genetic map The relative positions of genes on the chromosomes.

Genetic marker A characteristic of DNA that allows different versions of a locus to be distinguished from one another and followed through families in genetic studies.

Genome The complete DNA sequence containing the entire genetic information.

Genotype The genetic constitution of an individual.

Germline The cell line from which the gametes are derived.

Haploid The chromosome number of a normal gamete.

HGP Human genome project.

Housekeeping genes Genes expressed in most or all cells because their products provide basic functions.

Insertion A chromosomal abnormality in which a DNA segment from one chromosome is inserted into a non-homologous chromosome.

Intron A segment of a gene that is initially transcribed but then removed from within the primary RNA transcript by splicing together the exon sequences on either side.

Locus The position occupied by a gene on a chromosome.

Mitochondrial DNA The DNA in the circular chromosome of mitochondria that is maternally inherited.

mRNA Messenger RNA.

Mutation Any permanent heritable change in the sequence of genomic DNA.

Nucleotide A molecule composed of a nitrogenous base, a 5-carbon sugar and a phosphate group.

Pedigree A diagram of a family history indicating the family members, their relationship with the proband and their status with respect to a particular hereditary condition.

Penetrance The fraction of individuals with a genotype known to cause a disease who have any signs or symptoms of the disease.

Phenotype The observed characteristics of an individual as determined by his or her genotype.

Physical map A map showing the order of genes along a chromosome and their distances apart in units such as base pairs.

Pleiotropy Multiple phenotypic effects of a single gene or gene pair.

Point mutation A single nucleotide base-pair change in DNA.

Polygenic Inheritance determined by many genes at different loci.

Polymorphism The occurrence in a population of two or more alternative genotypes.

Positional cloning The molecular cloning of a gene on the basis of its map position, without prior knowledge of the gene product.

Promoter A DNA sequence located in the 5' end of a gene at which transcription is initiated.

Recessive A trait that is expressed only in homozygotes or hemizygotes.

RNA Ribonucleic acid. A nucleic acid formed upon a DNA template, containing ribose instead of deoxyribose. Messenger RNA is the template on which polypeptides are synthesized.

Sequence The order of nucleotides in a segment of DNA or RNA.

Sex chromosomes The X and Y chromosomes.

SNP Single nucleotide polymorphism.

Somatic mutation A mutation occurring in a somatic cell.

STR Short tandem repeat.

Transcription The synthesis of a single-stranded RNA molecule from a DNA template in the cell nucleus, catalyzed by RNA polymerase.

Translocation The transfer of a segment of one chromosome to another chromosome.

Trisomy The state of having three representatives of a given chromosome instead of the usual pair.

VNTR Variable number tandem repeat.

WGS Whole genome shotgun.

Suggested Reading

Botstein, D., White, R. L., Skolnick, M., and Davis, R. W. (1980) Construction of a genetic linkage map in man using restriction fragment length polymorphisms, Am. J. Hum. Genet. 32, 314–331.

Chumakov, I. M., Rigault, P., Le Gall, I., Ballanne-Chantelot, C., Billault, A., Guillon, S., et al. (1995) A YAC contig map of the human genome, Nature 377 (Suppl), 175–297.

Cohen, D., Chumakov, I., and Weissenbach, J. (1993) A first generation physical map of the human genome, Nature 366, 698–701.

Collins, F. S. (1992) Positional cloning: Let's not call it reverse anymore, Nat. Genet. 1, 3–6.

Deloukas, P., Schuler, G. D., Gyapay, G., Beasley, E. M., Soderlund, C., Rodriguez-Tome, P. et al. (1998) A physical map of 30,000 human genes, Science 282, 744–746.

Dib, C., Faure, S., Fizames, C., Samson, D., Drouot, N., Vignal, A., et al. (1996) A comprehensive genetic map of the human genome based on 5,264 microsatellites, Nature 380, 152–154.

Donis-Keller, H., Green, P., Helms, C., Cartinhour, S., Weifenbach, B., Stephens, K., et al. (1987) A genetic linkage map of the human genome, Cell 51, 319–337.

Dunham, I. N., Shimizu, N., Roe, B., Chissoe, S., Hunt, A. R., Collins, J. E., et al. (2000), The DNA sequence of human chromosome 22, Nature 404, 904–920.

Hudson, T. J., Stein, L. D., Gerety, S. S., Ma, J., Castle, A. B., Silva, J., et al. (1995) An STS-based map of the human genome, Science 270, 1945–1954.

International Human Genome Sequencing Consortium (2001) Initial sequencing and analysis of the human genome, Nature 409, 860–914.

Kerem, B., Rommens, J. M., Buchanan, J. A., Markiewicz, D., Cox, T. K., Chakravarti, A., Buchwald, M., and Tsui, L-C. (1989) Identification of the cystic fibrosis gene: Genetic analysis, Science 245, 1073–1080.

Riordan, J. R., Rommens, J., Kerem, B., Alon, N., Rozmahel, R.,Grzelczak, Z., et al. (1989) Identification of the cystic fibrosis gene: Cloning and characterization of complementary DNA, Science 245, 1066–1073.

Rommens, J. M., Iannuzzi, M. C., Kerem, B., Drumm, M. L., Melmer, G., Dean, M., et al. (1989) Identification of the cystic fibrosis gene: chromosome walking and jumping, Science 245, 1059–1065.

The Huntington's Disease Research Collaborative Group (1993) A novel gene containing a trinucleotide repeat is expanded and unstable on Huntington's disease chromosomes, Cell 72, 971–983.

Tsui, L-C. and Estivill, X. (1991) Identification of disease genes on the basis of chromosomal localization, Genome Anal. 3, 1–36.
Venter, J. C., Adams, M. D., Myers, E. W., Li, P. W., Mural, R. J., Sutton, G. G., et al. (2001) The sequence of the human genome, Science 291, 1304–1351.
Zielenski, J. and Tsui, L. C. (1995) Cystic fibrosis: Genotypic and phenotypic variations, Annu. Rev. Genet. 29, 777–807.

B. Clinical Human Genetics

10. Heredity
11. The Clinical Genetics Databases
12. Population Genetics

10 Heredity

C. A. Rupar

Introduction

Clinical geneticists classify human traits and genetic disorders on the basis of the patterns of inheritance in families: sporadic, autosomal dominant, autosomal recessive, X-linked, and mitochondrial. A compendium of genetic information, McKusick's Online Mendelian Inheritance in Man (OMIM) (*see* Website: http://www.ncbi.nlm.nih.gov/omim/), has been assembled primarily based on clinical observations as to how traits and disease states appear to be inherited.

Identification of the patterns of inheritance of genetic disorders has enabled geneticists to make significant contributions to health care. The recognition of the pattern of inheritance of a disorder in a family may be an important diagnostic aid, permit the identification of individuals in a family who are at risk to develop the disorder, and enable informed counseling of family members about the recurrence risks of having another affected child.

Early in 2001, the results of the publicly and privately funded human genome sequencing projects indicated that the human genome contains about 3 billion bases arranged in a genome, which encodes at least 35,000 genes. This represents considerably fewer genes than had been anticipated. As of September 22, 2001 the definitive catalog of human genes, OMIM listed a total of 12,954 loci with 7,441 mapped to specific sites in the genome. Clearly there are many more genes to be identified and the knowledge of how the expression of genes are regulated spatially and temporally is still in its infancy.

The majority of clinical genetics is devoted to the family, but genes are shared not only within families but also within populations. Many rare genetic traits affect individuals throughout the world, whereas other normally rare traits are much more prevalent in some populations. There are a number of reasons why a population may have a higher frequency of a particular allele that may be favorable or unfavorable. Individuals in populations whose gene pool has been relatively isolated for generations and populations whose gene pools originate from a small number of founder individuals are more likely to share alleles that may be rare outside that population.

In other situations one population may experience selective pressures that favour a particular allele but another population may not experience the same selective pressure. Perhaps the best example is heterozygosity, when an individual carries both alleles, for otherwise deleterious globin gene mutations it protects individuals in tropical climates against malaria.

Dominance and Recessiveness

Dominance and recessiveness refer to clinical phenotypes. A condition is recessive when the phenotype of a heterozygous individual is the same as the phenotype of homozygous normal individuals. However, upon closer inspection, heterozygous individuals in many recessive conditions may have a measurable biochemical difference when compared to homozygous normal individuals. For example, phenylketonuria (PKU) is most often due to mutations in the *PAH* locus, which codes for phenylalanine hydroxylase. Individuals with PKU are unable to convert phenylalanine to tyrosine and have plasma concentrations of phenylalanine much higher than normal individuals. Individuals who are heterozygous for PKU do not have a clinical phenotype but when plasma concentrations of phenylalanine and tyrosine are measured, heterozygotes may be distinguished from homozygous normal individuals.

In principle a condition is dominant when the clinical phenotype of heterozygous individuals is indistinguishable from homozygous affected individuals. There are probably few examples of true dominant disorders, with the most notable example being Huntington's disease. Most mutations are deleterious when compared to the wild-type or *normal* allele and behave in a recessive manner. It is unlikely that a newly and randomly introduced change in protein structure will result in a protein with improved function.

The explanation as to why a given disorder is inherited in a dominant or recessive manner is often not understood but there are observations that do provide clues. For example most enzyme deficiencies are inherited in a recessive manner with the heterozygous individual not having a phenotype. Presumably most enzymes are expressed in sufficient excess that a heterozygote who may have about half (to a first approximation) of the enzyme activity of a homozygous normal individual has a level of activity that prevents a phenotype.

Dominantly inherited disorders are often caused by genes that code for structural or developmentally important proteins where presumably half of the normal amounts of the gene product are inadequate. There are also examples of dominant mutations in regulatory enzymes. Porphobilinogen deaminase (PBG) is a notable example. PBG catalyses the first and rate-limiting step in heme biosynthesis. A deficiency in PBG deaminase results in the autosomal dominantly inherited condition, acute intermittent porphyria. Another type of example of dominant inheritance is familial hypercholesterolemia, owing to a deficiency of the low-density lipoprotein (LDL) receptor. This plays a key role in regulating cellular cholesterol metabolism.

Whether a given mutation behaves in a dominant or recessive manner is best explained by knowledge of the biochemistry and physiology of the gene product of specific mutations. Indeed, different mutations in the same gene may behave in dominant or recessive manners. An important concept is that of dominant negativeness, which describes the situation that occurs when a mutant protein from one chromosome interferes with the function of the normal protein from the other chromosome. There are elegant examples of dominant negativenss in disorders of the structural protein collagen and in some multimeric enzymes.

There are also examples of dominantly inherited mutations that result in a gain of function for a protein. This new function may be deleterious or even toxic to cells. An example is Huntington's disease, where there is a gain of function associated with the expansion of a CAG trinucleotide repeat. Other examples like hypermethioninema described below, cause loss of function.

Methionine Adenosyl Transferase OMIM #250850

Methionine adenosyl transferase (MAT) catalyses the synthesis of adenosylmethionine from methionine and ATP. Adenosylmethionine is an important methyl donor in transmethylation reactions and a deficiency of MAT results in hypermethioninemia. Most often the phenotype, hypermethioninemia, is inherited in an autosomal recessive manner with at least 17 mutations in *MAT1A* identified in the human population. However there are families in which the phenotype is inherited in an autosomal dominant manner. MAT exists in two forms MATI and MAT III. MATI and III are, respectively, homotetramers and homodimers of the peptide that is encoded by the *MATA1* gene. A mutation that results in the substitution of arginine with histidine at position 264 greatly reduced MATI/III activity by preventing homodimer formation that is essential for catalytic activity and is inherited in a dominant manner.

Understanding Pedigrees

Pedigrees are an important tool that geneticists use to understand the pattern of inheritance of a disorder or trait in a family. Pedigrees are drawn with standardized symbols and follow some simple conventions. Each generation is assigned a Roman numeral with the first or oldest generation of the pedigree numbered I. Each individual within a generation is assigned a number with number 1 being the individual at the left of the pedigree. Thus every individual in a pedigree has a unique number based on generation number and position within the generation. Within a family, the children are drawn in decreasing age from left to right. Figure 1 displays the various symbols used in the construction of pedigrees.

Autosomal Dominant Inheritance

An individual with an autosomal dominant condition has a mutation in only one allele, with the allele on the other chromosome being normal. Families with autosomal dominant disorders typically show vertical patterns of inheritance in pedigrees. The low frequency of most alleles that contain mutations makes the likelihood of an individual to inherit dominant mutant alleles from both parents quite low, but nevertheless, this has been observed. Typically individuals who are *double dominant* will have a more severe phenotype.

In autosomal dominantly inherited disorders a mutant gene may not always be expressed in a phenotype or the phenotype that is expressed may be variable in different individuals even in the same family. These concepts are referred to as reduced penetrance and variable expressivity. The underlying biological explanations of reduced penetrance and variable expressivity are generally not understood but presumably lies in the effects of other loci or environmental factors on the expression of the phenotype.

Often in the family of an affected individual there is no evidence of the previous presence of a dominant gene. This may be explained by the mutation in the affected

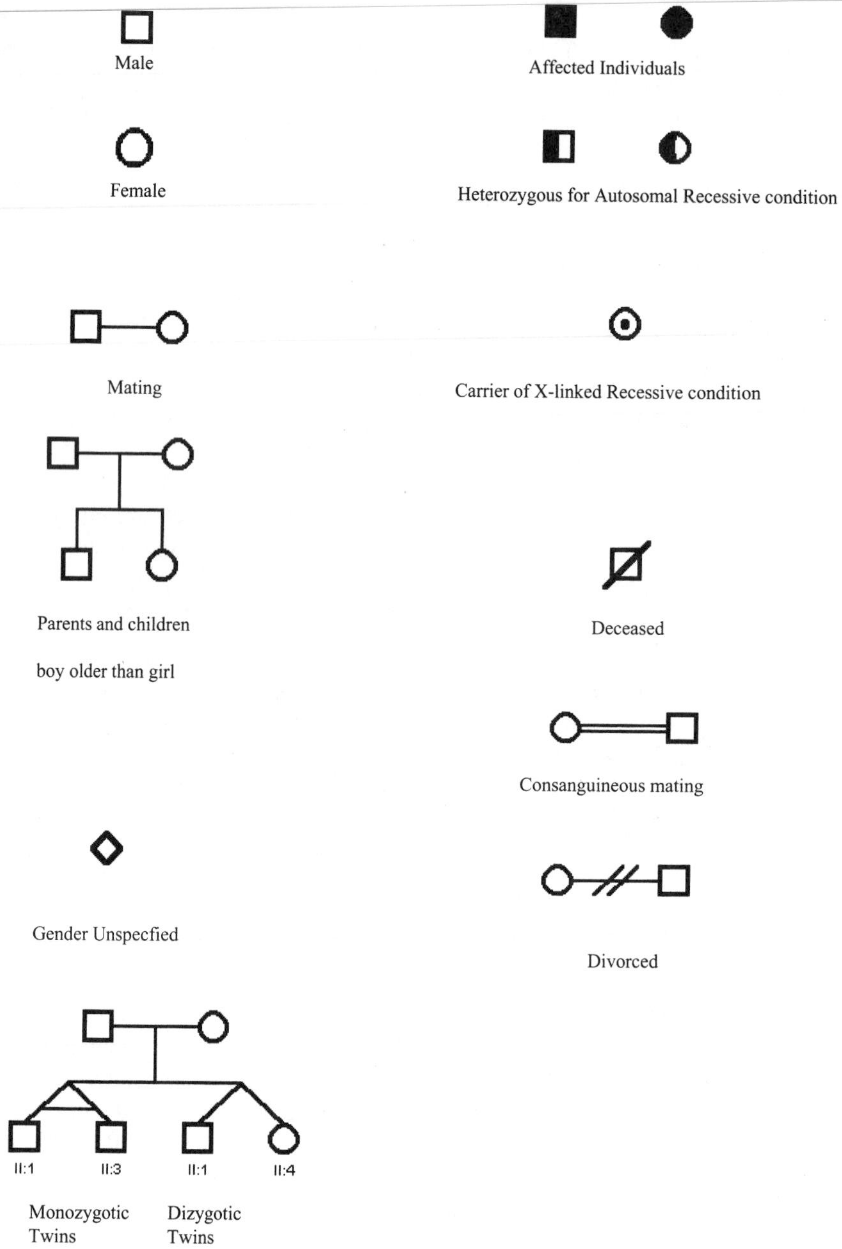

Fig. 1. The key to understanding pedigrees.

individual being a new mutation. New mutation rates have been determined for a number of disorders and typically occur in the range of 5×10^{-6} to 1×10^{-4} mutations per gamete per generation. Because a new mutation is a relatively rare event, it is unlikely to happen twice with the same couple. Empirical data gained by studying many families indicate that the recurrence risk of having another affected child is usually significantly greater than that of acquiring a new mutation. Those couples who do have another affected child are most easily explained by one of the parents being a *gonadal mosaic*. That is, a mutation has occurred in a germ-cell lineage and that parent may have a mixed population of sperm or ova with some cells having the normal allele and others having the mutation.

Trinucleotide repeat disorders are a particularly interesting group of dominantly inherited disorders. The underlying mutation is the expansion of a repetitious region of the gene. There are several triplet expansion disorders with many being primarily neurological. The following examines the clinical and genetic phenotype of muscular dystrophy.

Myotonic Dystrophy (OMIM # 160900)

Myotonic dystrophy is a fascinating example of a trinucleotide repeat as a mutation. Individuals with myotonic dystrophy have a progressive state of muscle tightness due to chronic spasms and other clinical features, including cataracts, early frontal hair loss, electrocardiographic changes, muscle wasting, and hypogonadism. Clinical geneticists have recognized for years the phenomena of *anticipation* in myotonic dystrophy: each successive generation has a more severe and earlier presenting disease. The gene for myotonic dystrophy is located at chromosome position 19q13.3 and codes for the protein dystrophia myotonia protein kinase. In the 3' untranslated region of the mRNA the sequence CTG is repeated from 5–35 times in tandem in unaffected individuals. In individuals with myotonic dystrophy, the repeat has expanded and may become as long as 5 kb. There is a rough correlation between the length of the repeat and the severity of disease. The repeat often becomes longer in successive generations although the opposite has also been observed. Often, the most severely affected individuals, those with congenital myotonic dystrophy, inherit the mutation from their mothers.

Characteristics of Autosomal Dominant Inheritance

- The trait often appears in every generation. Exceptions occur in the case of new mutations and with disorders that can have reduced penetrance or expressivity. Reduced penetrance occurs when some individuals who have inherited a particular geneotype do not express the typical phenotype. Penetrance can be described mathematically as the percentage of individuals who have the gene for a condition who actually show the trait. Expressivity of a phenotype is variable when different individuals with the same mutated gene express different phenotypes.
- Affected individuals will pass on the mutation to half of their children.
- Males and females are equally likely to inherit the trait.
- Unaffected members of the family will not pass on the trait to their children.

A typical pedigree for an autosomal dominant inherited disorder is shown in Fig. 2.

Autosomal Recessive Inheritance

An autosomal recessive trait is only expressed in homozygotes. Affected individuals have inherited a gene with a mutation from both parents. The parents, who are heterozygotes, are generally unaffected. Most inborn errors of metabolism, which are due to enzyme deficiencies, are inherited in an autosomal recessive manner. Recessive disorders are rare in most populations. However there are many groups where certain rare recessive disorders are relatively common because the population has been isolated by

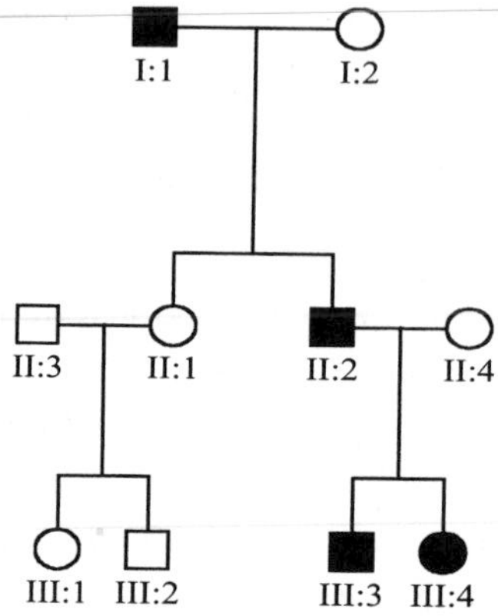

Fig. 2. An autosomal dominant pedigree.

geographical, cultural, religious, or linguistic barriers. Another situation that raises the risk for recessive disorders is when the parents are related, which is termed consanguinity. The more closely the parents are related, the greater the risk of sharing rare recessive alleles. In the extreme cases of parent-child and brother-sister matings, the children are homozygous at one quarter of their gene loci.

There are often many mutations in the population and it is of considerable interest to geneticists to establish genotype-phenotype correlations. Can the knowledge of an individual's genotype at a locus be used to predict the severity of disease? This becomes complex in autosomal recessive disorders where many affected individuals are compound heterozygotes, i.e., they inherited different mutations from each parent. Phenylketonuria, described below, is a classic example of an autosomal recessive disorder.

Phenylketonuria (OMIM # 261600)

Phenylketonuria is a classic example of an autosomal recessive disorder. Most individuals with phenylketonuria have mutations in the gene, which codes for phenylalanine hydroxylase (PAH). *PAH* converts phenylalanine to tyrosine and when it is dysfunctional the plasma and tissue concentrations of phenylalanine rise dramatically. This causes a devastating progressive neurological disorder that results in profound developmental delay with affected individuals dependent on others for their care. The incidence of PKU is about 1 in 15,000 births, which means nearly 1 in 60 in the population is a heterozygote carrying one *PAH* allele with a mutation. Many countries throughout the world screen newborn children for PKU because the profound developmental delay is preventable by a diet that is low in phenylalanine. PKU, like many other genetic disorders has a dedicated website. This provides information for families and a database for students and researchers (*see* Website: http://ww2.mcgill.ca/pahdb). Some mutations in the *PAH* locus have a relatively small impact on the function of phenylalanine hydroxylase and result in benign hyperphenylalaninemia, whereas other mutations have a severe impact on the presence or function of the enzyme and result in PKU. The presence of the phenotype is determined by the concentration of plasma phenylalanine. Benign hyperphenylalaninemia does not require dietary treatment.

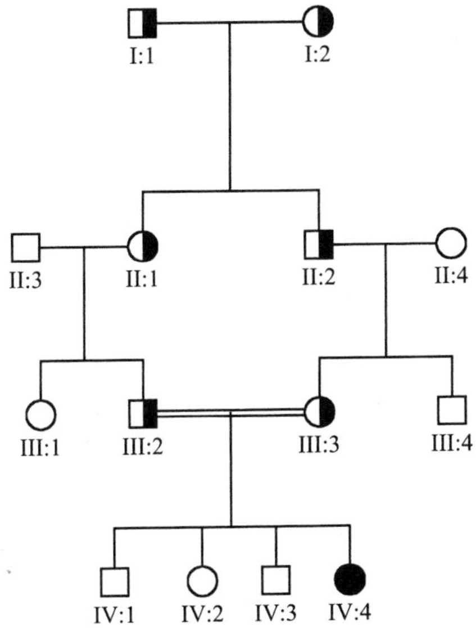

Fig. 3. An autosomal recessive pedigree.

Characteristics of Autosomal Recessive Inheritance

- Usually the phenotype is present in brothers and sisters not in parents.
- Statistically one-quarter of the sibs of an affected child will also be affected.
- Males and females are equally likely to be affected.
- Occurs more frequently in consanguineous relationships.

A typical pedigree for an autosomal recessive disorder is shown in Fig. 3.

X-linked Inheritance

Phenotypes of mutations in genes on the X chromosome are inherited in characteristic patterns that are determined by males having one X chromosome and females having two X chromosomes. Most disorders on the X chromosome are recessive in nature and are expressed primarily in males. Females are not always totally protected by the X chromosome with the normal allele because the Lyon hypothesis predicts random inactivation of one of the X-chromosomes early in embryonic development. Females with a mutation on one X chromosome then become mosaics with some cells inactivating the chromosome with the normal sequence gene, while others inactivate the X chromosome with the mutation. By random inactivation, some females inactivate a high proportion of the normal X chromosome. Even so, they essentially have a milder phenotype of the male disorder. In some disorders, a female may not have a phenotype, she may have a measurable biochemical abnormality as typified by X-inactivation of ornithine transcarbamylase as X described next.

Ornithine Transcarbamylase (OMIM # 311250)

Ornithine transcarbamylase catalyzes the synthesis of citrulline from ornithine and carbamyl phosphate in an early step in the urea cycle. The most common presentation

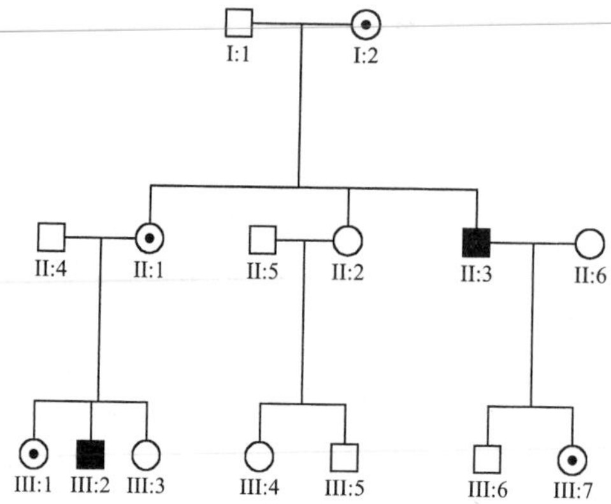

Fig. 4. An X-rated pedigree.

of affected males is an acute life-threatening hepatic encephalopathy brought on by very high levels of blood ammonium at a few days of age. Affected females usually present later in infancy or childhood with a less severe disease. These females have inactivated too great of a proportion of the X chromosomes carrying the normal allele in their livers. Like many X-linked disorders, many different mutations have occurred in the population. When parents of children with ornithine transcarbamylase deficiency are genotyped, it is apparent that frequency of new mutations in sperm is much higher than ova.

Characteristics of X-Linked Inheritance

- The incidence of the disorder is much greater in males than females.
- All the daughters of an affected male will be carriers of the mutant allele.
- A father can never transmit the mutant allele to his sons.
- Female carriers may show variable expression of the disorder.

A typical pedigree for an X-linked trait is shown in Fig. 4.

Mitochondrial Inheritance

Mitochondria, the powerhouse of the cell, are unique structures possessing their own DNA. The complete sequence of human mitochondrial DNA has been known since the early 1980s. It is a 16,569 nucleotide double-stranded molecule that codes for 13 polypeptides essential for oxidative phosphorylation, 22 tRNAs and 2 ribosomal RNAs. However, the vast majority of mitochondrial proteins are encoded in the nucleus. There has been intense interest in the contribution of mitochondria DNA to human disorders (*see* Website: http://www.gen.emory.edu/mitomap.html). This has enabled the identification of mutations that cause genetic disorders. Approximately 125 pathological point mutations have been identified in the mitochondrial DNA sequence. There have also been a large number of deletions characterized in patients with mitochondria DNA disorders. Distinguishing pathological mutations from benign polymorphisms is sometimes difficult. Unlike the nuclear encoded mutations, there are yet expression systems to study the effects of a mitochondrial DNA mutation on protein or cellular function.

At the time of conception all mitochondria originate from the ovum; the sperm makes no contribution in humans. Thus, any attribute or disorder that is a consequence of the mitochondrial genome is inherited along the maternal lineage. A mitochondrion may contain several copies of its genome and many cell types have large numbers of mitochondria; consequently, mitochondrial DNA is present in multiple copies within a cell.

A mutation in mitochondrial DNA, either inherited or a new mutation, can result in a mixed population of mitochondrial DNA consisting of normal sequence DNA and DNA with the mutation. This is called heteroplasmy. During mitosis, mitochondria in the parent cell are distributed to the daughter cells in a random manner resulting in daughter cell populations that may have different populations of mitochondrial DNA. These range from cells having only the normal sequence cells to cells that have a higher percentage of mutant DNA than the parent cell. The maternal pattern of inheritance mitochondrial DNA mutations provides a major clue as to whether a mitochondrial disorder is due to a mutation in a nuclear encoded or mitochondrial-encoded gene.

Mitochondrial DNA accumulates spontaneous mutations about 10 times faster than nuclear DNA. Two possible reasons for this sensitivity to damage are the presence of free radicals in mitochondria as a consequence of the electron transport chain and the lesser competence of mitochondria when compared to the nucleus to repair damage to DNA. Mitochondrial DNA mutations exhibit a threshold effect, in that, often about 85% of the mitochondrial DNA must contain a mutation before a clinically detectable phenotype occurs. An example of MELAS syndrome is described as follows.

MELAS Syndrome (OMIM # 540000)

MELAS syndrome, which is the acronym of mitochondrial myopathy, encephalopathy, lactic acidosis, and stroke-like episodes, is most frequently due to an A to G mutation at position 3243 of the mitochondrial genome. This region of the mitochondria codes for a leucine tRNA. Interestingly, many individuals with the nt 3243 mutation do not have MELAS syndrome but rather develop seemingly unrelated health problems such as bilateral sensorineural hearing loss and adult-onset diabetes. There are other mutations in the same leucine tRNA that also cause MELAS, but also mutations that cause seemingly unrelated disorders such as cardiomyopathy. Genotype-phenotype correlations within mitochondria DNA disorders are not often evident, making molecular diagnoses difficult. Presumably much of the variability reflects random segregation at cell division and threshold effects.

Characteristics of Mitochondrial Inheritance

- Inheritance is only along the maternal lineage. A male cannot pass the disorder to his children.
- There is no gender preference.
- Many, but not necessarily all, of an affected female's children will inherit the mutation but the clinical impact may be quite variable.

A typical pedigree for a mitochondrial inherited trait is shown in Fig. 5.

Multifactorial Inheritance

Although there are thousands of disorders that are inherited along recognisable Mendelian patterns of inheritance, most are relatively uncommon. Many common diseases such as schizophrenia, diabetes, alcoholism, coronary artery disease, and neural tube defects often "run in families" but are not inherited in a Mendelian pattern. These

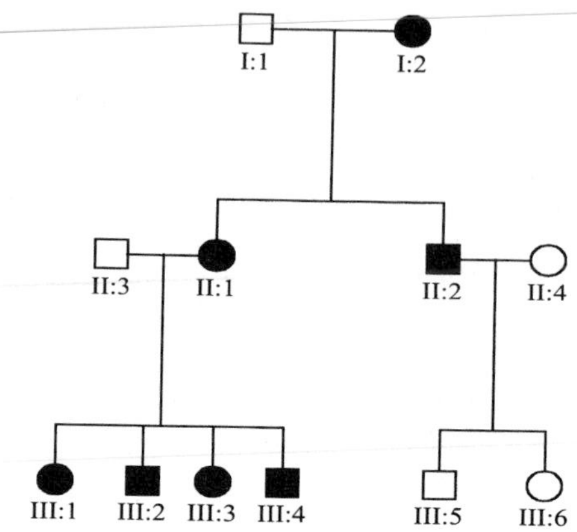

Fig. 5. Pedigree for a mitochondrial inherited trait.

common disorders are inherited in a multifactorial manner that includes the influences of multiple genetic and environmental factors. It will be one of the great accomplishments of human genetics to identify and quantify the contributions of genes to the risks of developing common disorders.

Studies using the incidence of disorder data in monozygotic (identical) and dizygotic (fraternal) twins, have made significant contributions to identifying the presence of a genetic susceptibility component to common diseases. As expected, disorders as diverse as cleft lip and palate, insulin-dependent diabetes, and coronary artery disease are more concordant in monozygotic than dizygotic twins.

In most cases, all the genetic and environmental contributions to the end point of a common disease have not yet been identified. However, there are models to help understand the principles of the roles of multiple contributions. The multiple additive locus model views phenotypes as the sum of the contribution of individual alleles. If at a given gene there are two possible alleles: a and b, then there are three possible genotypes: aa, bb, and ab. Alleles a and b may have different functional efficiencies and hence genotypes aa, bb, and ab may have quantitatively different contributions to a metabolic pathway. Applying the same logic to several genes whose gene product contributes to a phenotypic endpoint indicates how related individuals who share a number of alleles that may be less favorable, share an increased risk. It is easy to see how the multiple additive locus model can be applied to traits that are quantitative with endpoints that cover a continuum of values such as blood pressure.

Other multifactorial traits appear to be better explained by a threshold model of inheritance. The threshold model is particularly applicable to traits such as congenital malformations that tend to behave in an all-or-none manner. In the threshold model of multifactorial inheritance, when a combination of genetic and environmental factors reach a threshold value, the disorder is expressed. The threshold may be envisioned as having a constant value. The threshold may be exceeded in an individual by increasing either the genetic or environmental burden. Close relatives of an individual who exceeded the threshold for a congenital malformation, for example, share a greater percentage of genes than unrelated individuals and are more likely to exceed the threshold. A classic example of a multifactional genetic effect is typified by neural tube defects as described.

Neural Tube Defects

Neural tube defects in the absence of other congenital malformations are a heterogenous group of disorders that range from anencephaly to spina bifuda occulta, a benign form of spina bifuda. Neural tube defects are caused by the embryological failure of the neural groove to close and form the neural tube at about the third week after conception. The most familiar type of neural tube defect is spina bifuda in the lumbar region. This results in the tissues covering the spinal cord and often the spinal chord protrudes from the back. After surgical repair the infant will often be paralyzed below the hips. The world-wide incidence of neural tube defects is about 1 per 1000 live births with some populations such as in Great Britain having a much higher incidence. The genetic contributions to neural tube defects are illustrated by the fact that the occurrence of neural tube defects in first degree (parent or sibling) relatives is much greater than in the general population with a recurrence risk of about 3%. The environmental aspect to the etiology of neural tube defects is illustrated by the fact that the incidence of neural tube defects can be greatly reduced by supplementing the diet of women with folic acid prior to conception.

11 The Clinical Genetics Databases

Peter J. Bridge

Introduction

This introduction to Clinical Genetics reviews a selection of major internet resources drawn from the current large and growing listing. These include genetic variation, diagnostics, laboratory services, regulatory bodies and sequence data. Each of these sites can be regarded as the starting point for a journey to the wealth of information. Many sites provide a page of further links for those seeking additional or specific information. A selection of sites are shown in the figures and all referenced and linked websites are provided on the CD supplement.

OMIM (On-line Mendelian Inheritance in Man)

The principal catalog of genetic variation in humans has long been McKusick's Mendelian Inheritance in Man (MIM). This has been published in book form and revised approx every 2–3 yr by the Johns Hopkins University Press since 1966. An internet-based database and catalog called On-line Mendelian Inheritance in Man (OMIM) has now become available at Website: http://www.ncbi.nlm.gov/omim as part of the NCBI Entrez System. This curated database is updated daily and contains direct links to most of the other important clinical genetics databases as well as comprehensive hypertext links to other entries within OMIM.

The scale of OMIM is staggering. Great detail is provided on all known human phenotypes, and more recently, on many genes that have yet to be associated with any specific phenotype. When using OMIM it is important to be aware that the entries frequently have a significant historical component, from which outdated material is slowly purged. It is often difficult to be absolutely clear, which parts are a historical description vs current consensus.

See companion CD for color Figs. 1 and 2

Figure 1 shows the top of the entry page. Statistics concerning the database and the conventions used within it must be accessed through this entry page. As shown in Fig. 2, one can also proceed directly to the "searchomim.html" page for routine genetic searches. Try entering **cystic fibrosis** in the search box and clicking **title** in the field box. Several entries will be returned. Entry 602421 contains the gene and 219700 is the entry for the clinical phenotype. Either entry will also provide clickable boxes that contain direct links to the specific entry on cystic fibrosis in other databases.

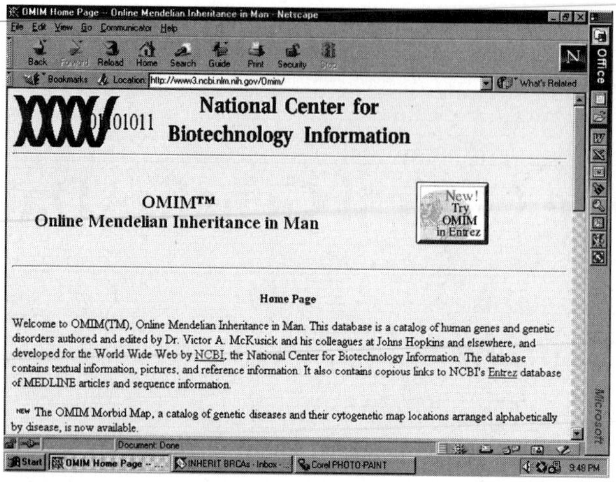

Fig. 1. OMIM: Online Mendelian Inheritance in Man home page.

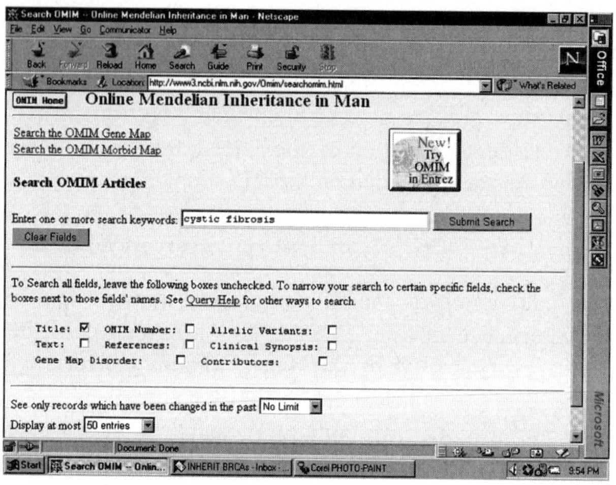

Fig. 2. Online Mendelian Inheritance in Man search page.

Databases of Human Mutations

Lists of mutations in each gene are compiled at the Human Gene Mutation Database (HGMD). This has a new web address (*see* Website: http://www.hgmd.org). Clicking on the **HGMD Search** link (top left, *see* Figure 3), permits progression to the search page where diseases or genes can be entered in a fashion similar to the OMIM search page. Remember that this site is based in the UK. Entering, for instance, a well-known disorder named hemochromatosis, returns nothing because in the UK it is spelled haemochromatosis. One might expect similar results from many other databases that are maintained outside North America like the Human Genome Variation Society (*see* Website: http://ariel.ucs.unimelb.edu.au:80/~cotton/mdi.htm), based at the University of Melbourne.

See companion CD for color Fig. 3

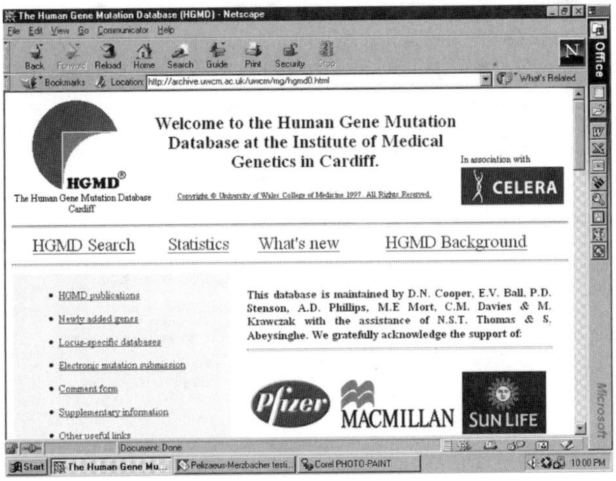

Fig. 3. Genetics Societies home page.

Gene-Specific Databases (Caution)

There are a great number of disease-specific mutation databases on the internet. Most are associated with research laboratories and it is difficult to judge the accuracy and completeness of many of these: user beware! A comprehensive listing of such sites is maintained at Cardiff (without warranty) by the Human Gene Mutation Database (*see* Website: http://archive.uwcm.ac.uk/uwcm/mg/docs/oth_mut.html). The Cardiff site also hosts a database called FIDD, which provides frequencies of inherited disorders around the world (*see* Website: http://archive.uwcm.ac.uk/uwcm/mg/fidd/).

Repositories of Sequence Data

The cDNA sequence of most genes can be conveniently accessed through the Human Gene Mutation Database. Genomic sequences are found at several sites including the Genome Database (GDB; *see* Website: http://gdbwww.gdb.org/) and the National Center for Biotechnology Information (NCBI; *see* Website: http://www.ncbi.nlm.nih.gov/). GDB links are provided through OMIM. One of the more comprehensive starting points is a site on the Human Genome Project Information page maintained for the Department of Energy by the Oak Ridge National Laboratory (ORNL) (*see* Fig. 4, *see* Website: http://www.ornl.gov/hgmis/links.html).

See companion CD for color Fig. 4

GeneClinics

Each entry in the GeneTests database is provides diagnostic and clinical management information. It curated by an expert or panel of experts on that particular disease. Clicking the **Find Disease-Specific Information** heading at the top right of the entry page (*see* Fig. 5), presents a disclaimer page that the user must indicate he/she has read before proceeding. As an example, if the term *cystic* is entered into the search box, you will retrieve cystic fibrosis, polycystic kidney disease, and autosomal recessive. Clicking on the **text info** box next to cystic fibrosis will lead to a long and very detailed article on the clinical aspects of cystic fibrosis. This database is partnered with the GeneTests database.

See companion CD for color Fig. 5

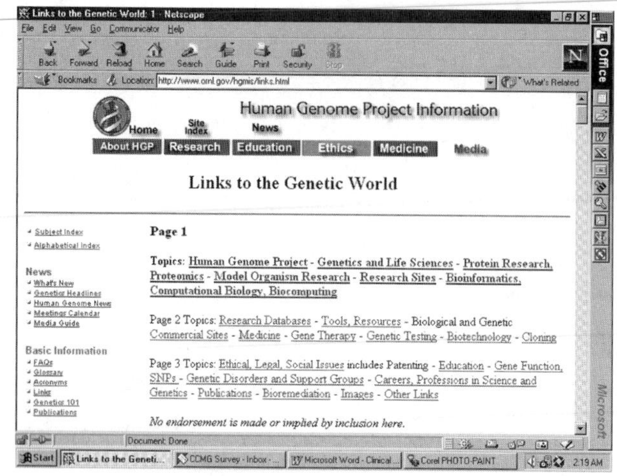

Fig. 4. Genetic Professional Societies home page.

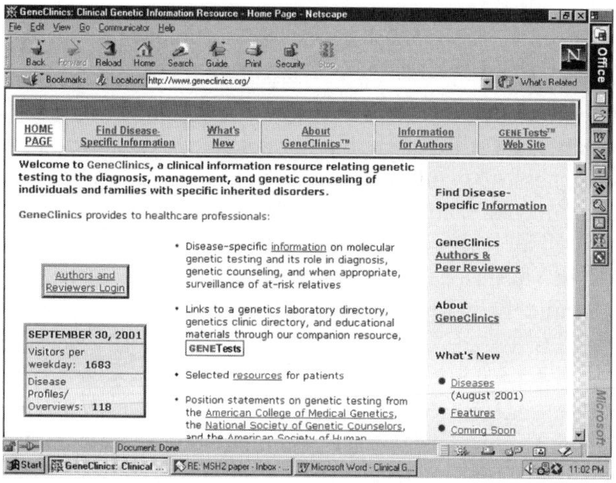

Fig. 5. HGMD Human Gene Mutation Database.

GeneTests

This is a comprehensive and well-curated database of genetic tests and testing laboratories in North America. It is necessary to have a password to enter the database, but this is readily available by following the instructions at the top left of the first page (*see* Fig. 6). Once a user ID and password have been established, entry is obtained by typing these in the boxes at the top left and clicking the **log in**. In the center of the next page, under the blue box, is a link to **Genetics Lab Directory** (*see* Fig. 7). This leads one through a disclaimer page, to a searchable database of genetic laboratories (*see* Fig. 8). Entering **achondro** will return several entries including achondroplasia. Achondroplasia has two boxes next to it **LAB List** and **TEXT Info**. Clicking the **LAB List** box will provide a list of laboratories that provide testing for achondroplasia (including mine in Canada and several in other countries). Clicking the **TEXT Info**

See companion CD for color Figs. 6, 7, and 8

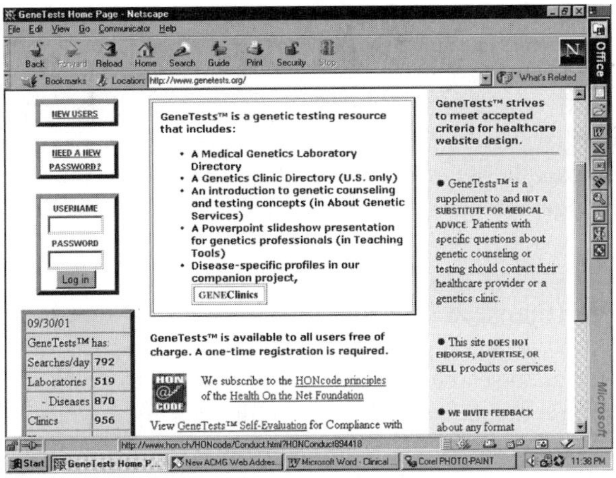

Fig. 6. Oak Ridge National Laboratory (ORNL) Links to the Genetic World.

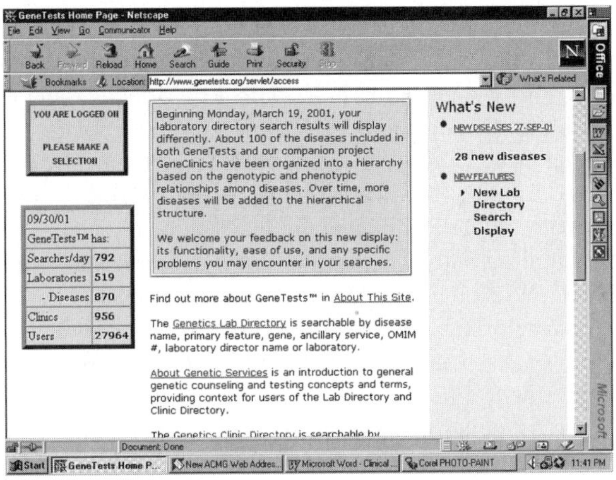

Fig. 7. GeneClinics.

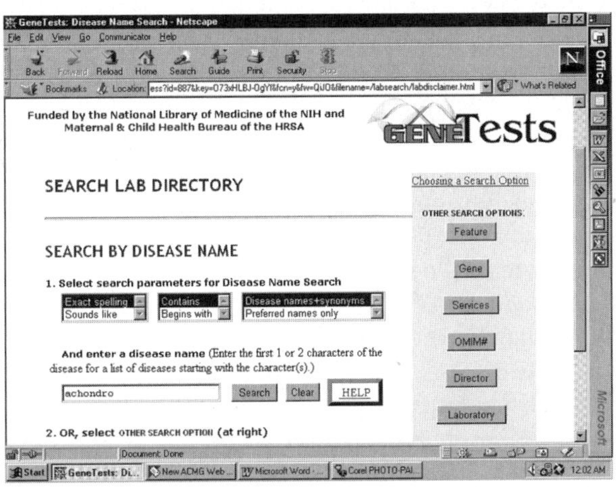

Fig. 8. GeneTests Login.

box will take you to the GeneClinics entry for achondroplasia in the database described earlier. On the right-hand side of the search page (*see* Fig. 8), are a series of boxes that give other search options. Clicking the **Director** box on the right and then entering **Bridge** describes this author's laboratory.

EDDNAL

EDDNAL (European Directory of DNA Labs) is a database of genetic tests and testing laboratories in Europe. Clicking the **Start a request** link at the left of the entry page allows one to search the database by entering a McKusick code, i.e., an OMIM number; disease name; contact; e.g., lab director; or country, to retrieve a list of all laboratories in that country (*see* Website http://www.eddnal.com/).

National Colleges

The national college governing the practice of medical genetics in the United States is the American College of Medical Genetics (ACMG). Founded in 1992, the ACMG has grown steadily both in numbers of members and in degree of influence (*see* Website: http://www.acmg.net/). This key website can be accessed for regulations and policy in the United States.

The national college governing the practice of medical genetics in the Canada is the Canadian College of Medical Geneticists (CCMG). Founded in 1975, the CCMG has a long history of leadership in the field of medical genetics. In Canada, the CCMG is also the examining body whereas in the United States this function is separate from the ACMG. (*see* Website: http://ccmg.medical.org/).

Genetic counselors in both the United States and Canada have a specific professional Society or Association. In the United States there is the National Society of Genetic Counselors (NSGC; *see* Website: http://www.nsgc.org/) and in Canada there is the Canadian Association of Genetic Counsellors (CAGC; *see* Website: http://www.cagc-accg.ca/).

Examining Boards

In the United States, the board examinations are administered by the American Board of Medical Genetics (ABMG; *see* Website: http://www.abmg.org), in Canada, it is administered by the Canadian College of Medical Geneticists (CCMG; *see* Website: http://ccmg.medical. org/), or the Royal College of Physicians and Surgeons of Canada (RCPSC; *see* Website: http://rcpsc.medical.org/). Examinations in genetic counseling are administered by the American Board of Genetic Counseling (ABGC; *see* Website: http://www.abgc.net/) and by the Canadian Association of Genetic Counsellors (CAGC; *see* Website: http://www.cagc-accg.ca/). Information about laboratory technologist certification is available through the Association of Genetic Technologists (AGT; *see* Website: http://www.agt-info.org/) in the United States, the Canadian Society for Medical Laboratory Science (CSMLS; *see* Website: http://www.csmls.org/) in Canada, and the Clinical Molecular Genetics Society (CMGS; *see* Website: http://www.ich.ucl.ac.uk/cmgs/cmgshelp.htm) in the UK. The latter also posts its curriculum on this website.

Learned Societies

See companion CD for color Fig. 9

There is a general starting point for several societies at the Federation of American Societies for Experimental Biology (FASEB; *see* Fig. 9, *see* Website: http://

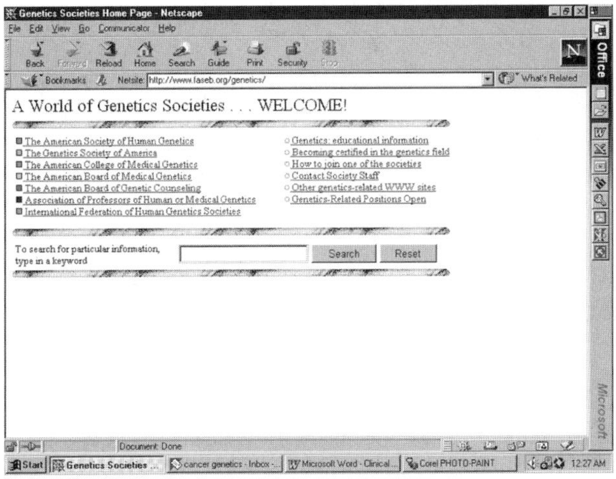

Fig. 9. GeneTests.

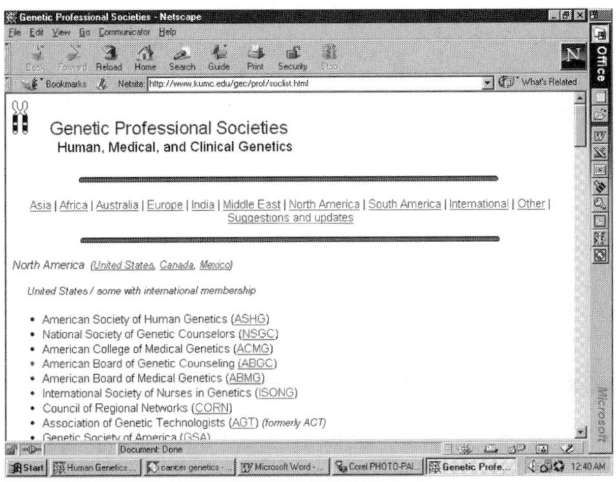

Fig. 10. GeneTests Search for clinical tests provided by various laboratories.

www.faseb.org/genetics/). This organization is still the host of the American Society of Human Genetics (ASHG; *see* Website: http://www.faseb.org/genetics/ashg/ashgmenu.htm) homepage and until very recently also hosted the American College of Medical Genetics (ACMG). A more global perspective can be found at the sites for the European Society of Human Genetics (ESHG; *see* Website: http://www.eshg.org/), the International Federation of Human Genetics Societies (IFHGS; *see* Website: http://www.ifhgs.org/), and the Human Genetics Society of Australasia (HGSA; *see* Website: http://www.hgsa.com.au/). There is a comprehensive listing of societies worldwide to be found at the Genetics Education Center, University of Kansas Medical Center (KUMC; *see* Fig. 10; *see* Website: http://www. kumc.edu/gec/prof/soclist.html).

See companion CD for color Fig. 10

12 Population Genetics

Jill S. Barnholtz-Sloan

Introduction

A species is comprised of many populations of individuals who breed with each other, each with their own unique set of genes (or loci) and alleles. Even so, the population as a whole shares a pool of all genes and alleles. *Evolution* is the change of frequencies of alleles in the total gene pool. Some genotypes, such as those associated with rare and sometimes deadly human diseases, are important to understand from a population genetics perspective so that changes in the incidence of disease can be predicted. Most individuals do not carry the genotypes that cause an extreme *phenotype* (or trait), but of the ones that do carry these rare genotypes or combination of genotypes, their phenotype varies greatly from the average person in the population.

Population genetics is the study of evolutionary genetics at the population level. We study the exchange of alleles and genes within and between populations and the forces that cause or maintain these exchanges. This exchange of genes and alleles causes changes in specific alleles and hence genotype frequencies within and between populations. Through the study of this evolution of alleles and hence, genotype frequencies, we can better understand how to use human populations as a data set to clarify genetic predisposition to disease. A glossary of terms and example calculations is provided at the end of the chapter.

Hardy-Weinberg and Linkage Equilibrium

A basic understanding of the equilibrium that exists in populations is needed in order to begin to understand these changes in allele frequencies over time and across generations. The two types of equilibrium assumed in populations are *Hardy-Weinberg Equilibrium* (HWE) within loci and *Linkage Equilibrium* (LE) between loci.

Fundamental to understanding these equilibria is the understanding that genotype frequencies are determined by mating patterns, with the ideal being random mating. *Random mating* assumes that mating takes place by chance with respect to the locus under consideration. With random mating, the chance that an individual mates with another having a specific genotype is equal to the population frequency of that genotype.

One's *genotype* at any *locus* is made up of two *alleles* (one of two or more forms that can exist at a locus), one allele from the mother and one allele from the father. A

Table 1
Observed and Expected Frequencies of the Genotypes *AA*, *Aa* and *aa* at Hardy-Weinberg Equilibrium After One Mating of Female and Male Gametes, for a Total Sample of *n* Individuals.

		Female Gametes Observed = $p = f(A)$	Observed = $q = f(a)$
Male Gametes	Observed = $p = f(A)$	Observed = $p^2 = f(AA)$ Expected = np^2	Observed = $pq = f(Aa)$ Expected = npq
	Observed = $q = f(a)$	Observed = $pq = f(Aa)$ Expected = npq	Observed = $q^2 = f(aa)$ Expected = nq^2

gene (or *locus*) is the fundamental physical and functional unit of heredity and will carry information from one generation to the next. (Note: Gene and locus will be used interchangeably in this chapter.) By definition, a gene encodes an RNA product that can be structured or encode a protein like an enzyme. The number of alleles that a gene may have can vary from two alleles, a bi-allelic locus, to a large number of alleles, a multi-allelic locus. A genotype can either be homogeneous, i.e., both alleles received from the mother and father are the same allele, or a genotype can be heterogeneous, i.e., the alleles received from the mother and the father are different.

As an example of random mating, consider the locus, *L*, with two alleles *A* and *a*. We would then have three possible genotypes, *AA*, *Aa*, and *aa*. If the population proportions of these genotypes were 0.20, 0.70, and 0.10, respectively, then the chance that a male with *AA* genotype would randomly mate with a female of genotype *AA*, *Aa*, or *aa* is 0.20, 0.70, or 0.10, respectively. These same proportions would apply to female mates with *Aa* or *aa* males. However, in human populations, mating seems to be random with respect to some traits, e.g., blood groups and nonrandom with respect to others, e.g., height, ethnicity, age, and other physical and cultural characteristics.

Independently in 1908, G. H. Hardy and W. Weinberg both published results showing that the frequency of particular genotypes in a sexually reproducing diploid population reaches equilibrium after one generation of random mating and fertilization with no selection, mutation, or migration. The population size is assumed to be very large and the generations are not overlapping. They then showed that the frequencies of the genotypes in the *equilibrium* population are just simple products of the allele frequencies. Again consider locus *L*, has alleles *A* and *a*, with p = frequency $(A) = f(A)$ and $q = f(a) = 1 - p$. Then, if members of the population select their mates at random, without regard to their genotype at the *L* locus, the frequencies of the three genotypes, *AA*, *Aa*, and *aa*, in the population can be expressed in terms of the allele frequencies: $f(AA)=p^2$; $f(Aa) = f(Aa) + f(aA) = 2pq$; $f(aa) = q^2$ (*see* Table 1).

Statistical tests for the presence or absence of HWE for each of the loci of interest are performed using either a *chi-square goodness of fit test* or an *exact test*, to test the null hypothesis that the locus is in HWE versus the alternative hypothesis that the locus is not in HWE. Both tests are testing the fit between the numbers observed and expected numbers, i.e., if the observed is similar enough to the expected, then we accept the null hypothesis of the locus being in HWE. Exact tests are used when there are small sample sizes and/or multi-allelic loci are involved.

Hence, for locus L, with alleles A and a, with frequencies, p and q, respectively, the observed number of the three possible genotypes are n_{AA}, n_{Aa}, and n_{aa}. Assuming the null hypothesis of HWE is true, we can calculate the expected number for each genotype, AA, Aa, and aa, which are np^2, $2npq$, and nq^2, respectively, where n is the total number of individuals in our sample (*see* Table 1). Hence, the chi-square goodness of fit test statistic for locus L with one *degree of freedom* (i.e., the total number of possible classes of data = 3, minus the number of parameters estimated from the data = 1, (i.e., the allele frequency p), – 1) is

$$\chi_1^2 = \sum_{genotypes} \frac{(Observed - Expected)^2}{Expected} \qquad \text{[Eq. 1]}$$

Exact tests for HWE are more computationally expensive and complicated then the chi-square goodness of fit test. This test is more powerful for multi-allelic loci and small sample sizes than the goodness of fit chi-square test, because it does not depend on large sample asymptotic theory. The exact test for HWE is permutation based and is based on the theory proposed by Zaykin, et al. (1995), and Guo and Thompson (1992). Zaykin, et al. (1995) proposed an algorithm that performs an exact test for disequilibrium between alleles within or between loci. The probability of the set of multi-locus genotypes in a sample, that is conditional on the allelic counts, is calculated from the multinomial theory under the null hypothesis of equilibrium being present. Alleles are then permuted and the conditional probability is calculated for the permuted genotype array. In order to permute the arrays, they employ a Monte-Carlo method. The proportion of permuted arrays that are no more probable than the original sample provides the significance level for the test. Because of the complexity of this testing procedure, a computer program must be used.

Hence, equilibrium refers to the concept that there are no changes in genotypic proportions in a population from generation to generation. This equilibrium will remain constant unless the frequencies of alleles in the population are disrupted. Distorting effects could be any one of the following: selection, migration, nonrandom (assortative) mating and inbreeding, population substructure or subpopulations, mutation or genetic drift.

When we consider a single locus we find two important random-mating principles: 1) genotype frequencies are simple products of the allele frequencies and 2) HWE is reached after one generation of random mating. However, independently, when we consider two or more loci, the first principle is correct for each locus, but not necessarily the second, because the alleles of one locus may not be in random association with the alleles of the second locus. Hence, the state of LE is defined by random allelic association between alleles at any loci. In other words, considering any two loci, the probability that the combination of alleles, one from each locus, is the same if the loci are in the same individual or in different individuals. This state of LE will be reached given enough time, but the approach to equilibrium is slow and highly dependent on the *recombination fraction*, θ.

The distance in centimorgans (cM) between two loci can be estimated from the recombination fraction, θ, between these loci, where θ can be calculated as the probability that the gamete transmitted by an individual is a recombinant, i.e., an individual whose genotype was produced by recombination. After DNA duplication, adjacent chromosomes can change parts, i.e., recombine (*see* Fig. 1), and it is this

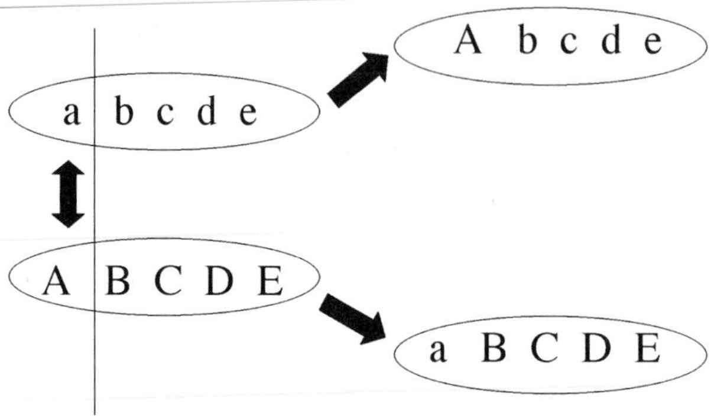

Fig. 1. A pictorial of recombination or crossing over between chromosomal segments (or loci).

genetic shuffling that enables species to have a rich diversity of phenotypic expression from generation to generation in a given population. If the loci are extremely close on the same chromosome, then the likelihood of a crossover between them and the recombination fraction will approach zero. If the loci are far apart or on different chromosomes, then recombination will occur by chance in 50% of meioses and the alleles at one locus will be inherited at random with respect to the alleles at the other locus. Loci with recombination fractions close to zero are tightly linked to each other and loci with recombination fractions of 0.5 are not linked to each other.

Thus, allelic *linkage disequilibrium* (*LD*) is measured by a statistic D, which is defined as $D = P_{ij} - P_i q_j$, where P_{ij} is the frequency of the gamete carrying i^{th} allele of one locus and the jth allele of another and p_i and q_j are the frequencies of the ith and j^{th} alleles of the two loci. D can be a positive or negative number or zero. In random mating populations with no selection, LD is reduced in every generation at a rate of θ (recombination fraction), $0 < \theta < 0.5$; leading to $D(t) = (1 - \theta)^t d(0)$, where $D(t)$ is the disequilibrium at generation t and $D(0)$ is the disequilibrium at generation zero.

Tests for significant allelic LD for combinations of alleles from two and three loci (different combinations of the alleles of the loci of interest that are adjacent to each other on a chromosome), are performed using a chi-square test to test the null hypothesis that $d(ij) = 0$ versus the alternative that $d(ij) = 0$. In order to calculate an allelic disequilibrium measure, $d(.)$, allele and genotype/haplotype (the combination of several alleles from multiple loci), frequencies must first be calculated. This can be done very simply by a direct counting method of the possible genotypes/haplotypes present in the population of interest, which can then be used to assess allele frequencies.

Let us assume that locus 1 has i alleles, locus 2 has j alleles, and locus 3 has k alleles and that the loci lie adjacent to each other. Then the calculations for combinations of alleles (haplotypes) at the three loci are as follows:

$$d(ij) = f(ij) - f(i)f(j) = f(jk) - f(j)f(k)$$
$$d(ijk) = f(ijk) - f(i)d(ij) - f(j)d(ik) - f(i)f(j)f(k)$$

where

$d(ij)$ = disequilibrium of allele i at locus 1, and allele j at locus 2;
$d(jk)$ = disequilibrium of allele j at locus 2, and allele k at locus 3;
$d(ijk)$ = disequilibrium of allele i at locus 1, and allele j at locus 2, allele k at locus 3;
$f(i)$ = frequency of allele i at locus 1, $f(j)$ = frequency of allele j at locus 2;

$f(k)$ = frequency of allele k at locus 3;
$f(ij)$ = frequency of haplotype ij (locus 1 and locus 2);
$f(jk)$ = frequency of haplotype jk (locus 2 and locus 3);
$f(ijk)$ = frequency of haplotype ijk (considering all three loci);

which would yield calculations for d (allele i at locus 1 and allele j at locus 2), d (allele j at locus 2 and allele k at locus 3) and d (alleles i, j, and k at loci 1, 2, and 3). The significance of the two locus disequilibrium is tested using an allele specific chi-square test, which tests whether or not d (allele i at locus 1 and allele j at locus 2) and d (allele j at locus 2 and allele k at locus 3) are significantly different from zero. The two-locus test used is the test proposed by Hill (1974), given by

$$\chi_{ij}^2 = \frac{n[d(ij)]^2}{f(i)\,[1-f(i)]\,f(j)\,[1-f(j)]} \qquad \text{[Eq. 2]}$$

which follows a χ^2 distribution with one degree of freedom.

For the three locus test, the test statistic used is the one suggested by Weir (1996), given by

$$\chi_{ijk}^2 = \frac{[d(ijk)]^2}{Var\,[d(ijk)]}\text{, with one degree of freedom}$$

where

$$Var[d(ijk)] = \frac{1}{n}\left[\begin{array}{l}\pi_i\pi_j\pi_k + 6d(ij)d(jk)d(ik) + \pi_i\left(\tau_j\tau_k d(jk) - [d(jk)]^2\right) + \pi_j\left(\tau_i\tau_k d(ik) - [d(ik)]^2\right)\\ + \pi_k\left(\tau_i\tau_j d(ij) - [d(ij)]^2\right) + d(ijk)\left[\tau_i\tau_j\tau_k - 2\tau_i d(jk) - 2\tau_j d(ik) - 2\tau_k d(ij) - d(ijk)\right]\end{array}\right]$$

in which

$$\begin{array}{l}\pi_i = f(i)[1-f(i)];\ \pi_j = f(j)[1-f(j)];\ \pi_k = f(k)[1-f(k)]\\ \tau_i = [1-2f(i)];\ \tau_j = [1-2f(j)];\ \tau_k = [1-2f(k)]\end{array} \qquad \text{[Eq. 3]}$$

which tests whether d (alleles i, j, and k at loci 1, 2, and 3) is significantly different from zero and also follows a chi-square distribution.

Linkage disequilibrium can be the result of many different circumstances. LD could have occurred in the founding population and because of a very small θ, has not had sufficient time (in generations of random mating) to disappear. The loci could be tightly linked, so that recombinants are rare, causing the approach to equilibrium to be slow. *Population admixture*, or the matings of different subpopulations with different allele frequencies, can also cause LD. Interaction between the loci of interest can cause LD to be present because of the proximity of the loci, i.e., the loci are closely linked. Selection of specific heterozygotes can also overcome the natural tendency for D to go to zero. Lastly, LD can be caused purely by chance, in that some loci may present themselves in a higher frequency in a population and stay at that frequency. For further information on estimating and testing of LD refer to Hill (1974) and Weir (1996).

Darwin and Natural Selection

The previously mentioned assumptions of equilibrium and hence allele and genotype frequencies, are all directly affected by the forces of evolution that exist all around us, such as natural selection, mutation, genetic drift and mutation, inbreeding, nonrandom mating, and population structure. The mechanism of evolution was the subject of speculation by several individuals in the early nineteenth century, but it was Charles Darwin who took up this problem. He proposed that the cause of evolution was natural selection in the presence of variation; *natural selection* is the process by which the environment limits population size.

He based this theory on three key observations: 1) When conditions allow individuals in a population to survive and reproduce, they will have more offspring than can possibly survive (population size increases exponentially); 2) Individuals will vary in their ability to survive and reproduce, most of the time because of a lack of available resources; and 3) No two individuals are the same because of variation in inherited characteristics, therefore they all vary in their ability to reproduce and survive. From these observations he deduced the following: 1) There is competition for survival and successful reproduction; 2) Heritable differences that are favorable will allow those individuals to survive and reproduce more efficiently as compared to individuals with unfavorable characteristics; i.e., elimination is selective; and 3) Subsequent generations of a population will have a higher proportion of favorable alleles present than previous generations. With the increase of these favorable alleles in the population, comes an increase of the favorable genotype(s), so that the population gradually changes and becomes better adapted to the environment. This is the definition of *fitness*; genotypes with greater fitness produce more offspring than less fit genotypes. Fitness of a gene or allele is directly related to its ability to be transmitted from one generation to the next.

Individuals are forced to compete for resources in order to stay alive and reproduce successfully, therefore, certain genotypes that are the genetic determinants for the more favorable characteristics in a population, will become more common than the less favorable genotypes. As a result, different genotypes will have different likelihoods of success. The effects of relative frequencies of the genotypes, group interactions and environmental effects can complicate this likelihood. Sexual selection is a key component to the likelihood of success and can be affected by direct competition between individuals of the same sex for a mate of the opposite sex or by mating success, which is a direct result of the choice of a mate.

There are three modes of natural selection (*see* Fig. 2): 1) *Stabilizing selection*: this removes individuals who deviate too far from the average and maintains an optimal population, i.e., selection for the average individual; 2) *Directional selection*: this favors individuals who are at one extreme of the population, i.e., selection of either of the extreme individuals; and 3) *Disruptive selection*: this favors individuals at both extremes of the population, which can cause the population to break into two separate populations.

Neo-Darwinism arose when it was realized that variation is a direct result of spontaneous mutation. The theoretical basis of Neo-Darwinism was then developed, based on a mathematical framework and has become essential to understanding molecular evolution. From the 1930s to the 1950s researchers worked to try to better understand the empirical basis of Neo-Darwinism, but this was met with great difficulty, because a human's lifetime is generally not long enough to be able to observe substantial changes in populations.

Types of Variation

Darwin's work and the work of the Neo-Darwinists helped us better understand that the variation within and between populations is caused and maintained by mutation, genetic drift, migration, inbreeding, and nonrandom mating, including the types of natural selection discussed in the previous section. A summary of whether or not each of these components of evolution increases or decreases variation within and between populations is given in Table 2.

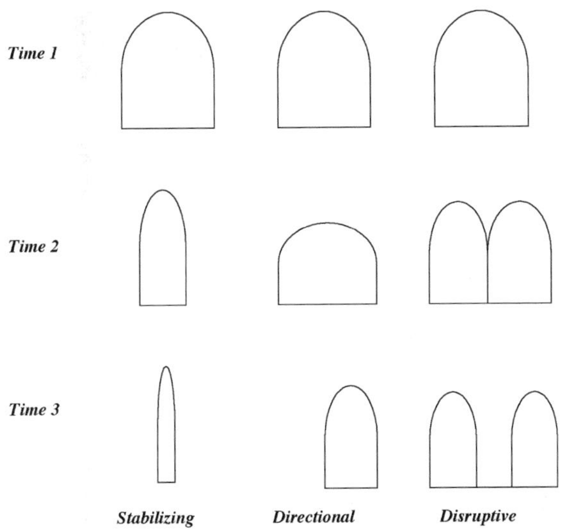

Fig. 2. Three types of natural selection—stabilizing, directional and disruptive—over the course of three different time periods 1, 2, and 3 (three subsequent generations of mating) and their effects on the normally distributed initial population in time period 1.

Table 2
The Effect of the Different Forces[a] of Evolution on Variation Within and Between Populations

Evolutionary component	*Within populations*	*Between populations*
Inbreeding and nonrandom mating	Decrease	Increase
Genetic drift	Decrease	Increase
Mutation	Increase	Decrease
Migration	Increase	Decrease
Selection		
– Stabilizing	Increase	Decrease
– Directional	Decrease	Increase and decrease
– Disruptive	Decrease	Increase

[a]Either an increase or decrease of variation within and/or between populations is shown for each force.

In 1953, the Watson-Crick model of DNA (deoxyribonucleic acid) was put forward, opening doors to the application of various molecular techniques in population genetics research. Because DNA is the chemical substance that encodes all genes, relationships between and within populations could now be characterized through the study of DNA. Now researchers could study the variation within a species instead of having to study the species as a whole. Researchers began by studying amino acid changes. With the advent of electrophoresis, a simpler method of studying protein variation, they then switched to studying genetic polymorphism within populations in the mid 1960s, Many other technical breakthroughs have since emerged such as restriction enzyme digestion, gene cloning, and rapid DNA sequencing. Together, these tools have uncovered many unexpected properties of the structure and organization of genes.

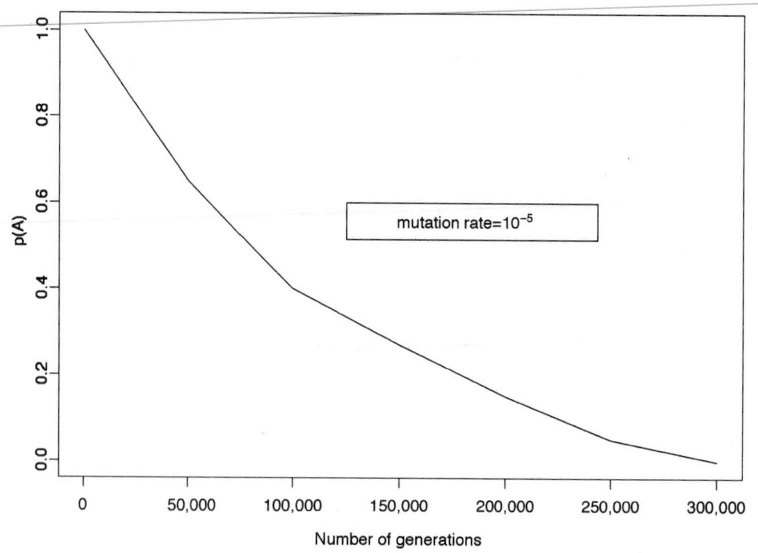

Fig. 3. The cumulative effect of mutation over generations of mating (over time) on the change in frequency of allele *A*, where the mutation rate for *A* to become *a*, is maintained at a constant rate of 10^{-5}.

Mutation

Through these new methods of molecular study, it was discovered that all new variation begins with a *mutation* or a change in the sequence of the bases in the DNA. A mutation in the DNA sequence caused by nucleotide substitution (e.g., sickle cell hemoglobin production), insertions/deletions (e.g., hemophilia A and B, cystic fibrosis, *cru-du-chat* syndrome), triplet expansion (e.g., Huntington's disease), translocation (e.g., Down's syndrome), etc., may be spread through the population by genetic drift and/or natural selection and eventually become fixed in a species. If this mutant gene produces a new phenotype, this new characteristic or trait will be inherited by all subsequent generations unless the gene mutates again. Some mutations will not affect the protein product and these are called silent mutations. Some mutations will occur in noncoding regions, which may or may not have regulatory roles. Hence, it is the regions where the sequence is important for function where variation is the most interesting in terms of effects on the population.

Spontaneous mutation rates are appreciably small, 10^{-4}–10^{-6} mutations per gene per generation, so it is the cumulative effects of mutation over long periods of time that become important (*see* Fig. 3). The simplest kind of mutation is when one nucleotide is replaced by another (a base substitution). These substitutions can be transitions, A to G or C to T, or transversions, all other types of substitutions. If a base substitution results in the replacement of an amino acid in the protein product, this is a missense mutation. Mutations can also result in a loss or gain of genetic material, deletion or insertion, which can result in frame-shift mutations. Genetic material can also be rearranged, by translocation, where pieces of different chromosomes change places with one another. Mutations owing to gene conversion come from the misalignment of DNA, which is associated with the unequal crossing over of parts of adjacent chromosomes.

Table 3
Genotypic Frequencies of the Three Genotypes Present in the *MN* Blood Group; *MM*, *MN* and *NN*, Calculated from a Total of 1419 Individuals

Genotype	*Number of Individuals*	*Genotypic Frequencies*
MM	543	543/1419 = 0.38
MN	419	419/1419 = 0.30
NN	457	457/1419 = 0.32
Total	1419	1.0

With the purpose of better grasping the concept of mutation, tabulating correct allele and genotype frequencies for a population under study is imperative. A basic understanding of polymorphisms, heterozygosity, and gene diversity is also critical.

Allele and Genotype Frequencies

The most fundamental quantitative variable in the study of population genetics is the allele frequency. In a population of N diploid individuals we have $2N$ alleles present. If the number of alleles i in the population is n_i, then the frequency of that allele in the population is defined as $p_i = n_i / 2N$. There is no limitation to the number of alleles that may exist at a single locus but their frequencies must always sum to one. When a locus has only two alleles we denote their frequencies as p and $q = 1 - p$. A biallelic locus, L, with alleles A and a, has three possible genotypes, AA, Aa, and aa. However, not all genotypes are necessarily present at all times in a population.

The genotype frequencies at a particular locus are defined similarly; the frequency of a particular genotype is the number of that genotype present in the population divided by the total number of genotypes present. Like the allele frequencies, genotype frequencies must sum to one over all genotypes present in the study population. However, the number of genotypes is constrained and equals $[m(m + 1)]/2$ if there are m alleles at the locus: m homozygotes and $[m(m - 1)]/2$ heterozygotes.

As an example of how to count alleles and genotypes in a population, the *MN* blood group will be used. Assume that a population consists of 543 *MM* (*phenotype M*), 419 *MN* (*phenotype MN*), and 457 *NN* (*phenotype NN*) individuals (total = 1419 individuals). We then need to determine the values of $p = f(M)$ and $q = f(N)$ and the genotype frequencies in the population. In this simple example, the values of p and q and the genotype frequencies can be determined by counting the genotypes and alleles. To determine the genotypic frequencies we simply divide the number of each genotype present in the population by the total number of individuals present in the population (*see* Table 3), where the genotypic frequencies will add to one. To determine the allelic frequencies we simply count the number of *M* or *N* alleles and divide by the total number of alleles. There are 543 *MM* individuals, which means there are $543 \times 2 = 1086$ *M* alleles being contributed. 419 *MN* individuals will contribute 419 *M* alleles and 419 *N* alleles. And there are 457 *NN* individuals contributing $457 \times 2 = 914$ *N* alleles. Therefore, there are $1086 + 419 = 1505$ *M* alleles total in the population and $419 + 914 = 1333$ *N* alleles total in the population. So, $p = f(M) = 1505/[2(1419)] = 0.53$ and $q = f(N) = 1333/[2(1419)] = 0.47 = 1 - p$.

Polymorphism

When a locus has many variants, or alleles, it is referred to as being *polymorphic*. Polymorphism is defined as the existence of two or more alleles with large relative frequencies in a population (occurrence of no less than 1–2%). The limiting frequency of the most common allele, and thus for the polymorphism, is set at 99%. The existence of these multiple alleles is generated by mutation(s) and recombination at a locus. Most are eliminated from the population by genetic drift or purifying selection and only a small number of them are incorporated into the population by chance or selection. The first human polymorphism discovered was the ABO blood group by Landsteiner (1900). Most polymorphisms are genetically simple, in that two alleles directly determine two versions of the same protein. Others can be highly complex, with multiple, related loci engaged in a complex system on a chromosome.

There are four primary ways to determine polymorphisms: Restriction Fragment Length Polymorphisms (RFLPs), *Minisatellites* or Variable Number of Tandem Repeats (VNTRs), *Microsatellites* or Short Tandem Repeats (STRs) or Single Nucleotide Polymorphisms (SNPs). RFLPs are DNA segments of different lengths generated by restriction enzyme digestion, targeted to specific base sequences. The different-sized DNA fragments can be separated using electrophoresis. Because RFLPs are based on single nucleotide changes, they are not very polymorphic in the population and usually have heterozygosities of less than 50%. Minisatellites or VNTRS are repeats of a relatively short oligonucleotide sequence that vary in number from one person to another. They are much more polymorphic than RFLPs. Micro-satellites or STRS are multiple (often 100 or more) repeats of very short sequences (2–4 nucleotides), e.g., $(CA)_n$ repeats that are amplified by polymerase chain reaction (PCR) and electrophoresed to score allele sizes. These are highly polymorphic in the population, with most individuals being heterozygous. Thousands of such markers are available, and are conveniently located throughout the genome. Tri- and tetranucleotide repeats are often easier to score than dinucleotide repeats. Microsatellites are often the markers of choice for genetic studies. SNPs are a class of recently identified markers characterized by variation at a specific nucleotide. Only 2 alleles exist for a given SNP in the population, therefore they are not as polymorphic as microsatellites. However, they are abundant throughout the genome.

Gene Diversity and Heterozygosity

When a large number of loci are examined in a population for variation, the amount of variation is usually measured by the proportion of polymorphic loci. This can be reported for a single locus, as an average over several loci or as the *average heterozygosity* per locus or *gene diversity*. The *heterozygosity* (the proportion of heterozygotes or polymorphic loci) is defined purely in terms of genotype frequencies in the population. If n_{ij} is the observed count of heterozygotes ij at locus L, where i and j are different alleles, in a sample of size n, then the sample heterozygosity for that locus L is given by

$$H_L = \sum_i \sum_{i \neq j} \frac{n_{ij}}{n} \qquad \text{[Eq. 4]}$$

Heterozygosity is calculated separately for each locus under study and then averaged over all loci under consideration (m), to give

$$\bar{H} = \frac{1}{m} \sum_{l=1}^{m} H_L \qquad \text{[Eq. 5]}$$

Average heterozygosity or gene diversity is a more useful measure of variation than the proportion of heterozygotes (heterozygosity) because it is not subject to bias caused by sample size, whether it be the size of the study sample or the number of loci being examined. Also, it is calculated from allele frequencies and not genotype frequencies. Assume that p_j is the frequency of the jth allele at the lth locus, then the gene diversity at this locus, L, is

$$D_L = 1 - \sum_j p_j^2 \quad \text{[Eq. 6]}$$

and as an average over m loci ,

$$\bar{D} = 1 - \frac{1}{m} \sum_l \sum_j p_{jl}^2 \quad \text{[Eq. 7]}$$

where $l = 1,...,m$. In a randomly mating population, $\bar{D}$ is equal to the average proportion of heterozygotes per locus. Hence, a very polymorphic locus will have a higher gene diversity, because, as more alleles are present at a locus, more heterozygotes will be possible.

However, it is not just mutation that is responsible for sustaining variation. Natural selection, genetic drift, and migration also play key roles in its maintenance, as well as inbreeding and nonrandom mating and the genetic structure of a population. Selection acts against the dysfunctional alleles that are continuously created by mutation. At equilibrium, the number of new dysfunctional mutations equals the number lost by selection. Selection, in fact, favors heterozygotes, because they maintain two different alleles in their genotypes and rare alleles are more common in a heterozygous individual. Hence, the heterozygous individual can carry more information than the homozygous individual.

Genetic Drift and Migration

Genetic drift is the change in allele frequency that results from the chance difference in transmission of alleles between generations. The gene pool changes at each generation, so that the frequencies of particular alleles will change (drift) through time, and these frequencies can go up or down, accumulating with time. Drift's largest effects are seen on small populations (larger samples will be closer to the average) and on rare alleles (the transmission frequency will be higher than the expected average frequency if it is a common allele). Drift is important because it has a greater effect on transmission of rare alleles than selection, as it helps remove or promote very rare alleles.

In small populations, drift can cause certain allele frequencies to be much larger or smaller than would likely occur in a large population. This is called the *founder effect*, when a small, underrepresented group forms a new colony. The Amish in the United States are a good example because the roots of this population can be traced to a small number of immigrant families. When a population is reduced to a small number, possibly because of disease, and later becomes the parents of a new large population, this is called *bottle-necking*. Drift can also cause small isolated populations to be very different from the norm, which can lead to the formation of new species and races.

The basic calibrator of genetic drift is *effective population size*, N_e. This is the size of a homogeneous population of breeding individuals, half of which are male and half are female, that would generate the same rate of allelic fixation as observed in the real population of total size N. Hence, in the real population of size N, the variance of the random deviation of allele frequencies is $[p(1-p)]/2N$ and the rate of decay is $1/2N$. A human population is structured in many different ways, i.e., its individuals are of different sexes, ages, and geographical and social groups. This does not match the "ideal" population. Accordingly, N_e is estimated indirectly to be $N/2$ to $N/3$, but can be estimated directly if the heterozygosity or the inbreeding coefficient of the population is known.

Migration also causes variation within populations, because of the possibility of mixing many populations together. Geographically defined populations generally show variation between each other and such variation can effect the fate of that population. Through migration, these populations subdivide and mix with new individuals to form new, sustainable populations. Population subdivision causes a decrease in homozygous individuals, known as *Wahlund's principle*, because it will increase variation in this newly formed population. In human populations, the main effect of this fusion of populations is that it will decrease the overall frequency of children born with genetic defects resulting from homozygous recessive genes that have a high frequency in one of the mixing populations.

Wright's Fixation Indices

Genetic structure of a species is characterized by the number of populations within it, the frequencies of the different alleles in each population and the degree of genetic isolation of the populations. The evolutionary forces previously discussed will cause differentiation within and between subpopulations within a larger species population. Wright (1931, 1943, 1951) showed that any species population has three levels of complexity, I, the individual; S, the various subpopulations within the total population and T, the total population. In order to assess this population substructure and test for allelic correlation within subpopulations, Wright defined three measurements called *fixation indices* that have correlational interpretations for genetic structure and are a function of heterozygosity. F_{IT} is the correlation of alleles within individuals over all subpopulations; F_{ST} is the correlation of alleles of different individuals in the same subpopulation; and F_{IS} is the correlation of alleles within individuals within one subpopulation. Cockerham (1969, 1973) later showed analogous measures for these three fixation indices, which he called the overall inbreeding coefficient, F (i.e., F_{IT}), the coancestry, θ (i.e., F_{ST}) and, the inbreeding coefficient within subpopulations, f (i.e., F_{IS}). These are all related by the following formula:

$$f = \frac{F - \theta}{1 - \theta} \qquad \text{[Eq. 8]}$$

In order to calculate the three fixation indices, we must first calculate the heterozygosities. H_I is the heterozygosity of an individual in a subpopulation and can be interpreted as the average heterozygosity of all the genes in an individual. H_S is the expected heterozygosity of an individual in another subpopulation and can be interpreted as the amount of heterozygosity in any subpopulation if it were undergoing random mating. H_T is the expected heterozygosity of an individual in an equivalent random mating total population and can be interpreted as the amount of heterozygosity in a total population where all subpopulations were pooled together and mated randomly.

Then if H_i is the heterozygosity in subpopulation i, and if we have k subpopulations,

$$H_I = \sum_{i=1}^{k} \frac{H_i}{k} \qquad \text{[Eq. 9]}$$

If p_{js} is the frequency of the jth allele in subpopulation s, then H_S is the expected Hardy-Weinberg heterozygosity in subpopulation s,

$$H_S = 1 - \sum_{i=1}^{h} p_{js}^2, \qquad \text{[Eq. 10]}$$

for a total of h alleles at that locus. $\bar{H}_s$ is the average taken over all subpopulations. Finally if $\bar{p}_j$ is the frequency of the jth allele, averaged over all subpopulations,

$$H_T = 1 - \sum_{i=1}^{k} \bar{p}_j^2, \qquad \text{[Eq. 11]}$$

for all k subpopulations. Thus, Wright's F statistics are

$$F_{IS} = \frac{\bar{H}_S - H_I}{\bar{H}_S}\,;\; F_{ST} = \frac{H_T - \bar{H}_S}{H_T}\,;\; F_{IT} = \frac{H_T - H_I}{H_T} \qquad \text{[Eq. 12]}$$

and these three equations are related by the following identity,

$$(1 - F_{IS})\,(1 - F_{ST}) = (1 - F_{IT}) \qquad \text{[Eq. 13]}$$

Genetic Distance

The degree of genetic isolation of one subpopulation from another can be measured by *genetic distance*, which can be interpreted as the time since the subpopulations that are under comparison diverged from their original ancestral population. Nei proposed the most widely used measure of genetic distance between subpopulations in 1972, even though the concept of genetic distance was first used by Sanghvi (1953). The mathematics of these measurements was later refined by Fisher (1963) and Mahalanobis (1963). Thus, Nei's standard genetic distance is given by $D = -ln(I)$, where I is called the genetic identity, which corrected for bias, is calculated using the following equation:

$$I = \frac{(2n-1)\sum_l \sum_j p_{j1} p_{j2}}{\sqrt{\sum_l \left(2n \sum_j p_{j1}^2 - 1\right) \sum_l \left(2n \sum_j p_{j1}^2 - 1\right)}} \qquad \text{[Eq. 14]}$$

where we are examining the jth allele at the lth locus for populations 1 and 2 and p_{j1} is the frequency of the jth allele at the lth locus for population 1 and p_{j2} is the frequency of the jth allele at the lth locus for population 2, from a total sample of n individuals.

Inbreeding and Non-Random Mating (Assortative Mating)

Inbreeding and other forms of *nonrandom mating*, or *assortative mating*, can also have a profound effect on variation within a population. Inbreeding refers to mating between related individuals. Inbreeding is when genetically similar (related) individuals mate more frequently than would be expected in a randomly mating population. Inbreeding mainly causes departures from HWE and as a consequence of this departure from equilibrium, an increase in homozygotes. Inbreeding can cause the offspring of the mating to have replicates of specific alleles present in the shared ancestor of the parents. Thus, inbred individuals may carry two copies of an allele at a locus that are *identical by descent* (IBD) from a common ancestor. The proportion of IBD is how frequently two offspring share copies of the same parental (ancestral) allele.

The amount of inbreeding in a population can be measured by comparing the actual proportion of heterozygous genotypes in the population that is inbreeding to the pro-

Table 4
Frequencies of Genotypes *AA*, *Aa*, and *aa* After One Generation of Inbreeding Where the Reference Population is the Preceding Generation Before the Inbreeding[a]

	Origin			
Genotype	*Independent*	*Identical by descent*	*Original frequencies*	*Frequency change after inbreeding*
AA	$p^2(1 - F)$	$+ pF$	$= p^2$	$+ pqF$
Aa	$2pq(1 - F)$		$= 2pq$	$- 2pqF$
Aa	$q^2(1 - F)$	$+ qF$	$= q^2$	$+ pqF$

[a] The inbreeding coefficient, *F* and the two different types of origin, independent and identical by descent, are incorporated in the calculations.

portion in a randomly mating population. Inbreeding alone cannot change allele frequencies, but it can change how the alleles come together to form genotypes.

In order to illustrate this change in genotype frequencies, a simple case of inbreeding will be examined, where the reference population will be the preceding generation so that the inbreeding coefficient, *F*, measures the increase in IBD from one generation to the next. If allele *A* has a frequency of p and allele *a* has a frequency of $q = 1 - p$, then the frequency of *AA* genotypes in an inbred gamete will be $f(AA) = p^2(1 - F) + pF = p^2 + pqF$. An individual of genotype *AA* can be formed by one of two ways, of independent origin, which has a probability of $p(1 - F)$ and identical by descent, which has a probability of F. Therefore, if $F > 0$, there will be an excess of *AA* homozygotes relative to what would be expected by HWE. If $F = 0$, then the frequency of the *AA* homozygotes will be as is expected by HWE. Similarly, the frequency of the homozygote *aa* would be $f(aa) = q^2(1 - F) + qF = q^2 + pqF$. And the same rules would hold for the relationship between the value of *F* and HWE. The probability of the heterozygote *Aa* is more complicated to calculate. But, we know that the frequencies of the genotypes must sum to one so, $f(Aa) = 1 - f(AA) - f(aa) = 2pq(1 - F) = 2pq - 2pqF$. Table 4 shows a summary of the changes in genotype frequencies after one generation of inbreeding.

If natural selection and inbreeding act together they can have a profound effect on the course of evolution because of the increase in the frequency of homozygous genotypes. Inbreeding in human populations can result in a much higher frequency of recessive disease homozygotes, since recessive disease alleles generally have low frequencies in humans. Inbreeding affects all alleles and hence, genes, in inbred individuals. This exposes rare recessive disorders that may not have presented if inbreeding did not occur.

Nonrandom mating or assortative mating is when a mate is chosen based on a certain phenotype. In other words, it is the situation when mates are more similar (or dissimilar) to each other than would be expected by chance in a randomly mating population. In positive assortative mating, a mate chooses a mate that phenotypically resembles himself or herself. In negative assortative mating, a mate chooses a mate that is phenotypically very different from himself or herself. Assortative mating will only affect the alleles that are responsible for the phenotypes affecting mating frequencies. The genetic variance (or variability) of the trait that is associated with the mating increases with more generations of assortative mating for that trait. In humans, positive assortative mating occurs for traits like intelligence (IQ score), height, or certain socioeconomic variables. Negative assortative mating occurs mostly in plants.

Conclusions

Even with the advances in molecular biology and genetics, all of this discovery in the field of population genetics and of the characteristics that cause population-based changes and their consequences, i.e., how they can affect human disease susceptibility, had until recently only been assessed one at a time by a technician in a laboratory. Now with the advent of the gene chips or microarrays, these new methods can be automated and carried out at a much larger scale, e.g., 10,000 genotypes can be determined using a single gene chip. These and other faster techniques will permit all genes to be tested for polymorphism within and between populations for many individuals in a population at a time and many populations at a time. This new technology will allow us even greater insight into the relationship between human genetic changes in populations and evolutionary forces.

Glossary of Terms

Allele One of two or more forms of a gene or locus that can exist at a locus (variants of a locus).

Average Heterozygosity (or Gene Diversity) The average proportion of heterozygotes in the population and the expected proportion of heterozygous loci in a randomly chosen individual.

Bottle-Necking When a population is reduced to a small number, possibly because of disease, and later becomes the parents of a new large population.

Chi-Square Goodness of Fit Test A statistical test used to test the fit between the observed and expected numbers in a population; the test statistic has a chi-square distribution.

Degrees of Freedom The number of possible classes of data, minus the numbers of parameters estimated from the data, minus 1.

Directional Selection Favors individuals who are at one extreme of the population, i.e., selection of either of the extreme individuals.

Disruptive Selection Favors individuals at both extremes of the population, which can cause the population to break into two separate populations.

Effective Population Size, N_e The size of a homogeneous population of breeding individuals, half male and half female, that would generate the same rate of allelic fixation as observed in real population of total size N.

Evolution The change of frequencies of alleles in the total gene pool.

Exact Test A statistical test used when the sample sizes are small or the locus under study is multi-allelic. It is more powerful than the chi-square goodness of fit test.

Fitness The ability of a gene or locus to be transmitted from one generation to the next; genotypes with greater fitness produce more offspring than less fit genotypes.

Founder Effect when a small, underrepresented group forms a new colony.

Gene (or locus) The fundamental physical and functional unit of heredity that will carry information from one generation to the next; generally encodes for some gene product, like an enzyme or protein. It is comprised of at least two alleles, a bi-allelic locus, to a large number of alleles, a multi-allelic locus. (Note: gene and locus are used interchangeably).

Genetic Distance The degree of genetic isolation of one subpopulation from another; interpreted as the time since the subpopulations that are under comparison diverged from their original ancestral population.

Genetic Drift The change in allele frequency that results from the chance difference in transmission of alleles between generations.

Genotype Composed of two alleles at a particular locus, one from the mother and one from the father. Homogeneous genotype, i.e., both alleles received from the mother and father are the same allele or heterogeneous genotype, i.e., the alleles received from the mother and the father are different.

Haplotype The combination of several alleles from multiple loci.

Hardy-Weinberg Equilibrium (HWE) The frequencies of the genotypes in the equilibrium population. Simple products of the allele frequencies.

Heterozygosity The proportion of heterozygotes or polymorphic loci in a population.

Identical by Descent (IBD) How frequently two offspring share copies of the same parental (ancestral) allele.

Inbreeding When genetically similar (related) individuals mate more frequently than would be expected in a randomly mating population.

Linkage Equilibrium (LE) Random allelic association between alleles at any loci. Considering any two loci. The probability of the combination of alleles, one from each locus, is the same if the loci are in the same individual or in different individuals.

Migration The movement of individuals within and between populations.

Mutation A change in the sequence of the bases in the DNA.

Natural Selection The process by which the environment limits population size.

Non-random Mating (or Assortative Mating) Mating does not take place at random with respect to some traits. Mates can chose each other based on height, ethnicity, age, and other physical and cultural characteristics.

Phenotype Trait or characteristic of interest.

Polymorphism The existence of two or more alleles with large relative frequencies in a population (occurrence of no less than 1–2%); limiting frequency is 99%; four ways to determine: Restriction Fragment Length Polymorphisms (RFLPs); *Minisatellites* or Variable Number of Tandem Repeats (VNTRs); *Microsatellites*, or Short Tandem Repeats (STRs), or Single Nucleotide Polymorphisms (SNPs).

Population Admixture The matings of different subpopulations with different allele frequencies.

Population Genetics The study of evolutionary genetics at the population level.

Random Mating Mating takes place by chance with respect to the locus under consideration. The chance that an individual mates with another having a specific genotype is equal to the population frequency of that genotype.

Recombination Fraction (θ) The probability that the gamete transmitted by an individual is a recombinant, i.e., an individual whose genotype was produced by recombination.

Stabilizing Selection Removes individuals who deviate too far from the average. It maintains an optimal population, i.e., selection for the average individual.

Wahlund's Principle A decrease in homozygous individuals in a population, caused by population subdivision.

Example Calculations

Disease Allele Frequency Calculations Based on Hardy-Weinberg Proportions

Example 1:
Tay-Sachs Disease (autosomal recessive; q is disease allele):

a. U.S. Ashkenazi incidence: $1/3{,}900 = q^2$
 $q = 0.016, p = 1 - 0.016 = 0.984$
 $p^2 = 0.968, 2pq = 0.031, q^2 = 0.00026$
 (Sum = 0.99926 ~ 1.0)

 Gene frequency = $q = 0.016$,
 Carrier frequency = $2pq \sim 2q = 0.032$
 Carriers/Affecteds = $2pq/q^2 \sim 2q/q^2 = 2/q = 125$

b. U.S. non-Ashkenazi Caucasian incidence: $1/112{,}000 = q^2$
 $q = 0.003, p = 0.997$
 $p^2 = 0.994, 2pq \sim 2q = 0.006, q^2 = 0.000009$

 Gene frequency = $q = 0.003$,
 Carrier frequency ~ $2q = 0.006$
 Carriers/Affecteds ~ $2/q = 667$

 Ashkenazi carriers/non-Ashkenazi Caucasian carriers = 0.032/0.006 = 5.3

Example 2:
Huntington Disease (Autosomal dominant; p is disease allele):

Incidence: $1/10{,}000 = p^2 + 2pq \sim 2pq \sim 2p$
$p = 1/20{,}000 = 0.00005, q = 1 - p = 0.99995$
Heterogygous Affecteds/Homozygous Affecteds ~ $2p/p^2 = 2/p = 40{,}000$

Determining if the Genotypes are in Hardy-Weinberg Equilibrium by a Chi-Square Goodness of Fit Test

(Using numbers from the example given under Subheading "Allele and Genotype Frequencies")

The MN Blood Group:
543 MM (phenotype M), 419 MN (phenotype MN), and 457 NN (phenotype N) individuals (total = 1419 individuals)

There are 543 *MM* individuals, which means there are 543 × 2 = 1086 *M* alleles being contributed. 419 *MN* individuals will contribute 419 *M* alleles and 419 *N* alleles. And there are 457 *NN* individuals contributing 457 × 2 = 914 *N* alleles.

Genotype	*Number of individuals*	*Genotypic frequencies*
MM (*phenotype M*)	543	543/1419 = 0.38
MN (*phenotype MN*)	419	419/1419 = 0.30
NN (*phenotype N*)	457	457/1419 = 0.32
Total	1419	1.0

Therefore, there are 1086 + 419 = 1505 *M* alleles total in the population and 419 + 914 = 1333 *N* alleles total in the population.

So, $p = f(M) = 1505/[2(1419)] = 0.53$ and $q = f(N) = 1333/[2(1419)] = 0.47 = 1 - p$.

A χ^2 test of "goodness of fit" is performed to determine if the population is in Hardy-Weinberg equilibrium proportions, given the values of p and q calculated above:

Phenotype	*Observed*	*Expected*
M	543	$p^2(1419) = (0.53)^2(1419) = 398.6$
MN	419	$2pq(1419) = 2(0.53)(0.47)1419 = 706.9$
N	457	$q^2(1419) = (0.47)^2(1419) = 313.4$

From subheading "Hardy-Weinberg and Linkage Equilibrium," the equation for the chi-square goodness of fit statistic, with one degree of freedom is:

$$\chi_1^2 = \sum_{genotypes} \frac{(Observed - Expected)^2}{Expected}$$

So, for this example,

$\chi_1^2 = (543 - 398.6)^2/398.6 + (419 - 706.9)^2/706.9 + (457 - 313.4)^2/313.4 = 235.36.$

Since the associated p-value < 0.0001, we reject the null hypothesis that the population is in Hardy-Weinberg equilibrium.

Allelic Linkage Disequilibrium Calculations for Two Simple, Biallelic Loci

Assume there are two biallelic loci, L_1 and L_2. L_1 has two alleles A and a and L_2 has two alleles B and b. The total sample size is 50 (n).

Hence, there are four possible haplotypes formed between the alleles of the two loci, L_1 and L_2: Ab, ab, AB and aB. The frequencies of these haplotypes are 20, 10, 5, and 15, respectively. Then

$f(Ab) = 20/50 = 0.40, f(\text{ab}) = 10/50 = 0.20, f(AB) = 5/50 = 0.10$ and $f(aB) = 15/50 = 0.30$ (Note: The sum of these frequencies equals one.) Then, $p_{L1} = f(A) = 20 + 5/50 = 0.50$,

which means that $q_{L1} = 1 - pL_1 = f(a) = 1 - 0.50 = 0.50$

and that $p_{L2} = f(\text{B}) = 5 + 15/50 = 0.40$,

which means that $q_{L2} = 1 - p_{L2} = f(b) = 1 - 0.40 = 0.60$.

Calculate the four allelic linkage disequilibria for L_1 and L_2.

The equation for two-locus LD, $d(ij)$, given in the Hardy-Weinberg and Linkage Equilibrium section,

$d(ij) = f(ij) - f(i)f(j)$

$d(ij)$ = disequilibrium of allele i at locus 1, and allele j at locus 2;

$f(i)$ = frequency of allele i at locus 1, $f(j)$ = frequency of allele j at locus 2;

$f(ij)$ = frequency of haplotype ij (locus 1 and locus 2);

Hence for loci L_1 and L_2, we will calculate $d(Ab)$, $d(\text{ab})$, $d(AB)$ and $d(aB)$.

$d(Ab) = 0.40 - (0.50)(0.60) = 0.10$

$d(ab) = 0.20 - (0.50)(0.60) = -0.10$

$d(AB) = 0.10 - (0.50)(0.40) = -0.10$

$d(aB) = 0.30 - (0.50)(0.40) = 0.10$

Then, the two locus chi-square test, with one degree of freedom, is given by

$$\chi_{ij}^2 = \frac{n[d(ij)]^2}{f(i)\,[1 - f(i)]\,f(j)\,[1 - f(j)]}$$

So, for the haplotype Ab, formed from allele A from the first locus and allele b from the second locus,

$\chi^2_{Ab} = \{[50(0.10)^2]/(0.50)(1-0.50)(0.60)(1-0.60)\} = 0.5/0.06 = 8.33.$

Since the associated p–value = 0.004, we reject the null hypothesis that the two loci are in linkage equilibrium at alleles A and b, i.e., reject the null hypothesis that $d(Ab) = 0$.

Suggested Reading

Hardy-Weinberg and Linkage Equilibrium

Hardy, G. H. (1908) Mendelian proportions in a mixed population, Science 28, 49–50.

Guo, S. W. and Thompson, E. A. (1992) Performing the exact test of Hardy-Weinberg proportion for multiple alleles, Biometrics 48, 361–372.

Hill, W. G. (1974) Disequilibrium among several linked neutral genes in finite populations. I. Mean changes in disequilibrium, Theor. Popul. Biol. 5, 366–392.

Hill, W.G. (1974) Estimation of linkage disequilibrium in randomly mating populations, Heredity 33, 229–239.

Li, C. C. (1955) Population Genetics, 1st ed., The University of Chicago Press, Chicago, IL.

Nei, M. (1987) Molecular Evolutionary Genetics, Columbia University Press, New York, NY.

Weinberg, W. (1908) Uber den Nachweis der Vererbung biem Menschen, Jh. Verein. f. vaterl. Naturk. Wurttemberg 64, 368–382.

Weinberg, W. (1909) Uber Verebungsgestze beim Menschen, Ztschr. Abst. U. Vererb. 1, 277–330.

Weir, B. S. (1996) Genetic Data Analysis II: Methods for Discrete Population Genetic Data, Sinauer Associates, Inc., Sunderland, MA.

Zaykin, D., Zhivotovsky, L., and Weir, B. S. (1995) Exact tests for association between alleles at arbitrary numbers of loci, Genetica 96, 169–178.

Darwin and Natural Selection

Darwin, C. (1859) On the Origin of Species, Murray, London, UK.

Darwin, C. (1871) The Descent of Man and Selection in Relation to Sex, D. Appleton and Company, New York, NY.

Fisher, R. A. (1930) The Genetical Theory of Natural Selection, 1st ed., Clarendon Press, Oxford, UK.

Haldane, J. B. S. (1932) The Causes of Evolution, Longmans and Green, London, UK.

Wright, S. (1931) Evolution in Mendelian populations, Genetics 16, 97–159.

Types of Variation

Ayala, F. J. and Kiger, J. A. (1984) Modern Genetics, 2nd ed., The Benjamin Cummings Publishing Company, Inc., San Francisco, CA.Watson, J. D. and Crick, F. H. C. (1953) Molecular structure of nucleic acids: A structure for Deoxyribase nucleic acid, Nature 4356, 737–738.

Hartl, D. L. and Clark, A. G. (1989) Principles of Population Genetics, 2nd ed., Sinauer Associates, Inc., Sunderland, MA.

Nei, M. (1987) Molecular Evolutionary Genetics, Columbia University Press, NY.

Vogel, F. and Motulsky, A. G. (1997) Human Genetics: Problems and Approaches, 3rd ed., Springer-Verlag, Berlin, Germany.

Weiss, K. M. (1993) Genetic Variation and Human Disease: Principles and Evolutionary Approaches, Cambridge University Press, Cambridge, MA.

POLYMORPHISM

Harris, H. and Hopkinson, D. A. (1972) Average heterozygosity per locus in man: an estimate based on the incidence of enzyme polymorphisms, Ann. Hum. Genet. 36, 9–20.

Landsteiner, K. (1900) Zur Kenntnis der antifermentativen, lytischen und agglutinierenden Wirkungen des Blutserums und der Lymphe, Zentralbl. Bakteriol. 27, 357–362.

Genetic Drift and Migration

Wahlund, S. (1928) Zuzammensetzung von Populationen und Korrelation-Erscheinungen vom Standpunkt der Vererbungslehre ausbetrachtet, Hereditas 11, 65–106.

Weiss, K. M. (1993) Genetic Variation and Human Disease: Principles and Evolutionary Approaches, Cambridge University Press, Cambridge, MA.

WRIGHT'S FIXATION INDICES

Cockerham, C. C. (1969) Variance of gene frequencies, Evolution 23, 72–84.

Cockerham, C. C. (1973) Analyses of gene frequencies, Genetics 74, 679–700.

Wright, S. (1931) Evolution in Mendelian populations, Genetics 16, 97–159.

Wright, S. (1943) Isolation by distance, Genetics 28, 114–138.

Wright, S. (1951) The genetic structure of populations, Ann. Eugen. 15, 323–354.

GENETIC DISTANCE

Fisher, R. A. (1936) The use of multiple measurements in taxonomic problems, Ann. Eugen. 7, 179–188.

Mahalanobis, P. C. (1936) On the generalized distance in statistics, Proc. Natl. Inst. Sci. India 2, 49–55.

Nei, M. (1972) Genetic distance between populations, Am. Nat. 106, 283–292.

Sanghvi, L. D. (1953) Comparison of genetical and morphological methods for a study of biological differences, Am. J. Phys. Anthrop. 11, 385–404.

Other General References of Interest

Cavalli-Sforza, L. L. and Bodmer, W. F. (1971) The Genetics of Human Populations, W.H. Freeman and Company, New York, NY.

Crow, J. F. (1986) Basic Concepts in Population, Quantitative, and Evolutionary Genetics, W.H. Freeman and Company, New York, NY.

Crow, J. F. and Kimura, M. (1970) An Introduction to Population Genetics Theory, Harper & Row, NY.

Falconer, D. S. and Mackay, T. F. C. (1996) Introduction to Quantitative Genetics, 4th ed., Longman Group Ltd., Essex, UK.

Felsenstein, J. (1981) Bibliography of Theoretical Population Genetics, Dowden, Hutchinson, and Ross, Stroudsburg, PA.

Hartl, D. L. (1980) Principles of Population Genetics, Sinauer Associates, Sunderland, MA.

Hartl, D. L. (1981) A Primer of Population Genetics, Sinauer Associates, Sunderland, MA.

Kimura, M. (1983) The Neutral Theory of Molecular Evolution, Cambridge University Press, Cambridge, MA.

Kimura, M. (1994) Population Genetics, Molecular Evolution, and the Neutral Theory, Selected Papers, (Takahata, N., ed.), The University of Chicago Press, Chicago, IL.

Lewontin, R. C. (1974) The Genetic Basis of Evolutionary Change, Columbia University Press, New York, NY.

Suzuki, D. T. Griffiths, A. J. F., and Lewontin, R. C. (1981) An Introduction to Genetic Analysis, 2nd ed., W.H. Freeman and Company, San Francisco, CA.

Winter, P. C., Hickey, G. I., and Fletcher, H. L. (1998) Instant Notes in Genetics, BIOS Scientific Publishers Limited, Oxford, UK.

Wright, S. (1968) Evolution and the Genetics of Populations, vol. 1, Genetics and Biometric Foundations, University of Chicago Press, Chicago, IL.

Wright, S. (1969) Evolution and the Genetics of Populations, vol. 2, The Theory of Gene Frequencies, University of Chicago Press, Chicago, IL.

Wright, S. (1970) Evolution and the Genetics of Populations, vol. 3,The Experimental Results and Evolutionary Deductions, University of Chicago Press, Chicago, IL.

Part III

The UNIX Operating System

A. Basics and Installation

13 Introduction to UNIX for Biologists

David D. Womble

Introduction

Much of the bioinformatics software described in the other chapters of this book (for example, the GCG or EMBOSS programs; e.g., *see* Chapters 18, 19, and 24) is installed on computers that have a UNIX operating system, such as Sun Solaris or Linux. In this chapter, the reader will receive an introduction to using computers with the UNIX operating system. This is not a comprehensive course in UNIX, but is written for general users who want to work with UNIX computers and UNIX software. Note that the perspective used for this chapter is that of a biologist, not a computer scientist. After a general introduction, the reader will be presented with examples and tutorials that will demonstrate several tasks, such as file management or text editing, on UNIX computers using either the command line or the graphical windows interface. A table of simple but useful UNIX commands is included in Appendix 3.

General Introduction to UNIX

A computer operating system is the program that allows a computer user to access the various resources, or parts, of the computer, such as memory, hard disks, or the display screen. It also provides the foundation for the user to install and run software or programs, to do work with the computer.

UNIX is a computer operating system that allows a computer to be shared providing secure simultaneous access for multiple users. It is a multitasking operating system, which means that a UNIX computer can carry out multiple tasks, such as commands or programs, all at the same time. UNIX allows the sharing of resources such as files and hardware across a network. Users can connect to a UNIX computer from anywhere on the network and operate the computer from a remote location.

Because UNIX is a multi-user operating system, a UNIX computer can be used by a group of users, either at different times or all at the same time. Each UNIX user has an account with a username and password that are used to *login* to the computer. Users can sit down in front of the computer and login using the keyboard, mouse, and monitor that are attached to the computer. This is called *logging onto the console*. Alternatively, users can connect to the UNIX computer from remote locations using terminals or terminal software on other computers connected via a network, such as Ethernet.

Note: The author has no affiliation with any of the software sources listed in this chapter.

There are several different versions of UNIX, and most of the larger computer vendors, such as Sun, IBM, and Compaq, ship their computers with their own versions of UNIX. Sun Solaris, a widely used version of UNIX, is one example that runs on computers sold by Sun Microsystems. Installation and systems administration of the Sun Solaris UNIX operating system are described in Chapters 14 and 15. Linux, an open source UNIX-like operating system, can be installed on personal computers with an Intel X86 processor. Most of the information in this chapter will be generally applicable to most any version of UNIX. However, Solaris will be the version that is used for the examples that follow.

On a UNIX computer, commands are used to instruct the computer to perform tasks. There is more than one way to issue commands. Most UNIX computers have a graphical windows interface that allows the user to use a mouse to select and execute various actions or to start programs. However, the most basic means to operate a UNIX computer is to use the command line to type the name of a command, followed by pressing the **return** or **enter** key to execute the command. The graphical windows interface and the command line of a UNIX computer can be used either at the console or remotely through the network.

UNIX commands instruct the computer to do something. The commands act on *input*, e.g., what the user types or is a file stored on the computer's hard disk. The result of the command is the *output*. The output is either displayed on the screen or is saved in a file.

Switches are additions to the UNIX command that change the way it performs its actions. Without a switch, the command will act in its *default* or normal mode. With a switch, it will act in a different, usually more complex, way. These switches apply to both the graphical interface and the command line. In the graphical interface, switches are often activated by using the mouse to check boxes next to various options. On the command line, the options are typed after the command before pressing the **return** key.

In the examples and tutorials that follow, it is assumed that the users will be connecting to and running programs on a UNIX computer called *genetics*, and that the genetics server is running the Sun Solaris operating system and is connected to the Internet. Other UNIX systems are similar, but some details may vary.

Logging on to a UNIX Computer

The first step is to have a user's account set up on the UNIX computer. The UNIX administrator, who has special privileges to manage the computer, manages the accounts including the creation of new accounts. Systems administration for the Sun Solaris operating system is described in Chapters 15 and 17. Once a user's account is set up, the user can either login at the console (i.e., at the computer itself) or from a remote location in the network.

The most basic method to connect to a UNIX computer from a remote location (such as from an office down the hall, from a laboratory across the campus, or from a hotel room across the country) is a program called *telnet*. Telnet is a computer program that allows the user to connect their local computer, such a personal computer, to the UNIX computer through the network to control the UNIX computer and run programs. A basic telnet program is currently included with most computer operating systems, and there are many examples of freeware or shareware telnet (or terminal) programs available. The user starts the telnet program like QVT/Term on the local computer, then connects to the remote server by typing **open genetics**.

In this case, the name of the remote UNIX computer is *genetics*, but it would most likely be in the format of an Internet address such as *genetics.myuniversity.edu* or something similar.

Once the connection is established, the login screen would appear, similar to:

login:

The user would then enter their username (e.g., janeuser), after which would appear:

Password:

The user would then type their password. For security reasons, the password itself does not appear on the screen. After entering the password, a UNIX command prompt would appear, similar to this:

genetics%

The UNIX command prompt is often the name of the computer followed by the percent sign (%). The command prompt will be at the left side of the screen on what is referred to as the command line and, as one would expect, commands are typed on that line to operate the computer.

Although any basic telnet program will work as described earlier, the author prefers to use a shareware program called QVT/Term, which can be downloaded from the Internet (*see* Website: http://www.qpc.com). QVT/Term is particularly good for connecting to UNIX servers running programs such as the GCG package (*see* Chapters 18, 19, 28, and 33), since it is easy to print the results from the GCG programs through the network. Printing works well for GCG programs operated either from the command line or from the graphical windows interface for GCG called SeqLab, both of which are described in Chapters 18, 19, 28, and 33. The QVT/Term telnet screen is shown in Fig. 1.

Other than using telnet, the login procedure described earlier also applies to logging onto the console. Either way, once the UNIX command prompt is displayed, the user can type the names of UNIX commands or programs.

Computer Files

In general, most operations that computers carry out are done with files. Files are pieces of information that are stored in directories (or folders) on the UNIX computer's hard disk(s). Files have names such as *my_dna_sequence.txt*. Files can contain data, such as a DNA sequence, or they can be programs, such as one of the GCG programs that will analyze the data in a sequence file. The following examples and tutorials describe how to manipulate files stored on the UNIX computer's hard disk(s).

Home Directory

After logging onto a UNIX computer, the user will be located in a folder on the computer's hard disk called the user's *home directory*. On a multi-user UNIX computer, each user will have their own home directory. The user is allowed to make changes to files located in their home directory (and subdirectories thereof), such as creating new files, editing existing files, or copying, renaming, or deleting existing files.

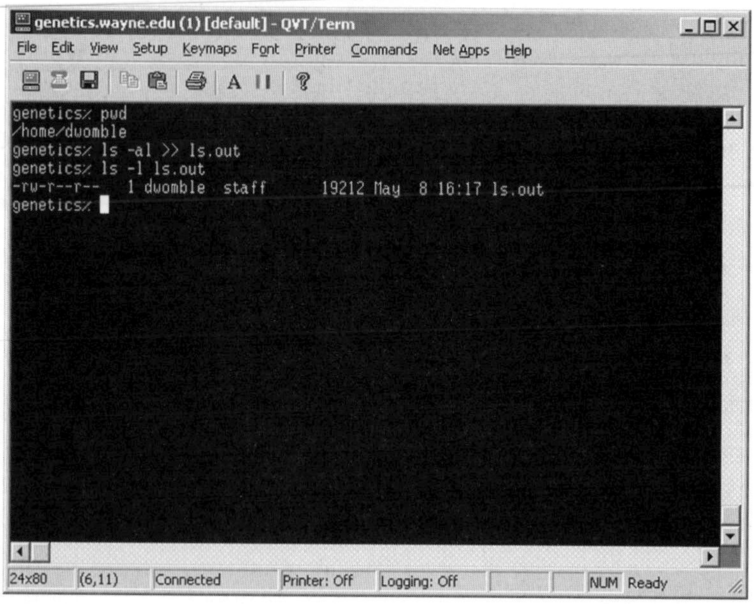

Fig. 1. The QVT/Term Telnet Screen Showing the UNIX Command Prompt.

Usually, users will not be able to make changes to files except those in their own home directories, so that one user cannot change files in another user's home directory. An exception is the *superuser*. The superuser is usually the owner or administrator of the UNIX computer who has special permissions to change all files on the computer, including those of the operating system itself or of the programs that are installed in the public areas of the computer for all users to run. Ordinary users cannot usually change operating system files, the publicly installed programs, or even other ordinary users' files.

Using the Command Line

The following examples and tutorials will demonstrate how to use the command line to operate on files and directories on a UNIX computer. The examples assume the user has logged into a UNIX server and has the **genetics%** command prompt available.

To get the most out of these examples and tutorials, they should be followed in sequence, as presented here. Please note that UNIX is case-sensitive, so it is important to type the commands exactly as indicated. For example, on a UNIX computer, the filenames *myfile* and *Myfile* indicate two different files, both of which may be located in the same folder.

Where Am I? (**pwd** command)

To see the name of the current directory in which the user is located, the user types: **pwd** and presses the **return** key. The result, or output, is the name of the current working directory, which will be displayed on the screen as:
/home/joeuser

That indicates that the user, whose username is *joeuser*, is currently located in their home directory. Their home directory is a folder named *joeuser*, and that folder is a subfolder of the main folder named *home*. The full directory path to their home directory is */home/joeuser*.

The details of the names of home directories and folders may vary depending on how the UNIX administrator has set up the user accounts, but the results shown earlier are typical.

In this first example of using the command line, the UNIX command was the **pwd** command, and the output was the name of the current working directory. This is typical of how commands are executed, and how the output is displayed on the screen. The other examples that follow are similar.

What Files Are In My Directory? (ls command)

To see a list of the files that are located in the user's current working directory, the user types the list files command **ls**. The result is an alphabetical list of the names of the files in the current working directory, similar to:

file1.txt file2.txt

Adding Switches to Change How a Command Operates

In the earlier example, the **ls** command was used in its default or normal mode. Most UNIX commands have switches that change the way the command operates. In the following examples, switches are added to the **ls** command to change the kind of information listed about the files in the current working directory.

To see more information about the files, such as their size and modification dates, the user would add the *longform* switch **-l** to the **ls** command. Switches are added to a UNIX command by typing a minus sign before the switch, **ls -l**. The user types the command, types a space, types a minus sign, then, without typing a space, types the switch, then presses the **return** key. The result is an alphabetical list of the files with all their longform information:

-rw-r--r-- 1 joeuser staff 10 May 7 15:51 file1.txt
-rw-r--r-- 1 joeuser staff 17 May 7 15:51 file2.txt

Although it is beyond the scope of this chapter to describe in detail all information, the basic pieces are, from right to left: the name of the file, the time and date it was last modified, the size in bytes, the name of the group to which the file's owner belongs, the username of the owner, the number of links to the file, and the read, write, and execute permissions associated with the file.

Hidden Files (dot files)

To see a list of all the files in the current working directory, including hidden (or *dot* files), the user would add the *all* switch **-a** to the **ls** command, **ls -a**. The result would be a list of all the files in the current working directory, including those filenames that begin with a period, or dot, for example:

./ ../ .dotfile1 .dotfile2 file1.txt file2.txt

Dot files located in a user's home directory are used to configure the operation of programs that the user runs. For example, files named *.cshrc* and *.login* are read by the operating system each time the user logs in. These files are required, so they should not be deleted. However, experienced users can edit the dot files to customize the way various programs operate according to their preferences.

Adding Multiple Switches to the Command Line

Switches can be combined in one command. An example would be to use the all and longform switches together with the **ls** command. That can be done either together or separately, such as:

\.ls -al

ls -a -l

The output might look similar to this:

```
drwxr-xr-x   2 joeuser  staff      512 May  7 15:54 ./
drwxr-xr-x  42 joeuser  staff     3072 May  7 15:53 ../
-rw-r--r--   1 joeuser  staff        0 May  7 15:54 .dotfile1
-rw-r--r--   1 joeuser  staff        0 May  7 15:54 .dotfile2
-rw-r--r--   1 joeuser  staff       10 May  7 15:51 file1.txt
-rw-r--r--   1 joeuser  staff       17 May  7 15:51 file2.txt
```

The UNIX Manual (man command)

In most cases, it does not matter in which order the switches are typed after a command. However, to see the details of what switches are available and how to use them, the user should consult the online UNIX manual by typing the **man** command. The user types the **man** command followed the name of the command of interest: **man ls**. That will display the manual about the **ls** command, which includes a list of all switches available, what they do, and how to use them. To see more of the manual, i.e., to advance to the next page, press the **Spacebar** key. To move to the previous page, press the **b** key. To quit reading the manual, press the **q** key.

Adding Arguments to a Command

In the earlier example of using the **man** command, some additional input was typed on the command line following the **man** command, i.e., the name of the command (**ls**) for which the manual was wanted. This additional input is called an *argument*. Some commands, such as the **man** command, require an argument on the command line. For other commands, such as the **ls** command, an argument may be optional. As an example, to list the files in the user's home directory, the user could type the whole name of the directory after the **ls** command: **ls /home/joeuser** . That would list all the files in the folder named */home/joeuser*.

Redirecting Output to a File (> symbol)

In the earlier examples for the **ls** command, the results (output) appeared on the screen. The results can be saved to a file instead. This is called *redirecting output to a file*. This is done by using the greater than symbol "**>**", the user types:

ls -al > ls.out

That will cause the results of the **ls -al** command to be saved into a file called *ls.out*. The ">" (greater than) symbol redirects the output of the command into the file. If two greater than symbols are used, like this: **ls -al >> ls.out** , the output from the **ls -al** command is appended onto the end of the file *ls.out*, saving the existing data in that file.

How Can I See What's In a File? (**more** and **cat** commands)

Use the **more** command to see the contents of a file, type:

more ls.out.

The **more** command displays the contents of a file one page at a time, e.g., the file named *ls.out* created in the previous section. To see more pages (if any) press the **spacebar** key. To move back a page, press the **b** key. To quit reading the file, press the **q** key.

Use the **cat** command to display the entire file contents scrolled across the screen. Type:

cat ls.out.

Using Multiple Commands on One Line (| symbol)

The **cat** command is not very useful by itself, but can be used in combination with other commands. To send the results from one command into another command, the user types the pipe symbol "|" like this: **cat ls.out | more**.

In this example, the results (output) of the **cat** command, instead of being displayed on the screen, are sent (piped) into the **more** command, i.e., the output of the **cat** command is used as input for the **more** command.

This example might seem a bit facile, since the **more** command could have been used directly, but it illustrates a powerful capability of the UNIX command line. Experienced users can write scripts that will automatically process large numbers of files or large amounts of data by sending the results of one command to be processed by other commands down the line.

How Do I Copy a File? (**cp** command)

Use the **copy** command to copy a file, type: **cp ls.out ls.copy**.

This will make a copy of the *ls.out* file and name it *ls.copy*. Note that in this case, two arguments are added to the **cp** command, the name of the file to copy, and the name of the destination file. The result is two files, the original and the copy. Other than its filename, it is identical to the original.

How Do I Rename a File? (**mv** command)

Use the **move** command to move a file to a new name, type: **mv ls.copy junk**. That will change the name of the *ls.copy* file to *junk*.

How Do I Delete a File? (**rm** command)

Use the **remove** command to delete a file, type: **rm junk**. That will delete the file named *junk*. Note that there is no **undelete** command in UNIX.

How Do I Create a New Folder? (mkdir command)

If the user is located in their home directory, the user can use the **make directory** command to create a new subfolder by typing:

mkdir Newfolder

That will create a new folder named *Newfolder*, and in these examples, it would have a complete name of:

/home/janeuser/Newfolder

How Do I Change to a Different Folder? (cd command)

To go to a different directory, use the **change directory** (**cd**) command to change from the current working directory to some other directory, for example type:

cd Newfolder

or

cd /home/janeuser/Newfolder

Either command line may take the user to the new folder. The first assumes that the user is already in their home directory. The second will change into the new folder from anywhere, no matter what the current working directory.

To change back to the user's home directory from any other directory, the user simply types the **cd** command without an argument.

How Do I Delete a Folder? (rmdir command)

Use the remove directory (**rmdir**) command to delete a folder, such as the one created in a previous section named *Newfolder*. The folder must not contain any files, i.e., it must be empty before it can be removed. Use the **cd** and **rm** commands to change into and delete the files in the folder. Then use the **cd** command to change to a different folder, such as the user's home directory. Then delete the folder by typing:

rmdir Newfolder

How Do I Edit a File?

Any text file in a user's home directory can be edited with a text editor. Which editor is used depends on which text editing programs are installed on the UNIX computer. Most UNIX computers have a standard text editor called *vi* that can be used to edit any text file. The vi editor is powerful and has many features, but it is also fairly difficult for a beginner to use.

An easy-to-use text editor that may be installed on many UNIX computers is called *pico*. The pico text editor is what is used to edit email messages in the popular pine email program—pico stands for pine composer. It is beyond the scope of this chapter to explain how to use either vi or pico. However, both can be started from the command line, similar to this example:

pico textfile.txt

This command would start the pico editor and open up a file named *textfile.txt*. If a file in the current working directory by that name already exists, it will open that file. If no such file exists, it will create a new file with that name. Once the file is opened, it can be edited by typing new text, deleting text, cutting and pasting. Other text editing procedures can also be applied. When finished editing, the user saves the edited file and quits the program.

How Do I Run the GCG Programs From the Command Line?

The main reason for logging onto a UNIX computer is to run programs to do useful work. One example is the GCG sequence analysis programs. These can be run by several different means, including the command line. Of course, the systems administrator must have already installed the GCG programs and made them publicly available to the ordinary users.

To start the GCG programs from the command line, the user usually types **gcg** and presses the **return** key. This initializes the GCG programs, so that the user can then type the names of GCG programs, including adding switches, just as if they were UNIX commands. To run the restriction mapping program, the user would type:

map

map mysequence.seq

The first method simply starts the mapping program, which will then ask the user for the name of the sequence data file to process. The second uses the name of the sequence file as an argument on the command line, and the map program will then run on that particular data file.

Command line use of the GCG programs, and many other kinds of programs, are described in Chapters 18 and 19.

How Do I Logout From a UNIX Computer? (**exit** command)

To courteously logout from a UNIX computer, or from a telnet session connected to a UNIX computer, type the **exit** command. This will shut down the login and exit the user from the UNIX computer. One should never just close the telnet program while connected to a remote UNIX computer, as the UNIX host might not realize the connection is finished and keep resources open that could better be used to serve other users.

What Other UNIX Commands are Available?

A table listing of a few simple and useful UNIX commands is included in Appendix 3. Many other commands are available, but those in the appendix are generally useful for the beginner. For those wishing to acquire more detailed information, there are many books devoted to using UNIX for users of all skill levels, including entire books dedicated to using the vi text editor. Additional information for UNIX systems administrators is presented (*see* Chapter 15).

Using the Graphical Windows Interface: X Windows

UNIX computers use a graphical windows interface called *X Windows*. A UNIX computer can display its X Windows on its own local display screen or on the display screen of some other remote computer connected via the network. Having the X Windows displayed remotely allows the remote user to control the UNIX computer through the graphical interface, using the mouse to select commands, programs, or files on which to operate. This is an alternative to using telnet and the command line, which some users may prefer. In the examples and tutorials that follow, X Windows will be used to operate files and folders on a remote UNIX computer, similar to the operations that were executed from the command line in the earlier sections of this chapter.

The key to having the remote computer display the X Windows locally is to have an X Windows server program installed on the local computer. Most UNIX (or Linux) computers have some kind of X Windows server installed by default. To display X Windows on an IBM personal computer (PC) or an Apple Macintosh (Mac), a third party X Windows server program is required. The author uses a commercial X Windows server program called *XWin-32*. There are more complex (and more expensive) programs available, but XWin-32 works well with the GCG or Staden programs (*see* Chapters 20, 24, 28, and 33). XWin-32 is available for download from the Internet (*see* Website: http://www.starnet.com/products/).

Setting Up Two Computers to Use X Windows

In the following examples, the user is assumed to be using a local computer that can connect to a remote UNIX computer through the network. The local computer can also be a UNIX or Linux computer, but it can also be a PC or Mac with X server software installed. The author prefers to use QVT/Term to connect and login to the remote UNIX computer, and start the X programs by typing them on the command line. The X Windows from the remote UNIX computer will be displayed on the user's local computer display screen.

There are three steps required to use X Windows: 1) set up the local computer to receive X Windows from a remote computer; 2) tell the remote UNIX computer where to display its X Windows; 3) run the X Windows programs on the remote computer.

For the first step, the user must install an X server program on their PC or Mac, or be using a UNIX or Linux computer with built-in X server software. On a local PC or Mac, the user then starts the X server program and leaves it running, ready to accept X Windows from a remote computer. From the console, often on a local UNIX or Linux computer, the user types the **xhost** command, example:

xhost +

That toggles on the *xhost* function. For more security, the user can add the Internet (IP) address of the remote computer to the **xhost** command line. This will restrict X displays to that particular computer. To turn off the xhost feature, the user types:

xhost –

The details of using the **xhost** command may vary, but are contained in the manual pages that are part of the operating system. They can be viewed by entering the **man xhost** command.

For the second step, the user must tell the remote UNIX computer the Internet (IP) address of their local computer. So, it is necessary to find out what that local IP address is. That usually can be done by looking in the network configuration control panel of the local computer, but it may require help from the local network administrator.

The easiest way to use X Windows programs on the remote computer is to first login to the remote computer using telnet as described earlier in this chapter. Once logged on, the user can tell the remote UNIX computer where to display its X Windows by setting the DISPLAY environment variable by typing on the command line:

setenv DISPLAY my.ip.address:0

Substitute the local PC's IP address, and don't forget the **:0** at the end. That sets an *environment variable* called *DISPLAY* to the value of the PC's IP address. If the user always connects from a PC with the same IP address, the user can put that line in their *.login* file.

Alternatively, one can set up the X server program on the PC to include all the display information along with the X program that will be remotely executed. Although that can be convenient, it does require extra effort.

It may also be necessary to set another environment variable, which can be done by adding this line to the user's .cshrc file:

setenv LD_LIBRARY_PATH /usr/openwin/lib

The details of what needs to be on that line may vary with the particular UNIX computer, so the user should consult with the UNIX systems administrator.

Running X Programs on the Remote UNIX Computer

Having accomplished the first and second steps needed to set up two computers to run X Windows as described earlier in this chapter, a user can type the name of any X program on the command line (of the remote computer), for example:

filemgr &

That will start the Sun graphical file manager program, which will display on the user's local computer screen. The user can then use their mouse to accomplish the tasks outlined in the examples and tutorials. The **&** on the end of the command line causes the *filemgr* program to run in the background, so that other commands can be typed from the command prompt.

Alternatively, the user could build an executable command icon on their local computer screen using the X server software. The icon would include the name of the remote host, the remote execution method, and the following command line:

/usr/openwin/bin/filemgr -display your.ip.address:0 &

Selecting this single icon will accomplish everything described above. Different icons can be created for each X program that the user wishes to run on the remote computer.

Using the Graphical File Manager

The Sun graphical file manager window is shown in Fig. 2. When *filemgr* starts, the user is located in a folder on the hard disk called their home directory. Their home directory is usually something like */home/joeuser*.

How Can I See Information About My Files?

There are several different ways to display information in the File Manager window. For example, using the mouse, right click on the **View** menu, then left click on **List by Name**. To see the hidden files as well, right click the **Edit** menu, left click

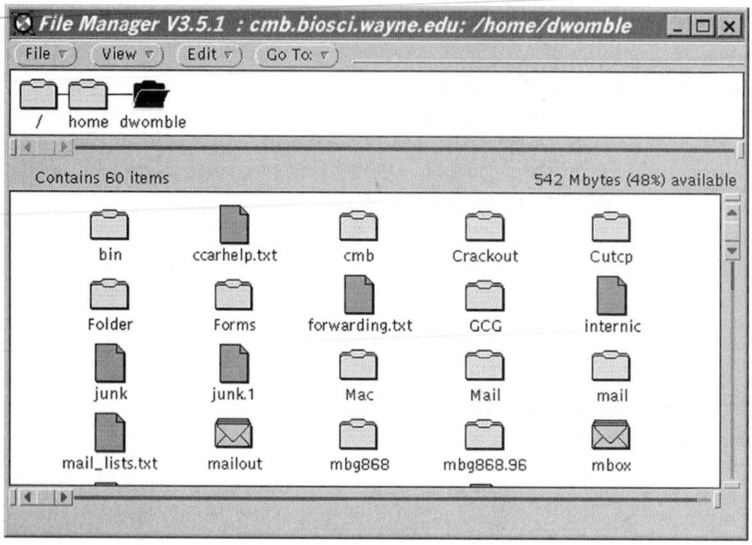

Fig. 2. The Sun Graphical File Manager Window.

on **Properties**, then in the new box, right click the **Category** button, then left click on **Current Folder Settings**, and click on **Show** next to Hidden Files, click the **X** in the upper right, then click on **Apply Changes** to apply the changes you just made. The user should see all the longform information about all their files in the File Manager window. Reverse the steps and click on **Icon by Name** under the **View** menu to return to the original view.

How Can I See What's In a File?

Using the mouse, left click once on a file to select it, then right click on the **File** menu, then left click on **Open in Editor**. The file will open in the X graphical text editor. Use the mouse to scroll through the contents. Left click the **X** in the upper right to close the file.

How Do I Copy a File?

Left click once on a file to select it, right click on the **Edit** menu, left click on **Copy**, right click on the **Edit** menu, left click on **Paste**, then click on **Alter name**. Type in a different name if desired.

How Do I Edit a File?

Left click once on a file to select it, then right click on the **File** menu, then left click on **Open in Editor**. Or if it is a plain text file, just double click on the file. Edit as you like, using the mouse to select text to cut, copy, or paste. To save the changes, right click on **File**, then left click on **Save** or **Save as**. Left click the **X** in the upper right to close the editor.

Alternatively, from the telnet and the UNIX command prompt, type **textedit &** to start the text editor program, independently of the File Manager. After the editor opens, right click on the **File** menu, left click **Open**, left click on the file to be edited, and left click on **Open**. Left click the **X** in the upper right to close the editor.

How Do I Rename a File?

Left click on the name of the file, then type the new name and press **enter**.

How do I Delete a File?

Left click once on a file to select it, right click on the **Edit** menu, left click on **Delete**. Note that unlike deleting a file from the command line, the deleted file is saved into the Waste Basket, from which it could be later retrieved.

How Do I Create a New Folder?

Right click on the **File** menu, left click on **Create Folder**, then type the name for the new folder and press **enter**. To create a new file, click on **Create Document**.

How Do I Change to Other Folders?

Double click on the folder you want to change to, or type the name of the folder on the *Go to* line. Alternatively, right click on the **Go to** menu, then click on one of the folders listed, or on **Home** directory.

How Do I Exit From the File Manger Window?

Left click on the **X** in the upper right, click on **Quit File Manager**, then click on **Yes** to empty the files from the waste.

How Do I Start the GCG SeqLab Interface?

Assuming that the GCG programs are installed on the remote UNIX computer, and that the user is connected via telnet and X Windows is configured as described, you first initialize the GCG programs from the command line by typing:

gcg

Once the GCG programs are activated, start the SeqLab program by typing:

seqlab &

That will start the SeqLab interface and display the SeqLab window on the user's local computer screen. The SeqLab Window is shown in Fig. 3.

The GCG SeqLab window allows the user to operate the GCG suite of sequence analysis programs by using the mouse to select sequences and programs. Using the GCG programs from both the command line and from SeqLab are described in subsequent Chapters 18, 19, 28, and 33.

Many users find using the X Windows interface easier than using the command line. However, experienced users may prefer to use the command line for several important reasons. For example, from the command line, it is possible to run programs reiteratively with the use of switches. This permits a high degree of automation that is not usually possible when running programs one by one from a graphical interface, or from the web.

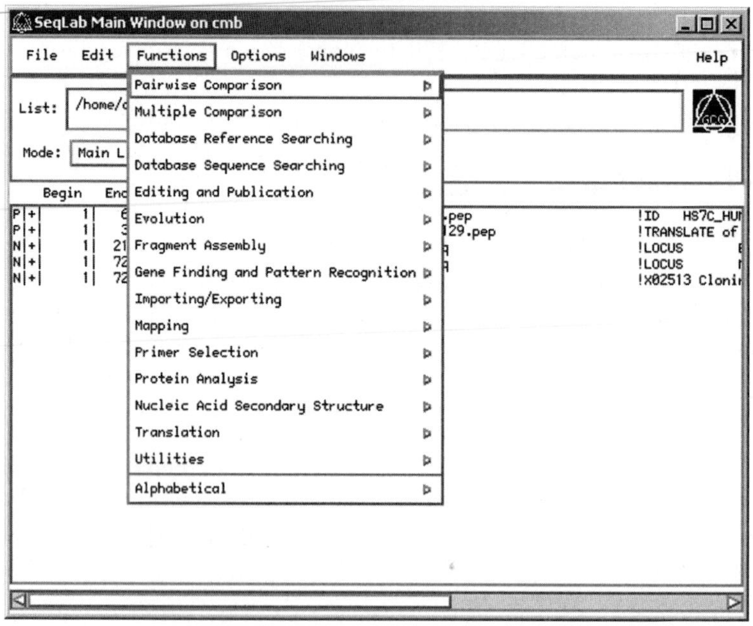

Fig. 3. The GCG SeqLab X Windows Interface.

Other Resources

As mentioned earlier, there are many books devoted to using UNIX available, for readers of all skill levels. In addition, for users of the GCG programs, the GCG manuals contain good basic introductions to using UNIX both from the command line and with X Windows, with particular emphasis on how to use UNIX for the purposes of running the GCG programs. The GCG manuals are usually available online at most installations, via the Internet in either HTML or in PDF format, or both, so the users can look up or print the information that is of interest to them.

14 Installation of the Sun Solaris™ Operating Environment

Bryon Campbell

Introduction

We will focus on the installation tasks for Solaris 8 on Intel® and SPARC® processor systems. Information for Sun Solaris™ running on SPARC® architecture is detailed at Website: http://www.sun.com/solaris and for Intel at Website: http://www.sun.com/intel. Additional documentation for Sun Solaris™ can be found at Website: http://docs.sun.com. As always, your User and System Administration Guides that are part of any Solaris purchase or locally available UNIX/Solaris™ experts are excellent resources.

Sun Solaris™ System Installation

Prior to installing the Solaris8 Operating Environment, fundamental system design decisions are required to ensure the installation process will be smooth.

- Define system use.
- Determine the SPARC® or Intel® hardware platform you will use.
- Determine how much disk space will be needed and how it will be partitioned.
- Determine how your system will be connected to your network.

System Use

Before you proceed you must determine how the system will be used. If the system will be used to develop applications, you will need plenty of processor speed and physical memory. If your intent is to have the system available for multiple users, you will need to plan for the correct amount of disk space to support their storage needs. If the system is also used as an application server, you will need to adjust the system hardware to meet the computational needs of the applications. Your local hardware vendor or Information Technology support organization can also assist you.

Hardware Platform

The Solaris™ operating system was first supported on the SPARC® platform. The first SPARC® systems were the SPARC® 5, 10, and 20. These systems were eventually replaced by faster UltraSPARC® systems that achieved speeds of 400 MHz and

Table 1
Software Distribution

Distribution	Size in MB
End User Support (smallest)	363 + swap space
Developer Support	801 + swap space
Entire Distribution	857 + swap space
Entire Distribution and OEM	900 + swap space

greater. It wasn't until Solaris™ version 2.1 that the Intel® architecture was supported, so that one could now install Solaris™ in dual boot mode on their Intel-based system. Potential Solaris Intel® x86 users should verify ISA, EISA, and PCI hardware compatibility in the Solaris 8 Operating Environment (*see* Website: http://access1.sun.com/drivers/hcl/hcl.html).

Disk Configuration

Before you decide on a disk-partition scheme, you will first need to decide the distributions that you will be installing. There are four distributions to choose from, *see* Table 1 for disk space recommendations.

The smallest distribution will work well for environments that do not require applications development. If you plan to develop applications it would be wise to install the entire distribution with the OEM (original equipment manager). Keep in mind that disk space is relatively inexpensive.

When partitioning the disk, there are five common partitions that will be created. These partitions should be a minimum of 300 MB and could extend in size to 1 GB +, depending on need. The partitions are as follows:

- **/–** This is the root partition. This is also the top-level directory. Root is where all files that support the OS reside.
- **/home** The partition contains the user files. Directories below the home level will contain user specific information for users with accounts on the system.
- **/opt** This location contains the optional applications. Depending on how many optional applications are stored, this area could require substantial disk space.
- **/usr** This partition contains the utilities used in the Solaris operating system. The /bin and /sbin directories are where most of these utilities are located.
- **/var** This directory contains the log files, mail files, and print files. If your system is providing print services, you will need to ensure this partition is quite large so that it may accomodate the spool files associated with printing.
- **/etc** This serves as the location for machine specific configuration files.

As emphasized, disk space has become relatively inexpensive. You should buy a large disk, containing 10's of GB's, to minimize future growth issues as you develop and or host additional users.

Network Connectivity

As you install the Solaris™ Operating Environment, you will be asked to provide network configuration parameters to complete the installation. The basic parameters that will be needed are:

- Hostname: The name you give to your system.
- IP Address: The Internet Protocol (IP) address that provides network access to your machine.
- Domain Name: The name that uniquely identifies your system on the Internet. The fully qualified format is *hostname.domainname.com.*
- Subnet Mask: In environments with multiple networks or systems, the *subnet mask* is required to connect to other systems outside of your subnet. Your network administrator can provide detailed information.
- Default Router (Gateway): This provides the network path to systems outside of your network or subnet. Your network administrator can provide detailed information.

Note: If your site utilizes the Dynamic Host Configuration Protocol (DHCP), your system would automatically configure everything except the *hostname*.

Methods for Installation

There are three options for installing the Solaris™ Operating Environment: Solaris Interactive Installation, Jumpstart, and WebStart.

The Solaris™ Interactive installation can be completed on both SPARC® and Intel® platforms. There are two modes for installation, graphical and text mode. Availability of these modes will depend on the capability of the monitor and the keyboard connected to the system you are installing. The installation procedures are identified for both platforms.

The Jumpstart installation is typically used for large Solaris™ installations, where another server has been pre-configured to install Solaris™ on new machines. You will want to work with your local system administrator to see if this is an option for you.

The WebStart installation provides a Java-based interface that walks you step by step through the installation process. The system requirements are higher than the minimum hardware requirements set forth by Sun. The Sun installation manual can provide additional WebStart information. A sample WebStart installation is presented below.

Installing the Solaris Operating Environment Using WebStart

There are two ways to accomplish a WebStart Installation. You can use the graphical user interface or the command line interface. The graphical installation requires a local or remote CD-ROM drive, network connection, keyboard, frame buffer, and graphics monitor.

With the command line interface, you have the same requirements except that a graphics monitor and frame buffer are not required. The sequence of instructions for both the graphical and command line interface installation are very similar. Figures 1 and 2 show sample screen shots.

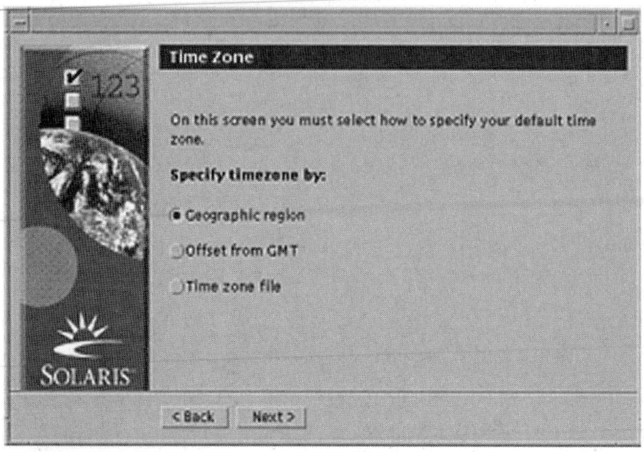

Fig. 1. Sample screen shot of the Graphical User Interface (GUI) Time Zone Dialog Box.

```
Please select how to specify your default time zone.
Specify Time Zone by:
1. Geographic region
2. Offset from GMT
3. Time zone file

Please enter the number corresponding to how you would like to
specify the time zone [1]:
```

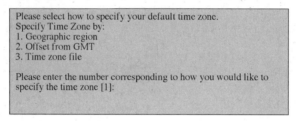

Fig. 2. Sample screen shot of Command-Line Interface (CLI) Time Zone Dialog Box.

Pre-Installation Steps

To determine how to install Solaris™, you will need to answer 5 key questions.

1. Where is the Solaris™ software source?
   In other words is there a CD-ROM drive attached to your system or a remote CD-ROM drive on the network.
2. Is the hardware platform you are installing supported on Solaris™?
   To answer this question, see the Solaris™ Hardware Platform Guide. Also, if your system is on the network, you will need to contact your system administrator to gather the information outlined in Table 2.
3. What Solaris™ components are you going to install?
   Disk space recommendations are listed in Table 3.
4. What language will you be using?
   Solaris™ Multilingual SPARC® supports the following languages: Chinese (simplified and traditional), English, French, German, Italian, Japanese, Korean, Spanish, and Swedish.
5. Is this an upgrade or a new installation?
   During the installation process you will be asked if this is an *initial* or *upgrade* installation.

Once the file copy process is complete you will see the following screen (Fig. 3).

Running WebStart

After the Welcome Screen, click the **Next** button on the graphical display. WebStart will start gathering information to complete the installation.

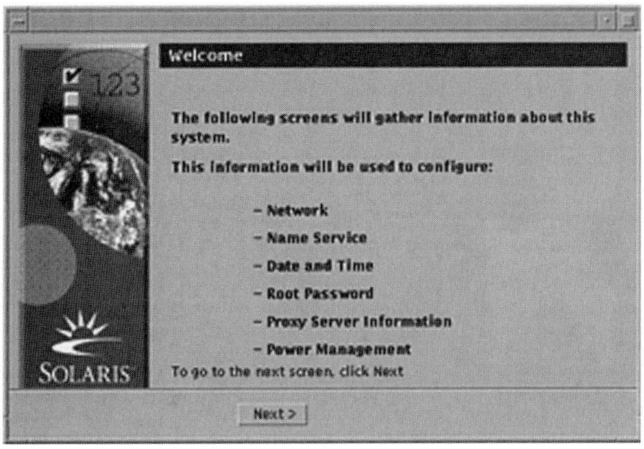

Fig. 3. Welcome Screen.

Table 2
Networking Parameters

Information	*Example*	*Solaris commands*
Host Name	jordan	uname -u
Host IP address	10.14.121.115	ypmatch system_*name hosts* or nismatch system_*nameHosts.org_dir*
Subnet mask	255.255.255.0	more /etc/netmasks
Type of name service (DNS, NIS, NIS+)	group: files nis passwd: files nis	cat /etc/nsswitch
Domain name	university.edu	domainname
Host name of the name server	brandan	ypwhich
Host IP address of the name server	10.14.110.5	Ypmatch names_*server hosts* or Nismatch name_*server hosts.org_dir*

Table 3
Disk Space Recommendations

Software	*Recommended disk space*
Distribution Plus OEM Support	2.4 Gbytes
Distribution Only	2.3 Gbytes
Developer Support	1.9 Gbytes
End User Support	1.6 Gbytes

The next few steps will configure, the network portion of the installation as shown in Figs. 4–20. Figure 4 begins the process with network connectivity.

If your system will not be connected to a network, then select **Non-networked**. If you select **Networked**, then you will be asked to answer a few more questions. You will need all the information in Table 2. At the screen shown in Fig. 5, you will type in the host name of your system. If you have questions with this step or other steps please see your site system administrator.

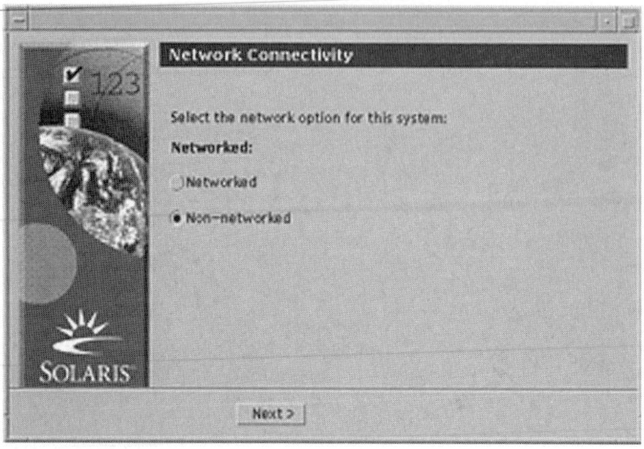

Fig. 4. Network Connectivity.

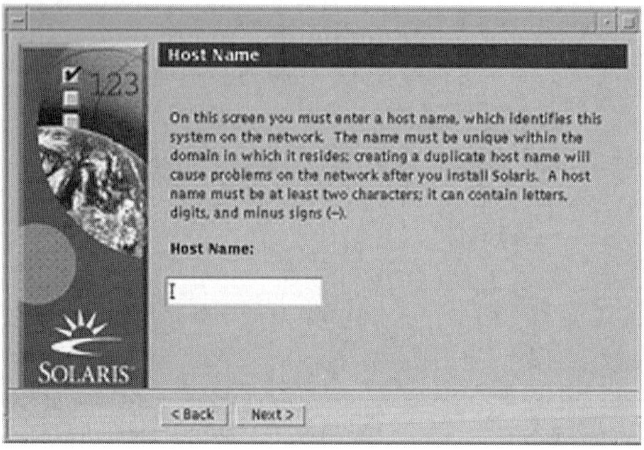

Fig. 5. Host Name.

The next step will configure network addressing. The dialog box (*see* Fig. 6), will ask if you wish to use Dynamic Host Control Protocol (DHCP). The advantage in using DHCP is that it configures the network settings automatically for you. This eliminates potential human error that may occur. If you select No at the DHCP Screen, you will be required to input all necessary network configuration values.

The next screen will require that you input the IP address for your system (*see* Fig. 7). Input the IP address that the system or network administrator has provided for your machine.

The next screen, shown in Fig. 8, specifies your net mask or subnet mask. Input the Netmask or Subnet mask for your system, the default value is 255.255.255.0. In some cases the subnet mask will be different depending upon the sites network configuration. This can be verified with your administrator.

The next screen (*see* Fig. 9), requires a yes/no response to enable the IPv6, the next generation Internet Protocol. It is suggested that you select **No** unless your site is using this new protocol.

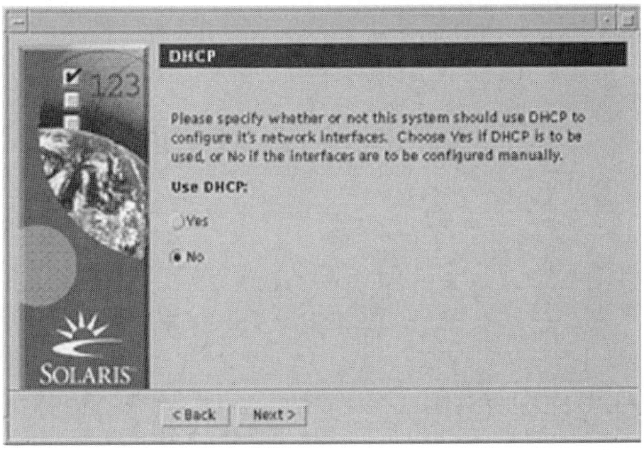

Fig. 6. Dynamic Host Control Protocol (DHCP).

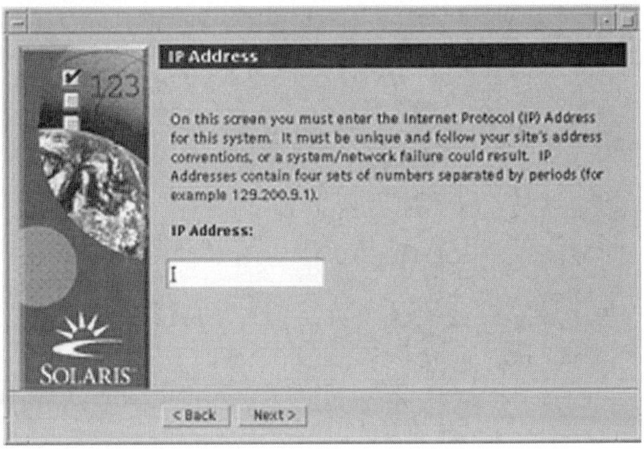

Fig. 7. IP address.

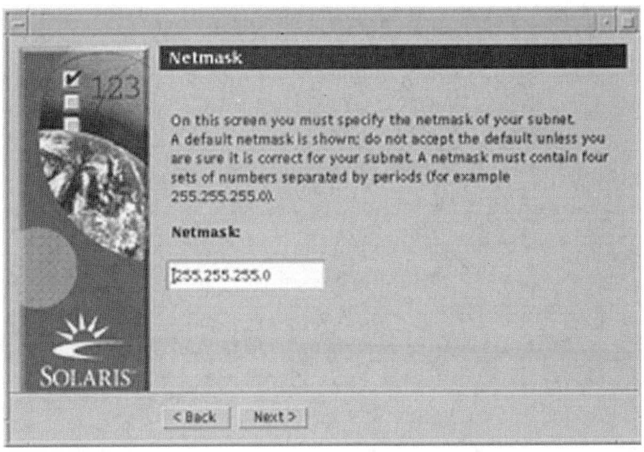

Fig. 8. Netmask or Subnet Mask.

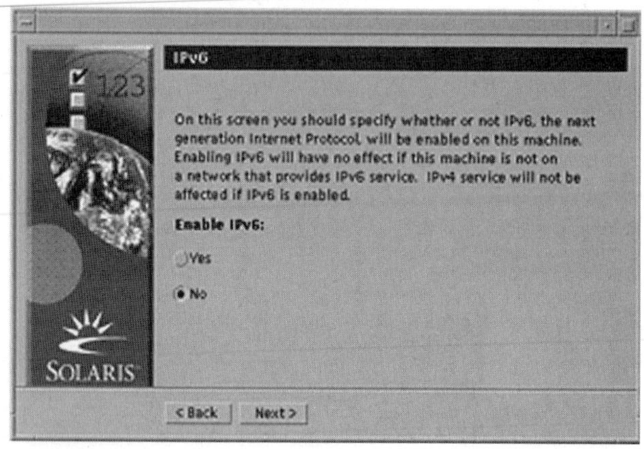

Fig. 9. IPv6, the next generation Internet Protocol.

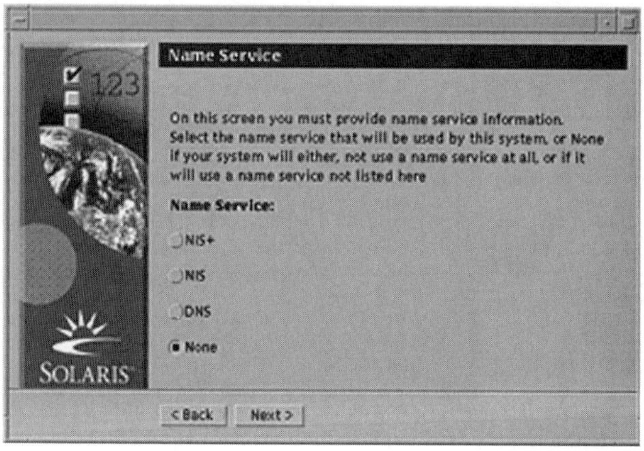

Fig. 10. Name Service.

The screen shown in Fig. 10 allows you to select the preferred name service for your system. The name service provides *friendly* name resolution to a physical IP (network) address.

As indicated, the domain name is requested next (*see* Fig. 11). Selecting **DNS**, **NIS**, or **NIS+** will require you to enter a *Domain Name*. An example of a domain name would be "university.edu". The fully qualified name of the machine would be "jordan.university.edu." with "jordan" as the hostname.

If you selected NIS or NIS+ you will be able to specify the name server or it will try to find a name server on your subnet (*see* Fig. 12).

If you selected DNS for the name service you will need to input the IP address of the DNS server. You can input as many as three different DNS server addresses (*see* Fig. 13). Primary and secondary servers are recommended to provide alternative access in case of a DNS server failure. Your network administrator can provide the IP addresses.

If you selected NIS or NIS+ you will need to input the *host name* and the *IP address* of the NIS or NIS+ server (*see* Fig. 14).

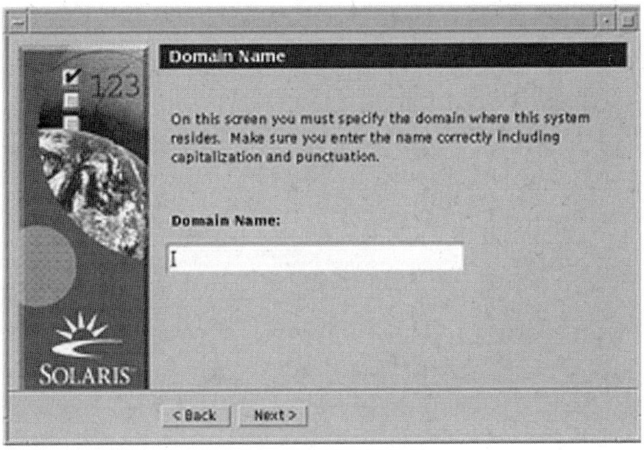

Fig. 11. Domain Name.

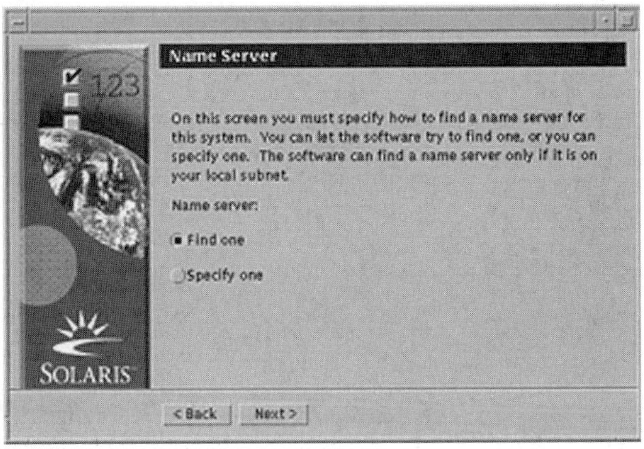

Fig. 12. Name Server, Find one.

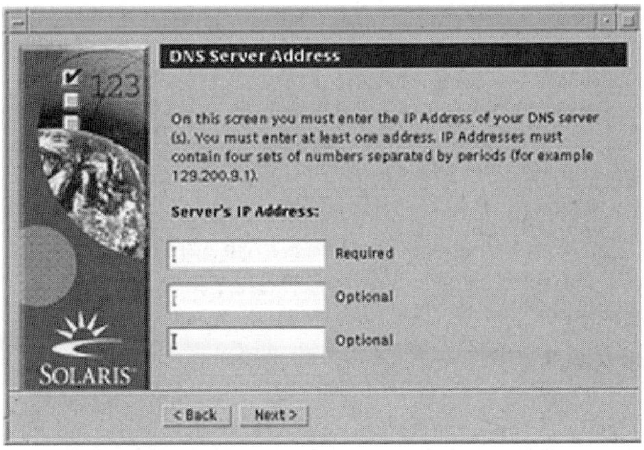

Fig. 13. DNS Server Address.

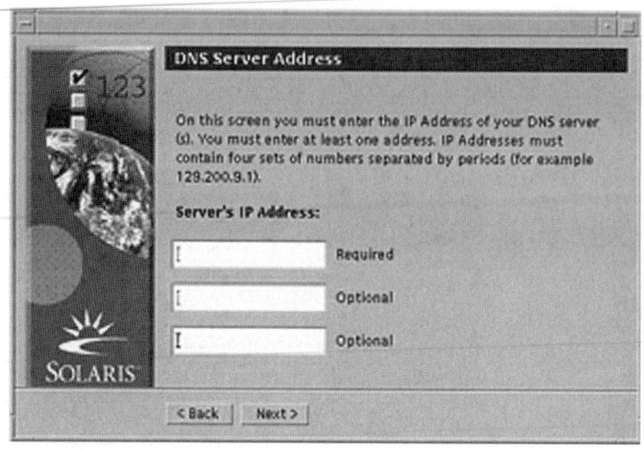

Fig. 14. Name Server Information.

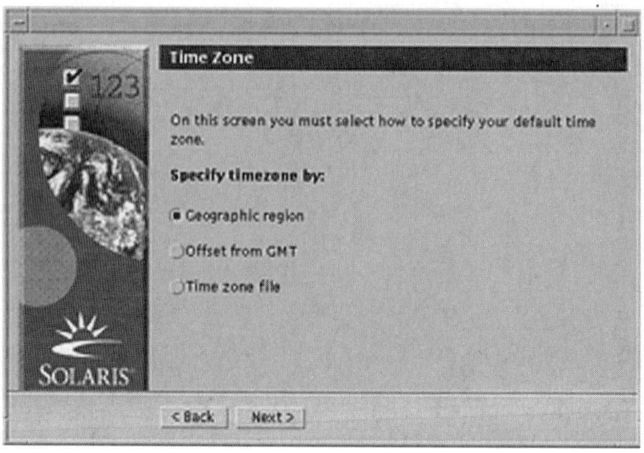

Fig. 15. Time Zone.

The screen shown in Fig. 15 will allow you to input the geographic region, offset from GMT or a Time Zone File. Time zone files are usually located in the /usr/share/lib/zoneinfo directory.

From the next screen you will need to input the year, month, day, hour, and minutes (*see* Fig. 16). This will set the local time for your system.

The screen in Fig. 17 is where you input the *superuser* password for your system. Please guard this password with the highest level of security. It is the highest level of access to the system. A typical password contains both letters and characters in both upper and lower case. Remember, the Solaris™ (UNIX) operating environment is case sensitive.

Power management software automatically saves the state of the system after it has been idle for 30 min. The software is installed by default and requires the user to either enable or disable the feature (*see* Fig. 18).

Next, there are two selections for connecting to the Internet, direct connection via a gateway or a proxy server. If you select proxy server, you need to provide the host

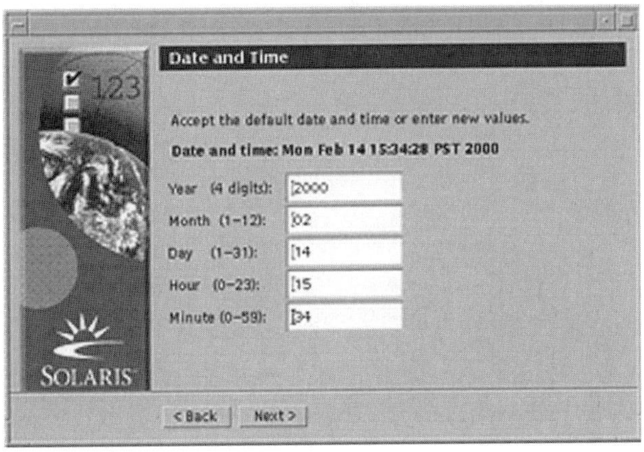

Fig. 16. Date and Time.

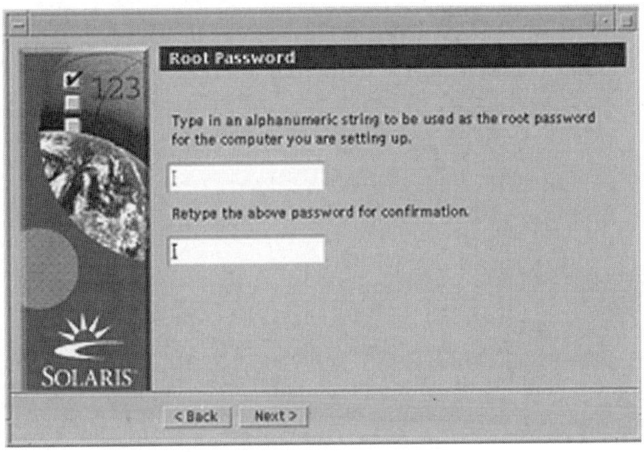

Fig. 17. Root Password.

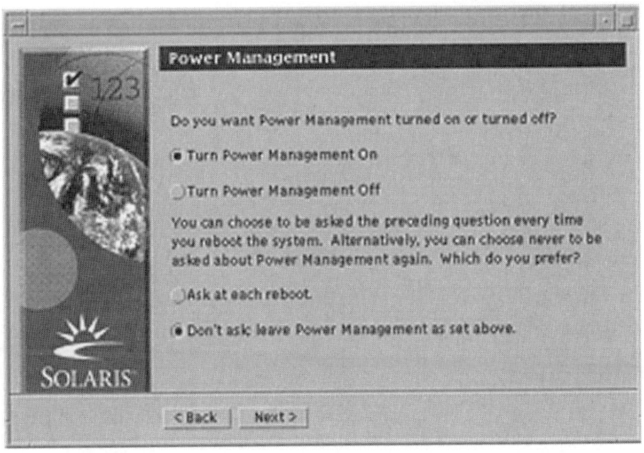

Fig. 18. Power Management.

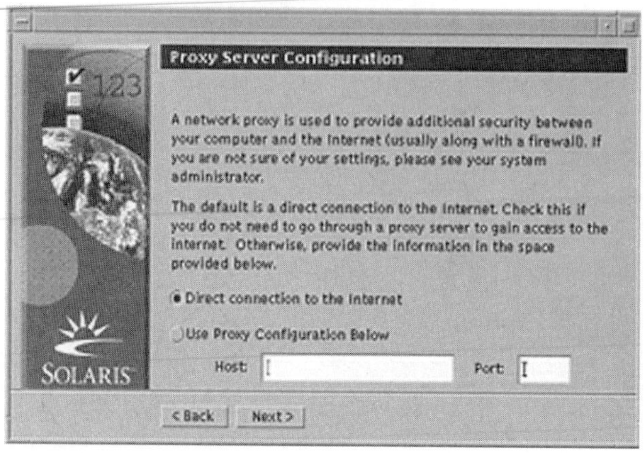

Fig. 19. Proxy Server Configuration.

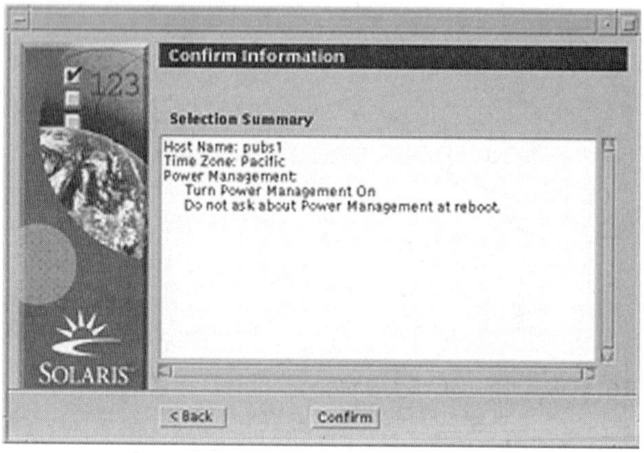

Fig. 20. Confirm Information.

Fig. 21. Main Menu.

name and the port your proxy server is on (*see* Fig. 19). Your local network administrator can advise.

The screen shown in Fig. 20 allows you to verify the settings before they are committed to the system. When you click on the **Confirm** button, the system will write the configuration information to the system. The **back** button permits scrolling to previous screens, to change configuration parameters.

Once you have confirmed your settings, you have completed the operating system installation (*see* Fig. 21). You are now ready to work in the Solaris™ Operating Environment.

Glossary and Abbreviations

Application Is a program designed to perform a specific function directly for the user or, in some cases, for another application program. (Examples of applications include word processors, database programs, Web browsers, development tools, drawing, paint, image editing programs, and communication programs).

CD-ROM (Compact Disc, read-only-memory) is an adaptation of the CD that is designed to store computer data in the form of text and graphics, as well as hi-fi stereo sound.

Command Line Interface (CLI) Is a user interface to a computer's operating system or an application in which the user responds to a visual prompt by typing in a command on a specified line, receives a response back from the system, and then enters another command, and so forth.

Default Router Is a device or, in some cases, software in a computer, that determines the next network point to which a packet should be forwarded toward its destination. The router is connected to at least two networks and decides which way to send each information packet based on its current understanding of the state of the networks it is connected to.

DHCP Dynamic Host Configuration Protocol. DHCP is a communications protocol that lets network administrators manage centrally and automate the assignment of Internet Protocol (IP) addresses in an organization's network. Without DHCP, the IP address must be entered manually at each computer and, if computers move to another location in another part of the network, a new IP address must be entered.

DNS The Domain Name System. DNS is the way that Internet domain names are located and translated into Internet Protocol addresses. A domain name is a meaningful and easy-to-remember "handle" for an Internet address.

Domain Name A domain name locates an organization or other entity on the Internet. For example, the domain name www.cnn.com locates an Internet address for "cnn.com" at Internet address: 64.236.24.20.

Dual Boot A dual boot system is a computer system in which two operating systems are installed on the same hard drive, allowing either operating system to be loaded and given control. When you turn the computer on, a boot manager program displays a menu, allowing you to choose the operating system you wish to use. A boot manager works by replacing the original Master Boot Record (MBR) with its own so that the boot manager program loads instead of an operating system.

EISA Is a standard bus (computer interconnection) architecture that extends the ISA standard to a 32-bit interface. It was developed in part as an open alternative to the proprietary Micro Channel Architecture (MCA) that IBM introduced in its PS/2 computers. EISA data transfer can reach a peak of 33 megabytes per second.

Giga Byte (GB) A gigabyte is a measure of computer data storage capacity and is "roughly" a billion bytes.

GMT Is the standard time common to every place in the world. Formerly and still widely called Greenwich Mean Time (GMT) and also World Time, This nominally reflects the mean solar time along the Earth's prime meridian. (The prime meridian is 0° longitude in the 360 lines of longitude on Earth.

Graphics Monitor A monitor that is capable of displaying graphics.

Hostname Any computer that has full two-way access to other computers on the Internet. A host has a specific "local or host number" that, together with the network number, forms its unique IP address. In this context, a "host" is a node in a network.

IP Internet protocol. The Internet Protocol (IP) is the method or protocol by which data is sent from one computer to another on the Internet. Each computer (known as a host) on the Internet has at least one IP address that uniquely identifies it from all other computers on the Internet. When you send or receive data (for example, an e-mail note or a Web page), the message gets divided into little chunks called packets. Each of these packets contains both the sender's Internet address and the receiver's address.

IP Address An IP address has two parts: the identifier of a particular network on the network and an identifier of the particular device (which can be a server or a workstation) within that network.

ISA Industry standard architecture. ISA is a standard bus (computer interconnection) architecture that is associated with the IBM AT motherboard. It allows 16 bits at a time to flow between the motherboard circuitry and an expansion slot card **IPv6** IPv6 (Internet Protocol Version 6) is the latest level of the Internet Protocol (IP) and is now included as part of IP support in many products including the major computer operating systems. IPv6 has also been called "IPng" (IP Next Generation). Network hosts and intermediate nodes with either IPv4 or IPv6 can handle packets formatted for either level of the Internet Protocol. The most obvious improvement in IPv6 over the IPv4 is that IP addresses are lengthened from 32 bits to 128 bits. This extension anticipates considerable future growth of the Internet and provides relief for what was perceived as an impending shortage of network addresses.

JAVA Java is a programming language expressly designed for use in the distributed environment of the Internet. It was designed to have the "look and feel" of the C++ language, but it is simpler to use than C++ and enforces an object-oriented programming model.

Name Server A server much like a DNS Server that translates Host Names to IP Address or IP Address to Host Names.

NIS Network Information System. NIS is a network naming and administration system for smaller networks that was developed by Sun Microsystems. NIS+ is a later version that provides additional security and other facilities. Using NIS, each host client or server computer in the system has knowledge about the entire system. A user at any host can get access to files or applications on any host in the network with a single user identification and password.

OEM An OEM (original equipment manufacturer) is a company that uses product components from one or more other companies to build a product that it sells under its own company name and brand. IBM is an example of a supplier to the OEM market (and IBM is also an OEM itself since it uses other companies' parts in some of its products).

PCI Peripheral component interconnect. PCI is an interconnection system between a microprocessor and attached devices in which expansion slots are spaced closely for high-speed operation.

Proxy Server A proxy server is a server that acts as an intermediary between a workstation user and the Internet so that the enterprise can ensure security, administrative control, and caching service. A proxy server is associated with or part of a gateway server that separates the enterprise network from the outside network and a firewall server that protects the enterprise network from outside intrusion.

SPARC® Scalable processor architecture. SPARC® is a 32- and 64-bit microprocessor architecture from Sun Microsystems that is based on reduced instruction set computing (RISC). SPARC® has become a widely used architecture for hardware used with UNIX-based operating systems, including Sun's own Solaris systems.

Solaris™ Solaris™ is the computer operating system that Sun Microsystems provides for its family of Scalable Processor Architecture-based processors as well as for -based processors.

Subnet Mask is an identifiably separate part of an organization's network. Typically, a subnet may represent all the machines at one geographic location, in one building, or on the same local area network (LAN).

Superuser A user that has administrative privileges on the system. The superuser account can perform any function on the system.

UNIX is an operating system that originated at Bell Labs in 1969 as an interactive time-sharing system. Ken Thompson and Dennis Ritchie are considered the inventors of UNIX.

x86 Is a generic name for the series of Intel® microprocessor families that began with the 80286 microprocessor. This series has been the provider of computing for personal computers since the 80286 was introduced in 1982. x86 microprocessors include the 386DX/SX/SL family, the 486DX/SX//DX2/SL/DX4 family, and the Pentium 3 family.

Suggested Readings

Watters, P. A. (2001) Solaris Administration: A Beginner's Guide, Osborne McGraw Hill, Berkeley, CA.

Kasper, P. A. and McCellan, A. (1995) Automating Solaris Installations: A Custom Jumpstart Guide with Disk, Prentice Hall, Upper Saddle River, NJ.

Wong, B. L. (1997) Configuration and Capacity Planning for Solaris Servers, Prentice Hall, Upper Saddle River, NJ.

Ledesma, R. (1994) PC Hardware Configuration Guide for DOS and Solaris, Prentice Hall, Upper Saddle River, NJ.

15 Sun System Administration

Bryon Campbell

Introduction

This chapter will describe the basic day-to-day administrative tasks necessary to manage a single or multi-user system. The primary source of information has been gathered from the Sun documentation website and the experience of the author (*see* Website: http://docs.sun.com). Additional and detailed information is always available as part of your Solaris™ User and System Administration Guides or local UNIX/Solaris™ experts.

User Administration

Managing User and Group Account Databases

One of the main tasks for the system administrator is to manage user access to the Solaris™ system(s). This includes the creation of user accounts, password changes, and user security. The file that contains this information is located in the directory: **/etc/passwd**.

The file format is text and utilizes single lines of information to define each user. The format for the information is: **username:x:uid:gid:commment:home_directory:login_shell**. Table 1 describes the field names for the **passwd** file.

In many cases there are system parameters that predefine the minimum and maximum values for user accounts and passwords.

The *User Account* is defined by the username that uniquely identifies the user who is logging into the system and accessing resources. The author recommends that the system administrator defines a standard for usernames. This will reduce the potential for problems as the user base grows.

The *Password* is the parameter that authenticates the user to permit access to the system. Again the author recommends defining a standard for passwords (e.g., minimum length and combination of characters and numbers). The location for the encrypted password file is in: **/etc/shadow**. This file is only accessible by the root user (highest level of access).

The format of the **/etc/shadow** file is much like that of the **/etc/passwd** file: **username:password:lastchg:min:max:warn:inactive:exprire:flag**. Table 2 describes the various fields.

Table 1
/etc/passwd File Fields

Field Name	*Description*
Username	Unique username
X	Locator for users encrypted password
Uid	**user id**entification number—used to define user system security
Gid	**group id**entification number—used to define the security group to which the user belongs
Comment	Holds additional information about the user or user account
home_dir	Directory that the user has been assigned for storing resources (e.g., files or programs)
login_shell	Defines the users default login shell (e.g., sh, csh, ksh)

Table 2
/etc/shadow File Fields

Field Name	*Description*
Username	Unique username
Password	13 character encrypted string—users password
Lastchg	Date password was last changed
Min	Minimum days required between password changes
Max	Maximum days the password is valid
Warn	Number of days the user is warned of password expiration
Inactive	Number of days the account can be inactive (no login). If left blank the account will always be active
Expire	Expiration of the account should be set for temporary or contract workers
Flag	Not in use

The *User ID* uniquely identifies each user on the system. This is analogous to the name, associated with the user's account. The range for UIDs is quite large, 0 to approx 2.1 billion. Solaris™ reserves ranges of IDs for administrative purposes as shown in Table 3.

The *Group IDs* are similar to the UID but it identifies a group of users. This allows a system administrator to apply security to resources to which a group of users have access. It minimizes the amount of administration that would be required to apply security privileges to each individual user (UID).

The GID information is stored in the **/etc/group** file as shown in Table 4. It emulates the format used in the **/etc/passwd** and **/etc/shadow** files: **groupname: password:gid:user_list**.

Table 3
Reserved Solaris™ UIDs

UID	*Description*
0	Root or *superuser*
1–99	Daemons and system maintenance processes
60001	Special user access *nobody*, used in specific maintenance activities
60002	Special user access *noaccess*, used in the same way as *nobody*
65534	Special user access *nobody4*, used for backward Solaris operating system compatibility.

Table 4
GID Parameters

Field Name	*Description*
Groupname	Symbolic name of the group (maximum of 8 characters)
Password	Not used in Solaris 8, carry over from previous Solaris operating systems
Gid	Unique numerical number
User_list	Comma separated list of users

Table 5
useradd or **usermod** Parameters

Option	*Parameter Name*	*Description*
-c	comment	User comment
-d	pathname	Path for user home directory
-g	groupname or GID	Default groupname or group ID for the user
-e	expire	Expiration for the user account
-f	inactive	Maximum inactivity period for a user account
-u	UID	UID to use for the user
-s	shell	Default login shell
-l	newname	Used to change user name

Managing User and Group Accounts

There are several commands that are used to manage user accounts. For illustrative purposes the use of a few commands will be demonstrated. All options are case-sensitive.

The **useradd "username"** command is executed by the root user (e.g., useradd christina). This command would create a user named "christina". There are several parameters that can be passed in the command line as shown in Table 5. These could also be used to change user parameters with the **usermod** command.

Table 6
passwd Parameters

Option	*Parameter Name*	*Description*
-f	username	Force the user to change password at next logon
-x	days username	Number of days the password is valid
-w	days username	Number of days before the password expires
-n	min username	Number of days a user has to wait to change their password
-l	username	Locks the specified user account

The **usermod "option" "username"** command permits the *root user* to change the characteristics associated with a specific user account. The parameters listed in Table 5 can be applied to **usermod** command.

The **userdel "username"** command is used to delete a specific user account. This command deletes the account from the system but does not remove any resources associated with the account.

The **passwd "option" "username"** command is used to change a users password. The **passwd** command can be executed by the account owner or the root user. An example of the parameters that can be used with the **passwd** command are shown in Table 6.

The **groupadd -g "gid" "groupname"** is similar to the **useradd** command. This command will create a group when provided a group ID (GID) and groupname.

The **groupmod -n "newname" "currentgroupname"** command will change the name of a current group.

The **groupdel "groupname"** deletes a group from the system.

System Process Administration

System processes are also known as *daemons*. Daemons are processes that allow the Solaris™ Operating Environment to be single and multi-user systems. They are the traffic cops of the operating system. These processes make computer resources available, manage interactions with other processes, in order to keep them from crashing into one another. They are the backbone of any operating system.

System Startup and Shutdown

There are several modes of operation when the Solaris system starts up. The *init* daemon is crucial to this process as *init* controls the initialization of the system. The initialization process and parameters are settable from the **/etc/inittab** file. The main function of *init* is to spawn the necessary daemon processes from the configuration file **/etc/inittab**.

Information stored in the **inittab** file handles many situations that arise during the boot process, (*see* Table 7).

Shutdown has been made easy with the **shutdown** command. The parameters for the shutdown command are: **#shutdown -i "run_level" -g "grace_period" -y**, where **-i** specifies the run level for the shutdown (*see* Table 8), **-g** specifies the period of time before the shutdown starts, and **-y** supplies the confirmation parameter for shutdown. If this is omitted the system will ask if you want to really shutdown.

Table 7
init Actions

Action	*Description*
boot	Initialization of a full reboot
bootwait	Transition from single-user to multi-user system
initdefault	Default run level (on all systems)
off	Ensures process termination
ondemand	Similar to re-spawn
powerfail	State when a power failure is detected
powerwait	Waits for process to terminate
respawn	Ensures specified process are running
sysinit	Safeguard to allow administrator to specify run level
wait	Starts a process and waits until it's started

Table 8
Solaris Run Levels

Run Level	*Init State*	*Type*	*Description*
0	Power Down	Power-down	Shutdown system to safely power off system
1	Administrative	Single-user	Access to user files with user logins
2	Multi-user	Multi-user	Normal operations, multiple users except the NFS daemon does not start
3	Multi-user with NFS	Multi-user	Normal operation with NFS daemon started
4	Alternative Multi-user	Multi-user	Currently not in use
5	Power Down	Power-down	Shutdown system to safely power off system with automatic power off if available
6	Reboot	Reboot	Shutdown system and reboot to multi-user state
s or S	Single-user	Single-user	Start as single user system with all resources available

Startup and Shutdown Run Levels

The systems *run level* or *init state* defines what services will be made available during startup or shutdown. Solaris™ has eight run levels defined in the **/etc/inittab** file. Table 8 describes the eight available run levels.

System Process Management

System processes are applications that run in support of the operating environment. These processes manage or control files, security, printing, network, and user applications. Solaris™ is a UNIX-based operating system and supports a multi-user

Table 9
ps Parameters

Parameter Name	*Description*
-a	Frequently requested processes
-e or -d	All processes
-c	Processes in scheduler format
-f or -l	Complete process information
-g or -G	Group information
-j	SID and PGID
-p	Processes for a specific process
-s	Session leaders
-t	Specific terminal process information
-u	Specific user process information

environment. These system processes ensure that everyone who is accessing the system is provided a secure portion of the environment enabling them to perform the tasks they are trying to accomplish.

There are many tools available in Solaris™ to assist system administrators with the management of the system. In the UNIX environment users have the ability to *spawn*, i.e., *create* new process. This sometimes creates problems and system administrators need tools that enable them to monitor or delete processes that are depleting system resources.

The most useful command is the **ps** command. There are many "case sensitive" parameters that can be passed with the **ps** command that will allow the system administrator to analyze the current state of the system. Table 9 shows a list of the parameters and what they provide.

Signals can also be sent to specific process that will stop or halt errant processes using the **kill** command. There are two parameters that are used to affect running processes. All signals are defined in the **<signal.h>** file. In **kill "signal_type" "pid"**, a **#kill -9 235** command would kill process 235, whereas a **#kill -3 236** command would kill process 236. Note: **-9** terminates any process; **-3** exits a process gracefully.

Network Basics

A network is the glue that connects systems together. The following basic networking concepts and commands are outlined.

Network Layers

There are several communication layers that achieve the connectivity that is needed to share information between one or more systems. Network protocols are the basic components that constitute the various network layers. These protocols are used to ensure that information is delivered via the network in a timely and accurately manner (*see* Table 10).

Table 10
Network Layers

Network Layers	*Layer Function*
Application Presentation Session	Application data
Transport Network	Host to host communications
Data Link Physical	Network access

As outlined in Table 10, each layer has a specific function as follows:

- Application, is where applications reside. It is the end user interface to the operating system (UNIX, LINUX, etc).
- Presentation, isolates the lower layers from the application data format. It converts data from the application into a common interchangeable format.
- Session, organizes and synchronizes the exchange of data between application processes. The session layer can be thought of as a timing and flow control layer.
- Transport, provides the transfer of data from a source end open system to a destination end open system. It establishes, maintains, and terminates communications between two machines while maintaining data integrity.
- Network, provides physical routing of the data, determining the path between the systems. The network layer handles all routing issues. The routing function will evaluate the network topology to determine the best route to send data.
- Data Link, monitors the signal interference on the physical transmission media. It also detects and in some cases corrects errors that occur, and provides the means to control the physical layer.
- Physical, is the lowest layer of the 7-layer OSI model representing the media and electrical components required for the transmission of data.

TCP/IP

The Transmission Control Protocol/Internet Protocol (TCP/IP) is the backbone of most networks today. It has become the standard for Internet-based network communications. This network protocol enables heterogeneous systems to communicate with one another. The Transmission Control Protocol (TCP) is a communications protocol that provides reliable exchange of data. It is responsible for assembling data passed from higher-layer applications into standard packets to ensure that the data is correctly transferred. Whereas the Internet Protocol (IP) moves the packets of data assembled by TCP across networks. It uses a set of unique addresses for every device on the network to determine its destinations and routing.

Network Addressing

The IP address is a 32-bit address that is divided into two sections: the prefix for network address and the suffix for host address. This is designed to make IP packet routing extremely efficient. IP addresses are presented in dotted decimal notation. The dotted decimal address range is from 0.0.0.0 through 255.255.255.255. IP Addresses are grouped in classes, as shown in Table 11.

With the expansion of the Internet there are currently only class 'C' addresses available and the standards committee is considering various means to extend the address space to meet the growing demand.

Network Services

There are other components of the TCP/IP Protocol that enable network administrators and users to monitor, troubleshoot, and easily share information. These tools are Kerberos (security), Simple Network Management Protocol (network management), Network File Server (UNIX File Systems), Remote Procedure Calls (programming tool), Trivial File Transfer Protocol, User Datagram Protocol (UDP), and Internet Control Message Protocol (ICMP).

There are several ports available to the TCP protocol that can be used for specific functions. The daemon processes on the remote system will monitor or listen to these ports for connection requests. A detailed list of the ports are available in the file /etc/services. Some of the more common ports are listed in Table 12.

Network Commands

There are several commands that allow users or administrators to manage network connections. A few of the common commands are described in Table 13. Additional Information is available in the user manuals or the "man" pages within the Solaris™ operating system.

FTP Administration

File Transfer Protocol (FTP) is a mechanism for transferring files between hosts. This common Internet protocol has been used for many years. FTP is a TCP/IP protocol that is referenced in RFC 959. This is one way to allow the sharing of publicly available files. Little or no security is required to access this information. There are various levels of security that can be incorporated to protect the information.

FTP Commands

FTP is a command rich environment that has made it extremely easy for users to upload and download files. Some of the FTP commands that are available are shown in Table 14.

FTP Access

The most common user of FTP is the *anonymous* account. This is typically a publicly accessible account and grants users access to public information.

FTP Interface

The interface can be command line or Graphical User Interface (GUI). The GUI interface is the most intuitive interface from a user's perspective. The command line

Table 11
IP Address Classes and Values

IP class	*Prefix bits*	*Number of networks*	*Suffix bits*	*Number of hosts*
A	7	126	24	16777214
B	714	16384	16	65532
C	21	2097152	8	254

Table 12
TCP Port Numbers

Port Number	*Service Name*	*Description*
7	echo	Echo's back from a remote host
21	ftp	Used to control the File Transfer Protocol (FTP)
22	ssh	Encrypted communications with remote systems
23	telnet	Terminal access to remote systems
25	smtp	Mail transfer protocol
514	shell	Executing programs on remote systems
80	http	Web server

Table 13
Network Commands

Tool	*Description*
arp	Address Resolution Protocol (ARP) is a cache table that is updated based on the presence of MAC address (network card physical address) in broadcast traffic.
ping	Tests the reach ability of remote systems. It uses ICMP, an echo request to test round trip connectivity.
snoop	You must run this as the root user. Snoop will monitor all network traffic passing by the system it is running on. The interface will be running in promiscuous mode to monitor all network traffic. You should contact your network administrator before you run snoop to ensure you will not be violating privacy policies.

interface can be difficult unless one is familiar with FTP. You can find freeware FTP products that will run on Solaris™ operating system on the Internet (*see* Website: http://www.sunfreeware.com).

Device Administration

One of the most important aspects of managing a system is managing the resources connected to the system. These resources are typically storage devices but other devices such as scanners, video, and audio devices can be attached to a system. Management of these devices is relatively simple in the Solaris™ environment. Solaris™

Table 14
FTP Command Options

FTP Command	Description
binary	Set file transfer type to binary
cd	Change remote working directory
close	Terminate current FTP session (don't exit from client)
delete	Delete specified file
debug	Set debugging mode to on
dir	List contents of remote directory
disconnect	Terminate current FTP session and exit client
form	Set file transfer type to binary or ASCII
get	Download specified remote file
help	Help with command usage
ls	List contents of remote directory
mget	Get multiple files from remote system
mkdir	Make directory on remote system
mode	Set transfer mode to binary or ASCII
open	Connect to a remote system
put	Upload a file to a remote system
pwd	Print the current working directory
quit	Terminate FTP session and exit
rename	Rename specified file
rmdir	Remove directory on remote system
send	Upload a file to the remote system
status	Show the current status of the FTP session
type	Set file type for file being transferred.
verbose	Echo detail information to screen
?	Print help on local system

supports dynamic configurations of devices on some of the SPARC® platforms. This makes it simple for administrators and users to manage large and small systems. Information for each device is stored in a *device file*, which is in the /dev directory (*see* Table 15).

Storage Devices

There are several storage devices supported in the Solaris™ operating system. CD-ROMs, Zip Drives, Jaz Drives, Tape Drives, Hard Drives, and Floppy Disks are just a few of the device types that are supported. Hard drives are the most common device. In some configurations it may be perferred to configure your hard disks with Redundant Array of Independent Disks (RAID) support. A RAID configuration will provide you an extra level of redundancy that will protect the data in the case of a

Table 15
/dev Directory

/dev	*Description*
/dev/console	Console device
/dev/null	Discarded output
/dev/hme	Network interface device
/dev/ttyn	Terminal devices attached to the system
/dev/dsk	Files for disk partitions

Table 16
Disk Partition

Partition Number	*Directory*
0	/ - Root level directory
1	Server *swap* space
2	Whole disk
3	/export
4	Client *swap* space
5	/opt
6	/usr
7	/export/home

hard disk failure. The most common RAID configurations are RAID-0 (disk mirroring) and RAID-5 (disk stripping with parity bit; *see* Glossary).

When a hard disk volume is created and configured the Solaris™ operating system will create several partitions. The partitions that are created on a SPARC® system are listed in Table 16.

List System Devices

To check for the type of devices connected to your system you can issue the **prtconf** command. If you see devices that are not connected, don't be concerned because Solaris loads device drivers based on the usage of the device. This allows the system to optimize resources, ensuring optimal performance.

Adding New Devices

Prior to adding a device to your system, there are several steps to be follow.

1. Purchase a device that is supported by the Solaris™ operating system.
2. Check your system to ensure you have physical capacity for the new device (internal and external).
3. Check your SCSI bus to ensure you have enough device locations to add the new device.
4. Follow the directions for installation provided by the vendor you purchased the device from.

Table 17
Physical Disk

Disk Area	*Description*
Platter	Magnetic disk that turns on a shaft.
Cylinder	A cylinder refers to the location of all the drive read and write heads, typically accessing multiple tracks.
Track	This refers to one of the concentric circles of data on disk media.
Block	A specific area within a track that data is written to.

File System Administration

Managing the file system will allow you to control the resource usage for any given system. You first need to understand how the file system is structured. The Solaris™ UNIX File System (UFS) came from the Berkley Software Design, Inc. (BSD) environment and allows single or multiple users to utilize the Solaris™ operating system. The following briefly describes how to utilize the partitions of the disk to store and retrieve information.

Basic Disk Structure

The disk is made up of four basic components as shown in Table 17. The typical disk geometry is composed of platters that are magnetically coated. This coating allows the system to write information to a very small area of the disk using 1's and 0's, binary notation (1 = on, 0 = off). There are typically several platters in a disk drive unit.

The Solaris™ UFS is segmented into specialized areas (*see* Table 18). This differs from the original format and creates a higher level of reliability than before.

Formatting A Disk Device

There are several steps that take place when a file system is created for the first time. How the disk space will be used will dictate how the file system should be configured. Typically larger partitions for data volumes are created to adjust capacity as users store data on the system.

When executing the format command Solaris™ will display the available devices on the system. If there is more than one disk, you will be prompted to enter the device to format. After selecting the device the system will display a menu that provides several options as shown in Table 19.

Note: If for some reason you select a device you don't want to format, you can stop the program by issuing the **ctrl-c** command.

Creating A File System

Upon formatting the new device, a new file system must be created. The command for creating a new file system is **#newfs devicename**. The device name is the logical device pathname on the device where the new files system will be created. An example is **#newfs /dev/dsk/c2t3d1s5**. (*See* Glossary for a description of **c2t3d1s5**.)

Table 18
UFS Disk Segments

Disk Segment	*Description*
Superblock	Contains information on disk geometry, free blocks, and inodes. Multiple copies are made to ensure reliability.
Inode	One inode per file. Ownership, time stamp, size and links are kept in this file.
Data Block	Data for the file being stored. The size of the block depends on how the disk was initialized (e.g., 512K block).

Table 19
Format Menu Commands

Menu Item	*Description*
Disk	Select the disk you want to format
Type	Define the type of disk your are formatting
Partition	Define the partition table
Current	Describe the current disk (disk name)
Format	Format and analyze the disk
Repair	Repair defective sectors
Label	Provide the label name for the disk
Analyze	Do a surface analysis of the disk
Defect	Defect management list (blocks)
Backup	Search for backup labels
Verify	Read and display labels
Save	Save the new disk partition definitions
Inquiry	Show vendor product and revision
Volname	Define eight character volume name
Quit	Leave format menu

Various switch options can be used with the **#newfs** command that allow you to manipulate the disk configuration after the file system is created.

The -m parameter permits one to adjust the amount of reserved space on the file system. The -o parameter permits one to specify whether the system should optimize the disk for space or allocation time. Depending upon your usage of the newly formatted device you may want to consider these options.

Having formatted the storage media the disk must be made either available or unavailable to the operating system. A device must be mounted as part of the system directory tree. There are many options for the **mount** command that may be considered as shown in Table 20. The two commands that assist with this operation are **mount** and **unmount**. The normal syntax for making the resource available is **#mount device directory**. An example is **#mount /dev/dsk/c2t3d1s5 /etc**.

Table 20
Mount Options

Mount Option	Description
rw	Mount device with read-write capability
ro	Mount device with read-only capability
nosid	Eliminates use of user or group identifier bits
remount	Remount an already mounted device

This command would mount the formatted disk in the /etc directory. The directory that mounts the device must exist. It should be noted that this superimposes the directory specified with the new system device.

To list the devices mounted on the current system, the mount command from the prompt is issued and the mounted devices on the system will be displayed. By issuing the **mount -v** (verbose) parameter with the mount command, the system will display detailed information on all mounted devices. In contrast, the unmount command makes devices or directories unavailable to the system. The **#unmount directoryname** command makes directory unavailable to the system and the **#unmount devicename** makes the device unavailable to the local system.

In Solaris™ the volume manager daemon manages access to CD-ROM and removable media. The *vold* daemon listens for insertion of media in these removable media devices. When the daemon detects that a CD-ROM has been inserted into the drive it invokes the **rmmount** command to mount the removable media. The vold daemon is also responsible for ejecting removable media for the user. If the vold daemon has frozen, the **eject** command can be used to eject removable media (CD-ROM, Floppy Disk, ZIP Drive).

There are two important maintenance activities that will enable the system administrator to manage storage resources more efficiently. The **#df** command displays device capacity information. This command provides:

- Filesystem: Name of the device or directory
- Kbytes: Total capacity of the device
- Used: Space used on the device
- Avail: Amount of space available on the device
- Capacity: Percentage of device space being used
- Mounted on: Directory mount point for the device

There are several optional parameters that can be passed with the **#df** command.

As a system administrator you also have the ability to define and set quotas on devices. This helps manage the utilization of storage space and prevents any one user from filling a volume and potentially disabling the system. Quotas can be set user by user for any given volume. To set quotas on a volume for a user, follow steps 1–7.

1. Find the etc/vfstab file as the root user.
2. Edit the etc/vfstab file and add the "rq" flag to the mount option field for the directory you want to establish quotas on (e.g., /usr/jordan).
3. Change to the directory you want quotas to be established (e.g., /usr/jordan).

4. Set the permissions on the /usr/jordan to read-write for *root* user only.
5. To set quotas on the directory, use the **edquota** command and set the *hard* and *soft* limits for storage space. The hard parameter sets the maximum limit. The soft parameter sets the overquota or temporary space for a user. An example is **#fs / usr/jordan blocks (soft=2500, hard=5000)**.
6. You can check to see if quotas are set by issuing the **quota** command.
7. To enable quotas once they have been defined, you can issue the **quotaon** command from *root user* ID.

Available storage space is something that you as an administrator need to be aware of and utilizing quotas is the easiest way to ensure you don't see problems with run-away storage from users or errant processes.

Backup Administration

System backup is critical to the stability/recoverability of the system. It allows restoration of files either deleted accidentally (user initiated) or corrupted. When defining the backup strategy consider disaster recovery if the system mission is critical to your operations. Disaster recovery plans are detailed in nature and should be tested at least once a year. This can also be a costly endeavor so be sure you can justify the additional cost associated with disaster recovery.

Backup Media

There are several ways to approach the selection of backup media. The amount/size of data you backup will dictate the best approach for your environment. There are 3 types of media you can direct your backup to:

1. Tape: Reliable and reasonable capacity (DLT: 40GB–80GB).
2. Optical: Could be used for near-line storage (CD-ROM and DVD).
3. Disk: More expensive but fast and readily available (RAID configuration ensures redundancy).

Backup Methodology

There are two methodologies utilized to backup systems. In *Full Backup*, a snapshot image of all the files on the system is created. This is typically executed on off-hours (evening) when the system is not being utilized. Alternatively, the *Incremental Backup* only effects those files that have changes since the last full backup. This is a time-saving and efficient process. An example schedule is a full backup on Saturday starting at 11:00 pm, and an incremental backup every day but Saturday, starting at 11:00 pm.

Note: If you have a database system running, you will need to consult your user/administrator guide for backup of the database. In many cases the database process will have to be stopped to ensure a complete backup. If the database file is open, the backup program may not be able to accurately backup the opened file. This is true for any file that maybe used by processes running on the system.

Backup Process

There are a few means to execute a backup of the system. The easiest way is with the **tar** command. **tar** is used to create and extract files from an archive file. However,

tar does not compress the file like other commercially available products. Compression can be achieved using the Solaris™ **compress** command.

Another method is using the Solaris™ **ufsdump** and **ufsrestore** utilities. These utilities only work on UNIX (UFS) file systems.

ufsdump allows you to create your full and incremental backup schedules. **ufsrestore** is easy to use and works much like the **ufsdump** command. You can utilize this utility in interactive mode by passing the "i" parameter with the **ufsrestore** command.

Commercially available backup products tend to be more feature rich than **ufsdump** and **ufsrestore**. For the Solaris™ Operating Environment there are two excellent choices, Legato® Networker (*see* Website: http://www.legato.com) and Veritas® Netbackup (*see* Website: http://www.veritas.com).

Each of these products have their benefits, so you and your system administrator need to decide if a commercially available product is the best choice for your system.

Web Server Administration

One of the most popular technologies today is web-based technology. This crosses all boundaries of information today, from research, business, consumer, and entertainment. The backbone protocol for the web is HyperText Transfer Protocol (HTTP), which uses Universial Resource Locators (URLs) embedded in HyperText Markup Language (HTML) files that display information in a web browser interface (Netscape Navigator® and Microsoft Explorer®). The combination of these components allows people to surf the World Wide Web (WWW) for anything you can imagine. The Solaris™ environment Apache Server is the component that will make your server WWW enabled.

Apache Web Server

The Apache Web Server product is free from the Apache website where the necessary components can be downloaded (*see* Website: http://www.apache.org). The downloaded file is in *tar* or *tar.Z* (compressed) format. Utilize the released version unless there are specific features in the beta version you need. You should also download or print the release notes specific to the product you have downloaded. These documents contain useful information such as vendor-specific bug fixes, installation procedures, and major application changes.

Installing Apache Web Server

Before installing the software on your system, the following pieces of information are required:

- Your IP Web Server Address (IP address for the Internet).
- Add your server to DNS (Name resolution for your web server).

Steps for Configuring Apache Web Server

1. Configure the application before installing on your system. This is accomplished with the **configure** command that is provided with the Apache server software distribution. The **configure** command program assesses your current system resources to ensure that the server will run reliably on your system.

2. After running the **configure** command, compile the software. The Apache software distribution provides the **make** command, which will compile the software according to the configuration information.
3. Now the complied software can be installed. To install the software you can run the **make install** command from the Apache software distribution directory. This command copies the *httpd* daemon and associated configuration files to the installation directory. The Apache software installation is now complete.

Now lets consider how the system process will startup and shutdown. This can be accomplished by copying the **apachectl** file to the /etc/init.d directory. With the **ln** command you can create a link to the operating system startup process so that Apache starts up and shuts down normally and doesn't require manual intervention every time a reboot is performed (*su* to root and then perform this command). Once the Apache server is running, you can *telnet* to port 80 to verify the server process is running.

Another important task before making your web server publicly available is to review and set the parameters in the **httpd.conf** file. There are three separate sections to the file:

1. Global Section
   - Location of files and directories. An example: ServerRoot **/home/http**
   - Network parameters. An example: Network Timeouts
2. Server Section
   - General server parameters. An example: **Port 80**
     (TCP - Port the daemon will be listening to)
   - Access control for file directories
   - Directory listings
   - Apache server logging process (audit control)
   - Web browser response parameters
3. Virtual Hosts
   - Enables you to configure multiple web aliases on the same server

Setting these parameters will ensure you have not compromised the system to intruders.

Other Considerations

As you offer web services from your system you will want to ensure that the setup and configuration of your system is of sufficient performance for the tasks. This is considered a function of *Static Pages* that provide information only. The *Application Services* that provide analytical services demands (memory and CPU) resources and the *Information Store* that allocates space for users to download information to their local machines (e.g., FTP)..

The simplest of scenarios is Static Pages. They usually do not require a large allocation of system resources to host. The Application Services and Information Store may require additional resources in the form of storage, CPU, memory or possibly additional systems. It is important to understand the expected usage and performance of the web server so you can scale the resources appropriately. Nothing is worse than visiting a website that has a poor response time. Because it is sometimes hard to define the use of the web server, you should plan for the worst case (budget and time will dictate capacity).

Glossary and Abbreviations

BSD Berkeley software distribution. BSD refers to the particular version of the UNIX operating system that was developed at and distributed from the University of California at Berkeley. BSD UNIX has been popular and many commercial implementations of UNIX systems are based on or include some BSD code.

Case Sensitive This term defines the operating systems sensitivity to alpha uppercase and lower case characters. (Example: If a password or username was created in all lowercase characters then the operating system would deny access if the user entered their password or username in uppercase characters).

c2t3d1s5 C = controller, t = target, d = disk, s = slice (c2 = controller 2, t3 = target SCSI ID 3, d1 = disk 1, s5 = slice number 5).

Command A command is a specific order from a user to the computer's operating system or to an application to perform a function.

CPU Central processing unit. CPU is an older term for processor and microprocessor, the central unit in a computer containing the logic circuitry that performs the instructions of a computer's programs.

Disk Quota The specific amount of disk space that a defined user or service is allow to use. This is done to prevent over utilization of disk resources.

Disk Mirror (RAID 1) Provides 100% redundancy of data. This means no rebuild is necessary in case of a disk failure, just a copy to the replacement disk. Transfer rates per block is equal to that of a single disk. Under certain circumstances, RAID 1 can sustain multiple simultaneous drive failures. This is the simplest RAID storage subsystem design.

Disk Stripping (RAID 0) RAID 0 implements a striped disk array, the data is broken down into blocks and each block is written to a separate disk drive. I/O performance is greatly improved by spreading the I/O load across many channels and drives. Best performance is achieved when data is striped across multiple controllers with only one drive per controller. No parity calculation overhead is involved. Not a "True" RAID because it is NOT fault-tolerant. The failure of just one drive will result in all data in an array being lost.

Disk Stripping with Parity Bit (RAID 3 to 6) Each entire data block is written on a data disk; parity for blocks in the same rank is generated on Writes, recorded in a distributed location and checked on Reads. RAID Level 5 requires a minimum of 3 drives to implement and is the most common RAID with Parity Bit used.

DVD Digital versatile disc. DVD is an optical disc technology that is expected to rapidly replace the CD-ROM disc (as well as the audio compact disc) over the next few years. The digital versatile disc (DVD) holds 4.7 gigabyte of information on one of its two sides, or enough for a 133-minute movie. The DVD can hold more than 28 times as much information as a CD-ROM.

Encryption The conversion of data (i.e., password) into a form called ciphertext, which cannot be easily understood. Decryption is the process of converting encrypted data back into its original form, so it can be understood.

FTP File transfer protocol. FTP is a standard Internet protocol and is the simplest way to exchange files between computers on the Internet.

GUI A graphical (rather than purely textual) user interface to a computer.

HTML Hypertext markup language. HTML is the set of markup symbols or codes inserted in a file intended for display on a World Wide Web browser page.

HTTP Hypertext transfer protocol. HTTP is the set of rules for exchanging files (text, graphic images, sound, video, and other multimedia files) on the World Wide Web.

ICMP Internet control message protocol. ICMP is a message control and error-reporting protocol between a host server and a gateway to the Internet.

IP Internet protocol. IP is the method or protocol by which data is sent from one computer to another on the Internet/network. Each computer (known as a host) on the Internet/network has at least one IP address that uniquely identifies it from all other computers on the Internet.

IP Address An IP address has two parts: the identifier of a particular network on the network and an identifier of the particular device (which can be a server or a workstation) within that network.

IP Packet A packet is the unit of data that is routed between an origin and a destination on the Internet or any other packet-switched network. When any file (e-mail message, HTML file, Graphics Interchange Format file, Uniform Resource Locator request, and so forth) is sent from one place to another on the Internet, the Transmission Control Protocol (TCP) layer of TCP/IP divides the file into "chunks" of an efficient size for routing. Each of these packets is separately numbered and includes the Internet address of the destination. The individual packets for a given file may travel different routes through the Internet. When they have all arrived, they are reassembled into the original file (by the TCP layer at the receiving end).

Kerberos Is a secure method for authenticating a request for a service in a computer network.

LINUX Is an UNIX-like operating system that was designed to provide personal computer users a free or very low-cost operating system comparable to traditional and usually more expensive UNIX systems.

Man Pages These are the help files associated with the Solaris™ operating system.

Multi-User System An operating system (e.g. UNIX or LINUX) that will support multiple user access at the same time. (Example: UNIX Operating System)

NFS Network file system. NFS is a client/server application that lets a computer user view and optionally store and update file on a remote computer as though they were on the user's own computer.

OSI Model Is a standard reference model for communication between two end users in a network. It is used in developing products that utilize network technology.

RAID Redundant array of inexpensive disks. This is a way of storing the same data in different places (thus, redundantly) on multiple hard disks. By placing data on multiple disks, I/O operations can overlap in a balanced way, improving performance. Since multiple disks increases the mean time between failure (MTBF), storing data redundantly also increases fault-tolerance.

Parameter Is an item of information such as: a name, a number, or a selected option that is passed to a program by a user or another program.

Reboot The process of restarting a computer operating system.

Power-down The process of shutting down a computer operating system to the point where power can be disconnected from the hardware.

RPC Remote procedure call. RPC is a protocol that one program can use to request a service from a program located in another computer in a network without having to understand network details.

SCSI Small computer system interface. SCSI is a set of ANSI standard electronic interfaces that allow personal computers to communicate with peripheral hardware such as disk drives, tape drives, CD-ROM drives, printers, and scanners faster and more flexibly than previous interfaces.

Server In general, a server is a computer that provides services to other computers and or multiple users.

Signal Messages sent to applications or the operating system to control system processes (i.e., start, stop, suspend, etc).

Single User System A computer operating system that supports only one user at a time (Example: Microsoft® Windows Desktop Operating System).

SNMP Simple network management protocol. SNMP is the protocol governing network management and the monitoring of network devices and their functions.

TCP Transmission control protocol. TCP is a set of rules (protocol) used along with the Internet Protocol (IP) to send data in the form of message units between computers over the Internet. While IP takes care of handling the actual delivery of the data, TCP takes care of keeping track of the individual units of data (called packets) that a message is divided into for efficient routing through the Internet or network.

Telnet Telnet is the way you can access someone else's computer, assuming they have given you permission.

TFTP Trivial file transfer protocol. TFTP is an Internet software utility for transferring files that is simpler to use than the File Transfer Protocol (FTP) but less capable. It is used where user authentication and directory visibility are not required.

UDP User datagram protocol. UDP is a communications protocol that offers a limited amount of service when messages are exchanged between computers in a network that uses the Internet Protocol (IP).

UFS The default disk based file system for the Sun Operating System 5.x environment.

UNIX is an operating system that originated at Bell Labs in 1969 as an interactive time-sharing system. Ken Thompson and Dennis Ritchie are considered the inventors of UNIX.

URL Uniform resource locator. URL is the address of a file (resource) accessible on the Internet. The type of resource depends on the Internet application protocol.

Suggested Reading

Nemeth, E., Snyder, G., Seebass, S., and Hein, T. R. (2000) UNIX System Administration Handbook, 3rd ed., Prentice Hall, Upper Saddle River, NJ.

Dimambro, B. (2000) Practical Solaris Administration: System Configuration and File Systems, MacMillan Technical Publishing, Indianapolis, IN.

Winsor, S. (1998) Advanced System Administrator's Guide, New Riders Publishing, Indianapolis, IN.

Watters, P. A. and Sumser, J. (2002) Solaris 8 Administrator's Guide, O'Reilly and Associates, Sebastopol, CA.

Howard, J. S. and Deeths, D. (2001) Boot Disk Management: A Guide for the Solaris Operating Environment, Prentice Hall, Upper Saddle River, NJ.

Winsor, J. (2002) Solaris Management Console Tools, Prentice Hall, Upper Saddle River, NJ.

Mulligan, J. P. (2001) Solaris 8 Essential Reference, New Riders Publishing, Indianapolis, IN.

Stringfellow, S., Barton, M., and Klivansky, M. (2000) Backup and Restore Practices for Sun Enterprise Servers, Prentice Hall, Upper Saddle River, NJ.

B. Managing Bioinformatics Tools

16 Installing Bioinformatics Software in a Server-Based Computing Environment

Brian Fristensky

Introduction

To support a diverse institutional program of genomics projects, it is often necessary to have an equally diverse and comprehensive software base. Although programs may come from many sources, it is important to make them easily accessible to the user community on a single computing platform. This chapter will outline the strategies for installing programs for a server-based molecular biology software resource, accessed by a large user base. It is assumed that the reader is familiar with basic UNIX commands and concepts, as described in the previous chapters. The approaches discussed here are implemented in the BIRCH system (*see* Website: http://home.cc.umanitoba.ca/~psgendb), but are generally applicable to any centralized multiuser software installation. The important parts of the process are described in either program documentation or UNIX documentation. The tricks and conventions that help to simplify the installation process will also be highlighted. This should give the novice an idea of what to expect before wading through the documentation.

Considerations

There are five guiding principles for installation and use that should be applied to help ensure a smooth operation.

1. Any user should be able to run any program from any directory simply by typing the name of the program and arguments. It should not be necessary to go to a specific directory to run a program.
2. System administration should be kept as simple as possible. This saves work for the Bioadmin[1], as well as increasing the likelihood that things will function properly.
3. Avoid interruption of service during installation and testing.
4. The Bioadmin should never have to modify individual user accounts.
5. Even if you have root access, do most of your work on a regular user account. Log in as root only when necessary.

[1]Since bioinformatics software may be installed by a specialist other than UNIX system staff, the term *Bioadmin* will refer to the person installing and maintaining bioinformatics software, distinct from system administrators.

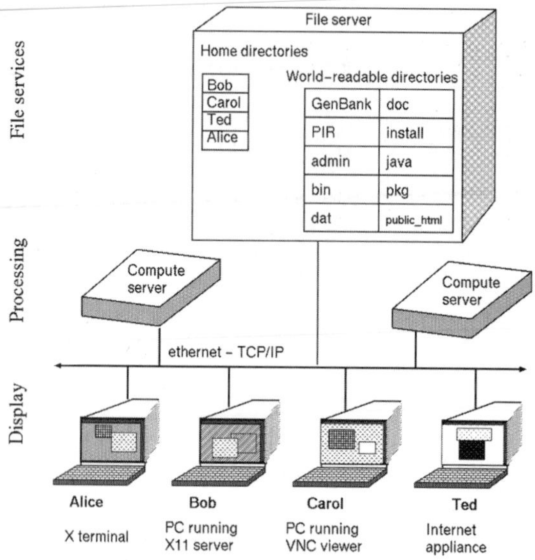

Fig. 1. Network-centric computing.

The Networked Computing Environment

The casual computer user learns only a narrow computing model: the PC model. PCs are based on the idea that each person has their own computer that is completely self-contained, with all hardware, software, and data residing physically on the desktop. Provisions for multiple users on a single machine (e.g., separate home directories, user accounts, file permissions) may exist, but are seldom taken into account by PC software developers. Each PC becomes a special case with special problems. The work of administration grows with the number of computers. Software has to be purchased and independently installed for each machine. Security and backup are often not practiced.

UNIX greatly simplifies the problem of computing with a network-centric approach, in which any user can do any task from anywhere. Figure 1 illustrates computing in a network-centric environment. All data and software reside on a file server, which is remotely mounted to one or more identically configured compute servers. Programs are executed on a compute server, but displayed at the user's terminal or PC. Regardless of whether one logs in from an X11 terminal, a PC running an X11 server, a PC using the VNC viewer (*see* Chapters 13 and 17) or an internet appliance, the user's desktop screen looks the same and opens to the user's $HOME directory. Consequently, any user can do any task from any device, anywhere on the Internet.

Leveraging the Multi-Window Desktop

The installation process involves moving back and forth among several directories, which is most effectively accomplished by viewing each directory in a separate window. One of the issues that makes the typical PC desktop awkward to use is the *one window owns the screen* model. In MS-Windows, most applications default to

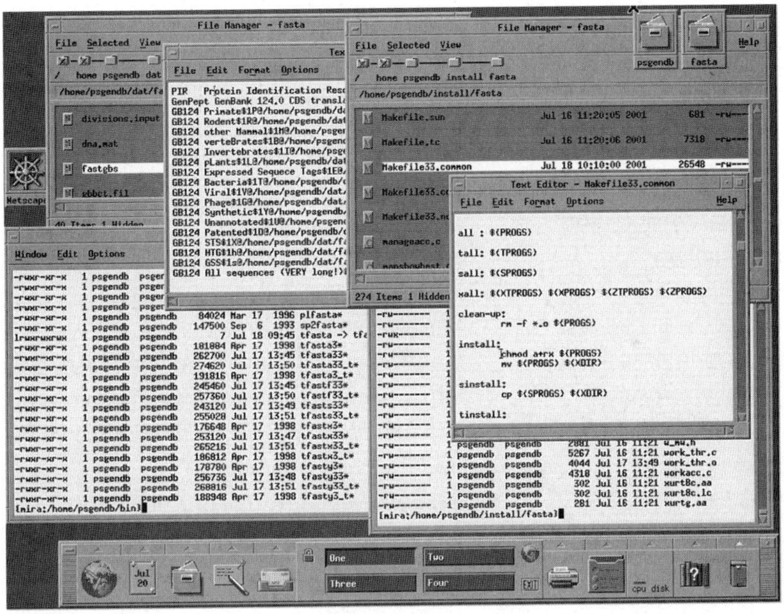

Fig. 2. Leveraging the multiwindow desktop. In the example, the environment variable $DB, which identifies the root directory for bioinformatics software, is set to /home/psgendb. Clockwise from top left: Double clicking on **fastgbs** in $DB/doc/fasta opens up a list of locations of database files in a text editor. Similarly, Makefile33.common has been opened up from $DB/install/fasta. This file contains Makefile commands that are compatible with all operating systems. A terminal window at lower right is used for running commands in $DB/install/fasta, while another terminal window at bottom left is used for running commands in $DB/bin. At bottom, the CDE control panel shows that the current screen, out of four screens available, is screen One.

Note: To get the C-shell to display the hostname and current working directory in the prompt, include the following lines in cshrc.source or your .cshrc file:

```
set HOSTNAME = `hostname`
set prompt="{$HOSTNAME":"$cwd"}
alias cd 'cd \!*; set prompt="{$HOSTNAME":"$cwd"}'
alias popd 'popd \!*; set prompt="{$HOSTNAME":"$cwd"}'
alias pushd 'pushd \!*; set prompt="{$HOSTNAME":"$cwd"}'
```

take up the entire screen. One moves between applications using the task bar. Although it is possible to resize windows so that many can fit on one screen, this is seldom done in MS-Windows. On Macintosh, even when multiple windows are present, they depend on the menu at the top of the screen. This requires the user to first select a window by clicking on it, and then to choose an item from the menu at the top of the screen. Even worse, the menus often look almost identical from program to program, so that it is not obvious when the focus has shifted to a new application.

On UNIX desktops, menus are found within the windows themselves. This decreases the amount of distance the eye has to cover. Focus moves with the mouse and does not need to be switched with the taskbar. The user simply moves from one window to another to work. Because UNIX tends to be oriented towards multiple windows, UNIX users tend to favor larger monitors. More screen real estate means more space for windows. The screen in Fig. 2 appears crowded because it was generated at

Table 1
Sources of Free Downloadable Software

Source	*URL*
IUBio Archive	http://iubio.bio.indiana.edu/
EMBOSS Software Suite	http://www.uk.embnet.org/Software/EMBOSS/
Open Source Bioinformatics Software	http://bioinformatics.org/
Linux for Biotechnology	http://www.randomfactory.com/lfb/lfb.html
Sanger Center Software	http://www.sanger.ac.uk/Software/
Staden Package	http://www.mrc-lmb.cam.ac.uk/pubseq/
NCBI FTP site	http://www.ncbi.nlm.nih.gov/Ftp/index.html
PHYLIP Phylogeny software	http://evolution.genetics.washington.edu/phylip.html
BIRCH, FSAP, XYLEM,GDE	http://home.cc.umanitoba.ca/~psgendb/downloads.html
FASTA package	ftp://ftp.uva.edu/pub/fasta/
Virtual Network Computing (VNC)	http://www.uk.research.att.com/vnc/

1024 × 768 resolution. Although this is a common resolution for PCs, the UNIX community tends to work with larger monitors, at 19" diagonal or larger, running at 1280 × 1000 or higher resolution. To provide further real estate, UNIX desktops such as CDE, KDE, and GNOME support switching between several desktops at the push of a button. Use of multiple windows during an installation is illustrated in Figure 2.

Finding and Downloading Software

Table 1 has a short and by no means exhaustive list of sites where freely available sequence analysis software can be downloaded. USENET newsgroups such as bionet.software contain announcements of new software and updates, as well as discussions on molecular biology software.

Usually, software is downloaded as a directory tree packed into a single archive file in various formats. Generally, files in these formats can recreate the original directory tree containing source code, documentation, data files, and often, executable binaries. Usually, the first step is to uncompress the file and then recreate the original directory. For example, the fasta package comes as a shell archive created using the **shar** command. Because you do not know in advance whether the archive contains a large number of individual files or a single directory containing files, it is always safest to make a new directory in which to recreate the archive, using the following commands:

mkdir fasta	create new directory
mv fasta.shar fasta	move fasta.shar into the new directory
cd fasta	go into the fasta directory
unshar fasta.shar	extract files from fasta.shar

Table 2 lists some of the most common archive tools and their usage.

Two goals when installing software are to 1) avoid interruption of service for users during installation and testing and 2) having the option of deleting programs after

Table 2
Archive Commands

File extension	*Utility*	*Archive command*	*Unarchive command*
.tar	UNIX tar	To create a tar file from a directory called source: **tar cvf source.tar source**	To recreate the directory: **tar xvf source.tar**
.zip	ZIP	To create a compressed archive file called source.zip: **zip source source**	To recreate the directory: **unzip source**
.shar	UNIX shar	To create a shar file from a directory named source: **shar source > source.shar**	To recreate the directory: **unshar source.shar** or **chmod u+x source.shar** or **sh source.shar** [a]
.gz	GNU zip	To compress a file with: **gzip source > source.gz**	To recreate the directory: **gunzip source**
.Z	compress	To compress source.tar: **compress source.tar**	To uncompress source.tar.Z: **uncompress source.tar.Z**
.uue	uuencode	To encode source.tar.Z using ASCII characters: **uuencode source.tar.Z source.uue**	To recreate the original binary file: **uudecode source.uue**

[a].shar files are actually shell scripts that can be executed to recreate the original directory.

evaluation. For example, a separate directory called *install* could hold separate directories for each package during the installation.

Understand the Problem Before You Begin

For many standard office tasks, it is possible to get by without ever reading the documentation. In molecular biology, the task itself often has enough complexity that it may not be possible to simply launch, point, and click. In practice, it is almost always faster to read the documentation before trying to install. Each program will have installation instructions. These will let you know about important options like where the final program files will reside and which environment variables must be set.

Reading the documentation at this stage gives you a chance to learn more about what the program does and to decide if it is really what you need. This weeding out phase can save a lot of unnecessary compiling, organizing, and testing.

Compilation

Programs distributed as source code, for which no binaries are available, will require compilation and linking steps. Although these procedures vary somewhat with the language in which they are written, most of the common packages use protocols of the C and C++ family of languages. In addition to source files (.c), code items such as

Table 3
Common File Types and File Extensions

File extension	File type
.c	C source code
.h	C header
.o	Compiled object file
no extension	Executable binary file
.1, .l	UNIX manual page
.makefile, .mak	Makefile

type definitions, which need to be shared, are found in header files (.h). When you compile, the code from the header files is inserted into C code, and the .c file translated to machine code, which is written as object modules (.o). Next, the compiler calls a linker, which links object modules into a final executable file. In most programs, object modules from standard libraries (e.g., Tcl/Tk) are also linked. These are typically linked dynamically, meaning that only a reference to the libraries is made and the actual library modules are loaded each time the program is run. Consequently, dynamic linking saves disk space. However, when a program depends on libraries that may not be found on all systems, static linking can be accomplished, in which object modules are written to the final executable code file. Static linking favors portability at the expense of disk space. A short list of the types of files frequently encountered during installation appears in Table 3.

Virtually all scientific program packages automate these procedures using the *make* program. The *make* program reads a Makefile, containing compilation, linking, and installation options. For cross-platform compatibility, it is common to include separate Makefiles for each platform (e.g., SGI, Linux, Windows, Solaris). For example, the fasta package has a file called Makefile.sun for Solaris systems. Copy Makefile.sun to Makefile, and edit Makefile as needed for your system. At the beginning of the Makefile, variables are often set to specify the final destinations for files. On our system, fasta's Makefile would be edited to change the line reading **XDIR = /seqprog/sbin/bin to XDIR = /home/psgendb/bin.** Because this directory is in the $PATH for all BIRCH users, the new programs become available to all users as soon as the files are copied to this location.

Typing **make** executes the commands in Makefile, compiling and linking the programs. It is best to run make in a terminal window that supports scrolling, so that all warning and error messages can be examined. This is particularly important because one can then copy error messages to a file to provide the author of the program with a precise description of the problem. If the authors do not receive this feedback, the problems do not get fixed. However feedback must be precise and detailed.

If **make** is successful, executable binary files, usually with no extension, are written to the target directory. This may or may not be the current working directory. Many Makefiles require you to explicitly ask for files to be copied to the destination directory by typing **make install**.

In some cases, testing can be carried out at this point, particularly if a test script is included with the package. In the fasta package several test scripts are found. For example, **./test.sh** will run most of the fasta programs with test datafiles.

Note: "./" forces the shell to look for test.sh in the current working directory. Unless "." was in your $PATH, it would not be found. However, it is generally considered insecure to include "." in your $PATH.

It is important to check test scripts to see where they look for executable files. For example, if the script sets $PATH to "." (the current directory), or if programs are executed with a statement such as **./fasta33**, then the shell will look for an executable file in the current directory. If the directory for the executable file is not explicitly set, the shell will search all directories in your $PATH to find an executable file. This could either result in a *Command not found* message, or if earlier copies of the programs were already installed, older programs will execute, not the newly compiled programs.

Installation

In the BIRCH system, all files and directories are found in a world-readable directory specified by the $DB environment variable. Thus, $DB/bin, $DB/doc, and $DB/dat refer to directories containing executable binaries, documentation, and datafiles used by programs, respectively, as summarized below.

$DB/bin

Although $DB/bin could in principle be set to refer to /usr/local/bin, it is probably best to keep the entire $DB structure separate from the rest of the system. This approach has the advantage that the Bioadmin need not have root privileges. All files in $DB/bin should be world-executable.

One practice for managing program upgrades is to create a symbolic link to point to the current *production* version of the program. For example, a link with the name *fasta* might point to fasta3:

lrwxrwxrwx 1 psgendb psgendb 6 Jul 18 09:45 /home/psgendb/bin/fasta3 -> fasta*

To upgrade to fasta33:

rm fasta
ln -s fasta33 fasta
lrwxrwxrwx 1 psgendb psgendb 6 Jul 18 09:45 /home/psgendb/bin/fasta33 -> fasta*

Aside from giving users a consistent name for the current most recent version of the program, this type of stable link eliminates the need to modify other programs that call the upgraded program.

$DB/doc

Documentation files for software should be moved to this directory. Ideally, the complete contents of this directory should be Web-accessible. Where a program or package has more than one documentation file, create a separate subdirectory for each program. All files should be world-readable.

$DB/dat

A program should never require that ancillary files such as fonts or scoring matrices be in a user's directory. These should always be centrally installed and administered, transparently to the user. Datafiles required for programs, such as scoring matrices, lists of restriction enzymes, and so forth should be moved to this directory. Generally, each program should have its own subdirectory. All files should be world-readable.

$DB/admin

This directory contains scripts and other files related to software administration. First time BIRCH users run the *newuser* script, to append a line to the user's .login file:

source /home/psgendb/admin/login.source

and to the .cshrc file:

source /home/psgendb/admin/cshrc.source

These files respectively contain commands that are executed when the user first logs in, and each time a program is started. All environment variables, aliases, and other settings required to run these programs are set in these files. Having run *newuser* once, a user should never have to do any setup tasks to be able to run new or updated programs. When a new program is added, the environment variables and aliases needed are specified in cshrc.source, and therefore become immediately available to the user community. The net effect is that the Bioadmin should never have to go to each user's account when a new program is installed.

Where programs require first-time setup, such as a configuration file being written to the user's $HOME directory, the program should be run from a wrapper script that checks for the presence of that file. If the file is not present, the script writes a default copy of the file to $HOME. The user should never have to explicitly run a setup script before using a program.

All directories that are to be accessible to users must be world searchable (world-executable), as well as world-readable. For example, to allow users to read files in $DB/doc/fasta, both $DB/doc and $DB/doc/fasta must be world executable. Use:

chmod a+rx $DB/doc/fasta

Special Considerations for Complex Packages

Some packages come as integrated units whose components can not be moved out of their directory structure to $DB/bin, $DB/dat, and $DB/doc. Packages of this type are installed in $DB/pkg. A good case in point is the Staden Package (*see* Table 1). The BIRCH login.source file contains the following lines:

Initialize Staden Package Settings
setenv STADENROOT $DB/pkg/staden
source $STADENROOT/staden.login

that cause the commands in staden.login to be executed when the user logs in. This script in turn sets several environment variables referencing files in the $STADENROOT directory. As well, login.source adds $DB/pkg/staden/solaris-bin to the $PATH. This illustrates that there are sometimes no simple solutions. On one hand, it would be desirable to simply copy all Staden binaries into $DB/bin. However this has the effect of making it difficult to identify the origin of specific programs in

$DB/bin as being part of the Staden Package. On the other hand, symbolic links from $DB/bin to each of the programs in $DB/pkg/staden/solaris-bin would provide a compromise. This would require that links be individually maintained.

Documentation and data can be linked more easily in $DB/doc. The following command:

ln -s $STADENROOT/doc staden

creates a link to the Staden documentation directory, while in $DB/dat, and

ln -s $STADENROOT staden

creates a link to the main Staden directory, from which the user can find several directories with sample datafiles. In this fashion, the $DOC and $DAT directories appear to contain *staden* subdirectories, whose contents are physically located elsewhere.

On Linux systems, complex packages are maintained using programs such as Red Hat Package Manager (RPM). RPM automates package installation, often requiring no user input. As files are copied to their destinations, their locations are recorded in the RPM database (/usr/lib/rpm). In addition to installation, RPM automates package updating, verification and de-installation. Tools such as RPM make it possible to install software in system directories such as /usr/local/bin or /usr/bin without making these directories unmanageable. The one disadvantage is that installation in system directories can only be accomplished with root permissions.

Special Considerations for Java Applications

Java applications should be installed in a central location, such as $DB/java. Ideally, all that should be required is the inclusion of $DB/java in the $CLASSPATH environment variable. The Java Virtual Machine (JVM) would search this location at runtime. However, the precise commands needed to launch an application vary, so that no single solution exists. For example, some applications are completely contained in a single .jar file, while others require a complex directory structure containing large numbers of objects and datafiles. Consequently, Java applications should be launched from wrappers: short scripts that reside in $DB/bin and call the application. For example, a script called $DB/bin/readseq runs the Java implementation of readseq (available from IUBio, *see* Table 1):

```
#!/bin/csh
# UNIX script file to run command line readseq

# Full path must be specified to enable us to
# launch readseq from any directory.
setenv CLASSPATH $DB/java/readseq/readseq.jar

# $argv passes command line arguments from the wrapper
# to the application
java -cp $CLASSPATH run $argv
```

Thus, typing **readseq** launches the wrapper, which in turn launches the Java readseq application. Readseq also has a method called *app* which runs readseq in a graphic interface. To run in this mode, the Xreadseq wrapper has the following line:

java -cp $CLASSPATH app

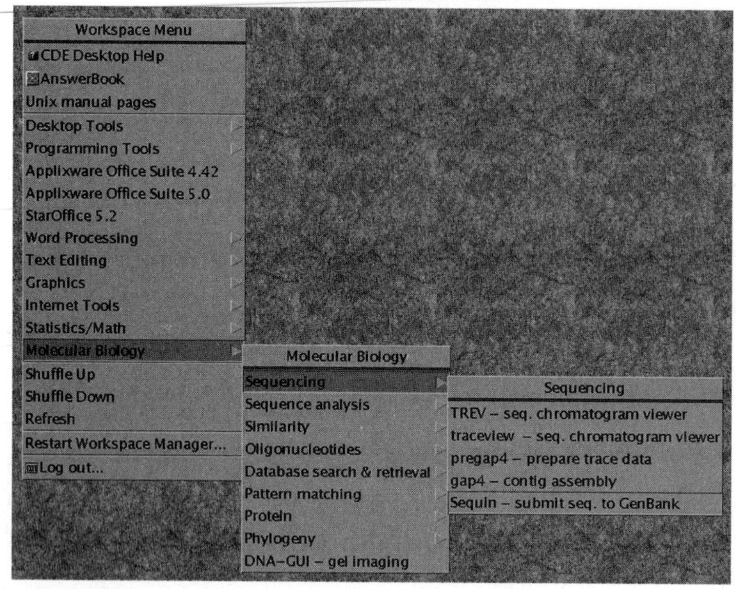

Fig. 3. The CDE Workspace Menu.

Calling Programs from a Graphic Front-End

Several options exist for unifying a large software base with a graphic front end. Programs such as GDE (*see* Table 1), SeqLab from the GCG package (*see* Website: http://www.accelrys.com), or SeqPup (*see* Table 1, IUBio) allow the Bioadmin to add external programs to their menus, as specified in easy-to-edit configuration files. In general, the user selects one or more sequences to work with, and then chooses a program from the main menu. A window pops up, allowing parameters to be set. The front end then generates a UNIX command to run the program with these parameters, using the selected sequences.

In many cases, it is best for the front end to call a wrapper that verifies and checks the parameters and sequences, then executes the program. This is especially important for programs from packages such as FSAP or PHYLIP (*see* Table 1), which operate through text-based interactive menus. If a prompt does not receive a valid response, programs of this type may go into an infinite loop that prompts for a response.

Launching Programs from the Workspace Menu

The *workspace* menu is yet another avenue through which users can find programs. Figure 3 shows a CDE workspace menu organized categorically. At the highest level are the main categories of programs, including standalone items for office packages. The *molecular biology* menu is further divided into submenus. For example, the *Sequencing* submenu contains programs that together cover all steps in the sequencing process, including reading the raw chromatograms, vector removal, contig assembly, and submission to GenBank. The downside of the workspace menu is that it is incomplete, as command line applications, cannot be launched from the workspace menu.

One should be able to launch GUI applications from the workspace menu, defaulting to the user's $HOME directory. In the CDE desktop, this is specified in the .dt directory. Most recent UNIX desktops, such as CDE 1.4 and GNOME use tree-structured directories to define the structure of the workspace menu. Again, it is important to avoid having to update individual user accounts. The easiest way is to create a directory for molecular biology programs on the Bioadmin's account, and have new users run a script creating a symbolic link from their workspace menu directory (e.g., .dt/Desktop) to the Bioadmin's directory. Subsequently, all updates to the Bioadmin's menu will become available to all users.

Testing

Testing should not be carried out using the account that owns the programs (e.g., root). Testing should always be done in a regular user account. One reason is that testing on a user account will uncover incorrect permissions. This is likely the single most common installation error. At the same time, it is probably also best to test in a subdirectory, rather than in the $HOME directory, to fully demonstrate that the program can be run from anywhere.

Using VNC (see Table 1), one can easily eliminate login/logout cycles between your Bioadmin account and your user account. The vncserver is an X11 server that runs on a networked UNIX host. It creates an X11 screen in memory. To display that screen, run vncviewer on your desktop machine. The complete UNIX desktop appears in a window. For example, the entire screen shown in Fig. 2 was run in a vncviewer window. Thus, switching back and forth between the user desktop and the Bioadmin desktop is as easy as switching between windows, facilitating rapid test-modify cycles. (See Chapter 17 for additional VNC insights.)

Installation Checklist

Before announcing updates or new programs, go through the package in a user account, checking the following:

- All files world-readable (**chmod a+r filename**)
- All binaries world-executable (**chmod a+x filename**)
- All directories world-searchable (**chmod a+x directoryname**)
- Environment variable set in cshrc.source
- Documentation and datafiles updated

Although installation should result in a *finished product*, there are often bugs that need to be worked out as the package or program gets used. At this point, the user base is probably the best group of testers, becuase they will make mistakes, and they will try a wider range of data than the Bioadmin would try.

Acknowledgments

Thanks to the Academic Computing and Networking staff at the University of Manitoba for UNIX system support. This work was made possible in part through hardware provided by the Sun Academic Equipment Grants Program.

Glossary and Abbreviations

Front end A user interface that executes other programs.

GUI Graphic user interface.

JVM Java virtual machine. JVM emulates a computer architecture in software. Java programs are compiled into pseudocode (P-code) which is executed by JVM. Consequently, compiled Java code runs on any computer for which JVM is available.

Thin client A display device that draws a screen as specified by the X-server. Thin clients are almost always diskless. Execution of the program occurs on the host, and the results are displayed on the client. X-terminals, SunRay(r) Internet Appliances, and even PC's running X11 server are all examples of thin clients.

Wrapper A script that automates startup tasks required for execution of a program. For example, wrappers often check for critical files and set environment variables.

X11 (X windows) Protocols and libraries for Unix graphic interfaces. The X-server (X) is a program that executes X11 calls from X-applications, and draws the specified screen.

Suggested Readings

Introduction

Fristensky, B. (1999) Building a multiuser sequence analysis facility using freeware, in: Bioinformatics Methods and Protocols, (Misener, S. and Krawetz, S., eds.), Humana Press, Totowa, NJ, pp. 131–145.

Sobell, M. G. (1995) A Practical Guide to the UNIX System, Benjamin/Cummings Publishing Co., Redwood City, CA.

The Networked Computing Environment

Fristensky, B. (1999) Building a multiuser sequence analysis facility using freeware, in: Bioinformatics Methods and Protocols, (Misener, S. and Krawetz, S., eds.), Humana Press, Totowa, NJ, pp. 131–145.

Compilation

Pearson, W. R. (1999) Flexible sequence similarity searching with the FASTA3 program package, in: Bioinformatics Methods and Protocols, (Misener, S. and Krawetz, S., eds.) Humana Press, Totowa, NJ, pp. 185–219.

Installation

Felsenstein J. (1989) PHYLIP Phylogeny Inference Package, Cladistics 5, 164–166.

Fristensky, B., Lis, J. T., and Wu, R. (1982) Portable microcomputer software for nucleotide sequence analysis, Nucl. Acids Res. 10, 6451–6463.

Fristensky, B. (1986) Improving the efficiency of dot-matrix similarity searches through use of an oligomer table, Nucl. Acids Res. 14, 597–610.

Fristensky, B. (1999) Building a multiuser sequence analysis facility using freeware, in: Bioinformatics Methods and Protocols, (Misener, S. and Krawetz, S., eds.), Humana Press, Totowa, NJ, pp. 131–145.

Smith, S., Overbeek, R., Woese, C. R., Gilbert, W., and Gillevet, P. M. (1994) The Genetic Data Environment: an expandable GUI for multiple sequence analysis, Comp. Appl. Biosci. 10, 671–675.
(*see* Website: http://megasun.bch.umontreal.ca/pub/gde/)

Staden R., Beal, K. F., and Bonfield, J. K. (1999) The Staden Package, in: Bioinformatics Methods and Protocols , (Misener, S. and Krawetz, S, eds.), Humana Press, Totowa, NJ, pp. 115–130.

17 Management of a Server-Based Bioinformatics Resource

Brian Fristensky

Introduction

The strategies for managing a server-based molecular biology software resource, accessed by a diverse user community has been discussed in the previous chapters. It assumes that the reader is familiar with basic UNIX commands and concepts. The approaches discussed here are implemented in the BIRCH system (*see* Website: http://home.cc.umanitoba.ca/~psgendb) but are generally applicable to any centralized multiuser software installation.

Most major UNIX distributions now come with graphic tools that simplify many administration tasks. It is therefore realistic to act as your own *sysadmin*. In fact many of the principles discussed are valid in the larger context of a general purpose multiuser system. Although general system administration is a broad field, particular attention should be paid to: daily and weekly backups, both onsite and offsite; security, including rapid installation of security patches; management of user accounts; and disk space to minimize the work and know-how needed on the part of the user. These topics are beyond the scope of this chapter, and are covered extensively in books on system administration, on USENET newsgroups in the comp.* section, and at various HOWTO websites.

The key factors and considerations when implementing the system are:

1. A user base with a diverse set of needs and usually minimal informatics training.
2. A diverse software base, comprised of programs from many authors, in many languages, and in many styles.
3. Documentation written in many formats and styles.
4. A complex networked server system.
5. Limitations of disk space and computing resources.

This chapter builds on the organizational scheme described in the previous chapter. To summarize, the resource is located in a world-readable directory tree referenced by the $DB environment variable. Program binaries, documentation, and ancillary datafiles are located in $DB/bin, $DB/doc, and $DB/dat, respectively. To use the resource, user accounts are set up by running the *newuser* script. This appends a set of configuration commands from $DB/admin/login.source and $DB/admin/cshrc.source to their .login and .cshrc files. The commands in these files are executed when a user logs in or starts a new shell. Thus, as the central configuration is updated, all users have immediate access to the updates. The means to implement this structure are described in the previous chapter.

Managing Documentation

Documentation is the user's entry point into the system. Keeping documentation organized, accessible, and updated accomplishes several tasks. First, it helps to bring out difficulties that users may face when running programs. Second, it forces the Bioadmin to see the software base from the user's perspective. Third, well-organized documentation works to the Bioadmin's advantage, making it easy to refer users to the appropriate documentation, rather than having to answer the same question over and over. While installation of documentation should be straightforward, there are a few considerations for providing a consistent web-accessible documentation library.

HTML

HTML is rapidly becoming the most common format for documentation because of its dynamic capabilities and universal availability. However, it is probably best to keep a local copy of the program documentation on your website, rather than simply linking to the author's website. An author's website will probably describe the most recent version of the software, which may not be installed on your system. If the author stops supporting a software package, he or she may no longer keep documentation on a website. Thus, installation of a local copy of the documentation that was obtained at the time the package was installed is guaranteed to accurately describe the version of the software currently installed.

UNIX Manual Pages

BIRCH has a directory for manual pages called $DB/manl. All files in this directory should be in the form name.l (where l stands for local). In login.source, the line

setenv MANPATH $MANPATH\:$DB

tells UNIX to look for the manual pages in this directory, as well as in any other directory specified in the system's $MANPATH. For example, to read the documentation for align, the user types **man align**, and the file $DB/manl/align.l will be displayed. To display on the web, UNIX manual pages can be converted to ASCII text by redirecting the output from the **man** command to an ASCII file, e.g.,

man fasta > fasta.txt

Postscript and PDF

Although PostScript viewers are usually available on most UNIX workstations, **acroread**, the Adobe Acrobat Reader, has been universally adopted. Therefore, it is probably safest to convert postscript files to PDF for web accessibility using **ps2pdf**, e.g., **ps2pdf primer3.ps**, will create a file called primer3.pdf. ps2pdf is included with most UNIX distributions.

ASCII Text

All web browsers can display ASCII text. It should be noted that file extensions such as .txt or .asc are probably best to use, because these are not commonly used by application software. ASCII files with .doc extensions should be changed to some other extension to avoid confusion with Microsoft WORD files.

Word Processor Documents

Import filters are often less than satisfactory. Therefore, when documentation is in a format specific to a word processor such as WordPerfect, StarOffice Writer, Applix Words, or Microsoft Word, it is best to convert it to the PDF format. Some programs can directly save or print to PDF, while others can only print to PostScript. For the latter, convert to PDF using **ps2pdf** as noted earlier.

Communicating with the User Base

Login Messages

Brief announcements can be printed at the user's terminal by including a statement such as **cat ~psgendb/admin/Login_Message** the in login.source, where Login_Message contains a few lines of text with the current announcements. This message is printed in each terminal window.

Web Site Organization

The BIRCH website provides a number of views to the system (*see* Fig. 1). The *New User* section provides documents that describe BIRCH, how to set up accounts, and how to learn the system. The *Documentation* section provides tutorials and other resources for users to develop their informatics skills while getting useful work done. Finally, the complete online documentation is available in the *Software* and *Database* sections, describing the full functionality of the system.

All login messages are archived in the file WHATSNEW.html, which can be viewed in a scrolling window entitled *BIRCH ANNOUNCEMENTS*. This file provides links to more detailed information than appears in login messages, so that even users who have been away from the system for a while won't miss important changes.

Discussion Groups

Although online discussions can be conducted through a mailing list, these often become an annoyance as the number of users increase and the number of lists one subscribes to increases. Most web browsers such as Netscape and Internet Explorer/Outlook Express, as well as third-party applications, can be used to read and participate in discussions on USENET newsgroups. Many users are familiar with worldwide groups, including the bionet.* groups (e.g., bionet.software, bionet.molbio.genearrays). However, it is also possible to have local newsgroups on any system that operates a newsserver, as do most campus UNIX systems. The local news Bioadmin can easily create a group such as *local.bioinformatics* or *local.genomics* that will be accessible to the local user community.

Remote Consultation Using VNC

Remote consultation on UNIX platforms is now greatly enhanced by Virtual Network Computing (VNC). VNC is a package of programs freely distributed by AT&T (*see* Website: http://www.uk.research.att.com/vnc/). In essence, vncserver creates an X11 desktop session on a remote login host, which keeps an image of the screen in

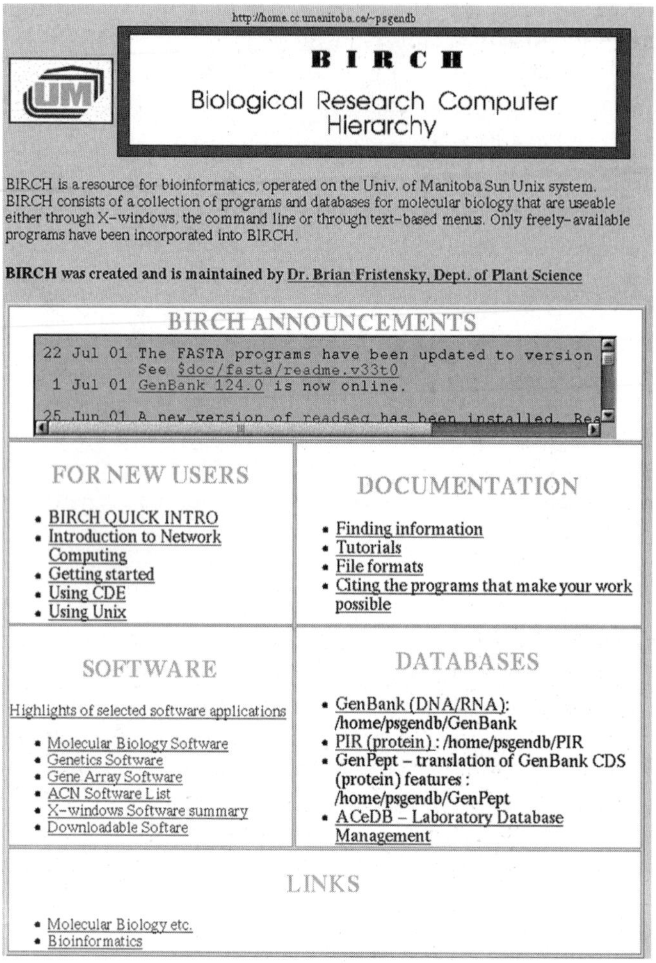

Fig. 1. Organization of web-based documentation on the BIRCH home page (*see* Website: http://home.cc.umanitoba.ca/~psgendb).

memory. A copy of vncviewer, running on a PC or workstation anywhere in the world with a high-speed Internet connection, can display and control the screen as if it were running locally. Figure 2 shows a screen in which a *vncviewer* window is displayed. VNC is available for MS-Windows, Macintosh, and UNIX. The vncviewer can also run as a Java applet in a web browser, so that vncviewer does not have to be installed on the local machine. Thus, regardless of where you are, your UNIX desktop looks and acts the same.

For remote consultation, assume that a user has phoned the Bioadmin with a problem. If it cannot be easily described over the phone, the user changes their VNC password using **vncpw**, and tells the Bioadmin the new password. Next the user starts up a copy of vncserver:

vncserver -alwaysshared
New 'X' desktop is mira:8

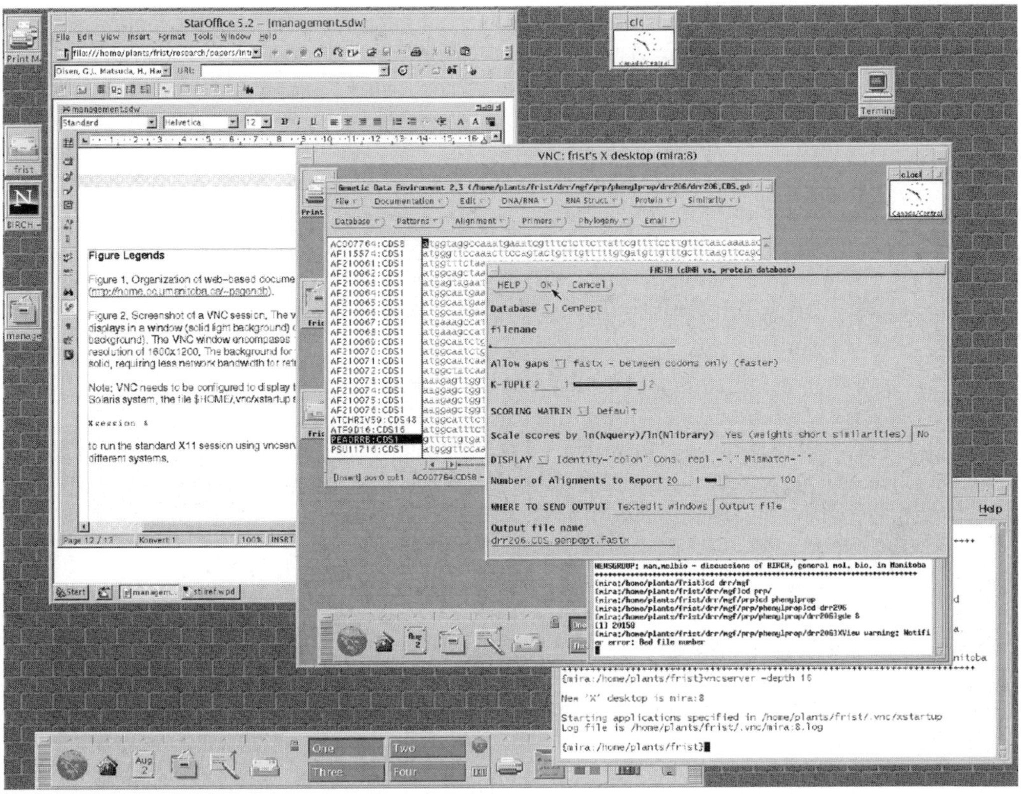

Fig. 2. Screenshot of a VNC session. The vncviewer VNC: frist's X desktop (mira:8) displays in a window (solid light background) on the local desktop (dark brick background). The VNC window encompasses 1024 × 768 pixels, against a screen at a resolution of 1600 × 1200. The background for the mira:8 desktop has been changed to solid, requiring less network bandwidth for refreshing the screen across a network.

Note: VNC needs to be configured to display the user's regular X11 desktop. On our Solaris system, the file $HOME/.vnc/xstartup should contain the line "Xsession &" to run the standard X11 session using vncserver. For the GNOME desktop, this line would read "gnome-session &."

The *-alwaysshared* option makes it possible for more than one user to simultaneously display the same desktop. The message tells the user that vncserver has created desktop 8 on host mira.

Next, the user and Bioadmin each type: **vncviewer mira:8** followed by the password, and the same vncviewer window will appear on both of their screens (*see* Fig. 2). If connecting via a browser, vncviewer would be launched by setting the URL to http://mira.cc.umanitoba.ca:5808, where the last two digits in 5808 indicate the screen number.

Now, both the user and Bioadmin can see and control the same desktop while discussing the various operations over the phone. The user can run a program that is causing difficulty, and the Bioadmin can see everything that happens. The Bioadmin can demonstrate in real time what the user should be doing, and if necessary, datafiles or configuration files such as .cshrc can be examined.

At the end of the session, the Bioadmin reminds the user to kill the VNC session by typing **vncserver -kill :8** and to change their VNC password.

The real value of VNC becomes apparent when traveling. For example, applications such as Powerpoint produce static presentations, and most people travel with their own laptop to ensure that it will work. Over the last 2 years, I have given real-time presentations across North America using VNC on any computer at hand. As long as a fast Internet connection is available, the full functionality of the desktop can be demonstrated anywhere there is a computer and a data projector.

Detecting, Handling and Preventing Problems

A multiuser system poses challenges in terms of managing shared resources, such as CPU time, memory, disk space, and network bandwidth. Usually it is possible to design a system that will minimize user errors, and in most cases UNIX is intrinsically protected from most catastrophes. For example, so that the permissions are explicitly set otherwise, a user can only read or modify files belonging to him, and usually these can only reside in the $HOME directory.

Disk Space

$HOME directories should always reside in a separate file system, and user quotas should be set, regardless of how much disk space exists. The one filesystem that is potentially troublesome is /tmp, which is writeable by all users. In the event that /tmp becomes full, programs that need to write temporary files may hang, resulting in a *filesystem full* error. The best way to avoid this problem is to have applications write temporary files to the current working directory, so that in the worst case, only the user is affected.

CPU Time

Monitoring CPU Usage

Keeping track of CPU usage is critically important. The **top** command gives you a real-time picture of the most CPU intensive jobs currently running on the host you are logged into. If you type **top** at the command line, your system will generate similar information to the following:

```
last pid: 13912; load averages: 2.61, 1.64, 1.31 13:48:41
504 processes: 488 sleeping, 1 running, 6 zombie, 7 stopped, 2 on cpu
CPU states: 16.4% idle, 65.7% user, 17.9% kernel, 0.0% iowait, 0.0% swap
Memory: 640M real, 17M free, 846M swap in use, 3407M swap free

  PID USERNAME THR PRI NICE  SIZE   RES STATE    TIME    CPU COMMAND
11371 umamyks   13  10    0   77M   71M cpu/0   23:19 64.27% matlab
27668 frist     10  58    0   97M   56M sleep    3:06  3.49% soffice.bin
13894 frist      1  33    0 3344K 1672K cpu/1    0:01  1.65% top
13898 umnorthv   1  58    0 6424K 4352K sleep    0:00  0.82% pine.exe
 1629 mills      7   0    0 9992K 7840K sleep    0:24  0.42% dtwm
13704 mhbasri    1  38    0 1464K 1360K sleep    0:01  0.31% elm.exe
 9797 syeung     1  58    0 1000K  816K sleep  267:53  0.28% newmail
 6914 umtirzit   8  58    0   13M 3992K sleep   26:38  0.23% dtmail
26524 mgarlich   1  58    0 9376K 6960K sleep    0:10  0.23% dtterm
29993 simosko    1  58    0 6824K 4528K sleep    0:21  0.23% pine.exe
 7937 jayasin    1  58    0 6112K 3816K sleep    6:55  0.22% Xvnc
 4483 francey    7  48    0 9904K 7920K sleep    0:24  0.21% dtwm
  206 root       6  58    0   76M 8024K sleep  458:13  0.20% automountd
27272 frist      7  58    0   11M 8376K sleep    0:35  0.20% dtwm
  580 syeung     1  48    0 2376K 1976K sleep    2:56  0.19% irc-2.6
```

This display is updated every few seconds in the terminal window. To quit, type **q**. The top command has many options. For example, you can sort jobs by memory used, or list only jobs under a given userid. The owner of a job can also kill that job using top. Type **man top** for full documentation.

The **ps** command with no arguments tells which jobs are running in the current shell (the current window):

```
ps
  PID TTY      TIME CMD
 2122 pts/104  0:00 dsdm
27401 pts/104  2:18 mozilla-
27376 pts/104  0:00 netscape
 2082 pts/104  0:00 zwgc
27384 pts/104  0:00 netscape
27396 pts/104  0:00 run-mozi
 2024 pts/104  0:18 Xvnc
 2041 pts/104  0:00 Xsession
27305 pts/104  0:01 csh
27381 pts/104  0:00 netscape
27457 pts/104  0:14 java_vm
```

while

ps -u userid

tells which jobs are running under a given userid on the host you are logged into.

The following list summarizes the types of tasks that tend to require a lot of processing time:

Jobs That Tend to be CPU-Intensive:

1. Phylogenetic Analysis
   a. Distance matrix methods (e.g., Neighbor Joining, FITCH): Very fast, the amount of time increases in a linear fashion with the number of sequences.
   b. Parsimony (e.g., DNAPARS, PROTPARS): Moderately efficient, the amount of time increases exponentially with the number of sequences
   c. Maximum likelihood (e.g., DNAML, PROTML, fastDNAML): Very slow, the amount of time increases according to a FACTORIAL function of the number of sequences.
2. Sequence database searches: The amount of time that is required is proportional to product of sequence length and database size; use high **k** values to speed up a search; protein searches are faster than DNA.
3. Multiple sequence alignments (e.g., CLUSTALX): Cluster type alignments scale linearly in proportion to the number of sequences.
4. Retrievals of large numbers of sequences: The time required is linear, related to number of sequences.
5. The efficiency of any sorting operation with a large number of items depends on the sort algorithm used.
6. Statistical and mathematical packages (e.g., SAS, MATLAB).

Jobs That Should Never Be CPU Intensive

If the following applications are using significant percentages of CPU time, they are not functioning normally, and are probably *runaway jobs*.

1. Graphic front ends: Programs such as GDE, SeqLab, or SeqPup by themselves do almost nothing. If you see one using a substantial amount of CPU time, it is probably a *runaway job*. One exception is when reading large sequence files, e.g., large numbers of sequences or very long sequences that are placed in memory for analysis.
2. Most user apps (e.g., word processors, mailers, spread sheets, drawing programs).
3. Desktop tools (e.g., text editors, filemanagers).
4. Most UNIX commands.
5. Web browsers: For short bursts browsers can be very CPU-intensive, but this should not persist for more than a minute or two.

Managing Long-Running Jobs

On any multitasking system, all jobs are assigned priorities that govern the amount of CPU time allocated to them. In UNIX, the nice command determines the priority. Most user commands default to a nice value of 0. This is especially important for applications run through a graphic interface, which need to work in real time. The higher the nice value, the less CPU time a job will be allocated, and the less of a load it puts on the system. Programs known to be CPU intensive can therefore be set to run at low priority. A higher nice value prevents the program from taking large amounts of time at high loads, but does not prevent it from utilizing CPU resources when the load on the system is light.

CPU-intensive tasks such as database searches or phylogenetic analysis should be run from wrappers, i.e., scripts that set parameters before running the program. The name of the program is preceded by the **nice** command. For example, to run fastDNAml at the default priority, a wrapper might contain the line:

nice fastDNAml arguments... &

The default priority for **nice** varies from system to system. In the BIRCH system, most sequence programs are launched from the GDE interface by calling wrappers that run programs using nice. As well, termination of the command line with an ampersand (&) tells the shell to run the task in the background. Thus, a user can launch a long-running job, quit GDE, and logout without terminating the job. When the program is completed, the output is written to the file, which the user can access when logged in during the next session.

In some cases, programs that use a graphic interface will perform analyses that require very long execution times. The problem with this design is that the user must remain logged in to the terminal from which the program was launched, because quitting the program would terminate the analysis. One can circumvent this problem by running jobs of this type from a vncviewer window. Killing a vncviewer window has no effect on the applications currently running, and the user can open up the same screen at any time from anywhere. This has the added benefit of making it easy to remotely monitor the progress of long-running jobs.

Killing Runaway Jobs

Sometimes a program will not correctly handle an error, and will begin using up large amounts of CPU time. Unless the Bioadmin has root permissions, it is necessary to ask either the owner of the job or a sysadmin to kill it. For example, a run-away netscape job might show up thus when running the top command:

```
PID    USERNAME  THR  PRI  NICE  SIZE  RES  STATE  TIME   CPU     COMMAND
25779  frist      13   22   0     24M  11M  cpu/0  23:19  64.27%  netscape
```

To kill the job, root or the owner would type: **kill -9 25779**.

Applications that do not normally use a lot of CPU time, but may be prone to run-away execution, could be contained by running them from a wrapper, in which the **ulimit** command is issued prior to running the program, e.g., **ulimit -t 900**, limiting CPU time in the current shell to 900 seconds (15 min).

Acknowledgments

Thanks to the Academic Computing and Networking staff at the University of Manitoba for UNIX system support. This work was made possible in part through hardware provided by the Sun Academic Equipment Grants Program.

Glossary and Abbreviations

ASCII Standard character set used by most computer operating systems, in which characters are represented by 8-bit numbers from 0 to 255.

PDF Portable document format. Platform-independent document rendering language for text and graphics. Files are more compact than PostScript. However, PDF viewers such as Adobe Acrobat typically generate PostScript, which is then printed. PDF was created by Adobe Systems Incorporated (*see* Website: www. adobe.com).

PostScript Standard control language used by virtually all laser printers for rendering text and graphics. Programs often create PostScript output which can be directly printed. PostScript was created by Adobe Systems Incorporated (*see* Website: www. adobe.com).

Suggested Readings

Introduction

Fristensky, B. (1999) Building a multiuser sequence analysis facility using freeware, in: Bioinformatics Methods and Protocols, (Misener, S. and Krawetz, S., eds.), Humana Press, Totowa, NJ, pp. 131–145.

Fristensky, B. (1999) Network computing: Restructuring how scientists use computers and what we get out of them, in: Bioinformatics Methods and Protocols, (Misener, S. and Krawetz, S., eds.), Humana Press, Totowa, NJ, pp. 401–412.

Sobell, M. G. (1995) A Practical Guide to the UNIX System, Benjamin/Cummings Publishing Co., Redwood City, CA.

Detecting, Handling and Preventing Problems

Felsenstein, J. (1989) PHYLIP Phylogeny Inference Package, Cladistics 5, 164–166.

Olsen, G. J., Matsuda, H., Hagstrom, R., and Overbeek, R. (1994) FastDNAml: a tool for construction of phylogenetic trees of DNA sequences using maximum likelihood, Comp. Appl. Biosci. 10, 41–48.

Smith, S., Overbeek, R., Woese, C. R., Gilbert, W., and Gillevet, P. M. (1994) The Genetic Data Environment: an expandable GUI for multiple sequence analysis, Comp. Appl. Biosci. 10, 671–675.
(*see* Website: http://megasun.bch.umontreal.ca/pub/gde/)

Thompson, J. D., Gibson, T. J., Plewniak, F., Jeanmougin, F., and Higgins, D. G. (1997) The CLUSTAL X windows interface: flexible strategies for multiple sequence alignment aided by quality analysis tools, Nucleic Acids Res. 25, 4876–4882.

C. Command Line Sequence Analysis

18 GCG File Management

Sittichoke Saisanit

Introduction

Users are most likely to encounter the Wisconsin Package (GCG) via the web interface as SeqWeb. As the name implies, SeqWeb is a web interface product that allows access to many programs in the GCG package. However, there are still a number of advantages for using GCG on the UNIX command line interface. First of all, the command-line interface is more amenable to batch processing of large datasets. Secondly, the command-line interface allows access to all programs not just the web interface subset. The use of GCG under the UNIX command line is presented in this chapter.

UNIX Commands and Overview

Familiarity with UNIXas presented in Chapter 13 and Appendix 3 is recommended prior to studying this chapter. Here are a few commands and rules in UNIX that can help you get started. Unlike DOS and VMS, UNIX is case-sensitive. For example, a file name *mygene.seq* is different from *Mygene.seq* or any other mixed case combinations. The **man** command is short for manual; it is equivalent to *help* in other operating systems and programs. For example, to find out how a certain UNIX command can be used, type **man** and the command of interest, then hit **Enter** at the command prompt %. For example: % **man cd**.

Manual pages for the command **cd** will be displayed. The **cd** command is used to change directory from one location to another. For example: % **cd /usr/home /usr/common/myproject**. This command changed the current working directory from /usr/home to /usr/common/myproject.

What if the command itself is not known? One powerful feature of the man pages is the ability to include a modifier *-k* to use a keyword feature for finding a command. For example, to find a command to delete a file, enter % **man -k remove**.

The command will list titles of man pages that contain the word *remove* in them. Introduction to UNIX is covered in Chapter 13 which includes descriptions of many UNIX commands.

In order to use GCG effectively with the command line interface, it is important to learn how to manipulate files and directories. This is fundamental to any operating system.

Using Database Sequences and Sequence Formats

The GCG package needs to be initialized by sourcing two scripts. This can be automated at the user log-in as the *.cshrc* file.

There are several formats of sequence data. Users may be familiar with GenBank or EMBL format. GCG has its own format. It also provides several program utilities to convert sequences from one format to another. The GCG format has one notable signature, i.e., 2 dots (..) to separate annotation and the sequence itself. The annotation proceeds the 2 dots followed by the sequence. In most cases, users should not worry about the GCG sequence format. All one needs to do is learn how to retrieve or specify a sequence from these databases when executing a GCG program. The GCG convention for specifying a sequence is *database:accession* or *database:locus_name*. The *database*, is the GCG logical name for a database. These names have been set by the GCG administrator. For example, it is customary to set **gb** for a logical name of GenBank database. To find out whether or not a local installation of GCG has **gb** as one of the logical names, issue the following command: % **name gb**.

To list the logical names, issue the command name without any database name.

Example: % **name**

To retrieve a sequence, the GCG **Fetch** command can be used.

Example: % **fetch gb:m97796**

Assuming that the GenBank database is installed locally and *gb* is set as its logical name, the above command will retrieve a GenBank sequence which has an accession number of M97796. The result will be written to a file with a default name unless a name is specifically given to the program.

The *Fetch* program can also work without database name specification.

Example: % **fetch m97796**

However, if the accession number appears in more than one database, *Fetch* will retrieve all of the sequence records. To ensure uniqueness and speed of retrieval, it is best to use *Fetch* with full specification of the database name and sequence accession number.

On the occasion that a GCG sequence is created or modified by a text editor and the checksum has been altered, GCG programs will not recognize this sequence. Users need to run a utility called *reformat* (shown below) to correct the checksum.

Example: % **reformat myseq.seq**

Another useful file format in GCG is the Rich Sequence Format (RSF). In SeqLab, which is a graphical user interface for GCG run under X Windows, RSF is particularly useful because sequence annotations such as domains and phosphorylation sites can be displayed for visualization. SeqLab can only be run from a UNIX workstation or an X Windows emulation program. There are two modes of working when inside SeqLab: *main list* and *editor*. The graphical sequence viewer is available in SeqLab *editor* mode. The **reformat** command can be used to convert a GCG sequence into an RSF format sequence by including the **-RSF** parameter in the command line: % **reformat -rsf myseq.seq**.

It is recommended that users name sequence files consistently. By default, GCG does not require consistent naming and UNIX does not insist on file types. In contrast, DOS and Windows usually require a 3-letter file type extension for files to be recognized correctly by the programs. However, after accumulating files it will be difficult to recognize older files. Users should make a habit of naming sequence files with meaningful names and consistent name extensions. Appending *.dna* or *.seq* extension for nucleic acid sequence files, or *.pep* or *.pro* extension for protein sequence files will help in recognizing these files. In addition, storing sequence files in specific directories for each project is generally a good idea. Once a certain project has been completed, the entire directory can be archived or removed.

Another file format users may encounter is the FASTA format. Most public sequence utilities on the web can accept or produce sequences in FASTA format. GCG has a utility to convert GCG sequences into FASTA format sequences and vice versa. This is useful because it allows one to use other available tools and external sequences. **Tofasta** converts a GCG sequence into a FASTA format sequence.

Example: % **tofasta gb:m97796**

FromFasta converts a FASTA sequence into a GCG format sequence.

Example: % **fromfasta pubseq.fasta**

Editing GCG Formatted Sequences

The need to edit sequences may come from users' own sequencing efforts. Additionally, users may want to track recombinant sequences such as products of mutagenesis. **SeqEd** is a utility to edit sequences in a much more efficient manner than a text editor. **SeqEd** has another advantage in that the edited sequence will be recognized by other GCG programs without the need to run the **reformat** command. Annotations to specific residues can also be placed within an edited sequence. **SeqEd** can be started by entering: % **seqed myseq.seq**.

Once inside a **SeqEd** editor, use **Control-D** to enter the editor command. Entering **help** in the editor brings up a list of commands that can be used inside the editor.

List File

When working with a family of gene or protein sequences, there is often a need to simultaneously manage a number of sequences. GCG provides a powerful function called a *list file*. A list file is simply a text file that contains a list of individual sequences beginning with 2 dots (..) and separated by new lines. The GCG programs ignore any text before the 2 dots and any text after an exclamation mark (!). Therefore, comments or descriptions of sequences can be added. An example of a list file:

Sequences of mammalian EGF receptors and related family members.
..
sw:EGFR_HUMAN
sw:EGFR_MOUSE
/usr/home/newdata/myseq.pep ! unpublished EGFR-related sequence

As shown in this example, a list file can contain either database sequences or local user sequences or both. A list file is accessed by preceding the file name with the @ symbol. For example, to retrieve all sequences in the list file named *egfr.list* to the current working directory, use the GCG **Fetch** command:

% **fetch @egfr.list**.

In addition to making a list file, multiple sequences can be aligned and written to a single Multiple Sequence Format (MSF) file. Several GCG programs can output files in an MSF format. For example, the **reformat** program with the **-MSF** parameter can be used to convert a group of sequences from a list file into an MSF formatted file.

Example: % **reformat -msf @egfr.list**

However, **reformat** does not align the input sequences. The file resulting from reformat can be named *egfr.msf*, for example. This MSF file can then be used as input for other GCG programs. One or a subset or all of the sequences in an MSF file can be used. To specify a single sequence from an MSF file, type the MSF file name followed by the sequence name in curly brackets, for example **egfr.msf{egfr1}**. To specify multiple sequences, an asterisk wildcard character must be used. For example, **egfr.msf{egfr*}** specifies sequences in the *egfr.msf* file with sequence names beginning with *egfr*. Similiary, **egfr.msf{*}** indicates that all sequences in the MSF file will be used. Note, plain file name specification is not sufficient to specify sequences from MSF files. Either a sequence name or wildcard in the curly brackets must be used with the file name.

SeqLab, the X Windows interface for GCG, can also output MSF files from a list of sequences. GCG command-line programs that can output MSF files are listed below. Programs that require **-MSF** parameter are listed accordingly.

- LineUp -MSF
- PileUp
- PrettyBox
- ProfileGap -MSF
- ProfileSegments -MSF
- Reformat -MSF

Below are two examples of how to use MSF files in a program without (PileUp) and with (LineUp) "-MSF" option requirement.

Example: % **pileup egfr.msf{*}**
% **lineup -msf egfr.msf**

Graphic Files

Several GCG programs have an option to generate output in a graphic format. In order to use the graphic feature, a graphical language and a graphic device must be defined. The command **ShowPlot** displays the current graphic device while the command **SetPlot** changes it. After setting the graphic device, the command **PlotTest** can generate a test graphic output. It is a quick and easy way to determine whether the device is properly configured.

Graphic files require specific applications in order to be displayed correctly. They can not be displayed from the command-line interface like plain text files. The *.figure* files are generally a graphic output from many GCG programs.

Graphics can be displayed directly on the screen. If an appropriate device is selected. For example, on an X Windows terminal, *ColorX* can be used. *ColorX* is a graphic language and a device for the X Windows environment.

File management in GCG requires knowledge of the operating system on which GCG runs. Most likely, it is one of many flavors of UNIX. Common sense should be applied to maintain naming consistency and to facilitate the task of file organization. This is helped by the various file utilities for creating sequence files and converting them into proper formats. Learning how to manage and use graphic files will be helpful to visualize the output from many GCG programs.

Glossary and Abbreviations

EMBL Nucleotide Database Europe's primary collection of all publicly available nucleotide sequences. It is maintain in collaboration with GenBank and DDBJ (Japan).

GCG Genetics Computer Group started in 1982 within the Department of Genetics at the University of Wisconsin. It went private in 1990 and was acquired by Oxford Molecular Group in 1997. In 2000, Oxford Molecular was acquired by Pharmacopeia resulting in a new company called Accelrys (*see* Website: http://www.accelrys.com) which is currently the commercial distributor of GCG(r) Wisconsin Package™.

GenBank An annotated collection of all publicly available nucleotide sequences. The protein sequence collection is referred to specifically as GenPept. GenBank is maintained by National Center of Biotechnology Information (NCBI), a unit of the US National Institute of Health (NIH).

SWISS-PROT An annotated protein sequence database maintained and curated by the Swiss Institute for Bioinformatics (SIB). The database designation is often abbreviated as SW in GCG.

Wisconsin Package A suite of tools and programs for Bioinformatics sequence analysis developed by GCG. It runs on various UNIX operating systems including SUN Solaris, SGI IRIX, Compaq Tru64 UNIX, IBM AIX, and Red Hat Linux.

19 GCG Sequence Analysis

Sittichoke Saisanit

Introduction

The strength of the Wisconsin Package (GCG) is that it contains a suite of programs that serve a wide range of sequence analysis needs. A selected number of these programs are described. Each GCG program has extensive modifiers or parameters available. Top-level online help contains a list of all programs and appendices in alphabetical order. Lists of IUPAC standard symbols for amino acids and nucleotides, including ambiguous symbols, can be found in Appendix 2. Program manuals organize the GCG programs into groups of related analyses or functions. The user's guide contains introductions and overviews that provide an excellent resource for those who are new to GCG. Release notes provide a list of new programs and existing programs with enhancements or bug fixes. To access top-level online help, program manuals, the user's guide and release notes, simply type **genhelp** without specifying a program name after the command prompt % (**genhelp**).

For specific help, i.e, to get help on the Map program, enter: % **genhelp map**.

Individual Sequence Analysis

Several programs in GCG can be used for analysis of individual DNA or protein sequences. These programs are divided into the functional groups of DNA restriction mapping, pattern recognition, secondary structure prediction, RNA secondary structure prediction, and other protein analysis.

DNA Restriction Mapping

Restriction digestions are routine laboratory techniques that many molecular biologists perform. There are related pattern-recognition programs in GCG that can facilitate the analysis or the preparation of a restriction digestion experiment. They are *Map*, *MapSort*, and *MapPlot*.

Map locates restriction sites within a given sequence. It also provides an optional protein translation along with the result. For example, upon entering the **Map** command, the program recognizes the sequence specification convention *database: accession number* (*gb:m97796*), and immediately uses the database sequence as an input. It then asks the user to enter specific restriction sites. All sites can be selected by hitting **return** key or none by hitting the **space bar**, followed by the **return** key. Next, the program asks the user to specify which frame is to be used for protein translation. Select a specific frame if known. If not known, select 3 forward frames, 3 reverse frames, or open reading frames. Otherwise, select the none option in order not to view any protein translation. Map then generates an output text file, which can be viewed by using the UNIX command **more** or by any other text viewer/editor.

All prompted parameters can also be entered in a single line of command. Following the interactive example earlier, the **map** command with needed parameters can be entered with the required parameters.

Example: % **map gb:m97796 -enzyme=* -menu=o -out=m97796.map -default**

The **-enzyme=*** parameter means that all restriction sites (*) are chosen. With the **-menu=o**, protein translation is performed for open reading frames (**o**) only. To save an output into a file named *m97796.map*, the parameter **-out=m97796.map** is supplied. Finally, the **-default** parameter tells the Map program to accept default values for any prompted parameter not specified. In this case, the start and the end positions of the sequence for the Map program to run are not specified. Therefore using the **-default** parameter, the entire sequence is analyzed.

Like the Map program example, any GCG command along with the necessary parameters can be submitted in a single line. This is very useful when using a GCG command inside a UNIX shell script. Note that it is a good idea to always append the *-default* option to any command in order to make sure that a default value is selected for only the parameter that was not specified. Running GCG in a shell script enables complex possibilities such as a multi-step analysis and repetitive or regularly scheduled processes.

Another related program for restriction mapping is MapSort. MapSort finds the restriction enzyme cuts in a given DNA sequence and sorts the fragments of the resulting theoretical digestion by size. MapSort can be used to predict how the fragments of a restriction enzyme reaction will separate on a gel. It is possible to concatenate a sequence of interest with its vector before running MapSort to determine if a single step isolation is possible. With the optional parameter **-circular**, the sequence will be analyzed in its circular form, otherwise the program considers the sequence as linear by default.

Example: % **mapsort myrecomb.seq -circular**

Lastly, the MapPlot program graphically displays restriction sites. In addition to a graphic output, MapPlot can write a text file that also approximates the graph. The program helps users visualize how the part of a DNA molecule of interest may be isolated.

Finding rare-cutter restriction enzymes in a given sequence is often a useful exercise. These enzymes can then be used to quickly test whether a clone or a polymerase chain reaction (PCR) product is likely to be correct. For example, if a *Eco*RI digestion of a 600 bp PCR product is predicted to produce 2 fragments of 400 and 200 bp each, it is prudent to digest a portion of the PCR product and examine it along side the undigested material using electrophoresis. Observing all three different size species will give confidence that the PCR product obtained is not an artifact. One optional parameter for mapping programs is **-six**. This option causes a program like Map to find only enzymes that have six base recognition sites (rare cutters). For subcloning experiments, it is often desirable to identify enzymes that cut only once in a sequence. Option **-once** is used to this end.

When using a mapping program, GCG provides a standard restriction enzyme site file (enzyme.dat) from the New England Biolabs for all commercially available enzymes. Single representatives of isoschizomers are defined in the file. However, there is an option to create a user-customized file. For example, it may be useful to run the Map program against a set of enzymes that are only available in the laboratory. In addition, there may be a preference for different isoschizomers not selected in the default *enzyme.dat* file. One way to create this customized file is to **Fetch** the **enzyme.dat** file and rename it to a personalized name, e.g., **labenzyme.dat**.

Example: % **fetch enzyme.dat**
% **mv enzyme.dat labenzyme.dat**

Starting with a list of all availble enzymes, the file **labenzyme.dat** can be modified to exclude enzymes not available in the laboratory. Inserting exclamation marks (**!**) in front of these enzymes will cause the mapping program to ignore them. In addition, preferred isoschizomers that were not selected as default can be chosen by removing the corresponding exclamation marks. To run the map program with this local data file, use option **-data** command to specify the file with:

% **map gb:m97796 -data=labenzyme.dat**

Pattern Recognition

Map and related programs are essentially pattern recognition programs. GCG also has a general purpose pattern finding program called *FindPatterns*. FindPatterns identifies sequences that contain short patterns like CANNTG or GCAATTGC. Ambiguous patterns can also be used. FindPatterns can recognize patterns with some symbols mismatched but not with gaps. For example, the optional parameter **-mis=1** allows 1 mismatch to occur in the search pattern. Patterns can be provided in a file or typed during an interactive session. It supports the IUPAC nucleotide code.

Example: % **findpatterns myseq.seq -data=pattern.dat**

The GCG formatted search patterns can be provided as a local file. Alternatively, the patterns can be individually entered from the command line. If using the command line to enter patterns, simply hit **return** when the last pattern has been entered and after the program has again prompted for the next pattern to be entered.

Output from FindPatterns is a text file that can be viewed by any text viewer/editor. This result shows only those sequences in which a pattern was found and its location. Use of the **-show** parameter will include a list of patterns not found.

FindPatterns works with either nucleotide or protein sequences. To search through proteins for sequence motifs as defined in the PROSITE Dictionary of Proteins Sites and Patterns, the program *Motifs* should be used. Motifs also displays a short literature summary for each of the motifs it finds in a given sequence. The program can recognize patterns with some of the symbols mismatched, but not with gaps.

Other pattern finding utilities can be quite useful when special analysis needs arise. The Map program can display open reading frames for the six possible translation frames of a DNA sequence. However, the program *Frames* was created specifically to find open reading frames. The program *Repeat* finds direct repeats in a sequence. A minimum repeat length (window), a stringency within the window, and a search range are required. Repeat then finds all the repeats of at least that size and stringency within the search range. The *Composition* program determines the composition of either DNA or protein sequences. To calculate a consensus sequence for a set of pre-aligned nucleic acid sequences, the program *Consensus* can be used. *Consensus* tabulates the percent of G, A, T, and C for each position in the alignment. *FitConsensus* can then use the output table as a query to search for patterns of the derived consensus in other DNA sequences.

Secondary Structure Prediction

Prediction of protein secondary structures is another suite of programs that is used quite frequently. The *PeptideStructure* program makes secondary structure predictions of an amino acid sequence. PeptideStructure calculates several predictions using the following methods:

- Secondary structure according to the Chou-Fasman method
- Secondary structure according to the Garnier-Osguthorpe-Robson method
- Hydrophilicity according to either the Kyte-Doolittle or Hopp-Woods method
- Surface probability according to the Emini method
- Flexibility according to the Karplus-Schulz method
- Glycosylation sites
- Antigenic index according to the Jameson-Wolf method

The results of PeptideStructure are written into a file for graphical presentation using a program called *PlotStructure*. The predicted structures can be shown with two main options: 1) parallel panels of a graph, or 2) a two-dimensional squiggly representation. With the first option, PlotStructure creates a one-dimensional, multi-paneled plot, in which the residues are numbered on the x-axis, and the attributes are represented as continuous curves in each of several different panels. The horizontal line across the surface probability panel at position 1.0 on the y-axis indicates the expected surface probability calculated for a random sequence. Values above this line indicate an increased probability of being found on the protein surface.

The *squiggly plot* option generates a two-dimensional representation of predicted secondary structures with different wave forms. Helices are shown with a sine wave, beta-sheets with a sharp saw-tooth wave, turns with 180 degree turns, and coils with a dull saw-tooth wave. Any of four different quantitative attributes (hydrophilicity, surface probability, flexibility, or antigenic index) can be superimposed over the wave with special symbols wherever the attribute exceeds a set threshold. The size of the symbols is proportional to the value of the attribute. In addition, possible glycosylation sites can be marked on the two-dimensional plot.

As with any computational prediction, users should be cautioned that they are just predictions and should be treated as such. They are not substitutes for experimental proof but can help to direct or focus experiments for validation.

Another program that determines peptide secondary structure is *PepPlot*. PepPlot calculates and plots parallel curves of standard measures for protein secondary structure. Most of the curves are the average, sum, or product of some residue-specific attribute within a window. In a few cases, the attribute is both specific to the residue and dependent on its position in the window. Throughout the plot, the blue curves represent beta-sheets and the red curves represent alpha-helices. Black indicates turns and hydropathy.

There are 10 different panels that can be plotted in any combination and in any order. The first part of the plot shows the sequence itself. This panel is extremely crowded if more than 100 residues per page are selected. When using PepPlot, consult the online help.

Other Protein Analysis

Numerous other programs can be used to analyze proteins. Short descriptions of each are given below. You should consult the online help for detailed descriptions and to find optional parameters for that analysis.

- *SPScan* can be used to predict secretory signal peptides (SPs) in protein sequences. For each sequence, SPScan prints a list of possible secretory signal peptides sorted by score.
- *Isoelectric* calculates the isoelectric point of a protein from its amino acid composition. Isoelectric plots the positive and negative charges and the charge of a protein as a function of pH.
- Hydrophobic *moment* is the hydrophobicity of a peptide measured for different angles of rotation per residue. The hydrophobic moment is calculated for all angles of rotation from 0–180 degrees.
- *HelicalWheel* plots a helical wheel representation of a peptide sequence. Each residue is offset from the preceding one by 100 degrees, the typical angle of rotation for an alpha-helix.
- Like *Map* for a nucleotide sequence, *PeptideMap* finds positions where known proteolytic enzyme or reagent might cut a peptide sequence.
- *PeptideSort* cuts a peptide sequence with any or all of the proteolytic enzymes and reagents listed in the public or local data file *proenzall.dat*. The peptides from each digestion are sorted by position, weight, and retention time as if subjected to high-performance liquid chromatography (HPLC) analysis at pH 2.1.

RNA Secondary Structure Prediction

Designing an anti-sense oligonucleotide is aided by folding predictions that would indicate single-stranded regions. There are 2 GCG programs that can be used. First, *StemLoop* searches for stems or inverted repeats in a sequence. However, StemLoop cannot recognize a structure with gaps, i.e., bulge loops or uneven bifurcation loops. The stems can be plotted with the *DotPlot* utility. Second, *MFold* predicts optimal and suboptimal secondary structures for an RNA or DNA molecule using the most recent energy minimization method of Zuker. PlotFold then displays the secondary structures predicted by Mfold.

Pairwise Analysis

Comparison of two sequences is undertaken to identify related segments. *Gap* and *Bestfit* are two GCG programs that can be used to compare 2 sequences of the same kind, i.e., two DNA sequences or two protein sequences. Gap creates a global alignment of the entire input, while *Bestfit*, as the name suggests, locally aligns the most similiar regions.

Gap uses the Needleman and Wunsch algorithm to create a global alignment of two sequences maximizing the number of matches and minimizing the number and size of gaps. Matching residues receive scoring value assignments. In addition, a *gap creation penalty* and a *gap extension penalty* are required to limit the insertion of gaps in the alignment. These parameters can be adjusted for best results. For example, the gap creation penalty and the gap extension penalty can be set low when two sequences are known to be only related in major domains, but to differ elsewhere. In this case, a gap between the domains is expected and therefore should not be significantly penalized. However, too low a penalty could allow too many gaps in the alignment. Depending on each case, several adjustments of the gap creation and gap extension penalties may be required before the best alignment is obtained.

Bestfit finds an optimal alignment of the best segment of similarity between two sequences using the Smith and Waterman algorithm. Optimal alignments are found by inserting gaps to maximize the number of matches. The two sequences can be of very different lengths and have only a small segment of similarity. If the relationship of two sequences is unknown, Bestfit is the most powerful method in the GCG Package for identifying the best region of similarity between sequences.

Gap and Bestfit normally produce output in plain text format. To display an alignment in a graphical format that shows the distribution of similarities and gaps, *GapShow* can be used. The two input sequences should be aligned with either Gap or Bestfit before they are given to GapShow for display. Gap and Bestfit can write the aligned sequences (with gaps inserted) into new sequence files. GapShow reads these files and plots the distribution of the differences or similarities in the alignment. The sequences are represented by horizontal lines. These horizontal lines have openings at points where there are gaps in either sequence. Regions of interest, such as coding regions, can be shown outside these lines. With appropriate options, a large vertical line between the sequences indicates either a difference or similarity.

FrameAlign can align a protein and the coding sequence, corresponding to the mRNA. FrameAlign creates an optimal alignment of the best segment of similarity (local alignment) between the protein sequence and the codons in all possible reading frames on a single strand of a nucleotide sequence. FrameAlign inserts gaps to obtain the optimal local alignment. Because FrameAlign can align the protein to codons in different reading frames of the nucleotide sequence, it can identify sequence similarity even when the nucleotide sequence contains reading frame shifts.

In standard sequence alignment programs, gap creation and extension penalties must be specified. In addition to these penalties, FrameAlign also has an option to specify a separate frameshift penalty for the creation of gaps that result in reading frame shifts in the nucleotide sequence. By default, FrameAlign creates a local alignment between the nucleotide and protein sequences. With the **-global** parameter, FrameAlign creates a global alignment where gaps are inserted to optimize the alignment between the entire nucleotide sequence and the entire protein sequence.

Developing a habit of consulting the online help prior to using any of these programs is a good idea. It will enable a full utilization of the programs and all of their options and flexibility.

Glossary and Abbreviations

Isoschizomers Different restriction enzymes that recognize and cut the same nucleotide sequence pattern.

PROSITE A database of protein families and domains. It consists of biologically significant sites, patterns and profiles that help to reliably identify to which known protein family (if any) a new sequence.

Suggested Readings

Individual Sequence Analysis

Zuker, M. (1989) On finding all suboptimal foldings of an RNA molecule, Science 244, 48–52.

Pairwise Analysis

Needleman, S. B. and Wunsch, C. D. (1970) A general method applicable to the search for similarities in the amino acid sequence of two proteins, J. Mol. Biol. 48, 443–453.

Part IV Computer Applications

A. Management and Analysis of DNA Sequencing Projects and Sequences

20 Managing Sequencing Projects in the GAP4 Environment

Rodger Staden, David P. Judge, and James K. Bonfield

Introduction

Methods for managing large scale sequencing projects are available through the use of our GAP4 package and the applications to which it can link are described. This main assembly and editing program, also provides a graphical user interface to the assembly engines: CAP3, FAKII, and PHRAP. Because of the diversity of working practices in the large number of laboratories where the package is used, these methods are very flexible and are readily tailored to suit local needs. For example, the Sanger Centre in the UK and the Whitehead Institute in the United States have both made major contributions to the human genome project using the package in different ways. The manual for the current (2001.0) version of the package is over 500 pages when printed, so this chapter is a brief overview of some of its most important components. We have tried to show a logical route through the methods in the package: pre-processing, assembly, contig[1] ordering using read-pairs, contig joining using sequence comparison, assembly checking, automated experiment suggestions for extending contigs and solving problems, and ending with editing and consensus file generation. Before this overview, two important aspects of the package are outlined: the file formats used, the displays and the powerful user interface of GAP4. The package runs on UNIX and Microsoft Windows platforms and is entirely free to academic users, and can be downloaded from Website: http://www.mrc-lmb.cam.ac.uk/pubseq.

The Data and Its Accuracy

The aim of a sequencing project is to produce a final contiguous sequence that satisfies certain accuracy criteria. During the project, the software should show which sequence positions fail to meet the accuracy standard and enable them to be dealt with efficiently. For us, the key to minimizing user interaction with sequence assembly data lies in the use of consensus algorithms, which employ base accuracy estimates or confidence values. Within GAP4 these algorithms are used when automatically locating problems that require an experimental solution and also during interactive tasks within the *Contig Editor* where they are used to guide the user only to those positions

[1] There is currently some confusion about the usage of the word *contig*. In this chapter the original meaning is used, a *contig* is defined to be a set of overlapping segments of DNA, Staden, R. (1980).

whose consensus accuracy falls below a given standard, and hence that require human attention. The consensus is updated on the fly for each change to the data. Because the same algorithm is used during editing and to create the final sequence, the user can ignore all apparent conflicts in the aligned readings, other than those that fail to produce A,C,G, or T in the consensus. Moreover, if the consensus at any point is a padding character (in GAP4 denoted by " * "), these too can be ignored as they will be removed from any consensus sequence file calculated by the program. The sole role of pads is to permit alignment of readings without the need to delete the original bases.

File Formats: SCF, ZTR, Experiment, Fasta Files, and the GAP4 Database

Suitable file formats for sequence related data can make it easier to write programs to process the data and can save a great deal of disk space. For storing traces, sequences and accuracy values, for data from fluorescence-based sequencing machines, we invented the SCF format. Later we moved to SCF version 3.0, which contains the same information as earlier versions but in a form that can be easily compressed, achieving a compression ration of around 10:1 using gzip on data converted from ABI files. Our programs automatically uncompress these files on the fly. More recently we have created the ZTR format, which produces even smaller files without the need for external compression programs. Experiment files are used for passing sequence readings and related data between processing programs. A list of some of the experiment file record types is shown in Fig. 1. Experiment files and FASTA format files can be used for output of the consensus sequence. The GAP4 program uses experiment files to import reading data for assembly and stores it in its own database. In addition to storing the items marked with asterisks (*) in Fig. 1, GAP4 records the positions of all the edits made to individual readings, and provides methods to check their validity. The database is designed so that in the event of system failure, although the most recent changes to it may be lost, it should not get corrupted.

Pre-assembly

Prior to assembly into a GAP4 database, sequence readings produced by automated sequencing instruments must be passed through several processes. Typically this will include conversion to SCF/ZTR format, calculation of base calling accuracy or confidence values, quality clipping, sequencing vector clipping, cloning (e.g., BAC) vector removal, and repeat tagging. A comprehensive set of operations is shown in the flowchart of Fig. 2. Using our package, each of these individual steps is performed by a separate and specific program. These routine operations, which generally require no user intervention, are configured and controlled by the program PREGAP4, which can pass any number of readings through each of these processes in a single run.

The input to PREGAP4 is a file containing the names of all the sequencing instrument files to process. The output is generally an SCF/ZTR file and an Experiment file for each of the input files processed, plus a new file of file names containing the names of all the newly created Experiment files, ready to be passed to GAP4. That is, PREGAP4 creates the initial Experiment file for each reading and then sends it, in turn, through each of the required processing steps. PREGAP4 is modular and very flexible, and can be tailored for compatibility with local working practices. It can be configured to work completely automatically, or to be partially interactive.

```
AC   Accession number
AP   Assembly Position
AQ   Average Quality for bases 100..200
AV   Accuracy values for externally assembled data **
BC   Base Calling software
CC   Comment line
CF   Cloning vector sequence File
CL   Cloning vector Left end
CN   Clone Name
CR   Cloning vector Right end
CS   Cloning vector Sequence present in sequence *
CV   Cloning Vector type
DR   Direction of Read
DT   DaTe of experiment
EN   Experiment Name
EX   EXperimental notes
ID   IDentifier *
LE   was Library Entry, but now identifies a well in a micro titre dish
LI   was subclone LIbrary but now identifies a micro titre dish
LN   Local format trace file Name *
LT   Local format trace file Type *
MC   MaChine on which experiment ran
MN   Machine generated trace file Name
MT   Machine generated trace file Type
ON   Original base Numbers (positions) for externally assembled data **
OP   OPerator
PC   Position in Contig for externally assembled data **
PN   Primer Name
PR   PRimer type *
PS   Processing Status
QL   poor Quality sequence present at Left (5') end *
QR   poor Quality sequence present at Right (3') end *
SC   Sequencing vector Cloning site
SE   SEnse (ie whether complemented) **
SF   Sequencing vector sequence File
SI   Sequencing vector Insertion length *
SL   Sequencing vector sequence present at Left (5') end *
SP   Sequencing vector Primer site (relative to cloning site)
SQ   SeQuence *
SR   Sequencing vector sequence present at Right (3') end *
SS   Screening Sequencing
ST   STrands *
SV   Sequencing Vector type *
TG   Gel reading Tag
TC   Consensus Tag *
TN   Template Name *
//   End of sequence records (SQ)
```

Fig. 1. Experiment file record types.

A screen dump from PREGAP4 is shown in Fig. 3. The program menus are at the top and the main window is occupied by the *Configure Modules* page. This page allows users to select and configure the modules they require: those selected are marked with a tick, the others with a cross. If a module is fully configured, it is labeled *ok*. Here the user is setting up the module that is used to locate and mark the sequencing vector. When everything is ready, the **Run** button at the bottom can be used to activate the processing.

Introduction to GAP4

GAP4 provides a comprehensive set of methods for: assembly; checking assemblies; finding joins between contigs by using read-pair data and/or poor quality data at

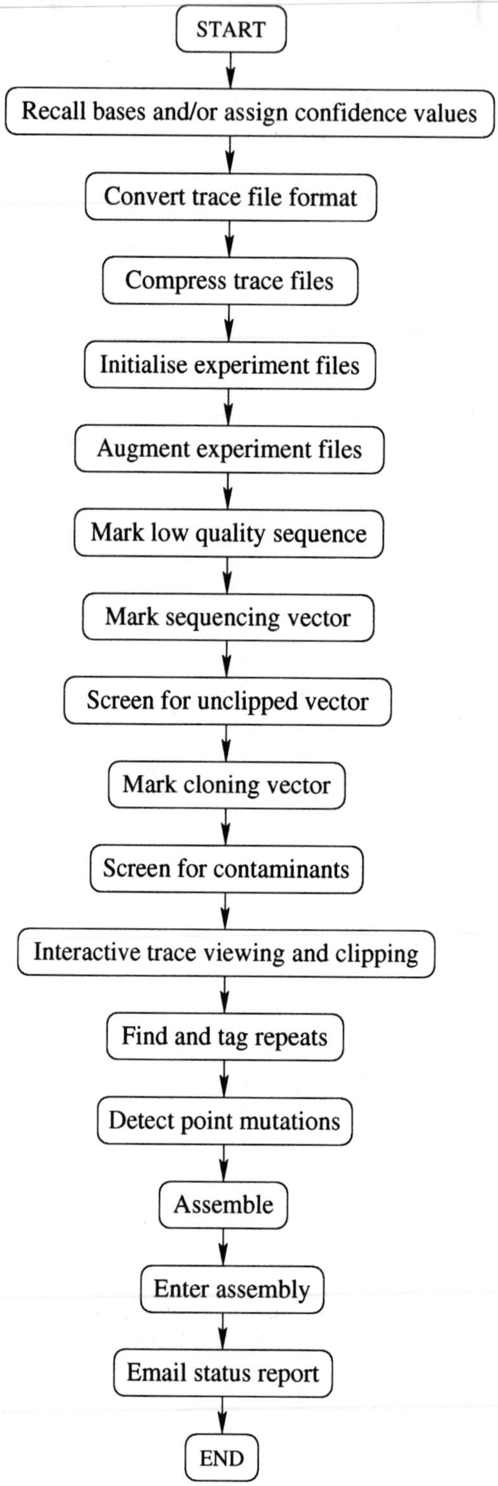

Fig. 2. A flowchart of the operations configured and carried out by PREGAP4.

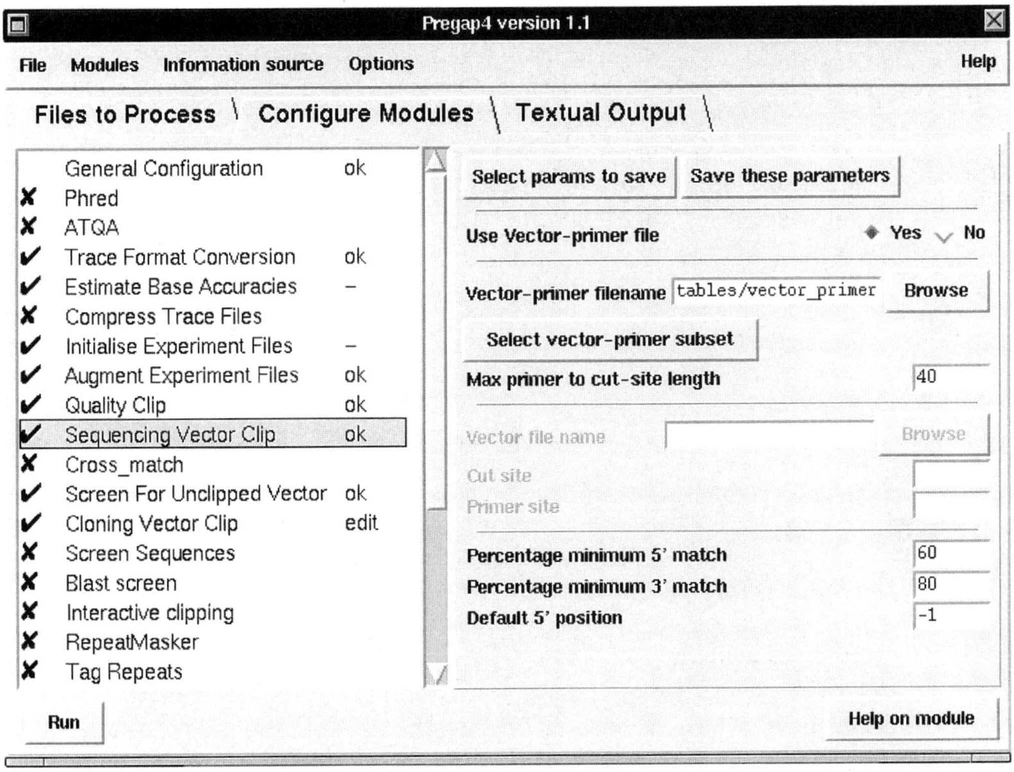

Fig. 3. The main PREGAP4 window.

the contig ends; suggesting additional specific sequencing experiments to join contigs or to overcome other deficiencies in the data; check the accuracy of the consensus; and edit contigs to the required level of confidence.

Files of File Names, Lists, Tags, Masking, Visible and Hidden Data

Files of file names are files that contain the names of other files that are to be processed as a batch. As already mentioned, PREGAP4 processes batches of files from sequencing instruments and the various GAP4 assembly engines process batches of experiment files. Both do this by being given the name of a file of file names. Lists are used internally by GAP4 for recording sets of readings or contigs, and to enable them to be processed in batches. Tags are labels that can be attached to segments of individual readings or consensus sequences. Each tag has an associated, editable text string and each tag type has an identifier and color. Tags can be used to record comments about segments of a sequence, or to denote the locations of specific features, such as primers or repeat elements. Within GAP4 tags can be displayed at all levels of resolution to provide visual clues, and can be used to mark segments of the sequence for special treatment by certain algorithms. For example, segments covered by selected tags can be *masked* during assembly. Our pre-processing programs do not actually remove vector sequences or poor quality data from the ends of readings, rather they add records to the experiment files to enable those segments to be treated in special ways within other programs such as GAP4. These end segments of readings are not normally revealed in the *Contig Editor* and other such places, and so they have come to be known as *hidden* data and the used parts of the readings as *visible*.

The GAP4 Scripting Language

GAP4 is composed of algorithms written in the C language, which have been added to the commands **understood** by the Tcl interpreter. Extended Tcl provides a scripting language for performing operations on sequence assembly data. For example, a simple script could open a GAP4 database, make a copy of it, and then assemble a new batch of readings listed in a file of file names. The design of GAP4 also makes it possible for others to add their own interactive modules, complete with dialogues and menu items.

The GAP4 User Interface

The graphical displays and user interface of GAP4 play an important role in enabling users to deal with difficult problems, and so help to simplify and speed up sequencing projects. The main points are summarised in the following sections.

The Main Window and Its Menus

An example of the main window of GAP4 is shown in Fig. 4. It consists of an area for receiving textual results, the *Output window*, and below that an area for displaying error messages. The output window is a searchable and has an editable text display, the contents of which can be saved to disk files. Along the top of the window is a row of menus: the file menu includes database opening and copying functions and consensus sequence file creation routines. The *Edit* menu contains options to alter the contents of the database such as **Edit Contig**, **Order Contigs**, **Join Contigs**, **Break Contig**, **Disassemble Readings**, **Complement Contig**, etc. The *View* menu provides functions that give different ways of examining the data that includes: **Contig Selector**, **Results Manager**, **Find Internal Joins**, **Find Read Pairs**, **Find Repeats**, **Check Assembly**, **Show Templates**, **Restriction Enzyme Map**, **Stop Codon Map**, **Quality Plot**, etc. The *Options* menu contains general configuration commands. The *Experiments* menu contains options to analyse the contigs and to suggest experiments to solve problems, including: **Suggest Primers**, **Suggest Long Reads**, **Compressions and Stops**, and **Suggest Probes**. The *List* menu contains options for creating and editing lists. The *Assembly* menu contains various assembly options including: **Normal Shotgun Assembly**, **Directed Assembly**, **Screen Only**, **Assemble Independently**, **CAP3 Assembly**, **FAKII Assembly**, and **PHRAP Assembly**.

Views of the Data and the Interactions Between Displays

GAP4 has several interactive displays to enable users to view and manipulate their data at appropriate resolutions. The graphical displays include the **Contig Selector**, the **Contig Comparator**, the **Template Display**, the **Quality plot**, the **Restriction Enzyme Map**, and the **Stop Codon Map**. For editing aligned readings the **Contig Editor** and the **Join Editor** are used. From each of these the trace data for readings can be displayed and scrolled in register with the editing cursors. The displays in GAP4 communicate with one another and have linked cursors. For example, if the **Contig Editor** is being used on a contig that is also being viewed in a **Template Display**, the position of the **Contig Editor's** cursor will be shown in

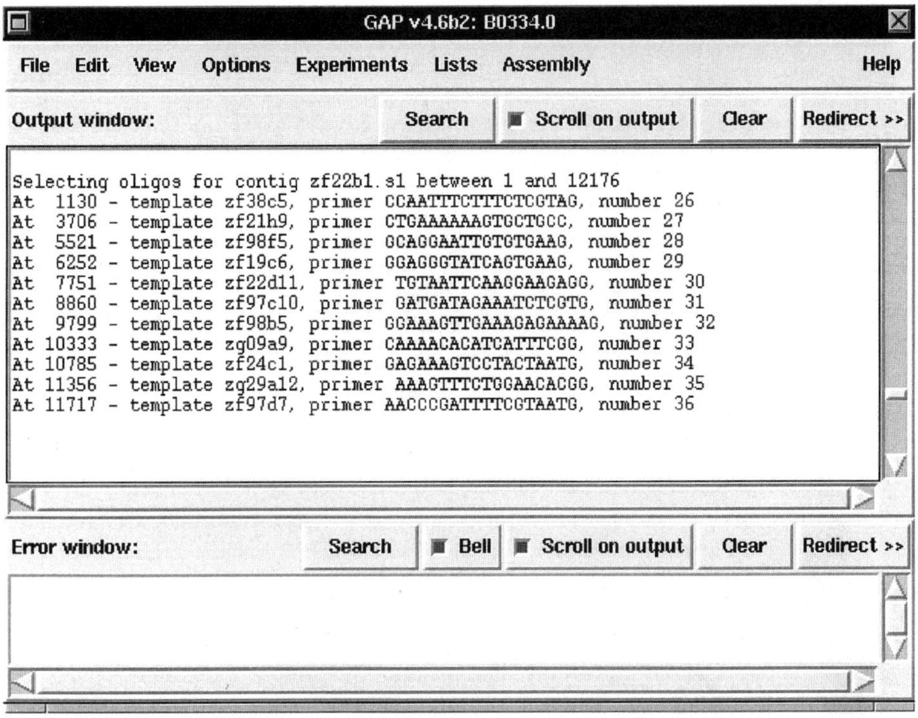

Fig. 4. The main GAP4 window.

the **Template Display**, and within the **Template Display** the user can use the mouse to drag the **Contig Editor's** editing cursor. Also, if the **Contig Editor** is displaying traces, they too will scroll under the control of the **Template Display**. Any number of displays of the same contig can be shown simultaneously, including several displays of the same type, such as several **Contig Editors**. Note that the GAP4 displays make good use of color to distinguish features of the assembly.

The Contig Selector

The GAP4 *Contig Selector* (*see* Fig. 5) is used to display, select, and reorder contigs. Within the display all the contigs are shown as colinear horizontal lines separated by short vertical lines. The lengths of the horizontal lines are proportional to the lengths of the contigs and their left to right order represents the current ordering of the contigs. This contig order is stored in the GAP4 database and users can change it by dragging the lines representing the contigs in the display. The *Contig Selector* can also be used to select contigs for processing and to display tags. As the mouse cursor is moved over a contig, it is highlighted and data about it displayed in the *Information Line* at the base of the display. At the top of the display are **File**, **View**, and **Results** menus. Below these are buttons for undoing zoom-in operations and toggling the crosshair display. The four text boxes to the right show the position of the crosshair. Figure 5 shows an example of the *Contig Selector* for a project currently comprising nine large contigs and a cluster of smaller ones. The crosshair is on the largest contig and the text box to the right of the crosshair toggle button gives its position in the contig and the next box

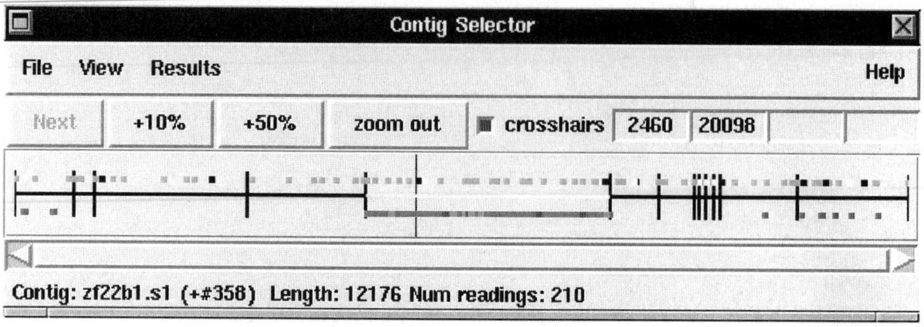

Fig. 5. The Contig Selector.

gives the position in the whole consensus. The boxes above and below the lines representing contigs show the location of tags. Those above the lines are on readings and those below are on the consensus. As can be seen the longest contig is tagged over its whole length.

The Contig Comparator

The *Contig Selector* is usually constantly in view while GAP4 is being used, but if the user selects one of the functions that in any way compares contigs, the *Contig Selector* is automatically transformed into a display known as the *Contig Comparator*. In this form it retains its *Contig Selector* functionality but can plot the results of contig comparison functions. The transformation process involves drawing an additional copy of the contig representations below and perpendicular to the original set in the *Contig Selector*, so as to produce a two dimensional area in which to plot comparative results.

An example of the *Contig Comparator* is shown in Fig. 6. Notice that the crosshair has both vertical and horizontal components and that the position of the horizontal component is reproduced as a short vertical cursor in the *Contig Selector* part of the display. Results are not duplicated and are only plotted in the top right half of the display and on its bounding diagonal. The results plotted in this example are those from **Find Internal Joins**, **Find Read Pairs**, and **Check Assembly**; the latter are shown along the main diagonal. Obviously each type of result is drawn in a different color. Results plotted parallel to the main diagonal show relationships between pairs of contigs that are in the same relative orientation, and those perpendicular to the main diagonal are for pairs that would require one of the contigs to be complemented before they could be joined. **Find Internal Joins** compares the sequences from the ends of contigs to see if they overlap. **Find Read Pairs** locates pairs of readings that are from the same template but are in separate contigs and hence give data about the relative orientations and approximate separations of the two contigs. **Check Assembly** checks the alignment of each reading with the consensus it overlaps, and plots the positions of those of doubtful quality. This is of most value if its results are displayed at the same time as those from a search for repeats; thus, if readings with poor alignment lie on the same horizontal or vertical projections as do repeats, it may indicate that they have been assembled into the wrong copy of the repeat.

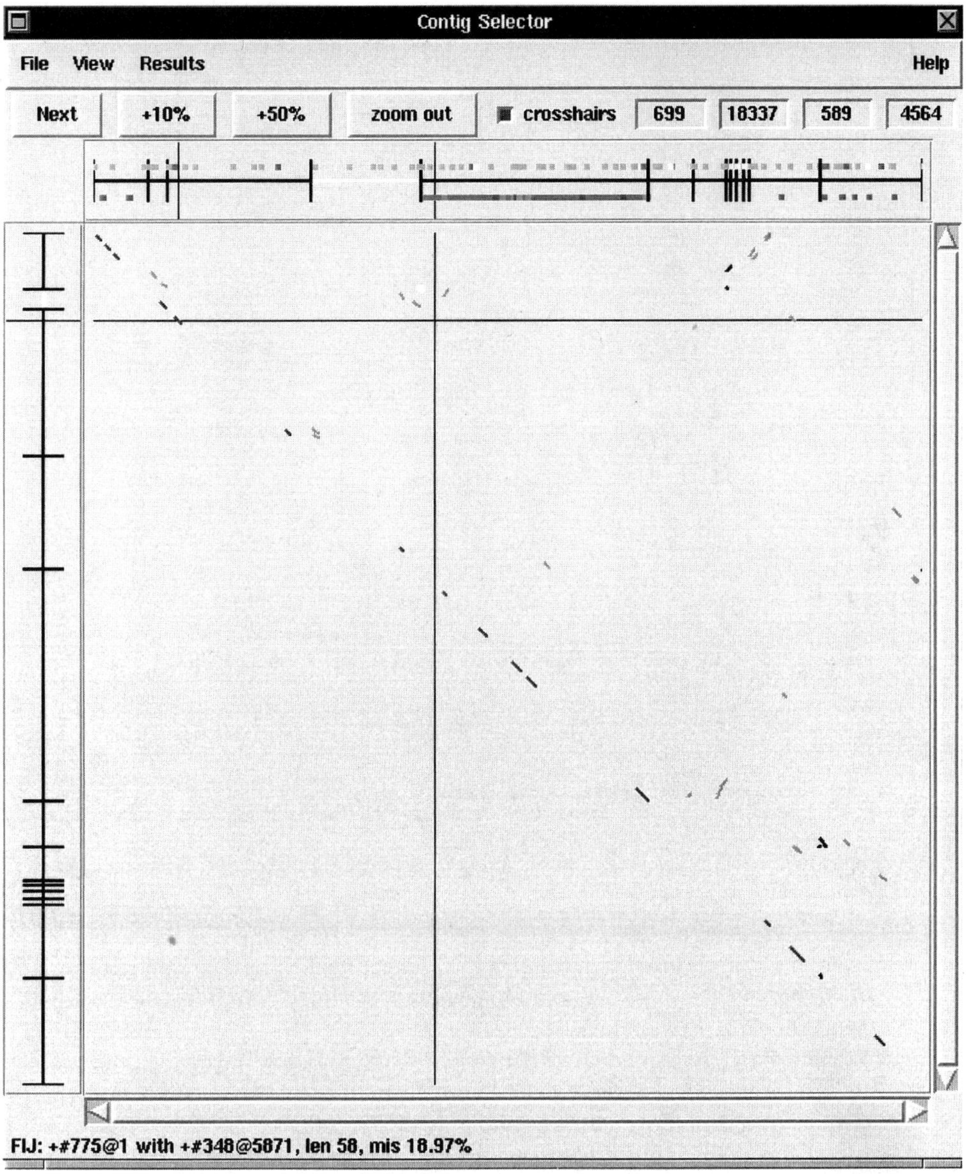

Fig. 6. The Contig Comparator.

Referring to Fig. 7, note the white dot, just above and to the left of the pair of crosshairs. Its whiteness indicates that it is the result that has most recently been touched by the crosshairs. The two contigs to which the result corresponds are also shown in white, and the *Information Line* contains relevant data. It gives the identity of the two contigs, the position and length of the overlap, and the percentage mismatch of the corresponding alignment. Near to the white dot are two diagonals showing that there are two templates, each with forward and reverse readings, spanning the same pair of contigs, which according to the **Find Internal Joins** result to have an apparent

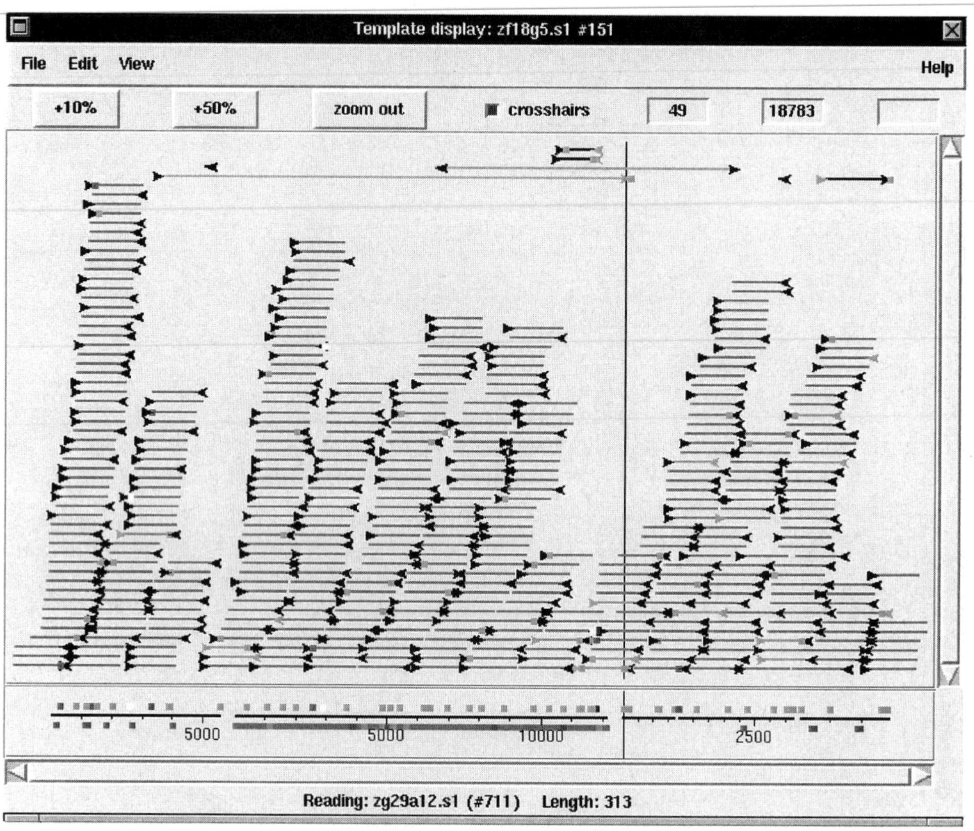

Fig. 7. Template Display of ordered contigs.

overlap. That is, there is independent evidence that these two contigs overlap and could be joined (*see* Fig. 8 and Subheading "Finding Joins Between Contigs Using Sequence Comparison").

Note that it is an interactive display. The lines representing contigs can be dragged to new locations or contigs can be complemented and their plotted results will move with them and all the others are automatically rearranged accordingly. Also, if a join is made using the **Join Editor**, the lines representing the contigs will be joined and the rest reorganized. Each type of result in the display can be operated on by a particular set of commands, and these can be invoked by moving the crosshair over the plotted line and pressing the right mouse button to pop up a menu.

The Template Display

The *Template Display* provides a graphical overview of either a set of contigs or a single contig. In our terminology, a *template* is the DNA insert from which a reading is obtained. In many laboratories, templates will be size-selected to have a length of around 2000 bases, and initial readings will be obtained from each of its ends to produce a *read-pair*. The information that can be displayed in the Template Display includes: readings, templates, tags, restriction enzyme sites, rulers, and consensus quality. As the mouse cursor is moved over any item in the display, textual data

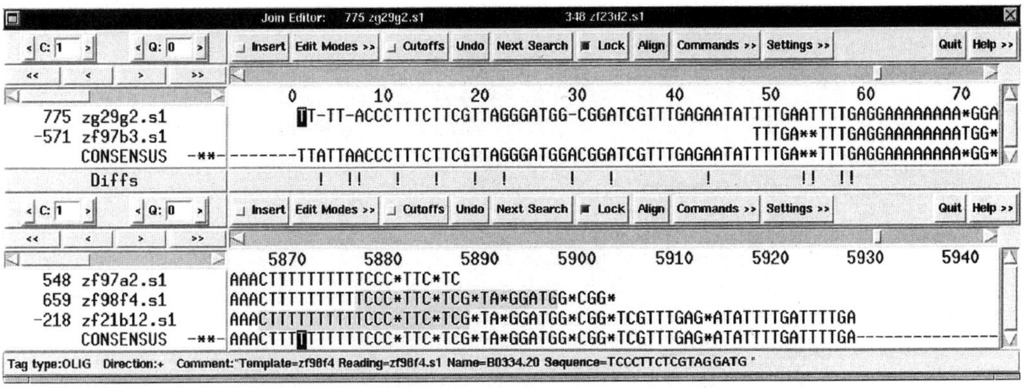

Fig. 8. The Join Editor.

about it will appear in the *Information Line*. The positions of a vertical crosshair, under the control of the mouse, are continuously displayed in two boxes at the top of the window. The left box shows the position in a contig and the right the position in the overall consensus. The order of the contigs can be changed by horizontally dragging the lines that represent them in the display, whereupon all their associated data will be redrawn.

In Fig. 7 we see that above the *Information Line* is a horizontal scrollbar that can be used if the plot has been magnified with the zooming mechanism. In the panel above the scrollbar are horizontal black lines representing 5 contigs, the longer ones having rulers marked on them. The boxes above and below these lines represent the positions of the respective tags on the readings and on the consensus. The longest contig contains a tag over its entire length. The vertical line cutting the contig to its right and reaching the top of the next panel, is the crosshair. This main panel contains lines representing individual templates and the readings derived from them. At the scale shown, the extent of each reading cannot be seen, and only their forward readings and gray-colored reverse readings arrow heads are visible. The templates are color coded: dark blue have only forward readings; red have both forward and reverse readings, are within the expected size range, and are in the same contig; yellow have both forward and reverse readings, in the correct relative orientation to one another, but which are in different contigs, and are within the expected size range; greenish yellow (*see* Fig. 7 on companion CD) have both forward and reverse readings, are in different contigs, but are outside their expected size range. These contigs have been processed through GAP4's automatic contig ordering function (*see* Subheading "Ordering Contigs Using Read-Pair Data"), and it may be possible to see that the gray scales of some of the templates between the contig ends are lighter, and that they have readings in each of the two contigs involved. Problem templates are separated out at the top of the display. With this ordering of the contigs, it can be seen that two of these problem templates would need to be many thousands of bases in length. In the panel containing the crosshair position boxes (the empty box is used to show the separations of restriction enzyme sites when their data are displayed), is a button for switching the crosshair on and off and a **zoom out** button, which reverts to the previous level of zoom when clicked. At the top of the display are menus that provide for closing the window, saving a changed contig order and selecting the features to be displayed.

Assembly

GAP4 can use several assembly engines including: *Normal shotgun assembly*, *Directed assembly*, *CAP3*, *FAKII*, and *PHRAP*. Particularly for repetitive data, the most reliable assembly will be achieved by global algorithms such as CAP3, FAKII, and PHRAP as they compare every reading against every other reading prior to aligning them into contigs. Later in a project, when new readings have been obtained to solve particular problems, *Directed Assembly* can be used (since their approximate location in the assembly is known). Obviously this can be very helpful if the readings have been determined to help with a difficult repeat; *Directed Assembly* will ensure that they are aligned in the correct places. Even if a global algorithm is used for assembling the initial shotgun, the *Normal shotgun assembly* algorithm is useful to enter readings obtained to help finish a project.

Ordering Contigs Using Read-Pair Data

GAP4 contains an option for automatic ordering of contigs based on read-pair data. The algorithm tries to find the most consistent orientations and left to right order for all the contigs in the database. The task is made more difficult by errors in the data owing to misnaming of readings and templates, which is usually caused by lane-tracking errors when processing the original gel data. This is becoming less of a problem with the increasing use of capiliary-based sequencing instruments. The output from the function is a list containing records giving the left to right orderings. When there are several records, this means that there is insufficient data to link all the contigs. If the user double-clicks on any of these records a *Template Display* showing their ordering will appear (*see* Fig. 7). Within this, if necessary, the order can be altered by using the mouse to move the lines representing the contigs.

Checking the Correctness of Assemblies

Prior to ensuring that the consensus sequence reaches a given standard of reliability it is advisable to check, at a coarser level, that readings have been correctly positioned. Within GAP4 there are several functions for checking on the reliability of an assembly and they all display their results in the *Contig Comparator* described earlier. We can ask: Is the read-pair data consistent? Do the quality clipped segments of readings align well with the consensus? Do the visible parts of readings align well? If not, do they match elsewhere?

As will be seen, the details of the read-pair data are most easily checked in the *Template Display*, but if these results are displayed in the *Contig Comparator* they can be viewed at the same time as other types of analysis. After the sequence is apparently completed, we need an external experimental check of its integrity, such as data from a restriction enzyme digest. GAP4 can produce a map of the restriction enzyme recognition sequences contained in the consensus sequence for comparison with experimental results.

Experiment Suggestion Functions

As a follow-up to the initial shotgun phase of a sequencing project, experiment suggesting functions are designed to help automate the task of choosing experiments to join contigs and to finish the sequence to the required level of accuracy. The package contains two programs for this purpose. Having located problems, the newest, PRE_FINISH (the details of program are outside the scope of this article), performs a sophisticated analysis of the benefits of applying a range of experiments to help to complete the project. It needs to be set up to fit the particular modes of operation of the laboratory where it is installed and hence is highly configurable. However, once set up, it is very effective.

An older and simpler set of experiment suggestion functions is available within GAP4. Here the options include **Suggest Primers**, **Suggest Long Gels**, **Suggest Probes**, and **Compressions and Stops**. One difference between these routines and PRE_FINISH is that in GAP4 the user must select the experiments type, whereas PRE_FINISH will choose the best of several types of experiments to solve the problems in each region. Figure 4 shows how the results are written to the GAP4 Output window. All of the experiment suggestion functions start by calculating the equivalent of a consensus sequence for the selected contigs, while at the same time encoding which segments contain data only on one strand. This encoding is then used to suggest suitable experiments, of the type requested by the user, to cover the single-stranded segments and extend the contigs. In the case of **Suggest Primers**, the function also adds the tag of *primer*, containing the template name and primer sequence, to the relevant reading. The **Contig Editor** also contains a primer selection function.

Finding Joins Between Contigs Using Sequence Comparisons

No assembly engine will make all the possible joins between contigs. As already mentioned, via the *Contig Comparator* GAP4 provides the user with views of the data that can reveal the safety or otherwise of making joins. The **Find Internal Joins** function compares the consensus sequences of the contigs in the database in both orientations to detect possible overlaps. It works in two modes: **quick** and **sensitive**. The quick mode is very rapid and should be applied before the sensitive mode is used to find any remaining overlaps. During large-scale sequencing where overlapping BAC clones are being sequenced, it is common practice to exchange readings from their GAP4 databases to help finish the projects. In this case **Find Internal Joins** may be employed to join the overlap between the two sets of readings. Here the quick mode is particularly useful, as it can find and align the overlaps between 100,000 base consensus sequences in a few seconds. The sensitive mode is slower, but will find weak matches between the ends of contigs.

For both modes, a number of options are available. The user can select to extend the contig consensus using segments of the hidden data near the contig ends. In conjunction with the sensitive mode this should find all possible joins. Users can also choose to mask any tagged regions in the contigs: typically regions tagged as being ALU or other repeat sequences. The aligments are displayed in the *Output Window* and the results are plotted in the **Contig Comparator** (*see* Fig. 6). A **Next** button will appear at the top of the **Contig Comparator**. The results are sorted in descending order of quality, and each time the user clicks on the **Next** button, the next best possible join will appear in a **Join Editor** window (*see* Fig. 8). As an alternative to the **Next** button, users can click on the results plotted in the **Contig Comparator** to bring up the **Join Editor**. The **Join Editor** is two **Contig Editors** sandwiched together with a horizontal strip between (labeled *Diffs*) to indicate disagreements in the consensus sequences. The **Join Editor** also has **Align** buttons for aligning the two consensus sequences and a **Lock** button for forcing the two contigs to scroll together. The join shown in Fig. 8 is obviously very poor, but it is confirmed by read-pair data as was discussed in the section on the *Contig Comparator*. Within the **Join Editor** users should align the contigs, making any necessary edits, and checking the trace data. When they exit the editor they can choose to make or reject the join. The **Join Editor** contains all the functionality of the **Contig Editor**, which is described next.

Checking and Editing Contigs with the Contig Editor

The GAP4 contig editor is designed to allow rapid checking and editing of characters in assembled readings. Very large savings in time can be achieved by its sophisticated problem-finding procedures, which automatically direct the user only to the bases that require attention.

Contig Editor Search Modes

The search modes available include the following:

1. **Search by problem** moves the cursor to the next position in the consensus that is not A,C,G, or T. The character in the consensus will depend on the consensus algorithm being employed and the thresholds set.
2. **Search by quality** moves the cursor to the next position in the sequence where the consensus characters, calculated separately for the two strands, disagree.
3. **Search by consensus quality** moves the cursor to the next position in the consensus where the confidence is below a set threshold.
4. **Search by discrepancies** moves the cursor to the next position where two readings contain aligned but disagreeing bases above a given confidence value.
5. **Search by edit** moves the cursor to the next position where an edit has been made, hence allowing all previous edits to be checked.
6. **Search by evidence 1** moves the cursor to the next edited position for which the consensus base is not supported by any evidence from the original data.
7. **Search by evidence 2** moves the cursor to the next edited position for which the consensus base is only supported by evidence from the original data on one of the two strands. *Search evidence* means that a base of the same type must appear at an equivalent position in an original, unedited reading.

These searches allow rapid checking of all the edits made. The other search modes provide more obvious operations such as: moving to a particular position, to a particular read, to the next occurrence of a given sequence, to the next tag of a given type, and to the next tag containing a given text string. It is also possible for the search to be controlled by a file containing commands.

The Contig Editor Window

In the *Contig Editor* window (*see* Fig. 9), reading numbers and names are on the left, sequences to their right, status lines are at the bottom, and controls are at the top. The buttons labeled **Settings**, **Commands**, and **Edit modes** reveal tear-off menus, and their contents are described below. The **Commands** menu contains a **Search** dialogue from which a search method appropriate to the data and current task can be selected. The editor display includes color coding of the base confidence values in the readings and in the consensus using gray scales, and marking of all the edits made; padding characters in green, changes in pink, deletions in red, and confidence value

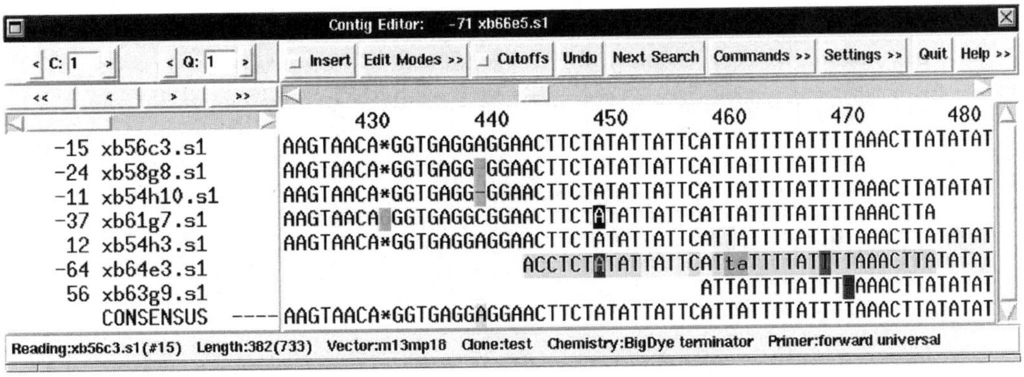

Fig. 9. The Contig Editor.

changes are highlighted in blue. Each time the **Next search** button is clicked, a search of the selected type is performed to locate the next problem in the sequence requiring visual inspection by the user. The **Undo** button will successively reverse all edits up to the last save. The **Cutoffs** button toggles on and off the visibility of the *hidden* data at the ends of readings. The final button along the top of the editor, **Insert**, toggles between insert and replace modes. The two text boxes with < and > symbols next to them are for altering the thresholds for the consensus algorithms. Just below these are more buttons that can be used to scroll the edit window. Below these is a scrollbar for viewing long reading names. The *Information Line* reveals data about the lengths of readings and the names of their vectors, or tags.

Editing Modes and Settings

Different laboratories have different working practices, and some wish to allow only particular people to perform certain types of editing operations. The **Contig Editor Edit modes** menu contains the following editing operations: 1) insert in read, delete in read, insert in consensus, delete dash (undetermined) in consensus, 2) delete any character type in consensus, 3) replace in consensus, reading shift, and 4) transposition.

Each of these may be switched on or off individually. The editor also has two preconfigured sets of edits: **Mode 1** and **Mode 2**, which define for example, a limited, safe set, and a powerful set for a more senior operator. Note that during editing the consensus is updated immediately for each edit made.

The **Contig Editor Settings** menu contains the following: **Status Line**, **Trace Display**, **Highlight Disagreements**, **Compare Strands**, **Toggle auto-save**, **3 character amino acids**, **Group Readings by Templates**, **Show reading quality**, **Show consensus quality**, **Show edits**, **Set Active Tags**, **Set Output List**, and **Set Default Confidences**. For example, the Status line can be configured to show if the contig has data on both strands, whether edits have been made, whether to show translation to amino acids. The **Trace Display** can be configured to automatically show traces relevant for each problem as revealed by the search command, by defining the number of rows and columns of traces to show at once.

The **Contig Editor Commands** menu includes commands: to operate on tags, to save the edits, to save the contents of the **Contig Editor** display as a text file, to create a *consensus trace*, and save it to a file; to select primers to align segments of readings,

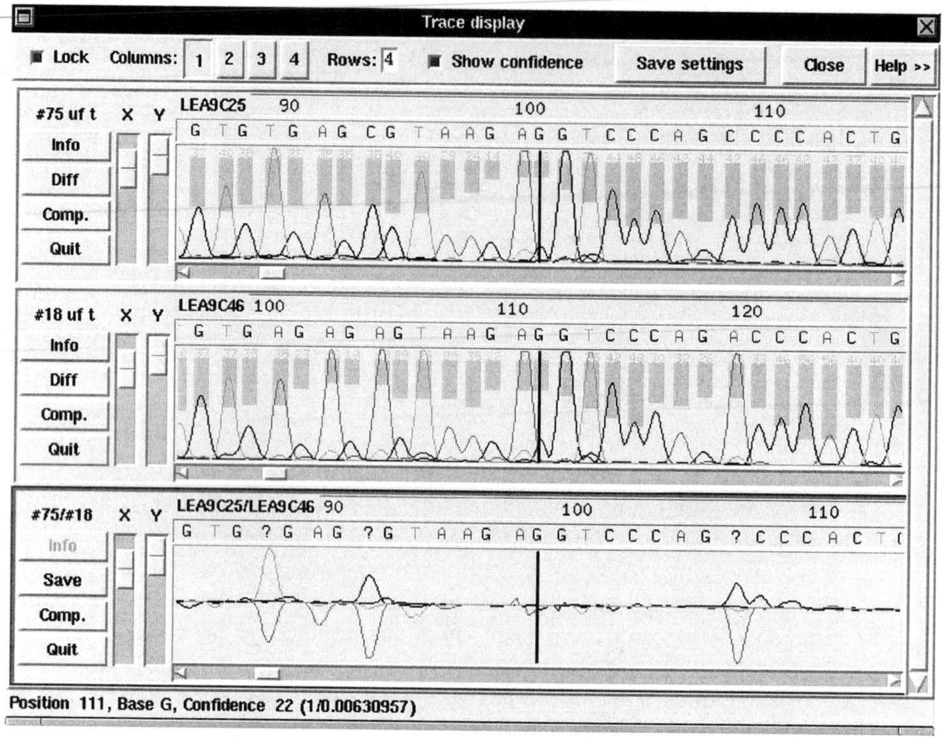

Fig. 10. The Trace Display including a difference plot.

to line up and remove padding characters, to remove readings, to break the contig, and to search the contig.

The Trace Display

Within the **Contig Editor** the **Trace Display** read can be invoked by double-clicking on a *base* in the read. By double clicking on the consensus, the traces for all the readings at that point will be displayed. An example of the GAP4 **Trace Display** is shown in Fig. 10. Here it has been configured to show up to four rows in one column, but it can be convenient to use more rows and multiple columns. In this example it is being used to show a pair of traces, with a plot of their differences below. For each reading the display can show the fluorescence amplitudes, the base calls and, as an inverted histogram, their confidence values. When the **Contig Editor** cursor is moved the traces scroll in register. Conversely, the **Contig Editor** can be scrolled from within the **Trace Display**. As shown here, individual confidence values can be shown on the Information Line at the base of the display and textual data about each reading can be viewed in a separate window. The traces can be zoomed in x and y using the scrollbars at the left edge. The difference plot is invoked using the **Diff button**. As can be seen in this example (bottom panel), in most positions the *signal* is quite low, but in three places there are coincident peaks and troughs, indicating possible mutations. Here these mutations are borne out by the base calls, but as automated in our trace_diff program, such analysis has been very helpful in distinguishing mutations from sequence differences due to base calling errors.

Creating a Consensus Sequence

GAP4 can calculate a consensus sequence and save it to a disk file in *FASTA* or *Experiment* file formats. *FASTA* is useful for programs such as *BLAST*. *Experiment* file format is very close to that of EMBL sequence library entries and can contain the text fields of selected tags added by the user during processing. If users follow our recommendation of making as few changes to their data as possible, the consensus will contain many padding characters, but users can choose to have these removed before the consensus sequence is written to the disk.

Glossary and Abbreviations

BAC Bacterial artificial chromosome used to clone segments of DNA up to 200 kbp.

Base Caller A computer program which interprets the fluorescence intensitites from a sequencing instrument to determine its sequence.

Basecall Confidence Values Numerical values assigned to each base in a sequence reading to predict its reliability. Confidence C = –10*log10(probability of error)

Consensus Sequence Multiple sequence alignments can be represented by a single consensus sequence derived by analyzing the frequency and confidence of the different character types aligned at each position.

Contig An ordered set of overlapping segments of DNA from which a contiguous sequence can be derived.

DNA Sequencing Traces In DNA sequencing, the chains of nucleotides are labeled with fluorescent dyes. The intensity of fluorescence measured as DNA fragments are electrophoresed in a sequencing instrument known as a chromatogram, or, more commonly, trace. The traces are processed to produce the DNA sequence.

DNA Template The segments of DNA inserted into a vector for sequencing. Also known as "fragments" and "inserts."

Experiment Files A file format used to transfer data between sequence assembly processing programs.

Forward Read A DNA sequence obtained from a single sequencing experiment using a primer for the forward strand of DNA.

Gap 4 A computer program for handling DNA sequencing projects.

PREGAP 4 A computer program for preparing DNA trace data for sequence assembly using gap4.

Primer A short (approx 20 bases) segment of single-stranded DNA of known sequence. The Sanger sequencing method and the Polymerase Chain Reaction are both initiated by a primer annealed to the DNA template.

Read-Pair A pair of sequence readings obtained from opposite ends of a DNA sequencing template.

Reading (Gel Reading) A DNA sequence obtained from a single sequencing experiment, typically around 500-800 bp.

Reverse Read A DNA sequence obtained from a single sequencing experiment using a primer for the reverse strand of DNA.

SCF A widely used, non-proprietary file format for storing DNA trace data.

Sequence Assembly The process of arranging a set of overlapping sequence readings into their correct order along the genome.

Sequencing Vectors Vectors designed to aid DNA sequencing.

VECTOR A DNA molecule into which foreign DNA can be inserted for introduction into a new host where it will be replicated, thus producing mass quantities. Depending on the type of vector, foreign DNA of lengths between 1 kb and 2 mb can be inserted.

ZTR The newest and most compact file format for storing trace data.

Suggested Readings

Sequence Assembly

Bonfield, J. K., Smith, K. F., and Staden, R. (1995) A new DNA sequence assembly program, Nucleic Acids Res. 23, 4992–4999.

Green, P. H. (1997) Personal communication.

Huang, X. and Madden, A. (1999) CAP3: A DNA Sequence Assembly Program, Genome Res. 9, 868–877.

Myers, E. W., Jain, M., and Larson, S. (1996) Internal report, University of Arizona, Tucson, AZ.

Staden, R. (1980) A new computer method for the storage and manipulation of DNA gel reading data, Nucleic Acids Res. 8, 3673–3694.

File Formats: SCF, ZTR, Experiment, Fasta Files, and the GAP4 Database

Bonfield, J. K. and Staden, R. (2002) ZTR: A new format for DNA sequence trace data, Bioinformatics 18(1), 3–10.

Bonfield, J. K. and Staden, R. (1996) Experiment files and their application during large-scale sequencing projects, DNA Sequence 6, 109–117.

Dear, S. and Staden, R. (1992) A standard file format for data from DNA sequencing instruments, DNA Sequence 3, 107–110.

Pearson, W. R. (1994) Using the FASTA Program to Search Protein and DNA Sequence Databases, in: Methods in Molecular Biology, (Griffin, A. M. and Griffin, H. G., eds.), vol. 25, Humana Press, Totowa, NJ, pp. 365–389.

Tool Kits

Free Software Foundation, 675 Mass Avenue, Cambridge, MA 02139.

Ousterhout, J. K. (1994) Tcl and the Tk toolkit, Addison-Wesley Publishing Company, Reading, MA.

Other Programs

Haas, S., Vingron, M., Poustka, A., and Wiemann, S. (1998) Primer design for large scale sequencing, Nucleic Acids Res. 26, 3006–3012.

Bonfield, J. K., Rada, C., and Staden, R. (1998) Automated detection of point mutations using flourescent sequence trace subtraction, Nucleic Acids Res. 26, 3404–3409.

Altschul, S. F., Gish, W., Miller, W., Myers, E. W., and Lipman, D. J. (1990) Basic local alignment search tool, J. Mol. Biol. 215, 403–410.

21 OLIGO Primer Analysis Software

John D. Offerman and Wojciech Rychlik

Introduction

Concurrent with the development of the polymerase chain reaction (PCR) in the late 1980s as an essential technique in the molecular biology laboratory, optimal design of PCR primers became an important part of the process. It was soon learned, for example, that inattention to secondary structure in synthetic primers could create primer-dimers and hairpins and could seriously reduce or eliminate the yield of the PCR product. The presence of priming sites in the template other than the intended target—so called *false priming* sites—were also found to interfere with PCR efficiency, by generating unwanted PCR products and *background* on the gel. Furthermore, the efficient PCR experiment required the proper concentrations of salt, buffer, and nucleic acid and the accurate determination of melting temperatures of the primers and the template. Cumbersome calculations were required to produce these values and their complexity often resulted in errors.

With limited success, PCR experimentalists trained their eyes to spot primer dimers, hairpins, and false priming sites in their DNA sequence. Many came to believe that they were exceptionally good at spotting these problems, when, in fact, it was the nature of PCR to proceed, after a fashion, despite poor oligonucleotide design. But most researchers understood early on that the development of a computer program was needed to quickly determine accurate values of oligonucleotide melting temperature (Tm) and to check the oligonucleotide sequence for the presence of secondary structure and PCR targets for the presence of false priming sites.

The first widely used program, OLIGO version 2, was developed by Dr. Wojciech Rychlik while doing PCR research at the University of Kentucky, and offered free through Nucleic Acids Research in 1989. The first commercial program, OLIGO v. 3 for the PC-DOS operating system, was released by Dr. Rychlik in 1989 and distributed through National Biosciences, Inc. (Minneapolis, MN). Version 3 provided both secondary structure and false priming analysis functions, and also aided the researcher in the design and selection of oligonucleotides for DNA sequencing.

Since version 3, there have been a number of competitive commercial applications offered, including several PCR/primer selection modules integrated into larger DNA sequence-analysis programs. These have been theoretical and algorithm-driven.

OLIGO's selection algorithms and assumptions have always been grounded in PCR laboratory research by the author and others, and fully referenced in the OLIGO manual.

Since OLIGO version 3, there have been three more PC as well as three more Macintosh releases of the program. The current OLIGO products are: version 6 for Windows, first released in 1999, and version 6 for Macintosh, released in 1998. New major versions are scheduled for release every 3 years. Single-user licenses provide for use on one to four computers under one principal investigator. Program network licenses are also available that offer from one to any number of simultaneous users of the program. There have been many new processes and procedures introduced to the molecular biology laboratory in the last 15 years, including many improvements to, and permutations of, PCR and DNA sequencing. OLIGO has, concurrently, added a range of new features that aid the researcher in improving the performance of these new tools. The features of OLIGO version 6, why they were needed, and how they simplify and optimize the selection and use of oligonucleotides in the laboratory, will be discussed in this chapter.

Program Organization

OLIGO 6 is organized into several major features and functions: the analysis functions under the **Analyze** menu, the search functions under the **Search** menu, edit/translation functions under the **Edit** menu, the oligo database functions, and the order form. The *Melting Temperature* and the *Internal Stability* windows (*see* Fig. 1), are the main analysis windows that open when a sequence file is loaded. These windows are the organizational center of the program. The melting temperature (Tm) window displays both DNA strands of the sequence, the translated protein sequence, and a histogram of the melting temperatures of every theoretical oligonucleotide in the file. Any oligo can be quickly analyzed in this window as well by selecting it as the **current oligo**, clicking the mouse on the **5' terminus**, and then applying the analysis functions. The current oligo can be selected as the upper (forward) primer by clicking the red UPPER button or lower (reverse) primer by clicking the LOWER button. Also, when primers are selected following the automated primer/probe searches, they are displayed as upper (or lower) primers in the melting temperature window.

The *Internal Stability* window displays free energy of DNA or RNA pentamers throughout the sequence visualizing GC clamps and AT-rich low Tm areas. It also displays the positive strand sequence and marked search-selected oligonucleotides, if any, on the bottom. The *current oligo* sequence, available in the **Analysis** menu, is highlighted (*see* Fig. 1).

PCR Primer Search and Selection

PCR has proven to be an amazingly robust laboratory procedure over the years, and has found a prominent place in most laboratories working with nucleic acids. However, there are a number of oligonucleotide design and other factors that can interfere with the optimization of the PCR process. OLIGO 6 searches DNA and RNA sequences to eliminate from consideration oligonucleotides that exhibit one or more of these interfering factors. Specifically, the program performs as many as nine different subsearches, eliminating oligonucleotides in each subsearch that fail to meet the threshold set by the program or the user. Potential PCR problems due to oligonucleotide design, and the subsearches that OLIGO uses to discard oligonucleotides containing these flaws, are discussed below.

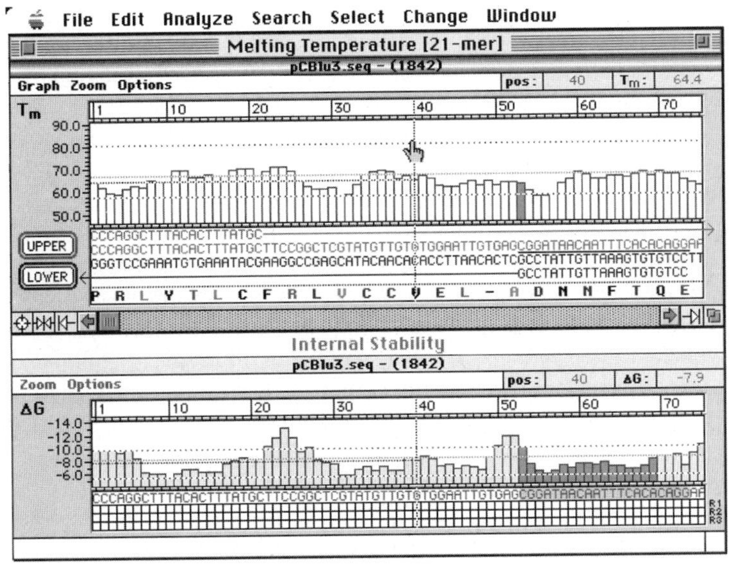

Fig. 1. The Melting Temperature and Internal Stability windows.

The most serious oligonucleotides design deficiency for PCR is certainly the stable 3' dimer, where the 3' end of the PCR primer binds strongly to itself or to its companion primer. If a 3' dimer is sufficiently stable so that it preferentially hybridizes to itself or its mate, rather than to the intended target on the template, the PCR product yield can be reduced essentially to zero.

Hairpin structures in oligonucleotides can also greatly reduce PCR yield. OLIGO discards primers with 3' dimers or hairpins (duplexes) based on the stability of the secondary structure, measured by the ΔG value, or alternatively, by the length of contiguous matching nucleotides. Because PCR has been shown to be adversely affected by 3' duplexes, OLIGO also includes a setting for the number of nucleotides on the 3' end to be checked (so as not to eliminate otherwise suitable oligonucleotides containing harmless 5' dimers). OLIGO performs the above checks in the **Duplex-free Oligonucleotides** subsearch. Another subsearch specifically for hairpins is also executed; this subsearch considers loop size while testing the entire set of oligonucleotides for hairpins. This subsearch is important in the search for *Hybridization Probes.*

OLIGO then searches for and discards *highly specific* oligonucleotides. Research by the author has determined that oligonucleotides that are too stable on their 3' ends (irrespective of dimer formation), are more likely to false prime randomly on unknown nucleic acid templates. This is because a shorter number of matching nucleotides on a stable 3' end are required to initiate priming on a false target than are required with a less stable 3' end. Statistically, a stable 3' end will create more false priming and unwanted background on the PCR gel.

The early convention was to design oligonucleotides with a *GC clamp* on the 3' end, in order to *clamp down* the oligo on its target. This practice would add stability but compromise specificity. OLIGO selects primers that are both specific and stable. It does this by employing subsearches that: 1) discard oligos that have excessively stable 3' ends, and 2) discard oligonucleotides that do not have one or more stable sections (a GC clamp) at the 5' end or central segment of the oligonucleotide. So the remaining oligonucleotides, following the **Highly Specific Oligos** subsearch and the **GC Clamp** subsearch, are both specific to their target and will hybridize with sufficient stability to permit priming.

False priming can create unwanted background, but are particularly problematic when they occur in or near the intended PCR product. OLIGO's false priming subsearch compares the 3' end of each potential primer with the active sequence file and discards any that are found to have false priming sites. Using another false priming subsearch, the researcher can also check each potential primer against other DNA or RNA sequence files on their computer. This is the **Continue False Priming Search in Other Files** subsearch. OLIGO employs a novel algorithm, developed experimentally, called the *priming efficiency* calculation, to predict priming and false priming. Priming efficiency (PE), determines whether an oligonucleotides will prime on a given site under a given set of conditions. This important feature of the OLIGO program is discussed on p. 351 (*see* Subheading "Priming Efficiency Measurements for Priming and False Priming").

The next subsearch used in OLIGO's PCR primer search is for *Oligonucleotides within Selected Stability Limits*. Oligonucleotides that have a high, but not excessively high, Tm, work best in PCR reactions. This subsearch discards all oligonucleotides that fall outside this Tm window. Another important feature of optimal PCR primers is the matching of Tms. False priming and unnecessarily high annealing temperatures can result when a PCR pair is selected having an excessive Tm difference. OLIGO automatically matches Tms of primer pairs following the PCR search and selection process by dropping nucleotides from the primer with the higher Tm until the Tms or priming efficiencies are in close agreement.

Homooligomers (i.e., GGGGG) and sequence repeats (i.e., GCGCGC), are eliminated in the **Eliminate Oligomers/Sequence Repeats** subsearch. Homooligomers and sequence repeat structure in primers can cause misalignment on the target and subsequently impair annealing kinetics or even cause synthesis of PCR products of different size.

The final subsearch of the PCR primer selection process, **Eliminate Frequent Oligos**, discards oligonucleotides that have 3' ends that occur frequently in the GenBank nucleic acid database. OLIGO 6 includes a table of frequencies of all 4,096 or 16,384 combinations of 6 or 7 nucleotide segments, respectively. When this subsearch is run, the 6-mer (or 7-mer) 3' ends of oligonucleotides in the active sequence are checked against the frequency table. As with the **Highly Specific Oligos** subsearch, this search further reduces the likelihood of false priming and background when using genomic DNA for PCR analysis.

However, when the PCR template is not to be run in genomic DNA or other complex substrates, the user can click off the **Complex Substrate** box in the search parameters window. This turns off the **Highly Specific Oligos** and **Frequent Oligos** subsearches, thereby saving otherwise suitable primers for use in plasmid DNA and other simple substrates.

When the researcher loads his/her nucleic acid sequence file of interest and selects the **Search for Primers and Probes - PCR Primers: Compatible Pairs**, the program activates the above subsearches and once the search is initiated, they are sequentially executed. When the full (composite) PCR search is complete, only those oligos that have met or exceeded the threshold settings for each subsearch are selected.

The upper (forward) and lower (reverse) primers are then compared for cross-compatibility (no 3' end interaction) and all cross-compatible pairs are compiled in the *Primer Pairs* table. Clicking on a given pair in the table brings up the PCR window, which displays PCR conditions, Tms, and other data for those primers, including a proportional schematic of the PCR product on the template. Primer pairs in the table can be sorted by position on the template, PCR product size, GC content, or PCR optimal annealing temperature. The functioning of each subsearch used in the PCR primer search depends, of course, on the threshold settings of the search parameters by which they are controlled. Because of the complexity of these parameters and the challenge of knowing where they should be set for any given search, the program includes an **expert system**. The program also allows the user to simply select one of 6 search stringencies ranging from *very high* to *very low*. The program will then insert the settings for each search parameter, based on the current understanding of the PCR process. However, users can set their own values for one or more of the search parameters and lock them in, overriding the expert system. In this way the program has maximum flexibility and adaptability to the users particular needs, while still being very easy to use.

Depending on the size and nature of nucleic acid sequences, it is hard to predict how many optimal primer pairs can be returned from a given search. The program includes a feature that will automatically drop the search stringency down one level and search again, if no primer pairs are found in the first search. A complete record of each PCR primer search is saved in the *Search Results* window. This includes all search settings and the specific results of each subsearch and primer pairings.

The Oligonucleotide Database and Order Form

The modern PCR laboratory can design and synthesize hundreds of primers per week or more. Keeping track of them all and their target templates can be a challenge, and transferring oligo sequences to synthesis providers can be cumbersome and time-consuming. The oligonucleotide database and order form features in OLIGO 6 can save researchers time and minimize transposition and data-maintenance errors. When a primers and probes search is selected in the OLIGO program, the primer database can be downloaded in a single operation into an oligonucleotide database window, using the **Import** function. Further, an entire group of primers selected in an OLIGO search can be imported in a single operation by using the **Multiplex Primers** option, as shown in Fig. 2.

When oligonucleotides are imported into a database, they are automatically dated and named. The naming convention is useful in keeping track of important oligonucleotide characteristics. The name includes the sequence file (template) name or the GenBank accession number, the position of the oligonucleotides on the template, whether it's an upper or lower primer, and its length.

In the database, the program also reports an oligonucleotide's Tm, its 3' end dimer status, its sequence, priming efficiency, and whether they are new entries in the database. There is also a reference field for the researcher to record pertinent notes. This window also allows for primer multiplexing, as discussed in the following.

Oligonucleotides in the database can be selected for export to an oligonucleotide order form. In the order form, the researcher can set up a template that includes ship to:/bill to: ordering information, including such specifications as synthesis scale, puri-

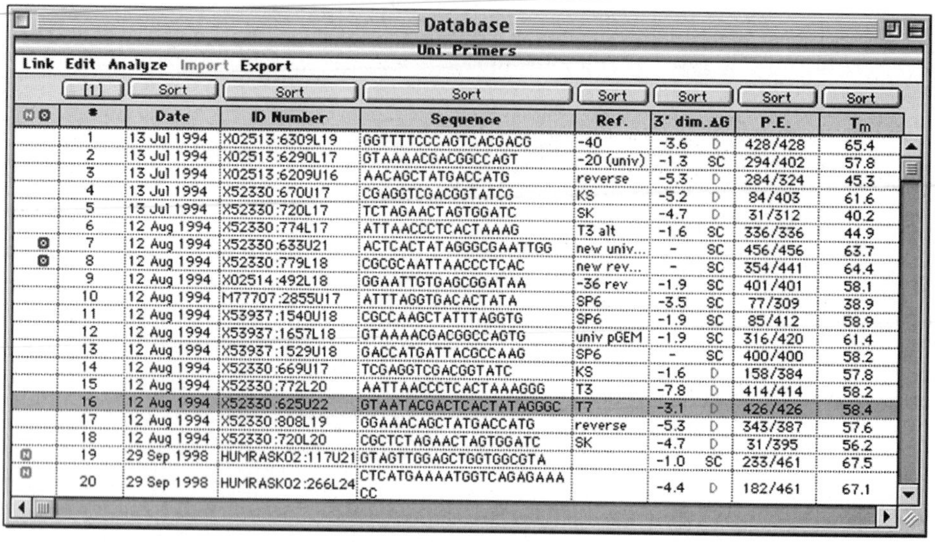

	#	Date	ID Number	Sequence	Ref.	3' dim. ΔG		P.E.	Tm
	1	13 Jul 1994	X02513:6309L19	GGTTTTCCCAGTCACGACG	-40	-3.6	D	428/428	65.4
	2	13 Jul 1994	X02513:6290L17	GTAAAACGACGGCCAGT	-20 (univ)	-1.3	SC	294/402	57.8
	3	13 Jul 1994	X02513:6209U16	AACAGCTATGACCATG	reverse	-5.3	D	284/324	45.3
	4	13 Jul 1994	X52330:670U17	CGAGGTCGACGGTATCG	KS	-5.2	D	84/403	61.6
	5	13 Jul 1994	X52330:720L17	TCTAGAACTAGTGGATC	SK	-4.7	D	31/312	40.2
	6	12 Aug 1994	X52330:774L17	ATTAACCCTCACTAAAG	T3 alt	-1.6	SC	336/336	44.9
	7	12 Aug 1994	X52330:633U21	ACTCACTATAGGGCGAATTGG	new univ...	-	SC	456/456	63.7
	8	12 Aug 1994	X52330:779L18	CGCGCAATTAACCCTCAC	new rev...	-	SC	354/441	64.4
	9	12 Aug 1994	X02514:492L18	GGAATTGTGAGCGGATAA	-36 rev	-1.9	SC	401/401	58.1
	10	12 Aug 1994	M77707:2855U17	ATTTAGGTGACACTATA	SP6	-3.5	SC	77/309	38.9
	11	12 Aug 1994	X53937:1540U18	CGCCAAGCTATTTAGGTG	SP6	-1.9	SC	85/412	58.9
	12	12 Aug 1994	X53937:1657L18	GTAAAACGACGGCCAGTG	univ pGEM	-1.9	SC	316/420	61.4
	13	12 Aug 1994	X53937:1529U18	GACCATGATTACGCCAAG	SP6	-	SC	400/400	58.2
	14	12 Aug 1994	X52330:669U17	TCGAGGTCGACGGTATC	KS	-1.6	D	158/384	57.8
	15	12 Aug 1994	X52330:772L20	AATTAACCCTCACTAAAGGG	T3	-7.8	D	414/414	58.2
	16	12 Aug 1994	X52330:625U22	GTAATACGACTCACTATAGGGC	T7	-3.1	D	426/426	58.4
	17	12 Aug 1994	X52330:808L19	GGAAACAGCTATGACCATG	reverse	-5.3	D	343/387	57.6
	18	12 Aug 1994	X52330:720L20	CGCTCTAGAACTAGTGGATC	SK	-4.7	D	31/395	56.2
	19	29 Sep 1998	HUMRASK02:117U21	GTAGTTGGAGCTGGTGGCGTA		-1.0	SC	233/461	67.5
	20	29 Sep 1998	HUMRASK02:266L24	CTCATGAAAATGGTCAGAGAAACC		-4.4	D	182/461	67.1

Fig. 2. Oligonucleotide Database window.

fication method, and end modifications. Then, with each synthesis order, one need only export the oligonucleotide sequences to be ordered from the database to the order form, which can then be faxed or e-mailed to the synthesis provider.

Multiplex PCR Design

PCR researchers often wish to amplify multiple PCR products in the same tube, in genetic test development or in other applications where operational efficiency is needed. In multiplex primer applications, it is necessary that all primers going into a PCR reaction be cross compatible, (dimers will not form between any 3' ends).

OLIGO 6 includes two multiplex primer selection features. One is designed for the selection of multiplex primers from a single gene or sequence file, such as the TaqMan probes selection. This multiplex selection feature is included under the **Analyze** menu. The second, more commonly used, multiplex feature provides for the selection of multiplex primers from two or more genes/exons (in separate sequence files). Users load and search target sequences for optimal PCR primers and then download them into an oligonucleotide database as described earlier. Downloading several primers can be accomplished using the **Import – Multiplex Primers** menu selection.

When primer groups from each sequence have been loaded into a database, the actual multiplex process can be initiated. The user selects a candidate primer from gene sequence #1, and then clicks **Analyze Multiplex**. This checks the 3' end of this primer against all the other primers in the database. The primers that are compatible with the multiplexed primer are identified with a *C* (in the **3' dimer Δ G** column of the database) and noncompatible primers with *NC*, along with the numeric value of free energy (Δ G). The second multiplex primer is then selected from the *C* (compatible) group, and multiplexed. Now, all remaining primers displaying a *C* are compatible with both primers #1 and #2. This process is continued until all the desired multiplex primers (all cross-compatible in all combinations) are selected.

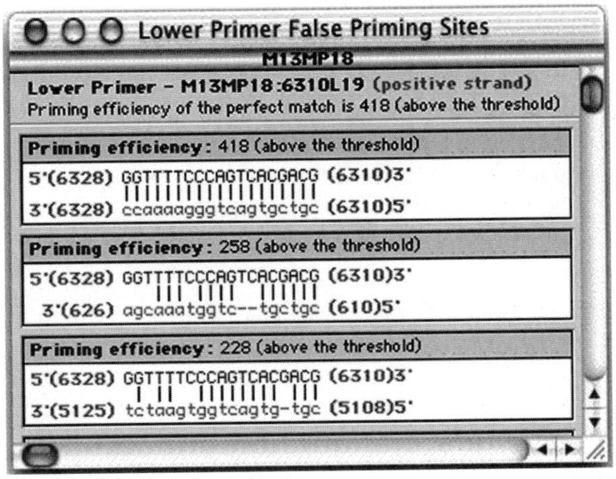

Fig. 3. False Priming Sites window. The site with priming efficiency of 258 points is the experimentally confirmed strongest false priming site of the universal M13 forward primer.

Numerous working multiplex PCR primer sets have been designed using the OLIGO 6 program. The best results in the design of large multiplexes are achieved by downloading as many optimal primers from each gene sequence as possible. Quite frequently, certain multiplex primer selections will prove to be incompatible with too many of the other primers in the database. When this occurs, the experienced user will deselect that problem primer and select another.

Priming Efficiency Measurements for Priming and False Priming

In early versions of OLIGO, and in most other programs even today, the search for false priming sites was (and is) carried out by comparing the 3' ends of potential primers with the template sequence to identify exact complementarity of 4, 5, 6, or (n) nucleotides. While this remains a simple search to perform, it is of limited use in determining whether a primer will actually false prime at a given site. For example, three complementary bases at the 3' end, followed by a mismatch, followed by 4 more complementary bases would be missed by the program as a false priming site when, in fact, it could false prime effectively.

The concept of *priming efficiency* was introduced to provide an accurate way to predict false priming. The proprietary algorithm takes into account mismatches, bulges, and loops and their positions relative to the 3' end of the primer. Priming efficiency (PE) is simple in concept, and is represented by a single number for each primer on a given target. A 21-mer with an average GC content of 50%, fully complementary with its target (no mismatches), will have a priming efficiency number of approx 400. A similar 30 mer will have a PE of approx 500. When such primers contain mismatches with a given target, such that they will marginally hybridize and prime, the priming efficiency will be approx 200 (*see* Fig. 3).

Priming efficiency is obviously useful in accurately predicting false priming. It has also proven valuable in the selection of *consensus primers* and *unique primers*, and it has been effective in selecting sequencing primers from a library of previously synthesized oligonucleotides. This eliminates the time and expense of a new synthesis.

Sequencing Primer and Hybridization Probe Selection

Along with its search for PCR primers, OLIGO includes comprehensive searches for DNA sequencing primers and hybridization probes. These searches are also initiated from the *Search for Primers & Probes* window.

When the sequencing primer search is chosen, the same subsearch group is selected as for PCR. The **Frequent Oligos** subsearch is not required for optimal sequencing primer performance. Although the subsearches used are almost the same as those for the PCR primer search, the threshold values are different in certain respects. First, there are advantages to using a sequencing primer with a very high Tm, so unlike PCR, the sequencing primer search selects high Tm oligos, including those with the highest Tms. The rest of the parameters are set close to those used for PCR, because the hybridization and priming requirements for both are very similar. After selecting the **Sequencing Primers** search, the user will set search stringency in the *Parameters* window as in the PCR search. The user will also check the **Complex Substrate** box (usual set off for sequencing in plasmids) and which strand (+ or –) to select the primer.

Once the search is initiated, it proceeds as it does with the PCR search. But the chosen (optimal) sequencing primers are displayed in a *Selected Oligos* window. This window displays the oligonucleotide number, position on the template, Tm, 3' terminal stability (specificity), and GC clamp stability. The user can sort by any one of these columns of data and, thereby further refine the primer selection to his or her liking. Sequencing primers can be exported to an oligonuclotide database and order form as can PCR primers.

The hybridization probe search is similar to the PCR and sequencing primer search, except that those subsearches that are designed to optimize the priming process are turned off, and those designed to enhance hybridization are turned on (and turned up). The probe search includes the **GC Clamp**, the **Stability**, the **Homo-oligomer/Sequence Repeats**, and the **Hairpin-free** subsearches. Once the probe search is complete, optimal probes are, again, listed in the *Selected Oligos* window. When a particular probe is selected, it is highlighted as the upper (or lower) primer on the OLIGO melting temperature screen. Along with standard probe selection, OLIGO can also be used to select optimal TaqMan probes and primers for this popular application.

Mutagenesis Primer Design

Site-specific mutagenesis is a very popular technique in the molecular biology laboratory. Perhaps the easiest way to insert a specific mutation into a gene is using primers containing mutagenic oligonuceotides. OLIGO 6 includes a mutagenesis feature that simplifies the design of the mutagenesis experiment. The *Mutagenesis* window displays a single line of 50–100+ bases at a time for viewing or editing, depending on the computer resolution. The user can switch from a nucleic acid sequence to a protein sequence in this edit mode by re-positioning the cursor. This window also displays the most stable hairpin, codon probabilities, and several other characteristics of the sequence displayed (*see* Fig. 4).

In addition to the Toolbar information, the window displays: sequence length, active reading frame, degeneracy, Tm, Δ G, hairpin loop Tm, and Δ G, reverse translation method, codon frequency for a given organism, nucleotide sequence with position numbers, translated protein sequence, the strongest hairpin loop of the displayed

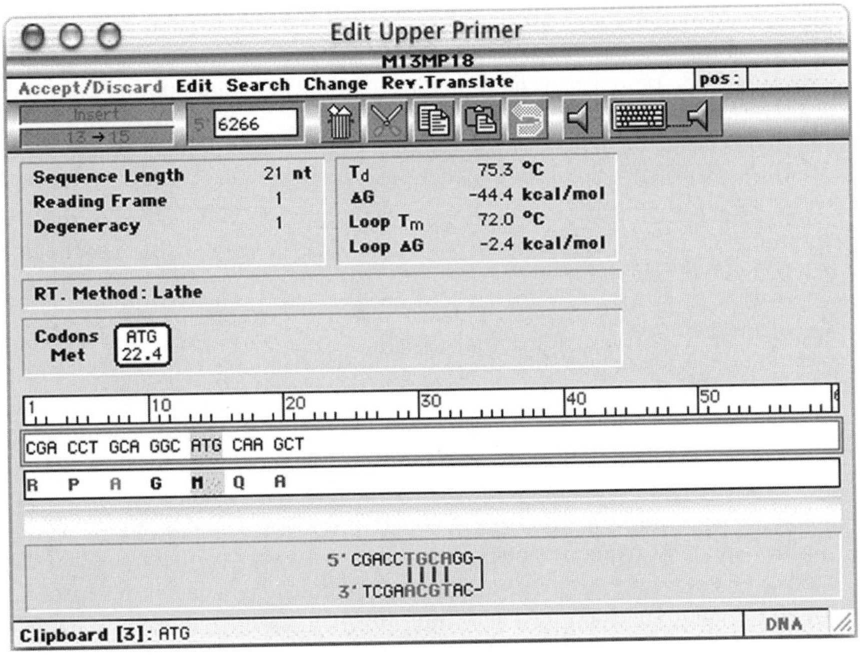

Fig. 4. Mutagenesis Edit window.

sequence, and the size and contents of the Clipboard; the sequence to be inserted with the **Paste** command (*see* Fig. 4).

The various colors of residues in the amino acid sequence represent the codon frequencies of each residue according to the codon table selected in the **Change** submenu. The information displayed in the mutagenesis window, allow the user to efficiently design mutagenetic primers with confidence.

Consensus Primers and Unique Primers Selection

PCR has become a universal tool used by molecular biologists, and is now being used in a wide variety of creative ways. Among them are consensus primer PCR and unique primer PCR. The **Consensus Primers** option is useful when the researcher wishes to select and synthesize a primer pair that can be used to amplify a number of homologous genes. Again, selecting a consensus primer pair would be difficult without the priming efficiency algorithm.

To begin the consensus primer selection function in OLIGO 6, the user sets up the standard PCR search, setting the search stringency and the minimum priming efficiency for the consensus primers in the parameters window. The files are then selected from which the consensus primers are to be selected, by clicking the **Consensus Primers** button on the main search window and then adding the files using the *Select Files* window. The search proceeds in the manner of the standard PCR search. The primer pairs displayed in the primer pairs window following the completion of the search will, by definition, prime in each of the consensus sequences with a priming efficiency at or above the threshold value set in the parameters window.

Unique primer selection is the reverse of the consensus primer-selection process. Here, the user wishes to selectively prime and amplify one particular gene in a PCR reaction from a number of homologous genes. The unique primer selection search can also be useful to differentiate between closely related bacterial or viral strains, or any group of closely related organisms. To initiate unique primer selection, the **Continue <False Priming> Search in Other Files** subsearch is selected instead of the **Consensus Primer** button. Here, it is the priming efficiency threshold for false priming (set in the parameters window) that determines whether a particular primer is selected as a *unique* primer.

Peripheral and Support Functions

In addition to the core features of the OLIGO program described earlier, a number of support features are included. For example, OLIGO 6, includes a search for restriction enzymes, with a cut table and map, a search for a sequence string (including wobbles and termination codons), a search for palindromes and a search for stems of hairpin loops. This specialized hairpin loop search can play a helpful role in the design of synthetic genes. It also has a number of functions that have been added to work with protein sequences. Protein sequences can be loaded into the oligo program, reverse translated (four different methods of reverse translation are provided, including degenerate and codon table methods) with oligo degeneracies displayed, and the protein sequence searched for potential restriction sites.

Under the **Analyze** menu, hybridization time can be calculated and the concentrations and volumes of the primers, PCR product, or the entire sequence can be quickly determined. The internal stability (free energy of pentamer subsequences) of an oligo can also be analyzed, assisting the user in choosing the ideal internal design of a primer-relatively unstable on the 3' end and stable elsewhere. DNA and protein sequence files from a number of formats open easily in OLIGO, including GenBank and PIR files, FASTA, and FASTN along with files from word processors saved as text files.

Suggested Readings

Oligo

Rychlik, W. and Rhoads, R. E. (1989) A computer program for choosing optimal oligonucleotides for filter hybridization, sequencing and in vitro amplification of DNA, Nucleic Acids Res. 17, 8543–8551.

Rychlik, W. (1999) Oligo Primer Analysis Software, v. 6, Molecular Biology Insights, Cascade, CO.

PCR Primer Search and Selection

Breslauer, K. J., Frank, R., Blocker, H., and Markey, L. A. (1986) Predicting DNA duplex stability from the base sequence, Proc. Natl. Acad. Sci. USA 83, 3746–3750.

Freier, S. M., Kierzek, R., Jaeger, J. A., Sugimoto, N., Caruthers, M. H., Neilson, T., and Turner, D. H. (1986) Improved free-energy parameters for predictions of RNA duplex stability, Proc. Natl. Acad. Sci. USA 83, 9373–9377.

Rychlik, W. (1995) Priming Efficiency in Polymerase Chain Reaction, Biotechniques 18, 84–90.

Priming Efficiency Measurements for Priming and False Priming

Steffens, D. L., Sutter, S. L., and Roemer, S. C. (1993) An alternate universal forward primer for improved automated DNA sequencing of M13, BioTechniques 15, 580–582.

22 Statistical Modeling of DNA Sequences and Patterns

Gautam B. Singh

Introduction

Of fundamental importance in bioinformatics are the mathematical models designed for modeling the biological sequence and to use that as the basis for detection of patterns. Patterns at the various levels of abstractions are the drivers of genomics and proteomics research. Starting at the fine level of granularity, the patterns are comprised of the splice sites, binding sites, and domains. These are subsequently utilized for the definition of patterns at a higher level of abstraction such as introns, exons, repetitive DNA, and locus-control regions.

DNA sequences are often modeled as probabilistic phenomena, with the patterns of interest being defined as samples drawn from the underlying random process. For example, the underlying DNA sequence is modeled as a Markov chain of random variables taking on the values (A, C, T, G). Given this underlying assumption, one may then model a splice site as a function P that assigns a sample sequence, S, of 8–10 nucleotides a value equivalent to their probability of being a splice site.

A pattern-detection algorithm would consider each substring from a DNA sequence that could potentially be a splice site and assign a probability to each candidate. The substrings scoring a high value may be further investigated using the appropriate wet-bench approaches. Although this is a simple illustration, it does bring forth an important point. The underlying models that define the DNA sequences and their accuracy are ultimately a determinant of the accuracy with which the patterns are subsequently detected. The modeling of the sequences and that of patterns are two complementary objectives. Sequence models provide a basis for establishing the significance of patterns observed, while the pattern models help us look for specific motifs that are of functional significance. Therefore we must consider both of these issues.

Sequence Models

The two main sequence models are the Independent Identically Distributed and Markov Chain models. Sequence models are needed to represent the background stochastic processes in a manner that enables one to analytically justify the significance of the observation. To provide an analogy, determinng the sequence model is similar to determining the probability of obtaining a *head* (H) while tossing a coin. (For a fair coin, this probability would be ½). In general however, we may estimate this probability by studying the strings of the heads and tail sequences that a given coin has produced in the past. Similarly, given the DNA sequence(s), we may induce the underlying model that represents the maximally likely automaton that produced the sequence.

Let us continue our analogy further. After the coin model has been induced, it would be possible to predict the probability of observing coin tossing pattern such as "three heads in a row," etc. Similarly, after inducing a DNA sequence model, it would be possible to deduce the expected frequency of occurrence of a DNA sequence pattern. This is helpful in classifying patterns in terms of their relative abundance in a sequence specific manner.

Independent Identically Distributed (IID)

The simplest of all the sequence models is the Independent Identically Distributed or IID model. In this model, each of the four nucleotides is considered to occur independent of each other. Furthermore, the probability of the occurrence of a given nucleotide at a given location is identical to the probability of its occurrence at another location. Thus, for example, assume that the sequence is defined using an IID random variable. It can take on the possible values defined by the DNA alphabet $\Sigma = (A, C, T, G)$. In this case, defining the individual probability values (p_A, p_C, p_T, and p_G) specifies the complete model for the sequence. The values may in turn be computed simply by considering the prevalence of each base in the given sequence. In statistical terms, the maximally likely or ML estimator for probability of occurrence of a given base is X is simply $\frac{n_x}{L}$ where n_x is the frequency of occurrence of the base X in a sequence of length L.

In general, the maximal likely estimator for the parameters may be used. Using the ML estimation, the probability of each base α, may be estimated as shown in Equation 1:

$$\hat{P}(\alpha) = \frac{n_\alpha(L)}{|L|} \qquad \text{[Eq. 1]}$$

This simply counts the relative frequency of nucleotide α in a sequence of length L. This estimator has the advantage of simplicity and usually works well when $|L|$ is large. It may not work well when $|L|$ is small.

Given the Model M_{IID} has been induced from the sequence data, the probability of an occurrence of a pattern x may be computed as shown in Equation 2.

$$P(x \mid M_{IID}) = \prod_{i=1,\dots,n(x)} P(x_i) \qquad \text{[Eq. 2]}$$

where $P(x_i)$ is the probability of nucleotide x_i at position i along the pattern. The model assumes that the parameters (probability of each of the four nucleotides) are independent of the position along the pattern.

Example 1:

Consider the following DNA Sequence of Length = 25.

SEQ = AACGT CTCTA TCATG CCAGG ATCTG

In this case the IID model parameters are $\left(\frac{6}{25}, \frac{7}{25}, \frac{7}{25}, \frac{5}{25}\right)$. This corresponds to the maximally likely estimation of the occurrence of each of the four bases given the alphabet S = (A, C, T, G). These are thus the IID parameters for the background sequence. The probability of finding the pattern CAAT on this sequence would be equal to $p_C \cdot p_A \cdot p_A \cdot p_T$ or $\left(\frac{7}{25}\right)\cdot\left(\frac{6}{25}\right)\cdot\left(\frac{6}{25}\right)\cdot\left(\frac{7}{25}\right) = 0.0045$.

Markov Chain Models

In a Markov chain the value taken by a random variable is dependent upon the value(s) taken by the random variable in a previous state(s). The number of historical states that influence the value of the random variable at a given location along the sequence is also known as the degree of the Markov process. The first-degree Markov chain model has $|\Sigma| + |\Sigma|^2$ parameters, corresponding to the individual nucleotide frequencies as well as dinucleotide frequencies. In this manner, this model permits a position to be dependent on the previous position. However, the frequencies are modeled in a position-invariant manner and thus may not be suitable for modeling signals.

This sequence model M is defined on the sample space Σ^* and assigns a probability to every sequence x of length $n(x)$ on Σ^* (*see* Equation 3):

$$P(x \mid M) = P_1(x_1) \prod_{i=2,\ldots,n(x)} P_2(x_i|x_{i-1}) \qquad \text{[Eq. 3]}$$

where P_1 is a probability function on Σ that models the distribution of α's at the first position in the sequence and P_2 is the conditional probability function on $\Sigma \times \Sigma$ that models the distribution of β's at position $i > 1$ on the alphabet symbol α at position $i-1$.

The parameter estimation using the *Maximally Likely* estimator proceeds in a manner analogous to the IID model estimation. The transition probabilities are however estimated using Bayes theorem as shown in Equation 4:

$$P_2(\beta|\alpha) = \frac{P(\alpha\beta)}{P(\alpha)} \qquad \text{[Eq. 4]}$$

In this manner, the conditional transitional probabilities of finding a base β at position (i) given that the base α was found at position ($i-1$) is computed by finding the abundance of the dinucleotide $\alpha\beta$ as a fraction of the abundance of the nucleotide α.

Example 2:

Consider once again the same 25-Nucleotide Sequence as shown earlier.

SEQ = AACGT CTCTA TCATG CCAGG ATCTG

While considering the first-degree Markov chain models, the 4-parameters corresponding to individual nucleotide frequencies, and the 4^2 parameters corresponding to the dinucleotide frequencies need to be computed. The Σ parameters are the same as before = $\left(\frac{6}{25}, \frac{7}{25}, \frac{7}{25}, \frac{5}{25}\right)$.

In order to compute P_2, the $\Sigma \times \Sigma$ conditional probability values, the dinucleotide frequencies and probabilities are computed from the sequence data. The dinucleotide frequencies and the probabilities are shown below (with the parenthesized numbers representing the probabilities):

freq (AA) = 1 $\left(\frac{1}{24}\right)$	freq (AC) = 1 $\left(\frac{1}{24}\right)$	freq (AT) = 3 $\left(\frac{3}{24}\right)$	freq (AG) = 1 $\left(\frac{1}{24}\right)$
freq (CA) = 2 $\left(\frac{2}{24}\right)$	freq (CC) = 1 $\left(\frac{1}{24}\right)$	freq (CT) = 3 $\left(\frac{3}{24}\right)$	freq (CG) = 1 $\left(\frac{1}{24}\right)$
freq (TA) = 1 $\left(\frac{1}{24}\right)$	freq (TC) = 4 $\left(\frac{4}{24}\right)$	freq (TT) = 0 $\left(\frac{0}{24}\right)$	freq (TG) = 2 $\left(\frac{1}{24}\right)$
freq (GA) = 1 $\left(\frac{1}{24}\right)$	freq (GC) = 1 $\left(\frac{1}{24}\right)$	freq (GT) = 1 $\left(\frac{1}{24}\right)$	freq (GG) = 1 $\left(\frac{1}{24}\right)$

Table 1
Conditional Nucleotide Probabilities for the 25-nt Example Sequence

$\downarrow S_{i-1}$ $S_i \rightarrow$	A	C	T	G
A	25/144	25/144	75/144	25/144
C	50/168	25/168	75/168	25/168
T	25/168	100/168	0	50/168
G	25/120	25/120	25/120	25/120

Table 2
Patterns and Probabilities Deduced Using IID and Markov Models

	Probability	
Pattern	*IID Model*	*Markov Model*
ATTTA	2.57×10^{-3}	2.0×10^{-3}
TGTTTTG	1.06×10^{-4}	1.64×10^{-4}
TTTTGGGG	1.40×10^{-5}	4.153×10^{-5}
CTTTTACCAAT	5.181×10^{-7}	7.596×10^{-7}
TCTTTATCTTTGCG	6.545×10^{-9}	1.968×10^{-9}
CTGAACATTGATGCA	1.238×10^{-9}	3.19×10^{-9}

The conditional probabilities are next computed using the Bayes theorem (*see* Equation 4). For example, the probability of finding "C" at position (i+1) given that an "A" has been found at position (i) is $P(C \mid A) = \frac{p_{AC}}{p_A} = \frac{1/24}{6/25} = \frac{25}{144}$. For large sequences the conditional probability $P(S_i|S_{i-1})$ approaches

$$\frac{freq(S_iS_{i-1})}{freq(S_{i-1})}$$

The conditional probabilities for the example sequence are shown in Table 1. Using these model parameters, the probability of finding the pattern CAAT in this sequence using the first order Markov model of the underlying sequence would be equal to $P(C) \cdot P(A|C) \cdot P(A|A) \cdot P(T|A)$ or $\left(\frac{7}{25}\right) \cdot \left(\frac{50}{168}\right) \cdot \left(\frac{25}{144}\right) \cdot \left(\frac{75}{144}\right) = 0.0075$. This is contrast to the ID sequence model probability of the pattern being 0.0045.

Example 3:

The sequence models described above were induced from a 76kb sequence from the beta-globin gene (L22754+HUMHBB). The pattern probabilities of the following patterns were computed for both sequence models. The patterns were carefully selected to be of varying lengths. A PERL program (*markov.pl*) for inducing sequence models and computing pattern probabilities is provided on the accompanying CD-ROM. Table 2 depicts the patterns as well as the probabilities of their occurrence deduced under the IID and Markov models.

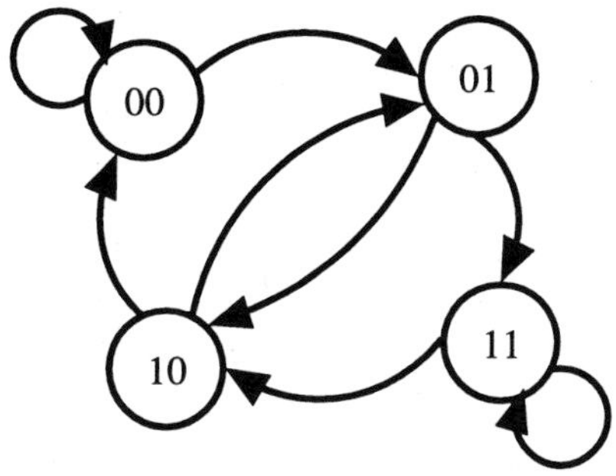

Fig. 1. The set of possibe transitions in a 2nd. Order Markov chain. Note that only 8 nonzero probabilities need to be estimated for this model, as not all of the 16 transitions are possible.

Higher-Order Markov Models

Higher-order Markov chains have been described. For example, the *nth* order Markov process has a memeory of n, and thus the occurrence of a nucleotide depends on the previous n nucloetides. The probability of observing a sequence x is defined in Equation 5, in a manner similar to the first order Markov chains.

$$P(x \mid M) = P_1(x_1) \prod_{i=2,\ldots,n(x)} P_2(x_i|x_{i-1},\ldots,x_{i-n}) \qquad \text{[Eq. 5]}$$

An *nth* order Markov chain over some alphabet A is equivalent to a first order Markov chain over the alphabet A^n of n-tuples. This follows from calculating the probability of A and B, given B is the probability of A given B, i.e., $P(x_k|x_{k-1},\ldots,x_{k-n}) = P(x_k,x_{k-1},\ldots,x_{k-n+1}|x_{k-1},\ldots,x_{k-n})$. That is, the probability of x_k given the n-tuple ending in x_{k-1} is equal to the probability of the n-tuple ending in x_k given the n-tuple ends in x_{k-1}.

Consider the simple example of a second order Markov chain for sequences of only two different characters "0" and "1". A sequence is translated to a sequence of pairs, so the sequence 011101 becomes 01-11-11-10-01. All transitions are not possible in this model, as only two different pairs can follow a given letter. For example, the state 01 can only be followed by the states 10 and 11, and not by the state 00 or 01. The set of possible transitions are shown in Fig. 1.

A second order model for DNA is equivalent to a first order model over the Σ^2 alphabet that is comprised of the 16 dinucleotedes. A sequence of five bases, CGACG would be treated as a chain of four states, CG-GA-AC-CG, with each symbol being drawn from the Σ^2 alphabet. Nonetheless, the framework of high order models is often preferable for analysis of higher order stochastic sequences.

Pattern Models

In the previous section our goal was to characterize the "sea" of data in which these biological "nuggets" of information are hidden. In contrast, our goal in this section is to model the nuggets themselves. Thus, this section describes the statistical modeling procedures for DNA patterns. We now focus on modeling motifs that are associated with certain biological functions.

Table 3
Weight Matrix for TATAA Box

T	6	49	1	56	6	22	6	20
C	14	6	0	0	3	0	1	2
A	8	4	58	4	51	38	53	30
G	32	1	1	0	0	0	0	8

There are a growing number of well-established patterns that we may wish to model and search for in DNA sequences. Often these patterns of functional significance are brought forth after an alignment of sequences belonging to a particular family. Such a multiple sequence alignment is often interspersed with gaps of varying sizes. However, there are sections in the final alignment that are free of gaps in all of the sequences. These fixed-size, ungapped, aligned regions represent the types of patterns that are modeled to permit their identification in an anonymous segment of DNA. The statistical techniques that may be employed for developing such a closed-form representation of a set of patterns are described in the following.

Weight Matrices

A DNA sequence matrix is a set of fixed-length DNA sequence segments aligned with respect to an experimentally determined biologically significant site. The columns of a DNA sequence matrix are numbered with respect to the biological site, usually starting with a negative number. A DNA sequence motif can be defined as a matrix of depth 4 utilizing a *cut-off* value. The 4-column/mononucleotide matrix description of a genetic signal is based on the assumptions that the motif is of fixed length, and that each nucleotide is independently recognized by a *trans*-acting mechanism. For example, the frequency matrix has been reported for the TATAA box (*see* Table 3).

If a set of aligned signal sequences of length L corresponds to the functional signal under consideration, then $F = [f_{bi}]$, $(b \in \Sigma),(j = 1.. L)$ is the nucleotide frequency matrix, where f_{bi} is the absolute frequency of occurrence of the *b-th* type of the nucleotide out of the set $\Sigma = (A, C, G, T)$ at the *i-th* position along the functional site.

The frequency matrix may be utilized for developing an ungapped score model when searching for sites in a sequence. Typically a log-odds scoring scheme is utilized for purpose of searching for pattern x of length L as shown in Equation 6. The quantity $e_i(b)$ specifies the probability of observing base b at position i. It is defined using the frequency matrix such as the one shown above. The quantity $q(b)$ represents the background probability for the base b.

$$S = \sum_{l=1}^{L} \log \frac{e_i(x_i)}{q(x_i)} \quad \text{[Eq. 6]}$$

The elements of $\log \frac{e_i(x_i)}{q(x_i)}$

behave like a scoring matrix similar to the PAM and BLOSUM matrices. The term Position Specific Scoring Matrix (PSSM) is often used to define the pattern search with matrix. A PSSM can be used to search for a match in a longer sequence by evaluating a score S_j, for each starting point j in the sequence from position 1 to $(N-L+1)$ where L is the length of the PSSM.

A method for converting the frequency matrix into a weight matrix has been proposed by Bucher (1990). The weights at a given position are proportional to the logarithm of the observed base frequencies. These are increased by a small term that prevents the logarithm of zero and minimizes sampling errors. The weight matrix is computed as shown in Equation 7. The term e_{bi} represents the expected frequency of base b at position i, c_i a column specific constant, and s, a smoothing percentage.

$$W(b,i) = \ln\left(\frac{f_{bi}}{e_{bi}} + \frac{s}{100}\right) + c_i \qquad \text{[Eq. 7]}$$

These optimized weight matrices can be used to search for functional signals in the nucleotide sequences. Any nucleotide fragment of length L is analyzed and tested for assignment to the proper functional signal. A matching score of

$$\sum_{i=1}^{L} W(b_i,i)$$

is assigned to the nucleotide position being examined along the sequence. In the search formulation, b_i is the base at position i along the oligonuclotide sequence, and $W(b_i,i)$ represents the corresponding weight-matrix entry for base b_i occurring along the ith. position in the motif.

Profiles are similarly defined for modeling functional motifs in amino-acid sequences. A profile is a scoring matrix $M(p,a)$ comprised of 21 columns and N rows, where N is the length of the motif. The first 20 scores represent the weight for each individual amino acid, and the 21st column specifys the cost associated with an insertion or deletion at that position. The value of the profile for amino acid "a" defined for position p is

$$M(a,p) = \sum_{b=1}^{20} W(b,p) \times Y(b,a)$$

where $Y(b,a)$ is Dayhoff's matrix and $W(b,p)$ is the weight for the appearance of amino acid b at position p. The position specific weight is defined by $\log(f[b,p]/N)$, or the frequency of occurrence of the amino acid as b as a fraction of the total N sequences utilized for construction of the profile, with a frequency of 1 being used for any amino acid that does not appear at position p.

Position-Dependent Markov Models

Markov models have been considered as a means to define the background DNA sequence. This model enabled us to define the probability of a nucleotide conditioned upon the nucleotides occurring in the previous position. However the modeled dependency is position-invariant. A position-dependent Markov model may be utilized for the representation of a sequence signal or motif. This model is defined on the sample space Σ^n and assigns a probability to every sequence x on Σ^n (*see* Equation 8):

$$P(x \mid M) = P_1(x_1) \prod_{i=2,\ldots,n} P_{2,i}(x_i \mid x_{i-1}) \qquad \text{[Eq. 8]}$$

This model has $|\Sigma| + (n-1)*|\Sigma|^2$ parameters. This model permits position-specific dependencies on the previous position by allowing the association of a unique set of transition probabilities with each position along the signal. This model assumes that sufficient training data is available to induce position specific Markov probabilities.

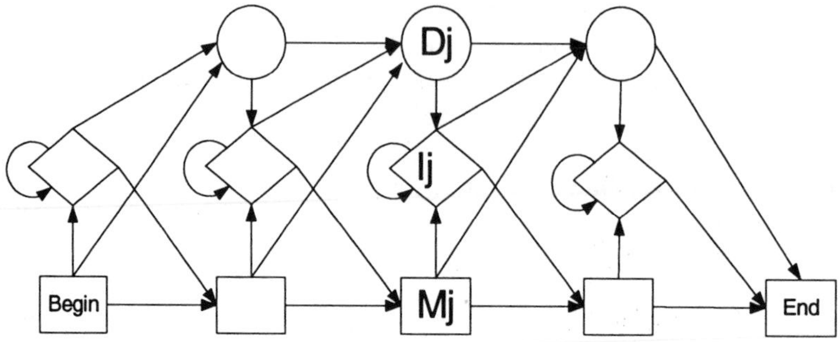

Fig. 2. A profile HMM utilizes the insert (diamond) and delete (circle) states. The delete states are *silent* and are not associated with the emissions of any symbols. The parameters of a profile HMM are learned from a multiple sequence alignment.

Hidden Markov Models

There are several extensions to the classical Markov chains. The Hidden Markov models (HMM) are one such extension. The rationale for building a HMM comes from the observation that as we search a sequence, our observations could arise from a model characterizing a pattern, or from a model that characterizes the background. Hidden Markov DNA sequence models are developed to characterize a model as an *island* within the sea of *nonisland* DNA. The Markov chain characterizing the *island* and *nonisland* need to be present within the same model, with the ability to switch from one chain to the other. In this manner, a HMM utilizes a set of hidden states with an emission of the symbols associated with each state.

From a symbol-generation perspective, the state sequence executed by the model is not observed. Thus, the state sequence must be estimated from the observed symbols generated by the model. From a mathematical perspective, the HMM is characterized by the following parameters:

- Σ is an alphabet of symbols.
- Q is a set of states that emit symbols from the alphabet Σ.
- $A = (a_{kl})$ is $|Q| \times |Q|$ matrix of state transition probabilities.
- $E = (e_k[b])$ is a $|Q| \times |\Sigma|$ matrix of emission probabilities.

Although a general topology of a fully connected HMM allows state transitions from any state to any other, this structure is almost never used. This is primarily due to the inadequacy of the available data for training a model with the large number of parameters needed for a fully connected HMM for any practical problem. Often, the over-generalized model produces sub-optimal results due to the lack of training data. Consequently, more restrictive HMMs that rely on the problem characteristics to suitably reduce the model complexity and the number of model parameters that are needed are utilized. One such model is defined to be the *profile-HMM*, which is induced from a multiple sequence alignment. The structure of a profile HMM is shown in Fig. 2.

The parameters of a profile HMM are estimated using the sample alignments of the sequences used for training. The transitions and the emissions of the symbols in the alignment are used to derive the Maximally Likely (ML) estimator of the HMM parameters. These values are assigned as shown in Equation 9. The actual transition and emission frequencies A_{kl} and $E_k(a)$ respectively, are used to define the transition and emission probabilities, A_{kl} and $E_k(a)$. Furthermore, pseudo-counts are added to the observed frequencies to avoid zero probabilities. The simplest pseudo-count method is Laplace's rule, which requires adding one to each frequency.

$$a_{kl} = \frac{A_{kl}}{\sum_X A_{kX}} \quad \text{and} \quad e_k(a) = \frac{E_k(a)}{\sum_Y E_k(Y)} \qquad \text{[Eq. 9]}$$

Example 4:

Consider the following multiple sequence alignment defined on amino acid residues for five globin sequences.

```
HBA_HUMAN        ... VGA--HAGEY ...
HBB_HUMAN        ... V----NVDEV ...
GLB3_CHITP       ... VKG------D ...
LGB2_LUPLU       ... FNA--NIPKH ...
GLB1_GLYDI       ... IAGADNGAGV ...
Match States         ***  *****
```

A HMM with 8 match states may be constructed based on this alignment. The residues **AD** in **GLB1_GLYD1** are treated as insertions, with respect to the consensus. In match state 1, the emission probabilities are (using Laplace's rule):

$$e_{M1}(V) = \frac{4}{25},\ e_{M1}(F) = \frac{2}{25},\ e_{M1}(I) = \frac{2}{25},\ \text{and } e_{M1}(a) = \frac{1}{25} \text{ for all others}$$

The transition probabilities from match state 1 are as follows:

$$a_{M1,M2} = \frac{5}{8},\ a_{M1,D2} = \frac{2}{8},\ a_{M1,I1} = \frac{1}{8},$$

corresponding to the one deletion in **HBB_HUMAN**, and no insertions. The emission probabilities for the state I_1 will be all equal to (1/20). The Viterbi algorithm yields the optimal path through the HMM, as well as the log-odds score for observing a given sequence using an HMM. It is commonly used to match a profile HMM to a sequence. The Viterbi algorithm is a recursively defined optimization procedure that is quite similar to the dynamic programming algorithm used for sequence alignment.

The various scores for matching a sequence to the profile HMM are defined in Equation 10. In this formulation, $V_j^M(i)$ represents the log-odds score of the best path matching subsequence $x_{1...i}$ to the submodel up to state j, ending with x_i being emitted by state M_j. Similarly $V_j^I(i)$ is the score of the best path ending in x_i being emitted by I_j, and $V_j^D(i)$ for the best path ending in state D_j.

$$V_j^M(i) = \log\frac{e_{M_j}(x_i)}{q_{x_i}} + \max\begin{cases} V_{j-1}^M(i-1) + \log a_{M_{j-1}M_j} \\ V_{j-1}^I(i-1) + \log a_{I_{j-1}M_j} \\ V_{j-1}^D(i-1) + \log a_{D_{j-1}M_j} \end{cases}$$

$$V_j^I(i) = \log\frac{e_{I_j}(x_i)}{q_{x_i}} + \max\begin{cases} V_j^M(i-1) + \log a_{M_jM_j} \\ V_j^I(i-1) + \log a_{I_jM_j} \\ V_j^D(i-1) + \log a_{D_jM_j} \end{cases} \qquad \text{[Eq. 10]}$$

$$V_j^D(i) = \max\begin{cases} V_{j-1}^M(i) + \log a_{M_jD_j} \\ V_{j-1}^I(i) + \log a_{I_{j-1}D_j} \\ V_{j-1}^D(i) + \log a_{D_{j-1}D_j} \end{cases}$$

Generally, there is no emission score $e_{I_j}(x_i)$ in the equation for $V_j^I(i)$ as it is often assumed that the emission distribution from the insert states I_j is the same as the background distribution. Also, the $D \rightarrow I$ and $I \rightarrow D$ transition terms may not be present, and those transition probabilities may be very close to zero.

Mixture Models

Mixture models are defined in relation to the sample space Σ^n. The mixture model M is a mixture of component models $M_i, i = 1,..., k$, and assigns a probability to every sequence x on Σ^n defined in Equation 11.

$$P(x \mid M) = \prod_{i=1,...,k} P(x \mid M_i)\, P(M_i) \qquad \text{[Eq. 11]}$$

where $P(M_i)$ is the weight of component model M_i in the mixture. Any probability model may be used as a component model, as the mixture model may have component models of a different type.

A mixture model is best suited for modeling data that is comprised of subgroups. In this manner, an observed data set may be assigned to a class if a high probability is assigned to it by at least one component model of sufficient weight. This may be considered to be a stochastic analog of a weighted OR function.

Consider for example a set D of short aligned sequences corresponding to some functional site. Further assume that we have a reason to believe that the observed sequences are characterized to belong to two categories. The goal to establish if an observed sequence x is similar to set D, may be achived by developing a mixture model for the set D. The mixture model is comprised of two constituent sub-models that are represented in the set.

Goodness of Fit

As described in the previous sections, there are often several methodologies for developing a model for a pattern. Consequently, the natural question to ask is: is there is a systematic methodology that may be utilized to evaluate which of the possible models is best suited for the data at hand? We may utilize the *goodness of fit* measure, described below, to estimate how well a given model represents the observed dataset. Generally, all data items d in the training, or another data set, D are considered to be independent.

Under the independence assumption, the likelihood that dataset D may be estimated as a product of all the probabilities of individual observations d is:

$$P(D \mid M) = \prod_{d \in D} P(d \mid M) \qquad \text{[Eq. 12]}$$

Rewriting Equation 11 in its log-likelihood form:

$$\log P(D \mid M) = \prod_{d \in D} \log P(d \mid M) \qquad \text{[Eq. 13]}$$

This is often desirable to prevent numeric underflows that are likely to occur when small numbers are multiplied. In this manner, one may choose a model instance M^* that best fits the dataset D according to the maximum likelihood principle defined in Equation 14.

$$M^* = \arg\max_M (P[D \mid M]) = \arg\max_M (P[D \mid M]) \qquad \text{[Eq. 14]}$$

Example Problems

The following examples and their solutions review the key concepts of this chapter.

1. Compute the background parameters for the following sequence:

```
ATTAG GCACG CATTA TAATG GGCAC CCGGA AATAA CCAGA GTTAC GGCCA
```

a. Assuming an IID model? Answer:

```
IID parameters

A : 17 (0.34)
B : 12 (0.24)
C : 12 (0.24)
T : 9 (0.18)
```

b. Assuming a 1st Order Markov model? Answer:

```
1-st Order Markov Probabilities Dinucleotide Frequencies

AA  4  (0.0816326530612245)
CA  5  (0.102040816326531)
AC  4  (0.0816326530612245)
CC  4  (0.0816326530612245)
GA  2  (0.0408163265306122)
TT  3  (0.0612244897959184)
AG  3  (0.0612244897959184)
GC  4  (0.0816326530612245)
CG  3  (0.0612244897959184)
GG  5  (0.102040816326531)
AT  5  (0.102040816326531)
TA  5  (0.102040816326531)
CT  0  (0)
TC  0  (0)
GT  1  (0.0204081632653061)
TG  1  (0.0204081632653061)
Prob X|Y is derived from Prob (XY)/Prob (Y)

Markov Probabilities (1-st Order)
A|C  5/12  (0.425170068027211)
C|A  4/17  (0.240096038415366)
C|C  4/12  (0.340136054421769)
A|G  2/12  (0.170068027210884)
T|T  3/9   (0.340136054421769)
G|A  3/17  (0.180072028811525)
C|G  4/12  (0.340136054421769)
G|C  3/12  (0.255102040816327)
G|G  5/12  (0.425170068027211)
A|T  5/9   (0.566893424036281)
T|A  5/17  (0.300120048019208)
C|T  0/9   (0)
T|C  0/12  (0)
T|G  1/12  (0.0850340136054422)
G|T  1/9   (0.113378684807256)
A|A  4/17  (0.240096038415366)
```

c. How many parameters would need to be estimated if a 2nd Order Markov model is assumed for the background sequence? Answer:

```
A second order Markov Process for modeling a sequence will have
the following transitions:

AA|AA AT|AA AC|AA AG|AA
CA|CC CC|CC CT|CC CG|CC
```

```
TA|TT TC|TT TT|TT TG|TT
GA|GG GC|GG GT|GG GG|GG
TA|AT TC|AT TT|AT TG|AT
CA|AC CC|AC CT|AC CG|AC
GA|AG GC|AG GT|AG GG|AG
....
....

64 transition probabilities will be defined, as
there are only 4 valid transitions from any of
the 16 states. (Note that we would have 16x6 = 256
possible transitions if all transitions were valid.
However, transitions such as AT|CG, etc. are not valid).
```

2. Compute the match scores (defined in Equation 5) generated by searching the above sequence using the weight matrix described for TATAA-box described in Table 1. Assume IID background model.

```
Pattern Length = 8
zero th order Markov model for the sequence
is used for the bakground computation.

A : 17 (0.34)
C : 12 (0.24)
T : 9  (0.18)
G : 12 (0.24)
------------------------------------------
zeros in the score matrix were changed to 1
as Eq. 5 requires taking a log (e-i(x-i)/q(x-i)).

Scores as computed using Equation (5):
Score[i] represents the score for pattern starting at position
"i".
Score[0]  = -11.164
Score[1]  =  -7.167
Score[2]  = -11.868
Score[3]  = -15.445
Score[4]  = -12.798
Score[5]  =  -5.578
Score[6]  =  -8.025
Score[7]  =  -5.836
Score[8]  =  -5.412
Score[9]  =   2.331
Score[10]  =   0.462
Score[11]  =  -1.943
Score[12]  =   3.863
Score[13]  =  -7.968
Score[14]  =  -6.633
Score[15]  =  -9.617
Score[16]  = -15.343
Score[17]  = -11.227
Score[18]  = -14.293
Score[19]  = -13.711
Score[20]  = -13.771
Score[21]  =  -9.305
Score[22]  = -13.624
Score[23]  = -11.255
Score[24]  =  -7.058
Score[25]  =  -3.244
Score[26]  =  -5.771
Score[27]  =   0.400
Score[28]  =  -2.515
```

```
Score[29]  =   -3.093
Score[30]  =  -10.722
Score[31]  =   -3.992
Score[32]  =   -7.183
Score[33]  =   -9.399
Score[34]  =  -10.319
Score[35]  =   -4.364
Score[36]  =   -8.227
Score[37]  =   -6.236
Score[38]  =   -5.188
Score[39]  =   -9.458
Score[40]  =  -10.690
Score[41]  =  -10.789

Maximum Score at Location 12.
Maximum Score = 3.863(12)
```

3. Use the HMMER program (URL provided in Subheading "Suggested Reading") to compute profile HMM for the following alignment.

```
A   C   G   A   C   G   A   C   G   A   C   G   .
.   .   G   G   G   A   A   A   G   G   .   G   A
ACG..AAATTT.A
```

a. Apply the Viterbi algorithm to compute the probability of observing the sequence "AATTAATTAA" from this model.

```
Step 1. Sequences were represented in Stockholm alignment format.

        #STOCKHOLM 1.0
        seq1 ACGACGACGACG.
        seq1 ..GGGAAAGG.GA
        seq1 ACG..AAATTT.A

Step 2. Program hmmbuild was run. This produced the following
        alignment HMM

HMMER 2.0 [2. 2g]
NAME  prb
LENG  13
ALPH  Nucleic
RF      no
CS      no
MAP   yes
COM   hmmbuild prb.hmm prb.slx
NSEQ  3
DATE  Fri Oct 12 14:38:44 2001
CKSUM 7915
XT      -9967     -1 -1000 -1000  -9967     -1 -9967     -1
NULT      -1  -9967
NULE       0      0      0      0
HMM        A      C      G      T
         m->m   m->i   m->d   i->m   i->i   d->m   d->d   b->m   m->e
         -412      *  -2011
     1   1007   -592   -592   -592      1
     -      0      0      0      0
     -    -21  -6687  -7729   -894  -1115   -701  -1378   -412      *
     2   -592   1007   -592   -592      2
     -      0      0      0      0
     -    -21  -6687  -7729   -894  -1115   -701  -1378      *      *
     3   -807   -807   1193   -807      3
     -      0      0      0      0
     -   -442  -7108  -1962   -894  -1115   -701  -1378      *      *
```

```
4    450    -592   387   -592     4
-      0       0     0      0
-    -21   -6687 -7729   -894  -1115 -1435    -666     *     *
5   -592     450   387   -592     5
-      0       0     0      0
-    -21   -6687 -7729   -894  -1115  -380   -2112     *     *
6    749    -807   234   -807     6
-      0       0     0      0
-    -16   -7108 -8150   -894  -1115  -701   -1378     *     *
7   1193    -807  -807   -807     7
-      0       0     0      0
-    -16   -7108 -8150   -894  -1115  -701   -1378     *     *
8    749     234  -807   -807     8
-      0       0     0      0
-    -16   -7108 -8150   -894  -1115  -701   -1378     *     *
9   -807    -807   792    171     9
-      0       0     0      0
-    -16   -7108 -8150   -894  -1115  -701   -1378     *     *
10   234    -807   171    171    10
-      0       0     0      0
-   -442   -7108 -1962   -894  -1115  -701   -1378     *     *
11  -592     450  -592    387    11
-      0       0     0      0
-   -629   -6687 -1541   -894  -1115  -380   -2112     *     *
12  -592    -592  1007   -592    12
-      0       0     0      0
-    -33   -6021 -7064   -894  -1115  -380   -2112     *     *
13   986    -571  -571   -571    13
-      *       *     *      *
-      *       *     *      *      *     *       *     *     0
//
```

b. Validate your results by comparing it to probability values generated by HMMER package.

```
Step 3. To evaluate tbe probability of matching a sequence to an
        profile HMM, we can run the program hmmpfam. This produced
        the following result for AATTAATTAA. The match score was
        -15.4 (E-value of 2, with anything less than 10 being
        considered significant match).

hmmpfam - search one or more sequences against HMM database
HMMER 2.2g (August 2001)
Copyright (C) 1992-2001 HHMI/Washington University School of Medi-
cine
Freely distributed under the GNU General Public License (GPL)
- - - - - - - - - - - - - - - - - - - - - - - - - - - - - - - - -
-
HMM file:           prb.hmm
Sequence file:               prb.seq
- - - - - - - - - - - - - - - - - - - - - - - - - - - - - - - - -
-
Query sequence: Query
Accession:      [none]
Description:    Sequence

Scores for sequence family classification score includes all do-
mains):
Model    Description                          Score    E-value  N
-------  -----------                          -----    ------- ---
prb                                           -15.4          2   1
```

```
Parsed for domains:
    Model     Domain  seq-f seq-t      hmm-f hmm-t      score  E-value
    -------- ------- ----- -----      ----- -----      -----  -------
    prb        1/1       1    10 []       1    13 []   -15.4        2

    Alignments of top-scoring domains:
    prb: domain 1 of 1, from 1 to 10: score -15.4, E = 2
                          *->acgacaaagacga<-*
                             a     aa++  a
           Query     1     AAT--TAATTA-A     10

    //
```

Glossary and Abbreviations

Alternative Hypothesis The alternative hypothesis, H1, is the conclusion that a statistical hypothesis test tries to establish. For example, in a new drug trial, the alternative hypothesis might be that the new drug has a different effect, on average, compared to that of the current drug.

Bayes' Theorem Bayes' Theorem allows new information to be used to update the conditional probability of an event.

Binomial Distribution A binomial random variable is typically used to model the number of successes in a series of trials, for example, the number of 'heads' occurring when a coin is tossed 100 times.

Conditional Probability The process of estimating the probability given the state of the environment. For example, the probability of an event E may be P_1 under one environment C_1, written as $P(E|C_1) = P_1$. While, the probability of the same event E may be P_2 under a different environment C_2, denoted as $P(E|C_2) = P_2$. In many situations, once more information becomes available, we are able to revise our estimates for the probability of further outcomes or events happening.

Continuous Random Variable A continuous random variable is characterized by its ability to take on an infinite number of possible values. Continuous random variables are usually measurements.

Cumulative Distribution Function All random variables (discrete and continuous) have a cumulative distribution function. It is a function giving the probability that the random variable X is less than or equal to x, for a given x.

Discrete Random Variable A discrete random variable may only take on a countable number of distinct values such as 0,1,2,3,... If a random variable can take only a finite number of distinct values, then it is discrete by definition. Discrete random variables are usually (but not always) counts.

Event An event is any collection of outcomes of an experiment.

Expected Value The expected value (or population mean) of a random variable indicates its average or central value. It is a useful summary value (a number) of the variable's distribution.

Independent Events Two events are independent if the occurrence of one of the events gives us no information about whether or not the other event will occur; that is, the events have no influence on each other.

Kolmogorov-Smirnov Test A test is used to establish if the sample of data is consistent with a specified distribution function. Alternatively, used to establish if two samples of data come from the same distribution.

Mutually Exclusive Events Two events are considered mutually exclusive (or disjoint) if it is impossible for them to occur together.

Normal Distribution Normal distributions is a probability distribution function of a class of continuous random variables. A normal random variable is capable of assuming any value on the real line.

Null Hypothesis The null hypothesis, H0, represents the default theory that is believed to be true or is the basis for argument. For example, in clinical trials, the null hypothesis might be that the new drug is no better, on average, than the current drug. In this case, we would write H0: there is no difference between the two drugs on average.

Poisson Distribution Poisson distribution is a probability distribution function for a class of discrete random variables. The corresponding Poisson random variable is the count of the number of events that occur in a certain time interval or spatial area. For example, the number of patterns found in a fixed size widows along the biological sequence.

Probability A probability provides a quantitative estimation of how likely or unlikely is the occurrence of a particular event. Probability is conventionally expressed on a scale from 0 to 1.

Probability Density Function Is defined for a continuous random variable. It may be integrated to obtain the probability that the random variable takes a value in a given interval.

Probability Distribution Is defined for discrete random variable. It is a list of probabilities associated with each of its possible outcome. It is also called the probability function or the probability mass function.

***p*-Value** The probability value (*p*-value) of a statistical hypothesis test is the probability of getting a value of the test statistic as extreme as or more extreme than that observed by chance alone, if the null hypothesis H0, is true.

Random Variable The outcome of an experiment need not be a number. For example, the outcome coin-toss is 'heads' or 'tails'. We often want to represent the outcomes as numbers. A random variable is a function that associates a unique numerical value with every outcome.

Significance Level The significance level of a statistical hypothesis test is a fixed probability of wrongly rejecting the null hypothesis H0, if it is in fact true.

Subjective Probability A subjective probability of an individual's estimation of how likely is the occurrence of a particular event. It is not based on any precise computation - simply a reasonable assessment by a knowledgeable person.

Test Statistic A test statistic is a quantity calculated from our sample of data. Its value is used to decide whether or not the null hypothesis should be rejected in our hypothesis test.

Variance The (population) variance of a random variable is a non-negative number providing an estimation of how widely spread the values of the random variable are likely to be. The larger the value of variance, the more scattered the observations.

Suggested Readings

Hidden Markov Models

Haussler, D., Krogh, A., Mian, I. S. and Sjolander, K. Protein modeling using hidden Markov models: analysis of globins, in: Proceedings of 26th Annual Hawaii

International Conference on System Sciences, IEEE Computer Society Press, vol. 1, pp. 792–802..
Krogh, A. An introduction to hidden Markov models for biological sequences, in: Computational Biology: Pattern analysis and machine learning methods, (Salzberg, S., Searls, D., and Kasif, S., eds.), Elsevier Press.
Ohler, U., Harbeck, S., Niemann, H., Noth, E., and Reese, M. G. (1999) Interpolated Markov chains for eukaryotic promoter recognition, Bioinformatics 15, 362–369.

HMMER (*see* Website: http://www.genetics.wustl.edu/eddy)
HMMPro (*see* Website: http://www.netid.com)
SAM (*see* Website: http://www.cse.ucsc.edu/research/compbio/sam.html)

Sequence Alignment

Smith, T. and Waterman, M. (1981) Identification of common molecular subsequences, J. Mol. Biol. 147, 195–197.

Quantitative Methods

Besemer, J. and Borodovsky, M. (1999) Heuristic approach to deriving models for gene finding, Nucleic Acids Res. 27, 3911–3920.
Feller, W. (1971) An introduction to probability theory and applications, vol. II, John Wiley and Sons, New York, NY.
Hayes, W. S. and Borodovsky, M. (1998) How to interpret an anonymous bacterial genome: machine learning approach to gene identification, Genome Res. 8, 1154–1171.

Weight Matrix and Profiles

Bucher, P. (1990) Weight matrix descriptions of four eukaryotic RNA polymerase II promoter elements derived from 502 unrelated promoter sequences, J. Mol. Biol. 212, 563–578.
Gribskov, M. and Veretnik, S. (1996) Identification of sequence patterns with profile analysis, Methods Enzymol. 266,198–212.
Gribskov, M., McLachlan, A., and Eisenberg, D. (1987) Profile analysis: Detection of distantly related protein, Proc. Natl. Acad. Sci. USA 87, 4355–4358,
Staden R. (1988) Methods to define and locate patterns of motifs in sequences, Comp. Appl. Biosci. 4, 53–60.
Staden R. (1988) Methods for calculating the probabilities of finding patterns in sequences, Comp. Appl. Biosci. 5, 89–96.

Substitution Matrices

Dayhoff, M. A., Schwartz, R. M., and Orcutt, B. C. (1978) A model for evolutionary change in proteins, in: Atlas of Protein Sequence and Structure, pp. 345–352.
Henikoff, S. and Henikoff, J. G. (1992) Amino acid substitution matrices from protein blocks, Proc. Natl. Acad. Sci. USA 89, 10,915–10,919.

23 Statistical Mining of the Matrix Attachment Regions in Genomic Sequences

Gautam B. Singh

Introduction

The functional role of a cell can be thought of as reflecting the partitioning of genes into compartments of those that can be expressed and those that cannot be expressed. Every cell contains the same genetic information and expresses the same subset of genes for basic cellular function. There is a second set of genes that are uniquely expressed in each cell type. The biological mechanism by which such differential gene expression is achieved and mediated is brought about by the presence of simple DNA sequence patterns that are predominantly found within the neighborhood of the gene locus. These simple sequence patterns are embedded within the majority of nuclear noncoding DNA (i.e., in direct contrast to the 2% of the genome that corresponds to the protein coding regions).

Noncoding DNA is comprised of special sequences of regulatory importance such as introns, promoters, enhancers, Matrix Association Regions (MARs), and repetitive elements. Many of these regions contain patterns that represent functional control points for cell-specific or differential gene expression. Others such as repetitive DNA sequence elements may serve as a biological clock. These and numerous other examples indicate that the patterns embedded in the eukaryote DNA may play a critical role for viability.

MARs: Background and Data Models

The Matrix or Scaffold Attachment regions are relatively short (100–1000 bp long) sequences that anchor the chromatin loops to the nuclear matrix. MARs are often associated with the origins of replication (ORI). They usually possess a concentrated area of transcription factor binding sites. Approximately 100,000 matrix attachment sites are believed to exist in the mammalian nucleus, where ~30,000–40,000 serve as ORIs. MARs have been observed to flank the ends of genic domains encompassing various transcriptional units. It has also been shown that MARs bring together the transcriptionally active regions of chromatin such that transcription is initiated in the region of the chromosome that coincides with the surface of nuclear matrix.

There are two potentiative states, i.e., open or closed, and two classes of potentiated open euchromatin, i.e., constitutive and tissue/cell-specific facultative. The constitutive class, e.g., those of the housekeeping genic domains, always maintain that segment of the genome in a transcriptionally favorable open chromatin conformation. In contrast, the tissue/cell-specific facultative class impose the open conformation onto a segment of the genome in a tissue/cell-specific manner. The two potentiative states, ready/open or off/closed, are correlated with the presence or absence of multiple factors interacting with element(s) that are far distal of their respective gene-specific promoters and enhancers at regions of locus control.

To date, three classes of elements that act as regions of locus control have been identified. This suggests that potentiation can be achieved by multiple and/or redundant means. The classes of elements are the Matrix Attachment Regions/Scaffold Attachment Regions (MARs/SARs); Specialized Chromatin Structures (SCSs); and Locus Control Regions (LCRs). These elements provide a dominant chromatin opening function that is an absolute requisite for transcription of this segment of the genome. In this manner phenotype is ultimately defined by gene potentiation.

MARs often flank the ends of genic domains encompassing various genic units. It is reasonable to propose that the remaining 30,000–35,000 pairs of the 100,000 MARs in each cell anchor the paired ends of the approx 12,000–30,000 genic domains to the nuclear matrix. It is likely that it is not a simple coincidence that this is also the number of genes transcribed in each cell. If MARs act, or participate as regions of locus control, then it is likely that their reiteration throughout the genome provides a means to specifically tag genes for potentiation in that cell.

The Human Genome Project (HGP) relies upon the availability of databases and tools that enable easy access, analysis, and comparison of genome information. Developing computational tools and algorithms that can assist in analysis, interpretation, and discovery of knowledge contained within these databases is critical. Specifically, these tools are expected to focus on completing the transcript map and understanding the functional significance of the sequenced genes. It is anticipated that elements of locus control, like MARs, will be sought during this phase given their key role in genetic processes and their localization to functional chromatin domains. Thus, a means to model these markers so that they could be placed on the genome sequence map would have significant ramifications.

Data mining and knowledge discovery techniques can be applied to genomic sequences to detect elements of locus control. MARs are one such type of locus-control element. Our limited knowledge of MARs has hampered formulating their detection using classical pattern recognition strategies where the existence of lower level constituent elements is used to establish the presence of a higher level functional block. However, MAR detection can be accomplished using the statistical estimation of "interestingness" of a sample. This detection strategy is of general utility for the detection of other classes of regulatory signals where a limited data set is available for describing the functional elements.

MARs have been experimentally defined for several gene loci, including, the chicken lysozyme gene, human interferon-β (IFN-β) gene, human β-globin gene, chicken α-globin gene, p53, and the human protamine gene cluster. Several motifs that characterize MARs have emerged, although a MAR consensus sequence is not apparent. The motifs that are currently utilized are functionally categorized and represented as AND-OR patterns described in the following.

The following characteristics of DNA known to be associated with the presence of Matrix Association Regions is summarized in Table 1.

- The Origin of Replication (ORI): It has been established that replication is associated with the nuclear matrix, and the origins of replication share the ATTA, ATTTA, and ATTTTA motifs.
- Curved DNA: Curved DNA has been identified at or near several matrix attachment sites and has been involved with DNA-protein interaction, such as recombination, replication and transcription. Optimal curvature is expected for sequences with repeats of the motif, $AAAAn_7AAAn_7AAAA$ as well as the motif *TTTAAA*.
- Kinked DNA: Kinked DNA is typified by the presence of copies of the dinucleotide TG, CA, or TA that are separated by 2-4 or 9-12 nucleotides. For example, kinked DNA is recognized by the motif TAn_3TGn_3CA, with TA, TG and CA occurring in any order.
- Topoisomerase II sites: It has been shown that Topoisomerase II binding and cleavage sites are also present near the sites of nuclear attachment. Vertebrate and Drosophila topoisomerase II consensus sequence motifs can be used to identify regions of matrix attachment.
- AT-Rich Sequences: Typically many MARs contain stretches of regularly spaced AT-rich sequences in a periodic manner.
- TG-Rich Sequences: Some T-G rich spans are indicative of MARs. These regions are abundant in the 3' UTR of a number of genes and may act as recombination signals.
- Consensus Motif: The sequence TCTTTAATTTCTAATATATTTAGAA defined as the nuclear matrix STAB-1 binding motif.
- ATC Rule: ATC rule (a stretch of 20 or more occurrences of H, i.e., A or T or C). The ATC rule was used in the analysis of Rice A1-Sh2 region by some researchers. This rule has shown to be an effective indicator of regions with marked helix destabilization potential.
- Bipartite Signal: A bipartite sequence signature has been reported to be associated with the MARs. This is composed of two degenerate sequences AATAAYAA and AWWRTAANNWWGNNNC within a close proximity.
- A-Box, T-Box, etc., and other motifs that have been associated with MARs.

Their sequence interdependency is not known, but in most cases multiple motifs are utilized to create a functional MAR. Our current state of analysis makes it clear that at least three and possibly four independent types of MARs can be detected. These are MARs utilized as ORIs, (identified by the ORI rule), AT-rich MARs (identified by the AT-Rich rule and ATC rule) typified by lysozyme, or β-interferon genes. MARs that are not AT-Rich as exemplified by those of the protamine locus and the MARs that are tissue-specific.

Patterns and Rule Definitions

In the general framework discussed previously, a pattern description language must be defined that has sufficient power to represent the variety of patterns likely to be discovered as our understanding about DNA-protein interactions and the control of genetic machinery reaches a higher level of maturity. One must remember, each motif (and pattern) is represented by the probability of its random occurrence. This value can be derived using the base composition of the sequence being analyzed.

When searching for patterns, one must strive for a balance between the specificity and generality of patterns sought. Thus a distinction is often drawn between the tasks

Table 1
Table of Sequence Level Motifs[a]

Motif	*Motif name*	*DNA Signature*
m_1	ORI Signal	ATTA
m_2	ORI Signal	ATTTA
m_3	ORI Signal	ATTTTA
m_4	TG-Rich Signal	TGTTTTG
m_5	TG-Rich Signal	TGTTTTTTG
m_6	TG-Rich Signal	TTTTGGGG
m_7	Curved DNA Signal	AAAANNNNNNNAAAANNNNNNNAAAA
m_8	Curved DNA Signal	TTTTNNNNNNNTTTTNNNNNNNTTTT
m_9	Curved DNA Signal	TTTAAA
m_{10}	Curved DNA Signal	AAA
m_{11}	Curved DNA Signal	AAAA
m_{12}	Kinked DNA Signal	TANNNTGNNNCA
m_{13}	Kinked DNA Signal	TANNNCANNNTG
m_{14}	Kinked DNA Signal	TGNNNTANNNCA
m_{15}	Kinked DNA Signal	TGNNNCANNNTA
m_{16}	Kinked DNA Signal	CANNNTANNNTG
m_{17}	Kinked DNA Signal	CANNNTGNNNTA
m_{18}	mtopo-II Signal	RNYNNCNNGYNGKTNYNY
m_{19}	dtopo-II Signal	GTNWAYATTNATNNR
m_{20}	topo-II Vert. Signal	NCNNCYNGKTNYNY
m_{21}	AT-Cluster Signal	WWWWWW
m_{22}	AT-Cluster signal	AATATTTT
m_{23}	AT-Cluster Signal	AATAAAYAAA
m_{24}	AT-Cluster Signal	ATATTT
m_{25}	ACBP-TF Signal	WTTTAYRTTTW
m_{26}	ARBP-TF Signal	ATTTCASTTGTAAAA
m_{27}	SAR-TF Signal	WWCAAWG
m_{28}	ARS 3'Consensus Signal	CTTTTAGCWWW
m_{29}	CEN Signal	TGTTTATGNTTTCCGAAANNNAAAA
m_{30}	HomProtcore Signal	TAATTA
m_{31}	YR-Richness Signal	YR
m_{32}	F/G Signal	AYCYRTRCAYYW
m_{33}	Bipartite AR Signal	AATAAYAA
m_{34}	Bipartite SAR Signal	AWWRTAANNWWGNNNC
m_{35}	MAMORI Signal	WAWTTDDWWWDHWGWHMAWTT
m_{36}	SAR Signal	WADAWAYAWW
m_{37}	SAR Signal	WWDAWAYAWW
m_{38}	SAR Signal	TWWTDTTWWW
m_{39}	T Box Signal	TTWTWTTWTT

[a]The set of motifs characterizing MARs constitute DNA-sequence signals or predicates upon which *rules* defining higher level patterns are constructed. Note that the IUPAC characters R, Y, W, and *k* are defined as: R = A or G, Y = T or C, *W* = A or T, and *k* = G or T.

of finding patterns and that of finding models or rules. The distinction between these two terms is rather arbitrary. Generally, a model is a global representation of a structure that summarizes components underlying the data that explain how the data may have arisen. In contrast, a pattern is a local structure, perhaps relating to a handful of variables and a few cases.

It is possible to employ a general set of DNA patterns using the AND-OR methodology. In such an AND-OR pattern specification methodology a disjunction (OR) of the conjunctions (AND) of the motifs detected in the sequence is used as the definition of the pattern being sought. The sequence level motifs serve as the lowest level predicates used to detect the presence of a higher level pattern. In general the following operations may be applied to the lower level motifs:

- Motif consensus sequence, m, represented as a regular expression of profile, or
- The logical OR of two motifs m_i and m_j, represented as $m_i \vee m_j$, or
- The augmented logical AND of two motifs m_i and m_j, represented as a $m_i \wedge_b^a m_j$ or
- The logical negation of a motif, m, represented as $\bar{m}$, specifying the absence of a given motif.

The pattern specification methodology must consider motif variability in its representation. Such variability may be captured using the AND-OR rules. As an example, consider the rule to define the Origin of Replication (OR) of DNA. This can be based on the OR operator applied to the three motifs m_1 =ATTA, m_2 = ATTTA, and m_3 = ATTTTA. The motif detectors bypass the AND layer in this case.

$$R_1 = m_1 \vee m_2 \vee m_3 \qquad \text{[Eq. 1]}$$

Similarly, the requirement for multiple motif occurrences can be specified using the AND operator. An additional parameter is incorporated when using the AND rule to constrain the allowable gap between the two co-occurring motifs. For example, the AT-Richness rule can be formulated as the occurrence of two hexanucleotide strings, m_4 = WWWWWW, that are separated by distance of 8–12 nt, using the augmented AND operator using $\wedge_{low}^{high}$ define the acceptable distance between the two motifs:

$$R_2 = m_4 \Lambda_8^{12} m_4 \qquad \text{[Eq. 2]}$$

The significance of the occurrence of a pattern in a DNA sequence is inversely related to the probability that the pattern will occur purely by chance. The probabilities of random occurrences of the underlying predicates are mathematically combined to evaluate the probability of the random occurrence of a pattern specified by a given rule. As an illustrative example, the random occurrence probabilities for the given patterns described by the above two rules can be computed. This value for the set of acceptable patterns described by rule R_2 is based on the occurrence of at least one motif within an acceptable distance from the reference motif. These probabilities are computed as shown in Tables 1 and 2.

In similar manner, the random occurrence probability rules are constructed on underlying predicates that are defined as profiles, can be computed using generating functions. As described, the rule probabilities are employed to estimate the statistical significance of matching the set of patterns that are detected in a given region of the DNA sequence.

Table 2
The Set of Biological Rules Defining Patterns That Were Used for Detecting Structural MARs.[a]

Rule	Name	Definition	Probability
R_1	ORI Rule	$m_1 \vee m_2 \vee m_3$	$p_1 = \Sigma_{i=1}^{3} \Pr(m_i)$
R_2	TG-Richness Rule	$m_4 \vee m_5 \vee m_6$	$p_2 = \Sigma_{i=4}^{6} \Pr(m_i)$
R_3	Curved DNA Rule	$m_7 \vee m_8 \vee m_9$	$p_3 = \Sigma_{i=7}^{9} \Pr(m_i)$
R_4	Kinked DNA Rule	$m_{12} \vee m_{13} \vee m_{14}$ $m_{15} \vee m_{16} \vee m_{17}$	$p_4 = \Sigma_{i=12}^{17} \Pr(m_i)$
R_5	Topoisomerase Rule	$m_{18} \vee m_{19} \vee m_{20}$	$p_5 = \Sigma_{i=18}^{20} \Pr(m_i)$
R_6	AT-Richness Rule	$m_{21} \wedge_8^{12} m_{21}$	$p_6 = \Pr(m_{21}) \cdot \{1 - \exp[-5 \cdot \Pr(m_{21})]\}$
R_7	MAR TF-Rule	$m_{25} \vee m_{26} \vee m_{27}$	$p_7 = \Sigma_{i=25}^{27} \Pr(m_i)$
R_8	AT Cluster Rule	$m_{21} \vee m_{22} \vee m_{23} \vee m_{24}$	$p_8 = \Sigma_{i=21}^{24} \Pr(m_i)$
R_9	Bipartite Rule	$m_{33} \wedge_{-200}^{+200} m_{34}$	$p_9 = \Pr(m_{33}) \cdot \{1 - \exp[-400 \cdot \Pr(m_{34})]\}$
R_{10}	SAR Rule	$m_{36} \vee m_{37} \vee m_{38}$	$p_{10} = \Sigma_{i=36}^{38} \Pr(m_i)$

[a]The table also specifies the relationship between the DNA-motif probabilities, $P(m_i)$, and the rule probabilities, p_j. These higher level statistical association forms the basis for mining MARs from DNA sequences.

Data Mining the MARs

There are two different data-mining methodologies. They are classified according to whether they seek to build models or find patterns. The methods aimed at building global models fall within the category of statistical exploratory analysis, which, for example, led to the rejection of conventional wisdom that long-term mortgage customers constitute a good portfolio. In a global sense, these customers constitute the group that were not able to find offers elsewhere and in fact may be the "not-so-good-customers." The second class of data-mining methods seeks to find patterns by sifting through the data seeking co-occurrences of specific values of specific variables. It is this class of strategies that has led to the notion of data-mining as seeking nuggets of information among the mass of data. The problem of detecting MARs from anonymous DNA sequence data falls within this category.

Data mining is the method employed to search for interesting patterns in data. Such a search often takes place in large data sets where the likelihood of finding such patterns is greater than expected. As described, the data-mining efforts aim at detecting statistically significant patterns, which are useful because they are not redundant, novel in regards to user's previous knowledge, simple for the user to understand, and sufficiently general to the referred population.

When searching for patterns, one must strive for a balance between the specificity and generality of the patterns sought. Thus, a distinction is often drawn between the tasks of finding *patterns* and that of finding *models*. The distinction between these two terms is rather arbitrary. Generally, a model is a global representation of a structure that summarizes components underlying the data that explain how the data may have arisen. In contrast, a pattern is a local structure, perhaps relating to a handful of variables and a few cases. Such local patterns are often sought in the time-series data analysis. One application of time series data analysis is the analysis of stock market data to detect interesting patterns that are novel, useful, and simple enough for the investors to understand.

There is a difference between the pattern-detection methods and the conventional diagnostic methods. One significant difference is that conventional diagnostic methods need a model to compare the data, while unsupervised pattern-detection does not require such a model. Another difference is the requirement in the pattern-detection context to search through very large collections of data and explore a large number of pattern shapes.

The search for MARs results from defining a group of patterns that are bonded together in order to form a biologically functional unit that is classified by similar function. After grouping, a search for the patterns from a given group in the query DNA sequence can be performed. If a large subset of members of a functionally related group of patterns is found in a specific region of the uncharacterized DNA sequence, one can begin to learn about its function. This process is called a *Functional Pattern Search* and is typified by the MAR-Wiz system that performs a search for the group of patterns that are associated with Matrix Attachment Regions (MARS).

It is quite intuitive to consider pattern-cluster density as a property defined along the span of a sequence. A *sliding window* algorithm can be applied for measuring this value, where the measurements are characterized by the two parameters, W and δ. The cluster-density is measured in a window of size W centered at location x along that sequence. Successive window measurements are carried out by sliding this window in the increments of δ nucleotides. If δ is small, linear interpolation can be used to join the individual window estimates that are gathered at x, $x + \delta$, ..., $x + k\delta$. In this manner, a continuous distribution of the cluster-density is obtained as a function of x.

The task of estimating the density of pattern clusters in each window can be statistically defined as a functional inverse of the probability of rejecting the null hypothesis, that states that the frequency of the patterns observed in a given window is not significantly different from the expected frequencies from a random W nucleotide sequence of the same composition as the sequence being analyzed. The inverse function chosen as, $\rho = -\log(\alpha)$, where the parameter α is the probability of erroneously rejecting H_0. In other words, α represents the probability that the set of patterns observed in a window occurred purely by chance. The value of ρ is computed for both the forward and the reverse DNA strands because we do not know which strand or if both strands will be bound, the average of the two values is considered to be the density estimate at a given location.

In order to compute ρ, assume that we are searching for k distinct types of patterns within a given window of the sequence. In general, these patterns are defined as rules $R_1, R_2,..., R_k$.The probability of random occurrence of the various k patterns is calculated using the AND-OR relationships between the individual motifs. Assume that these probabilities for k patterns are $p_1, p_2,...,p_k$. Next, a random vector of pattern frequencies, F, is constructed. F is a k-dimensional vector with components, $F = \{x_1, x_2,...,x_k\}$, where each component x_i is a random variable representing the frequency of the pattern R_i in the W base-pair window. The component random variables x_i are assumed to be independently distributed Poisson processes, each with the parameter $\lambda_i = p_i \cdot W$. Thus, the joint probability of observing a frequency vector $F_{obs} = \{f_1, f_2, ..., f_k\}$ purely by chance is given by:

$$P(F_{obs}) = \prod_{i=1}^{k} \frac{e^{-\lambda_i}\lambda^{f_i}}{f_i!} \quad \text{where} \quad \lambda_i = p_i \cdot W \qquad \text{[Eq. 3]}$$

The steps required for computation of α, the cumulative probability that pattern frequencies equal to or greater than the vector F_{obs} occurs purely by chance is given by Equation 4 below. This corresponds to the one-sided integral of the multivariate Poisson distribution and represents the probability that the H_0 is erroneously rejected.

$$\begin{aligned}\alpha &= P_r\,(x_1 \geq f_1, x_2 \geq f_2, \ldots, x_k \geq f_k)\\ &= P_r\,(x_1 \geq f_1) \cdot P_r\,(x_2 \geq f_2) \ldots\ldots P_r\,(x_k \geq f_k)\\ &= \sum_{x_1 = f_1}^{\infty} \frac{\exp^{-\lambda_1}\lambda_1^{x_1}}{x_1!} \cdot \sum_{x_2 = f_2}^{\infty} \frac{\exp^{-\lambda_2}\lambda_2^{x_2}}{x_2!}\\ &\quad \cdots\cdots \sum_{x_K = f_K}^{\infty} \frac{\exp^{-\lambda_K}\lambda_k^{x_K}}{x_k!}\end{aligned} \qquad \text{[Eq. 4]}$$

The p-value, α, in Equation 4 is utilized to compute the value of ρ or the cluster-density as specified in Equation 5 below:

$$\begin{aligned}\rho &= \ln \frac{1.0}{\alpha} = -\ln(\alpha) = \sum_{i=1}^{k} \lambda_i + \sum_{i=1}^{k} \ln f_i! - \sum_{i=1}^{k} f_i \ln \lambda_i\\ &\quad - \sum_{i=1}^{k} \ln\left(1 + \frac{\lambda_i}{f_i + 1} + \frac{\lambda_i^2}{(f_i + 1)(f_i + 2)} + \ldots\ldots + \frac{\lambda_i^t}{(f_i + 1)(f_i + 2)\ldots\ldots(f_i + t)}\right)\end{aligned} \qquad \text{[Eq. 5]}$$

The infinite summation term in Equation 5 quickly converges and thus can be adaptively calculated to the precision desired. For small values of λ_i, the series may be truncated such that the last term is smaller than an arbitrarily small constant, ε.

Using MAR-Wiz

Figure 1, presents the output from the analysis of the human β-globin gene sequence. In Fig. 1A Rules 1 through 6, or the core rules, were utilized for the detection of MARs in this sequence. All Rules 1 through 10 were utilzed for detection of MARs shown in Fig. 1B. This statistical inference algorithm based on the association of patterns found within the close proximity of a DNA sequence region has been incorporated in the MAR-Wiz tool. A java-enabled version of the tool is available for public access (*see* Website: http://www.futuresoft.org/MARWiz).

We observe that the results in Fig. 1A and B are in agreement. Fig. 1B appears noisy. A possible explaination for this is an interdependence between the some of the new rules, i.e., Rules 7 through 10, on the core rules. Thus, when a core rule is detected in the sequence, an associated new rule is also present. However, the MAR-potential assumed this event to be significant as independence of MAR rules is assumed. Consequently, the MAR-potential and noise increase. The interdependence of the MAR rules needs to be clarified.

MAR-Wiz was originally conceived to examine sequences from cosmid sized (~ 40 kb) sequencing projects, the initial backbone of human genome project. The program default values of window length (1000), step size (100), and run length (3), i.e., number of concurrent steps were implemented accordingly. For cosmid sized or larger sequences, step size should be maintained at 100 bp, to minimize noise while permitting sufficient discrimination.

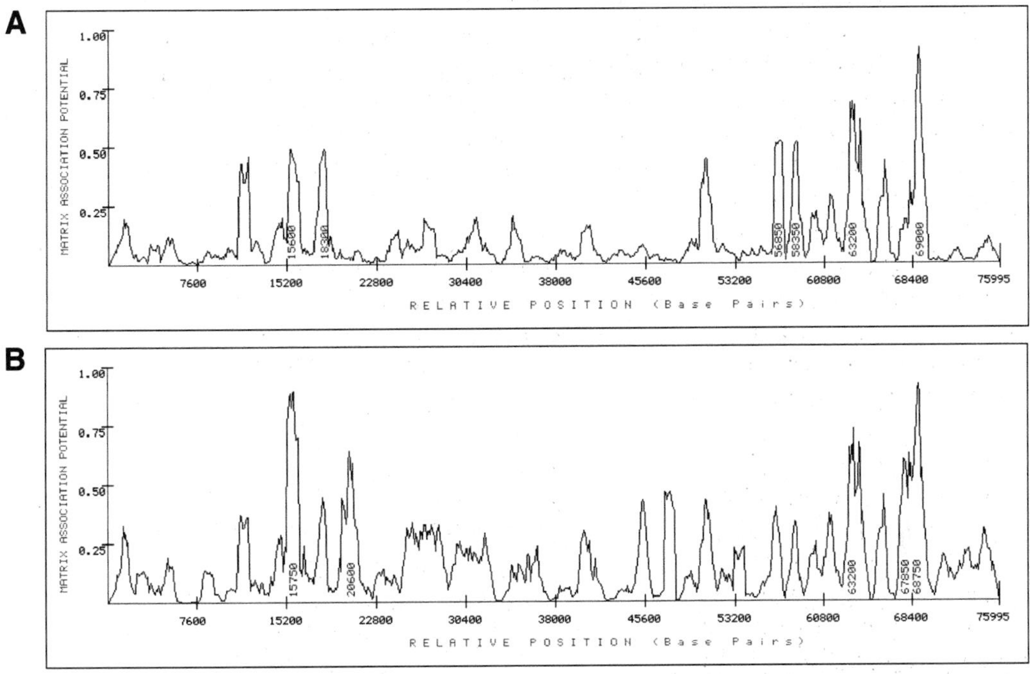

Fig. 1. The analysis of human beta-globin gene cluster using the MAR-Wiz tool. Default analysis parameters were used for generating the plot in **(A)**. Similar results are obtained when Rules R_7 through R_{10} were also included. These are shown in **(B)**. The results with all rules included tended to be more noisy, thereby indicating that the occurrence of the new rules was dependent on the old rules.

In the case of shorter sequences ranging in size from 1,000–10,000 bp, a window size of 100 with a step of 10 usually yields optimum results. This is best illustrated below in the analysis of the IFN-β gene shown in Fig. 2. The predicted locations of regions of matrix attachment correspond well with those experimentally determined and the predictions by SIDD (Stress Induced DNA Destabilization) program.

Several generalizations regarding the utility and interpretation of the data analysis by MAR-Wiz have become apparent over the course its development and use as an analytical tool. As discussed earlier, one of the significant contributions from these analyses has been the classification of candidate MARs as a function of the distribution of MAR sequence motifs they possess. This is best exemplified by AT-rich MARs and ORI MARs. Both are examples of MARs with different biological functions acting as either boundary elements or as origins of replication respectively. This has led to the strategy of initially scanning the query sequence with all available rules as a means to establish the potential class of MARs contained within the sequence selected for analysis. The distribution of identified elements and their local concentration can then be used to guide their initial classification and subsequent assessment of biological function. Experience has shown that the initial classification scan is most efficiently carried out in three phases. First, sequences are examined with all the core (default setting) rules selected to establish the overall distribution of motifs. This is subsequently followed by scanning with the ORI and AT-rich rules deselected in the presence and absence of the ATC rule. The relative contribution of each rule to the

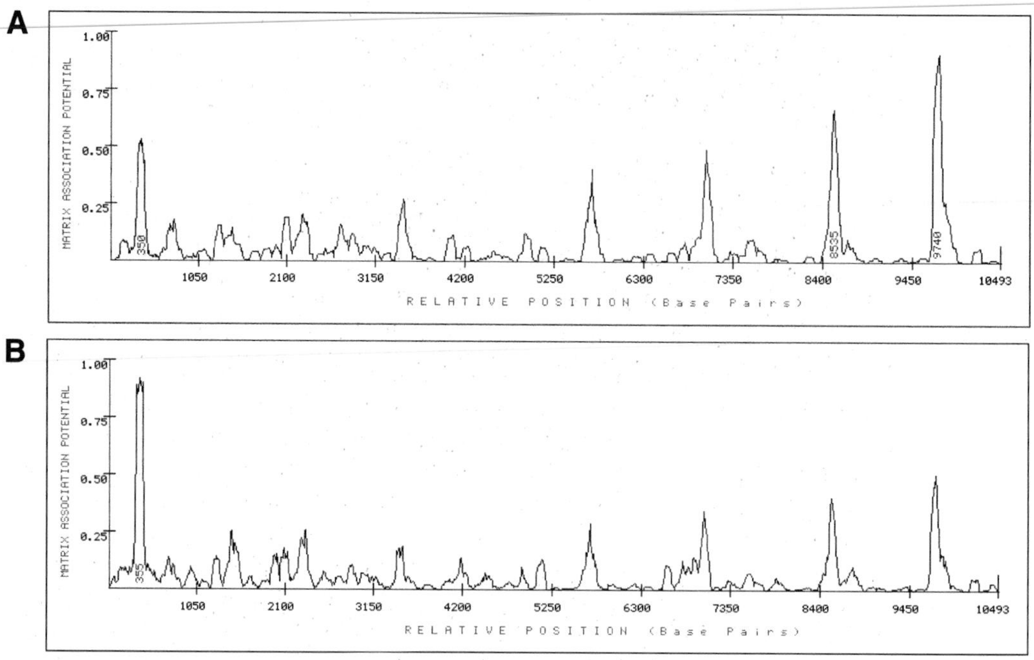

Fig. 2. For shorter sequences, such as the Human-interferon gene shown above, the window size of 100 and step size of 10 is optimal. In this case as well, the augmented Rule set in **(A)** does not indicate any additional regions with higher MAR potential. An increase in the strength of the first peak in **(B)** in fact relatively lowers the significance of the remaining peaks.

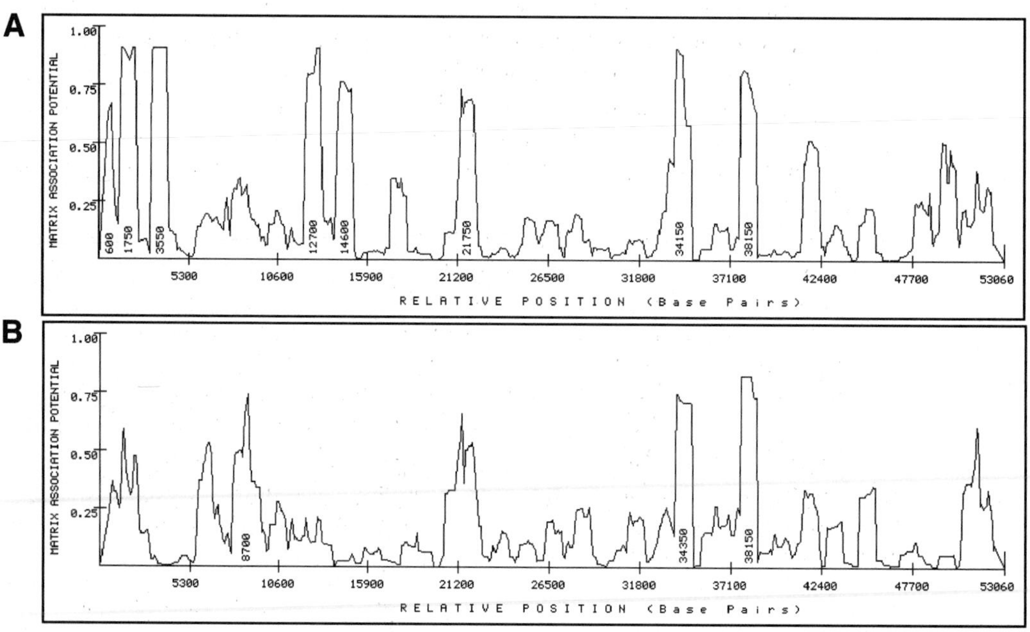

Fig. 3. The results of analyzing the human protamine gene cluster using the MAR-Wiz algorithm. **(A)** shows the potential with all core rules selected. **(B)** shows the analysis results with all default core rules selected, minus the ORI and AT-Richness rule.

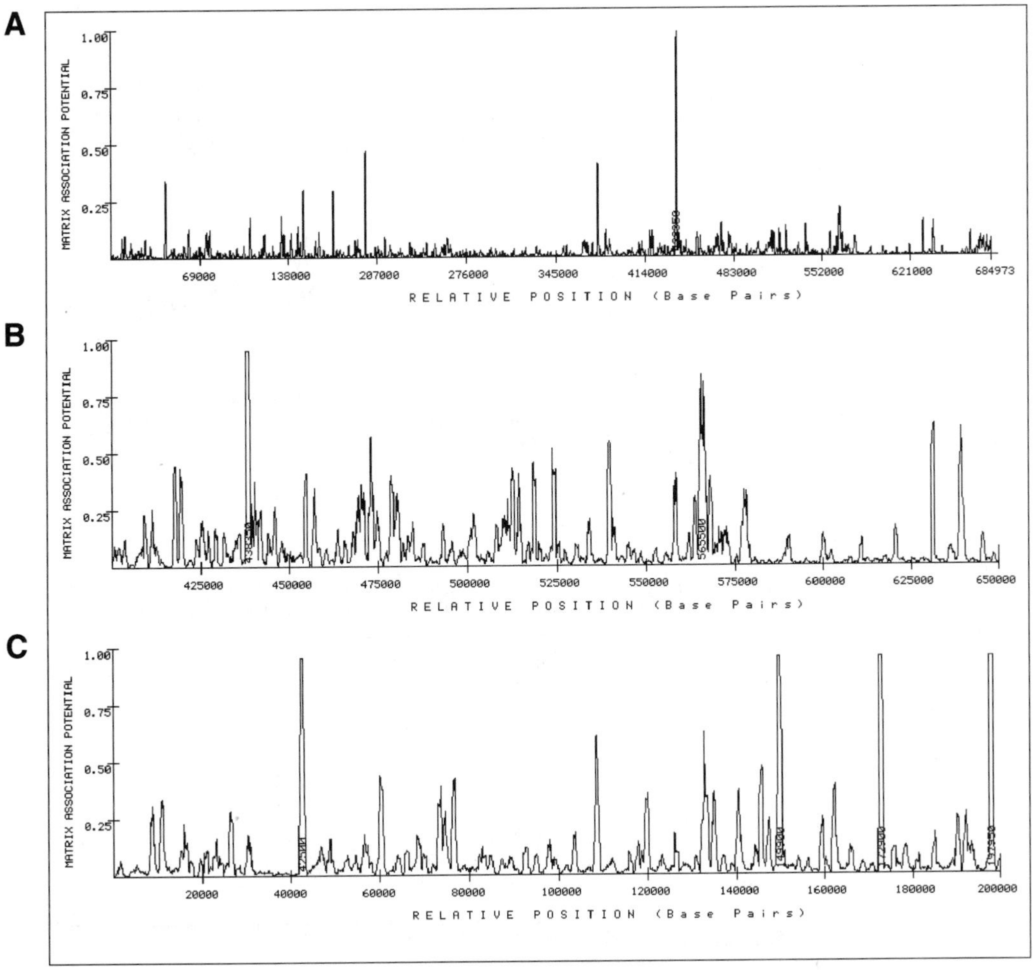

Fig. 4. The results of analyzing the human T-cell receptor gene with MAR-Wiz. In **(A)**, the large peak (with the absolute potential value of 120) overshadows the lower, albeit significant, peaks. This peak is clipped to a value of 30 and the other peaks normalized accordingly. This enables us to visualize the locations of other candidate MARs in the two ends of this locus, as shown in **(B)** and **(C)**.

detection of that motif within the query sequence can then be assessed. Having, used the rule parameter selection to initially categorize the MAR, one then examines the distribution of probabilities using a low-threshold of detection. While this strategy may yield a high false-positive rate, it ensures the detection of most MARs even when the individual MAR is at the limits of statistical detection (possess an expected value is at least e^{-8}).

As shown in Fig. 3, this strategy was effectively utilized to identify and classify the MARs of the PRM1 → PRM2 → TNP2 locus to the sperm-specific class. It must be emphasized that the predictions of MAR-Wiz can only provide a guide to biological verification.

As shown in Fig. 4A, a clustering of motifs with a low likelihood of occurrence by chance within any given region results in a single small region of very high MAR

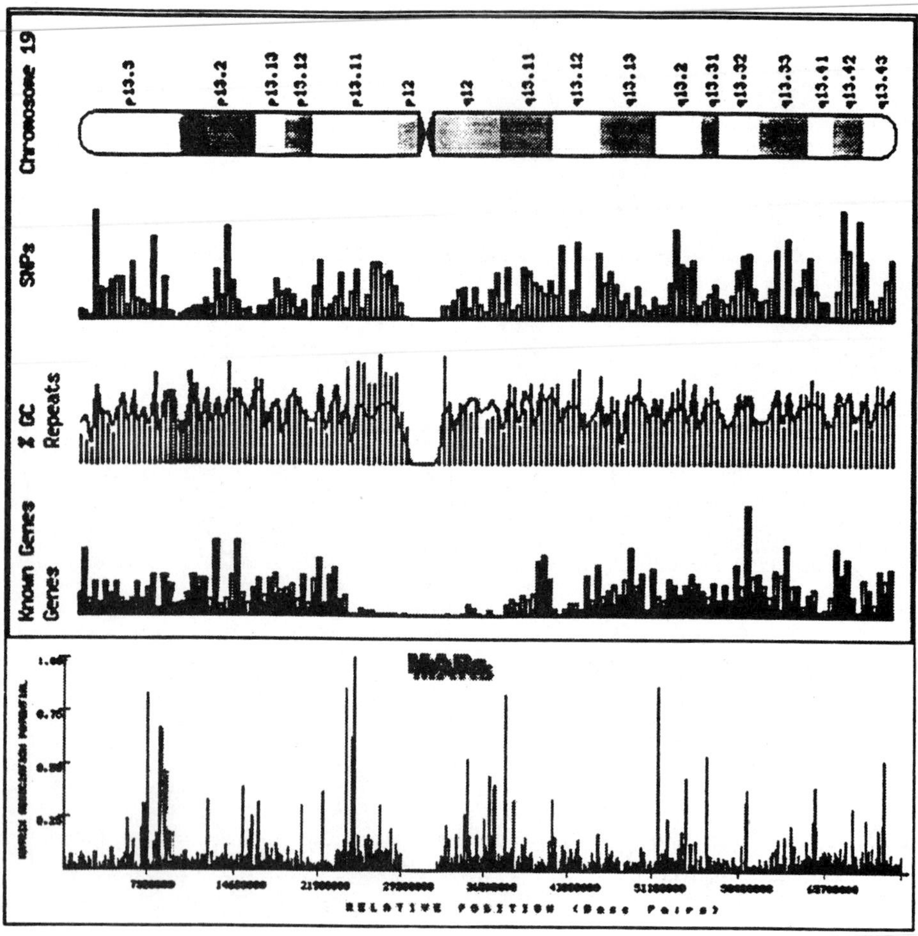

Fig. 5. Analysis of chromosome 19 using the MAR-Wiz software. The results have been aligned with the SNP, GC, Repeat, and data about the known genes available at ENSEMBL (*see* Website: www.ensembl.org). The examples in the chapter present applications of MAR-Wiz to classes of sequences where excellent correspondence when compared to the results obtained by wet-bench analysis was observed. However, there are cases where improvement is required.

potential. As is the case with the T-cell receptor gene locus, the one peak visible has an absolute potential value of 120. This corresponds to a chance occurrence of the observed motifs of approx 10^{-40}. During the normalization process, the other segments containing statistically significant candidate MARs are visually suppressed and upon initial inspection appear insignificant. This MAR-Wiz tool can effectively compensate for this artifact by adjusting the saturation value of the display, i.e., the peak height to which all values are clipped and result the saturation (i.e., 100%) of data values. The data is then scaled to 100% of this value and visualization of the previously masked segments is then apparent. This correction was performed for the two ends of the T-Cell receptor gene and is shown in Figs. 4B and Fig. 4C. In both of these cases, the potential values were clipped to 30, i.e., all values of MAR-Potential higher than 30 were saturated to this value. The remaining values were then normalized using this potential. The location of potential MARs has thus become apparent.

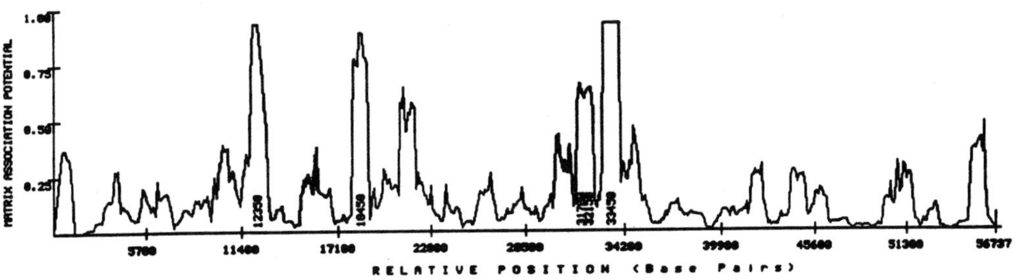

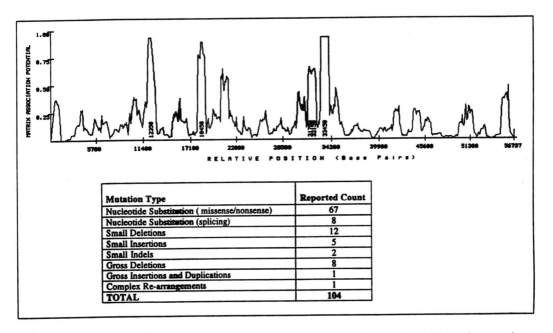

Mutation Type	Reported Count
Nucleotide Substitution (missense/nonsense)	67
Nucleotide Substitution (splicing)	8
Small Deletions	12
Small Insertions	5
Small Indels	2
Gross Deletions	8
Gross Insertions and Duplications	1
Complex Re-arrangements	1
TOTAL	104

Fig. 6. The analysis of the Lesch-Nyhan syndrome HPRT gene shows that additional research is required to identify MARs such as those embedded in introns (positions 5534-6107). Interestingly, most peaks are coincident with known mutations in this human gene (*see* Website: http://www.uwcm.ac.uk/uwcm/mg/search/119317.html).

Figure 5 presents the MAR-Wiz results of analyzing the chromosome 19. These results have been overlaid with the existing information available on chromosome 19 at ENSMBL (*see* Chapter 25; Website: http://www.ensembl.org).

To illustrate how Mar-Wiz can be applied, we will consider an example problem and its solution. Consider *hprt* gene known to be responsible for Lesch-Nyhan syndrome, a devastating self-mutilating disease. Analyze this gene sequence using MAR-Wiz at Website: http:///www.futuresoft.org/MARWiz. Correlate the existence of MARs with the known human mutations causing this disease (*see* Fig. 6).

In this case a MAR has been biologically defined to be contained within the first intron (positions 5534-6107), and has shown great promise when incorporated as an integral component of a gene therapy. However, this MAR region was not identified by the software. This may reflect the fact that this MAR functions as an ARS (Autonomously Replicating Sequence), which is yet another type of MAR.

Irrespective, other candidate MAR sequences have been identified by MAR-Wiz. It is interesting to note that most of these candidates are coincident with known human mutations causing this disease. This would suggest that their biological assessment is warranted.

Glossary and Abbreviations

CDNA Complementary DNA. Reverse transcriptase may be used to synthesize DNA that is complementary to RNA (e.g., an isolated mRNA).

Chromatin Stainable material of interphase nucleus consisting of nucleic acid and associated histone protein packed into nucleosomes.

Circular DNA DNA arranged as a closed circle. This causes serious topological problems for replication that are resolved by DNA topoisomerase.

DNA Deoxyribonucleic acid. The genetic material of all cells and many viruses. A polymer of nucleotides. The monomer consists of phosphorylated 2-deoxyribose N-glycosidically linked to one of four bases : adenine, cytosine, guanine or thymine. The sequence of bases encodes genetic information.

DNA Binding Proteins Proteins that interact with DNA, typically to pack or modify the DNA (e.g., Histones), or to regulate gene expression (e.g., transcription factors).

DNA Replication The process whereby a copy of a DNA molecule is made, and thus the genetic information it contains is duplicated.

DNA Topoisomerase An enzyme capable of altering the degree of supercoiling of double-stranded DNA molecules. Various topoisomerases increase or relax supercoiling, convert single-stranded rings to double-stranded rings, tie and untie knots, catenate and decatenate rings.

DNA Transfection This term is a hybrid of transformation and infection and generally denotes the introduction of other kinds of genes or gene fragments into cells as DNA. For example, introduction of activated oncogenes from tumours into tissue culture cells.

DNAse Deoxyribonuclease. An endonuclease with preference for DNA. In chromatin, the sensitivity of DNA to digestion by DNAase I depends on its state of organization, transcriptionally active genes being much more sensitive than inactive genes.

Enhancer A DNA control element frequently found 5' to the start site of a gene, which when bound by a specific transcription factor, enhances the levels of expression of the gene, but is not sufficient alone to cause expression.

Euchromatin The chromosomal regions that are diffuse during interphase and condensed at the time of nuclear division.

Facultative Heterochromatin That heterochromatin which is condensed in some cells and not in others, possibly representing differences in the activity of genes in different cells.

Gene Originally defined as the physical unit of heredity. Best defined as the unit of inheritance that occupies a specific locus on a chromosome. Given the occurrence of split genes, it might be re-defined as the set of DNA sequences (exons) that are required to produce a single polypeptide.

Gene Expression The full use of the information encoded in a gene via transcription and translation leading to production of a protein leading to the appearance of the phenotype determined by that gene. Gene expression is controlled at various points in this process. This control is thought to be the major determinant of cellular differentiation in eukaryotes.

Gene Locus The position of a gene in a linkage map or on a chromosome.

Gene Therapy Treatment of a disease caused by malfunction of a gene, by stable transfection of the cells of the organism with the normal gene.

Heterochromatin The chromosomal regions that are condensed during interphase and at the time of nuclear division.

Junk DNA Genomic DNA that serves, as yet, no known function.

Nuclear Envelope A membrane surrounding the nucleus of eukaryotic cells. Consists of inner and outer membranes separated by perinuclear space and perforated by nuclear pores.

Nuclear Lamina A fibrous protein-network lining the inner surface of the nuclear envelope. Proteins of the lamina are lamins A, B and C, which have sequence homology to proteins of intermediate filaments.

Nuclear Matrix Protein latticework filling the nucleus that anchors required for DNA replication and transcription complexes.

Promoter A region on the DNA that RNA polymerase binds to before initiating the transcription of DNA into mRNA. The nucleotide at which transcription starts is designated +1. Nucleotides positions with negative numbers indicate upstream nucleotides and with positive numbers indicate downstream nucleotides. Most factors that regulate gene transcription do so by binding at or near the promoter and affecting the initiation of transcription. RNA polymerase II, that transcribes all genes that code for polypeptides, recognizes many thousands of promoters. Most have the Goldberg-Hogness or TATA box centered around position –25 and has the consensus sequence 5'-TATAAAA-3'. Several promoters have a CAAT box around position –90 with the consensus sequence 5'-GGCCAATCT-3'. There is increasing evidence that all promoters for genes for housekeeping proteins contain multiple copies of a GC-rich element that includes the sequence 5'-GGGCGG-3'. Transcription by polymerase II is also affected by more distant elements known as enhancers.

Repetitive DNA Nucleotide sequences in DNA present in the genome in numerous copies. These sequences are not thought to code for polypeptides. One class of repetitive DNA, termed highly repetitive DNA, is found as short sequences (5–100 nucleotides in length) repeated thousands of times in a single long stretch. It typically comprises 3–10% of the genomic DNA and predominantly constitutes the satellite DNA. Another class, which comprises 25–40% of the DNA and termed moderately repetitive DNA, usually consists of sequences about 150–300 nucleotides in length that are dispersed evenly throughout the genome. This includes the Alu sequence and transposons.

Transcription mRNA synthesis mediated by RNA-Polymerases utilizing the DNA as a template.

Transcription Factor Protein required for recognition by RNA polymerases of specific stimulatory sequences in eukaryotic genes. Several are known that activate transcription by RNA polymerase II when bound to upstream promoters.

Suggested Readings

MARs: Background and Data Models

Benham, C., Kohwi-Shigematsu, T., and Bode, J. (1997) Stress-induced duplex DNA destabilization in scafold/matrix attachment regions, J. Mol. Biol. 274, 181–196.

Kramer, J. and Krawetz, S. (1997) PCR-Based assay to determine nuclear matrix association, Biotechniques 22, 826–828.

Kramer, J., Adams, M., Singh, G., Doggett, N., and Krawetz, S. (1998) Extended analysis of the region encompassing the PRM1→PRM2→TNP2 domain: genomic organization, evolution and gene identification, J. Exp. Zool. 282, 245–253.

Singh, G., Kramer, J., and Krawetz, S. (1997) Mathematical model to predict regions of chromatin attachment to the nuclear matrix, Nucleic Acid Res. 25, 1419–1425.

Singh, G., Stamper, D., and Krawetz, S. (1998) A web tool for detecting matrix association regions, Trends Genet. 14(2), 8.
Java version is available (*see* Website: http://www.futuresoft.org/MAR-Wiz).

van Drunen, C., Sewalt, R. G., Oosterling, R. W., Weisbeek, P. J., Smeekens, S. C., and van Driel, R. (1999) A bipartite sequence element associated with matrix/scaffold attachment regions, Nucleic Acids Res. 27, 2924–2930.

van Drunen, C., Oosterling, R. W., Keultjes, G. M., Weisbeek, P. J., van Driel, R., and Smeekens, S. C. (1997) Analysis of the chromatin domain organization around the plastocyanin gene reveals a MAR-specific sequence element in Arabidopsis thaliana, Nucleic Acids Res. 25, 3904–3911.

Staden, R. (1988) Methods for calculating the probabilities of finding patterns in sequences, Comput. Appl. Biosci. 5(2), 89–96.

The Biological Description of Matrix Attachment Regions

Bode, J., Stenger-lber, M., Kay, V., Schalke, T., and Dietz-Pfeilstetter, A. (1996) Scaffold/matrix attachment regions: Topological switches with multiple regulatory functions, Crit. Rev. Eukaryot. Gene Expr. 6(2,3), 115–138.

Deppert, W. (1996) Binding of MAR-DNA elements by mutant p53: Possible implications for oncogenic function, J. Cell. Biochem. 62, 172–180.

Farache, G., Razin, S., Targa, F., and Scherrer, K. (1990) Organization of the 3'-boundary of the chicken alpha globin gene domain and characterization of a CR 1-specific protein binding site, Nucleic Acid Res. 18, 401–409.

Jade, J., Rios-Ramirez, M., Mielke, C., Stengert, M., Kay, V., and Klehr-Wirth, D. (1995) Scaffold/Matrix attachment regions: structural properties creating transcriptionally active loci, Intl. Rev. Cytol. 162A, 389–454.

Jarman, A. and Higgs, D. (1988) Nuclear scaffold attachment sites in the human globin gene complexes, EMBO J. 7(11), 3337–3344.

Kramer, J. and Krawetz, S. (1996) Nuclear matrix interactions within the sperm genome, J. Biol. Chem. 271(20), 11619–11622.

Phi-Van, L. and Strätling, W. (1988) The matrix attachment regions of the chicken lysozyme gene co-map with the boundaries of chromatin domain, EMBO J. 7, 655–664.

Von Kries, J., Phi-Van, L., Diekmann, S., and Strätling, W. (1990) A non-curved chicken lysozyme 5' matrix attachment site is 3' followed by a strongly curved DNA sequence, Nucleic Acid Res. 18, 3881–3885.

MAR Sequence Patterns

Boulikas, T. (1993) Nature of DNA sequences at the attachment regions of genes to the nuclear matrix, J. Cell. Biochem. 52, 14–22.

Hartwell, L. and Kasten, M. (1994) Cell cycle control and cancer, Science 266, 1821–1828.

Sander, M. and Hsieh, T. (1985) Drosophila topoisomerase II double stranded DNA cleavage: analysis of DNA sequence homology at the cleavage site, Nucleic Acid Res. 13, 1057–1067.

Spitzner, J. and Muller, M. (1988) A consensus sequence for cleavage by vertebrate DNA topoisomerase II, Nucleic Acid Res. 16(12), 5533–5556.

Strissel, P., Espinosa, III, R., Rowley, J., and Swift, H. (1996) Scaffold attachment regions in centromere-associated dna, Chromosoma 105, 122–133.

Data Mining

Crecone, N. and Tsuchiya, M. (1993) Special issue on learning and discovery in databases, IEEE Trans. Knowl. Data Eng. 5(6).

Fayyad, U., Piatetsky-Shapiro, G., and Smyth, P. (1996) From data-mining to knowledge discovery: An overview, in: Advances in Knowledge Discovery and Data Mining, (Fayyad, U., Piatetsky-Shapiro, G., Smyth, P., and Uthuruswamy, R., eds.), AAAI Press, Menlo Park, CA, pp. 1–34.

Hand, D. (1998) Data mining: Statistics and more? The American Statistician 52(2), 112–118.

Klosgen, W. (1992) Problems for knowledge discovery in databases and their treatment in the statistics interpreter EXPLORA, Intl. J. Intell. Sys. 7(7), 649–673.

Klosgen, W. (1995) Efficient discovery of interesting statements in databases, J. Intell. Info. Sys. 4(1), 53–69.

Higher Order Control of Transcription

Kadonaga, J. (1998) Eukaryotic transcription: An interlaced network of transcription factors and chromatin-modifying machines, Cell 92, 307–313.

Kliensmith, L. and Kish, V. (1995) Principles of cell and molecular biology, 2nd ed, HarperCollins, Williamsport, PA.

Krawetz, S., Kramer, J., and McCarry, J. (1999) Reprogramming the male gamete genome: a window to successful gene therapy, Gene, 234, 1–9.

Roeder, R. (1998) The role of general initiation factors in transcription by RNA polymerase II, Trends Biochem. Sci. 21, 327–335.

24 Analyzing Sequences Using the Staden Package and EMBOSS

Rodger Staden, David P. Judge, and James K. Bonfield

Introduction

Since the beginning of big genome sequencing, initiated by the work on the nematode *Caenhorhabditis elegans*, the Staden group has concentrated on developing methods to increase the efficiency of these large-scale projects. In the course of this, we have designed and implemented a sophisticated and intuitive graphical user interface for use in our programs GAP4 and PREGAP4. This interface has also been used in our sequence analysis program SPIN, but as it has not been the main focus of our efforts, SPIN is still limited in the number and variety of the functions it contains. The EMBOSS project was initiated to provide a comprehensive set of sequence analysis tools that would be available free to all and has made rapid progress towards this goal. However, it did not have a graphical user interface and this limited its usefulness. It was felt that the combination of SPIN and EMBOSS would provide a powerful package.

To make it possible to have a single uniform graphical user interface to the programs in the EMBOSS package, we first combined our two sequence analysis programs NIP4 and SIP4. One dealt with analyzing individual nucleic acid sequences and the other comparing pairs of nucleic acid or protein sequences. Next we developed ways to launch EMBOSS programs and handle their output. Two features in the design of EMBOSS facilitated our work: 1) its flexibility in output formats and 2) its use of a language (ACD) for specifying the inputs to its programs. The first technical challenge was to parse the ACD to automatically produce suitable dialogue boxes for each EMBOSS program and to prepare SPIN to load the results into memory. The second problem was to parse these varying results files to display the results and allow users to interact with them as though they had been produced by internal SPIN functions.

SPIN is available free to academic sites for UNIX and for Microsoft operating systems (*see* Website: http://www.mrc-lmb.cam.ac.uk/pubseq/). EMBOSS is available for UNIX operating systems (*see* Website: http://www.hgmp.mrc.ac.uk/Software/EMBOSS/).

Introduction to SPIN

SPIN is an interactive and graphical program for analyzing nucleotide sequences. It contains functions to search for restriction sites, consensus sequences/motifs and protein coding regions. In addition, it can analyze the composition of the sequence and perform translations. It also has a good set of sequence comparison functions for both nucleic acid and proteins. Most functions produce both textual and graphical results.

Introduction to EMBOSS

EMBOSS is a free Open Source software analysis package specially developed for the needs of the molecular biology-user community. The software uses data in a variety of formats and even allows transparent retrieval of sequence data from the web. As extensive libraries are provided with the package, it is a platform that allows other scientists to develop and release software in true open source spirit. EMBOSS also integrates a range of currently available packages and tools for sequence analysis into a seamless whole. At the time of writing EMBOSS contained over 100 programs for: 1) sequence alignment; 2) rapid database searching with sequence patterns; 3) protein motif identification (including domain analysis); 4) nucleotide sequence pattern analysis, (for example to identify CpG islands or repeats); 5) codon usage analysis for small genomes; 6) rapid identification of sequence patterns in large scale sequence sets; and 7) presentation tools for publication.

Setting up EMBOSS for SPIN

Both SPIN and EMBOSS can be downloaded from their respective ftp sites and installed as independent packages. In order to use SPIN as an interface to EMBOSS, it is necessary to create dialogues for all EMBOSS programs. This is performed by the single command **create_emboss_files**, which is included with SPIN. The EMBOSS menu will then appear in SPIN and its programs will be available.

SPIN User Interface

Spin has a graphical user interface with four main displays. The first is a window from which all the main options are selected and which receives textual results. Most analytical functions add their graphical results either to a *Sequence Plot* window that is associated with the sequence being analysed, or for cases where two sequences are being compared, to a *Sequence Comparison Plot* window. (An exception is the restriction enzyme search that produces its own separate window.) Each of these graphical windows has an associated *Sequence Display* window for viewing the sequences. The main window contains an *Output* Window for textual results, an *Error* window for error messages and a series of menus arranged along the top. Figure 1 shows an example of the main window in which the *Output* Window contains a result from the tRNA gene search. The contents of the two text windows can be searched, edited and saved. Each set of results is preceded by a header containing the time and date when it was generated.

SPIN Sequence Plot

Figure 2 shows several graphical results displayed in a *Sequence Plot* overlaid with a *Sequence Display* window and a pop-up menu. The top four panels show results from protein gene prediction methods and below that are matches from a motif search. The first coding prediction method produces results for each of the three reading frames, which include short vertical lines showing the positions of

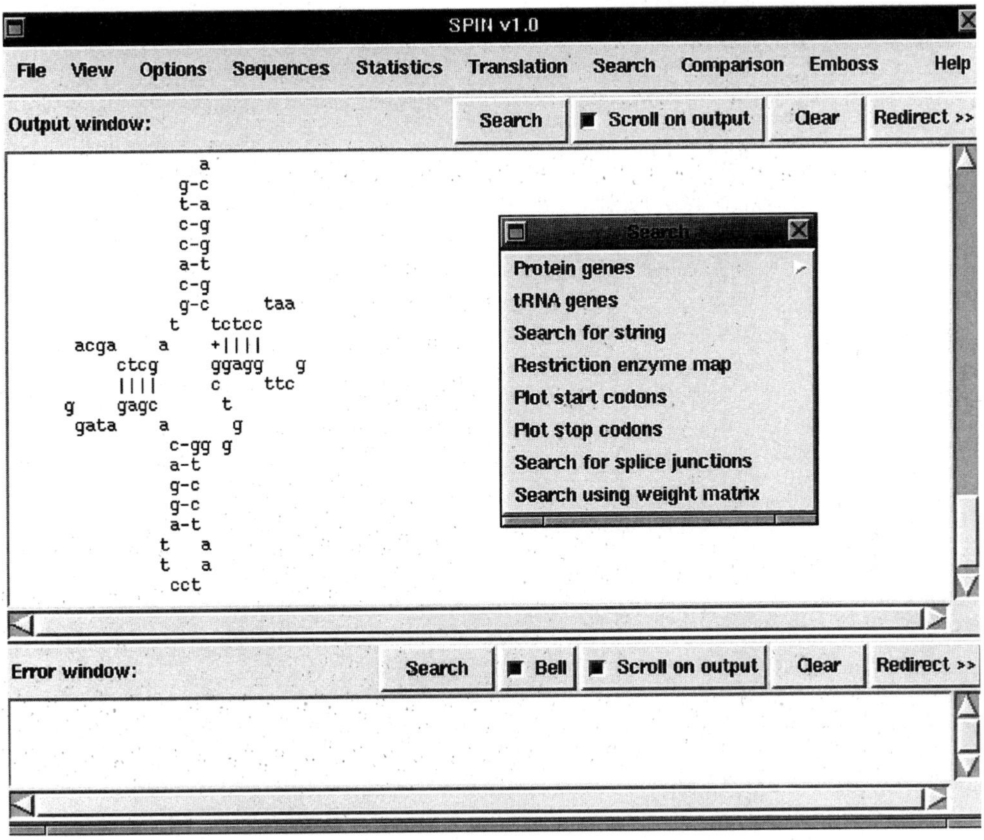

Fig. 1.The SPIN main window including the results from a tRNA gene search.

stop codons in each frame and a continuous line representing the likelihood of coding based on codon usage. Below is a coding prediction result that only has a single value for each position along the sequence. The bottom panel contains short vertical lines showing the positions and scores for a motif search. Each *Sequence Plot* has a cross-hair and scrollbars for zooming and moving the results in the x and y directions. The position of the cross-hair is shown in the boxes above the plot. The x position is shown in sequence base numbers in the left-hand box above the plot, and the y coordinate, expressed using the score values of the gene search, is shown in the right hand box. At the right hand side of each panel is a set of square boxes with the same colors as the lines drawn in the adjacent plot. These icon-like objects represent individual results and allow the user to operate on them via pop-up menus. As a minimum, these menus contain the commands: **Information**, **List results**, **Configure**, **Hide** and **Remove**, but as will be seen later, some sets of results have additional options. These icons can also be used to drag and drop the results to a new location.

As shown in Fig. 2, each Sequence Plot window also has an associated Sequence Display window which can be invoked by double clicking on the plot. The Sequence Plot contains a cursor that denotes the position of the cursor in the Sequence Display. The user can move the cursor and this will move the cursor in the Sequence Display and all other displayed cursors that relate to the sequence.

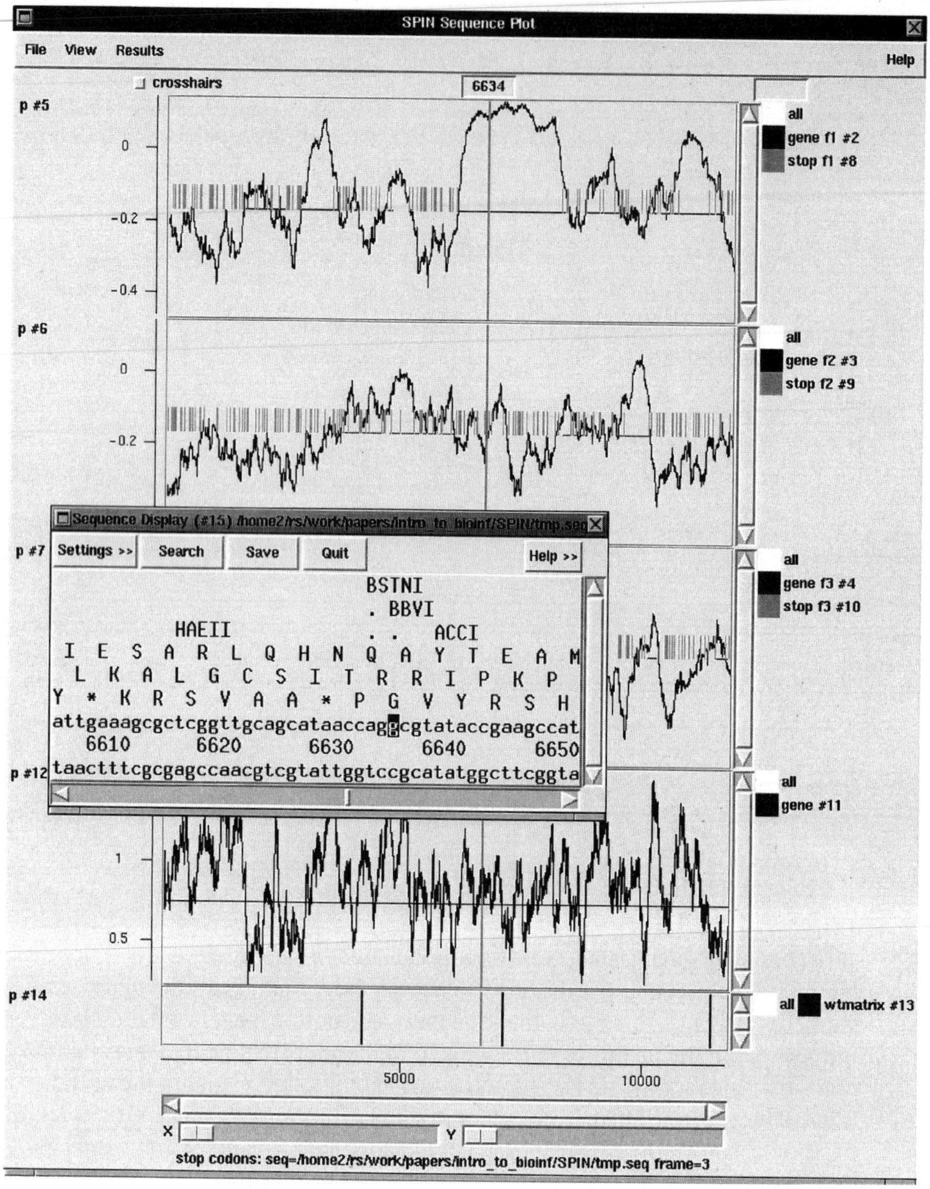

Fig. 2. The SPIN Sequence Plot including two protein gene search results, a motif search and a Sequence Display.

SPIN Sequence Display

From the Sequence Display (*see* Fig. 2), the user can view the sequence in textual form. For DNA, one or both strands can be shown as well as the encoded amino acids. Restriction enzyme sites can also be shown and simple text string searches performed to scroll the sequence. The position of the sequence display cursor is shown in the Sequence Plot, from where it can be driven using the mouse.

SPIN Sequence Comparison Plot

The *Sequence Comparison Plot* shows the results of comparison algorithms, including local and global alignments. Each match is represented as either a single dot or a line, depending on the analysis performed. As for the *Sequence Plot*, sets of matches from a single invocation of a comparison command are termed a *result*. Each result is plotted using a single color, which can be configured via the *Results Manager* (*see* Subheading "Spin Results Manager").

Vertical and horizontal rulers are plotted around the edge of the display and cross-hairs can be used to find the location of any position. It is possible within SPIN to compare many different sequences so there may be more than one horizontal or vertical sequence shown in the *Sequence Comparison Plot*. All the points are scaled to the largest sequence in each direction. As for the *Sequence Plot*, results can be dragged and dropped between plots. Each set of results has an associated *Sequence Comparison Display*, the cursors of which can be seen and controlled from within the *Sequence Comparison Plot*. An example *Sequence Comparison Plot* plus an overlaid *Sequence Comparison Display* is shown in Fig. 3. This contains the result of applying the **Find matching spans** algorithm and the **Align Sequences Globally** function to EMBL sequence library entries mysa_drome and mysa_human. This first algorithm finds and plots (as dots) similar segments of the two sequences and the second finds the best alignment between them and plots its path (as line segments). The results show that they are closely related. The figure also includes cross-hairs and the cursors from the *Sequence Comparison Display*.

SPIN Sequence Comparison Display

Figure 3 shows the Sequence Comparison Display superimposed on the Sequence Comparison Plot. The two sequences are shown one above the other with similarities marked in the intervening strip. The sequences can either be scrolled independently, or in register (by selecting the **Lock** button). As the display is associated with a particular set of results, the **Nearest match** and **Nearest dot** buttons can be used to jump the cursor to neighboring matches. This can make it much easier to examine the detail of individual aligned segments in the Sequence Comparison Plot. *Nearest match* means the match whose x,y coordinate in sequence character positions is closest, whereas *Nearest dot* means the match that appears closest in screen coordinates. (If the scaling is the same in both directions the *Nearest dot* and *Nearest match* will be equivalent.) The display can also be scrolled by dragging the cursor in the *Sequence Comparison Plot*.

SPIN Restriction Enzyme Map

The *SPIN* restriction enzyme map function finds and displays restriction sites found within a specified region of a sequence. As shown in Fig. 4, the results are plotted in a Restriction Enzyme Map. This window has some different capabilities from the other SPIN displays. Each record in the plot corresponds to a particular enzyme: their names are written to the left and their cut sites marked opposite as short vertical lines. The results can be scrolled vertically (and horizontally if the plot is zoomed in). A ruler is shown along the base and the current cursor (the vertical black line) position is shown in the left-hand box near the top right of the display. If the user clicks, in turn, on two restriction sites, their separation in base pairs will appear in the top right-hand box. Information about the last site touched is shown in the information line at the bottom

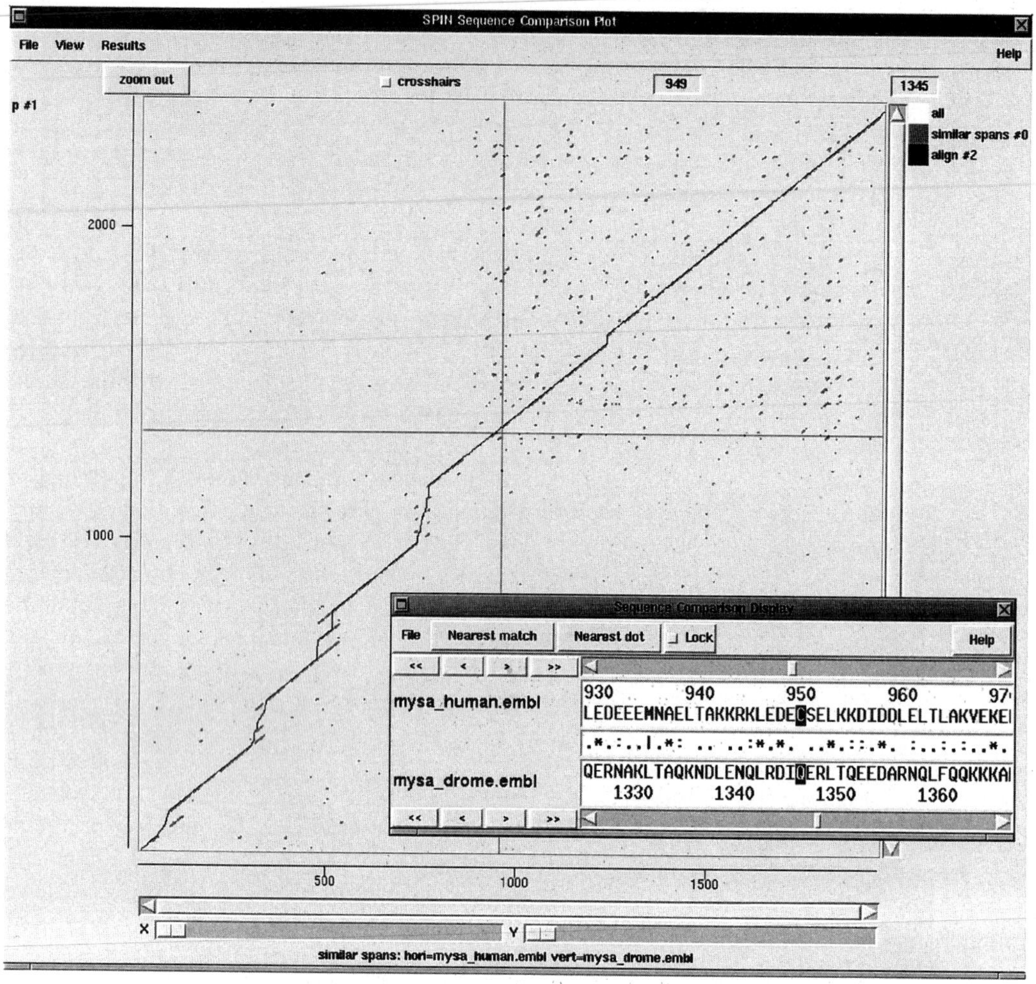

Fig. 3. The SPIN Sequence Comparison Plot including results for similar segments, an alignment path, and a Sequence Comparison Display.

of the display. The order of the records can be changed using drag and drop. As for the Sequence Plot, the Restriction Enzyme Map has an associated Sequence Display whose cursor can be seen and controlled in its display. From the View menu of the Restriction Enzyme map, the results can be written to the SPIN Output window.

SPIN Sequence Manager

SPIN manages sequences at two levels. First it provides for access to read sequences into the program, and second, it contains a range of facilities for deriving new sequences from them. For example, it can produce the complement of a DNA sequence, rotate it about any position, translate it, or scramble it. Each of these types of internal operations produces a new sequence that can be analyzed using the SPIN functions, or that can be saved to disk. SPIN is limited to reading sequences in plain text, EMBL, GenBank, PIR,

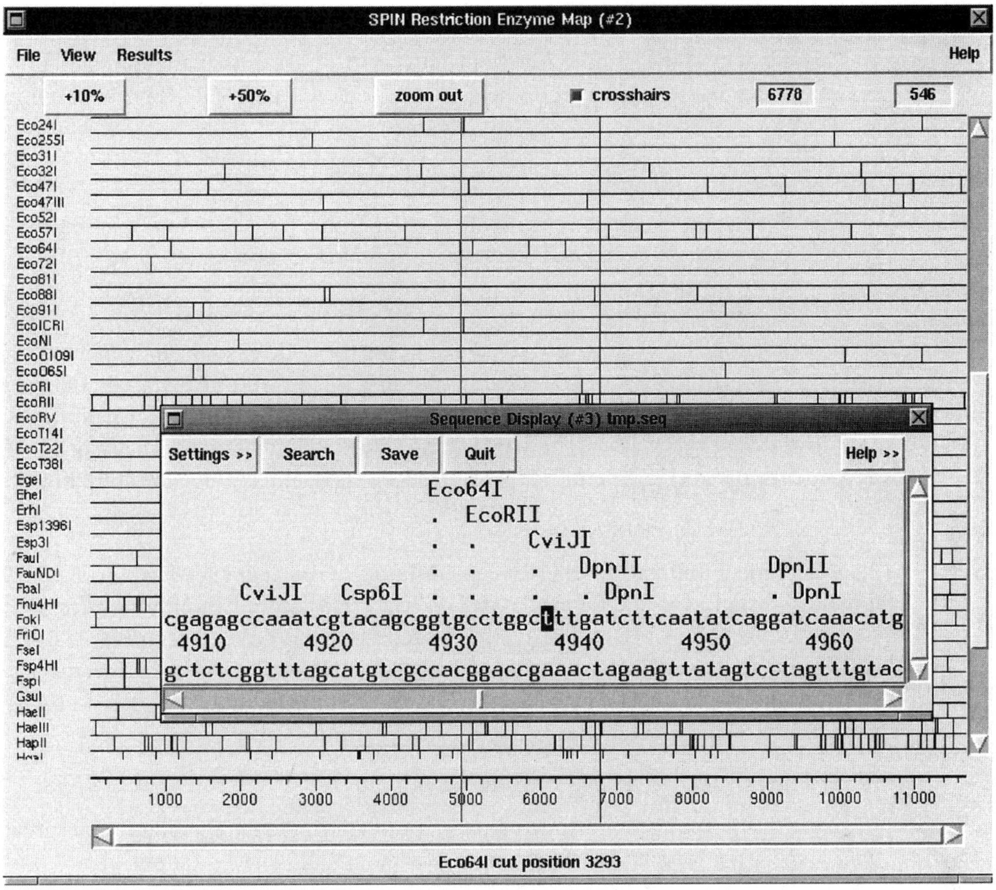

Fig. 4. The SPIN Restriction Enzyme Map including a Sequence Display.

and FASTA formats. Through its interface to EMBOSS, it can also read sequences from remote sequence libraries. Once loaded, the sequences are selected and manipulated using the *Sequence Manager*, which is available from the SPIN Sequences menu.

SPIN Results Manager

Most SPIN functions produce *results*. The *Result Manager*, which can be accessed from the main menu or the individual plots, provides a mechanism to interrogate and manipulate these results. Each result can be listed showing the time it was created, the name of the function that created the result, and a unique identifier. A pop-up menu can be used to obtain further information, list the results in the Output window, configure its plot (change its color, line width), hide or reveal its plot, or remove the result altogether.

SPIN Analytical Functions

SPIN's analytical functions are accessed through the following menus: 1) Statistics, 2) Translation, 3) Search, and 4) Comparison. The EMBOSS functions have their own separate menu.

SPIN Statistics Menu

This menu contains simple functions to write the base and dinucleotide composition of nucleic acid sequences to the Output Window and to plot their base composition to a Sequence Plot.

SPIN Translation Menu

This menu contains functions to set the genetic code, translate to protein sequences, to find open reading frames and to calculate and write codon tables to disk files.

SPIN Set Genetic Code Function

This function allows the user to change the genetic code used in all the options. The codes are defined in a set of codon table files distributed with the package, but calculated from those maintained by the National Center for Biological Information, USA. The user simply selects the list of code names from a dialogue box. The selection can be made for the current run of SPIN or made a permanent setting for future runs.

SPIN Translation Function

In addition to the translation that can be shown in the Sequence Display, SPIN can write a translation to the Output Window. This translation can either be for all six frames, or using an EMBL style feature table, limited to defined segments. The contents of the feature tables are displayed in a dialog box and the user can select which CDS records to translate. The translation is written to the Output Window in FASTA format, from where it can be saved to a file.

SPIN Find Open Reading Frames Function

Using the current genetic code, this function will find open reading frames greater than a specified length. As shown in Fig. 5 the results can be output in two ways, either in feature table format or FASTA format. The user can select the start and end points to do the search, which strand to search (either the forward, reverse, or both) and the minimum length of the open reading frame in codons. If the output is being written in the FASTA format, the name of a file is also required.

SPIN Codon Usage Function

Codon usage tables can be calculated and written to the Output window and written to disk. If required, the values found can be added to the counts in a pre-existing codon table, or when written out to disk they can be concatenated with an existing codon table file. In the first case the existing file will be read and added to the values calculated for the region defined by the user. In the latter, the values calculated for the region defined by the user will be written immediately after those from the existing table, hence producing a pair of tables joined end to end. The protein gene searches: **Codon Usage Method** and **Author Search** use single or double codon tables. The values in the table can be expressed as observed counts or as percentages of usage for the cognate amino acid.

SPIN Search Menu

The SPIN Search menu contains simple functions like the restriction enzyme, stop codon, start codon, and subsequence searches, plus some more complex functions for finding genes and motifs. It should be noted that these gene-finding methods, although

```
FT                     CDS 512..736
FT                     CDS 525..965
FT                     CDS 740..952

>512                   512..736
CLTLSLKESFIRHAAYLEGSRSEKRDVCVARESKRCSEASARSVTGGDSKWIAVQPQRPL
LGRLCNKRGPGSLSA*
>525                   525..965
ALKKVLYDTRHTSKGAGVKNVMSVSLVSRNVARKLLLVQLLVVIASGLLFSLKDPFWGVS
AISGGLAVFLPNVLFMIFAWRHQAHTPAKGRVAWTFAFGEAFKVLAMLVLLVVALAVLKA
VFLPLIVTWVLVLVVQILAPAVINNKG*
>740                   740..952
RFVYDICLASPGAYTSERPGGLDIRIWRSFQSSGDVGVTGGGVGGFKGGILAADRYVGFG
AGGSDTGTGCN*
```

Fig. 5. The SPIN Open Reading Frame Results in Feature Table and FASTA formats.

pioneering when invented, have since received little attention, and more recent methods may be more effective and better tested.

SPIN Restriction Enzyme Search

Files of restriction enzyme names, recognition sequences, and their cut sites are stored in disk files supplied with the package, but users can edit them to produce their own. Three default files, plus a browser for loading user files are made available from the function's dialogue box. Once loaded, the enzyme names are presented in a scrollable dialogue. The results are presented as shown in Fig. 4. A similar dialogue is used to configure the restriction enzymes shown in the Sequence Display. The results can be shown in textual form in the Output Window, from where they can be saved to disk.

SPIN Subsequence Search

Two subsequence or string searches are available in SPIN. The first is selected from the **Search** menu on the Output window, producing both graphical and textual output. The second is selected from the **Search** button in the Sequence display, it moves the cursor to the position of the next match. For DNA sequences, the user can define a subsequence using the IUPAC codes, set the percentage match required and which strand to search. The search can be made literal but is never case-sensitive. The results are plotted in a Sequence Plot and written to the Output Window.

SPIN Stop and Start Codon Search

A stop codons search can be carried out on either (or both) strands of the sequence. The stop codons are displayed graphically, with a different color used for each reading frame, and their positions can also be listed in the Output window. If any of the three phase gene search methods (described in the following) are currently being displayed, the stop codons will automatically be plotted on top of the corresponding frame. A similar function locates and plots the positions of start codons. These searches use the current set of genetic code tables.

SPIN Motif Search

Through the IUPAC symbols, the subsequence search described earlier allowed the use of special characters to encode permitted sets of sequence characters at each position in the search string. The SPIN Motif Search is more flexible in that it allows different

```
Mount acceptors
     18      15    0.0    10.0
P -14 -13 -12 -11 -10  -9  -8  -7  -6  -5  -4  -3  -2  -1   0   1   2   3
N 113 113 113 113 113 113 113 113 113 113 113 113 113 113 113 113 113 113
T  58  50  57  59  67  56  58  49  47  66  64  31  34   0   0  11  41  31
C  21  28  34  25  29  33  35  32  42  40  33  25  74   0   0  23  28  41
A  17  11  11  18   7  17  12  23  15   3  10  29   5 113   0  24  21  21
G  17  24  11  11  10   7   8   9   9   4   6  28   0   0 113  55  23  20
```

Fig. 6. A SPIN DNA Weight Matrix

scores to be assigned to each character type at each position along a subsequence or motif. These scores are stored in the form of *weight matrices*. These must be created beforehand from sets of aligned sequences that are known to contain the motif. This is usually done using the program *make_weights*, which is supplied with the package.

An example weight matrix file is shown in Fig. 6. It consists of a title record—a record defining the motif size, an offset and the score range—two records that need to be present but that are ignored; and four records (for DNA) defining the base counts calculated from trusted examples. These counts are converted into weights that are used during the searches. Any position in a sequence that scores at least as high as the minimum score is reported as a match, and if the results are plotted they are scaled to fit the range defined by the minimum and maximum scores. A typical plot is shown at the base of Fig. 2.

SPIN Splice Site Search

The SPIN splice junction search uses a pair of weight matrices to search for splice junctions. It differs from the Motif Search described above only in the way the results are plotted. The results are displayed in three colors, one color for each reading frame. The donors are plotted upwards from the base of the panel and the acceptors are plotted downwards from the top of the panel. The donors and acceptors with the same color are compatible; e.g., the same colored donors are compatible with the same colored acceptors. Of course it is the combination of reading frame and splice sites that really matters, so donors and acceptors drawn in different colors can be compatible if the reading frame changes. By default all the sites are drawn in the same plot (*see* Fig. 7). They can be separated by reading frame using the program's ability to reorganize the graphical results. This layout of the donors and acceptors is designed to add to the protein gene search methods and stop codon plots. The results are plotted as log-odds.

SPIN Codon Usage Gene Search

Although the codon usage gene search method contains some improvements over those of the original publication, this gene finding method is essentially that previously described by Staden (1984). For all protein gene-finding methods we are trying to decide if each segment of the sequence is coding or noncoding. Usually, each possibility is represented by a table of expected codon usage and the calculation finds the odds that each segment of the sequence fits either the coding or noncoding table and the results are presented as log odds in a Sequence Plot. At each position along the sequence the program also plots a single dot for the reading frame with the highest score. These dots appear at the midpoints of the three panels and will form a continuous line if one reading frame is consistently the highest scoring. An example is shown in Fig. 2.

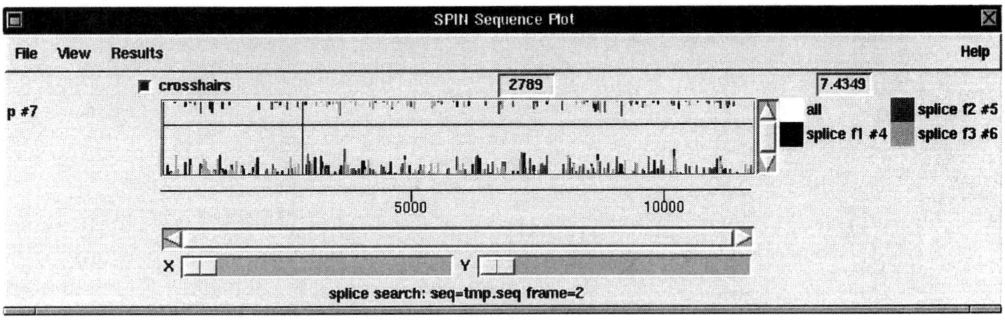

Fig. 7. The SPIN Splice Junction Search Plot.

The user supplies the name of a file containing two concatenated codon usage tables, the first being from coding sequence and the second from noncoding sequence. This double codon table can be calculated by SPIN using the Codon Usage function described earlier. If the user gives the name of a file that contains only a single codon table the algorithm will assume that it is from coding sequence and will generate a noncoding table that consists of the frequencies that would be expected if the sequence being analyzed was random but had the same base composition as the supplied codon table.

If no table is specified the program will generate a codon usage table corresponding to an average amino acid composition and then derive a noncoding table from its base composition. In addition the user can select to set the amino acid composition of the coding table to have an average amino acid composition, and/or to have no codon preference (i.e., for each amino acid the codon counts are equal, e.g., for the standard genetic code [TTT = TTC]; [TTA = TTG = CTT = CTC = CTA = CTG];...; [GGT = GGC = GGA = GGG]). In the latter case the search uses amino acid composition only.

SPIN Author Test Gene Search

This Codon Usage method uses a different mathematical treatment based on methods used to decide authorship of text, i.e., is the usage of words (codons) more like that of author A (coding) or that of author B (noncoding)? Again the main input is a pair of concatenated codon tables and the results are plotted in the same manner. However, the algorithm calculates the optimal weighting to give each codon to obtain the best discrimination between coding and noncoding sequence. The user sets the expected error rate as a percentage and the algorithm will choose the corresponding window length to use for the analysis.

SPIN Base Bias Gene Search

This method for finding protein genes, unlike the methods already described, does not attempt to say either which strand or frame is likely to be coding, only which regions of the sequence. The method analyzes the frequencies of each of the four base types in each of the three positions in long stretches of codons. Ficket (1982) showed that the bias in these measures can be used to indicate possible protein coding regions. The level of bias is plotted on a scale that shows the probability that the sequence is coding. An example is shown in the bottom panel in Fig. 2.

```
score   9 probability 1.73e-04 expected  365 observed 1772
score  10 probability 1.17e-05 expected   25 observed  601
score  11 probability 3.60e-07 expected    1 observed  149
```

Fig. 8. A SPIN Tabulate Scores Result

SPIN tRNA Gene Search

This method is used to find segments of a sequence that might code for tRNAs. It looks for potential cloverleaf forming structures and then for the presence of the expected conserved bases. It presents results in a graphic Sequence Plot in an identical manner to those for a motif search, and draws out the cloverleaf structures in the Output Window (*see* Fig. 1).

SPIN Comparison Menu

SPIN contains three functions for finding local segments of similarity between pairs of sequences (Find Similar Spans, Find Matching Words, and Local Alignment), plus a global alignment algorithm. It can also compare a nucleic acid sequence to a protein by automatically calculating a three-frame translation and can compare DNA against DNA at the protein level. In both cases the results are superimposed using a different color for each phase, hence avoiding the possibility of reading frame shifts obscuring any similarity. All of these functions produce results that are plotted in the Sequence Comparison Plot described earlier. Alignments and matching segments can be examined at the sequence level using the Sequence Comparison Display. The score matrices and other associated values can be configured in the SPIN Options menu. The combination of algorithms and graphical user interface make this one of the stronger features of SPIN. A further strength is that the program contains algorithms for calculating the probabilities of observing the hits found by two of its comparison functions.

Comparison Function Probabilities

For the *Find Similar Spans* and *Find Matching Words* functions, the program enables users to compare observed and expected hits to help assess the significance of their results. These probability calculations are also used to set the default scores for these methods. The probability depends on the composition of the two sequences, the cut-off score and for the Find Similar Spans algorithm, the score matrix. The probability calculated is the chance of finding the given score in infinitely long random sequences of the same composition as those that are being compared. The expected number of matches for any score is calculated by multiplying its probability value by the product of the lengths of the two sequences. The matches found for these two algorithms can be assessed by selecting the **Tabulate Scores** option from the pop-up menu in the Sequence Comparison Plot, which will write a list of observed and expected results in the Output Window (*see* Fig. 8). As shown in Fig. 8, there are clearly many more matches at each score level than would be expected by chance.

Find Similar Spans

This method calculates a score for each position in the plot by summing points found when looking forwards and backwards along a diagonal line of a given (window) length. The algorithm uses a score matrix that contains scores for every possible pair of character types. At each point that the score is above a minimum score, a match is plotted.

If one of the sequences is DNA and the other protein, the program will automatically calculate a 3-frame translation of the DNA and plot the results for each translation in a different color. The dialogue allows the user to set the window length and cut-off score. From the result icon pop-up menu available in the Sequence Comparison Plot the user can request: *Information*, *List results*, *Tabulate scores*, and *Rescan matches*; in addition to the standard *Display sequences*, *Configure*, *Hide*, and *Remove*. *Information* gives a brief description of the sequences used, the input parameters and the number of matches found. *List results* writes every segment of alignment in the Output Window. *Rescan* matches revisits each matching span and plots a dot for each residue pair whose score is above a given threshold. An example is shown in Fig. 3.

Find Matching Words

The *Find Matching Words* function finds regions of identical characters shared by the two sequences. Its main value is speed, being very much faster than the Find Similar Spans function. It is not very sensitive but is useful for long DNA sequences. Users set only the minimum word length. The pop-up from the Sequence Comparison Plot is the same as that for Find Matching Spans.

Align Sequences Locally

The SPIN local alignment routine is based on the program SIM by Huang and Miller. SIM finds the best nonintersecting alignments between two sequences or within a single sequence using dynamic programming. The algorithm requires space proportional to the sum of the input sequence lengths and the output alignment lengths. The user can either specify the number of alignments to find or that all alignments above a given score should be reported. Gap open and gap extend values are also required. The alignments are displayed in the Output Window and also on the Sequence Comparison Plot as a series of lines showing its path.

Align Sequences Globally

The SPIN global dynamic programming alignment algorithm is based on an algorithm of Huang, which is a linear space method. Users can supply gap open and gap extend penalties. The alignment is written to the Output Window and its path drawn in the Sequence Comparison Plot. An example is shown in Fig. 3.

EMBOSS Functions

EMBOSS contains a comprehensive set of programs for sequence analysis. In this section we give two illustrations of the SPIN interface and a shortened list of the EMBOSS applications. Using the EMBOSS programs through SPIN provides a uniform graphical interface through which applications can be selected, configured via appropriate dialogue boxes, and from which the results can be viewed and manipulated intuitively. The EMBOSS applications are selected from the SPIN EMBOSS menu.

An Example of SPIN EMBOSS Dialogue

Figure 9 shows the SPIN dialogue for the EMBOSS application **cpgplot**. It includes a browser for using the Sequence Manager (described earlier) to select the sequence to analyze, and boxes for setting its start and end points. Below are boxes for setting various parameters and output choices. The **Graphics output format** is selected using a pop-up menu by clicking on the arrow. The default value *data* will

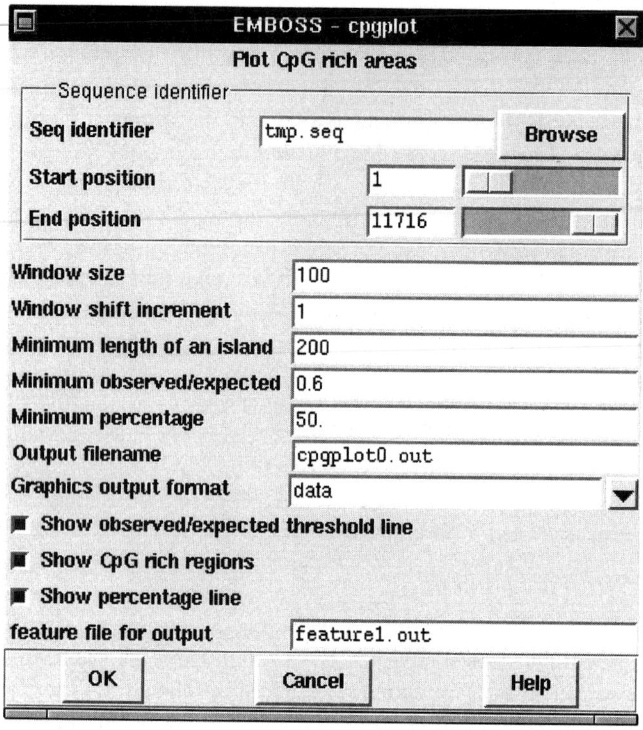

Fig. 9.The SPIN dialogue for the EMBOSS cpgplot program.

produce results that will be automatically loaded into SPIN, but other EMBOSS formats can be selected, for example, postscript output can be produced. Clicking the **OK** button will run cpgplot and the results will appear in a SPIN Sequence Plot.

An Example of SPIN EMBOSS Result

Figure 10 shows a SPIN Sequence Plot for two EMBOSS protein hydrophobicity analysis programs **octanol** and **pepwindow** applied to the SWISSPROT entry 5H1E_HUMAN, which is a member of family 1 of the G-protein coupled receptors. Here both programs have been applied twice and the results combined into a single Sequence Plot. The bottom two plots, partially obscured by the Sequence Display, are the individual results, and the top plot shows the two results superimposed. This superposition is achieved using SPIN's drag and drop functionality, that enables the user to compare the two analysis, a task which would be less straightforward without a graphical user interface.

A Summary of the Current EMBOSS Applications

Although many applications could be included in several categories, below we have divided the EMBOSS applications into separate lists: 1) Nucleic acid specific, 2) Protein specific, 3) Codons/Translation, 4) Alignment/Searching, and 5) Restriction Enzymes. Programs dealing with databases and those covering areas unrelated to sequences are not included.

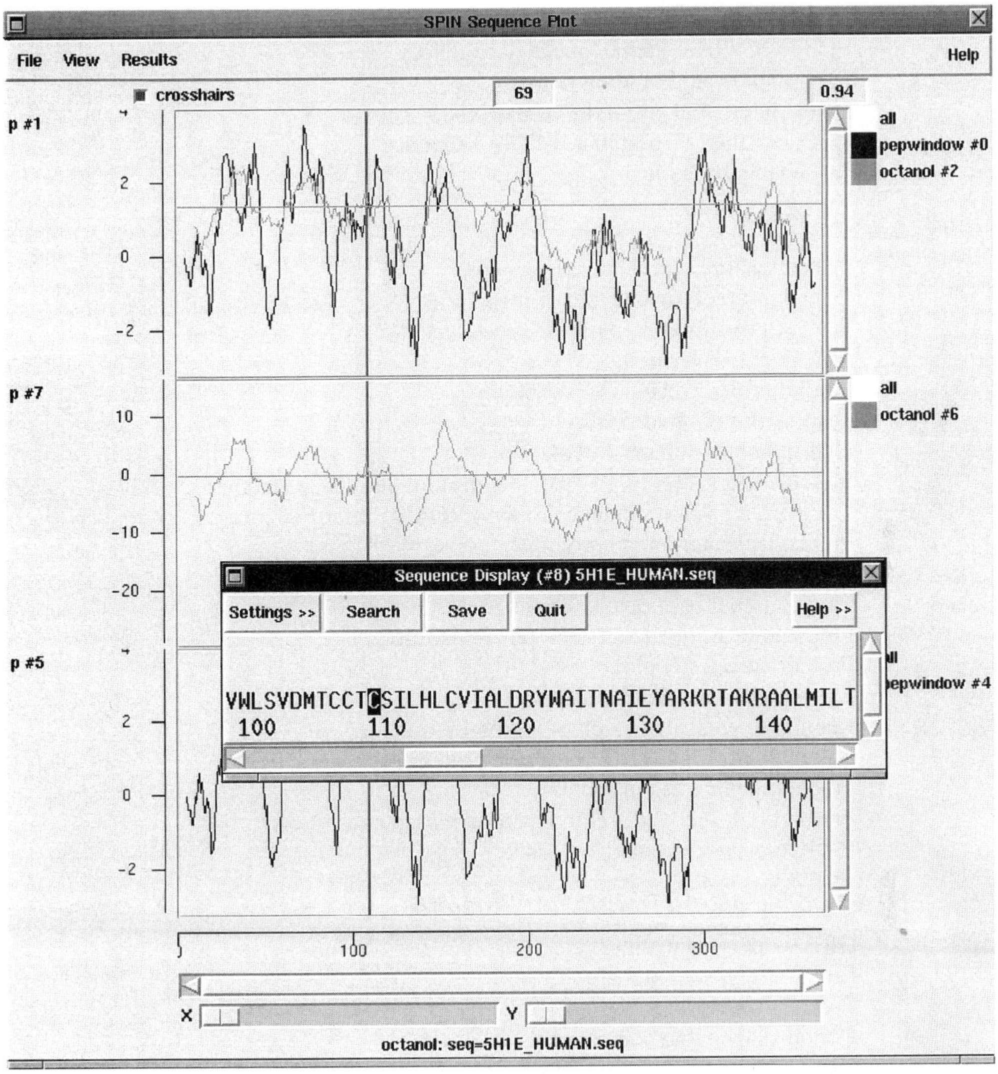

Fig. 10. A SPIN Sequence Plot for EMBOSS programs octanol and pepwindow.

EMBOSS Nucleic Acid Specific Programs

Find the linguistic complexity in nucleotide sequences.
Count words of a specified size in a DNA sequence.
Calculate the fractional GC content of nucleic acid sequences.
Plot/report CpG rich areas.
Plot isochores in large DNA sequences.
Plot melting temperatures for DNA.
Create a chaos plot for a sequence.
Look for inverted/tandem repeats in a nucleotide sequence.
Nucleic acid pattern search.
Regular expression search of a nucleotide sequence.

Scan DNA sequences for transcription factors.
Find MAR/SAR sites in nucleic sequences.
Find nucleic acid binding domains.
Plot bending and curvature in B-DNA.
Calculate the twisting in a B-DNA sequence.
Do wobble base plot.

EMBOSS Protein Specific Programs

Protein charge plot.
Protein proteolytic enzyme or reagent cleavage digest.
Protein identification by mass spectrometry.
Protein pattern search.
Predict protein secondary structure.
Display protein hydropathy.
Hydrophobic moment calculation.
Match a PROSITE motif against a Protein Sequence Database.
Compare a protein sequence to the PROSITE motif database.
Predict transmembrane proteins.
Predict coiled coil regions.
Predict signal peptide cleavage sites.
Plot simple amino acid properties in parallel.
Protein helical net plot.
Show protein sequences as helices.
Regular expression search of a protein sequence.
Calculate the isoelectric point of a protein.
Find antigenic sites in proteins.
Find protein sequence regions with a biased composition.
Back translate a protein sequence.

EMBOSS Codons/Translation Programs

ORF property statistics.
Codon usage statistics.
Create a codon usage table.
Codon usage table comparison.
Extract CDS, mRNA and translations from feature tables.
Find and extract open reading frames.
Do synonymous codon usage Gribskov statistic plot.

EMBOSS Alignment/Searching Programs

DNA Sequence Comparison Plot.
Local/global alignment of two sequences.
Plot the quality of conservation of a sequence alignment.
Display aligned sequences, with coloring and boxing.
Create a consensus from multiple alignments.
Find differences (SNPs) between nearly identical sequences.
Display a non-overlapping wordmatch dotplot of two sequences.
Align EST and genomic DNA sequences.
Do an all-against-all comparison of a set of sequences.
Display a multiple sequence alignment.
Find all exact matches of a given size between 2 sequences.

Scan a sequence or database with a matrix or profile.
Gapped alignment for profiles.
Select primers for PCR and DNA amplification.
Search DNA sequences for matches with primer pairs.

EMBOSS Restriction Enzyme Analysis Programs

Display a sequence with e.g., restriction enzyme cut sites, translation.
Find Restriction Enzyme Cleavage Sites.
Silent mutation restriction enzyme scan.
Find and remove restriction sites but maintain the same translation.
Find restriction enzymes that produce a specific overhang.
Draw circular maps of DNA constructs.
Draw linear maps of DNA constructs.

Concluding Remarks

At the time of writing (July, 2001) both SPIN and EMBOSS are quite new, and the interface between them even newer. By the time this book appears we expect them to have matured into a cohesive, comprehensive and easy to use combination.

Glossary and Abbreviations

CREATE_EMBOSS_FILES A computer program for creating a weight matrix from a set of sequence alignments.

Emboss A suite of programs for comparing and analyzing sequences.

Global Alignment A full-length alignment between a pair of sequences.

Local Alignment An alignment between segments of two sequences.

Score Matrix A table of values assigning a score for aligning each possible pair of bases or amino acids.

SPIN A computer program for comparing and analyzing DNA sequences.

Weight Matrix A table of values assigning a score for each character type at each position in a DNA or protein motif.

Suggested Readings

Sequence Assembly

Bonfield, J. K., Smith, K. F., and Staden, R. (1995) A new DNA sequence assembly program, Nucleic Acids Res. 23, 4992–4999.

The SPIN Analytical Functions

Detecting Signals in Sequences

Fickett, J. W. (1982) Recognition of protein coding regions in DNA sequences, Nucleic Acids Res. 10, 5303–5318.

Staden, R. (1984) Computer methods to locate signals in nucleic acid sequences, Nucleic Acids Res. 12, 505–519.

Staden, R. (1984) Measurements of the effects that coding for a protein has on a DNA sequence and their use for finding genes, Nucleic Acids Res. 12, 551–567.

Staden, R. (1980) A program to search for tRNA genes, Nucleic Acids Res. 8, 817–825.

Sequence Alignment and Significance

Huang, X. Q. and Miller, W. A. (1991) Time-Efficient, Linear-Space Local Similarity Algorithm, Adv. Appl. Math. 12, 337–357.

Huang, X. (1994) On global sequence alignment, CABIOS 10, 227–235.

Staden, R. (1989) Methods for calculating the probabilities of finding patterns in sequences, Comput. Applic. Biosci. 5, 89–96.

Staden, R. (1982) An interactive graphics program for comparing and aligning nucleic acid and protein sequences, Nucleic Acids Res. 9, 2951–2961.

B. The Genome Database: *Analysis and Similarity Searching*

25 Ensembl

An Open-Source Software Tool for Large-Scale Genome Analysis

James W. Stalker and Anthony V. Cox

Introduction

The completion of the human genome project (HGP) by the Human Genome Consortium provides research and computational biologists with the first *working draft* sequence of the human genome. The sequence consists of approximately three billion base-pairs of DNA sequence information, the sheer scale of which presents immense computational problems.

Biological sequence analysis is recognized as presenting computational challenges as great as those faced in existing *big science* projects such as particle physics and space exploration. Conventional methods of genome data curation and annotation cannot keep up with the rate at which data are accumulating. The gap will continue to widen. Ensembl was designed to meet the need for an automated annotation system capable of handling large volumes of finished and unfinished sequence data.

Ensembl, a joint project of the Sanger Center and the European Bioinformatics Institute, provides researchers with access to state-of-the-art automated annotation of genomic data. By its nature, this annotation is complete and consistent across the genome. Ensembl will be a foundation for the next generation of sequence databases that provide a curated, distributed, and nonredundant view of model organism genomes. Initial Ensembl development was concentrated on human genomic data, however the model is now applied to other organisms, including mouse, fly and worm.

Ensembl: An Open-Source Tool

One of the major successes of the HGP was to make the human genome sequence freely available to all. However, the computational resources necessary to analyze the data are not widely available outside of large private companies. This could have had the effect of confining the usefulness of the raw genome data to a small number of well-funded groups. Ensembl has aimed to bring these data to the widest possible audience.

A central tenet of the Ensembl philosophy is openness: all data, software, and associated information is freely available to all and without restriction. The project has enthusiastically embraced the open-source ethic, with all code released under an open-source licence, and contributors around the globe supplying expertise and time free of charge.

The Ensembl Analysis System

Ensembl consists of two main parts: 1) the analysis pipeline, which adds new data and analyses to the core database, and 2) the API (application programming interface), which gives structured access to these data. The website (*see* Website: http://www.ensembl.org) is simply one implementation of a graphical interface to the core database through the API. Other implementations, such as java clients, stand-alone applications, and so forth, are certainly possible and indeed encouraged.

The Analysis Pipeline

The Ensembl analysis pipeline is fed raw sequence data and subjects it to a battery of analysis programs. As the data passes through the pipeline these analyses produce supporting evidence for the gene predictions. At first all annotations are merely *in silico* predictions, with subsequent steps sorting predictions into the two groups of known genes and novel predictions. The result is a database containing DNA sequence, predicted features on that sequence and a complete body of evidence supporting these predictions. The database contains only the results of the pipeline analysis as no features are imported from external databases. Ensembl *known* genes therefore are simply those predicted genes that have high similarity to genes confirmed by experimental evidence.

The API

The Ensembl API provides a representation of the data in an Ensembl database in terms of model biological objects (genes, clones, contigs, etc.). This abstraction shields programmers from the underlying complexity of the data, making it easier to retrieve information in a meaningful form. This makes the API an extremely powerful tool for biologists. It is simple, for example, to extract a specific clone object from the database and query it for such biological properties as contigs, length, sequence, and any features added by the analysis pipeline such as genes, repeats, and CpG islands.

The API allows for the attachment of external databases to the Ensembl core data. In this way, a wide range of additional information, such as maps, gene expression data, and sequence features, can be superimposed onto the Ensembl predictions. The initial implementation of the API is in Perl, built upon a layer of Bio-Perl objects. Other implementations and language bindings such as Java and Python are under development.

Ensembl Data Concepts

The Ensembl data model revolves around two central ideas: a *golden path* and *virtual contigs*. Genomic sequence data is accumulated as a set of overlapping clones, each containing one or more sequence fragments called *contigs*. In *unfinished* data, the order and orientation of these contigs is often unknown. *Finished* data has been fully assembled, such that each clone comprises only a single contig, i.e., the clone has been fully sequenced. The clone overlap information, combined with data from genetic maps, can be used to assemble the clones into a continuous pathway along a chromosome. This pathway through the data, containing the nonredundant sequence, is often referred to as *the golden path*.

It is often desirable to be able to work with regions of an assembly that do not map exactly to a single clone or contig, for example, one might wish to examine the first megabase of a chromosome. The Ensembl API allows this manipulation of arbitrary regions by providing an abstraction of the underlying golden path assembly, called a *virtual contig*. A virtual contig behaves as if it was a real contig, but may actually be constructed behind-the-scenes from multiple real (or *raw*) contigs and fragments of contigs.

Virtual contigs smooth over the underlying complexity of the fragmentary, redundant nature of the assembly, and allow you to treat the data as one continuous sequence. Much of the power and flexibility of the Ensembl API comes from being able to manipulate virtual contigs. For example, virtual contigs provide a *handle* for accessing features, such as genes, that span contig or clone boundaries.

Ensembl Website

The Ensembl website (*see* Website: http://www.ensembl.org), is an interactive graphical interface to the Ensembl database, using Perl scripts that use the API (*see* Subheading "Using the Ensembl API"). In keeping with the Ensembl philosophy of openness, all source codes for the website can be freely downloaded, so you can install your own local copy, or just look at how it works.

The website offers a hierarchical interface to the human genome, so that a user can *drill down* into the data by selecting successively more detailed views. For example, clicking on a chromosome in **MapView** takes you to a high-level display of the region in ContigView, and from there to detailed displays of individual clones, genes, transcripts, proteins, and other sequence features. As well as drilling into the data, you can search for particular identifiers, or find data using alignment methods such as BLAST and SSAHA. The website also provides extensive facilities for exporting data in a variety of forms, including FASTA, EMBL, tab-delimited lists, and several image formats.

DAS (Distributed Annotation System)

With the rapid proliferation of databases of genome data from many research institutions around the world, it is becoming a Sisyphean task to keep up to date with the flood of data. Rather than each institution trying to maintain local copies of all data, with all the attendant issues of synchronisation and duplication, it makes sense for institutions to concentrate on their own areas of expertise and then share this with everyone else. This is the foundation of the Distributed Annotation System (DAS). DAS provides a distributed network of genome sequence servers that provide a consistent reference *backbone* upon which anyone can layer their own annotation data. This annotation data can, in turn, be served up via DAS to client applications worldwide.

The Ensembl website allows the users to extend the site by dynamically adding information provided via remote DAS servers. For example, a ContigView display served from the Ensembl site in the UK can easily be configured to display additional annotation information provided by a DAS server in the US. This enables users to mix-and-match their displays to suit their research needs.

In return, the Ensembl golden path data is served as a reference sequence via DAS (*see* Website: http://das.ensembl.org).

Website Tour

As a quick introduction to the Ensembl website we will investigate the BRCA2 gene. We will find the gene, look at its details, examine the region it occupies in the

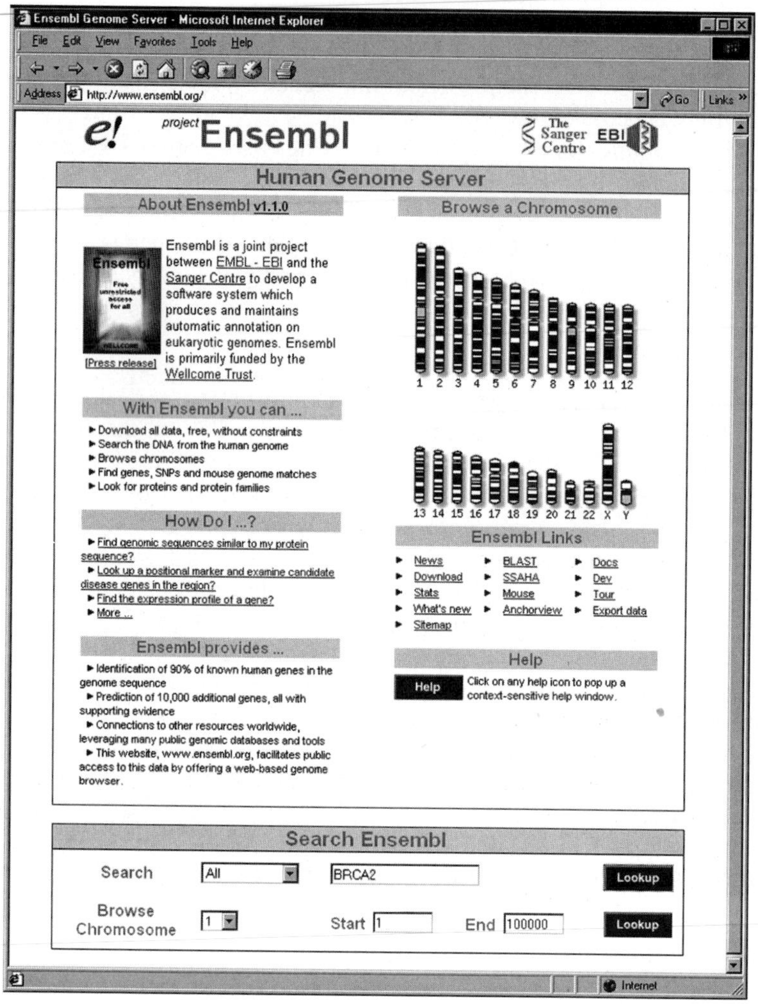

Fig. 1. The Ensembl Website home page.

genome, and then export some reference data. These are all tasks you can do in a script, of course, but the website puts an easy-to-use interface on top of all the code as shown in Fig. 1.

Searching for a Feature

The website uses the AltaVista search engine to provide a full index of the databases, enabling very fast and comprehensive searches. We will use this to find the BRCA2 gene by name.

Enter **BRCA2** into the search box on the home page. You can change the Search Type to limit the search to a particular type of feature, in this case gene, but we will leave it set to **All** to see everything that the database holds about the BRCA2 identifier.

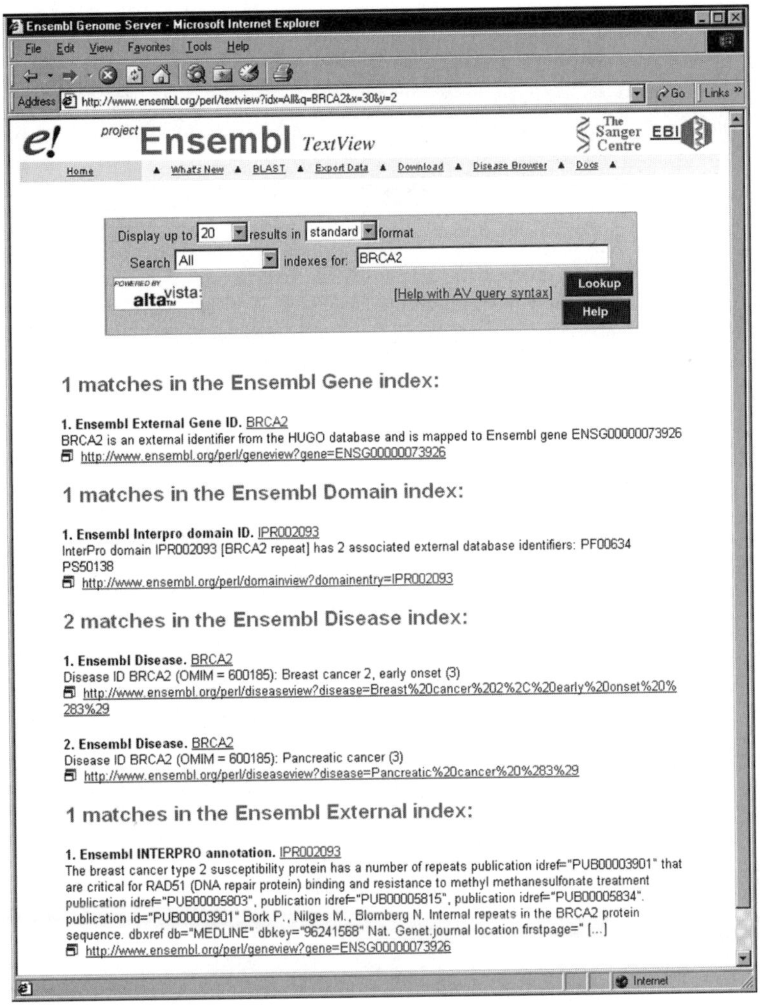

Fig. 2. Results of the search for BRCA2.

You should see more than one match for BRCA2, as Fig. 2. shows. The search currently matches the gene BRCA2, an InterPro protein domain, diseases associated with the gene, and also finds BRCA2 in some external annotation documentation. For now we are only interested in the gene, so click on the link from the match to the gene index. This will take us to a detailed view of the gene in GeneView.

GeneView

The GeneView page contains much detail and information about BRCA2 including its Ensembl identifier, description, DBLinks, and InterPro protein domain matches. This is shown in Fig. 3. Further down the page is the sequence of the corresponding transcripts, exons, and splice sites.

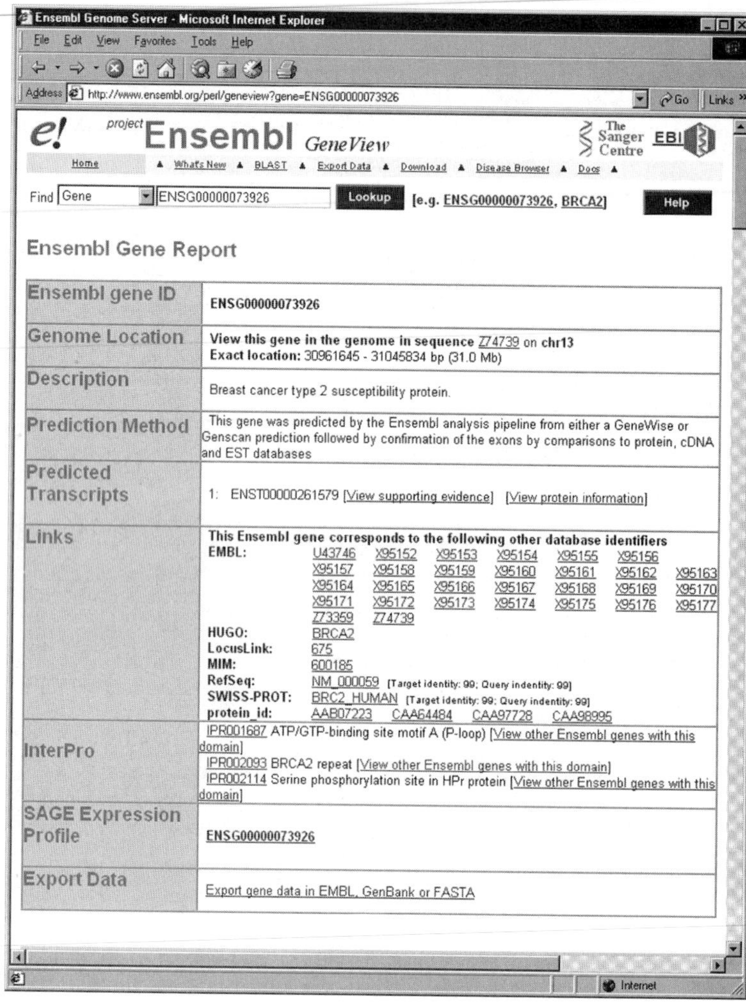

Fig. 3. The gene summary section of GeneView for BRCA2.

For each transcript, GeneView has diagrams showing the exon structure. These can be seen for a transcript of BRCA2 in Fig. 4. If we want to investigate the genomic location of the gene in more detail, there is a section in the gene summary called Genome Location. This specifies the clone, chromosome and base-pair coordinates where the gene is located. This information is linked into the detailed genome browser page using **ContigView**.

ContigView

ContigView is the main genome browser display for the Ensembl website. It allows the user to *walk* freely up and down any chromosome, and displays all the sequence features appropriate to the current region. There are a variety of navigation

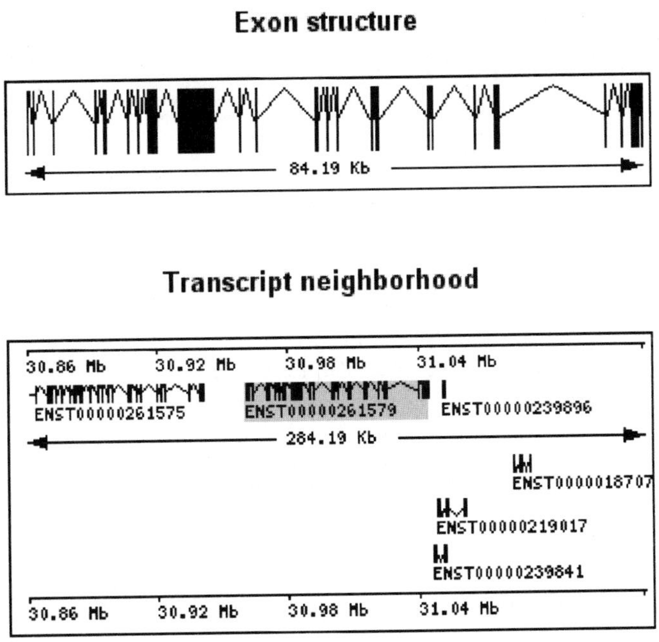

Fig. 4. Exon structure and transcript locale diagrams from GeneView.

tools provided to let the user move to any location, zoom in and out, and focus on a specific area.

The ContigView display is customizable. The user can toggle the display of any feature type, change how they are drawn, and even change their color. ContigView displays also show any DAS sources that the user has added. The page therefore can be customized precisely to show only the data needed for the task the user is working on.

Selecting any of the features by moving the mouse over the object on ContigView will display a drop-down menu. These menus contain more feature information, and links that jump to a detailed view of the specific feature.

As you can see from Fig. 5, ContigView shows a hierarchy of views. The topmost view shows the chromosome that we are looking at. A box surrounds the region that is represented in the next image: the overview display. The overview shows, by default, one megabase of DNA, and is a high-level view of the region. For this reason, the overview only shows landmark features such as markers and genes. Known genes, novel genes, curated EMBL genes, and pseudogenes are distinctively colored. Clicking anywhere on the overview will focus the detailed view on that point and this region of focus is displayed again.

The bottom view is the detailed display. It shows a relatively short region of the genome, but can display all the features present in that area. Only a few feature sets are turned on in Fig. 5, but you can see the large dark BRCA2 transcript in the center, and see that this prediction is supported by both EMBL and Genscan transcripts. SpTrEMBL protein homology matches are shown above these.

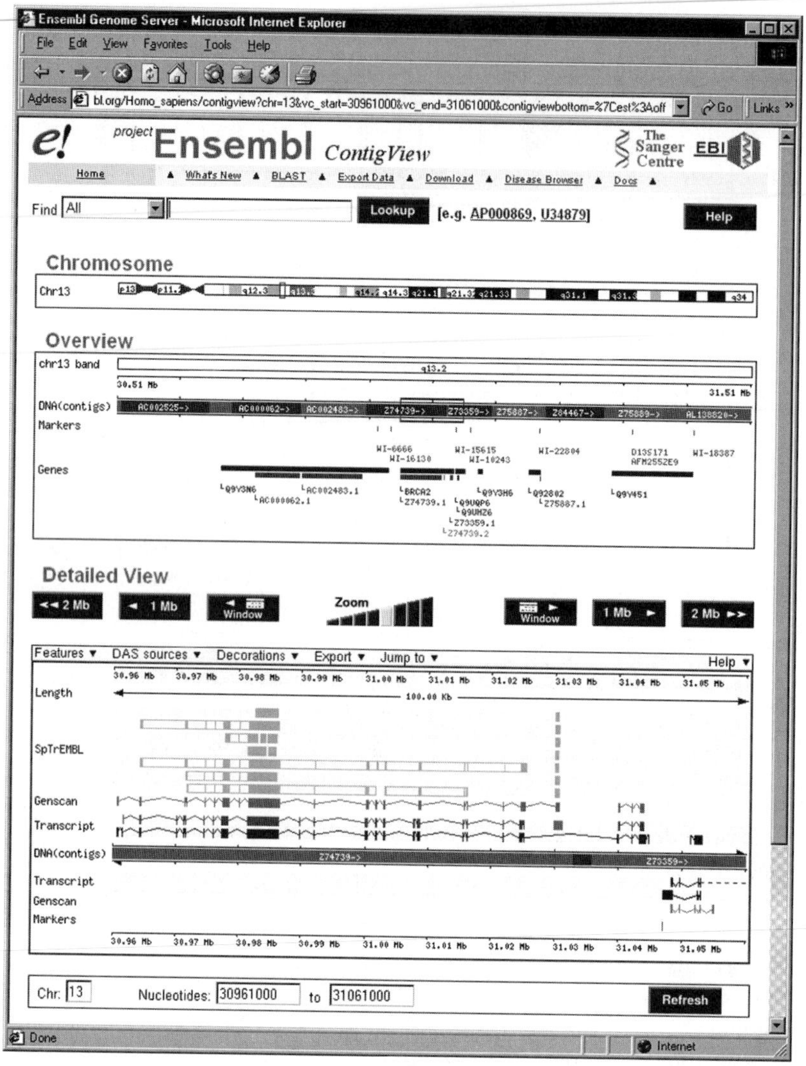

Fig. 5. ContigView centered around the BRCA2 gene.

The thick bar along the middle of the detailed display is a representation of the contigs in the golden path at that point. Features above the contigs are on the forward strand of the DNA at that point (as is our transcript), while those below are on the reverse strand.

The menus at the top of the detailed display provide additional customization options. The **Features** menu has checkboxes for the user to toggle the display of the different feature types. **Decorations** gives the same control over items on the display such as the length bar or a %GC plot. **DAS sources** is for toggling configured DAS sources, and also contains links for adding and removing sources. The **Jump to** menu lets you visit the equivalent region in the UCSC genome browser. Finally, the **Export** menu, as shown in Fig. 6, gives access to ExportView.

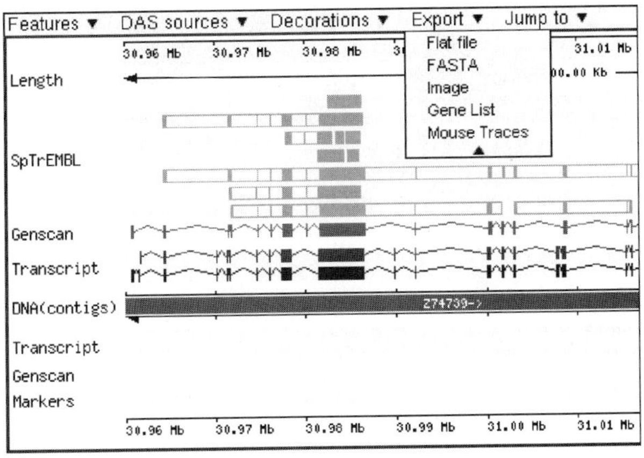

Fig. 6. The Export menu on the ContigView detailed display.

ExportView

ExportView is a tool for exporting data from a feature or region in a variety of formats. The page shows a tabbed dialog, with a different tab for each export format. At the time of writing, these were, as illustrated in Fig. 7, Flat File, FASTA, Image, Gene List, and Traces.

The **Flat File**, **FASTA**, **Gene List**, and **Traces** tabs all allow export of data as text (useful for cut and paste of data), HTML (the same data as text, but with links back into the website), or as a zipped text file for download. The Flat File tab allows you to export a feature or region in EMBL or GenBank format and the FASTA tab provides FASTA format.

Image exporting enables you to create a detailed image, similar to that shown at the bottom of ContigView, of any region of the genome. Images can be exported in GIF/PNG, PostScript, Scaleable Vector Graphics (SVG), and Windows MetaFile (WMF) formats. The Trace tab gives access to raw sequence traces that have been matched to the human genome, for example mouse traces.

The Gene List tab is extremely useful. It exports tab-delimited data that can be easily imported into other applications (such as spreadsheets) for further analysis. For example, if we click on the **Gene List** tab after coming from our BRCA2 region in contigview, the base-pair location fields will be filled in with the appropriate coordinates. The rest of the tab contains a large list of features we can include in or exclude from the export. As an example, check the **Ensembl gene id**, **known gene external id**, **chromosome start**, **chromosome end**, and **chromosome name** boxes. Click **export**, and the results should look like:

# gene_name	external_id	chrom_start	chrom_end	chrom_band
ENSG00000073926	BRCA2	30961645	31045834	q13.2
ENSG00000102832	Q9UQP6	31047843	31062857	q13.2
ENSG00000120702	Q9UHZ6	31052055	31053944	q13.2

This is a quick and powerful way to extract a lot of useful information from the Ensembl database.

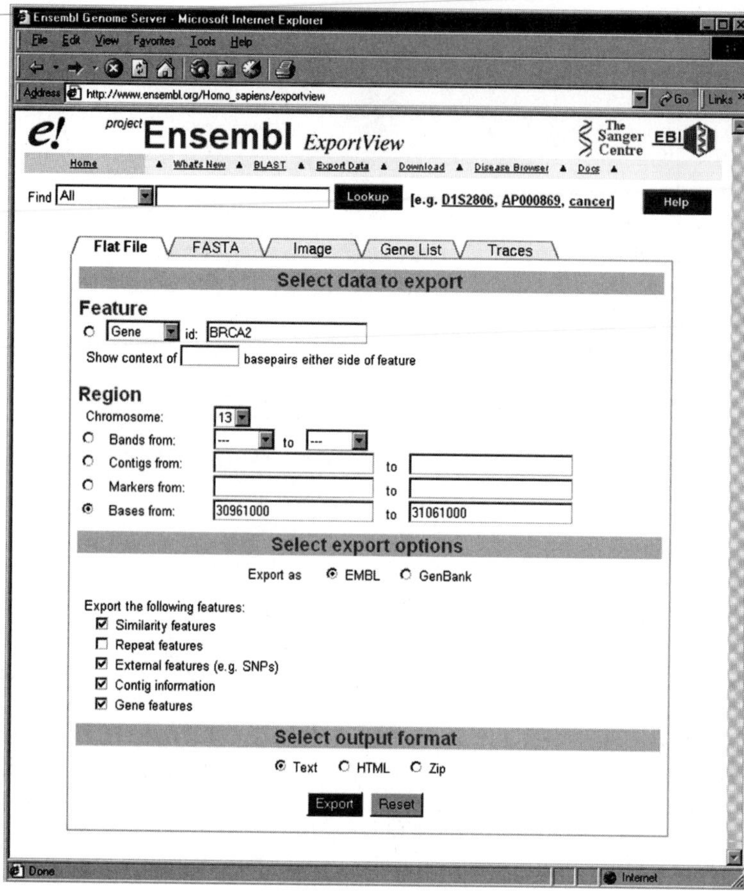

Fig. 7. ExportView.

Using the Ensembl API

Installation

Before using the Ensembl API, you must first obtain and install the Ensembl software modules. The components you will require for a basic installation are:

- Bioperl: Provides the foundation objects for Ensembl.
- Ensembl: The core functionality and database objects.

These components and instructions for retrieving and installing them, can be found on the Ensembl website. You will also need an Ensembl database to run your code. Again, the website provides instructions on obtaining and installing a freely available copy of the databases. If you do not have or do not want to install a local Ensembl database, you can direct your software to a publicly available copy at the Sanger Center. This is the database we will be using for these examples.

Finally, you will need a local installation of the Perl programming language, which is free to download (*see* Website: http://www.perl.com).

Set Up of the Ensembl Software Environment

Once you have installed Ensembl and Bioperl you need to configure your environment so that your Perl script will know where the modules are. The easiest way to do this is to add the location of the modules to the PERL5LIB environment variable.

For example, if you installed Ensembl and Bioperl into a directory called */home/bob*, then set the environment as follows:

In UNIX:

csh: **setenv PERL5LIB /home/bob/ensembl/modules:/home/bob/bioperl**

bash: **export PERL5LIB = /home/bob/ensembl/modules:/home/bob/bioperl**

On Windows:

set PERL5LIB c:\home\bob\ensembl\modules;c\home\bob\bioperl

Worked Examples

The following examples are intended to provide a brief introduction to using the Ensembl API for manipulating data in an Ensembl database. The code used here only scratches the surface; the API has many powerful features. Additional details are available at the website, which always contains the latest API documentation (*see* Website: http://www.ensembl.org).

Working with Clones and Contigs

As previously discussed (*see* Subheading "Ensembl Data Concepts"), we learned that a clone is a fundamental unit of a sequenced genome and is made up of one or more contigs. We are going to use the Ensembl API to retrieve a clone from the database, extract the contigs that make up that clone, and then look at their sequences.

Connecting to the Database

We will assume that you do not have a local Ensembl database installed and instead connect to a publicly available copy of the Ensembl databases on kaka.sanger.ac.uk. Of course, this is far slower than accessing a local copy, which is a must for any serious use.

We use a DBAdaptor module from the API to connect to the database:

```
use Bio::EnsEMBL::DBSQL::DBAdaptor;
```

To make the connection, we need to specify the host machine that is serving the database (kaka.sanger.ac.uk), the name of the database to connect to (the current database at time of writing is *ensembl110*), and the username to connect as (kaka accepts the user *anonymous*).

The code to make the connection is:

```
my $database = Bio::EnsEMBL::DBSQL::DBAdaptor->new( -host =>'kaka.sanger.ac.uk',
                                                    -user => 'anonymous',
                                                    -dbname => 'ensembl110' );
```

If the connection fails, you will get an error message. Otherwise, you are free to start working with the data in the database.

Fetching a Clone from the Database

It is very simple to retrieve a clone by its accession number by typing:

```
my $clone = $database->get_Clone('AP000869');
```

The variable $clone now contains an Ensembl clone object.

You can check it is the clone that you asked for by printing its identifier:

```
print "Clone id is ". $clone->id . "\n";
```

Getting the Contigs from a Clone

Now that we have a clone object, we can get the contigs that make up that clone:

my @contigs = $clone->get_all_Contigs;

@contigs is now an array that holds a list of all the contigs in the clone. We can loop over these contigs and print out some information about them:

foreach my $contig (@contigs) {
print "Contig ". $contig->id . " is ". $contig->length ." base-pairs long\n";
}

Getting the Sequence from a Contig

The method call *primary_seq* retrieves a sequence object from a contig. To get the DNA sequence from the contig, you ask the sequence object for its sequence string:

my $seqobj = $contig->primary_seq;
print $seqobj->seq . "\n";

This will print the correct sequence, but it is not exactly pretty output. Something like FASTA format would be much more useful. We could of course do this ourselves manually, but Bioperl already provides a way to do this via the *SeqIO* object.

use Bio::SeqIO;
my $seqio = Bio::SeqIO->new(-format => 'fasta');
$seqio->write_seq($seqobj);

Finished Example

Our completed script looks like this:

```
#!/usr/local/bin/perl

use strict;
use Bio::EnsEMBL::DBSQL::DBAdaptor;
use Bio::SeqIO;


my $database = Bio::EnsEMBL::DBSQL::DBAdaptor->new( -host => 'kaka.sanger.ac.uk',
                                                    -user=> 'anonymous',
                                                    -dbname=>'ensembl110');


my $clone = $database->get_Clone('AP000869');
print "Clone id is ". $clone->id . "\n";


my @contigs = $clone->get_all_Contigs;


foreach my $contig (@contigs){
    print "Contig ". $contig->id . " is ". $contig->length ." base-pairs long\n";
}


foreach my $contig (@contigs){
    my $seqio = Bio::SeqIO->new (-format => 'fasta');
    my $seqobj = $contig->primary_seq;
    $seqio->write_seq($seqobj);
}
```

To recap: this script connects to an Ensembl database, retrieves a clone object from the database by its identifier, collects all the contigs in that clone and prints their sequences in FASTA format.

The output should look something like this:

```
Clone id is AP000869
Contig AP000869.2.154917.155980 is 1064 base-pairs long
Contig AP000869.2.27859.38788 is 10930 base-pairs long
Contig AP000869.2.38889.50392 is 11504 base-pairs long
Contig AP000869.2.158624.159840 is 1217 base-pairs long
.
.
etc
```

Followed by the FASTA sequence of the contigs:

```
>AP000869.2.154917.155980
AGGGAAAAAAAAGTGATGGAGAAATGAGAACTTTCACCAACCCACCCAAATTGAGAGAAT
CTGTAGACCTGTCTTGCCAGAAGTATTTAAAAAAAAAACTTCTTCAGAGAAAAGAAAGAT
GATATAAGTTAGAAACTTTGAACTACATAAACAAGGGAAGAGCTTTAGAGAAGGAATAAG
.
.
etc
```

Working with a Virtual Contig

A virtual contig acts like the *raw* contigs that we have just been using. The calls we made on a contig will also work just as well on a virtual contig. Because genes are built on virtual contigs in the analysis pipeline, and because many genes span more than one contig, it is preferable (and often essential) to use virtual contigs to access them. In this example, we will build a virtual contig and look at the genes it contains.

Connecting to the Database

We connect to the database in exactly the same way as in the previous example, i.e., via a DBAdaptor. However, we are working with virtual rather than raw contigs and need access to the golden path (remember that a virtual contig is just a chunk of this continuous assembly). We access the golden path through another adaptor object — the *static golden path adaptor*. It is called static because the golden path has been pregenerated and stored in the database, rather than being generated dynamically when required (this is quite possible, but rather slow). The golden path we use in Ensembl is currently provided by UCSC. Ensembl has the capacity to store and use multiple different golden paths; first, the type of golden path is relayed to the DBAdaptor by typing:

$database->static_golden_path_type('UCSC');

and then get the static golden path adaptor:

my $sa = $database->get_StaticGoldenPathAdaptor;

We can now use the static golden path adaptor to assemble virtual contigs, much as we used the DBAdaptor to retrieve the raw contigs. In fact, we could get the same region as before, using the call:

my $vcontig = $sa->fetch_VirtualContig_of_clone('AP000869');

Building a Virtual Contig

There are several calls on the static golden path adaptor that retrieve virtual contigs. This can be queried by clone, contig, gene, and transcript identifiers. Probably the most interesting is to use the contiguous nature of the golden path to fetch an arbitrary region of sequence that might span multiple clones:

```
My $vcontig = $sa->fetch_VirtualContig_by_chr_start_end('chrX',1,500000);
```

$vcontig now contains a virtual contig built from the first half megabase of chromosome X. Even though it is constructed of many underlying contigs stitched together, it acts as though it were a single Ensembl contig, for example, we can extract the DNA sequence using the same method we used for a raw contig:

```
print $vcontig->primary_seq->seq;
```

With just this small snippet of code, we are already able to access the DNA sequence of any arbitrary region of a chromosome, as much or as little as is required.

Virtual Contig Properties

Because a virtual contig is created from a chromosomal assembly, it contains information about its absolute position in that chromosome. For example:

```
print "This virtual contig is from chromosome ". $vcontig->_chr_name. "\n";
print "Base-pairs ".$vcontig->_global_start. " to ". $vcontig->_global_end. "\n";
```

This information may not appear very useful when implemented on a virtual contig constructed by chromosomal position, but the clone identifier could use this to locate that clone within the golden path.

We can also examine the underlying structure of the virtual contig, by retrieving the contigs that comprise the contig. The call to do this is **each_MapContig**, and it gives us a list of contig objects, in a similar way in the previous example that the **get_all_Contigs** call on the clone did:

```
my @contigs = $vcontig->_vmap->each_MapContig;
print "Virtual Contig ".$vcontig->id. " is made up of the following contigs: \n";
foreach my $mapcontig (@contigs){
    print $mapcontig->contig->id."\n";
}
```

Retrieving Genes

We can access all the genes on a virtual (or raw) contig with:

```
my @genes = $vcontig->get_all_Genes;
```

As you should be coming to expect, this presents an array of gene objects. We can print their Ensembl identifiers with:

```
foreach my $gene (@genes){
    print "Gene ". $gene->id . "\n";
}
```

Ensembl identifiers do not yield a bounty of information about a gene. They are automated predictions of genes from the analysis pipeline, not experimentally confirmed genes. However, we can tell if an Ensembl gene has been matched to a known gene by checking the **is_known** property of the gene. If the gene is known, then we can look at the list of matches for that gene, and perhaps retrieve a more familiar name. The list is actually a list of matches against databases of known genes, and these connections between predictions and known genes are called *DBLinks*. In addition to the DBLink information, we can retrieve a description of known genes from the relevant SwissProt or RefSeq entry. For example:

```
if ($gene->is_known){
    print "Gene ". $gene->id. " : ". $gene->description."\n";
    foreach my $link ($gene->each_DBLink){
   print " Links:". $link->display_id. " from ". $link->database. "\n";
    }
}
else {
    print "Gene ". $gene->id. " is a novel prediction.\n";
}
```

Transcripts from Genes

Just as gene objects are retrieved from contig objects, transcript objects are retrieved from genes. A gene has one or more transcripts; one for each alternatively spliced mRNA. You can view the transcripts from a gene as follows:

```
my @transcripts = $gene->each_Transcript;
```

As you would expect, you can call the id method of a transcript object to retrieve its Ensembl identifier. Like Ensembl gene identifiers, these do not mean very much in themselves. Transcripts are most interesting for their structure and what they encode.

Exons from Transcripts

Like stacking Russian dolls, we can again extract more objects from the objects we already have. Transcripts are made up of exons, which can be pulled out with the familiar syntax:

```
my @exons = $transcript->each_Exon; }
```

We can query exons for their sequence and coordinates as:

```
foreach my $exon (@exons){
    print $exon->id. " : ". $exon->start ." - ". $exon->end. "\n";
    print $exon->seq->seq ."\n";
}
```

Notice again that the first call on the exon for that sequence retrieves a sequence object, this can be followed by a DNA string by asking for the sequence from the object.

Transcript Translations

The final manipulation of transcripts yields the peptide sequence from the translated transcript. The Bio::SeqIO module is used since it yields a nicely formatted output. We can retrieve the peptide object from the transcript by asking for its translation:

```
my $seqio = Bio::SeqIO->new (-format => 'fasta');
my $peptide = $transcript->translate;
$seqio->write_seq($peptide);
```

Finished Example

Our completed script looks like this:

```
#!/usr/local/bin/perl

use strict;
use Bio::EnsEMBL::DBSQL::DBAdaptor;
use Bio::SeqIO;

my $database = Bio::EnsEMBL::DBSQL::DBAdaptor->new(-host => 'kaka.sanger.ac.uk',
                                                   -user=> 'anonymous',
                                                   -dbname=>'ensembl110');

$database->static_golden_path_type('UCSC');
my $sa = $database->get_StaticGoldenPathAdaptor;

my $vcontig = $sa->fetch_VirtualContig_by_chr_start_end('chrX',1,500000);

print "Virtual contig: ". $vcontig->_chr_name. " base-pairs ";
print $vcontig->_global_start. " to ". $vcontig->_global_end. "\n";

print "is built from: \n";
foreach my $mapcontig ($vcontig->_vmap->each_MapContig){
    print "Raw contig: ".$mapcontig->contig->id."\n";
}

print "\n and contains the following genes: \n";
my @genes = $vcontig->get_all_Genes;

foreach my $gene(@genes){
    if ($gene->is_known){
        print "Gene ". $gene->id. " : ". $gene->description."\n";
        foreach my $link ($gene->each_DBLink){
            print " Links:". $link->display_id. " from ". $link->database."\n";
        }
        print "\n";
    }
    else {
        print "Gene ". $gene->id. " is a novel prediction.\n";
    }
}
print "\n";

foreach my $gene(@genes){
    print "Gene: ". $gene->id."\n";
    foreach my $transcript ($gene->each_Transcript){
        print "Transcript: ".$transcript->id."\n";
        print "Exons: \n";
        foreach my $exon ($transcript->each_Exon){
            print "\t".$exon->id. " : ". $exon->start. " - ". $exon->end. "\n";
        }
        print "Peptide:\n";
        my $seqio = Bio::SeqIO->new(-format => 'fasta');
        my $peptide = $transcript->translate;
        $seqio->write_seq($peptide);
        print "\n";
    }
}
```

This script connects to an ensembl database, retrieves a static golden path adaptor, and uses that to build a virtual contig of an arbitrary region of chromosome X. It then retrieves all the genes from the virtual contig, all the transcripts from the genes, and all the exons from the transcripts. Finally we print out the peptide translations of the transcripts in FASTA format are printed. As shown previously, the Ensembl API enables you to extract and manipulate biologically meaningful objects from the Ensembl database with a surprisingly small amount of code.

Future Developments

Ensembl is under active development. The already rich API is growing constantly to provide convenient access to a wider range of genome data resources. Each release of the database sees the inclusion of additional data of ever-increasing quality. The website is also being adapted to represent these underlying improvements in the API and data, and to meet the increasingly complex demands of the research community. Future developments currently being considered include:

- Extended support for DAS
- Cross-species data linking and comparison
- Multiple language bindings for the API, including Java & Python
- Remote object services via CORBA and SOAP

Contact List

The Ensembl project has a very active development mailing list called *ensembl-dev*. All of the Ensembl team participate in the list, so if you have a question or comment about Ensembl you can be sure it will be answered there. There is also a low traffic mailing list, ensembl-announce, which is used to announce major updates or a new release. To subscribe to these lists, send an email to: majordomo@ebi.ac.uk with either *subscribe ensembl-announce* or *subscribe ensembl-dev* in the body of the mail. These mailing lists are archived on the Ensembl website.

Ensembl also maintains a helpdesk facility that will answer any questions pertaining to the project. Either send an email to: helpdesk@ensembl.org, or use the form on the website.

The Ensembl web team is always interested in any feedback you might have on the site. Comments and suggestions are all carefully considered, and often make their way into the next version of the site. The web team can be contacted through the Ensembl helpdesk, or via webmaster@ensembl.org.

Suggested Readings

Ensembl: An Open-Source Tool

Raymond, E. S. (1999) The Cathedral and the Bazaar.
see Websites: http://www.ensembl.org/Download/ and http://www.ftp.ensembl.org
http://www.bioperl.org/
http://www.open-bio.org/

Ensembl Website

see Websites: http://www.sanger.ac.uk/Software/analysis/SSAHA/
http://www.biodas.org/

26 The PIR for Functional Genomics and Proteomics

Cathy H. Wu

Introduction

The human genome project has revolutionized the practice of biology and the future potential of medicine. Complete genomes continue to be sequenced *en masse*. Meanwhile, there is growing recognition that proteomic studies bring the researcher closer to the actual biology than studies of gene sequence or gene expression alone. High-throughput studies are being conducted and rapid advances being made in areas such as protein expression, protein structure and function, and protein-protein interactions. Given the enormous increase in genomic, proteomic, and molecular data, computational approaches, in combination with empirical methods, are expected to become essential for deriving and evaluating hypotheses. To fully explore these valuable data, advanced bioinformatics infrastructures must be developed for biological knowledge management. One major challenge lies in the volume, complexity, and dynamic nature of the data, which are being collected and maintained in heterogeneous and distributed sources. New approaches need to be devised for data collection, maintenance, dissemination, query, and analysis. The Protein Information Resource (PIR) aims to serve as an integrated public resource of functional annotation of proteins to support genomic/proteomic research and scientific discovery.

The PIR was established in 1984 as a resource to assist researchers in the identification and interpretation of protein sequence information. The PIR, along with the Munich Information Center for Protein Sequences (MIPS) and the Japan International Protein Information Database (JIPID), continues to enhance and distribute the PIR-International Protein Sequence Database. The database evolved from the first comprehensive collection of macromolecular sequences in the *Atlas of Protein Sequence and Structure* published from 1965–1978 under the editorship of Margaret O. Dayhoff, who pioneered molecular evolution research.

PIR provides many protein databases and data analysis tools employing a family classification approach to facilitate protein annotation and data integration. The PIR-International Protein Sequence Database (PSD) is the major annotated protein database in the public domain, containing about 283,000 sequences covering the entire taxonomic range. The PIR superfamily organization allows complete and nonoverlapping clustering of all proteins. Comprehensive protein information is available from iProClass, which includes family classification at the superfamily, domain, and motif levels; structural and functional features of proteins; as well as cross-references to over 50 databases of protein families, structures, functions, genes, genomes, literature, and taxonomy. The nonredundant reference protein database, PIR-NREF, provides timely and comprehensive data collected from PIR-PSD, Swiss-Prot, TrEMBL, GenPept, RefSeq, and PDB, with composite protein names and literature information for about 1,000,000 proteins. To promote database interoperability and improve annotation quality, we have adopted controlled vocabulary, standard nomenclature, and common ontologies, and distinguish experimentally determined from predicted protein features. We also provide open and modular database architecture and XML data distribution to assist data integration in a distributed networking environment. The PIR databases are implemented in the object-relational database system and are freely accessible from our web site (*see* Website: http://pir.georgetown.edu/). The site features data mining and sequence analysis tools for information retrieval and functional identification of proteins based on both sequence and annotation information. It supports the exploration of proteins and comparative studies of various family relationships. Such knowledge is crucial to our understanding of protein evolution, structure and function, and is important for functional genomic and proteomic research.

PIR-International Protein Sequence Database

The PIR-International Protein Sequence Database (PSD) is a nonredundant, expertly annotated, fully classified, and extensively cross-referenced protein sequence database in the public domain. Release 73.0, July 2002, contained about 283,000 protein sequences with comprehensive coverage across the entire taxonomic range, including sequences from publicly available complete genomes.

Superfamily Classification

A unique characteristic of the PIR-PSD is the superfamily classification that provides complete and nonoverlapping clustering of proteins based on global (end-to-end) sequence similarity. Sequences in the same superfamily share common domain architecture (i.e., have the same number, order and types of domains), and do not differ excessively in overall length unless they are fragments or result from alternate splicing or initiators. The automated classification system places new members into existing superfamilies and defines new superfamily clusters using parameters including the percentage of sequence identity, overlap length ratio, distance to neighboring superfamily clusters, and overall domain arrangement. Currently, over 99% of the sequences are classified into families of closely related sequences (at least 45% identical) and over two thirds of sequences are classified into >36,200 superfamilies. The automated classification is being augmented by manual curation of superfamilies, starting with those containing at least one definable domain, to provide superfamily names, brief descriptions, bibliography, list of representative and seed members, as well as domain and motif architecture characteristic of the superfamily. Sequences in PIR-PSD are also classified with homology domains and sequence motifs. Homology domains, which are shared by more than one superfamily, may constitute evolutionary building blocks, while sequence motifs represent functional sites or conserved regions.

The classification allows the systematic detection of genome annotation errors based on comprehensive superfamily and domain classification. Several annotation

See companion CD for color Fig. 1

errors originated from different genome centers have lead to the *transitive catastrophe*. Figure 1 illustrates an example where several members of three related superfamilies were originally misannotated because only local domain (not global superfamily) relationships were considered.

The classification also provides the basis for rule-based procedures that are used to propagate information-rich annotations among similar sequences and to perform integrity checks. These scripts use the superfamily/family classification system, sequence patterns and profiles to produce highly specific annotations. False-positives are avoided by applying automated annotations only to classified members of the families and superfamilies for which the annotation has been validated. Integrity checks are based on PIR controlled vocabulary, standard nomenclature (such as IUBMB Enzyme Nomenclature) and a thesaurus of synonyms or alternate names.

Evidence Attribution and Bibliography Submission

Attribution of protein annotations to validated experimental sources provides an effective means to avoid propagating errors that may have resulted from large-scale genome annotation. To distinguish experimentally verified from computationally predicted data, PIR-PSD entries are labeled with status tags such as *validated* or *similarity* in protein Title, Function and Complex annotations, as well as tags such as *experimental*, *predicted*, *absent*, or *atypical* in Feature annotations. The validated Function or Complex annotation includes hypertext-linked PubMed unique identifiers for the articles in which the experimental determination are reported.

Linking protein data to more literature data that describes or characterizes the proteins is crucial to increasing the amount of experimental information and improving the quality of protein annotation. We have developed a bibliography submission system for the scientific community to submit, categorize, and retrieve literature information for PSD protein entries. The submission interface guides users through steps in mapping the paper citation to given protein entries, entering the literature data, and summarizing the literature data using categories such as genetics, tissue/cellular localization, molecular complex or interaction, function, regulation, and disease. Also included is a literature information page that provides literature data mining and displays both references cited in PIR and submitted by users.

Integrated Protein Classification Database

See companion CD for color Fig. 2

The iProClass (Integrated Protein Classification) database (*see* Fig. 2), is designed to provide comprehensive descriptions of all proteins and to serve as a framework for data integration in a distributed networking environment. The protein information includes family relationships at both global (superfamily/family) and local (domain, motif, site) levels, as well as structural and functional classifications and features of proteins. A modular architecture organizes the information into multiple database components for Sequence, Superfamily, Domain, Motif, Structure, and Function.

See companion CD for color Fig. 3

The current version (Release 2.4, August 2002) consists of about 810,000 nonredundant PIR-PSD, Swiss-Prot, and TrEMBL proteins organized with more than 36,200 PIR superfamilies; 145,340 families; 3840 PIR homology and Pfam domains; 1300 ProClass/ProSite motifs; 280 PIR post-translational modification sites; and links to over 50 databases of protein families, structures, functions, genes, genomes, literature, and taxonomy. The Sequence report (*see* Fig. 3) provides detailed protein

H70468	SF001258	051440	phosphoribosyl-AMP cyclohydrolase (EC 3.5.4.19) / phosphoribosyl-ATP pyrophosphatase (EC 3.6.1.31) [similarity]	Aquifex aeolicus	Prok/other	594.3	4.8e-26	205	39.086	197	
S76963	SF001258	039935	phosphoribosyl-AMP cyclohydrolase (EC 3.5.4.19) / phosphoribosyl-ATP pyrophosphatase (EC 3.6.1.31) [similarity]	Synechocystis sp.	Prok/gram-	557.0	5.7e-24	230	39.175	194	
T35073	SF029243	005738	probable phosphoribosyl-AMP cyclohydrolase	Streptomyces coelicolor	Prok/gram+	399.3	3.5e-15	128	42.157	102	
S53349	SF001257	001188	phosphoribosyl-AMP cyclohydrolase (EC 3.5.4.19) / phosphoribosyl-ATP pyrophosphatase (EC 3.6.1.31) / histidinol dehydrogenase (EC 1.1.1.23)	Saccharomyces cerevisiae	Euk/fungi	384.1	2.5e-14	799	31.863	204	
E69493	SF029243	005738	phosphoribosyl-AMP cyclohydrolase (EC 3.5.4.19) [similarity]	Archaeoglobus fulgidus	Archae	396.8	4.8e-15	108	47.778	90	
G64337	SF006833	030827	phosphoribosyl-ATP pyrophosphatase (EC 3.6.1.31) [similarity]	Methanococcus jannaschii	Archae	246.9	1.1e-06	95	36.842	95	
D81178	SF006833	101491	phosphoribosyl-ATP pyrophosphatase (EC 3.6.1.31) NMB0603 [similarity]	Neisseria meningitidis	Prok/gram-	239.9	2.6e-06	107	35.227	88	
G81925	SF006833	101491	phosphoribosyl-ATP pyrophosphatase (EC 3.6.1.31) NMA0807 [similarity]	Neisseria meningitidis	Prok/gram-	245.2	1.4e-06	107	35.227	88	
S51513	SF001257	001188	phosphoribosyl-AMP cyclohydrolase (EC 3.5.4.19) / phosphoribosyl-ATP pyrophosphatase (EC 3.6.1.31) / histidinol dehydrogenase (EC 1.1.1.23)	Pichia pastoris	Euk/fungi	225.6	1.7e-05	842	29.670	182	

PIR ID	Imported	Corrected	Superfamily
H70468	3.6.1.31	3.5.4.19/3.6.1.31	SF001258
E69493	3.5.4.19/3.6.1.31	3.5.4.19	SF029243
G64337	3.5.4.19	3.6.1.31	SF006833

A

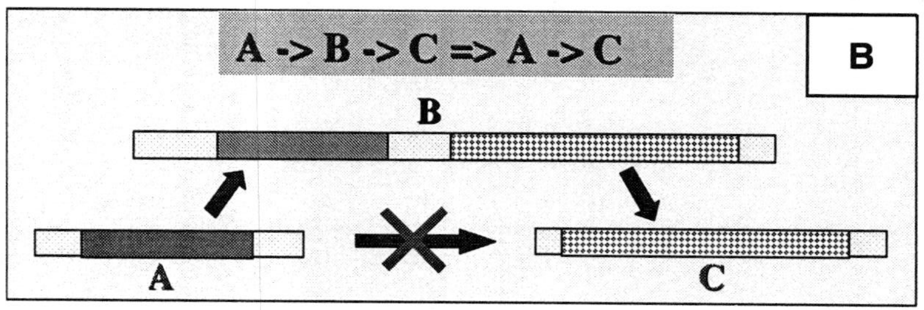

Fig. 1. Genome sequence annotation: transitive catastrophe. **(A)** Misannotation of three imported sequence entries is later corrected based on superfamily classification. **(B)** Transitive identification error, illustrated in entry G64337, often involves multi-domain proteins.

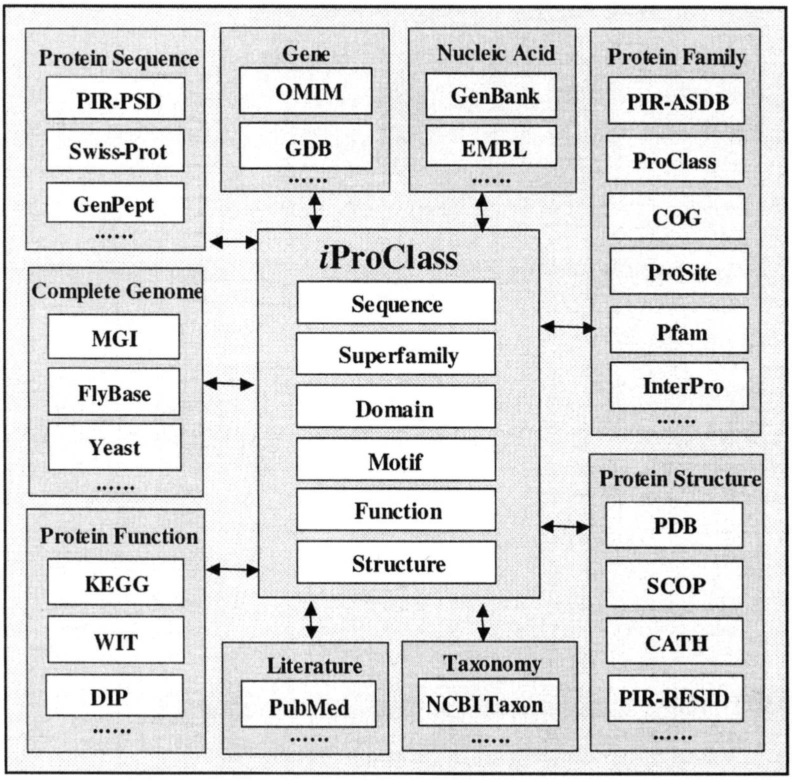

Fig. 2. iProClass database for data integration: modular database components and extensive links to molecular biology databases.

summary information in four sections: General Information, Cross-References, Family Classification, and Feature Display, with extensive hypertext links for further exploration and graphical display of domain and motif regions. The Superfamily report provides summaries including membership information with length, taxonomy, and keyword statistics; complete member listing separated by major kingdoms, family relationships, and structure and function cross-references.

Directly linked to the iProClass sequence report are two additional PIR databases, Annotation and Similarity DataBase (ASDB) and post-translational modification database (RESID). PIR-ASDB lists pre-computed, biweekly-updated FASTA sequence similarity researched neighbors of all PSD sequences with annotation information and graphical displays of sequence similarity matches. PIR-RESID documents over 280 post-translational modifications and links to PSD entries containing either experimentally determined or computationally predicted modifications with evidence tags.

To be implemented are the Domain-Motif components that represent domain and motif-centric views with direct mapping to superfamilies, the Function component that describes functional properties of enzymes and other activities and relationships such as families, pathways, and processes, as well as the Structure component that describes structural properties and relate structural classes to evolution and func-

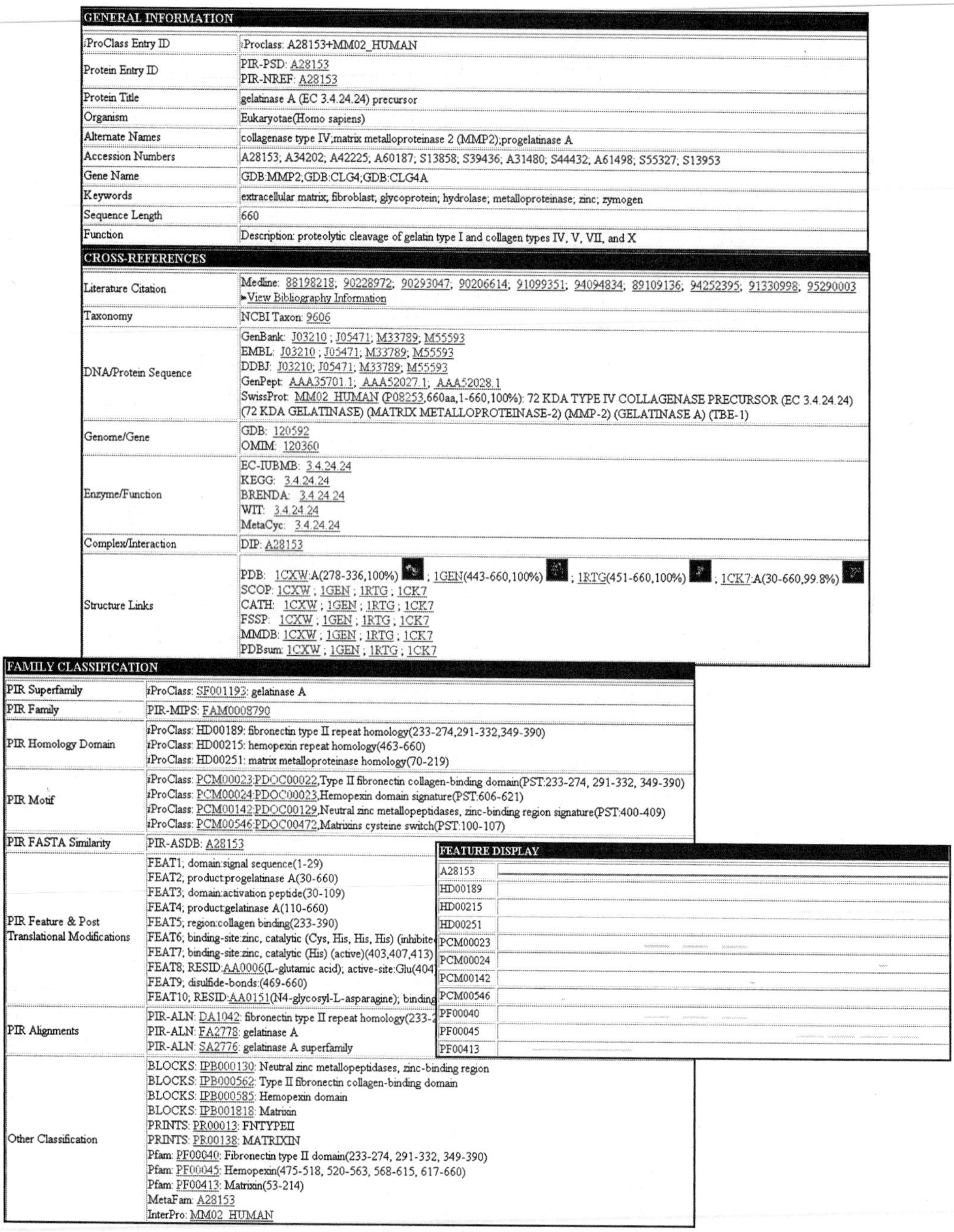

GENERAL INFORMATION	
iProClass Entry ID	iProclass: A28153+MM02_HUMAN
Protein Entry ID	PIR-PSD: A28153 PIR-NREF: A28153
Protein Title	gelatinase A (EC 3.4.24.24) precursor
Organism	Eukaryotae(Homo sapiens)
Alternate Names	collagenase type IV;matrix metalloproteinase 2 (MMP2);progelatinase A
Accession Numbers	A28153; A34202; A42225; A60187; S13858; S39436; A31480; S44432; A61498; S55327; S13953
Gene Name	GDB:MMP2;GDB:CLG4;GDB:CLG4A
Keywords	extracellular matrix; fibroblast; glycoprotein; hydrolase; metalloproteinase; zinc; zymogen
Sequence Length	660
Function	Description: proteolytic cleavage of gelatin type I and collagen types IV, V, VII, and X

CROSS-REFERENCES	
Literature Citation	Medline: 88198218; 90228972; 90293047; 90206614; 91099351; 94094834; 89109136; 94252395; 91330998; 95290003 ▸View Bibliography Information
Taxonomy	NCBI Taxon: 9606
DNA/Protein Sequence	GenBank: J03210 ; J05471; M33789; M55593 EMBL: J03210 ; J05471; M33789; M55593 DDBJ: J03210; J05471; M33789; M55593 GenPept: AAA35701.1; AAA52027.1; AAA52028.1 SwissProt: MM02_HUMAN (P08253,660aa,1-660,100%): 72 KDA TYPE IV COLLAGENASE PRECURSOR (EC 3.4.24.24) (72 KDA GELATINASE) (MATRIX METALLOPROTEINASE-2) (MMP-2) (GELATINASE A) (TBE-1)
Genome/Gene	GDB: 120592 OMIM: 120360
Enzyme/Function	EC-IUBMB: 3.4.24.24 KEGG: 3.4.24.24 BRENDA: 3.4.24.24 WIT: 3.4.24.24 MetaCyc: 3.4.24.24
Complex/Interaction	DIP: A28153
Structure Links	PDB: 1CXW:A(278-336,100%) ; 1GEN(443-660,100%) ; 1RTG(451-660,100%) ; 1CK7:A(30-660,99.8%) SCOP: 1CXW ; 1GEN ; 1RTG ; 1CK7 CATH: 1CXW ; 1GEN ; 1RTG ; 1CK7 FSSP: 1CXW ; 1GEN ; 1RTG ; 1CK7 MMDB: 1CXW ; 1GEN ; 1RTG ; 1CK7 PDBsum: 1CXW ; 1GEN ; 1RTG ; 1CK7

FAMILY CLASSIFICATION	
PIR Superfamily	iProClass: SF001193: gelatinase A
PIR Family	PIR-MIPS: FAM0008790
PIR Homology Domain	iProClass: HD00189: fibronectin type II repeat homology(233-274,291-332,349-390) iProClass: HD00215: hemopexin repeat homology(463-660) iProClass: HD00251: matrix metalloproteinase homology(70-219)
PIR Motif	iProClass: PCM00023:PDOC00022,Type II fibronectin collagen-binding domain(PST:233-274, 291-332, 349-390) iProClass: PCM00024:PDOC00023,Hemopexin domain signature(PST:606-621) iProClass: PCM00142:PDOC00129,Neutral zinc metallopeptidases, zinc-binding region signature(PST:400-409) iProClass: PCM00546:PDOC00472,Matrixins cysteine switch(PST:100-107)
PIR FASTA Similarity	PIR-ASDB: A28153
PIR Feature & Post Translational Modifications	FEAT1; domain:signal sequence(1-29) FEAT2; product:progelatinase A(30-660) FEAT3; domain:activation peptide(30-109) FEAT4; product:gelatinase A(110-660) FEAT5; region:collagen binding(233-390) FEAT6; binding-site:zinc, catalytic (Cys, His, His, His) (inhibite FEAT7; binding-site:zinc, catalytic (His) (active)(403,407,413) FEAT8; RESID:AA0006(L-glutamic acid); active-site:Glu(404 FEAT9; disulfide-bonds:(469-660) FEAT10; RESID:AA0151(N4-glycosyl-L-asparagine); binding
PIR Alignments	PIR-ALN: DA1042: fibronectin type II repeat homology(233-2 PIR-ALN: FA2778: gelatinase A PIR-ALN: SA2776: gelatinase A superfamily
Other Classification	BLOCKS: IPB000130: Neutral zinc metallopeptidases, zinc-binding region BLOCKS: IPB000562: Type II fibronectin collagen-binding domain BLOCKS: IPB000585: Hemopexin domain BLOCKS: IPB001818: Matrixin PRINTS: PR00013: FNTYPEII PRINTS: PR00138: MATRIXIN Pfam: PF00040: Fibronectin type II domain(233-274, 291-332, 349-390) Pfam: PF00045: Hemopexin(475-518, 520-563, 568-615, 617-660) Pfam: PF00413: Matrixin(53-214) MetaFam: A28153 InterPro: MM02_HUMAN

FEATURE DISPLAY	
A28153	
HD00189	
HD00215	
HD00251	
PCM00023	
PCM00024	
PCM00142	
PCM00546	
PF00040	
PF00045	
PF00413	

Fig. 3. iProClass protein sequence entry report (for a retrievable example *see* Website: http://pir.georgetown.edu/cgi-bin/iproclass/iproclass?choice=entry&id=A28153).

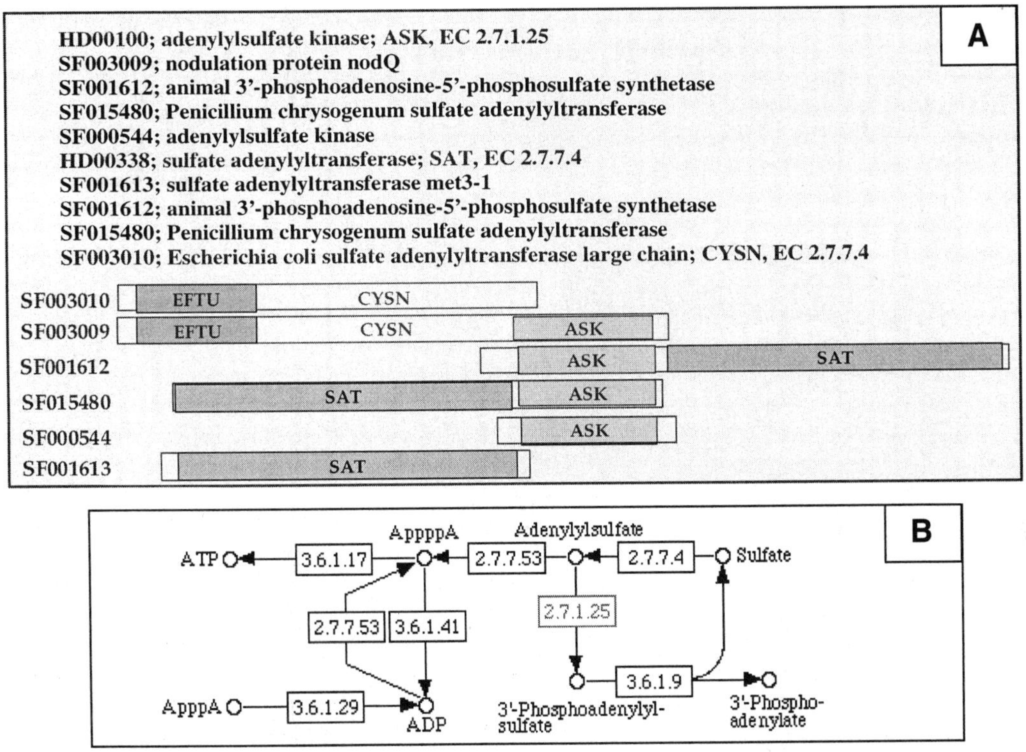

Fig. 4. Superfamily-domain-function relationship to reveal protein functional association beyond sequence homology. **(A)** Association of ASK (EC 2.7.1.25) and SAT/CYSN (EC2.7.7.4) in multi-domain proteins. **(B)** Association of ASK and SAT/CYSN in a metabolic pathway.

See companion CD for color Fig. 4

tion. Such data integration is important in revealing protein functional associations beyond sequence homology, as illustrated in the following example. As shown in Fig. 4A, the ASK domain (EC 2.7.1.25) appears in four different superfamilies, all having different overall domain arrangements. Except for SF000544, the other three superfamilies are bi-functional, all containing sulfate adenylyltrans-ferase (SAT) (EC 2.7.7.4). However, the same SAT enzymatic activity is found in two distinct sequence types, the SAT domain and CYSN homology. Furthermore, both EC 2.7.1.25 and EC 2.7.7.4 are in adjacent steps of the same metabolic pathway (*see* Fig. 4B). This example demonstrates that protein function may be revealed based on domain and/or pathway association, even without obvious sequence homology. The iProClass database design presents complex superfamily-domain-function relationships to assist functional identification or characterization of proteins.

PIR-Nonredundant Reference (PIR-NREF) Protein Database

As a major resource of protein information, one of our primary aims is to provide a timely and comprehensive collection of all protein sequence data that keeps pace with the genome sequencing projects and contains source attribution and minimal redundancy. The PIR-NREF protein database includes all sequences from PIR-PSD,

NREF Entry: NF00716203 *Last updated: 27-Sep-2001*

Protein Name	CYTOCHROME C-TYPE PROTEIN TORC
Source Organism	**Escherichia coli** *Lineage:* Bacteria; Proteobacteria; gamma subdivision; Enterobacteriaceae group; Enterobacteriaceae; Escherichia *NCBI Taxon ID:* 562: Escherichia coli *NCBI Taxon ID:* 83333: Escherichia coli K12
Bibliogaphy	PMID:9278503; PMID:8022286; PMID:8039676; PMID:8905232

Sequence Database

Database	Proein ID	Accession	Taxon ID	Protein Name
PIR	S34221	B64841; S43697; S34221	83333	membrane-bound tetraheme cytochrome torC
SwissProt	TORC_ECOLI	P33226 P77446	562	CYTOCHROME C-TYPE PROTEIN TORC
GenPept	1651488	BAA36138.1	562	Cytochrome c-type protein TorC
GenPept	1651494	BAA35763.1	562	Cytochrome c-type protein TorC
GenPept	1787230	AAC74081.1	83333	trimethylamine N-oxide reductase, cytochrome c-type subunit

Protein Sequence

```
MRKLWNALRRPSARWSVLALVAIGIVIGIALIVLPHVGIKVTSTTEFCVSCHSMQPVYEE
YKQSVHFQNASGVRAECHDCHIPPDIPGMVKRKLEASNDIYQTFIAHSIDTPEKFEAKRA
ELAEREWARMKENNSATCRSCHNYDAMDHAKQHPEAARQMKVAAKDNQSCIDCHKGIAHQ
LPDMSSGFRKQFDELRASANDSGDTLYSIDIKPIYAAKGDKEASGSLLPASEVKVLKRDG
DWLQIEITGWTESAGRQRVLTQFPGKRIFVASIRGDVQQQVKTLEKTTVADTNTEWSKLQ
ATAWMKKGDMVNDIKPIWAYADSLYNGTCNQCHGAPEIAHFDANGWIGTLNGMIGFTSLD
KREERTLLKYLQMNASDTAGKAHGDKKEEK
```

Sequence Length: 390

Fig. 5. PIR-NREF nonredundant reference protein database for timely and comprehensive collection of protein data with source attribution.

Table 1
Major PIR Web Pages for Data Mining and Sequence Analysis

Description	*Web Page URL*
PIR Home	http://pir.georgetown.edu
PIR-PSD	~/pirwww/search/textpsd.shtml
iProClass	~/iproclass
PIR-NREF	~/pirwww/search/prinref.shtml
PIR-ASDB	~/cgi-bin/asdblist.pl?id=CCHU
Bibliography submission	~/pirwww/literature.html
List of PIR databases	~/pirwww/dbinfo/dbinfo.html
List of PIR search tools	~/pirwww/search/searchseq.html
FTP site	ftp://nbrfa.georgetown.edu/pir_databases

~ = http://pir.georgetown.edu

Swiss-Prot, TrEMBL, RefSeq, GenPept, PDB, and other protein databases. The NREF entries, each representing an identical amino acid sequence from the same source organism redundantly represented in one or more underlying protein databases, can serve as the basic unit for protein annotation. The National Center for Biotechnology Information (NCBI) taxonomy is used as the ontology for matching source organism names at the species or strain (if known) levels. The NREF report (*see* Fig. 5) provides source attribution (containing protein IDs, accession numbers, and protein names from underlying databases), in addition to taxonomy, amino acid sequence, and composite literature data. The composite protein names, including synonyms, alternate names and even misspellings, can be used to assist ontology development of protein names and the identification of misannotated proteins. Related sequences, including identical sequences from different organisms and closely related sequences within the same organism are also listed. The database presently consists of about 800,000 entries and is updated biweekly. Future versions of iProClass and PIR-ASDB will be based on the PIR-NREF database.

See companion CD for color Fig. 5

PIR System Distribution

PIR Web Site

The PIR web site (*see* Website: http://pir.georgetown.edu) connects data mining and sequence analysis tools to underlying databases for exploration of protein information and discovery of new knowledge. The site has been redesigned to include a user-friendly navigation system and more graphical interfaces and analysis tools. The PIR-PSD, iProClass, and NREF pages represent primary entry points in the PIR web site. A list of the major PIR pages is shown in Table 1.

The PIR-PSD interface provides entry retrieval, batch retrieval, basic or advanced text searches, and various sequence searches. The iProClass interface also includes both sequence and text searches. The BLAST search returns best-matched proteins and superfamilies, each displayed with a one-line summary linking to complete reports. Peptide match allows protein identification based on peptide sequences. Text search supports direct search of the underlying Oracle tables using unique identifiers or combinations of text strings, based on a Java program running JDBC. The NREF database is searchable for BLAST searching, peptide matching, and direct report retrieval based on the NREF ID or the entry identifiers of the source databases. Other sequence searches supported on the PIR web site include FASTA, pattern matching, hidden Markov model (HMM) domain and motif search, Smith-Waterman pair-wise alignment, ClustalW multiple alignment, and GeneFIND family identification.

PIR FTP Site

The PIR anonymous FTP site (*see* Website: ftp://nbrfa.georgetown.edu/pir_databases) provides direct file transfer. Files distributed include the PIR-PSD (quarterly release and interim updates), PIR-NREF, other auxiliary databases, other documents, files, and software programs. The PIR-PSD is distributed as flat files in NBRF and CODATA formats, with corresponding sequences in FASTA format. Both PIR-PSD and PIR-NREF are also distributed in XML format with the associated Document Type Definition (DTD) file.

The PIR-PSD, iProClass, and PIR-NREF databases have been implemented in Oracle 8i object-relational database system on our Unix server. To enable open source distribution, the databases have been mapped to MySQL and ported to Linux. To establish reciprocal links to PIR databases, to host a PIR mirror web site, or to request PIR database schema, please contact Website: pirmail@nbrf.georgetown.edu.

The PIR serves as a primary resource for exploration of proteins, allowing users to answer complex biological questions that may typically involve querying multiple sources. In particular, interesting relationships between database objects, such as relationships among protein sequences, families, structures and functions, can be revealed. Functional annotation of proteins requires the association of proteins based on properties beyond sequence homology—proteins sharing common domains connected via related multi-domain proteins (grouped by superfamilies); proteins in the same pathways, networks or complexes; proteins correlated in their expression patterns and proteins correlated in their phylogenetic profiles (with similar evolutionary patterns). The PIR, with its integrated databases and analysis tools constitutes a fundamental bioinformatics resource for biologists who contemplate using bioinformatics as an integral approach to their genomic/proteomic research and scientific inquiries.

Acknowledgments

The PIR is supported by grant P41 LM05978 from the National Library of Medicine, National Institutes of Health. The iProClass and RESID databases are supported by DBI-9974855, DBI-0138188, and DBI-9808414 from the National Science Foundation.

Glossary

Domain An independently folded unit within a protein or a discrete portion of a protein with a unique function. Most proteins are multi-domain. The overall function of a protein is determined by the combination of its domains.

Motif A short conserved region in a protein sequence. Motifs are frequently highly conserved parts of domains.

Protein family classification Classification of proteins into groups with similar structure and/or function based upon comparisons of motifs, domains or family membership rather than pair-wise sequence comparisons.

Protein superfamily or family A set of proteins which share a common evolutionary ancestor as defined by sequence homology. Protein families can be arranged in a hierarchy, in which closely related proteins with a recent common ancestor comprise subfamilies, and larger groups of distant homologs comprise superfamilies.

Suggested Readings

Introduction—Protein Databases

Barker, W. C., Pfeiffer, F., and George, D. G. (1996) Superfamily classification in PIR-International Protein Sequence Database, Methods Enzymol., 266, 59–71.

Bateman, A., Birney, E., Cerruti, L., Durbin, R., Etwiller, L., Eddy, S. R., et al. (2002) The Pfam protein families database, Nucleic Acids Res. 30, 276–280.

Dayhoff, M. O. (1965–1978) Atlas of Protein Sequence and Structure, vol. 1–5, Suppl. 1–3, National Biomedical Research Foundation, Washington, DC.

Falquet, L., Pagni, M., Bucher, P., Hulo, N., Sigrist, C. J., Hofmann, K., and Bairoch, A. (2002) The PROSITE database, its status in 2002, Nucleic Acids Res. 30, 235–238.

Wu, C. H., Huang, H., Arminski, L., Castro-Alvear, J., Chen, Y., Hu, Z. Z., et al. (2002) The Protein Information Resource: an integrated public resource of functional annotation of proteins, Nucleic Acids Res. 30, 35–37.

Wu, C. H., Xiao, C., Hou, Z., Huang, H., and Barker, W. C. (2001) iProClass: An Integrated, Comprehensive, and Annotated Protein Classification Database, Nucleic Acids Res., 29, 52–54.

PIR-International Protein Sequence Database

Superfamily Classification

Enzyme Nomenclature, Nomenclature Committee of the International Union of Biochemistry and Molecular Biology (NC-IUBMB) in consultation with the IUPAC-IUBMB Joint Commission on Biochemical Nomenclature (JCBN). (*see* Website: http://www.chem.qmw.ac.uk/iubmb/enzyme/.)

Integrated Protein Classification Database

Garavelli, J. S., Hou, Z., Pattabiraman, N., and Stephens, R. M. (2001) The RESID database of protein structure modifications and the NRL-3D sequence-structure database, Nucleic Acids Res., 29, 199–201.

Huang, H., Xiao, C., and Wu, C. H. (2000) ProClass protein family database, Nucleic Acids Res., 28, 273–276.

PIR Nonredundant Reference Protein Database

Bairoch, A. and Apweiler, R. (2000) The Swiss-Prot protein sequence database and its supplement TrEMBL in 2000, Nucleic Acids Res., 28, 45–48.

National Center for Biotechnology Information (NCBI) taxonomy home page (*see* Website: http://www.ncbi.nlm.nih.gov/Taxonomy/taxonomyhome.html/)

Pruitt, K. D. and Maglott, D. R. (2001) RefSeq and LocusLink: NCBI gene-centered resources, Nucleic Acids Res., 29, 137–140.

Westbrook, J., Feng, Z., Jain, S., Bhat, T. N., Thanki, N., Ravichandran, V., et al. (2002) The Protein Data Bank: unifying the archive. Nucleic Acids Res. 30, 245–248.

PIR System Distribution

Altschul, S. F., Madden, T. L., Schaffer, A. A., Zhang, J., Zhang, Z., Miller, W., and Lipman, D. J. (1997) Gapped BLAST and PSI-BLAST: a new generation of protein database search programs, Nucleic Acids Res., 25, 3389–3402.

Eddy, S. R., Mitchison, G., and Durbin, R. (1995) Maximum Discrimination hidden Markov models of sequence consensus, J. Comp. Biol,. 2, 9–23.

McGarvey, P., Huang, H., Barker, W. C., Orcutt, B. C., and Wu, C. H. (2000) The PIR Website: new resource for bioinformatics, Bioinformatics, 16, 290–291.

Pearson, W. R. and Lipman, D. J. (1988) Improved tools for biological sequence comparision, Proc. Natl. Acad. Sci. USA, 85, 2444–2448.

Smith, T. F. and Waterman, M. S. (1981) Comparison of bio-sequences, Adv. Appl. Math., 2, 482–489.

Alignment Algorithms and Prediction

Marcotte, E. M, Pellegrini, M., Thompson, M. J., Yeates, T. O., and Eisenberg, D. (1999) A combined algorithm for genome-wide prediction of protein function, Nature, 402, 83–86.

Thompson, J. D., Higgins, D. G., and Gibson, T. J. (1994) CLUSTAL W: improving the sensitivity of progressive multiple sequence alignment through sequence weighting, position-specific gap penalties and weight matrix choice, Nucleic Acids Res., 22, 4673–4680.

Wu, C. H., Huang, H., and McLarty, J. (1999) Gene family identification network design for protein sequence analysis, Intl. J. Artificial Intelligence Tools (Special Issue Biocomput.) 8, 419–432.

27 Sequence Similarity and Database Searching

David S. Wishart

Introduction

Database searching is perhaps the fastest, cheapest, and most powerful experiment a biologist can perform. No other 10-s test allows a biologist to reveal so much about the function, structure, location or origin of a gene, protein, organelle, or organism. A database search does not consume any reagents or require any specific wet-bench laboratory skills; just about anyone can do it, but the key is to do it correctly. The power of database searching comes from not only the size of today's sequence databases (now containing more than 700,000 annotated gene and protein sequences), but from the ingenuity of certain key algorithms that have been developed to facilitate this very special kind of searching. Given the importance of database searching it is crucial that today's life scientists try to become as familiar as possible with the details of the process. Indeed, the intent of this chapter to provide the reader with some insight and historical background to the methods and algorithms that form the foundation of a few of the most common database searching techniques. There are many strengths, misconceptions and weaknesses to these simple but incredibly useful computer *experiments.*

Similarity Versus Homology

Considerable confusion still exists over the proper use of the terms, *similarity* and *homology*. Therefore, before we can begin any in-depth discussion on sequence similarity and databasae searching, it is important that we make a clear distinction between sequence similarity and sequence homology. Here are two definitions that should help:

- Similarity: In sequence analysis, this refers to the likeness or percent identity between any two sequences. Sequences are similar if they share a statistically significant number of amino acids or nucleotides in approximately the same positions. Similarity does not infer homology, it is only a descriptive term that carries no suggestion of shared ancestry or origin. Similarity is often enumerated by *percent identity* or an *expect (E) value*.
- Homology: In sequence analysis, this refers to a shared ancestry. Two sequences are homologous if they are derived from a common ancestral sequence or if one of the two sequences has diverged (through evolution) to be different in its amino acid or nucleotide sequence from its parent. Homology almost always implies

similarity, but similarity does not always imply homology. Homology is a *qualitative assertion* or *hypothesis*.

As these two definitions suggest, similarity can be quantified while homology has to be justified. Typically, to claim that two sequences are homologous, one usually needs more solid (i.e., experimental) evidence than just a sequence alignment and a high level of shared sequence identity. It is also important to remember that one cannot say two sequences are *X percent homologous* or *Y percent similar*. In fact, the only time a percentage can be given is when one speaks in terms of sequence identity, e.g., these two sequences are Z percent identical. It is OK, however, to say an alignment has a similarity score of X, just as long as one indicates what scoring matrix or scoring protocol was used.

DNA Versus Protein

Prior to performing any database search, a critical decision must be made: Should my query sequence be DNA or protein? The answer to this is clear, but may be surprising to many. Mathematicians have determined that sequence comparison is best carried out when the sequences exhibit *complexity*, meaning that they are composed of a large number of different characters. In this regard, protein sequences with their 20 letter alphabet are far more complex or informationally *richer* than DNA sequences, which only have a 4-letter alphabet. Consequently, database searches using DNA sequences are more likely to yield ambiguous results or potentially false alignments than database searches conducted against protein sequences. It is for this reason that most experienced bioinformaticians insist that DNA sequences be translated to protein sequences before they are submitted for database comparisons. Indeed, the only reasons why one would not want to translate a DNA sequence into the corresponding protein sequence are if the query sequence quality is low (as with ESTs), if the DNA does not code for any protein product (e.g., a DNA regulatory element) or if it corresponds to a tRNA or rRNA gene. *So always translate those DNA sequences!*

Dynamic Programming and Sequence Similarity

Dynamic programming lies at the heart of almost all sequence alignment and database searching routines. Strictly speaking dynamic programming is an efficient mathematical technique that can be used to find optimal *paths* or routes to multiple destinations or in locating paths that could be combined to score some maximum. The application of dynamic programming to sequence alignment was first demonstrated more than 30 years ago by Needleman and Wunsch (1970). The great strength of dynamic programming is that it actually permits a quantitative assessment of similarity, while at the same time showing how two sequences can be globally aligned. The great weakness of dynamic programming is that it is incredibly slow and extraordinarily memory intensive. Strictly speaking, dynamic programming is an $N \times M$ algorithm, meaning that the time it takes to execute and the amount of computer memory (RAM) required is dependent on both the length of the query sequence (N) and the cumulative length of the database sequence(s) (M). Given that databases today have an effective length of nearly 250 million amino acids or 4 billion bases, this obviously makes dynamic programming a rather slow approach to database searching. While the dynamic programming algorithm is inherently slow, it is still the most mathematically rigorous method for determining a pairwise sequence alignment. No other technique (not FASTA, nor BLAST) can offer a guaranteed mathematically optimal alignment. While this is a very strong statement, one must always remember that what is mathematically correct may not be biologically correct. In other words, one should always use common sense and a bit of biological intuition when evaluating any given sequence alignment.

Dynamic Programming: The Algorithm

In dynamic programming, pairwise alignments are calculated in two stages. The first stage is called the *scoring stage*. It involves putting the two sequences of interest (e.g., sequence A and sequence B) on the two axes of a table and then progressively filling that table from the upper left to the lower right with integer scores related to the pairwise similarity of each base or amino acid in the two sequences. These scores are initially obtained by comparing each letter in sequence A to each letter in sequence B using a scoring matrix such as the BLOSUM62 matrix. These similarity scores are then further modified using a special recursive scoring function shown in Equation 1.

$$S_{ij} = s_{ij} + \text{Max}\left\{\begin{array}{ll} s_{i-l,j-l} & \text{or} \\ \text{Max } s_{i-x,j-l} + w_{x-l}\ (2 < x < i) & \text{or} \\ \text{Max } s_{i-l,j-y} + w_{y-l}\ (y < 2 < i) & \end{array}\right\} \quad \text{[Eq. 1]}$$

Where S_{i-j} is the *net* score for the alignment ending at i in sequence A and j in sequence B, s_{ij} is the score for matching i with j, w_x is the score for making a x long gap in sequence A, and w_y is the score for making a y long gap in sequence B. Figure 1 illustrates how this table can be filled out using a simple scoring procedure where identical amino acids are given a score (s_{ij}) of 1 for a match, 0 for a mismatch and no gap penalty. In this figure we are attempting to align the sequence *GENES* (sequence A) with the sequence *GEMS* (sequence B).

Once this table is filled out, the second (*traceback*) stage is undertaken wherein one scans through the matrix in a diagonal fashion from the lower right to upper left to look for the highest scores entered in the matrix. The path that is chosen is actually a series of *maximum* numbers. When all the scores in this optimal path are added together, it gives a quantitative measure of the pairwise sequence similarity while at the same time defining which letters in sequence A should be matched with the letters in sequence B. The traceback route(s) along with the two possible alignments for the GENES vs GEMS example are shown in the lower part of Fig. 1. In this case the similarity score for both alignments was 3 + 2 + 2 + 1 = 8.

The original Needleman-Wunsch (NW) algorithm was specifically developed to perform global pairwise sequence alignments. In other words, the scoring function and traceback procedure implicitly assumes that the optimal alignment will be found by going from the lower right corner to the upper left corner of the matrix. A simple modification to the NW algorithm introduced by Smith and Waterman (1981) showed that dynamic programming could actually be adapted to perform local alignments. In other words, the path for the traceback procedure did not have to start and end at the edges of the search matrix, but it could start and end internally (i.e., within the search matrix). Such an alignment, once found, would be locally optimal. The advantage of identifying a locally optimal alignment, particularly for proteins, is that it may be possible to pull out small functionally related domains that would normally be missed by a global alignment algorithm. Because of their potential advantage in identifying remote or frequently missed sequence similarities, local alignment techniques have been the subject of considerable interest development over the past 15 years. Two fast local alignment methods in particular, namely FASTA and BLAST, arose from this work. These heuristic database search approaches will be discussed in more detail later on in this chapter.

Scoring Matrices

The scoring system illustrated in Fig. 1 used a simple match/mismatch scoring function. Such a scoring system can be described by a simple table where we place all 4 bases or all 20 amino acids on both the X and Y axes and indicate with a 1 or a 0 (inside the table) whether any two bases or any two amino acids match or do not match. This type of scoring table is commonly referred to as an *identity* or *unitary* scoring matrix and it is still the most commonly used scoring system for aligning or matching nucleic acid sequences. Scoring matrices are key to the success of dynamic programming. They are also its Achilles heel. Simply stated, scoring matrices try to capture billions of years of evolutionary information and tens of thousands of complex molecular interactions and reduce it all to a table of 200 integers. Perhaps this is scientific reductionism at its most extreme. Nevertheless, it seems to work (most of the time). Over the past 25 years more than a dozen amino acid scoring matrices have been described in the literature, however there are only two types of scoring matrices that seem to have survived the test of time: 1) PAM scoring matrices; and 2) BLOSUM scoring matrices. These scoring schemes are described in the following.

The Dayhoff (PAM) Scoring Matrices

Until recently the most common scoring matrices for protein sequence comparisons were based on the mutation data matrix (MDM_{78}) developed by Margaret Dayhoff and coworkers in 1978. These were derived using the Point Accepted Mutation (PAM) model of evolution originally proposed by Dayhoff. Using a set of proteins that were >85% identical, Dayhoff and her colleagues manually aligned these proteins, taking great pains to ensure the alignments were completely unambiguous. From these groups of alignments, an amino acid similarity ratio (R_{ij}) was calculated for each pair of amino acids as shown in Equation 2:

$$R_{ij} = q_{ij} / p_i p_j \qquad \text{[Eq. 2]}$$

Where q_{ij} is the observed frequency that residues i and j replaced each other in the set of aligned proteins and p_i and p_j are the observed frequencies of amino acids i and j in the complete set of proteins. Therefore, for conservative replacements (such as Y for F), R_{ij} would be expected to be greater than 1, while for unfavorable replacements, R_{ij} would be less than 1.

The initial PAM scoring matrix was calculated such that the probabilities in the scoring table would represent the average mutational change when one residue in 100 mutates (1% point accepted mutations or 1 PAM). This particular matrix was called the PAM-1 matrix. By assuming that the mutations that occur in a protein sequence are essentially not correlated with previous mutations, it is possible to use the mathematics of Hidden Markov Models to calculate a mutational probability matrix that has undergone N percent PAM's. To do so, the PAM-1 matrix is multipled by itself N times.

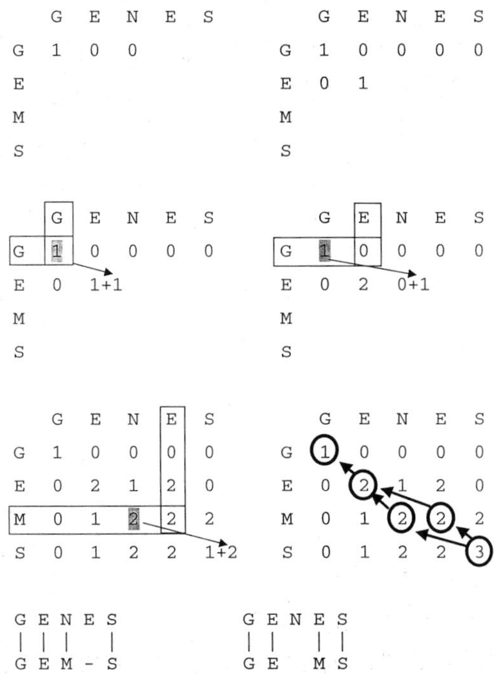

Fig. 1. A simple illustration of how dynamic programming is performed in the alignment of two short peptide sequences (sequence A = GEMS; sequence B = GENES). The upper tables illustrate the progressive filling of the scoring matrix using the recursion relationship in Eq. 1 and the following rules: a match =1, a mismatch = 0, and a gap insertion = 0 (i.e., w = 0). The lower right table illustrates the traceback procedure. The two possible alignments between GEMS and GENES, determined via dynamic programming, are shown at the bottom.

Using this simplified model of evolution Dayhoff created an entire family of scoring matrices, with the most useful being the PAM-120 and PAM-250 matrices. These matrices were created by multiplying the PAM-1 matrix by itself 120 and 250 times, respectively. As a general rule, to align sequences that are highly divergent, the best results are obtained with matrices having higher PAM values. PAM-120 and PAM-250 can be viewed as being the typical scoring matrices of proteins that have been separated by 120 million (PAM-120) and 250 million (PAM-250) years of evolution. Dayhoff also converted the PAM-120 and PAM-250 matrices into log-odds matrices. To do so, the natural log of these R_{ij} ratios were determined and the new numbers (S_{ij}) were substituted into the scoring matrix. The log-odds form of the PAM-250 matrix is called MDM_{78} and this is the one that Dayhoff recommended for use in general sequence comparisons. The MDM_{78} or PAM-250 matrix is shown in Fig. 2. As can be seen in this matrix, large positive values indicate a high level of conservation or chemical similarity between a pair of amino acids. Large negative values indicate very little chemical similarity and represent nonconservative mutations. In principle the sum of these log-odds scores over the length of any pair of aligned sequences is equal to the natural log of the probability that the two sequences are related.

	A	R	N	D	C	Q	E	G	H	I	L	K	M	F	P	S	T	W	Y	V
A	2																			
R	-2	6																		
N	0	0	2																	
D	0	-1	2	4																
C	-2	-4	-4	-5	4															
Q	0	1	1	2	-5	4														
E	0	-1	1	3	-5	2	4													
G	1	-3	0	1	-3	-1	0	5												
H	-1	2	2	1	-3	3	1	-2	6											
I	-1	-2	-2	-2	-2	-2	-2	-3	-2	5										
L	-2	-3	-3	-4	-6	-2	-3	-4	-2	2	6									
K	-1	3	1	0	-5	1	0	-2	0	-2	-3	5								
M	-1	0	-2	-3	-5	-1	-2	-3	-2	2	4	0	6							
F	-4	-4	-4	-6	-4	-5	-5	-5	-2	1	2	-5	0	9						
P	1	0	-1	-1	-3	0	-1	-1	0	-2	-3	-1	-2	-5	6					
S	1	0	1	0	0	-1	0	1	-1	-1	-3	0	-2	-3	1	3				
T	1	-1	0	0	-2	-1	0	0	-1	0	-2	0	-1	-2	0	1	3			
W	-6	2	-4	-7	-8	-5	-7	-7	-3	-5	-2	-3	-4	0	-6	-2	-5	17		
Y	-3	-4	-2	-4	0	-4	-4	-5	0	-1	-1	-4	-2	7	-5	-3	-3	0	10	
V	0	-2	-2	-2	-2	-2	-2	-1	-2	4	2	-2	2	-1	-1	-1	0	-6	-2	4

Fig. 2. The PAM-250 (or MDM_{78}) scoring matrix for amino acid substitutions.

	A	R	N	D	C	Q	E	G	H	I	L	K	M	F	P	S	T	W	Y	V
A	4																			
R	-1	5																		
N	-2	0	6																	
D	-2	-2	1	6																
C	0	-3	-3	-3	9															
Q	-1	1	0	0	-3	5														
E	-1	0	0	2	-4	2	5													
G	0	-2	0	-1	-3	-2	-2	6												
H	-2	0	1	-1	-3	0	0	-2	8											
I	-1	-1	-3	-3	-1	-3	-3	-4	-3	4										
L	-1	-1	-3	-4	-1	-2	-3	-4	-3	2	4									
K	-1	2	0	-1	-3	1	1	-2	-1	-3	-2	5								
M	-1	-1	-2	-3	-1	0	-2	-3	-2	1	2	-1	5							
F	-2	-3	-3	-3	-2	-3	-3	-3	-1	0	0	-3	0	6						
P	-1	-2	-2	-1	-3	-1	-1	-2	-2	-3	-3	-1	-2	-4	7					
S	1	-1	1	0	-1	0	0	0	-1	-2	-2	0	-1	-2	-1	4				
T	0	-1	0	-1	-1	-1	-1	-2	-2	-1	-1	-1	-1	-2	-1	1	5			
W	-3	-3	-4	-4	-2	-2	-3	-2	-2	-3	-2	-3	-1	1	-4	-3	-2	11		
Y	-2	-2	-2	-3	-2	-1	-2	-3	2	-1	-1	-2	-1	3	-3	-2	-2	2	7	
V	0	-3	-3	-3	-1	-2	-2	-3	-3	3	1	-2	1	-1	-2	-2	0	-3	-1	4

Fig. 3. The BLOSUM62 scoring matrix for amino acid substitutions.

The BLOSUM Scoring Matrices

A more recent addition and increasingly popular set of scoring matrices are the Block Substitution Matrix (BLOSUM) scoring matrices. A key difference between the BLOSUM and PAM matrices is that the BLOSUM matrices were constructed without an explicit model of evolution. In particular, the substitution probabilities or target frequencies were estimated from the BLOCKS database, which is a database of local (contiguous) multiple alignments for various distantly related sequence blocks or domains found in proteins. As with the PAM matrices there is a numbered series of BLOSUM matrices, such as BLOSUM30, BLOSUM62, and BLOSUM90, however the numbering scheme is essentially in reverse order relative to the PAM matrices. Specifically, the BLOSUM numbers refer to the maximum level of pairwise sequence identity in the selected sequence BLOCKS used to prepare the scoring matrix. The substitution frequencies for the BLOSUM62 matrix are influenced primarily by those sequences sharing less than 62% sequence identity. In general one would use the BLOSUM90 matrix to compare very similar sequences and the BLOSUM30 matrix to compare very different sequences or to detect more remote sequence similarities. The BLOSUM62 scoring matrix, which is the default scoring matrix used in BLAST, is shown in Fig. 3.

Gap and Gap Extension Penalties

In addition to scoring matrices, the use of gap and gap extension penalties can also increase the sensitivity of a sequence search and the utility of the resulting alignment. Gaps and gap extensions must often be introduced in alignments to accommodate deletions or insertions that may have occurred during the evolutionary divergence of one sequence from another.

Dynamic programming algorithms can be easily modified during the traceback step to include gap penalties and gap extension penalties. Most commonly, a fixed deduction is applied to the alignment score when a gap is first introduced then an extra deduction is added which is proportional to the length of the gap. Typically the gap opening penalty is called G and the gap extension penalty is called L. Therefore the total deduction for a gap of length n would be $G + Ln$. The selection of gap parameters is very empirical and this represents one of the greatest weaknesses in dynamic programming and in sequence alignment in general. For the BLOSUM62 matrix, it is usually recommended that a high gap penalty (G) of 10 to 15 be used along with a low value for L (1 or 2). As a rule of thumb, the gap penalty G should be approximately equal to the difference between the highest and the lowest number in the chosen scoring matrix.

Fast Local Alignment Methods

Dynamic programming is a superb method for comparing two sequences and obtaining a global (i.e., entire) sequence alignment. However, if one wishes to perform 700,000+ comparisons using this approach—typical of a database search—it could easily take several hours on a very fast computer. Given that most of us do not want to wait that long for an answer, there has been a great deal of effort over the past 15 years directed at developing methods to improve search speeds so that database searches could be done more quickly. However, improvements in speed usually come with a sacrifice in accuracy or sensitivity. Nevertheless, the advent of such

Query Sequence: 1 2 3 4 5 6 7 8 9 10 11 12 13
AMDEFGDEFGAMD...

Hash Table

k-tuple	position
AMD	1,11
MDE	2
DEF	3,7
EFG	4,8
FGD	5
GDE	6
FGA	9
GAM	10

Similarity Table

k-tuple	similar k-tuples				
AMD	AMD				
MDE	MDE	MDD	MDQ		
DEF	DEF	DEY	EEF	DQF	
EFG	EFG	QFG	DFG	EYG	
FGD	FGD	FGE	FGN	WGD	YGD
GDE	GDE	GDD	GDQ	GDK	GEE
FGA	FGA	FGS	YGA		
GAM	GAM				

Fig. 4. An example of a hash table (left) and a similarity table (right) prepared for a short peptide sequence (top). The numbering associated with each triplet (a word of length 3) is based on the position of the first residue. The sets of similar triplets were identified using similarity scores derived from the BLOSUM62 matrix. The cutoff score was 13.

fast, sensitive heuristic search algorithms such as FASTA and BLAST has revolutionized the process and frequency of sequence comparison and database searching. Their tremendous speed advantages seem to far outweigh their potential shortcomings in sensitivity.

Most fast local alignment algorithms are based on breaking the query sequence down into small overlapping subsequences, i.e., words or k-tuples (a k-tuple is a word or character string that is k letters long), and placing their relative sequence locations into what are called *hash tables*. Hash tables are lists of locations or addresses that allow computers to wade through and compare data more efficiently. Once this hash table is built, it is possible to compare other database sequences to the query sequence very quickly. In fact, it turns out that these hash-based methods scale linearly with the size of the database (i.e., they are M-type algorithms as opposed to N × M algorithms). This kind of algorithmic scaling makes them excellent choices to scan very large (and rapidly growing) databases with little cost in time. Figure 4 illustrates how a query sequence could be broken down into a hash table and how each k-tuple could be assigned to a group of similar k-tuples. This is typically the first step performed in a BLAST search.

BLAST

Basic Local Alignment Search Tool (BLAST) is the most commonly used sequence database search tool in the world. Since its introduction as a web-based service in 1995, BLAST has become *the standard* for sequence alignment and database searching. Key to BLAST's success, both as an algorithm and as a program, has been its use of statistical methods to simultaneously accelerate its search speed and to increase its

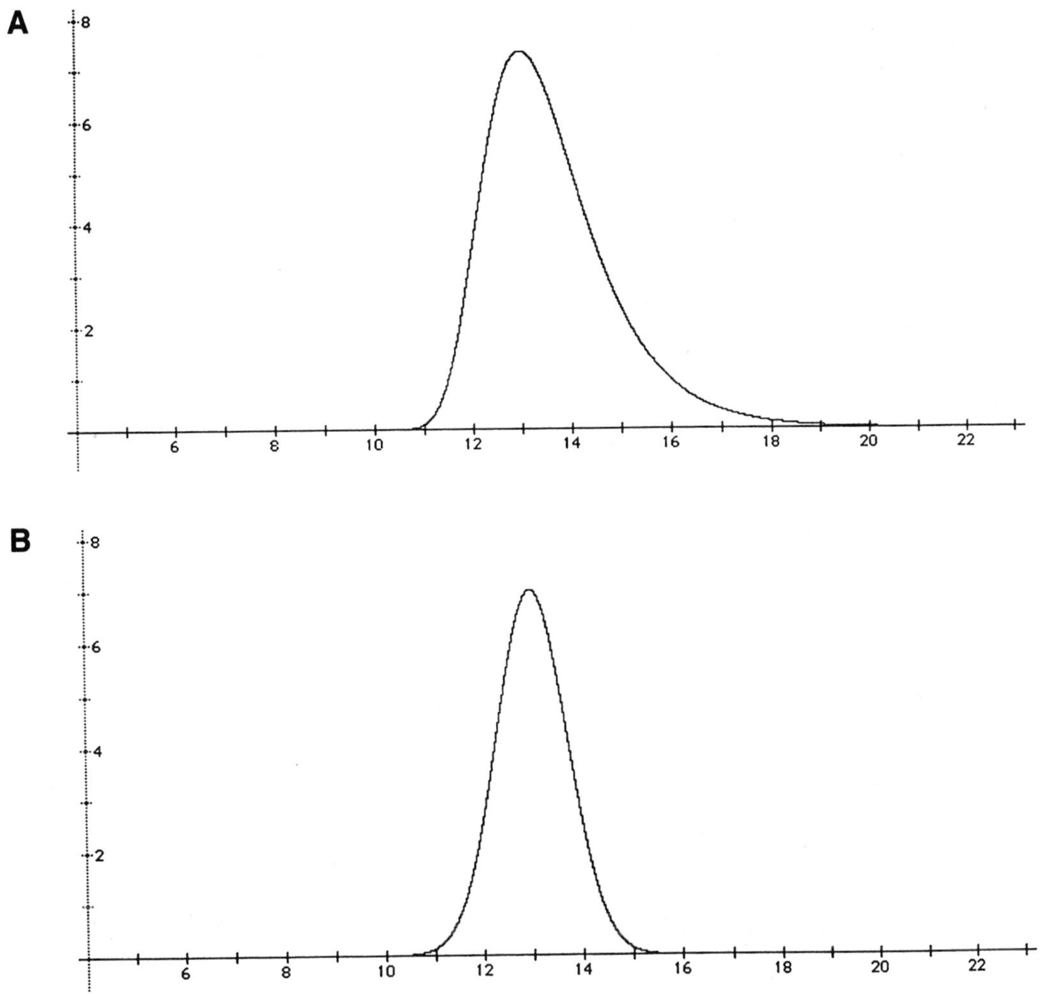

Fig. 5. A comparison between the shapes of an Extreme Value Distribution **(A)** and a Normal or Gaussian distribution **(B)**. The mean (μ) for both distributions is 13.

search sensitivity. In the late 1980s and early 1990s, Altschul and Karlin (two statisticians at Stanford) showed that the significance of pair wise sequence alignments could be rapidly determined or in essence, *predicted* using what is called an *Extreme Value distribution* (*see* Equation 3).

$$P(x) = e^{-x}e^{-e^{-x}} \qquad \text{[Eq. 3]}$$

Where P(x) is the probability of some event getting a score of x. This particular distribution appears reasonable at modeling the distribution of scores or events that are quite rare and which are slightly dependent (as opposed to independent) of each other. Consequently, the Extreme Value distribution differs from a Normal or Gaussian distribution by having a long tail (called a *right-handed skewness*) as shown in Fig. 5. This means that an alignment that scores high and is considered significant for a

Gaussian distribution would likely be considered insignificant in an Extreme Value distribution. By using this special kind of statistical distribution and the probabilities that could be calculated from it, Altschul and coworkers demonstrated that it was possible to rapidly identify, assess, and extend locally similar sequence blocks more quickly and more accurately than other competing alignment programs.

Simply stated, BLAST takes a query sequence and searches a given sequence database for high scoring k-tuples (words) or high scoring segment pairs (HSPs) that exceed a certain scoring threshold (T). This process is illustrated schematically in Fig. 6. Note that unlike earlier database searching algorithms, BLAST does not require HSPs to match exactly. Instead it refers to a precalculated look-up table of highly similar HSPs. This allows BLAST to use a longer word length (3 letters for proteins, 11 letters for DNA) without compromising sensitivity. After the HSPs are identified, BLAST attempts to identify locally dense regions of HSPs and then tries to extend them in either direction until the cumulative alignment score starts dropping (*see* Fig. 7). During the HSP identification and extension phases, BLAST uses rigorous statistical measures to assess significance. This improves on sensitivity and saves on time because the HSP search algorithm does not need to evaluate and extend false leads. In addition to these statistical *speed-ups* BLAST also takes advantage of several advanced programming techniques such as preloading the sequence database into RAM, incorporating finite state transition methods, and exploiting the large *word* size in modern computers to read and process data more quickly.

Historically, one of the key limitations of BLAST (version 1.4 and earlier) was the fact that its sequence alignments had to be broken down into collections of ungapped local alignments or sequence blocks. Thus the term *Local Alignment Search* was born. The difficulty in converting local alignments to more global alignments (which one typically gets with dynamic programming methods or FASTA searches) was overcome with the introduction of Gapped BLAST in 1997. This is now the default BLAST service offered by the NCBI and its mirror sites.

Gapped BLAST offers two key improvements over earlier versions of BLAST. First, an improvement in search speed was attained by requiring that at least two words had to occur in a given window length (A = 40 residues) in order for a given subsegment to be considered significant. This allows the program to ignore many other random HSP hits and to concentrate on the ones most likely to lead to an extended HSP. The second and most important improvement, however, lies in the fact that BLAST now handles gaps explicitly. The strategy adopted in gapped BLAST is to initially identify a HSP in the middle of the highest scoring window of 11 residues. Using this maximal segment pair, BLAST uses the Smith-Waterman algorithm to extend this alignment in both directions until it falls below a fixed percentage of the previous top score. This process is analogous to the way ungapped BLAST assembles HSPs. Another recent improvement in BLAST has been the introduction of composition statistics. This permits the E (expect) values to account for the differing amino acid or base composition of the query sequences and database hits. This little innovation effectively allows one to apply a *custom* scoring procedure for each sequence in the database. The net result is that the inclusion of composition statistics improves the sensitivity and specificity of the database search by reducing the number of false positives.

BLAST is under constant development and improvements to both the algorithm and its associated databases are continuing. A periodic check of the NCBI website will allow any user to stay current with the latest news on BLAST.

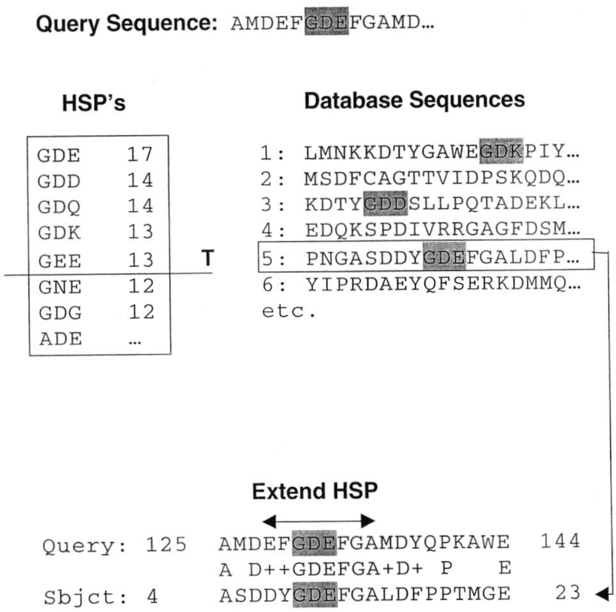

Fig. 6. A schematic illustration of how BLAST identifies and extends HSPs. The HSP in this case is centered around the triplet *GDE*. The Threshold (T) cutoff score in this case is 13, so only those triplets in the database set (right) with scores > 12 will be identified as HSPs. In the lower panel a sequence (sequence 5) has been chosen for further analysis and the initial HSP has been extended in both directions, producing the alignment seen here.

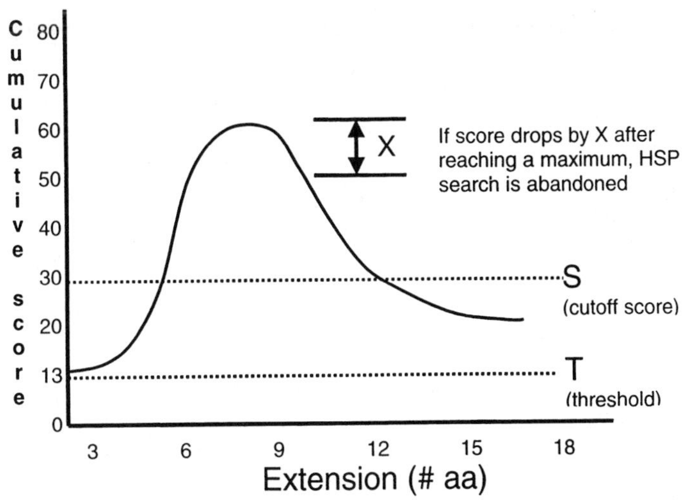

Fig. 7. During the HSP extension phase, a cumulative score is kept between the query and database sequence as the HSP is lengthened. If the HSP is of high quality the score will rapidly climb. Eventually the cumulative HSP score will reach a maximum as the similarity weakens at one end of the sequence or the other. BLAST stops the HSP extension once the cumulative HSP score drops by more than X (a drop-off parameter defined in BLAST).

Running BLAST (The Web Version)

BLAST can be freely and easily accessed from any number of websites from around the world. Some of these include the NCBI (*see* Website: http://www.ncbi.nlm.nih.gov/BLAST), the EBI (*see* Website: http://www.ebi.ad.uk/blastall/), or the Canadian Bioinformatics Resource (*see* Website: http://www.cbr.nrc.ca/blast). BLAST can also be downloaded and run locally or it can be accessed through a variety of commercial programs (most of which have customized front-ends to access the NCBI or EBI sites). For the purposes of this chapter, we will focus on the version of BLAST offered through the NCBI website.

Different Flavors of BLAST

When first logging onto the NCBI site, you will notice a rather large number of BLAST options. These represent the different *flavors* or variations of BLAST that have been developed to accommodate the different needs of users and the different settings required for different types of searches. Currently the NCBI offers at least eight different types of BLAST database searches:

1. BLASTP: Searches user-selected protein databases with protein sequence queries.
2. BLASTN: Searches user-selected nucleic acid databases with DNA/RNA queries.
3. BLASTX: Searches 6-frame translated DNA databases with protein queries.
4. TBLASTN: Searches protein databases with 6-frame translated DNA queries.
5. TBLASTX: Searches translated DNA databases with translated DNA queries.
6. PSI-BLAST: Searches user-selected protein databases with protein sequence profiles.
7. PHI-BLAST: Searches user-selected protein databases for protein sequence patterns.
8. MEGABLAST: Searches entire genome against user-selected nucleic acid databases.

BLASTP is useful for looking for moderate-to-distant relationships among protein sequences. BLASTN is primarily for identifying relatively strong matches between long DNA sequences. BLASTX is most commonly used for analyzing new DNA sequences and EST's (expressed sequence tags). TBLASTN is useful for finding undetected or unexpected protein coding regions (genes) in newly sequenced DNA. TBLASTX is often used in EST analysis. PSI-BLAST is particularly useful for identifying extremely distant or difficult-to-identify relationships between protein sequences. Indeed, with the introduction of PSI-BLAST, BLASTP has largely become obsolete. PHI-BLAST is used to look for user-specified protein sequence patterns. MEGABLAST is best used for whole genome comparisons at the nucleotide level. It is optimized for aligning sequences that differ only slightly and is up to 10 times faster than BLASTN.

BLAST Input

Once you have chosen your desired flavor of BLAST you are ready to submit your sequence request(s). The standard BLAST input window is illustrated in Fig. 8. In most cases you only need to paste in your sequence, choose your database and press the **Submit** button. A request ID (RID) number will be immediately assigned to you and a few seconds later you can press the **Format** button to obtain your search results. BLAST has been carefully designed so that its default values will generally provide a pleasing first-pass result. However, to properly use BLAST and to properly interpret its output, it is important to understand something about its input options. Here is a brief description of some of the key terms or parameters.

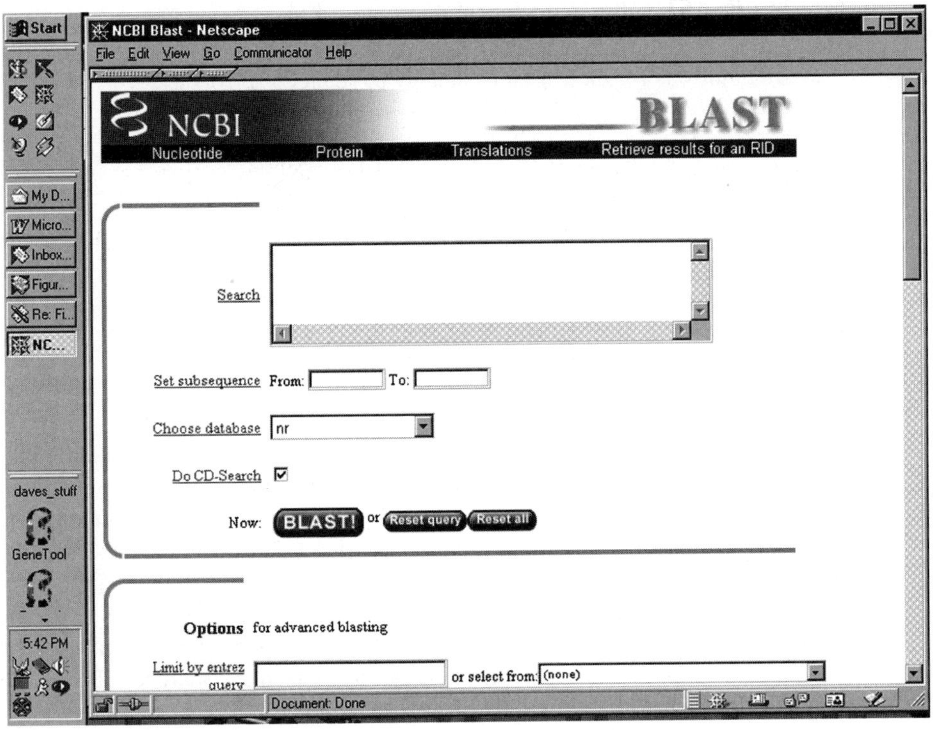

Fig. 8. A screen shot of the NCBI BLAST server. A description of the options and functions is given in the text.

The Sequence Window

This box allows users to type or paste a query sequence for searching. The sequence should be in FASTA format, which means that a > character must appear on one line (the sequence name is optional) and the sequence should appear on the other lines. Users may also type in a gene index (GI) or Genbank accession number, instead of a sequence. This latter option can save quite a bit of time.

Database Selection

NCBI and its mirror sites offer a wide range of both general and specialized databases of widely varying scope and quality. There are 8 different protein databases and 14 different DNA databases, both of which include several organism-specific databases (*E. coli*, yeast, drosophila), a patented sequence database (pat), and monthly updates (month). Outside of interchanging BLASTN with BLASTP, the most common error committed by BLAST users is in (inadvertently) choosing the wrong database. The NR (Nonredundant) database contains the most sequence data and is the default, however, it is not necessarily nonredundant and it certainly does not offer the most complete annotation (especially for proteins). In this regard, the SWISS-PROT database, which is a secondary or curated database, is the most fully annotated and perhaps the least redundant protein sequence database. The GenBank nr database is still the best database for genomic data although it, too, has its share of errors or omissions. The Sequence Tagged Site (STS), Expressed Sequence Tagged (EST), High Throughput Genomic Sequence (HTGS), and Genomic Survey Sequence (GSS) databases are notorious for their high frequency of sequence errors.

CD Search

The Conserved Domain (CD) search is a relatively new option that is particularly helpful for protein sequence searches. The CD search scans the Conserved Domain Database, which is a collection of preidentified functional or structural domains derived from the Pfam and Smart databases. It uses Reverse Position Specific BLAST to enhance the sensitivity of the search. When turned on, the CD search option can reveal many hidden domains and offer colorful structural insights through the Cn3D molecular viewer (*see* Chapter 32).

Filters

One can still encounter problems with sequence complexity, regardless of whether one chooses to work exclusively with proteins or not. This occurs when either the query sequence or the database sequence contains regions of biased sequence composition or low complexity regions (LCRs). Examples of LCRs are repeated stretches of the same amino acid or the same base (homopolymeric runs), short period repeats (such as CA repeats in DNA), and large repetitive elements (such as Alu repeats, LINEs and MERs). Wooton and Federhen (1996) have developed several approaches to identify these LCRs and to screen them out from database searches. The SEG program specifically looks at proteins and screens out their LCRs by replacing the amino acids in the suspect region with a series of Xs. The DUST program does the same for nucleic acids. In proteins, LCRs most likely exist as nonglobular regions and likely arise from errors in DNA replication (polymerase slippage) or unequal crossing over. The NCBI BLAST server and most of its mirror sites offer LCR screening as a default option. This option should always be kept on unless one is dealing with a special situation or an unusual query sequence.

Expect

This refers to the expected number of chance HSP alignments with scores equal to or greater than S (*see* following section "S - Alignment Score"). A very small value of E (something close to 0, say 2.1e-73) is characteristic of a highly significant match. A high E value (say greater than 1) is characteristic of an insignificant match. The default Expect value in BLAST is 10. For most sequences one should never trust an alignment that has an E value of more than 0.01

Word size

This is the length of the word or k-tuple that is scanned. Larger values for W (11–12) are typical for DNA searches. Smaller values (3–4) are typical for protein searches. The longer the word size, the faster the search. However, longer word sizes also reduce the sensitivity.

S - Alignment Score (Cutoff)

This is the score determined through comparing sequence matches of High Scoring Segment Pairs (HSPs) to the scoring matrix. S is also called the HSP cutoff score. For an alignment to be reported by BLAST it has to have an HSP with a score greater than or equal to S.

```
gi|7291930|gb|AAF47347.1| (AE003467) NitFhit gene product [Drosophila
melanogaster]

Length = 460

 Score = 99.0 bits (245), Expect = 1e-20
 Identities = 51/122 (41%), Positives = 72/122 (58%)

Query: 5   FGQHLIKPSVVFLKTELSFALVNRKPVVPGHVLVCPLRPVERFHDLRPDEVADLFQTTQR 64
            F  +++     +F ++E   FA  N + VV GHVLV   R   R   L   E+AD+F T
Sbjct: 318 FATNIVDKRTIFYESEHCFAFTNLRCVVKGHVLVSTKRVTPRLCGLDCAEMADMFTTVCL
377

Query: 65  VGTVVEKHFHGTSLTFSMQDGPEAGQTVKHVHVHVLPRKAGDFHRNDSIYEELQKHDKED
124
            V  ++EK +   TS T ++QDG +AGQTV HVH H++PR+ GDF  ND IY +L +  +E
Sbjct: 378 VQRLLEKIYQTTSATVTVQDGAQAGQTVPHVHFHIMPRRLGDFGHNDQIYVKLDERAEEK
437

Query: 125 FP 126
             P
Sbjct: 438 PP 439
```

Fig. 9. BLASTP output from a database search using Human Fragile Histidine Triad Protein (P49789) as the query sequence.

T - Threshold

This is the threshold score that a short word (HSP) or k-tuple must have in order for BLAST to consider it significant. T is a function of the scoring matrix used in the program. This is now automatically determined when the user selects their preferred scoring matrix.

Matrix and Gap Costs

These were detailed in the previous sections of this chapter.

BLAST Output and Assessing Sequence Similarity

An example of the alignment output of a typical BLAST run is shown in Fig. 9. BLAST also provides alignment lists and image-mapped *domain* graphs to facilitate querying or analyzing the results (not shown here). In addition to the name, accession number, and length of the protein, the alignment produced by BLAST includes data on the alignment score, the *Expect* value and other measures. The Bit Score (the first number) is a normalized score (S) derived from the raw score (given in parentheses). The raw score refers to the summed HSP scores (*see* S above) and is of course dependent on the scoring matrix used. The bit score is independent of the scoring matrix chosen, so one may use the bit score as a means of consistently comparing alignments obtained with different scoring matrices (e.g., BLOSUM62 vs BLOSUM30). While the bit score is generally quite useful, the key parameter to evaluating any BLAST output is the *Expect* value. This refers to the expected number of *chance* HSP alignments with scores equal to or greater than the bit score based on the size of the database, the length of the query sequence, and the scoring matrix used. Ideally this should be less than 1; otherwise this suggests that the alignment you have found could be just a spurious match. As a rule, one should not trust alignments with an Expect value

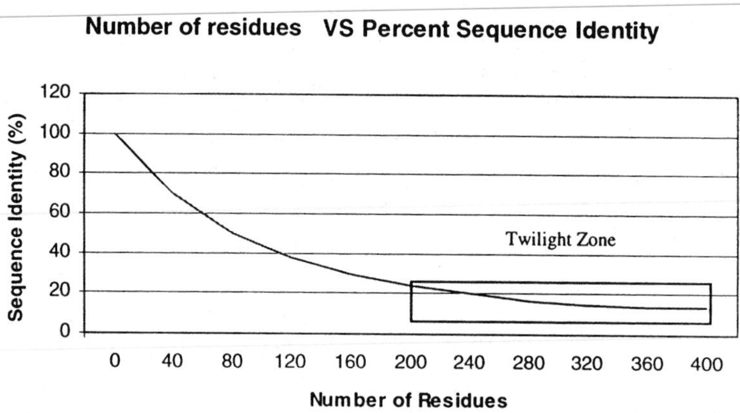

Fig. 10. A plot showing the relationship between sequence identity and sequence length for proteins. Sequences falling above this line are considered to be related (i.e., homologous), while sequences falling below this line are likely unrelated.

greater than 0.01. However, as with anything in sequence alignment, one should assess the alignment by taking into consideration the type and location of matching residues, the number of gaps and the biological or functional relationship between the query and matching sequence before making a decision.

In addition to the bit scores and Expect values, BLAST provides information on the number and percentage of matching residues (Identities) as well as the number and percentage of similar residues (Positives) and Gaps. These are very useful and can be critical to assessing the presumed relationship between two sequences. As a general rule, if two sequences are longer than 100 residues and are more than 25% identical after suitable gapping, it is very likely that they are related. If two sequences are 15–25% identical they may be related but it is usually necessary to perform further tests to confirm their putative relationship. If two sequences are less than 15% identical, they are probably not related. These rules (courtesy of R.F. Doolittle) are summarized in a graph shown in Fig. 10.

Most BLAST searches result in at least one or more significant matches. The determination of whether a match is significant is dependent not only on the numbers (Expect, bit score, %ID) that you obtain, but also on the type of relationship you are trying to identify. For example, if one is interested in finding out whether a query protein is structurally similar to something already in the database, then a match with very low sequence identity (<20%) or a modest Expect value (0.5) could very well exhibit a similar three-dimensional fold. However if one is trying to ascertain whether two proteins have the same function, one typically requires a much higher level of sequence identity (e.g., >50%) or a much lower Expect value. This simply reflects the fact that structure is generally more conserved than either function or sequence. With the rapid growth in whole genome sequence data, there is an unfortunate trend to use large-scale sequence alignments to ascertain the function or putative functions of thousands of proteins using very generous (i.e., low sequence identity) criteria. The result is that many proteins are being functionally misassigned (*see* Chapter 26). While sequence alignment is useful, it is important that alignment data be combined with experimental (structural, enzymatic, evolutionary) data to get the most complete and accurate picture possible.

Recommendations

If one is working with protein sequences or coding segments, the best approach to analyze a query sequence is by using PSI-BLAST. As a general rule, it is best to work with proteins greater than 50 residues, as smaller sequences can lead to spurious results. The default parameters for PSI-BLAST are usually sufficient for an initial search. In using PSI-BLAST it is important to remember to press the **Iterate** button. PSI-BLAST is an iterative process wherein each iteration allows the program to *learn* about the significant features of any previously identified set of matching sequences. Often one will have to press the **Iterate** button 3–4 times before the search converges. If no obvious homologs are apparent after a few iterations, try changing the scoring matrix to BLOSUM30 or PAM250. Once a set of proteins has been identified from this search (using the criteria discussed earlier), one should then ascertain whether the protein exhibits domain-like features. These features may be identified by looking for contiguous segments of the query protein (50–150 residues) matching distinctly different types or classes of proteins in the database. This is best observed through a visual inspection of the colored alignment graph at the top of the BLAST output window. It can also be seen using the CD search option. Once one has identified the different domains in a query protein, it is often a good idea to break the protein sequence into its constituent domains and to perform a PSI-BLAST search with each of these domains against the Protein Data Bank (PDB). This allows one to investigate whether the query protein may have some structural homologs. An equally good idea is to search the SWISS-PROT database (*see* Website: http://www.expasy.ch) as a means of retrieving additional annotation or information about the protein of interest. Further analysis, e.g., using multiple alignments, hydrophobicity analysis, signal site or PROSITE predictions, secondary structure prediction, or Medline searches. should always be carried out to help confirm or further identify important features of any newly sequenced protein.

However, bioinformatics and computer-based analysis can only take you so far. Indeed, database searching is essentially a computer experiment that helps generate (and sometimes confirm) a hypothesis. As with any experiment or hypothesis, it must be confirmed, controlled, and verified. If one neglects to use biological intuition or ignores the results of wet-bench experiments, or if one does not attempt to confirm the results with another laboratory measurement, then the results of a database search probably have little meaning or merit. Despite these cautions and caveats, it is perhaps safe to say that database searching is probably the fastest, easiest and most revealing experiment a biologist can perform.

Glossary and Abbreviations

Algorithm a defined sequence of actions or computational steps that perform a specific task.

Alignment the process of shifting letters in two character strings to create or highlight character matches between the two character strings.

BLAST a very fast and very powerful heuristic sequence alignment and database searching algorithm. BLAST uses well developed statistical methods to assess and identify significant matches and alignments.

Dynamic Programming an efficient mathematical technique that can be used to find optimal "paths" or routes to multiple destinations. Dynamic programming belongs to a special class of optimization or minimization techniques.

FASTA one of the first fast heuristic sequence alignment algorithms to be developed. FASTA made sequence searching through large sequence databases feasible.

Gap Penalty the numerical cost of opening or adding a gap to a sequence alignment. Gap penalties typically have values similar to those in a scoring matrix.

Heuristic an economical or intuitive strategy for determining a solution to a problem to which an exact solution is computationally impossible or intractable.

Homology in sequence analysis, this refers to a shared ancestry. Two sequences are homologous if they are derived from a common ancestral sequence or if one of the two sequences has diverged (through evolution) to be different in its amino acid sequence from its parent.

Scoring Matrix a table of numbers that provides the "cost" of substituting one amino acid or one base for another. Dynamic programming algorithms use scoring matrices to determine optimal sequence alignments.

Similarity in sequence analysis, this refers to the likeness or percent identity between any two sequences. Sequences are similar if they share a statistically significant number of amino acids in approximately the same positions.

Suggested Readings

DNA Versus Protein

Baxevanis, A. D. and Ouellette, B. F. F. (2001) Bioinformatics A Practical Guide to the Analysis of Genes and Proteins 2nd Edition, John Wiley & Sons, NY.

Doolittle, R. F. (1986) Of URFs and ORFs: A Primer on How to Analyze Derived Amino Acid Sequences, University Science Books, Mill Valley, CA.

Dynamic Programming and Sequence Similarity

Needleman, S. B. and Wunsch, C. (1970) A general method applicable to the search for similarities in the amino acid sequence of two proteins, J. Mol. Biol. 48, 443–453.

Dynamic Programming: The Algorithm

Altschul, S. F., Gish, W., Miller, W., Myers, E. W., and Lipman, D. J. (1990) Basic local alignment search tool, J. Mol. Biol. 215, 403–410.

Altschul, S. F., Madden, T. L., Schaffer, A. A., Zhang, J., Zhang, Z., Miller, W., and Lipman, D. J. (1997) Gapped BLAST and PSI-BLAST: a new generation of protein database search programs, Nucleic Acids Res. 25, 3389–3402.

Lipman, D. J. and Pearson, W. R. (1985) Rapid and sensitive protein similarity searches, Science 227, 1435–1441.

Pearson, W. R. and Lipman, D. J. (1988) Improved tools for biological sequence comparison, Proc. Natl. Acad. Sci. USA 85, 2444–2448.

Pearson, W. R. (2000) Flexible sequence similarity searching with the FASTA3 program package, Methods Mol. Biol. 132, 185–219.

Smith, T. F. and Waterman, M. S. (1981) Identification of common molecular subsequences, J. Mol. Biol. 47, 195–197.

Scoring Matrices

The Dayhoff (PAM) Scoring Matrices

Dayhoff, M. O., Barker, W. C., and Hunt, L. T. (1983) Establishing homologies in protein sequences, Methods Enzymol. 91, 534–545.

The BLOSUM Scoring Matrices

Henikoff, S. and Henikoff, J.G. (1992) Amino acid substitution matrices from protein blocks, Proc. Natl. Acad. Sci. USA 89, 10,915–10,919.

Henikoff, S. and Henikoff, J.G. (1991) Automated assembly of protein blocks for database searching, Nucleic Acids Res. 19, 6565–6572.

Fast Local Alignment Methods

Wootton, J. C. and Federhas, S. (1996) Analysis of compositionally biased regions in sequence databases, Methods Enzymol. 266, 554–571.

28 GCG Database Searching

David J. Heard

Introduction

The various programs available for searching GCG databases using text-based or sequence-based searches and the programs that allow the user create their own flat-file databases using the Genetics Computer Group (GCG) and the X-windows SeqLab interface will be described. When appropriate the equivalent command line options will be listed using the same format as given in the GCG program manual, for example *—WORDsize = 2*. It will also be assumed that the reader has access to GCG help documents either through the SeqLab or SeqWeb interfaces or the GCG Program Manuals that come with the software package.

Most users of GCG are well acquainted with at least one or two of the many programs available to search flat-file databases by keyword (Stringsearch, Lookup) or with query sequences (BLAST, FastA). But many people are confused as to the differences between programs and how to choose the best application for their search. For example BLAST seems to be the default program for most sequence-based searches because it is fast, but it may not always be the correct choice. We will review the pros and cons of each search program, how best to use them and how to interpret the output. A little known area of the GCG package will be described; i.e., the programs that allow scientists to create their own searchable databases using proprietary sequence data or extracts of public databases.

What Are Databases?

The definition of a database is simply a collection of records of similar content that can be easily accessed and managed. But there are two main types of databases, flat-file and relational. It is important to understand the difference between them and how this relates to GCG. Briefly, a flat-file is a file containing a number of records, or pieces of data that are not related to one another in a structured way. A typical GenBank record contains several pieces of information, such as the gene locus, accession number, organism name, the authors names, publications, features (i.e., the cds or coding sequence), and finally the DNA sequence itself. The GenBank flat-file database could theoretically be made up of a single large file containing several million sequence records (it is actually made of several large files containing different divisions of the

```
LOCUS       BH021105       191 bp    DNA             GSS       20-JUN-2001
DEFINITION  SP6 RPCI-1 55N16 RPCI-1 PAC library Homo sapiens genomic, DNA
            sequence.
ACCESSION   BH021105
VERSION     BH021105.1  GI:14495569
KEYWORDS    GSS.
SOURCE      human.
  ORGANISM  Homo sapiens
            Eukaryota; Metazoa; Chordata; Craniata; Vertebrata; Euteleostomi;
            Mammalia; Eutheria; Primates; Catarrhini; Hominidae; Homo.
REFERENCE   1  (bases 1 to 191)
  AUTHORS   Van Roy,N., Vandesompele,J., Berx,G., Staes,K., Van Gele,M., De
            Smet,E., De Paepe,A., Laureys,G., Versteeg,R., Van Roy,F. and
            Speleman,F.
  TITLE     Localisation of the 17q breakpoint of a constitutional 1;17
            translocation in a patient with neuroblastoma within a 50 kb
            segment located between the ACCN1 and TLK2 genes and near the
            distal breakpoints of two microdeletions in NF1 patients
  JOURNAL   Unpublished (2001)
COMMENT     Contact: Nadine Van Roy
            Dept Medical Genetics
            University Hospital Ghent
            De Pintelaan 185, 9000 Ghent, Belgium
            Tel: 3292405518
            Fax: 3292404970
            Email: nadine.vanroy@rug.ac.be
            Plate: 55  row: N  column: 16
            Seq primer: SP6
            Class: PAC end
            High quality sequence stop: 190.
FEATURES             Location/Qualifiers
     source          1..191
                     /organism="Homo sapiens"
                     /db_xref="taxon:9606"
                     /map="17"
                     /clone_lib="RPCI-1 PAC library"
BASE COUNT       47 a      33 c      62 g      43 t       6 others
ORIGIN
        1 ccctttgaan cccgttcngg cccngaatgt aggggtagag gagaggcagg ggacgctgct
       61 tgacctggag tgagggtcag tgagttttct aaatagctgt caataaattg tctgctgact
      121 gatatatcag ggtcaaggag aggacagcga ttctcgtacg aacggttacg attcgagaga
      181 ggngagagnt n
//
LOCUS       BH021106       359 bp    DNA             GSS       20-JUN-2001
DEFINITION  SP6 RPCI-1 266J21 RPCI-1 PAC library Homo sapiens genomic, DNA
            sequence.
ACCESSION   BH021106
VERSION     BH021106.1  GI:14495570
KEYWORDS    GSS.
SOURCE      human.
  ORGANISM  Homo sapiens
            Eukaryota; Metazoa; Chordata; Craniata; Vertebrata; Euteleostomi;
            Mammalia; Eutheria; Primates; Catarrhini; Hominidae; Homo.
REFERENCE   1  (bases 1 to 359)
  AUTHORS   Van Roy,N., Vandesompele,J., Berx,G., Staes,K., Van Gele,M., De
            Smet,E., De Paepe,A., Laureys,G., Versteeg,R., Van Roy,F. and
            Speleman,F.
  TITLE     Localisation of the 17q breakpoint of a constitutional 1;17
            translocation in a patient with neuroblastoma within a 50 kb
            segment located between the ACCN1 and TLK2 genes and near the
            distal breakpoints of two microdeletions in NF1 patients
  JOURNAL   Unpublished (2001)
COMMENT     Contact: Nadine Van Roy
            Dept Medical Genetics
            University Hospital Ghent
            De Pintelaan 185, 9000 Ghent, Belgium
            Tel: 3292405518
            Fax: 3292404970
            Email: nadine.vanroy@rug.ac.be
            Plate: 266  row: J  column: 21
```

Fig. 1. The GenBank flat file database format. Each sequence record begins with the LOCUS and ends with a double slash (//) on a separate line. There are many thousands of records in the GenBank flatfiles.

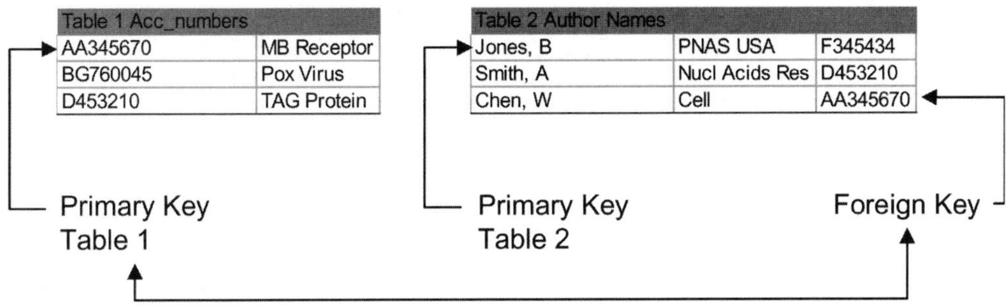

Fig. 2. An example of a simple relational database showing two tables and how they are related to one another. The foreign key in Table 2 of this figure relates this information to the information in Table 1 of this figure.

database). The individual records are separated from each other by a simple character (in GenBank a double slash, //, on a separate line), which indicates the end of one sequence record and the beginning of the next (*see* Fig. 1).

In contrast to flat-file databases, relational databases are made up of sets of formally described tables that are comprised of one or more columns containing different categories of data, i.e., species name or accession number, and rows of data for each unique record. The tables are related (hence the name relational) to one another by shared data fields called keys. For example in Fig. 2, two tables of a simple relational database are depicted. Table 1 of Fig. 2 contains accession numbers and sequence names and the key piece of information in this table is the accession number. Therefore this is called the *primary* key of that table. In Table 2 of Fig. 2, which contains author and journal names, the primary key is the author name. However, this table also contains a list of the accession numbers associated with each author. In Table 2 the accession number is called a *foreign* key and it is this information that *relates* the two tables.

The difference between the types of databases is obvious when you want to retrieve data from them. If one wanted to search the GenBank flat-file database for a specific gene one might have to search through every sequence record in the whole database, which could take days to finish. In contrast, the data in a relational database can be accessed and assembled in many different ways using a special programming language, the Structured Query Language (SQL). Using SQL queries one can limit the search to the tables containing the desired information, i.e., sequence names, ignoring all other information. However, it is important to note that while a relational database is more powerful and flexible than a flat-file database, it is much more complicated to construct, maintain, and query, and requires more computer resources. The standard release of the GCG program uses only flat-file databases. A special version of GCG was just released that can also interact with relational databases.

Searching By Keyword

Different pieces of data in a flat-file database can be extracted into separate files and individually searched. This process, called *database indexing*, makes flat-file database searching much faster and more efficient, providing many of the advantages of a relational database without the requirement of large amounts of system

Table 1
Relative Speed of the GCG Text-Based Search Tools Indicating Search Time and Results of a Search for the String: Estrogen Related Receptor[a]

Program	*Record searched*	*Time (hh:mm:ss)*	*Result of search*
Stringsearch	Definitions	00:00:27	Negative
Stringsearch	Full annotations	00:27:07	Negative
Lookup	Full annotations	00:00:06	Positive

[a]Performance on other machines will vary.

resources or knowledge of SQL. GCG contains a number of programs that perform database indexing and these are used to create the files searched by the GCG text-based search tools.

Stringsearch

To work with the GCG package, the GenBank flat-file database must be reformatted using one of the GCG database reformatting utilities (GenBanktoGCG) resulting in the sequence and the annotation information being split into different files called genbank.seq (sequence) and genbank.ref (annotation). Another program, Seqcat, indexes the database by extracting the locus name, accession number, definition line, date of submission and sequence length from genbank.ref into a genbank.seqcat file.

The GCG program Stringsearch performs simple text-based searches on the *dbname*.ref and *dbname*.seqcat files using queries (strings) typed by the user. In the SeqLab Stringsearch window you have the option of choosing to search the definition line contained in the *dbname*.seqcat file (—MENu=A) or the entire sequence annotation section in *dbname*.ref (—MENu=B). While searching the definition line alone is fast, only a limited amount of information is available. In contrast the entire sequence annotation may contain much more information but search times are many times longer (*see* Table 1).

The default setting in the program is to match **ALL** the words in the search string using the Boolean operator **AND** (—MATch=AND). In the example in Fig. 3, only records containing the words estrogen AND receptor would be returned. By selecting the **ANY** option (—MATch=OR) all records containing either estrogen **OR** receptor will be identified. Searches can be written in specific ways to make them more or less stringent. Wildcards (*), which allows one to search all spellings of a word, can make searches less stringent. For example, **hum*** would find entries with the words **hum**an or **hum**ans but may also find those containing the word **hum**mingbird. Quotation marks can be used to limit searches to specific word orders. A query for "*estrogen receptor*" would only find entries containing the words in the same order as typed and containing a space between them but would not find for example *estrogen-receptor* or *receptor estrogen*.

The output of the Stringsearch program is a GCG list file. This file can be imported into the SeqLab main or editor window enabling the user to access each sequence in the list through this interface. Alternatively, a list file can be used as input to other files including Stringsearch, BLAST, and FastA on the command line.

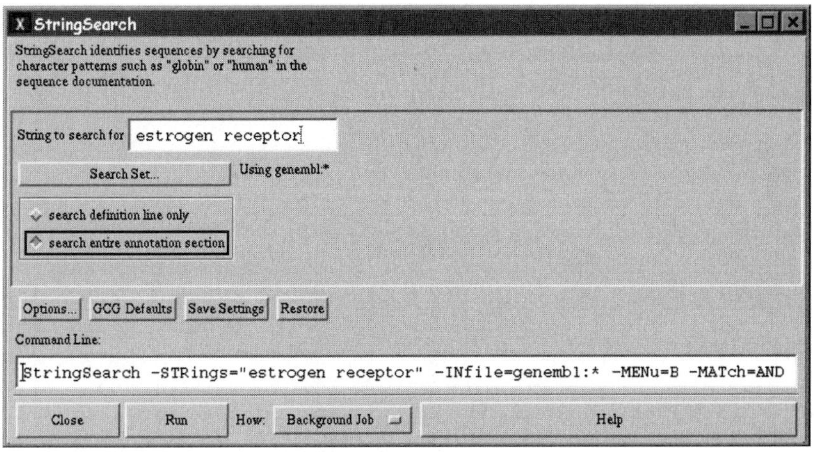

Fig. 3. The SeqLab Stringsearch window. Queries are typed or pasted into the *String to search for* window, (e.g., estrogen receptor). The database or list of sequences to search is chosen by clicking **Search Set...**. One can search only the definition or the entire sequence annotation. As in all SeqLab program windows, the various command line options can be chosen by clicking on the **Options** button. The **Help** button gives access to the complete program description and access to all other GCG help pages. The actual command as it would appear on the command line is indicated at the bottom of the window.

Lookup

The GCG package contains a suite of indexing programs, the Sequence Retrieval System (SRS) programs written for GCG by Etzold and Argos (1993) that extract and build the SRS indices used by the *Lookup* program. The different pieces of information extracted by SRS include: sequence name, accession number, definition, organism, keywords, author names, publication title, reference, features, sequence length, and date of entry into the database. Each individual piece of information is placed into a separate file so that each can be individually searched. Note that the complete SRS program in its present form (version 6) is an extremely powerful database search tool that is freely available on the internet (*see* Website: http://srs.ebi.ac.uk/). In order for *Lookup* to access a database it must have a format that is recognized by the SRS indexing software otherwise it will not be useful. (This is described in detail in the GCG System Support Manual).

Lookup is a much more powerful and faster text-based search program than Stringsearch (*see* Fig. 4). To gain full advantage of Lookup, it should be accessed from the SeqLab interface, as it is a little clumsy from the command line. The main advantage of Lookup compared to Stringsearch is that one can write database queries using boolean operators AND (**&**), OR (**|**), and BUT-NOT (**!**) in the same query allowing the creation of very complex queries. An example of a complex query might be: **(mrna | cdna | (complete & cds)) ! (promoter | *pseudogene* | *intron*)**. This is interpreted as "find entries containing the words mRNA or cDNA or complete cds but exclude those containing promoter or pseudogene in any spelling (including retropseudogene, pseudogenes or retro-pseudogenes) or intron in any spelling" (alternatively in bold or italics). Frequently typed queries can be saved in text files and copied and pasted into the appropriate fields on the interface. Another important aspect of

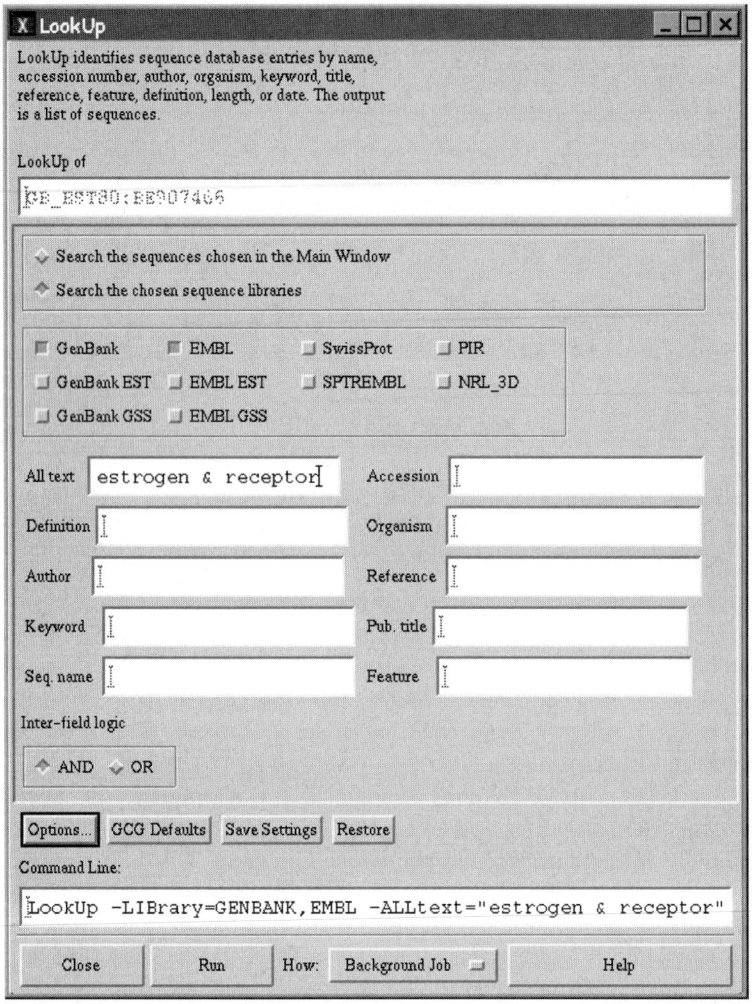

Fig. 4. The SeqLab Lookup interface allows you to click on one or all the databases that are formatted by the SRS tools. One can also limit the search to a group of sequences chosen in the main window (for example a List file of BLAST results). Text searches can be limited to certain parts of the annotation, (e.g., Author name) or to all the text in the annotation (All text). The Inter-field logic (AND/OR) buttons near the bottom of the window indicate the relationship between the different fields (e.g., Accession number: AF00* AND Organism: Homo sapiens).

Lookup is the ability to limit the search to specific parts of the sequence annotation, including organism, authors, and features. However, not all databases contain the same types of annotation. On occasion this can cause problems when searching different databases. One can routinely parse the GenBank database updates for specific subsets of genes that are of specific interest using Lookup with saved complex queries. For example, all the mammalian cDNAs that represent the complete coding sequence of a gene can be separated from all the other sequences using this tool. Alternatively one can parse the database for all sequences from a particular species (e.g., rabbit EST sequences) in one step.

The output from a Lookup query is a GCG list file, which can be imported into the main window or used in other GCG programs. This feature permits list refinement on a previous Lookup result, rather than searching the entire database again. For example, in a first Lookup query you asked for *all human EST sequences*. By importing the output of this search into the main window you can use Lookup again to find only those ESTs that are associated with prostate cancer. This combination of complex queries and list refinement make Lookup an extremely powerful database search and retrieval tool.

Lookup has a few disadvantages. One of the main drawbacks is that the files containing the indices require a substantial amount of disk space, for the full GCG database release of June 2001 the SRS indices require nearly 8 gigabytes of disk space. Also the indices are not as straightforward to create as those for Stringsearch and some databases will be incompatible with the SRS indexing software. However, as the example below will indicate, the performance of Lookup is superior compared to Stringsearch.

The example search summarized in Table 1 should illustrate the difference between Stringsearch and Lookup. A search for the string estrogen-related receptor was performed with both Stringsearch and Lookup using the Unix server with the aim of finding the accession number of the estrogen related receptor gamma (ERRgamma) gene. The Stringsearch of *definitions* in the GenEMBL database returned a result in 27 s but only found two entries for estrogen related receptor *alpha*, therefore neither was correct. A Stringsearch of the **entire** GenEMBL annotations with the same query took 27 min (or 60 times longer) and returned the same two genes. In contrast, using Lookup searched the **entire** GenEMBL annotations and returned a result in 6 s (270 times faster than Stringsearch) yielding 20 matches, amongst which was the gene of interest.

Searching with Query Sequences

GCG version 10.2 SeqLab contains the following sequence search programs: BLAST, NetBLAST, FastA, Ssearch, TFastA, TFastX, FastX, FrameSearch, HMMerSearch, MotifSearch, ProfileSearch, FindPatterns, Motifs, and WordSearch (*see* Fig. 5). The GCG package can be described as a toolbox, packed with tools of various shapes and sizes. The trick is to know which tool you need for the job. As shown in Table 2, the search tools can be divided into 3 basic types based on the type of search. In general BLAST, NetBLAST, (T)FastA/X, WordSearch, Ssearch, and FrameSearch are used to search databases with a single query sequence in order to find entries with similarity to the input sequence.

The programs HMMerSearch, MotifSearch, and ProfileSearch are similar in that groups of related sequences are first aligned to identify conserved motifs and the alignments are used to search the database for related sequences. Finally, Findpatterns and Motifs use simple word matching algorithms to find matches in short sequence patterns rather than searching full sequence databases. These will not be discussed further in this chapter.

It is important to understand how the search programs find and evaluate hits. The concept of scoring matrices is an important part of this task. A scoring matrix is a table that attempts to put a value on identities and substitutions in an alignment. For nucleotide-nucleotide comparisons the scoring matrices are rather simple. In BLAST any match is given a score of +1 and a mismatch of –3 by default but these numbers can be changed at the command line (—MATCH=2 and —MISmatch=5) or in the BLAST

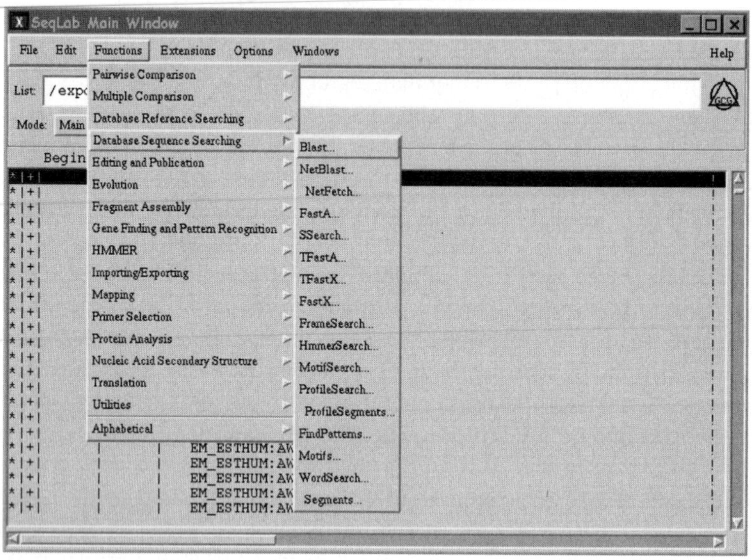

Fig. 5. The SeqLab main window showing all the Database Sequence Searching programs.

options window when using the SeqLab interface. In protein-protein comparisons scoring matrices are more complicated. When making an alignment the match or mismatch value of each alignment pair is obtained from a probabilistic model that considers the evolutionary conservation of amino acids at each position in related proteins. The original scoring matrices were determined by globally aligning highly conserved (85% identical) protein sequences from different organisms and determining the probability and type of amino acid substitutions in each position resulting in the percentage acceptable mutations (PAM) matrices described by Dayhoff et al. (1978). Matrices for more distantly related protein sequences were then extrapolated from these original scores. There are several different PAM matrices including PAM40, PAM70, and PAM250. Each refers to the evolutionary distance expressed as the percentage of positions that would be expected to mutate over a period of 10^8 y. The greater the value is, the greater the evolutionary distance. Therefore, PAM250 indicates a matrix for aligning proteins where 250% of all positions (or 2.5 substitutions at each position) would have changed over 100 million years.

However, as the PAM matrices were derived using global alignments on closely related sequences they are probably not the best choice to identify highly conserved protein domains in otherwise weakly related proteins. This problem was addressed by Henikoff and Henikoff (1992), who developed a new series of matrices called BLOCKS substitution matrices (BLOSUM, pronounced blossom) by comparing the ungapped, highly conserved protein sequences in the BLOCKS database. All BLOSUM matrices from BLOSUM 30 to BLOSUM 100 were derived from actual protein-protein alignments rather than being extrapolated mathematically. BLOSUM matrices have been found to be more reliable than PAM for aligning members of protein families. The numbers of the different BLOSUM matrices indicate the percent identity of the protein blocks used to generate the matrices. For example, BLAST, Ssearch, and FrameSearch all use the BLOSUM62 matrix by default, which was gen-

Table 2
The Characteristics of the Various GCG Search Tools and Their Major Advantages and Disadvantages

Program	*Nuc-Nuc*	*Nuc-Pro*	*Pro-Pro*	*Pro-Nuc*	*Gapped alignments?*	*Major advantages*	*Major disadvantages*
BLAST	Yes	Yes	Yes	Yes	Yes	Speed, gapped alignments, automatic detection of type of search.	Requires large local databases in a specific format. SeqLab can only use one database at a time.
NetBLAST	Yes	Yes	Yes	Yes	Yes	Searches NCBI Database over the internet.	Sequences submitted over internet therefore insecure.
FastA	Yes	No	Yes	No	No	Possibly more sensitive than BLAST in nuc-nuc searches. Flexible as you can search small groups of sequences rather than whole databases.	Slow and poor at aligning sequences with small gaps let alone cDNA vs Genomic sequence.
TFastA	No	No	No	Yes	No	See TFastX.	See TFastX.
TFastX	No	No	No	Yes	Frame-shifts only	Allows frameshifts.	Extremely slow. Poor at aligning sequences with gaps.
FastX	No	Yes	No	No	No	Allows frameshifts.	Slow and poor at aligning sequences with small gaps. Insensitive compared to BLAST.
WordSearch	Yes	No	Yes	No	No	Rapid.	Very insensitive compared to BLAST.
Ssearch	Yes	No	Yes	No	Small local gaps	Greater sensitivity.	Very slow.
FrameSearch	No	Yes	No	Yes	Frame-shifts only	More sensitive than BLAST or FastX.	Slower than BLAST and FastX.
HMMerSearch	Yes	No	Yes	No	No	Sensitive for finding weakly related sequences.	Slow, requires a number of related genes to build a profile.
MotifSearch	Yes	No	Yes	No	No	Useful for finding novel motifs in protein families.	Requires a number of related genes to build a profile.
ProfileSearch	No	No	Yes	No	No	Can find sequences with weak homology to the profile.	Slow, requires a number of related genes to build a profile. Not as sensitive as HMMerSearch.
FindPatterns	Yes	No	Yes	No	No	Finds short sequence patterns like restriction enzyme or proteolytic cleavage sites.	Restricted to short sequence patterns no database searching.
Motifs	No	No	Yes	No	No	Searches PROSITE database of protein sites and patterns.	Only finds motifs present in PROSITE cannot find novel motifs.

erated with BLOCKS with up to 62% identity. In principle lower numbered, e.g., BLOSUM40 matrices should be used with weakly conserved proteins and higher numbered, e.g., BLOSUM80 matrices with more conserved proteins.

An amino acid identity between query and subject gives a relatively large positive score: e.g., +4 (in BLOSUM62; *see* Fig. 6). A conservative amino acid substitution, such as leucine to isoleucine, results in a smaller positive score for that position (+2), whereas a nonconservative change, for example leucine to aspartate, results in a large negative score (–4). Changes that result in substitutions of hydrophobic for hydrophilic amino acids are penalized more than changes of amino acid polarity. The insertion of a gap has a large negative score (–8) by default in BLOSUM62 whereas the extension of a gap is penalized to a lower degree (–2 for each amino acid skipped). These numbers are then used to calculate the best alignment of the query sequence to that found in the database and to generate the sequence score. A description of all the scoring matrices available in GCG and how to manipulate them is found in the appendix VII of the GCG program manual.

BLAST/NetBLAST

The Basic Local Alignment Search Tool (BLAST) algorithm was described by Altschul, et al. (1990) and quickly became popular primarily because of its speed in comparison to other search algorithms. The current implementation of BLAST, called gapped BLAST or BLAST2 (Altschul, et al., 1990), was included in GCG beginning in version 10.0 (*see* Fig. 7A). This implementation allows gapped sequence alignments, meaning that more than one alignment is possible for each entry in the database. BLAST2 is approx three-fold faster than the original BLAST program and is faster than all other database searching tools (*see* Table 3). In our toolbox analogy BLAST2 is the handy adjustable wrench in your toolbox; if you could only have one wrench in the toolbox this would be the one to have. BLAST works well with several different types of databases from DNA to protein and EST to Genomic DNA. It rapidly answers the question: Which sequences in the database are related to my sequence, regardless of length, presence of large insertions or deletions, and sequence type. However, for serious protein function prediction BLAST is probably not the tool of choice.

NetBLAST is essentially identical to BLAST except NetBLAST uses the internet to query the databases maintained at the National Center for Biotechnology Information (NCBI). It is not recommended that you use NetBLAST with query sequences that you want to keep confidential. Be aware that sending a sequence on an insecure line may be considered public disclosure. If this is not a concern then there are two main advantages of using NetBLAST. The first is that the databases at NCBI are updated on a daily basis so you can query the most up-to-date sequence data. This is important as the public sequence databases are growing very rapidly. For example, the human EST database grew by over 14% in the 2 mo period between GenBANK release 121 and 122. This translates to the depositioned 391,652 human ESTs, an average of 6,528 sequences/day. The second advantage to NetBLAST is that you will not have to invest in disk space to have the public sequence data in-house.

BLAST is actually 5 different programs: BLASTN for nucleic acid queries of nucleic acid databases; BLASTP for protein queries of protein databases; BLASTX for translated nucleic acid queries of protein databases; TBLASTN for protein queries of translated nucleic acid databases, and finally TBLASTX for translated nucleic acid queries of translated nucleic acid databases. The decision as to which BLAST

```
!!AA_SCORING_MATRIX_RECT 1.0

BLOSUM62 amino acid substitution matrix.

Reference: Henikoff, S. and Henikoff, J. G. (1992). Amino acid
           substitution matrices from protein blocks.  Proc. Natl. Acad.
           Sci. USA 89: 10915-10919.

                     February 20, 1996 14:33   ..

{
GAP_CREATE 8
GAP_EXTEND 2
}
```

	A	B	C	D	E	F	G	H	I	K	L	M	N	P	Q	R	S	T	V	W	X	Y	Z	*
A	4	-2	0	-2	-1	-2	0	-2	-1	-1	-1	-1	-2	-1	-1	-1	1	0	0	-3	0	-2	-1	-4
B	-2	4	-3	4	1	-3	-1	0	-3	0	-4	-3	3	-2	0	-1	0	-1	-3	-4	-1	-3	1	-4
C	0	-3	9	-3	-4	-2	-3	-3	-1	-3	-1	-1	-3	-3	-3	-3	-1	-1	-1	-2	-2	-2	-3	-4
D	-2	4	-3	6	2	-3	-1	-1	-3	-1	-4	-3	1	-1	0	-2	0	-1	-3	-4	-1	-3	1	-4
E	-1	1	-4	2	5	-3	-2	0	-3	1	-3	-2	0	-1	2	0	0	-1	-2	-3	-1	-2	4	-4
F	-2	-3	-2	-3	-3	6	-3	-1	0	-3	0	0	-3	-4	-3	-3	-2	-2	-1	1	-1	3	-3	-4
G	0	-1	-3	-1	-2	-3	6	-2	-4	-2	-4	-3	0	-2	-2	-2	0	-2	-3	-2	-1	-3	-2	-4
H	-2	0	-3	-1	0	-1	-2	8	-3	-1	-3	-2	1	-2	0	0	-1	-2	-3	-2	-1	2	0	-4
I	-1	-3	-1	-3	-3	0	-4	-3	4	-3	2	1	-3	-3	-3	-3	-2	-1	3	-3	-1	-1	-3	-4
K	-1	0	-3	-1	1	-3	-2	-1	-3	5	-2	-1	0	-1	1	2	0	-1	-2	-3	-1	-2	1	-4
L	-1	-4	-1	-4	-3	0	-4	-3	2	-2	4	2	-3	-3	-2	-2	-2	-1	1	-2	-1	-1	-3	-4
M	-1	-3	-1	-3	-2	0	-3	-2	1	-1	2	5	-2	-2	0	-1	-1	-1	1	-1	-1	-1	-1	-4
N	-2	3	-3	1	0	-3	0	1	-3	0	-3	-2	6	-2	0	0	1	0	-3	-4	-1	-2	0	-4
P	-1	-2	-3	-1	-1	-4	-2	-2	-3	-1	-3	-2	-2	7	-1	-2	-1	-1	-2	-4	-2	-3	-1	-4
Q	-1	0	-3	0	2	-3	-2	0	-3	1	-2	0	0	-1	5	1	0	-1	-2	-2	-1	-1	3	-4
R	-1	-1	-3	-2	0	-3	-2	0	-3	2	-2	-1	0	-2	1	5	-1	-1	-3	-3	-1	-2	0	-4
S	1	0	-1	0	0	-2	0	-1	-2	0	-2	-1	1	-1	0	-1	4	1	-2	-3	0	-2	0	-4
T	0	-1	-1	-1	-1	-2	-2	-2	-1	-1	-1	-1	0	-1	-1	-1	1	5	0	-2	0	-2	-1	-4
V	0	-3	-1	-3	-2	-1	-3	-3	3	-2	1	1	-3	-2	-2	-3	-2	0	4	-3	-1	-1	-2	-4
W	-3	-4	-2	-4	-3	1	-2	-2	-3	-3	-2	-1	-4	-4	-2	-3	-3	-2	-3	11	-2	2	-3	-4
X	0	-1	-2	-1	-1	-1	-1	-1	-1	-1	-1	-1	-1	-2	-1	-1	0	0	-1	-2	-1	-1	-1	-4
Y	-2	-3	-2	-3	-2	3	-3	2	-1	-2	-1	-1	-2	-3	-1	-2	-2	-2	-1	2	-1	7	-2	-4
Z	-1	1	-3	1	4	-3	-2	0	-3	1	-3	-1	0	-1	3	0	0	-1	-2	-3	-1	-2	4	-4
*	-4	-4	-4	-4	-4	-4	-4	-4	-4	-4	-4	-4	-4	-4	-4	-4	-4	-4	-4	-4	-4	-4	-4	1

Fig. 6. The Blosum62 protein-protein scoring matrix indicating amino acid identity and substitution scores. Amino acids are indicated along the top and left side by their single letter codes.

A

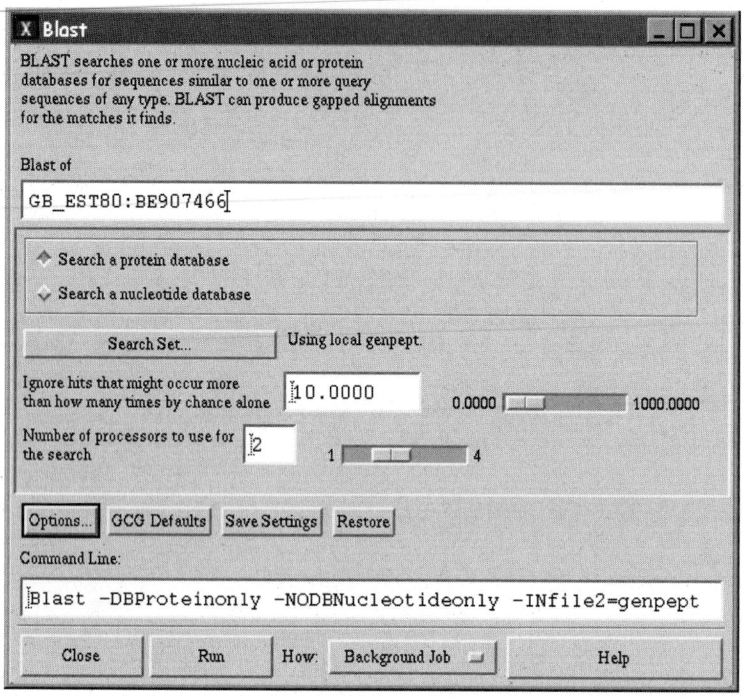

Fig. 7. **(A)** The BLAST window. In this example a DNA sequence is being used to search a protein database (genpept). The Ignore Hits slider changes the —EXPect variable, which determines the cutoff to show hits that would have occurred by chance alone (a higher number means more likely to occur by chance, or less significance). The number of processors slider tells the program how many processors that you are allowed to use for your search. Using more speeds up the program but slows down other applications running on the same computer. **(B)** *(opposite page)* The BLAST output in text format. Notice the line at the top of the output: *!!Sequence_List 1.0* —this tells GCG that this output is a valid list file that can be used to import the sequences into the SeqLab main window (note that this line appears in the output from all the GCG search programs described in this chapter). The score in bits and E-value scores appear on the right side at the top of the sequence list. An E-value of 0.0 means it is infinitely unlikely that this match occurred by chance alone. In the alignment portion the definition line of the database sequence is given followed by the scores and the orientation of the query and subject (database hit) strands. Plus equals forward direction, as the query sequence was entered into BLAST or the database sequence submitted to the database whereas "Minus" would indicate the reverse complement.

program to use is made automatically according to the type of input sequence (protein or nucleic acid) being used to search the type of database chosen. When using nucleotide sequences to query a protein database (BLASTX), the query sequence is translated in all six frames (3 forward and 3 reverse) and each resulting protein sequence is used to search the database. When using a protein sequence to query a DNA database (TBLASTN), the entire database is translated in all 6 frames and compared to the query peptide. The only BLAST program that has to be selected specifically by the user is TBLASTX. This program translates both the nucleic acid query sequence and the nucleic acid database in all 6 frames meaning that for each query sequence 36 different BLASTP searches must be performed. Note that TBLASTX is not capable of performing gapped alignments.

B

```
!!SEQUENCE_LIST 1.0
BLASTN 2.1.3 [Apr-1-2001]


Reference: Altschul, Stephen F., Thomas L. Madden, Alejandro A. Schaffer,
Jinghui Zhang, Zheng Zhang, Webb Miller, and David J. Lipman (1997),
"Gapped BLAST and PSI-BLAST: a new generation of protein database search
programs",  Nucleic Acids Res. 25:3389-3402.

Query= GB_PR:AB001636
         (3028 letters)

Database: genembl
           1,346,493 sequences; 3,479,015,987 total letters

Searching. . . . . . . . . . . . . . . . . . . . . . . . . . . . . . . . . . . . . . . .
. . . . . . . .done

                                                               Score     E
Sequences producing significant alignments:                    (bits)  Value ..

GB_PR:AB001636  Begin: 342 End: 2999
!AB001636 Homo sapiens mRNA for ATP-dependent RNA ...           5269  0.0
GB_PR:AB001636  Begin: 1 End: 296
!AB001636 Homo sapiens mRNA for ATP-dependent RNA ...
GB_PR:AF279891  Begin: 181 End: 2441
!AF279891 Homo sapiens dead box protein 15 mRNA, c...           4365  0.0
GB_PR:AF279891  Begin: 1 End: 135
!AF279891 Homo sapiens dead box protein 15 mRNA, c...
GB_RO:BC003745  Begin: 323 End: 2971
!BC003745 Mus musculus, Similar to DEAD/H (Asp-Glu...           3897  0.0
GB_RO:BC003745  Begin: 129 End: 273
!BC003745 Mus musculus, Similar to DEAD/H (Asp-Glu...
GB_RO:BC003745  Begin: 13 End: 42
!BC003745 Mus musculus, Similar to DEAD/H (Asp-Glu...
...
GB_PR:AB001601  Begin: 1482 End: 1524
!AB001601 Homo sapiens DBP2 mRNA for ATP-dependent...             62  2e-06
GB_PAT:AX013689  Begin: 157 End: 199
!AX013689 Sequence 9 from Patent WO9954460. 9/2000                62  2e-06
GB_PL:NCB208  Begin: 43364 End: 43436
!AL355930 Neurospora crassa DNA linkage group II BAC...           50  0.009
GB_IN:CET21B6  Begin: 20347 End: 20369
!Z68011 Caenorhabditis elegans cosmid T21B6, comple...            46  0.14
GB_IN:CELC02D5  Begin: 9310 End: 9332 Strand:-
!L16622 C. elegans cosmid C02D5. 10/1993                          46  0.14

\\End of List

>GB_PR:AB001636 AB001636 Homo sapiens mRNA for ATP-dependent RNA
            helicase #46, complete cds. 12/1997
          Length = 3028

 Score = 5269 bits (2658), Expect = 0.0
 Identities = 2658/2658 (100%)
 Strand = Plus / Plus


Query: 342   ttgcgagcttcaacaaatgctatgcttatcagtgctggattaccacccctgaaagcttcc 401
             ||||||||||||||||||||||||||||||||||||||||||||||||||||||||||||
Sbjct: 342   ttgcgagcttcaacaaatgctatgcttatcagtgctggattaccacccctgaaagcttcc 401


Query: 402   cattcagctcactcaacccactcagcacattcaacgcattctacacattctgctcattca 461
             ||||||||||||||||||||||||||||||||||||||||||||||||||||||||||||
Sbjct: 402   cattcagctcactcaacccactcagcacattcaacgcattctacacattctgctcattca 461
```

Table 3
Relative Speed of the GCG Query Sequence Search Tools

Search Type	*Program Name*	*Search Time (hh:mm:ss)*
Nuc-NucDB	BLASTN	00:00:31
Nuc-NucDB	BLASTN (wordsize=7)	00:12:38
Nuc-NucDB	FastA	00:29:32
Nuc-NucDB	SSearch	36:00:00[a]
NucX-TNucDB	TBLASTX	00:09:51
Nuc-ProDB	BLASTX	00:00:56
Nuc-ProDB	FastX	00:02:52
Nuc-ProDB	FrameSearch	00:41:17
Pro-ProDB	BLASTP	00:00:22
Pro-ProDB	FastA	00:02:29
Pro-ProDB	SSearch	00:08:12
Pro-NucDB	TBLASTN	00:04:58
Pro-NucDB	TFastX	01:39:03
Pro-NucDB	FrameSearch	36:00:00[a]

[a]Searched stopped due to drain on system resources. Performance on other machines will vary.
Nuc, GenBank Accession AB001636. NucDB, GenBank (release 123). NucX, AB001636 translated. TNucDB, translated GenBank (release 123). Pro, Swissprot Accession DD15_Human. ProDB, Swissprot (release 39).

The BLAST algorithm is complex (*see* the GCG manuals, Altschul, et al. (1997), and Chapter 27 for a detailed description). BLAST identifies words in the query sequence and searches for sequences with similar words in the database. The word size is the smallest region of 100% identity between a query sequence and the sequences in a database for a sequence to be identified as a potential hit. The default word size is 11 for nucleotide-nucleotide and 3 for protein-protein comparisons. This can be changed in the options menu or at the command line **(—WORDsize=n)**. When the program finds a similar word in a sequence in the database it tries to extend the alignment outwards in both directions creating a high scoring segment pair (HSP). Once an HSP is identified, the algorithm searches in both directions for other HSPs in the same sequence to generate the gapped alignments. It is often said that FastA is more sensitive in nucleotide-nucleotide searches than BLASTN. While this may be true using the default BLASTN settings, decreasing the wordsize to 7 results in BLAST being nearly as sensitive as FastA, but faster (*see* Table 3).

Unlike other GCG search algorithms, by default, BLAST filters or masks regions of low sequence complexity in the query sequence. Filtering removes a substantial amount of unwanted noise from the search output. A database search with a cDNA sequence containing a long poly-A stretch is a good example of the usefulness of a filter. Without filtering, or physically deleting the poly-A sequence, such a search would return thousands of statistically significant but uninteresting hits to the polyA region that could mask potentially interesting alignments. The filtering program for nucleic acid queries of nucleic acid databases (BLASTN) is called DUST and was written by Tatusov and Lipman (unpublished). DUST replaces low complexity nucleotide sequences with N's that are ignored by BLAST. All other BLAST programs use the SEG algorithm (Wootton and Federhen, 1996) to filter proteins for low complexity protein regions (for example stretches of glutamines or prolines) replacing those residues with an X (*see* the example in Fig. 8A). Note that filtering is only applied to the query sequence, not to database sequences. Filtering can be turned off when desired in both BLAST and NetBLAST. (For further discussion on the effects of filtering tools on database searching, *see* "Suggested Readings," Shpaer, et al.)

The BLAST output in GCG is essentially comprised of a text file containing a list of sequences and a number of alignments (*see* Fig. 7B). The length of the list and the number of alignments in the output can be controlled in the options menu **SeqLab** or at the command line **(—LIStsize=1000 —ALIgnments=500)**. The output also contains two different score values, which can aid evaluating aligned sequences. The first is called the bit score, which is presented as a whole number and represents the probability of finding the same alignment by chance. The bit score is the n in the formula $1/2^n$. If the bit score is 30 then the chance of finding the same sequence randomly would be 1 in 2^{30} or 1 in a billion. A higher bit score is better than a lower one. Importantly, the bit score is independent of the size of the database searched. This can be important when comparing hits in a small database such as your personal sequence database and a large database like the GenEMBL ESTs. The other score given is the expected (E) value, which is also an expression of the probability of finding the same match by chance and is expressed as a number such as 5e-48 (5×10^{-48}). The E value is however dependent on the size of the database being searched. A lower E value score indicates a better match, with 0 being a perfect match.

FastA Suite/SSearch/FrameSearch

In the toolbox analogy the FastA/SSearch/Framesearch programs would be like a set of crescent wrenches; they come in all different sizes, both metric and imperial, and one has to find the right wrench for the job at hand. These tools are best for comparing protein sequences (or translated nucleotides) with protein databases (or translated nucleotide databases). They are better than BLAST at answering the question: What sequences in the database are distantly related to my input sequence?

The reason FastA and SSearch/Framesearch are grouped together is that they are slower, yielding more sensitive searches of the databases, yet similar output. However, these programs are different in terms of the algorithms used to find sequence matches. The FastA programs use the algorithm of Pearson and Lipman (1988), whereas SSearch and FrameSearch use the Smith and Waterman (SW) algorithm. The Pearson-Lipman and SW algorithms have been extensively compared using different scoring matrices and in most instances the SW algorithm appears to be more sensitive than Pearson and Lipman for protein-protein searches. However, FastA programs are much faster than SW (*see* Table 3). It is possible to search subsets of sequences rather than entire databases. This can dramatically increase performance if one is interested in a particular protein family.

Like BLAST, FastA and Smith-Waterman (SW) searches come in several different flavors (*see* Table 3), specific to the type of search you want to execute. FastA and SSearch compare nucleotide queries against nucleotide databases and protein queries against protein databases. Both SSearch and FrameSearch are *extremely* slow when searching large databases for nucleotide-nucleotide comparisons (*see* Table 3). TFastA and TFastX compare protein queries against nucleic acid databases by translating the database sequences into all 6 frames (3 forward and 3 reverse). TFastX is probably more useful than TFastA in that it allows for frame-shifts in the alignment. Finally,

FastX compares a nucleic acid query, translated in all 6 frames, against a protein database. FrameSearch is similar to a combined FastX and TfastX search in that a translated nucleotide query can be compared to a protein database or a protein query can be compared to a translated nucleotide database.

The output of the FastA programs and SSearch are quite similar. At the top of the output is a histogram showing the distribution of z-scores between the query sequence and the database sequences (*see* Fig. 8A) followed by the sequence list and alignments in the same file (*see* Fig. 8B). The histogram illustrates the number of z-scores expected (indicated by an asterisk) and the actual scores observed (bars of equal signs) for each value. This may be useful in some cases to determine whether the observed similarity is statistically significant. The histogram search results usually show a normal distribution, with a small number of very high scores at the bottom. The majority of alignments to database entries will be in the random noise at lower z-scores (the large peak). A second peak, inset at the bottom right, indicates the same region as it overlaps on the main histogram but at a lower scale (*see* the histogram key to see how many sequences each equals sign represents). It is the inset peak that one should examine for the presence of sequence entries with significant z-scores (i.e., the asterisk appears to the left of the equals sign). In summary, the histogram is a visual summation of whether the alignments that appear below in the output may be significant. In the example used the histogram indicates a slightly higher than expected number of hits in the z-score range from 44–56 and 92–116 (*see* Fig. 8A). This reflects the low complexity regions of the query which identified more sequences in the database than would be expected statistically. However, by manually filtering the complexity regions using the GCG programs Xnu or Seg prior to searching one could ensure that these low complexity regions do not mask the truly interesting relationships (*see* Fig. 8C).

The remaining portion of the output appears very much like a BLAST output with a list of sequences sorted by score followed by the sequence alignments (*see* Fig. 8B). There are 3 scores reported in the sequence list: 1) the s-w score (in SSearch) or opt score (in FastA) is the Smith-Waterman pairwise alignment score derived from the sum of the scoring matrix values at each position in the alignment. 2) The z-score, which is calculated by linear regression of the s-w score with the natural log (ln) of the length of the matching sequence from the database. 3) The E-value score for each sequence indicates the number of sequences that would have to be searched to give a z-score equal to the z-score obtained for that sequence match by random chance. It is similar to the E-value score described for BLAST. The output is sorted by the E-value in the sequence list and alignments. It is stated in the GCG program manual that for searches of a protein database of 10,000 sequences, an E-value of less than 0.01 indicates similarity to the query sequence and that E-values between 1 and 10 may also indicate relatedness (homotogy). The Smith-Waterman program does a better job of aligning two DNA sequences than FastA therefore it is suggested that the option **Use**

Fig. 8. The SSearch/FastA output. **(A)** *(opposite page)* The histogram showing the distribution of z-scores over all the data in the database. The equal-signs indicate the actual scores whereas the asterisks indicate the expected. Note that in this search the actual score is higher than the expected for most of the z-scores. This is because the sequence contains low complexity regions that were not screened out before the search (*see* **C**). In the inset histogram (bottom right) the higher z-score values are indicated at a lower scale than the main histogram (Main: 1equals-sign represents 166 database sequences. Inset 1 "=" represents 3 database sequences). *(Continued on pages 480 and 481)*

A

```
!!SEQUENCE_LIST 1.0

(Peptide) SSEARCH of: o43143  from: 1 to: 795  August 13, 2001 13:56

ID   DD15_HUMAN     STANDARD;      PRT;   795 AA.
AC   O43143; Q9NQT7;

TO: SwissProt:*  Sequences:     98,739  Symbols:    36,175,283

Scoring matrix: GenRunData:blosum50.cmp
 Gap creation penalty: 12  Gap extension penalty: 2

Histogram Key:
 Each histogram symbol represents 166 search set sequences
 Each inset symbol represents 3 search set sequences
 z-scores computed from s-w scores

z-score obs    exp
        (=)    (*)
< 20    217      0:==
  22      2      0:=
  24      6      0:=
  26     19      2:*
  28     50     22:*
  30    232    136:*=
  32    554    525:===*
  34   1245   1422:========*
  36   2489   2921:===============  *
  38   4160   4828:==========================   *
  40   6081   6735:=====================================   *
  42   8017   8232:=================================================*
  44   9223   9081:======================================================*=
  46   9946   9249:=======================================================*====
  48   9245   8855:=====================================================*==
  50   8515   8080:================================================*===
  52   7519   7104:==========================================*===
  54   6390   6068:====================================*==
  56   5267   5069:==============================*=
  58   4219   4161:=========================*
  60   3270   3371:====================*
  62   2614   2702:================*
  64   2066   2149:============*
  66   1655   1699:==========*
  68   1240   1336:========*
  70    938   1047:======*
  72    758    818:====*
  74    567    638:===*
  76    431    497:==*
  78    316    386:==*
  80    271    300:=*
  82    225    229:=*
  84    181    182:=*
  86    138    141:*
  88    113    109:*
  90     83     84:*
  92     74     65:*          :=====================*===
  94     59     50:*          :================*===
  96     47     39:*          :============*===
  98     29     30:*          :=========*
 100     31     23:*          :=======*===
 102     26     18:*          :=====*===
 104     25     14:*          :====*====
 106     18     11:*          :===*==
 108     16      8:*          :==*===
 110     11      6:*          :=*==
 112     10      5:*          :=*==
 114      8      4:*          :=*=
 116      6      3:*          :*=
 118      3      2:*          :*
>120    114      2:*          :*=====================================

 Smith-Waterman (PGopt): reg.-scaled
```

B

```
The best scores are:                                         s-w    z-sc  E(98464)..

SW:DD15_HUMAN     Begin: 1   End: 795
! O43143 homo sapiens (human). putati...                    5316  5999.3        0
SW:DD15_MOUSE     Begin: 1   End: 758
! O35286 mus musculus (mouse). putati...                    4992  5632.9        0
SW:DD15_CAEEL     Begin: 9   End: 732
! Q20875 caenorhabditis elegans. puta...                    3548  3997.9  7e-216
SW:DD15_ARATH     Begin: 21  End: 717
! O22899 arabidopsis thaliana (mouse-...                    3316  3735.3  2.9e-201
SW:PR43_YEAST     Begin: 71  End: 747
! P53131 saccharomyces cerevisiae (ba...                    2914  3279.6  7.2e-176
SW:DD15_SCHPO     Begin: 54  End: 722
! O42945 schizosaccharomyces pombe (f...                    2863  3222.2  1.1e-172
SW:DD15_STRPU     Begin: 1   End: 455
! O17438 strongylocentrotus purpuratu...                    2666  3004.0  1.6e-160
SW:DDX8_HUMAN     Begin: 558  End: 1198
! Q14562 homo sapiens (human). atp-de...                    2250  2522.9  1e-133
SW:DDX8_ARATH     Begin: 461  End: 1101
...
! P34594 caenorhabditis elegans. hypo...                     111   117.4      9.7
SW:POLG_TEV    Begin: 1241  End: 1529
! P04517 t genome polyprotein [contai...                     134   117.4      9.7
\\End of List


o43143
SW:DD15_HUMAN

ID   DD15_HUMAN     STANDARD;       PRT;   795 AA.
AC   O43143; Q9NQT7;
DT   15-DEC-1998 (Rel. 37, Created)
DT   15-DEC-1998 (Rel. 37, Last sequence update)
DT   20-AUG-2001 (Rel. 40, Last annotation update)
DE   PUTATIVE PRE-MRNA SPLICING FACTOR RNA HELICASE (DEAH BOX PROTEIN 15) . . .

SCORES    z-score: 5999.3 E(): 0
>>SW:DD15_HUMAN                                          (795 aa)
 Z-score: 5999.3 expect():    0
Smith-Waterman score: 5316;    100.0% identity in 795 aa overlap
 (1-795:1-795)

                    10        20        30        40        50        60
o43143       MSKRHRLDLGEDYPSGKKRAGTDGKDRDRDRDREDRSKDRDRERDRGDREREREKEKEKE
             ||||||||||||||||||||||||||||||||||||||||||||||||||||||||||||
DD15_HUMAN   MSKRHRLDLGEDYPSGKKRAGTDGKDRDRDRDREDRSKDRDRERDRGDREREREKEKEKE
                    10        20        30        40        50        60

                    70        80        90       100       110       120
o43143       LRASTNAMLISAGLPPLKASHSAHSTHSAHSTHSTHSAHSTHAGHAGHTSLPQCINPFTN
             ||||||||||||||||||||||||||||||||||||||||||||||||||||||||||||
DD15_HUMAN   LRASTNAMLISAGLPPLKASHSAHSTHSAHSTHSTHSAHSTHAGHAGHTSLPQCINPFTN
                    70        80        90       100       110       120

                   130       140       150       160       170       180
o43143       LPHTPRYYDILKKRLQLPVWEYKDRFTDILVRHQSFVLVGETGSGKTTQIPQWCVEYMRS
             ||||||||||||||||||||||||||||||||||||||||||||||||||||||||||||
DD15_HUMAN   LPHTPRYYDILKKRLQLPVWEYKDRFTDILVRHQSFVLVGETGSGKTTQIPQWCVEYMRS
                   130       140       150       160       170       180

                   190       200       210       220       230       240
o43143       LPGPKRGVACTQPRRVAAMSVAQRVADEMDVMLGQEVGYSIRFEDCSSAKTILKYMTDGM
             ||||||||||||||||||||||||||||||||||||||||||||||||||||||||||||
DD15_HUMAN   LPGPKRGVACTQPRRVAAMSVAQRVADEMDVMLGQEVGYSIRFEDCSSAKTILKYMTDGM
                   190       200       210       220       230       240

                   250       260       270       280       290       300
o43143       LLREAMNDPLLERYGVIILDEAHERTLATDILMGVLKEVVRQRSDLKVIVMSATLDAGKF
             ||||||||||||||||||||||||||||||||||||||||||||||||||||||||||||
DD15_HUMAN   LLREAMNDPLLERYGVIILDEAHERTLATDILMGVLKEVVRQRSDLKVIVMSATLDAGKF
                   250       260       270       280       290       300
```

C

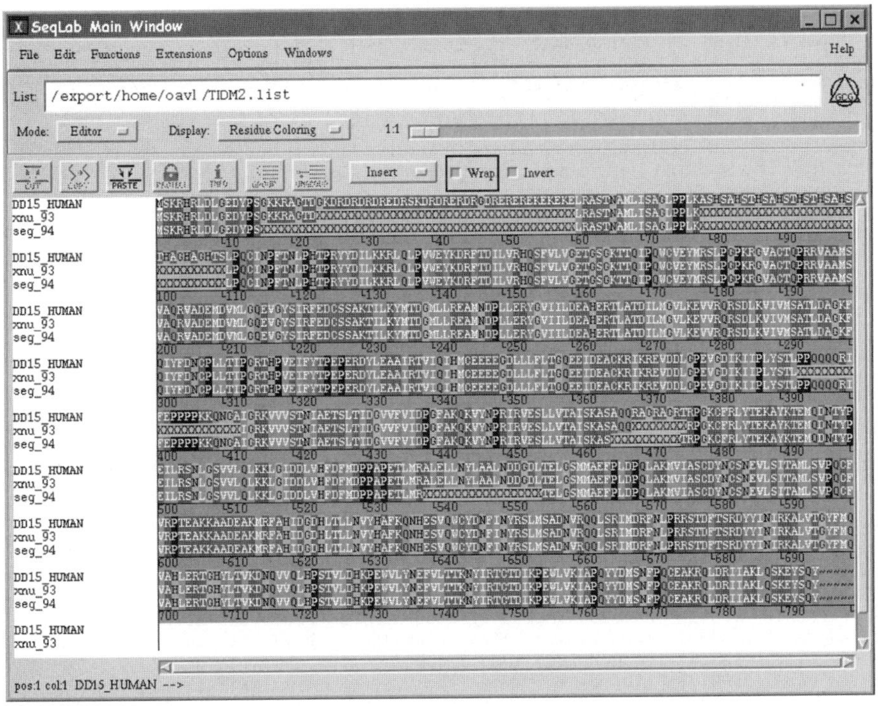

Fig. 8. *(Continued from page 478)* The SSearch/FastA output. **(B)** *(opposite page)* The list portion of the output showing the 3 significance scores. In FastA the s-w score is called the opt score. **(C)** The SeqLab editor window showing the protein sequence (single letter codes) used in this SSearch as it was retrieved from the database and after masking low complexity regions using the GCG programs Xnu (xnu_93) or Seg (seg_94). Two regions of low complexity sequence at the N-terminal portion of the protein were screened out (replaced by X's).

the Smith-Waterman algorithm for final DNA-DNA alignment be chosen when running this type of search in Fast A.

The alignments in the FrameSearch output (*see* Fig. 9A) show the alignment of codons (nucleic acid) aligned with amino acids (using the 3-letter code) with identities indicated by a line (|) and conservative changes indicated by a semi-colon (**:**) and a period (**.**) to indicate comparison values equal to at least +1. The problem with this type of alignment is that when the codon and amino acid residue are not identical it can be laborious to determine the identity of the amino acid in the nucleotide strand, unless of course you have memorized the entire codon table.

The histogram created by the Framesearch program appears in a separate file and looks quite different from the FastA/SSearch plots (*see* Fig. 9B). If you execute FrameSearch from the SeqLab interface, by default the output will not contain a histogram. It will only give a list of sequences sorted by the Smith-Waterman (s-w) score. However, the creation of a separate output file containing a histogram of the score distributions in the database can be selected in the options window (when run from the command line production of the histogram is on by default). The advantage of this graph is that an asterisk indicates the lowest scoring sequence in the list of returned hits and therefore allows one to rapidly determine if other sequences in the database may have significant similarity.

A

```
!!SEQUENCE_LIST 1.0
 FRAMESEARCH of: EM_ESTHUM:AW471468  check: 8916   from: 1  to: 280

ID   AW471468   standard; RNA; EST; 280 BP.
AC   AW471468;
SV   AW471468.1
DT   02-MAR-2000 (Rel. 62, Created)
DT   02-MAR-2000 (Rel. 62, Last updated, Version 1)
DE   xy53b04.x1 NCI_CGAP_Li8 Homo sapiens cDNA clone IMAGE:2856847 3' similar
 to


 TO: SwissProt:*  Sequences: 98,739  Total-length: 36,175,283  August 13, 2001 15:29

 Databases searched:
        SWISS-PROT, Release 39.2, Released on 20Jun2001, Formatted on 26Jun2001

 Scoring matrix: GenRunData:blosum62.cmp
 Translation table: GenRunData:translate.txt

  Gap creation penalty:      8
 Gap extension penalty:      2
    Frameshift penalty:      0

The best scores are:                                                         ..

SW:H4_VOLCA  P08436 volvox carteri. histone h4. 8/2001                       207
SW:H4_CHLRE  P50566 chlamydomonas reinhardtii. histone h4. 7/1999            205
SW:H4_PHACH  P35058 phanerochaete chrysosporium, and agaricus bispo...      203
SW:H4_YEAST  P02309 saccharomyces cerevisiae (baker's yeast). histo...      202
SW:H4_LYCES  P35057 lycopersicon esculentum (tomato). histone h4. 7...      202
SW:H4_WHEAT  P02308 triticum aestivum (wheat), zea mays (maize), pi...      199
SW:H4_HUMAN  P02304 homo sapiens (human), mus musculus (mouse), rat...      199
...
\\End of list

        Match display thresholds for the alignment(s):
                    | = IDENTITY
                    : =   2
                    . =   1

aw471468
H4_VOLCA

          Quality:   207            Length:   273
            Ratio:  2.407             Gaps:     6
 Percent Similarity: 68.235   Percent Identity: 64.706


                 .         .         .         .         .
      2 AAGGACGGAAAAGTGCTTGGGTG.AAGGGTG..AGTGCTAAAT..CGCCA 46
        |||   ||||||   ||||||  ||||||| ||   |||||| |||||||
      5 LysGlyGlyLysGlyLeuGly...LysGly...GlyAlaLys...ArgHi 18
                 .         .         .         .         .
     47 TCGTT..ATGGTGCTCCTGG..GATAACATCCACGGCATTACAAAACCGG 92
        |||| ||   ||||||    |||||||||||   ||||||||||||||||
     19 sArg...LysValLeuArg...AspAsnIleGlnGlyIleThrLysProA 33
                 .         .         .         .         .
     93 CTATTCGCCGTTTGGCTCGGCGCGGTGGCTGCAAGCGCATTTGCGGTCCT 142
        |||||||||||||||||||||||||||||   |||||||||   |||
     34 laIleArgArgLeuAlaArgArgGlyGlyValLysArgIleSerGlyLeu 49
                 .         .         .         .         .
    143 ATCTATGACGAGACTCTAAGTGAACTTAATGATCTCTTAAAGAAAACAAT 192
        ||||||:::||||||   ...   |||   ...   |||...      ||
     50 IleTyrGluGluThrArgThrValLeuLysAsnPheLeuGluAsnValIl 66
                 .         .         .         .         .
    193 AAGAAACAACGGCACTTATACGGCGCACGCCATGCGCAAAACTGGCACAA 242
        ||||......   |||||||||   ||||||   |||||||||   |||
     67 eArgAspSerValThrTyrThrGluHisAlaArgArgLysThrValThrA 83
                 .         .
    243 G.CTGAATATAGAATATAGCCTA 264
          :::...:::   |||...|||
     84 laMetAspValValTyrAlaLeu 90
```

B

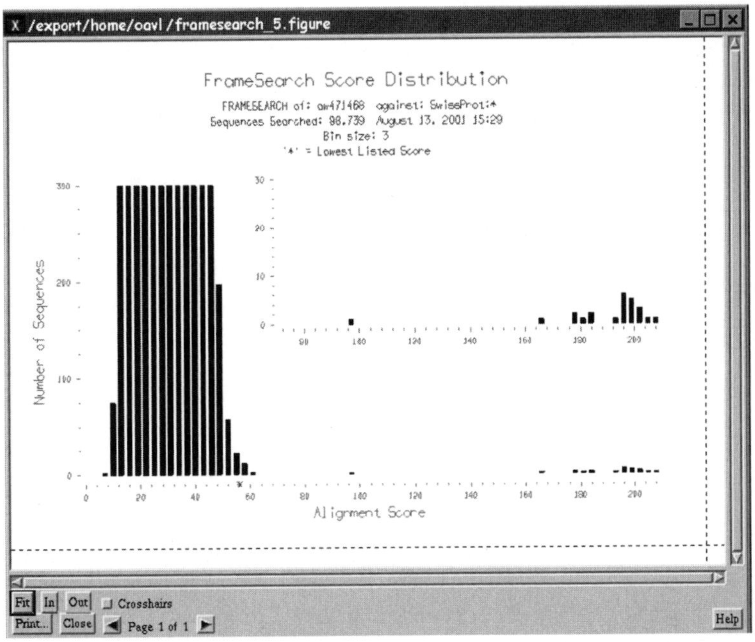

Fig. 9. Results of a FrameSearch of a DNA query vs a protein database. **(A)** *(opposite page)* Note that the query is indicated as a nucleotide sequence rather than a translated protein and the amino-acid sequence of the proteins found in the database is shown using the 3-letter code to overlap with each codon. **(B)** The distribution histogram of the FrameSearch in (A). The asterisk (*) indicates the lowest score in the list of sequence hits.

Rules for Effective Database Searching

Dr. William R. Pearson outlined a series of rules for database searching. These are paraphrased with additional comments and other useful rules:

1. To determine if your sequence already exists in the databases, use the BLAST program as it is by far the fastest and most flexible search program. When searching large eukaryotic genomic DNA or EST sequences with mRNA or cDNA queries, use gapped BLAST rather than FastA or SSearch. Eukaryotic genes are made up of both exons and introns and mature mRNA only contains the exons. Only gapped BLAST will return alignments for several exons spread over large areas of genomic DNA, whereas FastA and Ssearch will find only the single best local alignment.
2. Whenever possible compare sequences at the amino acid level. If the protein sequence is known, use it to search the protein databases (FastA, SSearch). Alternatively, use a translated nucleotide vs protein search (FastX, BLASTX). Searching protein vs. protein will allow the discovery of more evolutionary related distant sequences than DNA vs DNA.
3. Search the smallest, best annotated sequence database before the large poorly annotated sequence databases. I refer to these databases as information rich vs information poor databases. Information rich databases tend to be well-curated, highly annotated, and nonredundant (i.e., Swissprot, PIR, GenBANK refseq) and have fewer partial sequence fragments, sequence errors, redundancies as

high-throughput or low quality sequence found in the whole GenEMBL, dbEST, or High Throughput Genomic (HTG) databases. In some instances it may be worthwhile to create subsets of existing databases (i.e., GeneEMBL coding sequences) using tools such as the Lookup program to improve the chance of success and performance.

4. Use statistics rather than percent similarity scores to judge the quality of a sequence match. Sometimes a sequence can be 100% identical but still insignificant if it is short, or consists of low sequence complexity. Matches with 50% similarity over regions of 20–40 amino acids occur often by chance.
5. For protein query sequences use sequence-masking programs such as Seg or Xnu to remove regions of low complexity before running your search using FastA or SSearch.
6. When evaluating the search results of sequences with a low similarity score, check that the statistical analysis is accurate by randomizing the query sequence using the GCG program Shuffle. Randomized sequences should have a lower E-value than the query sequence.
7. Try using different scoring matrices, gap opening, or extension penalties. When searching with long query sequences, changing the scoring matrix will not dramatically alter the results. However when using shorter sequences to query the database, use of more stringent matrices (Blosum 80, PAM 30) may help identify similar sequences.

Putting the Search Output to Work for You

The output files of all the database search programs described in this chapter are in a special GCG format called a *list file*. List files can be used to enter all the sequences in a list directly into the SeqLab Main or Editor windows and can be used as input to many different GCG programs. In SeqLab, when a database search result appears in the Output Manager window one simply selects the file of interest and clicks the button **Add to Main List**. Alternatively, the list can be opened from the main window by clicking the **File** pull down menu and **Open List** or used directly from the command line of different GCG programs. Now all the sequences identified by your search program are available for further GCG sequence analysis, using programs like *multiple sequence alignment* and *pairwise alignment*. An example of how to utilize this capability to full advantage is to perform a BLAST search with a sequence of interest, import the BLAST output into the GCG main window, and execute a multiple sequence alignment on the BLAST results. One can then import the file of aligned sequences into the SeqLab Editor window to view the alignment in color.

Another important but virtually unknown feature of the GCG software is that the list files (and other GCG files including rich sequence format, RSF, files) can be used to create personal databases. The program Dataset converts a group of sequences into a GCG-formatted database. The databases thus created are compatible with other GCG programs including Stringsearch, FastA/SSearch, the DatabaseBrowser, and many others. In the SeqLab interface the DataSet program appears in the menu **Functions>Utilities>Database Utilities**. To use this program, one simply selects the sequences from the main window and opens the dataset window. Once the database is created, it appears automatically in your personal SeqLab interface. Dataset can also be used from the command line and the newly created database specified at the command line for any GCG search except BLAST. Note that both Lookup and BLAST programs require databases in specific formats distinct from the normal GCG-formatted flat-file database. A database created using Dataset can be made available to everyone using the GCG software, however the systems administrator has to update certain GCG system files. The 6 files created by Dataset appear in the current working directory or can be sent to another directory using the program options or command line. Once created the files cannot be moved or renamed unless their location is edited in your *.datasetrc* file, which appears in your home directory. See the GCG Program Manual or GCG help for a more complete description of this program.

The BLAST program requires a database with a different format than a normal GCG database. GCG has provided a program similar to dataset to create BLAST databases. The program, GCGtoBLAST, is found in the same menu as dataset and works in much the same manner. However, unlike dataset, GCGtoBLAST does not automatically update the SeqLab files so that you can use your personal BLAST database. It is very likely that in order to access this database you will have to ask your systems administrator to update the file BLAST.lbds in the GCG directory (the path to this file is **../gcg/gcgcore/data/rundata/BLAST.lbds**). To install the new BLAST database called, for example, **cancer_genes_BLAST**, the full path to the database and the database name must be entered into this file in the following format **path/databasename database-type** (**protein = p, nucleotide = n**), and any comment you want. For example my database would have the following entry in the BLAST.lbds file:

/export/home/david/databases/cancer_genes_BLAST n Genes involved in cancer

This database will be visible to anyone using GCG but may not be readable by them if the Unix file permissions are set that only you can read from the files. It is probably easier to set up your own GCG-formatted databases rather than BLAST databases, but if you are undertaking very large sequence projects or only searching subsets of the GenBANK databases it may be worthwhile.

Acknowledgments

I would like to thank Dr. Jonathan Kearsey for critical reading of the manuscript; Dr. Brian Golding, Fabien Rouet, and Diego Pallares for their helpful discussions.

Glossary and Abbreviations

Algorithm A step-by-step procedure for solving a problem or accomplishing some end especially by a computer.

Bit score Used in BLAST searches the bit score represents the probability of finding the same alignment by chance. The bit score is the n in the formula 1/2n. A higher bit score indicates a better alignment. Bit scores are independent of the size of the database being searched.

Database A collection of records of similar content that can be easily accessed and managed.

Database Indexing The process of extracting different pieces of data in from flat-file database into separate files that can be searched individually and used to find the original record.

Database Records Pieces of data that are not related to one another in a structured way.

E-value The E-value score for each sequence indicates the number of sequences that would have to be searched to give a similar bit or z-score score obtained for that sequence match by random chance. A lower score is better with 0 being the best. The E-value takes into account the size of the database being searched.

Flat-file A database file containing a number of database records.

Foreign Key A piece of data in a relational database table that is the primary key of another table in the same database.

Global Alignment The detection of global similarities over the entire length of two or more sequences.

Local Alignment The detection of local or short regions of similarities in portions of two or more sequences.

Low Complexity Complexity is the probability of finding a particular amino acid at a particular position in a protein and is proportional to the composition of the whole sequence. For example in a complex protein, 10 prolines in a row are unlikely and therefore of low complexity. The same idea can apply to nucleotide sequences.

Primary Key The most important piece of data in a relational database table.

Suggested Reading

Searching by Keyword

Bailey, T. L. and Gribskov, M. (1998) Combining evidence using p-values: application to sequence homology searches, Bioinformatics 14, 48–54.

Lookup

Etzold, T. and Argos, P. (1993) SRS: an indexing and retrieval tool for flat file data libraries, Comp. Appl. Biosci. 9(1), 49–57.

Searching with Query Sequences

Dayhoff, M. O., Schwartz, R. M., and Orcutt, B. C. (1978) Altas of Protein Sequence Research and Structure, vol. 5, Suppl. 3 (Dayhoff, M. O., ed.) National Biomedical Research Foundation, Washington, DC, pp. 345–352.

Henikoff, S. and Henikoff, J. G. (1992) Amino acid substitution matrices from protein blocks, Proc. Natl. Acad. Sci. U S A. 89(22), 10,915–10,919.

BLAST/NetBLAST

Altschul, S. F., Gish, W., Miller, W., Myers, E. W., and Lipman, D. J. (1990) Basic local alignment search tool, J. Mol. Biol. 215, 403–410.

Altschul, S. F., Madden, T. L., Schaffer, A. A., Zhang, J., Zhang, Z., Miller, W., and Lipman, D. J. (1997) Gapped BLAST and PSI-BLAST: a new generation of protein database search programs, Nucleic Acids Res. 25, 3389–3402.

Shpaer, E. G., Robinson, M., Yee, D., Candlin, J. D., Mines, R., and Hunkapiller, T. (1996) Sensitivity and selectivity in protein similarity searches: a comparison of Smith-Waterman in hardware to BLAST and FastA, Genomics 38, 179–191.

Wootton, J. C. and Federhen, S. (1996) Analysis of compositionally biased regions in sequence databases, Methods Enzymol. 266, 554–571.

FastA Suite/Ssearch/FrameSearch

Pearson, W. R. and Lipman, D. J. (1988) Improved tools for biological sequence comparison, Proc. Natl. Acad. Sci. USA, 85(8), 2444–2448.

Pearson, W. R. (1995) Comparison of methods for searching protein sequence databases, Protein Sci. 4, 1145–1160.

Smith, T. F. and Waterman, M. S. (1981) Comparison of Bio-Sequences, Adv. Appl. Math. 2, 482–489.

Rules for Effective Database Searching

Pearson, W. R. (1996) Effective protein sequence comparison, Methods Enzymol. 266, 227–258.

Pearson, W. R. (2000) Flexible sequence similarity searching with the FastA3 program package, Methods Mol. Biol. 132, 185–219.

C. Identifying Functional and Structural Sequence Elements

29 Pattern Discovery

Methods and Software

Broňa Brejová, Tomáš Vinar, and Ming Li

Introduction

A pattern is a feature that occurs repeatedly in biological sequences, typically more often than expected at random. Patterns often correspond to functionally or structurally important elements in proteins and DNA sequences. Pattern discovery is one of the fundamental problems in bioinformatics. It has applications in multiple sequence alignment, protein structure and function prediction, drug target discovery, characterization of protein families, and promoter signal detection.

Regions important to the structure or function of the molecule tend to evolve more slowly. In particular an occurrence of a conserved motif in a protein may imply that this region may be involved in the interaction with some other protein, may comprise the active site of an enzyme, or may be important for the tertiary structure of the protein. Attempts have been made to organize proteins and protein domains from different organisms into families based on their evolutionary relations, and structural and functional similarity. Sequences in one family often share one or several common motifs and these motifs are used to characterize the family. Several databases containing motifs characterizing protein families have been established. Newly discovered proteins can be assigned to a family by searching a database of motifs. We may then associate the function or structure to the new protein based on the knowledge we have about the other members of the family.

Nucleotide sequences outside of protein coding regions tend to be less conserved, except where they are important for function, that is, where they are involved in the regulation of gene expression. Some regulatory elements are located in promoter regions upstream from genes. Identifying promoters in genomic sequences is difficult, especially in eukaryotic genomes because they do not have a common core promoter, but rather consist of multiple regulatory factors distributed over long distances. Adding to the complexity is low number of availab le annotated promoters. The best programs are only able to identify about half of eukaryotic promoters.

If a pattern characteristic for a binding site of a certain transcription factor is known, we can find occurrences of this pattern in promoter regions of known genes. This helps us to understand how these genes are regulated, under which conditions they are transcribed, and may even help to infer a function of a gene.

New binding motifs of transcription factors can be discovered by considering upstream regions of co-regulated genes and identifying motifs that occur in these regions more frequently than elsewhere. For example groups of co-regulated genes can be identified by analyzing gene expression data. Provided that a transcription factor is conserved between two species, we may discover its binding sites by identifying conserved sequences in promoter regions of these two genomes.

Related molecules, usually proteins or RNA, sometimes do not display significant similarity at the sequence level. However, significant similarity can be found in their secondary or tertiary structure. Discovery of structural motifs in proteins and RNA molecules has also been studied, but this work is beyond the scope of this chapter.

The availability of several fully sequenced genomes has enabled scientists to identify homologies shared between two genomes. Such conserved regions are likely to correspond to functionally important elements. This information has been applied to predict genes, discover new regulatory elements, and reveal evolutionary relationships between species and types of evolutionary changes to genome organization. Identifying possibly long similarities between two long sequences can be considered a special case of pattern discovery, yet the large amounts of data require special consideration from the computer science point of view.

In this chapter, we introduce the basics of algorithms used to discover patterns. We also discuss the goals of such algorithms and how to statistically verify their results. Many programs for pattern discovery and databases of biologically relevant patterns are available. We provide an overview and links to these important tools in a supplement located in the accompanying CD-ROM.

Pattern Discovery

What is a Pattern

A pattern is an element that has multiple occurrences in a given set of biological sequences. In this section we outline how to represent a pattern. Probably the simplest representation of a pattern is a list of its occurrences in the given sequences which is sufficient to specify the pattern. However, it is not convenient for further use as it is difficult to decide whether or not a new sequence contains occurrences of the pattern. Therefore we usually represent a pattern by describing properties shared by all its occurrences. Such representation is more succinct and allows easier searches for new occurrences.

Deterministic Patterns

The simplest kind of a pattern is a *consensus sequence*. For example *TATAAAA* is the TATA box consensus sequence. Whenever we find string *TATAAAA* we say it is an occurrence of this pattern. Of course not all such occurrences correspond to a real TATA box and not every TATA box perfectly matches the consensus. The latter of these two problems can be solved by allowing a certain degree of flexibility in the pattern. This can be achieved by adding some of the following frequently used features.

Let Σ be the alphabet of all possible characters occurring in the sequences (i.e., $\Sigma = \{A,C,G,T\}$ for DNA sequences and Σ is a set of all 20 amino acids for protein sequences).

- An ambiguous character matches any character from a subset of Σ. Such a subset is denoted by a list of its elements enclosed in square brackets. For example, *[LF]* is a set containing L and F. *A-[LF]-G* is a pattern in a notation used in PROSITE database. This pattern matches 3-character subsequences starting with A, ending with G and having either L or F in the middle.

For nucleotide sequences there is a special letter for each set of nucleotides, where:

R = [AG], Y = [CT], W = [AT], S = [GC], M = [AC], K = [GT], B = [CGT], D = [AGT], H = [ACT], V = [ACG], N = [ACGT]

- *Wildcard* or *don't care* is a special kind of ambiguous character that matches any character from Σ. Wildcards are denoted *N* in nucleotide sequences, *X* in protein sequences. They may also be denoted by a dot '.'. A group of one or several consecutive wildcards is called a *gap* and patterns allowing wildcards are often called *gapped patterns*.
- *Flexible gap* is a gap of variable length. In the PROSITE database it is denoted by $x(i,j)$ where i is the lower bound on the gap length and j is an upper bound. Thus $x(4,6)$ matches any gap with length 4, 5, or 6. Fixed gap of length i is denoted $x(i)$ (e.g., $x(3) = xxx$). Finally * denotes a gap of any length (possibly 0).

String *F-x*(5)-*[LF]-x*(2,4)-*G*-*-H is an example of a PROSITE pattern containing all of the above features.

Patterns with Mismatches

One can further extend the expressive power of deterministic patterns by allowing a certain number of mismatches. The most commonly used type of mismatches are substitutions. In this case subsequence S matches pattern P with at most k mismatches, if there is a sequence S' exactly matching P that differs from S in at most k positions. Sometimes we may also allow insertions or deletions, i.e., the number of mismatches would be an edit distance between the substring S and a closest string matching the pattern P.

Position Weight Matrices

So far we have explored only deterministic patterns. A deterministic pattern either matches the given string or not. However, even the most complicated deterministic patterns cannot capture some subtle information hidden in a pattern. Let us assume we have a pattern. The first position is C in 40% cases and G in 60% cases. The ambiguous symbol [*CG*] gives the same importance to both nucleotides. It does not matter in strong patterns, but it may be important in weak patterns, where we need to use every piece of information to distinguish the pattern from a random sequence.

Probabilistic patterns are probabilistic models that assign a probability to each sequence that was generated by the model. The higher the probability, the better the match between the sequence and the pattern.

The simplest type of probabilistic pattern is a *position-weight matrix* (PWM). PWMs are also sometimes called a *position-specific score matrix* (PSSM), or a *profile* (however, term *profile* is also used for more complicated patterns allowing gaps). PWM is a simple ungapped pattern specified by a table. This table shows the relative frequency of each character at each position of the pattern (*see* Fig. 1 for an example).

Assume that the pattern (i.e., PWM) has length k (number of columns of the table). The score of a sequence segment $x_1 \ldots x_k$ of length k is

$$\prod_{i=1}^{k} \frac{A[x_i, i]}{f(x_i)}$$

PWM with relative frequencies

A	0.26	0.22	0.00	0.00	0.43	1.00	0.11
C	0.17	0.18	0.59	0.00	0.26	0.00	0.35
G	0.09	0.15	0.00	0.00	0.30	0.00	0.00
T	0.48	0.45	0.41	1.00	0.00	0.00	0.54

PWM with log-odd scores (using $f(c) = \frac{1}{4}$)

A	-3.94	-4.18	$-\infty$	$-\infty$	-3.22	-2.00	-5.18
C	-4.56	-4.47	-2.76	$-\infty$	-3.94	$-\infty$	-3.51
G	-5.47	-4.74	$-\infty$	$-\infty$	-3.74	$-\infty$	$-\infty$
T	-3.06	-3.15	-3.29	-2.00	$-\infty$	$-\infty$	-2.89

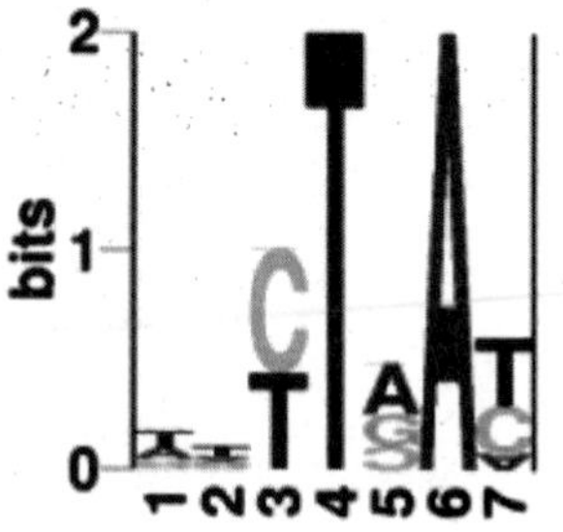

Fig. 1. Position weight matrix of vertebrate branch point in the form of a table and corresponding visual representation as a sequence logo. The sequence logo was created using RNA Structure Logo, an on-line tool available at Website: http://www.cbs.dtu.dk/gorodkin/appl/slogo.html.

where $A[c,i]$ is the entry of position weight matrix corresponding to position i of the pattern and character c, and $f(c)$ is the background frequency of character c in all sequences considered. This product represents the odd-score that the sequence segment $x_1 \ldots x_k$ belongs to the probability distribution represented by the PWM. In order to simplify the computation of the score we can store log-odd scores $A'[c,i] = \log_2 A[c,i]/f(c)$ in a table, in place of using frequencies $A[c,i]$. Then the following formula yields the log-odd score:

$$\sum_{i=1}^{k} A'[x_i,i]$$

Position-weight matrices can be visualized in the form of sequence logos (*see* Fig. 1). Each column of a sequence logo corresponds to one position of the pattern. Relative heights of the characters in one column are proportional to the frequencies $A[c,i]$ at the corresponding position of the pattern. At each position, the characters are ordered according to their frequency, with the most frequent character on top. Each column is scaled so that its total height is proportional to the information content of the position, computed as:

$$\log_2 |\Sigma| + \sum_c A[c,i] \log_2 A[c,i]$$

Note: $\log_2 |\Sigma|$ is added to obtain positive values. It is dependent on the size of alphabet Σ. Sequence logos have been developed further to consider background distribution and to invert characters that occur less frequently than expected.

An examination of a sequence logo reveals the most conserved positions (highest columns) and consensus characters at all positions (highest letter in the column). The size of characters in different columns cannot be directly compared.

Stochastic Models

The patterns discussed thus far are explicit in the sense that the user can easily see important characteristics of the occurrences of a pattern. Sometimes it is advantageous to represent a pattern in a more implicit form, usually as a discrimination rule, to decide whether a given sequence is an occurrence of the modeled pattern or not. It can be based on a stochastic model, such as *Hidden Markov Model* (HMM), or can employ machine learning methods, such as neural networks.

It is questionable whether such rules constitute a pattern at all. Obviously, they can be trained (pattern discovery) and then they can be used for discrimination (pattern matching). Therefore, they are applicable in pattern-related tasks such as protein family classification and binding site discovery. In some cases (such as HMMs with simple topology) it is even possible to obtain some information about the pattern modeled. For example, the relative frequencies of characters at individual conserved positions.

Pattern Discovery vs Pattern Matching

There are two fundamentally different tasks related to identifying new patterns in biological sequences. The first one is called *pattern matching*. This finds new occurrences of a known pattern. Many consensus sequences are known in biology and it is important to have tools that will allow one to find occurrences of known patterns in new sequences.

There are specialized software tools for pattern matching. Some are quite general, i.e., they allow the user to specify a pattern as part of the input in a specific form. Others are built to recognize only one pattern. Many specialized tools are available for recognizing splicing signals, different regulatory elements, and special structural elements. Authors of such specialized tools fine-tune the parameters of the system to increase the accuracy of the prediction.

Although pattern matching is very important, we will concentrate on a different kind of pattern-related problem, called *pattern discovery*. The task is to identify a new pattern in a set of several sequences.

The input for pattern discovery programs consists of several sequences, expected to contain the pattern. Input sequences are typically related in some way, e.g., they are members of the same protein family, functionally related sequences, or upstream regions of co-regulated genes.

Goals of Pattern Discovery

The goal of pattern discovery is to identify an unknown pattern in a given set of sequences. There are a great number of potential patterns and it is often difficult to decide which of them are the most promising. Defining the *best* pattern depends on the intended use of the pattern. We will consider two possible scenarios: 1) classification, i.e., we want to characterize members of some sequence family and distinguish them from nonmembers, and 2) identification of significant patterns, i.e., we want to discover patterns that are unlikely to occur by chance and would therefore probably have functional or structural significance.

Classification

In a classification scenario we want to identify motifs that best characterize a given protein family. The motifs thus identified are then used as classifiers. For example, given an unknown protein we can classify it as a member or nonmember of a family, based on whether it contains the motifs characteristic for that family. This is a typical machine learning problem: given a set of sequences belonging to the family (positive examples) and a set of sequences not belonging to the family (negative examples), find a function f, which decides for each protein whether or not it belongs to the family. In the context of motif discovery we consider classes of functions f, that match some discovered patterns against the unknown sequence. Note, that negative examples are simply other known proteins taken from protein databases such as SWISS-PROT.

The common strategy in pattern discovery is to use only positive examples. The most significant motif in the family is found in a hope that it will not occur elsewhere. Negative examples are only used to evaluate the prediction. Thus, the task is converted to the second scenario, described in the following.

Identifying Significant Patterns

Motif discovery is not always formulated as a classification problem. For example let's identify a regulatory element in a set of regions likely to contain this element. However, it does not mean that this element cannot occur in other places in the genome or that all of these sequences must contain a common regulatory element. We are also interested in identifying conserved regions (protein family motifs) that may indicate structurally or functionally important elements, regardless of whether they have enough specificity to distinguish this family from other families. In this context it is more complicated to precisely formulate the question.

The usual approach is to find the *highest scoring* pattern within a well-defined class of patterns (e.g., PROSITE patterns, *see* Subheading "What is a Pattern?"), that has sufficient *support*. Various approaches use different scoring functions and support measures and consider different classes of patterns. Support of a pattern is usually the number of sequences in which the pattern occurs. We can require that the pattern should occur in all sequences or there is a minimum number of occurrences specified by the user. In some cases the number of occurrences is not specified but it is a part of the scoring function. A longer pattern with fewer occurrences is sometimes more interesting than a shorter pattern with more occurrences. The situation is more complicated in the case of probabilistic patterns, such as HMMs. Deterministic patterns either match the sequence or not (zero or one), whereas probabilistic models give a probability between 0 and 1. Therefore, there are different degrees of *matching*. It is necessary to set some threshold on what should be considered a match or to integrate these matching probabilities to the scoring scheme.

Methods for scoring patterns also differ. A score can reflect the pattern itself only (e.g., its length and degree of ambiguity), or it can be based on the occurrences of the pattern (their number, how much these occurrences differ from the pattern). Scoring functions are sometimes based on statistical significance. For example, we may ask: what is the probability that the pattern would have so many occurrences if the sequences were generated at random? If this probability is small, the pattern is statistically significant. (For a more detailed discussion of statistical significance of patterns, *see* "Assessment of Pattern Quality" in this chapter.) The goal of an algorithm is to find the highest scoring pattern, or to find several best scoring patterns, or all patterns with some predefined level of support and score.

Algorithms for Pattern Discovery

Exhaustive Search

Many computer science problems related to pattern discovery are computationally hard tasks. One cannot hope to find a fast algorithm that would guarantee the best possible solution. Thus, many approaches are based on the exhaustive search. Although such algorithms in the worst case may run in exponential time, they often use sophisticated pruning techniques that make the search feasible.

Enumerating All Patterns

The simplest exhaustive search works as follows. All possible patterns satisfying constraints given by the user are enumerated. For each pattern the program finds each occurrence in the input sequences and based on these occurrences assigns a score or statistical significance to the pattern. We can then output patterns with the highest score or all patterns with scores above some threshold. For example, if we want to identify the most significant nucleotide pattern of length 10 with at most 2 mismatches, we can enumerate all possible strings of length 10 over the alphabet $\{A,C,G,T\}$ (there are $4^{10} = 1{,}048{,}576$ such strings). Each string is a potential pattern. We find all occurrences with at most 2 mismatches in the input sequences and compute the score. We report the pattern with the highest score.

This method is suitable only for short and simple patterns, because the running time increases exponentially with the length of the pattern. The number of possibilities is even larger if we allow patterns to contain wildcards, ambiguous characters, and gaps. On the other hand, the advantage of this method is that with increasing length of the input sequences the running time usually increases linearly. Therefore the enumeration approach is suitable for identifying short patterns in large data sets.

An exhaustive search is guaranteed to identify the best pattern. We may easily output an arbitrary number of high scoring patterns, we may also choose relatively complicated scoring functions, providing that they can be easily computed based on the pattern and its occurrences. We can also allow mismatches, even insertions and deletions.

Application of Enumerative Methods

Many protein binding sites in DNA are actually short ungapped motifs, with certain variability. They can be quite well-modeled with simple patterns allowing a small number of mismatches. Therefore we can apply exhaustive searches to identify these types of binding sites. Simplicity of the exhaustive search allows one to develop sophisticated methods for pattern statistical significance estimation.

Enumerating Gapped Patterns

In some contexts it is more reasonable to search for patterns with gaps. MOTIF is an example of such system. MOTIF finds patterns with 3 conserved amino acids separated by two fixed gaps (for example $A\ldots Q\ldots.I$). The gaps can have length $0,1,\ldots,d$ where d is a parameter specified by the user. The number of possible patterns is 20^3d^2. MOTIF does not allow any mismatches, but the pattern does not need to occur in all sequences.

If the sequences contain a conserved region of more than 3 positions, there will be many patterns, each containing a different subset of the conserved positions from this region. Therefore, in the following step the algorithm removes the patterns occurring close to each other. For each of the remaining patterns all occurrences of the pattern are aligned. Based on the alignment the pattern is extended by finding a consensus in the columns of the alignment. Patterns are also extended to both sides where possible.

Pruning Pattern Enumeration

If we want to identify longer or more ambiguous patterns, we cannot use a straightforward exhaustive search. For example, assume that we want to identify a long ungapped pattern occurring (possibly with some mismatches) in at least k sequences. We will start from short patterns (for example patterns of length 1) that appear in at

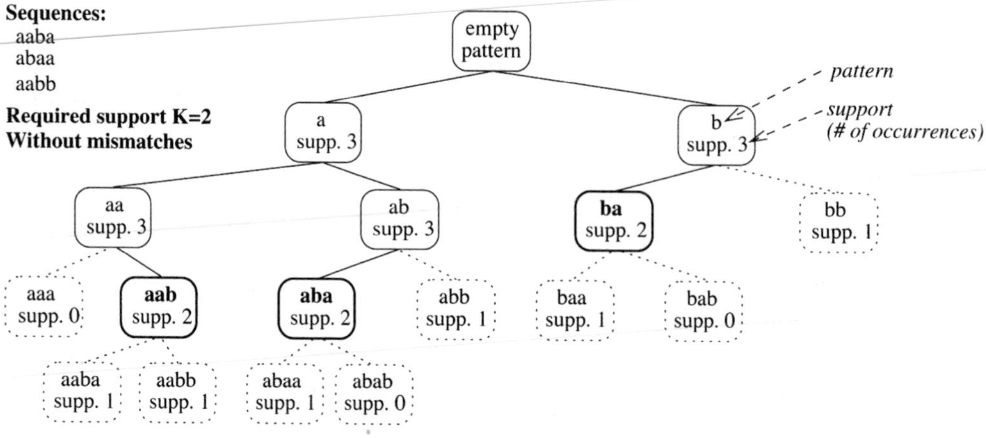

Fig. 2. One way to improve an exhaustive search is to search in a tree of all possible patterns. When we discover a node corresponding to a pattern that does not have enough support, we do not continue to search its subtrees. Dashed nodes do not have enough support. Bold nodes are patterns that cannot be further extended.

least *k* sequences and extend them while the support does not go below *k*. In each step we extend the pattern in all possible ways and check whether the new patterns still occur in at least *k* sequences. Once we obtain a pattern that cannot be extended without loss of support, this pattern is maximal and can be written to the output. This search strategy is actually a depth first search of a tree of all possible sequences (*see* Fig. 2). We prune branches that cannot yield supported patterns.

Improvements of this kind perform well in practice. However, in the worst-case scenario the running time can still be exponential. The main advantage of such improvements is that they allow a search for longer and more complicated patterns than a simple exhaustive search. Examples of this strategy include the Pratt algorithm described in detail below and the first scanning phase of TEIRESIAS algorithm.

Pratt

Pratt is an advanced algorithm based on applying the depth first search to a tree of patterns. Pratt discovers patterns containing flexible gaps (with a lower and upper bound of the gap length) and ambiguous symbols. Each pattern discovered is required to exactly match at least some predetermined number of sequences. The user has to specify several parameters that restrict the type of patterns. These include the maximum total length of the pattern, maximum number of gaps, maximum number of flexible gaps, and set of allowed ambiguous symbols.

To reduce the size of the output and the running time, the program does not report patterns that are less specific than other discovered patterns. Here pattern *A* is more specific than pattern *B*, if any sequence that matches *A* must also match *B* (for example, *B* is less specific if it can be obtained from *A* by replacing nonambiguous characters with ambiguous characters, or making a gap more flexible). This is achieved by a special scoring function that gives a higher score to more specific patterns.

In each step of the depth first search, we take an existing pattern with sufficient support and we add a gap (possibly of length 0) and another character or ambiguous character. All such possibilities are tried. New patterns without sufficient support are then discarded. This uses a special data structure that makes the search faster. Additional optimizations are carried out by discarding patterns that cannot be extended to the most significant pattern.

The Pratt algorithm is guaranteed to find the pattern with the highest score when no flexible gaps are allowed. If we allow flexible gaps, the returned pattern may not be the highest scoring since a heuristic is used to speed up the search.

Exhaustive Search on Graphs

Not all exhaustive search methods enumerate all relevant patterns. It is also possible to enumerate all combinations of substrings of given sequences that can be possible occurrences of a pattern. Assume we have n sequences and we want to identify a pattern of given length L, that occurs in all sequences with at most d mismatches. Then any two occurrences of such a pattern differ at most in $2d$ positions, because they both differ from the pattern in at most d positions. Therefore, we can identify the pattern by finding a group of n substrings of length L, each from a different sequence, such that any two substrings differ in at most $2d$ positions.

This can be formulated as a problem in graph theory as follows. Each substring of length L will be a vertex of a graph G. Vertices corresponding to two substrings will be connected by an edge if the substrings are taken from different sequences and differ in at most $2d$ positions (*see* Fig. 3A). This graph is n-partite. This means that it can be partitioned to n partitions so that there is no edge between vertices in the same partition. In this case partitions correspond to individual sequences. We want to find a set of n vertices such that any two vertices are connected by an edge. Such a set of vertices is called a *clique*.

The problem of finding a clique is known to be NP-hard. NP-hard problems are computationally difficult problems. There is no known algorithm for solving an NP-hard problem in polynomial time. One way to find a clique is to enumerate combinations of vertices and test each combination for being a clique. Such an approach has an exponential running time because there are many possible combinations. In order to make the software practical we need to add careful pruning. This eliminates large groups of vertex combinations that are guaranteed not to contain a clique.

The WINNOWER algorithm eliminates combinations by first modifying the graph itself. It attempts to reduce the number of edges in the graph, removing only edges that cannot be part of any clique of size n. In this way we may obtain a graph with less edges that will be easier to search for a clique.

Even if we find a combination of n substrings of length L, each pair differing in at most $2d$ positions, it does not guarantee that we have found a pattern. For example assume that we want a pattern of length $L = 4$ with at most one mismatch and we have found the following 3 occurrences: AAAA, BBAA and CCAA. Any two occurrences differ in exactly $2 = 2d$ positions, but there is no pattern that would differ from each occurrence in at most one position. However, we may assume that this would not happen very often and that most combinations found will actually correspond to a pattern.

Usually the user wants to know the set of occurrences and the corresponding pattern. One way to identify the pattern is to enumerate all patterns that occur within distance d from one chosen occurrence. There are at most $\binom{L}{d}(|\Sigma| - 1)^d$ such patterns. This number is exponential in d but not in L and d is typically small. For each possible pattern we verify whether it is within distance d from all other occurrences as well.

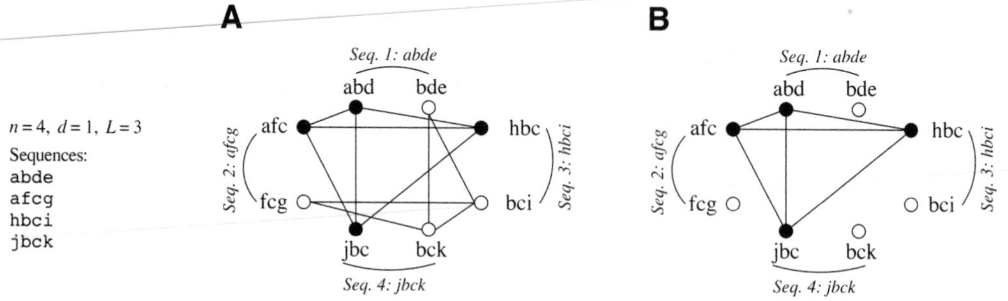

Fig. 3. **(A)** shows the graph corresponding to the depicted set of sequences. **(B)** shows the same graph after removing edges with the WINNOWER algorithm. This graph contains exactly one clique corresponding to pattern abc.

The search can be further pruned by using knowledge about the other occurrences. Alternatively we can use the set of occurrences as a starting point for Gibbs sampling or other iterative methods (*see* "Gibbs Sampling" and "Other Iterative Methods"). This is of course not guaranteed to find the pattern with specified parameters, even if one exists.

Creating Long Patterns from Short Patterns

A pattern cannot be significant unless it is sufficiently long. However long patterns are more difficult to identify using enumerative techniques. One possible approach to identifying long patterns is to start with shorter patterns and then combine them together. Perhaps the most elegant example of such an algorithm is TEIRESIAS. This algorithm is based on a well-organized exhaustive search through possible combinations of shorter patterns. In the worst case the algorithm runs in exponential time, but in practice it works very well. Further effort has yielded a different algorithm that runs in polynomial time (*see* "Improvement of Running Time").

TEIRESIAS Algorithm

TEIRESIAS searches for so-called (L,W) patterns (L and W are constants specified by the user). Pattern P is an (L,W) pattern if it meets the following criteria:

- P consists of characters from Σ and wildcards '.'
- P starts and ends with a character from Σ (i.e., non-wildcard)
- Any substring of P that starts and ends with a non-wildcard and contains exactly L non-wildcards has a length W at most (this condition is called *density constraint*).

The density constraint eliminates patterns with long stretches of wildcards. Consider for example $L = 3$ and $W = 5$. String $AF..CH..E$ is a valid (3,5) pattern, however string $AF.C.H..E$ is not (substring $C.H..E$ has length 6).

Maximal Patterns

TEIRESIAS discovers all (L,W) patterns that occur in at least K input sequences ($K \geq 2$ is also specified by the user). However, out of several patterns having the same set of occurrences it outputs only one pattern. This is selected as follows.

Pattern P is said to be more specific than pattern Q if Q can be derived from P by removing several (possibly 0) characters from both ends of P and replacing several (possibly 0) non-wildcards with wildcards. For example $AB.CD.E$ is more specific than $AB..D$.

If pattern P is more specific than pattern Q, then every occurrence of P is also an occurrence of Q. If Q has the same number of occurrences as P, it is not useful to report both P and Q because they have the same set of occurrences and P contains more information. Therefore the algorithm only outputs pattern P if a more specific pattern with the same number of occurrences does not exist. Patterns reported by the algorithm are called *maximal*.

Note that if P is more specific than Q and Q has more occurrences than P, i.e., Q has greater support, Q is outputted as well. Although Q has a smaller specificity, it has greater support.

ALGORITHM

The TEIRESIAS algorithm is based on the concept that if a pattern P is a (L,W) pattern occurring in at least K sequences, then its subpatterns are also (L,W) patterns occurring in at least K sequences. Therefore the algorithm assembles the maximal patterns from smaller subpatterns.

TEIRESIAS works in two phases. In the first phase (called *scanning phase*), it finds all (L,W) patterns occurring in at least K sequences that contain exactly L non-wildcards. This is carried out by a pruned exhaustive search (*see* "Enumerating All Patterns"). In the second, *convolution phase* these elementary patterns are extended by gluing them together. In order to determine whether two patterns P and Q can be glued together we compare the suffix of P containing exactly $L - 1$ non-wildcards to the prefix of Q containing exactly $L - 1$ non-wildcards. If the suffix and the prefix are equal, P and Q can be glued together so that the $L - 1$ non-wildcards overlap. The list of occurrences of the resulting pattern can be constructed from the lists of occurrences of P and Q (we do not need to scan all sequences). Only when the resulting pattern occurs at least K times, is it retained.

For example let $P = AB.CD.E$ and $Q = DFE.G$ (with $L = 3$, $W = 5$). In this case P and Q cannot be glued together, because $D.E \neq DF$. However if $Q = D.E.G$ we can glue them together obtaining $AB.CD.E.G$. If occurrences of P are (1,1), (2,3), (2,6), (4,7) (each pair gives a sequence and a position in the sequence) and occurrences of Q are (1,5), (2,8), (2,10), then the list of occurrences for the new pattern is (1,1), (2,6).

In the convolution phase we take each elementary pattern, and we try to extend it on both sides by gluing it with other elementary patterns in all possible ways (depth first search). Any pattern that cannot be extended without loss of support can potentially be maximal. However we can still obtain non-maximal patterns in the output and some patterns can be generated more than once. Therefore a list of patterns written to the output is maintained. In this manner we can check any newly generated pattern with the list and if the list contains a more specific pattern with the same set of occurrences we simply discard the new pattern.

The TEIRESIAS algorithm is an exact algorithm. It is guaranteed to find all (L,W) maximal patterns supported by at least K sequences. The number of such patterns can be exponential. In such cases TEIRESIAS will require exponential time to complete. However, such a situation is not likely to occur with real data. For example, the entire GenPept database with 120 million amino acids contains only 27 million maximal patterns. Experimental studies suggest that the running time of TEIRESIAS algorithm is linear in the number of patterns it outputs.

Patterns discovered by the TEIRESIAS algorithm are not very flexible. First of all, the only mismatches allowed are wildcard characters. Newer versions of TEIRESIAS can now also identify patterns containing ambiguous characters representing pre-specified groups of characters from Σ. Second, TEIRESIAS patterns do not allow gaps with flexible length. This problem can be addressed by the post-processing phase, where the patterns found are combined into larger patterns separated by flexible gaps. However, such methods do not guarantee that all patterns of the specified form will be found.

Improvement of Running Time

Irredundant Patterns

One of the drawbacks of TEIRESIAS is the potential exponential size of the output and thus exponential running time. A new algorithm has recently been developed that computes only a subset of maximal patterns, called *irredundant patterns*. Any maximal pattern can be easily obtained from the set of irredundant patterns. The main advantage of the new method is that in any input of length n there are at most $3n$ irredundant patterns and these patterns can be found in $O(n^3 \log n)$ time. This is a substantial theoretical improvement compared to traditional exponential algorithms. However neither implementation of this algorithm, nor experimental study demonstrating the application of this approach is available to date.

Iterative Heuristic Methods

So far we have considered algorithms guaranteed to identify the best pattern. However for more complicated types of patterns we cannot hope to do so. We have to use heuristic approaches that may not find the best pattern, but may converge to a local maximum. The most important example of such technique is Gibbs sampling.

Gibbs Sampling

In its simplest version (the Gibbs sampling method), we are looking for the best conserved ungapped pattern of fixed length W in the form of a position weight matrix. We assume that the pattern occurs in all sequences.

The algorithm is carried out in iterations. The result of each iteration is a set of subsequences of length W: one from each sequence. This set of subsequences represents the occurrences of the pattern. We can compute a position weight matrix characterizing the pattern from this set of occurrences. The algorithm works as follows:

- Randomly select one subsequence of length W from each input sequence. These subsequences will form our initial set of occurrences. Denote o_i occurrence in sequence i.
- Iteration step.
- Randomly select one sequence i.
- Compute the position weight matrix based on all occurrences except o_i. Denote this position weight matrix P.
- Take each subsequence of sequence i of length W and compute a score of this subsequence according to matrix P.
- Select a new occurrence o_i' randomly among all subsequences of i of length W using the probability distribution defined by the scores (a higher score means higher probability).

- Replace o_i with o_i' in the set of occurrences.
- Repeat iteration, until a stop condition is met.

The Gibbs sampling algorithm does not guarantee that the position weight matrix and set of occurrences giving the best score will be found. Instead, the algorithm can converge to a local maximum. The method is fast, making it suitable for many applications.

Several problems related to Gibbs sampling have been identified and addressed in subsequent work.

- **Phase shifts.** Assume that the optimal set contains occurrences starting at positions 8, 14, 22, and 7 of the corresponding sequences. If we start with position 21 in the third sequence, the whole system is likely to converge to the set of occurrences 7, 13, 21, and 6 instead.

  The problem was addressed by introducing an additional randomized step. In this step, scores of the occurrences shifted by several characters are computed. One random shift is selected with a probability distribution corresponding to the scores. Authors of PROBE reduce or extend patterns on both sides in a similar manner.
- **Multiple patterns.** Sometimes it is appropriate to define a pattern as a sequence of several consecutive subsequences of fixed length separated by variable length gaps. In this case each occurrence is represented by several short subsequences in the sequence rather than one. It is possible to identify such patterns using a modified Gibbs sampling approach that employs dynamic programming in the process of ranking and choosing a new candidate occurrence. Lengths of subsequences and their number are specified beforehand.
- **Pattern width.** We have assumed, that the pattern width is fixed and is specified by the user. Most of the time it is not a reasonable assumption, especially if we are looking for multiple patterns separated by variable length gaps.

  In PROBE a genetic algorithm is used to determine the parameters of patterns (i.e., the number of subsequences and their lengths). Two sets of parameters can be recombined (take part of the first and part of the second set) and in this manner a better set of parameters may be obtained. Sets of parameters for recombination are chosen at random with a distribution proportional to their score (called *fitness*). Fitness of the set of parameters is determined by the Gibbs sampling procedure.
- **Gapped patterns.** Not all positions within a continuous block of length W are necessarily important for the function of this block. Rather we want to create a pattern which is gapped, i.e., only $J < W$ positions are used to form the model. This problem can be addressed by introducing yet another randomized step, in which we replace one of the J positions included in the pattern by one of the $W - J + 1$ positions, which are not included in the pattern. The choice is again random with a distribution of probabilities proportional to the corresponding scores.

Other Iterative Methods

Several other approaches use iterative methods similar to Gibbs sampling. Typically the algorithm starts with some pattern and finds the best fitting occurrence of this pattern in each sequence. Based on these occurrences it builds a pattern that best matches the occurrences. This process is then repeated with the new pattern until no improvement is obtained. The main difference between this algorithm and Gibbs sampling is that all sequences are used to define the new pattern and subsequently the position of the new pattern is refined in all sequences. The process is completely deterministic, and of course has no guarantee to find the global optimum.

This strategy was used to identify ungapped deterministic patterns of a given length that matches all sequences with mismatches. The goal is to minimize the total number of mismatches. By using different methods a set of occurrences of some unknown candidate pattern is obtained that can be refined by an iterative method. In each step a new pattern is computed by taking the most frequent character in each position (based on the frequencies in the occurrences). The method is further improved to remove nonsignificant columns from consideration to obtain a gapped pattern.

An iterative method has also been used to detect coiled coil regions in histidine kinase receptors. Coiled coils were previously detected in other protein families; therefore, the statistical properties of such regions are known, although they may be somewhat different for this family. In this example the goal was to identify the distribution of residues and pairs of residues at different distances in a sliding window of fixed length, provided that the window is from a coiled coil region. The process started with taking the known distribution from other families. Based on this information each position of the sliding window was scored and the best scoring positions were the candidates for coiled coil regions. A random sample of these candidates was used to compute a new distribution. This process was iterated. In each step a pseudocount from the known distribution of other families was added. In contrast to the previous method, this is randomized, and due to pseudocounts the result cannot extensively diverge from the original pattern.

The iterative approach can be also used to improve position weight matrices. For example a PWM for splice-site signals computed from vertebrate genomes can be iteratively refined to obtain a PWM specific for human.

In general it seems that the simple iterative methods are suitable for improvement of patterns obtained by other methods or from different data. However, this approach is not sufficient to discover patterns without any prior knowledge.

From Iteration to PTAS

The Consensus Pattern problem is another formulation of pattern discovery. The problem is defined as follows: find a pattern P and one occurrence of P in each sequence so that the total number of mismatches over all occurrences is minimized.

The Consensus Pattern problem is NP-hard. It is unlikely that any polynomial time algorithm for such problems exists.

Because there is no algorithm guaranteed to find the best solution of the Consensus Pattern problem in a reasonable time, we may wish to have a guarantee that the cost of the found pattern (i.e., the total number of mismatches) is at most α times the cost of the optimal pattern. The *approximation ratio* is termed α. For example, if $\alpha = 2$ we are guaranteed to find a pattern that has at most twice as many mismatches as the best possible pattern.

For some problems it is possible to construct an algorithm that works for any α supplied. However, the smaller the approximation ratio, the longer the algorithm runs. This type of algorithm is called the *polynomial approximation scheme*, or PTAS. The PTAS for a Consensus Pattern problem is based on a simple iterative idea repeated many times with different initial patterns.

The PTAS requires input sequences, the desired length L of a pattern, and a parameter r. It finds all possible combinations of r substrings of length L taken from input sequences. Each combination may contain zero, one, or several substrings from each sequence, some substrings may even repeat more than once. If the total length of all sequences is N, there are $O(N^r)$ combinations. For each combination of r substrings the following steps are performed:

- The majority pattern P of the r substrings is computed. This pattern has in each position the character occurring most frequently in this position in the r substrings.
- Find the best occurrence of P in each input sequence.
- Compute a new majority pattern P'.
- Find the best occurrences of P' in all sequences and compute the number of mismatches (cost of P').

The result will be the pattern P', which achieves the minimum cost. Notice, that the algorithm performs one step of iteration with the pattern obtained from each possible combination. The running time of the algorithm is $O(N^{r+1} L)$ and its approximation ratio is $1 + (4|\Sigma|A - 4) / \left[\sqrt{e}\left(\sqrt{4r+1} - 3\right)\right]$ for $r \geq 3$.

This result is very interesting from the point of view of theoretical computer science. However the algorithm is not very practical. For example, if we choose $r = 3$ and $\Sigma = \{A,C,G,T\}$, the algorithm will identify the pattern with at most 13 times as many mismatches as the optimal pattern. The running time is $O(N^4L)$, impractical for large inputs. In order to achieve $\alpha = 2$, r needs to be at least 21. This gives an algorithm a prohibitive running time $O(N^{22})$. Of course, the approximation ratio is only an upper bound of the possible error. For some inputs the optimal or close-to-optimal results can be obtained even for small r, however there is no guarantee.

A program called COPIA is based on the ideas of PTAS. Several changes considerably reduce the running time. The enumeration of all possible combinations of r substrings is replaced by randomly sampling combinations. The consensus pattern obtained from each randomly chosen combination of substrings is improved by the iterative method until there is no further improvement. COPIA runs in reasonable time for real data but it does not have the same guarantees of pattern quality as the PTAS algorithm.

Machine Learning Methods

Sometimes a pattern cannot be described well by a simple deterministic pattern and one may wish to express it in a form of a stochastic model, such as Hidden Markov Model or position weight matrix (which is a simpler version of HMM). This kind of pattern is discovered using iterative expectation maximization techniques that do not necessarily converge to the global maximum.

Expectation Maximization

First we will consider a simpler case of position weight matrices. A simple learning algorithm called *expectation maximization* (EM) is used to estimate parameters of the stochastic model of a pattern that occurs once at an unknown position in each input sequence. The algorithm can be easily extended to more complicated models, e.g., patterns with flexible gaps, a finite mixture model.

The algorithm is iterative. It starts with some initial model parameters (usually randomly set). Each iteration consists of two steps as follows:

- **E step.** For every sequence s and for every position in s compute the probability that the occurrence of the pattern in s starts at this position. The probability is based on the model from the previous iteration (or initial model for the first iteration).

- **M step.** For every position in the pattern compute new probabilities for characters at this position. This is based on all possible occurrences of the pattern weighted by probabilities computed in E step. These values will form new parameters of the model.

Notice that the algorithm uses all possible occurrences of the pattern to obtain a new matrix, instead of only one occurrence in each string. Similarly to other iterative methods, the EM algorithm converges to a local maximum depending on the initial parameters of the model, instead of the global maximum likelihood. There is the additional assumption that every pattern occurs exactly once in every sequence.

These are addressed in the MEME algorithm, which is a modification of EM algorithm. The algorithm is based on the assumption that the pattern found should closely resemble at least one subsequence found in the dataset. Several or no possible occurrences of the pattern in a sequence could be considered. The algorithm proceeds as follows:

1. Form an initial model for each subsequence in the dataset. The initial model is a position weight matrix. For every position the character at the corresponding position in the subsequence has probability p (p is usually between 0.5 and 0.8), and all other characters have probability $(1 - p) / (|\Sigma| - 1)$.
2. One iteration of the EM algorithm is performed on each initial model. The likelihood score is computed for the resulting models.
3. The model with the largest likelihood score is selected as an initial model for the EM algorithm.

The algorithm can be forced to report more patterns by erasing all occurrences of the found pattern from the dataset and rerunning the entire process.

Hidden Markov Models

Hidden Markov Models (HMMs) can be used to model a family of sequences. Given an HMM and a sequence, it is possible to compute the most probable path through the model for this sequence in $O(nm)$ time using the Viterbi algorithm, where n is the length of the sequence and m is the number of states in the model. This path represents the most probable occurrence of the pattern in the sequence. The probability P that the sequence was generated by the model can also be computed in $O(nm)$ time using the forward algorithm. Value $-\log P$ is called a *NLL score of the sequence* with respect to the model. A higher probability of generating the sequence corresponds to a lower NLL score of the sequence.

There are three issues that need to be addressed if HMMs are used to represent a sequence family:

- **Topology of HMM.** Topology specifies the scheme of the Hidden Markov model that is used to represent a sequence family.
- **Training process.** The training process is needed to estimate the parameters of the model so that the sum of scores of sequences in the family is optimized.
- **Search for sequences.** The searching process should allow one to distinguish between sequences that belong to the family and sequences that do not.

Topology of HMM

A common HMM topology for sequence analysis is depicted in Fig. 4. The model consists of three types of states. *Match motif states* model conserved parts of the sequence. Match states specify the probability distribution of characters at each conserved position. There can be any number of match states in the model. We assume that the user gives this number beforehand. *Insertion states* model possible gaps between match states. Gaps can be arbitrarily long. The probability assigned to a self-loop in an insertion state determines probability distribution of possible gap lengths. The probability distribution is geometric, and the mean value can be easily computed. Finally, *deletion states* permit one to model occurrences of the pattern that do not contain some of the conserved positions.

Training of the Model

Given a topology of an HMM and a family of sequences to be modeled by the HMM, we can estimate the parameters of the model so that the model will generate sequences similar to those in the family with high probability.

The Baum-Welch algorithm can be used to perform this task. It is an iterative algorithm very similar to the EM algorithm used to estimate parameters of PWMs. We start with arbitrary parameters. If we have some prior knowledge of the sequence family, we can use this knowledge to set the initial parameters. Then in each step, the probabilities of all paths for all sequences are computed, and the model parameters are reestimated to minimize the NLL score of the training sequences to maximize the probability.

The algorithm does not guarantee a global optimum. It converges to a local minimum dependent on the initial parameter settings.

Search for Sequences

Searching for the pattern in the form of HMM is more complicated than in the case of simpler patterns. Given a sequence one can efficiently compute the most probable alignment of the sequence to the pattern and compute its NLL score. The NLL score gives a measure of how well the sequence can be aligned to the pattern. However, NLL scores depend highly on sequence length. In general, shorter sequences have smaller NLL scores than longer ones. Therefore, we cannot use a fixed threshold on an NLL score to discriminate between members and nonmembers of the family. This is possible only if all the input sequences have approximately the same length. Fortunately it was observed that sequences, that do not belong to the sequence family, form a line corresponding to a linear dependency. NLL scores for family members drop well below this line. Thus, it is possible to identify members of the family by a statistical test using a z-score for some window of sequence length. In order to estimate parameters needed to determine the z-score we need to compute the NLL score for many background sequences of different lengths not belonging to the family.

Enhancing HMM Models

Reducing the Number of Parameters

The greater the number of parameters of the model, the greater the amount of data required to properly train the model. Too many parameters can cause overfitting, where the model fits the training data very well but does not generalize to new sequences. There are several ways to reduce the number of parameters of the model. These include model surgery and different initial topology.

- **Model surgery.** Model surgery adjusts the model topology during the training in order to reduce the number of parameters of the model. In particular, this technique avoids two common problems that arise during training:

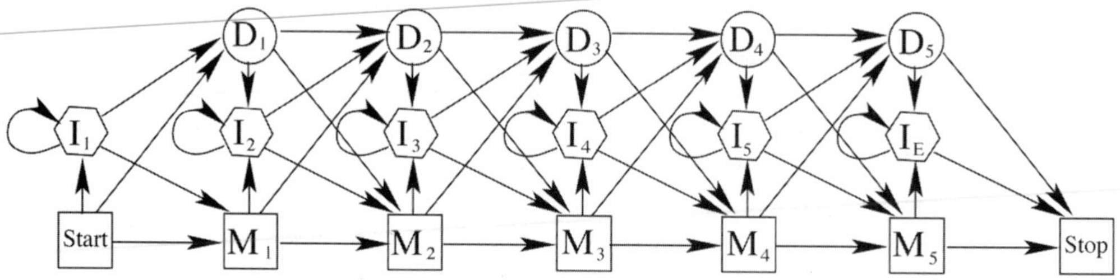

Fig. 4. A common HMM topology for pattern discovery. States $M_1, \ldots, M_5$ are match states, $I_1, \ldots, I_E$ are insertion states, and $D_1, \ldots, D_5$ are deletion states.

- Some match states are used only by a few sequences. If the number of sequences using a match state drops below a given threshold (typically one-half), the state is removed. In this way we force sequences to either use the insertion state at this point, or significantly change their alignment.
- Some insertion states are used by too many sequences. If an insertion state is used by more sequences than a given threshold (typically one-half), then the state is replaced by a chain of match states. The number of inserted match states is equal to the expected number of insertions in the replaced insertion state.

• **Different initial topology.** Meta-MEME uses a different program to report simple short patterns in the sequence. These patterns are transformed into matching states in HMM. The patterns are combined together using insertion states as shown in Fig. 5.

Discovering Subfamilies

Sometimes a family of sequences consists of several subfamilies. In such cases the family is represented by several motifs rather than by one. This problem can be solved by combining several HMMs with standard topology to one larger HMM as shown in Fig. 6.

If we do not have any preliminary knowledge of how to set the initial parameters of this model, it might be difficult to accurately train the model. In this case it is appropriate to use the Viterbi algorithm for training. The Viterbi training algorithm uses only the best path to reestimate the parameters, in contrast to the Baum-Welch algorithm that uses all paths weighted by their probabilities. Therefore, once the parameters of a part of the model reflect a bias to one subfamily, only sequences in this subfamily are used to train this part of the model in the Viterbi algorithm.

Methods Using Additional Information

Many biologically significant patterns are difficult to discover in sequences. In such cases additional sources of information can be used to guide the search.

Identifying Motifs in Aligned Sequences

Pattern discovery and multiple local alignments are closely related tasks. One can easily obtain a pattern (e.g., in a form of consensus sequence and PWM) from a given local alignment by taking each column of the alignment as one position of the pattern. The question begins to be interesting if we assume that the input contains errors (i.e.,

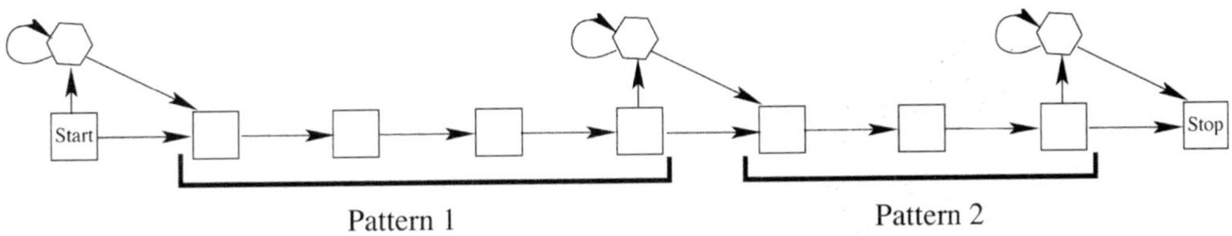

Fig. 5. Meta-MEME uses much simpler initial topology. Patterns found by other programs are connected together by insertion states.

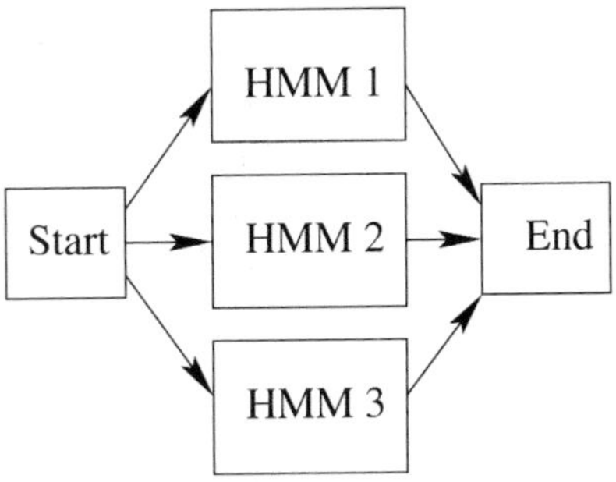

Fig. 6. Topology of HMM suitable for representing families of sequences with several subfamilies. HMM 1, 2, and 3 are models representing individual subfamilies.

some sequences are not aligned correctly) or it contains several subfamilies. In this case we may try to identify a pattern that does not match all sequences. This task is addressed by EMOTIF.

EMOTIF searches for motifs containing characters, ambiguous characters, and wildcards. The set of possible ambiguous characters is fixed. Each character (normal, ambiguous, or wildcard) corresponds to one column of the local alignment. It is possible to compute the specificity of each pattern of this form (how likely it is to occur by random) and sensitivity (how many training sequences it covers). EMOTIF identifies many motifs with different values of specificity and coverage. For several motifs with the same specificity, only the motif with the greatest coverage is reported and vice versa. Motifs are found by a pruned exhaustive search.

Global Properties of a Sequence

Computational recognition of eukaryotic promoters is a difficult task. In addition to local information in the form of transcription factor binding sites, it is also necessary to consider global properties of the DNA in the surrounding regions. One example are CpG islands: 1–2 kb long regions with higher frequency of CpG than found elsewhere in the genome. CpG islands often demarcate the 5' region flanking constitutively expressed vertebrate genes. In addition, regions downstream of genes usually have low flexibility (flexibility or bendability of DNA can be estimated from sequence-based models of DNA structure).

In the pattern matching problem we can use global information, such as CpG islands and flexibility, to distinguish random occurrences of a pattern from those that have functional significance. In pattern discovery we may use this kind of prior knowledge to choose appropriate parts of the genome as our input set to search for patterns.

Using Phylogenetic Tree

One of the basic assumptions in identifying patterns in biological sequences is that regions conserved in evolution are functionally important. Therefore it is natural to use known phylogenetic relations among sequences to guide the pattern search.

Assume we want to identify a regulatory element. Instead of using regulatory regions from many co-regulated genes of the same species, we will use regulatory regions of the same gene taken from many related species. We assume that the evolutionary tree of these species is known. Now we may try to identify the short pattern best conserved during evolution.

The best-conserved pattern can be identified using a parsimony measure as follows. We are given the length of pattern k. We want to associate a sequence t_w of length k with each node w. In internal nodes, t_w can be an arbitrary string. In each leaf, t_w is required to be a subsequence of the input sequence and corresponds to an occurrence of the pattern. We want to minimize the sum of $d\,(t_v,t_w)$ over all tree edges (v,w), where $d\,(t_v,t_w)$ is a distance between strings t_v and t_w (in this case the number of substitutions).

The algorithm works as follows. First the tree is rooted in an arbitrary internal node. For each node w and each possible string t of length k let $d^*_w(t)$ be the best possible parsimony score that can be achieved in the subtree rooted at w provided that $t_w = t$ (i.e., string t is stored in node w). Scores $d^*_w(t)$ can be computed in a leaves-to-root fashion.

The scores are easily found for leaf nodes: if t is a substring of the input string associated with the leaf w, then $d^*_w(t) = 0$, otherwise the score will be ∞. Once we know all scores for both children w_1 and w_2 of a certain internal node w, we can compute the scores for w. If we assume that the node w_1 stores sequence t_{w_1}, w_2 stores t_{w_2} and w stores t_w, then the parsimony of the subtree rooted at w will be:

$$\left[d^*_{w_1}(t_{w_1}) + d(t_{w_1},t_w)\right] + \left[d^*_{w_2}(t_{w_2}) + d(t_{w_2},t_w)\right]$$

For each possible t_w we want to find t_{w_1} and t_{w_2} that minimize this sum and store the sum as $d^*_w(t_w)$. After we compute scores for all nodes, we can retrieve the overall minimum parsimony as the smallest score computed for the root. We can use the stored intermediate results to reconstruct the entire optimal solution in a root-to-leaves manner. Strings of t_w stored in the leaves represent the occurrences of the pattern.

With additional optimizations the algorithm can be implemented to run in time $O(nk|\Sigma|^k)$, where n is the number of leaves. This is exponential in k but the problem is NP-hard, so we cannot hope to find a polynomial solution.

The use of phylogenetic tree can help to find patterns which are hard to find otherwise. For example, if the input contains several families of sequences, other methods may discover patterns characteristic for the sequences in the largest family instead of the patterns shared by all sequences. In practice, this problem is often solved by a preprocessing step: sequences are first clustered to separate families and then a single member is chosen from each family for further processing. If we use the phylogenetic tree, this step is not necessary and we keep information from all sequences. Because close homologs are grouped together in the phylogenetic tree, their weight is not so great, as the pattern still has to agree with other parts of the tree.

Use of Secondary/Tertiary Structure

Positions important to the secondary and tertiary structure of proteins are usually well conserved. If we know the structure of proteins in question, we can try to locate regions important for achieving this structure. These regions are good candidates to identify occurrences of our pattern. One possibility is to choose points of contact between two secondary structure elements as candidate spots for conserved positions. This approach has been used to construct a sparse deterministic pattern containing ambiguous characters and flexible gaps. If possible, sequences are aligned so that the points of contact align together. In such an alignment we can choose positions that are well-preserved among those columns that contain many points of contact.

Secondary structure and motif searching are also closely knit together in algorithms that identify conserved patterns in RNA sequences. RNA molecules are more related in their structure than in their sequence. Identifying RNA secondary structure of a set of related RNA sequences is best accomplished by first aligning the sequences. Alignment is then used to discover similarities. The process can be iterated resulting in simultaneous discovery of the alignment, secondary structure features, and conserved patterns.

Finding Homologies Between Two Sequences

Finding homologies between two DNA or protein sequences is a special case of the general pattern discovery problem. Here, the problem becomes simpler in principle but with larger amounts of data, the challenge shifts to efficiency and scalability. It is not our intention to survey the entire field of similarity searching, we will only consider the specific problem of comparing two very long genome sized DNA sequences, to shed some light on this problem.

In theory, this problem is easily solved by standard Smith-Waterman dynamic programming algorithm. However, when sequences are long, the dynamic programming and FASTA strategies become too expensive. Scalable heuristics are required.

Two strategies have lead to improvements. The first is exemplified by the popular Blast family of algorithms. This approach finds short exact *seed* matches (hits), which are then extended into longer alignments. However, when comparing two very long sequences, most programs in this category such as SIM, Blastn (BL2SEQ), WU-Blast, and Psi-Blast run slowly and require large amounts of memory. SENSEI is somewhat faster and uses less memory than the above, but it is currently limited to ungapped alignments. MegaBlast runs quite efficiently without a gap open penalty and a large seed length of 28 yielding much lower sensitivity.

Another strategy, exemplified by MUMmer, QUASAR, and REPuter, uses suffix trees. Suffix trees suffer from two problems: They were designed to deal with precise matches and are limited to comparing highly similar sequences. MUMmer and QUASAR have implemented various ways of linking precisely matched neighboring blocks. The second problem with suffix trees is that they have an intrinsic large space requirement.

A new program PatternHunter has recently been developed. PatternHunter uses optimized spaced seeds for high sensitivity and improved search and alignment algorithms. It is implemented in Java and runs at the speed of MegaBlast and the suffix tree program family while producing output at default Blastn sensitivity. PatternHunter was tested against the newly improved Blastn (using BL2SEQ) and MegaBlast, downloaded from the NCBI website on July 9, 2001. Program compari-

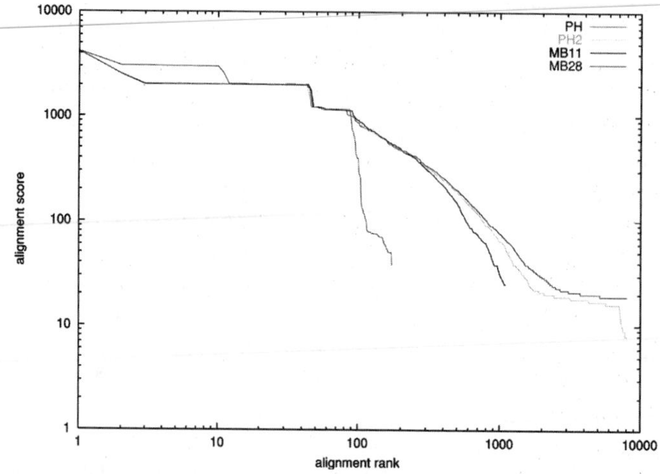

Fig. 7. Input: *H. influenza* and *E. coli*. The score is plotted as a function of the rank of the alignment, with both axes logarithmic. MegaBlast (MB28) misses over 700 alignments of score at least 100. MB11 is MegaBlast with seed size 11 (it is much slower and uses more memory), indicating the missed alignments by MB28 are mainly due to seed size.

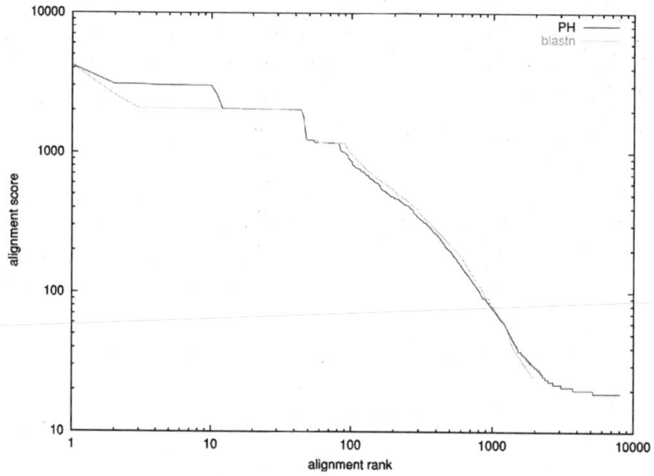

Fig. 8. Input: *H. influenza* and *E. coli*. PatternHunter produces better quality output than Blastn while running 20 times faster.

sons were performed on a 700 MHz Pentium III PC with 1 gbyte of memory. Experiments were performed on the following datasets: *M. pneumoniae* vs *M. genitalium*, *E. coli* vs *H. influenza*, and *A. thaliana* chromosome 2 vs *A. thaliana* chromosome 4 were then undertaken. All programs were run without filtering (bl2seq option –F F) to ensure identical input to the actual matching engines. With filter, Figs. 7 and 8 essentially remained the same. All comparisons were based on same scoring reward and penalties to insure the output results were comparable. MB28 is MegaBlast with seed size 28. PH is PatternHunter at sensitivity similar to Blastn seed size 10 , and PH2 is PatternHunter at sensitivity similar to Blastn seed size 11. Figures 7–9 show the output quality of PatternHunter vs Blastn and MegaBlast. In Fig. 7, MegaBlast using seed

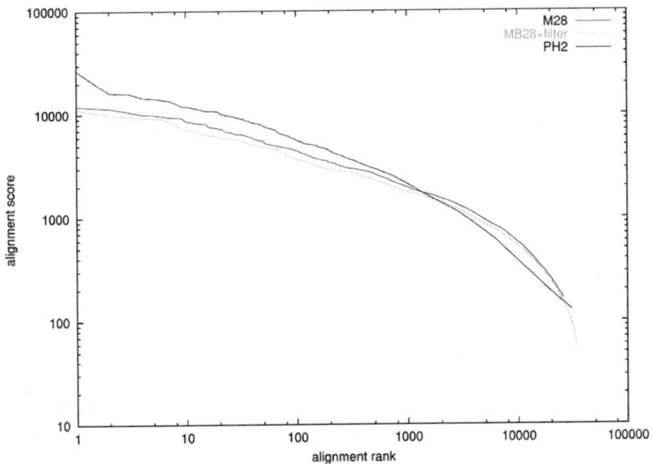

Fig. 9. Input: *A. thaliana* chr 2 and chr 4. PatternHunter (PH2) outscores MegaBlast in one sixth of the time and one quarter the memory. Both programs used MegaBlast's non-affine gap costs (with gapopen 0, gapextend –7, match 2, and mismatch –6) to avoid MegaBlast from running out of memory. For comparison we also show the curve for MegaBlast with its default low complexity filtering on, which decreases its runtime more than sixfold to 3305 seconds.

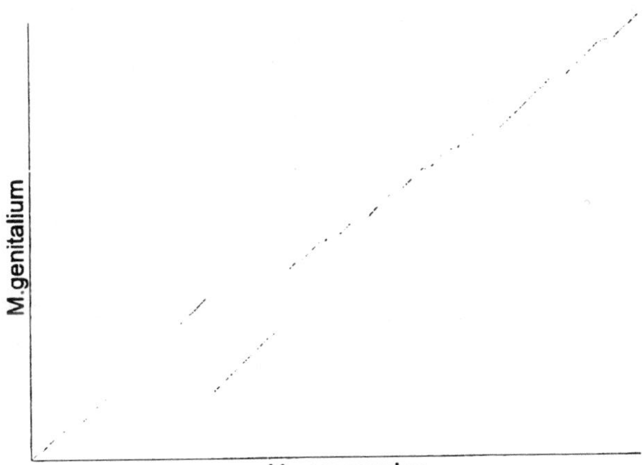

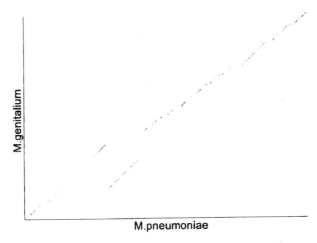

Fig. 10. Highscoring Segment Pairs plot of *M. Pneumoniae* vs *M. Genitalium*.

weight 28 (MB28) misses over 700 high scoring alignments. Using the same parameters, PatternHunter results are comparable or better than results obtained by Blastn. It is 20 times faster and uses one tenth the memory (*see* Fig. 8). Figure 9 shows that MegaBlast produces alignments with significantly lower scores compared to PatternHunter (PH2), which uses only one sixth the time and one quarter the space, on arabidopsis chromosomes. Figure 10 shows a genome alignment of *M. Pneumoniae* vs *M. Genitalium*, by PatternHunter and MUMmer. The table in Figure 11 compares the time and space used by PatternHunter (PH2). For example, the comparison of human chromosome 22 (35M bases) vs human chromosome 21 (26.2M bases) only required 1 h to complete.

Seq1	*Size*	*Seq2*	*Size*	*PH*	*PH2*	*MB28*	*Blastn*
M. pneumoniae	828K	*M. genitalium*	589K	10s/65M	4s/48M	1s/88M	47s/45M
E. coli	4.7M	*H. influenza*	1.8M	34s/78M	14s/68M	5s/561M	716s/158M
A. thaliana chr 2	19.6M	*A. thaliana* chr 4	17.5M	5020s/279M	498s/231M	21720s/1087M	∞

Fig. 11. Performance comparison: If not specified, all with match 1, mismatch –1, gap open –5, gap extension –1. Table entries under PH, PH2, MB28 and Blastn indicate time (seconds) and space (megabytes) used; ∞ means out of memory or segmentation fault.

Assessment of Pattern Quality

A wide variety of pattern discovery methods are available. They differ in what they consider to be the best pattern and most are not guaranteed to identify the best pattern. Thus we need to evaluate the quality of the discovered patterns. Various statistical methods have been employed to address the question: how likely is it that the pattern occurs in our sequences merely by chance? The smaller the likelihood the bigger the chance that the pattern discovered has biological meaning. Statistical significance of a pattern is used to evaluate the performance of different algorithms, but also as a scoring function to rank discovered patterns for a user, or to guide a search for the most significant pattern.

Although statistical significance is an important tool that allows one to distinguish artifacts of search algorithms from significant patterns, one must keep in mind that the goal of pattern discovery is to identify elements of certain biological importance. Even a very significant pattern may not be what we are looking for. For example we may want to discover functionally important sites but the pattern was conserved because it was essential for structure instead. Therefore it is important to verify patterns by appropriate biological experiments. For example, mutagenesis or another appropriate biological assay can be used to verify the function of a protein, x-ray crystallography or nuclear magnetic resonance (NMR) to determine the structure of a protein, and DNA footprinting to verify binding sites.

Background Model

If we want to understand what the probability is that a pattern occurs by random we need to define *random*. In other words, we need to select a background model. The simplest background model assumes that all possible characters of the alphabet are equally likely and the individual positions of the sequence are independent. Therefore all possible sequences of characters of the same length are equally likely.

This model is usually not adequate because different characters of the alphabet, i.e., individual nucleotides or amino acids, occur in biological sequences with different frequencies. For example in an AT rich sequence we can expect that the string 'TAATA' will be more frequent that 'CGGCG'. We can solve this problem using the *Bernoulli model*. In this model each character of the alphabet potentially has a different probability but individual positions of the sequence are still independent.

An even more complicated model is *Markov chain*. In this case, the probability of each character at position j depends on the characters at positions $j-1, j-2, \ldots, j-k$, where k is a parameter called the order of the Markov chain. A Markov chain of order 0 is identical to the Bernoulli model. Markov chains take into account the fact that some combinations of characters occur less or more frequently than expected based on the frequencies of their constituents.

Parameters of background models, i.e., probabilities of individual characters, can be estimated as a function of the observed frequencies in the input sequences or in some larger databases.

Pattern Significance

Given a deterministic pattern P and a sequence of length L we can simply count the number of occurrences of P in the sequence. Denote this number N_P. Let $E(X_{P,L})$ be the expected number of occurrences of pattern P in a sequence of length L generated by a background model. If the observed number of occurrences N_P is much higher than the expected value $E(X_{P,L})$, P is then a significant pattern. The standard measure used in this context is the z-score:

$$z_P = \frac{N_P - E(X_{P,L})}{\sigma(X_{P,L})}$$

where $\sigma(X_{P,L})$ is the standard deviation of the number of occurrences of P in a random sequence of length L. This measure gives the number of standard deviations by which the observed value N_P differs from the expected value.

The simplest approach towards computing the z-score is to generate a large number of sequences using the chosen background model, count the number of occurrences of the pattern, then estimate the expected value and standard deviation from this random sample. This works for any kind of background model and pattern but it has a high running time (especially if we need to evaluate the z-score for many patterns). The values obtained are only estimates.

Another approach is to compute the mean and variance of the distribution of the number of occurrences of a given pattern exactly. For example, algorithms are available for a large class of patterns when the background distribution is a Markov chain of order k.

Information Content

In case of probabilistic models such as position weight matrices we do not have strictly defined occurrences but rather a score between 0 and 1 for any string. One can set a threshold on what we consider to be an occurrence and then evaluate the z-score or other appropriate statistical measures. Alternatively when evaluating position weight matrices an *information content* (also called *relative entropy*) measure is used. This tells how much the distribution defined by the PWM differs from the (Bernoulli-type) background distribution. Relative entropy is computed as follows:

$$\sum_i \sum_c A[c,i] \log_2 \frac{A[c,i]}{f(c)}$$

where $A[c,i]$ is the frequency of character c in column i of the matrix and $f(c)$ is the background frequency of the character c. Relative entropy has two disadvantages. First, it does not depend on the number of occurrences of the pattern in the sequences. A strong pattern with very many occurrences has higher relative entropy than a weaker pattern with few occurrences. Therefore, it is an appropriate measure only in situations where the pattern is required to occur in all sequences. This is often the case in Gibbs sampling methods. Second, relative entropy of one column is always non-negative and therefore if we add columns that are not well-conserved to the pattern, we can obtain a better score. Therefore relative entropy is not suitable for comparing patterns of different lengths. This can be solved by subtracting the appropriate term from the contribution of each column so that the expected contribution of a column is zero.

Sensitivity and Specificity of Classification

One application of the various methods of pattern discovery is to identify patterns that characterize a given family of related sequences. In this context we need to measure how well we can distinguish members of the family from nonmembers based on the occurrence of the pattern. For this purpose a test set consisting of sequences of a known family is required. We find all occurrences of the motif in the test set and compute the following four scores: TP (true positives) are sequences that contain the motif and belong to the family in question, TN (true negatives) are sequences that do not belong to the family and do not contain the motif, FP (false positives) are sequences that contain the motif but do not belong to the family and FN (false negatives) are sequences that do not contain the motif but belong to the family. Thus $TP + TN$ is the number of correct predictions and $FN + FP$ is the number of wrong predictions. Based on counts of TP, TN, FP, FN we can define various measures. Sensitivity (also called *coverage*) is defined as $TP/(TP + FN)$ and specificity is defined as $TN/(TN + FP)$. A pattern has maximum sensitivity, if it occurs in all proteins in the family (regardless of the number of false positives) and it has maximum specificity, if it does not occur in any sequence outside the family. A score called *correlation coefficient* gives an overall measure of prediction success:

$$C = \frac{TP \cdot TN - FP \cdot FN}{\sqrt{(TP + FP)(TP + FN)(TN + FN)(TN + FP)}}$$

This expression grows from –1 to 1 as the number of correct predictions increases.

Concluding Remarks

An overview of methods available for pattern discovery was presented. The tools developed by computer scientists are common today in many biological laboratories. They are required to handle large-scale tasks, including the annotation of newly sequenced genomes, organization of proteins into families of related sequences, or identifying regulatory elements in co-expressed genes. They are also important in smaller-scale projects because they can be used to detect possible sites of interest and assign putative structure or function. Thus, they can be used to guide biological experiments in *wet labs*, decreasing the time and money spent in discovering new biological knowledge.

Indeed, there are many examples, where computational tools have helped biologists to make important discoveries. For example, pattern-discovery tools helped to identify a number of putative secretory proteins in *Mycobacterium tuberculosis* genome. Subsequently, 90% of the predicted candidates were experimentally confirmed. Identification of *M. tuberculosis* secretory proteins is a first step to the design of more effective vaccines against tuberculosis.

In order to fully understand the meaning of the output of a pattern-discovery tool, biologists need to understand the basics of the algorithm used in the tool. It is very useful to know the performance guarantees of the algorithm. Tools that cannot guarantee finding the best or all patterns, might find only low-scoring patterns in sequences which contain high-scoring patterns as well.

The pattern discovery process is often a computationally intensive task. Therefore many databases are maintained and updated containing results of pattern discovery applied to particular tasks. These databases often contain experimental evidence from biological literature and other useful information. On the accompanying CD-ROM, we provide a list of such databases together with related links and short descriptions of database contents. An overview of the software tools is also included on the CD-ROM.

Acknowledgments

Parts of this chapter are based on technical report of Brejová et al. (2000) and some material from paper of Ma et al. (2002). We would like to thank co-authors of the report Chrysanne DiMarco, Sandra Romero Hidalgo, Gina Holguin, and Cheryl Patten and co-authors of the paper Bin Ma and John Tromp for cooperation and helpful discussion. We want to also thank Stephen Krawetz, Jonathan Badger, Paul Kearney, and Marthenn Salazar who kindly reviewed parts of the material.

Suggested Readings

Biological Motivation and Introductory Reading

Batzoglou, S., Pachter, L., Mesirov, J. P., Berger, B., and Lander, E. S. (2000) Human and mouse gene structure: comparative analysis and application to exon prediction, Genome Res. 10(7), 950–958.

Fickett, J. W. and Hatzigeorgiou, A. G. (1997) Eukaryotic promoter recognition, Genome Res. 7(9), 861–868.

Gelfand, M. S., Koonin, E. V., and Mironov, A. A. (2000) Prediction of transcription regulatory sites in Archaea by a comparative genomic approach, Nucleic Acids Res. 28(3), 695–705.

Gomez, M., Johnson, S., and Gennaro, M. L. (2000) Identification of secreted proteins of Mycobacterium tuberculosis by a bioinformatic approach, Infect. Immun. 68(4), 2323–2327.

Hardison, R. C., Oeltjen, J., and Miller, W. (1997) Long human-mouse sequence alignments reveal novel regulatory elements: a reason to sequence the mouse genome, Genome Res. 7(10), 959–966.

Hughes, J. D., Estep, P. W., Tavazoie, S., and Church, G. M. (2000) Computational identification of cis-regulatory elements associated with groups of functionally related genes in Saccharomyces cerevisiae, J. Mol. Biol. 296(5), 1205–1214.

Linial, M., Linial, N., Tishby, N., and Yona, G. (1997) Global self-organization of all known protein sequences reveals inherent biological signatures, J. Mol. Biol. 268(2), 539–546.

Mironov, A. A., Koonin, E. V., Roytberg, M. A., and Gelfand, M. S. (1999) Computer analysis of transcription regulatory patterns in completely sequenced bacterial genomes, Nucleic Acids Res. 27(14), 2981–2989.

Riechmann, J. L., Heard, J., Martin, G., Reuber, L., Jiang, C., Keddie, J., et al. (2000) Arabidopsis transcription factors: genome-wide comparative analysis among eukaryotes, Science 290(5499), 2105–2110.

Yada, T., Totoki, Y., Ishii, T., and Nakai, K. (1997) Functional prediction of B. subtilis genes from their regulatory sequences, in: Proceedings of the 5th International Conference on Intelligent Systems for Molecular Biology (ISMB) (Gaasterland, T., Karp, P., Ouzounis, C., Sander, C., and Valencia, A., eds.) The AAAI Press, Halkidiki, Greece, pp. 354–357.

Related Books and Surveys

Brazma, A., Jonassen, I., Eidhammer, I., and Gilbert, D. (1998) Approaches to the automatic discovery of patterns in biosequences, J. Comp. Biol. 5(2), 279–305.

Brejová, B., DiMarco, C., Vinar, T., Hidalgo, S. R., Holguin, G., and Patten, C. (2000) Finding Patterns in Biological Sequences, Technical Report CS-2000-22, Dept. of Computer Science, University of Waterloo, Ontario, Canada.

Gusfield, D. (1997) Algorithms on strings, trees and sequences: computer science and computational biology, Chapman & Hall, New York, NY.

Pevzner, P. A. (2000) Computational molecular biology: an algorithmic approach, The MIT Press, Cambridge, MA.

Rigoutsos, I., Floratos, A., Parida, L., Gao, Y., and Platt, D. (2000) The emergence of pattern discovery techniques in computational biology, Metabolic Eng. 2(3), 159–167.

Pattern Discovery

Gorodkin, J., Heyer, L. J., Brunak, S., and Stormo, G. D. (1997) Displaying the information contents of structural RNA alignments: the structure logos, Comp. Appl. Biosci. 13(6), 583–586.

Schneider, T. D. and Stephens, R. M. (1990) Sequence logos: a new way to display consensus sequences, Nucleic Acids Res. 18(20), 6097–6100.

Algorithms for Pattern Discovery

Exhaustive Search Methods

Jonassen, I. (1996) Efficient discovery of conserved patterns using a pattern graph, Technical Report 118, Department of Informatics, University of Bergen, Norway.

Parida, L., Rigoutsos, I., Floratos, A., Platt, D., and Gao, Y. (2000) Pattern discovery on character sets and real-valued data: linear bound on irredundant motifs and an efficient polynomial time algorithm, in: Proceedings of the 11th Annual ACM-SIAM Symposium on Discrete Algorithms (SODA), ACM Press, San Francisco, CA, pp. 297–308.

Pevzner, P. A. and Sze, S. H. (2000) Combinatorial approaches to finding subtle signals in DNA sequences, in: Proceedings of the 8th International Conference on Intelligent Systems for Molecular Biology (ISMB), (Bourne, P., Gribskov, M., Altman, R., Jensen, N., Hope, D., Lengauer, T., et al., eds.) The AAAI Press, San Diego, CA, pp. 269–278.

Rigoutsos, I. and Floratos, A. (1998) Combinatorial pattern discovery in biological sequences: The TEIRESIAS algorithm, Bioinformatics 14(1), 55–67.
Published erratum appears in Bioinformatics, 14(2), 229.

Rigoutsos, I. and Floratos, A. (1998) Motif discovery without alignment or enumeration (extended abstract), in: Proceedings of the 2nd Annual International Conference on Computational Molecular Biology (RECOMB), (Istrail, S., Pevzner, P., Waterman, M., eds.) ACM Press, New York, NY, pp. 221–227.

Smith, H. O., Annau, T. M., and Chandrasegaran, S. (1990) Finding sequence motifs in groups of functionally related proteins, Proc. Natl. Acad. Sci. USA 87(2), 826–830.

Tompa, M. (1999) An exact method for finding short motifs in sequences, with application to the ribosome binding site problem, in: Proceedings of the 7th International Conference on Intelligent Systems for Molecular Biology (ISMB),

(Glasgow, J., Littlejohn, T., Major, F., Lathrop, R., Sankoff, D., and Sensen, C., eds.) The AAAI Press, Montreal, Canada, pp. 262–271.

van Helden, J., Andre, B., and Collado-Vides, J. (1998) Extracting regulatory sites from the upstream region of yeast genes by computational analysis of oligonucleotide frequencies, J. Mol. Biol. 281(5), 827–832.

Iterative Methods

Lawrence, C. E., Altschul, S. F., Boguski, M. S., Liu, J. S., Neuwald, A. F., and Wootton, J. C. (1993) Detecting subtle sequence signals: a Gibbs sampling strategy for multiple alignment, Science 262(5131), 208–214.

Li, M., Ma, B., and Wang, L. (1999) Finding Similar Regions in Many Strings, in: Proceedings of the 31st Annual ACM Symposium on Theory of Computing (STOC), Atlanta, ACM Press, Portland, OR, pp. 473–482.

Liang, C. (2001) COPIA: A New Software for Finding Consensus Patterns in Unaligned Protein Sequences. Master thesis, University of Waterloo.

Liu, J. S., Neuwald, A. F., and Lawrence, C. E. (1995) Bayesian Models for Multiple Local Sequence Alignment and Gibbs Sampling Strategies, J. Am. Stat. Assoc. 90(432), 1156–1170.

Neuwald, A. F., Liu, J. S., Lipman, D. J., and Lawrence, C. E. (1997) Extracting protein alignment models from the sequence database, Nucleic Acids Res. 25(9), 1665–1667.

Singh, M., Berger, B., Kim, P. S., Berger, J. M., and Cochran, A. G. (1998) Computational learning reveals coiled coil-like motifs in histidine kinase linker domains, Proc. Natl. Acad. Sci. USA 95(6), 2738–2743.

Zhang, M. Q. (1998) Statistical features of human exons and their flanking regions, Human Mol. Genet. 7(5), 919–922.

Machine Learning Methods

Bailey, T. L. and Elkan, C. (1994) Fitting a mixture model by expectation maximization to discover motifs in biopolymers, in: Proceedings of the 2nd International Conference on Intelligent Systems for Molecular Biology (ISMB), (Altman, R., Brutlag, D., Karp, P., Lathrop, R., and Searls, D., eds.) The AAAI Press, Stanford, CA, pp. 28–36.

Bailey, T. L. and Elkan, C. (1995) Unsupervised learning of multiple motifs in biopolymers using expectation maximization, Machine Learning 21(1/2), 51–80.

Lawrence, C. E. and Reilly, A. A. (1990) An expectation maximization (EM) algorithm for the identification and characterization of common sites in unaligned biopolymer sequences, Proteins, 7(1), 41–51.

Hidden Markov Models

Durbin, R., Eddy, S. R., Krogh, A., and Mitchison, G. (1998), Biological Sequence Analysis, Cambridge University Press, Cambridge, UK.

Grundy, W. N., Bailey, T. L., Elkan, C. P., and Baker, M. E. (1997) Meta-MEME: motif-based hidden Markov models of protein families, Comp. Appl. Biosci. 13(4), 397–406.

Hughey, R. and Krogh, A. (1996) Hidden Markov models for sequence analysis: extension and analysis of the basic method, Comp. Appl. Biosci. 12(2), 95–107.

Krogh, A., Brown, M., Mian, I. S., Sjolander, K., and Haussler, D. (1994) Hidden Markov models in computational biology. Applications to protein modeling, J. Mol. Biol. 235(5), 1501–1501.

Pattern Discovery Using Additional Information

Blanchette, M., Schwikowski, B., and Tompa, M. (2000) An exact algorithm to identify motifs in orthologous sequences from multiple species, in: Proceedings of the 8th International Conference on Intelligent Systems for Molecular Biology (ISMB), (Bourne, P., Gribskov, M., Altman, R., Jensen, N., Hope, D., Lengauer, T., et al., eds.) The AAAI Press, San Diego, CA, pp. 37–45.

Chiang, D. Y., Brown, P. O., and Eisen, M. B. (2001), Visualizing associations between genome sequences and gene expression data using genome-mean expression profiles, Bioinformatics 17(S1), S49–S55.

Eidhammer, I., Jonassen, I., and Taylor, W. R. (2000) Structure comparison and structure patterns, J. Comp. Biol. 7(5), 685–716.

Gorodkin, J., Heyer, L. J., and Stormo, G. D. (1997b) Finding the most significant common sequence and structure motifs in a set of RNA sequences, Nucleic Acids Res. 25(18), 3724–3732.

Ison, J. C., Blades, M. J., Bleasby, A. J., Daniel, S. C., Parish, J. H., and Findlay, J. B. (2000) Key residues approach to the definition of protein families and analysis of sparse family signatures, Proteins 40(2), 330–331.

Nevill-Manning, C. G., Wu, T. D., and Brutlag, D. L. (1998) Highly specific protein sequence motifs for genome analysis, Proc. Natl. Acad. Sci. USA 95(11), 5865–5871.

Pedersen, A. G., Baldi, P., Chauvin, Y., and Brunak, S. (1999) The biology of eukaryotic promoter prediction-a review, Comp. Chem. 23(3–4), 191–207.

Finding Homologies Between Two Sequences

Altschul, S. F., Madden, T. L., Schaffer, A. A., Zhang, J., Zhang, Z., Miller, W., and Lipman, D. J. (1997) Gapped BLAST and PSI-BLAST: a new generation of protein database search programs, Nucleic Acids Res. 25(17), 3389–3392.

Altschul, S. F., Gish, W., Miller, W., Myers, E. W., and Lipman, D. J. (1990) Basic local alignment search tool, J. Mol. Biol. 215(3), 403–410.

Burkhardt, S., Crauser, A., Ferragina, P., Lenhof, H.-P., Rivals, E., and Vingron, M. (1999) q-gram based database searching using a suffix array (QUASAR), in: Proceedings of the 3rd Annual International Conference on Computational Molecular Biology (RECOMB), ACM Press, Lyon, France, pp. 77–83.

Delcher, A. L., Kasif, S., Fleischmann, R. D., Peterson, J., White, O., and Salzberg, S. L. (1999) Alignment of whole genomes, Nucleic Acids Res. 27(11), 2369–2376.

Gish, W. (2001) WU-Blast website (*see* Website: http://blast.wustl.edu/).

Huang, X. and Miller, W. (1991) A time-efficient, linear-space local similarity algorithm, Adv. Appl. Math. 12(3), 337–357.
(*see* SIM Website: http://www.expasy.ch/tools/sim.html)

Kurtz, S. and Schleiermacher, C. (1999) REPuter: fast computation of maximal repeats in complete genomes, Bioinformatics 15(5), 426–427.

Lipman, D. J. and Pearson, W. R. (1985) Rapid and sensitive protein similarity searches, Science 227(4693), 1435–1441.

Ma, B., Tromp, J., and Li, M. (2002) PatternHunter faster and more sensitive homology search, Bioinformatics 18(3), 440–445.

Smith, T. F. and Waterman, M. S. (1981) Identification of common molecular subsequences, J. Mol. Biol. 147(1), 195–197.

States, D. J. and Agarwal, P. (1996) Compact encoding strategies for DNA sequence similarity search, in: Proceedings of the 4th International Conference on Intelligent Systems for Molecular Biology (ISMB), (States, D. J., Agarwal, P.,

Gaasterland, T., Hunter, L., and Smith, R. F., eds.) The AAAI Press, St. Louis, MO, pp. 211–217.
(*see* SENSEI Website: http:<stateslab.wustl.edu/software/sensei/).

Tatusova, T. A. and Madden, T. L. (1999) BLAST 2 Sequences, a new tool for comparing protein and nucleotide sequences, FEMS Microbiol. Lett. 174(2), 247–250.

Zhang, Z., Schwartz, S., Wagner, L., and Miller, W. (2000) A greedy algorithm for aligning DNA sequences, J. Comp. Biol. 7(1–2), 203–204.

Assessment of Pattern Quality

Nicodème, P., Salvy, B., and Flajolet, P. (1999) Motif statistics, in: Algorithms — ESA '99, 7th Annual European Symposium, vol. 1643, Lecture Notes in Computer Science, (Nesetril, J., ed.), Springer, Prague, pp. 194–211.

Pesole, G., Liuni, S., and D'Souza, M. (2000) PatSearch: a pattern matcher software that finds functional elements in nucleotide and protein sequences and assesses their statistical significance, Bioinformatics 16(5), 439–440.

Rocke, E. and Tompa, M. (1998) An algorithm for finding novel gapped motifs in DNA sequences, in: Proceedings of the 2nd Annual International Conference on Computational Molecular Biology (RECOMB), (Istrail, S., Pevzner, P., and Waterman, M., eds.), ACM Press, New York, NY, pp. 228–233.

30 The Role of Transcription Factor Binding Sites in Promoters and Their *In Silico* Detection

Thomas Werner

Introduction

Transcription is the general process of copying part of the genomic DNA into RNA. This RNA either has functions of its own or is used to produce proteins. This is a multi-step process requiring the coordinated interaction of a plethora of proteins with the genomic DNA at various loci. The major regions of DNA involved in transcription are the regulatory regions like locus control regions, enhancers, and promoters.

Regulatory regions have to fulfill several requirements in order to serve a biological function in transcriptional control. The general chromatin status is a major determinant of sequence accessibility and is dependent on special protein complexes known as nucleosomes and their higher-order organization. On the molecular level, DNA methylation is of crucial importance and all processes discussed below can only occur after chromatin structure as well as DNA methylation have achieved a state where regulatory sequences are accessible for protein binding.

The basic principles of the interaction of proteins with DNA in transcriptional control are identical for all of these regions, so it is possible to focus on one representative region. The promoter is the best-studied of all regulatory regions and will be reviewed.

The Promoter

In general, the promoter is an integral part of the gene and often makes sense only in the context of its own gene, especially if important parts of the regulation are determined outside of the promoter (e.g., by an intron enhancer). The function of a promoter is to mediate and control initiation of transcription of that part of a gene that is located immediately downstream of the promoter (3'). This can be achieved either in an unregulated permanent manner (constitutive transcription) or in a highly regulated fashion by which transcription is subjected to the control of various extracellular and intracellular signals (regulated transcription). The DNA region required to fulfill this function can be determined by assays for promoter function in a heterologous context. I will refer to a promoter mainly as the region that is necessary to achieve transcriptional initiation, although this region may not be sufficient to completely determine the regulation of a gene. The promoter by definition marks the beginning of the first exon of a gene (*see* Fig. 1). The functional setup of promoters is intimately coupled

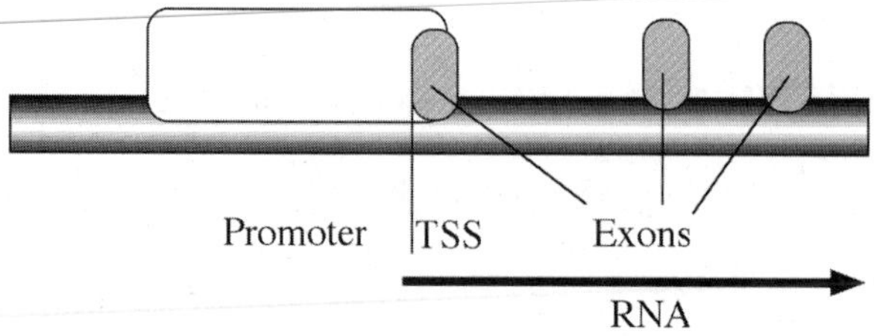

Fig. 1. Location of the promoter in genomic DNA. The promoter overlaps with the first exon and contains the transcription start site (TSS) where the transcription of genomic DNA into the nuclear RNA starts.

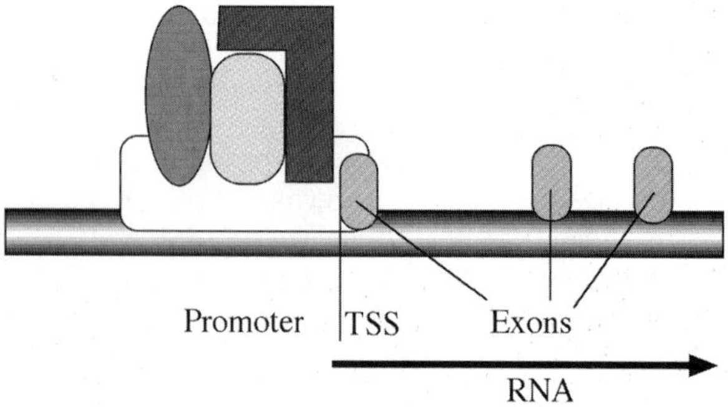

Fig. 2. Binding of transcriptional activators to the upstream promoter. The transcription factors bind to the promoter sequence and form the *"activation complex,"* which attracts the polymerase complex to the promoter.

with the basic events of transcriptional initiation. The focus throughout this chapter will be on polymerase II responsive promoters, which are controlling the vast majority of cellular genes encoding proteins in higher eukaryotes.

Transcription can only proceed after a competent transcription complex consisting of RNA polymerase II (pol II) and several general transcription factors (GTFs) have been recruited to the promoter. Usually, pol II is not capable of functionally interacting with a promoter alone and initiating transcription by itself and requires a host of cofactors. The polymerase complex is mainly concerned with accurately copying the DNA into RNA and not with determining where to start this process. This is the job of other types of proteins, called *activators*, that help to recruit the RNA polymerase to the correct location on the genomic DNA. Basically, there are two different phases in transcriptional activation of a gene. The first step includes a variety of transcription factors (TFs), that bind to upstream promoter and enhancer sequences to form a multiprotein complex (*see* Fig. 2). In the second step this complex directly or indirectly recruits a pol II complexed with GTFs to the core promoter and the transcription start site (TSS) located within the core promoter. Subsequently, transcription is initiated by this initiation complex, which itself is subject to regulatory influences of TFs.

Once the complete complex including the polymerase complex is assembled on the promoter (called the *initiation complex*), it is now competent to initiate RNA

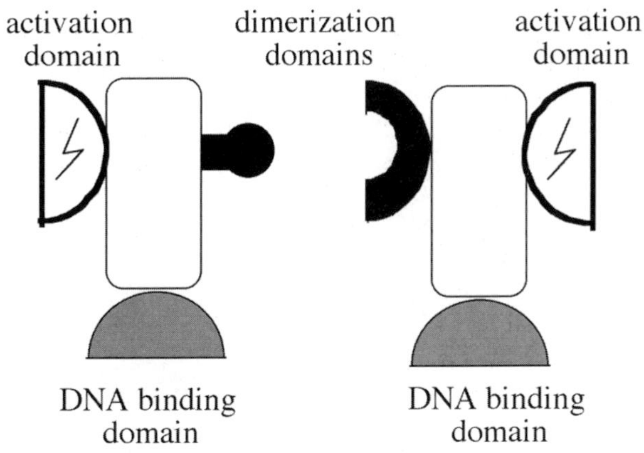

Fig. 3. Schematic representation of two transcription factors that can dimerize. The DNA binding domains may have different specificities as well as the activation domains that do not need to be of the same kind. The dimerization domains determine which factors can form dimers.

synthesis. The promoter can be defined as the minimum region of DNA that allows the formation of a functional initiation complex. This can be reduced to a core promoter or may include one or several upstream and/or downstream elements. Other regions directly upstream to this minimum promoter are termed *upstream regulatory regions* as long as they cannot be clearly identified as separate functional units (e.g., enhancers). There is a gradual transition from upstream promoter elements to enhancer elements (position and orientation independent activator regions), which is not necessarily obvious from inspecting the sequence. Similarly, the elements located downstream of the minimal promoter may also be downstream of the promoter elements and may constitute part of enhancers.

Transcription Factors

As evident, the key players in promoter activation are specialized proteins called *transcription factors*. Although there is a large variety of transcription factors in a single cell, at least several hundred if not a thousand, share some very basic features.

All transcription factors (TFs) contain a DNA binding domain enabling them to bind to genomic DNA as well as an activator domain, which has either an activating or suppressing activity. Many transcription factors have the ability to form specific homo- or hetero-dimers with other TFs. Such factors contain an additional domain, called a *dimerization domain* completing the generic structure of a TF shown in Fig. 3.

The function of a transcription factor is very simple and by itself not directly coupled to transcriptional control. The factor brings its action domain into a specific location by binding to the genomic DNA at selected sites. Whether this has consequences for transcription of a gene is determined by the functional context, i.e., by what other factors are bound or brought close enough to interact with the particular factor. Only a larger complex of transcription factors that often contain regulatory proteins that do not bind directly to DNA (so called *mediators of transcription*) have the ability to recruit the DNA polymerase complex to the promoter and thus influ-

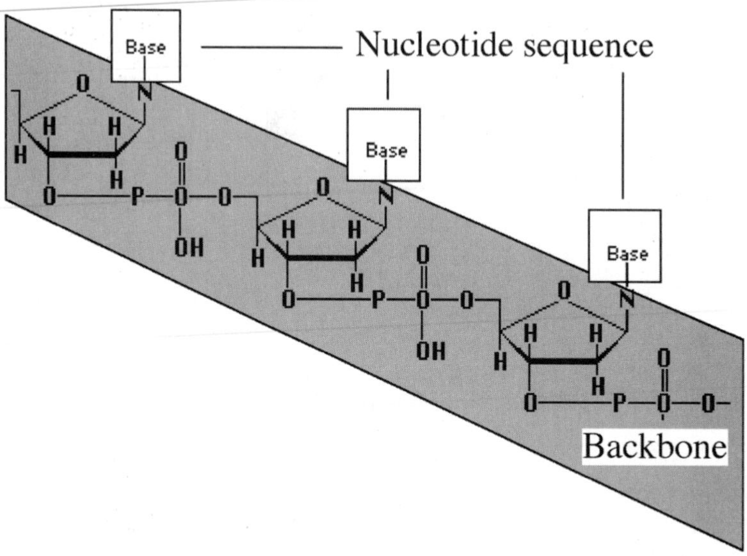

Fig. 4. Basic structure of a single DNA strand. The gray area represents the sugar-phosphate backbone supporting general protein contacts. The white boxes represent the bases that form sequence-specific contacts with proteins.

ence transcription. Transcription is a very dynamic process. Aggregate binding of a variety of factors to genomic DNA form an active initiation complex and the timely dissociation of the initiation complex, and even release of transcription factors from the DNA is crucial to transcription. This push/pull complicates considerably the process of optimization of binding site detection. It has very important consequences on the nature and detection of TF binding sites as will become evident below.

How Transcription Factors Bind to DNA

Transcription factors bind to DNA via a multitude of atomic interactions that are either van der Waals hydrophobic contacts or supported by juxtaposition of oppositely charged amino acids and DNA components. The two basic modes of molecular interactions can be distinguished:

1. The first mode involves nonspecific contacts between the protein side chains and the so-called *backbone* of the DNA, consisting of the sugar-phosphate structure that links the bases together. Such contacts can form anywhere on a DNA (double) strand and are responsible for the general tendency of TFs to associate with DNA.
2. The second mode is sequence-specific recognition. This is achieved by the direct contact of the amino acid side chains with the DNA bases. Therefore, these contacts can only be formed where there is a suitable succession of bases, i.e., a specific nucleotide sequence (*see* Fig. 4).

The apparent binding affinity of a TF to a particular DNA sequence is the sum of the nonspecific and the specific binding:

$$\text{Affinity} = \text{Sum (general contacts)} + \text{Sum (specific contacts)}$$

This shows that specific contacts only account for part of the binding affinity and that sequence variation has a quantitative effect on the binding affinity of TFs.

However, proteins as well as DNA are three-dimensional structures. There are sterical dependencies for each of the individual contacts. For example, a bulky side chain can only form a very limited number of sterical arrangements with respect to the DNA. This has direct consequences for the selection of neighboring positions in the DNA sequence. Due to such restrictions individual exchanges of nucleotides can have dramatically different effects on the binding affinity. This is not a simple linear function of sequence fit. The contribution of a DNA protein contact is a function of the sterical neighborhood and is easily represented by the nucleotide sequence. Taking this into consideration, the affinities are calculated as:

$$\text{general contact}_i = E_i * f(S_i) \quad \text{and} \quad \text{specific contact}_j = E_j * f(S_j)$$

where i and j are the position within the binding site, S_i is the sequence context of position i, and E_i is the energy of the interaction at position i.

The Characteristics of TF Binding Sites

TF binding sites are usually short 8–20 nucleotide stretches of DNA that are covered by the protein upon binding. Surprisingly, at first glance, the sequences for the binding sites for the same protein vary considerably in different locations. Nevertheless, the binding affinity may be comparable and all of these sites are part of a functional context. Interestingly, the average binding affinity of natural binding sites is often suboptimal, that is, there are other sequences that would bind with a much higher affinity to the protein. There are several reasons for these very general observations.

First, TFs have to bind to DNA during a lifetime of an individual or on a larger scale, until evolution has changed that particular regulatory event. Therefore, TF binding is faced with the inevitable mutations that occur over time in genomic DNA. By allowing a variety of slightly different sequences to be bound, TFs can reduce the risk of losing their ability for DNA binding due to point mutations in binding sites. Second, with regard to TF function, they not only need to specifically bind to DNA, but they must dissociate correctly in order to complete each transcriptional cycle.

The observed flexibility of TF binding sites has quite favorable consequences for biological function and fitness. However, how is this limited flexibility achieved on a molecular basis? This is important in order to design optimal algorithms for the detection of real binding sites by *in silico* methods. Detailed analysis of individual TF binding sites, binding the same factor, revealed that sequence variations are not evenly distributed over the binding site sequence. On one hand, there are a few highly conserved nucleotide positions within the binding site that are never or rarely changed. Mutations at such sites often have deleterious effects on DNA binding of the protein and have been shown in many cases to represent positions that are contacted by the protein in a sequence-specific manner. On the other hand, many binding sites contain positions that are covered by the protein as evident from footprint studies, but where there is low or no sequence conservation. Those *internal* spacers are usually not contacted in a base-specific manner and may or may not contribute back-bone contacts to binding (*see* Fig. 5).

The series of three-dimensional interactions can impart a mutual dependency of pairs of nucleotides within a binding site. This is evidenced as correlated positions.

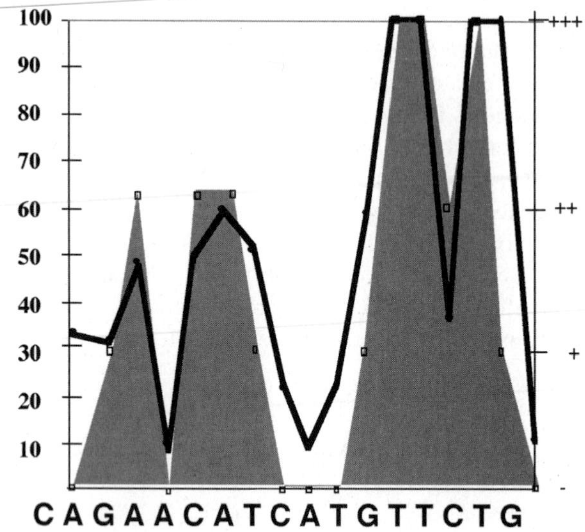

Fig. 5. Comparison of calculated importance (consensus index based on Shannon entropy) and experimental evidence for the Glucocorticoid Receptor Binding site. The scale on the left side shows the normalized consensus index derived from the nucleotide weight matrix of the GRE. The experimental evidence is given as follows: – = no DNA contact by the protein; + = backbone contact; ++ = unspecific base contact; +++ = sequence specific base contact.

These are different from conserved positions because correlated positions do vary in the nucleotide from sequence to sequence but in a coordinated manner (e.g., if position A contains an A then position B contains a G, if position A contains a T then position B contains an A). Thus, TF binding sites can be viewed as collections of closely related but distinct sequences that can be described in a collective manner. Thus, TF binding sites sequences only carry the potential to bind their cognate protein. They occur everywhere in the genome and are by no means restricted to regulatory regions. This complicates their recognition because there are always a large number of potential binding sites that have absolutely no function in transcriptional control. It is therefore almost impossible to discriminate functional from nonfunctional sites (usually referred to as *false positive matches*) based solely on the analysis of the individual binding sites.

The Principles of *In Silico* TF Binding Site Detection

The question becomes how does one identify these TF binding sites in nucleotide sequences? The first and obvious approach would be to collect known TF binding sites and then simply use a string matching algorithm to find new locations of the series of letters in question. Allowing for one or two mismatches to the known sites could mimic the sequence variations. As intriguing as this simple approach appears, it is so flawed in its practical application that it can only serve as a negative example. First, it can only identify binding sites already known if no mismatches are allowed. When mismatches are permitted this algorithm will return an overwhelming number of sequence matches, most of which may not even be binding sites for the factor in question.

A = A	**C** = C	**G** = G	**T** = T (U)
W = A or T	**S** = C or G	**K** = G or T	
M = A or C	**Y** = C or T		
R = A or G			
B = C, G, T **= (non A)**	**D** = A, G, T **= (non C)**	**H** = A, C, T **= (non G)**	**V** = A, C, G **= (non T)**
N = A, C, G,			

Fig. 6. The 15 letter IUPAC ambiguity code.

This illustrates the problem of this approach, ignoring the well-known variety of binding sites. Rather than using individual sequences, one can compile a consensus from all known binding sites and then search with this consensus to eliminate this problem. This is accomplished by aligning the binding sites by optimizing the number of matching positions then transforming this alignment into a single description. This can be accomplished by employing the International Union of Pure and Applied Chemistry (IUPAC) code that is an extended alphabet of nucleotides of 15 letters including symbols for alternative nucleotides (R = A or G). The first successful algorithms to locate TF binding sites in DNA have used this IUPAC string representation and they are still in use (*see* Fig. 6).

These approaches have limitations. First the IUPAC strings are absolutely unforgiving for sequences that were not part of the training set, i.e., the sequences used to derive the IUPAC consensus string. For example, if all training sequences contained either an A or a G at a particular position, a C at this position would cause all candidates to be rejected, even if they were identical to the IUPAC in all other positions. This may be correct in case of a sequence-specific recognition at this position but is unacceptable if this position is located within an internal spacer. IUPAC string matching yields a binary decision only; match or no match. There is no way to quantitatively distinguish between the candidates. In addition, the use of the IUPAC strings allows sequences to be identified that would not contain a functional binding site because the combinations of individual positions were not restricted by any means (allowing the accumulation of *rare* nucleotides throughout the binding site). Currently, the most reliable way to detect TF binding sites in DNA sequences is based on nucleotide weight matrices.

The Nucleotide Weight Matrix

The concept of nucleotide weight matrix (NWM) descriptions were developed in the 1980s. A weight matrix uses the complete composition of nucleotides for each position of the alignment to achieve a more differentiated rating of a matching sequence. For example, a single position of an alignment of 12 sequences containing (T,T,T,T,T,T,T,A,A,A,C,C; each letter representing one sequence at this position) would be assigned T in the IUPAC consensus. A new sequence with a T at this position would be considered a match while an A at the same place would cause the sequence to be dismissed as no match. Even a simple nucleotide distribution matrix would assign a weighted score (in this case proportional to the percentage of the nucleotide) of 0.58 to the T and still 0.25 to an A. In this manner, weight scores represent

Table 1
Internet Accessible Methods to Detect Promoter Elements (Transcription Factor Binding Sites)

Program	*Availability*	*Comments*
MatInspector	http://www.genomatix.de/cgi-bin/matinspector/matsearch.pl	MatInspector matrix library (includes matinspector.pl TRANSFAC matrices)
SIGNAL SCAN	http://wwwbimas.dcrt.nih.gov/molbio/signal/	IUPAC consensus library based on TFD
MATRIX SEARCH	http://wwwbimas.dcrt.nih.gov/molbio/matrixs/	IMD matrix library (TRANSFAC+TFD)
TFSearch	http://pdap1.trc.rwcp.or.jp/research/db/TFSEARCH.html	TRANSFAC matrices
TESS	http://agave.humgen.upenn.edu/utess/tess/	TRANSFAC Matrices

the similarity of the tested sequence to all of the sequences in the alignment much better than IUPAC consensus sequences. Most weight matrix-based methods use additional weighting. This is achieved by comparison of the actual nucleotide distribution with random values (log odds methods) or by other statistical measures. (e.g., information content).

The widespread use of weight matrices was delayed for almost a decade because only a few special matrices had been defined. In 1995 two (overlapping) matrix libraries for TF sites were compiled for the first time and became widely available. They still represent the only libraries of their kind and are used in several bioinformatics tool sets. Some of the tools are available through the world-wide-web (WWW) (*see* Table 1).

Available methods for TF binding site definition and detection have been surveyed and an extensive comparison of their capabilities was also published (*see* Suggested Reading).

The Hidden Markov Model

Consider tossing coins. There are just two possibilities for the outcome: heads or tails. You may attempt to find out what the probability is that either side will show up during the next coin toss given the outcome of the last event. This would constitute a simple Markov chain. Now consider, there is somebody behind a curtain (so you cannot observe the actual action) tossing coins and telling you the outcome. Again you attempt to predict the outcome from the previous result. However, this time things are complicated by the fact that the person behind the curtain has several coins to choose from and will not tell you which one was tossed. You are only told the final result while you do not know the start condition (i.e., which coin was tossed). If the selection of the coins is a stochastic background process, which cannot be observed directly (hidden) then calculating the probabilities for the various outcome scenarios from the previous outcome involving such a hidden background process constitutes a Hidden Markov Model (**HMM**).

If the selection of actual sequences used for the alignment of binding sites is considered a stochastic background process, then the probability of the occurrence of

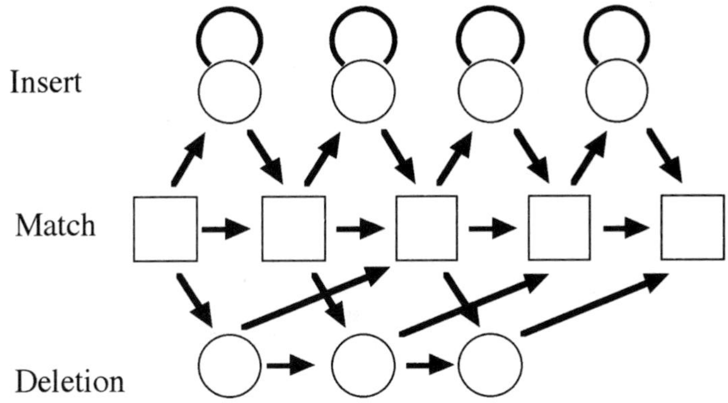

Fig. 7. Schematic architecture of a HMM describing the alignment of sequences with a length of five nucleotides. The square boxes indicate matching positions. The circles above the boxes indicate insertions and the circles below indicate deletions. Note that each sequence can feed through a different path in this HMM. The bold arrows represent the transitions and carry the parameters determining the relative probabilities for these transitions.

each of the four nucleotides at the next position of the alignment (of a new sequence to the existing alignment) can be calculated by a HMM. A schematic of a HMM is shown in Fig. 7.

As illustrated in Fig. 7., the parameters of the HMM are being trained from the existing alignment. In this manner any new candidate can be checked against the HMM describing a known binding site and quantitatively scored. HMMs have the advantage that they can account for almost all of the variability occurring in real sequences including the variable length of spacers within binding sites (not common but possible). Unfortunately, HMMs require a high number of parameters to describe binding sites with the required flexibility. Optimal training of all these parameters would require training sets of hundreds or even thousands of known binding sites for each factor. This is the sole reason why weight matrices still dominate the field of binding-site recognition although in theory HMMs are superior.

Frequent Problems with Practical Application of Search Programs

All search programs attempting to locate potential TF binding sites in genomic DNA face similar challenges. The most notorious, is incomplete data that prevents the generation of high quality descriptions by any means. For example, it is meaningless (but not impossible) to construct a weight matrix if only two examples for a specific binding site are available. Even a simpler IUPAC string will not be very useful. This is very close to the next most frequent problem, i.e., the *nonexistent description.* One must remember that if an IUPAC or matrix that describes a binding site is not available, it does not mean that a specific binding site for that protein does not exist.

Now, let us consider the case where there is a sufficiently well-defined weight matrix and this is used to scan sequences. Regardless of the matrix there will always be a disappointingly large number of matches in long sequences. Most of these matches will have no function in transcriptional control. The majority of the same matches may bind the cognate protein. The dilemma results not from the software, but from the confusion of two different topics. Transcriptional function only arises from TF binding sites located within the correct functional context. Accordingly, examination of the individual binding sites can never yield information about transcriptional function. This may seem trivial after the previous introduction. However, this incorrect expectation is very common among researchers and accounts for at least 95% of all concerns raised about TF binding site-detection programs.

The question then becomes, why are nonfunctional candidate sites identified that are obviously out of context? This can be addressed by considering that DNA sequences are used to encode many functions beyond transcription factor binding. For examples, the AP-1 binding site (IUPAC consensus TGASTCA) is several fold over-represented in coding regions as compared to promoter regions. This puzzling observation has a very simple explanation. This combination of nucleotides encodes a series of frequently used amino acids. Occurrence of the AP-1 binding site is therefore a consequence of the coding potential of these sequences and has absolutely nothing to do with transcriptional regulation. However, there is no rule without an exception. There are coding regions that contain functional AP-1 binding sites.

How to Define Unknown Transcription Factor Binding Sites

In light of an ever-growing number of full-scale genomic sequencing projects it is very important to discover new, previously unknown binding sites. However, the question becomes how can a weight matrix be created for an unknown binding site when it requires a set of known binding sites?

It is difficult to identify transcription factor binding sites in a large totally anonymous sequence. However, there are several, at least partial ways out of this dilemma. Some previous level of knowledge is required to use pattern definition algorithms to produce new patterns that can be used as IUPAC consensus sequences or nucleotide weight matrices. A very effective and relatively simple approach is experimental determination of the binding site spectrum for a given protein. This is called *SELEX* that is actually the in vitro selection of binding sequences from a large collection of random oligonucleotides. Only sequences with sufficient affinity to the protein will be bound. The rest can be washed away. Sequencing of the bound oligonucleotides reveals individual binding sequences that can be used to derive a nucleotide weight matrix. However, before that can be done an extensive purification of the protein has to be carried out.

Another experimentally oriented approach is the evaluation of expression array data. Here, large amounts of gene probes are arrayed onto a filter or glass chip. This array is then hybridized to RNA (via complementary DNA) isolated from cells that have undergone some treatment. The amount of signal over each spot indicates the approximate level of RNA present for this gene. By comparing such values with a parallel experiment, e.g., with untreated cells, it is possible to detect which genes changed their RNA levels under treatment. Is is then possible to cluster genes according to their expression patterns. Analyzing promoter regions from the corresponding genes with a very similar expression pattern can be used to identify common patterns, many of which are transcription factor binding sites. Brazma, et al. (1998) have demonstrated this approach successfully in the yeast system. Unfortunately, promoters in higher eukaryotes, like mammals, are not as readily available as in yeast, but this will change in the near future. Regardless of the means by which promoter sequences are acquired, the sequences need to be analyzed for unknown motifs hidden in the set. There are many programs available to define the patterns in a set of sequences. The most popular methods are the Gibb's sampler reviewed in expectation maximization algorithms. A variety of other approaches are reviewed in Chapter 29 (*see* Suggested Reading).

Some Rules of Thumb for Application

It is most important to clearly define which kind of analysis makes sense and which does not. In contrast, the particular algorithm being used to detect TF binding sites is not as important. The rules of application are outlined below:

1. The first criterion is the length of the sequences to be analyzed. A binding site that appears to be a significant finding in a hundred base pairs may turn out to be matching every few hundred base pairs even in long random sequences. The smaller region selected for analysis (this can be localized, e.g., by experimental results or annotation), the more informative are results from TF binding site analysis.
2. Another important factor is the threshold to be used for the analysis. A very high threshold will most likely prevent the occurrence of false matches (those not binding to the protein). However, it will also suppress some true matches that just do not reach the high threshold. Optimal binding may not be the biological optimum, as dissociation must also occur at some time.
3. Using a low threshold will faithfully record all positive matches but will also collect a huge number of false matches. There are two solutions to this problem. First , observe the limitations of the sequence length: If it is not possible to restrict the length of the sequence to less than one kb then in most cases a low threshold will return substantially more data than is useful. One could look for binding sites within a larger context (at least another binding site near by), which allows for both lower thresholds as well as analysis of larger sequences.
4. If it is necessary to identify individual binding sites with low thresholds, sequence length should be 500 bp or less. It is worthwhile to concentrate one's efforts on meeting such conditions before carrying out the actual analysis for TF binding sites. Otherwise the results are usually not interpretable and the whole endeavor becomes a waste of time.

Nevertheless, even when observing the aforementioned conditions, results often contain more matches than desired. Evaluation of the matches is then required to select the most likely candidates for further analyses. Match scores are of limited use since scores do not necessarily reflect the binding affinities correctly and *weak* binding sites may be perfectly suitable within the correct context. Biological evidence should be used to evaluate the matches. Examples are correlation with other features (e.g., TSS, the closer the more likely involved in the promoter), conserved occurrence of sites in orthologous sequences in other species (indicative of functional conservation), or correlation with another binding site in promoters of coexpressed genes (indicative of promoter modules).

An example would be the development of a promoter model describing the histone H1 genes. In order to generate this model the following strategy was used: collecting suitable promoters for a set of histone H1 genes. We used the homology group 6.1.2.1.1 from the Eukeryotic Promoter Database (EPD) yielding the promoter sequences as seen in Table 2.

Table 2
Promoter Sequences from EPD Homology Group 6.1.2.1.1.

EPD AC	*EMBL AC (ID)*	*Description*
EP27002	M17019 (GGH1PL)	Gg histone H1-a 11L
EP27003	M17020 (GGH1PR)	Gg histone H1-a` 11R
EP27004	M17021 (GGH103)	Gg histone H1-b 03
EP27005	M17018 (GGH1LH)	Gg histone H1-c .10
EP07047	U18782 (GG18782)	Gg histone H1-c` 01
	J00863 (GGH11A1)	
EP33001	X06128 (APHISH1)	Cm histone H1
EP11065	X01752 (GGHISH1)	Gg histone H1-d 02
EP48019	Y12292 (MMHISTH14)	Mm histone H1-E
	L26163 (MMH1EH2B)	

Table 3
H1t and H1a Alignment Carried Out by CLUSTAL with Default Parameters

```
The following sequences are too divergent to be aligned:
hs_h1a and hs_h1t (distance 1.637)
(All distances should be between 0.0 and 1.0)
This may not be fatal but you have been warned!

hs_h1t        --GAAAATC-GAGGGCTTTCTCGAATAGTTTTGGCATCCAGGGT-CATTTTTCATTAAAA
hs_h1a        ATGAAAAGCTGAAGGGATTTTTTAAAATATCTTTCATCAATTGCACAAGATTCTTGAAAA
                ***** * ** **  ** *   ** *  * *  **** *  *  **   *** * ****

hs_h1t        -AGAGAAAAGTCATGTCAAATATGAATTTCCGCAGATTATTCAGCACTAGACCCTGGGAG
hs_h1a        CACAAACAAGT-ATGTGAACCTGGAGGCTGTTTTCCTCCTTTGGAGCTTCAAAGTGCCAA
               * * * **** **** **     **    *        *  **  *  **  *   **  *

hs_h1t        ATTCTGTAAAGAGGGGTTTTGT-TATACTCAACTTTTCCGGGTAAAACAAACACAAAT--
hs_h1a        ATTCTGTACCATTGTTTTAAGCATTTAATCAAATTTTGAGGACTAA-CAAACACAATTTG
              ********       *  **  *  * ** **** ****  **   ** ********* *

hs_h1t        --ACTCCTCCTCCAAGG-GGCGG-----GGGCGGTGCCTAGGT-GATGCACCAATCACAG
hs_h1a        GGAGTCCAACGCGAGCGCGGCGGCCAGAGGGCGGTGGATTGGACGCTCCACCAATCACAG
                * ***  * * *  * *****     ********  * **  * * ************

hs_h1t        CGC-GCCCTACCCTATATAAGGCCCCGAGGCCGCCCGGGTGTTTCATGCTTTTCGCTGGT
hs_h1a        GGCAGCGCCGGCTTATATAAG--CCCGGGCCCGAGCATAGCAGCAACGCAAAAC-CTGCT
               ** ** *   * ********  **** * ***   *          * **   * *** *

hs_h1t        TATTACATCTTGCGTTTCT-CTGTTGTTATGTCTGAAACCGTGCCTGCAGCTTCTGCCAG
hs_h1a        CTTTAGATTTCGAGCTTATTCTCTTCTAGCAGTTTCTTGCCACCATGNNNNNNNNNNNNN
                *** ** * * * ** * ** ** *       *      *   * **

hs_h1t        TGCTGGTGTAGCCGCTATGGAGAAAC
hs_h1a        NNNNNNNNNNNNNNNNNNNNNNNNNN
```

The term *homology group* is a bit misleading as the sequences only share sequence similarity around the TSS (by defintion position 500 in EPD promoters). This can be illustrated by an alignment of the best conserved part of two human histone H1 promoters, H1t and H1a (carried out by CLUSTAL with default parameters) as shown in Table 3.

Fig. 8. Promoter Model.

Table 4
Transcription Elements Conserved in Histone H1 Promoters

Element	*Name*	*Strand*	*Parameters*	*Dist. to next element*
Matrix	V$E2FF	(+/–)	Min. core sim.: 0.750 Min. matrix sim.: optimized-0.07	0 to 75 bp
Matrix	V$HEPA	(–)	Min. core sim.: 0.800 Min. matrix sim.: optimized-0.07	10 to 100 bp
Matrix	V$SP1F	(+)	Min. core sim.: 0.750 Min. matrix sim.: 0.800	5 to 50 bp
Matrix	V$PCAT/ CAAT_01	(+)	Min. core sim.: 0.800 Min. matrix sim.: 0.860	20 to 30 bp
Matrix	V$TBPF	(+)	Min. core sim.: 0.800 Min. matrix sim.: 0.890	
			Total length: 35 – 255 bp	

As clearly evident from the alignment there is some limited similarity that may be insufficient for recognition of the promoters. However, as pointed out, promoter function is encoded by a particular arrangement of transcription elements, in this case transcription factor binding sites. The next step is to format all of these promoter sequences for use as a training set, into one FASTA file and to analyze this file with GEMS Launcher (Genomatix software GmbH, Munich, Germany) for a conserved framework of binding sites.

See companion CD for color Fig. 8

This analysis results in a closely related framework, which can be summarized into the promoter model (*see* Fig. 8). This model consists of five binding sites in a linear arrangement with the characteristics described in Table 4.

It is interesting to note that E2F is known to be involved in cell-cycle regulation while the presence of a hepatic factor (HEPA) does not make immediate sense. Subsequently, one evaluates the specificity of the new model. For that purpose database searches were carried out using the EMBL database (*see Table 5*)

The complete results included 59 matches. The list shows the 30 histone gene promoters found by the model in one search. Most of the matches that were not shown were located in unannotated sequences. This shows that the model is quite specific (about 1 match every 12 million basepairs) and indeed locates new histone genes that were not in the training set (indicating that specificity is not just a trivial consequence of overtraining). As a negative control we purged EPD for histone promoters, result-

Table 5
Sequences Matched by Histone Promoter Model

Sequence Identifier [acc. #]	*Sequence Name*
MMHISH1T [M97756]	Macaca mulatta histone H1t gene
APHISH1 [X06128]	Duck histone H1 gene
GG18782 [U18782]	Gallus gallus histone H1 gene
GGH103 [M17021]	Chicken H1 histone gene lambda-Ch03 H1
GGH11A1 [J00863]	Chicken histone H1 gene
GGH1LH [M17018]	Chicken H1 histone gene lambda-H1.10
GGH1PL [M17019]	Chicken H1 histone gene pCH11.5E left
GGH1PR [M17020]	Chicken H1 histone gene pCH11.5E right
GGHISH1 [X01752]	Chicken histone H1 gene
-MM06232 [U06232]	Mus musculus CD-1 histone H1t (H1t) gene
MMH1EH2B [L26163]	Mouse histone H1e gene
-MMH1T [X72805]	M.musculus gene for testicular histone H1
-MMH1X [L26164]	Mouse histone H1
MMHIS1 [J03482]	Mouse histone H1 gene
-MMHIST431 [Y12290]	M.musculus genes encoding histone H1.1
-MMHISTA [L28753]	Mus musculus histone H1t (Hist) gene
MMHISTH12 [Y12291]	M.musculus genes encoding histone H1.2
MMHISTH14 [Y12292]	M.musculus genes encoding histone H1.4
MMU62922 [U62922]	Mus musculus histone H1b gene
RNH1D2B [X67320]	R.norvegicus genes for H1d-histone
RNH1TH4T [M28409]	Rat testis-specific histone H1t
RNHIS1D [M31229]	Rat histone H1d gene
RNHIS1TP [M13170]	Rat testis-specific H1 histone variant H1t gene
HS193B12 [Z98744]	Human histone H1.5 gene
HSH1FNC1 [X06757]	Human H1 histone gene FNC16 promoter region
HSH1T [M60094]	Human testicular H1 histone (H1) gene
HSHISAC [M60748]	Human histone H1 (H1F4) gene
HSHISH1T [M97755]	Human histone H1T gene
HSHISTN15 [X83509]	H.sapiens gene for histone H1.5.
HSU91328 [U91328]	Human histone 2A-like protein gene

ing in a total of 808,200 bp of 1347 non-histone H1 but functional promoters. The model had no false positive matches in this control set further supporting the extraordinary specificity.

Summary

Transcription factor binding sites are important elements in transcriptional control. TF binding sites per se only have the function of binding their cognate protein(s). The function in transcription control only arises within the appropriate context. TF binding sites represent a collection of variable sequences and are currently best described by nucleotide weight matrices. Since potential TF binding sites are not restricted to regulatory DNA regions, matches to search programs are best evaluated by looking at the functional context of candidates.

Glossary and Abbreviations

For a complete list of terms, *see* Website: http://www.genomatix.de/genomics_tutorials/basic_terms/basic_terms.html.

Enhancer DNA regions which are usually rich in *transcription factor binding sites* and/or repeats. They enhance transcription of the responsive *promoter* independent of orientation and position.

Expression Array Assessment of the expression of a gene in various cells/tissues or under specific conditions (stimulation by signals, development or differentiation) using *DNA-chips* and labeled hybridization probes.

Gene An entity of a genome consisting of sequences defining the gene product (RNA or protein) and additional sequences directing expression of the gene (regulatory sequences for transcriptional and post-transcriptional control). The human genome contains about 60,000 ± 30,000 genes.

Promoters DNA regions which are rich in *transcription factor binding sites* similar to enhancers, but also contain elements that allow specific initiation of transcription (core promoter).

Transcription Factor Binding Site Short stretches of DNA, sufficiently conserved to allow specific recognition by the corresponding transcription factor.

Suggested Readings

The Promoter

Sauer, F. and Tjian, R. (1997) Mechanisms of transcriptional activation: Differences and similarities between yeast, Drosophila, and man, Curr. Op. Gen. Dev. 7, 176–181.

Stamatoyannopoulos, J. A., Clegg, C. H., and Li, Q. (1997) Sheltering of gamma-globin expression from position effects requires both an upstream locus control region and a regulatory element 3' to the (A)gamma-globin gene, Mol. Cell. Biol. 17, 240–247.

The Characteristics of TF Binding Sites

Frech, K., Herrmann, G., and Werner, T. (1993) Computer-Assisted prediction, classification, and delimitation of protein binding sites in nucleic acids, Nucleic Acids Res. 21, 1655–1664.

Quandt, K., Frech, K., Karas, H., Wingender, E., and Werner, T. (1995) Matlnd and Matlnspector: New fast and versatile tools for detection of consensus matches in nucleotide sequence data, Nucleic Acids Res. 23, 4878–4884.

Risse, G., Jooss, K., Neuberg, M., Brüller, H.-J., Müller, R. (1989) Asymmetrical recognition of the palindromic AP1 binding site (TRE) by Fos protein complexes, EMBO J. 8, 3825–3832.

The Nucleotide Weight Matrix

Bucher, P. (1990) Weight matrix description of four eukaryotic RNA polymerase II promoter elements derived from 502 unrelated promoter sequences, J. Mol. Biol. 212, 563–578.

Chen, Q. K., Hertz, G. Z., and Stormo, G. D. (1995) Matrix Search 1.0: A computer program that scans DNA sequences for transcriptional elements using a database of weight matrices, Comp. Appl. Biosci. 11, 563–566.

Frech, K., Quandt, K., and Werner, T. (1997) Finding protein-binding sites in DNA sequences: The next generation, Trends Biochem. Sci. 22, 103–104.

Frech, K., Quandt, K., and Werner, T. (1997) Software for the analysis of DNA sequence elements of transcription, Comp. Appl. Biosci. 13, 89–97.

Ghosh, D. (1993) Status of the transcription factors database (TFD), Nucleic Acids Res. 21, 3117–3118.

Heinemeyer ,T., Wingender, E., Reuter, I., Hermjakob, H., Kel, A.E., Kel, O. V., et al. (1998) Databases on transcriptional regulation: TRANSFAC, TRRD and COMPEL, Nucleic Acids Res. 26, 362–367.

Naitou, M., Hagiwara, H., Hanaoka, F., Eki, T., and Murakami, Y. (1997) Expression profiles of transcripts from 126 open reading frames in the entire chromosome VI of Saccharomyces cerevisiae by systematic northern analyses, Yeast 13, 1275–1290.

Nagase, T., Ishikawa, K., Miyajima, N., Tanaka, A., Kotani, H., Nomura, N., and Ohara, O. (1998) Prediction of the coding sequences of unidentified human genes. IX. The complete sequences of 100 new cDNA clones from brain, which can code for large proteins in vitro, DNA Res. 5, 31–39.

Quandt, K., Frech, K., Karas, H., Wingender, E., and Werner, T. (1995) Matlnd and Matlnspector: New fast and versatile tools for detection of consensus matches in nucleotide sequence data, Nucleic Acids Res. 23, 4878–4884.

Stormo, G. D. and Hartzell, III, G. W. (1989) Identifying protein-binding sites from unaligned DNA fragments, Proc. Natl. Acad. Sci. USA 86, 1183–1187.

How to Define Unknown Transcription Factor Binding Sites

Brazma, A., Jonassen, I., Vilo, J., and Ukkonen, E. (1998) Predicting gene regulatory elements in silico on a genomic scale. Genome Res. 8, 1202–1215.

Cardon, L. R. and Stormo, G. D. (1992). Expectation maximization algorithm for identifying protein-binding sites with variable lengths from unaligned DNA fragments, J. Mol. Biol. 223, 159–170.

Neuwald, A. F., Liu, J. S., and Lawrence, C. E. (1995). Gibbs motif sampling: Detection of bacterial outer membrane protein repeats, Prot. Sci. 4, 1618–1632.

Scherf, M., Klingenhoff, A., and Werner, T. (2000) Highly specific localization of promoter regions in large genomic sequences by PromoterInspector: A Novel Context Analysis Approach, J. Mol. Biol. 297, 599–606.

Wolfertstetter, F., Frech, K., Herrmann, G., and Werner, T. (1996) Identification of functional elements in unaligned nucleic acid sequences by a novel tuple search algorithm, Comp. Appl. Biosci. 12, 71–80.

31 An Introduction to Multiple Sequence Alignment and Analysis

Steven M. Thompson

Introduction

Given the nucleotide or amino acid sequence of a biological molecule, what do we know about that molecule? We can find biologically relevant information in sequences by searching for particular patterns that may reflect some function of the molecule. These can be catalogued motifs and domains, secondary structure predictions, physical attributes such as hydrophobicity, or even the content of DNA itself as in some of the gene-finding techniques. What about comparisons with other sequences? Can we learn about one molecule by comparing it to another? Yes, naturally we can; inference through similarity is fundamental to all the biological sciences. We can learn a tremendous amount by comparing our sequence against others.

The comparative method is a cornerstone of the biological sciences. Multiple sequence alignment is the comparative method on a molecular scale and is a vital prerequisite to some of the most powerful biocomputing techniques available. Many methods are available for aligning more than two sequences. Understanding the algorithms and the program parameters of each is the only way to rationally know what is appropriate. Several methods are even available on the Internet over www servers. Knowing and staying well within the limitations of this route will avert much frustration. However, realizing these limitations and being able to do something about them are very different things.

The power and sensitivity of sequence based computational methods dramatically increases with the addition of more data. More data yields stronger analyses if carefully carried out! Otherwise, it can confound the issue. The patterns of conservation become clearer by comparing the conserved portions of sequences among a larger and larger dataset. As in pairwise comparisons and database searching, those areas most resistant to change are functionally the most important to the molecule. The basic assumption is that those portions of sequence of crucial functional value are most constrained against evolutionary change. They will not tolerate many mutations. Not that mutations do not occur in these portions, just that most mutations in the region are lethal and thus not observed. Other areas of sequence are able to drift more readily being less subject to evolutionary pressure. Therefore, sequences become a mosaic of quickly and slowly changing regions over evolutionary time. We can use those constrained portions as *anchors* to create a sequence alignment allowing comparison. It is easy to see that two sequences are aligned when they have identical symbols at identical positions, but what happens when symbols are not identical or the sequences are not the same length? How can we know that the most similar portions of the sequences are aligned, when is an alignment optimal and does optimal mean biologically correct? Part of the solution is the dynamic programming algorithm.

Dynamic Programming

Let's review pairwise dynamic programming. Follow the example below. We will consider matching symbols to be worth one point, nonmatching symbols to be worth zero points, and we will use a very simple gap-penalty function. We will penalize the scoring scheme by subtracting one point for every gap inserted unless they are at the beginning or end of the sequence. In other words, end gaps will not be penalized, i.e., both sequences do not have to begin or end at the same point in the alignment. This zero penalty end-weighting scheme is the default for most alignment programs, but can often be changed with a program option. However, the gap function described here and used in the example below is a much simpler gap penalty function than used in most alignment programs. Normally an *affine*, i.e., a linear, function is used; the standard $y = mx + b$ equation:

total penalty = gap opening penalty + [(length of gap) · (gap extension penalty)]

To execute most alignment programs with this simple DNA gap penalty, you have to designate a gap *creation* or *opening* penalty of zero and a gap *extension* penalty of whatever counts in that particular program as an identical base match for DNA sequences.

As we will see, the oversimplified gap function used in this example does have a rather unusual effect. The solution occurs in two stages. The first begins very much like a dot matrix method while the second is totally different. A simple representation is used here. Instead of calculating the *score matrix* on the fly as you proceed through the graph, as is often done in illustrations of dynamic programming, I like to completely fill in an original *match matrix* first, and then add points to those positions that produce favorable alignments next. Points are added based on a "*looking back over-your-left-shoulder*" algorithm rule where the only allowable trace-back is diagonally behind and above. Follow the example in Table 1.

There will probably be more than one best path through the matrix. This time, starting at the top and working down as we did, then tracing back, I found two optimum alignments:

```
cTATAtAagg          cTATAtAagg
|  |||||            |   ||||
cg.TAtAaT.          cgT.AtAaT.
```

Each of these solutions yields a trace-back total score of 22. This is the number optimized by the algorithm, not any type of a similarity or identity score! Even though one of these alignments has six exact matches and the other has five, they are both optimal according to the rather strange gap-penalty criteria in which we solved the algorithm. Do you have any ideas about how others could be discovered? Often if you reverse the solution of the entire dynamic programming process, other solutions are found! In other words, reverse the sequences in software programs to see alternative alignments. Some programs also offer a highroad/lowroad option to help explore this solution space. To summarize, an optimal pairwise alignment is defined as an arrangement of two sequences, the first of length i and the second of length j, such that:

Table 1
Dynamic Programming Example[a]

a. First complete a match matrix using one point for matching and zero points for mismatching between bases:

	c	*T*	*A*	*T*	*A*	*t*	*A*	*a*	*g*	*g*
c	1	0	0	0	0	0	0	0	0	0
g	0	0	0	0	0	0	0	0	1	1
T	0	1	0	1	0	1	0	0	0	0
A	0	0	1	0	1	0	1	1	0	0
t	0	1	0	1	0	1	0	0	0	0
A	0	0	1	0	1	0	1	1	0	0
a	0	0	1	0	1	0	1	1	0	0
T	0	1	0	1	0	1	0	0	0	0

b. Now add and subtract points based on the best path through the matrix, working diagonally, left to right and top to bottom. When you have to jump a box to make the path, subtract one point per box jumped, except at the beginning or end of the alignment. Fill in all additions and subtractions and calculate the sums and differences as you go:

	c	*T*	*A*	*T*	*A*	*t*	*A*	*a*	*g*	*g*
c	1	0	0	0	0	0	0	0	0	0
g	0	0+1=1	0+1–1=0	0+0–0=0	0+0–0=0	0+0–0=0	0+0–0=0	0+0–0=0	1+0–0=1	1+0=1
T	0	1+1–1=1	0+1=1	1+1–1=1	0+0–0=0	1+0–0=1	0+0–0=0	0+0–0=0	0+0–0=0	0+1–0=1
A	0	0+0–0=0	1+1=2	0+1=1	1+1=2	0+1–1=0	1+1=2	1+1–1=1	0+0–0=0	0+0–0=0
t	0	1+0–0=1	0+1–1=0	1+2=3	0+1=1	1+2=3	0+2–1=1	0+2=2	0+1=1	0+0–0=0
A	0	0+0–0=0	1+1=2	0+2–1=1	1+3=4	0+3–1=2	1+3=4	1+3–1=3	0+2=2	0+1=1
a	0	0+0–0=0	1+0–0=1	0+2=2	1+3–1=3	0+4=4	1+4–1=4	1+4=5	0+3=3	0+2=2
T	0	1+0–0=1	0+0–0=0	1+1=2	0+2=2	1+3=4	0+4=4	0+4=4	0+5=5	0+5–1=4

c. Clean up the score matrix next. I'll only show the totals in each cell here:

	c	*T*	*A*	*T*	*A*	*t*	*A*	*a*	*g*	*g*
c	1	0	0	0	0	0	0	0	0	0
g	0	1	0	0	0	0	0	0	1	1
T	0	1	1	1	0	1	0	0	0	1
A	0	0	2	1	2	0	2	1	0	0
t	0	1	0	3	1	3	1	2	1	0
A	0	0	2	1	4	2	4	3	2	1
a	0	0	1	2	3	4	4	5	3	2
T	0	1	0	2	2	4	4	4	5	4

d. Finally, convert the score matrix into a trace-back path graph by picking the bottom-most, furthest right and highest scoring coordinates. Then choose the highest scoring trace-back route, to connect them all the way back to the beginning using the same 'over-your-left-shoulder' rule:

	c	*T*	*A*	*T*	*A*	*t*	*A*	*a*	*g*	*g*
c	①	0	0	0	0	0	0	0	0	0
g	0	①	0	0	0	0	0	0	1	1
T	0	1	①	①	0	1	0	0	0	1
A	0	0	2	1	②	0	2	1	0	0
t	0	1	0	3	1	③	1	2	1	0
A	0	0	2	1	4	2	④	3	2	1
a	0	0	1	2	3	4	4	⑤	3	2
T	0	1	0	2	2	4	4	4	⑤	4

[a]This example uses two randomly generated sequences that happen to fit the TATA consensus regions of eukaryotes and prokaryotes. The most conserved bases within the consensus are capitalized. The eukaryote promoter sequence is along the X-axis, the prokaryote along the Y-axis. Circled digits indicate trace-back route.

1. You maximize the number of matching symbols between 1 and 2;
2. You minimize the number of gaps within 1 and 2; and
3. You minimize the number of mismatched symbols between 1 and 2.

Therefore, the actual solution can be represented by:

$$S_{ij} = s_{ij} + \max \left\{ \begin{array}{ll} S_{i-1\ j-1} & \text{or} \\ \max S_{i-x\ j-1} + w_{x-1} & \text{or} \\ 2 < x < i & \\ \max S_{i-1\ j-y} + w_{y-1} & \text{or} \\ 2 < y < i & \end{array} \right\}$$

where S_{ij} is the score for the alignment ending at i in sequence 1 and j in sequence 2,
s_{ij} is the score for aligning i with j,
w_x is the score for making a x long gap in sequence 1,
w_y is the score for making a y long gap in sequence 2,

allowing gaps to be any length in either sequence.

Just because dynamic programming guarantees an optimal alignment, it is not necessarily the only optimal alignment. Furthermore, the optimal alignment is not necessarily the correct or biologically relevant alignment! As always, question the results of any computerized solution based on what you know about the biology of the system. The above example illustrates the Needleman and Wunsch (1970) global solution. Later refinements, like Smith and Waterman (1981), demonstrate how dynamic programming could also be used to find optimal local alignments. Programs use the following two means to solve dynamic programming using local alignments.

1. An identity match matrix that uses negative numbers for mismatches is incorporated. Therefore, bad paths quickly become very bad. This leads to a trace-back path matrix with many alternative paths, most of which do not extend the full length of the graph.
2. The best trace-back within the graph is chosen. This does not have to begin or end at the edges of the graph; it is looking for the best segment of the alignment!

Scoring Matrices

What about protein sequences, conservative replacements and similarities, as opposed to identities? This is definitely an additional complication to consider. Certain amino acids are very much alike, structurally, chemically, and genetically. How can we take advantage of the similarity of amino acids in our alignments? Margaret Dayhoff (1979) unambiguously aligned closely related protein datasets with no more than 15% difference available at that point in time. She noticed that certain residues, if they mutate at all, are prone to change into certain other residues. These propensities for change fell into the same categories that chemists had known for years, those chemical and structural classes, conserved through the evolutionary constraints of natural selection. However, Dayhoff's empirical observation quantified these changes. Based on the multiple sequence alignments that revealed a level of divergence between the sequences considered, the assumption that estimated mutation rates in closely related proteins can be extrapolated to more distant relationships was born. Using matrix and logarithmic mathematics that smooth out the statistics of the system,

Table 2
BLOSUM62 Scoring Matrix

	A	B	C	D	E	F	G	H	I	K	L	M	N	P	Q	R	S	T	V	W	X	Y	Z
A	4	–2	0	–2	–1	–2	0	–2	–1	–1	–1	–1	–2	–1	–1	–1	1	0	0	–3	–1	–2	–1
B	–2	6	–3	6	2	–3	–1	–1	–3	–1	–4	–3	1	–1	0	–2	0	–1	–3	–4	–1	–3	2
C	0	–3	9	–3	–4	–2	–3	–3	–1	–3	–1	–1	–3	–3	–3	–3	–1	–1	–1	–2	–1	–2	–4
D	–2	6	–3	6	2	–3	–1	–1	–3	–1	–4	–3	1	–1	0	–2	0	–1	–3	–4	–1	–3	2
E	–1	2	–4	2	5	–3	–2	0	–3	1	–3	–2	0	–1	2	0	0	–1	–2	–3	–1	–2	5
F	–2	–3	–2	–3	–3	6	–3	–1	0	–3	0	0	–3	–4	–3	–3	–2	–2	–1	1	–1	3	–3
G	0	–1	–3	–1	–2	–3	6	–2	–4	–2	–4	–3	0	–2	–2	–2	0	–2	–3	–2	–1	–3	–2
H	–2	–1	–3	–1	0	–1	–2	8	–3	–1	–3	–2	1	–2	0	0	–1	–2	–3	–2	–1	2	0
I	–1	–3	–1	–3	–3	0	–4	–3	4	–3	2	1	–3	–3	–3	–3	–2	–1	3	–3	–1	–1	–3
K	–1	–1	–3	–1	1	–3	–2	–1	–3	5	–2	–1	0	–1	1	2	0	–1	–2	–3	–1	–2	1
L	–1	–4	–1	–4	–3	0	–4	–3	2	–2	4	2	–3	–3	–2	–2	–2	–1	1	–2	–1	–1	–3
M	–1	–3	–1	–3	–2	0	–3	–2	1	–1	2	5	–2	–2	0	–1	–1	–1	1	–1	–1	–1	–2
N	–2	1	–3	1	0	–3	0	1	–3	0	–3	–2	6	–2	0	0	1	0	–3	–4	–1	–2	0
P	–1	–1	–3	–1	–1	–4	–2	–2	–3	–1	–3	–2	–2	7	–1	–2	–1	–1	–2	–4	–1	–3	–1
Q	–1	0	–3	0	2	–3	–2	0	–3	1	–2	0	0	–1	5	1	0	–1	–2	–2	–1	–1	2
R	–1	–2	–3	–2	0	–3	–2	0	–3	2	–2	–1	0	–2	1	5	–1	–1	–3	–3	–1	–2	0
S	1	0	–1	0	0	–2	0	–1	–2	0	–2	–1	1	–1	0	–1	4	1	–2	–3	–1	–2	0
T	0	–1	–1	–1	–1	–2	–2	–2	–1	–1	–1	–1	0	–1	–1	–1	1	5	0	–2	–1	–2	–1
V	0	–3	–1	–3	–2	–1	–3	–3	3	–2	1	1	–3	–2	–2	–3	–2	0	4	–3	–1	–1	–2
W	–3	–4	–2	–4	–3	1	–2	–2	–3	–3	–2	–1	–4	–4	–2	–3	–3	–2	–3	11	–1	2	–3
X	–1	–1	–1	–1	–1	–1	–1	–1	–1	–1	–1	–1	–1	–1	–1	–1	–1	–1	–1	–1	–1	–1	–1
Y	–2	–3	–2	–3	–2	3	–3	2	–1	–2	–1	–1	–2	–3	–1	–2	–2	–2	–1	2	–1	7	–2
Z	–1	2	–4	2	5	–3	–2	0	–3	1	–3	–2	0	–1	2	0	0	–1	–2	–3	–1	–2	5

[a]Values whose magnitude is ≥ ± 4 are drawn in outline characters to make them easier to recognize. Notice that positive values for identity range from 4 to 11 and negative values for those substitutions that rarely occur are as low as –4. The most conserved residue is tryptophan with an identity score of 11; cysteine is next, with a score of 9; histidine, 8; both proline and tyrosine have scores of 7. The hydrophobic substitutions: isoleucine, leucine, valine, and to a lesser extent, methionine, easily swap places.

she was able to empirically specify the relative probabilities that different residues mutate into other residues through evolutionary history. This is the basis of the famous PAM (corrupted acronym of accepted point mutation) 250 (meaning that the matrix has been multiplied by itself 250 times) log odds matrix. Since Dayhoff's time, other biomathematicians, (*see* Henikoff and Henikoff's BLOSUM series of tables) have created newer matrices with more or less success than Dayhoff. Dayhoff's original PAM 250 table remains a classic as historically the most widely used.

Collectively these types of tables are known as symbol comparison tables, log odds matrices, or scoring matrices and they are fundamental to all sequence comparison techniques. The standard default scoring matrix for many protein similarity comparison programs is now the BLOSUM62 table. It appears in Table 2.

Rather than using the one/zero match function shown in the simple dynamic programming used for nucleic acids, protein sequence alignments use the match function provided by a scoring matrix. The concept of similarity becomes very important with some amino acids being *more similar* than others! A common misnomer in this area is the concept of homology vs similarity: there is a huge difference! Similarity is merely a statistical parameter that describes how two sequences, or portions of them, are alike according to some set scoring criteria. It can be normalized to ascertain statistical significance as seen in the database searching methods. Homology, in contrast and by definition, implies an evolutionary relationship. You need to be able to demonstrate lineage between the organisms or genes of interest in order to claim homology or provide experimental evidence, e.g., morphological, genetic, or fossil, that corroborates your assertion. The term *percent homology* does not exist; something is either homologous or it is not. The famous molecular evolutionist Walter Fitch likes to relate the joke, "homology is like pregnancy; you can't be 45% pregnant, just like something can't be 45% homologous. You either are or you are not." Do not make the all too commonly made mistake of calling any sequence similarity homology. Highly significant similarity can be used to argue homology, but never the other way around.

Multiple Sequence Dynamic Programming

As seen in pairwise dynamic programming, a *brute force* approach, looking at every possible position by sliding one sequence along every other sequence, is just not practical for alignment. Even without considering the introduction of gaps, the computation required to compare all possible alignments between just two sequences requires time proportional to the product of the lengths of the two sequences. Therefore, if the two sequences are approx the same length (N), this is a N^2 problem. To include gaps, the calculation would be repeated 2N times to examine the possibility of gaps at each position within the sequences. This is now a $N4^N$ problem! Dynamic programming reduces the problem to N^2.

How do you work with more than just two sequences at a time? You could painstakingly manually align all your sequences using some type of editor, and many people do that, but an automated solution is desirable, at least as a starting point to manual alignment. However, solving the dynamic programming algorithm for more than just two sequences rapidly becomes intractable. Dynamic programming's complexity, and hence its computational requirements, increases exponentially with the number of sequences in the dataset being compared [complexity = $(\text{sequence length})^{\text{number of sequences}}$]. Mathematically this is an N-dimensional matrix, quite complex indeed. As we have seen, pairwise dynamic programming solves a two-dimensional matrix and the complexity of the solution is equal to the length of the longest sequence squared. A three-member standard dynamic programming sequence comparison would be a matrix with three axes, the length of the longest sequence cubed, and so forth. You can at least draw a three-dimensional matrix, but more than that becomes difficult, if not impossible, to even visualize. It quickly boggles the mind.

Several different heuristics have been employed over the years to simplify the complexity of the problem. One program, MSA, attempts to globally solve the N-dimensional matrix equation using a bounding box trick. However, the algorithm's complexity precludes its use in most situations, except with very small datasets. One way to globally solve the algorithm and yet reduce its complexity is to restrict the search space to only the most conserved *local* portions of all the sequences involved. This approach is used by the program PIMA. MSA and PIMA are both available through the Internet.

How the Algorithm Works

The most common implementations of automated multiple alignment modify dynamic programming by establishing a pairwise order in which to build the alignment. This modification is known as pairwise, progressive dynamic programming. Originally attributed to Feng and Doolittle (1987), this variation of the dynamic programming algorithm generates a global alignment, but restricts its search space at any one time to a local neighborhood of the full length of only two sequences. Consider a group of sequences. First, all pairs are compared to each other, using normal dynamic programming. This establishes an order for the set, most to least similar. Similarly, subgroups are clustered together. Then, take the top two most similar sequences and align them using normal dynamic programming. Now create a consensus of the two and align that consensus to the third sequence using standard dynamic programming. Now create a consensus of the first three sequences and align that to the forth most similar. This process continues until it has worked its way through all sequences and/or sets of clusters. The pairwise, progressive solution is implemented in several programs including Des Higgins' and Julie Thompson's Clustal (1994) (a copy of which is available on this volume's accompanying CD) and the GCG PileUp program.

See companion CD

As seen with pairwise alignments and sequence database similarity searching, all of this is much easier with protein sequences vs nucleotide sequences. Twenty symbols are easier to align then only four; the signal-to-noise ratio is far better. Furthermore, the concept of similarity applies to amino acids but generally not to nucleotides. If at all possible, multiple sequence alignment should always be carried out at the protein level. Therefore, translate nucleotide sequences to their protein counterparts if you are aligning coding sequences before performing multiple sequence alignment. The process is much more difficult if you are forced to align nucleotides because the region does not code for a protein. Automated methods may be able to provide a starting point, but there is no guarantee that the alignment will be biologically correct. The resulting alignment will probably require extensive editing, if it works at all. Success will largely depend on the similarity of the nucleotide dataset.

One liability of the global progressive pairwise methods is they are entirely dependent on the order in which the sequences are aligned. Fortunately, ordering them from most similar to least similar usually makes biological sense and works very well. However, the techniques are very sensitive to the substitution matrix and specified gap penalties. Programs that allow *fine-tuning* areas of an alignment by re-alignment with different scoring matrices and/or gap penalties can be extremely helpful. However, any automated multiple sequence alignment program should be thought of as only a tool to offer a starting alignment that can be improved upon, not the *end-all-to-meet-all* solution, guaranteed to provide the *one-true* answer.

Reliability

To help assure the reliability of the sequence alignment, always use comparative approaches. A multiple sequence alignment is a hypothesis of evolutionary history. To insure that you have prepared a reasonable alignment, be sure it makes sense. Think about it, a sequence alignment is a statement of positional homology. It establishes the explicit homologous correspondence of each individual sequence position, each column in the alignment. Therefore, devote considerable time and energy toward developing the most satisfying multiple sequence alignment possible. Editing alignments is encouraged. Specialized sequence editing software helps achieve this, but any editor will do as long as the sequences are properly formatted. After some automated solution has offered its best guess, go into the alignment and use your own brain to improve it. Use all available information and understanding to insure that all columns are homologous. Look for conserved functional sites to help guide your judgement. Assure that known enzymatic, regulatory, and structural elements all align. The results of subsequent analyses are absolutely dependent on the alignment.

Researchers have successfully used the conservation of co-varying sites in ribosomal and other structural RNA alignments to assist refinement. That is, as one base in a stem-structure changes the corresponding Watson-Crick paired base will change in a corresponding manner. The Ribosomal Database Project at the Center for Microbial Ecology at Michigan State University has used this process extensively to help guide the construction of their rRNA alignments and structures (*see* Website: http://rdp.cme.msu.edu/html/index.html).

Be sure an alignment makes biological sense. Beware of comparing *apples and oranges*. If creating alignments for phylogenetic inference, either make *paralogous* comparisons (i.e., evolution via gene duplication) to ascertain gene phylogenies within one organism, or *orthologous* (within one ancestral loci) comparisons to ascertain gene phylogenies between organisms, which should imply organismal phylogenies. Try not to mix them up without complete data representation. A substantial amount of confusion can arise, especially if you do not have all the data and/or if the nomenclature is contradictory; extremely misleading interpretations can result. Be wary of trying to align genomic sequences with cDNA when working with DNA, the introns will cause all sorts of headaches. Similarly, do not align mature and precursor proteins from the same organism and loci. It does not make evolutionary sense, as one has not evolved from the other, rather one is the other. These are all easy mistakes to make, try your best to avoid them.

Some general guidelines to remember include the following:

- If the homology of a region is in doubt, then throw it out (or *mask* it).
- Avoid the most diverged parts of molecules, they are the greatest source of systematic error.
- Do not include sequences that are more diverged than necessary for the analysis at hand.

Practical consideration: remember the old adage: “garbage in—garbage out!”

Applicability

The question arises, what are the uses of multiple sequence alignments? They are:

- Very useful in the development of PCR primers and hybridization probes;
- Great for producing annotated, publication quality, graphics and illustrations;
- Invaluable in structure/function studies through homology inference;
- Essential for building “Profiles” for remote homology similarity searching;
- Required for molecular evolutionary phylogenetic inference programs such as those from Phylogenetic Analysis Using Parsimony (and other methods) (PAUP*) and PHYLogeny Inference Package (PHYLIP).

The results from a multiple sequence alignment are useful for probe and primer design. They allow you to visualize the most conserved regions of an alignment. This technique is invaluable for designing phylogenetic specific probes as it clearly localizes areas of high conservation and high variability in an alignment. Depending on the dataset that you analyze, any level of phylogenetic specificity can be achieved. Areas of high variability in the dataset can be used to differentiate between universal and specific probe sequences. After localizing these general target areas, you can then use any of a number of primer discovery programs to find the best primers within those regions and to test those potential probes for common PCR conditions and problems.

Graphics prepared from multiple sequence alignments can dramatically illustrate functional and structural conservation. These can take many forms of all or portions of an alignment, shaded or colored boxes or letters for each residue, cartoon representations of features, running line graphs of overall similarity, overlays of attributes, various consensus representations. All can be printed with high-resolution equipment, in color or gray tones. These can make a big difference in a poster or manuscript presentation.

Conserved regions of an alignment are functionally important. In addition to the conservation of primary sequence and function, structure is also conserved in these crucial regions. In fact, recognizable structural conservation between true homologs extends way beyond statistically significant sequence similarity. An often-cited example is in the serine protease superfamily. *S. griseus* protease A demonstrates remarkably little similarity when compared to the rest of the superfamily (Expectation-values $E \geq 10^{1.8}$ in a typical search) yet its three-dimensional structure clearly shows its allegiance to the serine proteases (Pearson, W.R., personal communication). These principles are the premise of *homology modeling* and it works remarkably well.

As originally described by Michael Gribskov (1987), profiles are a position specific weight matrix description of an alignment or a portion of an alignment. Gap insertion is penalized more heavily in conserved areas than in variable regions, and the more highly conserved a residue is, the more important it becomes. Later refinements have added more statistical rigor. Generally, a profile is created from an alignment of related sequences and then used to search databases for remote sequence similarities. Profile searching is tremendously powerful and can provide the most sensitive, albeit extremely computationally intensive, database similarity searches possible.

We can use multiple sequence alignments to infer phylogeny. Based on the assertion of homologous positions in an alignment, several algorithms can estimate the most reasonable evolutionary tree for that alignment. Always remember that regardless of the algorithm used, parsimony, any distance method, or even maximum likelihood, all molecular sequence phylogenetic inference programs make the absolute validity of your input alignment their first and most critical assumption.

The most important factor to infer reliable phylogenies is the accuracy of the multiple sequence alignment. The interpretation of your results is utterly dependent on the quality of your input. In fact, many experts advice against using any parts of the sequence data that are at all questionable. Only analyze those portions that assuredly align. As a general rule, if any portions of the alignment are in doubt, throw them out. This usually means trimming down or masking the alignment's terminal ends and may require internal trimming or masking as well. Biocomputing is always a delicate balance—signal against noise—and sometimes it can be quite the balancing act.

Complications

One of the biggest problems in computational biology is that of sequence format. Each suite of programs seems to require its own different sequence format. The major databases all have their own. Clustal has its own; even the database similarity searching program FastA has a sequence format associated with it. The GCG Package sequence format exists both as single and *Multiple Sequence Format* (MSF) forms, and GCG's SeqLab has its own format called *Rich Sequence Format* (RSF) that contains both sequence data and reference and feature annotation. PAUP* has a required format called the *NEXUS* file and PHYLIP has its own unique input data format requirements. The PAUP* interfaces in the GCG Package, PAUPSearch, and PAUPDisplay, automatically generate their required NEXUS format directly from the GCG formatted files. Most systems are not nearly so helpful. Several different programs are available to convert formats back and forth between the required standards, but it all can get quite confusing. One program, ReadSeq by Don Gilbert at Indiana University (1993), allows for the back and forth conversion between several different formats. I would heartily recommend installing it on all of your computers. It is available as a C version or a new JAVA version with a graphical interface. Alignment gaps are another problem. Different program suites may use different symbols to represent them. Most programs use hyphens, "-", the GCG Package uses periods, ".". Furthermore, not all gaps in sequences should be interpreted as deletions. Interior gaps are probably okay to represent this way, as regardless of whether a deletion, insertion, or a duplication event created the gap; they will be treated the same by the algorithms. These are called *indels*. However, end gaps should not be represented as indels because a lack of information beyond the length of a given sequence may not be due to a deletion or insertion event. It may have nothing to do with the particular stretch being analyzed at all. It may just not have been sequenced. These gaps are just place holders for the sequence. Therefore, it is safest to manually edit an alignment to change leading and trailing gap symbols to +, *unknown amino acid,* or n, *unknown base*, or ?, which is supported by many programs and means *unknown residue or indel*. This will ensure that the programs do not make incorrect assumptions about your sequences.

The Protein System

The Elongation Factors are a vital protein family crucial to protein biosynthesis. They are ubiquitous to all of cellular life and, in concert with the ribosome, they must have been one of the very earliest enzymatic factories in life. The Elongation Factor subunit known as 1-Alpha (EF-1α) in Eukaryota and Archaea and called *Elongation Factor Tu* in [Eu]Bacteria (and Euk and Arch plastids) will be used as an example. It is essential in the universal process of protein biosynthesis and promotes the GTP-dependent binding of aminoacyl-tRNA to the A-site of the intact ribosome. GTP is hydrolyzed to GDP in the process. Because of strong evolutionary pressure resulting in very slow divergence and because of its ubiquity, it is an appropriate gene to estimate early life questions. In fact, a series of papers in the early 1990s, notably those by Iwabe, et al. (1989), Rivera and Lake (1992), and Hasegawa, et al. (1997) all base *universal* trees of life on this gene. Iwabe, et al. used the trick of aligning the α gene paralog EF-1β to their α dataset to root the tree. Elongation Factor 1α/Tu has guanine nucleotide, ribosome, and aminoacyl-tRNA binding sites. There are three distinct types of elongation factors that all work together to help perform the vital function of protein biosynthesis, as seen in Table 3.

Table 3
The Three Elongation Factors in Eukayota and Bacteria

Eukaryota	*[Eu]Bacteria*	*Function*
EF-1α	EF-Tu	Binds GTP and an aminoacyl-tRNA; delivers the latter to the A site of ribosomes.
EF-1β	EF-Ts	Interacts with EF-1α/EF-Tu to displace GDP and thus allows the regeneration of GTP-EF-1α/EF-Tu
EF-2	EF-G	Binds GTP and peptidyl-tRNA and translocates the latter from the A site to the P site.

[a]In [Eu]Bacteria and Eukaryota they have the names as described. The nomenclature in Archaea is still under consideration.

In EF-1α, a specific region is involved in a conformational change mediated by the hydrolysis of GTP to GDP. This region is conserved in both EF-1α/EF-Tu and EF-2/EF-G and seems to be typical of GTP-dependent proteins, which bind noninitiator tRNAs to the ribosome.

In *E. coli* EF-Tu is encoded by a duplicated loci; tufA and tufB. They are located at positions 74.92 and 90.02 of the chromosome. In humans at least 20 loci on seven different chromosomes demonstrate homology to this gene. However, only two are potentially active. The remainder appear to be retropseudogenes. The gene is encoded in both the nucleus and mitochondria and chloroplast genomes in eukaryotes and is a globular, cytoplasmic enzyme in all life forms.

See companion CD for color Fig. 1

The three-dimensional structure of elongation factor 1α/Tu has been solved in about 15 cases. Partial and complete *E. coli* structures have been resolved and deposited in the Protein Data Bank (1EFM, 1ETU, 1DG1, 1EFU, and 1EFC). The complete *Thermus aquaticus* and *thermophilus* structures have been determined (1TTT, 1EFT, and 1AIP), and even the cow EF-1α has been determined (1D2E). Most of the structures show the protein in complex with its nucleotide ligand, some show the terniary complex. The *T. aquaticus* structure is shown in Fig. 1. The *T. aquaticus* structure has six well-defined helices that occur from residue 24 through 38, 86 through 98, 114 through 126, 144 through 161, 175 through 184, and 194 through 207. There are also two short helices at residues 47 to 51 and 54 to 59. The guanine nucleotide-binding site involves the following regions: residues 18 to 25, residues 81 to 85, and residues 136 to 139. Residue 8 is associated with aminoacyl-tRNA binding. Multiple sequence alignment with this dataset can be used to explore these functional and structural regions as well as discover other interestingly conserved sites. To illustrate the various principles, we will restrict the example to a subset of *lower* eukaryotic EF-1α sequences. These will include many protists and algae but will exclude much of the *Crown* group, including all of the higher plants, true fungi, and metazoans. As such it may be an appropriate dataset with which to ask early branching order questions deep in eukaryotic evolution.

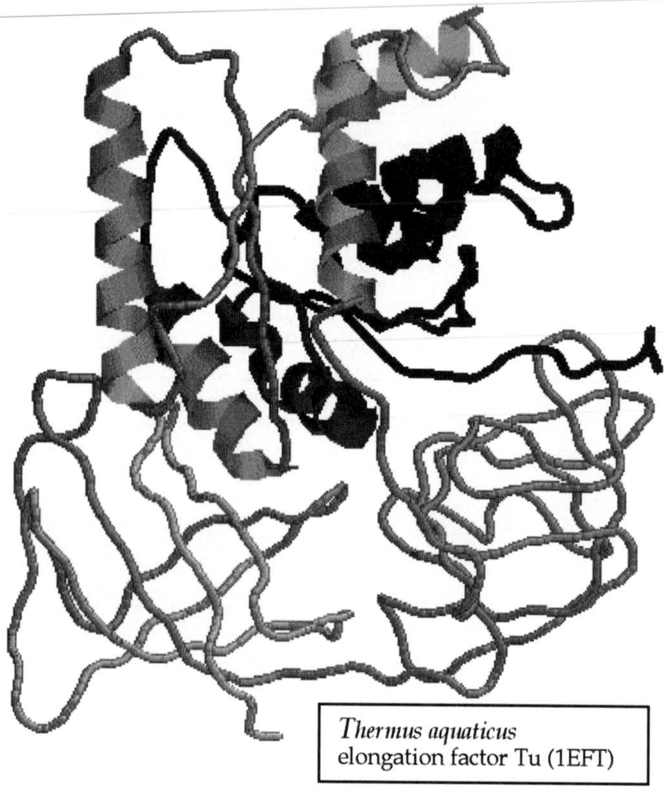

Fig. 1. The *Thermus aquaticus* elongation factor Tu structure, 1EFT. Notice that half of the protein has well-defined alpha helices and the rest consists of rather unordered coils. GTP/GDP fits right down in amongst all the helices in the pocket.

What is Available

A large range of programs is available for performing multiple sequence alignment on your own computer or on server computers. Many of the client/server applications are web-based so the only program requirement on your part is a Web browser. Specialized programs such as the global MSA and local PIMA software are generally not loaded onto personal machines, most are run over Web links. However, running a general purpose, progressive, pairwise implementation for multiple alignment directly on your own computer can often be very helpful. This is especially true if your Internet connection is slow or unreliable. Perhaps the most popular of the general purpose multiple sequence alignment programs is Clustal. The current version, ClustalW and its multi-platform, graphical user interface ClustalX can be found at biocomputing sites around the globe and on the CD accompanying this volume, and installed on your own machine. ClustalX has versions available for most graphical computer Operating Systems; including UNIX, Microsoft Windows, and Macintosh. The ClustalX home-site guarantees the latest version (*see* CD and Website: http://www-igbmc.u-strasbg.fr/BioInfo/ClustalX/). Complete documentation comes with the program and is accessed through a *Help* menu.

See companion CD

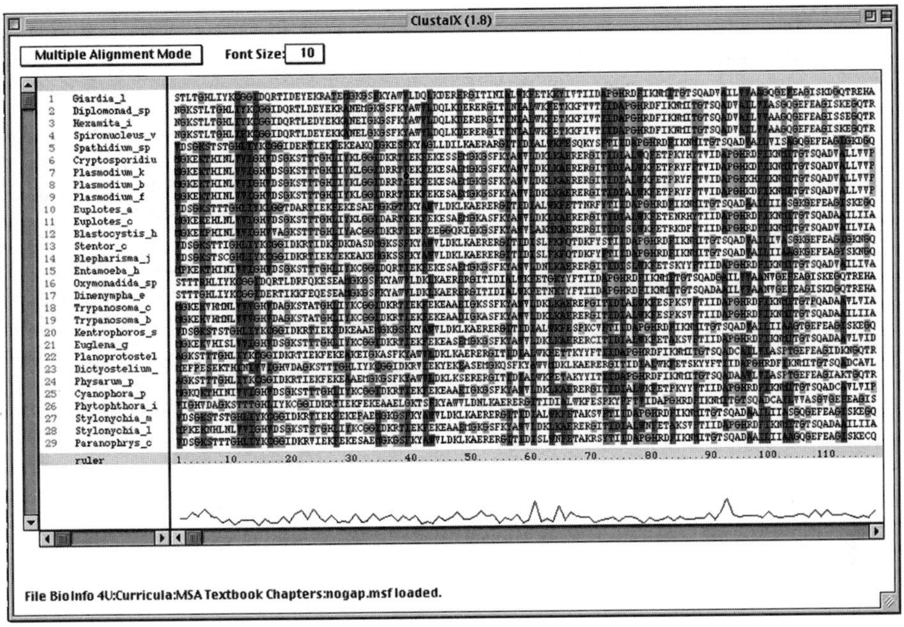

Fig. 2. The ClustalX interface with a newly loaded dataset ready to be aligned.

Running ClustalX on Your Machine, Briefly

Sequences are entered into the program through the *File* menu *Load Sequences* choice. They must all be in one of the following file formats: NBRF/PIR, EMBL/SWISSPROT, Pearson's FastA, Smith's GDE, GCG's MSF, or RSF, or its own native Clustal format. The GenBank format cannot be used. Therefore, if you are saving sequences from the National Center for Biotechnology Information (NCBI), the home of GenBank, be careful to switch the default saved sequence format to be compatible with ClustalX. However, be careful of FastA format files downloaded from NCBI. For example, ClustalX will not properly load FastA format sequences, uploaded from a Mac running Netscape using Entrez at NCBI. NCBI encodes UNIX style carriage returns in the file and Mac ClustalX requires Mac style hard returns. If you run into this problem, BBEdit can be used to change the return type to Mac style globally in the file and it will work fine thereafter.

The collection of sequences used in the example contains representative EF-1α sequences from many *lower* eukaryotes. This dataset was assembled using GCG's LookUp program, a Sequence Retrieval System (SRS) derivative. These sequences can also be collected using Entrez at NCBI, either through the Web or installed as their client/server NetEntrez application, or SRS on the Web, available at all EMBL and many other biocomputing sites around the world (*see* Website: http://srs.ebi.ac.uk/). After the sequences are properly loaded into ClustalX, the window should look similar to Fig. 2.

See companion CD for color Fig. 2

Colors are based on the physical properties of the amino acids and can easily be modified by changing the default color parameter file. The plot along the bottom shows positional conservation within the dataset. Since this dataset is not yet aligned, there is little positional conservation at this point.

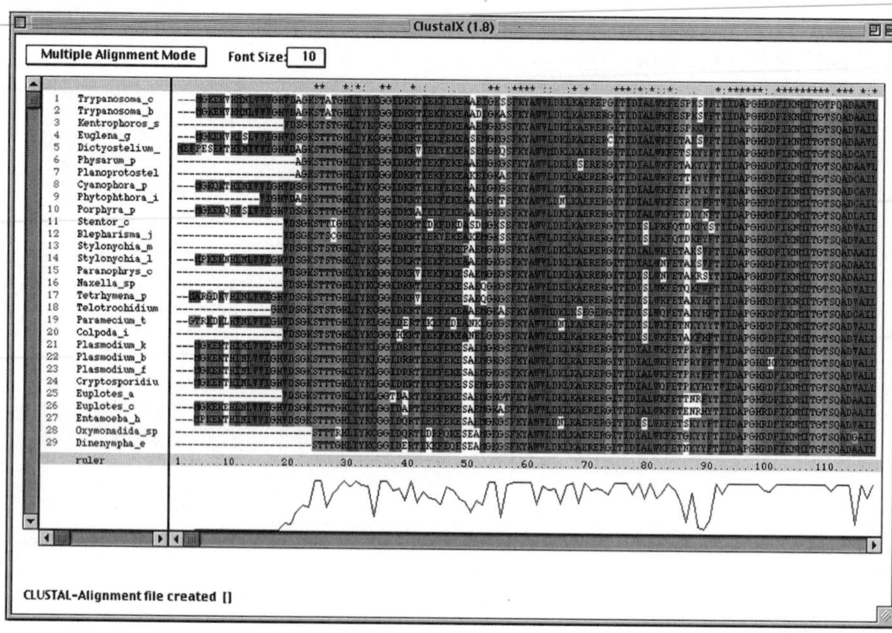

Fig. 3. An aligned dataset in ClustalX. Notice the columns of color, as well as the similarity plot along the bottom, and the similarity symbols along the top of the display.

The ClustalX interface is not an editor. You can select entire sequence entries and cut and paste them from the alignment or change their order but you can not change any characters within the alignment including gaps. The exception is you can globally remove gaps, either all of them or just common columns of gaps. Any manual editing of the alignment is not possible. This can only be done with a dedicated sequence editor, such as GCG's SeqLab editor (*see* Chapters 28 and 33).

The *Help* pages within the program are quite valuable. Documentation on the Web, including tutorials (*see* Website: http://www.may.ie/academic/biology/james/ClustalX_tutorial.html as an example) are also available. ClustalW uses an enhanced progressive, pairwise, dynamic, programming-alignment algorithm. Enhancements include the addition of an alternative fast heuristic-alignment method, differential sequence weighting, the use of a neighbor-joining guide tree rather than a UPGMA and the use of several additional protein parameters over and above the built in scoring matrices, such as different gap penalties associated with runs of hydrophilic amino acids or other structural attributes. Look through all of the program parameters and think about each before you run your alignments.

To create an alignment using default parameters **Select All Sequences** using the **Edit** menu and then **Do Complete Alignment** from the **Alignment** menu. However, take a moment to review the **Alignment Parameters** from the **Alignment** menu before starting the process. Your machine will dedicate itself to solving the alignment after pressing **ALIGN** from the *Complete Alignment* window. This dataset took under 5 min on a 300 MHz G3 Macintosh computer to compute using the default slow alignment method. The results are shown in Fig. 3.

See companion CD for color Fig. 3

Now the colors align nicely and a line appears along the top where asterisks (*) indicate absolute residue conservation, semi-colons (:) denote strong conservation, and periods (.) show weak conservation. The cutoff value between strong and weak amino acid relationships is ± 0.5 from the built-in Gonnet PAM250 scoring matrix. The plot along the bottom of peaks indicates those areas of sequence conservation and valleys show areas of sequence divergence (or misalignment). Alignment quality can also be gauged with the options **Calculate**, **Show Low-Scoring Segments**, and **Show Exceptional Residues** that highlight residues in black and gray respectively. Regions of low quality can be realigned by selecting across their columns, lowering the **Multiple Alignment Parameters**, **Gap Opening** penalty and then using the **Realign Selected Residue Range** option. This can be very effective for *cleaning* up problem areas of the alignment.

Clustal also lets you manipulate two alignments, or an existing alignment and other unaligned sequences, all at once in the *Profile Alignment Mode*. A Clustal profile is just a multiple sequence alignment, but it does provide an efficient and effective means for combining alignments or adding to an existing alignment. To run ClustalX in this manner switch from *Multiple Alignment Mode* to *Profile Alignment Mode*. This can be illustrated by adding the *T. aquaticus* EF1-Tu sequence to the example dataset. After switching modes, **Load Profile 2** to the empty lower panel, then **Align Profile 2 to Profile 1** from the **Alignment** menu. If you have changed any alignment parameters, while refining some region, e.g., you may have lowered gap penalties, you may want to reset them for this step. After pressing **ALIGN**, the new sequence will be aligned to the existing multiple alignment. The **Lock Scroll** button allows you to simultaneously scroll through both alignments with one scroll bar. *Profile Alignment Mode* is displayed in Fig. 4. To merge the pregapped 1EFT sequence with the existing alignment, you need to use the **Edit** menu to **Add Profile 2 to Profile 1** and then **Save Profile 1 As...** a new alignment file. Increasing an alignment's size in this manner is not nearly as powerful and accurate as the true profile methods. However, it is certainly an easy-to-use alternative that works quite well as long as Profile 1 and Profile 2 are sufficiently similar.

See companion CD for color Fig. 4

The World Wide Web and Multiple Sequence Alignment

Web resources for multiple alignments are not as easy to use nor as powerful as locally performing the multiple alignment, on either your own office machine or on a local dedicated sequence analysis server. Some of the difficulty comes from limits in Web interface scripting and forms capabilities, and cut-and-paste errors, but also just the unreliability of Internet connections. In spite of that warning, it is possible, and straightforward to take advantage of multiple sequence resources available on the Internet through the www. Naturally, if you are not willing to install and use any local tools for multiple alignment, www resources can be invaluable. However, problems with very large datasets make multiple sequence alignment on the Web impractical after your data has reached a certain size.

One of the most comprehensive multiple sequence alignment resource collections on the www are at the Bielefeld University Virtual School of Natural Sciences BioComputing Division (VSNS-BCD) in Germany. This is part of an extensive Web site developed, starting in 1995, for teaching bioinformatics over the Internet. Exploring all of their pages is very worthwhile as it contains incredibly informative lectures, demonstrations, and tutorials. The VSNS-BCD multiple alignment URL home page

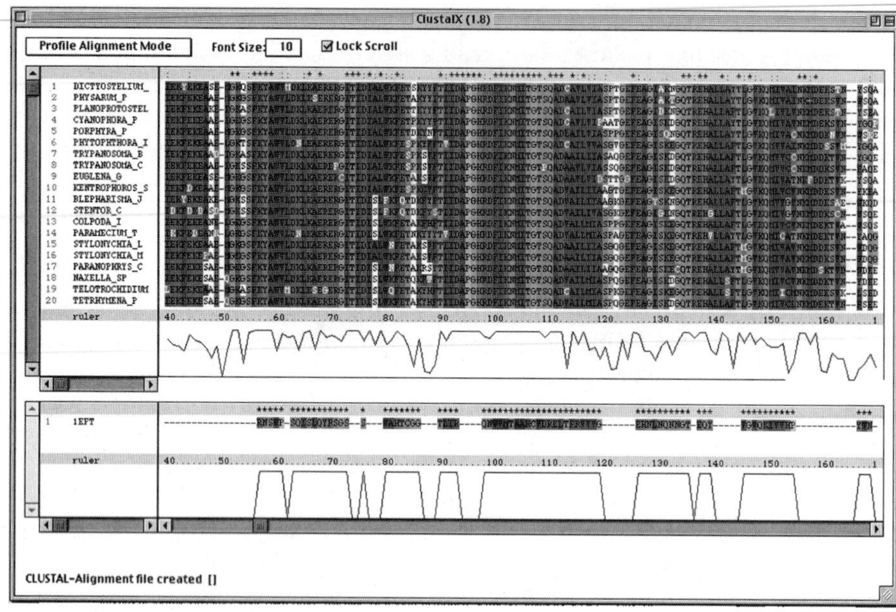

Fig. 4. ClustalX in *Profile Alignment Mode*. A new elongation factor sequence is merged with the existing alignment in this example.

(*see* Website http://www.techfak.uni-bielefeld.de/bcd/Curric/MulAli/welcome.html) is shown in Fig. 5. Another very good multiple alignment resource is at the PBIL (Pôle Bio-Informatique Lyonnais) World Wide Web server in Lyon, France (*see* Website: http://pbil.univ-lyon1.fr/alignment.html). Developed in association with the Laboratory of Biometry and Evolutionary Biology and the Institute of Biology and Chemistry of Proteins, the PBIL multiple alignment page has some of the same URLs as the VSNS page, but the differences merit a look. Its multiple alignment section is displayed in Fig. 6.

See companion CD for color Figs. 5 and 6

ClustalW on the Web

The European Molecular Biology Laboratory's European Bioinformatics Institute (EMBL EBI) in Hinxton UK provides an interface to ClustalW. All program parameters are set from the main forms window (*see* Website: http://www.ebi.ac.uk/clustalw/), and are shown in Fig. 7. To run ClustalW through a Web server in the USA go to the Baylor College of Medicine Search Launcher (*see* Website: http://searchlauncher.bcm.tmc.edu/). The Baylor Search Launcher provides a single, powerful Web portal to many different types of sequence analysis services available on the WWW. Functions are organized according to what type of analysis is offered, e.g., protein vs DNA similarity searches. The welcome page is displayed in Fig. 8.

See companion CD for color Figs. 7 and 8

Click on **Multiple sequence alignments** to get the correct form and paste your unaligned sequence set in the box. Many popular formats are accepted, though the FastA format is probably the most reliable. Select the **Most ReadSeq formats accepted** link to read the help file for all of your input choices. Program Help files are displayed, Options are set, default Parameters are listed, and Examples are shown, respectively, by

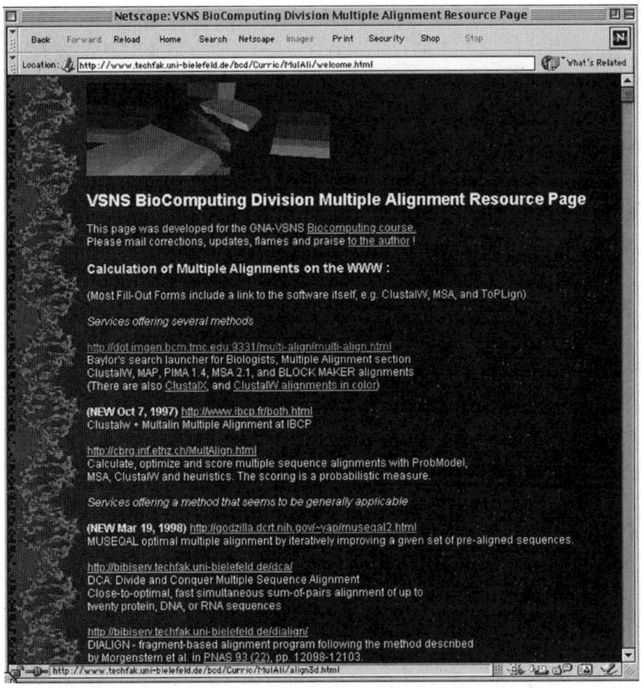

Fig. 5. The VSNS-BCD multiple sequence alignment home page (*see* Website: http://www.techfak.uni-bielefeld.de/bcd/Curric/MulAli/welcome.html).

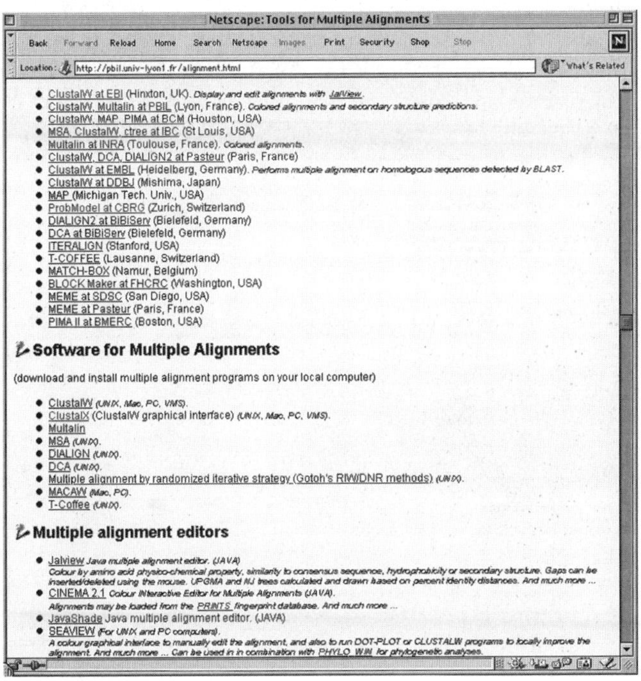

Fig. 6. The Pôle Bio-Informatique Lyonnais (PBIL) World Wide Web server's alignment page (*see* Website: http://pbil.univ-lyon1.fr/alignment.html).

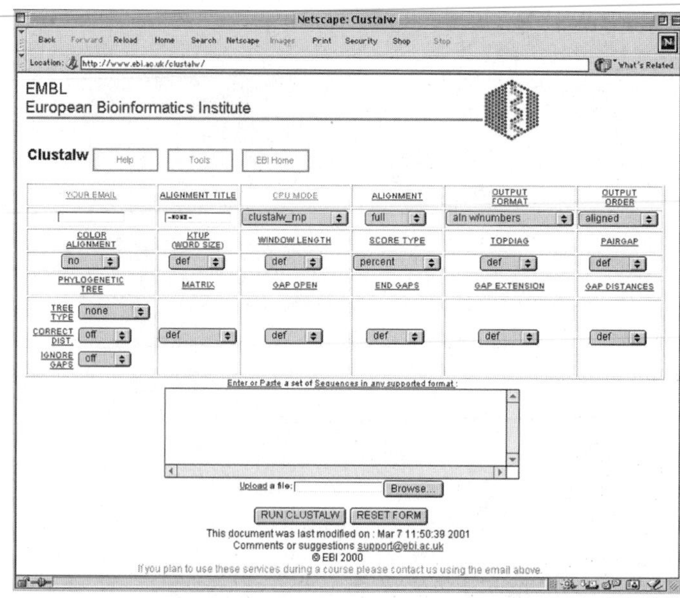

Fig. 7. The European Molecular Biology Laboratory's European Bioinformatics Institute's World Wide Web interface to ClustalW. Program parameters are all set right from the main form window (*see* Website: http://www.ebi.ac.uk/clustalw/).

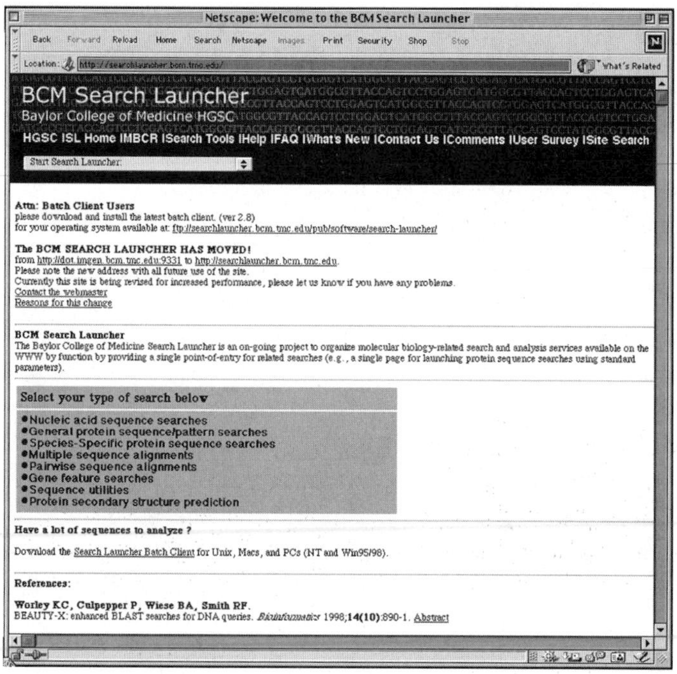

Fig. 8. The Baylor College of Medicine's BCM Search Launcher welcome page (*see* Website: http://searchlauncher.bcm.tmc.edu/). The Baylor Search Launcher organizes commonly used search functions according to what type of analysis is offered, e.g. protein versus DNA similarity searches.

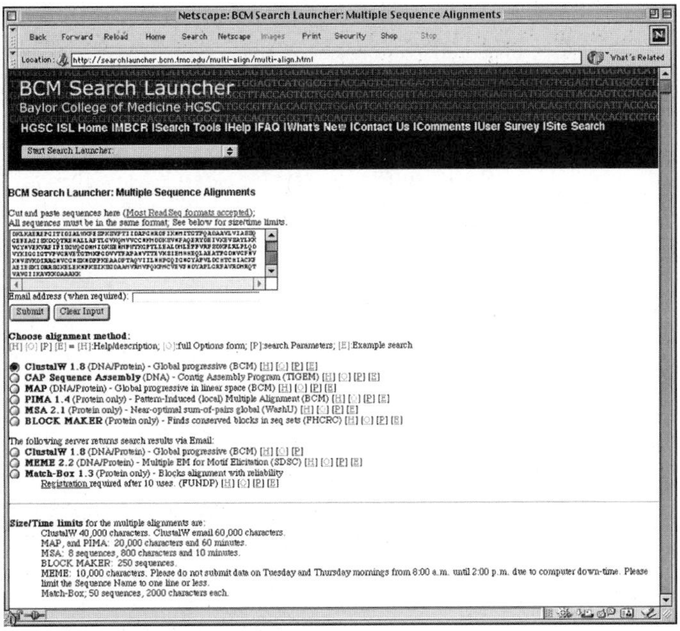

Fig. 9. The Baylor College of Medicine's BCM Search Launcher's multiple sequence alignment input form.

See companion CD for color Fig. 9

clicking the *HOPE* buttons next to every service: **[H]** **[O]** **[P]** **[E]**. The default multiple alignment program choice is ClustalW. The screen will look similar to that shown in Fig. 9 after you've pasted your dataset into the form. Press the **Submit** button when ready. The Search Launcher screen will go away and be replaced by the following text:

```
ClustalW Multiple Sequence Alignment Results
Courtesy of the BCM Search Launcher
Your job has been accepted. Please DO NOT submit it again. Thanks.
Click here to check your job cw18-3028 status.
```

The sample dataset was aligned in less than 5 min. It is returned in an easy-to-read interleaved format as well as a standard FastA format section that you can cut-and-paste into subsequent applications. The alignment is very similar to that derived on the desktop. There are some interesting differences though. In particular the Baylor ClustalW alignment is considerably shorter, 471 residues and gaps long, vs 498. One significant difference, ClustalX uses the Gonnet scoring matrix series by default whereas ClustalW through the Baylor Search Launcher uses the BLOSUM matrix series by default.

Web Alternatives to ClustalW

MSA and PIMA are both very specialized programs. Generally, they would not be used for most standard datasets and in fact, both have quite limited input capacities. So why would anyone want to use either? It is largely a matter of local vs global similarity and dissatisfaction with standard algorithms. PIMA is very good at finding local *patches* of similarity between sequences and aligning those patches independent of high background dissimilarity. MSA globally aligns the full length of sequences but does so *all-at-the-same-time*, it does not use a pairwise process, it explores an n-dimensional trace-back matrix. So, PIMA is valuable for aligning domains of proteins where full-length alignments just will not work, and MSA is good for aligning the full lengths of proteins in situations where pairwise, progressive techniques leave too much ambiguity. However, both programs are limited to small datasets. The PIMA limit at the Baylor Search Launcher is 20,000 total characters and 60 min of computation time whereas the MSA limit is 8 sequences, 800 characters, and 10 min of computation time.

Multiple Sequence Alignment and Structure Prediction

Structural inference is fraught with difficulties. However, it becomes possible using comparative multiple sequence approaches. One of the best predictors of secondary structure is on the World Wide Web (*see* Website: http://www.embl-heidelberg.de/predictprotein/predictprotein.html). This uses multiple sequence alignment profile techniques along with neural net technology. PredictProtein is a service offered by the Protein Design Group at the European Molecular Biology Laboratory, Heidelberg, Germany. A multiple sequence alignment is created with the MaxHom weighted dynamic programming method and a secondary structure prediction is produced by the profile network method (PHD). PHD is rated at an expected 70.2% average accuracy for the three states helix, strand, and loop. This Web page provides default, advanced, and expert submission forms. One powerful advanced and expert option is the ability to submit your own multiple alignments. Their automated search and alignment procedure is very good, but if you have been working for months on a multiple alignment, and you know it is the best it can be, you may want to force PredictProtein to use that information, rather than it's own automated alignment. The welcome page shown in Fig. 10 presents a wealth of informational links.

See companion CD for color Fig. 10

Three-dimensional modeling without crystal coordinates is even possible. This is *homology modeling*. It will often lead to remarkably accurate representations if the similarity is great enough between your protein and one with an experimentally solved structure. Automated homology modeling is available through the Web as GlaxoSmithKline's SWISS-MODEL at Amos Bairoch's ExPASy server in Switzerland (*see* Website: http://www.expasy.ch/swissmod/SWISS-MODEL.html). As with PredictProtein, using the *First Approval Mode* you can submit an individual sequence and the server will perform a database search. In this case it will search against all of the sequences from the three-dimensional Protein Data Bank. It will then create a multiple alignment of the significant hits, to provide a structural inference. Alternatively, using the *Optimise (project) mode* you can submit your own customized and carefully scrutinized multiple sequence alignment. Naturally, your template sequences must have solved structures. Swiss-PdbViewer must be used to format and submit your data. Swiss-PdbViewer is an interactive molecular structure viewer and editor developed at GlaxoSmithKline. Swiss-PdbViewer allows superpositioning of both structures and their corresponding sequences, that you install on your own computer. It has versions for many of the major operating systems. An extensive menu and help system is provided by the SWISS-MODEL home page as shown in Fig. 11.

See companion CD for color Fig. 11

Results are returned via e-mail in one of three modes, Swiss-PdbViewer mode, normal mode, or short mode. Normal mode and short mode both return PDB format coordinates for the model, normal with a complete log file of all the server actions,

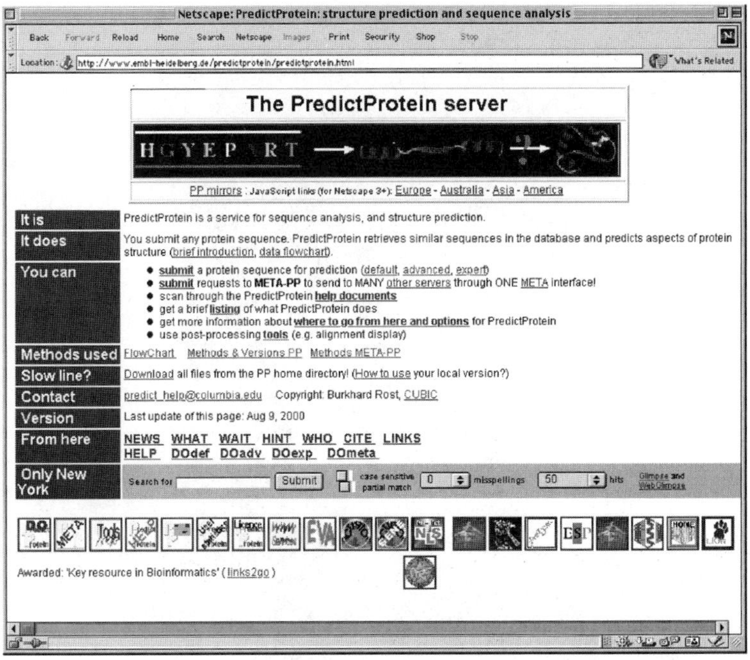

Fig. 10. The PredictProtein secondary structure prediction server home page in Heidelberg, Germany (*see* Website: http://www.embl-heidelberg.de/predictprotein/predictprotein.html).

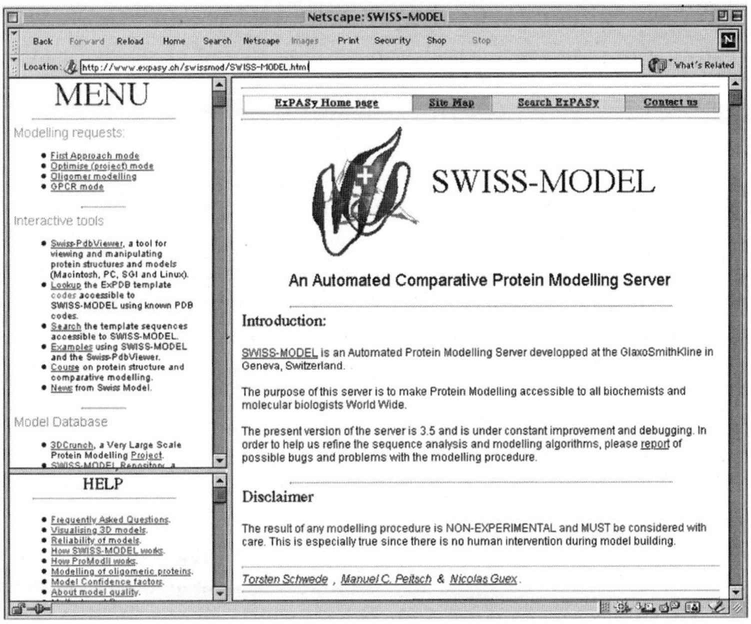

Fig. 11. GlaxoSmithKline's SWISS-MODEL automated homology modeling home page at Amos Bairoch's ExPASy server in Switzerland (*see* Website: http://www.expasy.ch/swissmod/SWISS-MODEL.html).

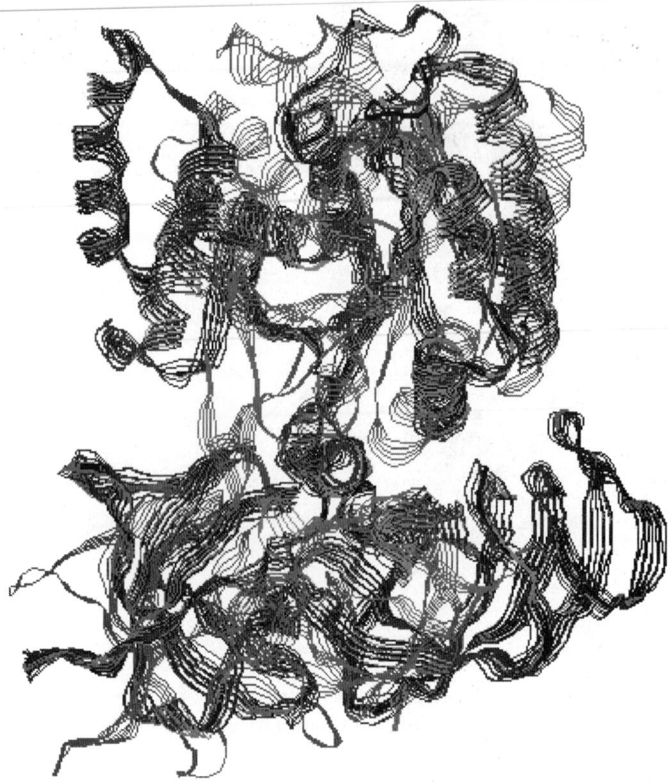

Fig. 12. A RasMac *Strands* graphic of the *Giardia* EF1α structural model superimposed over eight other chains (*see* Website: http://www.umass.edu/microbio/rasmol/).

See companion CD for color Fig. 12

short without. Swiss-PdbViewer mode returns a project file containing PDB formatted coordinates for the model and all templates superimposed, formatted for Swiss-PdbViewer, and a complete log file. The results from submitting the *Giardia lamblia* elongation factor 1α sequence to SWISS_MODEL in *First Approach mode* were e-mailed back in less than 5 min. Figure 12 displays a RasMac (*see* Website: http://www.umass.edu/microbio/rasmol/) *Strands* graphic of the *Giardia* EF1α structural model superimposed over eight other chains.

Glossary and Abbreviations

Affine An affine function is a linear function, described by the algebraic formula: y = mx + b.

Anchor An anchor in the context of a multiple sequence alignment is a region across all the sequences of the alignment that is very highly conserved and thus can help guide alignment by constraint of that region.

Crown Group In the context of the universal tree of life, the Crown group refers to the 'explosion' of diversity that occurred relatively late in the history of life on earth and includes all animals, plants, true fungi, algae, and many protists.

Gap Penalties The creation or opening penalty is how many points a dynamic programming algorithm is penalized for imposing a gap in an alignment. The extension or lengthening penalty describes how many additional points the algorithm is penalized for each additional gap added to the first one, after that first gap, the gap creation penalty, is introduced.

Global Alignment As opposed to local alignment, which is the alignment of only the best regions within sequences, global alignment is the alignment of the full length of your sequence set and generally applies to the multiple sequence alignment problem. However, it should be realized that global alignment can be restricted to subsequences within sequences, the distinction being that local alignment 'picks' the best regions for you, whereas global alignment uses the full length of whatever is specified.

Homology Homology, as opposed to sequence identity and similarity, can have no level. A sequence and, in fact, a position within an alignment, is either demonstrably related via evolution to another or it is not. Statistically significant similarity can argue for homology; however, a lack of statistically significant similarity can not be used to argue against homology.

Homology Modeling The secondary and often tertiary, three-dimensional structure of proteins can be inferred by alignment with proteins whose structure has been experimentally determined. Obviously the more similar the sequences are, the more successful the model will be.

Indel An indel is a gap introduced into a sequence alignment necessary to reconcile differing lengths and evolutionary histories. It is impossible to ascertain whether an insertion or a deletion event created the discrepancy, hence the term indel.

Lower or Primitive Eukaryotes Both terms are misnomers as they imply evolutionary 'progress' and these organisms are no less successful than the 'higher' eukaryotes of the Crown group, but the terms persist and are descriptive of the more basal placement of this assemblage of protists in the universal tree of life.

Matrices A match matrix is the first step in solving the dynamic programming algorithm. Its cells contain the value each position receives for matching (aligning) respective X and Y axis characters. A score matrix can have two meanings. In the context of dynamic programming it is the matrix in which cell values have received initial match values adjusted by gap penalties and trace back paths. The alternative meaning describes the values that amino acid residues or bases receive for aligning with one another, e.g. the PAM and BLOSUM matrix series. The trace-back path matrix delineates the alignments discovered by the dynamic programming algorithm; it illustrates the path through the matrix.

Orthology One of the two major classes of sequence homology exist. Orthology describes homologous sequences present in different organisms as a result of speciation processes. Major confusion can result from mixing paralogues and orthologues in the same analysis.

Paralogy One of the two major classes of sequence homology exist. Paralogy describes homologous sequences within the same organism as a result of gene duplication. As stated above, major confusion can result from mixing paralogues and orthologues in the same analysis.

Universal Tree of Life A phylogenetic tree, i.e. a graph that illustrates the relations of organisms through evolutionary time, that attempts to establish the placement of all earth's extant cellular life.

Suggested Readings

Dynamic Programming

Needleman, S. B. and Wunsch, C. D. (1970) A general method applicable to the search for similarities in the amino acid sequence of two proteins, J. Mol. Biol. 48, 443–453.

Smith, T. F. and Waterman, M. S. (1981) Comparison of bio-sequences, Adv. Appl. Math. 2, 482–489.

Scoring Matrices

Henikoff, S. and Henikoff, J. G. (1992) Amino acid substitution matrices from protein blocks, Proc. Natl. Acad. Sci. USA 89, 10,915–10,919.

Schwartz, R. M. and Dayhoff, M. O. (1979) Matrices for detecting distant relationships, in: Atlas of Protein Sequences and Structure, vol. 5, (Dayhoff, M. O., ed.), National Biomedical Research Foundation, Washington DC, pp. 353–358.

Multiple Sequence Dynamic Programming

Feng, D. F. and Doolittle, R. F. (1987) Progressive sequence alignment as a prerequisite to correct phylogenetic trees, J. Mol. Evol. 25, 351–360

Genetics Computer Group (GCG), a part of Accelrys Inc., a subsidiary of Pharmacopeia Inc. (©1982-2002) Program Manual for the Wisconsin Package, Version 10.3. (http://www.accelrys.com/products/gcg-wisconsin-package).

Gupta, S. K., Kececioglu, J. D., and Schaffer, A. A. (1995) Improving the practical space and time efficiency of the shortest-paths approach to sum-of-pairs multiple sequence alignment, J. Comp. Biol. 2, 459–472.

Higgins, D. G., Bleasby, A. J., and Fuchs, R. (1992) CLUSTALV: improved software for multiple sequence alignment, Comp. Appl. Biol. Sci. 8, 189–191.

Smith, R. F. and Smith, T. F. (1992) Pattern-induced multi-sequence alignment (PIMA) algorithm employing secondary structure-dependent gap penalties for comparative protein modeling, Protein Eng. 5, 35–41.

Thompson, J. D., Higgins, D. G., and Gibson, T. J. (1994) CLUSTALW: improving the sensitivity of progressive multiple sequence alignment through sequence weighting, positions-specific gap penalties and weight matrix choice, Nucleic Acids Res. 22, 4673–4680.

Thompson, J. D., Gibson, T. J., Plewniak, F., Jeanmougin, F., and Higgins, D. G. (1997) The ClustalX windows interface: flexible strategies for multiple sequence alignment aided by quality analysis tools, Nucleic Acids Res. 24, 4876–4882.

Applicability

Alignment Profiles

Eddy, S. R. (1996) Hidden Markov models, Curr. Opin. Struct. Biol. 6, 361–365.

Eddy, S. R. (1998) Profile hidden Markov models, Bioinformatics 14, 755–763

Gribskov, M., Luethy, R., and Eisenberg, D. (1989) Profile analysis, in: Methods in Enzymology, vol. 183, Academic Press, San Diego, CA, pp. 146–159.

Gribskov M., McLachlan M., and Eisenberg, D. (1987) Profile analysis: detection of distantly related proteins, Proc. Natl. Acad. Sci. USA 84, 4355–4358.

Complications

File Formats

Gilbert, D. G. (1993 [C release] and 1999 [Java release]) ReadSeq, public domain software, Bioinformatics Group, Biology Department, Indiana University,

Bloomington, IN.
(*see* Website: http://iubio.bio.indiana.edu/soft/molbio/readseq/)

The Protein System

Phylogenetic Relaionships

The *E. coli* Database Collection (ECDC) The K12 chromosome, Justus-Liebig-Universitaet, Giessen, Germany.
(*see* Website: http://www.uni-giessen.de/ngx1052/ecdc.htm)

Hasegawa, M., Hashimoto, T., Adachi, J., Iwabe, N., and Miyata, T. (1993) Early branchings in the evolution of Eukaryotes: ancient divergence of Entamoeba that lacks mitochondria revealed by protein sequence data, J. Mol. Evol. 36, 380–388.

Iwabe, N., Kuma, E.-I., Hasegawa, M., Osawa, S., and Miyata, T. (1989) Evolutionary relationship of archaebacteria, eubacteria, and eukaryotes inferred from phylogenetic trees of duplicated genes, Proc. Natl. Acad. Sci. USA 86, 9355–9359.

Madsen, H. O. Poulsen, K., Dahl, O., Clark, B. F., and Hjorth, J. P. (1990) Retropseudogenes constitute the major part of the human elongation factor 1 alpha gene family, Nucleic Acids Res. 18, 1513–1516.

Rivera, M. C. and Lake, J. A. (1992) Evidence that eukaryotes and eocyte prokaryotes are immediate relatives, Science 257, 74–76.

What is Availble

Running ClustalX on Your Machine, Briefly

Etzold, T. and Argos, P. (1993) SRS–an indexing and retrieval tool for flat file data libraries, Comp. Appl. Biosci. 9, 49–57.

Gonnet, G. H., Cohen, M. A., and Benner, S. A. (1992) Exhaustive matching of the entire protein sequence database, Science 256, 1443–1145.

CLUSTALW ON THE WEB

Smith, R. F., Wiese, B. A., Wojzynski, M. K., Davison, D. B., and Worley, K. C. (1996) BCM Search Launcher–an integrated interface to molecular biology data base search and analysis services available on the World Wide Web, Genome Res. 6, 454–62.

Multiple Sequence Alignment and Structure Prediction

ALIGNMENT SECONDARY STRUCTURE

Guex, N., Diemand, A., and Peitsch, M. C. (1999) Protein modeling for all, Trends Biochem. Sci. 24, 364–367.

Guex, N. and Peitsch, M. C. (1997) SWISS-MODEL and the Swiss-PdbViewer: an environment for comparative protein modeling, Electrophoresis 18, 2714–2723.

Rost, B. and Sander, C. (1993) Prediction of protein secondary structure at better than 70% accuracy, J. Mol. Biol. 232, 584–599.

Rost, B. and Sander, C. (1994) Combining evolutionary information and neural networks to predict protein secondary structure, Proteins 19, 55–77.

Sander, C. and Schneider, R. (1991) Database of homology-derived structures and the structural meaning of sequence alignment, Proteins 9, 56–68.

Sayle, R. A. and Milner-White, E. J. (1995) RasMol: biomolecular graphics for all, Trends Biochem. Sci. 20, 374–376.

32 3D Molecular Visualization with Protein Explorer

Eric Martz

Introduction

Visualization of macromolecular structure in three dimensions is becoming ever more important for understanding protein structure-function relationships, functional consequences of mutations, mechanisms of ligand binding, and drug design. Free molecular visualization software of excellent quality is now available. Protein Explorer is featured because it is easiest to use, yet quite powerful. It is compared with Cn3D, WebLab Viewer Lite and DeepView (SwissPDB-Viewer). In brief, among these four packages, Protein Explorer is best for visualization, WebLab is best for publication-quality printed graphics, and DeepView is the only freeware package capable of modeling operations such as mutation, homology modeling, and structural alignments. Other packages that have strong features, but are not covered here, include DINO, MAGE, PyMOL, and VMD. Chime and RasMol are discussed in the next subheading.

Protein Explorer is freeware, for Windows or Macintosh, designed to make 3D macromolecular visualization as easy as possible. Its basic features are designed for students and educators, but it also has powerful, yet easy to use features appreciated by protein structure specialists and crystallographers. Although the majority of uses for Protein Explorer involve protein structure visualization, it is also well suited to visualization of other macromolecules, such as RNA, DNA, and polysaccharides, as well as complexes, such as those between transcriptional regulatory proteins and DNA.

Protein Explorer can operate directly from the web (*see* Website: http://www.proteinexplorer.org), or can be downloaded for off-line use. Either Netscape Communicator or Internet Explorer is required along with a plug-in called MDL Chime. If you have not downloaded and installed Chime, when you attempt to use Protein Explorer, it will direct you where to do so. Table 1 provides a list of associated websites.

Protein Explorer vs Chime and RasMol

Because of its greater ease of use and power, Protein Explorer has superceded Chime and RasMol for interactive exploration of macromolecular structure in most situations (*see* Website: http://www.umass.edu/microbio/chime/explorer/pe_v_ras.htm). Protein Explorer is, in part, a user interface to MDL Chime that would not be possible without the visualization power and chemical intelligence built into Chime. Protein

Table 1
Major Websites

Website name	*Location*
Protein Explorer[a]	http://www.proteinexplorer.org
World Index of Molecular Visualization Resources (including tutorials using Chime, dedicated to specific molecules)	http://www.molvisindex.org
PDB Lite (search interface for novices)	http://www.pdblite.org
Protein Data Bank (source of all published macromolecular structure data)	http://www.pdb.org
Nature and Limitations of 3-D Structural Data	http://www.rcsb.org/pdb/experimental_methods.html
Cn3D (*see* category "Free Software")	http://www.molvisindex.org
DeepView (SwissPDB-Viewer)	http://www.molvisindex.org
WebLab Viewer Lite	http://www.molvisindex.org

[a]Consult Protein Explorer's Help, Index and Glossary to find how to access specific features of Protein Explorer. It is linked to Protein Explorer's FrontDoor under About PE.

Explorer's purpose is to make the power in Chime accessible and to extend it by adding higher level capabilities (*see* Website: http://www.umass.edu/microbio/chime/explorer/why_pe.htm).

Chime is a Netscape plugin that renders images of molecules. Chime's name is derived from *Chemical* and *MIME*, where MIME denotes the method used to categorize information sent through the Internet (Multi-part Internet Mail Extension). Chime is freeware created at MDL Information Systems (*see* Website: http://www.mdlchime.com), and is built upon the rendering and command language source code of RasMol (*see* Website: http://www.umass.edu/microbio/rasmol), a brilliant and deservedly popular, open-source, stand-alone molecular visualization program generously put in the public domain by its author, Roger Sayle. In addition to its browser plugin functionality, Chime's visualization capabilities go considerably beyond those of RasMol, to include surfaces and animation support.

Those willing to acquire some programming skills can create user-friendly web pages in Chime. Examples of excellent, molecule-specific tutorials in Chime, as well as methods for building these tools are indexed (*see* Website: http://www.molvisindex.org).

Sources of Macromolecular Structure Data: The Protein Data Bank (PDB)

PDB Files and Codes

In order to display a macromolecule, Protein Explorer like the other programs, requires an *atomic coordinate data file*, that specifies the positions of each atom in space with Cartesian coordinates. There are many formats for such data files, but the most common is the Protein Data Bank (PDB) format. These files are often referred to simply as *PDB files* rather than the generic name, atomic coordinate files. A PDB file is a plain text file that can be edited with a text editor or word processor. An introduction to the PDB format is available (*see* Website: http://www.umass.edu/microbio/rasmol/pdb.htm), along with the official PDB format specification (*see* Website: http://www.pdb.org and click on **File Formats**).

Each entry deposited at the PDB is assigned a unique four-character identification code. The first character of the code is always a numeral; the last three characters can be either letters or numerals. Examples of PDB identification codes are given in Table 2. These codes can be entered in the slot on the FrontDoor page of Protein Explorer to see the corresponding molecules.

The PDB file format is antiquated and inadequate in many respects. Therefore, the International Union of Crystallography has adopted a new format called *macromolecular Crystallographic Information File Format* or *mmCIF*. However, many software packages depend on the old PDB format. To accommodate the transition, the Protein Data Bank will continue to provide all entries in PDB format for the foreseeable future. The Chime plugin cannot read mmCIF, and because Protein Explorer is built upon Chime, Protein Explorer cannot read mmCIF files. RasMol (version 2.7 or later) can read mmCIF files, but WebLab Viewer Lite, Cn3D, and DeepView cannot.

Contents of the Protein Data Bank

The Protein Data Bank is the internationally accepted repository of all published 3D macromolecular structures. Currently, there are over 15,000 PDB files available from the Protein Data Bank (PDB). This number is growing rapidly due to streamlining of structure determination methods. However, many of the entries are mutations or different experiments with the same molecule. Depending on how stringent your criteria, the number of sequence related molecules in the PDB with good resolution is only a few thousand (*see* Website: http://www.fccc.edu/research/labs/dunbrack/culledpdb.html). Less than two thousand are human proteins. Since the human proteome is encoded by approx 35,000 genes, the 3D structures that are available only represent a small percentage of human proteins. Moreover, a large percentage of the PDB files are solutions for single domains and not entire proteins.

Certain categories of proteins are underrepresented at the PDB. In most cases, the protein must be crystallized to enable its structural determination (*see* the following section). Proteins with hydrophobic surfaces, notably transmembrane proteins, tend to precipitate in an amorphous mass, rather than forming regular crystals. Therefore, transmembrane proteins are underrepresented, but several are listed in Table 2. In addition, large proteins are also underrepresented due to difficulties in crystallization. Often, single domains can be crystallized when intact proteins cannot. Nevertheless, some astounding successes have been achieved with large molecules, like the nucleosome and the entire ribosome (*see* Table 2).

Origins and Limitations of Empirical 3D Structure Data

X-ray crystallography or nuclear magnetic resonance is empirically the most reliable way to determine the 3D conformation of a macromolecule. Crystallographic results are characterized by an average resolution value given in Ångstroms. On the average, the uncertainty in the position of an atom is roughly one-fifth to one-tenth of

Table 2
Some Interesting Molecules and Their PDB Identification Codes[a]

Molecule	*Identification code*
Acetylcholinesterase with inhibitor	1VOT
Alpha hemolysin transmembrane heptamer	7AHL
Antibody (intact IgG)	1IGT
Antibody Fab bound to lysozyme	1FDL
Bacteriorhodopsin	1C8R
Calcineurin (ser/thr phosphatase), FKBP, FK506	1TCO
Calcium transporting ATPase including transmembrane	1EUL
Calmodulin (NMR ensembles)	1CFC (slight flexibility) or 2BBN (much flexibility)
Green fluorescent protein	1EMB
Hemoglobin, deoxy	1HGA
Hemoglobin, oxy	1HHO
Hemoglobin, sickle	1HBS
Hemolysin transmembrane (mushroom)	7AHL
HIV protease with inhibitor	1OHR
Lipase	1LPM vs 1TRH
Lysozyme, human	1LZR
Major Histocompatibility I (with virus peptide)	2VAB
Myoglobin, oxy	1MBO
Nucleosome (histones + DNA)	1AOI
Potassium channel	1BL8
Ribosome with tRNAs and mRNA	1GIX plus 1GIY[b]
RNA Polymerase, T7	1QLN
Transcriptional regulator, Gal4 + DNA	1D66
Transfer RNA, Phenylalanine	1TRA
Trypsin (porcine pancreatic) complexed to soybean trypsin inhibitor	1AVX
To search for other molecules *see* Website: http://www.pdblite.org	

[a](PDB codes are case-independent: 1VOT is the same as 1vot.)

[b]The ribosome is too big to fit in a single PDB file when all side chains are included. A PDB file containing only the phosphorus atoms for the rRNA, and only the alpha carbons for proteins, is available (*see* Website: http://www.molvis.sdsc.edu/pdb/1gix1giy.pdb). This URL can be entered in the long slot on the FrontDoor of Protein Explorer.

the resolution value for high-quality data. However, uncertainty varies in different parts of the molecule as a result of the varying degrees of disorder in the crystal. In Protein Explorer's QuickViews, this can be visualized by applying the *Temperature* color scheme. Most published crystallographic results have resolutions in the range of 1.8–2.5 Å. Small values of resolution, such as 1.2 Å, mean very high resolution. Even hydrogen atoms may be resolved while large values, e.g., 5.0 Å, mean low resolution, such that only the general outlines of the backbone, but not details of side chain positions could be resolved.

Nuclear magnetic resonance (NMR) has the advantage that the protein molecules are in aqueous solution while measurements are made. In fact, the molecules need to tumble rapidly in order to achieve high resolution. This limits NMR experiments to proteins of approx 30 kD or less in size. While the result of crystallography is a single model that best fits the diffraction results, the result of a successful NMR determination is an ensemble of models all consistent with the data. Protein Explorer has excellent support for viewing such ensembles, e.g., *see* calmodulin in Table 2. About 15% of the results in the PDB are from NMR, the remainder being largely from X-ray crystallography. There are a few theoretical models in the PDB and these are much less reliable.

Protein crystals used in X-ray diffraction contain approx 50% water. Some proteins have been determined both by X-ray crystallography and by NMR, with consistant results. This gives confidence that crystallographic results reflect the conformations of proteins in aqueous solution. A more detailed introduction to the origins and limitations of macromolecular structural data is available on-line (*see* Website: http://www.rcsb.org/pdb/experimental_methods.html).

Theoretical Models of Proteins

When empirical structural data are lacking, one can turn to theoretical models. These are attempts to predict the 3D conformation from the amino acid sequence. There are two categories of theoretical models; *ab initio* models and homology models. *Ab initio* modeling attempts to predict the folded conformation of a protein using general principles of protein structure. It is moderately successful for predicting secondary structure, but poor for predicting tertiary or quaternary structure.

Homology modeling requires that an empirical structure be available for a protein with greater than 25% sequence identity. The amino acid sequence is then threaded into the template structure, following a carefully constructed sequence alignment. Homology models are more reliable than *ab initio* models at predicting the general fold of a protein, especially when the sequence identity with the template is high. However, neither method is capable of predicting side-chain positions reliably, and even homology models based on >80% sequence identity occasionally have major errors in tertiary structure. Protein Explorer includes detailed instructions on how to use existing web resources for homology modeling, notably Swiss-Model, DeepView, with links to tutorials for the latter by Gale Rhodes.

Finding Your Molecule

As explained earlier, in many cases, no empirical 3D structure is available for a molecule of interest. Nevertheless, structures are available for thousands of interesting molecules. There are many search interfaces for the Protein Data Bank, and each has its strengths and weaknesses. If you are having trouble finding a molecule, be sure to try several search interfaces. Sometimes one search interface fails to identify the relevant entries that exist in the PDB, while another succeeds.

If you have a specific molecule of interest and you have little experience searching the PDB, a good place to start is with PDB Lite. This interface is simple, avoids unnecessary jargon, explains the terms it uses, and provides detailed instructions for saving PDB files to your disk. A more sophisticated search form is provided at SearchFields (*see* Website: http://www.pdb.org) or OCA (*see* Website: http://www.bioinfo.weizmann.ac.il:8500).

If you want to browse general categories of molecules, try PDB At A Glance (*see* Website: http://www.cmm.info.nih.gov/modeling/pdb_at_a_glance.html). For further sources of PDB files; for both large and small molecules, including lipid bilayers and micelles, *see* Website: http://www.molvisindex.org.

Molecular Visualization Needs Satisfied by Protein Explorer

Ease of Use

Protein Explorer offers three tiers of interaction designed for beginners, intermediate users, and advanced users. These tiers correspond to sections in the software named *FirstView*, *QuickViews*, and *Advanced Explorer* respectively. FirstView shows a highly informative first image of the molecule together with an explanation. QuickViews provide menus and buttons that enable moieties of interest to be rendered and colored interactively to answer additional questions about the molecule. Finally, Advanced Explorer offers powerful features that require more experience to use effectively, including sections that give increased control over some visualization modes available as less flexible one-click operations in QuickViews.

Following a two-day Protein Explorer workshop, a high school biology teacher commented, "It is the most user-friendly program I have ever encountered." The visualization tools that Protein Explorer offers you at the outset are designed for nonspecialists and people who need visualization on an occasional basis. Knowledge of basic biochemistry is assumed, but beyond that, Protein Explorer is designed to be self-explanatory. An introductory overview of its capabilities is built in as the *One-Hour Tour*. Protein Explorer's menu system, *QuickViews*, automatically displays contextual help and access to relevant resources whenever a menu or button is clicked. When you do not know how to do something, or how best to accomplish your objective, consult the *Help/Index/Glossary*. For those planning to use Protein Explorer often, an extensive Tutorial is provided. All of these resources are accessible from Protein Explorer's *FrontDoor* page (*see* Website: http://www.proteinexplorer.org). This remains open in a background window while one or more Protein Explorer sessions are running.

Getting Started Quickly and Smoothly

To try Protein Explorer, *see* Website: http://www.proteinexplorer.org and click on the large *Quick-Start* link near the top of the first page, which is called the *FrontDoor*. Printing and following the *One-Hour Tour* that is prominently linked on the *FrontDoor* screen is the recommended way to begin.

Protein Explorer works in the Netscape browser (Windows or Macintosh) or in the Microsoft Internet Explorer browser (Windows only). At Website: http://www.proteinexplorer.org, when you click on **QuickStart**, Protein Explorer will tell where to get the free Chime plugin if needed. It will refuse to start until Chime is installed. If you have problems getting Protein Explorer to display the *QuickStart* molecule, use the *Troubleshooting* link at the *FrontDoor*.

FirstView: Informative and Friendly

See companion CD for color Fig. 1

The first view of a molecule offered by Protein Explorer is designed to be maximally informative (*see* Fig. 1). Protein Explorer's *FirstView* page describes this image and offers extensive background information on how protein and nucleic acid back-

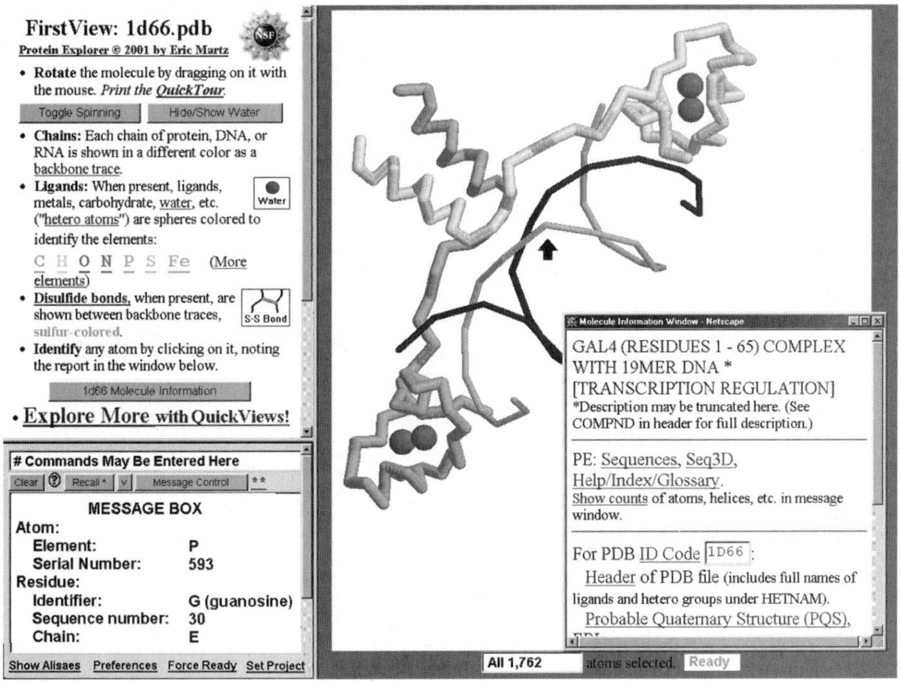

Fig. 1. Protein Explorer's *FirstView* strives to be maximally informative. The molecule shown, PDB identification code 1D66, is the DNA-binding domain of Yeast Gal4 complexed to a 19 base pair DNA double helix. Rotating the image with the mouse makes 3D relationships clear, difficult to appreciate in this static screenshot. FirstView enables you to observe how many chains are in the molecule, which are protein and which are nucleic acid, and whether disulfide bonds or ligands (spacefilled) are present. Protein chains have been made thicker than DNA chains in this figure; normally all chains are the same thickness and can be distinguished by color. Extensive background information is available through hyperlinks on this screen. For example, backbone traces and simplified disulfide bond rendering are explained graphically (not shown). Clicking on any atom reports its identification in the message box, hence protein chains can be easily distinguished from nucleic acid chains. The arrow indicates the atom clicked for this figure. Water, currently hidden, is shown by default (configured in *Preferences*), but can be shown or hidden with the button **Hide/Show Water**. The window at the lower right can be closed or reopened at any time by pressing the **Molecule Information** button.

bone traces and disulfide bonds are rendered, on water in protein crystals, and a key to the standard Corey-Pauling-Koltun color scheme used to identify elements in ligands. You are ready to leave the *FirstView* page when you know how many chains are present in the molecule, whether each chain is protein or nucleic acid, and whether disulfide bonds or ligands are present.

QuickViews: Easy but Powerful Interactivity

The most fundamental need in any molecular visualization software is the ability to interactively render and color components of the molecule as desired. Often hiding some portions of the molecule helps to visualize the moieties of interest. Protein Explorer provides these basic visualization capabilities in its *QuickViews* menu system.

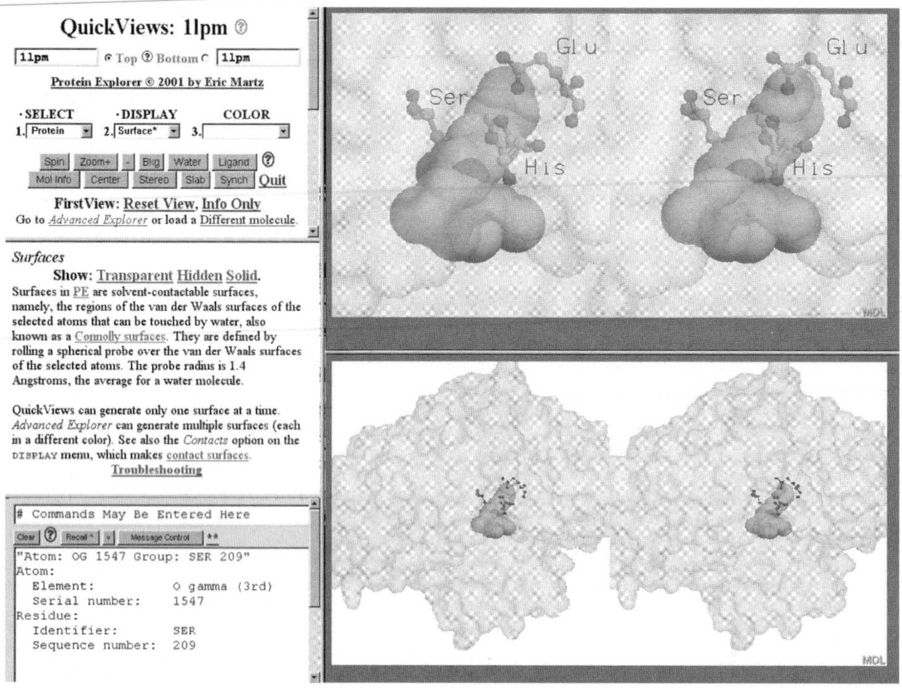

Fig. 2. The *QuickViews* menu system is the heart of the user-friendly power of Protein Explorer. Select, Display, and Color menus (*see* Fig. 3) and buttons make it unnecessary to learn any RasMol-style commands. However, Rasmol commands may be entered freely by those who have learned them. Buttons include **Spin**, **Zoom**, **Background** (toggles between black and white), **Water**, **Ligand**, **Molecule Information**, **Center** (clicked atom or currently selected atoms), **Stereo**, **Slab**, and **Synch**. Each menu or button action automatically displays help in the left middle frame. Sometimes the help includes submenus. In this case, there are links to make the protein surface transparent, hidden, or solid (it is currently transparent). This image shows an inhibitor (spacefilled) bound to the catalytic site of lipase (divergent stereo pair). The catalytic triad (ball and stick) is visible inside the transparent surface of the protein. This screenshot is of *Protein Comparator*, which is identical to ProteinExplorer except that two molecules can be compared, one above the other. All menus and buttons work on one molecule at a time, selected by the **Top** — **Bottom** radio buttons. In this case, the same molecule was loaded in both top and bottom positions, but is shown at different zoom levels.

Basic Rendering, Coloring, and Hiding

See companion CD for color Fig. 2

Most rendering needs are met by QuickViews' DISPLAY menu (*see* Figs. 2–4). To keep the QuickViews menus compact to fit in the available space, short keyword identifiers are used for most menu options; however, a detailed explanation is automatically displayed in the middle *help* frame when any option is chosen. Therefore, the way to become familiar with the menu options and what they mean is to try them out. In an important enhancement that goes beyond RasMol, molecular surfaces, constructed with a rolling solvent probe, can be created quickly and displayed and rotated in real time (*see* Figs. 2 and 4).

In order to apply different renderings and color schemes to different parts of the molecule, subsets of atoms must first be selected. Protein Explorer's SELECT menu (*see* Fig. 3) offers many commonly used subsets of atoms, including each chain, and ligand. When multiple ligand molecules or chains are present, an arbitrary subset can

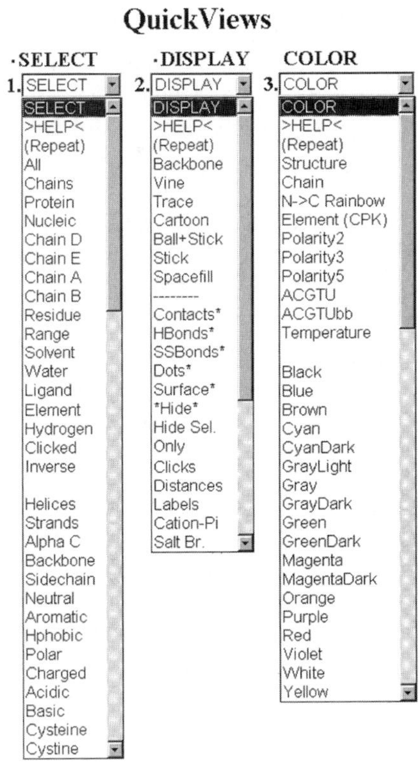

Fig. 3. QuickViews menus expanded to show all options. These menus and associated features enable sophisticated interactive visualization without learning the RasMol command language. The paradigm for modifying the image of the molecule, adopted from RasMol, is to select a subset of the atoms, display or render them as desired (or hide them), and color them if desired. Repeating these three steps on different subsets of atoms produces complex displays. Choosing **Clicked** on the SELECT menu changes the action of the mouse clicks to selection, rather than the default (atom identification). Using mouse clicks facilitates selection of arbitrary subsets of atoms, residues, or chains. (A separate window not shown, *Seq3D*, enables selecting arbitrary residues or ranges by clicking on a sequence listing.) Every menu selection automatically displays help, or for color schemes, a color key, in the left middle frame shown in Fig. 2. A section of QuickViews called *QuickViews Plus* (not shown) enables Boolean operations between items on the SELECT or DISPLAY menus (access by scrolling down in the upper left frame in Fig. 2). For example, one can select **Protein**, then subtract from the selection **Helices** and **Strands**; or one can add a ball and stick rendering to a backbone rendering. Some options on the DISPLAY menu invoke complex command scripts, notably **Contacts** (*see* Fig. 4), **Cation-Pi**, and **Salt Br**. Nevertheless, from the perspective of the user, these are one-click operations.

be selected by clicking with the mouse. The number of currently selected atoms is always shown in a slot beneath the molecular image (*see* Fig. 1).

See companion CD for color Fig. 3

A color scheme to reveal each of the following is a one-click operation from the COLOR menu (*see* Fig. 3): locating the amino and carboxy termini (with a rainbow color sequence, N->C Termini); secondary structure (alpha helices, beta strands, and turns); distribution of hydrophobic vs. polar amino acid side chains (**Polarity2**, two colors); charged residues (**Polarity5**, 5 colors); nucleotides (A, C, G, T and U); and regions of higher disorder in the crystal (temperature).

Sequences: Detecting Gaps and Identical Chains

Protein Explorer can display the sequences of the chains in your molecule. The *Sequences* and *Seq3D* (*see* following section) pages are accessed through the Molecule Information Window, available by clicking the **Mol. Info.** link that is present on all tiers of Protein Explorer. This display is especially useful for spotting whether the structure has gaps because the sequences are taken directly from the atomic coordinates. Leading and trailing ends of a chain are often unresolved in protein crystals because they are disordered. Sometimes, surface loops are missing for the same reason. These gaps are difficult to detect by looking at the 3D structure. Another use of the sequences display is to discover whether there are multiple copies of chains with identical sequences. Protein sequences are displayed in one-letter amino acid code, but touching any residue with the mouse pointer displays the corresponding three-letter code.

Sequence to 3D Mapping

In addition to an annotated full-screen sequences display, Protein Explorer offers a more compact listing of sequences that can be viewed alongside the 3D image. In this window, called *Seq3D*, clicking on a residue (or range of residues) highlights the positions in the 3D structure. It also leaves them selected, so they can be rendered and colored as desired. *Seq3D* includes the option to *scrutinize a range*. This highlights a range of amino acids so it is easy to tell whether a gap in the results from the sequence absence of residues in the structure, due to disorder or is merely a residue numbering artifact with no residues actually missing.

Measurements and Labels

Identification labels, distances between atoms, dotted lines between atoms labeled with distances (*monitor lines*), or simple and dihedral angle values can be displayed using the **Distances**, **Labels**, or **Clicks** options of the *QuickViews* DISPLAY menu. Identification labels may be customized as in the example at top of Fig. 2, by entering arbitrary text onto a form. These can then be applied to the atoms by clicking on them. All these are done from menus and forms. Knowledge of command language syntax is not required. The current action of mouse clicks is always shown in a one-line message at the top of the middle help frame, unless it is the default messaging atom identification.

Zooming, Centering, Stereo

It is important to be able to easily enlarge (zoom) or reduce the size of the image, at will. A cluster of convenience buttons is accessible on all pages (except *FirstView*) including zoom and centering. Centering can operate on the currently selected atoms, or on a single atom designated by clicking. Centered atoms remain centered during rotation and zooming. A stereo button toggles the split image stereo on and off. This also provides a link to the help frame, for instructions for learning how to view stereo. Convergent (cross-eyed) vs divergent (wall-eyed) stereo is set with a preference checkbox.

Contact Surfaces Reveal Interfacial Bonds

Contact surface displays are one of the most unique and powerful displays offered by Protein Explorer (*see* Fig. 4). One-click on DISPLAY **Contacts** shows the atoms that are likely noncovalently bonded to the currently selected group of atoms on the contact surfaces. Interfacial bonds can be shown for an entire chain, a single secondary structure element (helix or strand), a ligand molecule, a single residue, a single

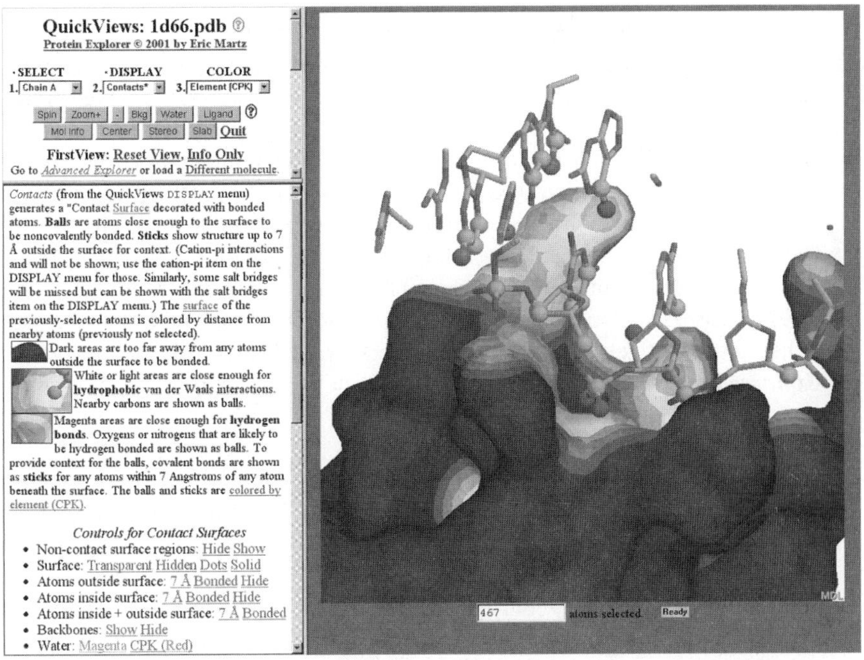

Fig. 4. The *Contacts* surface display. Two clicks reveal noncovalent bonding relationships across any interface. The user selects the moiety to be surfaced, then DISPLAY **Contacts**. In this case, **Chain A** (one of the two homodimer protein chains in the DNA-binding domain of Gal4, 1D66) was selected, and is shown as a surface. The surface is rendered and automatically decorated with small spheres (*balls*), which represent atoms close enough to appropriate atoms beneath the surface to be noncovalently bonded. Sticks are added to the balls to show all covalent bonds up to 7 Ångstroms from the surface. All portions of the structures outside the surface that are farther than 7 Å from the surface are hidden. (The DNA backbone can be shown for context using **Backbones: Show** in the lower left frame.) The surface is colored by distance from the nearest atoms. Dark areas of the surface are too distant from any atoms to be noncovalently bonded. Light areas are at distances suitable for van der Waals interactions, and magenta areas (*see* companion CD for color) are close enough for hydrogen bonds or salt bridges. The *finger* of this member of zinc-finger superfamily can be seen protruding upwards, where it contacts several DNA bases in the major groove. In color (*see* companion CD), it is immediately apparent that the noncovalently bonded atoms (balls) include oxygens and nitrogens, hence that the protein is recognizing a specific base sequence. Clicking on the nucleotide base rings that include balls, from left to right (in the rearmost chain D), reports CGG, the published recognition sequence for Gal4.

See companion CD for color Fig. 4

atom, or any other selected subset of atoms. The surface of the selected subset of atoms is shown, decorated with the atoms noncovalently bonded to it (*see* Fig. 4). Putatively noncovalently bonded atoms, shown as balls, are defined as oxygen or nitrogen atoms within 3.5 Å of an oxygen or nitrogen beneath the surface and carbon or sulfur atoms within 4.5 Å of a carbon or sulfur beneath the surface. After displaying a contact surface, the middle help frame offers a submenu with many options for modifying the initial image. Such modifications include hiding noncontacted regions of the surface, rendering the surface transparent and showing the likely noncovalently bonded atoms beneath the surface. Together with centering and zooming, these make it easy to visualize and identify noncovalent bonding interactions.

Cation-Pi Orbital Interactions and Salt Bridges

Interactions between cations and the faces of aromatic rings (pi orbitals) typically make an energetically significant contribution to the stability of a folded protein. They can be displayed in one click. At the time of this writing, they are identified with approximate distance-based criteria. Energetically significant cation-pi interactions can be confirmed by consulting Gallivan and Doherty's CaPTURE server, which can be accessed through the link automatically shown in the middle help frame in *QuickViews*. It is planned that a future release of Protein Explorer will display only the energetically significant cation-pi interactions, obtained directly on-line from the CaPTURE server. Anions and cations within 4.0 Å of each other may be highlighted as likely salt bridges with a one-click operation (DISPLAY Salt Bridges). *Advanced Explorer* enables ions or aromatic rings within ligands to be included in the cation-pi and salt bridge displays.

Advanced Explorer

The Advanced Explorer section within Protein Explorer offers increased flexibility for some operations available in *QuickViews*, and some additional capabilities discussed below. An example of increased flexibility is the option to include aromatic rings of ligands, or charged atoms, in the displays of cation-pi interactions or salt bridges and to adjust the distances used to identify and highlight these interactions. Another section offers more control over construction of contact surface displays than is available in QuickViews. The *Surfaces* section of Advanced Explorer enables multiple surfaces to be concurrently shown. This enables the probe radius to be adjusted and offers molecular electrostatic potential and molecular lipophilicity potential color schemes.

The *Noncovalent Bond Finder* (NCBF) is an alternative to the *Contact Surface* display of *QuickViews*. Whereas a *Contact Surface* shows an overview of all noncovalent interactions at an interface, the NCBF allows a more detailed exploration of noncovalent bonding, better suited to large interfaces. It displays the atoms closest to any selected moiety, stepping out in 0.1 Å shells with each click on the **Find** button. To simplify the view, the display can be limited to subsets of noncovalent bonds, such as only hydrophobic, or only hydrophilic bonds.

Animation and NMR Ensembles

Multiple models of the same molecule may be contained in a single PDB file. NMR experiments result in an ensemble of alternative models, all consistent with the data (*see* Website: http://www.rcs.org/pdblexperimental_methods.htm). *Advanced Explorer* has an *NMR Models* section with numerous buttons and form slots to facilitate visualization of the models in an NMR ensemble. NMR ensembles can also be animated, simulating thermal motion.

Two different conformations of a protein are sometimes observed experimentally. When there are large differences between the conformations, animation of the transition with a *morph* helps the eye to visualize the changes in specific regions. These morphs include at least a dozen intermediate models interpolated between the experimental models. *Advanced Explorer's Animation* control page enables such morphs to be shown as *movies*. However, such animations differ from true movies in being able to be played from any rotational perspective or magnification on an arbitrary center. Moreover, these animations can be played in a variety of renderings, e.g., backbone,

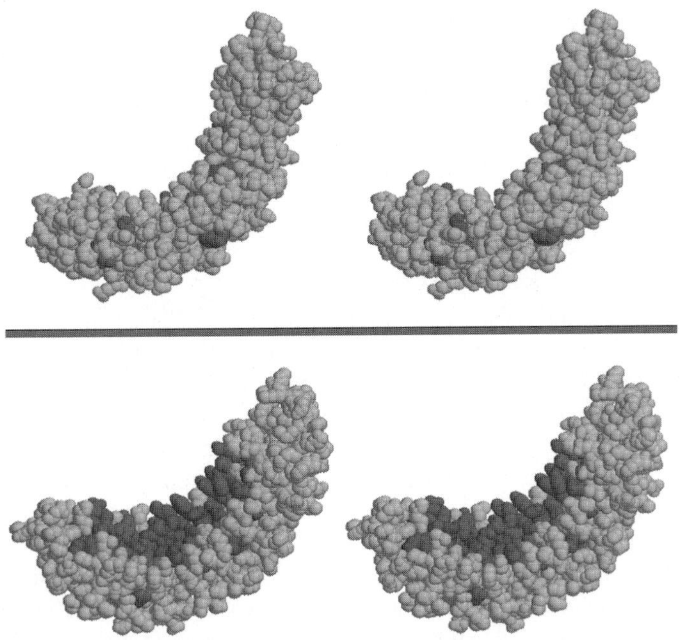

Fig. 5. Conserved regions (dark) of the surface of the PUF translation repressor Pumilio 1 (1LB2) revealed by Protein Explorer's MSA3D (divergent stereo). There is little conservation on the convex surface (top), but a large conserved patch in the concave surface of the same molecule (bottom) is believed to bind to the 3′ untranslated region of the mRNA. A multiple protein sequence alignment was constructed (outside of Protein Explorer) that included sequences from human, *Xenopus*, *Drosophila*, Yeast (2), *Dictylostelium*, and *C. elegans*. A 3D crystallographic structure is available for the human sequence (1LB2). The sequence alignment (in FASTA or PIR format) was pasted into a form box in **MSA3D**, the consensus requirement set to 80% for the seven aligned sequences. With one click of a button, **MSA3D** produced a text listing of the alignment (not shown) assigning three colors representing identity, similarity, and difference. The colors were then automatically applied to the 3D molecular model. (Thanks to David S. Bernstein for providing this alignment and example.)

cartoon, wireframe, spacefilled, and color schemes. By clicking on the animated icon at the upper left of Protein Explorer's FrontDoor, the conformational change of a protein EF hand upon binding calcium will be presented.

Coloring by Multiple Sequence Alignment (MSA3D)

See companion CD for color Fig. 5

Multiple protein sequence alignments reveal patterns of conservation or mutation during evolution. *Advanced Explorer's MSA3D* feature assigns colors to the alignment, representing conservation or mutation, and then applies these colors to the 3D image (*see* Fig. 5). Conserved regions in the 3D structure can then be visualized. The requisite sequence alignments must be prepared outside of Protein Explorer with appropriate websites or software. MSA3D includes ready-made built-in examples and a tutorial with instructions for preparing an alignment at the *Biology Workbench* (*see* Website: http://workbench.sdsc.edu).

Side by Side Comparisons

Protein Comparator is available from the FrontDoor of Protein Explorer. It is a full-featured mode of Protein Explorer that shows two molecules side by side. In Windows, rotations with the mouse can be synchronized so that both molecules rotate together when one is dragged.

Molecular Visualization Needs Not Satisfied by Protein Explorer

Limitations to Visualization

Protein Explorer's ability to display hydrogen bonds is inadequate. Currently, it can only display protein, backbone-to-backbone hydrogen bonds, and in DNA or RNA, only canonical Watson-Crick base-pair hydrogen bonds. Thus, it cannot automatically display nonstandard hydrogen bonds in nucleotides, nor hydrogen bonds in proteins that involve solvent or side chains. Better visualization of hydrogen bonds is possible in DeepView. Protein Explorer is not the best option for publication quality images, although in some cases it can suffice. This results from a compromise between image quality and speed of rendering, enabling Protein Explorer's images to be rotated smoothly in real time on ordinary personal computers. This is a feature of the Chime plugin and is unlikely to be changed. Among freeware, WebLab Viewer Lite easily produces images suitable for publication. However, interactive rotation of its high quality images is much slower, making depth perception problematic unless images are viewed in split image stereo. But unlike Protein Explorer, WebLab Viewer Lite can show alpha helices as cylinders, or nucleotide bases as cartoons.

No Modeling

Protein Explorer is limited to visualization; it cannot do modeling. Modeling, in the strict sense, means building models, or making chemical or conformational changes in existing models. Covalent bonds cannot be formed nor broken in Protein Explorer, nor can atoms be moved relative to each other. Thus, Protein Explorer cannot do *docking*, that is, for example, it cannot move a ligand into a favorable binding position on a protein. It cannot mutate amino acid side chains, or do energy minimization. However, DeepView is the only freeware package capable of substantial modeling.

Comparisons with Other Freeware Visualization Packages

Chime and RasMol

As explained in the section Protein Explorer vs Chime and RasMol, because of its substantially greater ease of use and power, Protein Explorer is preferable to Chime (by itself) or RasMol for most common visualization purposes. For a detailed comparison *see* Website: http://molvis.sdsc.edu/protexpl/pe_v_ras.htm

Cn3D from NCBI

Cn3D is the visualization freeware offered by the US National Center for Biotechnology Information (NCBI; *see* Weblinks). Its main goals include showing the user an informative first view of a molecule (an excellent feature which was released in Cn3D well before Protein Explorer was designed), and enabling interactive exploration, similar to Protein Explorer. It is a well-developed package with many strong features. It works on unix as well as Windows and Macintosh platforms, and has open source code. Cn3D accepts atomic coordinate files only in the ASN.1 format peculiar to the NCBI; it cannot read PDB format. The advantage is that the ASN.1 atomic coordinate files have better internal consistency and fewer errors than do PDB files; one disadvantage is that there is a lag between when a PDB file is first released, and when it becomes available in ASN.1 format.

Cn3D is, in my opinion, not as easy to use as Protein Explorer, especially for beginners. It has no context-sensitive help (in contrast with QuickViews in Protein Explorer). Cn3D has no presentation capabilities; such capabilities are under development for Protein Explorer at the time of this writing (*see* Website: http://www.umass.edu/microbio/chime/pipe).

Cn3D's image quality is higher than Protein Explorer's, and as a consequence, rotation of the molecule is slower and jumpier. Its sequence-to-structure interface is superior to Protein Explorer's in that it is clickable in both directions (sequence to structure and structure to sequence) and it maintains the same colors in both the sequence and structure displays. Rendering and coloring operations are generally at the residue level; it is less able to operate at the atomic level than is Protein Explorer. It can render helices as Cylinders (unlike Protein Explorer), but cannot render surfaces (Protein Explorer can). All views are customized from menus; there is no scripting or command language. A file can easily be saved that will restore the same view of a molecule in a later session; this is more difficult to do in Protein Explorer. Many PDB files give alternative conformations for amino acid side chains; Cn3D handles these very well, while Protein Explorer handles them badly. Cn3D's support for coloring a 3D structure according to a multiple sequence alignment appears to be more fully developed (more color schemes) than Protein Explorer's, but more difficult to use. Cn3D lacks the kind of generalized animation capability present in Protein Explorer, and has nothing equivalent to the Contact Surfaces, Noncovalent Bond Finder, Cation-Pi, or Salt-Bridge displays in Protein Explorer.

WebLab Viewer Lite

WebLab Viewer Lite is the free version of the commercial WebLab Viewer Pro from Accelrys Inc. (formerly Molecular Simulations, Inc.). Both Pro and Lite versions are available for Windows; Lite is available for Macintosh. The Pro version has extensive modeling capabilities lacking in the Lite version (which can however add hydrogen atoms, and change torsion angles). Image quality is higher in WebLab than in Protein Explorer, with the consequence that images rotate much more slowly, making it difficult to perceive depth without using split-image stereo. Because of the high image quality, WebLab is especially suited to printing publication-quality images. It can simplify alpha helices to cylinders (unlike Protein Explorer). In addition to the usual renderings, WebLab can show surfaces, and color them by molecular electrostatic potential (MEP). Its MEP-colored surfaces are strikingly better-looking than those of Protein Explorer (*see* Website: molvis.sdsc.edu/protexpl/mep.htm).

WebLab has some unusual features. It can display all hydrogen bonds, label centers of chirality with "R" or "S", and show "bumps" (atoms that are too close, namely less than 70% of the sum of their covalent radii). It has a Crystal Builder that fills out crystallographic unit cells and neighbors (but this is a great deal slower than the comparable feature in DeepView).

In my opinion, WebLab Lite's ease of use is not as great as that of Protein Explorer, but is fair. There is no context sensitive help, and color keys do not appear for the numerous color schemes available. There is no tutorial, but there is an extensive reference manual (in the form of a Windows help file).

Modeling with DeepView Freeware

DeepView, also known as SwissPDB-Viewer, is a powerful modeling and visualization package for Windows, Macintosh, SGI and linux. It is a closed-source freeware program from GlaxoWellcome. For purely visualization purposes, its images are not as attractive or compelling as those of Protein Explorer, Cn3D, or WebLab. Many useful components of the images disappear during rotation, making stereo viewing especially important. DeepView's user-friendliness is at the low end of the scale, but Gale Rhodes has written a number of excellent tutorials for it (accessible through the DeepView section of molvisindex.org), and procedures for mutating, structural alignment, or building crystal contacts in DeepView are built into Protein Explorer (see below).

DeepView's modeling capabilities are powerful and extensive, and include energy minimization, and integration with the SWISS-MODEL web server for homology modeling. A comprehensive overview of DeepView's capabilities is beyond the scope of this chapter. However, DeepView's capabilities complement the visualization capabilities of Protein Explorer nicely, and below are summarized some of the most popular uses of DeepView for producing models to be visualized in Protein Explorer.

As mentioned above, if no empirical structure is available for a protein, the best way to visualize its 3D structure is with a **homology model**. Construction of a homology model requires that an empirical template structure be available with at least 25% sequence identity. Homology modeling is beautifully automated by SWISS-MODEL working in concert with DeepView. Protein Explorer provides orientation to homology modeling using SWISS-MODEL and DeepView (look for "homology modeling" in the Help/Index/Glossary).

People using Protein Explorer often want to know how to **mutate** selected residues in a published PDB structure. DeepView makes this very easy (look for "mutation" in Protein Explorer's Help/Index/Glossary; *see* the Major Websites box above). It is sometimes important to examine contacts between molecules in a crystal, to evaluate whether they have affected the conformations of surface features. **Crystal contacts** can be constructed using DeepView for visualization in Protein Explorer. For instructions, in Protein Explorer, open the Molecule Information Window and click on **Crystal Contacts**. Finally, DeepView provides the easiest way to create structural alignments of two or more molecules, even with multiple chains, while retaining hetero atoms. For instructions, look up "alignments" in Protein Explorer's Help/Index/Glossary.

Challenges to Help You Learn Protein Explorer

Do the QuickTour

See Website: http://proteinexplorer.org and take a careful look at the *FrontDoor* page. It is important to know about the resources that can be accessed here. Before you can begin to use Protein Explorer effectively, you will need to spend an hour or two completing the *QuickTour*. Go to proteinexplorer.org and click on the large link to the *QuickTour*. Once you have finish the *QuickTour*, it will be very worthwhile to continue into the section entitled *Beyond the QuickTour*.

Generic Questions for Any Molecule

Using a molecule of your choice from the *Interesting Molecules* from Table 2 or a search, (e.g., *see* Website: http://www.pdblite.org), go to Website: http://www.proteinexplorer.org and enter the PDB identification code in the slot at the *FrontDoor* of Protein Explorer. A good place to start is the set of questions applicable to any molecule available on-line as *Discovery in Protein Explorer* (*see* Website: http://molvis.sdsc.edu/protexpl/discover.htm, linked under *Lesson Plans*). It is important to have completed the *QuickTour* before you attempt to answer these questions. You may wish to print the questions and record your answers as a record of your progress. You will learn the most if you try to answer these questions before you look at the hints on how to answer them in Protein Explorer (*see* Website: http://molvis.sdsc.edu/protexpl/genhints.htm).

Heme and Water in Myoglobin

Myoglobin is a protein within muscle cells that stores and transports oxygen for use in oxidative metabolism. Oxygen is bound by an embedded heme group, identical to that found in the hemoglobin of red blood cells. Heme gives myoglobin a reddish-brown color. The muscles of animals that need to store unusually large amounts of oxygen, such as marine mammals, are brown due to the large amounts of myoglobin present. Myoglobin was the first protein for which a 3D structure was obtained by X-ray crystallography, in work done by John Kendrew and coworkers in the 1950's.

Assuming you have completed the *QuickTour* and are familiar with the techniques learned, load **1MBO** into Protein Explorer. Use the generic questions (linked under *Lesson Plans*) to become familiar with this molecule. You may wish to print the questions and record your answers as a record of your progress. Myoglobin-specific questions follow.

Speed Up Performance by Saving Your PDB File to Disk

If you have a slow connection to the Internet, it will help to have a copy of the myoglobin PDB file on your local disk. After loading 1MBO from the Internet once, while it is visible in Protein Explorer, click on **MDL** to the lower right of the molecule, then use the menu that pops up for *File, Save Molecule As*, naming the file **1mbo.pdb**. You may want to create a new folder named **PDB Files** to put it in. To speed up the performance of Protein Explorer, return to the *FrontDoor*, and start **Bare Protein Explorer**. Use the Browse button to find and load **1mbo.pdb** from your disk. As a result, using **Reset View** (which reloads the molecule) will be much faster. Also, when you start another session of Bare Explorer, 1mbo.pdb will be on the menu of recently loaded molecules.

You can further speed up performance by downloading Protein Explorer itself, using the **download** link on the FrontDoor.

Myoglobin-Specific Questions

Is heme an amphipathic molecule?

That means: Does it have a largely hydrophobic (nonpolar, carbon) end and a more hydrophilic (polar) end? In QuickViews, SELECT **Ligand**, DISPLAY **Only**. (Use the **Center** and **Zoom** buttons.) (Spacefill the heme, and color it by element.)

HOW MANY IRON ATOMS ARE IN ONE HEME MOLECULE?
WHAT HOLDS THEM IN PLACE?

DISPLAY **Ball + Stick**. Protein Explorer does not show the bonds that hold the iron in place, but with a basic knowledge of chemistry you can deduce that the atoms closest to the iron have lone electron pairs facing the electron-hungry metal ion (Fe^{+++}). The molecular oxygen, O_2, bound to the iron is not covalently bound and can be released. (Bonds shown by Protein Explorer are often incorrect around metals due to limitations in Chime.)

IS ANY PORTION OF THE HEME IN CONTACT WITH WATER?

Examine the surface of the protein. In QuickViews, use **FirstView: Reset View**. Return to QuickViews, then SELECT **Protein**, DISPLAY **Surface**. Use the **Water** toggle button to examine the protein surface with water hidden, then with water showing.

HOW MUCH WATER IS INSIDE THE PROTEIN?

Click **FirstView: Reset View**, return to QuickViews, DISPLAY **Spacefill** (for all atoms). Color water green to distinguish water oxygens from nonwater oxygens. SELECT **Water**, COLOR **Green**. Press the **Slab** button. Rotate the molecule, looking carefully for water that is buried in the inside of the protein.

WHAT KINDS OF PROTEIN ATOMS CONTACT THE HEME?

Click **FirstView: Reset View**. In QuickViews, SELECT **Ligand**, then DISPLAY **Ball + Stick**. Now, DISPLAY **Contacts**, using the step by step option. After you click the 5th checkbox (**Show likely noncovalently-bonded atoms as balls**), zoom in and notice the elements that are noncovalently bonded, and their distribution. Click checkbox 2 (**Show surface as opaque**) to uncheck it, making the surface transparent again so you can see the relations between the bonded elements and the heme elements.

HOW MANY POLAR PROTEIN ATOMS CONTACT THE HEME?

Click the 8th checkbox (skipping the 6th and 7th checkboxes). Scroll down in the middle frame until you see the *Controls for Contact Surfaces*. At the bottom of the block of control links, click **Water: Magenta**.

Now you can tell water oxygens from protein oxygens. To count the contacting protein atoms, enter **select protein and balled** in the command entry slot (pressing the Enter/Return key). The report of the number of atoms selected appears in the message box so that the atoms display as small spheres.) To verify that this command selected the correct atoms, COLOR **Black**. To restore the color scheme, COLOR **Element** (CPK). To confirm the number of protein carbon atoms contacting the heme, enter the command **select protein and balled and carbon**.

Lipase

One type of lipase cleaves fatty acids from triacylglycerol. Such lipases are used both in digestion of food and for harvesting of fatty acids in fat cells, i.e., adipocytes. They are also used by microbes, a fungus *Candidia rugosa*. Load the lipase **1LPM** into Protein Explorer. Complete the QuickTour, and answer the generic questions (linked under "Lesson Plans") before proceeding.

Lipase-Specific Questions

Is the entire surface of lipase polar? How does this relate to the function of this enzyme?

Is this lipase monomeric or oligomeric?

Open the Molecule Information Window and check the report at the Probable Quaternary Structures (PQS) website. (If you need help, click on the circled green question mark at the top, to access the Help/Index/Glossary.) When you have answered the question, close the PQS windows, returning to the Polarity2-colored lipase.

Is water excluded from the hydrophobic surface patch?

Use the **Water** button to display water. Do you see any bound to hydrophobic areas? If you do, try the Polarity3 color scheme to find out if such water is in fact bound to the polar backbone within stretches of hydrophobic side chains. You may also try Polarity5 to see whether charges occur in the hydrophobic patch. Then return to Polarity2.

Where is the catalytic site (Part 1)?

SELECT **Ligand**, COLOR **Green**. (Click the **Ligand** button if nothing green is visible.) Four green items are on the surface. More interestingly, one green molecule is centered in the hydrophobic patch, in a depression. Hide it by clicking the **Ligand** button, and you will see that it is inserted into a tunnel extending deep into the core of the protein. This molecule is an inhibitor of the enzyme that binds to the catalytic site. It has a fatty acid-like tail, but a phosphonate where the ester bond would be. What does "MPA" stand for? (Hint: consult the HET records in the PDB file header.)

Where is the catalytic site (Part 2)?

With protein selected, DISPLAY **Hide Selected**, so the protein disappears. Now **DISPLAY, Surface**, and make it transparent. With the green inhibitor showing, you can see how it penetrates into the core of the protein. Lipases are serine esterases with a catalytic triad of amino acids, in this case, Ser209, Glu341, and His449. Use Seq3D to highlight these three residues. (Help finding or using Seq3D can be found in the Help/Index/Glossary.)

Which atom of which member of the catalytic triad is covalently bonded to the phosphonate (based on a distance of less than 1.6 Å)?

SELECT **Ligand**, COLOR **Element**. Because the enzyme cannot hydrolyze the inhibitor, it cannot be released. (This enabled it to be crystallized in the active site!)

Are the residues of the catalytic triad in alpha helices or beta strands?

Interestingly, some of the crystals of this lipase formed in a *closed* conformation, with the hydrophobic patch and catalytic site obscured, e.g., 1TRH. Thus, the enzyme may be closed when soluble, and may open to engage a fat droplet at the catalytic site. At Protein Explorer's FrontDoor, click on the small animated EF hand image at the top left. On this page about Animations, one of the examples near the bottom is a *morph* from the closed form of lipase to the open form. To look at it, click on the link to Lipase on this Animations page.

Identifying Conserved Regions

Choose a molecule of interest and follow the tutorial in Protein Explorer's MSA3D to construct a multiple protein sequence alignment using Biology Workbench. Use the resulting alignment in MSA3D to identify conserved regions of your protein. Note: This project will take several hours to complete.

Answers to Questions

Myoglobin file 1MBO is a single protein chain of 153 amino acids with no gaps. Bound to the protein are 334 water molecules, one heme molecule to which is bound molecular oxygen and one sulfate ion. The protein has no disulfide bonds and no cysteine residues. The other 19 amino acids are present. The secondary structure is all alpha, with most helices contacting the heme. The amino and carboxy termini are on the surface, and over 20 Å apart. The protein surface is largely polar and the core is entirely hydrophobic except for two histidines that contact the iron of the heme. The surface appears to have more positively charged amino acids than negatively charged. This is confirmed by the isoelectric point of 9.3 (charge of +3 at pH 7.0).

Myoglobin-Specific Questions

Heme is an amphipathic molecule because one end is made entirely of carbon, while the other end has two organic acid groups. Each heme molecule contains a single iron atom (Fe^{+++}), held into place by the lone electron pairs of four nitrogens. The hydrophobic end of heme is buried in the hydrophobic protein core, while the hydrophilic carboxyls protrude from the protein surface and contact water. There are only a few water molecules buried in the protein. For example, HOH305 is bound to the oxygen molecule that is bound to the heme iron. The vast majority (51 of 56) of the protein atoms that contact heme are carbons that form van der Waals interactions with the carbon predominant in heme; there are also one oxygen and four nitrogens, three of which are in separate histidine side-chains.

Lipase

Triacylglycerol hydrolase 1LPM consists of a single protein chain of 534 amino acids with no gaps. There are two disulfide bridges, plus one cysteine. There are two carbohydrate adducts on the surface consisting entirely of NAG (N-acetyl-D-glucosamine). They are covalently linked to Asn 314 and 351. These linkages can be seen by displaying the ligand contact surfaces. Although the covalent bonds between the Asn nitrogen and sugar carbon are not shown due to a technicality, their positions can be confirmed by the inter-atomic distances of less than 1.5 Å. Two calcium ions are bound to the protein surface, one to the side chain of Asp260 and one to the oxygen of Gly326. Of greatest interest, one ligand molecule is buried deeply within the protein. It is the inhibitor, a substrate analog, menthyl hexyl phosphonate. The protein has an alpha plus beta secondary structure, with most beta strands in a single large beta sheet. The amino and carboxy termini are on the surface at opposite sides of the protein. The carboxy terminus is near the inhibitory ligand (5.4 Å). The core of the protein is largely hydrophobic, but includes a number of polar and even charged side chains. Consistent with this, there are quite a few water molecules distributed about the interior. The protein has a largely polar surface, except for a large hydrophobic pocket, in the bottom of which sits the inhibitor. The protein surface appears to have more negatively charged side chains than positively charged. This is confirmed by the pI of 4.5, with a charge of -19 at pH 7.0.

LIPASE-SPECIFIC QUESTIONS:

The hydrophobic surface pocket fits with function, because the substrate (fat) is hydrophobic and needs a surface region suitable for binding. Probable Quaternary Structures confirms that lipase is monomeric. The hydrophobic surface pocket has no water bound (except to protein backbone), and no charged side chains. The surface ligands were identified earlier, as was MPA. The side-chain oxygen of Ser209 is covalently bound to the phosphonate of the inhibitor. The catalytic triad residues are in neither helices nor strands. The catalytic site is centered at the edge of the large beta sheet, surrounded on the other side by loops without secondary structure, outside of which are alpha helices.

Acknowledgments

I am grateful to the Division of Undergraduate Education of the National Science Foundation for grant support, and to Joel Sussman and Philip Bourne for encouragement. Thanks to Roger Sayle for RasMol, and to Tim Maffett, Bryan van Vliet, Jean Holt, and others at MDL for Chime, without which PE would not have been possible. Thanks to Frieda Reichsman for a critical reading of the manuscript and many clarifying suggestions, and to Byron Rubin for introducing me to lipase.

Suggested Readings

Protein Explorer vs. Chime and RasMol

Bernstein, H. J. (2000) Recent changes to RasMol, recombining the variants, Trends Biochem. Sci. 25, 453–455.

Sayle, R. A. and Milner-White, E. J. (1995) RASMOL: Biomolecular graphics for all, Trends Biochem. Sci. 20, 374–376.

Contents of the Protein Data Bank

Berman, H. M., Westbrook, J., Feng, Z., Gilliland, G., Bhat, T. N., Weissig, H., Shindyalov, I. N., and Bourne, P. E. (2000) The Protein Data Bank, Nucleic Acids Res. 28, 235–242.

Origins and Limitations of Empirical 3D Structure Data

Branden, C. and Tooze, J. (1999) Introduction to Protein Structure, 2nd ed., Garland Publishers, New York, NY.

Rhodes, G. (1999) Crystallography Made Crystal Clear, Academic Press, New York, NY.

Cation-Pi Orbital Interactions and Salt Bridges

Gallivan, J. P. and Dougherty, D. A. (1999) Cation-pi interactions in structural biology, Proc. Nat'l. Acad. Sci. USA, 96, 9459.

Cn3D from NCBI

Wang, Y., Geer, L. Y, Chappey, C., Kans, J. A., and Bryant, S. H. (2000) Cn3D: sequence and structure views for Entrez, Trends Biochem. Sci. 25, 300.
See Website: http://www.ncbi.nlm.nih.gov/Structure/CN3D/cn3d.shtml.

Modeling with DeepView Freeware

Guex, N. and Peitsch, M. C. (1997) SWISS-MODEL and the Swiss-PdbViewer: An environment for comparative protein modeling, Electrophoresis 18, 2714.
See Website: http://www.expasy.ch/spdbv

Lipase

Rubin, B. (1994) Grease pit chemistry exposed, Structural Biol. 1, 568.

33 Multiple Sequence Alignment and Analysis

The SeqLab Interface: A Practical Guide

Steven M. Thompson

Introduction

SeqLab is based on Steve Smith's (1994) GDE (Genetic Data Environment) and is a part of Accelrys' Genetics Computer Group Wisconsin Package. This comprehensive package of sequence analysis programs is used worldwide and is an *industry-standard.* The GCG Package only operates runs on server computers running the UNIX operating system but it can be accessed from any networked terminal. Specialized *X-server* graphics communications software is required to display GCG's SeqLab GUI. X server emulation software needs to be installed separately on personal style Microsoft Windows/Intel or Macintosh machines but genuine X Windowing comes standard with most UNIX operating systems. *Wintel* machines are often set up with either XWin32 or eXceed to provide this function; Macintoshes are often loaded with either MacX or eXodus software.

The details of X and of connecting to a GCG server are briefly described in Chapters 13 and 17. They are machine-specific, however, there are a few useful hints that are common to all machines. X-windows are only active when the mouse cursor is in that window and buttons are turned on when they are pushed in and shaded. Rather than holding mouse buttons down, to activate items, just click on them. Do not close windows with the X-server software's close icon in the upper right- or left-hand window corner, rather, always use GCG's **Close** or **Cancel** or **OK** button located near the bottom of the window.

After logging on to your UNIX GCG user account, issue the command **gcg** to initialize the software suite. This initialization process activates all of the programs within the package and displays the current version of both the software and all of its accompanying databases. Issue the command **seqlab &** in your terminal window to start the SeqLab interface. The ampersand, **&**, instructs the command to launch SeqLab as a background process so that you can retain control of your initial terminal window. This should produce two new windows, the first, an introduction with an **OK** box; check **OK.** You should now be in SeqLab's List mode. Before beginning any analyses, go to the **Options** menu and select **Preferences . . .** A few of the options should be verified to insure that SeqLab runs in its most intuitive manner. The defaults are usually fine, but changes can be made. Remember, buttons are turned on when they are pushed in and shaded.

First notice that three different **Preferences** settings can be changed: **General, Output,** and **Fonts;** start with **General.** The **Working Dir . . .** setting will be the directory from which SeqLab was initially launched. This is where all SeqLab's working files will be stored. It can be changed in your accounts if desired. Be sure that the **Start SeqLab in:** choice has **Main List** selected and that **Close the window** is selected under the **After I push the Run button:** choice. Next select the **Output** Preference. Be sure that **Automatically display new output** is selected. Finally, take a look at the **Fonts** menu. If you are analyzing very large alignments, then selecting a smaller Editor font point size may be desirable in order to view more of your alignment on the screen at once. Click **OK** to accept any changes.

LookUp a Protein in the Database

Given interest in a particular biological molecular sequence, you can use any text string searching tool, such as NCBI's Network Entrez or EMBL's SRS on the World Wide Web, to find that entry's name in a sequence database. GCG's LookUp, an SRS derivative, was used to retrieve the Elongation Factor 1α dataset. After an entry has been identified, the next step is to use a sequence similarity searching program to help prepare a list of sequences to be aligned. One of the challenges in creating a multiple alignment is knowing what sequences should align. Any list from any program should be restricted to only those sequences that actually should be aligned. To generate a meaningful alignment, make sure that the group of sequences that you align belong to the same gene or related gene family.

To use entries of interest in the GCG sequence databases we need to know their proper database names or accession codes. There are several methods. The NCBI Entrez program either over the Web or installed locally in the network client/server mode is one of the more powerful. GCG's LookUp program can also be used, creating an output file that can be used as an input list file to other GCG programs. To start be sure that the **Mode: Main List** choice is selected in your main window and then launch **LookUp** through the **Functions Database Reference Searching** menu. In the new **LookUp** window be sure that **Search the chosen sequence libraries** is checked and then select **SwissProt** as well as **SPTREMBL** for the libraries to search. The representative set of elongation factor entries are all from *primitive* Eukaryotes, i.e., any Eukaryote excluding Fungi, Metazoans, and true Plants. Therefore, under the main query section of the window, type the words and symbols **elongation & factor & alpha** following the category **Definition** and the words and symbols **eukaryota ! (fungi | metazoa | viridiplantae)** in the **Organism** category; next press the **Run** button. You need to use the Boolean operator symbols to connect the individual query strings because the databases are indexed using individual words for most fields. The **Organism** field is an exception, it will accept *Genus species* designations as well as any other single word supported level of taxonomy, e.g., *fungi.* The Boolean operators supported by LookUp are the ampersand, **&**, meaning *AND,* the pipe symbol, | , to denote the logical *OR,* and the exclamation point, **!** , to specify *BUT NOT.* Other LookUp query construction rules are case insensitivity, parenthesis nesting, * and ? wildcard support, and automatic wildcard extension. This query should find most of the elongation factor alpha's from the *lower* eukaryotes in the SwissProt and SPTREMBL databases and will provide a reasonable and interesting starting dataset for the chapter. The **LookUp** window should look similar to Fig. 1.

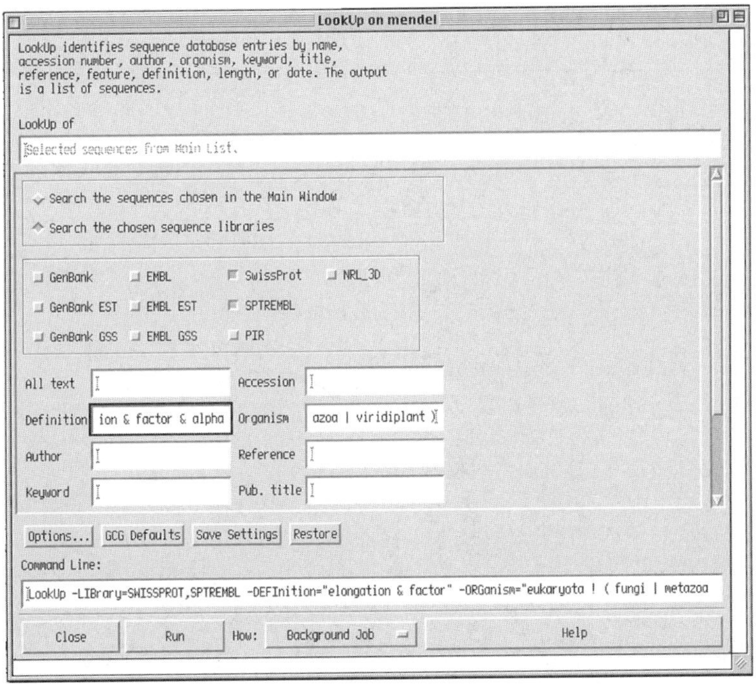

Fig. 1. The GCG Package SeqLab LookUp window. LookUp is an SRS derivative that allows one to construct complex text-based sequence database queries. It produces GCG list file format output.

The program will display the results of the search. Scroll through the output and then **Close** the window. The beginning of the LookUp output file from the example follows in Table 1. Be careful that all of the proteins included in the output from any text searching program are appropriate. All may look correct here, but improper nomenclature and other database inconsistencies can cause problems. If you find inappropriate proteins upon reading the output, you can either edit the output file to remove them, or *CUT* them from the SeqLab Editor display after loading the list. If you use an editor, you can comment out the undesired sequences by placing an exclamation point, ! , in front of the unwanted lines.

Select the LookUp output file in the **SeqLab Output Manager.** This is a very important window and will contain all of the output from your current SeqLab session. Files may be displayed, printed, saved in other locations with other names, and deleted from this window. Press the **Add to Main List** button in the **SeqLab Output Manager** and **Close** the window afterwards. Next, be sure that the LookUp output file is selected in the **SeqLab Main Window** and then switch the **Mode:** to **Editor.** This will load the file into the SeqLab Editor to permit further analyses. Notice that all of the sequences now appear in the Editor window with the amino acid residues color-coded. The nine color groups are based on a UPGMA clustering of the BLOSUM62 amino acid scoring matrix, and approximate physical property categories for the different amino acids. Expand the window to an appropriate size by *grabbing* the bottom-left corner of its *frame* and *pulling* it out as far as desired. Use the vertical scroll bar to

Table 1
LookUp Output File[a]

```
!!SEQUENCE_LIST 1.0
LOOKUP in: swissprot,sptrembl of: "([SQ-DEF: elongation* & factor* & alpha*] &
[SQ-ORG: eukaryota* ! ( fungi* | metazoa* | viridiplant* )])"
 79 entries May 10, 2001 16:08 ..
SWISSPROT:EF11_EUPCR ! ID: ef470001
! DE ELONGATION FACTOR 1-ALPHA 1 (EF-1-ALPHA-1).
! GN EFA1.
SWISSPROT:EF12_EUPCR ! ID: f8470001
! DE ELONGATION FACTOR 1-ALPHA 2 (EF-1-ALPHA-2).
! GN EFA2.
SWISSPROT:EF1A_BLAHO ! ID: 0d480001
! DE ELONGATION FACTOR 1-ALPHA (EF-1-ALPHA).
SWISSPROT:EF1A_CRYPV ! ID: 14480001
! DE ELONGATION FACTOR 1-ALPHA (EF-1-ALPHA).
SWISSPROT:EF1A_DICDI ! ID: 16480001
! DE ELONGATION FACTOR 1-ALPHA (EF-1-ALPHA) (50 KDA ACTIN-BINDING PROTEIN)
! DE (ABP-50).
! GN EFAA.
SWISSPROT:EF1A_EIMBO ! ID: 17480001
! DE ELONGATION FACTOR 1-ALPHA (EF-1-ALPHA) (FRAGMENT).
SWISSPROT:EF1A_ENTHI ! ID: 18480001
! DE ELONGATION FACTOR 1-ALPHA (EF-1-ALPHA).
SWISSPROT:EF1A_EUGGR ! ID: 19480001
! DE ELONGATION FACTOR 1-ALPHA (EF-1-ALPHA).
! GN TEF.
SWISSPROT:EF1A_GIALA ! ID: 1a480001
! DE ELONGATION FACTOR 1-ALPHA (EF-1-ALPHA) (14 NM FILAMENT-ASSOCIATED
! DE PROTEIN) (FRAGMENT).
! GN TEF1.
SWISSPROT:EF1A_PLAFK ! ID: 2a480001
! DE ELONGATION FACTOR 1-ALPHA (EF-1-ALPHA).
! GN MEF-1.
SWISSPROT:EF1A_STYLE ! ID: 35480001
! DE ELONGATION FACTOR 1-ALPHA (EF-1-ALPHA).
! GN EFAA.
SWISSPROT:EF1A_TETPY ! ID: 38480001
! DE ELONGATION FACTOR 1-ALPHA (EF-1-ALPHA) (14 NM FILAMENT-ASSOCIATED
! DE PROTEIN).
SWISSPROT:EF1A_TRYBB ! ID: 3d480001
! DE ELONGATION FACTOR 1-ALPHA (EF-1-ALPHA).
! GN TEF1.
SWISSPROT:EF1C_PORPU ! ID: 54480001
! DE ELONGATION FACTOR 1-ALPHA C (EF-1-ALPHA).
! GN TEF-C.
//////////////////////////////////////////////////////////////////////////
```

[a]Abridged screen trace of GCG's LookUp output file. Notice the *list file* format that can be read by Wisconsin Package interfaces and programs, such as SeqLab and PileUp.

See companion CD for color Fig. 2

view the entire collection. Any portion of, or the entire alignment loaded, is now available for analysis by any of the GCG programs (*see* Fig. 2).

Alternatively, one can import sequences into SeqLab using the **Add sequences from Sequence Files. . .** choice under the **File** menu. Only GCG format compatible sequences or list files are accessible through this route. Using SeqLab's Editor **File** menu **Import** function, one can directly load GenBank sequences or ABI binary trace files. You can also directly load sequences from the online GCG databases with the **Databases. . .** choice under the **Add sequences** menu if you know their proper identifier name or accession code. The **Add Sequences** window's **Filter** box is very important! By default files are filtered such that only those that end with the extension *.seq* are displayed. To view all files, delete the **.seq** extension in the **Filter** box (including the period); be sure to leave the * wild card. Press the **Filter** button to display all of the files in your working directory. Select the file that you want from the **Files** box, and then check the **Add** and then **Close** buttons on the bottom of the window to put the desired file into your current list, if you're in List Mode, or directly into the Editor, if you're in **Editor Mode.**

Each protein sequence is listed by its official SwissProt or SPTREMBL entry name (ID identifier). The scroll bar at the bottom allows you to move through the sequences linearly. The side scroll bar allows you to scroll through all of your entries vertically.

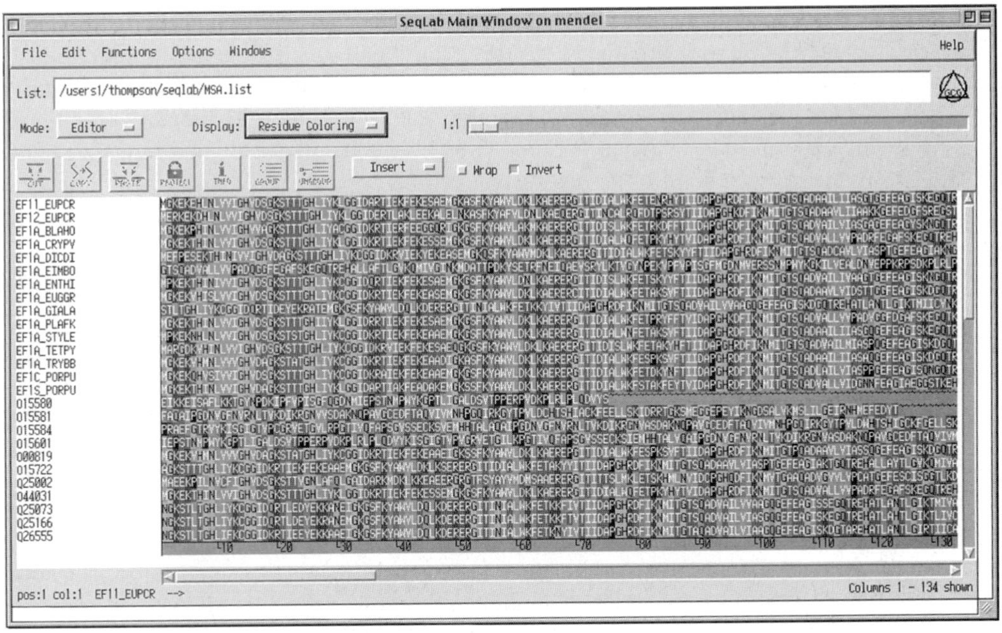

Fig. 2. The SeqLab Editor window with a LookUp dataset loaded and ready to analyze.

Double-clicking on the various entry names or a single click on the **INFO** icon with the sequence entry name selected will provide the database and documentation. This is the same information that you can get with the GCG command **typedata -ref** at the command line. You can also change the sequences' names and add any documentation that you want in this window. Change the **Display:** box from **Residue Coloring** to **Feature Coloring** and then to **Graphic Features.** The display will show a schematic of the feature information from each entry with colors based on the information from the database Feature Table for the entry. **Graphic Features** present features using the same colors but in a *cartoon* fashion. Double-click on one of the various colored regions of the sequences (or use the **Features** choice under the **Windows** menu) to produce a new window that describes the features located at the cursor. Selecting the feature will show the detailed entry. All the features are fully editable through the **Edit** check box in this panel and new features can be added with desired shapes and colors through the **Add** check box.

Nearly all GCG programs are accessible through the **Functions** menu. To perform different analyses, select the entry of interest and then go to the **Functions** menu. You can select sequences in their entirety by clicking on their names or you can select any position(s) within sequences by *capturing* them with the mouse. You can select a range of sequence names by <shift><clicking> the top-most and bottom-most name desired, or <ctrl><click> sequence entry names to select noncontiguous entries. The **pos:** and **col:** indicators show you where the cursor is located on a sequence without including gaps and with including gaps respectively. The **1:1** scroll bar near the upper right-hand corner allows you to **zoom** in or out on the sequences; move it to 2:1 and beyond and notice the difference in the display.

It is a good idea to save the sequences in the display at this point and multiple times as you work on an alignment. Do this occasionally while you are in SeqLab just in case there is an interruption of service. Go to the **File** menu and choose **Save As.** Accept the default *.rsf* extension but give it any file name and directory specification you choose. Rich Sequence Format (RSF) contains all the aligned sequence data as well as all the reference and feature annotations associated with each entry. It is *Richer* than many other multiple sequence formats and is SeqLab's default format.

Similarity Searching to Increase (or Decrease) Dataset Size

A logical next step to preparing a multiple sequence alignment can be a similarity search to add similar sequences from the database to the dataset. Similarity searching can be carried out within SeqLab several ways. The BLAST and FastA family of programs are some of the more frequently used programs. An advantage to running any similarity search within the context of GCG is the results are immediately available for further analyses without the need for any sequence downloading or reformatting. This is achieved by virtue of the GCG list file format and the fact that all of the databases are mounted locally.

Database similarity searching can also be helpful by allowing one to sort a collection of sequences in order of alignment significance. This allows one to remove undesired sequences from the bottom of a list. But, be warned, on some systems you cannot run FastA in GCG on too small of a dataset without causing core dumps! To avoid this problem you can add another small database such as NRL_3D to your Search List Set as well as the list file that you would like to sort. This provides the necessary background randomization for normalization. Another point to remember, BLAST programs cannot be used to search against any sequence set that has not been preformatted into a BLAST compatible database.

In this example, the *Giardia* sequence will be used as a search query because many researchers consider *Giardia*'s most ancient ancestor to be rooted near the base of the universal tree of life on the eukaryote lineage. This is appropriate when examining *lower* eukaryotes. Select the **EF1A_GIALA** sequence entry name in the Editor display and launch FastA from the **Functions Database Sequence Searching** menu. If a **Which selection** window pops up asking if you want to use the **selected sequences** or **selected region,** choose **selected sequences** to execute the program on the full length of the selected protein. At most sites, the default protein database to search, **Search Set. . .** will be **Using pir:***. To specify the my LookUp output list file instead, push the **Search Set. . .** button, select **pir:*** in the **Build FastA's Search Set** box that pops up and then **Remove from Search Set.** Next, press the **Add Main List Selection. . .** button and then select your previous LookUp output list file from the **List Chooser** window that pops up, press **Add to Search Set.** Repeat this process using the **Add Database Sequences. . .** button and specify **NRL_3D** as discussed earlier. **Close** the **List Chooser** and the **Build Search Set** windows. The other parameters in the main **FastA** window are usually fine at their default settings, though you may want to decrease their cutoff Expectation-value to reduce the output list size. Press the **Options. . .** button, some of which can be helpful. Scroll down the window and notice the **Show sequence alignments in the output file** button. This toggles the command line option **-NoAlign** off and on to suppress the pairwise alignment section. This can be helpful if you are not interested in the pairwise alignments and wish to produce smaller output files. Restricting your search by the database sequence length or by date of their deposition in the database can also be useful. **Close** the **Options** window, be sure that the **FastA** program window shows **How: Background Job,** and then press the **Run** button. To check on the progress of the job you can go to SeqLab's **Windows** menu and choose **Job Manager.** Select the **FastA** entry to see its progress and then close the window.

The output is a GCG list file that can serve as input to other GCG programs such as PileUp, complete with beginning and ending attributes and complementary strand attributes when necessary, if using DNA. As in BLAST reports, the Expectation function, *E()*, is the most important statistic on the output. It is the likelihood (Expectations) that the match was observed by chance. Similar to BLAST *E-values*, the value in parenthesis describes the number of search set sequences that would be needed to obtain a *z-score* greater than or equal to the *z-score* obtained in any search purely by chance. The entries are sorted by this *z-score* parameter based on a normalization of the opt scores and their distribution from the rest of the database. However, this *z-score* is different from a Monte Carlo-style Gaussian distribution Z score. It is calculated as a simple linear regression against the natural log of the overall search set sequence length. Just like BLAST *E-values*, the smaller the number, the better and more significant the match. As a conservative rule-of-thumb, for a search against a random protein database of approx 10,000 sequences, as long as optimization is not turned off, *E()* scores much less than 0.01 are probably homologous, and scores from 0.01 to 1 may be homologous, whereas scores between 1 to 10 are only perhaps homologous, and scores above 10 are most probably not homologous. These guidelines can be skewed by compositional biases of the query and/or of the database. You should observe a demarcation where the scores drop off between the significant hits and background noise. Many significant E values can be seen in the output with scores of 10^{-100} or less, then there is a gradual increase in values from 10^{-99} through 10^{-75}, and finally many scores not quite as significant are seen with E values of 10^{-40} and above. A histogram of the score distribution is also displayed in the FastA outputs. This can be helpful to understand the statistical significance of the search and to ascertain whether the search list was of sufficient size. For the search statistics to be valid, the expected distribution, as indicated by the line of asterisks, should approximate the actual distribution, as shown by the equal signs. You want your list size big enough to include some random low scores to ascertain the significance of the alignments. The default FastA Expectation cutoff of 10.0 assures this. Table 2 shows a blowup of the highly significant score end of the graph—these are the best alignments found by the program, not the worst! The histogram can be suppressed with the **-NoHistogram** option if desired. FastA output also shows a sequence alignment for each pair up to a set number, unless you suppress this with the **-NoAlign** option, as in Table 2.

Use the **Output Manager** to load the dataset into the SeqLab Editor. Select the FastA output file in the **Output Manager** window and then press the **Add to Editor** button. Specify **Overwrite old with new** in the **Reloading Same Sequence** window when prompted, to take the FastA output and merge it with the sequences already in the open Editor. Click **Interrupt Loading** in the **Loading sequences** window after thirty or so sequences to prevent the entire file from loading. They are loaded in order of the FastA file and are, therefore, in order of similarity to your query. You are asked whether to **Modify the sequences** or **Ignore all attributes** in the **List file attributes set** window. The answer will depend on the type of alignment you are creating and the biological questions that you are asking. In many cases, especially if you are

Table 2
FastA Output List File[a]

```
!!SEQUENCE_LIST 1.0
(Peptide) FASTA of: input_25.rsf{ef1a_giala} from: 1 to: 396 May 14, 2001 12:43
Description: Q08046 Giardia lamblia (Giardia intestinalis). elongation factor
 1-alpha (ef-1-a Accession/ID: Q08046
===================General comments===================
ID EF1A_GIALA STANDARD; PRT; 396 AA.
 TO: @/users1/thompson/.seqlab-mendel/fasta_ss1_25.list Sequences: 23,370
Symbols: 4,555,867 Word Size: 2
 Databases searched:
 SWISS-PROT, Release 39.0, Released on 15Jun2000, Formatted on 18Sep2000
 SPTREMBL, Release 14.0, Released on 15Jun2000, Formatted on 20Sep2000
 NRL_3D, Release 27.0, Released on 30Mar2000, Formatted on 20Oct2000
 Scoring matrix: GenRunData:blosum50.cmp
 Variable pamfactor used
 Gap creation penalty: 12 Gap extension penalty: 2
Histogram Key:
 Each histogram symbol represents 39 search set sequences
 Each inset symbol represents 3 search set sequences
 z-scores computed from opt scores
z-score obs exp
 (=) (*)
 20 745 0:===================
 22 0 0:
 24 0 0:
 26 0 0:
 28 1 5:*
 30 6 31:*
 32 92 120:===*
 34 371 325:========*=
 36 571 668:============== *
 38 1711 1104:===========================*==============
 40 1537 1540:=====================================*
 42 1997 1883:==============================================*===
 44 1775 2077:============================================ *
 46 1782 2116:============================================ *
 48 2290 2025:=================================================*=======
 50 1475 1848:==================================== *
 52 1702 1625:=======================================*==
 54 1490 1388:=================================*===
 56 948 1159:======================== *
 58 898 952:=======================*
 60 935 771:==================*====
 62 708 618:==============*===
 64 365 492:========== *
 66 402 389:=========*=
 68 419 306:=======*===
 70 343 240:======*==
 72 187 187:====*
 74 98 146:===*
 76 87 114:==*
 78 76 88:==*
 80 63 69:=*
 82 42 52:=*
 84 28 42:=*
 86 23 32:*
 88 25 25:*
 90 4 19:*
 92 0 15:* : *
 94 12 12:* :===*
 96 30 9:* :==*=======
 98 12 7:* :==*=
 100 5 5:* :=*
 102 4 4:* :=*
 104 1 3:* :*
 106 4 2:* :*=
 108 3 2:* :*
 110 0 1:* :*
 112 0 1:* :*
 114 0 1:* :*
 116 0 1:* :*
 118 0 1:* :*
>120 103 0:=== *================================
Joining threshold: 37, opt. threshold: 25, opt. width: 16, reg.-scaled
The best scores are: init1 initn opt z-sc E(22522)..
SWISSPROT:EF1A_GIALA Begin: 1 End: 396
! Q08046 Giardia lamblia (Giardia int... 2696 2696 2696 3151.0 2.4e-169
SP_INVERTEBRATE:Q25166 Begin: 4 End: 399
! Q25166 diplomonad atcc50330. elonga... 2318 2318 2318 2709.5 9.3e-145
SP_INVERTEBRATE:Q25073 Begin: 4 End: 399
! Q25073 hexamita inflata. elongation... 2125 2125 2125 2484.1 3.3e-132
SP_INVERTEBRATE:O36039 Begin: 4 End: 401
! O36039 spironucleus vortens. elonga... 1071 2074 2083 2435.0 1.8e-129
SP_PLANT:O82788 Begin: 21 End: 417
! O82788 blastocystis hominis. elonga... 1017 1825 1830 2138.9 5.6e-113
SP_INVERTEBRATE:O97109 Begin: 4 End: 405
! O97109 naegleria andersoni. elongat... 802 1803 1827 2135.9 8.2e-113
SP_INVERTEBRATE:Q26913 Begin: 1 End: 395
! Q26913 trypanosoma cruzi. elongatio... 1003 1791 1815 2122.1 4.8e-112
SWISSPROT:EF1C_PORPU Begin: 21 End: 419
! P50256 porphyra purpurea. elongatio... 952 1786 1801 2104.8 4.4e-111
//////////////////////////////////////////////////////////////////////////
```

Table 2 *(continued)*
FastA Output List File[a]

```
SP_INVERTEBRATE:O96975 Begin: 6 End: 398
! O96975 euplotes aediculatus. transl... 935 1618 1693 1979.4 4.3e-104
SP_INVERTEBRATE:O77447 Begin: 21 End: 413
! O77447 plasmodium knowlesi. elongat... 928 1637 1684 1968.3 1.8e-103
SWISSPROT:EF1A_PLAFK Begin: 21 End: 413
! Q00080 plasmodium falciparum (isola... 922 1624 1671 1953.1 1.3e-102
SP_INVERTEBRATE:O77478 Begin: 21 End: 413
! O77478 plasmodium berghei. elongati... 915 1615 1662 1942.6 4.8e-102
SP_INVERTEBRATE:O44031 Begin: 21 End: 397
! O44031 cryptosporidium parvum. elon... 938 1453 1650 1929.2 2.7e-101
SP_INVERTEBRATE:O96976 Begin: 6 End: 398
! O96976 euplotes aediculatus. transl... 850 1578 1635 1911.7 2.5e-100
SP_INVERTEBRATE:Q9UAF6 Begin: 1 End: 346
! Q9uaf6 pyrsonympha grandis. elongat... 959 1518 1520 1778.5 6.6e-93
SP_INVERTEBRATE:Q9UAF5 Begin: 1 End: 346
! Q9uaf5 pyrsonympha grandis. elongat... 959 1515 1517 1775.0 1e-92
SP_INVERTEBRATE:Q9Y1W1 Begin: 1 End: 346
! Q9y1w1 pyrsonympha grandis. elongat... 955 1497 1499 1754.0 1.5e-91
SWISSPROT:EF12_EUPCR Begin: 22 End: 412
! Q27140 euplotes crassus. elongation... 581 1398 1483 1733.6 2.1e-90
//////////////////////////////////////////////////////////////////////////
SP_PLANT:O82555 Begin: 1 End: 290
! O82555 blastocystis hominis. elonga... 894 1233 1244 1457.5 5.1e-75
SP_INVERTEBRATE:O36034 Begin: 1 End: 178
! O36034 hexamita inflata. elongation... 901 901 901 1059.7 7.2e-53
SP_INVERTEBRATE:O36038 Begin: 1 End: 179
! O36038 spironucleus muris. elongati... 466 754 785 925.0 2.3e-45
SP_INVERTEBRATE:Q94839 Begin: 1 End: 406
! Q94839 glugea plecoglossi. elongati... 386 869 780 912.5 1.1e-44
SP_INVERTEBRATE:Q25002 Begin: 21 End: 426
! Q25002 glugea plecoglossi. peptide ... 386 869 780 912.2 1.2e-44
SP_INVERTEBRATE:O15600 Begin: 18 End: 169
! O15600 entamoeba histolytica. elong... 730 756 773 911.1 1.4e-44
SP_INVERTEBRATE:O15601 Begin: 1 End: 157
! O15601 entamoeba histolytica. elong... 699 699 723 853.5 2.2e-41
SWISSPROT:EF1S_PORPU Begin: 21 End: 460
! P50257 porphyra purpurea. elongatio... 492 1281 666 778.3 3.4e-37
SP_INVERTEBRATE:O15584 Begin: 9 End: 166
! O15584 entamoeba histolytica. elong... 582 627 631 745.7 2.3e-35
NRL_3D:1EFT Begin: 50 End: 323
! translation elongation factor EF-Tu... 202 431 508 595.5 5.2e-27
NRL_3D:1TUIC Begin: 42 End: 315
! translation elongation factor EF-Tu... 202 431 507 594.5 5.9e-27
NRL_3D:1TUIA Begin: 42 End: 315
! translation elongation factor EF-Tu... 202 431 507 594.5 5.9e-27
NRL_3D:1TUIB Begin: 42 End: 315
! translation elongation factor EF-Tu... 202 431 507 594.5 5.9e-27
//////////////////////////////////////////////////////////////////////////
SP_INVERTEBRATE:O15581 Begin: 3 End: 107
! O15581 entamoeba histolytica. elong... 407 407 435 518.9 9.7e-23
SP_INVERTEBRATE:O15580 Begin: 1 End: 74
! O15580 entamoeba histolytica. elong... 239 239 281 342.7 6.3e-13
NRL_3D:1D2EC Begin: 29 End: 337
! elongation factor tu (ef-tu), chain... 187 449 255 300.2 1.5e-10
NRL_3D:1D2ED Begin: 29 End: 337
! elongation factor tu (ef-tu), chain... 187 449 255 300.2 1.5e-10
NRL_3D:1D2EB Begin: 29 End: 337
! elongation factor tu (ef-tu), chain... 187 449 255 300.2 1.5e-10
NRL_3D:1D2EA Begin: 29 End: 337
! elongation factor tu (ef-tu), chain... 187 449 255 300.2 1.5e-10
NRL_3D:1DG1H Begin: 41 End: 335
! elongation factor tu, chain H - bac... 168 369 240 282.9 1.3e-09
NRL_3D:1DG1G Begin: 41 End: 335
! elongation factor tu, chain G - bac... 168 369 240 282.9 1.3e-09
NRL_3D:1EFCA Begin: 42 End: 336
! elongation factor, chain A - bacteria 168 369 240 282.9 1.3e-09
NRL_3D:1EFCB Begin: 42 End: 336
! elongation factor, chain B - bacteria 168 369 240 282.9 1.3e-09
NRL_3D:1ETU2 Begin: 1 End: 79
! translation elongation factor EF-Tu... 153 208 208 252.9 6.4e-08
NRL_3D:1EFM2 Begin: 1 End: 78
! elongation factor Tu (trypsin-modif... 148 203 203 247.6 1.2e-07
NRL_3D:1EFUA2 Begin: 16 End: 280
! translation elongation factor EF-Tu... 126 327 192 228.0 1.5e-06
NRL_3D:1EFUC2 Begin: 16 End: 280
! translation elongation factor EF-Tu... 126 327 192 228.0 1.5e-06
\End of List
! Distributed over 1 thread.
! Start time: Mon May 14 12:43:00 2001
! Completion time: Mon May 14 12:43:39 2001
! CPU time used:
! Database scan: 0:00:11.4
! Post-scan processing: 0:00:03.0
! Total CPU time: 0:00:14.4
! Output File: /users1/thompson/seqlab/ef1a_giala_25.fasta
```

[a]An abridged output list file from GCG's implementation of FastA. A histogram of score distributions is plotted preceding the list portion of the file where *hits* are ranked statistically by Expection-value. Normally a pairwise alignment section would follow the list, but that was turned off in this run with the -NoAlign option.

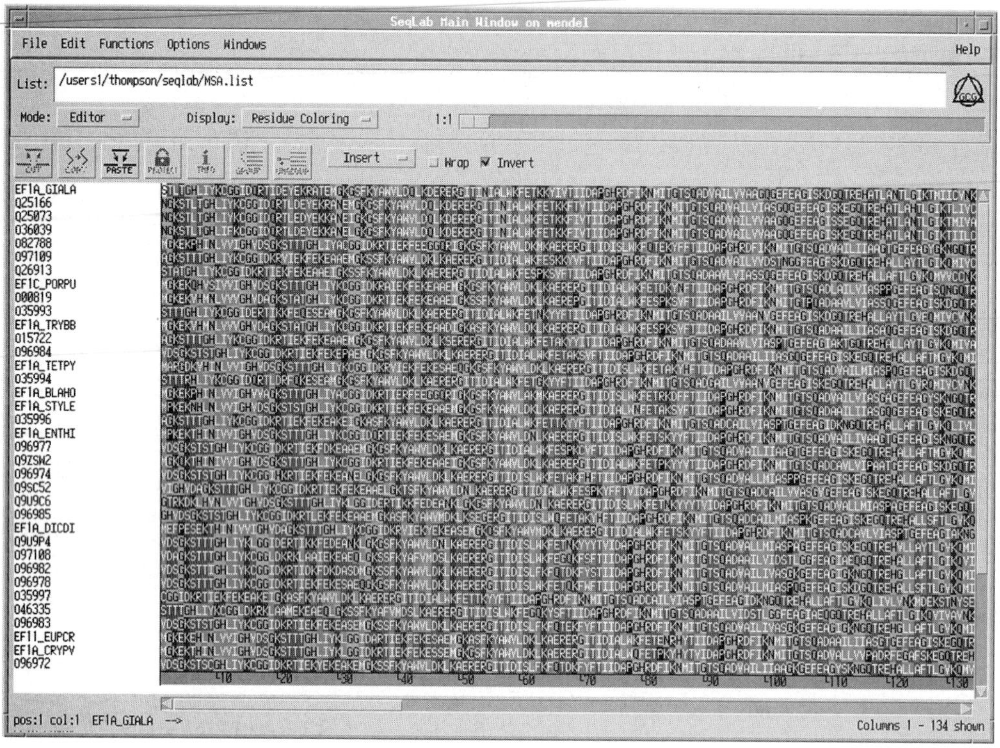

Fig. 3. The SeqLab Editor loaded with sorted FastA output. FastA can be used as a tool to sort a list into ranked order based on similarity to a particular query. Any desired portion of this output can then be loaded into the SeqLab editor for further analysis.

See companion CD for color Fig. 3

asking phylogenetic questions, you will not want to modify the sequences. Load their full length to maximize the available signal. However, if you are using extremely diverse sequences and/or domains of sequences, then trimming the sequences to the most conserved portions identified by FastA can be very helpful. Figure 3 shows the Editor display after loading the top part of my FastA file. At this juncture go to the **File** menu and save the RSF file. **Overwrite** in the **File exists** box if you have used the same name for this file earlier. RSF files are quite large and there is no need to save all the versions of the data.

MEME

A powerful *de novo* motif discovery algorithm can be run before actually performing multiple sequence alignment. The Expectation Maximization algorithm uses Bayesian probabilities and unsupervised learning to identify conserved motifs among a group of unaligned, ungapped sequences. The motifs do not have to be in congruent order among the different sequences, i.e., it has the power to discover *unalignable* motifs between sequences. This characteristic differentiates MEME from most other profile building techniques. It is implemented as the MEME program and it produces output containing a multiple profile file as well as a readable report file. The profile output serves as input to MotifSearch.

Select all of the sequences in the Editor window to run MEME. Several methods are available for selecting multiple sequence entry names. Either drag the mouse through them all if they are all visible at once in the display, or **<shift><click>** on the top- and bottom-most entries (select nonadjacent entries with <ctrl><clicks>), or select **Select All** from the **Edit** menu. Launch **MEME** from the **Functions Multiple Comparisons** menu. A **Which selection** window may pop up, asking whether you want to use either the **selected sequences** or **selected region**; choose **selected sequences** to run the program on the entire set of sequences. The algorithm can be sped up at the cost of sensitivity by decreasing the number of motifs to be found, by restricting the number of motifs found to exactly one in each sequence, and/or by decreasing the allowable motif window size.

MEME output consists of two files; a **.meme** readable text file and a **.prf** multiple profile text file. MotifSearch will scan any dataset specified with the multiple profile file that MEME produced. Scanning the original *training* dataset will annotate those regions that MEME discovered in your SeqLab Editor RSF file. After alignment the MEME motifs that are alignable will all line up. Go to the **Database Sequence Searching** menu and select **MotifSearch. . .** Specify your **query profile(s),** the one you just made, and change the **Search set** to the RSF dataset that is loaded in the Editor. Be sure to activate **Save motif features to the RSF file.** The output will return a .rsf file on top. This file contains the SeqLab format feature data discovered by MEME in your dataset. The .ms file contains the readable results of the search in list file format with the Expectation-value statistics and the number of motif hits for each hit. After the list file portion a *Position diagram* schematically describes the hits in each sequence. This can be viewed by pressing the **Display** button in the Output Manager.

The Output Manager can be used to merge the motifsearch.rsf feature file with the existing data already open in the SeqLab Editor. This will add the feature annotation created with the MotifSearch-**RSF** option. The location of each motif will be included in the Editor sequence display. Use the **Add to Editor** Output Manager function. As noted earlier, specify **Overwrite old with new** in the next window when prompted. **Close** the **Output Manager** after loading the new RSF file. Change **Display:** to **Graphic Features** and check out the additional annotation. Figure 4 illustrates **Graphic Features** display at a **4:1** zoom ratio.

See companion CD for color Fig. 4

Searching PROSITE—GCG's Motifs

Many features have been described and catalogued in biological sequences over the years. Most have consensus patterns that allow one to screen an unknown sequence for their occurrence. One database of catalogued structural, regulatory, and enzymatic consensus patterns is Amos Bairoch's protein signature database, the *PROSITE Dictionary of Protein Sites and Patterns*. It is one of the quickest and easiest databases to search with a peptide sequence. The GCG program Motifs performs this search. The program can tolerate mismatches with a -MisMatch option and it displays an abstract with selected references for each motif signature found. In many cases this can be a tremendous aid that can suggest the function of an unknown peptide sequence. It can often lead to immediate answers and routes of investigation.

Start the Motifs program by selecting all of the protein entry names in SeqLab, then go to the **Functions Protein Analysis** menu and select **Motifs. . ..** The **Motifs** program window will be displayed. Check the **Save results as features in file motifs.rsf**

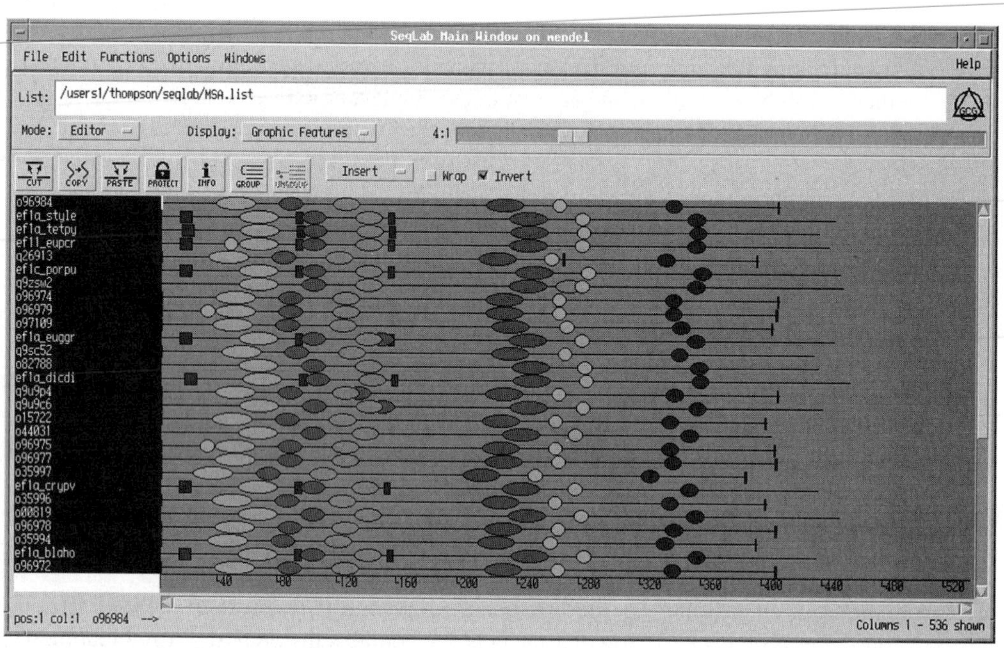

Fig. 4. Graphic Features display, MEME results. SeqLab can use *cartoons* to graphically display the feature annotation contained in sequence database entries and produced by programs such as MotifSearch. SeqLab merges this annotation with existing datasets with the **Add to Editor** and **Overwrite old with new** function. It also allows the user to *zoom in or out* on a dataset to see its entire length at once.

button in the **Motifs** program window. This file contains annotation discovered by the program. After running the program, the **motifs.rsf** file displayed. **Close** it and use the **Output Manager** to display the file with the **.motifs** extension. Notice the sites in the Motifs output file in Table 3 that have been characterized in these sequences and associated bibliography. This information can save a tremendous amount of work! Each site is shown with its sequence location below each consensus pattern. Post-translational modification sites found in many proteins, such as glycosylation, phosphorylation, amidation, and myristylation, will only be listed if the -Frequent option is specicifed. Realize that sites may be false positives. This is always a danger with simple consensus style searches. Notice that Motifs discovered the truly positive GTP-binding elongation factor signature and the ATP/GTP-binding P-loop site, yet it also found two probable false positives, the Prokaryotic membrane lipoprotein lipid attachment site and the FGGY family of carbohydrate kinases signature.

Close the **Motifs** output window, then load the motifs.rsf file into SeqLab. This will add the feature annotation created with the **RSF** option. The location of the PROSITE signatures will now be included in the Editor sequence display. Again use the **SeqLab Output Manager**. Select the file **motifs.rsf**, then press the **Add to Editor** button and specify **Overwrite old with new** to take the new motifs.rsf feature file and merge it with the old RSF file in the open Editor. **Close** the **Output Manager** after loading the RSF file. To display the new annotation, use **Features Coloring** or **Graphic Features**. Figure 5 shows the dataset using **Features Coloring** now annotated with its original database features as well as MEME discoveries and Motifs patterns.

See companion CD for color Fig. 5

Table 3
Abridged Motifs Output[a]

MOTIFS from: @/users1/thompson/.seqlab-mendel/motifs_54.list
Mismatches: 0 May 17, 2001 10:25 ..
input_54.rsf{GIARDIA_L} Check: 6084 Length: 475 ! In situ PileUp of: @/users 1/thompson/.seqlab-mendel/pileup_36.list

---

```
Efactor_Gtp D(K,R,S,T,G,A,N,Q,F,Y,W)x3E(K,R,A,Q)x(R,K,Q,D)(G,C)(I,V,M,K)(S,T)(I,V)x2(G,S,T,A,C,K,R,N,Q)
            D(Q)x{3} E(R)x(R)(G)(I)(T)(I)x{2} (A)
  64: YAWVL DQLKDERERGITINIA LWKFE
******************************************
* GTP-binding elongation factors signature *
******************************************
```

Elongation factors [1,2] are proteins catalyzing the elongation of peptide chains in protein biosynthesis. In both prokaryotes and eukaryotes, there are three distinct types of elongation factors, as described in the following table:

Eukaryotes	Prokaryotes	Function
EF-1alpha	EF-Tu	Binds GTP and an aminoacyl-tRNA; delivers the latter to the A site of ribosomes.
EF-1beta	EF-Ts	Interacts with EF-1a/EF-Tu to displace GDP and thus allows the regeneration of GTP-EF-1a.
EF-2	EF-G	Binds GTP and peptidyl-tRNA and translocates the latter from the A site to the P site.

The GTP-binding elongation factor family also includes the following proteins:

- Eukaryotic peptide chain release factor GTP-binding subunits (3). These proteins interact with release factors that bind to ribosomes that have encountered a stop codon at their decoding site and help them to induce release of the nascent polypeptide. The yeast protein was known as SUP2 (and also as SUP35, SUF12 or GST1) and the human homolog as GST1-Hs.
- Prokaryotic peptide chain release factor 3 (RF-3) (gene prfC). RF-3 is a class-II RF, a GTP-binding protein that interacts with class I RFs (see ERROR[Unused arguments - too many, or wrong type] in:<PDOC00607>) and enhance their activity (4).
- Prokaryotic GTP-binding protein lepA and its homolog in yeast (gene GUF1) and in Caenorhabditis elegans (ZK1236.1).
- Yeast HBS1 (5).
- Rat statin S1 (6), a protein of unknown function which is highly similar to EF-1alpha.
- Prokaryotic selenocysteine-specific elongation factor selB (7), which seems to replace EF-Tu for the insertion of selenocysteine directed by the UGA codon.
- The tetracycline resistance proteins tetM/tetO (8,9) from various bacteria such as Campylobacter jejuni, Enterococcus faecalis, Streptococcus mutans and Ureaplasma urealyticum. Tetracycline binds to the prokaryotic ribosomal 30S subunit and inhibits binding of aminoacyl-tRNAs. These proteins abolish the inhibitory effect of tetracycline on protein synthesis.
- Rhizobium nodulation protein nodQ (10).
- Escherichia coli hypothetical protein yihK (11).

In EF-1-alpha, a specific region has been shown (12) to be involved in a conformational change mediated by the hydrolysis of GTP to GDP. This region is conserved in both EF-1alpha/EF-Tu as well as EF-2/EF-G and thus seems typical for GTP-dependent proteins which bind non-initiator tRNAs to the ribosome. The pattern we developed for this family of proteins include that conserved region.

-Consensus pattern: D-[KRSTGANQFYW]-x(3)-E-[KRAQ]-x-[RKQD]-[GC]-[IVMK]-[ST]- [IV]-x(2)-[GSTACKRNQ]
-Sequences known to belong to this class detected by the pattern: ALL, except for 11 sequences.
-Other sequence(s) detected in SWISS-PROT: NONE.
-Last update: November 1997 / Text revised.

[1] Concise Encyclopedia Biochemistry (1988) 2nd ed., Walter de Gruyter, Berlin, NY.
[2] Moldave, K. (1985) Annu. Rev. Biochem. 54, 1109-1149.
[3] Stansfield, I., Jones, K. M., Kushnirov, V. V., et al. (1995) EMBO J. 14, 4365-4373.
[4] Grentzmann, G., Brechemier-Baey, D., Heurgue-Hamard, V., Buckingham, R. H. (1995) J. Biol. Chem. 270, 10,595-10,600.
[5] Nelson, R. J., Ziegelhoffer, T., Nicolet, C., Werner-Washburne, M., Craig, E.A. (1992) Cell 71, 97-105.
[6] Ann, D. K., Moutsatsos, I. K., Nakamura, T., et al. (1991) J. Biol. Chem. 266, 10,429-10,437.
[7] Forchammer, K., Leinfeldr, W., Bock A. (1989) Nature 342, 453-456.
[8] Manavathu, E. K., Hiratsuka, K., Taylor, D. E. (1988) Gene 62, 17-26.
[9] Leblanc, D. J., Lee, L. N., Titmas, B. M., Smith, C. J., Tenover, F. C. (1988) J. Bacteriol. 170, 3618-3626.
[10] Cervantes, E., Sharma, S. B., Maillet, F., Vasse, J., Truchet, G., Rosenberg, C. (1989) Mol. Microbiol. 3, 745-755.
[11] Plunkett, III, G., Burland, V. D., Daniels, D. L., Blattner, F. R. (1993) Nucleic Acids Res. 21, 3391-3398.
[12] Moller, W., Schipper, A., Amons, R. (1987) Biochimie 69, 983-989.

^^

//

input_54.rsf{CRYPTOSPORIDIUM_P} Check: 6774 Length: 475 ! In situ PileUp of: @/users1/thompson/.seqlab-mendel/pileup_36.list

---

```
Atp_Gtp_A               (A,G)x4GK(S,T)
                         (G)x{4} GK(S)
          17: NLVVI       GHVDSGKS      TTTGH
****************************************
* ATP/GTP-binding site motif A (P-loop) *
****************************************
```

From sequence comparisons and crystallographic data analysis it has been shown [1,2,3,4,5,6] that an appreciable proportion of proteins that bind ATP or GTPshare a number of more or less conserved sequence motifs. The best conserved of these motifs is a glycine-rich region, which typically forms a flexible loop between a beta-strand and an alpha-helix. This loop interacts with one of the phosphate groups of the nucleotide. This sequence motif is generally referred to as the 'A' consensus sequence [1] or the 'P-loop' [5].

(continued)

Table 3 *(continued)*
Abridged Motifs Output[a]

There are numerous ATP- or GTP-binding proteins in which the P-loop is found. We list below a number of protein families for which the relevance of the presence of such motif has been noted:
- ATP synthase alpha and beta subunits (see <PDOC00137>).
- Myosin heavy chains.
- Kinesin heavy chains and kinesin-like proteins (see <PDOC00343>).
- Dynamins and dynamin-like proteins (see <PDOC00362>).
- Guanylate kinase (see <PDOC00670>).
- Thymidine kinase (see <PDOC00524>).
- Thymidylate kinase (see <PDOC01034>).
- Shikimate kinase (see <PDOC00868>).
- Nitrogenase iron protein family (nifH/frxC) (see <PDOC00580>).
- ATP-binding proteins involved in 'active transport' (ABC transporters) [7] (see <PDOC00185>).
- DNA and RNA helicases [8,9,10].
- GTP-binding elongation factors (EF-Tu, EF-1alpha, EF-G, EF-2, etc.).
- Ras family of GTP-binding proteins (Ras, Rho, Rab, Ral, Ypt1, SEC4, etc.).
- Nuclear protein ran (see <PDOC00859>).
- ADP-ribosylation factors family (see <PDOC00781>).
- Bacterial dnaA protein (see <PDOC00771>).
- Bacterial recA protein (see <PDOC00131>).
- Bacterial recF protein (see <PDOC00539>).
- Guanine nucleotide-binding proteins alpha subunits (Gi, Gs, Gt, G0, etc.).
- DNA mismatch repair proteins mutS family (See <PDOC00388>).
- Bacterial type II secretion system protein E (see <PDOC00567>).

Not all ATP- or GTP-binding proteins are picked-up by this motif. A number of proteins escape detection because the structure of their ATP-binding site is completely different from that of the P-loop. Examples of such proteins are the E1-E2 ATPases or the glycolytic kinases. In other ATP- or GTP-binding proteins the flexible loop exists in a slightly different form; this is the case for tubulins or protein kinases. A special mention must be reserved for adenylate kinase, in which there is a single deviation from the P-loop pattern: in the last position Gly is found instead of Ser or Thr.

- Consensus pattern: [AG]-x(4)-G-K-[ST]
- Sequences known to belong to this class detected by the pattern: a majority.
- Other sequence(s) detected in SWISS-PROT: in addition to the proteins listed above, the 'A' motif is also found in a number of other proteins. Most of these proteins probably bind a nucleotide, but others are definitively not ATP- or GTP-binding (as for example chymotrypsin, or human ferritin light chain).
- Expert(s) to contact by email: Koonin E.V.; koonin@ncbi.nlm.nih.gov
- Last update: July 1999 / Text revised.

[1] Walker, J. E., Saraste, M., Runswick, M. J., Gay, N. J. (1982) EMBO J. 1, 945-951.
[2] Moller, W., Amons, R. (1985) FEBS Lett. 186, 1-7.
[3] Fry, D. C., Kuby, S. A., Mildvan, A. S. (1986) Proc. Natl. Acad. Sci. USA 83, 907-911.
[4] Dever, T. E., Glynias, M. J., Merrick, W. C. (1987) Proc. Natl. Acad. Sci. USA 84, 1814-1818.
[5] Saraste, M., Sibbald, P. R., Wittinghofer, A. (1990) Trends Biochem. Sci. 15, 430-434.
[6] Koonin, E. V. (1993) J. Mol. Biol. 229, 1165-1174.
[7] Higgins, C. F., Hyde, S. C., Mimmack, M. M., Gileadi, U., Gill, D. R., Gallagher, M. P. (1990) J. Bioenerg. Biomembr. 22, 571-592.
[8] Hodgman, T. C. (1988) Nature 333, 22-23, Nature (Errata) 333, 578-578.
[9] Linder, P., Lasko, P., Ashburner, M., et al. (1989) Nature 337, 121-122.
[10] Gorbalenya, A. E., Koonin, E. V., Donchenko, A. P., Blinov, V. M. (1989) Nucleic Acids Res. 17, 4713-4730.

```
^^^^^^^^^^^^^^^^^^^^^^^^^^^^^^^^^^^^^^^^^^^^^^^^^^^^^^^^^^^^^^^^^^^^^^^^^^^^^^^^^^^^^^^^^^^^^^^^^^^^^^^^^^^^
////////////////////////////////////////////////////////////////////////////////////////////////////////////
input_54.rsf{BLASTOCYSTIS_H} Check: 172 Length: 475 ! In situ PileUp of: @/users1/thompson/.seqlab-mendel/
pileup_36.list

Atp_Gtp_A              (A,G)x4GK(S,T)
                       (G)x{4} GK(S)
         17: NLVVI       GHVVAGKS      TTTGH

Find reference above under sequence: input_54.rsf{CRYPTOSPORIDIUM_P} , pattern: Atp_Gtp_A.
------------------------------------------------------------------------------------------------------------
Prokar_Lipoprotein ~(D,E,R,K)6(L,I,V,M,F,W,S,T,A,G)2(L,I,V,M,F,Y,S,T,A,G,C,Q) (A,G,S)C
                   ~(D,E,R,K){6} (L,I){2} (Y)(A)C
         24: VVAGK                        STTTGHLIYAC
      GGIDK

********************************************************
* Prokaryotic membrane lipoprotein lipid attachment site *
********************************************************
```

In prokaryotes, membrane lipoproteins are synthesized with a precursor signal peptide, which is cleaved by a specific lipoprotein signal peptidase (signal peptidase II). The peptidase recognizes a conserved sequence and cuts upstream of a cysteine residue to which a glyceride-fatty acid lipid is attached [1].

Some of the proteins known to undergo such processing currently include (for recent listings see [1,2,3]:
- Major outer membrane lipoprotein (murein-lipoproteins) (gene lpp).
- Escherichia coli lipoprotein-28 (gene nlpA).
- Escherichia coli lipoprotein-34 (gene nlpB).
- Escherichia coli lipoprotein nlpC.
- Escherichia coli lipoprotein nlpD.
- Escherichia coli osmotically inducible lipoprotein B (gene osmB).
- Escherichia coli osmotically inducible lipoprotein E (gene osmE).
- Escherichia coli peptidoglycan-associated lipoprotein (gene pal).
- Escherichia coli rare lipoproteins A and B (genes rplA and rplB).
- Escherichia coli copper homeostasis protein cutF (or nlpE).
- Escherichia coli plasmids traT proteins.
- Escherichia coli Col plasmids lysis proteins.
- A number of Bacillus beta-lactamases.

Table 3 *(continued)*
Abridged Motifs Output[a]

```
- Bacillus subtilis periplasmic oligopeptide-binding protein (gene oppA).
- Borrelia burgdorferi outer surface proteins A and B (genes ospA and ospB).
- Borrelia hermsii variable major protein 21 (gene vmp21) and 7 (gene vmp7).
- Chlamydia trachomatis outer membrane protein 3 (gene omp3).
- Fibrobacter succinogenes endoglucanase cel-3.
- Haemophilus influenzae proteins Pal and Pcp.
- Klebsiella pullulunase (gene pulA).
- Klebsiella pullulunase secretion protein pulS.
- Mycoplasma hyorhinis protein p37.
- Mycoplasma hyorhinis variant surface antigens A, B, and C (genes vlpABC).
- Neisseria outer membrane protein H.8.
- Pseudomonas aeruginosa lipopeptide (gene lppL).
- Pseudomonas solanacearum endoglucanase egl.
- Rhodopseudomonas viridis reaction center cytochrome subunit (gene cytC).
- Rickettsia 17 Kd antigen.
- Shigella flexneri invasion plasmid proteins mxiJ and mxiM.
- Streptococcus pneumoniae oligopeptide transport protein A (gene amiA).
- Treponema pallidium 34 Kd antigen.
- Treponema pallidium membrane protein A (gene tmpA).
- Vibrio harveyi chitobiase (gene chb).
- Yersinia virulence plasmid protein yscJ.
- Halocyanin from Natrobacterium pharaonis (4), a membrane associated copper-binding protein. This is the first
  archaebacterial protein known to be modified in such a fashion).
From the precursor sequences of all these proteins, we derived a consensus pattern and a set of rules to identify this
type of post-translational modification.
-Consensus pattern: {DERK} (6)-[LIVMFWSTAG](2)-[LIVMFYSTAGCQ]-[AGS]-C [C is the lipid attachment site]
 Additional rules: 1) The cysteine must be between positions 15 and 35 of the sequence in consideration.
                   2) There must be at least one Lys or one Arg in the first seven positions of the sequence.
-Sequences known to belong to this class detected by the pattern: ALL.
-Other sequence(s) detected in SWISS-PROT: some 100 prokaryotic proteins. Some of them are not membrane
 lipoproteins, but at least half of them could be.
-Last update: November 1995 / Pattern and text revised.
[1] Hayashi, S., Wu, H. C. (1990) J. Bioenerg. Biomembr. 22, 451-471.
[2] Klein, P., Somorjai, R. L., Lau, P. C. K. (1988) Protein Eng. 2, 15-20.
[3] von Heijne, G. (1989) Protein Eng. 2, 531-534.
[4] Mattar, S., Scharf, B., Kent, S. B. H., Rodewald, K., Oesterhelt, D., Engelhard M. (1994) J. Biol. Chem. 269,
    14,939-14,945.
^^^^^^^^^^^^^^^^^^^^^^^^^^^^^^^^^^^^^^^^^^^^^^^^^^^^^^^^^^^^^^^^^^^^^^^^^^^^^^^^^^^^^^^^^^^^^^^^^^^^^^^^^^^^^^^^
////////////////////////////////////////////////////////////////////////////////////////////////////////////////
input_54.rsf{PHYTOPHTHORA_I} Check: 9509 Length: 475 ! In situ PileUp of: @/users1/thompson/.seqlab-mendel/
pileup_36.list
Atp_Gtp_A              (A,G)x4GK(S,T)
                        (G)x{4} GK(S)
           17: ...VI    GHVDAGKS    TTTGH
Find reference above under sequence: input_54.rsf{CRYPTOSPORIDIUM_P} , pattern: Atp_Gtp_A.
Efactor_Gtp            D(K,R,S,T,G,A,N,Q,F,Y,W)x3E(K,R,A,Q)x(R,K,Q,D)(G,C)(I,V,M,K)(S,T)(I,V)x2(G,S,T,A,C,K,R,N,Q)
                       D(N)x{3} E(R)x(R)(G)(I)(T)(I)x{2} (A)
            64: YAWVL DNLKAERERGITIDIA LWKFE
Find reference above under sequence: input_54.rsf{GIARDIA_L} , pattern: Efactor_Gtp.
________________________________________________________________________________
Fggy_Kinases_1         (M,F,Y,G,S)x(P,S,T)x2K(L,I,V,M,F,Y,W)xW(L,I,V,M,F)x(D,E,N,Q,T,K,R)(E,N,Q,H)
                       (G)x(T)x{2} K(Y)xW(V)x(D)(N)
            53: EAAEL GKTSFKYAWVLDN LKAER
**************************************************
* FGGY family of carbohydrate kinases signatures *
**************************************************
It has been shown [1] that four different type of carbohydrate kinases seem tobe evolutionary related. These
enzymes are:
 - L-fucolokinase (EC 2.7.1.51) (gene fucK).
 - Gluconokinase (EC 2.7.1.12) (gene gntK).
 - Glycerokinase (EC 2.7.1.30) (gene glpK).
 - Xylulokinase (EC 2.7.1.17) (gene xylB).
 - L-xylulose kinase (EC 2.7.1.53) (gene lyxK).
These enzymes are proteins of from 480 to 520 amino acid residues. As consensus patterns for this family of kinases
we selected two conserved regions, one in the central section, the other in the C-terminal section.
-Consensus pattern: [MFYGS]-x-[PST]-x(2)-K-[LIVMFYW]-x-W-[LIVMF]-x-[DENQTKR]- [ENQH]
-Sequences known to belong to this class detected by the pattern: ALL, except for lyxK.
-Other sequence(s) detected in SWISS-PROT: 5.
-Consensus pattern: [GSA]-x-[LIVMFYW]-x-G-[LIVM]-x(7,8)-[HDENQ]-[LIVMF]-x(2)-[AS]-[STAIVM]-[LIVMFY]-[DEQ]
-Sequences known to belong to this class detected by the pattern: ALL.
-Other sequence(s) detected in SWISS-PROT: 11.
-Expert(s) to contact by email: Reizer J.; jreizer@ucsd.edu
-Last update: November 1997 / Patterns and text revised.
[1] Reizer, A., Deutscher, J., Saier, Jr., M. H., Reizer, J. (1991) Mol. Microbiol. 5, 1081-1089.
^^^^^^^^^^^^^^^^^^^^^^^^^^^^^^^^^^^^^^^^^^^^^^^^^^^^^^^^^^^^^^^^^^^^^^^^^^^^^^^^^^
//////////////////////////////////////////////////////////////////////////////////
```

[a]PROSITE patterns found by the GCG Motifs program in the example elongation factor dataset.

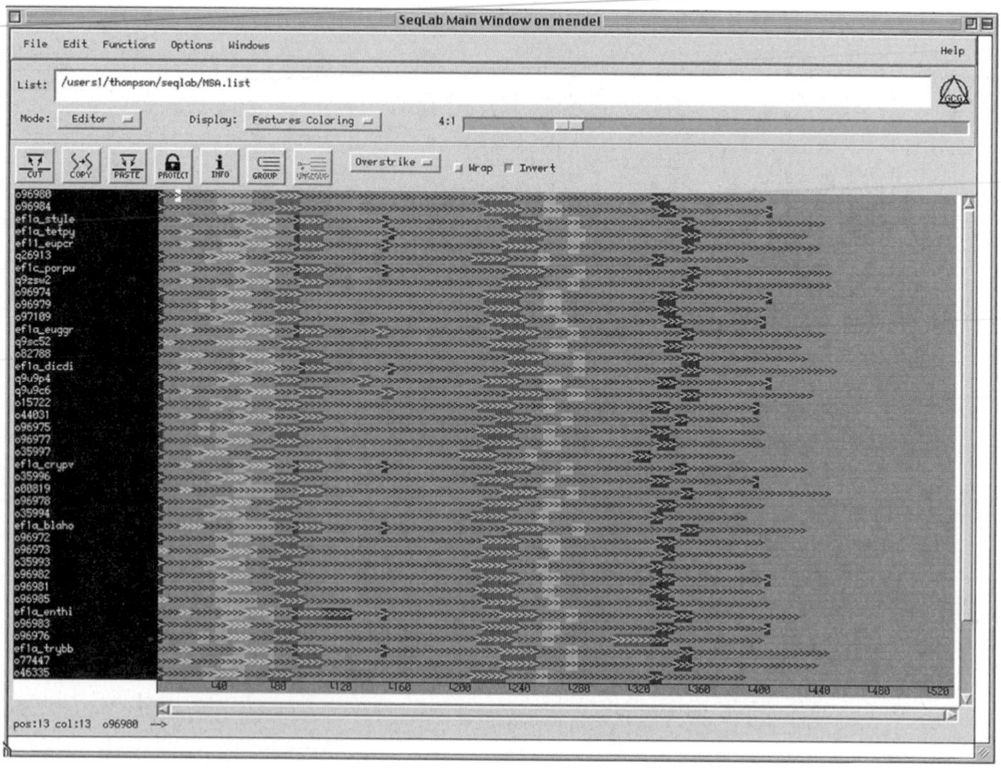

Fig. 5. Motifs RSF annotation displayed by SeqLab. Motifs can create an RSF file with the location of PROSITE patterns annotated by color and shape. The display now shows annotation from the database, from the program pair MEME/MotifSearch, and from the program Motifs using **Features Coloring**.

Performing the Alignment Using the PileUp Program

To align all of these protein sequences, select all of the entries in the Editor window using one of the methods discussed. Once all of the sequences are selected, go to the **Functions** menu and select **Multiple comparison.** Click on **PileUp. . .** to align the entries. A new window will appear with the parameters for running PileUp. Be sure that the **How:** box indicates a **Background Job.** Often you'll accept all of the program defaults on a first run by pressing the **Run** button. As a default this would use the BLOSUM62 scoring matrix. However, the BLOSUM30 matrix can be helpful for aligning more divergent sequences. Depending on the level of divergence in a data set, better multiple sequence alignments can often be generated with alternate scoring matrices (the -Matrix option, specifies the desired matrix from the GCG logical directory GenMoreData) and/or different gap penalties. Beginning with GCG version 9.0, the BLOSUM62 matrix file, blosum62.cmp, is used as the default symbol comparison table. Furthermore, appropriate gap creation and extension penalties are now coded directly into the matrix, though they can still be adjusted within the program if desired. This is greatly improved over the normalized Dayhoff PAM 250 table and the program encoded penalty values formerly used. The BLOSUM series ranges from BLOSUM30 being appropriate for the most divergent datasets, to the BLOSUM100 table for the conserved datasets.

Click on the **Options** button. To specify the BLOSUM30 matrix select the check button next to and click on the **Scoring Matrix . . .** box in the **Pileup Options** window. This will launch a **Chooser for Scoring Matrix** window from which you can select the BLOSUM30 matrix file, **blosum30.cmp.** Double-click the matrix's name to see what it looks like; click **OK** to close both windows. Scroll through the rest of the **PileUp Options** window to see all the available options. **Close** it when finished and press **Run** in the **PileUp** window to launch the program.

The program first compares every sequence with every other one. This pairwise comparison will progressively merge the sequences into an alignment in order of similarity, from most to least similar. The window will disappear and then, depending on the complexity of the alignment and the load on the server, display a series of new output windows. The top window will be the Multiple Sequence Format (MSF) output from your PileUp run. Notice the BLOSUM30 matrix specification and the default gap introduction and extension penalties associated with that matrix, 15 and 5 respectively. As mentioned above, in most cases the default gap penalties will work fine with their respective matrices, though they can be changed if desired. As shown in the example in Table 4, notice the interleaved character of the sequences. They all have unique identities, addressable through their MSF filename together with their own name in braces, {name}.

The listing of sequence names near the top of the file contains the checksum. All GCG sequence programs use this number as a unique sequence identifier. There is a checksum line for the alignment as well as individual checksum lines for each member of the alignment. If any two of the checksum numbers are the same, then those sequences are identical. If they are, an editor can be used to place an exclamation point, ! at the start of the checksum line in the duplicate sequence. Exclamation points are interpreted by GCG as remark delineators, therefore, the duplicate sequence will be ignored in subsequent programs. Or the sequence could be **CUT** from the alignment with the SeqLab Editor. Similarly, the *Weight* designation determines how each sequence contributes to the alignment profile. Sometimes it is worthwhile to adjust these values so that the contribution of a collection of very similar sequences does not overwhelm the signal from the more divergent sequences.

Use the **Output Manager**, **Add to Editor**, and **Overwrite old with new** to take the new MSF output and merge it with the old RSF file in the open Editor. This will keep all of the database feature annotation intact, yet renumber all of the reference locations based on the gaps in the alignment. **Close** the **Output Manager** after loading the new alignment. The next window will contain PileUp's cluster dendrogram, in the EF-1α example, as shown in Fig. 6.

See companion CD for color Fig. 6

PileUp automatically creates this dendrogram of clustering similarity between the sequences. It can be very helpful for adjusting the sequence Weight values, to average the contribution of each sequence to a profile. The lengths of the vertical lines are proportional to the differences in similarity between the sequences. This tree is not an evolutionary tree, and it should never be presented as one. It is akin to an uncorrected Unweighted Pair Group Method with Arithmetic Mean (UPGMA) tree, prone to all the same UPGMA errors. If the rates of evolution for each lineage were exactly the same, then it could represent a *true* phylogenetic tree, but this is seldom the case in nature. No phylogenetic inference optimization criteria algorithm, such as maximum likelihood, least-squares fit, or parsimony, nor any molecular substitution, multiple hit correction models, such as Jukes-Cantor, Kimura, or any other subset of the

Table 4
GCG PileUp Output, Abridged[a]

```
!!AA_MULTIPLE_ALIGNMENT 1.0
PileUp of: @/users1/thompson/.seqlab-mendel/pileup_28.list

 Symbol comparison table: /usr/gcg/gcgcore/data/moredata/blosum30.cmp CompCheck: 8599

                   GapWeight: 15
             GapLengthWeight: 5

 pileup_28.msf MSF: 472 Type: P May 14, 2001 14:35 Check: 2476 ..

 Name: ef1a_giala Len: 472 Check: 8631 Weight: 1.00
 Name:     q25166 Len: 472 Check: 6209 Weight: 1.00
 Name:     q25073 Len: 472 Check: 2914 Weight: 1.00
 Name:     o36039 Len: 472 Check: 7560 Weight: 1.00
 Name:     o96981 Len: 472 Check: 3858 Weight: 1.00
 Name:     o96980 Len: 472 Check: 3082 Weight: 1.00
 Name:     o44031 Len: 472 Check: 851 Weight: 1.00
 Name: ef1a_crypv Len: 472 Check: 2406 Weight: 1.00
 Name:     o77447 Len: 472 Check: 9210 Weight: 1.00
 Name:     o77478 Len: 472 Check: 1123 Weight: 1.00
 Name: ef1a_plafk Len: 472 Check: 1436 Weight: 1.00
/////////////////////////////////////////////////////////////
 Name:     o96978 Len: 472 Check: 6796 Weight: 1.00
 Name: ef1c_porpu Len: 472 Check: 6199 Weight: 1.00
 Name:     o46335 Len: 472 Check: 7668 Weight: 1.00
 Name:     o97108 Len: 472 Check: 5669 Weight: 1.00
 Name:     o97109 Len: 472 Check: 6457 Weight: 1.00

//

           1                                                   50
ef1a_giala ~~~~~~~~~~ ~~~~~~~~~~ ~~~STLTGHL IYKCGGIDQR TIDEYEKRAT
    q25166 ~~~~~~~~~~ ~~~~~~~~~~ NGKSTLTGHL IYKCGGIDQR TLDEYEKRAN
    q25073 ~~~~~~~~~~ ~~~~~~~~~~ NGKSTLTGHL IYKCGGIDQR TLEDYEKKAN
    o36039 ~~~~~~~~~~ ~~~~~~~~~~ NGKSTLTGHL IFKCGGIDQR TLDEYEKKAN
    o96981 ~~~~~~~~~~ ~~~~~~~~VD SGKSTSTGHL IYKCGGIDER TIEKFEKEAK
    o96980 ~~~~~~~~~~ ~~~~~~~~VD SGKSTSTGHL IYKCGGIDER TIEKFEKEAK
    o44031 ~~~MGKEKTH INLVVIGHVD SGKSTTTGHL IYKLGGIDKR TIEKFEKESS
ef1a_crypv ~~~MGKEKTH INLVVIGHVD SGKSTTTGHL IYKLGGIDKR TIEKFEKESS
    o77447 ~~~MGKEKTH INLVVIGHVD SGKSTTTGHI IYKLGGIDRR TIEKFEKESA
    o77478 ~~~MGKEKTH INLVVIGHVD SGKSTTTGHI IYKLGGIDRR TIEKFEKESA
ef1a_plafk ~~~MGKEKTH INLVVIGHVD SGKSTTTGHI IYKLGGIDRR TIEKFEKESA
    o96975 ~~~~~~~~~~ ~~~~~~~~VD SGKSTTTGHL IYKLGGTDAR TIEKFEKESA
    o96976 ~~~~~~~~~~ ~~~~~~~~VD SGKSTTTGHL IYKCGGIDAR TIEKFEKESA
ef11_eupcr ~~~MGKEKEH LNLVVIGHVD SGKSTTTGHL IYKLGGIDAR TIEKFEKESA
    o82788 ~~~MGKEKPH INLVVIGHVD SGKSTTTGHL IYACGGIDKR TIERFEEGGQ
ef1a_blaho ~~~MGKEKPH INLVVIGHVV AGKSTTTGHL IYACGGIDKR TIERFEEGGQ
    o96982 ~~~~~~~~~~ ~~~~~~~~VD SGKSTTIGHL IYKCGGIDKR TIDKFDKDAS
    o96983 ~~~~~~~~~~ ~~~~~~~~VD SGKSTSTGHL IYKCGGIDKR TIEKFEKEAS
    o96972 ~~~~~~~~~~ ~~~~~~~~VD SGKSTSCGHL IYKCGGIDKR TIEKYEKEAK
    o96973 ~~~~~~~~~~ ~~~~~~GHVD SGKSTSCGHL IYKCGGIDKR TIEKYEKEAN
ef1a_enthi ~~~MPKEKTH INIVVIGHVD SGKSTTTGHL IYKCGGIDQR TIEKFEKESA
    o35994 ~~~~~~~~~~ ~~~~~~~~~~ ~~~STTTRHL IYKCGGIDQR TLDRFQKESE
    o35993 ~~~~~~~~~~ ~~~~~~~~~~ ~~~STTTGHL IYKCGGIDER TIKKFEQESE
    q26913 ~~~~~~~~~~ ~~~~~~~~~~ ~~~STATGHL IYKCGGIDKR TIEKFEKEAA
    o00819 ~~~MGKEKVH MNLVVVGHVD AGKSTATGHL IYKCGGIDKR TIEKFEKEAA
ef1a_trybb ~~~MGKEKVH MNLVVVGHVD AGKSTATGHL IYKCGGIDKR TIEKFEKEAA
    o96977 ~~~~~~~~~~ ~~~~~~~~VD SGKSTSTGHL IYKCGGIDKR TIEKFDKEAA
ef1a_euggr ~~~MGKEKVH ISLVVIGHVD SGKSTTTGHL IYKCGGIDKR TIEKFEKEAS
    o35997 ~~~~~~~~~~ ~~~~~~~~~~ ~~~~~~~~~~ ~~~CGGIDKR TIEKFEKEAK
    o35996 ~~~~~~~~~~ ~~~~~~~~~~ AGKSTTTGHL IYKCGGIDKR TIEKFEKEAK
ef1a_dicdi MEFPESEKTH INIVVIGHVD AGKSTTTGHL IYKCGGIDKR VIEKYEKEAS
    o15722 ~~~~~~~~~~ ~~~~~~~~~~ AGKSTTTGHL IYKCGGIDKR TIEKFEKEAA
    q9zsw2 ~~~MGKQKTH INIVVIGHVD SGKSTTTGHL IYKCGGIDKR TIEKFEKEAA
    q9sc52 ~~~~~~~~~~ ~~~~VIGHVD AGKSTTTGHL IYKCGGIDKR TIEKFEKEAA
    o96984 ~~~~~~~~~~ ~~~~~~~~VD SGKSTSTGHL IYKCGGIDKR TIEKFEKEPA
ef1a_style ~~~MPKEKNH LNLVVIGHVD SGKSTSTGHL IYKCGGIDKR TIEKFEKEAA
    o96979 ~~~~~~~~~~ ~~~~~~~~VD SGKSTTTGHL IYKCGGIDKR VIEKFEKESA
ef1a_tetpy ~~MARGDKVH INLVVIGHVD SGKSTTTGHL IYKCGGIDKR VIEKFEKESA
    o96985 ~~~~~~~~~~ ~~~~~~GHVD SGKSTSTGHL IYKCGGIDKR TLEKFEKEAA
    q9u9p4 ~~~~~~~~~~ ~~~~~~~~VD SGKSTTTGHL IYKLGGIDER TIKKFEDEAN
    q9u9c6 ~~GTRKDKLH VNLVVIGHVD SGKSTTTGHL IYKLGGIDER TIKKFEDEAN
    o96974 ~~~~~~~~~~ ~~~~~~~~VD SGKSTSTGHL IYKCGGIHKR TIEKFEKEAN
    o96978 ~~~~~~~~~~ ~~~~~~~~VD SGKSTTTGHL IYKCGGIDKR TIEKFEKESA
ef1c_porpu ~~~MGKEKQH VSIVVIGHVD SGKSTTTGHL IYKCGGIDKR AIEKFEKEAA
    o46335 ~~~~~~~~~~ ~~~~~~~~~~ ~~~STTTGHL IYKCGGLDKR KLAAMEKEAE
    o97108 ~~~~~~~~~~ ~~~~~~~~VD AGKSTTTGHL IYKCGGLDKR KLAAIEKEAE
    o97109 ~~~~~~~~~~ ~~~~~~~~~~ AGKSTTTGHL IYKCGGIDKR VIEKFEKEAA

           51                                                 100
ef1a_giala EMGKGSFKYA WVLDQLKDER ERGITINIAL WKFETKKYIV TIIDAPGHRD
    q25166 EMGKGSFKYA WVLDQLKDER ERGITINIAL WKFETKKFTV TIIDAPGHRD
    q25073 EIGKGSFKYA WVLDQLKDER ERGITINIAL WKFETKKFIV TIIDAPGHRD
    o36039 ELGKGSFKYA WVLDQLKDER ERGITINIAL WKFETKKFIV TIIDAPGHRD
    o96981 QIGKESFKYA WVLDKLKAER ERGITIDIAL WKFESQKYSF TIIDAPGHRD
    o96980 QIGKESFKYA GLLDILKAER ARGITIDIAL WKFESQKYSF TIIDAPGHRD
    o44031 EMGKGSFKYA WVLDKLKAER ERGITIDIAL WQFETPKYHY TVIDAPGHRD
ef1a_crypv EMGKGSFKYA WVLDKLKAER ERGITIDIAL WQFETPKYHY TVIDAPGHRD
    o77447 EMGKGSFKYA WVLDKLKAER ERGITIDIAL WKFETPRYFF TVIDAPGHKD
    o77478 EMGKGSFKYA WVLDKLKAER ERGITIDIAL WKFETPRYFF TVIDAPGHKH
ef1a_plafk EMGKGSFKYA WVLDKLKAER ERGITIDIAL WKFETPRYFF TVIDAPGHKD
    o96975 EMGKGTFKYA WVLDKLKAER ERGITIDIAL WKFETTNRFY TIIDAPGHRD
    o96976 EMGKGSFKYA FVLDNLKAER ERGITIDIAL WKFETPKRFY TIIDAPGHRD
ef11_eupcr EMGKASFKYA WVLDKLKAER ERGITIDIAL WKFETENRHY TIIDAPGHRD
    o82788 RIGKGSFKYA WVLDKMKAER ERGITIDISL WKFQTEKYFF TIIDAPGHRD
ef1a_blaho RIGKGSFKYA WVLAKMKAER ERGITIDISL WKFETRKDFF TIIDAPGHRD
//////////////////////////////////////////////////////////////////
```

[a]An abridged GCG PileUp output MSF file. The format holds the file name, type, date, and checksum, sequence names, checksums, lengths, and weights, and the aligned sequence data in an interleaved fashion.

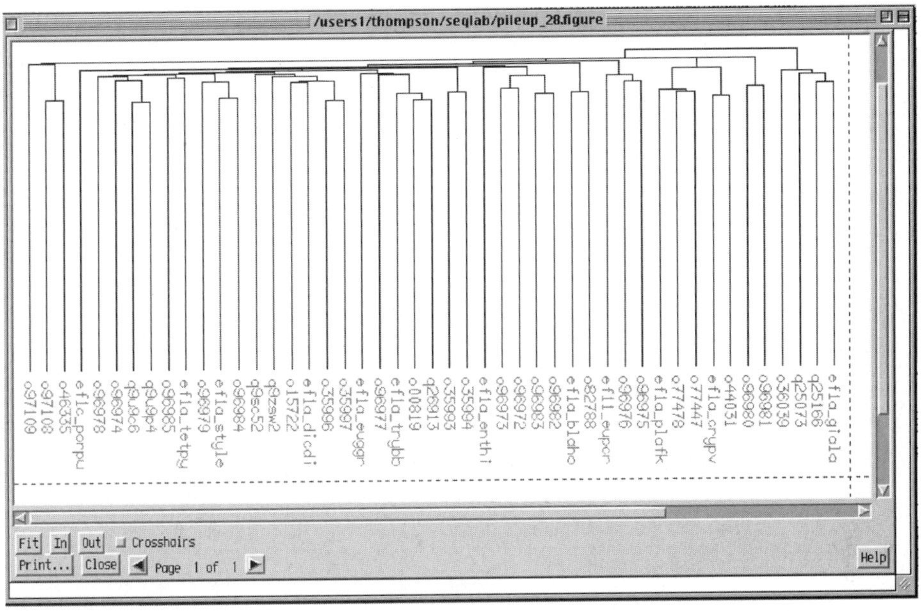

Fig. 6. PileUp's similarity dendrogram. The PileUp program automatically plots a cluster dendrogram of the similarities between the sequences of your dataset. The lengths of the vertical lines are proportional to those similarities.

General Time Reversible (GTR) model, nor any site rate heterogeneity models such as a Gamma correction, are used in its construction. PileUp's dendrogram merely indicates the relative similarity of the sequences based on the scoring matrix used and, is the clustering order used to create the alignment.

If desired, you can directly print from a SeqLab graphics Figure window to a PostScript file by selecting **Print . . .** Be sure that the **Output Device:** is **[Encapsulated] PostScript File.** You can rename the output file. Click **Proceed** to create an EPS file output in your current directory. To actually print this file you may need to transfer the file to a local machine attached to a PostScript printer unless you have direct access to the UNIX system printer and it is PostScript compatible. All Macintosh compatible laser printers use PostScript by default. Carefully check any laser printer connected to a Wintel system to be sure that it is PostScript compatible. **Close** the dendrogram window to return to the Editor.

See companion CD for color Figs. 7 and 8

After loading the MSF file using **Residue Coloring** and a **1:1** zoom ratio, the Editor display looks like Fig. 7 with the residues aligned by color. The columns of color represent columns of aligned residues. By changing the **Display:** box from **Residue Coloring** to **Graphic Features,** the display shows a schematic of the feature information from each entry, as well as all of the motifs discovered by the programs Motifs and MotifSearch, as in Fig. 8. Quick double-clicks on any of the color-coded feature regions in the Editor display will produce a **Features** window. Selecting the Feature entry in the new window reveals more information for that particular feature. Clicking once in the colored region and then using the **Features** option from the **Windows** menu will also produce the **Features** window. You should save this work as an updated RSF file!

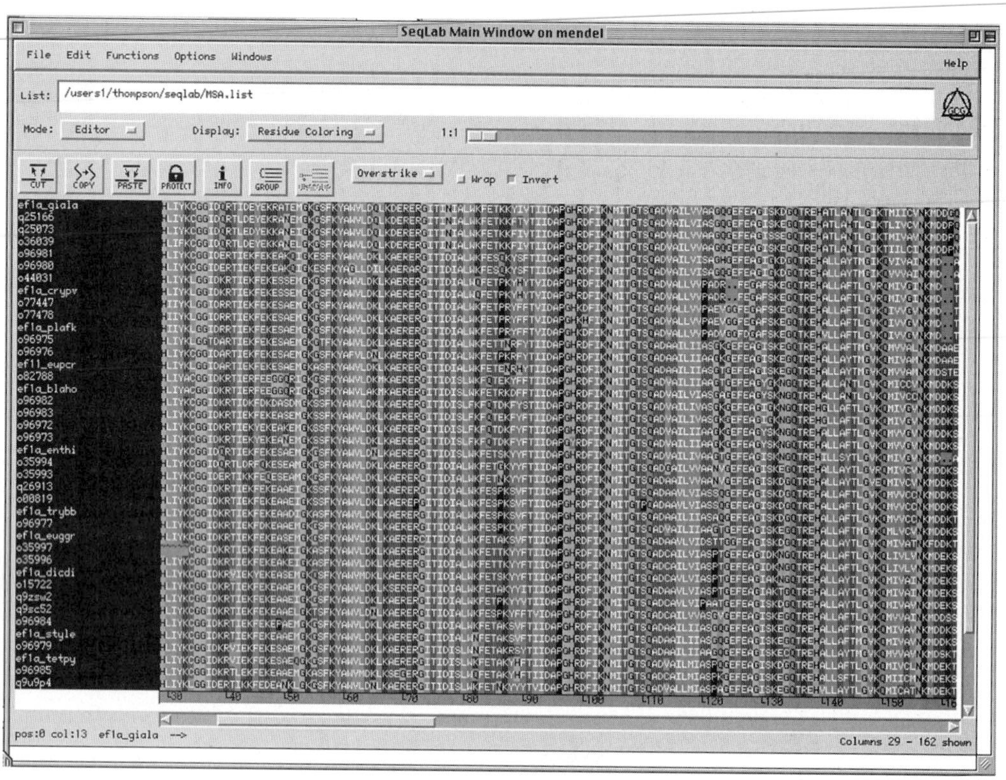

Fig. 7. Elongation Factor alignment displayed by the SeqLab Editor. The PileUp alignment loaded into the SeqLab Editor, displayed using **Residue Coloring** and a **1:1** zoom ratio.

Visualizing Conservation in Multiple Sequence Alignments

The most conserved portions of an alignment are those most resistant to evolutionary change, which often arise from structural constraint. The graphics program PlotSimilarity can be used to visualize positional conservation of a multiple sequence alignment. The program draws a graph of the running average similarity along with a group of aligned sequences (or of a profile with the **-Profile** option). The PlotSimilarity peaks of a protein alignment represent the areas that are most conserved and most resistant to evolutionary change. PlotSimilarity can also be helpful for ascertaining alignment quality by noting changes in the overall average alignment similarity and in those regions of conservation within the alignment, as it is adjusted and refined.

As before, select all of the sequence names and then go to the **Functions** menu and select **Multiple comparison PlotSimilarity . . . .** Check **Save SeqLab colormask to** and **Scale the plot between:** the **minimum and maximum values calculated from the alignment.** The first option's output file will be used in the next step. The second specification launches the program's command line **-Expand** option. This scales the plot, between the maximum and minimum similarity values observed, so that the entire graph is used, rather than just the portion of the Y axis that the alignment occupies. The Y-axis of the resulting plot uses the similarity values from the scoring matrix that was used to create the alignment unless you specify an alterna-

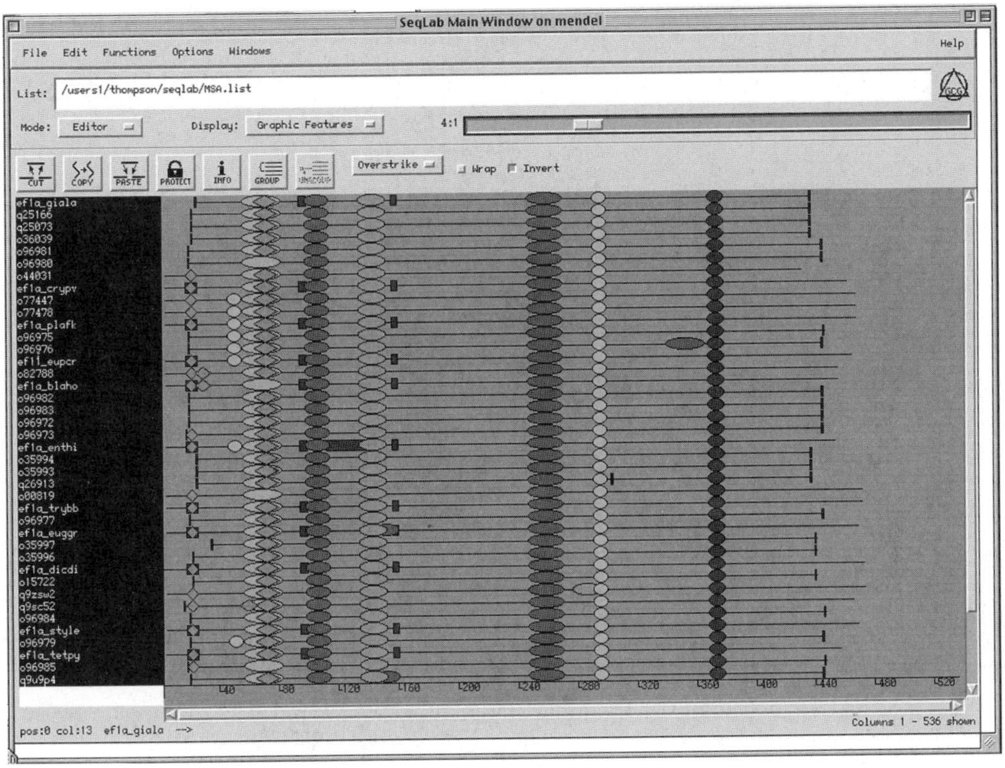

Fig. 8. The PileUp aligned dataset visualized with SeqLab's **Graphic Features** annotation and a **4:1** zoom ratio. Aligned annotation now includes database features, plus Motifs and MotifSearch patterns.

See companion CD for color Fig. 9

tive. The default matrix, BLOSUM62, begins its identity value at 4 and ranges up to 11 with mismatches as low as –4. **Close** the **Options** window; the **Command Line:** box now reflects updated options. Click the **Run** box to launch the program. The output will quickly return as shown in Fig. 9. **Close** the plotsimilarity.cmask display and the **Output Manager**.

Strong peaks of sequence similarity are seen centered around positions 30, 100, and 375. The dashed line across the middle shows the average similarity value for the entire alignment, approx 4.4. As before, to print a SeqLab graphics Figure to a PostScript file: select **Print . . .** from the Figure window, choose **Output Device: [Encapsulated] PostScript File,** and click **Proceed,** to create EPS file output. Take note where the similarity significantly falls off. In this example, the deepest valleys are the least similar regions of the alignment. They lay in the first 25 residues, a region around 190 and 220, around 390, and about the last 25 residues. **Close** the PlotSimilarity window. Go to the **File** menu and click on **Open Color Mask Files.** This will produce another window from which to select the new **plotsimilarity.cmask** file; click on **Add** and **Close** the window. This will produce a gray scale overlay on the sequences that describes their regional similarity where darker gray corresponds to higher similarity values as shown in Fig. 10. Notice the strong conservation peak near column 100 in the alignment, one of EF-1α's GTP binding regions.

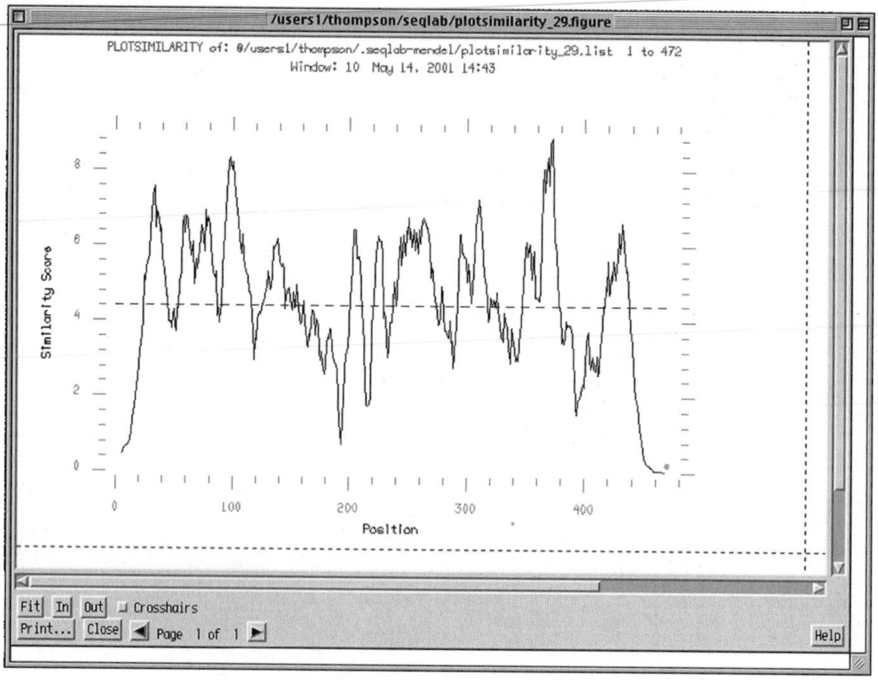

Fig. 9. The GCG PlotSimilarity graphic. PlotSimilarity draws a graph of the running similarity along the length of a multiple sequence alignment using a window averaging approach. Peaks are conserved regions; valleys are dissimilar areas.

Improving Alignments within SeqLab

You can now select those regions of low similarity to try to improve their alignment using the **-InSitu** option that realigns regions within an alignment. Be sure that all of your sequences are selected, then zoom back in your alignment to 1:1 so that you can see individual residues and scroll to the carboxy end. It is best to start at the carboxy termini so that the low similarity regions do not become skewed as you proceed. Select a region of low similarity across the complete sequence set. This can be accomplished using the mouse if it's all on the screen. Otherwise, use the **Edit Select Range** function. Determine the positions by placing your cursor at the beginning and end of the range to be selected and noting the column number in the lower left-hand of the Editor display. Once all of the sequences and the region that you wish to improve are selected, go to the **Functions** menu and again select **Multiple comparison.** Click on **PileUp . . .** to realign all of the sequences within that region. The **Windows** menu also contains a *shortcut* listing of all of the programs that have been accessed in the current session. You will be asked whether you want to use the **Selected sequences** or **Selected region**. It is very important to specify **Selected region.** This will produce a new window with the parameters for running PileUp. Next, be sure to click on **Options . . .** to change the way that PileUp will perform the alignment. In the **Options** window check the gap creation and extension boxes and change their respective values to much less than the default. Changing them to about a third of the default value works well. For the BLOSUM30 matrix change the values to 5 and 2. Most impor-

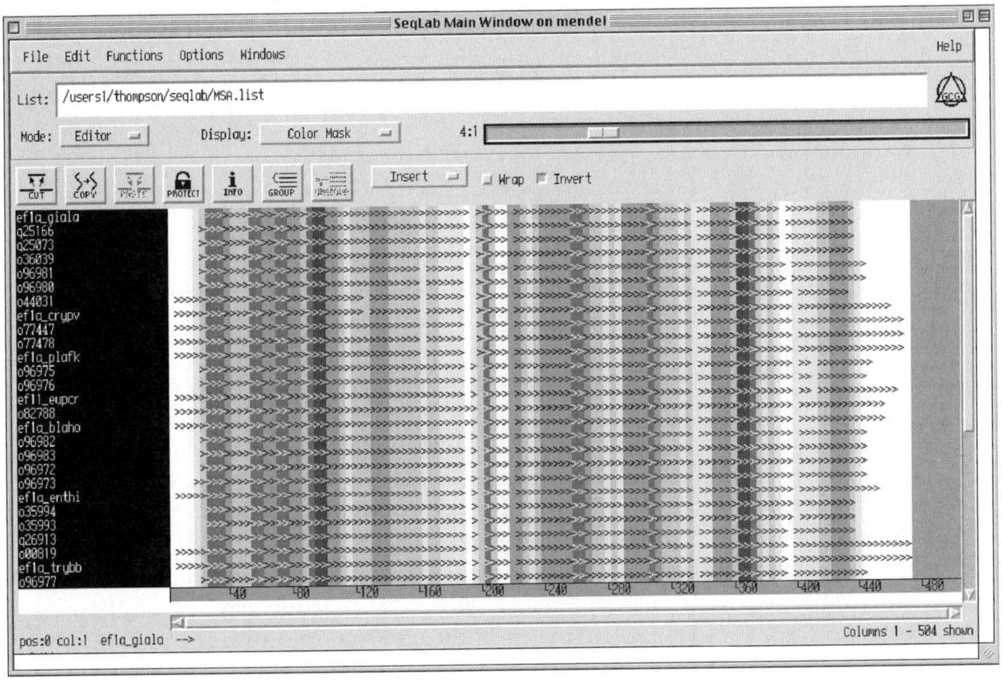

Fig. 10. PlotSimilarity Color Mask on an alignment. PlotSimilarity can produce a Color Mask that can be superimposed over an open alignment in the Editor. Dark regions now correspond to conserved peaks, whereas valleys are represented with white areas.

tantly, check **Realign a portion of an existing alignment**. This calls up the command line **-InSitu** option. Otherwise only that portion of the selected alignment will be retained in the output. Furthermore, deselect the **Plot dendrogram** box. **Close** the window and notice the new options in the PileUp Command Line: **Run** to improve your alignment. The window will disappear and your results will be returned quickly since you are only realigning a portion. The top window will be the MSF output from your PileUp run. Notice the BLOSUM30 matrix specified (others available through the Options menu) and the lowered gap introduction and extension penalties of 5 and 2. Scroll through the alignment then **Close** the window. The next window will be the **Output Manager**. Just as before, click on **Add to Editor** and then specify **Overwrite old with new** in the new **Reloading Same Sequences** window to merge the new alignment with the old alignment and retain all feature annotation. This feature information may help guide your alignment efforts in subsequent steps. **Close** the **Output Manager** window after loading the new alignment.

The alignment should now be a bit better within the specified region. Repeat this process in all areas of low similarity, working from the carboxy termini toward the amino end. Notice that all of the options that were specified are retained by the program. You can also save these run parameters so that they will come up in subsequent sessions by clicking on the **Save Settings** box in any of the program run windows. You may want to periodically go to the **File** menu to save your work using the

Save as . . . function in case of a computer or network problem. It is also a good idea to reperform the PlotSimilarity and color mask procedure after going through the entire alignment to see how things have improved after you have finished the various InSitu PileUps. If you discover an area that you cannot improve through this automated procedure, then it is time to either manually *correct* it or *throw it away.* Note those *problem* areas, then switch back to **Residue Coloring**. This will ease manual alignment by allowing your eyes to work with columns of color.

Other tools that can help manual alignment are **GROUP**ing and **Protections**. The **GROUP** function allows you to manipulate *families* of sequences as a whole. Any change in one will be propagated throughout all. To *GROUP* sequences, select those that you want to behave collectively and then click on the **GROUP** icon right above your alignment. You can have as many groups as required. The space bar will introduce a gap into the sequence and the delete key will take a gap away. However, you can not delete a sequence residue without changing that sequence's or the entire alignment's **Protections**. Click on the padlock icon to produce a **Protections** window. Notice that the default protection allows you to modify **Gap Characters** and **Reversals** only. Check **All other characters** to allow you to *CUT* regions out of your alignment and/or delete individual residues and then click **OK** to close the window. This very powerful manual alignment function can be thought of as the *abacus* function. To take advantage of this function select the region that you want to slide and then press the shift key as you move the region with the right or left arrow key. You can slide residues greater distances by prefacing the command keystrokes with the number of spaces that you want them to slide.

Make subjective decisions regarding your alignment. Is it satisfactory? Do the sequences line up the way that they should? If, after all else, you decide that you just cannot align some region, or even an entire sequence, then perhaps get rid of it with the **CUT** function. Cutting out an entire sequence may leave some columns of gaps in the alignment. If this is the case, then reselect all of your sequences and go to the **Edit** menu and select **Remove Gaps . . . Columns of gaps**. Amino and carboxy termini seldom align properly and are often jagged and uncertain. This is common in multiple sequence alignments and subsequent analyses should probably not include these regions. If loading sequences from a database search, then allowing SeqLab to trim the ends automatically based on beginning and ending constraints considerably improves this situation. Overall, consider strongly conserved residues such as tryptophans, cysteines, and histidines; important structural amino acids such as prolines, tyrosines, and phenylanines, and the conserved isoleucine, leucine, valine triumvirate; make sure they all align. After tweaking, evaluating, and readjusting the alignment, change back to **Feature Coloring Display**. Those features that are annotated should now align perfectly. This is another way to assure that your alignment is as biologically *correct* as possible. Everything you do from this point on, e.g., if you use alignments to ascertain molecular phylogenies, is absolutely dependent on the quality of the alignment! You need a very clean, unambiguous alignment with a very high confidence level in a truly biologically meaningful alignment. Each column of symbols must actually contain homologous characters.

Many other alignment editors are available. However, using a GCG compatible editor like SeqLab, assures that the format will not be corrupted. If you do make any changes to a GCG sequence data file with a non-GCG compatible editor, you must reformat the alignment. Reformatting GCG MSF or RSF files requires a certain level

of expertise. If you do need to do this for any reason, you must use the appropriate Reformat option (either -MSF or -RSF, respectively), and you must specify all the sequences within the file using the brace specifier, i.e.,{*} , for example:

> reformat -msf your_favorite.msf{*}

SeqLab Editor On-Screen Annotation

Adding text annotation to the display and changing the names of the entries for presentation purposes may be helpful. Double-click on an entry's name to reveal the **Sequence Information** window and directly edit the name. Selecting the entry name and then pressing the **INFO** icon can also be used. To put text lines directly into your display go to the SeqLab **File** menu **New sequence . . .** entry and select the **Text** button to the **What type of sequence?** question. This will put a *NewText* line at the bottom of the Editor display allowing the annotation to be inserted. You can also add customized **Graphic Features** and **Features Coloring** annotation with the **Windows Features** window. Select a desired region across an alignment and launch the **Features** window. Press **Add** to get a **Feature Editor** window where you can designate the feature's **Shape: Color:** and **Fill:** as well as giving the region a **Keyword:** and **Comments:**. You can add feature annotation to a region across an entire alignment, but you cannot delete or edit the annotation from the whole region afterwards. You can only edit or delete feature annotation from an RSF file with the SeqLab Editor one sequence feature at a time!

Profile Analysis: Position-Specific, Weighted Score Matrices of Multiple Sequence Alignments

After refining the alignment as much as possible, a powerful approach to suggesting function of distantly related proteins and structural motifs is the Profile suite. This strategy works best when one has prepared and refined a multiple sequence alignment of significantly similar sequences or regions within sequences. A good plan is to identify similar sequences in a newly sequenced section of DNA using traditional database searching techniques and then align all of the significantly similar sequences or domains. Next, run the aligned sequences through the Profile package to generate a profile of the family, a very sensitive probe for further analysis. Searching sequence databases with this probe is tremendously powerful.

Profile methods enable the researcher to recognize features that may otherwise be invisible to individual sequence members. Profile analysis uses the full information content of an alignment. Compared to that of individual sequences, this enhanced information content has the potential to find similar motifs in sequences that are only distantly related. All other methods of describing an alignment such as consensus or pattern description either through away too much information or become too ambiguous. Profiles achieve additional sensitivity with a two-dimensional weight matrix approach, in which conserved areas of the alignment receive the most importance and variable regions the least.

A distinct advantage is that further manipulations and database searches consider evolutionary issues by virtue of their Profile algorithms. The creation of gaps is highly discouraged in conserved areas and occurs easily in variable regions in subsequent profile alignments and searches. This occurs because gaps are penalized more heavily in conserved areas than in variable regions. Furthermore, the more highly conserved a residue, the greater its position-specific matrix score. These two factors give the profiles power. The matrix and its associated consensus sequence are not based merely on the positional frequency of particular residues, but rather utilize the evolutionary conservation of amino acid substitutions within the alignment based on the specified scoring matrix. The BLOSUM62 table is used by default although other substitution matrices can also be specified. Therefore, the resultant consensus residues are the most evolutionarily conserved, rather than just the most statistically frequent.

Traditional Profiles, ala Michael Gribskov

A profile, and its inherent consensus, is created with the GCG program ProfileMake. When a profile is created, all of its members should be appropriately weighted to evenly distribute each contribution. The profile refinement procedure, including repeatedly searching the databases and including or excluding members and adjusting their weights as well as adjusting the profile's length, is known as validating the profile. If you use Profile analysis in your own research, the validation procedures outlined in the GCG Program Manual in the ProfileScan description is prudent. A *motif* style profile library based on the PROSITE Dictionary of Protein Sites and Patterns has been prepared by Gribskov and made available within the GCG system. The program ProfileScan searches the query protein sequence against this library. The present version of GCG has 629 validated profiles in its ProfileScan library.

To run ProfileMake be sure that all of your aligned sequences are selected. Based on your previous observations and your experimental objectives, select the longest, most conserved, sequence length available. Restrict the length of the profile so that the jagged ends in the alignment are excluded. In SeqLab use the **Edit Select Range . . .** menu. **Select** and then **Close** the box. Another effective strategy is to develop multiple shorter profiles centered about the peaks of similarity. These most likely correspond to functional or structural domains. After the range is selected use the **Functions Multiple Comparison ProfileMake** menu and reply **Selected region** in the **Which selection** dialog box. You can also use the **Options. . .** menu from the **ProfileMake** dialog box to specify the **-SeqOut** command option by checking **Write the consensus into a sequence file**, giving it an appropriate name. This will generate a consensus sequence file and a profile file. After running ProfileMake, the top window returned will display the profile consensus sequence. All positions will be filled, because the Profile algorithm selects the most conserved residue for each position. The header contains information relating to the sequence's creation through ProfileMake. **Close** the consensus window. The **Output Manager** will also list a **.prf** file. This is the profile itself which other programs can read and interpret to perform very sensitive database searches and further alignments, using the information within the matrix that penalizes misalignments in conserved areas more than in variable regions. **Save As . . .** the profile giving it an appropriate name that you can recognize and retain the **.prf** extension. **Close** the **Output Manager.**

ProfileSearch is launched from SeqLab with the **Functions** menu; select **Database Sequence Searching ProfileSearch.** Specify the **Query profile. . .** in the **File Chooser** and click **OK.** Search whichever protein database you prefer. ProfileSegments can be run separately after ProfileSearch. The ProfileSearch output file can then be delimited so that ProfileSegments only makes pairwise or multiple alignments of the sequences of interest. Therefore, uncheck **ProfileSegments. . .** to prevent ProfileSearch's output from automatically being passed to ProfileSegments. Under **Options. . . .** use the **-MinList** option by changing **Lowest Z score to report in output list** from 2.5 to 3.5 or higher. -MinList sets a list Z score cut-off value providing a means to limit the output list size. **Close** the **Options** window and be sure that **How: Background Job** is selected and then click **Run.**

As in BLAST and FastA searches, ProfileSearch estimates a significance parameter. In this case it is a Z score based on the distance, that is the number of standard deviations, from the rest of the *insignificant* database matches. ProfileSearch Z scores are normalized and reflect the significance of the results. Rather than randomizing sequences to evaluate a Z score, as in Monte Carlo approaches, it is calculated based on all of the nonsimilar sequences from the database search. As with Monte Carlo approaches, Z scores below 3 are probably not worth considering, from around 4 to 7 may be interesting, and above 7 are most probably significant and should definitely be examined. You can find remote similarities that all other methods will miss using Profile analysis.

Interpreting Profile Analysis

ProfileSearches do require some work to setup and run. They are CPU intensive, and together with HmmerSearch they are some of the most intensive in the GCG package. Be sure to submit them as a batch job as early as possible. If launched from the command line, use the -Batch option. When you examine a ProfileSearch output, take a careful look, there is a good chance that other search algorithms will have missed some of the sequences listed as significant matches. If launched from SeqLab, the output will be located in your working directory and it will have a cryptic name of the form profilesearch_some-number.pfs.

In this example, ProfileSearch finds all of the Elongation Factors in the PIR/NBRF protein database plus other interesting nucleotide binding proteins near the end of the list, all with Z Scores >4. The nucleotide binding motifs in the EF-1α profile are among the most highly conserved portions of the alignment; therefore, greater importance is placed on them by the search. This strategy helps to identify other proteins with similar domains. An abridged screen trace of this ProfileSearch output is shown in Table 5.

The program ProfileSegments constructs BestFit alignments of the results of a ProfileSearch. The MSF option in ProfileSegments allows one to prepare a multiple sequence alignment of the ProfileSearch segments. This can be very helpful for merging ever-increasingly distant sequences into an alignment. The full information content of the profile including the importance of the conserved portions of the alignment is used in this alignment procedure. When running ProfileSegments be sure to set the list size large enough to include all of the relevant sequences in the ProfileSearch output. The -Global option will force full-length alignments, which may be more informative if you are trying to construct a multiple sequence alignment. Figure 11 shows a screen snapshot centered about the t-RNA binding region of a ProfileSegments -MSF -Global alignment, made from the remaining entries in the example in Table 5 aligned against the EF-1α profile.

See companion CD for color Fig. 11

Notice the difference between this alignment and examples seen with other algorithms. Profile alignments often include more gaps than those from other programs. The conserved portions of the profile do not allow the corresponding portion of align-

Table 5
ProfileSearch Output, Abridged[a]

```
!!SEQUENCE_LIST 1.0
(Peptide) PROFILESEARCH of: /users1/thompson/seqlab/primitive.prf Length: 428 to: pir:*

        Scores are not corrected for composition effects

                Gap Weight: 60.00
         Gap Length Weight: 0.67
        Sequences Examined: 188196
        CPU time (seconds): 2713

*   *   *   *   *   *   *   *   *   *   *   *   *   *   *   *

Profile information:
(Peptide) PROFILEMAKE v4.50 of:
 @/users1/thompson/.seqlab-mendel/profilemake_63.list Length: 428
 Sequences: 38 MaxScore: 1798.78 July 11, 2001 20:11
                      Gap: 1.00            Len: 1.00
                 GapRatio: 0.33       LenRatio: 0.10
     input_63.rsf{GIARDIA_L} From: 19 To: 446 Weight: 1.00
 input_63.rsf{DIPLOMONAD_SP} From: 19 To: 446 Weight: 1.00 . . .

*   *   *   *   *   *   *   *   *   *   *   *   *   *   *   *

Normalization:                    July 11, 2001 21:21

        Curve fit using 49 length pools
        0 of 49 pools were rejected

        Normalization equation:

                Calc_Score = 66.96 * ( 1.0 - exp(-0.0023*SeqLen - 0.6191) )

        Correlation for curve fit: 0.973

        Z score calculation:
        Average and standard deviation calculated using 99616 scores
        384 of 100000 scores were rejected

                Z_Score = ( Score/Calc_Score - 1.010 ) / 0.164

         Sequence Strd ZScore   Orig Length ! Documentation ..
PIR2:A49171        + 158.30 1454.17    435 ! translation elongation factor e
EF-1 alpha chain - Tetrahymena pyriformis
PIR2:A54760        + 157.48 1458.18    449 ! translation elongation factor e
EF-1 alpha chain - Trypanosoma brucei
PIR2:S11665        + 156.90 1458.53    456 ! translation elongation factor e
EF-1 alpha chain - slime mold (Dictyostelium discoid
PIR2:S16308        + 156.81 1449.85    446 ! translation elongation factor e
EF-1 alpha chain - Stylonychia lemnae
PIR2:JC5117        + 155.73 1442.59    449 ! translation elongation factor e
EF-1 alpha - Trypanosoma cruzi
PIR2:T43890        + 154.38 1385.87    395 ! translation elongation factor e
EF-1 alpha [similarity] - Dinenympha exilis (fragmen
PIR2:T43892        + 154.08 1383.28    395 ! translation elongation factor e
EF-1 alpha [similarity] - unidentified Oxymonadida A
PIR2:A60491        + 152.65 1425.02    462 ! translation elongation factor e
EF-1 alpha chain - African clawed frog
PIR2:JU0133        + 152.61 1424.67    462 ! translation elongation factor e
EF-1 alpha chain - Chinese hamster
PIR2:S21055        + 152.61 1424.67    462 ! translation elongation factor e
EF-1 alpha chain - rat
PIR2:I50226        + 152.35 1422.28    462 ! translation elongation factor e
EF-1 alpha - chicken
PIR2:S50143        + 152.24 1421.33    462 ! translation elongation factor e
EF-1 alpha chain - zebra fish
PIR1:EFHU1         + 152.17 1420.67    462 ! translation elongation factor e
EF-1 alpha-1 chain - human
///////////////////////////////////////////////////////////////////////////////
PIR2:S37283        +   9.80 154.03     639 ! tetracycline resistance protein
tetM - Neisseria meningitidis
PIR2:S03268        +   9.80 154.03     639 ! tetracycline resistance protein
tetM - Ureaplasma urealyticum
PIR2:A24333        +   9.69 153.00     639 ! tetracycline resistance protein
tetM - Enterococcus faecalis transposon Tn1545
PIR2:E70827        +   9.66 155.56     701 ! probable fusA protein - Mycobact
erium tuberculosis (strain H37RV)
PIR2:G83052        +   9.66 160.60     840 ! translation initiation factor IF
-2 PA4744 [imported] - Pseudomonas aeruginosa (stra
PIR2:H81430        +   9.44 159.24     871 ! translation initiation factor IF
-2 Cj0136 [imported] - Campylobacter jejuni (strain
PIR2:F70556        +   9.35 149.14     628 ! hypothetical protein Rv1165 - My
cobacterium tuberculosis (strain H37RV)
PIR2:S75863        +   9.28 151.39     691 ! translation elongation factor EF
-G.sll1098 - Synechocystis sp. (strain PCC 6803)
///////////////////////////////////////////////////////////////////////////////
PIR2:S53707        +   4.99 110.33     727 ! translation initiation factor eI
F-2 - bovine
```

Table 5 *(continued)*
ProfileSearch Output, Abridged[a]

```
PIR2:T21621          +    4.98 113.85       878 ! hypothetical protein F32A7.5 - C
aenorhabditis elegans
PIR2:E83344          +    4.98 90.86        317 ! probable adhesion protein PA2407
 [imported] - Pseudomonas aeruginosa (strain PAO1)
PIR2:C69308          +    4.97 93.48        355 ! immunogenic protein (bcsp31-1) h
omolog - Archaeoglobus fulgidus
PIR2:I40701          +    4.97 89.04        294 ! glyceraldehyde-3-phosphate dehyd
rogenase (EC 1.2.1.12) - Citrobacter freundii (frag
PIR2:T38897          +    4.96 82.42        216 ! hypothetical protein SPAC513.02
- fission yeast (Schizosaccharomyces pombe)
PIR2:C75581          +    4.96 105.14       580 ! malate oxidoreductase - Deinococ
cus radiodurans (strain R1)
PIR2:I40603          +    4.96 82.02        212 ! hypothetical protein A - Clostri
dium acetobutylicum
PIR2:T17237          +    4.96 85.14        247 ! hypothetical protein DKFZp434P10
6.1 - human (fragment)
PIR2:S65758          +    4.96 110.29       737 ! nitrate reductase (EC 1.7.99.4)
chain A narB - Oscillatoria chalybea
PIR2:A46241          +    4.95 87.60        277 ! interferon response element-bind
ing factor IREBF-2 - mouse (fragment)
////////////////////////////////////////////////////////////////////////////////
```

[a]A greatly abridged GCG ProfileSearch output list file. Most of the known elongation factors have been edited from the file; several distant homologues are left intact.

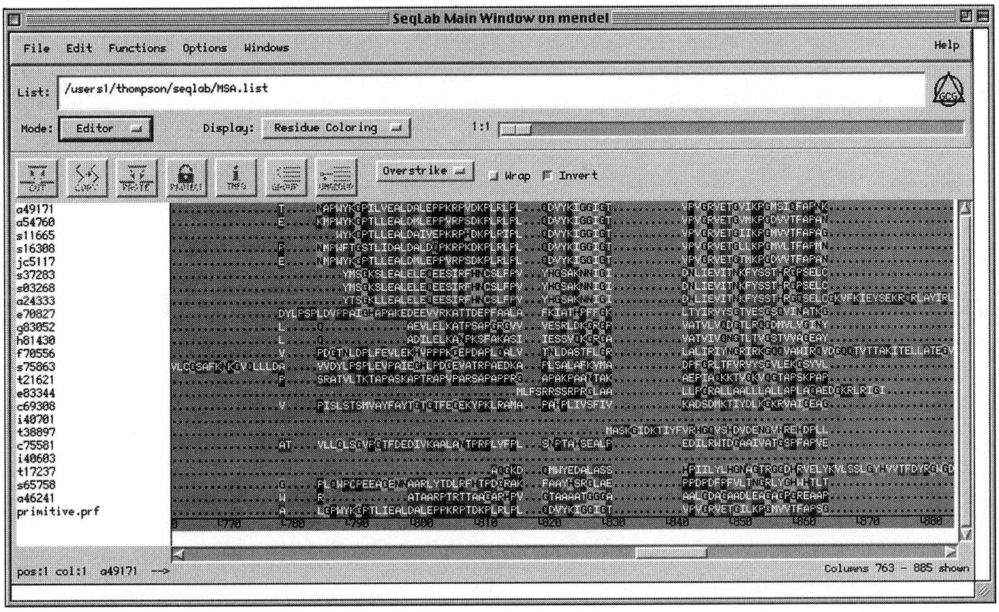

Fig. 11. ProfileSegments -MSF -Global output loaded into SeqLab. The t-RNA binding region of a ProfileSegments -MSF -Global alignment of selected near and distant EF-1α homologues aligned against my example EF-1α profile.

ment to gap; yet gaps are easily placed in the nonconserved regions of the alignment. *Clustering* is more Profile analyses than other methods, because of these variable gap penalties. This can be a very useful strategy for pregapping new sequences when introducing them into existing alignments.

HMMER: Hidden Markov Modeling and Profiles

As powerful as the heuristics based Gribskov profiles are, they require a lot of time and skill to prepare and validate. An excess of subjectivity and a lack of formal statistical rigor contribute to their limitations. To address these concerns, GCG incorporated the HMMER (pronounced "hammer") package into GCG version 10.2. HMMER uses Hidden Markov modeling, with a formal probabilistic basis and consistent gap insertion theory, to build and manipulate HMMER profiles and profile databases, to search sequences against HMMER profile databases, and to easily create multiple sequence alignments using HMMER profiles as a *seed.* HMMER profiles are much easier to build than traditional profiles and they do not require as many sequences in their alignments to be effective. They offer a statistical rigor not available in Gribskov profiles and they have all the sensitivity of any profile technique.

Like Gribskov profiles, HMMER profiles are constructed from a set of pre-aligned sequences. However, it is not as important that the alignment be as comprehensive and perfect. To construct a SeqLab HMMER profile alignment, select all of the relevant sequences and perhaps a region within them to exclude, e.g., jagged, unalignable ends. Do not select a Mask sequence, as profiles need to include all of the ambiguity of the alignment within the region being used. Go to the **Functions HMMER** menu and pick **HmmerBuild.** Specify **Selected region** rather than **Selected sequences** if restricting the length of the profile. Accept the default **create a new HMM** and specify an **Internal name for profile HMM.** Specify the **Type of HMM to be Built** as the default is **multiple global**. When the profile is built you need to specify the type of alignment it will be used with, rather than when the alignment is run. The HMMER profile will either be used for global or local alignment and it will occur multiply or singly on a given sequence. Weighting is also considered differently in HMMER than it is with Gribskov profiles. To use a custom weighting scheme, e.g., if you have modified your RSF file weight values for ProfileBuild, select the **-Weighting=N** option. Otherwise HmmerBuild's internal weighting algorithm will calculate the best weights based on a cluster analysis of sequence similarities. It again becomes important to understand the types of biological questions that you are asking to rationally set many of the program parameters.

HmmerCalibrate is checked by default. The completion of HmmerBuild automatically launches a calibration procedure that increases the speed and accuracy of subsequent analyses with the resultant profile. Other HmmerBuild options can be explored, but first read the Program Manual. For now accept the default HmmerBuild parameters and press **Run.** The output is an ASCII text profile representation of a statistical model, a Hidden Markov Model, of the consensus of a sequence family, deduced from a multiple sequence alignment. A utility program, HmmerConvert, can change HMMER style profiles into Gribskov profiles, but information is lost. In most cases the new HMMER profile is used as either a search probe for extremely sensitive database searching or as a template upon which to build ever-larger multiple sequence alignments.

To use the HMMER profile as a search probe go to the **Functions** menu and select **HMMER**, then **HmmerSearch.** Specify the new HMMER profile by clicking **Profile HMM to use as query . . .** and using the **File Chooser** window to select the correct HMMER profile. Either accept the default **Sequence search set . . . PIR:*** specification or choose other sequences to search. HmmerSearch has similar cutoff parameters as other GCG database searches. You can restrict the size of the output based on significance scores to limit the number of pairwise alignments displayed. HmmerSearch is very slow because it is, as a ProfileSearch, a comprehensive, non-heuristic, dynamic programming implementation. So run this program in the background when using SeqLab or, if at a terminal session, use the -Batch command line option. If the server has multiple processors, HmmerSearch supports the multithreading -Processors=x option. **Run** the program when you have the appropriate options selected. The output is extensive and informative, based on significance Expectation-value scores. The top portion is a list of best hits on all domains, the second section is the GCG list file portion of the best domain hits, next pairwise alignments are given, and finally a score distribution is plotted. Since it is a GCG list file, it can be read by other GCG programs, like HmmerAlign.

HmmerAlign can help when working with very large multiple alignments and when adding newly found sequences to an existing alignment regardless of size. Somewhat similar in concept to the -MSF option of ProfileSegments, it takes a specified profile, in this case a HMMER profile, and aligns a specified set of sequences to it, to produce a multiple sequence alignment based on that profile. Unlike ProfileSegments, HmmerAlign takes any GCG sequence specification as input, not just the output from its own database searching program. It is much faster to create very large multiple alignments this way, rather than using PileUp over and over. The rationale being, take the time to make a good small alignment and HMMER profile, then use that to build upon the original. The alignment procedure used by HmmerAlign is a recursive, dynamic programming implementation. It compares the profile's matrix individually against every sequence, until an entire alignment is constructed. HmmerAlign can also use its profile to align one multiple alignment to another and produce a merged result of the two. A heuristic solution is provided in those cases where the original alignment is not one of the two, although optimalization is not guaranteed. To use this option choose **Combine output alignment and ...**, then **another alignment** in the SeqLab **HmmerAlign Options** window. This will launch the command line **-Heuristic=some.msf{*}** option. Aligning the original alignment that was used to construct the profile with another sequence set is very fast and non-heuristic though, using the **-MapAlignment=some.rsf{*}** option. Launch HmmerAlign from the **Functions HMMER** menu by selecting **HmmerAlign.** Specify the correct HMMER profile with the **profile HMM to use...** button and pick the sequences that you want to align to the profile with the **Sequences to align...** button. For example, 1EFT is one of the most similar Elongation Factor 1α homolog to the *lower* eukaryote EF-1α profile example that has a solved structure. Therefore, an alignment of its primary sequence with structural annotation against this sample dataset should allow the inference of secondary structure across the entire alignment. This is the basis of homology modeling. The inferred alpha helices are highlighted in red as shown on the accompanying CD. Figure 12 illustrates the inferred secondary structure based on an alignment of 1EFT, the EF-Tu structure from *Thermus aquaticus*, against the EF-1α HMMER profile.

See companion CD for color Fig. 12

HmmerPfam

As with Motifs and MotifSearch, HmmerPfam can supplement annotations of an RSF file. This program scans sequences against a library of HMMER profiles, by default the Pfam library (A database of protein domain family alignments and HMMs, 1996–2000 The Pfam Consortium). Its output lists Pfam domain matches ranked by

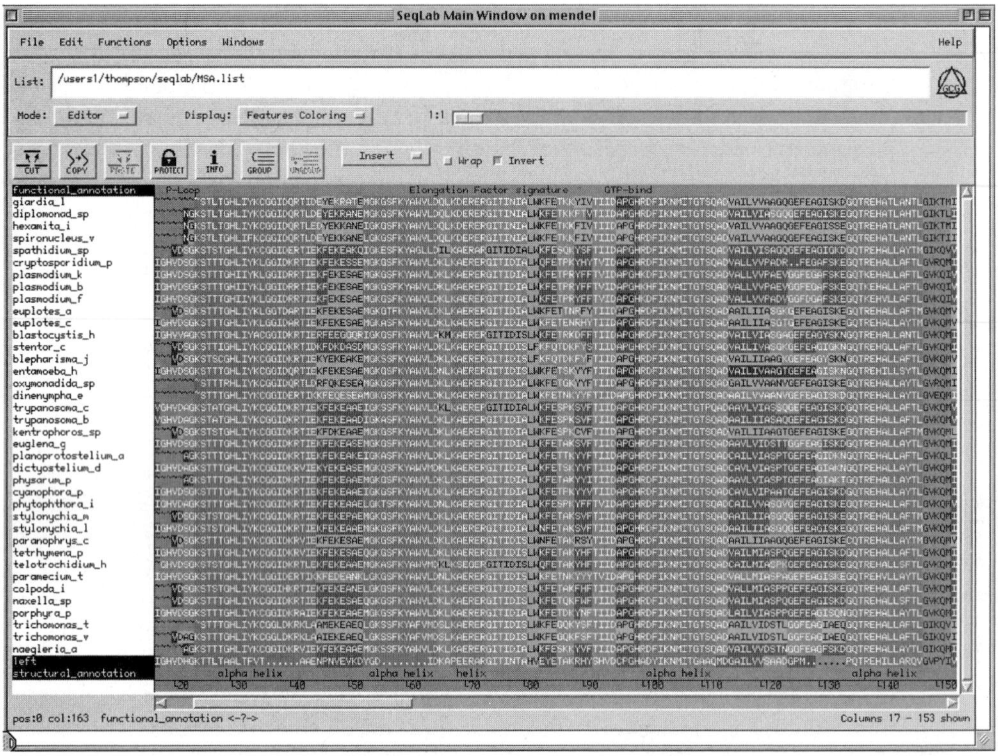

Fig. 12. EF-1α *primitive* dataset aligned to the *Thermus aquaticus* EF-Tu sequence by HmmerAlign. Inferred alpha helices based on the *Thermus* structure are gray in this **Features Coloring** display. Text annotation lines have also been added to the display.

See companion CD for color Fig. 13

Expectation-values and with the -RSF option writes the domain identification and Expectation-value as a feature in an RSF file. The screen snapshot in Fig. 13 shows a sample alignment over the same span as Fig. 12, but includes additional HmmerPfam annotation using **Graphic Features Display:** mode.

Consensus and Masking Issues

Consensus methods are another powerful way to visualize similarity within an alignment. The SeqLab **Edit** menu allows one to easily create several types of consensus representations. To create a standard protein sequence consensus select all sequences and use the **Edit Consensus . . .** menu and specify **Consensus type: Protein Sequence.** When constructing a sequence consensus of a protein alignment you can generate figures with black highly similar residues, gray intermediate similarities, and white non-similar amino acids. The default mode is to create an identity consensus at the two-thirds plurality level (*percent required for majority*) with a threshold of 5 (*minimum score that represents a match*). Different plurality and threshold values as well as different scoring comparison matrices can be used to highlight the difference in the alignment. Be sure that **Shade based on similarity to consensus** is checked to generate a color mask overlay on the display to help in the

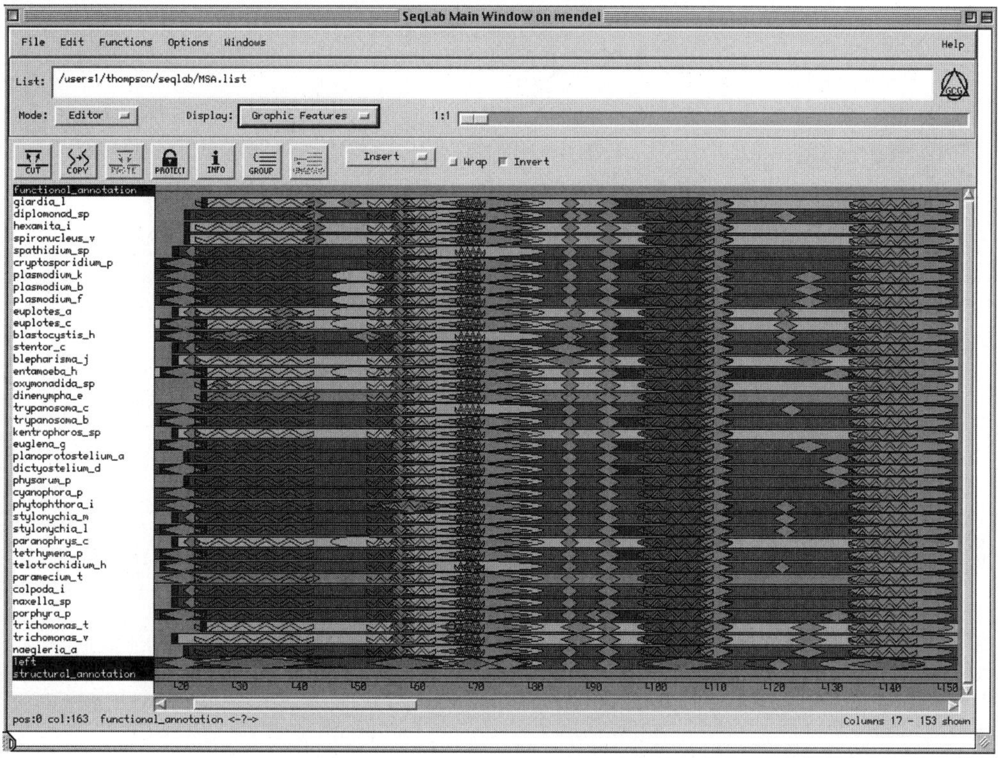

Fig. 13. Screen snapshot of the sample alignment showing the same region as Figure 12 but now including additional HmmerPfam annotation and displayed with **Graphic Features**. Inferred alpha helices are now seen as transparent medium gray coils.

visualization process. Figure 14 illustrates a region near the carboxy termini using the BLOSUM30 matrix, a *Percent required for majority* (plurality) of 33%, and a *minimum score that represents a match* (threshold) cutoff value of 4.

When you have identified an optimum plurality combination, select the **File Print . . .** command and change the **Output Format:** to **PostScript** to prepare a PostScript file of your SeqLab display. Whatever color scheme is displayed by the Editor will be captured by the PostScript file. As you change the font size the number of pages to be printed varies. In the **Print Alignment** menu specify **Destination . . . File** and give it an appropriate filename and then click **OK.** This command will produce a PostScript language graphics file in the directory from which SeqLab was launched. This PostScript file can be sent to a color PostScript printer, or to a black and white laser printer that will simulate the colors with gray tones, or it can be imported into a PostScript compatable graphics program for further manipulation.

In addition to standard consensus sequences using various similarity schemes, SeqLab also allows one to create consensus *Masks* that screen specified areas of your alignment from further analyses by specifying 0 or 1 weights for each column. A SeqLab Mask allows the user to differentially weight different parts of alignment to reflect confidence. Masks can be modified by hand or they can be created manually

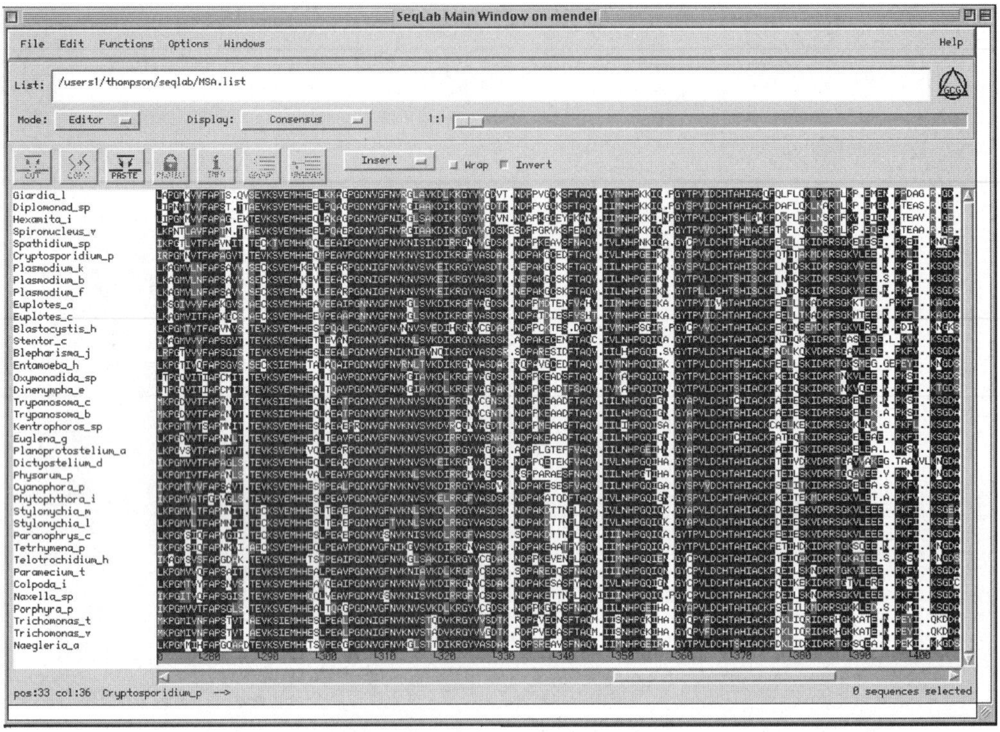

Fig. 14. SeqLab **Consensus** display of a region near the carboxy termini of my EF-1α example using the BLOSUM30 matrix, a 33% **Percent required for majority** (plurality), and a cutoff value of 4 for the **Minimum score that represents a match** (threshold).

using the **New Sequences** menu. They can have position values up to 9. Masking is helpful for phylogenetic analysis as it can exclude less reliable columns in the alignment without actually removing the data. Once a Mask has been created in SeqLab, most of the programs available through the **Functions** menu will use that Mask, if the Mask is selected along with the desired sequences, to weight the columns of the alignment data matrix appropriately. This only occurs through the **Functions** menu.

To create a Mask style sequence consensus select all sequences and then use the **Edit Consensus . . .** menu and specify **Consensus type: Mask Sequence.** As noted earlier, the default mode uses an identity consensus at the two-thirds plurality level with a threshold of 5. These stringent values will likely mask much of the phylogenetically informative data. One can try using lower pluralities, threshold values, and scoring comparison matrices. Figure 15 illustrates the carboxy terminal end using a weight Mask generated from the BLOSUM30 matrix, a plurality of 15%, and a threshold of 4. Few areas are excluded by the Mask in this alignment because of the high similarity of this group of sequences. Excluding more columns would likely leave nearly identical sequences. It would be impossible to ascertain how they are related.

Coding DNA Issues

It is often useful to align DNA sequences along with their corresponding proteins. This is because many investigators prefer to run phylogenetic analyses on DNA rather

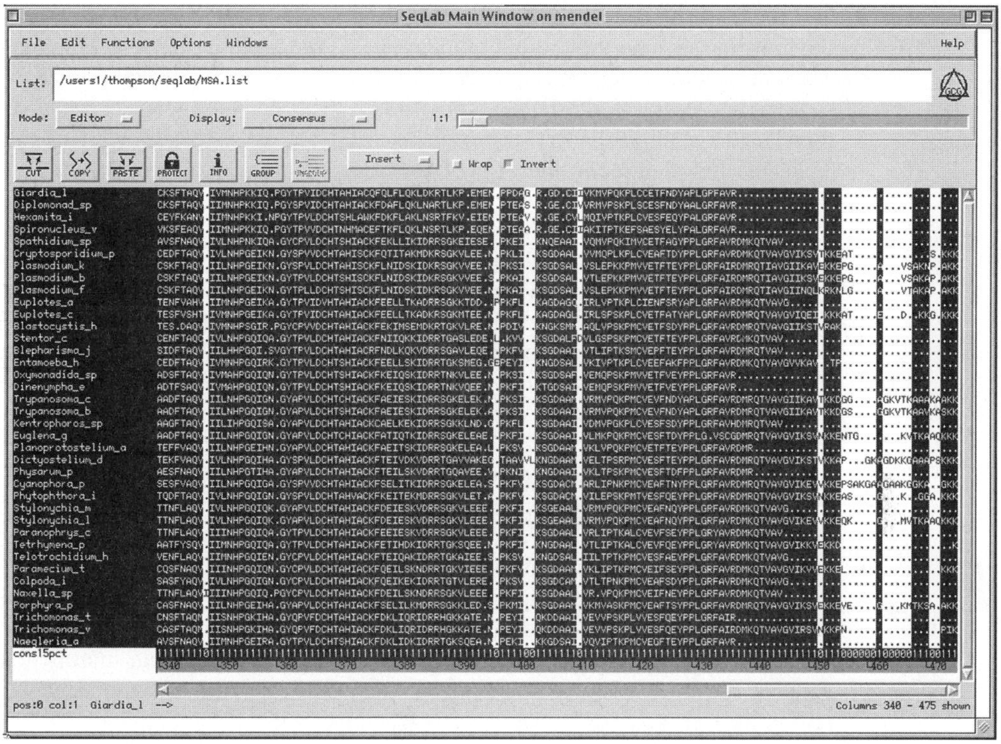

Fig. 15. SeqLab **Consensus** Mask display of the carboxy terminal region of my EF-1α example using a weight Mask generated from the BLOSUM30 matrix, a plurality of 15%, and a threshold of 4.

than protein, as the multiple substitution models are more robust for DNA. In fact, many phylogenetic inference algorithms do not even take advantage of amino acid similarity when comparing protein sequences; they only consider identities! However, the more diverged a dataset becomes, the more random third and eventually first codon positions become. This introduces noise and error into the analysis. Therefore, often third positions and sometimes first positions are masked. One is always balancing signal against noise. Too much noise or too little signal both degrade the analysis to the point of nonsense.

The logic to this paired protein and DNA alignment approach is as follows:

1. Directly align the DNA. If the DNA sequences are quite similar, then merely create your DNA alignment. Next use the **Edit** menu **Translate** function and the **align translations** option to create the corresponding alignment of the protein sequences. Select the region to translate based on the CDS reference as per each DNA annotation. Be careful of CDS entries that do not begin at position 1; the GenBank CDS feature annotation **/codon_start=** identifies the start position within the first codon listed. You may also have to trim the sequences to contain only the relevant gene, especially if they are genomic. This can be accomplished with appropriate protections (padlock icon). **Group** each protein with its corresponding DNA sequence so that subsequent manipulations will keep them together.

2. Use the protein sequences to create the alignment if the DNA alignment is not obvious. In this case the protein sequences are first used to create an alignment. The corresponding DNA sequences are then loaded. You can find the DNA sequence accession codes in the annotation of the protein sequence entries. Next translate the unaligned DNA sequences into new protein sequences with the Edit-Translate function using the **align translations** option and **Group** these with their corresponding DNA sequences, just as noted earlier. The DNA along with their translated sequences will not be aligned as a set, just the other protein set is aligned. **Group** all of the aligned protein dataset together, but separately from the DNA/aligned translation set. Rearrange your display to place the DNA, its aligned translation and the original aligned protein sequence side-by-side and then manually slide one set to match the other. Use the **CUT** and **PASTE** buttons to move the sequences. When pasting, remember the **Sequence clipboard** contains complete sequence entries, whereas the **Text clipboard** only contains sequence data, amino acid residues or DNA bases. The translated sequence entries can be **CUT** away after they are aligned to the set. Merge the newly aligned sequences into the existing alignment Group. It sounds difficult, but you are matching two identical protein sequences, the DNA translation, and the original aligned protein. The **Group** function keeps everything together so that you do not lose your original alignment as you space residues apart to match their respective codons. Some codons may become spaced apart in this process and will require adjustment. Figure 16 shows a sample dataset in an intermediary stage of alignment. The complete sample data RSF file with all annotation, protein sequences, and DNA sequences is available in the accompanying CD.

See companion CD for color Fig. 16

Multiple Alignment Format and Phylogenetics

Multiple sequence alignment is a necessary prerequisite for biological sequence based phylogenetic inference, and phylogenetic inference guides our understanding of molecular evolution. The famous Darwinian Theodosius Dobzhansky summed it up succinctly in 1973. It is provided as an inscription on the inner cover of the classic organic evolution text *Evolution*: "Nothing in biology makes sense except in the light of evolution." These words ring true. Evolution provides the single, unifying, cohesive force that can explain all life. It is to the life sciences what the long sought holy grail of the unified field theory is to astrophysics.

*GCG Interface to PAUP**

GCG implements David Swofford's **PAUP*** (usually pronounced "pop star") phylogenetic analysis package with the paired programs **PAUPSearch** and **PAUPDisplay.** These interface programs provide an easy to use access to **PAUP***. However, you may want to consider running PAUP* exterior to GCG by getting the latest version, containing many bug fixes and enhancements, directly from Sinauer Associates (*see* Website: http://www.sinauer.com/Titles/frswofford.htm), and installing it on your own machine. Version 4.0.0d55 PAUP* is included in GCG version 10.3 and runs in native mode or through the PAUPSearch and PAUPDisplay programs. Use the following command in a terminal window to read the license agreement with GCG, if you are curious:

> typedata paup-license.txt

The PAUP package was originally written to only perform parsimony analysis with either DNA sequences or morphological character data using a Macintosh computer.

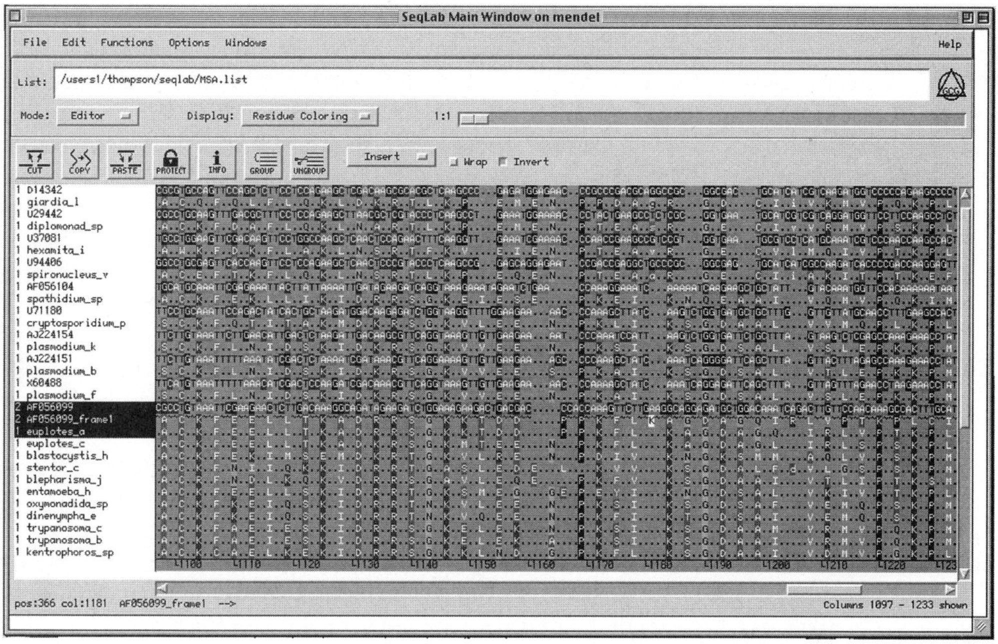

Fig. 16. Using SeqLab to align a set of DNA sequences against an already aligned dataset of their translational products.

The package's name changed in version 4.0 by adding the asterisk which means *and other methods,* referring to the incorporation of the minimum evolution distance method and the maximum likelihood method. It was also expanded to a *portable* package capable of being run on many different platforms using a command line interface in addition to its original Macintosh graphical user interface. PAUP* does not include any protein models of evolution other than a crude like/not-like model. Sophisticated protein models can be used by embedding the necessary commands and matrices in the NEXUS file used as input to the package. PAUP*'s DNA models are perhaps the most sophisticated available in any molecular phylogenetic inference software.

NEXUS Format

Within the context of GCG, NEXUS format files are most easily and reliably built from alignments with GCG's own interface to the PAUP* package. PAUPSearch within SeqLab can be used to generate NEXUS format files that can then be directly fed to any version of PAUP*.

Begin NEXUS conversion by selecting all relevant sequences and weight Mask, in the **Main Window** display. Select **PAUPSearch. . .** from the **Functions Evolution** menu to launch the dialogue box. To generate a NEXUS file, run PAUPSearch in its fastest mode without performing a search. Accept the default **Tree Optimality Criterion . . . maximum parsimony** and the **heuristic tree search (fast) . . . Method for Obtaining Best Tree(s).** Be sure that the **perform bootstrap replications. . .** button is not pressed and then launch the **Options** menu by pressing the appropriate button. In the **PAUPSearch Options** menu check the top box to save the PAUPscript file. This is not required for running the programs but is essential to generate a NEXUS file. You can change or leave the file name as you wish. The PAUPscript output file results from the automatic conversion of the alignment to NEXUS format and contains all the PAUP commands as well as their alignment. If needed, the PAUPlog file keeps track of all that happened during the program run and is a good place to look for any error messages. Uncheck the next box, **Perform the analysis.** The program does the conversion and generates the NEXUS script but is prevented from performing the heuristic search for the best tree. This is equivalent to the command line option -NoRun. Scroll through the options menu, leaving the rest of the options at their default settings. **Close** the options menu. Normally PAUP-Search and PAUPDisplay are linked to each other when they are run from the SeqLab interface. Therefore, uncheck the **PAUPDisplay. . .** button in PAUPSearch's main window to turn PAUPDisplay off. Be sure that **How: Background Job** is specified on the main PAUPSearch menu and then press **Run** there. After a moment the output PAUPscript file will be displayed. An abridged protein dataset example is shown in Table 6.

The PAUPscript file contains the NEXUS format file that was generated by GCG to run PAUP*. Notice that the masked columns of the alignment contain zeroes and are excluded from the NEXUS alignment. This file can be used to run the latest version of PAUP*, if it is available. Using a Macintosh may be desirable in order to take advantage of PAUP*'s very friendly Macintosh interface. GCG automatically creates this file, correctly encoding all of the required format data. When using this file as input to native PAUP*, remove any inappropriate commands within the command block near the end of the file with a simple text editor.

PHYLIP Format

Joseph Felsenstein's PHYLogenetic Inference Package (PHYLIP) from the University of Washington (*see* Website: http://evolution.genetics.washington.edu/phylip.html) is a comprehensive freeware suite of thirty different programs for inferring phylogenies that can handle molecular sequence, restriction digest, gene frequency, and morphological character data. Methods available in the package include parsimony, distance matrix, and likelihood, as well as bootstrapping and consensus techniques. A menu controls the programs and asks for options to set and start the computation. Data is automatically read into the program from a text file in a unique PHYLIP format called *infile*. If it is not found, the user types in the proper data file name. Output is written to special files with names like *outfile* and *treefile*. Trees written into *treefile* are in the Newick format, an informal standard agreed to in 1986 by authors of a number of phylogeny packages.

To generate PHYLIP format input from GCG alignments in SeqLab, a combination approach of GCG's ToFastA and Don Gilbert's ReadSeq will be used. First, go to the **SeqLab Main Window File Export** menu; click **Format** and notice that **MSF, GenBank,** and **GDE2.2** are all available for saving a copy of an RSF file in an alternative format. At this point do not export any of these formats. **Cancel** the window. This export routing does not use the Mask data option that would include or exclude columns from your alignment. To take advantage of the Mask data for subsequent phylogenetic analyses, export your alignment using another method. Make sure that all of the relevant sequences, as well as any Mask that you wish to test, are selected. Next, go to the **Functions** menu, where all choices will be affected by the Mask that you have chosen and select **Importing/Exporting ToFastA. . ..** Press **Run** to convert the portion of the alignment that is not masked in the FastA format. FastA is a good inter-

Table 6
An Abridged NEXUS File from PAUPSearch NoRun[a]

```
#NEXUS

[! Aligned sequences from GCG file(s) '@/users1/thompson/.seqlab-mendel/paupsear ch_51.list' ]

[Length: 441  Type: P May 15, 2001 15:07]

[ Name: GIARDIA_L       Len: 441 Check: 2966 Weight: 1.00]
[ Name: DIPLOMONAD_SP   Len: 441 Check: 4608 Weight: 1.00]
[ Name: HEXAMITA_I      Len: 441 Check: 9530 Weight: 1.00]
[ Name: SPIRONUCLEUS_V  Len: 441 Check: 2245 Weight: 1.00]
[ Name: SPATHIDIUM_SP   Len: 441 Check: 2937 Weight: 1.00]
[ Name: CRYPTOSPORIDIUM_P Len: 441 Check: 7665 Weight: 1.00]
[ Name: PLASMODIUM_K    Len: 441 Check: 9956 Weight: 1.00]
[ Name: PLASMODIUM_B    Len: 441 Check: 9937 Weight: 1.00]
[ Name: PLASMODIUM_F    Len: 441 Check: 796 Weight: 1.00]
[ Name: EUPLOTES_A      Len: 441 Check: 8831 Weight: 1.00]
[ Name: EUPLOTES_C      Len: 441 Check: 8653 Weight: 1.00]
[ Name: BLASTOCYSTIS_H  Len: 441 Check: 9014 Weight: 1.00]
[ Name: STENTOR_C       Len: 441 Check: 5386 Weight: 1.00]
[ Name: BLEPHARISMA_J   Len: 441 Check: 7915 Weight: 1.00]
[ Name: ENTAMOEBA_H     Len: 441 Check: 8365 Weight: 1.00]
[ Name: OXYMONADIDA_SP  Len: 441 Check: 8531 Weight: 1.00]
[ Name: DINENYMPHA_E    Len: 441 Check: 5471 Weight: 1.00]
[ Name: TRYPANOSOMA_C   Len: 441 Check: 9945 Weight: 1.00]
[ Name: TRYPANOSOMA_B   Len: 441 Check: 960 Weight: 1.00]
[ Name: KENTROPHOROS_SP Len: 441 Check: 1567 Weight: 1.00]
[ Name: EUGLENA_G       Len: 441 Check: 492 Weight: 1.00]
[ Name: PLANOPROTOSTELIUM_A Len: 441 Check: 8843 Weight: 1.00]
[ Name: DICTYOSTELIUM_D Len: 441 Check: 6233 Weight: 1.00]
[ Name: PHYSARUM_P      Len: 441 Check: 320 Weight: 1.00]
[ Name: CYANOPHORA_P    Len: 441 Check: 4176 Weight: 1.00]
[ Name: PHYTOPHTHORA_I  Len: 441 Check: 804 Weight: 1.00]
[ Name: STYLONYCHIA_M   Len: 441 Check: 2825 Weight: 1.00]
[ Name: STYLONYCHIA_L   Len: 441 Check: 1254 Weight: 1.00]
[ Name: PARANOPHRYS_C   Len: 441 Check: 196 Weight: 1.00]
[ Name: TETRHYMENA_P    Len: 441 Check: 4061 Weight: 1.00]
[ Name: TELOTROCHIDIUM_H Len: 441 Check: 1239 Weight: 1.00]
[ Name: PARAMECIUM_T    Len: 441 Check: 3452 Weight: 1.00]
[ Name: COLPODA_I       Len: 441 Check: 8135 Weight: 1.00]
[ Name: NAXELLA_SP      Len: 441 Check: 6970 Weight: 1.00]
[ Name: PORPHYRA_P      Len: 441 Check: 1559 Weight: 1.00]
[ Name: TRICHOMONAS_T   Len: 441 Check: 6212 Weight: 1.00]
[ Name: TRICHOMONAS_V   Len: 441 Check: 6532 Weight: 1.00]
[ Name: NAEGLERIA_A     Len: 441 Check: 7736 Weight: 1.00]

begin data;
     dimensions ntax=38 nchar=441;
     format datatype=protein interleave gap=.;
     matrix
[                      1                                                 50]
          GIARDIA_L  .......... .......... STLTGHLIYK CGGIDQRTID EYEKRATEMG
      DIPLOMONAD_SP  .......... .......NGK STLTGHLIYK CGGIDQRTLD EYEKRANEMG
         HEXAMITA_I  .......... .......NGK STLTGHLIYK CGGIDQRTLE DYEKKANEIG
     SPIRONUCLEUS_V  .......... .......NGK STLTGHLIFK CGGIDQRTLD EYEKKANELG
      SPATHIDIUM_SP  .......... .....VDSGK STSTGHLIYK CGGIDERTIE KFEKEAKQIG
  CRYPTOSPORIDIUM_P  MGKEKTHINL VVIGHVDSGK STTTGHLIYK LGGIDKRTIE KFEKESSEMG
       PLASMODIUM_K  MGKEKTHINL VVIGHVDSGK STTTGHIIYK LGGIDRRTIE KFEKESAEMG
       PLASMODIUM_B  MGKEKTHINL VVIGHVDSGK STTTGHIIYK LGGIDRRTIE KFEKESAEMG
       PLASMODIUM_F  MGKEKTHINL VVIGHVDSGK STTTGHIIYK LGGIDRRTIE KFEKESAEMG
         EUPLOTES_A  .......... .....VDSGK STTTGHLIYK LGGTDARTIE KFEKESAEMG
         EUPLOTES_C  MGKEKEHLNL VVIGHVDSGK STTTGHLIYK LGGIDARTIE KFEKESAEMG
     BLASTOCYSTIS_H  MGKEKPHINL VVIGHVVAGK STTTGHLIYA CGGIDKRTIE RFEEGGQRIG
          STENTOR_C  .......... .....VDSGK STTIGHLIYK CGGIDKRTID KFDKDASDMG
      BLEPHARISMA_J  .......... .....VDSGK STSCGHLIYK CGGIDKRTIE KYEKEAKEMG
        ENTAMOEBA_H  MPKEKTHINI VVIGHVDSGK STTTGHLIYK CGGIDQRTIE KFEKESAEMG
     OXYMONADIDA_SP  .......... .......... STTTRHLIYK CGGIDQRTLD RFQKESEAMG
       DINENYMPHA_E  .......... .......... STTTGHLIYK CGGIDERTIK KFEQESEAMG
      TRYPANOSOMA_C  MGKEKVHMNL VVVGHVDAGK STATGHLIYK CGGIDKRTIE KFEKEAAEIG
      TRYPANOSOMA_B  MGKEKVHMNL VVVGHVDAGK STATGHLIYK CGGIDKRTIE KFEKEAADIG
    KENTROPHOROS_SP  .......... .....VDSGK STSTGHLIYK CGGIDKRTIE KFDKEAAEMG
          EUGLENA_G  MGKEKVHISL VVIGHVDSGK STTTGHLIYK CGGIDKRTIE KFEKEASEMG
PLANOPROTOSTELIUM_A  .......... .......AGK STTTGHLIYK CGGIDKRTIE KFEKEAKEIG
    DICTYOSTELIUM_D  MESEKTHINI VVIGHVDAGK STTTGHLIYK CGGIDKRVIE KYEKEASEMG
         PHYSARUM_P  .......... .......AGK STTTGHLIYK CGGIDKRTIE KFEKEAAEMG
       CYANOPHORA_P  MGKQKTHINI VVIGHVDSGK STTTGHLIYK CGGIDKRTIE KFEKEAAEIG
     PHYTOPHTHORA_I  .......... .VIGHVDAGK STTTGHLIYK CGGIDKRTIE KFEKEAAELG
      STYLONYCHIA_M  .......... .....VDSGK STSTGHLIYK CGGIDKRTIE KFEKEPAEMG
      STYLONYCHIA_L  MPKEKNHLNL VVIGHVDSGK STSTGHLIYK CGGIDKRTIE KFEKEAAEMG
      PARANOPHRYS_C  .......... .....VDSGK STTTGHLIYK CGGIDKRVIE KFEKESAEMG
       TETRHYMENA_P  M.GDKVHINL VVIGHVDSGK STTTGHLIYK CGGIDKRVIE KFEKESAEQG
   TELOTROCHIDIUM_H  .......... ...GHVDSGK STSTGHLIYK CGGIDKRTLE KFEKEAAEMG
       PARAMECIUM_T  G.KDKLHVNL VVIGHVDSGK STTTGHLIYK LGGIDERTIK KFEDEANKLG
          COLPODA_I  .......... .....VDSGK STSTGHLIYK CGGIHKRTIE KFEKEANELG
```

(continued)

Table 6 *(continued)*
An Abridged NEXUS File from PAUPSearch NoRun[a]

```
            NAXELLA_SP  .......... .....VDSGK STTTGHLIYK CGGIDKRTIE KFEKESAEQG
            PORPHYRA_P  MGKEKQHVSI VVIGHVDSGK STTTGHLIYK CGGIDKRAIE KFEKEAAEMG
         TRICHOMONAS_T  .......... .......... STTTGHLIYK CGGLDKRKLA AMEKEAEQLG
         TRICHOMONAS_V  .......... .....VDAGK STTTGHLIYK CGGLDKRKLA AIEKEAEQLG
           NAEGLERIA_A  .......... .......AGK STTTGHLIYK CGGIDKRVIE KFEKEAAEMG
////////////////////////////////////////////////////////////////////////////////
[                       401                                        441]
             GIARDIA_L  CCETFNDYAP LGPFAVR... .......... .......... .
          DIPLOMONAD_SP SCESFNDYAA LGRFAVR... .......... .......... .
            HEXAMITA_I  CVESFEQYPA LGRFAVR... .......... .......... .
       SPIRONUCLEUS_V   SAESYELYPA LGRFAVR... .......... .......... .
        SPATHIDIUM_SP   VCETFAGYPP LGRFAVRDMK QTVAV..... .......... .
    CRYPTOSPORIDIUM_P   CVEAFTDYPP LGRFAVRDMK QTVAVGVIKS VKKE....KK K
         PLASMODIUM_K   VVETFTEYPP LGRFAIRDMR QTIAVGIIKA VKKEAAKNAK K
         PLASMODIUM_B   VVETFTEYPP LGRFAIRDMR QTIAVGIIKS VKKEAAKAAK K
         PLASMODIUM_F   VVETFTEYPP LGRFAIRDMR QTIAVGIINQ LRKNAAKAAK K
           EUPLOTES_A   CIENFSRYAP LGRFAVRDMK QTVAVG.... .......... .
           EUPLOTES_C   CVETFATYAP LGRFAVRDMR QTVAVGVIQE IKKKE.KKKK K
       BLASTOCYSTIS_H   CVETFSDYPP LGRFAVRDMR QTVAVGIIKS TRAK...... .
            STENTOR_C   CVETFTEYPP LGRFAVRDMK QTVAV..... .......... .
        BLEPHARISMA_J   CVEPFTEYPP LGRFAVRDMR QTVAV..... .......... .
          ENTAMOEBA_H   CVEEFAKFPP LGRFAVRDMK QTVAVGVVKA V.TP...... .
       OXYMONADIDA_SP   VVETFVEYPP LGRFAVR... .......... .......... .
          DINENYMPHA_E  VVETFVEYPP LGRFAVR... .......... .......... .
        TRYPANOSOMA_C   CVEVFNDYAP LGRFAVRDMR QTVAVGIIKA VKKDAAAAAK K
        TRYPANOSOMA_B   CVEVFNDYAP LGRFAVRDMR QTVAVGIIKA VKKDGAAVSK K
      KENTROPHOROS_SP   CVESFSDYPP LGRFAVHDMR QTVAV..... .......... .
            EUGLENA_G   CVESFTDYPP LG.VSCGDMR QTVAVGVIKS VKKE.TKAKK K
  PLANOPROTOSTELIUM_A   CVETFTEYPP LGRFAVRDMR .......... .......... .
       DICTYOSTELIUM_D  CVESFTEYPP LGRFAVRDMR QTVAVGVIKS TKKAAAAAKK K
            PHYSARUM_P  CVESFTDFPP LGRFAVRDMR .......... .......... .
          CYANOPHORA_P  CVEAFTNYPP LGRFAVRDMR QTVAVGVIKE VKKEAGKAGK K
        PHYTOPHTHORA_I  TVESFQEYPP LGRFAVRDMR QTVAVGVIKS VKKEG.GGKK K
         STYLONYCHIA_M  CVEAFNQYPP LGRFAVRDMK QTVAVG.... .......... .
         STYLONYCHIA_L  CVEAFNQYPP LGRFAVRDMK QTVAVGVIKE VKKEGTKAKK K
         PARANOPHRYS_C  CVEVFSEYPP LGRYAVRDMK QTVAV..... .......... .
          TETRHYMENA_P  CVEVFQEYPP LGRYAVRDMK QTVAVGVIKK VKKD...... K
      TELOTROCHIDIUM_H  CVESFAEYPP LGRFAVRDMK QTVAVG.... .......... .
          PARAMECIUM_T  CVEIFSEYPP LGRFAVRDMK QTVAVGVIKV VKKE....KK K
             COLPODA_I  CVEAFSDYPP LGRFAVRDMK QTVAVG.... .......... .
            NAXELLA_SP  CVEIFNEYPP LGRFAVRDMK QTVAV..... .......... .
            PORPHYRA_P  CVEAFTSYPP LGRFAVRDMR QTVAVGVIKS VKKEGTKSAK K
         TRICHOMONAS_T  VVESFQEYPP LGRFAIR... .......... .......... .
         TRICHOMONAS_V  VVESFQEYPP LGRFAIRDMK QTVAVGVIRS VKKP....PI K
           NAEGLERIA_A  CVEGFTEYPP LGRFAVR... .......... .......... .

      ;
endblock;

begin paup;
set errorstop;
set criterion=parsimony;
set increase=no;
pset collapse=maxbrlen;
hsearch start=stepwise addseq=simple swap=tbr;
savetrees /brlens file='/users1/thompson/seqlab/paupsearch_51.pauptrees' replace;
quit;
endblock;
```

[a]The PAUPSearch program can reliably and quickly extract NEXUS format from GCG multiple sequence alignments using the -NoRun option. Zero Mask weighted columns are excluded from the file.

mediate format on the way to PHYLIP's required format. The new file will be displayed by SeqLab. The very first part of the protein dataset FastA format output file is shown in Table 7. Notice that it excludes those positions that were masked with zero and that it now follows all FastA format conventions including the automatic conversion of all GCG style gap periods and tildes to the more universal gap hyphen representation. This circumvents the common *dot to dash* problem that is often encountered in sequence format conversion. **Close** the ToFastA output window. You may want to use the **Output Manager** to save the file under a name you recognize using the **Save As . . .** menu.

Table 7
GCG ToFastA Output[a]

```
>GIARDIA_L In situ PileUp of: @/users1/thompson/.seqlab-mendel/pileup_36.list
--------------------STLTGHLIYKCGGIDQRTIDEYEKRATEMGKGSFKYAWVL
DQLKDERERGITINIALWKFETKKYIVTIIDAPGHRDFIKNMITGTSQADVAILVVAAGQ
GEFEAGISKDGQTREHATLANTLGIKTMIICVNKMDDGQVKYSKERYDEIKGEMMKQLKN
IGWK-EEFDYIPTSGWTGDNIMEKSDKMPWYEGPCLIDAIDGLKAPKRPTDKPLRLPIQD
VYKISGVGTVPAGRVETGELAPGMKVVFAPTS-QSEVKSVEMHHEELKKAGPGDNVGFNV
RGLAVKDLKKGYVVGDVTNDPPVGCKSFTAQVIVMNHPKKIQ-PGYTPVIDCHTAHIACQ
FQLFLQKLDKRTLKP-EMENPPDAR-GD-CIVKMVPQKPLCCETFNDYAPLGPFAVR--
-------------------
>DIPLOMONAD_SP In situ PileUp of: @/users1/thompson/.seqlab-mendel/pileup_36.list
-----------------NGKSTLTGHLIYKCGGIDQRTLDEYEKRANEMGKGSFKYAWVL
DQLKDERERGITINIALWKFETKKFTVTIIDAPGHRDFIKNMITGTSQADVAILVIASGQ
GEFEAGISKEGQTREHATLAHTLGIKTLIVCVNKMDDPQVNYSEARYKEIKEEMQKNLKQ
IGYK-DEFDFIPTSGWTGDSIMEKSPNMPWYSGPCLIDAIDGLKAPKRPTDKPLRLPIQD
VYKINGVGTVPAGRVESGLLIPNMTVVFAPST-TAEVKSVEMHHEELPQAGPGDNVGFNV
RGIAAKDIKKGYVVGDTKNDPPVGCKSFTAQVIIMNHPKKIQ-PGYSPVIDCHTAHIACK
FDAFLQKLNARTLKP-EMENPTEAR-GE-CIVRMVPSKPLSCESFNDYAALGRFAVR--
-------------------
>HEXAMITA_I In situ PileUp of: @/users1/thompson/.seqlab-mendel/pileup_36.list
-----------------NGKSTLTGHLIYKCGGIDQRTLEDYEKKANEIGKGSFKYAWVL
DQLKDERERGITINIALWKFETKKFIVTIIDAPGHRDFIKNMITGTSQADVAILVVAAGQ
GEFEAGISSEGQTREHATLANTLGIKTMIVAVNKMDDPQVNYSEARYTEIKTEMQKTFKQ
IGFK-EEFDFVPLSGWTGDNIMEASPKTPWYKGKCLIECIDGLKAPKRPNDKPLRLPIQD
VYKINGVGTVPAGRVESGELIPGMMVVFAPAG-ETEVKSVEMHHEQLAKAGPGDNVGFNI
KGLSAKDIKKGYVVGDVNNDAPKGCEYFKANVIIMNHPKKI-NPGYTPVLDCHTSHLAWK
FDKFLAKLNSRTFKV-EIENPTEAR-GE-CVMQIVPTKPLCVESFEQYPALGRFAVR--
-------------------
>SPIRONUCLEUS_V In situ PileUp of: @/users1/thompson/.seqlab-mendel/pileup_36.list
-----------------NGKSTLTGHLIFKCGGIDQRTLDEYEKKANELGKGSFKYAWVL
DQLKDERERGITINIALWKFETKKFIVTIIDAPGHRDFIKNMITGTSQADVAILVVAAGQ
GEFEAGISKEGQTREHATLANTLGIKTIILCINKMDDPNVNYSKDRYNEIKTEMTKTLVA
IGYK-PEFNYIPTSGWTGLNIMEKTEKTGWYDGPCLIEAIDSLKPPKRPTDKCLRLPIQD
VYKINGVGTVPAGRVESGCLKPNTLAVFAPTN-TAEVKSVEMHHEELPQAEPGDNVGFNV
RGIAAKDIKKGYVVGDSKSDPPGRVKSFEAQVIIMNHPKKIQ-PGYTPVVDCHTNHMACE
FTKFLQKLNSRTLKP-EQENPTEAR-GE-CIAKITPTKEFSAESYELYPALGRFAVR--
-------------------
>SPATHIDIUM_SP In situ PileUp of: @/users1/thompson/.seqlab-mendel/pileup_36.list
----------------VDSGKSTSTGHLIYKCGGIDERTIEKFEKEAKQIGKESFKYAGLL
DILKAERARGITIDIALWKFESQKYSFTIIDAPGHRDFIKNMITGTSQADVAILVISAGQ
GEFEAGIGKDGQTREHALLAYTMGIKQVVVAINKMD-AVQYNEERFTDIKKEVIDYLKK
MGSKKKMLMSLPISGFMGDNLIEKSDKMPWYKGDTILEALDRVERPKRPVAKPLRLPLQD
VYKITGVGTVPVGRVETGVIKPGTLVTFAPVNITTECKTVEMHHQQLEEAIPGDNVGFNV
KNISIKDIRRGNVVGDSKNDPPKEAVSFNAQVIVLNHPNKIQA-GYCPVLDCHTSHIACK
FEKLLIKIDRRSGKEIESE-PKEIKNQEAAIVQMVPQKIMVCETFAGYPPLGRFAVRDMK
```

[a]The GCG ToFastA program reliably converts GCG multiple sequence alignments into Pearson FastA format. This conversion takes advantage of the Mask sequence and changes gap periods to hyphens.

Next, ReadSeq is used to convert this FastA format file to a PHYLIP compatible format. Exit SeqLab with the **File** menu **Exit** choice, or temporarily switch to your background terminal window. If you exit, you will probably be asked if you want to save your RSF file and any changes in your list. Accept the suggested changes with appropriate names and SeqLab will close. This will return you to your terminal window, formerly behind the SeqLab display, where ReadSeq can be run. This program can be used to change your FastA format file into a PHYLIP formatted file. ReadSeq does not allow you to only choose a portion of an alignment, nor does it automatically convert dots and tildes to hyphens. These issues were resolved in SeqLab. Begin ReadSeq by typing **readseq** at your command prompt in the terminal window. ReadSeq first prompts you for an appropriate output file name, not an input file. Do not make a mistake in this step by giving the name of your input file first. If you do, you will overwrite the input file while running the program, and then when it tries to read the input, there will be nothing left to read! Next choose the current PHYLIP format and then designate the input sequence. Do not use the GCG {*} designator; this is not a GCG program. After the program has read all of the input sequences, specify

Table 8
A ReadSeq Screen Trace[a]

```
> readseq
readSeq (1Feb93), multi-format molbio sequence reader.

Name of output file (?=help, defaults to display):
EF1A.phy

        1. IG/Stanford              10. Olsen (in-only)
        2. GenBank/GB               11. Phylip3.2
        3. NBRF                     12. Phylip
        4. EMBL                     13. Plain/Raw
        5. GCG                      14. PIR/CODATA
        6. DNAStrider               15. MSF
        7. Fitch                    16. ASN.1
        8. Pearson/Fasta            17. PAUP/NEXUS
        9. Zuker (in-only)          18. Pretty (out-only)

Choose an output format (name or #):
12

Name an input sequence or -option:
EF1A.tfa
Sequences in EF1A.tfa (format is 8. Pearson/Fasta)
  1) GIARDIA_L In situ PileUp of: @/users1/thompson/.seqlab-mendel/pileup_36.list
  2) DIPLOMONAD_SP In situ PileUp of: @/users1/thompson/.seqlab-mendel/pileup_36.list
  3) HEXAMITA_I In situ PileUp of: @/users1/thompson/.seqlab-mendel/pileup_36.list
  4) SPIRONUCLEUS_V In situ PileUp of: @/users1/thompson/.seqlab-mendel/pileup_36.list
  5) SPATHIDIUM_SP In situ PileUp of: @/users1/thompson/.seqlab-mendel/pileup_36.list
  6) CRYPTOSPORIDIUM_P In situ PileUp of: @/users1/thompson/.seqlab-mendel/pileup_36.list
  7) PLASMODIUM_K In situ PileUp of: @/users1/thompson/.seqlab-mendel/pileup_36.list
  8) PLASMODIUM_B In situ PileUp of: @/users1/thompson/.seqlab-mendel/pileup_36.list
  9) PLASMODIUM_F In situ PileUp of: @/users1/thompson/.seqlab-mendel/pileup_36.list
  10) EUPLOTES_A In situ PileUp of: @/users1/thompson/.seqlab-mendel/pileup_36.list
  11) EUPLOTES_C In situ PileUp of: @/users1/thompson/.seqlab-mendel/pileup_36.list
  12) BLASTOCYSTIS_H In situ PileUp of: @/users1/thompson/.seqlab-mendel/pileup_36.list
  13) STENTOR_C In situ PileUp of: @/users1/thompson/.seqlab-mendel/pileup_36.list
  14) BLEPHARISMA_J In situ PileUp of: @/users1/thompson/.seqlab-mendel/pileup_36.list
  15) ENTAMOEBA_H In situ PileUp of: @/users1/thompson/.seqlab-mendel/pileup_36.list
  16) OXYMONADIDA_SP In situ PileUp of: @/users1/thompson/.seqlab-mendel/pileup_36.list
  17) DINENYMPHA_E In situ PileUp of: @/users1/thompson/.seqlab-mendel/pileup_36.list
  18) TRYPANOSOMA_C In situ PileUp of: @/users1/thompson/.seqlab-mendel/pileup_36.list
  19) TRYPANOSOMA_B In situ PileUp of: @/users1/thompson/.seqlab-mendel/pileup_36.list
  20) KENTROPHOROS_SP In situ PileUp of: @/users1/thompson/.seqlab-mendel/pileup_36.list
  21) EUGLENA_G In situ PileUp of: @/users1/thompson/.seqlab-mendel/pileup_36.list
  22) PLANOPROTOSTELIUM_A In situ PileUp of: @/users1/thompson/.seqlab-mendel/pileup_36.list
  23) DICTYOSTELIUM_D In situ PileUp of: @/users1/thompson/.seqlab-mendel/pileup_36.list
  24) PHYSARUM_P In situ PileUp of: @/users1/thompson/.seqlab-mendel/pileup_36.list
  25) CYANOPHORA_P In situ PileUp of: @/users1/thompson/.seqlab-mendel/pileup_36.list
  26) PHYTOPHTHORA_I In situ PileUp of: @/users1/thompson/.seqlab-mendel/pileup_36.list
  27) STYLONYCHIA_M In situ PileUp of: @/users1/thompson/.seqlab-mendel/pileup_36.list
  28) STYLONYCHIA_L In situ PileUp of: @/users1/thompson/.seqlab-mendel/pileup_36.list
  29) PARANOPHRYS_C In situ PileUp of: @/users1/thompson/.seqlab-mendel/pileup_36.list
  30) TETRHYMENA_P In situ PileUp of: @/users1/thompson/.seqlab-mendel/pileup_36.list
  31) TELOTROCHIDIUM_H In situ PileUp of: @/users1/thompson/.seqlab-mendel/pileup_36.list
  32) PARAMECIUM_T In situ PileUp of: @/users1/thompson/.seqlab-mendel/pileup_36.list
  33) COLPODA_I In situ PileUp of: @/users1/thompson/.seqlab-mendel/pileup_36.list
  34) NAXELLA_SP In situ PileUp of: @/users1/thompson/.seqlab-mendel/pileup_36.list
  35) PORPHYRA_P In situ PileUp of: @/users1/thompson/.seqlab-mendel/pileup_36.list
  36) TRICHOMONAS_T In situ PileUp of: @/users1/thompson/.seqlab-mendel/pileup_36.list
  37) TRICHOMONAS_V In situ PileUp of: @/users1/thompson/.seqlab-mendel/pileup_36.list
  38) NAEGLERIA_A In situ PileUp of: @/users1/thompson/.seqlab-mendel/pileup_36.list

Choose a sequence (# or All):
all
Name an input sequence or -option:<rtn>
```

[a]A ReadSeq sample screen trace with user responses highlighted in bold.

All the sequences by typing the word **all.** When the program again asks for an input sequence, press return and the file conversion will begin. Table 8 illustrates a sample terminal session screen trace.

The **. . . padded to fit** error message is not cause for concern. However, if a GCG MSF file was used as the input, then an essential change would be required before it would be correct for PHYLIP. The periods and tildes would need to be changed to hyphens (dashes). To make these changes the following UNIX command works well:

> tr \~\. \- < infile.phy > outfile.phy

Table 9
PHYLIP Format[a]

```
 38 439
GIARDIA_L   ---------- ---------- STLTGHLIYK CGGIDQRTID EYEKRATEMG
DIPLOMONAD  ---------- -------NGK STLTGHLIYK CGGIDQRTLD EYEKRANEMG
HEXAMITA_I  ---------- -------NGK STLTGHLIYK CGGIDQRTLE DYEKKANEIG
SPIRONUCLE  ---------- -------NGK STLTGHLIFK CGGIDQRTLD EYEKKANELG
SPATHIDIUM  ---------- -----VDSGK STSTGHLIYK CGGIDERTIE KFEKEAKQIG
CRYPTOSPOR  MGKEKTHINL VVIGHVDSGK STTTGHLIYK LGGIDKRTIE KFEKESSEMG
PLASMODIUM  MGKEKTHINL VVIGHVDSGK STTTGHIIYK LGGIDRRTIE KFEKESAEMG
PLASMODIUM  MGKEKTHINL VVIGHVDSGK STTTGHIIYK LGGIDRRTIE KFEKESAEMG
PLASMODIUM  MGKEKTHINL VVIGHVDSGK STTTGHIIYK LGGIDRRTIE KFEKESAEMG
EUPLOTES_A  ---------- -----VDSGK STTTGHLIYK LGGTDARTIE KFEKESAEMG
EUPLOTES_C  MGKEKEHLNL VVIGHVDSGK STTTGHLIYK LGGIDARTIE KFEKESAEMG
BLASTOCYST  MGKEKPHINL VVIGHVVAGK STTTGHLIYA CGGIDKRTIE RFEEGGQRIG
STENTOR_C   ---------- -----VDSGK STTIGHLIYK CGGIDKRTID KFDKDASDMG
BLEPHARISM  ---------- -----VDSGK STSCGHLIYK CGGIDKRTIE KYEKEAKEMG
ENTAMOEBA_  MPKEKTHINI VVIGHVDSGK STTTGHLIYK CGGIDQRTIE KFEKESAEMG
OXYMONADID  ---------- ---------- STTTRHLIYK CGGIDQRTLD RFQKESEAMG
DINENYMPHA  ---------- ---------- STTTGHLIYK CGGIDERTIK KFEQESEAMG
TRYPANOSOM  MGKEKVHMNL VVVGHVDAGK STATGHLIYK CGGIDKRTIE KFEKEAAEIG
TRYPANOSOM  MGKEKVHMNL VVVGHVDAGK STATGHLIYK CGGIDKRTIE KFEKEAADIG
KENTROPHOR  ---------- -----VDSGK STSTGHLIYK CGGIDKRTIE KFDKEAAEMG
EUGLENA_G   MGKEKVHISL VVIGHVDSGK STTTGHLIYK CGGIDKRTIE KFEKEASEMG
PLANOPROTO  ---------- -------AGK STTTGHLIYK CGGIDKRTIE KFEKEAKEIG
DICTYOSTEL  MESEKTHINI VVIGHVDAGK STTTGHLIYK CGGIDKRVIE KYEKEASEMG
PHYSARUM_P  ---------- -------AGK STTTGHLIYK CGGIDKRTIE KFEKEAAEMG
CYANOPHORA  MGKQKTHINI VVIGHVDSGK STTTGHLIYK CGGIDKRTIE KFEKEAAEIG
PHYTOPHTHO  ---------- -VIGHVDAGK STTTGHLIYK CGGIDKRTIE KFEKEAAELG
STYLONYCHI  ---------- -----VDSGK STSTGHLIYK CGGIDKRTIE KFEKEPAEMG
STYLONYCHI  MPKEKNHLNL VVIGHVDSGK STSTGHLIYK CGGIDKRTIE KFEKEAAEMG
PARANOPHRY  ---------- -----VDSGK STTTGHLIYK CGGIDKRVIE KFEKESAEMG
TETRHYMENA  M-GDKVHINL VVIGHVDSGK STTTGHLIYK CGGIDKRVIE KFEKESAEQG
TELOTROCHI  ---------- ---GHVDSGK STSTGHLIYK CGGIDKRTLE KFEKEAAEMG
PARAMECIUM  G-KDKLHVNL VVIGHVDSGK STTTGHLIYK LGGIDERTIK KFEDEANKLG
COLPODA_I   ---------- -----VDSGK STSTGHLIYK CGGIHKRTIE KFEKEANELG
NAXELLA_SP  ---------- -----VDSGK STTTGHLIYK CGGIDKRTIE KFEKESAEQG
PORPHYRA_P  MGKEKQHVSI VVIGHVDSGK STTTGHLIYK CGGIDKRAIE KFEKEAAEMG
TRICHOMONA  ---------- ---------- STTTGHLIYK CGGLDKRKLA AMEKEAEQLG
TRICHOMONA  ---------- -----VDAGK STTTGHLIYK CGGLDKRKLA AIEKEAEQLG
NAEGLERIA_  ---------- -------AGK STTTGHLIYK CGGIDKRVIE KFEKEAAEMG

            KGSFKYAWVL DQLKDERERG ITINIALWKF ETKKYIVTII DAPGHRDFIK
            KGSFKYAWVL DQLKDERERG ITINIALWKF ETKKFTVTII DAPGHRDFIK
            KGSFKYAWVL DQLKDERERG ITINIALWKF ETKKFIVTII DAPGHRDFIK
            KGSFKYAWVL DQLKDERERG ITINIALWKF ETKKFIVTII DAPGHRDFIK
            KESFKYAGLL DILKAERARG ITIDIALWKF ESQKYSFTII DAPGHRDFIK
            KGSFKYAWVL DKLKAERERG ITIDIALWQF ETPKYHYTVI DAPGHRDFIK
            KGSFKYAWVL DKLKAERERG ITIDIALWKF ETPRYFFTVI DAPGHKDFIK
            KGSFKYAWVL DKLKAERERG ITIDIALWKF ETPRYFFTVI DAPGHKHFIK
            KGSFKYAWVL DKLKAERERG ITIDIALWKF ETPRYFFTVI DAPGHKDFIK
            KGTFKYAWVL DKLKAERERG ITIDIALWKF ETTNRFYTII DAPGHRDFIK
            KASFKYAWVL DKLKAERERG ITIDIALWKF ETENRHYTII DAPGHRDFIK
            KGSFKYAWVL AKMKAERERG ITIDISLWKF ETRKDFFTII DAPGHRDFIK
            KSSFKYAWVL DKLKAERERG ITIDISLFKF QTDKFYSTII DAPGHRDFIK
            KSSFKYAWVL DKLKAERERG ITIDISLFKF QTDKFYFTII DAPGHRDFIK
            KGSFKYAWVL DNLKAERERG ITIDISLWKF ETSKYYFTII DAPGHRDFIK
            KGSFKYAWVL DKLKAERERG ITIDIALWKF ETGKYYFTII DAPGHRDFIK
            KGSFKYAWVL DKLKAERERG ITIDIALWKF ETNKYYFTII DAPGHRDFIK
            KSSFKYAWVL DKLKAEREPG ITIDIALWKF ESPKSVFTII DAPGHRDFIK
            KASFKYAWVL DKLKAERERG ITIDIALWKF ESPKSVFTII DAPGHRDFIK
            KGSFKYAWVL DKLKAERERG ITIDIALWKF ESPKCVFTII DAPGHRDFIK
            KGSFKYAWVL DKLKAERERC ITIDIALWKF ETAKSVFTII DAPGHRDFIK
            KASFKYAWVL DKLKAERERG ITIDIALWKF ETTKYYFTII DAPGHRDFIK
            KQSFKYAWVM DKLKAERERG ITIDIALWKF ETSKYYFTII DAPGHRDFIK
            KGSFKYAWVL DKLKSERERG ITIDIALWKF ETAKYYITII DAPGHRDFIK
            KGSFKYAWVL DKLKAERERG ITIDIALWKF ETPKYYVTII DAPGHRDFIK
            KTSFKYAWVL DNLKAERERG ITIDIALWKF ESPKYFFTVI DAPGHRDFIK
            KGSFKYAWVL DKLKAERERG ITIDIALWKF ETAKSVFTII DAPGHRDFIK
            KGSFKYAWVL DKLKAERERG ITIDIALWNF ETAKSVFTII DAPGHRDFIK
            KGSFKYAWVL DKLKAERERG ITIDISLWNF ETAKRSYTII DAPGHRDFIK
//////////////////////////////////////////////////////////////////
```

[a]The beginning of the sample dataset in PHYLIP format produced by ReadSeq from a FastA format file. ToFastA stripped zero weight columns and changed gap periods to hyphens reflected in the PHYLIP file.

The first part of the example PHYLIP output file is displayed in Table 9.

Notice that the file begins with two numbers. The first shows the number of sequences in the matrix and the second lists the length of the matrix including any gaps and ambiguities. The next section lists the names of the sequences truncated to ten characters, if necessary, along with all the sequences printed in an *interleaved* fashion. Only the first sequence block lists the names, all others just give the sequence data itself.

Remember to evaluate the terminal ends of the data matrix. If any of the implied *indels* are uncertain (if the sequence lengths were different), then question marks, **?**, are usually more appropriate than hyphens. The hyphens represent gaps caused by an insertion or deletion; this could be misleading. Therefore, edit the output from ReadSeq to replace leading and trailing hyphens in the alignment with question marks or the unknowns characters **n** or **x** depending on which is appropriate. This is also an excellent point to verify that the sequence names are exactly as you wish in the final PHYLIP plots. PHYLIP sequence names can contain very limited punctuation and mixed capitalization and can be up to ten characters in length. Be very careful with these edits so that the alignment does not shift out of phase.

One vital point that can not be repeated often enough is the dramatic importance of your multiple sequence alignments. Subsequent analyses are absolutely dependent upon them. If you are building multiple sequence alignments for phylogenetic inference, do not base an organism's phylogeny on just one gene. Many complicating factors can make interpretation difficult. Unusual phylogenies can result from bad alignments, insufficient data, abjectly incorrect models, saturated positions (homoplasy), compositional biases, and/or horizontal gene transfer. Use several genes, e.g., the Ribosomal Database Project (RDP) (*see* Website: http://rdp.cme. msu.edu/html/) to provide a good, largely accepted, alignment and phylogenetic framework from which other phylogenies can be compared. The complete RDP can be installed on a local GCG server in aligned GCG format. Otherwise desired data subsets can be downloaded from RDP and loaded into SeqLab. Anytime the orthologous phylogenies of organisms based on two different genes do not agree, there is either some type of problem with the analysis, or you have found a case of lateral transfer of genetic material. Paralogous gene phylogenies are altogether another story and if possible should be based on sequences all from the same organism.

There are many situations that will present vexing alignment problems and difficult editing decisions. Most datasets that you will encounter will not have many homologs or related domains, or you will be working on a paralogous system. These are the times that you will really have to think.

Gunnar von Heijne in his quite readable but somewhat dated treatise, *Sequence Analysis in Molecular Biology; Treasure Trove or Trivial Pursuit* (1987), provides an appropriate conclusion:

> "Think about what you're doing; use your knowledge of the molecular system involved to guide both your interpretation of results and your direction of inquiry; use as much information as possible; and do not blindly accept everything the computer offers you."

He continues:

> ". . . if any lesson is to be drawn . . . it surely is that to be able to make a useful contribution one must first and foremost be a biologist, and only second a theoretician . . . . We have to develop better algorithms, we have to find ways to cope with the massive amounts of data, and above all we have to become better biologists. But that's all it takes."

Glossary and Abbreviations

Expectation value (E-value) The likelihood that a particular sequence alignment is due to chance. The value is dependent on sequence and database composition and size and on how often a researcher performs database searches. Most modern sequence database similarity programs such as the BLAST and FastA programs provide this statistic based on the Extreme Value Distribution. The closer the value is to zero, the more significant the match.

Mask In the context of a multiple sequence alignment a mask can be used to create variants of your dataset that ignore certain columns and/or over emphasize other columns of the data, without having to actually duplicate the original dataset and edit it into the desired variants.

Motif A motif is a described and catalogued region of a sequence, usually shorter than a domain, and often, but not always, associated with some biological structural, functional, or regulatory role. Motifs are commonly represented as consensus patterns, but are often described by profiles as well.

Profile A profile is a statistical description of a multiple sequence alignment, commonly of a region or a motif within a multiple sequence alignment. Profiles take many forms associated with the particular programs that create them, e.g. ProfileBuild, HMMer, MEME, but always increase the importance of conserved residues or bases and decrease the importance of variable areas.

Rich Sequence Format (RSF) GCG's proprietary multiple sequence format contains sequence data, sequence names, and sequence annotation, and is read and displayed by their SeqLab Graphical User Interface (GUI). The annotation includes all database reference information, if the sequences come from a database.

Seed In the context of multiple sequence alignments and profiles, a seed refers to a profile that can be used to easily create larger and larger alignments.

Wintel This is a contraction of Microsoft's Windows Operating System (OS) and the Intel brand central processor unit (cpu) that usually exists on computers running that OS.

X-server The X display system is the 'way' that UNIX OS computers pass graphics back and forth. This standard was established back in the early days of computing and seems somewhat backwards in that X windows are 'served' up on your terminal from a 'client' program on the UNIX server computer. Therefore to display X windows on personal, non-UNIX computers, you need to install emulation software for the X-server function.

Z-score and **z-score** The Z-score is based on a normal Gaussian Distribution and describes how many standard deviations a particular score is from the distribution's mean. This is confusingly in contrast to Bill Pearson's z-score in the FastA programs that is a linear regression of the opt score against the natural log of the search set sequence length. The two values, Z and z, have entirely different magnitudes and should not be correlated.

Suggested Reading

SeqLab and Multiple Sequence Reading

Etzold, T. and Argos, P. (1993) SRS—an indexing and retrieval tool for flat file data libraries, Comp. Appl. Biosc. 9, 49–57.

Genetics Computer Group (GCG), a part of Accelrys Inc., a subsidiary of Pharmacopeia Inc. (©1982-2002) Program Manual for the Wisconsin Package, Version 10.2, Madison, WI.
(*see* Website: http://www.accelrys.com/products/gcg-wisconsin-package)

Gilbert, D. G. (1993 [C release] and 1999 [Java release]) ReadSeq, Bioinformatics Group, Biology Department, Indiana University, Bloomington, IN.
(For public domain software, *see* Website: http://iubio.bio.indiana.edu/soft/molbio/readseq)

National Center for Biotechnology Information (NCBI) Entrez, National Library of Medicine, National Institutes of Health, Bethesda, MD.
(For public domain software, *see* Website: http://www.ncbi.nlm.nih.gov/Entrez)

Smith, S. W., Overbeek, R., Woese, C. R., Gilbert, W., and Gillevet, P. M. (1994) The Genetic Data Environment, an expandable GUI for multiple sequence analysis, Comp. Appl. Biosci. 10, 671–675.

von Heijne, G. (1987) Sequence Analysis in Molecular Biology; Treasure Trove or Trivial Pursuit, Academic Press, San Diego, CA.

Similarity Searching

Altschul, S. F., Gish, W., Miller, W., Myers, E. W., and Lipman, D. J. (1990) Basic Local Alignment Tool, J. Mol. Biol. 215, 403–410.

Altschul, S. F., Madden, T. L., Schaffer, A. A., Zhang, J., Zhang, Z., Miller, W., and Lipman, D. J. (1997) Gapped BLAST and PSI-BLAST: a new generation of protein database search programs, Nucleic Acids Res. 25, 3389–3402.

Pearson, W. R. and Lipman, D. J. (1988) Improved tools for biological sequence analysis, Proc. Natl. Acad. Sci. USA 85, 2444–2448.

Pearson, W. B. (1998) Empirical statistical estimates for sequence similarity searches, J. Mol. Biol. 276, 71–84.

Indentifying Motifs

Bailey, T. L. and Elkan, C., (1994) Fitting a mixture model by expectation maximization to discover motifs in biopolymers, in: Proceedings of the Second International Conference on Intelligent Systems for Molecular Biology, AAAI Press, Menlo Park, CA, pp. 28–36.

Bailey, T. L. and Gribskov, M. (1998) Combining evidence using p-values: application to sequence homology searches, Bioinformatics 14, 48–54.

Bairoch, A. (1992) PROSITE: A dictionary of sites and patterns in proteins, Nucleic Acids Res. 20, 2013–2018.

Gribskov, M., Luethy, R., and Eisenberg, D. (1989) Profile analysis, in: Methods in Enzymology, vol. 183, Academic Press, San Diego, CA, pp. 146–159.

Gribskov, M., McLachlan, M., and Eisenberg, D. (1987) Profile analysis: detection of distantly related proteins, Proc. Natl. Acad. Sciences USA 84, 4355–4358.

The Scoring Matrix

Henikoff, S. and Henikoff, J. G. (1992) Amino acid substitution matrices from protein blocks, Proc. Natl. Acad. Sci. USA 89, 10,915–10,919.

Schwartz, R. M. and Dayhoff, M. O. (1979) Matrices for detecting distant relationships, in: Atlas of Protein Sequences and Structure, vol. 5 (Dayhoff, M. O., ed.), National Biomedical Research Foundation, Washington, DC, pp. 353–358.

Phylogenetics

Dobzhansky, T., Ayala, F. J., Stebbins, G. L., and Valentine, J. W. (1977) Evolution, W. H. Freeman and Co., San Francisco, CA.

The source of the original 1973 quote is obscure though it has been cited as being transcribed from the American Biology Teacher (1973) 35, 125–129.

Felsenstein, J. (1980–2001) Phylogeny Inference Package (PHYLIP) version 3.5+, Department of Genetics, University of Washington, Seattle, WA.

(For public domain software *see* Website: http://evolution.genetics.washington.edu/phylip.html)

Feng, D. F. and Doolittle, R. F. (1987) Progressive sequence alignment as a prerequisite to correct phylogenetic trees, J. Mol. Evol. 25, 351–360

Sogin, M. L., Morrison, H. G., Hinkle, G., and Silberman, J. D. (1996) Ancestral relationships of the major eukaryotic lineages, Microbiolgia Sem. 12, 17–28.

Swofford, D. L. (1989–2001) PAUP* (Phylogenetic Analysis Using Parsimony and other methods), version 4.0+, Illinois Natural History Survey (1994), Smithsonian Institution (1998), Florida State University (2001).

(*see* Website: http://paup. csit.fsu.edu)

Distributed through Sinaeur Associates, Inc., Sunderland, MA.

(*see* Website: http://www.sinauer.com/)

Hidden Markow Models

Eddy, S. R. (1996) Hidden Markov models, Curr. Opin. Struct. Biol. 6, 361–365.

Eddy, S. R. (1998) Profile hidden Markov models, Bioinformatics 14, 755–763

D. Analysis of Gene Expression: *Microarrays and Other Tools*

34 Overview of the Tools for Microarray Analysis

Transcription Profiling, DNA Chips, and Differential Display

Jeffrey A. Kramer

Introduction

In the infancy of the computer revolution of the 1960s, Moore's law, which stated that personal computer speeds would double every 18–24 mo, was coined. A similar law of genomic data could be stated today. The genomic revolution has changed the way that molecular biology is carried out and has necessitated a brand new field of scientific endeavor, bioinformatics. With the increasing number of whole genome sequences being completed, including the recent reports of the completion of the human genome sequence and that of the mouse, it is becoming increasingly possible to study the effects of multiple perturbations on several complex and interconnected gene-signaling pathways. As molecular biology moves to this systems approach to understanding the complex control mechanisms mediating growth, development, and differentiation, the amount of data generated is staggering. Bioinformatics is, among other things, the science of building novel approaches and new tools capable of sorting through vast quantities of genomic data and enabling molecular biologists to draw meaningful conclusions from their data.

The science of genomics can be divided into three main areas, specifically, DNA sequencing, transcription profiling, and proteomics. DNA sequencing is the cornerstone upon which the entire genomic revolution is built. Transcription profiling (TxP) is the study of the response that multiple messenger RNA species present in a given tissue or cell type to specific conditions or treatments. Proteomics is the study of changes in part or all of the protein species present in a given tissue or cell type, including post-translational modifications such as phosphorylation and glycosylation. The three branches of genomics deal with three different macromolecules: DNA, RNA, and proteins. Sequencing aims to unravel the genetic information contained within the genome (DNA). Transcription profiling seeks to understand a tissue or cell's transcriptional response to its environment by identifying all or many of the individual species of messenger RNA and how they change as the cell's environment changes. Proteomics studies the changes in the protein complement present in a specific tissue or cell type under a particular set of conditions. As such, each of the three branches of the science of genomics has specific informatics problems often requiring unique solutions. An understanding of the biological and technical specifics of the questions asked and the answers being sought by scientists in each of the three branches of genomics is necessary to ensure that bioinformatic solutions are of maximum utility. This chapter will attempt to describe the theory and the biology underlying some of the techniques presently being used in transcription profiling.

As detailed earlier, genomic DNA sequencing seeks to identify all of the genes present in a given organism's genome. Bioinformatic approaches have been generated that are capable of predicting genes based solely on genomic sequence data. However, final verification of each predicted gene relies on the identification of a transcription product (a messenger RNA molecule) corresponding to the predicted gene sequence at some point in the lifetime of the organism being studied. Similarly, changes in the occurrence and level of individual mRNA molecules in a particular cell will not always directly correlate with the levels of translation products (proteins) present. Finally, the identity and relative levels of individual proteins present in a cell may not be an adequate predictor of protein activity, as numerous post-translational modifications and protein interactions may effect the activity and localization of proteins within a tissue or cell. For all these reasons, simply identifying all of the mRNA species present, and the levels at which they are present at a particular time, will not yield a complete picture of what is happening inside a particular population of cells. Still, elucidating those mRNA species present and identifying those genes whose expression levels change the most in response to specific conditions or treatments is a useful way to begin to unravel the cellular mechanisms of disease and of drug response. As such, TxP holds the promise of identifying new targets for disease intervention. For this reason the academic community, pharmaceutical and biotechnology industries have embraced transcription profiling as a vital technology.

Transcription profiling, the identification of a profile or fingerprint of some or all of the genes present in a given tissue or cell population at a particular time, need not involve all of the genes in a particular population. Indeed, as the human genome was only recently completed and since the full complement of human genes remains to be determined, true profiling of every human gene in any given experiment is impossible, at least for the time being. However, any attempt to study the transcriptional response of multiple genes can be said to be transcription profiling. As such, there are several experimental approaches to TxP. In general, the experimental methods can be divided into two categories, open and closed. Open methods do not rely on previous knowledge of the sequence or even the identity of the genes that comprise the genome of the organism being studied. Instead, open methods seek to identify mRNA species that demonstrate the most striking or the most interesting response to the experimental conditions utilized and then characterize those species at a sequence level. Closed systems rely on the previous identification and isolation of each RNA species being assayed, and as such, only those genes for which sequence information is available can be studied. Examples of both open and closed methods of transcription profiling and the bioinformatic issues surrounding these activities will be discussed. Differential Display, an example of an open transcription profiling methodology is briefly discussed below. DNA microarrays will be discussed at more length as the primary example of a closed transcription profiling technique.

Differential Display

Open transcription profiling approaches have a clear advantage over closed methodologies since they do not require extensive knowledge of the sequence of the genes that make up the genome. However, these technologies tend to be somewhat labor

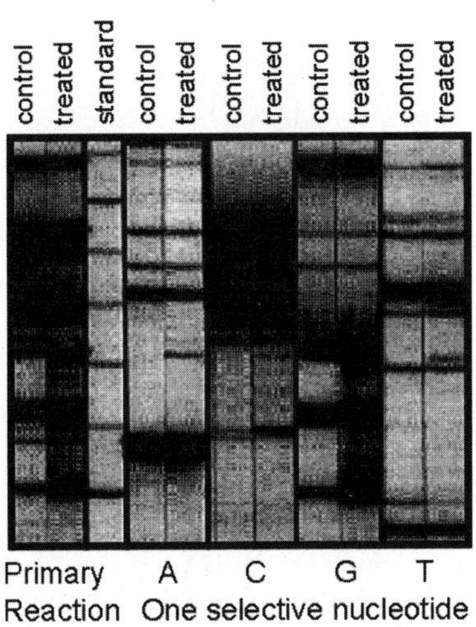

Fig. 1. Polyacrylamide gel electrophoresis is used in differential display to identify fragments of regulated genes. Double-stranded complementary DNA is prepared from populations of RNA, then fragmented with restriction endonucleases. Linkers are attached to the ends of the fragments, then the fragments are amplified using the polymerase chain reaction (PCR). The PCR products are separated by polyacrylamide gel electrophoresis. Differentially expressed genes will yield restriction fragments of different intensity in the treated vs control samples. The primary treated and control samples give a complex mixture of unaffected and differentially expressed fragments. For this reason, fragments are often *parsed* or selectively amplified using one or more degenerate nucleotide at the 3'-position of one or both PCR primers to deconvolute the mixture of amplified species. Addition of a single degenerate nucleotide in one of the PCR primers results in a partial deconvolution of the sample, allowing differentially expressed fragments to be separated and excised more easily.

intensive and are often quite expensive. Perhaps the most widely used open transcription profiling approach is differential display. There are several permutations of differential display, including Celera's Amplified Fragment Length Polymorphism (AFLP)® and Millennium Pharmaceutical's Rapid Analysis of Differential Expression (RADE)™. All differential display methods seek to deconvolute the highly complicated contents of the biological samples being studied in an effort to facilitate the identification of those species most highly affected by the conditions or treatments being studied. Differential display techniques begin with the preparation of RNA from two or more cell populations, such as diseased and normal, or treated and untreated. The first step is often the preparation of double-stranded cDNA. Upon preparation of double-stranded cDNA various methods are employed to identify those species that are differentially expressed. In the differential display technique known as AFLP® the double-stranded cDNA molecule is digested with restriction endonucleases, enzymes that cleave double-stranded DNA at specific sequences. Double-stranded linkers are annealed to the ends of the cDNA molecules and used as priming sites for amplification using polymerase chain reaction (PCR). By using a PCR primer that differs in its final 3'-most nucleotide it is possible to separate the complex mixture of amplified products into four different populations. This tends to reduce the complexity of the amplified products that are subjected to polyacrylamide gel for electrophoresis (*see* Fig. 1). Upon separation by gel electrophoresis, bands that correspond to differentially expressed genes (i.e., those that change in intensity on the gel) are excised, purified, and sequenced. In this way, beginning with no prior knowledge of the sequence of the genes expressed in the biological samples being studied, the researcher generates a sequence of only those genes that are of interest (i.e., those that are differentially expressed). The informatics issues surrounding differential display data analysis are largely the same as the issues surrounding DNA sequencing. That is, the role of the bioinformatician in analyzing differential display data comes close to the end of the technique, and consists largely of database mining and repetitive element masking.

DNA Microarrays

Perhaps the most visible transcription profiling methodology is the DNA microarray, or gene chip. DNA microarrays consist of an array of oligonucleotides or complementary DNA molecules of known composition affixed to a solid support, typically nylon or glass. Gene chips are usually categorized into one of two classes, based on the DNA actually arrayed onto the support. An oligo array is comprised of synthesized oligonucleotides, whereas a cDNA array contains cloned or PCR-amplified complementary DNA molecules. Although the purpose of either type of array is the same, specifically, to profile changes in the expression level of many genes in a single experiment, the two types of arrays present unique bioinformatic challenges. However, most microarray data analysis methods share common themes and goals. As such, the challenges and approaches to data mining are often common between all TxP platforms. The bioinformatics tasks required to complete a thorough analysis of even a single DNA microarray experiment are broken down into four main categories. The four categories are microarray quality control, data visualization and reporting, data analysis, and project organization. Many tools have been developed that simultaneously address several of these categories. For the sake of simplicity, each tool is mentioned only once, but the full utility of each tool may be significantly greater than can be described in a single chapter.

Microarray Quality Control

The two main varieties of microarrays, oligo arrays and cDNA arrays, present different challenges for data QC. These two general classes of array and their unique features will be described in detail in the following. However, regardless of what type of array is used, the data must first pass minimum quality control parameters before any analysis of TxP results can be performed. Microarray experiments involve numerous multi-step procedures at the laboratory bench, both in preparing the actual array and in preparing the labeled probes, as well as hybridizing the probes then washing and reading the microarrays. As such, there are myriad sources of potential error and variability in a microarray experiment and microarrays are often prone to high rates of false-positive and false-negative results. It is therefore vital that all microarray data be passed through several quality control steps. Even after extensive measures are taken to ensure high-quality data, it is imperative that key results be validated by alternative methods. Failure to address these issues will result in significant loss of time and resources spent chasing down numerous false leads. However, as an informatics problem the solution to many of these issues is often trivial. For this reason, the bioinformatician must be adept at applying statistical approaches to ensure that suboptimal quality data is omitted from further consideration. The first-quality control activity after the microarray has been read is to ensure that adequate signal/background and balance was achieved for each array hybridization experiment. This involves an inspection of total average signal and total average background, as well as calculating local signal to background for each element on the array. Elements with signals outside the linear range of the reader, or elements with a very low signal to background should be omitted from further consideration. This is vital to ensure that the resulting data report contains only valid values. Additional quality control metrics are frequently specific for the type of microarray being used. Therefore, a description of the differences between oligonucleotide and cDNA arrays is pertinent.

Oligonucleotide arrays contain short, synthesized oligonucleotides affixed to a solid matrix. Perhaps the best-known commercially available oligonucleotide microarray is the Affymetrix GeneChip®. Individual Affymetrix arrays typically contain 16–20 oligonucleotides for each of up to ~12,000 genes arrayed onto a glass slide approx the size of a microscope slide. Oligos are selected from multiple regions of the gene sequence from which they are derived (*see* Fig. 2). The oligos are typically 25 nucleotides long, and attempts are made in their design to maintain similar GC content, ensuring similar kinetics of binding to the labeled probe. A theoretical difficulty in using short oligonucleotides is the potential for cross-hybridization with other mRNA species. The human genome contains more than 30,000 genes and ~3 billion nucleotides. It is therefore difficult to design short oligonucleotides that are specific to their individual target gene and do not cross hybridize with multiple cDNA probes. To address this, each gene represented on the Affymetrix GeneChip® has several oligos designed to be a perfect match to the target gene to address the potential lack of specificity of short oligonucleotides. Additionally, each perfect match oligo has a paired oligo designed to be identical to the perfect match oligo except for a single nucleotide mismatch (*see* Fig. 2). Many of the mismatched probes and indeed some of the perfect-match probes may cross-react with closely related cDNA species. If a mismatched probe gives a significant signal, both it and its perfect match partner may be excluded from consideration. With the potential for cross reactivity in mind, oligonucleotides that are arrayed are designed to regions of low sequence conservation with genes that are closely related to the target gene. Additionally, Affymetrix array analysis considers signal intensity and signal to background levels for every perfect match/mismatch pair spotted onto the array. Pairs of perfect match/mismatch elements that give significantly more signal than the mismatch element are considered to have a *high average difference* (*see* Fig. 3). Pairs with approximately the same degree of signal are referred to as *low average difference* and a *negative average difference* refers to pairs in which the mismatch oligonucleotides signal is greater than that of the perfect match oligonucleotides. Only those perfect match elements with relatively high signal intensities, and a high average difference are used to make a *present* or *absent* call. As well as investigating each element, data concerning all of the perfect match/mismatch pairs that correspond to a gene are considered. Minimum requirements with respect to the positive/negative ratio (pairs where the perfect match is greater than the mismatch vs those where the mismatch is greater), positive fraction, and log average signal ratio are considered. Those elements that do not meet minimum signal intensity and cutoffs are referred to as *absent*. The signal from these elements is typically not considered in the subsequent analyses. These elements that meet the requirements can be evaluated against other arrays, to assess *increase*, *decrease* or *no change* in signal.

See companion CD for color Fig. 3

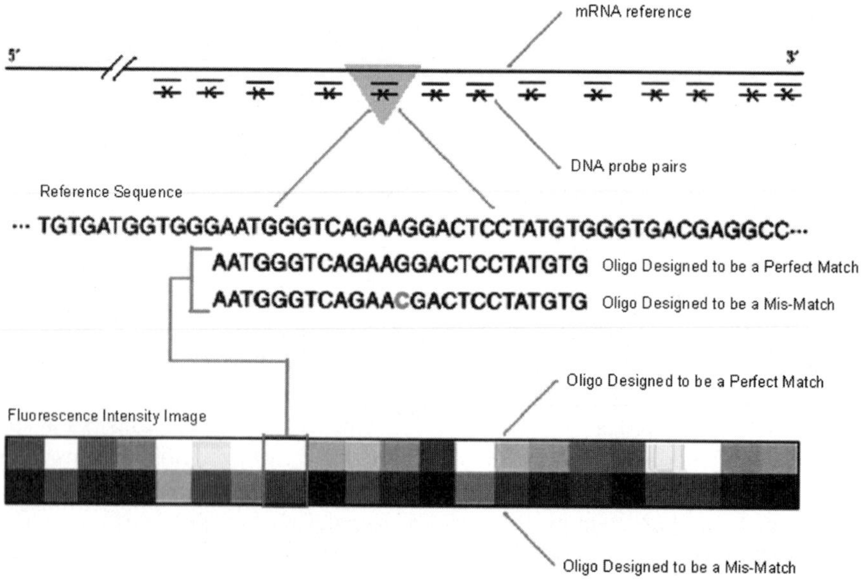

Fig. 2. Affymetrix uses several oligonucleotides to get broad coverage of individual genes. Each gene is represented by oligos designed to be a perfect match to the target sequence, as well as oligos designed to contain a single mismatch. Pairs of perfect match and single nucleotide mismatch oligonucleotides are designed to different regions of each gene. Typically 16 or 20 oligo pairs are arrayed for each gene represented on the GeneChip®. The oligonucleotides are typically 25 bases in length.

Because the oligonucleotides are designed to be similar with respect to length, GC content and melting temperature (T_M), the kinetics of binding of the labeled probe are highly reproducible from one element to the next. For this reason, oligonucleotide arrays are often referred to as *single-channel arrays*. That is, a labeled cDNA population from a single biological source can be hybridized onto each microarray. Because the kinetics of hybridization are effectively identical for all of the elements on an oligonucleotide array, samples hybridized onto separate arrays can be compared with only minimal mathematical signal balancing. In this way, each individual control sample, and each treated or affected sample is used to prepare a labeled probe, then hybridized onto an individual microarray. This means that within each individual array, it is theoretically possible to compare one element (for example an element corresponding to acyl CoA oxidase, or ACOX) with each other element (such as one corresponding to fatty acid synthase, or FAS). The signal at one element relative to any other element may contain information about the environment and response of the biological sample from which the probe was generated. For example, a liver from a rat treated with a novel chemical entity might have an increased level of ACOX and decreased level of FAS signal relative to an untreated rat liver. The increase in ACOX and the concomitant decrease in FAS, might suggest something about the new compound to an investigator. Additionally, the values at each element, after some minimal balancing based upon signal intensity of a number of control elements, can be compared to each matched element on a second microarray. The values that result from these comparisons can be expressed a number of ways.

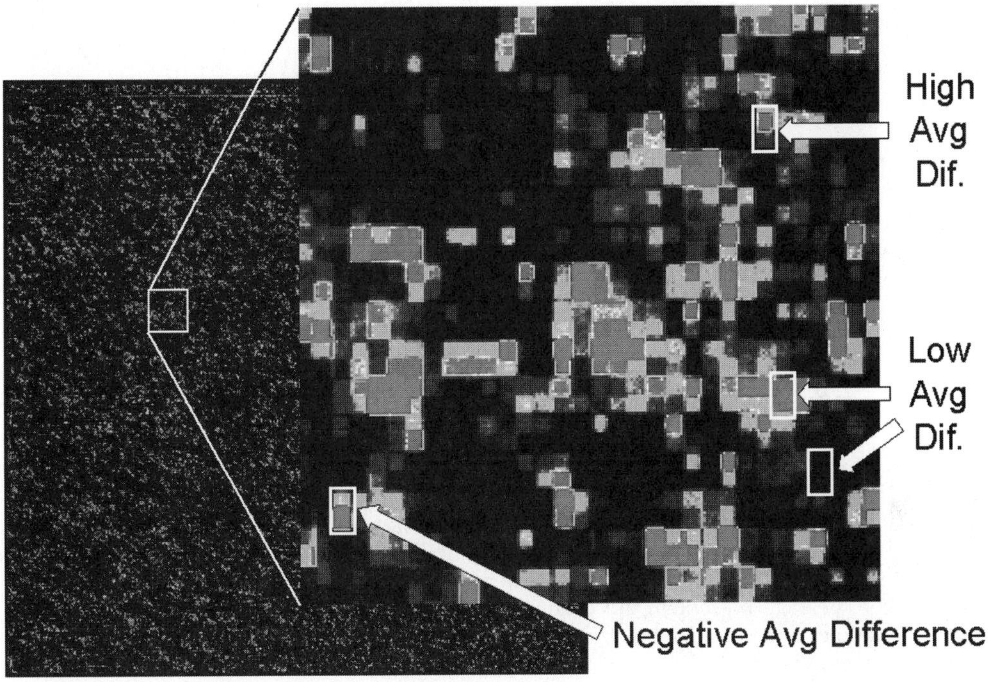

Fig. 3. False color images demonstrate signal intensity on an Affymetrix GeneChip®. Signal intensity at each element is indicated by color, with lighter, *hotter* colors representing greater signal intensities. Many single-channel, oligonucleotide arrays, including Affymetrix arrays, include several oligonucleotides for each gene. For this reason, there tend to be clusters of elements with similar signal intensity, representing all the elements that comprise a single gene. In the expanded region of the array, individual Perfect match/mismatch paired elements can be visualized. Perfect match/mismatch pairs for which the signal intensity of the perfect match oligo is greater than for the mismatch oligo (high average difference pairs), are used when comparing arrays to make calls regarding differential expression.

Unlike oligonucleotide arrays, cDNA array elements contain longer cloned or PCR amplified cDNAs. Often the length of the cDNA species arrayed onto a cDNA array varies considerably. Additionally, the GC content varies, and the T_M can vary significantly from element to element. For this reason, the time required for the hybridization of a labeled probe onto the microarray to come to a steady state is often greater than the stability the labeled probes would allow. For this reason cDNA arrays tend to be hybridized for preset durations according to standard operating procedures. As a result of the short hybridization times relative to steady state, most species of labeled cDNA in the probe do not adhere to steady state binding kinetics, and the binding at each element varies according to the T_M of the probe specific for each element. Because of this, the signal at any element on an individual cDNA microarray cannot be reliably compared with an other element on that array in a meaningful way. To continue the previous example, if the signal at the ACOX element is greater than that for the FAS element, it may be a function of the composition and T_M of the two arrayed elements and not due the amount of each message present in the labeled probe.

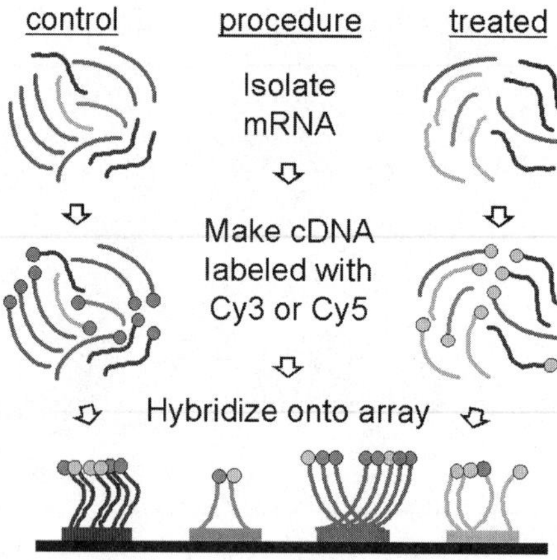

Fig. 4. Experiments using cDNA microarrays require two-channel hybridizations. Two channel or cDNA arrays contain cloned or PCR amplified fragments of genes. Two separate populations of RNA are labeled with different fluorescent dyes. The dye-labeled samples are applied to the array, and differential hybridization is measured by recording fluorescence in both channels at each element. Single-channel signal intensity at any element on a cDNA array may not accurately reflect the amount of the message present in the original biological sample relative to any other message. Instead, the ratio of Cy5 vs Cy3 labeled cDNA probe at each element contains information regarding differential expression.

The way to address this issue is through the use of differential or 2-channel hybridization. Two populations of mRNA (i.e., treated and untreated, diseased vs normal, and so on) are labeled and hybridized onto an individual cDNA microarray. A control sample is used to prepare cDNA labeled with one fluorescent label (such as Cy3), and a treated or affected sample is labeled with an alternate fluor (such as Cy5). Both labeled cDNA populations are then mixed and applied to the microarray for hybridization (*see* Fig. 4). If there was twice as much of a particular RNA species present in the Cy5 labeled probe as in the Cy3 labeled probe, twice as much of the Cy5 probe will hybridize to the corresponding element on the array, regardless of the T_M of the arrayed element or the probes. Thus, although the single-channel data in either the Cy5 or the Cy3 channel on a cDNA array may not be informative, the ratio of signal intensities in both channels is. For this reason, cDNA array experiments are often referred to as *2-channel hybridizations*.

See companion CD for color Fig. 4

The main deliverable for the biologist using microarrays is information regarding the differential expression of genes. This differential expression is determined by comparing two oligo arrays, or the two channels of a cDNA array. In order to compare the two channels in a 2-channel array, or to compare two single-channel arrays, the signal intensities must first be balanced. The simplest approach to balancing uses the total average signal in one channel divided by the total average signal in the other channel to generate a balance coefficient. This can be demonstrated graphically using an expression histogram (*see* Fig. 5), where the two lines on the histogram represent either the two channels in a cDNA array experiment, or two single-channel oligo arrays. Slight differences in the amount of probe, or in the labeling reaction efficiency can result in higher total signal intensities on one channel than on another.

See companion CD for color Fig. 5

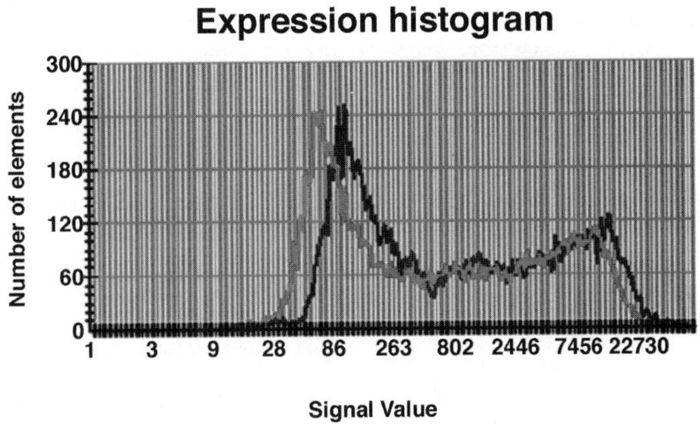

Fig. 5. An expression histogram from a two-channel hybridization reveals how well the channels are balanced. An expression histogram is a convenient way to visualize differences in input material and/or labeling efficiency for a two-channel hybridization. After balancing the array data using a balance coefficient, the two lines should largely overlap. Balance coefficients can be determined in a number of ways. The simplest way to calculate a balance coefficient relies on a ratio of total average signal in both channels.

A balancing coefficient will even out such experimentally derived sources of error. The balance coefficient is used to correct the signal in one channel (or on one array) at all of the elements on the array. If the total average signal were 2500 in the Cy3 channel, and 2000 in the Cy5 channel, the balance coefficient would be 1.25 (2500/2000). The Cy5 signal for each element would be multiplied by 1.25 to generate a balanced Cy5 signal. Alternatively, the Cy3 signal at each element could be corrected by a factor of 0.8 (2000/2500) to generate a balanced Cy3 signal.

Other more complex methods of balancing 2-channel arrays have been used. One difficulty with simply using total average signal is that it ignores the biology of the samples being assayed. For example, if a scientist is comparing an untreated cell population with a population of cells treated with a potent transcriptional activator, the treated cell population may have significant increases in the levels of many genes. The increased signal in the treated sample may be due to real and significant increases in transcription. Applying a balance coefficient based solely upon signal intensity may over *correct* many of the biologically relevant changes in expression. Additionally, balancing simply by total average signal fails to account for changes in signal and signal to background across a microarray. If the signal and the background in both channels are similar and evenly distributed across the entire array (*see* Fig. 6), a simple balancing approach is adequate. However, if the background intensity in the two channels is very different, or not evenly distributed, other approaches may be needed. For example, it is not unusual to see differences in signal and background due to different labeling efficiencies and gradient effects. Figure 7 shows an example of a 2-channel array with both a gradient effect and a large difference in signal and background between the two channels. Although this array experiment has significant issues, there may still be some useful data present. However, care must be taken before trusting any expression data resulting from this array.

See companion CD for color Figs. 6 and 7

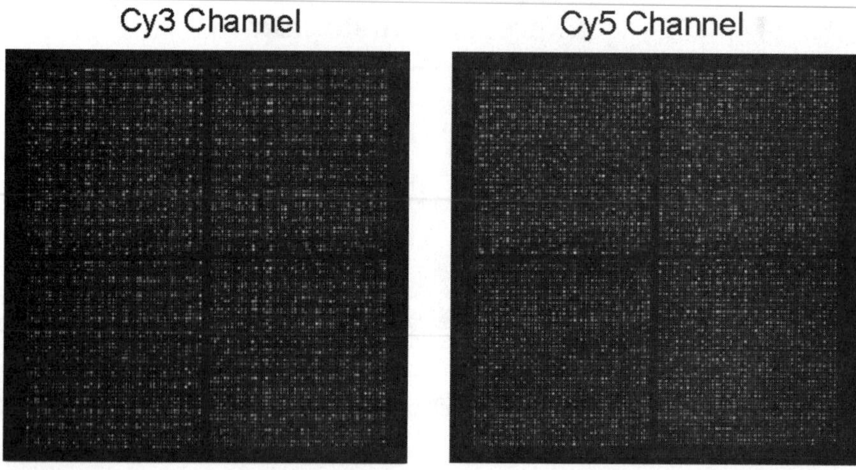

Fig. 6. False color images can be used to demonstrate signal intensity in both channels of a two-channel array hybridization. Signal intensity at each element in either channel is indicated by color, with lighter, *hotter* colors representing greater signal intensities. After balancing, elements that give greater intensity in one channel than in the other are considered to represent differentially expressed genes.

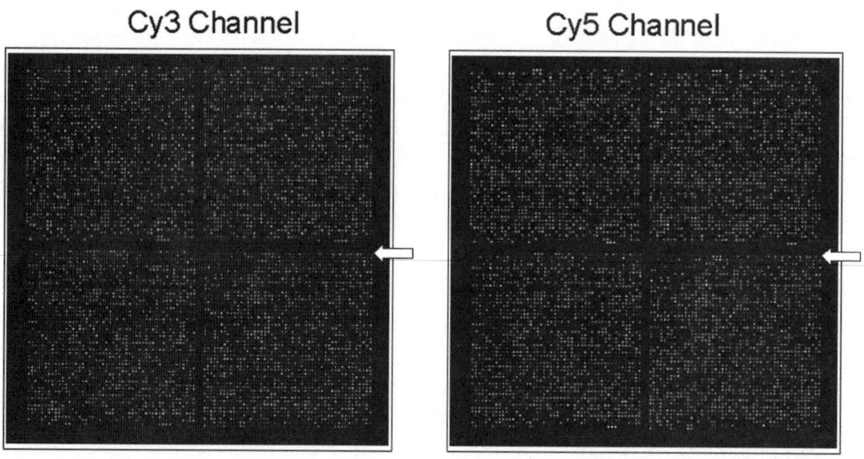

Fig. 7. Unacceptable hybridization on a two-channel array is determined by careful examination of several parameters. In some cases, total average signal intensity, total average background, or both are very different between the two channels of a two-channel hybridization. If the background is uniform in each channel or if a gradient is present in both channels, it can often be corrected. If, as in the example shown, there is a gradient effect in one channel and not the other, it may be very difficult to achieve reliable expression data from the microarray.

First, note that there appears to be a gradient in the background of the Cy3 channel that is not present in the Cy5 channel. That is, the background is greater on the left side of the array. Simply balancing based on the total average signal ignores the fact that the higher background on the left part of the array may cause the signal intensities of the elements on that portion of the array to be affected differently than elements on the right side of the array. Balancing elements individually by signal to

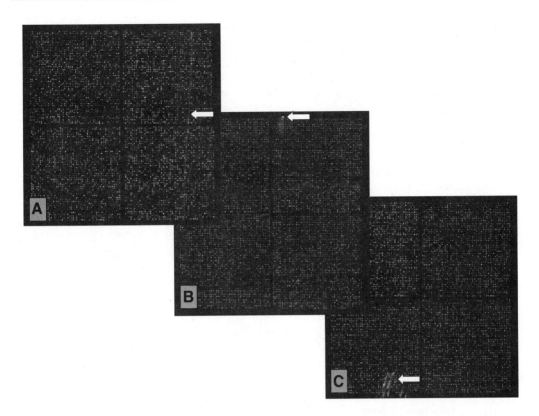

Fig. 8. Imperfections and impurities that affect hybridization and therefore expression data may occur on microarrays. **(A)** Some microarrays may contain imperfections that occur during the fabrication process. **(B)** Elements can also be affected by impurities introduced at the time of the hybridization. The *comet-like* imperfection seen here is most likely due to a dust particle. **(C)** It is uncertain what caused the impurity on the lower portion of this array. It may be an artifact from the scanning process. Regardless of the cause, the affected elements may need to be discarded from further consideration.

local background may address this problem. An additional problem with this array is that the balance coefficient will be unusually large. A very large or a very small balance coefficient may bring seemingly meaningful signals from noise, or mute signals beyond the linear range of the reader used to read the hybridized array. However, re-running this experiment may not be an option owing to the prohibitive costs often associated with running many microarrays. Additionally, there may be some useful and reliable information in this experiment. For example, the arrows point to an element that may be differentially expressed in the Cy5-labeled population when compared to the Cy3-labeled population. Therefore, new approaches to glean useful data from such an experiment, without providing false or misleading data is a key challenge.

See companion CD for color Fig. 8

Another type of problem that often occurs on both single and 2-channel array experiments is caused by imperfections or impurities on the array. Figure 8 shows several examples. In Fig. 8A, the line running across the array will change the signal to background of elements along its course. Additionally, elements along the course of the line may appear to have a signal that is significantly above the global average background. The array in Fig. 8B appears to contain a bit of dust on the top of the array. The elements in the *tail* of the comet-like feature will be affected similarly to those near the linear imperfection in Fig. 8A. The array in Fig. 8C has an unusual pattern of unknown cause. The affected elements should be omitted from further consideration. Such impurities may occur on either single-channel or 2-channel arrays. If they are faint and if they occur similarly in both channels of a 2-channel array, they might be corrected for. But in general, the elements affected by these features should usually be discarded from the final data report.

Software Tools for Microarray Analysis

Several proprietary software tools exist that allow scientists to select individual elements or groups of elements for masking from further analysis. However many of these tools tend to be designed to work with only one type of array. A general tool capable of working with all types of arrays that a laboratory might use has yet to be made available. The Institute for Genome Research (TIGR) (*see* Website: http://www.tigr.org/), has a software tool called the *TIGR Spotfinder* available to academic users at no charge. TIGR Spotfinder is a PC/Windows compatible software tool written in C/C++. It was designed for Microarray image processing using 16-bit gray-scale TIFF image files generated by most microarray scanners. Spotfinder allows for manual and automatic grid drawing, and spot detection can be adjusted for use with arrays with multiple size spot and spacing. One particularly useful feature of the TIGR Spotfinder software tool is that it allows the user to adjust the grid to be sure that an entire spot is included in the reference field (*see* Fig. 9). It is not uncommon for spots on a microarray to be off center, and spot finding software using a static grid may often cut off portions of spots. Spotfinder provides a local background correction for each spot, and calculates ratios using one of several user-preferred criteria. One other interesting feature of the TIGR Spotfinder software is the ability to remove saturated pixels from intensity calculations. This feature helps calculate accurate differential expression values for extremely abundant messages, the fluorescent signal for which may be beyond the linear range of the detector. Finally, Spotfinder allows the data to be exported as an excel file and into a format compatible with other TIGR software tools.

The National Human Genome Research Institute (NHGRI) microarray project, (*see* Website: http://www.nhgri.nih.gov/) is also developing a microarray analysis tool, called *ArraySuite*. This suite is a collection of extensions written for IPLab, an image-processing package by Scanalytics (*see* Website: http://www.scanalytics.com/). The NHGRI approach to microarray image analysis is divided into several discreet tasks, including array segmentation and spot identification, background intensity determination, target detection and signal-intensity determination, and ratio calculation. The various capabilities being designed into the ArraySuite tool set will also permit ratio analysis, a comparison of the intensities of a number of *housekeeping* genes, as well as multiple image analysis. The NHGRI is also working on tissue arrays, a method of arraying up to 1000 fixed tissue samples onto a glass slide for high throughput *in situ* analysis of DNA, RNA or protein. This novel approach requires additional new bioinformatic approaches to data acquisition and analysis.

Data Visualization and Reporting

After the quality of the microarray data has been confirmed, the data must be reported in a way that facilitates the rapid determination of significant results. This is a significant challenge, as the amount of data provided by a single microarray

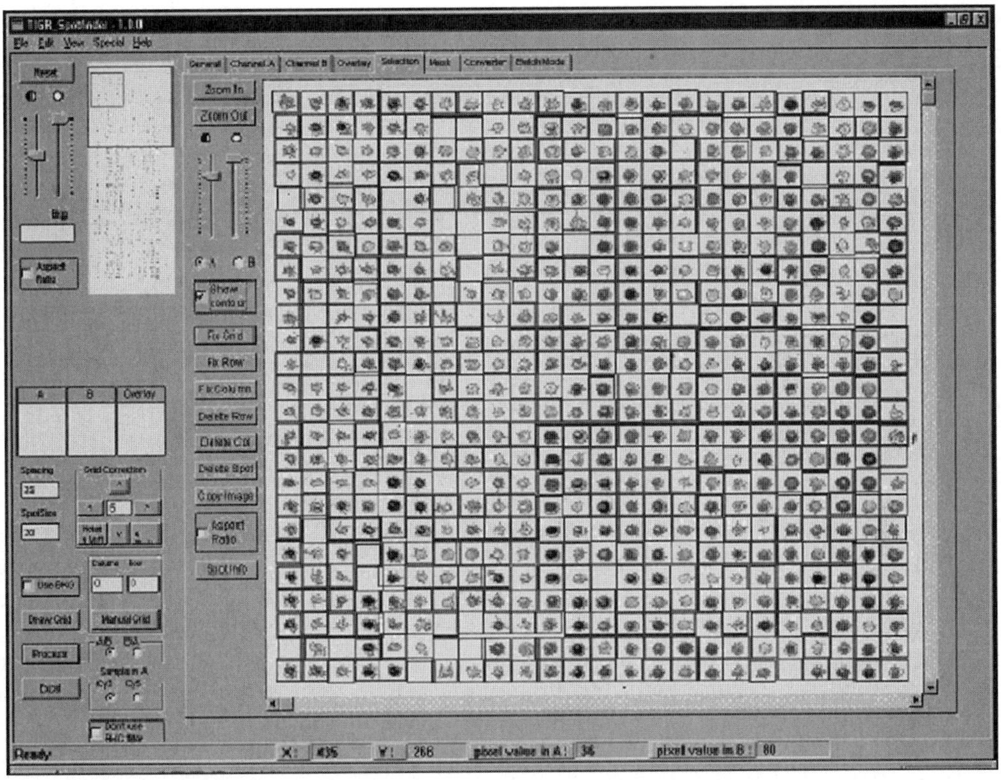

Fig. 9. The TIGR Spotfinder tool allows the user to adjust the grid to be sure that an entire spot is included in the reference field. It is not uncommon for spots on a microarray to be off center. Spot finding software that uses a static grid may often cut off portions of spots, resulting in a loss of useful information. Additionally, badly off-center spots may result in a portion of one spot appearing in the grid of an adjacent spot, resulting in *false-positive* gene expression values.

experiment is very large. Simply reporting the data as a list of signal intensities and element IDs is inadequate. As microarrays are prone to error, it is often desirable to verify microarray findings using other molecular biological methodologies. Data must be expressed in a way that can be compared to results from other molecular techniques. Typically, the purpose of running microarray experiments is to identify new targets for intervention into disease; new molecular markers and predictors of disease, toxicity, or clinical outcome; or a better understanding of molecular mechanisms. In all of these applications, the purpose for the experiment cannot be met by simply providing a list of regulated genes. However, as a first step, it is necessary to express the results in a format that is both intuitive and amenable to further analysis. Most array analysis software packages calculate differential expression values from the elements that pass quality-control parameters. Several methods of relating differential expressions exist. The simplest is a ratio of treated sample intensity divided by control intensity for each element. If the Cy3 channel of a 2-channel array contained the control sample probe and the Cy5 channel contained the treated sample probe, the Cy5 signal intensity is divided by the Cy3 signal. One difficulty with the

Table 1
Differential Expression

Gene ID	*Control (Cy3)*	*Treated (Cy5)*	*bCy5*	*Ratio*	*Log ratio*	*BDE*	*fBDE*
a	500	800	1000	2.00	0.30	2.00	1.00
b	500	200	250	0.50	−0.30	−2.00	−1.00
c	500	100	125	0.25	−0.60	−4.00	−3.00
d	500	80	100	0.20	−0.70	−5.00	−4.00
e	500	2000	2500	5.00	0.70	5.00	4.00
f	500	404	505	1.01	0.00	1.01	0.01
g	505	400	500	0.99	0.00	−1.01	−0.01
h	250	600	750	3.00	0.48	3.00	2.00
i	2500	3800	4750	1.90	0.28	1.90	0.90

expression ratio is obvious when the data is graphed. Down regulated genes tend to be collapsed between 0 and 1 on the graph, making it difficult to distinguish among down regulated genes. This is easily alleviated by using a log scale when graphing, however the degree of down regulation is not as intuitive as using simple ratios. Some researchers use an arithmetic log of the expression ratio instead of a simple ratio. A difficulty with this approach is that significantly regulated genes yield deceptively small log ratio values (*see* Table 1). Another way to report differential expressions is with the use of the balanced differential expression value (BDE). The BDE is calculated using Equation 1, assuming that Cy5 is the treated and Cy3 is the control sample.

$$\text{If Cy5} \geq \text{Cy3, then BDE} = \text{Cy5/Cy3, else BDE} = -1 \times (\text{Cy3/Cy5}) \quad \text{[Eq. 1]}$$

A difficulty with the BDE value is that it leaves a gap between 1 and –1. That is, it is impossible to calculate a BDE of 0. This causes a problem when trying to compare expression values with phenotypes, or when trying to calculate a meaningful average BDE for a group of similarly affected or similarly treated biological samples. Additionally, two elements that are effectively identical may appear to be significantly different from one another (*see* example genes *f* and *g* in Table 1). For this reason, some bioinformatic scientists use a fractional Balanced Differential Expression (fBDE) value, essentially is a BDE collapsed by 1. It is calculated using Equation 2 where:

$$\text{fBDE} = (\text{Cy5} - \text{Cy3})/\text{MIN (Cy5, Cy3)} \quad \text{[Eq. 2]}$$

the Cy3 (control sample signal intensity) is subtracted from the Cy5 treated sample intensity), and this value is divided by the smaller of the two values. Table 1 shows several theoretical control and treated signal intensities, and the values calculated using these four methods of showing differential expression. The hypothetical data in Table 1 is first corrected using a balance coefficient of 1.25 to generate a balanced Cy5 (bCy5) signal intensity.

Another issue that must be considered when reporting microarray data is the significance of fold induction values. Simply stating a differential expression value does not reveal anything about the reliability of that value. For example, genes *d* and *e* are both regulated fivefold. However, the signal intensity for the two channels (or on the

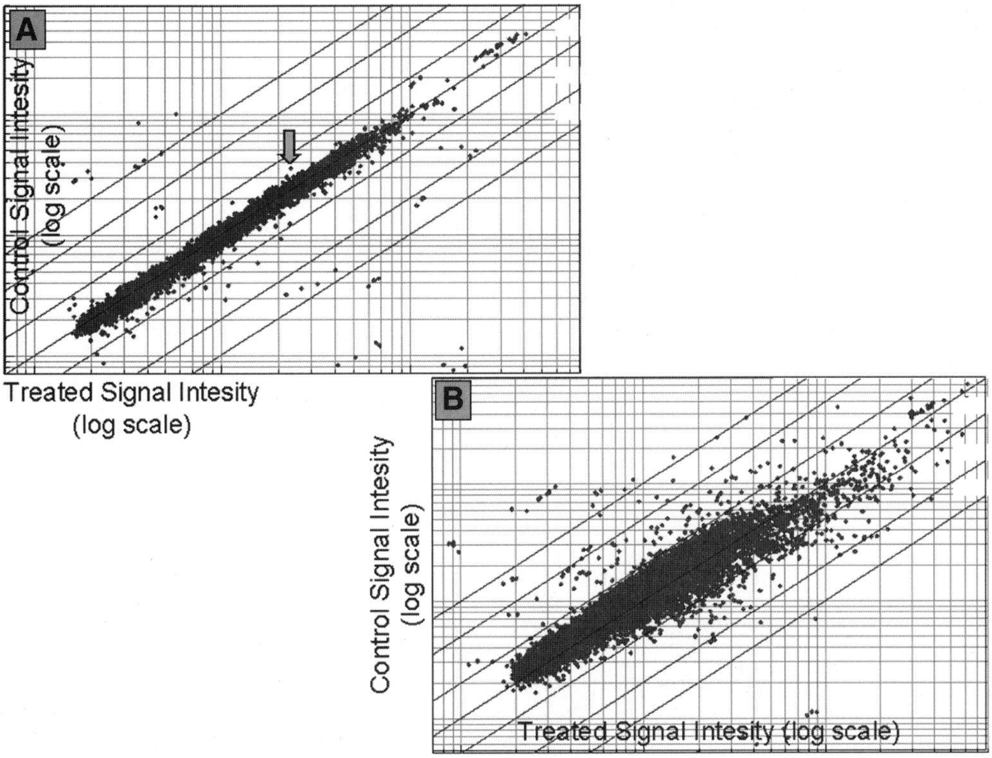

Fig. 10. Scatter plots can be generated from a two-channel hybridization or from any two single-channel hybridizations, after data is balanced with respect to signal intensity. Signal intensity for each element from 2 oligo arrays, or from both channels of a cDNA array is graphed on a logarithmic scale. Genes lying on the slanted line with a slope of one are not regulated. Those elements that demonstrate differences in signal intensity in the two channels (or on two different oligo arrays) after balancing may be differentially expressed. The differential expression value for the element marked in **(A)** may be reliable, even though it represents only a 1.6-fold difference in the signal intensities of the two samples. A similar differential expression value in **(B)** would almost certainly be meaningless.

See companion CD for color Fig. 10

two arrays if this were an oligonucleotide array experiment) for gene *e* is significantly higher than for gene *d*. Similarly, although gene *i* has a smaller differential expression value than gene *h*, the signal intensity at element *i* is strong, whereas that for element *h* is more questionable. This issue can be envisioned by examining a scatter plot from two microarray experiments (*see* Fig. 10). In the examples shown, the first scatter plot shows very tight clustering of elements around the 1 X line. The second scatter plot shows significant deviation from the 1 X line. This does not mean that useful data cannot be attained from the second array. However, the cut-off of reliable differential expression values will be different for the two experiments. The arrow in Fig. 10A points to a gene with a balanced differential expression value of approx 1.6. This gene is clearly separated from the background *noise* of unregulated genes, and the value of 1.6 can be trusted with a good degree of comfort. Statistically, the confidence that this value represents an actual gene regulation event is strong. In the experiment shown in Fig. 10B, a BDE of 1.6 is clearly not significant. If a researcher were to give attention

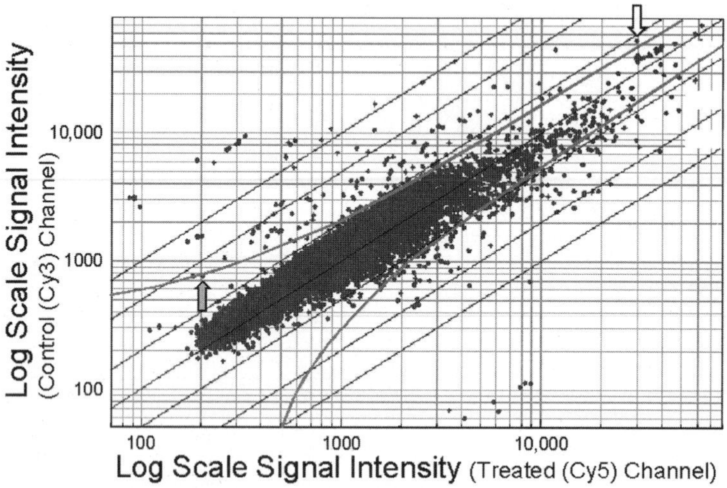

Fig. 11. Confidence limits may be placed on microarray data. The lines parallel to the diagonal represents a reasonable cut-off based upon signal strength and differential expression. Elements with lower signal intensity must be highly differentially expressed to be considered reliable, owing to the increased error at the lower edge of the signal range. RNA quality, time since fabrication of the array, hybridization conditions and numerous other factors can all affect the final outcome of a microarray experiment. Reproducibility and reliability of differential expression values are affected by these variables (*see* Fig. 9). Therefore, confidence limits should be adjusted to reflect better or worse hybridizations.

See companion CD for color Fig. 11

to every gene regulated at 1.6-fold or more, the list of regulated genes would be difficult to manage. Statistical methods to calculate meaningful expression values for each individual microarray experiment would provide valuable confidence limits for the expression values. Among the criteria that must be addressed in such a statistical confidence limit are the signal intensity and the ratio of signal to background. Simply reporting a BDE does not reveal the strength of the data upon which the expression value is based. Figure 11 shows a graphical demonstration of one approach to this issue. Any points within the two lines closest to the diagonal are not considered to be significantly different. For example, the element marked with a gray arrow is not considered reliable, due to low signal intensity, even though the BDE is about four-fold. However, the element marked with a white arrow may reflect a legitimate change in expression of that gene. Although the BDE is only about 1.8, the high signal intensity suggests a more reliable result. There are several statistical methods to generate confidence limits. As described earlier and as demonstrated in Fig. 10, it is important that the methods be flexible, to reflect scatter plots with more or less noise.

See companion CD for color Fig. 12

Upon calculating meaningful expression values, there is still the problem of visualizing all of the data in an intuitive way. Several approaches to this problem exist. One simple way is to port the data into a spreadsheet and color cells in the spreadsheet based upon the expression values. A brief inspection of the spreadsheet informs the viewer of up and down regulated genes (*see* Fig. 12). The scientist can then zoom in to see the identity of the gene whose expression pattern stands out. Of course, it is very difficult to view such a spreadsheet generated on a single page from even a modestly

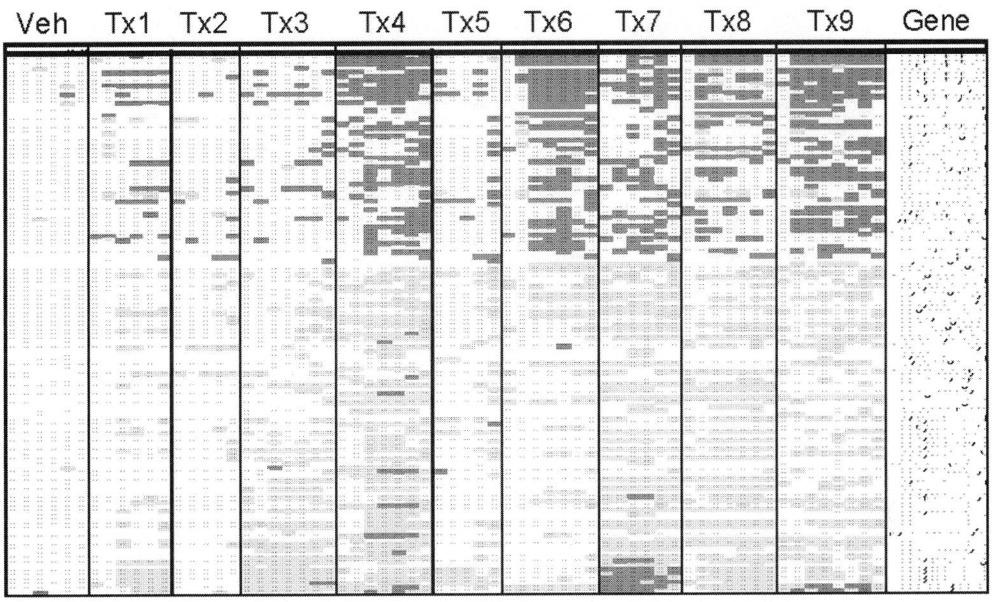

Fig. 12. The application of color gradients to differential expression values aids in rapid visualization of differential expression. The use of color gradients also permits the identification of genes that are differentially regulated by multiple treatments, and may also help identify experimental outliers. In the example shown, data from several microarrays hybridized with RNA from cells treated with vehicle (*veh*) and one of nine compounds (*Tx1–9*) is used. This approach can be used with a simple spreadsheet. However, many software tools exist that facilitate this type of data visualization.

See companion CD for color Fig. 13

sized TxP experiment. For this reason, other commercially available tools such as Spotfire™ have been created specifically for this purpose (*see* Fig. 13). Many of these tools also have data analysis features. However assigning a color gradient, with intensity or brightness corresponding to signal intensity or BDE is essentially the basis of how these data viewers work.

The TIGR Array Viewer is a software tool designed to accommodate both presentation and analysis of microarray data. Array Viewer has the ability to use data from flat files or from an array database and provides links between the elements to the underlying gene information. The software allows for the selection of a subset of elements, for example differentially expressed genes, or genes from a specific region of the array. The subset of genes can be visualized independently, or with the rest of the data but in different colors. This feature is useful if a researcher suspects regional variations on an array. For example, the elements on the left side of the array shown in Fig. 6 can be selected and colored differently from the elements on the right side of the array on a scatter plot. If all or most of the differentially regulated genes are from one or the other region, it is immediately obvious that there are subarray variations and that the BDE values may not be reliable. Although simple inspection of the pseudo color image in Fig. 7 would have revealed this, the subset selection feature of tools like the TIGR Array Viewer would help identify more subtle discrepancies. Finally, Array Viewer allows the export of all or a subset of the data to flat files, databases, or other tools, such as Spotfire. Numerous other similar tools exist. Most

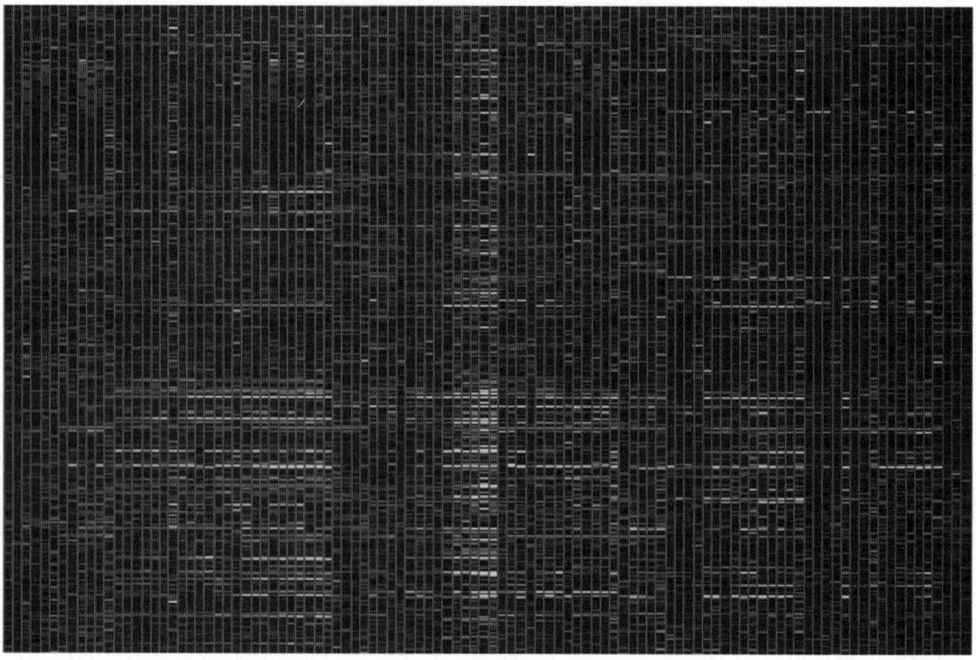

Fig. 13. Heat maps aid in the visualization of transcription profiling data. A heat map such as this one produced by Spotfire™, may be used to visually identify broad patterns of gene expression. Typically genes above and below user-defined thresholds are colored red (induction) and green (repression), respectively. Individual microarray experiments are organized on the X-axis, while individual genes are organized along the Y-axis. Several large groups of similar microarrays may be observed in this example. One might reasonably infer that similar gene expression patterns suggest similar mechanisms of action for the compounds used in these studies.

array platforms provide similar tools with at least some of the basic features provided by TIGR's Array Viewer. Many of these are proprietary and must be purchased, or are only available with purchase of that company's array products. Still others have been developed within pharmaceutical and biotechnology companies and are not generally available.

Data Analysis

Visualization of the data is a useful way to identify those genes that are most highly regulated. It is also a useful way to quickly discard uninteresting data, in order to generate a list of regulated genes. However, generating a list of regulated genes is only the first step in the analysis of TxP data and it is an inadequate use of microarray-derived experimental data. The purposes for running microarray experiments typically require advanced analysis of the TxP data. For example, simply asking what genes are expressed differently in an arthritic knee compared to a normal knee does little to help advance the effort to treat arthritis. Instead, identifying those genes whose expression correlates temporally and responds proportionally to the onset and severity of arthritic symptoms may help to identify a new target for intervention. Simply asking which genes are expressed in the liver in response to treatment with a pharmaceutical cholesterol lowering agent will do nothing to identify new targets for intervention

Table 2
Clustering Expression Data

ID	Array 1	Array 2	ID	Array 1	Array2
Gene 1	1200	700	Gene 9	630	1140
Gene 2	1050	750	Gene 10	600	470
Gene 3	990	730	Gene 11	540	140
Gene 4	700	500	Gene 12	420	480
Gene 5	690	1200	Gene 13	380	490
Gene 6	660	120	Gene 14	260	220
Gene 7	650	450	Gene 15	200	180
Gene 8	640	1090	Gene 16	190	250

into hypercholesterolemia. Identifying genes whose expression pattern clusters with the known targets of a cholesterol lowering drug may help identify mechanistic details of the body's cholesterol metabolism pathways. This could lead to the identification of new genes and gene products whose manipulation may also reduce dangerously high cholesterol levels. For these reasons, simply preparing a list of genes resulting from a microarray experiment falls short of the goal of understanding the science behind a particular signaling pathway of a disease mechanism.

Two general approaches were touched upon in the above paragraph, that of *clustering* and *correlation*. Both approaches can be applied to microarray data. Clustering expression data can help to identify co-regulated genes likely to be in common biochemical pathways. For example, proinflammatory agents such as tumor necrosis factor (TNF)-α, interleukin (IL)-1β, and lipopolysaccharide (LPS) are known to increase the expression of the cyclooxygenase (COX) 2 gene, which encodes a key enzyme involved in inflammation. The mechanism(s) by which these pro-inflammatory agents act is not completely understood. All of these agents are typically present outside the cell. Receptors on the surface of the cell detect their presence and initiate a signaling pathway that results in transcription factors inducing transcription of COX-2 mRNA. Even a carefully designed experiment including treatment with proinflammatory agents at several dose levels and/or time points would likely result in a large list of genes whose expression was affected. However clustering genes with similar expression patterns might identify novel genes with expression patterns similar to known members of the intracellular signaling pathway. Such novel genes may encode proteins that could be valuable points of intervention to block inflammation.

There are a number of approaches to clustering large sets of data. It would be difficult to describe each and new approaches are being developed regularly. One such common way to cluster microarray data is to use Euclidean distance in n dimensional space, where n is the number of variables for each microarray element. A very simple example will help visualize this approach. Imagine that two microarrays, each containing 16 elements that have been used to evaluate RNA from the livers of two rats treated with different carcinogenic compounds. The researcher might wish to cluster elements into groups of similar genes. Each element on the microarray has two variables, the signal from experiment or treatment 1, and the signal from experiment or treatment 2 (*see* Table 2). Simple visualization of the data may help to place the genes into several clusters, but it is not immediately clear how. However, graphing the data in n dimensional space, where n = 2 (for the number of variables for each element), will make clustering easier (*see* Fig. 14). Measuring a simple linear (Euclidean) distance between each point yields elements that are close to one another in this experimental space.

In this simplified example, one may not have been required. However, suppose a researcher performs TxP using a microarray with 10,000 elements on liver RNA from 12 rats fed 3 different diets resulting in different levels of fasted serum triglycerides. Using Euclidean distance, the researcher would graph each microarray element in 12-dimensional space. Clearly this must be done in virtual space using a computer, as the researcher cannot simply measure the linear distance between 10,000 points on a theoretical 12-dimensional graph. For this reason, methods have been developed to mathematically cluster the data points. One approach is to use a kth nearest neighbors strategy, where constant k equals a small integer. The computer program begins with a single data point, and finds it's 3 (if $k = 3$) nearest neighbors, that is, those points with the smallest Euclidean distance between them and the first, randomly selected element. Those 3 elements are the nearest neighbors of the first element, and they are all placed in the same *neighborhood.* The program then goes on finding the 3 nearest neighbors of each of the 3 neighbors it just added to the neighborhood. Each of these is then added into the neighborhood. The program does this iteratively until all of the nearest neighbors identified are already in that neighborhood. That neighborhood is a cluster. The program then goes on to another element not in the first neighborhood, and begins building the next neighborhood—the next cluster. In this example, the researcher could identify novel genes or known genes with no known function that are in the same cluster as genes known to be related to serum triglyceride levels.

There are several commercially available tools that enable the advanced analysis of microarray data, including clustering by several methods. As with microarray data, many visualization and reporting tools are proprietary and are not generally available. Increasingly, some of these tools are being made available to academic scientists. The TIGR Multi Experiment Viewer is a tool designed to facilitate the analysis of microarray data and is freely available to academics. It is a flexible and expandable tool capable of identifying patterns of gene expression and differentially expressed genes. TIGR Multi Experiment Viewer includes several data normalization, clustering and distance algorithms as well as a variety of graphical display features. Multi Experiment Viewer is fully compatible with TIGR's Array Viewer and represents a higher level of data visualization and analysis.

The European Bioinformatics Institute (EBI) also provides tools for genomic data analysis. The EBI Expression Profiler is a set of tools for the visualization and analysis of gene expression data. Their aim is to provide a complete and fully integrated set of analysis methods for expression data as well as sequence data. The value of including sequence data analysis capabilities with TxP data analysis tools lies in the fact that similar expression profiles of a set of genes may lead to the identification of sequence pattern profiles in the regulatory regions of these genes. Similarly, the relevance of shared sequence elements found in the promoters of a number of genes can be evaluated by comparing the expression profiles of those genes under multiple experimental conditions. Expression Profiler also allows for clustering of microarray data from multiple experiments (*see* Fig. 15). Genes whose expression patterns most closely match one another across many experiments cluster more closely than genes whose expression patterns are not closely matched. A dendogram, much like a phylogenetic tree is generated for each element, with branch points representing clusters.

See companion CD for color Fig. 15

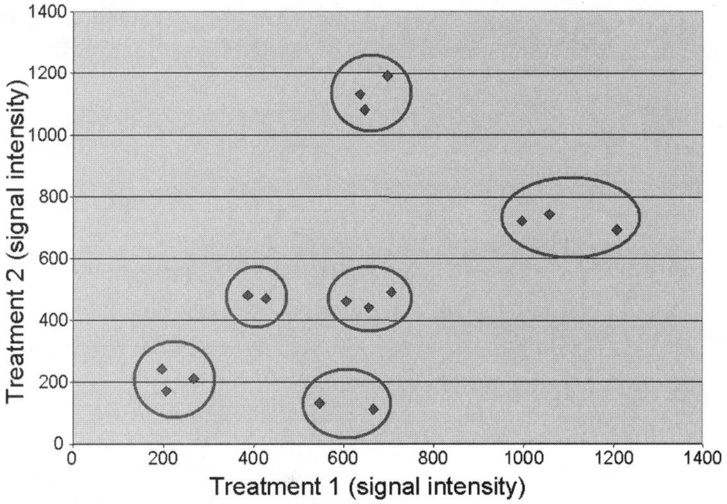

Fig. 14. Clustering of microarray data can be performed using a number of different techniques. Euclidean distance in n-dimensional space applies a variable derived from each microarray (a differential expression value or signal intensity) to every element present on the microarray. Each point on this graph represents an element on the microarray utilized. Elements in the same *neighborhood* are circled, representing six gene clusters.

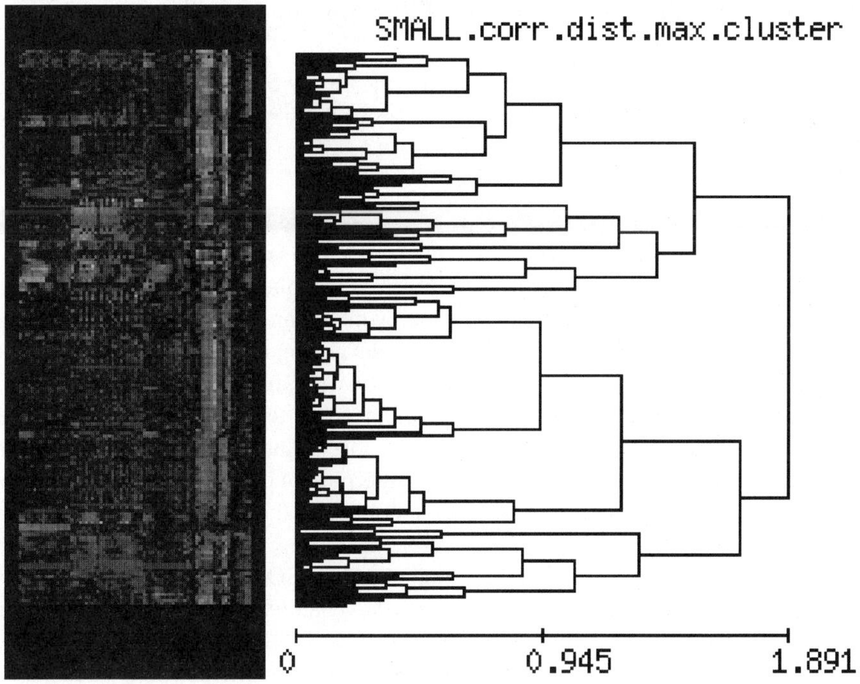

Fig. 15. The European Bioinformatics Institute's Expression Profiler tool allows users to cluster microarray data from multiple experiments. Genes whose expression patterns most closely match one another across many experiments cluster more closely than genes whose expression patterns are not closely matched. A dendogram is generated for each element, with branch points representing clusters.

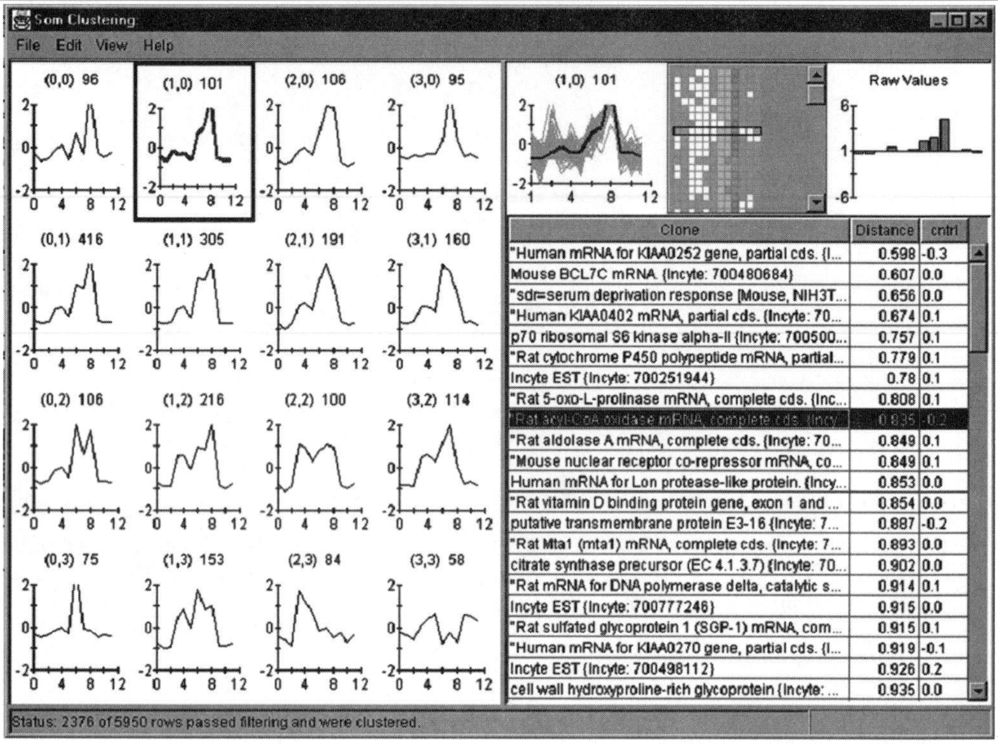

Fig. 16. Self-organizing maps represent to cluster microarray data into groups of similarly regulated genes. Millennium Pharmaceuticals and others provide tools that enable scientists to generate self-organizing maps from their TxP data.

Another clustering approach that has been taken is the self-organizing map (SOM). Self-organizing maps were developed by Teuvo Kohonen (1995) as a way to visualize high-dimensional data. The self-organizing map is an unsupervised learning algorithm that attempts to reduce the dimensions of data using self-organizing neural networks. The SOM algorithm finds vectors representative of the input data set. At the same time the algorithm creates a continuous map from the input space mapped onto a 2-dimensional lattice. The preliminary vectors of the SOM are initialized to random values. With iteration of each training pattern the winning *neurone* is found by comparing input (data) vectors and weight vectors of the neurones using Euclidean distance. The weights of the winning neurone and its nearest neighbors are moved toward the input vector using a learning rate factor. The SOM can also be used as a starting point for additional analyses. Figure 16 shows an example of a self-organizing map output generated by Millennium Pharmaceutical's SOM tool. The data was divided into four groups of four patterns. The highlighted cluster contains 101 genes, one of which, acyl CoA oxidase, is highlighted in the right panel. The individual expression pattern for this gene is overlaid upon the expression patterns of the other members of the group in the upper middle panel (*see* Fig. 16).

See companion CD for color Fig. 16

Higher order statistical analysis of transcription profiling data is another valuable means to sort through the thousands of data points that result from TxP experiments.

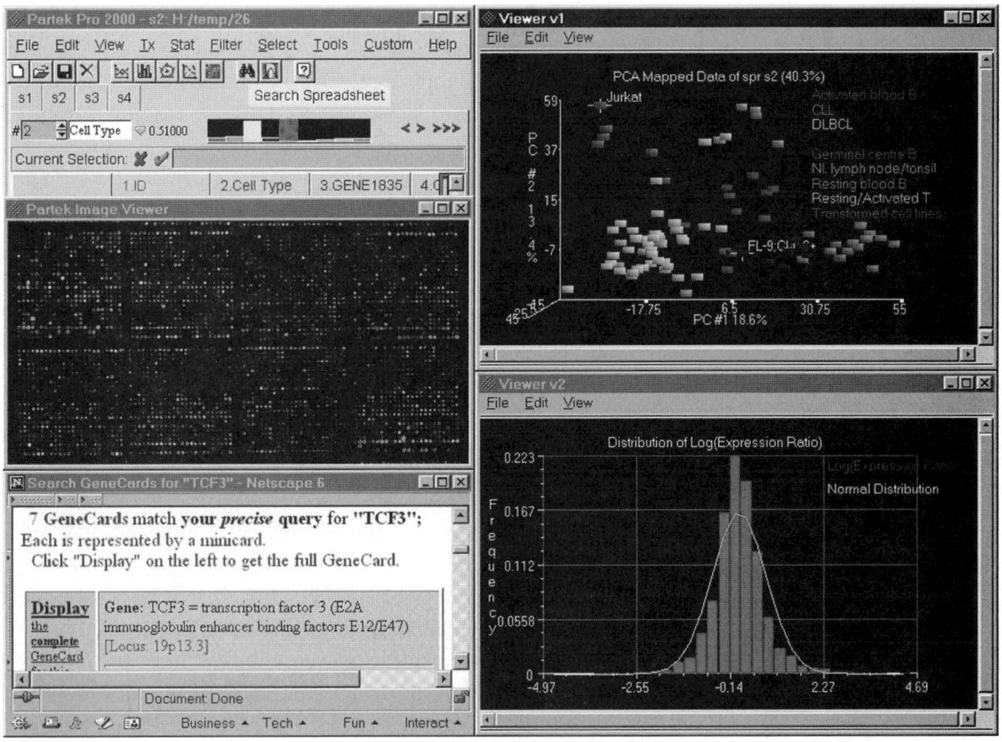

Fig. 17. Partek Pro 2000 allows scientists multiple data analysis options. Principal component analysis, multidimensional scaling, and inferential analysis can all be performed by tools such as Partek Pro. These higher-order statistical analyses of microarray results are vital to avoid false-positives and false-negatives. The costs of following up on false results can be staggering. As transcription profiling finds application in medical diagnostics, false results may even endanger patients.

See companion CD for color Fig. 17

Partek Pro 2000 (*see* Website: http://www.partek.com/) is a comprehensive data visualization and data-analysis tool for performing statistical analyses on many types of data. Partek Pro 2000 is not limited to TxP data, but can also be used for high throughput screening data, proteomic data, and nonbiological data. The software can be adapted to work with numerous databases and data formats and has been used by many large pharmaceutical, biotechnology, and bioinformatics companies. Partek Pro includes modules that permit high-level statistical analysis such as principal component analysis, multidimensional scaling, and inferential analysis (*see* Fig. 17). The tool can be used to apply statistical rigor to experimental design, normalization, chip-to-chip scaling, and other activities performed during the analysis. One difficulty in applying statistics to TxP data lies in the small sample size. That is, due to financial and biological constraints, it is not uncommon to have only a very small number of samples subjected to microarray analysis. Statisticians typically require high *n*, that is a high number of experimental repetitions to determine statistically significant values with any precision. If an experiment includes only three animals per treatment group, only very large differential expression values may be statistically significant. Additionally, comparing 10,000 elements with only a small number of biological samples will yield many seemingly significant relationships due to chance alone. Partek Pro 2000 and similar tools can be used to apply rigorous statistical tests to determine whether seemingly relevant relationships between two or more elements might be occurring simply by chance.

As well as clustering genes by similar expression patterns, correlating the expression of genes with one or more relevant phenotypes is another way to identify important and interesting genes. This approach may be particularly useful for pharmacogenomic studies, in which one or more genes are sought with a causative role in a specific measurable response or phenotype within a large population. For example, if a small but significant population does not respond to a particular pharmaceutical agent, transcription profiling may identify a gene or pathway whose regulation is different in the unresponsive population than in the responsive population. When studying thousands of genes at once using microarrays, such a simple pattern of expression would be very difficult to identify by simple visual inspection. Furthermore, clustering may not help, as known reference genes may not be available. One approach to this issue would be to express the phenotypes as a balanced differential expression, then cluster this value phenotype with the entire microarray dataset. In this way, identification of those genes that occur in the same cluster as the phenotype of interest ought to display expression patterns that correlate to the phenotype.

Another approach is to calculate a correlation score based upon a number of parameters. A simple correlation coefficient can be generated for each microarray element compared to one or more phenotypic values. This score may be adjusted to reflect signal intensities and significant differential expression values, to weight the scores in favor of reliable genes. All of these clustering and correlation approaches assume that all of the differential expression values are genuine, even those within the noise (*see* Fig. 10B). By weighting signal intensity, the correlation score approach is less likely to identify genes whose expression lies within the more nebulous range of differential expression values. Such an approach will identify genes that are both highly regulated in at least some of the experimental conditions, and correlative with the phenotype of interest. It is important to note that, just because an element has a small BDE that occurs within the noisy region of the scatter plot, does not mean that the value is not an accurate reflection of the expression of the gene that the element represents. However, owing to the general lack of a large number of replicates, TxP results should be validated by alternative methods, such as RT-PCR or the Quantigene™ (Bayer Diagnostics) assay. Genes with large changes in their expression are more reliably and more easily verified by secondary methods. Additionally, genes with very small changes in expression will be difficult to measure and verify without significant experimental repetition, making them poor choices for markers of efficacy. Since the purpose of TxP experiments is often the identification of molecular markers of disease or efficacy, or the identification of new targets for intervention, tracking changes in the expression of the genes identified will be key to additional experiments.

With these caveats in mind, the ability to identify genes whose expression correlates with a phenotype of interest, and whose expression under at least some of the experimental conditions is highly regulated is a valuable way to identify interesting genes. In a theoretical experiment described earlier, TxP was performed using liver RNA from 12 rats fed three different diets. The dietary regimens resulted in differ-

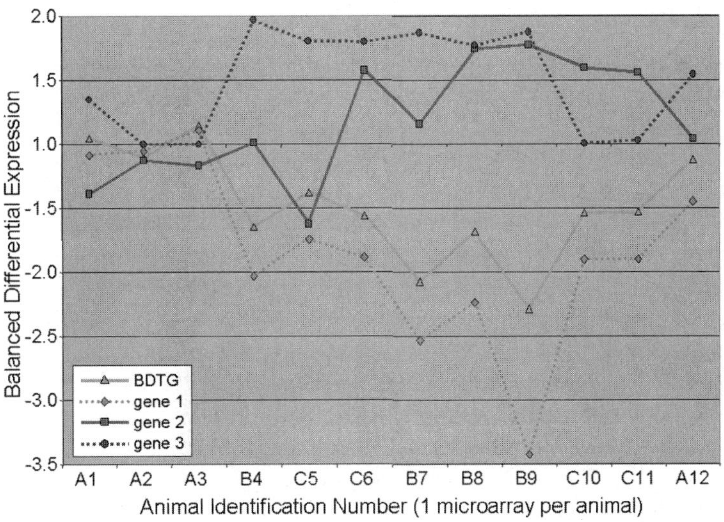

Fig. 18. Correlation analysis can be used to identify genes whose expression correlates with a specific phenotype of interest. In the experiment shown, 12 rats were randomly assigned to one of three diet groups, A, B, or C for 4 wk. Fasted serum triglycerides were measured in individual rats prior to sacrifice. Liver RNA was used to prepare probes for hybridization onto microarrays. The triglyceride phenotype was used to calculate a balanced differential triglyceride (BDTG) value, using the same equation to determine differential expression values for the array elements. The BDTG value was then compared to each element. In this example, the expression of gene 1 correlates well with the measured phenotype.

ences in fasted serum triglycerides relative to one another. A researcher knowing nothing about gene products involved in the dietary regulation of serum triglycerides might wish to identify genes whose expression is directly proportional to this phenotype, which is a risk factor in humans for cardiovascular disease. Figure 18 shows a graphical representation of three genes and the serum triglyceride phenotype from such an experiment. The serum triglycerides were first expressed as a Balanced Differential TriGlyceride (BDTG) value, using Equation 1 detailed earlier. Instead of a treated and control, the average TG value for the four rats fed the control diet (diet group A) was used as the control *signal intensity*. Individual TG values were used as the treated *signal intensities*, and compared to the pooled control, much as individual rat liver RNA samples would be compared to a pooled control sample on the microarray. A correlation score could be calculated for each element compared to one or more phenotype. High scoring genes, such as gene 1 in Fig. 18, would correlate well with the phenotype. That is, those animals with the lowest serum triglyceride levels relative to control have the largest decreases in the expression of gene 1 relative to the control group. Poorly scoring genes, such as genes 2 and 3 (*see* Fig. 18) correlate poorly with the phenotype. Without the ability to rapidly generate correlation scores for each element on the array, it would have been necessary to graph each element along with the phenotype until those with similar graphs were identified. Clearly this is not feasible when performing experiments using thousands of arrayed elements. Software that automates this approach would enable a researcher to rapidly identify genes with *interesting* expression patterns.

Project Organization

The final type of informatic task required to maximize the value of microarray experiments is project organization. Every microarray has many features, many pieces of associated data that must be stored, linked, and made available to the scientists performing and analyzing the experimental results. There are a number of organizations currently building data repositories for microarray experimental results. The National Center for Biotechnology Information (NCBI) has developed a gene expression data repository and online resource for the retrieval of gene expression data called the gene expression omnibus (*see* Website: http://www.ncbi.nlm.nih.gov/geo/). The gene expression omnibus supports multiple types of expression data, including microarray data and SAGE (Serial Analysis of Gene Expression) data. Additionally, the International Life Sciences Institute (ILSI) (*see* Website: http://www.ILSI.org/) in collaboration with the European Bioinformatics Institute (EBI) has developed both a database and a standardized reporting format for microarray data. Among the challenges facing such efforts are ways to ensure that minimal data quality standards are met and the need to include sufficient experimental information, perhaps including actual .tiff files, without taxing servers to the point of making data downloads prohibitive.

Databases that simply store microarray data are a valuable way of ensuring public access to a significant body of microarray data. However, many organizations are developing database and analysis software suites that allow for interactive data analysis on all or a subset of data stored in a database. Links are also included to associated histopathological images from every tissue for which profiling data has been acquired. The Phase-1 product is aimed toward the field of toxicogenomics, the use of genomic and microarray technology in toxicology and preclinical safety assessment, but their approach to an interactive data repository has clear advantages over a simple data repository from which information must be exported prior to data analysis.

Another application of informatics to the field of genomics that has not been fully appreciated by the scientific community is the need for rational, statistically informed experiment planning. There are many types of microarrays. A complete statistical analysis of the performance of the type of array being used in a laboratory is vital. For example, knowing the sensitivity and reproducibility of profiling results on the array platform being used can inform decisions regarding the number of samples required, and the reliability of the results of each array experiment are. An array platform that gives consistently noisy results may require large groups or many duplicates to provide useful data. Alternatively, if only small amounts of biological material are available for microarray analysis, the confidence limits may require that only genes with very large differential expression values are reliable. In such cases, correlations with phenotypic parameters would be unreliable. These issues date back to quality control issues. At this time, this author is unaware of any tool that seeks to address this issue. However tools such as Partek Pro 2000 can allow the higher-level statistical analysis necessary to evaluate the experimental parameters of TxP experiments and direct planning of future experiments. There are several books that detail statistical approaches to experimental design. One such book is *Biostatistics and Experimental Design,* by James Zolman (1993). The area of statistical experimental design tends to be overlooked by many biologists, to the detriment of their experiments. With the large number of elements that can be arrayed, the probability of relationships that may seem significant occurring simply by chance is very large. The lack of rigorous statistical evaluation of study designs *prior to* the inception of the studies will result in a significant loss of time and money trying to validate questionable TxP results.

Glossary and Abbreviations

BDE Balanced differential expression. A way of expressing fold changes in expression.

Bioinformatics A field of study encompassing statistical and computational approaches to gathering, archiving, annotating, visualizing, analyzing and reporting genomic data.

cDNA Complementary DNA. Generated by reverse transcription of RNA.

Cy3 Cyanine 3 dye. A fluorescent dye used to label cDNA or cRNA populations.

Cy5 Cyanine 5 dye. A fluorescent dye used to label cDNA or cRNA populations.

fBDE Fractional increase balanced differential expression. A way of expressing changes in gene expression.

Genomics An emerging scientific field encompassing the large scale study of the informational content and regulatory mechanisms of entire genomes.

mRNA Messenger RNA. Typically encodes proteins, often regulated by environmental conditions.

PCA Principal components analysis. A method of clustering complex data sets.

Proteomics The study of the content and regulatory mechanisms the entire complement of proteins encoded by an organism's genome.

RT-PCR Reverse transcriptase polymerase chain reaction. A method of evaluating changes in gene expression.

SOM Self-organizing map. A method of clustering complex data sets.

Transcription Profiling A technique whereby changes in the expression of many genes are measured in a single experiment.

Suggested Readings

Kohonen, T. (1995) Self-Organizing Maps, Springer, NY.

Zolman, J. (1993) Biostatistics and Experimental Design, Oxford University Press, New York, NY.

35 Microarrays

Tools for Gene Expression Analysis

Sorin Draghici

Introduction

A particular tool that has been shown to be very useful in genomics is the DNA microarray. In its most general form, the DNA array is a substrate (nylon membrane, glass, or plastic) on which DNA is deposited in localized regions arranged in a regular, grid-like pattern. Two main approaches are used for microarray fabrication: *in situ* synthesis and deposition of DNA fragments. *In situ* manufacturing can be further divided into photolithography, ink jet printing, and electrochemical synthesis. The photolithographic approach (Affymetrix) is similar to the VLSI fabrication process: photolithographic masks are used for each base. If a region should have a given base, the corresponding mask will have a hole allowing the base to be deposited at that location. Subsequent masks will construct the sequences base by base. This technology allows the fabrication of very high-density arrays but the length of the DNA sequences constructed is limited[1]. The ink jet technology (e.g., Agilent and Protogene) is similar to the technology used in ink jet color printers. Four cartridges are loaded with the A, C, G, and T nucleotides. As the print head moves across the array substrate, specific nucleotides are deposited where they are needed. The electrochemical synthesis (CombiMatrix) uses small electrodes embedded into the substrate to manage individual reaction sites. Solutions containing specific bases are washed over the surface and the electrodes are activated in the necessary positions. In the deposition-based fabrication (e.g., Clontech and Corning), the DNA is prepared away from the chip. Robots dip thin pins in the solutions containing the desired DNA and then touch the pins onto the surface of the arrays. Small quantities of DNA are deposited as spots on the array. Unlike *in situ* manufacturing, spotted arrays can use small sequences, whole genes, or polymerase chain reaction (PCR) products.

The DNA array is subsequently probed with complementary DNA (cDNA) obtained by reverse transcription of mRNA extracted from a tissue sample. This DNA is fluorescently labeled with a dye and subsequent illumination with an appropriate

[1]This is because the probability of introducing an error at each step is very small but not zero. In order to limit the overall probability of an error, one needs to limit the length of the sequences. To compensate, many short sequences from the same gene can be synthesized on a given array. The particular sequences must be carefully chosen to avoid cross-hybridization.

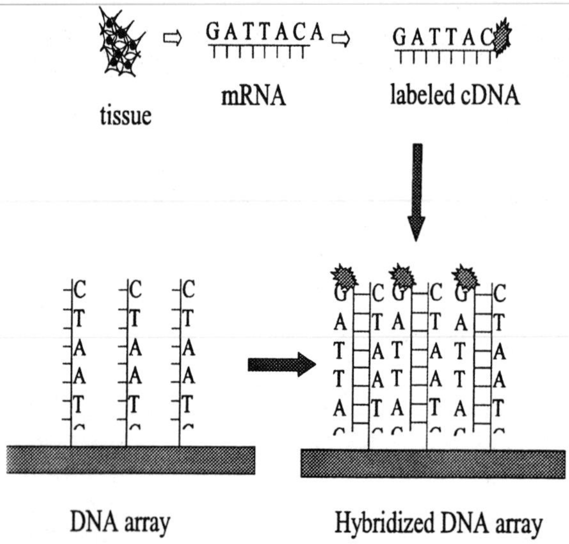

Fig. 1. A general overview of the DNA array use. The mRNA extracted from tissue is transformed into cDNA which is hybridized with the DNA previously spotted on the array.

light source will provide an image of the array. The intensity of each spot or the average difference between matches and mismatches can be related to the amount of mRNA present in the tissue which in turn is usually correlated with the amount of protein produced by the gene corresponding to the given region. The labeling can also be done with a radioactive substance. Figure 1 illustrates the microarray process. In a multichannel experiment, several probes are labeled with different dyes and used at the same time in a competitive hybridization process. A large number of expression values are obtained after processing the image(s) of the hybridized array. Typically, one DNA chip will provide expression values for thousands of genes.

Although microarrays have been used successfully in a range of applications including sequencing and single nucleotide polymorphism (SNP) detection, most applications are related to gene expression. Typical examples include comparing healthy and malignant tissue, studying cell phenomena over time or studying the effect of various factors on the global pattern of gene expression.

Challenges

Compared to other molecular biology techniques, microarrays are relatively new and a number of issues and challenges remain. Such issues include:

Noise

Due to their nature, microarrays tend to be very noisy. Even if an experiment is performed twice with exactly the same materials and under exactly the same conditions, it is likely that after the scanning and image-processing steps, many of the same genes will probably be characterized by different quantification values. Noise is introduced at each step of various procedures[2]: mRNA preparation (tissues, kits,

[2]Not all steps apply to all types of arrays.

and procedures vary), transcription (inherent variation in the reaction, enzymes), labeling (type and age of label), amplification, pin type (quill, ring, ink-jet), surface chemistry, humidity, target volume (fluctuates even for the same pin), slide imperfections (slide production), target fixation, hybridization parameters (e.g., time, temperature, buffering), nonspecific hybridization (labeled cDNAs hybridized to areas that do not contain perfectly complementary sequences), nonspecific background hybridization (e.g., bleeding with radioactive materials), artifacts (dust), scanning (gain settings, dynamic range limitations, inter-channel alignment), segmentation (feature/background separation), and quantification (mean, median, percentile of the pixels in one spot).

The challenge appears when comparing different tissues or different experiments. Is the variation of a particular gene due to the noise or is it a genuine difference between the different conditions tested? Furthermore, when looking at a specific gene, how much of the measured variance is due to the gene regulation and how much to noise? The noise is an inescapable phenomenon and the only weapon that the researcher seems to have against it is replication.

Normalization

The aim of the normalization is to account for systematic differences across different data sets, e.g., overall intensity and eliminate artifacts, e.g., nonlinear dye effects. Normalization is crucial if results of different experimental techniques are to be combined. While there is a general consensus that normalization is required, there is little if any such consensus regarding how normalization should be accomplished. Normalization can be necessary for different reasons such as different quantities of mRNA (leading to different mean intensities), dye nonlinearity, and saturation toward the extremities of the range.

Experimental Design

The experimental design is a crucial but often neglected phase in microarray experiments. If the experiments are not adequately designed, no analysis method will be able to obtain valid conclusions. It is very important to provide data for a proper comparison for every major source of variation. In a classical example from agriculture, one wishes to compare two strains of corn. If each strain is planted on a different field, there will be no way to distinguish the effect of the field including more nutrients or more sun, from the effect of the corn strain. This is a typical example of a confounding experimental design. A better design would have planted opposite halves of each field with both strains of corn such that an analysis of the results would allow a distinction between the two effects. Experimental design in the microarray context has been thoroughly explored.

Large Number of Genes

The fact that microarrays can interrogate thousands of genes in parallel is one of the features that led to the wide adoption of this technology. However, this characteristic is also a challenge. The classical metaphor of the needle in the haystack can easily become an accurate description of the task at hand when tens of thousands of genes are investigated. Furthermore, the sheer number of genes can change the quality of the phenomenon and the methods that need to be used. The classical example is that of the p-values in a multiple testing situation.

Significance

If microarrays are used to characterize specific conditions, a crucial question is whether the expression profiles differ in a significant way between the groups considered. The classical statistical techniques that were designed to answer such questions, e.g., chi-square tests, cannot be directly applied because the number of variables, usually thousands of genes, is much greater than the number of experiments, usually tens of experiments.

Biological Factors

In the normal cell, the RNA polymerase transcribes the DNA into mRNA which carries the information to ribosomes where the protein is assembled by tRNA during translation. Most microarrays measure the amount of mRNA specific to particular genes and the expression level of the gene is associated directly with the amount of mRNA. However, the real expression of the gene is the amount of protein produced not the amount of mRNA. Although in most cases, the amount of mRNA accurately reflects the amount of protein, there are situations in which this may not be true. If nothing else, this is a fundamental reason why microarray results usually require verification. Microarrays are tools for screening many genes and focusing hypothesis. However, conclusions obtained with microarrays must be validated with independent assays using different techniques from various perspectives.

Array Quality Assessment

It is useful if data analysis is not seen as the last step in a linear process of microarray exploration but rather as a step that completes a loop and provides the feedback necessary to fine tune the laboratory procedures that produced the microarray. Thus, array quality assessment is an aspect that should be included among the goals of the data analysis. It would be very useful if in addition to the expression values the analysis provides some quality assessment of the arrays used. Such quality measures will discard the data below a standard as well as the identity of possible causes of failure in the process.

Current Issues in Microarray Data Analysis

Normalization

We assume that each spot is represented by a value computed from the pixel intensities. A first pre-processing step is the background correction. This can be done locally[3], using a group of spots (e.g., a subgrid)[4] or blank spot[5]. Once the background correction has been applied, a usual step in two-channel experiments is to consider the ratio between the two channels (e.g., experiment/reference). Subsequently, one should apply a logarithmic function (log). There are several reasons for this. First, the log makes the distribution symmetrical. Consider the values 100,

[3]Only the background local to the spot is considered; good when the background varies considerably from spot to spot.

[4]Suitable for high density arrays where there are not enough pixels around a single spot to produce a reliable value.

[5]Some researchers have noted that a spot containing DNA that is not supposed to hybridize will often have an intensity lower than the background suggesting that subtracting the background might overcorrect the values. In order to control this more accurately, one can use spots containing no DNA or spots containing foreign DNA that should not hybridize.

1000, and 10,000 (a 16-bit tiff file can contain values between 1 and 65,536). If one considers the difference (distance) between the middle values and the two extremes, one is tempted to consider the difference to the right more important than the difference to the left ($10{,}000 - 1000 = 9000 >> 1000 - 100 = 900$). However, from a biological point of view the phenomenon is the same, namely there is a ten fold change in both cases. The log will transform the values into $log(100)$, $log(1000)$, and $log(10{,}000)$, which for log base 10 are 2, 3, and 4, rejecting the fact that the phenomena are the same only that they happen in different directions. Second, if the log is taken in base 2, subsequent analysis is facilitated, e.g., selecting genes with a four-fold variation can be done by cutting a ratio histogram at the value $log(ratio) = 2$. Furthermore, the log partially decouples the variance and the mean intensity and makes the distribution almost normal. Replicate genes can be combined by calculating mean, median, or mode and coefficients of variance (cv). This will produce the average-log-ratios.

One important problem is that various dyes produce different results due to different biochemical properties. The idea of a flip dye experiment was introduced in order to control such phenomena. In a flip dye experiment, the two samples of mRNA, A and B are labeled first with cy3 (A) and cy5 (B) and then with cy5 (A) and cy3 (B). Subsequent hybridization and image analysis will produce two sets of data that represent the same biological sample. A plot of the expression levels registered on the two channels for the same mRNA should produce a straight line $cy3 = cy5$. One is prepared to accept a small number of genes that are off the straight line of reference but any general trend suggests a non-negligible influence that should be corrected. Similar expectations even hold for experiments involving all or most genes in a genome. It is assumed that most genes will not change. Such expectations are not warranted if a small subset of genes is considered, especially if the genes are known to be functionally related.

The final normalization step tries to obtain values that are independent of the experiment and hopefully can be compared with other values. This can be carried out in different alternative ways as follows.

Method 1

Divide the values of each channel/experiment by their mean[6]. This corrects global intensity problems, such as one channel being more intense than the other, but does not address nonlinearity of the dye. Variations of this strategy eliminate the values in the upper and lower 10% of the log ratio distribution (corresponds to differentially regulated genes) divided by the mean of the remaining genes. The rationale being that few genes will be differentially regulated but most genes will remain the same. Eliminating the tails of the log ratio distribution theoretically eliminates the differentially regulated genes and dividing by the mean of the remaining genes bring the two sets of measurements to a common denominator.

Method 2

Modify the values of each channel/experiment such that certain control spots in both experiments have the same or similar values. The control spots should span the entire intensity range.

[6]The mean can be substituted with the median, mode or percentile if the distribution is noisy or skewed. One could also subtract the mean and divide by the standard deviation.

Method 3

Apply iterative linear regression as follows: apply linear regression, find residuals, eliminate spots that have residuals more than 2 SD away from zero (potential differentially regulated genes), apply regression and continue until the residuals become less than a given threshold.

Method 4

Apply a parametric nonlinear normalization with or without the previous division by mean, median or percentile. The exponential normalization fits an exponential decay of the form: $y = a + b \cdot e^{-cx}$ to the $log(Cy3/Cy5)$ vs $log(Cy5)$ curve[7]. Subsequently, the values are normalized by subtracting the fitted log ratio from the observed log ratio. This normalization essentially relies on the hypothesis that the dye effect can be described by an exponential curve, which may not be true for other dyes. Furthermore, the fitting of the exponential is computationally intensive involving a least-mean-square (LMS) minimization.

Method 5

Apply a general nonlinear normalization such as Loess: the values are modified in order to obtain a linear variation of the two channels (in a flip dye experiment). This is usually computationally intensive. An excellent correction for the dye nonlinearity without the high computational cost of Loess can be obtained using an adaptive piecewise linearization method.

Figure 2 illustrates the importance of pre-processing and normalizing the cDNA data labeled with cy3/cy5. The array contains 944 genes spotted in triplicates. The raw data is present in Fig. 2A. Owing to the different properties of the two dyes, the intensities measured on one channel are consistently higher than the intensities measured on the other channel. In these conditions, it is likely that any analysis method will yield erroneous results. Taking the logarithm helps greatly, as illustrated in Fig. 2B, but the overall intensity difference between the two channels is still present. Dividing by the mean brings most points in the vicinity of the reference line finally aligning the data with the reasonable expectation that most genes will not change between the two experiments. The steps taken here would be an example of the very minimum preprocessing necessary for two-channel cDNA data. Note that there is no correction for dye nonlinearity, which is rejected in the curvature of the data points distribution. Correcting this nonlinearity would further enhance the accuracy of any subsequent analysis.

It is important to note that the measured variance is dependent on the mean intensity having high variance at low intensity levels and low variance at high intensities. This can be corrected by using an iterative algorithm that gradually adjusts the parameters of a probabilistic model. This approach can be further refined using a Gamma-Gamma-Bernoulli model.

Normalization is slightly different for oligonucleotide arrays (e.g., Affymetrix's GeneChips) designed for gene expression analysis. Here, a gene is represented by a number of probe pairs (short oligonucleotide sequences) with each pair containing a perfect match and a mismatch (the same sequence but for a different nucleotide). The

---

[7]The reference line in a $log(cy3/cy5)$ vs $log(cy5)$ plot is $y = 0$ because $log(cy3/cy5) = log(cy3) - log(cy5) = 0$ if cy3 equal to cy5, as expected for the same mRNA labeled differently.

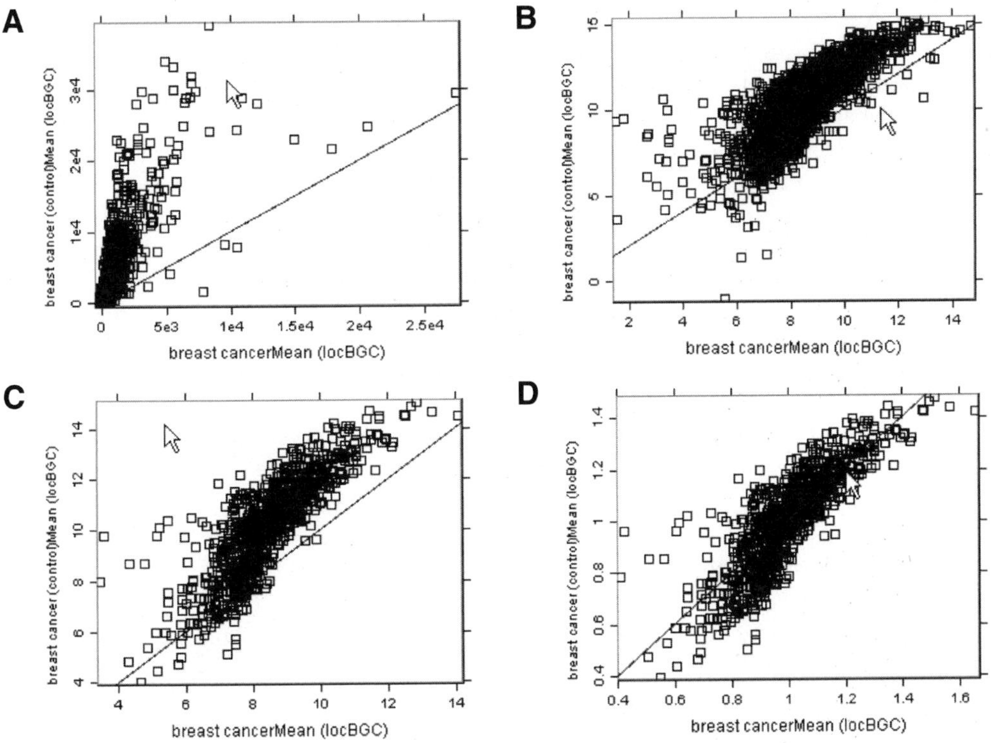

Fig. 2. The effects of data normalization. The data represents a *cy3/cy5* cDNA array with 944 genes printed in triplicates. **(A)** Raw data; the data is far from the reference and the scales are different on the two axes. **(B)** After log; the data is closer to the reference line but still above it. **(C)** Replicates are combined; each gene is represented as the mean of its replicates. **(D)** Subtracting the mean finally centers the data; however, the data are still curved reflecting the nonlinearity of the dyes.

amount of hybridization on the mismatched sequence is thought to be representative of non-specific hybridization and its intensity is usually subtracted from the intensity of the perfect match. Subsequently, such differences are averaged for all probes corresponding to a gene and an average difference (AD) is calculated. The higher this AD, the higher the expression level of the gene. The software provided by Affymetrix also calculates a *call*, i.e., a ternary decision about the gene: absent (A), marginally present (M), and present (P). A conundrum can occur if absent genes have average difference higher than present genes. Options include ignoring the calls and using only the average differences of all genes, considering only genes that are declared present, ignoring the calls and considering only genes with the average difference larger than a threshold or calculating the expression values according to some other model.

Selection of Differentially Regulated Genes and Significance Analysis

The measurements obtained from microarray experiments have multiple sources of variation. There is approx a 5% probability that the hybridization of any single spot containing complementary DNA will not reject the presence of the mRNA and a 10% probability that a single spot will provide a signal even if the mRNA is not present.

Given this, it is crucial to distinguish between interesting variation caused by differential gene expression and variation introduced by other causes. Using replicates at any or all levels (e.g., spots, arrays, mRNA preparations) is the only known method that allows subsequent discrimination.

Selecting interesting genes can be done in various ways. Two selection methods are widely used. The first selection method is the *fold method*. This method involves a simple comparison between the expression levels in the experiment and the control. Genes having different values in experiment vs control will be selected. Typically, a difference is considered significant if it is at least two- or three-fold.

The second widely used selection method is the *ratio method*. This method involves selecting the genes for which the experiment/control ratio is a certain distance, e.g., 2 SD, from the mean experiment/control ratio. Other ad hoc thresholding procedures have also been used. For example, one can select genes with at least a two-fold change and for which the difference between the duplicate measurements does not exceed half their average. These criteria can be expressed in terms of a ratio mean and SD and therefore this is a variant of the ratio method. An alternative method selects the genes for which the absolute difference in the average expression intensities is much larger than the estimated standard error.

More complex methods such as analysis of variance (ANOVA), maximum likelihood approach, gene shaving, assigning gene confidence or significance, bootstrap, and Bayesian approaches have also been proposed but are not widely used. Other interesting methods take into consideration that the variance depends on the intensity. Intensity dependency can be reduced to defining some curves in the green-red plane corresponding to the two channels. The points inside these curves correspond to genes that change little between the control and experiment while the points that fall outside the curves correspond to differentially regulated genes.

If several arrays are available for each condition, differentially expressed genes can be identified by ranking the genes according to their similarity to an expected expression profile. False-positives can be controlled through random permutations that allow the computation of suitable cut-off thresholds.

Another possible approach to gene selection is to use univariate statistical tests (e.g., *t*-test) to select differentially expressed genes. Regardless of the particular test used (e.g., *t*-test if normality is assumed), one needs to consider the fact that when many genes are analyzed at one time, some genes will appear as being significantly different just by chance.

Let us assume we are considering a gene with a value (e.g., log-ratio) v situated in the tail of the histogram of all such values, possibly indicating that the gene is regulated. The p value provided by the univariate test is the probability that v is where it is just by chance. If we call this gene differentially regulated based on this value and the value is there by chance, we will be making a mistake. Therefore, p is *the probability of making a mistake*. The probability of drawing the right conclusion in this one experiment will be $1 - p$. If there are R such experiments, we would like to draw the right conclusion from *all* of them. The probability of this will be $prob(right) = (1 - p)^R$. The probability of making a mistake will be $prob(wrong) = 1 - prob(right) = 1 - (1 - p)^R$. This is called *Sidák correction*. Bonferroni noted that for small p, $1 - (1 - p)^R \approx Rp$ and proposed $\tilde{p} = p/R$. Both Bonferroni and Sidák corrections are not suitable for gene expression analysis because for large number of genes R, no gene will be below the corrected p value (e.g., $\tilde{p} = p/R$ for Bonferroni).

A family of methods that allow less conservative adjustments of the p-values without the heavy computation involved in resampling is the Holm step-down group of methods. These methods order the genes by increasing order of their p-value and make successive smaller adjustments.

Bonferroni, Siák and Holm's step-down adjustment assumes that the variables are independent. This may not be true for expression data since genes influence each other in complex interactions. The Westfall and Young (W-Y) step-down is a more general method which adjusts the p-value while taking into consideration the possible correlations. Duplication, together with a univariate testing procedure (e.g., t-test or Wilcoxon) followed by a W-Y adjustment for multiple testing are proposed.

Another technique that considers the correlation is the bootstrap method. This method samples with replacement the pool of observations to create new data sets and calculates p-values for all tests. For each data set, the minimum p-value on the resampled data sets is compared with the p-value on the original test. The adjusted p-value will be the proportion of resampled data where the minimum pseudo-p-value is less than or equal to an actual p-value. Bootstrap used with sampling without replacement is known as the permutation method. Both bootstrap and permutation are computationally intensive.

Data Analysis Techniques

Scatterplots

The scatterplot is probably the simplest tool that can be used to analyze expression levels. In a scatterplot, each axis corresponds to an experiment and each expression value of a given gene is represented as a point. If a gene G has an expression level of e_1 in the first experiment and that of e_2 in the second experiment, the point representing G will be plotted at coordinates (e_1, e_2) in the scatterplot (*see* Figs. 2 and 3). In such a plot, genes with similar expression levels will appear somewhere near the line ($y = x$). The further from the diagonal, the more significant the variation between experiments.

The main disadvantage of scatterplots is the fact that they can only be applied to a very small number of dimensions since they can only be plotted in two or three dimensions. Dimensionality reduction techniques such as Principal Component Analysis are generally used to extend the usefulness of scatterplots.

Principal Component Analysis

One very common difficulty in many problems is the large number of dimensions. A natural approach is to try to reduce the number of dimensions and thus, the complexity of the problem, by eliminating those dimensions that are not "important." Of course, the problem now shifts to defining what is an important dimension. A common statistical approach is to pay attention to those dimensions that account for a large variance in the data and to ignore the dimensions in which the data does not vary much.

This is the approach used by Principal Component Analysis (PCA). The PCA approach is shown in Fig. 4. The data that includes patterns from two classes, red crosses and blue circles, is given in the original coordinate system with axes x_1 and x_2. If the data is projected on each of the two axes, the clusters corresponding to the two classes overlap and the classes cannot be separated using any single dimension.

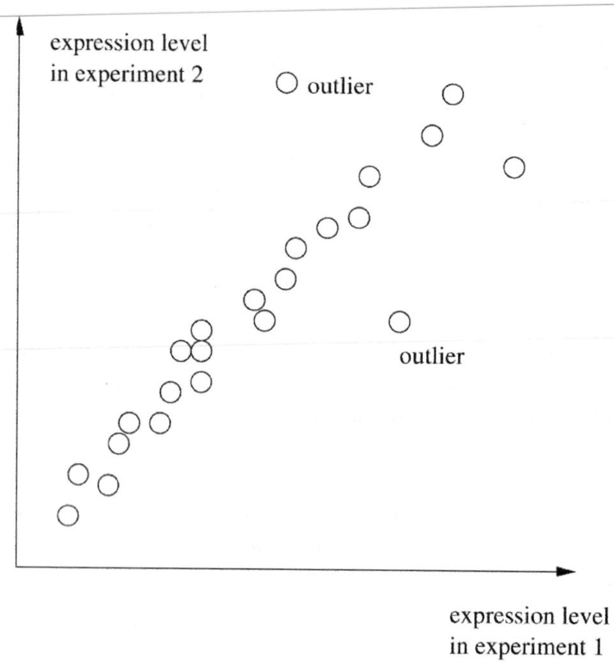

Fig. 3. Expression levels in two experiments visualized as a scatterplot. Points above the first diagonal represent genes with expression levels higher in the second experiment whereas points below the diagonal represent genes with expression levels higher in the first experiment. It is very easy to identify genes that behave differently from one experiment to another.

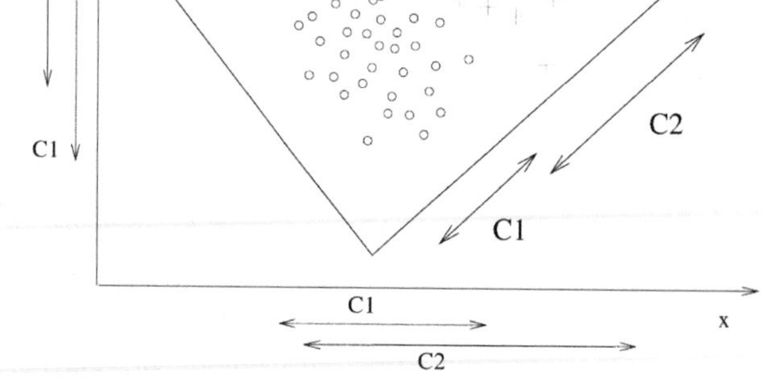

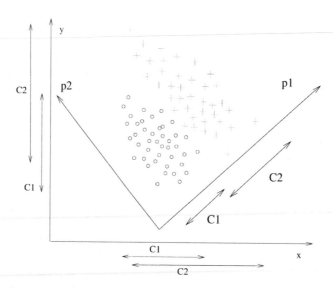

Fig. 4. Principal Component Analysis (PCA). If one of the two original axes *x* or *y* is eliminated, the classes cannot be separated. The co-ordinate system found by PCA ($p1, p2$) allows the elimination of $p2$ while preserving the ability to separate the given classes. It is said that PCA performs a dimensionality reduction.

A dimensionality reduction is not possible since both x_1 and x_2 are required to separate the classes.

However, the PCA approach can analyze the data to extract a new coordinate system with axes p_1 and p_2. If the two clusters are projected on the axes of the new coordinate systems one can notice that the situation is different. The projections of the classes on p_2 overlap completely. However, the projections of the two classes on p_1 yield two clusters that can be easily separated. In these conditions, one can discard the second coordinate p_2. In effect, we have achieved a dimensionality reduction from a space with two dimensions to a space with just one dimension while retaining the ability to separate the two classes.

PCA has been shown to be effective in many practical problems including gene expression data and is currently available in a number of software tools. The main limitations of PCA are related to the fact that it only takes into consideration first-order statistical characteristics of the data. The axes of the new coordinate system are the eigenvectors[8] of the covariance matrix of the patterns. In effect, the transformation provided by the change from the original coordinate system to PCA, is only a rotation followed by a scaling proportional to the eigenvalues of the covariance matrix. PCA only considers the variance and not the classes of data so its results are not always as useful as in the earlier example.

Cluster Analysis

Two frequently posed problems related to microarrays are finding groups of genes with similar expression profiles across a number of experiments and finding groups of individuals with similar expression profiles within a population. The technique most commonly used for such purposes is cluster analysis.

Cluster analysis techniques are essentially dependent on the definition of a metric in the multidimensional space of interest. In practice this means establishing a way to quantitatively calculate how similar two given expression profiles are. Distances such as Euclidean, correlation, squared Euclidean or Manhattan are frequently used. Once such a distance is chosen, one can use it to derive a set of clusters including the given data points. Traditionally, microarray data have been analyzed using hierarchical clustering. Such techniques yield trees of clusters also known as dendrograms. Different genes are grouped together in clusters using the distance chosen. Different clusters are also linked together to form the dendrogram based on a cluster distance such as the average distance between all pairs of objects in the clusters. A combined dendrogram with gene clustering plotted horizontally and experiment clustering plotted vertically is presented in Fig. 5.

K-Means Clustering

The k-means algorithm is often used because it is very simple and very fast. Like any clustering, it can be used to group genes or experiments or any set of homogeneous entities described by a vector of numbers. We shall denote such entities as patterns. Similar patterns grouped together by the algorithm are clusters. A set of clusters including all genes or experiments considered form a clustering.

---

[8]An eigenvector of a matrix A is defined as a vector x such as $Ax = \lambda x$ where λ is a scalar. Eigenvectors represent a set of directions of the space that are only scaled (i.e., not rotated) by the linear transformation represented by the matrix.

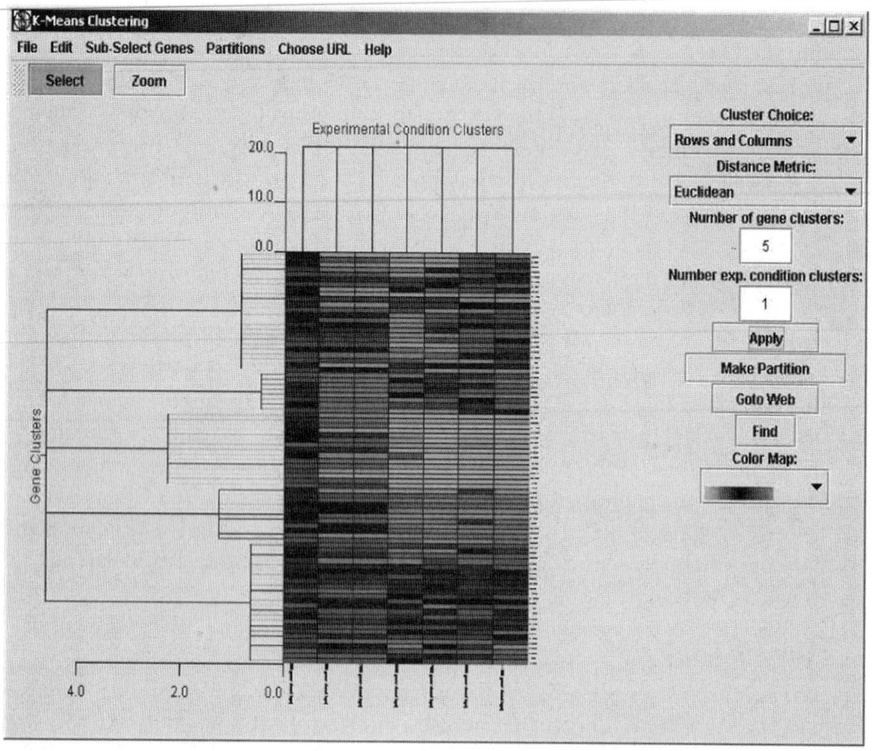

Fig. 5. K-means clustering in GeneSight. The user can choose the number of clusters as well as the distance used. The colors of the rectangular cells represents the expression values while the colors of the tree branches are associated to specific gene functions. The program also allows inferring gene function for previously unknown genes by functional enrichment analysis.

In k-means clustering the user chooses the value of *k*, which is the number of clusters to be formed. The program starts by randomly choosing *k* points as the centers of the clusters (*see* Fig. 6A). For each pattern, the program will calculate the distance from it to all cluster centers. The pattern will be associated with the closest cluster center. A first approximate clustering is obtained after allocating each pattern to a cluster. However, because the cluster centers were chosen randomly, it is not said that this is the correct clustering. The second step starts by considering all patterns associated to one cluster center and calculating a new position for this cluster center (*see* Fig. 6B). The coordinates of this new center are usually obtained by calculating the mean of the coordinates of the points belonging to that cluster. Since the centers have moved, the pattern membership needs to be updated by recalculating the distance from each pattern to the new cluster centers (*see* Fig. 6C, two patterns move from one cluster to the other). The algorithm continues to update the cluster centers based on the new membership and update the membership of each pattern until the cluster centers are such that no pattern moves from one cluster to another. Since no pattern has changed membership, the centers will remain the same and the algorithm can terminate (*see* Fig. 6D).

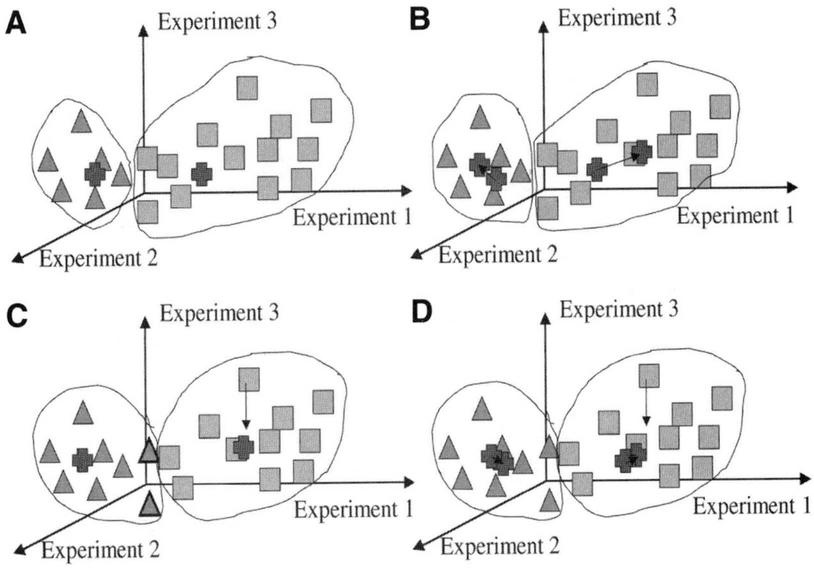

Fig. 6. The k-means algorithm with $k = 2$. **(A)** Two cluster centers are chosen randomly and patterns are assigned to each cluster based on their distance to the cluster center. **(B)** New centers are calculated based on the patterns belonging to each cluster. **(C)** Patterns are assigned to new cluster centers based on distance. Two patterns move from the right cluster to the left cluster. **(D)** New cluster centers are calculated based on the patterns in each cluster. The algorithm will continue trying to reassign patterns. No pattern will be moved between clusters. In consequence, the centers will not move in the next update and the algorithm will stop.

The k-means algorithm has several important properties. First of all, the results of the algorithm, i.e., the clustering or the membership of various patterns to various clusters, *can change* between successive runs of the algorithm (*see* Fig. 7). Furthermore, if some clusters are initialized with centers far from all patterns, no patterns will fall into their sphere of attraction and they will produce empty clusters. In order to alleviate these problems, care should be taken in the initialization phase. A common practice initializes centers with *k* points chosen randomly from the existing patterns. This ensures that: 1) the starting cluster centers are in the general area populated by the given data, and 2) each cluster will have at least one pattern. This is because if a pattern is initialized as a center of a cluster, it will probably remain in that cluster.

A natural question arises regarding the meaning of the k-means clustering results: if k-means can produce different clusters every time, what confidence can one have in the results of the clustering? This question can be refined into a number of questions that will be briefly considered in the following.

One such question is how good is a particular cluster? One way to assess the goodness of fit of a given clustering is to compare the size of the clusters with the intercluster distance. If the intercluster distance is much larger than the size of the clusters, the clustering is deemed to be more trustworthy (*see* Fig. 8). Therefore, for each cluster, the ratio between the distance *D* to the nearest cluster center and its diameter *d* can be used as an indication of the cluster quality. In the dendrogram plotted by

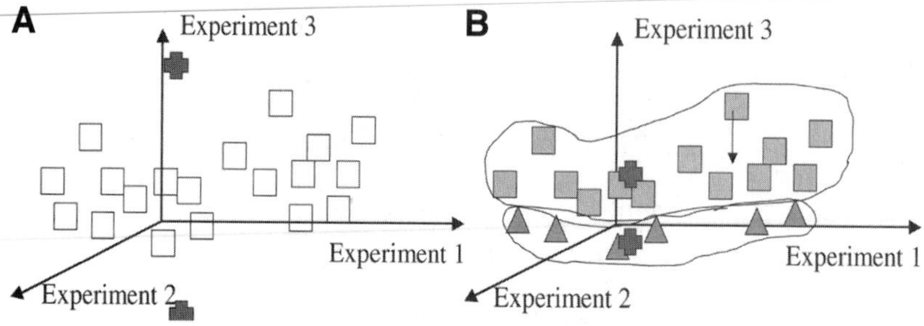

Fig. 7. K-means can produce different results in different runs depending on the initialization of the cluster centers. For instance, **(A)** if the clusters are initialized, **(B)** the final result will be very different from the one obtained previously (in Fig. 6.).

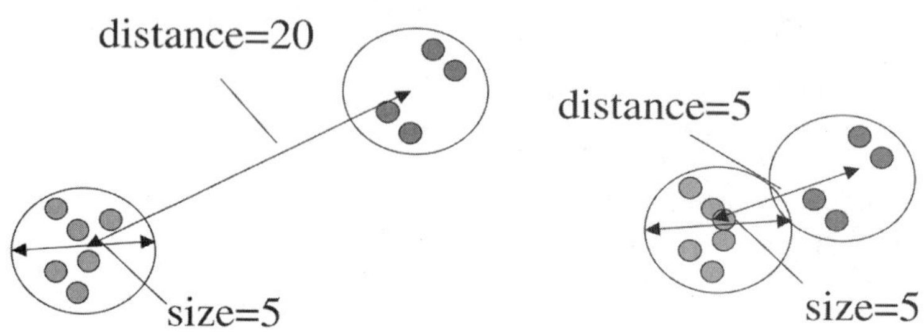

Fig. 8. Cluster quality assessment: clusters for which the nearest adjacent cluster is situated at a distance much larger than their own size are more trustworthy.

GeneSight (*see* Fig. 5), the length of the branches of the tree are proportional to the ratio $D = d$. Thus, *taller* clusters are better than *short* clusters[9].

Another interesting question is how confident can one be that a gene that fell into a cluster will fall into the same cluster if the clustering is repeated? This question can be addressed by repeating the clustering several times and following the particular gene of interest. In GeneSight, this can be achieved by generating a partition based on a given clustering. Such a partition will have all genes in a cluster coded with the same color (*see* Fig. 9). Repeating the clustering several times will reveal whether the colors remain grouped together. Those genes that are clustered together repeatedly are more likely to have a genuine connection. This idea can be taken further to its natural extension that is bootstrapping.

Bootstrapping is a general technique that allows the computation of some goodness of fit measure based on many repeats of the same experiment on slightly different datasets all constructed from the available data. The bootstrap is a very powerful method but is computationally intensive often requiring hours or days of computing time on state-of-the-art machines.

[9]Note that this is specific to GeneSight. Other data analysis programs may not calculate such quality information and therefore the length of the branches in many publications may have no particular significance.

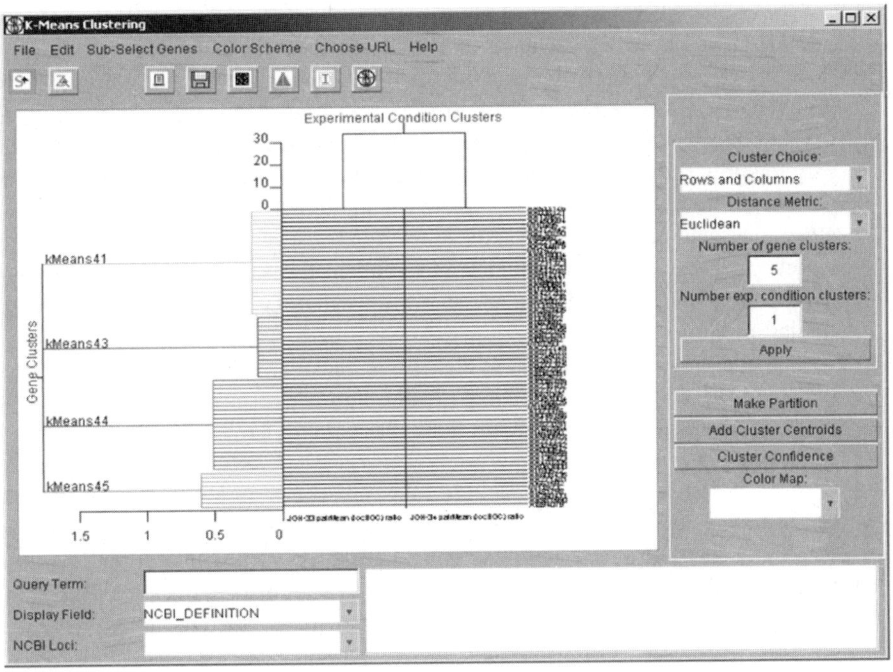

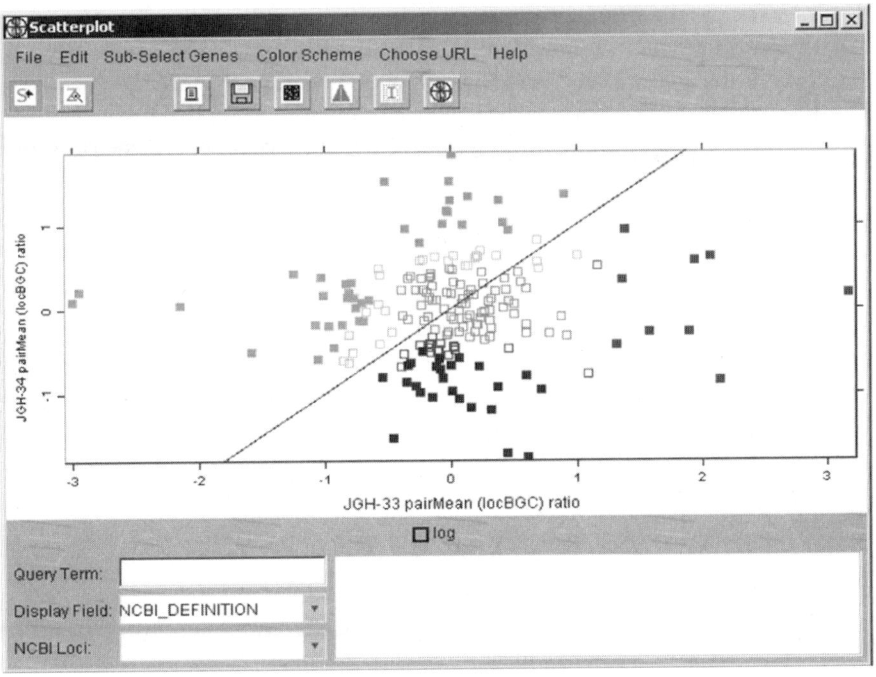

Fig. 9. An example of a partition defined by a clustering. Genes falling in one cluster are coded with the same color. Repeating the clustering and choosing those colors that tend to stay together increases the confidence that those genes truly share important features.

The choice of the number of clusters is another issue that needs careful consideration. If it is known in advance that the patterns to be clustered belong to several different classes, e.g., benign and malignant, one should then cluster using the known number of classes. Thus, if there are features that clearly distinguish between the classes, the algorithm might use them to construct meaningful clusters. It is not necessary to know which pattern belongs to each class but only that there are two different classes. If the number of existing classes is not known and the analysis has an exploratory character, one could repeat the clustering for several values of k and compare the results, i.e., track the genes that tend to fall in the same cluster all the time. This approach is heuristic in nature and its utility will vary widely depending on the particular problem studied.

The complexity of the k-means algorithm must also be considered. It can be shown that the k-means algorithm is linear in the number of patterns, e.g., genes, N. This means that the number of computations that need to be performed can be written as $p \cdot N$, where p is a value that does not depend on N but does depend on the number k of clusters chosen by the user as well as the number of iterations. However, the number of clusters is very small, e.g., 10–20 clusters, in comparison with the number of patterns, e.g., 30,000 genes. One can conclude that k-means has a very low computational complexity which translates directly into a high speed.

Hierarchical Clustering

Hierarchical clustering aims at the more ambitious task of providing *the* clustering that characterizes a set of patterns in the context of a given distance metric. The result of the clustering will be a complete tree with individual patterns, genes or experiments as leaves and the root as the convergence point of all branches. The tree can be constructed in a bottom-up fashion, starting from the individual patterns and working upwards towards the root[10] or following a top-down approach, starting at the root and working downwards towards the leaves. The bottom-up approach is sometimes called agglomeration because it works by putting smaller clusters together to form bigger clusters. Analogously, the top-down approach is sometime called division because it works by splitting large clusters into smaller ones.

Unlike k-means, a hierarchical clustering algorithm applied on a given data set and using a chosen distance will always produce the same tree. However, different hierarchical clustering algorithms, e.g., bottom-up and top-down, may produce different trees. In general, algorithms working by division require less computation and are therefore faster. However, obtaining the results quicker may not necessarily be a reason for joy because a hierarchical clustering algorithm working by division, or top-down, may produce results worse than an algorithm working by agglomeration. This can happen because in dividing the clusters the most important splits, affecting many patterns, are performed at the beginning before accumulating enough information and two patterns inadvertently placed in different clusters by an early splitting decision will never be put together again.

The bottom-up method works as follows. Start with n clusters, each consisting of a single point (gene or experiment). Calculate a table containing the distances from each cluster to every other cluster (for n points this will be of the order of n^2 computations). Then repeatedly merge the two most similar clusters into a single superclus-

[10]Unlike the real trees, classification trees are usually drawn with the root on top and the branches developing underneath.

ter until the entire tree is constructed. A cluster distance is required to assess the similarity between clusters.

The distance between clusters can be taken to be the distance between the closest neighbors (known as single linkage clustering) furthest neighbors (complete linkage), the distance between the centers of the clusters (centroid linkage), or the average distance of all patterns in each cluster (average linkage). Clearly, the total complexity of the algorithm and therefore its speed is very much dependent on the linkage choice. Single or complete linkages require only choosing one of the distances already calculated while more elaborated linkages such as centroid, require more computations. Such further computations are needed *every time two clusters are joined*, which greatly increases the total complexity of the clustering. However, cheap is not always better. Simple and fast methods such as single linkage tend to produce long stringy clusters, when e.g., using a Euclidean distance, while more complex methods such as centroid linkage or neighbor joining tend to produce clusters that more accurately reflect the structure present in the data but are extremely slow. The complexity of a bottom-up implementation can vary between n^2 and n^3 depending on the linkage chosen. In the context of gene expression, one should try to prune the set of genes of interest as much as possible before attempting to apply bottom-up clustering with a more complex linkage.

The top-down approach starts by considering the whole set of patterns to be clustered. Subsequently, the algorithm uses any of a large number of nonhierarchical clustering algorithms to divide the set into two clusters. A particular choice of such a nonhierarchical algorithm is k-means with $k = 2$. Subsequently, the process is recursively repeated on each of the smaller clusters as they are obtained. The process stops when all small clusters contain a single pattern.

The top-down clustering tends to be faster but the clusters produced tend to less accurately reflect the structure presented in the data. Theoretically, the results of a hierarchical clustering should only depend on the data and the metric chosen. However, a top-down approach will essentially rely on the qualities of the partitioning algorithm. For example, if k-means is chosen to divide clusters into subclusters, the overall result may be different if the algorithm is run twice with the same data. This can be due to the random initialization of the cluster centers in the k-means division. The complexity of the top-down approach can require between $n \log n$ and n^2 computations and is therefore intrinsically faster than the bottom-up approach especially when a complex linkage is involved.

Finally, another approach to building a hierarchical cluster uses an incremental method. This approach can be even faster than the top-down approach. Such methods build the dendrogram by adding one point at a time, with minimal changes to the existing hierarchy. In order to add a new gene, the gene under consideration is compared with each cluster in the tree, starting with the root and following always the most similar branch according to the distance used. When finding a cluster containing a single gene, the algorithm adds a branch containing the gene under consideration. This approach can be lightning fast compared to the others. However, the weakness is that the results can depend not only on the distance metric (as any clustering) or the distance metric and some random initialization (as the top-down approach) but also on the *order* in which the points are considered.

A few conclusions can be drawn from this discussion of various hierarchical clustering methods. First, various implementations using the same data and the same metric can still produce different dendrograms if they use different approaches. Second, merely obtaining a clustering is not, nor is the dendrogram itself the answer to the researcher's desires. A dendrogram connecting various genes in a graphically pleasant way can be obtained relatively quickly even if thousands of genes are involved. The real problem is to obtain a clustering that reflects the structure of the data. A clustering that reflects well the properties of the data may require more computations. Therefore, various implementations of hierarchical clustering should not be judged simply by their speed. Many times, slower algorithms may simply be trying to do a better job of extracting the data features.

ANOVA

In order to account for the multiple sources of variation in a microarray experiment, Kerr and Churchill used an ANOVA approach and proposed the following model:

$$\log(y_{ijkg}) = \mu + A_i + D_j + V_k + G_g + (AG)_{ig} + (VG)_{kg} + \varepsilon_{ijkg} \qquad \text{[Eq. 1]}$$

In this model, μ is the overall mean signal of the array, A_i is the effect of the ith array, D_j represents the effect of the jth dye, V_k represents the effect of the kth variety (a condition such as healthy or malignant), G_g represents the variation of the gth gene, $(AG)_{ig}$ is the effect of a particular spot on a given array, $(VG)_{kg}$ represents the interaction between the kth variety and the gth gene and ε_{ijkg} represents the error term for array i, dye j, variety k, and gene g. The error is assumed to be independent and of zero mean.

The ANOVA method uses a classical optimization algorithm to find numerical values that fit the given data. ANOVA is usually followed by a residual analysis, in which one studies the residuals, i.e., the differences between the measured values and the values given by the model. The purpose of this analysis is to show that the model is appropriate. If the distribution of the residuals is consistent with a random distribution, the approach is considered to be successful and the model used suitable for the given phenomenon. If the residuals show any particular shape that is not consistent with a random distribution, the model is considered to be inadequate for the given phenomenon. The rationale behind this analysis is that if the model is accurately representing the phenomenon, the differences between the predicted values and the real values should be only due to the noise that is random. If the residuals are not random, the data contained some feature that is not properly represented in the model and thus is visible in the residuals.

The ANOVA has several important advantages. First, it provides an explicit quantitative term for each factor considered in the noise. Thus, differences between different arrays as well as dye effects can be precisely assessed and normalization becomes unnecessary. Second, it is easy to find differentially regulated genes in a rigorous manner because there is an explicit term that relates to the expression level of the genes.

Among the disadvantages, ANOVA is very sensitive to the experimental design. If the experiment is not carried out in a manner that is consistent with the model, various factors will be confounded. In spite of this, the ANOVA is one of the best methods currently in use for analysis of microarray data.

Supervised Learning

Cluster analysis is currently by far the most frequently used multivariate technique to analyze gene sequence expression data. Clustering is appropriate when there is no *a priori* knowledge about the data. In such circumstances, the only possible approach is to study the similarity between different samples or experiments. In a machine learning framework, this process is known as unsupervised learning since there is no known desired answer for any gene or experiment.

However, we are now starting to understand the way genes function. The information has started to be organized and there are public databases storing functional information and pathways describing gene interactions. Such information may be used in the data analysis process. For example, the clustering step can be followed by a step in which one attaches functional labels to various clusters. This can be based on the members of the clusters whose function is known. Subsequently, one can construct a number of hypotheses that attach functionality to genes whose function is not currently known. Such hypotheses can then be tested. This mechanism is an effective way to construct a set of reasonable hypotheses from a large number of expression values and may be the key to establishing structure-function relationships. Furthermore, this approach permits the construction of metabolic pathways and the discovery of previously unknown functional relationships.

The disadvantage of clustering techniques is related to the fact that there are no guarantees that the clusters obtained make sense from a biological point of view. In other words, there is no guarantee that there is a clear biological function attached to each cluster.

Recently, a number of laboratories addressed the issue of using gene expression to distinguish between classes of conditions such as leukemia, colon cancer, malignant melanoma, and B-cell lymphoma. In a machine learning framework, this modus operandi is known as supervised learning and is very suitable for identifying the function of new genes.

Reviews of various supervised and unsupervised techniques are presented as well as other results using supervised learning (*see* Suggested Readings). Other classical machine learning techniques such as nearest neighbor, boosting, Bayesian classifiers, support vector machines, singular value decomposition have shown to be successful in microarray data analysis.

Other Existing Research and Tools

Several recent review articles discuss computational methods and challenges in this field. Various data analysis methods have been used to extract functional information. One favorite target for such studies is the yeast genome.

Some software tools have already been developed for the visualization, manipulation and analysis of gene expression data. GenExplore (Applied Maths) can do cluster analysis, PCA, discriminant analysis, and SOFMs. ImaGene and GeneSight (Biodiscovery) offer everything from image processing to data analysis including clustering and PCA. XDotsReader (Cose, France) offers calibration, normalization, and statistic analysis for DNA grids. WorkBench, Phylosopher, Impressionist, and Expressionist (GeneData AG) offer gene expression, sequence comparison, protein expression analysis, and data management tools. GeneCluster (MIT's Whitehead Genome Center); ArrayVision (Imaging Research Inc.); arraySCOUT (LION Bioscience AG); Stingray (Affymetrix); ArrayAnalyzerDB (MolecularWare, Inc.); Resolver (Rosetta Inpharmatics); the MicroArray Suite (Scanalytics Inc.); GeneSpring (Silicon Genetics); Array-Pro (Spotfire Inc.); Cluster, Xcluster, and TreeView (Stanford); ArrayViewer (TIGR); Axeldb; and MUMmer and Glimmer (IGR) are few other tools offering various visualization and analysis tools for DNA data analysis.

DNA array databases and on-line tools include: GeneX, Arrayexpress, SAGEmap, μArray, ArrayDB, ExpressDB, SMD, KEGG, and MGED (*see* Suggested Readings).

This wealth of software and resources clearly shows the amount of effort currently directed towards developing new tools for microarray data analysis. Microarrays have already proven invaluable tools able to shed new light on subtle and complex phenomena that happen at the genetic level. However, in order to realize its full potential, the laboratory work using microarrays needs to be complemented by a careful and detailed analysis of the results. The early years of this technology were characterized by a wealth of spectacular results obtained with very simple data-analysis tools. Those were some of the low-hanging fruits of the field. A careful analysis performed with suitable tools may reveal that those low-hanging fruits were only a very small fraction of the potential crop. Furthermore, it is likely that the most spectacular results, deeply affecting the way we currently understand the genetic mechanism, are further up in the knowledge tree and their gathering will require a close symbiosis between biologists, computer scientists and statisticians.

Suggested Readings

Microarrays: Tools for Gene Expression Analysis

Alizadeh, A., Eisen, M., Davis, R., Ma, C., Lossos, I., Rosenwald, A., et al. (2000) Distinct types of diffuse large b-cell lymphoma identified by gene expression profiling, Nature 6769(403), 503–511.

Alon, U., Barkai, N., Notterman, D. A., Gish, K., Ybarra, S., Mack, D., and Levine, A. J. (1999) Broad patterns of gene expression revealed by clustering of tumor and normal colon tissues probed by nucleotide arrays, Proc. Natl. Acad. Sci. USA 96, 6745–6750.

Bittner, M., Meltzer, P., Chen, Y., Jiang, Y., Seftor, E., Hendrix, M., et al. (2000) Molecular classification of cutaneous malignant melanoma by gene expression profiling, Nature 406(6795), 536–540.

Der, S., Williams, B., and Silverman R. (1998) Identification of genes differentially regulated by interferon alpha, beta, or gamma using oligonucleotide arrays, Proc. Natl. Acad. Sci. USA 26(95), 15,623–15,628.

Efron, B. and Tibshirani, R. J. (1993) An introduction to Boostrap, Chapman and Hall, London, UK.

Eisen, M., Spellman, P., Brown, P., and Botstein, D. (1998) Cluster analysis and display of genome-wide expression patterns, Proc. Natl. Acad. Sci. USA 95, 14,863–14,868.

Fan, J.-B., Chen, X., Halushka, M., Berno, A., Huang, X., Ryder, et al. (2000) Parallel genotyping of human SNPs using generic high-density oligonucleotide tag arrays, Genome Res. 10, 853–860.

Golub, T. R., Slonim, D. K., Tamayo, P., Huard, C., Gaasenbeek, M., Mesirov, J. P., et al. (1999) Molecular classification of cancer: class discovery and class prediction by gene expression monitoring, Science 286(5439), 531–537.

Khan, J., Saal, L. H., Bittner, M. L., Chen, Y., Trent, J. M., and Meltzer, P. S. (1999) Expression profiling in cancer using cDNA microarrays, Electrophoresis 20(2), 223–229.

Lockhart, D. J., Dong, H., Byrne, M., Folletie, M., Gallo, M. V., Chee, M. S., et al. (1996) DNA expression monitoring by hybridization of high density oligonucleotide arrays, Nat. Biotech. 14, 1675–1680.

Perou, C., Sorlie, T., Eisen, M., van de Rijn, M., Jeffrey, S., Rees, C., et al. (2000) Molecular portraits of human breast tumors, Nature 406(6797), 747–752.

Schena, M. (2000) Microarray Biochip Technology, Eaton Publishing, Natik, MA.

Schena, M., Shalon, D., Davis, R., and Brown, P. (1995) Quantitative monitoring of gene expression patterns with a complementary DNA microarray, Science 270, 467–470.

Shalon, D., Smith, S. J., and Brown, P. O. (1996) A DNA microarray system for analyzing complex DNA samples using two-color fluorescent probe hybridization, Genome Res. 6, 639–645.

Spellman, P. T., Sherlock, G., Zhang, M. Q., Iyer, W., Anders, K., Eisen, M. B., et al. (1998) Comprehensive identification of cell cycle-regulated genes of the yeast Saccharomyces cerevisiae by microarray hybridization, Mol. Biol. Cell 9(12), 3273–3297.

Tamayo, P., Slonim, D., Mesirov, J., Zhu, Q., Kitareewan, S., Dmitrovsky, E., Lander, E. S., and Golub, T. R. (1999) Interpreting patterns of gene expression with self-organizing maps: Methods and application to hematopoietic differentiation, Proc. Natl. Acad. Sci. USA 96, 2907–2912.

Wang, D. G., Fan, J. B., Siao, C., Berno, J. A., et al. (1998) Large-scale identification, mapping, and genotyping of single-nucleotide polymorphisms in the human genome, Science 280(5366), 1077–1082.

Zhu, H., Cong, J., Mamtora, G., Gingeras, T., and Shenk, T. (1998) Cellular gene expression altered by human cytomegalovirus: global monitoring with oligonucleotide arrays, Proc. Natl. Acad. Sci. USA 24(95), 14,470–14,475.

Experimental Design

Draghici, S., Kuklin, A., Hoff, B., and Shams, S. (2001) Experimental design, analysis of variance and slide quality assessment in gene expression arrays, Curr. Opin. Drug Disc. Dev. 4(3), 332–337.

Fisher, R. (1951) The Design of Experiments, Oliver and Boyd, London, UK.

Kerr, M. K. and Churchill, G. A. (2001) Analysis of variance for gene expression microarray data, J. Comp. Biol. 7(6):819–837.
(*see* Website: http://www.jax.org/research/churchill/pubs/index.html)

Kerr, M. K. and Churchill, G. A. (2001) Experimental design for gene expression analysis, Biostatistics 2, 183–201.
(*see* Website: http://www.jax.org/research/churchill/pubs/index.html)

Kerr, M. K. and Churchill, G. A. (2001) Statistical design and the analysis of gene expression, Genet. Res. 77, 123–128.
(*see* Website: http://www.jax.org/research/churchill/pubs/index.html)

Schuchhardt, J., Beule, D., Wolski, E., and Eickhoff, H. (2000) Normalization strategies for cDNA microarrays, Nucleic Acids Res. 28(10), e47i–e47v.

West, M., Nevins, J., Marks, J., Spang, R., Blanchette, C., and Zuzan, H. (2000) Bayesian regression analysis in the "large p, small n" paradigm with application in DNA microarray studies, Technical report, Duke University Medical Center, Durham, NC.

Data Normalization

Arabidopsis (2001) Normalization method comparison, Technical report, Stanford University, Stanford, CA.
(*see* Website: http://www.afgc.stanford.edu/ finkel/talk.htm)

Bouton, C., Henry, G. W., and Pevsner, J. (2001) Database referencing of array genes online—DRAGON. Technical report, Kennedy Krieger Institute, Baltimore, MD. (*see* Website: http://www.pevsnerlab.kennedykrieger.org/dragon.htm)

Chen, Y., Dougherty, E. R., and Bittner, M. L. (1997) Ratio-based decisions and the quantitative analysis of cDNA microarray images, J. Biomed. Optics 2(4), 364–374.

Cheng, L. and Wong, W. (2001) Model-based analysis of oligonucleotide arrays: Expression index computation and outlier detection, Proc. Natl. Acad. Sci. USA 98, 31–36.

Dudoit, S., Yang, Y. H., Callow, M., and Speed, T. (2000) Statistical models for identifying differentially expressed genes in replicated cDNA microarray experiments, Technical Report 578, University of California, Berkeley, CA.

Hedge, P., Qi, R., Abernathy, K., Gay, C., Dharap, S., Gaspard, R., et al. (2000) A concise guide to cDNA microarray analysis, Biotechniques 29(3), 548–562.

Houts, T. M. (2000) Improved 2-color Exponential normalization for microarray analyses employing cyanine dyes, in: Proceedings of CAMDA, Critical Assessment of Techniques for Microarray Data Mining, (Lin, S., ed.), December 18–19, Duke University Medical Center, Durham, NC.

Kepler, T., Crosby L., and Morgan, K. (2001) Normalization and analysis of DNA microarray data by self-consistency and local regression, Nucleic Acids Res., submitted.

Long, A., Mangalam, H., Chan, B., Tolleri, L., Hatfield, G. W., and Baldi, P. (2001) Improved statistical inference from DNA microarray data using analysis of variance and a Bayesian statistical framework, J. Biol. Chem. 276(23), 19,937–19,944.

Schadt, E. E., Cheng, L., Su, C., and Wong, W. H. (2000) Analyzing high-density oligonucleotide gene expression array data, J. Cell. Biochem. 80, 192–202.

Speed, T. P. (2000) Hints and prejudices—always log spot intensities and ratios, Technical report, University of California, Berkeley, CA.
(*see* Website: http://www.stat.berkeley.edu/users/terry/zarray/Html/log.html)

Yang, Y., Buckley, M. J., Dudoit, S., and Speed, T. P. (2000) Comparison of methods for image analysis on cDNA, Technical report, University of California, Berkeley, CA.
(*see* Website: http://www.stat.berkeley.edu/users/terry/zarray/Html/log.html)

Yang, Y., Dudoit, S., Luu, P., and Speed, T. P. (2000) Normalization for cDNA microarray data, Technical report, University of California, Berkeley, CA.
(*see* Website: http://www.stat.berkeley.edu/users/terry/zarray/Html/normspie.html)

Yue, H., Eastman, P., Wang, B., Minor, J., Doctolero, M., Nuttall, R. L., et al. (2001) An evaluation of the performance of cDNA microarrays for detecting changes in global mRNA expression, Nucleic Acids Res. 29(8), e41.

(2001) Imagene User's manual, Technical report, BioDiscovery Inc., Marina del Rey, CA.
(*see* Website: http://www.BioDiscovery.com)

Selection of Differentially Regulated Genes and Significance Analysis

Aharoni, A., Keizer, L. C. P., Bouwneester, H. J., Sun, Z., Alvarez-Huerta, M., Verhoeven, H. A., et al. (1975) Identification of the SAAT gene involved in strawberry avor biogenesis by use of DNA microarrays, Plant Cell 12, 647–661.

Audic, S. and Claverie, J.-M. (1998) Vizualizing the competitive recognition of TATA-boxes in vertebrate promoters, Trends Genet. 14, 10–11.

Baldi, P. and Long, A. D. (2001) A Bayesian framework for the analysis of microarray expression data: regularized t-test and statistical inferences of gene changes, Bioinformatics 17(6), 509–519.

Bonferroni, C. E. (1935) Il calcolo delle assicurazioni su gruppi di teste, chapter Studi in Onore del Professore Salvatore Ortu Carboni, Rome, Italy, pp. 13–60.

Bonferroni, C. E. (1936) Teoria statistica delle classi e calcolo delle probabilità, Pubblicazioni del Istituto Superiore di Scienze Economiche e Commerciali di Firenze 8, 3–62.

Brazma, A. and Vilo, J. (2000) Gene expression data analysis, Feder. Euro. Biochem. Soc. Lett. 480(23893), 17–24.

Brown, C. C. and Fears, T. R. (1981) Exact significance levels for multiple binomial testing with application to carcinogenicity screens, Biometrics, 37, 763–774.

Claverie, J.-M. (1999) Computational methods for the identification of differential and coordinated gene expression, Human Mol. Genet. 8(10), 1821–1832.

DeRisi, J. L., Iyer, V. R., and Brown, P. O. (1997) Exploring the metabolic and genetic control of gene expression on a genomic scale, Science 278, 680–686.

DeRisi, J. L., Penland, L., Brown, P. O., Bittner, M. L., Meltzer, P., Ray, M., et al. (1996) User of a cDNA microarray to analyse gene expression patterns in human cancer, Nature Genet. 14(4), 457–460.

D'haeseller, P. (2000) Genetic Network Inference: From Co-Expression Clustering to Reverse Engineering, PhD Thesis, University of New Mexico, Albuquerque, NM.

D'haeseller, P., Liang, S., and Somogyi, R. (2000) Genetic network inference: From co-expression clustering to reverse engineering, Bioinformatics 8(16), 707–726.

Draghici, S., Cumberland, L., and Kovari, L. C. (2000) Correlation of HIV protease structure with Indinavir resistance, a data mining and neural network approach, Proc. SPIE 4057.

Felsenstein, J. (1985) Confidence limits on phylogenies: an approach using the bootstrap, Evolution 39, 783–791.

Galitski, T., Saldanha, A. J., Styles, C. A., Lander, E. S., and Fink, G. R. (1999) Ploidy regulation of gene expression, Science 285, 251–254.

Hastie, T., Tibshirani, R., Eisen, M. B., Alizadeh, A., Levy, R., Staudt, L., et al. (2000) 'Gene shaving' as a method for indentifying distinct sets of genes with similar expression patterns. Genome Biol. 1(2), 1–21.

Heyse, J. and Rom, D. (1988) Adjusting for multiplicity of statistical tests in the analysis of carcinogenicity studies, Biometr. J. 30, 883–896.

Hill, A. A., Hunter, C. P., Tsung, B. T., Tucker-Kellogg, G., and Brown, E. L. (2000) Genomic analysis of gene expression in *C. elegans*, Science 290, 809–812.

Hochberg, Y. and Tamhane, A. C. (1987) Multiple comparison procedures, John Wiley and Sons, New York, NY.

Holland, B. and Copenhaver, M. D. (1987) An improved sequentially rejective Bonferroni test procedure, Biometrica 43, 417–423.

Holm, S. (1979) A simple sequentially rejective multiple test procedure, Scand. J. Statistics 6, 65–70.

Kerr, M. K. and Churchill, G. A. (2001) Bootstrapping cluster analysis: assessing the reliability of conclusions from microarray experiments, Proc. Natl. Acad. Sci. USA 98(16), 8961–8965.
(*see* Website: http://www.jax.org/research/churchill/pubs/index.html)

Lee, M.-L. T., Kuo, F. C., Whitmore, G. A., and Sklar, J. (2000) Importance of replication in microarray gene expression studies: statistical methods and evidence from repetitive cDNA hybridizations, Proc. Natl. Acad. Sci. USA 97(18), 9834–9839.

Manduchi, E., Grant, G. R., McKenzie, S. E., Overton, G. C., Surrey, S., and Stoeckert, C. J. (2000) Generation of patterns from gene expression data by assigning confidence to differentially expressed genes, Bioinformatics 16(8), 685–698.

Newton, M., Kendziorski, C., Richmond, C., Blattner, F. R., and Tsui, K. (1999) On differential variability of expression ratios: improving statistical inference about gene expresison changes from microarray data, Technical report, University of Wisconsin, Madison, WI.
(*see* Website: http://www.biostat.wisc.edu/geda/eba.html)

Richmond, C. S., Glasner, J. D., Mau, R., Jin, H., and Blattner, F. R. (1999) Genome-wide expression profiling in *Escherichia coli* K-12, Nucleic Acids Res. 27(19), 3821–3835.

Roberts, C. J., Nelson, B., Marton, M. J., Stoughton, R., Meyer, M. R., Bennett, H. A., et al. (2000) Signaling and circuitry of multiple MAPK pathways revealed by a matrix of global gene expression profiles, Science 287, 873–880.

Sapir, M. and Churchill, G. A. (2000) Estimating the posterior probability of differential gene expression from microarray data, Technical Report, Jackson Labs, Bar Harbor, ME.
(*see* Website: http://www.jax.org/research/churchill/pubs/)

Schena, M., Shalon, D., Heller, R., Chai, A., Brown, P., and Davis, R. (1996) Parallel human genome analysis: microarray-based expression monitoring of 1000 genes, Proc. Natl. Acad. Sci. USA 93, 10,614–10,519.

Shaffer, J. P. (1986) Modified sequentially rejective multiple test procedures, J. Am. Statistical Assoc. 81, 826–831.

Shaffer, J. P. (1995) Multiple hypothesis testing, Ann. Rev. Psychol. 46, 561–584.

Sudarsanam, P., Iyer, V. R., Brown, P. O., and Winston, F. (2000) Whole-genome expression analysis of snf/swi mutants of *Saccharomyces cerevisiae*, Proc. Natl. Acad. Sci. USA 97(7), 3364–3369.

Tao, H., Bausch, C., Richmond, C., Blattner, F. R., and Conway, T. (1999) Functional genomics: expression analysis of *Escherichia coli* growing on minimal and rich media, J. Bacteriol. 181(20), 6425–6440.

ter Linde, J. J., Liang, H., Davis, R. W., Steensma, H. Y., Dijken, J. P., and Pronk, J. T. (1999) Genome-wide transcriptional analysis of aerobic and anaerobic chemostat cultures of *Saccharomyces cerevisiae*, J. Bacteriol. 181(24), 7409–7413.

Tusher, V. G., Tibshirani, R., and Chu, G. (2001) Significance analysis of microarrays applied to the ionizing radiation response, Proc. Natl. Acad. Sci. USA 98(9), 5116–5121.

Wellmann, A., Thieblemont, C., Pittaluga, S., Sakai, A., Jaffe, E. S., Seibert, P., and Raffeld, M. (2000) Detection of differentially expressed genes in lymphomas using cDNA arrays: identification of *clusterin* as a new diagnostic marker for anaplastic large-cell lymphomas, Blood 96(2), 398–404.

Westfall, P. H. and Young, S. S. (1993) Resampling-Based Multiple Testing: Examples and Methods for *p*-Value Adjustment, John Wiley and Sons, New York, NY.

White, K. P., Rifkin, S. A., Hurban, P., and Hogness, D. S. (1999) Microarray analysis of Drosophila development during metamorphosis, Science 286, 2179–2184.

Data Analysis Techniques

Aach, J., Rindone, W., and Church, G. M. (2000) Systematic management and analysis of yeast gene expression data, Genome Res. 10, 431–445.
(*see* Website: http://www.arep.med.harvard.edu/ExpressDB)

Ben-Dor, A., Shamir, R., and Yakhini, Z. (1999) Clustering gene expression patterns, J. Comp. Biol. 6(3/4), 281–297.

Brazma, A. (1998) Mining the yeast genome expression and sequence data, BioInformer (4).
(*see* Website: http://www.bioinformer.ebi.ac.uk/newsletter/archives/4/lead article.html)

Ewing, R. M., Kahla, A. B., Poirot, O., Lopez, F., Audic, S., and Claverie, J.-M. (1999) Large-scale statistical analyses of rice ESTs reveal correlated patterns of gene expression, Genome Res. 9, 950–959.

Getz, G., Levine, E., and Domany, E. (2000) Coupled two-way clustering analysis of gene microarray data, Proc. Natl. Acad. Sci. USA 97(22), 12,079–12,084.

Herwig, R., Poustka, A., Muller, C., Bull, C., Lehrach, H., and O'Brien, J. (1999) Large-scale clustering of cDNA-fingerprinting data, Genome Res. 9(11), 1093–1105.

Heyer, L. J., Kruglyak, S., and Yooseph, S. (1999) Exploring expression data: identification and analysis of coexpressed genes, Genome Res. 9, 1106–1115.

Hilsenbeck, S., Friedrichs, W., Schiff, R., O'Connell, P., Hansen, R., Osborne, C., and Fuqua, S. W. (1999) Statistical analysis of array expression data as applied to the problem of Tamoxifen resistance, J. Natl. Cancer Inst. 91(5), 453–459.

Pietu, G., Mariage-Samson, R., Fayein, N.-A., Matingou, C., Eveno, E., Houlgatte, R., et al. (1999) The Genexpress IMAGE knowledge base of the human brain transcriptome: a prototype integrated resource for functional and computational genomics, Genome Res. 9, 195–209.

Raychaudhuri, S., Stuart, J. M., and Altman, R. (2000) Principal components analysis to summarize microarray experiments: application to sporulation time series, Proc. Pacific Symp. Biocomp. 5, 452–463.

Sidák, Z. (1967) Rectangular confidence regions for the means of multivariate normal distributions, J. Am. Statistical Assoc. 62, 626–633.

Souvaine, D. L. and Steele, J. M. (1987) Efficient time and space algorithms for least median of squares regression, J. Am. Statistical Assoc. 82, 794–801.

Tsoka, S. and Ouzounis, C. A. (2000) Recent developments and future directions in computational genomics, Feder. Euro. Biochem. Soc. Lett. 23897, 1–7.

van Helden, J., Rios, A. F., and Collado-Vides, J. (2000) Discovering regulatory elements in non-coding sequences by analysis of spaced dyads, Nucleic Acids Res. 28(8), 1808–1818.

Wang, M. L., Belmonte, S., Kim, U., Dolan, M., Morris, J. W., and Goodman, H. M. (1999) A cluster of ABA-regulated genes on *Arabidopsis Thaliana* BAC T07M07, Genome Res. 9, 325–333.

Zhang, M. Q. (1999) Large-scaled gene expression data analysis: a new challenge to computational biologists, Genome Res. 9, 681–688.

Zhu, J. and Zhang, M. (2000) Cluster, function and promoter: analysis of yeast expression array, Pac. Symp. Biocomp., 476–487.

Supervised Learning

Alter, O., Brown, P., and Botstein, D. (2000) Singular value decomposition for genome-wide expression data processing and modeling, Proc. Natl. Acad. Sci. USA 97(18), 10,101–10,106.

Ashburner, M., Ball, C. A., Blake, J. A., Botstein, D., Butler, H., Cherry, J. M., et al. (2000) Gene ontology: tool for the unification of biology, Nature Genet. 25, 25–29.

Ben-Dor, A., Bruhn, L., Friedman, N., Nachman, I., Schummer, M., and Yakhini, Z. (2000) Tissue classification with gene expression profiles, in: Proceedings of the Fourth Annual Interternational Conference on Computational Molecular Biology (RECOMB 2000), Tokyo, Japan, pp. 54–64.

Brazma, A., Jonassen, I., Eidhammer, I., and Gilbert, D. (1998) Approaches to the automatic discovery of patterns in biosequences, J. Comp. Biol. 5(2), 279–305.

Brown, M. P. S., Grundy, W. B., Lin, D., Christianini, N., Sugnet, C. W., Ares, M., and Haussler, D. (1999) Support vector machine classification of microarray gene expression data, Technical report, University of California, Santa Cruz, CA.

Brown, M. P. S., Grundy, W. B., Lin, D., Cristianini, N., Sugnet, C. W., Furgey, T. S., et al. (2000) Knowledge-based analysis of microarray gene expression data by using support vector machines, Proc. Natl. Acad. Sci. USA 97(1), 262–267.

Butte, A. and Kohane, I. (2000) Mutual information relevance networks: Functional genomic clustering using pairwise entropy measurements, Pac. Symp. Biocomp., 418–429.

Butte, A., Tamayo, P., Slonim, D., Golub, T., and Kohane, I. (2000) Discovering functional relationships between RNA expression and chemotherapeutic susceptibility using relevance networks, Proc. Natl. Acad. Sci. USA 97(22), 12,182–12,186.

Celis, J. E., Kruhoffer, M., Gromova, I., Frederiksen, C., Ostergaard, M., Thykjaer, T., et al. (2000) Gene expression profiling: monitoring transcription and translation products using DNA microarrays and proteomics, Fed. Euro. Biochem. Soc. Lett. 23892, 1–15.

Cho, R., Huang, M., Campbell, M., Dong, H., Steinmetz, L., Sapinoso, L., et al. (2001) Transcriptional regulation and function during the human cell cycle, Nat. Genet. 27, 48–54.

Cortes, C. and Vapnik, V. (1995) Support-vector networks, Machine Learn. 20(3), 273–297.

Duda, R. and Hart, P. (1973) Pattern Classification and Scene Analysis, John Wiley and Sons, New York, NY.

Freung, Y. (1997) A decision-theoretic generalization of on-line learning and an application to boosting, J. Comp. System Sci. 55, 119–139.

Furey, T., Cristianini, N., Duffy, N., Bednarski, D., Schummer, M., and Haussler, D. (2000) Support vector machine classification and validation of cancer tissue samples using microarray expression data, Bioinformatics 16(10), 906–914.

Keller, A., Shummer, M., Hood, L., and Ruzzo, W. (2000) Bayesian classification of DNA array expression data, Technical report UW-CSE-2000-08-01, University of Washington, Seattle, WA.

Stitson, M. O., Weston, J. A. E., Gammerman, A., Vovk, V., and Vapnik, V. (1996) Theory of support vector machines, Technical report CSD-TR-96-17, Royal Holloway University, London, UK.

Tavazoie, S., Hughes, J. D., Campbell, M. J., Cho, R. J., and Church, G. M. (1999) Systematic determination of genetic network architecture, Nat. Genet. 22, 281–285.

(2001) Gene Ontology, Technical report, Gene Ontology Consortium.
(*see* Website: http://www.geneontology.org/)

(2001) Kyoto Encyclopedia of Genes and Genomes, Technical report, Kyoto University, Kyoto, Japan.
(*see* Website: http://www.genome.ad.jp/kegg/)

(2001) National Center for Biotechnology Information (NCBI), Technical report, National Library of Medicine, National Institutes of Health, Bethesda, MD.
(*see* Website: http://www.ncbi.nlm.nih.gov/)

Other Existing Research and Tools

Anderson, J. S. J. and Parker, R. (2000) Computational identification of cis-acting elements affecting post-transcriptional control of gene expression in *Saccharomyces cerevisiae*, Nucleic Acids Res. 28(7), 1604–1617.

Bassett, Jr., D., Eisen, M. B., and Boguski, M. S. (1999) Gene expression informatics—it's all in your mind, Nat. Genet. 21(suppl), 51–55.

Brazma, A., Jonassen, I., Vilo, J., and Ukkonen, E. (1998) Predicting gene regulatory elements in silico on a genomic scale, Genome Res. 8, 1202–1215.

Colello, G., Stewart, J., Zhou, J., Montoya, L., Mangalam, H., Pear, M. R., and Peterson, T. (2001) GeneX, Technical report, National Center for Genome Research, Sante Fe, NM.
(*see* Website: http://www.ncgr.org/genex/team.html)

Hieter, P. and Boguski, M. (1997) Functional genomics: it's all how you read it, Science 278(5338), 601–602.

Hughes, T. R., Marton, M. J., Jones, A. R., Roberts, C. J., Stoughton, R., Armour, C. D., et al. (2000) Functional discovery via a compendium of expression profiles, Cell 102, 109–126.

Jansen, R. and Gerstein, M. (2000) Analysis of the yeast transcriptome with structural and functional categories: characterizing highly expressed proteins, Nucleic Acids Res. 28(6), 1481–1488.

Kal, A. J., van Zonneveld, A. J., Benes, V., van den Berg, M., Koerkamp, M. G., Albermann, K., et al. (1999) Dynamics of gene expression revealed by comparison of serial analysis of gene expression transcript profiles from yeast grown on two different carbon sources, Mol. Biol. Cell 10, 1859–1872.

Lash, A. E., Tolstoshev, C. M., Wagner, L., Shuler, G. D., Strausberg, R. L., Riggins, G. J., and Altschul, S. F. (2000) SAGEmap: a public gene expression resource, Genome Res. 10, 1051–1060.

Nierras, C. R. and Warner, J. R. (1999) Protein Kinase C enables the regulatory circuit that connects membrane synthesis to ribosome synthesis in *Saccharomyces cerevisiae*, J. Biol. Chem. 274(19), 13,235–13,241.

Pollet, N., Schmidt, H., Gawantka, V., Neihrs, C., and Vingron, M. (2000) In silico analysis of gene expression patterns during early development of *Xenopus Laevis*, Proc. Pacific Symp. Biocomput. 5, 440–451.

Shemaker, D. D., Lashkari, D. A., Morris, D., Mittmann, M., and Davis, R. W. (1996) Quantitative phenotypic analysis of yeast deletion mutants using a highly parallel molecular bar-coding strategy, Nat. Genet. 14, 450–456.

Shi, L. (2001) DNA microarray—monitoring the genome on a chip, Technical report, (*see* Website: http://www.gene-chips.com/)

Winzeler, E. A., Shoemaker, D. D., Astromoff, A., Liang, H., Dow, S. W., Friend, S. H. et al. (1999) Functional characterization of the *S. cerevisiae* genome by gene deletion and parallel analysis, Science 285, 901–906.

(2001) ArrayDB, Technical report, National Human Genome Research Institute, Bethesda, MD.
(*see* Website: http://genome.nhgri.nih.gov/arraydb/schema.html)

(2001) ArrayExpress, Technical report, European Bioinformatics Institute, Cambridge, UK.
(*see* Website: http://www.ebi.ac.uk/arrayexpress/index.html)

(2001) Microarray Databases, Technical report, Centre National de la Recherche Scientifique, Paris, France.
(*see* Website: http://www.biologie.ens.fr/en/genetiqu/puces/bddeng.html)

(2001) Microarray Gene Expression Database Group, Technical report, European Bioinformatics Institute, Cambridge, UK.
(*see* Website: http://www.mged.org/)
(2001) Stanford Microarray Database (SMD) Technical report, Stanford University, Stanford, CT.
(*see* Website: http://genome-www5.Stanford.EDU/MicroArray/SMD/)

36 Knowledge Discovery from the Human Transcriptome

Kousaku Okubo and Teruyoshi Hishiki

Introduction

The practical definition of a *transcriptome* is the entire population of mRNAs from a defined source, such as a cell, cells, tissue, or an organism. The population structure, the species of mRNA and their abundance in a transcriptome, varies widely depending on the source. This variation is thought to reflect phenotypic differences between sources. Therefore, the population structure is crucial to understanding the information in the transcriptome data.

The classic analysis of transcriptomes involved liquid hybridization (Rot analysis) in 1970s (*see* Suggested Readings, Lewin [1999]), when most transcripts were anonymous. Nevertheless, important knowledge was extracted regarding a population structure. The population appeared to contain three abundance classes and the number of different transcripts per cell was suggested to be 10,000–20,000.

The situation has changed since the initiation of the human genome project early in the 1990s. Increasing amounts of data regarding the human transcriptome have been generated. In these data, many transcripts are no longer anonymous as they have names or identification codes (IDs), enabling us to compile different data sets and characterize individual genes as well as the transcriptome as a mass.

There are two categories of transcriptome data available in the public domain today. One is population analysis data generated by random sampling identification, and the other is the collection of the ratio of thousands of individual transcripts across different populations. The former is usually carried out by determining short sequences of randomly selected cDNA clones from a library. The latter is generated by microarray hybridization. We will focus on the available random sampling of public data as an example of data structure analysis with the goal of building a framework for such an analysis. Application of the mathematical analysis package, MATLAB (The MathWorks Inc., Natick, MA, *see* Website: http://www.mathworks.com/) that enhances the flexibility in data analysis of transcriptome data will also be discussed.

Data Preparation

To begin mining data for transcriptomes deposited in various forms in the public domain, we must extract population information from the raw data and transform that information into a format that we can apply our statistical analysis and visualization techniques. The desired data format for a transcriptome is a list of component transcript IDs paired with their abundance values in a specific source. If we compile such data from multiple sources, we will have a matrix of abundance values arranged coordinates of transcript ID × source material (Gene Expression Matrix). To simplify the analysis, we do not consider variations in splicing patterns and alternative polyadenylation sites, because discriminative observation is usually not possible. The methods for extracting population data from each type of data are described in the following sections.

EST

An expressed sequence tag (EST) is a short stretch, usually 200–500 bp, of nucleotide sequence from a clone picked randomly from a cDNA library. On one hand the tagged portion usually represents the 3' end of cDNA, because cDNA is usually synthesized with primers annealing to the poly(A) stretch at the 3' end of the mRNA. On the other hand the 5' end of cDNA represents the start site of the transcription. This is only observed when the mRNA remains intact until cDNA synthesis and when it has no strong internal structure that stops reverse transcription. Large numbers of ESTs have been generated (thousands of ESTs per library) from the various projects and deposited into a single public directory, *dbEST*, maintained by the National Center for Biotechnology Information (NCBI). Similar to GenBank, the dbEST data exist as multiple individual nucleic acid sequences with notations of the source material, method for data generation, authors and any citations (for the file formats *see* Websites: http://www.ncbi.nlm.nih.gov/Sitemap/samplerecord.html and http://www.ncbi.nlm.nih.gov/dbEST/). When EST data is used for transcriptome analysis, one first sorts all human EST entries according to their library of origin by using the respective annotations as keys. As shown, some libraries are noted as *normalized*. This means that differences in the representational frequencies between clones were intentionally diminished prior to sampling.

Examples of libraries noted as *normalized*:

NCI_CGAP_Brn41 (Adult brain)
NCI_CGAP_Brn50 (Adult brain)
NCI_CGAP_Brn52 (Adult brain)

You can obtain details about dbEST libraries from the UniGene web pages (*see* Website: http://www.ncbi.nlm.nih.gov/UniGene/lib.cgi?ORG=Hs&LID=816). Library ID (LID)—library source is available from Hs.lib.info, as part of the UniGene files available from the NCBI ftp website.

Other procedures that will alter the representational frequency and population structure include the elimination of abundant clones by prescreening with cDNA probes, and subtraction between two similar libraries to enhance any interpopulation differences. In commercially available libraries, the population of clones may be biased in favor of those that do not interfere with proliferation of host bacteria. ESTs contained within these representationally altered libraries are not suitable for transcriptome analysis. If this information is not noted, we must refer to the original publications to determine if the data are suitable for transcriptome analysis.

To transform the EST records from each library into the population analysis format of transcript ID and abundance, we must cluster ESTs from one library into cognate sequence classes. This process is similar to shotgun sequence assembly using overlap-

Table 1
A Part of the Gene × Tissue Matrix in the BodyMap Database[a]

Blood					*Connective/Muscular*					*Epithelial*					*Cluster ID*		
B01	*B02*	*B03*	*B04*	*B05*	*C01*	*C02*	*C03*	*C04*	*C05*	*E01*	*E02*	*E03*	*E04*	*E05*	*BodyMap*	*UniGene*	*Gene name*
											55				GS08025		cytokeratin 12
											2	23			GS06283	Hs.74070	cytokeratin 13
					3		3	2							GS03142	Hs.195851	a-actin, vascular
	14	1	4	3	2	1	2	11		4	2	2	10	7	GS00244	Hs.180952	b-actin
1	5	1		4	4	1	3	9	9	2	2		4	9	GS00114	Hs.215747	g-actin
					1		11	4							GS02049	Hs.172928	COL1A1
				2			26	13							GS02285	Hs.179573	COL1A2

[a]B01 through E05 represents different libraries.

ping sequences. The results are contained in the UniGene database. In this database, all EST entries and full-length cDNA entries for major organisms have been clustered into cognate sequence classes with unique class IDs (e.g., Hs numbers for human). The correspondence between the UniGene IDs and EST IDs is available (for human *see* Website: ftp://ncbi.nlm.nih.gov/repository/UniGene/Hs.data.Z). Thus, beginning with the EST IDs for a library, we can generate a list of gene IDs with frequency values. Because UniGene has sequence variants registered separately, some UniGene IDs represent the same gene. LocusLink maps UniGene entries to unique gene loci and can be used to integrate multiple UniGene IDs for one gene.

BodyMap

The BodyMap database (*see* Website: http://bodymap.ims.u-tokyo.ac.jp/) is an EST database containing a data set for the purpose of population analysis. The libraries analyzed in the process of building the database are not normalized or amplified. All the ESTs represent the most 3'cDNA fragments created by cleavage with the restriction enzyme *Mbo*I (GATC). The data in BodyMap are summarized as a gene × tissue abundance matrix that shows how frequently a particular gene sequence is represented in a specific source. Table 1 shows a part of such a gene expression matrix that covers approx 20,000 genes × 60 tissues. In BodyMap, the corresponding gene IDs and UniGene IDs are also provided.

SAGE

The serial analysis of gene expression (SAGE) database (*see* Website: http://www.ncbi.nlm.nih.gov/SAGE/) is a collection of very short site-directed tags from cDNA libraries. The sequence tags consist of the 10 bases that follow the 3'-most GATC (MboI) or CATG (NlaIII) restriction site of a cDNAs. Tags are read by sequencing plasmid inserts containing 10–20 concatenated tags to enhance the efficiency of tag collection. The resultant sequences are separated into 10-base tags by separator sequences that are introduced before concatenation. The 10-base tags are counted using a 100% match basis because any 10 bases could represent a gene. If the experiments are carried out as planned and the sequences after the cleavage sites are random, the 10 bases should be long enough to discriminate among the 30,000–50,000+ human genes.

The publicly available SAGE data (*see* Website: ftp://ftp.ncbi.nlm.nih.gov/pub/sage/) is stored in multiple files, each containing a list of 10-base tags with their frequencies in a specific transcriptome. The corresponding Hs number for each tag is provided in the same directory. Because the tags are counted on a perfect-match basis, a sequence alignment program is not necessary, and a simple **sort** command followed by **uniq -c** provided by the UNIX shell is sufficient. Tag frequency and tag-Hs correspondence tables can be used to create a gene × source matrix.

Sources of Confusions and Errors in Data

Random Fluctuation Errors

The difficulty with interpreting the data arises from the random fluctuations or chance errors that are inherent in tag counting. Because the number of clones for a gene is small relative to the size of the sample, the probability to observe x clones for one gene transcript, $p(x)$, should follow the Poisson distribution:

$$p(x) = exp(-\lambda) \cdot \lambda^x / x! \qquad \text{[Eq. 1]}$$

where λ is the actual (though unknown) number of clones for a gene per N sampled clones. Figure 1 shows a series of plots of $p(x)$ for $x = 0$ to 10, with λ increasing from 1 to 15. The MATLAB **poisspdf** command has been used. Each curve shows the distribution of the probability to observe x counts for each λ value. For example, given $x = 3$, there could be several values for λ with probability larger than 5%.

The confidence limits for λ, for the observation of x clones of a gene may be obtained as follows. Let α be a significance level (e.g., 0.01), and the lower $1 - \alpha$ confidence limit is

$$L_1 = \chi^2 \{[1 - (\alpha/2)], 2 \cdot x\}/2, \qquad \text{[Eq. 2]}$$

where $\chi\ (p, \nu)$ is the chi-square value for the probability p and the degree of freedom ν, and the upper $1 - \alpha$ confidence limit is

$$L_2 = \chi^2 [\alpha/2, 2 \cdot (x + 1)]/2. \qquad \text{[Eq. 3]}$$

Chi-square values from standard statistical tables for critical values of the chi-square distribution, the Excel function **CHIINV**(p, ν) or the MATLAB function **chi2inv**(p',ν) (you should use **1** – p for p'), can be used. If $x = 3$ and $\alpha = 0.01$, then

$$L_1 = chi2inv\{1 - [1 - (0.01/2)], 2 \cdot 3\}/2 = 0.3379,$$

and

$$L_2 = chi2inv[1 - 0.01/2, 2 \cdot (3 + 1)]/2 = 10.9775.$$

Therefore, rounding the values yields a 99% confidence interval between 0 and 10 for the count. The expected ranges of actual counts for different observed counts for α = 0.01 and 0.05, and the results are presented in Table 2.

Confusion in Tag Counting and in Tag to Gene Correspondence

Cluster errors must also be considered because we count the number of unique tags by clustering the alignments when we use EST data. Errors in clustering have various causes. First, tag sequences containing repetitive sequences may lead to joining different clusters. In addition to repetitive sequences such as Alu or L1, contaminating vector sequences may similiarly act as repetitive units. An example of the inclusion of a repetitive sequence in a representative cDNA set is shown in Table 3. Therefore, sequences are clustered after intensive filtering of repetitive sequences. Nevertheless, there may still be some unmasked repetitive sequence left.

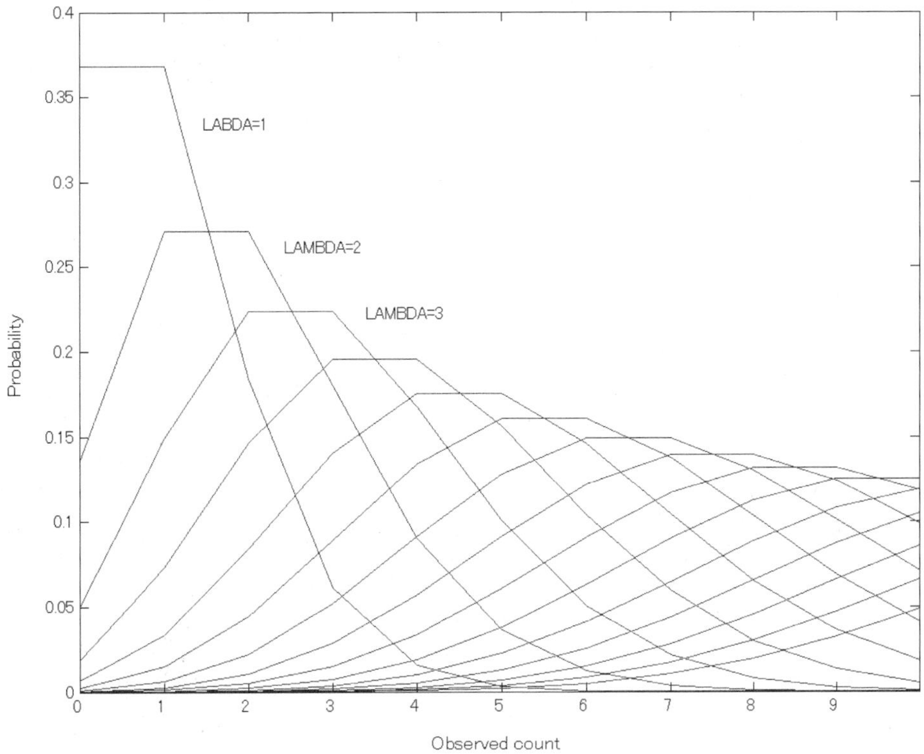

Fig. 1. Possible observations under Poisson distribution.

Table 2
Confidence Intervals of Possible Actual Occurrence (___) for Observed Counts (x).

Observed counts		*1*	*2*	*3*	*4*	*5*	*6*	*7*
Actual occurence (λ)	α = 0.05	0–5	0–7	0–8	2–10	2–11	2–13	3–14
	α = 0.01	0–7	0–9	0–10	0–12	2–14	2–15	3–17
8	9	10	11	12	13	14	15	16
4–15	5–17	5–18	6–19	7–20	7–22	8–23	9–24	10–25
3–18	4–19	4–21	5–22	5–24	6–25	7–26	7–28	8–29
17	18	19	20	21	22	23	24	25
10–27	11–28	12–29	13–30	13–32	14–33	15–34	16–35	17–36
9–30	9–32	10–33	11–34	12–35	12–37	13–38	14–39	14–41

It must be remembered that exhaustive attempts to remove repetitive sequences with long margins may lead to loss of unique tags.

Second, clustering errors can be caused by chimeric clones resulting from the connection of two independent cDNA fragments at the cloning steps. Chimeric clones can only be identified when an assembly of cognate tags or an alignment to genomic sequence is made.

The third source of error is contamination by genomic fragments. The canonical polyadenylation signal (AAUAAA) does not assure distinction from genomic

Table 3
Inclusion of a Repetitive Sequence in a Representative cDNA Set

```
A representative sequence containing a repetitive sequence (GS5406):
GANNNNNNNNNNNNNNNNNNNNNNNNNNNNNNNNNNNNNNNNNNNNNNNNNNNNNNNNNN
NNNNNNNNNNNNNNNNNNNNNNNNNNNAAAGAAGAAAAAAAAGAGAAAAATAACTCTTTT
GAACAAACAGACAAATTAGCTAGTAGTATGGAGATGTATACCCTCTATTACACACATAAA
ACCGTAACAAAATTCATTGTGGTGTATTATAATTAGTTTTGTGAATAGAAAAATAAAGCA
CTTATGTTTAAATTTGTTACAGTTGACTTTTAAAGGATAATGTTGAATCACATTGTCAGA
ATTTTTTCCNCCCCCCGTTCAATTTTGTTNTTTTTACCCCCNAAAATGAAATTCNCAAAT
TTATACNTTTTNTTTTGTTTGAANAATNATCCNCCCNTTTAAAAAAA
The masked part includes a repetitive sequence as follows:
TCGGGTTGAGCCCAGGAGGTTGTGGCTGCAGTNAGCTGTGATGTGCCCTTATGCTATAGCCTGGGCA
AGAGCGTGAGACCCTGTCTCAAAGAAGAAAA
```

sequences. Approximately 10% of the transcripts completely lack this hexanucleotide even if one-base is substituted. A stretch of Ts in 3' ESTs representing poly (A)s may help distinguish such cDNAs; however, when 3' EST sequences are read beyond the poly (A) tail in the antisense direction, the sequences in such a region are often of poor quality and are therefore eliminated from the submitted sequences.

The fourth source of errors is the misidentification of SAGE tags. Sequencing errors are difficult to detect because tags for different genes may differ at only one base. If the sequence quality is 99.0%, the probability of obtaining a 10-bp sequence free from error is 90%. Therefore, there is one incorrect tag in every 10 tags. For example, for 286,089 human SAGE tags, reliable correspondence to an Hs member was found for less than one third (89,230). The remaining tags could be derived from a different region of a partially registered transcript, a novel transcript, or an artifact. This is an excellent example of the inevitable trade-off between efficiency and robustness of random noise in the information transmission.

In SAGE and BodyMap, transcripts without *Mbo*I or *Nla*III cleavage sites are not represented in the data. For example, among 13,739 sequences in the RefSeq database, 398 full-length cDNAs lack *Mbo*I sites and 145 sequences lack *Nla*III sites.

Analyzing Data for a Single Transcriptome

One of the most commonly asked questions about a population of mRNAs is: what are its characteristics? Typical answers have included information such as: the most abundant is gene A, which represents 10% of total tags, followed by B representing 5%; or the 30 most abundant genes comprise 50% of the population; or 500 gene species were found in 1000 tags. These are informative values, but they are not as comprehensive as the classical Rot curves because each value only represents a small fraction of the characteristics of that population.

By introducing a secondary feature to each gene, the abundance rank, we can graphically represent the entire population. The abundance rank is the relative amount of a transcript in a transcriptome, i.e., rank = 1 for the most abundant, rank = 2 for the second most abundant, and so on. The rank is not an inherent feature of a gene, however, it provides a unique description of a gene in a population.

To obtain a graph called the *gene expression profile* the frequencies of genes can be plotted as a function of their abundance ranks. A *virtual Rot curve* can be derived

See companion CD for color Fig. 2

by plotting the accumulated sum of the frequencies of the sequence tags in a population as a function of their frequency rank. These curves look similar for all transcriptomes because the plotted genes are always distributed in small areas close to the coordinates on a logarithmic scale (*see* Fig. 2). These log-rank vs log-frequency plots, or Zipf's plots, were named after a linguist George Kingsley Zipf, who found a beautiful constraint in the frequency of words in English texts. In either case, the continuity of abundance across ranks, rather than clustering to form abundance classes, was suggested. This permits us to easily visualize the difference in mRNA populations between various transcriptomes.

Interestingly, with populations of differentiated and homogeneous cells, such as liver and muscle, the curve is very close to the line representing $F = 0.1/r$, where F is the frequency and the r is the abundance rank. If this holds true for transcripts with the lowest rank, an estimate of the number of transcribed genes in liver or muscle is obtained as a natural number N such that the accumulated sum of $0.1/r$ with r from 1 to N equals 1. For $N = 12{,}367$, the sum equals 1.0000. Although the value may easily be affected by attitude of rare transcripts (tail of the curve), such a prediction is the beauty of the discovery of the constraint.

Useful Tools for Expression Data Analysis of Microarray Data

A set of expression data is essentially a gene by source (e.g., cells and tissues) matrix of frequency data. Therefore, tools to manipulate large matrices efficiently facilitate flexible exploration, rather than having tools specialized in expression profiling. MATLAB, a widely used mathematical computing tool in science and engineering, it is one of the best of its kind. The first version of MATLAB was written in the late 1970s at the University of New Mexico and Stanford University and was intended for use in courses in Matrix Theory. Version 6 (Release 12) contains collections of tools (toolboxes) built on the MATLAB environment, including Statistics Toolbox and Signal Processing Toolbox, have been developed. Student versions are sold at a very reasonable price and provide essentially the same environment, but limit the matrix size.

What is MATLAB?

MATLAB is a software package (*see* Website: http://www.mathworks.com/search) that can be used to define and solve mathematical problems. Its application areas include all fields where problems are defined mathematically. MATLAB provides the flexibility equivalent to problem specific environments written in languages such as Fortran or C. Compatibility with these languages and coverage of computing tasks from data acquisition and analysis to applications development minimizes the learning curve for applying this tool to gene-expression analysis.

MATLAB integrates mathematical computing, visualization, and a powerful technical language. It provides users with a combination of a very intuitive interface, language, and built-in math and graphics functions. For example, let **A** and **B** represent matrices $m \times n$ and $n \times k$. The product of the two matrices is obtained by simply writing the mathematical expression **A * B**. To join the rows (horizontal concatenation) of matrices **A** and **B** to make a wider matrix enter **[A B]**. To display a colored map that represents the distribution of values over the whole matrix A requires only that the user run a command **pcolor(A)**.

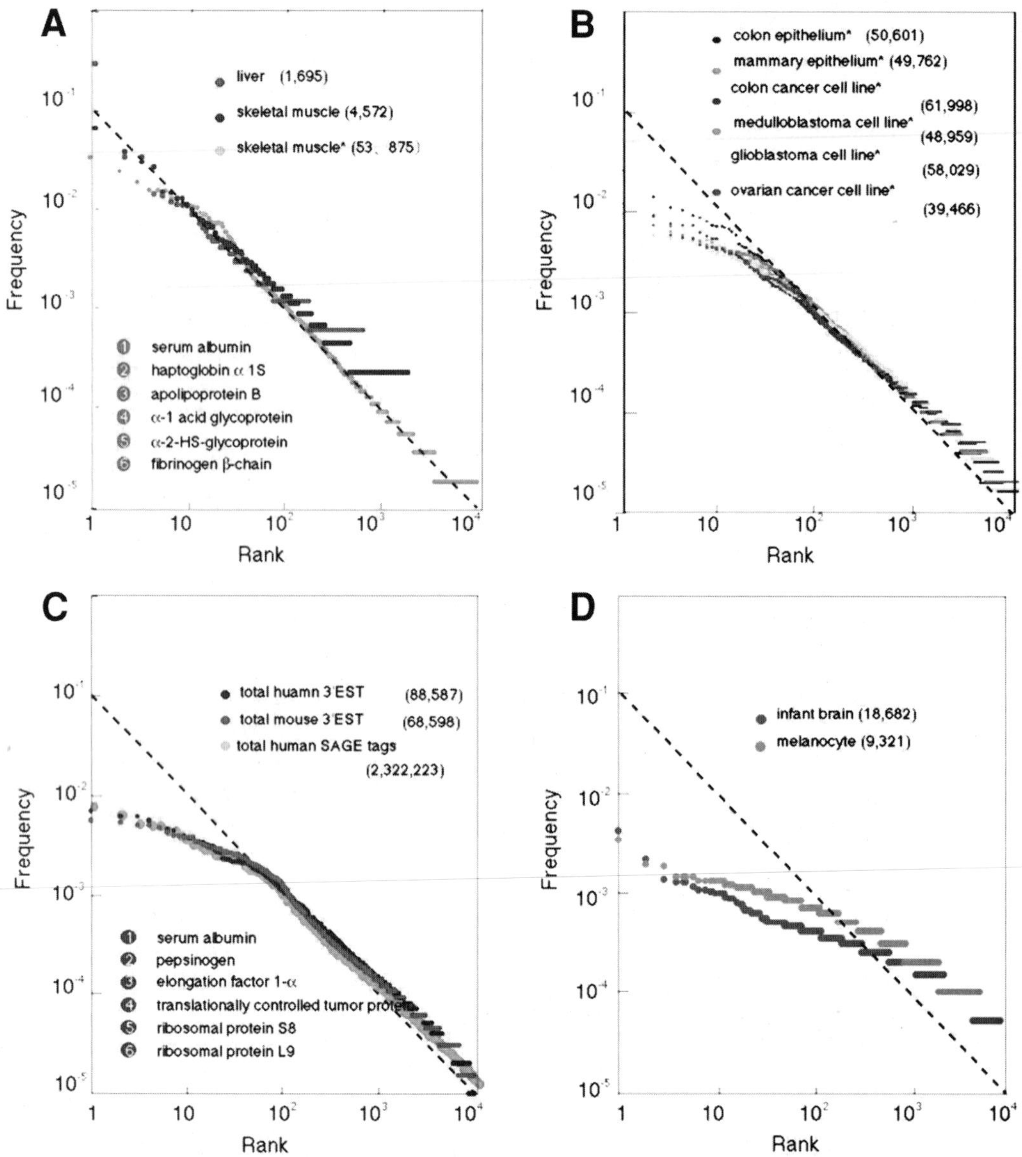

Fig. 2. The frequency of occurrence (*f*) of each transcript in 3'EST and SAGE tag (*) collections of various transcriptomes plotted against the abundance rank (*r*). The broken line represents $f = 0.1/r$. **(A)** Organs with homogeneous populations of differentiated cells. Gene names for $r = 1 - 6$ in liver are given. **(B)** Cell lines and complex tissues. **(C)** Compiled data from 51 human EST sets, 31 mouse EST sets, and 64 SAGE tag sets. Gene names for $r = 1 - 6$ in compiled human transcriptome (3'EST) are given. **(D)** Occurrence of 3'ESTs in normalized libraries. The total tag occurrence for each data set is given in parentheses. The frequency data were obtained from websites (*see* Websites: http://bodymap.ims.u-tokyo.ac.jp/datasets/index.html (3'EST) and ftp://ncbi.nlm.nih.gov/pub/sage/ (SAGE). The data for liver are the combined data for two human liver libraries. The frequencies of total SAGE tags are from re-analysis of all available human SAGE tags. Clustering 3'ESTs for two representative normalized libraries in dbEST, 1N1B and 2NbHM, yielded the data for normalized libraries.

Expression Analysis with MATLAB

This section provides an example of the use of MATLAB to determine various expression patterns. In this example, we will use supplemental data (Fig. 2 clusters; **fig2data.txt**) that were originally reported in Iyer et al. (1999). This can be downloaded from Stanford Genomic Resource (*see* Website: http://genome-www.stanford.edu/).

Import and Display Matrix Data

First, import and display an entire matrix. The raw matrix data should be a text delimited file with tabs or other delimiters (e.g., spaces and |). The command **help formats** shows other compatible file formats. Pull down the **File** menu, start the Import Wizards and load **fig2data.txt** The file **fig2data.txt** has several comment lines that provide an explanation of the origin of the file. These lines should be removed. Some text files are impossible to import because of format errors, that are often hard to detect. In such a case, importing these files into Excel and exporting the files as a tab-delimited text file is often effective. The wizards will separate the text file into a data matrix named *data* and row/column titles named *textdata*.

The command **pcolor(data)** will display the matrix. Often only a black window is visible because the panel is too small to both draw mesh lines and paint matrix cells. Pull down the **Edit** menu, start the Current Object Property Editor, and remove the mesh lines by setting the line style to **none**. The color-value table (color bar) for the matrix cells is shown as the **colorbar** command. Only a blue field will be visible as the values in the cells are the red/green ratio scanned from the microarrays. The lower limit of the ratio is 0 while the upper limit may be more than 100. It is necessary to use a logarithmic scale as most matrix cells are in the blue (near 1) area. Let Fig2 represent a new data matrix, and make a statement **Fig2 = log2(data)** to make a properly scaled matrix. Figure 3 shows the column 1 (0 h) to 13 (unsync) of Fig. 2 in Iya et al. (1999).

Let *X* be a matrix, which has been extracted from *Fig2* by **X = Fig2(:,1:13);**. Run **pcolor(X)** to display the figure. To reverse the direction of the Y-axis, type **set(gca,'YDir', 'reverse')**. The direction can be changed again by **set(gca, 'YDir', normal')**. The background color of the figure can be changed to white using the **set gcf,'color','white'** command.

Manipulating the Color Map

Readers may want to change the color bar to the familiar red/green representation, because it is rational to use only two colors rather than to use all three (red, green, and blue) to show the ratio between two mRNA levels. This is possible by changing the color map or a table that relates the order in the value to a color. A color map is a matrix of three columns, where each row represents a color, and the first, second, and third columns represent the intensities of the red, green, and blue components, respectively.

We will make a color map with the same number of rows, 64, as the default, but it will have a red column with a continuum of zeros from the start to the middle and then increase linearly from 0 to 1. The color map will have a green column that starts at 1 and diminishes from 1 to 0 in the middle, with a continuum of zeros to the end, and a blue column with all zeros. Lower values correspond to the intensity of green, whereas higher values correspond to the intensity of red. The color map has a black

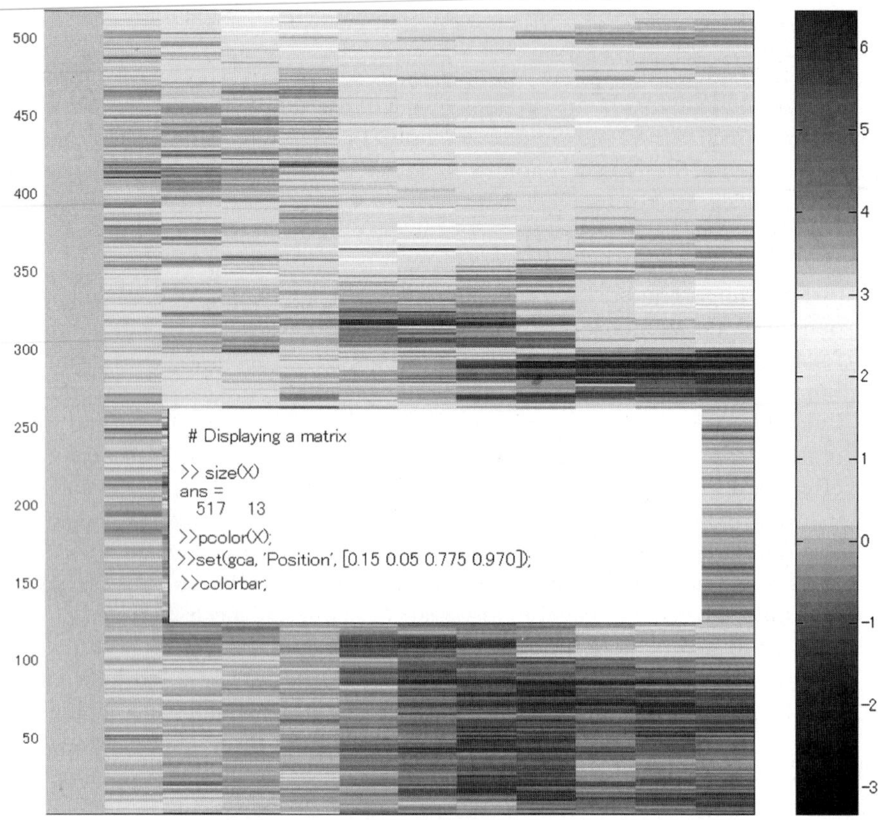

Fig. 3. Displaying a matrix.

row with all zeros in the middle, and this can be adjusted so that cells with red/green ratios close to 1.0 are black. Name the color matrix **MAP**. To use the color map, display the figure and then execute **colormap(MAP)**. Figure 4 shows the resultant representation.

Preparation Before Clustering

MATLAB can be used to cluster by rebuilding a clustered matrix of expression patterns. In this section, a random permutation (ordering) of the rows is generated from the original clustered matrix. To start, make a random permutation array of length 517 or the number of rows. A permutation array is a reordered list of serial numbers indicating the order of the numbered objects. If the i-th element of a permutation array is j, the j-th object occupies the i-th position in the new list. Let the array **p_1 = randperm(517)**. With this array, a row permutation matrix that reorders the rows of a matrix can be simply defined by **X_rowrand = X(p_1,:)**. An example of a matrix with permutated rows of X is shown in Fig. 5.

Clustering Expression Data

There are two purposes to clustering the data: 1) to search for a set of genes showing similar expression patterns, and 2) to search for similar cells or tissues showing

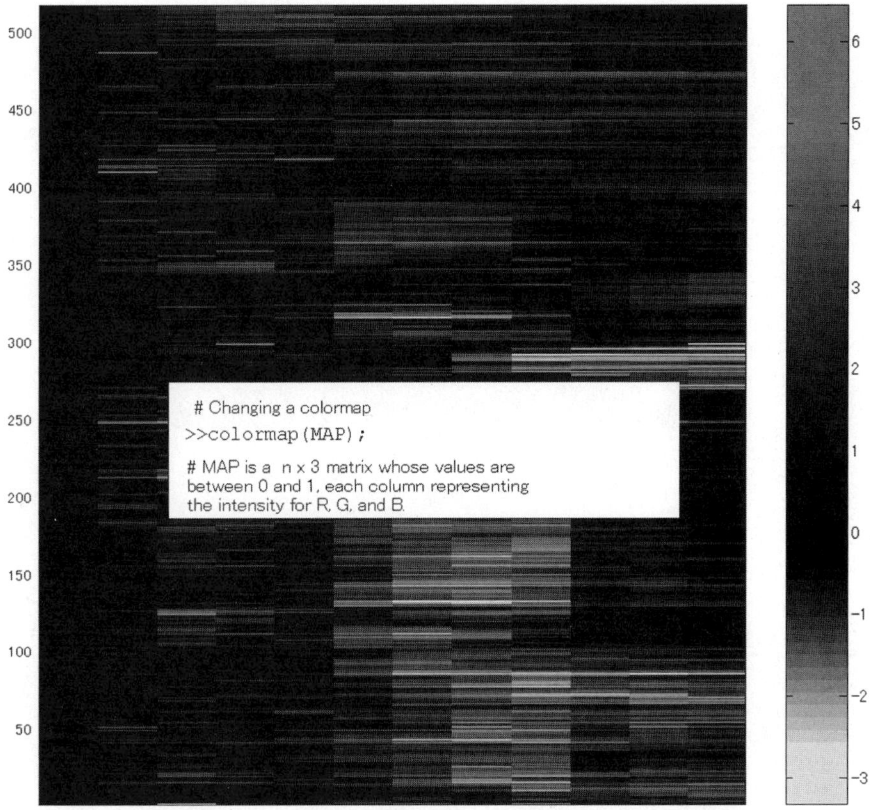

Fig. 4. Changing the color map.

similar patterns of expression. The first is referred to as *row clustering*, and the second *column clustering*.

This example has time-ordered, noncategorical columns and therefore, only row clustering will be considered. Column clustering can be done independently and is accomplished the same way as row clustering after the matrix is transposed. The MATLAB expression of the transposed matrix A is *A*.

One of the methods to cluster the rows is hierarchical clustering. This is accomplished in three steps: 1) calculating pairwise distances between data points (row vectors); 2) linking the nearest data point or group of data points hierarchically (to make a tree) with some alternative methods of defining the distance between groups; 3) cutting the tree into clusters according to a dissimilarity threshold within a cluster or the desirable number of clusters.

MATLAB users can easily define these tasks and make tests. For example, the pairwise distance calculation task is carried out with Euclidian distance by **Y = pdist(X_rowrand, 'euclid')**, and the linkage and tree generation task with average distance between data points in two groups as the distance between the groups by **Z = linkage(Y, 'average')**. If the dissimilarity threshold is set to 0.95, cutting the tree or the clustering is **T = cluster(Z, '0.95')**. The array *T* has a length of the number of rows of *X*, and the *i*-th element corresponds to the *i*-th row of *X_rowrand*; the value of the

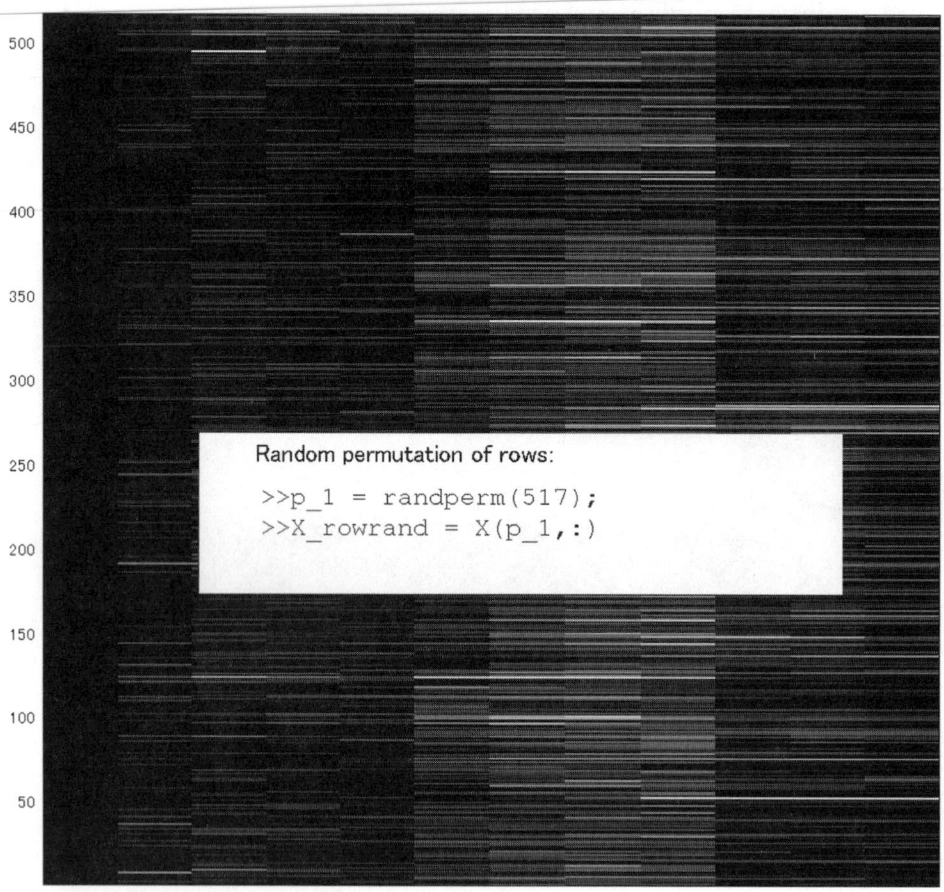

Fig. 5. A randomly row-permutated matrix.

element is the cluster to which the corresponding row is assigned. The number of clusters is obtained by **max(T)**.

Sort the randomized rows by the cluster array *T* with **[X_14cols index]= sortrows([T X_rowrand], [1]);**. The resultant clustered matrix is obtained by **X_rebuilt = X_14cols(:,2:14);**. The **sortrows** command sorts the rows of a matrix **[T X_rowrand]** by the columns indicated by a list **[1]**. The matrix **X_rebuilt** is shown as Fig. 6. The **index** array directs the permutation of rows of the randomized matrix, **X_rowrand**.

See companion CD for color Fig. 6

To see how similar the reclustered matrix is to the original, a matrix describing the correspondence of rows between the matrices can be generated by **P2 = spconvert([(1:517)' p_1(index)' ones(517,1)]);**. The command **spy(P2);** plots the matrix as shown in Fig. 7.

The closer the points are to the diagonal line that run from the upper left to the lower right of the plot, the greater the similarity between matrices. The figure shows that the positions of some clusters are interchanged each other but the set of clusters as a whole is preserved after reclustering.

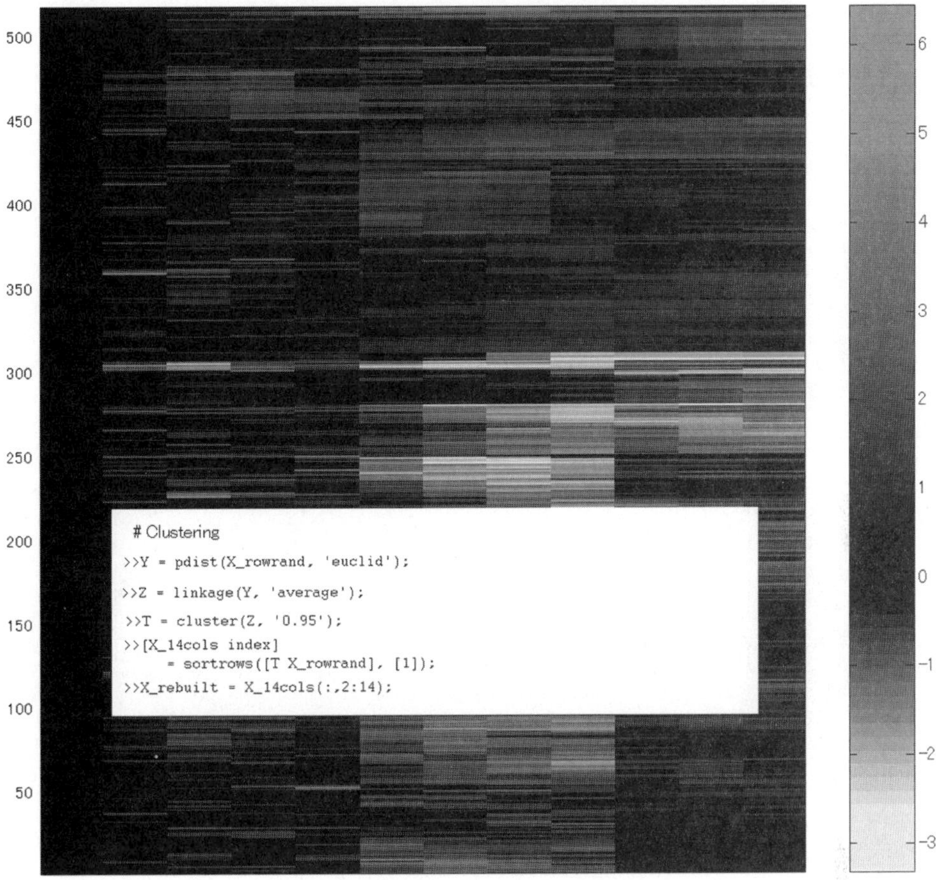
500
450
400
350
300
250
200
150
100
50
Clustering
>>Y = pdist(X_rowrand, 'euclid');
>>Z = linkage(Y, 'average');
>>T = cluster(Z, '0.95');
>>[X_14cols index]
= sortrows([T X_rowrand], [1]);
>>X_rebuilt = X_14cols(:,2:14);
6
5
4
3
2
1
0
−1
−2
−3

Fig. 6. The re-clustered matrix.

Displaying a Part of the Matrix

To examine the expression matrix more closely, extract a part of the matrix and attach titles to the rows. For example, extract rows 271–320 from the rebuilt matrix and rows 251–300 from the original matrix. Correspondence between these rows is indicated in Fig. 7. Display the rebuilt matrix with **pcolor(X_rebuilt(271:320,:))**. However, before running that command the value range to adjust the color map must be defined.

By default, the MATLAB color map allocates the smallest value to the first row of the color map matrix and the largest to the last row without considering the absolute value. Therefore, when a small part of the matrix is displayed, the range of the value in the whole data must be explicitly defined. Display the original matrix *X* by **pcolor(X)**. Run the **cax = caxis** command. If a semicolon is not included at the end of the statement, the command will show the content of the *cax* array, which is the range of the values of the cells in the whole matrix. Now display the partial matrix and run **colormap(MAP)**. The colors will change. Type **caxis(cax)** to adjust the range of colors. To include more areas of the matrix, run a command such as **set(gca, 'Position', [0.15 0.05 0.775 0.970]);**.

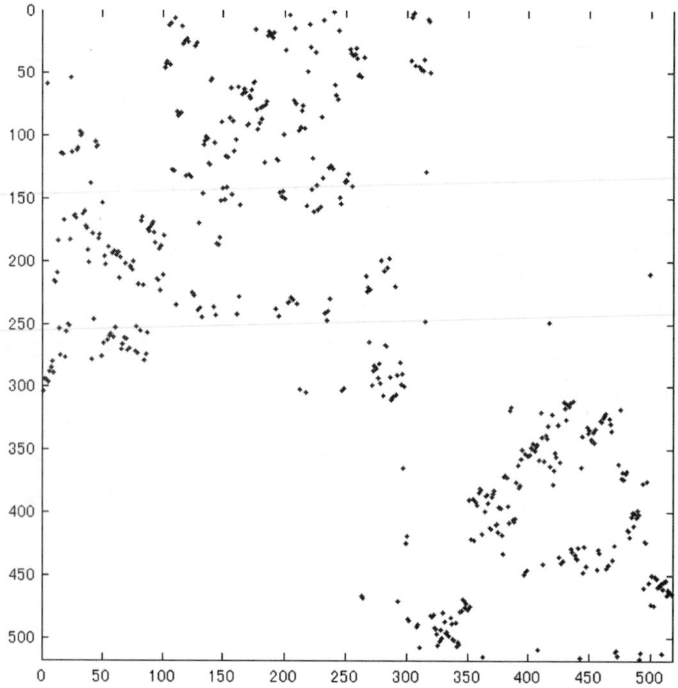

```
# Comparing two indices

# Compare the order between 1:517 and its permutation by p_1 followed by index.
>>P2 = spconvert([(1:517)' p_1(index)' ones(517,1)]);
>>spy(P2);
```

Fig. 7. Comparison of two indices.

To assign titles to each row, make titles from the *textdata* array that was separated when importing. To obtain an array of GenBank EST accession numbers for the genes, extract the second column as **acc = textdata(2:518,2:2)**". A version that has gone through randomization and clustering, *acc_rebuilt*, can be obtained with **acc_rebuilt = acc(p_1(index))**. The labels and their locations on the Y-axis can be changed. Define a label set and the order of labels by **set(gca, 'YtickLabel', acc_rebuilt(271:320))**. Set the number of labels to 50 by **set(gca, 'Ytick', 1:50)**. The font size can be changed to 8 points with **set(gca,'Fontsize',8)**. Now display the color bar by **colorbar**. Compare Fig. 8, which shows the original matrix with Fig. 9, which shows the rebuilt matrix.

Rows can also be extracted by cluster. As an example, rows that belong to clusters whose serial numbers are larger than 150 will be extracted. Use the array *T* that relates rows of the randomized matrix *X_rowrand* to the cluster serial number as the result of **cluster** function. Let an array *T_sort* represent row-to-cluster correspondence in *X_rebuilt*. It is obtained by **T_sort = sort(T);**. An array of the row indices for clusters with a serial number larger than 150 is obtained by **find(T_sort > 150);**. With this array, rows are extracted by **X_rebuilt(find(T_sort > 150),:)**, and the titles are extracted by **acc_rebuilt(find(T_sort > 150));**.

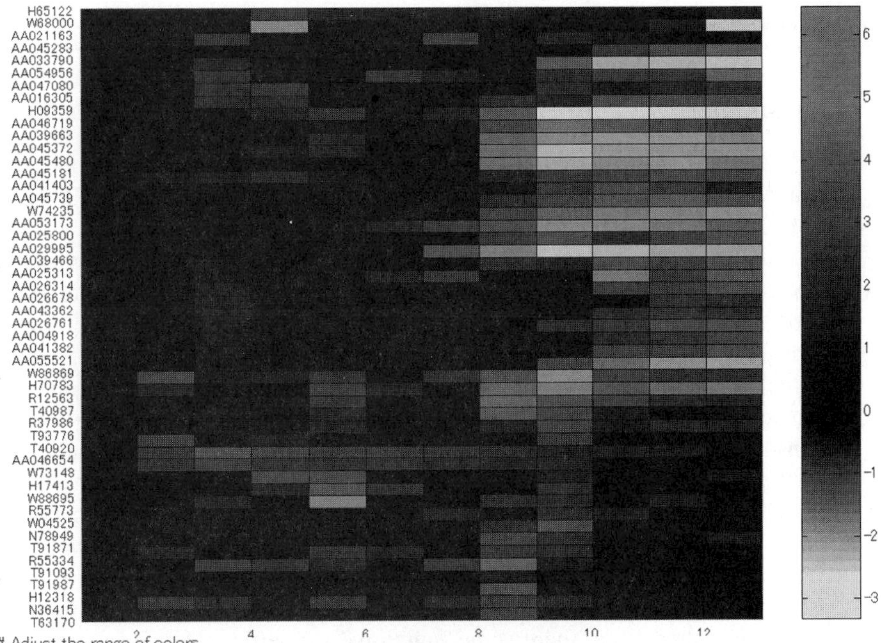

Adjust the range of colors

```
>>pcolor(X);
>>colormap(MAP);
>>cax = caxis
>>pcolor(X(251:300,:));
>>colormap(MAP);
>>caxis(cax);
```

Add titles to rows

```
>>acc=textdata(2:518,2:2);
>>set(gca,'YTickLabel',acc(251:300));
>>set(gca,'YTick',1:50);
>>set(gca,'Fontsize',8);
```

Fig. 8. A portion of the original matrix.

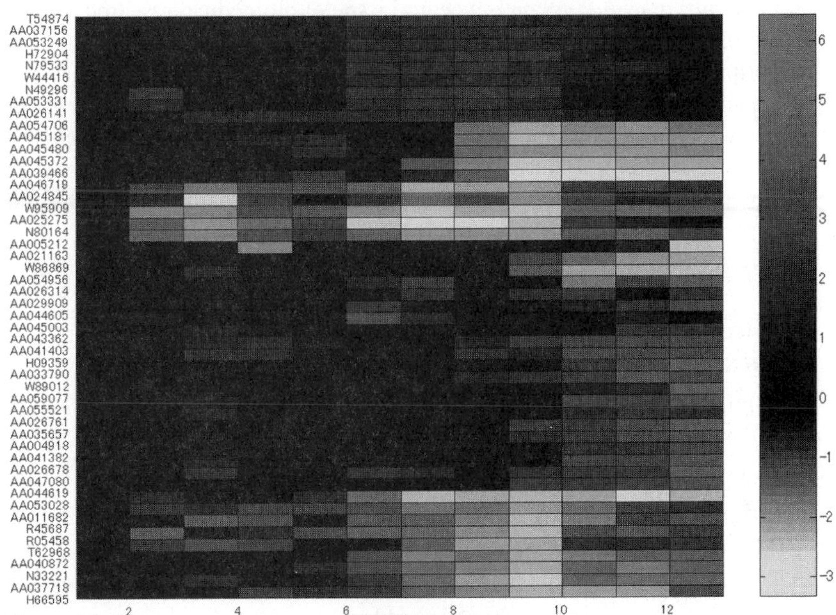

Adjust the range of colors
(Re-clustered matrix)

```
>>pcolor(X_rebuilt);
>>cax = caxis
>>pcolor(X_rebuilt(271:320,:));
>>colormap(MAP);
>>caxis(cax);
```

Add titles to rows

```
>>acc_rebuilt=acc(p_1(index));
# permute acc by p_1 and then by index
>>title = acc_rebuilt(271:320);
>>set(gca,'YTickLabel',title);
>>set(gca,'YTick',1:50);
>>set(gca,'Fontsize',8);
```

Fig. 9. The corresponding portion of the re-clustered matrix.

Analyzing Data for Multiple Transcriptomes and Future Prospects

Abundance matrices constructed from random sampling data are typically of very sparse low sensitivity. For example, matrices constructed from the dbEST and SAGE only contain values in approx 5% of the cells. This makes the random sampling data unsuitable for clustering of genes by source distribution patterns and clustering of sources by mRNA. Nevertheless, the entire matrix is useful for selecting genes on the basis of distribution patterns especially for transcripts with high ranks in some tissues. Absolute abundance data is more reliable than the absolute intensities of hybridization signals because hybridization signals are dependent both on the concentration of labeled cRNA/cDNA molecules and their stereostructure in solution. For these reasons, total abundance levels of transcripts obtained from random sampling data will continue to provide reliable clues for predicting gene functions from expression patterns. Examining correlations between absolute abundance levels and gene characteristics such as GC content and primary transcript length may be worthwhile.

One goal of transcriptome data mining is the systematic annotation of gene functions. Microarray experiments have revealed that transcripts with high similarity in tissue distributions share some functional properties. However, discovering the properties shared by a group of known transcripts is experts' work, and such human efforts cannot keep pace with the rate of production of transcriptome data. Moreover, manual annotations are typically not reproducible or objective and must be repeated because the knowledge available regarding genes increases daily.

To overcome the inconvenience of manual annotation, developing a system for *computing with function* is a central issue of biomedical research. Computing with function is defined as executing computation operations whose inputs or outputs are descriptions of the functions of biomolecules. Efforts for formal representation of biochemical knowledge by KEGG and EcoCyc have pioneered this effort. Gene Ontology (*see* Website: http://www.geneontology.org) also facilitates such computations by introducing controlled and structured terminology for describing gene function. Although such efforts have proven effective for simple organisms, the same task in complex organisms represents ontological challenges where most proteins are embedded in regulatory networks that cannot be represented as lower order structures.

Suggested Readings

Transcript Abundance

Bishop, J. O., Morton, J. G., Rosbash, M., and Richardson, M. (1974) Three abundance classes in HeLa cell messenger RNA, Nature 250, 199–204.

Lewin, B., (1999) Genes VI, Oxford University Press, New York, NY.

Model Transcriptome Analysis

Alizadeh, A. A., Eisen, M. B., Davis, R. E., Ma, C., Lossos, I. S., Rosenwald, A., et al. (2000) Distinct types of diffuse large B-cell lymphoma identified by gene expression profiling, Nature 403, 503–511.

Gilbert, D. R., Schroeder, M., and Helden, J. (2000) Interactive visualization and exploration of relationships between biological objects, Trends Biotechnol. 18, 487–494.

Iyer, V. R., Eisen, M. B., Ross, D. T., Schuler, G., Moore, T., Lee, J. C., et al. (1999) The transcriptional program in the response of human fibroblasts to serum, Science 283, 83–87.

Okubo, K., Hori, N., Matoba, R., Niiyama, T., Fukushima, A., Kojima, Y., and Matsubara, K. (1992) Large scale cDNA sequencing for analysis of quantitative and qualitative aspects of gene expression, Nat. Genet. 2, 173–179.

Perou, C. M., Jeffrey, S. S., van de Rijn, M., Rees, C. A., Eisen, M. B., Ross, D.T., et al. (1999) Distinctive gene expression patterns in human mammary epithelial cells and breast cancers, Proc. Natl. Acad. Sci. USA. 96, 9212–9217.

Ross, D.T., Scherf, U., Eisen, M. B., Perou, C. M., Rees, C., Spellman, P., et al. (2000) Systematic variation in gene expression patterns in human cancer cell lines, Nat. Genet. 24, 227–235.

Velculescu, V. E., Zhang, L., Vogelstein, B., and Kinzler, K. W. (1995) Serial analysis of gene expression, Science 270, 484–487.

Data Preparation

EST

Adams, M. D., Kelley, J. M., Gocayne, J. D., Dubnick, M., Polymeropoulos, M. H., Xiao, H., et al. (1991) Complementary DNA sequencing, expressed sequence tags and human genome project, Science 252, 1651–1656.

Boguski, M. S., Lowe, T. M., and Tolstoshev, C. M. (1993) dbEST—database for "expressed sequence tags", Nat. Genet. 4, 332–333.

Pruitt, K. D., Katz, K. S., Sicotte, H., and Maglott, D.R. (2000) Introducing RefSeq and LocusLink, curated human genome resources at the NCBI, Trends Genet. 16, 44–47.

Schuler, G. D., Boguski, M. S., Stewart, E. A., Stein, L. D., Gyapay, G., Rice, K., et al. (1996) A gene map of the human genome, Science 274, 540–546.

Organism Transcriptome Maps

Hishiki, T., Kawamoto, S., Morishita, S., and Okubo, K. (2000) BodyMap: a human and mouse gene expression database, Nucleic Acids Res. 28, 136–138.

Kawamoto, S., Yoshii, J., Mizuno, K., Ito, K., Miyamoto, Y., Ohnishi, T., et al. (2000) BodyMap: a collection of 3' ESTs for analysis of human gene expression information, Genome Res. 10, 1817–1827.

Lash, A.E., Tolstoshev, C. M., Wagner, L., Schuler, G. D., Strausberg, R. L., Riggins, G. J., Altschul, S. F. (2000) SAGEmap: A public gene expression resource, Genome Res. 10, 1051–1060.

Sese, J., Nikaidou, H., Kawamoto, S., Minesaki, Y., Morishita, S., and Okubo, K. (2001) BodyMap incorporated PCR-based expression profiling data and a gene ranking system, Nucleic Acids Res. 29, 156–158.

Microarrays, Expression and Statistical Analysis Techniques

Ashburner, M., Ball, C. A., Blake, J. A., Botstein, D., Butler, H., Cherry, J. M., et al. (2000) Gene ontology, tool for the unification of biology, The Gene Ontology Consortium, Nat. Genet. 25, 25–29.

Brenner, S. E. (1999) Errors in genome annotation, Trends Genet. 15, 132–133.

Eisen, M. B., Spellman, P. T., Brown, P. O., and Botstein, D. (1998) Cluster analysis and display of genome-wide expression patterns, Proc. Natl. Acad. Sci. USA 95, 14,863–14,868.

Kanehisa, M. and Goto, S. (2000) KEGG: Kyoto Encyclopedia of Genes and Genomes, Nucleic Acids Res. 28, 27–30.

Karp, P. D. (2000) An ontology for biological function based on molecular interactions, Bioinformatics 16, 269–285.

Karp, P. D., Riley, M., Saier, M, Paulsen, I. T., Paley, S. M., and Pellegrini-Toole, A. (2000) The EcoCyc and MetaCyc databases, Nucleic Acids Res. 28, 56–59.

MathWorks, Inc. (1997) The Student Edition of MATLAB, User's Guide, version 5, Prentice-Hall, Upper Saddle River, NJ.

Southern, E., Mir, K., and Shchepinov, M. (1999) Molecular interactions on microarrays, Nat. Genet. 21(1 Suppl), 5–9.

Velculescu, V. E., Madden, S.L., Zhang, L., Lash, A. E., Yu, J., Rago, C., et al. (1999) Analysis of human transcriptomes, Nat. Genet. 23, 387–388.

Zar, J. H., (1999) Biostatistical Analysis, 4th ed., Prentice-Hall International, Upper Saddle River, NJ, p. 574.

Zipf, G. K. (1949) Human behavior and the principle of least effort, Addison-Wesley, Cambridge, MA.

Part V

Appendices

1. **CD Contents**
2. **A Collection of Useful Bioinformatic Tools and Molecular Tables**
3. **Simple UNIX Commands**

1

Appendix

CD Contents

What is Included on the CD?

The CD that comes with this book includes:

1. All Figures and Tables with legends from the various chapters, many of which are in color. This is an excellent source of illustrative material for presentations.
2. Several bioinformatics software packages that the readers can install on their own computer workstations or servers.
3. Several useful basic tables and charts for understanding genome properties.

The CD is organized into folders and subfolders. The readers should be able to load the CD into the CD-drive of any IBM-Personal Computer or Apple Macintosh and browse through the folders.

The color figures can be found in the **Color Figures** folder, organized into subfolders by chapter.

The software packages can be found in the **Programs** folder, organized into subfolders by the name of each package. For each program subfolder, there is a **ReadmeCD** file that provides further information about the software, including how to install it, use it, and where up-to-date versions can be downloaded from the Web. There is also information on licensing and registration, and restrictions that may apply.

BioDiscovery

This folder contains software packages for microarray analysis that may be installed on IBM-PC computers. Installation instructions are included in the file named **Readme.pdf.** You will need to use the Acrobat Reader utility to read the file (*see* Section "Adobe Acrobat Reader"). The BioDiscovery software was kindly provided by Sorin Draghici, author of Chapter 35.

ClustalX

This folder contains the graphical interface versions of the Clustal multiple sequence alignment program. Versions for both IBM-PC (clustalx1.81.msw.zip) and Macintosh (clustalx1.81.PPC.sea.Hqx) are included. The files in the packages will need to be unpacked with common unzipping utilities. ClustalX versions for various flavors of UNIX are also available from the original source FTP website (*see* Website: ftp://ftp-igbmc.u-strasbg.fr/pub/ClustalX/), described in the readme file. Permission to include ClustalX on this CD was kindly provided by Julie Thompson and is described by Steven Thompson in Chapter 31.

Ensembl

This folder contains the files needed to install the Ensembl package on a UNIX server. Installation instructions are located in the **additional docs** subfolder in the file named **EnsemblInstall100.pdf**. You will need to use the Acrobat Reader utility to read the file (*see* Section "Adobe Acrobat Reader"). The **source code** subfolder contains the required source code for both Ensembl and Bioperl. Note that the files in the source code folder are in UNIX format. Please use BINARY FTP mode to transfer those files to your UNIX server. Up-to-date versions of Ensembl and Bioperl are available at their respective Websites (*see* Websites: http://www.ensembl.org/ and http://www.bioperl.org). The Ensembl software was kindly provided by James Stalker, author of Chapter 25.

MicroAnalyser

This folder contains a software package for microarray analysis that may be installed on Macintosh computers. Up-to-date versions of the software are available (*see* Website: http://imru.bham.ac.uk/MicroAnalyser/). Permission to include the MicroAnalyser software on this CD was kindly provided by Adrian Platts.

Oligo

This folder contains demo versions of the *Oligo* primer design and analysis software for both IBM-PC and Macintosh computers. This software was kindly provided by Wojciech Rychlik, author of Chapter 21.

Sequencealign

This folder contains a PowerPoint demonstration of sequence alignment. It was kindly contributed by David S. Wishart, author of chapter 27.

Singh_perl_scripts

This folder contains perl scripts for statistical analysis that were generously contributed by Gautam Singh, author of Chapters 22 and 23. They can be used for solving the problems described in Chapter 23.

Staden

This folder contains the Staden Sequence Analysis Package and the Gap4 Viewer software that can be installed on an IBM-PC computer. For up-to-date versions *see* Website: http://www.mrc-lmb.cam.ac.uk/pubseq/. This software was kindly provided by Roger Staden, author of Chapters 20 and 24.

TreeView

This folder contains the TreeView tree drawing software for both IBM-PC and Macintosh computers. TreeView is a free program for displaying phylogenies. Up-to-date versions, including UNIX versions, can be found (*see* Website: http://taxonomy.zoology.gla.ac.uk/rod/treeview.html). Please visit the Website to register TreeView if you wish to use it. Permission to include TreeView on this CD was kindly provided by Roderic D. M. Page.

Adobe Acrobat Reader

In several of the folders on the CD, there are information files that may be in PDF format. To read PDF format files, you will need to have the free Acrobat Reader utility installed on your computer. If you do not already have Acrobat Reader installed, you can download it (*see* Website:: http://www.adobe.com/products/acrobat/readstep.html).

Other Sources for Bioinformatics Software

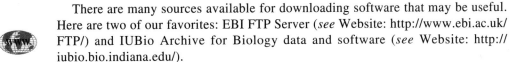

There are many sources available for downloading software that may be useful. Here are two of our favorites: EBI FTP Server (*see* Website: http://www.ebi.ac.uk/FTP/) and IUBio Archive for Biology data and software (*see* Website: http://iubio.bio.indiana.edu/).

2 Appendix

A Collection of Useful Bioinformatic Tools and Molecular Tables

The Genetic Code

1st Position	*2nd Position* U	C	A	G	*3rd Position*
U	UUU Phe	UCU Ser	UAU Tyr	UGU Cys	**U**
	UUC Phe	UCC Ser	UAC Tyr	UGC Cys	**C**
	UUA Leu	UCA Ser	**UAA** Stop	**UGA** Stop	**A**
	UUG Leu	UCG Ser	**UAG** Stop	UGG Trp	**G**
C	CUU Leu	CCU Pro	CAU His	CGU Arg	**U**
	CUC Leu	CCC Pro	CAC His	CGC Arg	**C**
	CUA Leu	CCA Pro	CAA Gin	CGA Arg	**A**
	CUG Leu	CCG Pro	CAG Gin	CGG Arg	**G**
A	AUU Ile	ACU Thr	AAU Asn	AGU Ser	**U**
	AUC Ile	ACC Thr	AAC Asn	AGC Ser	**C**
	AUA Ile	ACA Thr	AAA Lys	AGA Arg	**A**
	AUG Met	ACG Thr	AAG Lys	AGG Arg	**G**
G	GUU Val	GCU Ala	GAU Asp	GGU Gly	**U**
	GUC Val	GCC Ala	GAC Asp	GGC Gly	**C**
	GUA Val	GCA Ala	GAA Glu	GGA Gly	**A**
	GUG Val	GCG Ala	GAG Glu	GGG Gly	**G**

The codons are read as triplets in the 5' → 3' direction, i.e., left to right.
Termination codons are in bold.

IUPAC Nucleotide Codes

Code	*Members*	*Nucleotide*
A	A	Adenine
C	C	Cytosine
G	G	Guanine
T	T	Thymine (DNA)
U	U	Uracil (RNA)
Y	C or T(U)	pYrimidine
R	A or G	puRine
M	A or C	aMino
K	G or T(U)	Keto
S	G or C	Strong interaction (3 H bonds)
W	A or T(U)	Weak interaction (2 H bonds)
H	A or C or T(U)	not-G
B	G or T(U) or C	not-A
V	G or C or A	not-T
D	G or A or T(U)	not-C
N	G,A,C or T(U)	aNy base

IUPAC Amino Acid Codes

3-Letter Code	*1-Letter Code*	*Amino Acid*
Ala	A	Alanine
Arg	R	Arginine
Asn	N	Asparagine
Asp	D	Aspartic acid
Cys	C	Cysteine
Gln	Q	Glutamine
Glu	E	Glutamic acid
Gly	G	Glycine
His	H	Histidine
Ile	I	Isoleucine
Leu	L	Leucine
Lys	K	Lysine
Met	M	Methionine
Phe	F	Phenylalanine
Pro	P	Proline
Ser	S	Serine
Thr	T	Threonine
Trp	W	Tryptophan
Tyr	Y	Tyrosine
Val	V	Valine
Asx	B	Aspartic acid or Asparagine
Glx	Z	Glutamic acid or Glutamine
Xaa	X	Any amino acid

Converting Base Size of a Nucleic Acid → Mass of Nucleic Acid

Number of Bases	*Mass of Nucleic Acid*
1 kb ds DNA (Na^+)	6.6×10^5 Da
1 kb ss DNA (Na^+)	3.3×10^5 Da
1 kb ss RNA (Na^+)	3.4×10^5 Da
1.52 kb ds DNA	1MDa ds DNA (Na^+)
Average MW of a dsDNA	660 Da
Average MW of a ss DNA	330 Da
Average NW of an RNA	340 Da

Converting Base Size of a Nucleic Acid → Maximum Moles of Protein

DNA	*Molecular Weight (Da)*	*Amino Acids*	*1 μg*	*1 nmol*
270 bp	10,000	90	100 pmol or 6×10^{13} molecules	10 μg
1.35 Kbp	50,000	450	20 pmol or 1.2×10^{13} molecules	50 μg
2.7 Kbp	100,000	900	10 pmol or 6×10^{12} molecules	100 μg
4.05 Kbp	150,000	1350	6.7 pmol or 4×10^{12} molecules	150 μg

Average MW of an amino acid = 110 (Da).
3 bp are required to encode 1 amino acid.

Sizes of Common Nucleic Acids

Nucleic Acid	*Number of Nucleotides*	*Molecular Weight*
lambda DNA	48,502 (dsDNA)	3.2×10^7
pBR322 DNA	4361 (dsDNA)	2.8×10^6
28S rRNA	4800	1.6×10^6
23S rRNA (*E. coli*)	2900	1.0×10^6
18S rRNA	1900	6.5×10^5
16S rRNA (*E.coli*)	1500	5.1×10^5
5S rRNA (*E. coli*)	120	4.1×10^4
tRNA (*E. coli*)	75	2.5×10^4

Mass of Nucleic Acid ↔ Moles of Nucleic Acid

Mass	*Moles*
1 μg/ml of nucleic acid	3.0 μM phosphate
1 μg of a 1 kb DNA fragment	1.5 pmol; 3.0 pmol ends
0.66 μg of a 1 kb DNA fragment	1 pmol

Sizes of Various Genomes

Organism	*Approximate Size (million bases)*
Human	3000.0
M. Musculus (mouse)	3000.0
Drosophila (fruit fly)	135.6
Arabidopsis (plant)	100.0
C. elegans (round worm)	97.0
S. cerevisiae (yeast)	12.1
E. coli (bacteria)	4.7
H. influenzae (bacteria)	1.8

Genomic Equivalents of Species

Organism	*Source of DNA*	*pg/haploid*[a] *Genome*	*Avg.*[b]	*μg quantity for Genome Equivalence*	*Number of Genomes* $\times 10^6$
Human	diploid	3.50	3.16	10.0	2.86
Mouse	diploid	3.00	3.21	8.57	2.86
Rat	diploid	3.00	3.68	8.57	2.86
Bovine	haploid	3.24	3.24	9.26	2.86
Annelid	haploid	1.45	1.45	4.14	2.86
Drosophila	diploid	0.17	0.18	0.486	2.86
Yeast	haploid	0.016	0.0245	0.0457	2.86

[a]pg/haploid genome was calculated as a function of the tissue source. Genomic equivalence was calculated given that 10 μg of human genomic DNA contains 2.86×10^6 genome copies.

[b]Average of all values given in each tissue for that species.

3 Appendix

Simple UNIX Commands

The following tables contain a brief list of simple but useful UNIX commands[1]. These commands can be used to move around the file system, examine files, and copy, delete, or rename files. They can also be used to do housekeeping on a user's account, and to communicate with other users on the local system or on remote systems.

Directory Operations

Command	*Action*
pwd	present working directory (show directory name)
cd	change directory: **cd /path/name**
cd	change to your home directory: **cd**
mkdir	make (create) new directory: **mkdir Name**
rmdir	remove directory (if empty): **rmdir Name**
quota	check disk space quota: **quota -v**

File Operations

Command	*Action*
ls	list files
cp	copy files: **cp /path/name newname**
rm	remove (i.e. delete) files: **rm name**
mv	move or rename files: **mv name newname**
more	page file contents (spacebar to continue): **more name**
cat	scroll file contents: **cat name**
less	better pager than more? (**q** to quit): **less name**
vi	visual text editor (**:wq** to save and quit): **vi name**
pico	pico text editor (**Ctrl-X** to quit): **pico name**
chmod	change mode of file permissions: **chmod xxx name**

[1]Most commands have options. To see what options are available, use the **man** command to open the manual pages for that command, e.g. type **man ls** to open the manual for the **ls** command.

Manual Pages

Command	*Action*
man	open the man pages for a command: man command

Communications

Command	*Action*
write	write messages to another user's screen
talk	talk split-screen with another user: **talk username**
mail	UNIX email command
pine	send or read E-mail with pine mail system
telnet	connect to another computer via the network
ftp	file transfer over the network
lynx	text-based Web browser

System Operations

Command	*Action*
df	show free disk space
du	show disk usage
ps	list your processes
kill	kill a process: **kill ###**
passwd	change your password
date	show date and time
w	who is doing what on the system
who	who is connected to the system
ping	ping another computer (is it alive?)
finger	get information on users
exit	exit, or logout, from the system

X Windows

Command	*Action*
clock &	display a clock (&: run in background)
cmdtool &	command tool window
filemgr &	file manager
mailtool &	email program
perfmeter &	system performance meter
seqlab &	SeqLab interface for GCG
setenv DISPLAY	for setting the DISPLAY environment variable
shelltool &	shell tool window
textedit &	text editor
xterm &	X terminal window

Index

A

B

C

D

E

F

G

H

I

J

K

L

M

N

O

P

Q

R

S

T

U

V

W

X

Z